The Memoirs of Cordell Hull

THE MACMILLAN COMPANY
NEW YORK · BOSTON · CHICAGO · DALLAS
ATLANTA · SAN FRANCISCO
MACMILLAN AND CO., Limited
LONDON · BOMBAY · CALCUTTA · MADRAS
MELBOURNE
THE MACMILLAN COMPANY
OF CANADA, Limited
TORONTO

The Memoirs of

Cordell Hull

IN TWO VOLUMES

VOLUME II

New York

THE MACMILLAN COMPANY

1948

History

First Printing

Contents

VOLUME II

Part Five THE YEAR OF WAR (1941)

66: SELF-DEFENSE 919
67: BATTLE OF THE ATLANTIC 935
68: STRUGGLE WITH VICHY 948
69: CRISIS AT VICHY 958
70: WE HELP RUSSIA 967
71: WE TALK WITH JAPAN 982
72: ARMS BREAK OFF TALKS 1000
73: ROOSEVELT-KONOYE MEETING 1016
74: WAR CABINET IN JAPAN 1028
75: WEYGAND OUSTED 1038
76: CONFLICT IN THE ATLANTIC 1046
77: WARLORDS RULE JAPAN 1054
78: JAPAN'S ULTIMATUM 1069
79: ZERO HOUR 1083
80: JAPAN STRIKES 1095

Part Six DIPLOMACY IN WAR (1942–1943)

81: UNITED NATIONS JOIN FOR WAR 1109
82: TROUBLES OVER FRANCE 1127
83: NEIGHBORS AND WAR 1139
84: LAVAL VERSUS DE GAULLE 1154
85: STALIN'S AMBITIONS 1165
86: PRELUDE TO AFRICAN INVASION 1181
87: AFTERMATH OF AFRICAN LANDING 1195
88: CHURCHILL AND EDEN 1211
89: FIRST QUEBEC CONFERENCE 1227
90: STALIN THE SPHINX 1247
91: RUSSIA VERSUS POLAND 1265
92: MOSCOW CONFERENCE BEGINS 1274
93: BIRTH OF THE UNITED NATIONS ORGANIZATION 1292
94: STALIN AGAINST JAPAN 1308

Part Seven THE LAST YEAR (1944)

95: PROLOGUE TO 1944 1321
96: IBERIA AND THE WAR 1324

v

97: SWEDEN, SWITZERLAND, EIRE 1345
98: TURKEY ON THE EDGE OF WAR 1365
99: THE BAD NEIGHBOR 1377
100: BREAK WITH ARGENTINA 1390
101: AN UNWORTHY MEMBER 1400
102: BRITAIN AND ARGENTINA 1409
103: THE GOOD NEIGHBORS 1420
104: FRANCE REGAINED 1427
105: QUESTION OF RUSSIA 1436
106: RUSSIA—CONCLUSIONS 1451
107: WORKING WITH BRITAIN 1472
108: INDEPENDENCE FOR INDIA 1482
109: THE NEAR EAST LOOMS BIG 1498
110: NEAR EAST AND OIL 1511
111: THE PROBLEM OF JEWS AND ARABS 1528
112: ITALY: ENEMY AND FRIEND 1548
113: UNCONDITIONAL SURRENDER 1570
114: TOWARD VICTORY IN THE ORIENT 1583
115: PLAN FOR GERMANY 1602

Part Eight PEACE AND AFTER (1939–1945)

116: WE BEGIN TO PLAN 1625
117: ROOSEVELT-CHURCHILL IDEAS 1634
118: PLANNING INTENSIFIES 1649
119: NONPARTISAN POLICY 1656
120: DUMBARTON OAKS 1671
121: HANDS OFF UNITED NATIONS 1686
122: CORNERSTONE OF UNITED NATIONS 1700
123: FOURTH TERM AND RESIGNATION 1714
124: WHAT OF THE FUTURE? 1729

INDEX 1743

Part Five

THE YEAR OF WAR

(1941)

66: Self-Defense

AS THE YEAR of war, 1941, dawned, we intensified our diplomatic and material assistance to the Allies throughout the world. Wherever it was possible, whether in Vichy France, Latin America, the Balkans, Africa, the Atlantic islands, or the Far East, to bolster the Allies either by exerting our influence or pressure or by furnishing concrete aid, we were quick and wholehearted in making the necessary moves.

Our position toward the conflict was clear. We were convinced that an Allied victory was possible and we were determined to do everything we could to bring it about, short of actually sending an expeditionary force to Europe or the Orient. We were equally convinced that an Axis victory would present a mortal danger to the United States. Those nations that supported the Allies could count on our friendship, those that supported the Axis on our opposition.

We were acting no longer under the precepts of neutrality, but under those of self-defense. In conversations with the President, with my associates and with Congressmen in those weeks I used to state our attitude in this homely narrative:

"A citizen sees an avowed outlaw coming to meet him on the highway and he folds up and says: 'I'm neutral. I have nothing to say as between you and the officers of the law. I'm harmless. Don't bother me.' And he thinks that ought to protect him.

"But the outlaw goes up to him and taps him on the side of the head with the butt of his pistol and takes his watch and valuables and then moves on.

"Down a hundred and fifty yards in front of him is another fellow looking at this incident very closely, and with increasing concern. The outlaw marches straight on in his direction. So this fellow pulls out and holds in his hand a little derringer pistol. When I was a boy, I saw a fellow shoot another fellow right in the stomach with one of those derringers, and the bullet buried in and then bounced out.

"On the other hand, we have a six-inch Colt. After you've passed the stage where every chance of neutrality protection is exhausted, then the question is whether you are going to use your derringer in the hope that, after all, it will take care of you, or whether you will use your Colt that plows through the outlaw's guts and tears him to pieces when it hits him.

"We could stick neutrality out in front between us and the outlaw. That would obstruct any serious plans of ours beyond our boundary line —and it would not protect us. Because of the imminence of danger, only the law of self-defense and self-preservation is left to us."

The President stated our position forcefully in his address to Congress on January 6, 1941, when he said that "at no previous time has American security been as seriously threatened from without as it is today." He said we were committed to three propositions: all-inclusive national defense; full support of all those resolute peoples, everywhere, who were resisting aggression and thereby keeping war away from our hemisphere; and no acquiescence in a peace dictated by aggressors and sponsored by appeasers.

In this address the President stated the four freedoms upon which the world should be founded: freedom of speech and expression, freedom of worship, freedom from want, and freedom from fear.

In the few preceding weeks the President had been reading and studying a fifteen-page letter from Prime Minister Churchill, dated December 7, 1940, vigorously stating Britain's position and needs and the war prospects for 1941. Ambassador Lothian had sent this to me on December 8, with a copy for myself, and asked that I send it by seaplane to the President, then cruising in the Caribbean, which I did.

The Prime Minister said he was strongly and confidently placing his estimate before the President because "it seems to me that the vast majority of American citizens have recorded their conviction that the safety of the United States as well as the future of our two democracies and the kind of civilization for which they stand are bound up with the survival and independence of the British Commonwealth of Nations. Only thus can those bastions of sea-power, upon which the control of the Atlantic and the Indian oceans depends, be preserved in faithful and friendly hands. The control of the Pacific by the United States Navy and of the Atlantic by the British Navy is indispensable to the security of the trade routes of both our countries and the surest means to preventing the war from reaching the shores of the United States."

The Prime Minister said that Britain was unable to match the immense armies of Germany in any theater where their main power could be brought to bear, but, by using sea and air power, could meet the German armies in regions where only comparatively small forces could be brought into action. Britain had to do her best to prevent German domination of Europe spreading into Africa and into southern Asia, and also had to maintain in constant readiness in the United Kingdom armies strong enough to make the problem of an overseas invasion insoluble. The danger of Britain being destroyed by a swift, overwhelming blow, he said, had for the time being very greatly receded, but in its place there was an equally deadly danger, the steady and increasing diminution of sea tonnage.

"Even if the United States was our ally instead of our friend and indispensable partner," he said, "we should not ask for a large American expeditionary army. Shipping, not men, is the limiting factor and the power to transport munitions and supplies claims priority over the movement by sea of large numbers of soldiers. . . .

"The decision for 1941 lies upon the seas; unless we can establish our ability to feed this island, to import munitions of all kinds which we need, unless we can move our armies to the various theatres where Hitler and his confederate Mussolini must be met, and maintain them there and do all this with the assurance of being able to carry it on till the spirit of the continental dictators is broken, we may fall by the way and the time needed by the United States to complete her defensive preparations may not be forthcoming. [He estimated two years.] It is therefore in shipping and in the power to transport across the oceans, particularly the Atlantic Ocean, that in 1941 the crunch of the whole war will be found."

But he pointed out that Britain's shipping losses—the figures for which he appended—had been on a scale almost comparable to that of the worst years of the last war, and that the relative battleship strength in home waters was approaching an unsatisfactory level. He pointed to a "second field of danger"—the possibility that the Vichy Government might assist Hitler—and to a third—indications that the Japanese were thrusting southward.

He suggested four methods by which the United States could help. The first was a reassertion of the doctrine of the freedom of the seas from illegal and barbarous warfare. The second was protection of shipping by United States naval and air forces. He did not think such protection would provoke a declaration of war by Germany, since Hitler had shown himself inclined to avoid the Kaiser's mistake. The third, if the second could not be granted, was the gift, loan, or supply of a large number of American vessels of war, above all, destroyers. The fourth was United States influence toward getting naval and air facilities in Eire for Britain.

In connection with this last suggestion, he said: "If it were proclaimed an American interest that the resistance of Great Britain should be prolonged and the Atlantic route kept open for the important armaments now being prepared for Great Britain in North America, the Irish in the United States might be willing to point out to the Government of Eire the dangers which its present policy is creating for the United States itself."

Here he gave an intimation of future union of Northern Ireland and Eire by saying: "I do not doubt that if the Government of Eire would show its solidarity with the democracies of the English-speaking world at this crisis, a Council of Defence of all Ireland could be set up out of which the unity of the island would probably in some form or other emerge after the war."

Mr. Churchill finally appealed for some method whereby Britain could receive from the United States the immense supplies he specified she needed, without paying cash for them. "The moment approaches," he said, "when we shall no longer be able to pay cash for shipping and other supplies. While we will do our utmost and shrink from no proper sacrifice to make payments across the exchange, I believe that you will agree that it would be wrong in principle and mutually disadvantageous in effect if, at the height of this struggle, Great Britain were to be divested of all salable assets so that after victory was won with our blood, civilisation saved and time gained for the United States to be fully armed against all eventualities, we should stand stripped to the bone. Such a course would not be in the moral or economic interests of either of our countries."

In the following weeks this letter received the earnest consideration of the President, myself, and other officials of the Government. Though not all its suggestions were adopted, it proved a powerful advocate for the policy of Lend-Lease.

A few hours before the President's address to Congress on January 6, Harry Hopkins left for London to establish a direct liaison between Mr. Roosevelt and Prime Minister Churchill and to make a firsthand survey of Britain's war needs so that our efforts to help her could be better coordinated.

Now began Hopkins's career on a world scale. Until 1941 he had been engaged in the service of other Departments or agencies of the Government. Beginning in 1941, his chief cooperation with the President related mainly to the conduct of military affairs and included his work in administering the Lend-Lease Act and several highly important missions to confer with Churchill and Stalin as the personal representative of the President. He rendered efficient, admirable service in all these respects so far as I was aware. He was constantly at the President's elbow in private conferences at the White House during this period, and no doubt rendered much important aid to Mr. Roosevelt.

Although Hopkins's work was now on an international scale, I never had any friction, much less clashes, with him. He professed toward me a friendly attitude. To the best of my knowledge, he did not undertake to interfere with any important policies of the State Department. He often called on me at the Department on questions of mutual interest, and our agreeable working relations thus continued to the end. He visited me a number of times while I was in the Naval Hospital following my resignation, making his last call just a day or two before his final departure for New York, where he soon died.

While I and many others differed with Hopkins's views on numerous domestic questions prior to 1941, my later estimates of him were that he possessed splendid ability and rendered valuable service during the war.

The Lend-Lease Bill was introduced in the House and Senate on January 10. About that day the President called for me. He said Morgenthau had expected to lead the fight for the bill in Congress, but that considerable opposition could be expected from the isolationists and waverers, and he wanted me to take charge of and handle the bill as the best means of getting it through. Specifically he requested that I appear personally before the House Committee on Foreign Affairs and the Senate Committee on Foreign Relations, which would hold hearings on the bill. I agreed.

On the day after the bill's introduction I saw Sir Frederick Phillips, British Under Secretary of the Exchequer, in my office. I said to him that, although I had had virtually nothing to do with the formal drafting of the bill, which had been in the hands of the President and Morgenthau, I had suggested three or four points that I thought would facilitate its passage and preserve favorable public opinion in support of aid to Britain. One of these suggestions, I explained, was that, if Britain intended to make any kind of payment during the next twelve months or so for military supplies, now was the one time for her to do so in the form of collateral of a billion and a half or two billion dollars. "This action," I commented, "would go further to disarm critics and keep the whole movement on a favorable basis than anything else that might be said or done."

But I made no impression whatever on the British Under Secretary so far as I could see. Britain's argument at that time was that she was at the end of her tether, and that the foreign securities she still possessed were pledged or needed elsewhere. Yet this became one of the major weapons in the hands of opponents of Lend-Lease who argued that Britain still could and should pay cash for her purchases here.

When the House committee began its hearings on January 15, I opened with an extensive statement to the committee in support of the legislation. My approach was to analyze not the bill in detail but the international situation that made the bill necessary. I examined the menace presented to us by each of the Axis countries. As to the Oriental member, I said: "It has been clear throughout that Japan has been actuated from the start by broad and ambitious plans for establishing herself in a dominant position in the entire region of the western Pacific. Her leaders have openly declared their determination to achieve and maintain that position by force of arms and thus to make themselves masters of an area containing almost one half of the entire population of the world."

Italy I dismissed briefly except to point out her responsibility as the first of the European Powers to commit one of the recent series of breaches of the world order.

After outlining Hitler's preparations for war, his broken promises, his aggressions, and our many efforts to prevent war from coming, I said:

"It has become increasingly apparent that mankind is today face to face not with regional wars or isolated conflicts, but with an organized, ruthless, and implacable movement of steadily expanding conquest. We are in the presence of forces which are not restrained by considerations of law or principles of morality; which have fixed no limits for their program of conquest; which have spread over large areas on land and are desperately struggling now to seize control of the oceans as an essential means of achieving and maintaining their conquest of the other continents."

The most serious question for the United States, I emphasized, was whether the control of the high seas should pass into the hands of powers bent on a program of unlimited conquest. It was in this light, above all, that we should order our thinking and action with respect to the amount of material assistance that we were prepared to furnish Great Britain.

As was expected, the debate in Congress on Lend-Lease aroused the last-ditch opposition of isolationists and those who resented any additional grant of authority to the President. They brought to the stand persons of note such as Colonel Charles A. Lindbergh to propagate the thought that our safety would not be affected even if Germany won.

In the State Department we prepared arguments against some of the amendments that were introduced to cripple the application of Lend-Lease or to hamstring our foreign policy. In particular we worked against a proposed amendment stating that the Act conferred no additional powers to authorize the employment of our armed forces beyond the limits of the Western Hemisphere. I believed this amendment, although it did not change the constitutional powers of the President, would have a bad psychological and political effect on our own people and on other Governments. We also opposed an amendment that specifically named the countries to be assisted.

The Act, as it finally was passed and became law on March 11, was substantially what my associates and I wanted. It was one of the most revolutionary legislative actions in American history. I felt a sharp sense of relief that Congress had so signally recognized the strong interest of the United States in seeing to it that Britain did not fall and Hitler triumph.

I then had a long discussion with the President on what he might say following the passage of Lend-Lease. I felt he should make it the kernel of a vigorous statement to warn the Axis that we were engaging in active rather than passive defense. In consequence, he said, in an address to the White House Correspondents' Association on March 15: "Let not dictators of Europe and Asia doubt our unanimity now. . . . The world has been told that we, as a united nation, realize the danger which confronts us—and that to meet that danger our democracy has gone into action."

The Act authorized the transfer of $1,300,000,000 worth of materials already on hand, and a fortnight later the President signed a bill appropriating $7,000,000,000 for Lend-Lease purposes. Again at the President's request that I rather than the Secretary of the Treasury take the lead, I had supported this bill in arguments to the House Committee on Appropriations.

The Lend-Lease Act overthrew what seemed to have been one of Hitler's basic hopes in promoting the Axis Tripartite Pact of the previous September. Our Embassy in Berlin had cabled me on December 20, a few days after the President stated the concept of Lend-Lease in his press conference, that one of the few plausible explanations for concluding the Tripartite Pact was a conviction in upper circles in Berlin that the

United States would be so alarmed at the prospect of war with Japan and Germany simultaneously that we would abandon assistance to England rather than face this possibility.

The new British Ambassador, the former Foreign Secretary Lord Halifax, had arrived while Lend-Lease was before Congress. He received an unprecedented welcome in that the President went down to Annapolis to meet him as he came in aboard the battleship *King George V*. Halifax paid his first call on me on January 25 to present a copy of his credentials, and we had a general interchange of information. While I keenly regretted Lothian's death, I saw at once that I could work on the same effective, cordial terms with his tall, thin, ascetic-looking successor. Halifax, who possessed unusual ability, engaged in prodigious, fruitful labors while serving in Washington, and the extent and importance of his accomplishments were unexcelled by any other foreign representative during my tenure in office.

Britain and we exchanged new ambassadors at almost the same time, John G. Winant going to London as United States Ambassador to replace Kennedy, who had resigned. Winant had achieved a fine background as a broad-gauged public servant while occupying the office of Governor of New Hampshire. Possessing vision and a constructive mind, he proved alert and active in his work as Ambassador to Great Britain and made us many useful suggestions.

Lend-Lease came at a critical psychological moment. Hitler's armies had occupied Bulgaria on March 1, 1941, after previously taking over Rumania. The Nazis were bringing overwhelming pressure on Yugoslavia to join the Axis, which pressure the President and I, working along parallel lines with Great Britain, were striving to counterbalance. Our own relations with the Axis were becoming ever more strained.

I instructed Ambassador Phillips in Rome on February 28 to inform the Italian Government that we wished its consulates in Seattle, Detroit, and Newark closed and its personnel in those posts withdrawn. This was our reaction to the request of the Italian Government on February 12 that the consulates of all Governments except Germany be moved from Palermo and Naples to Rome or farther north and away from the seacoast. The Italian consulates in Detroit and Newark were duly closed, even as were ours at Palermo and Naples. Seattle was omitted from this action on Phillips's suggestion since other countries had consulates there under career officers, and to single out the Italian consulate might result in retaliatory action against our other consulates in Italy.

Our relations with the Axis became further exacerbated when, on March 30, 1941, the Coast Guard took into protective custody the German, Italian, and Danish ships lying idle in United States ports following evidence that the German and Italian ships were being sabotaged. Coast Guardsmen found that the machinery of many Axis ships had been drastically damaged. Of the twenty-seven Italian ships in our ports, twenty-five had been so badly damaged that extensive repairs would be necessary if they were to sail.

During the previous December I had handed the President a memorandum written by several of my associates, including Jesse Saugstad, the Department's shipping expert, recommending that the German, Italian, and Danish ships in our ports be taken into protective custody lest the vessels of the first two nationalities be sabotaged or sunk by their crews and the Danish vessels be damaged by Axis agents. The President thought this action too drastic at that time.

We at the State Department, however, had continued to study the subject. During the first part of March we had an exchange of notes with the German Embassy which, apprehensive lest we requisition Axis ships in our ports, had claimed that this right could be exercised only by a belligerent state and then only under conditions of "urgent public emergency." I approved an *aide-mémoire* to the German Chargé, Dr. Hans Thomsen, in which we refused to enter into a discussion with Germany of the circumstances under which the right of a sovereign state to requisition foreign shipping found within its jurisdiction might be exercised.

The German, Italian, and Danish Governments all protested our action, but Danish Minister de Kauffmann, whose loyalty to the Allied cause never faltered, said to Assistant Secretary Long that he was not unhappy that it had happened.

I sent strong replies on April 3 to the German and Italian Embassies. I pointed out that their crews, in damaging their vessels to the detriment of navigation and the safety of our harbors, had committed felonies under United States law, in disregard of the hospitality we had extended to them.

The Italian side of the incident was aggravated by the fact that we received, through the Treasury, documentary evidence that the Italian Naval Attaché in Washington, Admiral Lais, had directed that the machinery of five Italian ships at Norfolk, Virginia, be put out of commission. After getting the President's approval, I sent a note to Italian Ambassador Prince Colonna on April 2 stating that his naval attaché was *persona non grata* and should be immediately recalled.

We informed the other American Republics of our taking the Axis and Danish ships into protective custody, so that they might take similar action with regard to the ships of the same nationalities tied up in their ports. Many of the Axis ships in Latin American ports were also being sabotaged.

When Hitler invaded Yugoslavia and Greece on April 6, the intense diplomatic effort we had been making to solidify the Balkans against this eventuality came to an end. Ever since the beginning of January, from all the capitals concerned, cables had come to my desk reporting the probability that Hitler would attack Greece to aid his failing partner, Mussolini.

From Belgrade our Minister Arthur Bliss Lane cabled me on January 24 and 25 that he and Colonel William J. Donovan, who was sent by Secretary of the Navy Knox, on behalf of the President, to the Balkans to stimulate their resistance, had been assured by the Regent, Prince Paul, and by Prime Minister Cvetković that Yugoslavia would not permit troops or war materials to pass through her territory and would resist aggression.

Lane also said it was thought in Belgrade that if Bulgaria and Turkey would adopt a similar attitude, the three countries together might successfully protect themselves. He suggested the possibility of informally pointing out to the three countries the desirability of a joint defense policy. He thought, however, that mutual distrust among the three might prevent a joint policy, and that steps would have to be taken by us to dispel this mistrust.

I cabled Lane on January 29 that, while it was not our practice directly to initiate a policy such as he suggested, we were losing no opportunity to bring our position relative to the war to the attention of the Balkan representatives in Washington. I also commented that we were placing particular emphasis on our aid to Greece and Britain.

I gave virtually the same answer to Lord Halifax when he called upon me on February 5 to request our support of the British in encouraging conversations between Turkey and Yugoslavia toward a policy of mutual defense.

As reports came to us that a movement of German troops into Bulgaria was imminent, Lane cabled me from Belgrade on February 8 that the Regent considered Yugoslavia's situation desperate. He said that the Prime Minister, along with Foreign Minister Cincar-Marković, who Lane thought had Axis leanings, might shortly go to Berlin at Hitler's invitation, and that the Regent was disposed to avoid the possibility of war at all costs.

After talking this situation over with the President, I sent Lane in Belgrade and Ambassador John V. A. MacMurray in Ankara, Turkey, identical cables on February 9 to be communicated to the Yugoslav and Turkish Governments. After quoting a statement by the President that "we are planning our own defense with the utmost urgency and in its vast scale we must integrate the war needs of Britain," I said, in effect:

"This position continues to be the keystone of the national defense policy of the United States and this effort has been intensified by the developing situation. That Britain will win we are convinced. Already war-material production in America has been undertaken on the vast scale indicated, and the provision of facilities to meet the requirements of the British will continue until the final victory ever increasingly. On several occasions the President has pointed out that from this policy there can be no deviation, as in his own words: 'We know now that a nation can have peace with the Nazis only at the price of total surrender.' "

I asked the Bulgarian Minister in Washington to come to the State Department, where he was given the substance of the cables to the Turkish and Yugoslav Governments.

Five days later I went personally to the Yugoslav Legation and handed Minister Fotitch a message from the President to be transmitted to his Government. The President had not asked Fotitch to come to the White House because of speculation that might have been aroused by the visit. The message said:

"The President . . . is convinced that any victory on behalf of the predatory powers, even if it only be in the diplomatic field, would but pave the way for fresh demands accompanied by threats of force against the very independence of the nation thus menaced. The President also desires it to be realized that the so-called Lend-Lease Bill now before Congress and which has been passed by the House of Representatives and by the Committee on Foreign Relations of the Senate permits . . . the President to supply the materials of war to those nations that are now the victims of aggression or which might be threatened with aggression."

I cabled Ambassador MacMurray the same day instructing him, at the President's direction, to convey to the Turkish Prime Minister an almost identical message. MacMurray cabled on February 18 that the Turkish Prime Minister, without making any definite commitment, had expressed his cordial appreciation of the President's message and his Government's wholehearted support of the ideals of the United States and Great Britain.

Lane cabled me on the same day that the Regent was very grateful for the President's message and the manner of its delivery to Minister Fotitch. Prince Paul said Yugoslavia would fight if attacked. He added, however, that, if German troops occupied Bulgaria, Yugoslavia's position would not be tenable and, if Yugoslavia were attacked by Germany, her resistance could not continue for more than two weeks. He felt that any United States aid would come too late to help Yugoslavia. However, the Regent had confidence in the ultimate victory of the Allies.

I sent Minister Lane's cable to the President for his information. After Mr. Roosevelt read it he sent me a memorandum dated February 20 in which he said: " I think we should find some means of getting across to the Prince Regent and others that the United States is looking not merely to the present but to the future, and that any nation which tamely submits on the grounds of being quickly overrun would receive less sympathy from the world than a nation which resists, even if this resistance can be continued for only a few weeks."

He pointed to Abyssinia, China, Greece, and Norway as examples on the good side. "Abyssinia," he said, "won world sympathy by a brief though useless resistance—and Abyssinia will be restored in some way not now foreseeable.

"China seemed capable of making no resistance in the modern sense of the word—but after four years China is still resisting and has the sympathy of the world—with an excellent chance of being reconstituted in her independence in some way at some date.

"The Greek cause looked completely hopeless in view of an Italian army and air force of overwhelming proportions. Even if Greece goes down fighting in the next few weeks, the cause of Greek independence will win in the end.

"The rear-guard action fought by Norway for two or three months means that all of us will work for the restoration of Norwegian independence."

With specific reference to Yugoslavia and Turkey, he said:

"Our type of civilization and the war in whose outcome we are definitely interested, will be definitely helped by resistance on the part of Yugoslavia and, almost automatically, resistance on the part of Turkey—even though temporarily Yugoslavia and Turkey are not successful in the military sense.

"How can we best get these thoughts across?"

We thereupon prepared a telegram to Minister Lane based on the memorandum, with some necessary changes, and sent it on February 22.

The following day Lane cabled that the Prince Regent's mood, while not optimistic, seemed much more determined after he had read the message. Prince Paul said Yugoslavia would sign with Germany no political agreement impairing Yugoslav sovereignty and would resist aggression. Under no conditions would Yugoslavia sign the Tripartite Pact or participate in the "new order in Europe," which amounted to the same thing.

Then, on March 1, Bulgaria signed the Axis pact and German troops began immediately to occupy that country, and to move toward the Greek border. The cables we now received from our diplomatic missions showed that Turkey would not undertake any military action even if Greece were invaded; that no progress had been made toward a Turkish-Yugoslav understanding; that Greece would not submit to the German threat and would receive all possible aid from the British; and that Yugoslav resistance was uncertain.

Lord Halifax came to me on March 3 to inquire whether we would supply Turkey with war materials direct or whether this should be done by or through Britain. I replied that it was my understanding that my Government would cooperate to the fullest possible extent in supplying war materials to Turkey under appropriate circumstances.

The following day the President froze Bulgarian credits in the United States. In reply to a request from Minister Lane, I authorized him on March 5 to make the President's February 22 message to the Regent known to the Prime Minister, and the substance of it to other Government leaders, in an effort to bolster Yugoslav resistance.

Prime Minister Churchill cabled the President on March 10 that the "concerted influence" of our Chiefs of Mission at Moscow, Ankara, and Belgrade would be of enormous value at the moment. Mr. Churchill hoped we could induce the Soviet Government to give assurances to Turkey which would assist its Government in withstanding German penetration.

I thereupon sent the President a memorandum on March 12, in which I recited the various actions we had already taken in the Balkans and said: "I am satisfied that we here, and our representatives in that area have done everything that could possibly be done to bolster up the resistance of the Balkan Governments to penetration and occupation by the German forces." I informed Mr. Roosevelt that I had been told by Balkan representatives here—and I believed it to be true—that the only further step that would be of real help would be the promise by the British Government to lend material military aid with air and ground forces to the Yugoslav and Turkish Governments in the event they found it necessary to resist the entrance or passage of German troops.

I added that I had already transmitted this suggestion to British Ambassador Halifax when I saw him several days previously.

Turkish Ambassador Mehmet Münir Ertegün called on me on March 15 to inform me of certain assurances that the President of Turkey had received from Hitler relative to the German occupation of Bulgaria. Although I thanked the Ambassador for his information, I remarked:

"Hitler took this communication out of his stock on hand of similar communications. He has been sending these to each of the dozen countries he has occupied or conquered. He seems to contemplate sending them to countries whose seizure he has in mind for the future."

The Ambassador smiled and promptly agreed.

On the same day Minister Lane cabled from Belgrade that the Prime Minister had indicated to the British Minister in Belgrade that Yugoslavia would sign a nonaggression pact with Germany, but would not sign the Tripartite Pact with its clause permitting the military occupation of Yugoslavia. The following day Lane cabled that Prince Paul had taken the same position.

But German pressure was increasing, the Yugoslav Government's resistance decreasing. Lane cabled on March 19 a statement by Assistant Foreign Minister Smiljanić that adherence to the Tripartite Pact was under consideration. He cabled again on March 21 that adherence to the Axis pact, excluding any military clauses, was imminent. Two days later he reported that the Yugoslav Government had decided to sign the pact, with reservations, and on March 24 he cabled that Yugoslavia would sign the pact in Vienna the following day. Lane argued forcefully with the Regent and the Prime Minister, using again the various points we had made in our telegrams to Belgrade, but without being able to change their conviction that signing the pact could not be avoided.

The President issued an order freezing Yugoslav assets in this country on March 24, when it became clear that Yugoslavia would sign with Germany.

The Yugoslav Government duly entered the Tripartite Pact—but an adverse popular reaction broke out almost immediately. Britain's and our various representations of support in case Yugoslavia resisted had seemingly had the effect only of postponing the Yugoslav Government's acceptance of the Axis pact, but they undoubtedly had the further effect of helping to solidify popular resistance to that acceptance. A *coup d'état* occurred early in the morning of March 27, young King Peter assumed control of the country, the Regent resigned, and General Simović became Premier. Yugoslavia had regained her independence, if only for the moment.

President Roosevelt the following day cabled his best wishes to King Peter.

Ten days after the *coup d'état* the Germans launched their attack on Yugoslavia and Greece. On that day, April 6, I issued a public statement, saying: "The barbaric invasion of Yugoslavia and the attempt to annihilate that country by brute force is but another chapter in the present planned movement of attempted world conquest and domination. Another small nation has been assaulted by the forces of aggression and is further proof that there are no geographical limitations or bounds of any kind to their movement for world conquest."

I emphasized the sympathy of the American people for Yugoslavia and our intention to send military and other supplies to Yugoslavia as speedily as possible. The President spoke to the same effect in a message to King Peter on April 8.

I cabled our Legations in Sofia, Bucharest, and Budapest on April 7 to make clear to the Bulgarian, Rumanian, and Hungarian Governments, respectively, how we would regard their support of any aggressive acts against Yugoslavia. I said that we here were directing all our efforts under existing law toward helping those nations that were defending themselves against aggression, and I assumed our representatives were using all information coming to them from this country to stress the scope of our determination. Subsequently, however, Hungary attacked Yugoslavia, and Bulgaria attacked both Greece and Yugoslavia.

Hitler's rapid conquest of Yugoslavia and Greece is a matter of record. Important, however, was the fact that Yugoslavia resisted. German divisions therefore had to be employed in the Balkans that could have made considerable difference during the invasion of Russia two months later. Had we not taken the strong diplomatic steps we took, and had Britain not sent an expeditionary force to Greece, Yugoslavia might have given in without a struggle, and the Nazi occupation divisions tangled in the Balkans might have been thrown decisively into the climactic struggle in the December snows at the gates of Moscow.

Germany's might now touched the shores of the Aegean and the

Adriatic. At about the same time the British forces in Libya, weakened by the dispatch of troops to Greece, were sent reeling back toward Egypt. It looked as if Hitler might extend himself across North Africa and come out upon the Atlantic.

We therefore had to face new problems at once in our contribution to the winning of the Battle of the Atlantic.

67: Battle of the Atlantic

AS HITLER INTENSIFIED his sea war against Britain in the Atlantic by using more and better underwater and surface warships, it became incumbent upon us to take a series of important steps in the diplomatic field to aid in defeating his efforts to strangle the United Kingdom.

It was evident to the President and me and to American military authorities that the year 1941 was perhaps the crucial one for Britain. Shipping losses were averaging twice and thrice her capacity to replace them. Our production of war materials was increasing by leaps and bounds, but the increase meant little unless it could be transported to the United Kingdom for use.

We knew that Germany was exerting ever greater pressure on the Vichy Government to obtain bases in French North and West Africa from which German submarines could operate. She was bringing pressure on the Spanish Government toward a similar end. At the same time a Nazi threat to Greenland became evident.

The whole question of the defense of Greenland had been under discussion at the White House, at the State, War, and Navy Departments, and with the British and Canadians during a large part of 1940 and into 1941, but it was not until April 9, 1941, three days after Hitler's invasion of Yugoslavia and Greece, that it came to a head with the signing of an agreement for our protection of the gigantic island.

The British and Canadians had been pressing us to establish an airfield in Greenland to assist in the transport of warplanes, under their own power, from Canada to the United Kingdom, or to agree that they themselves should do so. In March, with the approval of the President, we agreed to send a survey expedition to Greenland for this purpose. We had had prior consultation with Danish Minister de Kauffmann and with Greenland authorities, who urged us to proceed.

On March 12 I addressed a letter to Secretary of the Navy Knox enclosing a general letter of instruction for the guidance of the senior officer of the expedition. I outlined our political thinking toward Greenland, saying:

"As a result of Greenland's geographical location in the Western Hemisphere and inclusion within the general scope of the Monroe Doctrine, and by reason of obligations toward the Western Hemisphere arising out of the adherence by this Government to the Act of Havana in July, 1940, the United States also has a certain dominant interest in Greenland arising out of considerations of national and hemispheric defense. Under the Monroe Doctrine and the Act of Havana, the United States could not tolerate an attack upon Greenland by any non-American power or an attempt by such a power to alter the present political status of the island. Accordingly, since the outbreak of the present war in Europe, the United States has endeavored to guard against Greenland's being drawn into the sphere of belligerent activities and at the same time to maintain scrupulous respect for Danish sovereignty in Greenland which has long been recognized by our Government."

We next drew up the draft of a projected agreement between the United States and Denmark entitling us to lease certain airfields in Greenland. This Assistant Secretary Berle handed the Danish Minister on March 28.

I cabled our Consul James K. Penfield at Godthaab, Greenland, on April 4, informing him of the decision we had arrived at that the construction and subsequent protection of Greenland's defense facilities should be under United States jurisdiction solely. I added that, by reason of recent European developments affecting the North Atlantic and the security of this country and this continent, we had exchanged views informally with Minister de Kauffmann relative to steps not inconsistent with Denmark's sovereignty over Greenland which we might take to protect Greenland against being used as a point of attack on the American continent by a non-American Power.

The President on the following day authorized the allocation of $5,000,000 for the construction of aviation bases in Greenland.

When the Danish Minister signed the agreement on April 9, he knew and we knew he was performing a brave act, because the reaction from his Government, under the influence of the Germans occupying Denmark, might be serious. De Kauffmann said he believed that in executing the agreement he was doing the best thing possible for his King and his country.

The reaction was not long in coming. On April 12, our Chargé in Copenhagen, Mahlon F. Perkins, cabled a note from Danish Foreign Minister Eric Scavenius protesting the agreement and stating that Minister de Kauffmann had been recalled.

Two days later the Danish Minister handed me a note informing us of his Government's attitude toward the agreement, of his own recall, and of his own attitude. He stated his belief that his Government, in conveying this reaction, was acting under duress from the German occupying forces.

I replied at once that my Government likewise considered that the Danish Government was acting in this respect under duress. Consequently, I said, we did not recognize the order of recall and would continue to recognize him as the Minister of Denmark in Washington.

De Kauffmann said that, in the light of the military occupation of Denmark, he considered it his duty as a loyal envoy to continue to represent the interests of his country as he saw them, rather than the mere paper orders which might proceed from Copenhagen. I replied: "We consider this to be the true representation of Denmark."

Chargé Perkins cabled me from Copenhagen on April 13 his opinion that the general Danish reaction to the Greenland agreement was one of relief and satisfaction. On April 16 he reported that our action had caused great satisfaction among all classes in Denmark since it was regarded as enabling Denmark to make some contribution to the struggle against the forces of aggression as well as insuring Danish sovereignty in Greenland.

Obviously the Germans were enraged at the action of Minister de Kauffmann in agreeing that we could establish airfields in Greenland, and were bringing all the pressure they could on the Danish Government to get his head. For, on April 16, Chargé Perkins cabled me a note from the Danish Foreign Minister transmitting a letter from King Christian of Denmark to President Roosevelt recalling De Kauffmann. On the following day I received a cable from the Danish Foreign Minister informing me of the King's letter to the President and of the appointment of a Chargé d'Affaires (Mr. Blechingberg, Counselor of the Danish Legation here) to care for Danish interests in this country until De Kauffmann could be replaced.

I was then studying a long memorandum the President had sent me on April 15. He began this by saying: "Here is a thought. What is your comment? I should like to send a telegram from me personally to the King of Denmark personally along the following lines."

He then recalled the occupation of Denmark on April 9, 1940, and our recognition of the duress under which the Government of Denmark was compelled to act. That Government, in his judgment, had ceased to retain full independence of views and of actions.

The President reviewed the respect maintained by the United States during more than a century for the Danish possessions in the Western Hemisphere. He stated that the use of Greenland for military, air, or naval purposes by any non-American nation, except Denmark, would violate the integrity of the Western Hemisphere, and that efforts toward such use had been made by Germany, as indicated by the fact that German planes had already flown over Greenland.

He promised: "Just as soon as the untrammeled sovereignty of Denmark is reestablished, full control of Greenland will return to Denmark with our approval and blessing. In the meantime, it is necessary for the United States to act in a sense as the trustee for Denmark during the period of duress.

"We are seeking to save Greenland from the control of a different non-American nation which has never had any color of interest or sovereignty in Greenland and which in any event must be excluded from such sovereignty."

He concluded with the hope that the Danish people would before long return to full independence.

After the cable came in from the King of Denmark recalling De Kauffmann, the President sent me a further memorandum on April 18, asking me to let him have a draft of a reply at the earliest possible moment.

Mr. Roosevelt commented in this memorandum that the appointment of Minister de Kauffmann was a free and untrammeled act on the part of the King, whereas most unfortunately, since April 9, 1940, the actions of the Danish Government must be considered as taken under the duress of German occupation.

He stated that the United States recognized the sovereignty of Denmark over Greenland, but the United States could not agree to a change of sovereignty to another European nation. German planes, he added, had been flying over Greenland and, in the light of the history of the past year and a half, there could be no assurance against German occupation of Greenland.

We drafted a reply, following closely the lines of the President's memoranda, and I sent it on April 19 to the President who was then at Hyde Park. I received his "O.K." the same day and cabled the note that evening to Copenhagen.

The previous day I had already cabled Chargé Perkins my reply to Foreign Minister Scavenius, which embraced much the same arguments we stated in the President's reply to King Christian.

The German pressure at Copenhagen, however, was too strong for mere argument. Perkins cabled on April 26 a second message from King

Christian to the President. The King said De Kauffmann had exceeded his authority in signing the Greenland agreement, the agreement was invalid, and our continued recognition of him as Danish Minister would be tantamount to making impossible diplomatic contact in Washington between Denmark and the United States. Foreign Minister Scavenius elaborated these points in a message to me at the same time.

At the State Department we drew up a reply for the President, which he approved on May 5, and we cabled it to Copenhagen. The President expressed his great distress that the King had found it necessary to characterize as unjustified the measures our Government deemed essential, no less in the interests of Danish sovereignty over Greenland than for the protection of the Western Hemisphere. He likewise regretted the King's statement with regard to De Kauffmann. He said he was confident that the Danish Government would find it possible to maintain completely friendly relations with us through our Chargé in Copenhagen.

In my reply on the following day to Foreign Minister Scavenius I amplified what the President had said, and emphasized that we would not withdraw recognition of De Kauffmann. The Danish Foreign Minister replied on May 17, saying that relations maintained through our Chargé in Copenhagen would not afford adequate protection to Danish interests in this country. Again asking that we accept a Danish career officer as Chargé d'Affaires ad interim in Washington, he said that otherwise Denmark would be forced to entrust the representation of its interests in the United States to another neutral country.

I replied on June 3 that we would find it out of the question to recognize any other person, or any other Danish diplomatic officer, or any third country, as having the capacity to represent Danish interests in the United States. I countered his opinion that relations through our Chargé in Copenhagen would be inadequate by recalling that the Danish Government had used that channel satisfactorily to present its views on various occasions, including the present situation.

And thus the matter rested. In our eyes De Kauffmann continued to be the Danish Minister in Washington, but not in the official eyes of his Government. What relations we had with the Danish Government were conducted through our Legation in Copenhagen.

Our diplomatic action in the Battle of the Atlantic had to envisage the possibility that Hitler might occupy Spain and Portugal and their Atlantic islands, including the Canaries and the Azores. Persistent reports came to us from many sources during the spring of 1941 concerning Hitler's ambitions in that direction.

I sent telegrams on April 10 to our Ambassador in Madrid, Alexander W. Weddell, and our Minister in Lisbon, Bert Fish, stressing the obligation of all this Government's representatives abroad, at this crucial time in the fight against totalitarian aggression on a world-wide scale, to make the greatest contribution within their power to the successful outcome of the fight. I said it had been made abundantly clear by the people and the Government of this country that "we do not intend to stand on the sidelines but that on the contrary we do intend to play our part in resistance against the forces of aggression."

Therefore, I emphasized, our representatives, and in fact all American citizens abroad, were called upon to reflect in their conversation and in their bearing our absolute determination to follow this struggle through until a successful conclusion was reached. I said the President depended on our Chiefs of Mission to make clear to public opinion in Spain and Portugal, respectively, and to the civil and military Government leaders of those countries the extent of our national determination and effort to resist the aggressive powers.

I expressed my confidence that the Chiefs of Mission would lose no opportunity, when talking with these Government leaders and in any other possible way, to stress again and again the significance of our stand and to emphasize our certainty that the aggressive forces would lose. I added that the Chiefs of Mission should feel no hesitancy in setting forth our convictions and our determination in the strongest terms.

I concluded that it was our conviction that a forceful and continuous setting forth of our position and of the extent of our effort against aggression would have a salutary effect in such countries as Portugal and Spain which so far had taken no direct part in the conflict, and would greatly assist in offsetting the cumulative effect of Axis propaganda.

Later that month I sent similar telegrams to our Missions at Helsinki and Stockholm, and also to Rome for the guidance of our Mission to the Vatican.

As rumors spread that the United States intended to occupy the Azores to keep them from falling into German hands, I assured the Portuguese Minister on April 18 that these reports were entirely without foundation. Nevertheless, if Germany had made a move to take the Azores, we were prepared to occupy them, and the President gave instructions to this effect to Admiral Stark, Chief of Naval Operations, on May

22, 1941. The President soon thereafter had exchanges of views with Prime Minister Churchill, Prime Minister Salazar of Portugal, and President Vargas of Brazil (Portugal being the mother country of Brazil) on this subject. We were in general agreement with Britain that we would occupy the Azores if Hitler sought to seize them. President Vargas was approached to learn whether Brazil would send a token force along with ours in the event occupation of the Azores became necessary. We felt that a Brazilian force alongside ours would have a beneficial effect on Portuguese public opinion in such case and would offset German propaganda against us in Portugal.

In May we approached the Latin American countries to inquire whether, on their own initiative, they would appeal to the Spanish Government to remain out of the war. When British Ambassador Lord Halifax suggested to me on May 21, however, that a joint statement be made by Great Britain, the United States, and the Latin American countries appealing to Spain not to enter into an alliance with Germany, I said I doubted the wisdom of it at this time, but that each country might well proceed in its own way.

Along with the President, I sought to point out to Americans what the Battle of the Atlantic meant to us, and what our role in it should be. Many Americans were still saying that it made no difference to the United States whether Germany or England won out.

Speaking to the thirty-fifth annual meeting of the American Society of International Law, of which I was president, I said on April 24: "Some among us . . . still contend that our country need not resist until armed forces of an invader shall have crossed the boundary line of this hemisphere. But this merely means that there would be no resistance by the hemisphere, including the United States, until the invading countries had acquired complete control of the other four continents and of the high seas, and thus had obtained every possible strategic advantage, reducing us to the corresponding disadvantage of a severely handicapped defense. This is an utterly shortsighted and extremely dangerous view."

I continued that events had shown beyond possible question that the safety of the hemisphere and of the United States called for resistance wherever resistance would be most effective. "In my judgment," I said, "our safety and security require that, in accordance with the declared policy of the legislative and executive branches of the Government, aid must be supplied without hesitation to Great Britain and those other countries that are resisting the sweep of the general conflagration. This policy means, in practical application, that such aid must reach its destination in the shortest of time and in maximum quantity. So ways must be found to do this."

Replying to those who said it made no difference to us who won the war, I pointed out that evidence had been piling up over several years which made it perfectly plain that one group of powers actually had designs both upon the New World and upon the principles, the possessions, and the way of life that were ours. Our freedom and wealth inevitably made us magnets for their machine of force.

"Yes," I concluded, "it makes a difference who wins—the difference between whether we stand with our backs to the wall with the other four continents against us and the high seas lost, alone defending the last free territories on earth, or whether we keep our place in an orderly world."

The President in a radio address on May 27 pointed out the dangers to us inherent in the Battle of the Atlantic. Simultaneously he proclaimed the existence of an unlimited national emergency requiring the strengthening of our defenses to the extreme limit of our national power and authority. He had discussed this proclamation with me in preceding days, and I was in agreement that the time had come to issue it. The Nazis, he said in his address, "have the armed power at any moment to occupy Spain and Portugal; and that threat extends not only to French North Africa and the western end of the Mediterranean, but also to the Atlantic fortress of Dakar, and to the island outposts of the New World—the Azores and the Cape Verde Islands. The Cape Verde Islands are only seven hours distant from Brazil by bomber or troop-carrying planes. They dominate shipping routes to and from the South Atlantic. The war is approaching the brink of the Western Hemisphere itself. It is coming very close to home."

Part of our contribution in the Battle of the Atlantic was to obtain more shipping with which to get our war materials and other supplies to the United Kingdom. The President asked Congress on April 10 for authority to requisition foreign ships lying idle in our ports. These had already been taken into protective custody by the Coast Guard. We at the State Department assisted in the preparation of his message and in the drafting of the legislation. Congress passed the bill, which became law on June 6.

While the bill was pending, I received protests against it from the German and Italian Embassies on the ground that it would constitute a breach of neutrality and represent the seizure of foreign-owned private property contrary to law. In a reply to the German Chargé, Dr. Thomsen, I said: "The right of a Government to requisition for public use private property within its jurisdiction, whether owned by nationals or by aliens, subject to the payment of just compensation, is not open to question. . . . Determination of the needs of the national defense of the United States is not a matter to be passed upon by a foreign government; rather it is a sovereign prerogative of the United States."

After negotiations with the British Government, which had held out since April, 1940, against the use of the forty Danish ships in our ports unless they flew the British flag, we requisitioned the vessels and put them to work, largely with their own crews. The new shipping we thus acquired was vitally needed because of the desperate character of the war in the Atlantic. We did not make use of the Axis ships until after Pearl Harbor.

The question whether to ask Congress to repeal parts of the Neutrality Act so as to permit American ships to be armed and to carry cargoes directly to Britain was much under discussion in and out of the Administration during the spring of 1941. However desirable the repeal would be, I believed it inadvisable to make the request of Congress at that time because the isolationist sentiment in both the Senate and the House was still strong. I felt that these influential isolationists would take advantage of the debate to delay action perhaps for many months and still further divide public opinion. Following my April 24 speech I had received 1,700 telegrams and letters, of which 600 were favorable, while 1,100 opposed further action on our part, a considerable number of them severely criticizing me for being too warlike. The strength of this sentiment in the House was proven in August when the extension of the Selective Service Act was approved by one lone vote—203 to 202.

The President, in our discussions on this point, felt as I did. He had also talked with Attorney General Jackson who believed that some provisions of the Neutrality Act were open to liberal interpretation which would permit us to assist Britain without obtaining their repeal.

In May Secretaries Stimson and Knox delivered speeches in which they both came out publicly for repeal of the Neutrality Act. At the following Cabinet meeting I spoke out strongly against these speeches on the grounds that they would stir up public controversy and arouse unnecessary opposition to the Administration. The President backed me up and agreed that the time had not yet come to request repeal of the Act.

We took a series of actions, however, to accelerate our aid to Britain.

As British forces in Libya were thrown back toward Egypt, it became evident that if the British were to hold Egypt the United States had to rush military supplies to that area, and the only way to get a sufficient quantity there was to send them in American ships. At that time, however, a combat area under the Neutrality Act existed at the mouth of the Red Sea which excluded American vessels.

I therefore wrote the President on April 10, enclosing for his consideration a proclamation modifying the combat area proclamation of June 11, 1940, in such a way as to eliminate this combat zone and permit American vessels to proceed to Suez. Mr. Roosevelt agreed immediately, and we issued the proclamation the following day.

On that day, April 11, I sent the President another memorandum submitting for his approval our reply acquiescing in a British request of April 7 that British merchant ships equipped with fighter aircraft for purely defensive purposes be permitted to enter our ports. The President returned this with his O.K.

Senator George, acting chairman of the Senate Foreign Relations Committee, wrote me on April 16 requesting my comment on a joint resolution introduced in Congress to prohibit the use of American armed forces, vessels, and aircraft for transporting, delivering, or conveying articles or materials to belligerent countries. I did not believe the time had yet come to modify the Neutrality Act, but I also did not believe it wise for Congress to pass a prohibition of this kind. It would discourage the Allies, encourage the Axis. I replied to Senator George on April 29, recommending against passage. I said it was "manifest that its passage would be misunderstood abroad."

German attacks on American shipping in the Atlantic began to create a new situation under which repeal of certain sections of the Neutrality Act became possible later in the year. The first of these incidents was the sinking of the American merchantman *Robin Moor* by a German submarine in the South Atlantic on May 21, 1941. The sinking was atrocious because the German submarine commander knew from the *Robin Moor* markings, flag, and the statements of her crew that she was American, en route from New York to Capetown, with a general cargo none of which was war materials. The crew and passengers were forced to put out in small boats many hundreds of miles from shore.

The President sent a message to Congress on June 20 concerning the sinking, in which he said: "We must take the sinking of the *Robin Moor* as a warning to the United States not to resist the Nazi movement of world conquest. It is a warning that the United States may use the high seas of the world only with Nazi consent."

We took other actions stronger than words. The President issued an Executive Order on June 14 freezing all German and Italian assets in the United States, as well as those of the European occupied countries not already frozen, such as Albania, Austria, Czechoslovakia, Danzig, and Poland. In the next few days we ordered the closing of all German and Italian Consulates and certain other Axis agencies in the United States on the ground that their personnel had been engaging in improper activities. These activities included espionage, propaganda, and interfering in our internal affairs.

We sent a circular telegram on June 19 to the other American Republics pointing out that the German personnel were *persona non grata* because of their improper activities, some of which fell within the meaning of a resolution adopted by the Havana Conference in 1940 regarding activities against domestic institutions directed from abroad. We said we hoped that, if any of these Germans sought admission to any of the other American Republics, the dangerous character of their activities would be taken into consideration by the Governments concerned.

Naturally the German and Italian Governments reacted by closing our Consulates in their countries. We agreed, but we categorically rejected the Axis allegations that our consular officials had acted in a manner incompatible with their duties.

As the German submarine menace came closer to our side of the world in the summer of 1941, our patrol activities in the Atlantic increased in intensity. A portion of the Pacific fleet came to the Atlantic during the spring. These patrol activities were still for information only. We avoided clashes with the Germans, but at the same time we wanted to keep German submarines from Western Hemisphere waters and to protect American and other shipping in this area. The isolationist element in the United States, of course, violently opposed any movements of American naval vessels out into the Atlantic for this purpose.

The Western Hemisphere Neutrality Zone which the President and Welles had evolved and the Panama City Conference had agreed to in 1939 had fizzled out because it was impossible to maintain a definitely demarcated zone under international law or to obtain the belligerents' consent to it. The President, however, had agreed to my idea of a flexible zone. I maintained to him that we and the other American Republics had the right under self-defense to send our naval patrols out to any distance from our coast we felt necessary to protect the security of the hemisphere. That distance might be greater or less, depending on the intensity of belligerent activities near the Western Hemisphere.

The acquisition of our ninety-nine-year leases to British bases in Newfoundland, the western Atlantic, and the Caribbean gave us added reason to move our patrols farther out to sea. Gradually our patrols extended to Newfoundland. The British soon moved up to Newfoundland their ships protecting the Canadian coast and generally operated to the north and east, while we patrolled the waters south of our Newfoundland base on down to South America.

Later, as the German submarine menace increased, I suggested that the flexible patrol line running south from the American base in Newfoundland could, without publicity, be gradually moved out into the North Atlantic. The President agreed, and this course was pursued until Pearl Harbor. Our outside line then ran south from a point due east of our Newfoundland base and skirted the Azores.

In the North Atlantic we took a major step in our own protection by sending an occupation force to Iceland at the beginning of July, to release the British troops there. This matter had been under discussion for many months. As early as December 24, 1940, Consul Bertel E. Kuniholm in Reykjavik sent me a request from Icelandic Foreign Minister Stefán Jóhan Stefánsson for our reaction to a possible appeal by the Althing (Parliament) for American protection of the island. Stefánsson said he was concerned over the possibility that, should the British position deteriorate, Iceland might be subject to conquest by Germany.

I replied on January 18 that we sympathized with his apprehension and would continue to give most serious consideration to our relations with Iceland, but that we wished to make no commitments at that time. We wanted to retain our full freedom of action so that we might be in position effectively to meet any situation affecting our interests that might arise.

During the following months Consul Kuniholm sent a series of reports indicating an increasing amount of German air and submarine activity in the vicinity of Iceland. British Ambassador Halifax gave me on May 7 a report that Iceland was threatened by German occupation. I told him the entire matter was receiving attention at the Navy Department.

The Icelandic Althing announced on May 17 that it did not intend to renew the union with Denmark, and that it would elect a regent to function until the union could be formally dissolved. We would therefore not face in Copenhagen the same difficulties over Iceland we had experienced over Greenland. We could now deal directly with Reykjavik.

In June the British indicated to us that they were prepared to see their troops in Iceland replaced by American forces. The President then decided to go through with the operation. It would be a material contribution to the winning of the Battle of the Atlantic.

After the decision was reached, Prime Minister Churchill sent the President a message on June 14 saying: "I am much encouraged by . . . your marines taking over that cold place and I hope that once the first instalment has arrived you will give full publicity to it. It would give us hope to face the long haul that lies ahead. It would also produce the best effects in Spain, Vichy France, and Turkey."

Here was striking support for the belief I had entertained for years that events throughout the world were closely interwoven, and that a major development in one country could not but influence other countries however far removed. It was rather startling to reflect that what we did in Iceland might have an effect in far-off Turkey, but I fully realized it could.

As for Vichy France, I knew that the various steps we took in the Battle of the Atlantic could not but affect this difficult area of our foreign relations.

68: Struggle with Vichy

OUR RELATIONS WITH the Vichy Government plunged to a low and dangerous depth in the first half of 1941. As the year began, the British opened their offensive against the Italians in Libya, and soon further confirmation was given to the demonstration already made in Greece that Mussolini's vaunted might was boast and show. But the defeat of the Italians in North Africa nourished the well grounded fear in London and Washington that Hitler would either invade French North Africa or bring the utmost pressure on Vichy to grant him vantage points from which to aid the Italians in Libya. Ceaselessly we devoted our diplomatic efforts both at Vichy and in French North Africa to preventing the Pétain Government from succumbing to Hitler's pressure.

At the opening of 1941 we were acting as a channel for discussions between the British and Vichy. Britain was hoping to induce the Pétain Government to resume the fight against Germany from North Africa. On December 29, 1940, we had transmitted to Vichy on Britain's behalf a formal proposal that, if the French Government decided to cross to North Africa, or to resume the war there against Italy and Germany, Britain would send a strong expeditionary force up to six divisions and an air force to aid in defending Morocco, Algeria, and Tunisia.

As the Vichy Government paid little heed to this proposal, I cabled Leahy on January 13 that Churchill had informed the President he was concerned lest Pétain had not realized the concrete importance of the British proposal. Later, on January 29, I cabled Leahy again that Britain would facilitate the mobilization and departure of the French naval squadron at Alexandria if the French Government would cross to North Africa and resume the fight from there.

Britain's proposals came to naught. But it is interesting to note—in view of the criticism that came from British sources in 1940 and 1941 against our policy of maintaining relations with Vichy—that Britain herself was in frequent contact with Vichy. Furthermore, the British regularly studied our diplomatic reports from Vichy, which we turned over to them, although they did not always believe them.

Leahy's first cables to the President and me, following his arrival at Vichy, were none too encouraging. Darlan was convinced that Germany would win and that France's future lay with Hitler, not with Britain whom he violently disliked. Pétain was physically unable to perform the work he had assumed, and was very sensitive to German pressure. The Germans were using every means to return Laval to the Cabinet since they calculated he would collaborate 100 per cent with them; but here Pétain, who entertained a bitter hatred toward Laval, was adamant. Darlan, who in February became Vice Premier, Foreign Minister, and Minister of the Interior, in addition to Minister of Marine which he already was, held frequent and suspicious conversations with the Germans.

We had two weapons in the arsenal of our diplomacy toward Vichy, in addition to the constant representations we made on the possibility of Vichy's exceeding the terms of the armistice with Germany. One was relief supplies to unoccupied France, and the other was economic relations with French North Africa, built around General Weygand.

Almost immediately after his arrival in Vichy, Admiral Leahy urged that we dispatch food and clothing to unoccupied France so that the Germans might not use the widespread misery of the people as a lever to swing the Pétain Government to open collaboration.

To do so, however, we would have to obtain a relaxation of the British blockade, and Britain had formally stated on December 10, 1940, that she could not consent to food shipments to France since they would indirectly aid the Germans and thereby postpone the liberation of the very people they were designed to help. We had already accepted this view in principle, but through the Red Cross we did make shipments of medical supplies and food for children in unoccupied France. These were gratefully received and proved to the French people and Government that the United States would be a friend as long as Vichy did not make us an enemy.

When British Ambassador Halifax came to my office on February 10, I said that the food situation in unoccupied France would gradually become more acute. "It's the hope of my Government," I added, "that the British Government will not be too inflexible in their attitude toward this matter." We were then prospecting the idea of sending several shiploads of food to unoccupied France.

Our policy of limited relief to unoccupied France, however, was much less important in its long-range effects than our economic policy toward French North Africa. Robert D. Murphy, whom we had sent from Vichy to North Africa in December, spent a month there and made me a comprehensive report of his findings. Weygand, as well as Pierre Boisson, Governor General of French West Africa, both assured him repeatedly that they wanted a British victory but that, in any event, they were determined to oppose any German effort to dominate French Africa, although at the same time they were resolved to remain loyal to Pétain. Weygand and his associates furnished Murphy an elaborate analysis of their economic needs. They said the United States alone could bring salvation—the sooner the better because they feared lest the Germans should force the issue of North Africa in the spring and they wanted North Africa to be strong enough to resist effectively.

Both before and after Murphy's report, we held conversations at the State Department with representatives of the British Embassy to obtain a sufficient lifting of the blockade to permit the carrying out of an economic accord with North Africa. At first the British strongly demurred. Finally we handed the British, on January 27, a written statement of our proposal. We said that resumption of trade with French Morocco was desirable since without it the internal political situation might disintegrate. Also, it would keep the door open to a possible move of the French Government from France to Morocco, and would better enable General Weygand to maintain his position of opposition to a German invasion of French North Africa.

Britain replied with a note on February 7, agreeing in principle with our proposal, and also expressing her willingness to include Tunisia and Algeria along with Morocco—but adding a number of conditions. Among these was that we should press for the release of British and neutral shipping in Moroccan ports and get written undertakings from General Weygand as to his future attitude.

We were not too cordial to Britain's reply. Since our thought was to fortify French Morocco economically, we did not relish the conditions Britain sought to attach to our project. Seeing Halifax on February 10, I said to him point-blank that this Government was going forward with its arrangements to send gasoline, sugar, and certain other staple commodities to French Africa.

When Halifax remarked that Britain had hoped we would agree with her that our shipments should be made contingent on the turning over to the British of six or eight vessels in the Tangier-Moroccan area, I replied: "I believe we can be of more help to Britain in this matter by pursuing our course of conciliation and offering relief of food and goods than we could by making the turning over of the ships a condition precedent." I added that Britain, of course, could pursue her own policy in this respect.

Three days later we sent the British Embassy a note stating flatly that, in our opinion, it was urgently necessary to resume trade relations on a restricted basis with French North Africa if we were to prevent an economic breakdown in that area which might have far-reaching, perhaps disastrous, consequences. We had therefore decided to authorize at once the unblocking of the necessary funds to permit the shipment of a tanker of petroleum products to Casablanca. This would be the first step in a program the United States Government proposed to pursue with a view to furnishing minimum and urgently needed supplies to French North Africa.

We immediately instructed Murphy to work out an agreement with Weygand for the shipment of petroleum, sugar, tea, coal, and other products urgently needed, for which sufficient French funds in the United States would be unblocked. These products would be entirely for local consumption. Weygand initialed an agreement on February 26, and Vichy approved on March 10.

Under the accord the United States would supply French North Africa with needed American products, provided they were consumed locally and were not allowed to accumulate. They would be carried by French ships now tied up in our ports, thus avoiding any diversion of shipping from the all-important route to Britain, and the vessels would be returned to the United States after each voyage. American officials would be sent to North Africa to supervise the shipments in North African ports and on the railroads.

The accord was concluded at a moment when dispatches were reaching my desk telling of ever increased infiltration of German officials and agents in North Africa. The German Armistice Commission was rapidly replacing the Italian Commission and seemed likely to take control of the carrying out of the armistice terms.

Consequently the clause permitting us to send American officials to North Africa to superintend the execution of the economic accord was of immense value to us. We immediately recognized its great possibilities extending well beyond the economic accord into the political and military fields. We suggested to the War and Navy Departments that they send officers who could observe the military and naval situation in North Africa while carrying on their control work under the economic accord. As a result, various officers in civilian clothes went to North Africa as vice consuls to serve as "technical assistants." We instructed Robert D. Murphy to remain in Algiers to supervise the control organization and the consulates, reporting on all matters of political, economic, or military interest.

In due course we had an efficient staff of control officials in North Africa, watching events like a thousand hawks. They were indispensable in preparing the ground for our invasion of North Africa in November, 1942.

The British came to approve our accord with North Africa and to urge us to further steps in this direction. But they failed to appreciate that our policy toward North Africa was only part of our over-all policy toward Vichy. They raised obstacles to our project of sending relief supplies to unoccupied France. The President and I felt that, if we were really to influence the conduct of Vichy foreign policy, we had to accede, at least in part, to Vichy's incessant requests for some relief. We could go along with the British attitude of no relief to the rest of France and the Low Countries, where the Germans were in occupation; but something had to be done, under rigid supervision, for unoccupied France or we would find Darlan and his group, aided by Laval, using our lack of help to embitter still further the relations between Vichy and Britain, and pushing Vichy closer to Hitler.

When French Ambassador Henry-Haye on March 7 repeated to me his usual impassioned plea for the relief of Vichy France, I said I intended to present earnestly all aspects of the question to Ambassador Halifax who was due to call at my office within a few minutes. I reminded him we were doing the very best possible without undertaking to bludgeon the British.

A little later, when Halifax came to my office, I said to him emphatically: "Unless the British allow a little flexibility in this matter, the French will become further inflamed against you and against us as well, and we cannot then be responsible for keeping the French fleet out of German hands. We have been working day and night with respect to the fleet and other problems, including that of discouraging actual fighting between France and Britain."

Adding that the French were making frequent representations, I said: "There may be an early explosion, and I feel that you should know this. Lazarus, in a state of great hunger, felt extremely grateful to the rich man when he was permitted to pick up a few crumbs that fell from the table—and this is still human nature today."

Halifax agreed to give the matter further attention and to let me hear from him soon.

The volcanic state of feeling in Vichy France over our failure to extend them relief was almost immediately demonstrated when Vice Premier Darlan, in a statement reported by press and radio, threatened to use French warships to break the British blockade.

Prime Minister Churchill thereupon appealed to the President on March 13 to attempt to reach a working agreement between Britain and France. Thereby Britain would allow a monthly ration of wheat to go through to unoccupied France and something to French North Africa in exchange for Vichy's limiting the infiltration of German officials into Morocco and French North African ports to the bare armistice terms and permitting an increasing number of French warships to move gradually from Toulon, in France proper, to Casablanca or Dakar.

A further communication from Britain asked us to send to French North Africa the greatest possible number of American observers, who should be of sufficiently high standing to counteract German infiltration and to discuss with the French the possibility of armed resistance.

With the exception of the observers, the British proposals did not seem to us acceptable. So far as we could see, there was little chance that Pétain would dare to engage in such open moves as would rouse Hitler's ire and reprisal.

I gave Ambassador Halifax on March 15 our views on Darlan's threat and Britain's proposals, as well as on our desire to get limited relief to unoccupied France. Relations between Britain and France, I said, were very delicate and there was danger that the situation might get out of hand. I commented that Darlan's threat, whether in earnest or a bluff, seemed to be more a move to secure favor with Hitler than to get relief for the French people. "The one supreme purpose of the Laval-Darlan groups," I added, "seems to be to whipsaw French sentiment around by utilizing the food-relief question in a most dastardly way. They thereby want to get the upper hand at Vichy, and with the support of changed French sentiment, turn the navy over to Hitler, and in many other disastrous ways deliver the best interests of France to Germany—as was contemplated by Laval before he was discovered and thrown out by Marshal Pétain."

The Ambassador, I said, could therefore readily understand the great concern of my Government in the question of relief to unoccupied France under the most rigid supervision, and why we had held repeated discussions with the British Government on this subject.

"We have purposely not undertaken to stand for an important *quid pro quo* formula," I explained, "for the reason that Darlan might turn away and charge that the British are more interested in the *quo* than in the *quid*. He might seek to make large capital of it on the charge of lack of sympathy for the distressed people of France."

The solution, I said, seemed to me that we should carry forward the proposal for some relief as a separate project, and carry on parallel conversations with the French with regard to the concessions the British wanted.

Halifax said his country was coming around slowly to our view. I replied that I thoroughly understood the psychology of the British in view of their dangerous situation.

On the same day I suggested to French Ambassador Henry-Haye that Britain and France should approach each other in a spirit of moderation and mutual concession so as to work out their difficulties. "The two countries," I said, "can well afford to select one outstanding man in each country who has the confidence of both countries and who could function together from day to day to promote understanding and to facilitate the solution of many or most of these questions."

When Henry-Haye again raised the question of relief for unoccupied France, I said that the American people continued to cherish their ancient friendship for the French and desired to serve them in every way feasible. But we also intended to aid the British as best we could in their efforts to defeat Hitler, and in doing so we were serving the cause of liberty of all the conquered countries of Europe as well as ourselves.

"We profoundly believe," I said, "that our friendship and aid to Britain are in complete harmony with our every desire to cooperate with the French to the fullest practical extent."

I pointed out, however, that we did not know just how far certain members of the French Government desired to go beyond the terms of the armistice. I commented that just before Admiral Darlan had made his loud threat against Great Britain a few days before, I had been making real progress in my discussions with the British on relief for unoccupied France, but that I had been seriously handicapped since then.

Saying that I felt we were again making progress, I added that it was important in my opinion for the French to indicate a spirit of cooperation in case Great Britain should permit the proposed boatloads of wheat to go to unoccupied France. This might include assurances of noninfiltration by Germans into North Africa, the working out by all countries concerned of a rigid supervision over the distribution of the wheat, any reasonable courtesies that could possibly be extended to the British regarding ship-ments in French boats, and the moving of French naval vessels from continental France to French African ports.

Through the Red Cross we went ahead with our plans for two ship-loads of wheat. Prime Minister Churchill, in a message to the President on March 29, agreed that the ships should go through. At this moment, however, violent criticism broke out in London on the part of a large segment of Government officials and Government-inspired newspapers, charging that the United States, in trying to send relief to unoccupied France even to this limited extent, lacked sufficient interest in the British cause and was aiding Darlan in his efforts to assist Hitler.

I called this to the attention of Lord Halifax on April 8 and said that to cancel the shipments would probably result in complete severance of anything like friendly working relations between the United States and France, with the result that the Pétain and Weygand elements in the Government would be superseded by the forces of Darlan bent primarily on aiding Hitler.

Halifax said he would favor going forward with the shipments, but asked for a little time in which to check his Government's final attitude.

I took this occasion to emphasize to him the connection between our policy toward French North Africa, which Britain had finally approved, and our policy of relief to Vichy France, which Britain had been oppos-ing. "If Pétain," I said, "should be overridden by the Darlan-Hitler forces, the whole structure of British-American plans for North Africa will crash to the ground. Weygand takes orders from Pétain. For this reason, it is vitally necessary to hold up the hands of the Pétain branch of the French Government at Vichy. We have been struggling almost daily since the French Government left Paris to uphold that element in the French Gov-ernment which opposes Hitlerism and Hitler. It is very tedious and delicate work, especially when many leading Britishers seem to have no comprehension of its nature and importance to them."

Britain undoubtedly was being influenced by the flood of rumors coming from many quarters in Europe that Hitler was about to advance into North Africa through Spain or through Italy to Libya. The British forces in Libya, weakened by the dispatch of troops to assist the Greeks, were being driven back toward Egypt by a combined German and Italian army.

Admiral Leahy was making wonderful progress in establishing close relations with Marshal Pétain, but all signs pointed to the fact that Darlan was acting more and more on his own and was maintaining suspiciously intimate contacts with the Germans. Pétain and Darlan continued to give Leahy full assurances that neither the fleet nor French North Africa would be turned over to the Germans, but we could have little faith in Darlan himself.

For my part I kept in the back of my mind the very definite information I had received in January that Hitler was making the most elaborate plans to attack Russia (see Chapter 70). It did not seem to me logical that he would extend himself in the western Mediterranean at the very moment he should be marshaling all his forces for an attack in the East.

Nevertheless I cabled Admiral Leahy on April 18 to protest very earnestly against German infiltration in French North Africa. And on the following day I discussed with Lord Halifax the possible steps that might be taken if Pétain should yield to the pro-Hitler influences in his Government. I said there might be left three courses for this and the British Government to pursue: "First, either we or the British protest strongly. Second, we or the British take definite action with the use of force to establish ourselves at Dakar or Casablanca."

Halifax interposed that neither of us was in position to do that. I nodded.

"Third, an attempt be made to get General Weygand to invite the British or some other force to come in and aid him against German invasion."

The third possibility seemed to me the most likely. "Weygand," I said, "has softened considerably toward the British-American viewpoint. Weygand has repeatedly said he would fight Germany if she came in. He has not only requested our cooperation in the sale and shipment of certain staple commodities to French North Africa for local use, but he has also earnestly requested the sale and shipment of certain munitions so that he might more effectively resist invasion by Germany or by any other country."

Halifax read to me a letter from Churchill in which the Prime Minister appeared mildly optimistic about North Africa. I said I was looking for still more reassurance.

The British Government, alarmed by the numerous reports of imminent danger to Syria and North and West Africa, and further reports that Hitler intended marching south through Spain, asked us on April 29 to transmit a strong message for them to Vichy asking the Vichy Government to join actively with them in resisting such movements and to permit the British and French fleets to act together in the eastern Mediterranean. The British also asked us to send naval units to Dakar and Casablanca.

As we studied the British message, it seemed to us that, since the Germans would inevitably learn of it from Vichy, it might provoke the very movements Britain feared. I asked Welles to inform Halifax that we preferred simply to have Leahy express strongly to Pétain our hope that he would reject any demand that went beyond the armistice terms. Halifax agreed.

We also informed Halifax that we had decided to negotiate directly with Vichy for the delivery of two shiploads of wheat to unoccupied France. We believed it was wise policy to assist Pétain in relieving distress in unoccupied France because we thereby made it easier for him to maintain his own position and prestige and, with the support of the French people, to resist German demands. We pointed out to Britain that all she was proposing was for us to continue to deliver sharp and often menacing messages for her to Pétain. We did not feel that our policy would be advanced by limiting ourselves to transmitting messages of this nature.

The wheat ships duly sailed, and arrived at Marseille on May 14.

69: Crisis at Vichy

VICE PREMIER DARLAN was already conducting a series of ominous negotiations with the Germans when our food ships reached Marseille. He had gone to Paris on May 3, 1941, and made a dangerous agreement with Hitler's representative, Otto Abetz. To assist the Germans in supporting the Nazi-instigated uprising against the British in Iraq, which had just broken out, France would make available to the Iraq rebels munitions and planes from near-by Syria. France would also permit German planes to use an airfield in northeastern Syria and would refuel and repair German planes in transit across Syria. France would supply General Rommel, the German commander in Libya, with a quantity of trucks from Tunisia. In return the French would receive a number of concessions, including a substantial reduction in the costs of occupation.

As we became aware, in general, of the French concessions, I sent Leahy on May 8 a personal message from the President to Pétain urging the latter to defend the French colonies against attack. Because Pétain was away, Leahy did not see him until May 13. Meantime Darlan had conferred with Hitler at Berchtesgaden on May 11 and 12. Pétain told Leahy he did not know what Darlan had accomplished, but promised in no event to give any voluntary active military aid to Germany.

Such vague assurances satisfied us not a whit. We had every reason to be apprehensive when Marshal Pétain made an extraordinary broadcast on May 15, following Darlan's return to Vichy. Pétain, prefacing that he approved Darlan's negotiations with the Germans in principle, said: "If, through our close discipline and our public spirit, we can conduct the negotiations in progress, France will surmount her defeat and preserve in the world her rank as a European and colonial power."

I went to the White House, accompanied by Welles, to talk this new situation over with the President. In consequence, the President issued a public statement recalling Pétain's past assurances, and concluding: "The people of the United States can hardly believe that the present Government of France could be brought to lend itself to a plan of voluntary alliance, implied or otherwise, which would apparently deliver up France and its colonial Empire, including French African colonies and their Atlantic coasts with the menace which that involves to the peace and safety of the Western Hemisphere."

On the same day the President ordered the Coast Guard to take custody of the French merchantmen in American ports.

I then suggested to the President that in the near future we should proceed along three main lines:

"First, endeavor to ascertain just what can be salvaged through the Vichy Government by every kind of practicable, wise treatment. Second, in the same connection, examine all aspects of the matter thoroughly to ascertain what can be developed to our advantage from Weygand and the situation in Africa generally in return for cooperation by us. Third, keep in constant conference with the British."

I restated these points to Lord Halifax when he came to see me on May 19. I said to Halifax it was manifestly important for us to ascertain the probable relations of the British to the French while we were going forward with points one and two. "If the British get into open war with the French," I commented, "it would mean that this country would be directly influenced thereby, and naturally any effort to salvage much from the French situation would be rendered more or less impossible."

Halifax said he could not state what the future attitude of his Government would be, but he expressed his personal belief that the Vichy Government had not agreed to give Germany as much aid as Germany was seeking.

Darlan, however, went on with his negotiations with Abetz in Paris.

At this point Welles, who was somewhat in disagreement with my policy of proceeding cautiously though constantly, talked the President into agreeing to send a message to Congress which, in effect, would have placed within the Monroe Doctrine all of West Africa north of the Equator, belonging to Britain, France, Spain, Portugal, and Liberia, as well as the Atlantic islands. The President asked Welles on May 19 to draw up the draft of such a message. Welles did so and sent it to him the following day. This stated that "the seizure of, or control over, these areas, some of which are barely sixteen hundred miles from the coast of South America, by powers which are bent on world conquest, would constitute so immediate a threat to the peace and safety of the Western Hemisphere that the situation arising therefrom could not be regarded passively by the United States."

Welles showed me this draft before sending it to the President, and I at once said emphatically that such a message to Congress at that time would be most unwise. I then went to the President and argued against it. I said it would be an invitation to Germany to go into those African possessions. The Germans would say that, if the territory was as vital to our strategy as the President made out to Congress, they would have to occupy it. I also said that the message would provoke the fiercely vociferous resentment of the isolationists in and out of Congress. Mr. Roosevelt saw the validity of these arguments and abandoned the idea.

French Ambassador Henry-Haye on May 20 protested to me, on behalf of his Government, against our taking custody of the French ships. I replied that, in the light of the recent portentous announcement by Marshal Pétain, I had not even thought of shipping matters, and little would be done about it until we obtained a thorough clarification of the full significance of that announcement. Recalling Pétain's last assurances to us, I said:

"You can imagine the astonishment of peoples here and everywhere when they saw Pétain's announcement with its clear, express, and implied meanings. The definite belief was created in every nation of the world that the French Government at Vichy has gone straight into Hitler's arms, with all the implications of such a step, and that the well known pro-Hitler officials in the French Government have finally taken over control, their first thought being to deliver France body and soul to Hitler."

I emphasized that French officials, attempting to justify this new attitude, were referring to comparatively microscopic considerations such as food supplies, reducing the expenses of occupation, and the failure of somebody to aid France in 1940. These considerations, I pointed out, were but infinitesimal contrasted with the single important question of saving the liberties of all free countries by successfully resisting Hitler's march of devastation across the earth.

I added that the United States was thoroughly dedicated to the success of the British. "Therefore," I said, "any military aid rendered to Germany beyond the strict terms of the armistice is an attempt to slit the throat of the United States indirectly. Hence the deep feeling this country has in the reported new plan of 'collaboration' between the Vichy Government and Germany."

As for Syria, Henry-Haye asserted that the armistice terms had authorized the Germans to control the air bases there. I recalled to him that when France assumed the mandate over Syria she signed a pledge to the United States not to permit any interference with the sovereignty of Syria by any other nation.

"This obligation by France," I said, "was not even raised by her at the time of the armistice. Furthermore, the retention by Germany of control over French air bases in Syria would ordinarily contemplate control to prevent their undesirable use to the detriment of Germany. It does not mean a complete license to Germany to transport any and all kinds of implements and supplies anywhere over Syria, which is exactly what Germany needs to establish a great base of operations against the British throughout the Middle Eastern area."

We nevertheless decided to go ahead with our economic accord with French North Africa as Robert D. Murphy reported to me from Algiers that Weygand's attitude was unchanged. The General reiterated the assurances he had already given that he would do his best to defend North Africa against any aggression, and that the supplies we had agreed to send him under the accord were more urgently needed than ever.

The British took our decision with some disappointment, but we pointed out that, if Weygand were now to lose the assistance we had promised, he obviously would believe that no help of any kind could possibly come from the United States, no matter what his attitude was, and in that event he might materially change his present stand.

The President and I now met with heavy pressure from various quarters, both in Britain and in the United States, to recognize General de Gaulle's Free French movement as the Government of France. This pressure reached an emotional climax when the British and American press carried many dispatches reporting Darlan's meetings with the Germans and the pro-German utterances of Darlan and his followers.

Neither the President nor I, however, could see any benefit to be derived from recognizing De Gaulle. Such recognition would have meant the repudiation of our universal policy of noninterference in the internal affairs of another country. It would have meant a complete break with Vichy, the withdrawal of our diplomatic mission there and of our consular staffs in cities of metropolitan France. It would have left the field clear for the collaborationists. It would have resulted in a rupture of the fruitful contact we were maintaining with Weygand in North Africa and the recall of all our officials in Morocco, Tunisia, Algeria, and French West Africa.

The Free French propagandists, at De Gaulle's urging or with his acquiescence, acted at times as if the United States were their enemy, and brought us under the bitterest attack. During my period in office, De Gaulle showed few signs of political acumen, being more likely than not to go off on tangents. Desperately temperamental, he was withal keen and, when he acted normally, he had excellent capacities. The President and I early adopted the view that we should do nothing that would impose De Gaulle upon the French as their future ruler. We determined that the French themselves must be left with full freedom, when the appropriate time came, to choose their own Government. According to dispatches from our Embassy in Vichy at the time, there was more popular support in unoccupied France for Marshal Pétain than for De Gaulle, even though a great majority of the people wanted Britain to win the war.

As the pressure on the President and me reached a peak of intensity, British Ambassador Halifax came to my office on May 21 and asked whether we felt we could recognize De Gaulle in any more conspicuous way than heretofore.

"We are trying, of course, to salvage whatever we can," I replied, "from Weygand's situation in Africa, and from the Government at Vichy. If Weygand stands up, De Gaulle will have to become subordinate." To this Halifax agreed.

With concentrated pressure being exerted on the Administration to recognize De Gaulle's movement and break with Vichy, I said to my associates at the State Department that it might be necessary—although I would fight against it—to adopt the attitude of the colored youth who boasted that he could ride any horse in the community. "He was given a prompt tryout," I said. "When he got astride the horse and started him off, the animal immediately reared up into the air in different directions. The rider was pitched across a fence into a plowed field. He promptly got up and as he clawed the dirt out of his eyes, ears, and mouth, he said: 'Now you see, gentlemen, when I discover that a horse is going to throw me, I just get off.' "

The pressure and propaganda on the part of De Gaulle's friends continued in waves of intensity, as such pressure usually does, throughout the war, but the President and I were able to hew consistently to the line we early adopted.

Darlan and Abetz, after some days of negotiation, reached an agreement on May 28. It fulfilled our worst expectation. In addition to the use of Syria, provided for in the earlier agreement, France agreed to let the Germans use the port of Bizerte in Tunisia and the railroad from Bizerte to Gabès for transport to Libya; French merchantmen, convoyed by French warships, would carry supplies across the Mediterranean; French trucks and guns were to be sold to the Germans; and Dakar in West

Africa was to serve as a supply base for German submarines, warships, and planes.

After Darlan returned to Vichy and the substance of his agreement with the Germans leaked out, there began one of the most fateful discussions of the war. Pétain appeared at first to know nothing about Darlan's concessions, but when he learned that Bizerte and Dakar were to be made available to the Germans, he agreed to summon Weygand and Boisson to Vichy for conference. As Admiral Leahy learned of what Darlan had agreed to, he brought all the pressure he possibly could upon any member of the French Cabinet with whom he had contact, while keeping in close touch with the State Department. The Cabinet members were almost entirely with Darlan, believing his argument that Hitler would take North Africa by force through Spain if France rejected the agreement.

Leahy cabled me a conversation with Darlan on June 4, quoting him as saying that if Germany attacked Russia the offensive would last no longer than the Greek and Yugoslav "affairs"; there was no likelihood of starving Germany; German manpower was immense; Britain could not win; and if the war continued Communism would prevail in Europe. He said France was like a prostrate man with a great stone on his chest which, if he were to live, he had to push off by all means in his power.

But now we were to see the ripening of the fruits of our many months spent in carefully developing closer and substantial relations with French Africa. Weygand and Boisson threw all their weight against the Darlan agreement. They bluntly refused to allow the Germans to take over Bizerte or Dakar. Weygand predicted a popular uprising both in France and North Africa if the agreement went into effect. Leahy added his influence to theirs, and Pétain began to see that carrying out the agreement would possibly mean a break of diplomatic relations with the United States and war with Great Britain.

I made a public statement of our position on June 5. After reviewing our many efforts to help France, including the sending of food to unoccupied France and supplies to the African colonies, and the preservation of France's possessions in the Western Hemisphere, I said:

"It would seem scarcely believable that the French Government at Vichy should adopt the policy of collaboration with other powers for the purpose of aggression and oppression, despite indications appearing in our preliminary reports. Such action would not only be yielding priceless rights and interests beyond the requirements of a harsh armistice but it would at once place France in substantial political and military subservience and would also make her, in part, the instrument of aggression against many other peoples and nations. This could only be utterly inimical to the just rights of other countries, to say nothing of its ultimate effects on the liberties, the true interests, and the welfare of the people of France."

Finally, on the following day, Pétain swung away from the majority of his Cabinet and decided that the agreement had to be reconsidered. What could well have been an unsurmountable crisis in our relations with Vichy was averted.

The agreement previously negotiated with regard to Syria, however, went into effect, and, as the Germans began using Syria as a base for supporting the rebellion in Iraq, the British, aided by the Free French, invaded Syria on June 8.

French Ambassador Henry-Haye came to see me the following day. He at once pointed with theatrical sadness to the spectacle of the British attacking the French in Syria without, in his opinion, any justification whatever.

I remarked that, ever since the French capitulation, my Government and I had worked incessantly for a betterment of relations between the British and the French. We had pleaded the French cause so strongly that in many instances we had obtained reversals of decisions by the British Government with respect to blockade measures and other conditions affecting the lives of Frenchmen.

"We will continue most diligently our effort to better the conditions under which the French people are now living," I added. "And there is no force on earth that can move us from our determination to continue this policy except if the French Government itself turns its back upon the friendly cooperation we are offering and adopts closer collaboration with the forces of conquest that are seeking to destroy Great Britain and endanger the security of our own country."

As for Syria, I emphasized that the French had not defended themselves in Syria against the Germans when the Nazis made use of Syrian airports beyond the requirements of the armistice and in violation of the agreement of 1924 between the French and American Governments to preserve the sovereignty of Syria.

"A distinction must be made," I added, "between the small, local aspect—the Syrian developments—and the larger issue, which is that

Germany must have Syria in connection with her military operations toward Iraq and the Suez Canal. Any action by the French authorities in permitting the use of facilities in Syria for the further extension of German military operations in the Near East affects the fundamental position of the British. It is most regrettable that France cannot see the larger element in this new development, which is far more important to French interests and the future of all Frenchmen than the smaller, more immediate, and local issue of Syria. I feel that the French Government should realize that this is an issue that touches upon the very foundation of the future continuance of French life, independence, and civilization."

The campaign in Syria lasted five weeks, ending on July 14. We played an important part in the negotiations leading to the armistice, acting as a channel for communications between the British and French Governments and permitting Cornelius Van H. Engert, our Consul General at Beirut, to serve as intermediary between the British and French commanding generals. Syria had been pulled from the hands of the Germans.

We had also taken strong diplomatic action in Bagdad to help the British smooth out their difficulties with Iraq. We received the thanks of Churchill's Government both for this assistance and for our work in Syria.

But an invasion of far greater moment than that of Syria had begun two weeks after the British crossed the Syrian frontier. Hitler was pouring his troops into Russia, and the whole emphasis of the war shifted for the time being to the East. It therefore seemed less likely that Hitler would dispatch an army to French North Africa. Vichy France had a breathing spell, and we as well.

What was probably the most dangerous period of our relations with Vichy, culminating in our narrow escape when Marshal Pétain almost agreed to Darlan's sweeping agreement with the Germans, had come and gone. This period provided ample justification for our policy toward Vichy France, particularly that toward Weygand and French North Africa. Britain alternately approved and disapproved of our stand on Vichy and North Africa, but the President and I never wavered in adopting and sticking to a consistent policy. On the one hand we resisted the emotional wave in favor of breaking with the legal Government at Vichy and recognizing as the Government of France General de Gaulle's group which as yet had apparently won comparatively little following among the French. And on the other we passed by no opportunity to show Pétain and his group how we felt about any concessions to the Germans, while

THE MEMOIRS OF CORDELL HULL

at the same time demonstrating through concrete actions what assistance they might expect from us if they lived within the terms of the armistice. The United States came through the crisis as the strongest foreign influence in Vichy.

70: We Help Russia

I WAS ILL AT HOME when word of Hitler's invasion of Russia on June 22 reached me. Immediately I telephoned the President and then Under Secretary Welles. To each I said, in effect:

"We must give Russia all aid to the hilt. We have repeatedly said we will give all the help we can to any nation resisting the Axis. There can be no doubt for a moment that Russia comes within that category."

I also telephoned some of my associates in the State Department to emphasize to them the same point of view. I would have gone to the Department, but my doctor refused to allow it. He insisted that I leave Washington for a rest, which I did the following day, going to White Sulphur Springs, West Virginia.

From there I kept in touch with the State Department by long-distance telephone and by courier. I emphasized again and again to my associates that we should take every step to aid the Soviets. I knew that some military experts both here and abroad were predicting that Hitler would eliminate Russia from the war in a matter of a few weeks. But I could not believe it any more than I had believed the statements of so many that, with the fall of France, the collapse of Britain would be a matter of a few weeks. I had felt that, in rushing vast quantities of weapons to Britain in the summer of 1940, we were taking no real risk that they would fall into German hands. And similarly I believed we could send Russia all weapons and supplies possible without real risk that the Germans would overrun and capture them. If the President and I had doubted Russia's ability to resist Germany, it would have been foolhardy to send her arms that would only have fallen into Hitler's hands.

For half a year we had had excellent reason to believe Hitler would attack Russia, hence the event of June 22 did not surprise us. In January, 1941, there came to me a confidential report from Sam E. Woods, our commercial attaché in Berlin. Woods had a German friend who, though an enemy of the Nazis, was closely connected with the Reichs ministries, the Reichsbank and high Party members. As early as August, 1940, this friend informed Woods that conferences were then taking place at Hitler's headquarters concerning preparations for war against Russia. This information became more concrete after some weeks, when Hitler reportedly said he intended to have "only my soldiers from Vladivostok to Gibraltar."

Woods used to meet this friend in a Berlin motion-picture house. By buying reserved seats from an agency and sending a ticket to Woods, the friend managed to sit alongside him and in the semidarkness slipped notes into Woods's coat pocket.

The information from Woods was in marked contrast to the considerable evidence that Hitler was planning an invasion of Britain, but the contacts of Woods's friend said that the air raids against England served as a blind for Hitler's real and well calculated plans and preparations for a sudden, devastating attack on Russia.

Later Woods's friend informed him that an organization of the Wehrmacht for the old twenty-one Russian Czarist regional governments had been formed, and that the economic staffs for these territories had been appointed. Bales of banknotes in rubles had been printed.

Finally, through a contact this friend had on the German General Staff, Woods learned the chief points of Hitler's strategic plan: the three wedges, those of the North and the South and the decisive third one in the center, direct against Moscow. All preparations had to be completed in the spring of 1941.

When Woods's report embracing all this information came to me it was so circumstantial that, at first, I believed it a German "plant." I turned it over to J. Edgar Hoover, Chief of the Federal Bureau of Investigation, for his comment. Hoover thought it authentic. Woods having told us of a method of confirming the standing and contacts of the source by checking with a prominent German exile in the United States, I asked Assistant Secretary of State Breckinridge Long to see him and obtain this confirmation, which he did. I also talked over the report with the President.

I then decided that the contents of the report should be communicated to Soviet Ambassador Oumansky. Such a step, I believed, was in keeping with the proper attitude this country should take toward Russia. I requested Welles, who at my suggestion had been holding a series of conversations with Oumansky to straighten out the differences between our two countries, to call this information to the Ambassador's attention. This Welles did.

When further information from the same source came to me, I again turned it over to Welles, requesting him to communicate it to Oumansky. This he did on March 20.

Oumansky no doubt forwarded this information to his Government, as he said he would. It is difficult to say what precise effect it had on

Soviet policy. Only three weeks later, however, Stalin suddenly concluded a nonaggression treaty with Japanese Foreign Minister Matsuoka at a moment when Matsuoka believed such a treaty impossible. There is no doubt that Stalin made the treaty to protect himself in the Far East in the belief that Hitler intended attacking him in Europe. Furthermore, Russia was adopting a stronger policy toward the Balkan countries than might have been expected in the face of Hitler's plans to absorb them into the Axis.

Although the Russo-German nonaggression pact had stimulated Hitler in August, 1939, to embark on the European War, and although Russia had shared with Germany the spoils in Eastern Europe, she nevertheless had interfered with and obstructed Hitler's purposes in many ways since June, 1940. We knew that Molotov's visit to Berlin in November, 1940, had served to exacerbate rather than improve relations between the two countries.

The information we had that Hitler was planning an invasion of Russia was particularly useful to me in my conversations with the Japanese. It ruled out any likelihood of an alliance between Russia and Japan, and it enabled us to adopt a firmer attitude toward Japan than would otherwise have been the case.

We on our part were constantly pressing for better relations with Russia. On January 21 we lifted the moral embargo against her which had been in effect since her invasion of Finland in December, 1939. Actually, this comported no material difference since the articles previously embraced in the moral embargo were now included within the licensing system by virtue of the Act of July 2, 1940, and their exportation was therefore strictly controlled. However, it was designed to have a psychological effect.

To me it was evident that, even if Russia were standing asleep like a piece of statuary, she would still be a powerful influence in the war. She was keeping Hitler guessing, notwithstanding the agreements they had for closer relations. When Hitler made any kind of military move that looked bad for Russia, Moscow became meek. But when Hitler failed to invade Britain or overcome her in the air, and when Italy failed in the campaigns in Greece and North Africa, then Russia persuaded Bulgaria temporarily to resist Hitler's pressure to join the Axis. No one could tell what Russia would do, except that she would prepare to defend herself and at the same time do everything in her power to avoid an attack from Germany.

One of the first questions Lord Halifax took up with me after his arrival in this country as British Ambassador was a suggestion from his Government that we ration our exports to Russia. He said to me on February 5 that Britain feared that considerable supplies were passing through Russia to Germany. He handed me a memorandum which noted increased Russian purchases in the United States.

I informed Halifax that we had been observing our trade situation with Russia on a weekly basis and thus far it was our opinion that, while certain exports to Russia had considerably increased, there had not been an alarming increase.

"Russia," I added, "whether very active or sound asleep, is and will continue to be a tremendous factor in the war and likewise in questions affecting peace generally, both in Europe and in Asia. Russian officials are very sensitive when prodded, and Russia is calculated to go some distance in showing her displeasure—much farther, in fact, than she would ordinarily go to indicate her pleasure and satisfaction with respect to some favor done her.

"Since Russia entered into the agreement with Germany leading up to the war and since she occupied the Baltic, Polish, and other areas, she has consistently pursued her policy of seeking to drive hard bargains, especially with Germany and Japan or in areas where they are immediately interested. The sum total of her course and attitude during past months has been to obstruct and to cause miscarriage of many elaborate plans of Hitler or the Japanese, or their joint plans. Of course, the Russians are not thinking of aiding any of us while thus seriously slowing down and disrupting Hitler's plans, especially with respect to the Mediterranean and Suez Canal areas."

Since London had published the fact that Britain planned to ask the United States to impose embargoes against Russia, I said: "I doubt whether your Government is now receiving as much information from Moscow as before, and doubtless not as much cordiality, although the period through which we are passing renders it all-important that Great Britain should be on as good relations as possible with Russia."

I then rehearsed to Halifax the course we had been pursuing with the Soviet Union since the summer before, carrying on frequent conferences with the Soviet Ambassador to remove many small grievances on both sides. "Our purpose," I said, "is to give less occasion for Soviet officials to feel unkindly toward this Government, especially in the event of some pivotal development where the slightest influence might tip the scales at

Moscow against us in a most damaging, far-reaching way." And I added frankly: "I feel that Britain is tipping the scales when she presents publicly such proposals as calling on this Government to impose an embargo against Russia." The Ambassador seemed to agree entirely.

When Halifax came back to see me five days later, I said I must again refer to the lack of disposition on the part of Great Britain to endeavor to promote better relations with France and Russia. "I don't say this by way of criticism," I commented, "but, as you well know, this Government is intensely interested in the course of France and Russia during coming months. This is especially so at highly critical or pivotal stages where their action or attitude might tip the scales of war either way.".

Unfortunately, the discussions between Oumansky and Welles broke down, or rather blew up in an explosive, acrimonious exchange between them. Oumansky, who thought that firmness meant rudeness, was difficult to deal with at best. Moreover, he was put on the spot by his Government, which demanded much more in purchases of key materials than we could release in view of our commitments to Britain, and looked to Oumansky to obtain them.

Oumansky came to me in a dark mood on May 14 and spent the first twenty minutes of our conversation in rehearsing the differences between our two Governments which he said he had vainly discussed with Welles twenty-two times since the preceding summer. He then handed me a communication signed by himself, referring to a delay in the departure of a shipload of material to Russia. His note spoke of our "hostile attitude" toward his Government and threatened that his Government would "draw all necessary conclusions" from our attitude. He then repeated orally two or three times that our action was due to hostility to his Government and was a personal act due to personal hostility.

I halted him at that point by saying: "When I think of a country I think of the people more than of the government. Neither I nor my Government has the least hostility toward the people of any country. In the case of the Soviet Union and its Government I have not the slightest feeling of personal hostility, nor has my Government. It is not only entirely inaccurate but grossly unfair to impute personal considerations in the slightest extent to actions of this Government. I don't propose that you shall get away from my office with any thought that you have successfully fastened that charge on this Government since it is absolutely without basis."

I then restated our position toward Hitler's world-wide movement of conquest and our determination to exert ourselves to the utmost to see that Hitler did not get control of the high seas, which would include Britain. Amidst all our preparations for our own defense and our aid to Britain, it was not possible to deal normally with neutral countries in a commercial way.

"We've suffered great losses of our regular exports to Great Britain," I continued, "in the way of apples, tobacco, cotton, and other agricultural products, due to Britain's war measures. While we felt this to be a painful experience, we never thought of treating such a thing as personal any more than did the many countries in Europe whose assets we have frozen. The Soviet Government has suffered less and complained more about the unavoidable difficulties incident to opposing Hitler than any other two or three countries whose assets we've frozen or whose commerce we've interrupted under compelling war conditions."

I reminded Oumansky that his country was maintaining commercial relations with Germany but failed to recognize this fact when my Government sought to prevent military supplies from filtering through Russia to Germany.

Oumansky asserted that Russia, being a neutral, had all the privileges of a neutral.

I recalled to him that during the First World War the best friends the United States had anywhere were the Scandinavian countries. They assured us we could sell any quantities of materials to them and they would be sure to let no amount above normal exports get across to Germany. Later, however, we discovered that merchants were still shipping vast quantities through to Germany, with the result that we embargoed all exports to those countries above the prewar level. "But," I added, "they were the last people to think for a moment about taking offense— much less treating it as personal."

As Oumansky did not argue further, I ended the conversation by saying we had been friends of the Russian people both before and after our recognition of the Soviet Union in 1933. The discussion had been a little animated.

On the eve of Hitler's invasion of Russia, our policy toward the Soviet Union embraced these points:

Make no approaches to Russia.

Treat any approaches toward us with reserve until the Russians satisfied us they were not maneuvering merely to obtain unilateral concessions for themselves.

Reject any Soviet suggestions that we make concessions for the sake of improving American-Soviet relations, and require a strict *quid pro quo.*

Make no sacrifices of principle in order to better relations.

Let Russia understand that we considered an .improvement in relations to be just as important, if not more so, to Russia than to the United States.

Make the principle of reciprocity the basis of our day-to-day relations.

In general our policy toward Russia was one of firmness but friendliness.

The first week in June we received convincing cables from our Legations in Bucharest and Stockholm that Germany would invade Russia within a fortnight. The Department sent these reports to Ambassador Steinhardt in Moscow.

Eight days before Hitler marched into Russia, Prime Minister Churchill sent the President a message saying that, from every source at his disposal, it looked to him as if a vast German onslaught on Russia were imminent. If the new war broke out, he said, Britain would of course give all encouragement and any help she could spare to the Russians, on the principle that Hitler was the foe she had to beat. He said he did not expect any class political reactions in England and trusted that a German-Russian conflict would not cause us any embarrassment.

The conflict caused us no embarrassment, and gave us renewed hope of overcoming Hitlerism. From White Sulphur Springs I was in constant touch with the President and Welles, urging that we give Russia the most vigorous assurances of all the help we could extend. The President sent Harry Hopkins from London to Moscow to survey Russia's military needs. Mr. Roosevelt released Soviet blocked funds, and decided not to apply the Neutrality Act. On August 2 Acting Secretary Welles and Ambassador Oumansky exchanged letters, we promising "to give all economic assistance practicable for the purpose of strengthening the Soviet Union in its struggle against armed aggression."

Immediately upon my return to Washington on August 4, I issued a statement saying that "no rational person needs any argument to convince him that during the weeks of my absence the most clinching demonstration has been given of what some of us for some years have insisted was being planned. That is, that there is a world movement of conquest by force, accompanied by methods of governing the conquered peoples that are rooted mainly in savagery and barbarism. That situation calls for . . . ever increasing production of military supplies both for ourselves and for those who are resisting the would-be world conquerors. . . . I feel very strongly that with unity of purpose, maximum effort, and firm determination, the remaining free peoples of the world will win."

At about the same hour I saw Oumansky, who brought with him Soviet General Golikov. Oumansky's attitude was now quite different from what it had been at our last interview. I told him of the interest I had taken while I was away, and especially since my return, in seeing that Russia got all the military supplies we could spare. General Golikov said he had presented the needs of his Government to the State Department two weeks before, but the only result had been the shipment of sixty planes to Russia, and that Russia needed antiaircraft and antitank guns most of all. I offered to redouble my efforts to aid in speeding the delivery of these weapons.

As I talked to my Soviet visitors, the President was engaging in his Atlantic Conference with Prime Minister Churchill. Russia attracted an important segment of attention at the Atlantic Conference. After Harry Hopkins, who was present at the meeting, made an optimistic report on the Soviet Union's ability to resist Hitler's invasion, the President and the Prime Minister agreed on a statement to be given Stalin. The President wirelessed this to me on August 13, asking me to cable it to Moscow.

The two leaders assured Stalin: "We are at the moment cooperating to provide you with the very maximum of supplies that you most urgently need. Already many shiploads have left our shores and more will leave in the immediate future." They proposed a conference in Moscow to analyze Russia's needs, with high representatives of the United States and Britain going to Russia for this purpose.

The story of the Atlantic Conference has been narrated elsewhere at various times. While it was being prepared I was recuperating at White Sulphur Springs, and when I returned to Washington the President was already en route to his rendezvous. Mr. Roosevelt had cherished for several months the idea of a personal conference with Churchill. I first became aware of it the end of May.

Welles wrote me at White Sulphur Springs on July 28, stating that the conference had been arranged for August 8, 9, and 10, and telling me that he intended to urge the President, if he expected to discuss more than purely military problems, to take someone with him who could keep a precise record of the conversations and of the agreements that might be reached.

Much was accomplished at the conference in the way of bringing the President and the Prime Minister into close personal touch with each other's ideas. On the British battleship *Prince of Wales* and on our cruiser *Augusta* began that unique intimate relationship between two great men which did so much to speed the outcome of the war.

Their statement of the aims of the two countries set us a high goal. These aims embraced the right of peoples to choose their own form of government; no aggrandizement; no territorial changes opposed by the peoples concerned; access to trade and raw materials; improved labor standards, economic advancement, and social security; international security; freedom of the seas; and disarmament.

I publicly stated my reaction to the Atlantic Charter on August 14 by saying: "It is a statement of basic principles and fundamental ideas and policies that are universal in their practical application. They have heretofore been generally accepted by all civilized nations and were being strongly supported until certain countries decided to launch a universal movement to destroy the whole structure of civilized relations. . . . They are the basic doctrines and policies that have received the support of all civilized nations and should continue to receive their support until they are completely restored throughout the world."

I felt that our two nations could go no further in their statement of war or peace aims. In preceding months I had been asked frequently to bring pressure by this Government on Britain to make a formal statement of her war aims. I invariably replied to this effect: "If you see a peacefully disposed citizen engaged in a death grapple with another person, with pistols drawn and dirks raised, can you tap the peaceful man on the shoulder and ask him to stop and state his purposes before he goes any further defending himself?"

I was keenly disappointed, however, in the fourth article of the Atlantic Charter, referring to international trade. This stated that the two nations would endeavor, with due respect for their existing obligations, to further the enjoyment by all States, great or small, victor or vanquished, of access, on equal terms, to the trade and to the raw materials of the world which were needed for their economic prosperity. Unfortunately the phrase "with due respect for their existing obligations" deprived the article of virtually all significance since it meant that Britain would continue to retain her Empire tariff preferences against which I

had been fighting for eight years. Mr. Churchill had insisted on this qualification; Welles had argued for a stronger declaration; but Churchill said
he could not abandon Empire preference and, in any event, he would have
to communicate on this point with the Dominions, which fact would delay
the issuance of the Atlantic Charter. The President gave in.

After I learned the background of this article, I began negotiations
with Britain, through Halifax here and Ambassador Winant in London,
to work out a better understanding on this point. These negotiations bore
fruit in the Lend-Lease agreement with Britain in 1942 which promised
the elimination of all forms of discriminatory treatment in international
commerce.

The Atlantic meeting stimulated yet more our efforts to get military
supplies to Russia. The President and I were carefully following the cables
telling of the extent of Hitler's advances into Russia. Already our original
estimate that the Russians could hold out seemed likely to be proven true.

At this point Russia and Britain on August 25 jointly occupied Iran
as it became evident that Nazi propaganda and other means had under-
minded some of the leaders of the Iranian Government. The Allies could
not permit this dangerous situation to continue because of Iran's strategic position in the Middle East to the south of Russia.

I felt it was important, however, that Russia and Britain should make
clear to the world that they had no intention to occupy Iran permanently.
On August 27 I spoke to Soviet Ambassador Oumansky and to British
Chargé Sir Ronald Campbell on this score. Referring to the assurances
Britain and Russia had given to the Iranian Government that they were
in Iran solely because of the war with Hitler, with no purpose of infring-
ing on Iran's sovereignty or of remaining longer than military necessity
required, I suggested: "Russia and Britain should repeat this same assurance to all peaceful nations and all other nations opposed to aggression. Such a statement would have a very healthy and wholesome effect
on the entire Moslem world, even as it would be stimulating to the peoples
of small countries everywhere."

This suggestion was duly carried out by Britain and Russia.

The question of credits for Russia to enable her to cover large
purchases in the United States proved a difficult one at the beginning.
When Oumansky asked to see the President on this subject, Mr. Roosevelt asked Harry Hopkins and me to take part in the discussion on September 11.

The President frankly explained to Oumansky the extreme difficulty of getting the necessary Lend-Lease appropriations from Congress for Russia because of the unpopularity of Russia among large groups in the United States which exercised great political power in Congress. Referring to the fact that Russia did have churches and did permit religious worship under the 1936 Constitution, the President suggested that if Moscow could get some publicity back to this country regarding freedom of religion it might have a fine educational effect. He added the further suggestion that this publicity begin before the next Lend-Lease appropriations bill came up in Congress and before the mission he had named, headed by W. Averell Harriman, arrived in Moscow to discuss Soviet needs. Oumansky said he would attend to it.

(Harriman was bringing to the public service a vast experience in our business and industrial life. In working for the Government he exhibited a ready grasp of the important phases of international problems, and this equipment stood him and the Government in good stead when in 1943 he went to Moscow as United States Ambassador.)

The President said also to Oumansky that, to get a Lend-Lease proposal for Russia through Congress, we should have to have an official statement showing Russian assets, the amount of gold on hand, and also the barter that could be carried on between the two countries. He offered to purchase the maximum quantities of Russian manganese, chromium, and other commodities with the understanding that production and delivery need not take place until after the war.

Oumansky said he preferred a direct credit, but, if this were not possible, then his Government very earnestly would ask for Lend-Lease aid. We finally agreed on a credit and barter arrangement for $75,000,000 through the Reconstruction Finance Corporation to cover a few months during which adequate arrangements for Russian military supplies could be worked out.

We sought to aid Russia in another way by pulling off the two little countries that were clawing at her sides—Finland in the north and Rumania in the south. We had previously brought what pressure we could on Japan, through a message from President Roosevelt to Premier Konoye on July 6, to induce Japan to refrain from driving at Russia's back.

Finland and Rumania had entered the war against the Soviet Union on the side of Germany and were now advancing well into Russia. The Rumanians soon assured us they intended only to occupy the territories Russia had acquired from Rumania the year before, take up a strategic defensive position along the Dniester River, and then consider their obligations to Germany fulfilled. But the Finns offered us a greater problem, as well as a more important one, because a large portion of our aid to the Soviet Union would have to go to northern Russian ports that might be interfered with or blocked from Finnish territory.

I called Finnish Minister Hjalmar Procopé to my office on September 8 and, after expressing my gratification that Finland had regained possession of the territory Russia took from her in the war of 1939–1940, I said I had noted a statement reportedly made by General Mannerheim, Commanding General of the Finnish Army, that Finland would fight on until the end of the war between Germany and other countries. I said I felt justified in inquiring about this statement in view of our friendly relations and of the United States' concern over world conditions.

Procopé spoke vaguely about Finland's ambitions, giving his personal opinion that the Finns were occupying Russian territory only for the purpose of safeguarding their own lands, and that his Government did not intend to fight on to the conclusion of the general war.

I emphasized to the Minister our conviction that Hitler planned to conquer the world, and that therefore the United States could not remain quiet from the viewpoint of our own self-defense. As for Finland, if Hitler won, Finland would find herself entirely subject to his whims and dictates as the only friend she had left. And she would find that this so-called friend was demonstrably faithless and utterly disposed to disregard the rights and freedoms of all peoples coming under his control.

I pointed out to Procopé that Finland's position was similar to that of Rumania, and that Rumania had informed us that she would cease active hostilities against the Soviet Government when Odessa had fallen and the former Rumanian territory had been regained.

Procopé promised to report our conversation fully to his Government. However, he then launched into a series of relatively minor arguments against Communism and Stalin. Of an emotional nature, he could scarcely control himself.

I finally interrupted him by saying: "We have a record of opposition to Communism with which we are pleased. This record will always be continued in the future. But Hitler, instead of peacefully disseminating Hitlerism, which is very closely related to Communism and Fascism, proceeded for more than six years to assemble the greatest army and air force that has ever been organized in history. This was not for the purpose of defending himself but for conquering peaceful nations everywhere and securing control of the high seas without geographical limit."

I added that no desperado, individual or official, had ever been known voluntarily to abandon his occupation, and Hitler would not stop until somebody stopped him by force. "It is equally clear now to all rational countries," I went on, "that when Hitler is stopped—and I firmly believe he'll be stopped—some organized system involving the use of navies and aircraft, and so on, must be established to preserve the peace of the world against uprisings or movements of conquest by international bandits of the 100-per-cent stripe of Hitler. This long view is the only view for peace-loving nations to adopt if the world is to offer anything worthwhile to any country in the future; it is the only course that will make life worth while in any country, in Finland, and in all other peacefully inclined nations."

I remarked casually that, when Hitler was stopped, the United States might show a far greater and more important interest in Finland than we had at any time in the past.

When Procopé asked if we were going to war with Germany, I replied: "Hitler would like an answer to that question." The Minister agreed that was true. "We have shown considerable interest in resisting Hitler," I remarked, "and if you have any doubt on that score Hitler himself can assure you."

At the time I was bringing pressure on the Finnish Minister here, we were simultaneously bringing pressure on the Finnish Government through our Legation in Helsinki.

A few days later the Finnish Minister of Commerce and Industry made a statement in Helsinki that the Finns would soon be able to cease hostilities; they would stand on a defensive line they hoped soon to reach and would not take part in an attack against Leningrad. I felt sure this was a result of our representations to the Finns.

Therefore, when British Chargé Campbell handed me a note from his Government on September 17, suggesting that the United States might ask Russia for terms of peace for Finland and pass them on to Helsinki, I demurred. Under Secretary Welles had already, on August 18, notified Procopé that Russia was prepared to negotiate a peace with Finland which would involve territorial concessions by Russia, but this step had produced no results. I said I thought our present course of action was most likely to produce the best results, and commented that the Finns were in no mood to accept any assurances from the Soviet Government in view of the treatment they had received from the hands of that Government in the last two years.

Finland, however, became too impressed with the extent of the German advance into Russia, and continued her own operations. I called in Procopé on several additional occasions and emphasized how shortsighted I considered such a course. "Finland's advances," I said on October 3, "will signify exactly nothing at the peace table. It all depends on who wins the war. If Finland persists in these excesses, then you and your Government must understand clearly and definitely that the United States is with Great Britain in every sense, and any other course for us would be suicidal."

I sent the Finnish Government formal notes on October 25 and 28 so strong that they fell just short of a breach of relations. I said that Finnish military operations were giving infinitely valuable military aid to Nazi world aggression and, without contributing to Finland's future security, were thus a direct threat to our own security. If Finland did not desist, she must clearly understand that she would forfeit our friendly support in the future difficulties that would inexorably arise from her course of action. Furthermore, any attack made from Finnish-controlled territory on war material dispatched from the United States via the Arctic Ocean to northern Russia would create an immediate crisis in Finnish-American relations.

The following day British Ambassador Halifax came to see me and stated that Russia desired Britain to declare war against Finland. He asked our opinion. I informed him of our note to Finland and said this paved the way for further action at any time. However, I could not express an opinion as to what Britain should do in the situation.

I made a public statement of our attitude on November 28. The Finnish Foreign Minister having recently journeyed to Berlin to join with Hitler's puppet governments over Europe in signing the Anti-Comintern Pact, I said this was highly significant and could not be explained away by propaganda attacks on nations engaged in defending themselves. Every recent act of the Finnish Government, I concluded, "has confirmed our apprehensions that it is fully cooperating with the Hitler forces."

In later months, after Britain had declared war on Finland and we were on the verge of severing diplomatic relations, Finland came to realize the wisdom of our advice and limited her military activities to holding a defensive line. It was then too late, however, for her to secure the advantages that she could have obtained from Russia had she acted earlier on our suggestions.

Our relations with Russia became ever closer in the autumn of 1941.

American and British missions—ours headed by W. Averell Harriman— met with the Russians at Moscow from September 29 to October 1 and made arrangements to fill practically all Soviet requests for supplies. The President extended initial Lend-Lease aid to Russia in the amount of $1,000,000,000.

In token of Russia's appreciation of the importance of United States aid in her desperate struggle to resist the German advances, Stalin named a new Ambassador to the United States, the former Foreign Commissar Maxim Litvinov, whom I had come to know on several occasions. He arrived in Washington at almost the hour of the attack on Pearl Harbor.

71: We Talk with Japan

JAPAN ENTERED THE YEAR 1941 determined to wrest what further gain she could from the war in Europe, but still undecided as to when and where. In continental Europe she saw Hitler undisputed master, though his partner Mussolini was suffering serious setbacks in Greece and North Africa, and Britain was gaining strength. In Asia she saw her troops in China still tied down in inconclusive fighting. To the north she saw Russia, of unpredictable strength, maintaining an alert neutrality that required Japan to keep large armies along the Manchurian and Mongolian borders. In the New World she saw the United States engaged in a stupendous program of rearmament and assistance to the Allies.

There was one element of certainty in this situation. As long as the European countries were enmeshed in their own struggle and the United States was aiding Britain to the fullest extent possible, the Western nations had neither the power nor the inclination to throw their main weight into the Orient. But there were also elements of uncertainty. Russia was one, although it was a safe conclusion that Stalin would do all he could to refrain from getting into war with either Germany or Japan. The United States was another and the most important.

In January, 1941, our position as a Government had been made clear. We regarded Japan as an ally of Hitler and Mussolini, a signatory to an alliance aimed at us. We considered Japan's expansionist ambitions an eventual danger to our own safety.

"Previous experience and current developments," I said to the House Foreign Affairs Committee on January 13, "indicate that the proposed 'new order' in the Pacific area means, politically, domination by one country. It means, economically, employment of the resources of the area concerned for the benefit of that country and to the ultimate impoverishment of other parts of the area and exclusion of the interests of other countries. It means, socially, the destruction of personal liberties and the reduction of the conquered peoples to the role of inferiors.

"It should be manifest to every person that such a program for the subjugation and ruthless exploitation by one country of nearly one-half of the population of the world is a matter of immense significance, importance, and concern to every other nation wherever located."

Though the Japanese Government knew the President's feelings and mine, it did not know how far the United States Government would go in using pressure or force to oppose Nipponese plans for absorbing the entire Western Pacific. It was this uncertainty, as much as any other reason, that had kept her from launching out to seize the greatest opportunity of her history when France and Holland fell and Britain seemed about to fall.

Japan knew that our economic pressure was growing. By the beginning of 1941, shipments to her from the United States of iron, steel, most other important metals, high-octane gasoline, and plants for producing it had virtually ceased. We still permitted shipments of petroleum lest Japan use such an embargo as an excuse for taking over the oil production of the Netherlands East Indies. She also knew that our aid to China was growing. Beginning in January, the American Volunteer Group of airmen with American-made planes began to give the Chinese aerial support. And she also knew that the major portion of our fleet was still in the Pacific.

What Japan did not know was whether and in what circumstances we would use force. Isolationist sentiment in the United States was still strong, as the Lend-Lease debate in Congress showed. But she also saw that the Administration was acting with determination, and that an increasing number of Americans were coming to realize the dangers threatening us in both the Atlantic and the Pacific.

Members of the Japanese Government were giving vent to ever more bellicose statements, with Foreign Minister Matsuoka as their bellwether. Perhaps they hoped they could cow the United States, already preoccupied with Europe, into agreeing to a Japanese East Asia so as to avoid war. A Japanese East Asia meant Nipponese predominance in China, Malaya, French Indo-China, the Dutch East Indies, and the Philippines. Matsuoka said to the Japanese Diet on January 21 that he wanted the United States to realize the vital concern to Japan of the establishment of an East Asia "co-prosperity sphere," to agree to her supremacy in the Western Pacific, and to cease our economic restrictions against her. He aimed his speech at the statement I had made to the House Foreign Affairs Committee six days before.

In reply I issued a press statement on the following day, saying: "We have threatened no one, invaded no one, and surrounded no one. We have freely offered and now freely offer cooperation in peaceful life to all who wish it. This devotion to peaceful and friendly processes naturally warrants no implication of a desire to extend frontiers or assume hegemony. Our strategic line must depend primarily on the policies and courses of other nations."

Ambassador Grew cabled me from Tokyo on January 27 that the Peruvian envoy there said to him he had heard from many quarters, including a Japanese one, "that a surprise mass attack on Pearl Harbor was planned by the Japanese military forces in case of 'trouble' between Japan and the United States; that the attack would involve the use of all the Japanese military facilities." The Peruvian said to Grew he was prompted to pass this on because it had come to him from many sources, although the plan seemed fantastic. On the following day we communicated the contents of the cable to the War and Navy Departments.

It was at about this time and in these circumstances that two Catholic priests, Bishop James Edward Walsh, Superior General of the Catholic Foreign Mission Society, at Maryknoll, New York, and Father Drought, returned to the United States from Japan. They reported that they had talked to many highly placed Japanese, including Matsuoka; they realized that relations between the two countries were strained and that worse might follow, and they had a laudable desire to do whatever they could as private citizens to avert the prospect of war.

They saw on the one hand Postmaster General Frank C. Walker, one of the most prominent Catholics in the Administration, and on the other several members of the Japanese Embassy. Walker obtained an interview with the President for them late in January at which Walker and I were present. Bishop Walsh and Father Drought said it was their understanding, from their talks with highly placed Japanese, that the Japanese Government would welcome a chance to alter its political ties with the European Axis and its attitude toward China. They gave the opinion of the Japanese that, if Japan could obtain an agreement with the United States which would afford her security, the "moderate" elements there could gain predominance over the military elements. These Japanese thought there was sufficient support in the Japanese Government to bring about an agreement with the United States whereby Japan would recognize the "Open Door" in China provided she received similar treatment everywhere in the Far East. They believed that most Japanese, weary of the war in China, were prepared to see Japan reorient her policies toward peace.

The President and I, of course, had heard such opinions emanating from the liberal group in Japan before. Whatever the intentions of the liberals, the military group had virtually always been too strong for them. It was true enough that the Japanese people were tired of the war in China, but were they already too imbued with the propaganda of the jingoists to want to ignore the Heaven-sent opportunity of the war in Europe to create a Japanese East Asia? What the Catholic priests were telling us was in drastic contrast to what Matsuoka and many official leaders of Japan were proclaiming to the world.

At that very moment the Japanese were manifestly gaining control over the Government of Thailand. A border dispute between Thailand and French Indo-China, in the northern part of which lay a Japanese army, afforded them the chance they wanted. Seeing the Thai Minister, Mom Rajawongse Seni Pramoj, on January 13, I expressed my belief that Japan would "swallow up" both countries in due course, and urged the Thai Government to compose its differences with Indo-China at once.

When the British Chargé, Neville Butler, handed me on January 22 an *aide-mémoire* from his Government asking us to use our influence with both sides to end the border dispute, I promised Butler we would give his request every consideration. But I added: "I am not sure whether this Government will be able to do anything more than it is now doing. Japan probably is directing and controlling the course and attitude of Thailand toward Indo-China, and in these circumstances it may be very difficult to get the ear of the Thai Government."

We could therefore view the approach of Bishop Walsh and Father Drought only with caution. But they insisted that the proposal they had outlined was acceptable to many high Japanese officials and could be agreed to in Japan. The President and I were in accord that, for our part, we could not afford to neglect any chance to avoid a war in the Pacific. The menace of Hitlerism from across the Atlantic was sufficient to induce us to take any steps we could to keep our other flank peaceful.

Accordingly the President and I agreed that Bishop Walsh and Father Drought, along with Postmaster General Walker, should continue their contacts with the Japanese Embassy on a purely private basis and seek to reduce to writing what the Japanese had in mind. We felt, however, that we ourselves could not take any action until the new Japanese Ambassador, Admiral Kichisaburo Nomura, arrived in Washington.

Prior to Ambassador Nomura's arrival, I went over with the President in great detail the whole of our relations with Japan, and the prospects for reaching an agreement with Tokyo. I estimated right at the outset that there was not one chance of success in twenty or one in fifty or even one in a hundred. Japan's past and present record, her unconcealed ambitions, the opportunity for aggrandizement lying before her while embroiled Europe demanded a large part of our attention, and the basic divergence between our outlooks on international relations, were all against the possibility of such an accord.

The President and I agreed that the existing treaties relating to the Far East were sufficient, provided the signatories, meaning especially Japan, lived up to them. There was no real need for new agreements—but if new agreements would contribute to peace in the Pacific, we believed we should not throw the chance away, however microscopic it was.

We realized that the danger in the Far East was constantly growing. We appreciated the gravity of the situation in Europe and on the Atlantic. We knew that the territory we had to defend was vast, that our armaments had to be built up, that at the same time we had to supply war materials for the defense of the Western Hemisphere, the British Isles, the Near East, and the Far East. We took cognizance of the fact that our own public opinion was divided on the issues confronting us in Europe and the Orient. We had in the forefront of our minds the advice repeatedly given us by our highest military officers that they needed time to prepare the defenses vital to ourselves as well as to the countries resisting aggression. We had before us the statements made to us by the British, Australian, and Netherlands Governments that they were dangerously vulnerable in the Far East. We foresaw the far-reaching consequences to the whole world that would follow the outbreak of war in the Pacific.

Consequently, the President and I agreed that we would do whatever we could to bring about a peaceful, fair, and stabilizing settlement of the whole Pacific question. We knew we would have to be patient, because the Japanese Government could not, even if it wished, abruptly put into reverse Japan's march of aggression. Implementation of promises Japan might make in any peaceful agreement would demand much time. But we also agreed that, while carrying no chip on our shoulders in our negotiations with Japan, we could not sacrifice basic principles without which peace would be illusory.

Ambassador Halifax reflected the British Government's view of relations with Japan when he said to me on February 20 that his Government was increasingly concerned over the dangerous outlook and hoped the United States might find further means of deterring the Japanese from a military and naval drive south to the Dutch East Indies and the Singapore area. I went over with Halifax the various steps we had already taken and told him we were watching the situation from every possible viewpoint.

Ambassador Nomura paid his first call on me on February 12. He was tall, robust, in fine health, with an open face, differing considerably in physique from the average Japanese. He spoke a certain—sometimes an uncertain—amount of English. His outstanding characteristic was solemnity, but he was much given to a mirthless chuckle and to bowing. I credit Nomura with having been honestly sincere in trying to avoid war between his country and mine.

In our first conversation we made no effort to go into the relations between our countries, reserving that for a triangular conversation with the President two days later. Mr. Roosevelt received Nomura most cordially, recalled their first meeting some twenty-odd years before, remarked that he proposed to call him Admiral rather than Ambassador, and said they were friends and could at all times talk candidly as friends. Then the President said that relations between our two countries were not good and in fact were getting worse. He pointed out that the American people were seriously concerned over Japan's movement southward and over her entry into the Tripartite Pact which seemed to give Hitler the power to decide whether she should enter the war.

The President also made the point that, while the American people were peace-minded and peace-observing, it would be extremely easy for an incident like the sinking of the *Maine* or of the *Panay* to cause an overnight uprising of American sentiment, more or less explosive, against the authors. He added that if he and I had not instantly dealt with the *Panay* incident in a calm manner there would probably have been a terrific inflammation of public sentiment in this country.

He then suggested that Nomura might find it advisable—as he himself did—to sit down with me and other State Department officials and review the important phases of relations between the two countries, at least during the previous four or five years, frankly discuss all their aspects, ascertain just when and how points of divergence developed and what their effects were, and bring the whole situation up to date to see if our relations could not be improved.

The President concluded by saying there was plenty of room in the Pacific for everybody, and that it would not do this country or Japan any good, but harm to both, to get into war.

Nomura kept nodding his head as the President spoke and promised to do anything he could to improve our relations. He frankly said, however, that his chief obstacle would be the military group in control in Tokyo.

Lord Halifax and Australian Minister Casey came to see me the following day to inquire about the conversation of the day before. I gave them a general outline of what had been said. I mentioned that I had told Nomura this:

"There is a real possibility of danger that cannot be overlooked by any of the peaceful countries. This is that the military group in control in Japan, by a sudden, unannounced movement, could any day send an expedition to the Netherlands East Indies and Singapore. Or they could, inch by inch and step by step, get down to advanced positions in and around Thailand and the harbor of Saïgon, Indo-China. This would leave the peacefully disposed elements in Japan, including the Japanese Ambassador to the United States, to express their amazement and to say that such actions were without their knowledge or consent."

I held my first extended conversation with Nomura on March 8 in my apartment at the Carlton Hotel. This was the first of some forty to fifty conversations between us until Pearl Harbor. They were invariably at night, in the study of my apartment, first at the Carlton and then at the Wardman Park Hotel. Nomura preferred to come to my apartment rather than to the State Department so as to keep our conversations as free as possible from publicity.

During the course of these discussions many blunt words were spoken point-blank, but our voices never rose from the level of a conversational tone. Nomura was very gentlemanly. As between us personally, relations were amicable.

These conversations were to prove very tiring to me since they went into detail after detail of our relations and were usually conducted at night after I had already put in a full day at the State Department. Our first several conversations were limited to ourselves. Later they embraced my advisers and Nomura's.

Joseph W. Ballantine, an outstanding Japanese expert of the Department, used to appear at my apartment at seven-forty-five, bring whatever documents were necessary, and talk them over with me. Nomura and his advisers came in shortly before eight-thirty, and the conversations usually went on until ten o'clock, sometimes ten-thirty. Ballantine then returned to the State Department to prepare a memorandum of the conversation.

My principal advisers throughout these conversations were Dr. Stanley K. Hornbeck, Political Adviser on Far Eastern Affairs; Maxwell M.

Hamilton, Chief of the Division of Far Eastern Affairs; and Ballantine. These officers had had long experience and training in oriental affairs, and were especially equipped for the work they performed in the Department.

In my first direct talk with Nomura I referred to the discussions Bishop Walsh and Father Drought had been conducting and said that, while I deeply appreciated their efforts and purposes and had told them so, I had also made it clear that on all official questions between our two Governments I could deal only with and through the duly authorized Ambassador of Japan. I added that I had informed them that I could not confer with them individually unless the Ambassador assumed the responsibility and initiative to that end.

I then outlined to Nomura the efforts I had made ever since 1933 to organize some forty nations into a movement toward liberal commerce, which efforts had been impeded by movements of military conquest in various parts of the world. I said I hoped Nomura might have something definite in mind that would offer a practical solution.

But Nomura had no concrete suggestions to offer. He said Japan would be very glad to make a peace with China that would combine something of the puppet Government at Nanking with Chiang Kai-shek's Government, but when I asked on what basis, he was silent. He did not clarify his Government's position in the Tripartite Pact with reference to the United States. On this point I said to him:

"The American people, who were long complacent with respect to dangerous international developments, have of late become very thoroughly aroused over movements by Japan and Germany presumably to take charge of the seas and continents for their own personal arbitrary control and profit at the expense of all other peoples. These apprehensions, of course, will continue as long as Hitler continues his avowed course of unlimited conquest and tyrannical rule and as long as the Japanese Army and Navy increase their occupation by force of other and distant areas."

Nomura said several times that Japan was not committed to courses of conquest, but I emphatically replied:

"As long as Japanese forces are all over China, and Japanese troops, planes, and warships are as far south as Thailand and Indo-China, accompanied by such threatening declarations as Japanese statesmen are making week after week, there can only be increasing concern by nations vitally interested in halting world conquest by force and barbaric methods of government."

Nomura commented that, if our embargoes continued to press his Government and the military group in control, the latter might well feel forced to proceed further in a naval or military way.

"I don't believe," I replied, "that that question should arise because the whole responsibility for military conquest rests entirely on your Government." It was Japan's movement of conquest that produced the embargoes; the embargoes did not produce the movement.

I pointed out that few nations ever enjoyed more friendly relations than our two countries for two generations until about the beginning of the 1930's. I revealed to him that, when I came to the State Department, one of my greatest ambitions was to work out a mutually satisfactory arrangement with respect to Japanese immigration into the United States— one of the bitterest points of Japanese resentment against us—so that Japanese could come into the United States on a basis of equality.

Two or three times I asked Nomura whether he were agreeable to pursuing the President's suggestion of our talking over past relations between our two Governments in an effort to reach a settlement. He indicated he was favorably disposed, but had nothing specific to suggest.

I concluded our conversation by emphasizing that it was the opinion of the President and others in the Administration that the British, beyond any reasonable doubt, would be able successfully to resist Hitler.

Less than a week later, on March 14, I took Nomura, at his request, to see the President. Nomura repeated to us that none of his people, with few exceptions, desired war with us. Matsuoka, he said, talked loudly for home consumption because he was ambitious politically, but Japan herself could not maintain such ambitious plans. He said Japan desired three things in China: good will, economic cooperation, and defense against Communism. She also wanted raw materials from neighboring countries. Remarking that the situation in Europe was increasingly disastrous, he said Japan and the United States should cooperate for peace.

Picking up Nomura's reference to Communism in China, the President remarked that the people of China were constituted very differently from those of Russia and had a philosophy that stabilized and guided them along much broader lines. China, he said, was not really communistic in the same sense as Russia, and Japan had an undue fear of Communism in China.

He commented that the Tripartite agreement had upset the American people because they thought a concerted effort was being made by Germany and Italy to reach the Suez Canal and by Japan to approach

Singapore, the Netherlands Indies, and the Indian Ocean. Nomura strongly expressed his belief that his country would not go south.

Matsuoka was now en route to Berlin, issuing bellicose statements as he went, but Nomura said his trip to Berlin was merely a compliment to the German Government. After the President remarked that matters between our two countries could undoubtedly be worked out without a military clash, and that the first step in this direction would be the removal of suspicion and fear regarding Japan's intentions, I added:

"Of course, with Matsuoka astride the Axis on his way to Berlin and talking loudly as he goes, and with Japanese naval and air forces in the vicinity of Indo-China and Thailand, with no explanation but with serious inferences concerning their presence there, you must realize how acute the feeling in this country has become. Since Japan has departed from the course that most other countries have been pursuing, the initiative and responsibility are hers to suggest what, how, and when she is willing to undertake serious discussions with us. Above all, she must make it clear by words and acts whether her intentions in this direction are serious."

Japan having mediated the border dispute between Indo-China and Thailand and awarded the latter a liberal slice of territory, Lord Halifax came to my office on April 8 and handed me two memoranda from his Government asking our help to keep Thailand in line.

"I myself," I replied, "am not at all convinced that the present Thai Government is a real friend of this Government or any other government except the Japanese. It went into collusion with the Japanese to secure Tokyo's aid which enabled it to obtain much territory from Indo-China. In my opinion Japanese-Thai alliances already exist in the military, political, and economic fields."

The informal conversations conducted by Bishop Walsh, Father Drought, and Postmaster General Walker with Japanese representatives, including Ambassador Nomura, reached a head on April 9. On that day I received from them a draft proposal on which the participants had agreed. During the next few days I went over this carefully with the experts on Far Eastern affairs in the State Department.

As we studied the proposal, our disappointment was keen. It was much less accommodating than we had been led to believe it would be, and most of its provisions were all that the ardent Japanese imperialists could want.

With regard to the Tripartite Pact, Japan would state that her military obligation under the Axis alliance came into force only when one of the parties of the alliance was aggressively attacked by a power not at present involved in the European War. But this still left Japan the right to decide what constituted an aggressive attack. The war in the Atlantic between the British Navy and German submarines and surface raiders was growing yet more acute. To the President and me it was becoming ever more apparent that it was not enough to manufacture war goods for Britain and pass them on to her under Lend-Lease. We should also have to ensure that they got to Britain, for no matter how much supplies we produced, they could not help the Allies if they lay at the bottom of the sea. If incidents then rose between Germany and ourselves in the Atlantic, Japan was free under the draft proposal to decide that we were making an aggressive attack and to declare war against us.

With regard to China, the draft proposal stated that the President would request Chiang Kai-shek to negotiate peace with Japan on a basis of China's independence, withdrawal of Japanese troops from China in accordance with an agreement to be reached between Japan and China; no acquisition of Chinese territory; no imposition of indemnities; resumption of the "Open Door," the interpretation and application of which would be agreed upon at some future, convenient time between the United States and Japan; coalescence of the Chiang Kai-shek and Wang Ching-wei Governments; no large-scale or concentrated immigration of Japanese into Chinese territory; and recognition of Japan's possession of Manchukuo.

If Chiang Kai-shek agreed to the President's request, Japan would submit peace terms within the above limits and along the line of neighborly friendship, joint defense against communistic activities, and economic cooperation. If Chiang Kai-shek did not agree, the United States would discontinue assistance to the Chinese.

The proposal provided that the United States and Japan would assure the supply to each other of such commodities as were available and were required by either. Normal trade relations were to be resumed. The United States would give Japan a gold credit. The United States would give Japan cooperation and support in the production and procurement of natural resources such as oil, rubber, tin, and nickel.

A conference between President Roosevelt and Premier Konoye at Honolulu was suggested.

Nothing was mentioned about Japanese troops in Indo-China.

Numerous questions at once rose to our minds. To what extent and

when would Japan evacuate her troops from China? How would she interpret and apply the "Open Door"? What did the coalescence of the Chiang
Kai-shek and the puppet Nanking regimes mean? How could we require
China to recognize Manchukuo which we ourselves did not recognize?
How could we request Chiang Kai-shek to negotiate when there were so
many loopholes for Japanese interpretation, and how could we agree to
discontinue aid to China if he refused?

While our study of these proposals went on, Matsuoka, returning
through Moscow from Berlin, signed a neutrality pact with Stalin on
April 13. We knew that negotiations for an agreement of this nature had
been in course between Tokyo and Moscow for several months. Japan
had wanted a stronger agreement, but Russia had held off. Suddenly
Stalin gave a last-minute assent to a limited agreement, as Matsuoka
was about to leave Moscow. It was obvious to us that Stalin was worried
over the possibility of an attack by Hitler and wanted to protect his
Far Eastern flank. We ourselves had already given Russia two warnings
that Hitler was planning an attack.

On the day following this announcement, I publicly stated our reaction to the agreement. "The significance of the pact between the Soviet
Union and Japan relating to neutrality, as reported in the press today,
could be overestimated," I said. "The agreement would seem to be
descriptive of a situation which has in effect existed between the two
countries for some time past. It therefore comes as no surprise, although
there has existed doubt whether the two Governments would or would
not agree to say it in writing. The policy of this Government, of course,
remains unchanged."

Ambassador Steinhardt in Moscow cabled us on April 11 an account
of a conversation he had with Matsuoka. The Japanese Foreign Minister
said he had made no commitments in Berlin or Rome; Japan was not
obligated to go to war with the United States but if the United States
declared war on Germany the situation might be different; Matsuoka did
not expect Germany to declare war on the United States, but if so he
hoped we would make no move in the Pacific until Japan had made its
position clear; Japan would adhere to its obligations under the Tripartite
Pact; Hitler and Ribbentrop had said to him they had no desire to become
involved in a war with us; Hitler expected to win the war by submarine
and air activities against Britain and would attempt an invasion of Britain
only if necessary.

After our Far Eastern experts and I completed our examination of the proposals sent me through Postmaster General Walker, I concluded that, however objectionable some of the points might be, there were others that could be accepted as they stood and still others that could be agreed to if modified. The state of our relations with Japan was such, and the requirements of our policy of extensive aid to Britain were such, that I felt no opportunity should be overlooked that might lead to broad-scale conversations with Japan. I therefore asked Nomura to see me in my apartment at the Wardman Park Hotel, to which I had recently moved.

I mentioned to Nomura that I had received the unofficial proposals for a settlement between our two countries, and added that I had been told that the Ambassador himself had participated in and associated himself with these plans. I repeated what I had said before, that we could deal only with the Ambassador in considering the problems outstanding between our Governments, and I wanted to clear up the question of the extent of his knowledge of the document containing the proposals and whether it was his desire to present it officially as a first step in negotiations.

Nomura promptly replied he knew all about the document, he had collaborated to some degree with the various Japanese and American individuals who drew it up, and he would be disposed to present it as a basis for negotiations. He had not yet forwarded it to his Government, however, but he thought his Government would be favorably disposed toward it.

I said there were certain points my Government would desire to raise prior to negotiations, such as the integrity and sovereignty of China and the principle of equality of opportunity in China, and he could then communicate these to his Government and ascertain whether it agreed that there was a basis for negotiations.

Two days later I handed Nomura at my apartment a statement of four basic principles which I said would have to underlie any agreement we reached. Before doing so, I said: "The one paramount preliminary question about which my Government is concerned is a definite assurance in advance that your Government has the willingness and ability to go forward with a plan for settlement. Is it willing to abandon its present doctrine of military conquest by force and of taking title to all property and territories seized? Is it ready to give up the use of force as an instrument of policy and adopt the principles that my Government has been proclaiming as the foundation on which all relations between nations should properly rest?"

The four principles I laid before Nomura were these:

"(1) Respect for the territorial integrity and the sovereignty of each and all nations;

"(2) Support of the principle of noninterference in the internal affairs of other countries;

"(3) Support of the principle of equality, including equality of commercial opportunity;

"(4) Nondisturbance of the status quo in the Pacific except as the status quo may be altered by peaceful means."

I said to Nomura that, with these four points accepted, if he submitted to his Government the informal document prepared by the individual Americans and Japanese, and if his Government approved it and instructed him to propose it to us, it would afford a basis for starting conversations. We would thereupon offer counter proposals and independent proposals. We would then discuss these with Nomura, along with the Japanese proposals, and talk them out to a conclusion one way or the other in the friendly spirit that unquestionably should and would characterize the conversations.

After Nomura studied our four points he suggested that the principle of equality might well be discussed during our talks.

"This is impossible," I promptly replied. "We could not think of entering into negotiations if your Government should even hesitate in agreeing to this point. No country in the world would get more from the doctrine of equality than Japan. You yourself know how successfully this doctrine has operated between the United States and the Latin American countries."

Nomura remarked that the United States had special relations with Latin America which Japan would not be permitted to have with countries in the Orient.

"There's great misunderstanding on this point," I responded. "The truth is that the chief South American countries produce large surpluses of wheat, corn, and meat, such as we produce, with the result that we have never had more than a limited trade relationship with them, as compared with their trade with the rest of the world.

"When I went to Montevideo eight years ago, I sought to institute a system of closer relations among our countries. The largest purpose I had in mind was the common defense of the hemisphere. If I had not cultivated closer relations in lieu of the embittered relations that existed prior to 1933, there would probably be several Hitler puppet governments in

Central and South America now. And they might be conceding naval and airplane bases to Hitler and performing other acts under his instructions."

As for Japan, I said she could carry on all social, educational, economic, and political relations with nations in the Pacific with a view to cultivating them in the same way. But, I added: "She will get nowhere if she surrounds herself and them by preferences, or asserts zones of special controlling influence, or carries out movements such as are not dreamed of in this country or in this hemisphere."

Nomura wanted me to indicate whether I would largely approve the proposals contained in the document handed me on April 9. I said we could give ready approval to several, while others would have to be modified or eliminated, and we would offer some proposals ourselves. "But if your Government is in real earnest about changing its course," I continued, "I can see no good reason why ways could not be found to reach a fairly satisfactory settlement of all the essential questions presented."

Nomura's command of English was so marginal that I frequently doubted whether he understood the points I was making. I took care to speak slowly and often to repeat and reemphasize some of my sentences. In the following month I introduced Joseph W. Ballantine into our conferences so that, with his excellent knowledge of Japanese (he is the author of a grammar of that language) he could go over again some of the vital points in the Ambassador's own tongue.

Nomura duly sent to Tokyo the document of April 9, along with my four points and other observations, and we sat down to await the Japanese reply.

Lord Halifax and Australian Minister Casey brought me on April 22 a telegram reporting a Japanese concentration of twelve to fifteen divisions at Formosa, Canton, and Hainan, with the apparent object of attacking Malaya direct or through Thailand. Halifax handed me also an *aide-mémoire* from his Government suggesting that a declaration be made by the United States, the British, and Netherlands Governments jointly or separately stating that should Japan make any further major move to the south their interest would be jointly and individually affected.

I reminded the Ambassador of the statements I had made when Japan was expressing a suspicious interest in the Dutch East Indies. "Those statements," I said, "declared that interference with the Dutch East Indies by Japan would raise the whole question of peace throughout the

Pacific area. They were much stronger than the one your Government now proposes."

I added that I did not concur in the idea of a joint statement, but would give thought to the possibility of a parallel statement.

Halifax also gave me an *aide-mémoire* from his Government asking our help in weaning Thailand away from Japan. I said, as I had before, that we would do anything practicable, but that I was very much afraid that Thailand was already in the clutches of Japan.

Many days of waiting for Japan's reply to Nomura's cable now ensued. Nomura came to my apartment on May 2 and, pleading for patience, said there was politics in the situation back in Japan and implied that this was the cause of the "hitch" in his receiving the instructions he had requested. The "politics in the situation," of course, was Foreign Minister Matsuoka, who had returned to Tokyo aflame from his talks with Hitler and Mussolini and opposed any negotiations with the United States that would infringe on the Tripartite Pact. (According to Premier Konoye's memoirs, Matsuoka went directly to the Emperor over Konoye's head to urge support of the Axis, and Konoye had to go to the Emperor to urge proceeding with the talks with the United States.)

The President on May 6 declared China eligible for assistance under the Lend-Lease Act.

The following day Nomura came again to my apartment. He made a suggestion, as coming from his Government, that our two countries sign a nonaggression pact. Without hesitation I promptly brushed this aside. "This is an entirely different matter from the proposals contained in your document of April 9," I said. "My Government is not thinking of considering anything except basic principles as a foundation for any negotiations."

This idea of a Japanese-American nonaggression pact was a hoary one that had been presented to me several times in the past. It would have meant our agreeing to refrain from war with Japan no matter what she did in the Far East.

Nomura also said he had received a telegram from Matsuoka, but there were many things in it that "were wrong." He asked if he might hand it to me. I studied a moment and then said that, since it had many things in it that were wrong, he might just as well retain it, if he had the authority to do so, because, as he indicated, it would seem to negate most or much of the document of April 9, and hence no progress could be made. Nomura accordingly kept the telegram.

Actually, we already knew the contents of the message. It contained a statement from Matsuoka to me that the German and Italian leaders were confident of victory, that American participation in the European War would merely prolong it and bring about the destruction of civilization, and that Japan could not injure the position of her allies.

We knew this because of the fact that our Navy and Army cipher experts, with remarkable ingenuity, had broken the Japanese code and were deciphering Government messages from Tokyo to Washington and other capitals, translating them and sending them to the State Department for our information.

These intercepts, bearing our code name "Magic," played little part in our early negotiations, but were of great importance during the final phases. They enabled us to know many of the instructions the Japanese Foreign Minister was sending to Nomura and to other Japanese representatives; they gave us a check on what Nomura was reporting to Tokyo concerning the conversations he was holding with me; and they showed that the Japanese Government was going ahead with its plans of conquest even while talking of peace with us. I looked upon them as I would upon a witness who was testifying against his own side of a case.

I naturally had to be careful never to give Nomura the slightest impression of this special knowledge. I had to take care to keep our conversation limited to the knowledge I might have gained from him or from normal diplomatic sources. So as to safeguard the security of these messages, I named one of my secretaries to handle them, keep track of them, and make sure they were either returned to the Navy or destroyed.

After strongly complimenting Nomura on his conscientious efforts to promote better relations between our two countries, and remarking that he knew I had been patient thus far, I said: "I would not be candid with you if I did not say that I cannot give any assurances of further patience in the event of more delay. There are influences at work that cannot be held back. This country, as I have already said to you, is determined that Hitler shall not get control of the high seas—and this means not one sea but the seven seas. We do not propose, therefore, to delay all necessary steps of resistance and defense until it is too late. As you know, things are moving fast in the direction of resistance, just as Hitler is endeavoring to move fast in his course of aggression."

This was at a moment when Hitler had completed his invasion of Yugoslavia and Greece, when we knew he was concluding his preparations to invade Russia, when it seemed that Vichy France was moving toward collaboration with Germany, and when we ourselves were taking even broader steps to make our assistance to Britain effective.

Four days later Nomura called at my apartment and left with me a series of documents. These included a draft for an agreement between the United States and Japan; a paper containing a series of explanations of the draft; the text of the agreement between Japan and the puppet regime at Nanking signed November 30, 1940; a copy of a "Joint Declaration by the Governments of Japan, Manchukuo, and China," and a copy of a declaration by Premier Konoye on December 22, 1938. But the following day Nomura returned in some confusion and said he had made a mistake in leaving with me the copies of the Nanking agreement, the Joint Declaration, and Konoye's statement. He asked for the return of all the documents he had handed me the day before, and I duly gave them back to him.

Nomura then handed me a complete new set of documents; namely, Japan's draft for an agreement and a paper containing an "oral explanation" of the proposals.

We were now in possession of Japan's official propositions. A basis was laid, as of May 12, for the discussions that went on, with one interruption, up to Pearl Harbor.

72: Arms Break Off Talks

ONCE WE HAD Japan's formal proposals of May 12 before us, we began to study them intensively. We analyzed each point in itself and in its relation to the other points. We sought to ascertain what we could accept outright, what we had to reject outright, and what lay in the twilight zone where the change of a word or a phrase would mean the difference between acceptance or rejection.

Very few rays of hope shone from the document. What Japan was proposing was mostly to her own advantage. In effect, it called for a species of joint overlordship of the Pacific area by Japan and the United States, with Japan the baron of the part that embraced nine-tenths of the population and the wealth, and with little consideration for the rights and interests of other nations.

The first portion of the document was in the nature of a preamble, containing abstract affirmations of peaceful intent and international co-operation. Our first hurdle occurred in Section Two, relating to the attitude of the two Governments toward the European War.

Here Japan stated that her alliance with the Axis Powers was "designed to prevent the nations which are not at present directly affected by the European War from engaging in it." This was clearly an effort to coerce the United States.

As for us, Japan presented this proposal: "The Government of the United States maintains that its attitude toward the European War is, and will continue to be, directed by no such aggressive measures as to assist any one nation against the other." In other words it was questionable whether we could any longer assist Britain. Also, what was Japan's definition of aggressive measures?

Finally, this section contained another clause whereby Japan and the United States agreed to act jointly "speedily to restore peace in Europe." Any speedy restoration of peace in Europe, with Hitler in possession of most all the Continent, meant a peace on Nazi terms.

As for the war in China, the document called for our Government to request Chiang Kai-shek to negotiate peace with Japan on terms approximately those contained in the document of April 9. In the explanatory note accompanying the document, Japan requested "an understanding, in a separate and secret document, that the United States would discontinue her assistance to the Chiang Kai-shek regime if Chiang Kai-shek does not accept." Failing this, she wanted a definite pledge by "some highest authorities."

Japan also proposed that the two countries supply, as far as possible, commodities that the other required, and take steps to resume normal trade relations. The United States would help Japan to produce and obtain natural resources such as oil, rubber, tin, and nickel. Other provisions called for a joint guarantee of the independence of the Philippines and a nondiscriminatory basis for Japanese immigration to the United States.

Japan deleted the suggestion in the April 9 document that the President and Premier Konoye meet at Honolulu. Instead she suggested it would be better to arrange, by an exchange of letters, that the conference would be considered after the results of the agreement had been studied.

As I communicated to the President our impressions of the draft agreement, we had to decide whether to begin the conversations with the Japanese. As the document stood, it offered little basis for an agreement, unless we were willing to sacrifice some of our most basic principles, which we were not. Nevertheless, it was a formal and detailed proposal from Japan. To have rejected it outright would have meant throwing away the only real chance we had had in many months to enter with Japan into a fundamental discussion of all the questions outstanding between us.

The President and I figured that if there were the slightest possibility of inducing Japan to withdraw from the Axis alliance, we should pursue it, for this would be a sharp blow to Hitler and a fillip to the Allies. Even a gradual withdrawal of Japan would have its worth.

Consequently, we decided to go forward on the basis of the Japanese proposals and seek to argue Japan into modifying here, eliminating there, and inserting elsewhere, until we might reach an accord we both could sign with mutual good will.

Nomura came to my apartment two days after he presented Japan's proposals, and we discussed the factors embraced in our concept of self-defense in the light of Hitler's movement of conquest. Nomura said his view and that of his Government was that the United States was in no danger from Europe.

"We have irrefutable evidence," I replied, "that this hemisphere and this country would be and are in serious and imminent danger. It all depends on whether Hitler conquers Great Britain. If he should, he would probably or possibly come into control of the high seas and would make his first attack in South America."

On that same day, May 14, Foreign Minister Matsuoka said to Ambassador Grew in Tokyo that Konoye and he were determined that Japan's southward advance should be carried out by peaceful means— "unless," he added significantly, "circumstances render this impossible." When Grew asked what circumstances, Matsuoka pointed to the concentration of British troops in Malaya. Grew replied that this was purely defensive, but Matsuoka countered that the Japanese public considered it provocative and might bring pressure on the Government to act.

Matsuoka's attitude was therefore not very heartening to our preliminary conversations. Japan had been "threatened" by China, hence she invaded China. She had been "threatened" by British, Chinese or De Gaullist agents in Indo-China, hence she invaded Indo-China. These sophistries were those of Hitler. The implications were those of conquest.

Nevertheless, we went forward with our conversations. Our Far Eastern experts and I prepared an informal series of written observations which I handed to Nomura on May 16. This included excerpts from my address of April 24 explaining the position of our Government toward Hitler's movement of world conquest and the steps we were taking in self-defense. "Hitler," I further stated, "is the one person who can promptly remove the necessity for efforts at effective self-defense by this country and other countries similarly situated, whereas for any other nation to request that the United States desist from any such resistance would in its actual effect range the country making such request on the side of Hitler and his movement of aggression by force."

I also handed Nomura our redraft of certain sections of the agreement, particularly those relating to the Tripartite Pact and to China. On the first point, we sought to limit Japan to entering the war under the Axis alliance only if one of the Axis nations were aggressively attacked by a power not at present involved in hostilities; but at the same time we wanted Japan to declare that she was under no commitment to the Axis inconsistent with the terms of the agreement under discussion. As for ourselves, we declared our attitude toward the European War to be solely that of self-protection and self-defense.

As to China, we agreed that, if Japan and the United States approved the agreement, the President would suggest to the Governments of Japan and China that they enter into peace negotiations on a basis that would include neighborly friendship, mutual respect of sovereignty and territorial integrity, withdrawal of Japanese troops in accordance with a schedule to be agreed upon, no annexation or indemnities, equality of commercial opportunity for all concerned, parallel measures of defense against subversive activities from without, and the question of Manchuria to be dealt with by friendly negotiations. There was no provision for our ceasing to aid China if Chiang Kai-shek refused these terms.

I asked Lord Halifax to come to my office on that same day, May 16, and mentioned that rumors were current that the United States was negotiating peace between Japan and China. I said I had not thus far treated them seriously.

"There are two groups in Japan," I remarked. "One is pro-German, the other is a peace group among high officials. According to one report, this latter group really wants to turn Japan's policy toward law and order and away from military conquest, move their troops out of China, pledge China's independence and the principle of nondiscrimination to all nations dealing with her, and oppose war being brought into the Pacific. But I have not taken this too seriously."

Halifax replied he thought I should explore this possibility even though there might not be one chance in twenty-five to develop it successfully.

I met again with Nomura at my apartment on the evening of May 20 to discuss the various proposals put forth by both sides. Nomura had already introduced to me the two advisers who had come from Japan to assist him and who now appeared with him for most of our conferences. They were Colonel Hideo Iwakuro, representing the Japanese Army, and Tadao Wikawa, an official of the Cooperative Bank of Japan, who was close to the most influential civilian group in the Japanese Government. From now on I had with me at most of these conferences the State Department Far Eastern experts, Hamilton and Ballantine.

Iwakuro and Wikawa had been in Washington for some weeks, and had taken part in the discussions with Bishop Walsh and Father Drought. They had been sent especially from Japan for these conversations. Their hope, however, had been that the President would appoint someone outside the State Department expressly to negotiate with them.

Iwakuro had all the virtues and shortcomings of a Japanese Army officer. He was a very fine type, honest, calmly poised, very sure of himself without being annoyingly self-confident. He could, of course, see only his Army's viewpoint, not ours or the real interest of Japan. Wikawa was of the "slick politician" type whom the Japanese themselves did not seem to respect for integrity.

When I asked Nomura how the prospects for agreement now looked to him, he replied that the Japanese Army and Navy, as well as the Foreign Office and the whole Cabinet, had approved the agreement, that it had been referred to the Emperor, and that it would have unanimous support in Japan. He was referring, of course, to Japan's proposals, not our counter proposals. He said that if now we should fail to carry the proposals through, he would be in a very embarrassing position with regard to his Government. I drew the impression from that that he had already indicated to his Government that the approval of our Government was assured. He therefore said it would be a pity if we failed to reach an understanding "through disagreement on words."

I brought up two points in regard to China. One was Japan's proposal that China and Japan join in defense against Communism. The other was the stationing of Japanese troops in certain parts of China. I said that if and when my Government approached Chiang Kai-shek on the matter of negotiating with Japan, I should have to tell him on what basis Japan proposed to negotiate. "This basis," I said, "should be one on which Chiang could carry his country with him. If the Chinese Government should be unwilling to proceed with negotiations on the basis proposed, I would be in a very embarrassing position."

I suggested that the two points be covered under a broader provision such as special measures of protection for Japanese nationals and property against lawlessness in areas where such measures were necessary. This meant measures to be undertaken by the Chinese Government. It was intended to do away with any necessity for retaining Japanese troops in China.

Colonel Iwakuro spoke up to say he was surprised I had brought up these points. It was his conception, he said, that the central objective of the agreement we were discussing was peace in the Pacific between Japan and the United States, and the settlement of the "China affair" was incidental and concerned only China and Japan.

"I agree," I replied, "that our central objective is peace in the Pacific between Japan and the United States. But a peaceful settlement between Japan and China is an essential element in the situation." I later pointed out that, if the United States were to suggest that Chiang Kai-shek enter into negotiations with Japan, my Government could not divest itself of some responsibility for the basis of the proposed negotiations and for seeing that they conformed to the principles we supported.

Colonel Iwakuro then and in later conversations made clear what Japan had in mind regarding evacuation of troops from China. These would be gradually removed from Central and Southern China over a period of some years. But they would not be removed at all from Inner Mongolia and the adjacent regions of China proper, including lines of communication to the sea as far south as Tsingtao. This meant Japanese military domination of the five North China provinces of Hopeh, Shantung, Shansi, Chahar, and Suiyuan, with an area of more than 400,000 square miles and a population estimated at more than 80,000,000 persons.

From time to time Nomura varied in his opinions on evacuation of Japanese troops from China; but Iwakuro never changed his view that the stationing of Japanese troops in northern China was an absolute condition of any settlement with China. And it was likely that Iwakuro's views on this point would prevail since he was the representative of the Japanese Army, which was determined to remain in China.

This subject rose again in a further discussion I had with Nomura alone at my apartment on the evening of May 28. Nomura said he did not know exactly what the Japanese Army had in mind regarding evacuation of troops from China, and this would be dealt with in direct negotiations between Japan and China. He said his personal opinion was that negotiations on this point might be protracted possibly over a period of six months and that two years would be required before evacuation could be effected. In response to my specific questions, Nomura said such evacuation would not include troops retained in China for "cooperative defense against communistic activities." He did not know how many troops would be stationed in China.

"It seems important to me," I remarked, "that relations between China and Japan should be adjusted on a basis that would offer permanent promise of friendship between the two countries. The continued presence of Japanese troops in China would be a factor operating against such friendship, since the presence of these troops tends to produce incidents and friction. We found from our experience in Latin America that a policy of sending troops to settle claims does not pay." I recommended our policy in Latin America as an example Japan could use with regard to China.

Nomura said he personally agreed with me, but he did not think the Far East had progressed to a point where my suggestions would be feasible.

Nomura and I had kept our discussions on an informal basis. Written documents had passed between us, but they were marked "unofficial and informal." I now remarked to him that, before entering into any official negotiations, and before approaching the Chinese Government, it was my intention to talk over in strict confidence with the Chinese Government the proposals we had under discussion.

Nomura commented he did not expect that our Government would negotiate with the Chinese Government but would merely serve as a bridge to bring the Chinese and Japanese together into direct negotiations. When I asked Nomura how he thought Chiang Kai-shek would react to the proposal to station troops in China "for cooperative defense against communistic activities," he replied that Chiang Kai-shek was largely relying on American aid to sustain him, and, if we should discontinue our aid, he would be forced to come to terms with Japan.

I had already called the Chinese Ambassador, Dr. Hu Shih, to my office on May 23 and talked to him about the current rumors of peace negotiations between Japan and China.

"Recently," I said, "the war situation in Europe has been getting worse [German occupation of the Balkans, British retreat in North Africa]. I have at all times treated the Far Eastern and the European wars as one combined movement so far as our defense is concerned. We, of course, are standing absolutely firm on all our basic policies and principles in both the West and the East."

Adding that, if the situation in Europe became more dangerous, I could not be certain whether a large segment of our Navy still at Pearl Harbor might not be sent to the Atlantic, I said: "Hence the question of peace reports naturally arises, even though matters have not reached a stage where negotiations would be undertaken."

Hu Shih discounted the possibility of peace between Japan and China, but said he would give the matter thought in the light of the increasing dangers I had mentioned.

"In any event," I said, "I shall not take matters into a serious stage without first fully consulting with you and your associates in the Government." He expressed his appreciation.

I tried to get through Nomura, during our May 28 conversation, clarification of his Government's attitude toward the Tripartite Pact. "Since Matsuoka's return from Europe," I said, "he has been making declarations on every occasion regarding Japan's obligations under the Tripartite Alliance and saying Japan would support Germany in the event of American entry into the war. If we reached an agreement with you, critics would assert—unless your Government should clarify its attitude—that we had received no assurance as to Japan's position."

Nomura said he doubted very much whether his Government would be willing to add anything to what it already proposed because it would be placed in a very difficult position vis-à-vis Germany and Italy, and the pro-Axis group in Japan would create domestic difficulties.

I sent Nomura on May 31 a new draft of the proposals, incorporating certain changes we wished to make. In the section relating to the Tripartite Pact we inserted a sentence: "Obviously, the provisions of the pact do not apply to involvement through acts of self-defense." In the section relating to China, we provided for withdrawal of Japanese military and naval forces from Chinese territory and waters as promptly as possible and in accordance with an agreement to be concluded between Japan and China. We made cooperative defense by China and Japan against Communism subject to further discussion.

Nomura came to see me on June 2 and said he thought he and his associates were in agreement on our document of May 31, "with the exception of some of the phraseology." Since he was going to New York for a few days, we agreed that his and my associates should discuss this phraseology.

Speaking very slowly and deliberately, I asked Nomura: "Is it your considered judgment that your Government seriously desires to enter into a settlement for peace, nondiscriminatory commercial relations, and friendship generally in the Pacific?"

Nomura promptly replied that was his judgment.

"The loud statements that Matsuoka and others are making daily," I went on, "sharply raise the question I just put to you. I'm forced to inquire whether Japan really is seeking this sort of agreement, or whether she is only seeking a way to get out of China and then go forward in other directions with methods and practices entirely contrary to the principles that would have to underlie our settlement."

Nomura repeated his view that Japan earnestly desired a fair settlement.

British Ministers Nevile Butler and Noel Hall called on me the following day to ask my impression as to a strong statement the British Government proposed to issue to back up a broadcast made by Netherlands Foreign Minister E. N. van Kleffens regarding joint defense of the Netherlands Indies.

"I have never made it a practice," I said, "to make a threat without being ready to back it up. Therefore I would not offer a statement too challenging or too threatening, but one of such moderation, firmness, and definiteness as would adequately meet the situation."

In the conversations that ensued between Nomura's assistants and mine, the Japanese manifested an ever greater reluctance to agree to cleancut provisions, capable of no equivocation, that would guarantee peace in the Pacific. What they had in mind when they said they could agree to our proposals "with the exception of some of the phraseology" was soon apparent. They wanted provision after provision changed to such indefinite wording that it would be capable of various interpretations, including the one Japan intended giving it. Their original proposals were none too conciliatory, but as the discussions progressed and Nomura and his assistants began to receive reactions and instructions from Tokyo, their attitude became yet more grudging.

In our initial exchanges Japan had disclaimed any intention to continue an economic monopoly for herself in China. But Nomura and his assistants made it clear that Japan intended to retain a preferred economic position in China and at the same time obtain economic rights in the Southwest Pacific such as she was unwilling that other nations should enjoy in China. For my part I had fought for so many years, in Congress and in the State Department, for nondiscrimination and equality of treatment in international commerce, that I could not agree to any claim by Japan to a preferred position in China.

In general, with regard to Japan's insistence on "phraseology," I emphasized that my Government was seeking a basic, comprehensive agreement that would speak for itself as an instrument of peace. I said I was not interested in an agreement of a temporizing character that would not offer promise for future stability along sound progressive lines.

I brought the divergencies of view between us to a head on June 6 when I handed Nomura an "oral statement."

"It is disappointing," I said, "to note a vast difference between the proposal as it now stands with these revisions and the original document on which earlier discussions were based. The successive Japanese revisions appear to have gradually narrowed down the extent of the advances in the direction of a liberal policy and to have carried the proposal away from the fundamental points which the Government of the United States considers are involved in establishing and preserving peaceful conditions in the Pacific area."

I then stated three basic observations: "The impression that the Secretary of State derives from the proposed revisions as a whole and from recent manifestations of the Japanese Government's attitude, is that they evince a disposition (1) to stress Japan's alignment with the Axis, (2) to avoid giving a clear indication of an intention to place Japan's relations with China on a basis which in the opinion of the Government of the United States would contribute to a lasting peace and thus to future stability in the Far East, and (3) to veer away from clear-cut commitments in regard to policies of peace and of nondiscriminatory treatment which are the fundamentals of a sound basis for peace in the Pacific area."

Nomura, of course, insisted that his Government really wanted peace and sincerely desired to conclude an understanding with us as speedily as possible. But in the same breath he made a proposal that showed how little he and his Government appreciated the nature of the understanding we wished. He asked whether it would not be possible for the President, having in view not merely America's own interest but a wider interest in world peace, to act on his own initiative in proposing to the Chinese Government that it enter into negotiations with Japan.

Colonel Iwakuro forthwith chimed in to say Nomura's suggestion was prompted by the idea that it would better befit Japan's dignity as a great Power if there could be avoided any appearance that Japan was coming to the United States in a suppliant attitude asking the United States to help in settling difficulties between Japan and China.

Here was another manifestation of the necessity for "saving face" with which we had already had to deal in our relations with Japan in the past. I replied to Nomura and Iwakuro that the President should have an agreement of the character we had in mind to stand on before undertaking to make an approach to the Chinese Government.

"We need," I said, "to draw up an agreement in clear-cut and unequivocal terms so that it will speak for itself. This is especially important at this time when the world has had so much experience with bad faith in international dealings and when there is so much skepticism and suspicion among the public in regard to international relations."

What had happened thus far was the opposite of what the President and I had hoped would happen. We had been willing to accept the Japanese proposals of May 12 as a basis for discussion, knowing full well they could not be accepted as they stood, but hoping that our subsequent discussion would bring about modifications that would make them acceptable. But as soon as the Japanese Government realized we were willing to use the May 12 proposals as a basis for discussion, they began instantly to move, not in our direction with more conciliatory proposals, but in the opposite direction with changes that brought the proposals more into line with their imperialistic ambitions and their Axis alliance.

Nomura handed me a new draft of proposals on June 15. This deleted the sentence our previous proposals contained, to the effect that Japan would not be obliged to act under the Tripartite Pact if we became involved in the European War through measures of self-defense. The new draft was as far as ever from being acceptable to us.

Then on June 21 I handed Nomura a document containing revisions of his draft of June 15 so as to bring it into focus with our views. In addition, I gave him an "oral statement" to emphasize our attitude on several main points.

In this latter I said I had no reason to doubt that many Japanese leaders shared the desire of Nomura and his associates to bring about a better understanding between our two countries and to establish peace in the Pacific. "Unfortunately," I pointed out, "accumulating evidence reaches this Government from sources all over the world . . . that some Japanese leaders in influential official positions are definitely committed to a course which calls for support of Nazi Germany and its policies of conquest and that the only kind of understanding with the United States which they would endorse is one that would envisage Japan's fighting on the side of Hitler should the United States become involved in the European hostilities through carrying out its present policy of self-defense." This attitude, I said, we could not ignore.

I added that we also had misgivings over the Japanese Government's desire to provide in the agreement for the stationing of Japanese troops in Inner Mongolia and North China. Our liberal policies would not permit this Government to associate itself with any course inconsistent with these policies. "Furthermore," I added, "although in matters affecting only this country there might be some latitude of decision as to the qualifying of rights, the matter under discussion affects the sovereign rights of a third country, and accordingly it is felt that this Government must be most scrupulous in dealing with such a matter."

I amplified orally to Nomura the point I had made on the Tripartite Pact in the statement I handed him. "At a time when Nazi Germany has invaded some fifteen or so countries," I said, "the Japanese Minister for Foreign Affairs is declaring in effect that measures of resistance by countries not already actually invaded would call for action by Japan under the Tripartite Pact. This is like saying that, if a tiger should break loose in the countryside and if a villager living a mile or so away from where the tiger is committing depredations and killing neighbors should go out and attack the tiger in order to protect his own family, his action would constitute aggression."

The following day Nomura came back to see me a few hours after I had received word that Hitler had launched his invasion of Russia. I asked Nomura point-blank whether it was Matsuoka's intention on the one hand to have us subject China to pressure to come to an agreement with Japan and on the other hand to free Japan to take action with reference to the European War as indicated in a message Matsuoka had sent Mussolini. Matsuoka had endorsed the Italian's statement that "Japan will not remain indifferent in the face of American aggression against the Axis."

Nomura replied, as he had on previous occasions, that Japan did not want war with the United States, but that she did not wish to bind herself in advance with regard to some future eventuality.

I commented I might have difficulty in the United States over the proposed understanding unless the Japanese Government could find some way of clarifying its attitude in view of the public statements that had been made in Japan. "I wonder," I said, "whether Germany's declaration of war against the Soviet Union might not affect the situation in such a way as to render it easier for the Japanese Government to find some way of doing this."

But Nomura said his Government did not wish to be placed in the position of repudiating its obligations under the Tripartite Pact.

At this very moment Japanese espionage agents were working in the United States to ferret out the secrets of our national defense. The Department of Justice asked the State Department on June 13 whether we agreed to the prosecution of a number of Japanese agents in Hawaii who had not registered with the State Department, as agents of a foreign government were required to do. We consented.

The Federal Bureau of Investigation had communicated to us in May that they had uncovered espionage activities by Lieutenant Commander Tachibana, a language officer of the Japanese Government, and asked our attitude toward his arrest. We agreed on May 27, and Tachibana was arrested at Los Angeles. Ambassador Nomura besought us on June 14, in the interest of promoting friendly relations between our two Governments, to permit Tachibana to be deported immediately without trial.

I went carefully into this case and decided to grant Nomura's request, out of consideration for him and also having in mind that our conversations with the Japanese were at a crucial stage. Tachibana left San Francisco on June 21 with the proviso that he would never return to the United States. Shortly thereafter it developed that two other Japanese naval language officers, Lieutenant Commander Okada and Lieutenant Yamada, had been associated with Tachibana in espionage. They were sent out of the United States on July 5. The effects of all three officers were carefully examined by the FBI for confidential material relating to our defenses before they were permitted to sail.

The same procedure was followed in the case of Lieutenant Commander Ezima, a Japanese officer attached to the Japanese Naval Inspector's Office, New York City, who was transmitting information to Germany via Japan on behalf of a group of German spies.

I left Washington on June 23 for White Sulphur Springs, West Virginia, to rest from an illness. The conversations, however, went on between my associates and Nomura and his associates, and I followed them daily through telephone and pouch.

As reports came in that Japan contemplated an attack on Soviet Russia, now desperately resisting the German onslaught, the President had a message sent on July 6 to Konoye expressing the earnest hope that Japan would not enter into hostilities against the Soviet Union. The following day Konoye replied through Matsuoka that they had "not so far considered the possibility of joining the hostilities against the Soviet Union." They asked whether it was "really the intention of the President or the American Government to intervene in the European War." Our reply to this, delivered on July 16, was that our policy toward Nazi Germany's movement of world conquest was solely that of self-defense and we could not be expected to permit Germany to obtain control of the seas or any other strategic advantages that would directly threaten our security.

We had, in fact, very definite knowledge of what Japan was planning. On the surface, an Imperial Conference was held in Tokyo on July 2, following which military steps of an alarming nature began to be taken. Between one and two million men were called to the armed forces, Japanese merchant vessels were suddenly recalled from the Atlantic, travel restrictions and strict censorship of mails and communications were imposed in Japan. The various steps taken were indicative of preparations for a major war.

Under the surface, our intercepts of Japanese Government messages gave us equally alarming information. A message from Tokyo to Berlin on July 2 contained these ominous paragraphs on policy:

"(1) Imperial Japan shall adhere to the policy of contributing to world peace by establishing the Great East Asia Sphere of Co-Prosperity, regardless of how the world situation may change.

"(2) The Imperial Government shall continue its endeavor to dispose of the China incident, and shall take measures with a view to advancing southward in order to establish firmly a basis for her self-existence and self-protection."

A message from Matsuoka to Nomura on the same day added: "Preparations for southward advance shall be reenforced and the policy already decided upon with reference to French Indo-China and Thailand shall be executed. As regards the Russo-German War, although the spirit of the three-Power Axis shall be maintained, every preparation shall be made at the present and the situation shall be dealt with in our own way. In the meantime, diplomatic negotiations shall be carried on with extreme care. Although every means available shall be resorted to in order to prevent the United States from joining the war, if need be Japan shall act in accordance with the three-Power pact and shall decide when and how force will be employed."

Shortly thereafter Japanese troops on July 21 occupied the southern portions of Indo-China and were now in possession of the whole of France's strategic province, pointing like a pudgy thumb toward the Philippines, Malaya, and the Dutch East Indies.

Welles telephoned me at White Sulphur Springs on July 23 to talk over with me what he should say to Nomura who had requested an interview with him. We knew that the topic Nomura had in mind was the invasion of Indo-China.

Nomura had come to see me at White Sulphur Springs ten days before, on July 13. He arrived without making an appointment, and I refused to see him. I was not well, and I knew Nomura had nothing new to offer. Furthermore, my associates and I thought it a good idea psychologically not to be too eager to see Nomura each time he requested an interview. Too much evidence on our part that we were anxious to reach a settlement with Japan induced the Japanese to narrow their concessions and enlarge their demands.

When Welles telephoned me, I said to him that the invasion of Southern Indo-China looked like Japan's last step before jumping off for a full-scale attack in the Southwest Pacific. Since it came in the midst of the conversations we were holding with Japan, I said I could see no basis for pursuing the conversations further.

Welles made these comments forcefully to Nomura and gave him my decision that our conversations had come to an end.

On the following day the President, receiving Nomura, proposed that if the Japanese Government would withdraw its forces from French Indo-China, he would seek to obtain a solemn declaration by the United States, Britain, China, and The Netherlands to regard Indo-China as a "neutralized" country, provided Japan gave a similar commitment. Japan's explanation for occupying Indo-China having been that she wanted to defend her supplies of raw materials there, the President's proposal took the props from under this specious reasoning. A week later the President extended his proposal to include Thailand.

Indicating our reaction to Japan's latest act of imperialist aggression, the President froze Japanese assets in the United States on July 26. I agreed to this step by telephone. All financial, import, and export transactions involving Japanese interests came under Government control, and thereafter trade between the United States and Japan soon dwindled to comparatively nothing.

Shortly before the occupation of southern Indo-China, Foreign Minister Matsuoka had been forced to resign. The sudden German invasion of Russia only two months after Matsuoka had signed a neutrality pact with Stalin's Government, plus the concessions he had had to make to Stalin to obtain his signature, plus the fact that Hitler invaded Russia without notifying Tokyo in advance, plus Matsuoka's habit of going over Konoye's head to the Emperor to plead for all-out collaboration with the European Axis, all combined to make his continuance in the Cabinet impossible. He was succeeded by Admiral Teijiro Toyoda.

With the conversations between Nomura and myself and our associates broken off, Colonel Iwakuro and Mr. Wikawa left the United States late in July to return to Japan.

This first act of the drama of our dialogue with Japan ended in failure, just as the second act was destined to end. It showed us, however, what we had to face. Japan would readily and instantly have signed a straight nonaggression pact with the United States. She would as readily have signed a general agreement with us on the basis of her own proposals. But neither pact would have given us peace for more than a short time. And either one would have meant a betrayal of China, Britain, Russia, and The Netherlands, and of our own future security.

From now on our major objective with regard to Japan was to give ourselves more time to prepare our defenses. We were still ready—and eager—to do everything possible toward keeping the United States out of war; but it was our concurrent duty to concentrate on trying to make the country ready to defend itself effectively in the event of war being thrust upon us.

73: Roosevelt-Konoye Meeting

"BOTH YOU AND I are deserving of sympathy because of the developments that broke up our efforts to bring about a better understanding between the United States and Japan."

With these words I resumed contact with Nomura on August 6, two days after my return from White Sulphur Springs. Nomura had come to my apartment at his request to hand me a new set of proposals from his Government, purportedly in answer to the President's proposal of July 24 on Indo-China.

Nomura read his document to me, then handed me a copy, which I put into my pocket without reading. I suggested we postpone discussion until we had had a chance to study the propositions, but I said, "Frankly, I'm pessimistic over the prospect of getting anywhere with proposals such as you've read me."

Japan proposed that we remove our restrictions upon trade with her, suspend our military measures in the Southwest Pacific area, and exercise our good offices to bring about direct negotiations between Japan and China. Still understood was the idea that, if Chiang Kai-shek did not agree to negotiate, we would discontinue aid to China.

Japan proposed the withdrawal of her troops from Indo-China after a settlement had been reached between Japan and China, but we would have to recognize her special position in Indo-China even after the withdrawal.

As I analyzed Japan's proposition with the Department's Far Eastern experts, it was obvious to me that Tokyo had moved further away than before from a basis for possible negotiations. The proposals did not even mention the President's suggestion for the neutralization of Indo-China. Under this provision, the United States would have to lift her trade restrictions against Japan, discontinue making defensive preparations in the Philippines and furnishing aid to Great Britain and the Netherlands in the Far East, and to China, and agree to Japan's special military position and preferential political and economic status in Indo-China.

She was willing to agree not to station her troops in regions of the Southwest Pacific other than Indo-China. But from Indo-China she could menace the Philippines and the British and Dutch Far Eastern possessions.

Two days later, when Nomura came back to see me at my request, I handed him a note in which I said that Japan's proposals were "lacking in responsiveness to the suggestion made by the President."

I said to Nomura that my Government had been prepared to be patient and to move gradually and to help the Japanese Government assert control over all groups in Japan and thus bring the Government as a whole and public opinion into line to support policies such as Nomura and I had in mind.

I commented on the Japanese press statement that Japan was being encircled by the Western powers, particularly the United States. "There is no occasion," I said, "for any nation in the world that is law-abiding and peaceful to become encircled by anybody except itself."

British Ambassador Halifax came to me the following day with an inquiry as to the amount of aid this Government might give in case Singapore or the Dutch East Indies were attacked.

"I myself have visualized the problem in a broader way," I said. "The issue is presented by the plan of the Japanese to invade the whole of the Indian Ocean and the islands and continents adjacent thereto, sail probably to the mouth of the Suez Canal, to the Persian Gulf oil area, and to the Cape of Good Hope—thereby blocking the trade routes and supply sources to the British. This would be more damaging to British defense in Europe perhaps than any other step short of a German crossing of the Channel.

"My Government is visualizing these broad conditions and the problem of resistance they present. Our activities in the way of discouraging and resisting this Japanese movement will be more or less affected by Britain's defensive position in Europe and hence the number of American naval vessels and other American aid that may be needed by Great Britain at the same time."

I added that, in the event of further Japanese movements to the south, the American and British Governments should naturally have a conference at once. At that time we should be able to determine more definitely and in detail our possibilities of resistance.

President Roosevelt was away at this time attending the Atlantic Conference with Prime Minister Churchill. On August 12 I received a wireless message from him asking me to alert Ambassador Nomura to be ready to come to the White House Saturday or Sunday of that week. The President said it seemed highly desirable to him that he and I should see Nomura as soon as he, Mr. Roosevelt, got back.

Welles returned to Washington from the Atlantic Conference ahead of the President, arriving on Friday August 15, and bringing a document that had been agreed upon by the President and Mr. Churchill as a statement each Government would make to the Japanese.

As I went over this with our Far Eastern experts it at once seemed to me dangerously strong, and in need of toning down. Its conclusion read:

"The Government of the United States, therefore, finds it necessary to state to the Government of Japan that if the Japanese Government undertakes any further steps in pursuance of the policy of military domination through force or conquest in the Pacific region upon which it has apparently embarked, the United States Government will be forced to take immediately any and all steps of whatsoever character it deems necessary in its own security notwithstanding the possibility that such further steps on its part may result in conflict between the two countries."

I felt that this statement might be misinterpreted in Japan and treated as a challenge. The military element there could seize upon it to incite the people of Japan against us, possibly leading them to war at that very time.

We accordingly redrafted the document. The conclusion now read:

"Such being the case, this Government now finds it necessary to say to the Government of Japan that if the Japanese Government takes any further steps in pursuance of a policy or program of military domination by force or threat of force of neighboring countries, the Government of the United States will be compelled to take immediately any and all steps which it may deem necessary toward safeguarding the legitimate rights and interests of the United States and American nationals and toward insuring the safety and security of the United States."

On Saturday, when we went over this redraft, it still appeared to us too provocative, unless it were balanced by a more friendly gesture. Hence my associates and I decided to split the substance of the document into two statements. One would be the warning. The other, an olive branch, would inform Japan that our Government would be prepared to continue its conversations with the Japanese Government and thereby offer Japan a reasonable and just alternative to the course upon which she was launched. I decided to recommend to the President that he hand both statements to Nomura when he saw him on Sunday.

When I saw Nomura later that day, he brought up the old argument that Japan did not have enough foodstuffs and had gone into Indo-China to secure such needed commodities as rice.

"If Japan had been willing," I replied, "to go forward with a peaceful settlement in the Pacific area in line with the principles and policies you and I have discussed, she would have been able peacefully and without the use or threat of force to have equal access with every other nation to world markets for rice and all other foodstuffs."

I saw the President the following morning. He readily agreed to the changes we had made in the document Welles had brought back from the Atlantic Conference, and said he would present both statements to Nomura that afternoon. I went over in detail with him the ground likely to be covered during the interview.

When Nomura and I met with the President that Sunday afternoon, Mr. Roosevelt said to the Ambassador that our attitude of opposition to Japan's course had been made well known, and that the next move was now up to Japan.

Nomura thereupon drew out of his pocket an instruction he said was from his Government. In it Premier Konoye said he felt so earnestly about preserving peaceful relations between our two countries that he would be disposed to meet the President midway between our two countries and sit down and talk out our difficulties in a peaceful spirit.

Without commenting directly on this proposal, the President replied that he wanted to bring the questions between the two Governments up to date, and would therefore offer certain observations. He regretted the need to do so, but he had no other recourse. He then read the first of the two statements, that containing the warning. This also recalled the President's proposal relating to Indo-China and pointed out that, notwithstanding our efforts to reach an agreement with Tokyo, Japan had continued her military activities at various points in the Far East and had occupied Indo-China.

The President then paused, to let the warning sink in. He next turned to Nomura's request made to me the day before that our conversations should be resumed. He said we could not think of reopening the conversations if the Japanese Government were to continue its present movement of force and conquest supported by its bitter press campaign against the United States.

He then read to Nomura, however, the second statement. This reviewed the conversations up to the time they were shattered by Japan's occupation of southern Indo-China. It concluded with:

"In case the Japanese Government feels that Japan desires and is in position to suspend its expansionist activities, to readjust its position, and to embark upon a peaceful program for the Pacific along the lines of the program and principles to which the United States is committed, the Government of the United States would be prepared to consider resumption of the informal exploratory conversations . . . it would be helpful if the Japanese Government would be so good as to furnish a clearer statement than has yet been furnished as to its present attitude and plans, just as this Government has repeatedly outlined to the Japanese Government its attitude and plans."

The President handed both statements to Nomura, who said he would communicate them to his Government.

Nomura's suggestion for a meeting between the President and Konoye, which he had made on instructions from his Government, recurred again and again during the following weeks, both in conversations between the Ambassador and me and in conversations between Foreign Minister Toyoda and Ambassador Grew in Tokyo. The President was agreed in principle to the meeting, but in his conversation of August 17 he had suggested that Japan make a clearer statement of her position before we proceeded with preparations for it. He had indicated that, if such a meeting were to be held, it might be arranged for about October 15.

Nomura came back to me on August 23 to say that his Government would like to hold the Roosevelt-Konoye meeting at an earlier date than October 15. He said frankly that this desire was due to the military conferences that would be held shortly in Moscow. He was referring to the missions Britain and the United States were sending to Moscow to coordinate Russia's military supply needs. He indicated that his Government was afraid that some agreements might be reached at Moscow detrimental to Japan.

"Don't you think," I asked with some irony, "that the neutrality pact signed in April between Japan and Russia will undoubtedly give Japan all the assurance of Russia's peaceful attitude toward Japan that you could desire?"

Nomura contented himself with laughing very heartily.

Specifically he brought up the question of shipments of American supplies to Russia via the Far Eastern Soviet port of Vladivostok. He said that, while no diplomatic incident had developed thus far, the shipment of oil to Vladivostok through "Japanese waters" would naturally give the Japanese real concern at an early date. Japan was faced with large Russian forces in the Vladivostok area, he added, and could not be satisfied to see what she would firmly believe would be a great building up of Russian military supply bases just across the line from Japan.

"My Government," I replied, "is concerned only with seeing that Russia gets these and other military supplies to use in European Russia to resist the German armies. We have no other purpose than that. Hence the question of building up supplies for the Russian Army in the Far East is not in any sense in view. Of course, if Japan should project herself militarily into the Russo-German situation—which I hope she will not —an entirely different question would be presented."

Four days later Nomura protested to me against two oil-tanker shipments from the United States to Russia through Vladivostok.

I replied that the shipments were entirely legitimate under all laws of commerce, and that they were comparatively microscopic in quantity.

At the same time Nomura handed me a copy of his Government's reply to the President's notes of August 17. I thereupon arranged to take the Ambassador to see Mr. Roosevelt the following day, August 28.

Nomura gave the President two communications. The first, from Konoye to Mr. Roosevelt, dealt with their proposed meeting. It clearly stated Japan's idea that the meeting should be held as quickly as possible, and that negotiations for an agreement should follow rather than precede it. Konoye said the present situation was developing swiftly and might produce unforeseen contingencies.

The President complimented Konoye, through Nomura, on the spirit of his communication. He then spoke of the difficulty of going as far as Hawaii and suggested Juneau, Alaska. He said he would be keenly interested in having three or four days with Konoye.

In the second communication Nomura handed the President the Japanese Government assured us of its peaceful intentions and of its search for a program for the Pacific consistent with American principles— with several qualifications. These were:

Japan would withdraw her troops from Indo-China "as soon as the China Incident is settled or a just peace is established in East Asia." Japan would take no military action against Russia so long as Russia observed the neutrality pact and did "not menace Japan or Manchukuo." Japan had no intention of using "without provocation" military force against any neighboring country.

That evening Nomura came to my apartment to discuss the proposed meeting. He thought that Konoye would be assisted by a staff of about twenty—five each from the Foreign Office, the Army, the Navy, and the Embassy in Washington. He suggested September 21 to 25 as the date, and said his Government was anxious that the meeting be held at the earliest possible moment in view of the efforts to disturb Japanese-American relations on the part of a third country—meaning Germany—and of fifth columnists in Japan who were backing a press campaign against the United States.

After saying I would refer these points to the President, I commented that it was desirable to reach an agreement in principle on major questions prior to the meeting.

"Serious consequences from the viewpoint of both Governments," I said, "would ensue if the meeting failed to result in an agreement. The meeting should therefore have as its purpose the ratification of essential points already agreed to in principle."

Nomura went over the three principal points on which we had encountered difficulties in our conversations—Japan's relations to the Axis, retention of Japanese troops in North China and Inner Mongolia, and the application of the principle of nondiscrimination in international commercial relations. He thought that only with regard to Japanese troops in China and Mongolia would there be real difficulty.

Nomura emphasized that it was the idea of his Government that we should exercise our good offices to bring China and Japan together, leaving them to reach a direct settlement among themselves. Our idea was to discuss with Japan the basic terms on which peace might be firmly maintained.

"We should be involved in this matter," I explained, "through Japan's requesting us to exercise our good offices. In order to exercise such good offices, we need to have the confidence and friendship of the Chinese Government before and after. We can't propose that the Chinese negotiate with Japan until we know what Japan's basic terms are. You can imagine what a difficult situation would arise if, after a meeting between Prince Konoye and the President, an explosion should occur in China over dissatisfaction with the results of the meeting.

"We can't afford to have the Chinese think we are ignoring their interests in going ahead with any arrangements. It is our idea to help the Japanese establish friendship with China on a solid basis. In this way we can work together, Japan and the United States, in order to develop the trading potentialities of 500,000,000 Chinese."

Nomura asked if other questions pending between Japan and the United States could not be settled at the meeting, apart from the China question, so as to tide over a critical situation in our relations.

"It's quite true," I said, "that there are other questions pending that

must be settled; but the China question is one of the pivotal ones. If this
remains unsettled to the satisfaction of all, the roots of future instability
and trouble would remain."

Nomura thought our attitude in regard to self-defense vis-à-vis Germany was "entirely reasonable"; but he remarked that to ask that Japan
give a blank check for any action the United States might take against
Germany in the name of self-defense was equivalent to asking for nullifi-
cation of the Tripartite Pact.

Sir Ronald Campbell, British Chargé, brought me on August 30
copies of two alternative drafts of a warning Britain intended to send
Japan, and asked for my comment on them. Both forms contained the
concluding sentence of the draft drawn up by the President and Mr.
Churchill which my associates and I had considered undesirable. I went
over the situation in the Far East with Sir Ronald, particularly the
domestic political situation in Japan which I thought in an explosive stage,
so that his Government could form its own conclusions about presenting
its ultimatum at this time. I said that, in any event, it should be presented
confidentially and in a way that would not tend to upset the present
Japanese Cabinet.

When I saw Nomura again at my apartment on September 1, I asked
him to suggest to his Government that it exercise its influence with the
Japanese press.

"If the Japanese Government," I said, "finds it difficult to influence
the Japanese public and press against agitation for a policy of conquest
and against a campaign prejudicial to the success of a peaceful settlement
with the United States, there's no assurance that your Government
could obtain public support for any such settlement after it had been
concluded—and then a new political crisis in Japan might occur."

Nomura promised to communicate this to his Government. In due
course we did notice a diminution in the press attacks against us.

My associates and I were now analyzing the Japanese notes Nomura
had handed the President on August 28, and were preparing the replies.
Our attention concentrated on the point that seemed uppermost in the
mind of the Japanese Government—the proposed Roosevelt-Konoye
meeting.

The more we analyzed the possibilities and dangers of the conference,
the more we became convinced that no meeting should be held until the
heads of the two Governments were ready to sign an agreement. We

wanted an agreement on fundamental principles—and on their application.

Japan's insistence on holding the meeting and leaving the "details" to be worked out later was in itself significant. It seemed to us that Japan was striving to push us into a conference from which general statements would issue—and Japan could then interpret and apply these statements to suit her own purposes, as she had always done in the past. Moreover, she could then say she had the President's endorsement of her actions.

It was difficult to believe that the Konoye Government would dare to agree to proposals we could accept. Konoye, Toyoda, and Nomura were insisting that their suggestion for the meeting be kept strictly secret, for the reason that, if premature publicity occurred, the elements in Japan hostile to any such move would defeat it. This indicated to us—what we knew already—that a substantial opposition existed in Japan to any efforts to improve relations with the United States. Included in this opposition were powerful military officials and many other Japanese who were being whipped up by the incessant activities of the German Embassy in Tokyo.

Even while our preliminary conversations with the Konoye Government were in progress, that Government restricted and narrowed the concessions it had originally been willing to make. It was not likely that Konoye, in a personal meeting with Roosevelt, would be able to move completely in the opposite direction.

We had no real assurance that Konoye himself would desire to carry out an agreement that would turn Japan into the paths of real peace. We could not forget that Konoye had been Premier when Japan invaded China in 1937; he had signed the Axis Alliance in 1940 and had concluded the treaty with the puppet Government in Nanking designated to give Japan the mastery of China.

We could not overlook the fact that the very holding of the meeting between the President and Konoye, following so soon on the Atlantic Conference, would cause China grave uneasiness, unless an agreement had already been reached that would protect China's sovereignty.

Unless the President were willing to agree to vague generalities that would all be to Japan's advantage, there was every likelihood that the meeting would end in failure. In that event Japan's military officials could declare to the Japanese that the United States was responsible for the failure and proceed to prepare public opinion for war in the Pacific.

We knew, of course, that the Konoye Government was beginning to encounter internal difficulties and might be in danger of collapse. This was one evident reason why Konoye was pressing so strongly for the meeting with the President. If he could present the country with the accomplished fact of an agreement with the United States he might be able to stay in power. We knew, too, that if the Konoye Government fell it would be replaced in all likelihood by a military Government with which it would be more difficult to deal. Unsatisfactory as the Konoye Government was from our point of view, it still seemed better than what was likely to follow it; and it was therefore to our own interest to cooperate as far as we could to keep it in power. But we could not do so at the expense of our own principles and interests, those of China, and those of the other nations concerned in the Far East.

During the next few weeks we received numerous appeals from Tokyo to hasten the Roosevelt-Konoye conference. Ambassador Grew recommended it. But Grew, who had an admirable understanding of the Japanese situation, could not estimate the over-all world situation as we could in Washington.

President Roosevelt would have relished a meeting with Konoye, and at first he was excited at the prospect. But he instantly agreed that it would be disastrous to hold the meeting without first arriving at a satisfactory agreement.

At no time did we return a refusal to Japan's proposal for a meeting. We simply laid down the condition that we should arrive at a basic agreement before the meeting. Japan could have had the conference at any time by negotiating an agreement that would really have brought peace in the Pacific and prosperity to her as well as to the other countries interested in the Orient.

As for me, I was thoroughly satisfied that a meeting with Konoye, without an advance agreement, could only result either in another Munich or in nothing at all. I was opposed to the first Munich and still more opposed to a second Munich.

We did not know it at the time, but four years later, with the uncovering of Premier Konoye's memoirs, there came a striking confirmation of the wisdom of our refusal to hold the conference unless an agreement had been reached. Konoye sets forth in his memoirs that on August 4, 1941, he presented his project for the meeting to the Japanese War and Navy Ministers. He proposed that, if the President failed to "understand" the Japanese position, he would quit the meeting, and that the Japanese people would then understand that war was inevitable and would consequently have a firmer determination. He felt that haste was necessary because Germany might not come out well with her war in Russia, in which event the United States might take a stronger attitude toward Japan.

Konoye's memoirs say further that the Navy supported his view. The Army, however, made a conditional acceptance in writing, to which Konoye would have to agree before setting out to meet the President. The Army first stated that the meeting would be calculated inevitably to weaken the Empire's diplomacy founded on the Tripartite Alliance and was likely to cause considerable domestic ripples, and was therefore considered by the Army to be inappropriate. Then came this condition:

"If the Prime Minister intends, while attending the conference, to adhere to the fundamental policy contained in the Japanese revised plan and, in the event that the American President fails to understand the real intentions of this country and is resolved to go on with his present policy, to quit the place of rendezvous with a determination to make war on the United States, the Army will not oppose the Prime Minister's having a direct talk with the President."

Konoye thus had to promise to go to the meeting and demand a Yes or No answer from the President to the Japanese proposals which would have given Japan the overlordship of the Orient; and, if the President said No, to return to Japan determined to make war on the United States.

I took Nomura to the President on September 3 to receive our replies to the Japanese notes of August 28. The President, in his answer to Konoye's proposal for a meeting, pointed out that he could not avoid taking cognizance of indications that concepts existed in some quarters in Japan which, if widely entertained, would hinder successful collaboration between him and Konoye. He therefore suggested that they "take precaution, toward ensuring that our proposed meeting shall prove a success, by endeavoring to enter immediately upon preliminary discussion of the fundamental and essential questions on which we seek agreement."

In a second communication which the President handed Nomura we asked Japan to clarify her attitude with regard to the fundamental questions still outstanding between us.

I saw Chinese Ambassador Hu Shih the following day and informed him that I was having exploratory conversations with the Japanese, but that no common basis for negotiations had yet been revealed. I repeated what I had told him in May, that, before considering negotiations with

Japan affecting China, we should expect to discuss the entire subject with China, Britain, The Netherlands, and Australia.

Hu Shih seemed to feel that Japan was showing signs of weakening, and that within a reasonable time she would be obliged to abandon any aggressive military activities and seek peace.

I pointed out four possible developments: first, the collapse of Japan mentioned by the Ambassador; second, Japan's adoption and application of the basic principles for which the United States stood; third, Japan's endeavoring to face both ways by entering into an agreement whereby, under an implied reservation, she would contend that she had the right to exercise force against other countries in given circumstances; fourth, refusal of the governments opposed to Japan, including the United States, to enter into a settlement at the present time.

A few days later I instructed Clarence E. Gauss, our Ambassador at Chungking, to inform the Chinese Foreign Minister that, in our conversations with the Japanese, no consideration had been or would be given to any arrangement permitting the continuance of aggression in China, and that we had no intention of sacrificing the fundamental principles and policies which this Government had long believed constituted the only sound basis for stable relations between nations. Gauss was also to say that we would continue our policy of aiding nations resisting aggression.

We now awaited new proposals from Japan, in answer to the President's request for clarification of Japan's position on the issues before us. They were soon forthcoming. We received them from Grew on September 5, and Nomura handed his copy of them to me on September 6.

74: War Cabinet in Japan

JAPAN'S PROPOSALS, on the basis of which she expected a meeting between President Roosevelt and Premier Konoye to be held, fell far short of any possibility of acceptance. They were much narrower than we had reason to expect from the comparatively generous assurances communicated to the President on August 28. They thereby followed the pattern of the earlier conversations in that, as soon as Japan saw we were interested in a set of proposals sufficiently to want to discuss them, she began to back-pedal and to narrow and limit them.

Japan promised not to make any military advance from French Indo-China against any adjoining area and not to resort to military action against any regions south of Japan without justifiable reason. We took particular note of this qualifying phrase, also of the fact that Japan still evaded the President's suggestion that she withdraw her troops from Indo-China in exchange for neutralization of that colony.

Japan stated that interpretation and execution of the Tripartite Pact by her would be "independently decided." This meant that Japan herself would judge what constituted self-defense on the part of the United States if we became involved in the European War.

She set forth that she would endeavor to bring about normal relations with China, after which she would be ready to withdraw her armed forces from China as soon as possible in accordance with the agreements between Japan and China. Here was no commitment as to the terms Japan would offer China, no assurance of any intention by Japan to respect China's sovereignty and integrity or to refrain from stationing Japanese troops indefinitely in certain areas of China.

Japan stated that the economic activities of the United States in China would not be restricted "so long as pursued on an equitable basis." She obviously would be the judge of what constituted an "equitable basis."

We on our part were to abstain from any measures or actions that would be prejudicial to Japan's endeavor to settle the "China Affair." This meant, of course, that we would cease giving aid to Chiang Kai-shek and thus force him into an agreement with Japan.

We were also to suspend any military measures in the Far East and in the Southwest Pacific. This would naturally include our ceasing to strengthen the Philippines and to give aid to the British and Dutch in strengthening their possessions in the same area.

Also, both countries were to suspend the application of the freezing acts, and the United States was to remove the prohibition against the passage of Japanese vessels through the Panama Canal. Likewise, the two countries were to resume their normal trade relations.

The effect of this last provision would have been to deprive us of the weapon of economic pressure through which we had been able to indicate to Japan our attitude toward her successive moves of expansion.

On the day Nomura handed me these new proposals, Premier Konoye, in a conversation with Grew in Tokyo, said that the Japanese Government fully subscribed to the four principles I had set forth in my memorandum to the Japanese on April 16—respect for the territorial integrity and sovereignty of all nations, noninterference in the internal affairs of other countries, the principle of equality, including equality of commercial opportunity, and nondisturbance of the status quo in the Pacific except as it might be altered by peaceful means.

Konoye's affirmation of complete adherence to these principles looked to us like an attempt to make his other proposals more palatable. In any event, Foreign Minister Toyoda stated one month later that Konoye had accepted these four points only "in principle," and that in applying them to actual conditions certain "adjustments" would be necessary. That meant, of course, that the Japanese Government might accept these principles, but the Japanese Army would apply them in its own way.

British Chargé Campbell called upon me two days later to inquire about our conversations with the Japanese. I told him that Government officials in Japan were putting out reports that an agreement could be expected this week or some time in the near future, presumably hoping this publicity would enlist the support of public opinion and check the efforts of Japanese extremists to carry public opinion in the opposite direction.

"The negotiations," I said, "are still in an exploratory stage. A number of basic matters will have to be discussed and settled before we shall be in position to take them up in earnest with China, Britain, and other interested countries.

"I doubt if that situation ever will develop. In my opinion, delaying the possible expansion movements of Japan—which I have had in mind since last spring—is still the primary consideration."

To me it seemed there was still only one chance in fifty of reaching a real agreement with Japan. My major hope was to hold off Japan's next advance, which would probably bring war in the Pacific, as long as possible.

Our discussions with Japan now encountered numerous difficulties, only part of which related to the points under discussion. First of these was the desire of Foreign Minister Toyoda to transfer the conversations to Tokyo, and there to rush us into an agreement on Japanese terms. I objected, however, for two reasons. One was that the President was closely following our conversations in Washington. I was in contact with him several times a week on this subject. The other was that we wished to keep the conversations close to ourselves who had the world picture in mind. We realized that there were basic differences between our two countries. If these had been resolved, we could have transplanted the conversations to Tokyo to work out the details there; but they still existed, and Japan's successive proposals tended to accentuate them.

Toyoda thereupon began to draw Grew into the negotiations on his own account. He handed Grew copies of the various Japanese proposals and statements, while at the same time cabling Nomura to hand me the same copies. Owing to the necessity for paraphrasing in both cases, we in Washington found ourselves scrutinizing documents that were intended to be identical but contained serious differences of words and phrases.

One version of the proposals of September 6 stated that Japan would not take military action against regions to the south of her. The other read, to the north of her. We asked for clarification repeatedly but, up to the time of Pearl Harbor, had not received it.

Nomura himself was a serious difficulty. He was not a professional diplomat, and his assistants who should have given him adequate technical help were not equal to their task. I believe he was serious and honest, but he made blunders that embarrassed his Government. He mentioned to White House correspondents on August 28 that he had given the President a message from Konoye; this started a wave of speculation on both sides of the Pacific. He handed me on September 4 a new set of proposals, without the authority of his Government, which he had worked over himself. He later had to withdraw them.

I was never completely sure that Nomura understood our points, even when I had Joseph Ballantine repeat them to him in Japanese. He and his assistants did not keep as full a record of our conversations as they should have. In consequence, Toyoda was obliged gently to reprimand him and to demand that Nomura cable the full minutes of our meetings as quickly as possible.

At times we were not sure that Nomura understood some of his own Government's points, since he seemed vague in explaining them.

We on our side kept our conversations perfectly documented. We knew at all times the exact status of the conversations, what proposals had been made, and what explanations offered when and by whom. This was owing to Dr. Hornbeck's precise draftsmanship and analysis of documents, Hamilton's infinite capacity for detail, and Ballantine's skillful industry in returning to the State Department after my night talks with Nomura and putting down on paper precisely what had been said.

There were two difficulties connected with the terms of our conversations. One was the disposition of the Konoye Government to wave aside the idea of preliminary discussions and to insist again and again that a Roosevelt-Konoye meeting would settle everything. The other was the Japanese Government's undue preoccupation with formulas. Konoye, Toyoda, and Nomura recognized our well known desire for peace and our determination to stick by our principles. Their efforts therefore centered on finding a formula that would satisfy that desire and determination in principle, while still giving them an outlet for their ambitions. This accounts for the belief they often affirmed that our two countries were not really far apart, and that it was merely "a question of phraseology," or clever draftsmanship.

In the background of all these difficulties in our discussions lay a series of menacing Japanese developments. Japan increased the number of troops in Indo-China, began to prepare new airports there, and entered actively into the administration of the colony. She speeded up her military preparations at home, to the tune of constant agitation in the Japanese press in support of extremist policies and the bellicose utterances of Japanese leaders. In China, Japanese bombings of civilian populations went on incessantly.

A series of discussions followed Nomura's presentation of the September 6 proposals. I conducted some with Nomura; Grew conducted others with Toyoda. There was an element of eagerness on both sides. Konoye and his Cabinet wanted to bring about the meeting with the President. We wanted to do what we could to reach an agreement so that the Konoye Government could stay in power rather than be ousted by a military Government. But there was little progress, if any, in overcoming our differences.

Nomura handed me on September 23 a statement from his Government defining Japan's peace terms for China, for which we had asked specifically. These continued to retain the provision for the stationing of Japanese troops in certain areas of China, and the equivocal provision that economic activities of other Powers in China would not be restricted so long as they were pursued "on an equitable basis."

Then on September 27 Nomura gave me, as from his Government, a new redraft of the Japanese proposals. There were a few minor changes but no evidence of any modification of Japan's attitude on fundamental points.

When Nomura came back to my apartment on September 29 to press for an answer, I commented that, just as the Japanese Government had its difficulties, we had our difficulties too, and we could not accept any agreement other than a broad-gauge one. "The whole effort of our conversations," I said, "has been to narrow the gap between our respective views, and we have felt that time is necessary in order to enable the Japanese Government to educate its public opinion to accept a broad-gauge program such as we advocate."

Nomura remarked that he himself was in favor of a broad-gauge program, but he knew the Japanese Army's psychology very well. Even the highest-ranking generals, he said, had a simplicity of mind that made it difficult for them to see why the United States, on the one hand, should assert leadership in the Western Hemisphere with the Monroe Doctrine and, on the other, want to interfere with Japan's assuming leadership in Asia.

"Why can't the Japanese Government educate the generals?" I asked.

Nomura replied this would take twenty years.

"A number of our marine guards don't want to leave China," I said, "and I suppose there are many Japanese troops in China who don't want to be recalled."

Nomura laughingly replied this was true. He said that when an army general in China was clothed with the authority of a viceroy, naturally he did not welcome the prospect of being shorn of that authority.

Nomura handed me a statement by Foreign Minister Toyoda that the ship to carry Konoye to the meeting with Roosevelt was ready, the members of his suite, including a full general and a full admiral, had been secretly appointed, and the date of October 10–15 would be suitable. He added that any delay would put his Government in a very delicate position. If the present Cabinet were to fall, the opportunity for a Japanese-American rapprochement was likely to be lost for some time to come.

But, in view of Japan's attitude, the opportunity Toyoda mentioned seemed to me very small, as I informed Chinese Ambassador Hu Shih on October 1. I said that the chances of reaching a stage of formal negotiations with Japan had at all times been one out of twenty-five or fifty or even a hundred. And I repeated our firm purpose to discuss all pertinent questions fully with China if that stage should be reached. In any event, I said, we intended to continue to aid China until a satisfactory settlement should be made.

After many conversations and exchanges with the Japanese I began to prepare with my associates a comprehensive communication to Japan on our position. As always throughout the discussions with Japan, I kept in close contact with the President as we drafted it. Occasionally I jotted down thoughts in pencil and sent them to him in this form. On September 28 he sent me from Hyde Park a memo in answer to such a note concerning the document under preparation.

"I wholly agree," he said, "with your penciled note—to recite the more liberal original attitude of the Japanese when they first sought the meeting, point out their much narrowed position now, earnestly ask if they cannot go back to their original attitude, start discussions again on agreement in principle, and reemphasize my hope for a meeting."

I handed our document to Nomura on October 2, my seventieth birthday. In it I pointed out that the Japanese proposals of September 6 had been "a source of disappointment" to us in that they narrowed down the application of the general assurances Konoye had given us on August 28.

I emphasized that what this Government envisaged was a comprehensive program calling for the application uniformly to the entire Pacific area of liberal and progressive principles. "From what the Japanese Government has so far indicated in regard to its purposes," I added, "this Government derives the impression that the Japanese Government has in mind a program which would be circumscribed by the imposition of qualifications and exceptions to the actual application of those principles."

As for the Roosevelt-Konoye meeting, I said this had engaged, and continued to engage, the President's close and active interest. "It is the President's earnest hope that discussion of the fundamental questions may be so developed that such a meeting can be held," I concluded.

During the next two weeks we continued discussions in Washington and Tokyo to narrow the gap between our fundamentally different viewpoints, with no success. Various new arguments were advanced, such as Nomura's that, since the Japanese public had suffered the sacrifices of four years of war in China, his Government would necessarily have to present to the Japanese people some reward for that sacrifice or an attractive alternative gain. But there was no meeting of minds.

Foreign Minister Toyoda informed Grew on October 10 that, since he had the impression that Nomura was very fatigued, he was considering sending a diplomat of wide experience to Washington to assist the Ambassador. This was our first intimation of the sending to Washington of Ambassador Saburo Kurusu in November.

Kaname Wakasugi, Minister-Counselor of the Japanese Embassy, returning to Washington after a two-weeks visit to Japan, said to us that all the high Japanese officials with whom he talked wanted peace with us, but that a small but very powerful group had placed its fortunes on the Axis and was determined to go to any length to prevent an understanding with the United States and to bring Japan actively into Germany's camp. He added that his Government would have to show some results and could not continue conversations with the United States indefinitely. In the event the Government fell, he said, it would in all probability be replaced by a Cabinet of military representatives responsive only to German pressure; and thereupon hope of adjusting relations with the United States must vanish.

We knew from our intercepts of Japanese Government messages how strong was the German pressure being applied in Tokyo. One such message, of October 16, from Toyoda to Nomura, stated that the German authorities were demanding that the Japanese Government submit a note of warning to the United States. The Germans were aroused over the President's "shoot on sight" order of September 11, the incidents that had already occurred between German and American vessels, and the possibility that the Neutrality Act would be amended. They wanted the Japanese Government to state to us that, if the Roosevelt Administration continued to attack the Axis Powers increasingly, a belligerent situation would inevitably arise between the European Axis and the United States which might lead Japan, under the provisions of the Tripartite Alliance, to join immediately in the war against the United States.

Toyoda did send Nomura a message along these lines on the same day, but considerably watered down.

It was one of Toyoda's last official acts. For on that very day the Konoye Cabinet fell, to be replaced on the following day by the Tojo military Cabinet that later carried Japan through Pearl Harbor down the path of disaster.

Our conversations with the Konoye Government had continued for six months. I had had dozens of long talks with Nomura, and we had exchanged scores of telegrams with Tokyo. On our part we had been truly anxious to reach an agreement that would make peace in the Pacific possible, not for a few months but for years or generations. Yet when the Konoye Cabinet fell the area of difference betwen us was wider than at the start of the discussions.

Rather than edging closer to our point of view once they had stated their original proposals on May 12, the Japanese Government steadily moved in the opposite direction. They became more inflexible on their basic demands even as they became more aggressive in the military field.

We had to take into consideration the fact that for years Japanese leaders and writers had been preaching territorial aggrandizement. They said it was essential to Japan's security that she control additional sources of war materials so as to make herself economically and militarily self-sufficient. Many of Japan's civilian as well as military leaders were disciples of this doctrine. Konoye himself had made clear-cut statements in this direction.

It was plain to us therefore that, if through adverse developments in the war in Europe we had to divert our principal naval strength from the Pacific to the Atlantic, the Japanese Government would find it almost impossible to refrain from essaying new conquests.

The conversations of the previous six months, and the limited commitments that Konoye and his Government were willing to make, showed clearly that Japan was not prepared to make a general renunciation of aggression. She was adamant in refusing to withdraw her troops from northern China and Inner Mongolia, because the presence of her armed forces in those territories gave her control over them. And she was equally adamant in refusing to state that she would not declare war on us if we became engaged in war with Germany as a result of our measures of self-defense. She was also insistent on qualifications and interpretations that would continue to give her a preferred economic position in the Far East.

Our primary problem, therefore, was to obtain unequivocal evidence from Japan that she honestly wished to abandon her course of aggression and to resume a peaceful policy. Until we had secured this evidence, any agreement with Japan would have been worth less than the ink expended in signing it.

We had repeatedly pointed out to Japan that her position with regard to the Axis Alliance and her professed desire for peace with the United

States in the Pacific were in open contrast. Even had we worked out an agreement for peace in the Pacific in the most minute detail, that peace could have been shattered if Hitler chose to make our measures of self-defense a cause for war and Japan had felt obliged to observe the Axis Alliance pact. Japan wanted to make herself the sole judge as to what constituted self-defense on our part.

In an agreement such as the Konoye Government proposed, Japan might have taken several years to carry out her side of the bargain, as in China. We, on the other hand, were obliged to perform certain acts immediately. From the moment of signing we should have to lift all our economic restrictions against Japan. She also would lift her economic restrictions against us—except in China; but our restrictions were the ones that counted, since they virtually cut off Japan's supplies of strategic materials from this country. Japan's proposals provided for no method whereby we could have removed economic pressure against her step by step as and when she moved step by step away from conquest toward peace.

Right at the outset, furthermore, we should have had to discontinue sending further troops and war materials to the Philippines, and military aid to China, British Malaya, and the Dutch East Indies. Japan suggested no counter provision whereby she would instantly have reduced her military establishments in the Far East.

Japan was willing to give general assurances that she would not continue her movement of conquest, but these were not enough. We had to have definite evidence of her willingness and ability to pursue policies conforming to the principles to which we adhered. And she was giving us the opposite.

We realized, of course, that the Japanese Government could not, even if it wished, reverse overnight a trend toward conquest that had been going on for ten years—that is, since her invasion of Manchuria in 1931—to say nothing of her earlier movements of aggression. We knew that considerable time would be involved in any such change of direction, and we were willing to be patient, as we repeatedly informed Tokyo. The Konoye Government, however, was very impatient. It wanted quickly to reach an agreement that would keep it in power and at the same time offer sufficient loopholes and escapes to enable it to take advantage of the opportunities that seemed to lie ahead because of the war in Europe.

The President and I knew that any agreement we signed had to be acceptable to the American people. Such an agreement could not, and should not, be kept secret. It was manifest to us that the American people would scrutinize with minute care an agreement so vital to their future, and would rise up against any accord that sacrificed the basic principles essential for sound international relations. We could certainly count on the Japanese giving it their own "slant" throughout the Far East, as they had done with previous agreements like the Lansing-Ishii accord of 1917.

We could easily have had an agreement with the Konoye Government at any time by signing on the dotted line. Mr. Roosevelt and Konoye could have met, and from their meeting might have flowed vague generalities on undying peace. But we should have negated principles on which we had built our foreign policy and without which the world could not live at peace. We should have betrayed China and the Philippines and abandoned Britain and Holland. Japan might have gone into Russia and so weakened her that Hitler might have won over Stalin.

And on the ladder of an agreement such as the Japanese demanded, a mightier Japan would have climbed to become a greater danger to us than ever before.

75: Weygand Ousted

WHEN JAPAN INVADED southern Indo-China and Vichy France concurred, our relations with the Pétain Government became yet more difficult. This invasion was one of three main factors that influenced our contact with Vichy in the six months between Hitler's invasion of Russia and Pearl Harbor. The other two were the uncertainty over whether the Germans would invade French North Africa during the inactivity induced by the Russian winter, and the dismissal of General Weygand.

In July, 1941, Pétain summoned Weygand to Vichy for a conference. Since it seemed again that the possibility of German bases in French North and West Africa would be discussed, President Roosevelt sent a message to Pétain and the State Department a message to Weygand, urging them to stand firm.

Leahy asked to see Pétain alone to present the President's message; but indicative of Vice Premier Darlan's influence was Pétain's statement to Leahy that Darlan had insisted on being present. Darlan, in fact, assumed virtual control of the interview. He assured Leahy that, as long as the present armistice arrangement with Germany continued, no foreign Power would be permitted to use the African bases. That left the supposition wide open that he expected a change in that arrangement.

Darlan gave Leahy advance information that Japan would in the immediate future occupy bases in Indo-China, from which it could undertake further military operations to the South. Leahy believed that this information was deliberately given to us with the knowledge and approval of Germany in the hope that it would get us heavily involved in the Pacific and thus limit our efforts in the Atlantic.

We reacted strongly when Vichy France concurred in Japan's occupation of southern Indo-China on the specious grounds that it was carried out to forestall a similar move by the British and the De Gaullists. Welles, after talking over the situation with me by long-distance telephone when I was absent from Washington, stated our position publicly on August 2 by saying we were now impelled to question whether the Pétain Government in fact proposed to maintain its declared policy to preserve for the French people the territory both at home and abroad which had been under French sovereignty.

We would not, of course, have expected the Vichy Government to offer any effective resistance to the Japanese. But we could have expected it to refrain from giving the Japanese occupation its legal sanction and from falling in with Tokyo's propaganda line that the British and the De Gaullists were about to seize Indo-China.

Popular reaction here to the occupation seemed more bitter against Vichy France for legalizing the move than against Japan for making it. We again received a wave of demands that we break relations with Vichy and occupy Dakar. This wave rose when Pétain made a radio address on August 12 that seemed to pull the last underpinnings out from under whatever remained of democracy in France, placed all power in the hands of the Government, and doubled the police force. He did not, however, mention collaboration with Germany.

Ambassador Henry-Haye came to me on August 20 to explain Pétain's address and to protest the press criticism against it in this country. He said Pétain had spoken merely to quiet the French internal situation without intending to make any change in Vichy's relations with Berlin.

"So many things," I replied, "have occurred at Vichy that people feel Marshal Pétain is being dragged along toward collaboration with Hitler. Without disparaging his great military career, they feel he is only a general and a soldier, not a statesman, and naturally he would be over-reached by oily-tongued demagogues posing as statesmen. The uppermost purpose of the Laval-Darlan groups seems to be to deliver France body and soul to Hitler."

Weygand's attitude, however, continued highly satisfactory, and nothing had occurred to change the basic points on which the President and I were resolved to maintain diplomatic ties with the Pétain Government. Weygand's associates suggested to our representative, Robert Murphy, that we state what military aid the United States could give Weygand for the purpose of resisting Axis aggression, and when. In a letter to me of July 15, Murphy suggested it would have an important effect if he could inform Weygand that a program of substantial military aid was under discussion in Washington.

We were not ready in 1941, however, to send military supplies to North Africa; nor did it seem wise to do so, since this very act might provoke a German invasion of the French colonies. Furthermore, the situation did not seem to demand it. The Russian invasion was not going according to Hitler's plan, and it seemed likely that French North Africa might enjoy a longer breathing spell. We could never be sure, however, and Ambassador Leahy reported to the President that indications at Vichy pointed to a German move against the Mediterranean upon the completion of the current Russian campaign, regardless of the outcome. Now that Indo-China had been abandoned to Japan, he thought it would be particularly hard for the French to resist German demands for African bases.

The most we wanted to do in French North Africa at the time was to continue the closest possible contact with Weygand and other authorities, supported by the economic accord we had signed with him. Actually we had considerable difficulty living up to that accord. By July 1 we had dispatched only two tankers with petroleum products to North Africa. By October only one more tanker and four cargo vessels, carrying principally sugar, tea, coal, cotton goods, and tobacco, had gone. Delay was occasioned by trouble over priorities, by opposition to our program on the part of some other Departments and agencies of the Government, and by difficulties with the British over navicerts.

On the other hand, the advantages we expected from the accord were accruing to us in full. The vice consuls we had sent to North Africa to control the distribution and consumption of our shipments, and above all to keep an eye on the situation there, were sending us excellent intelligence and were making useful contacts with local authorities and the army. Our relations with Weygand and his assistants were of the best. The people in the colonies seemed to want the economic connection with the United States to continue. From the surveys we received, German infiltration in North and West Africa did not appear serious. Consul Wasson reported in October that he had been unable to find any Germans at all at Dakar, except a few Jewish refugees.

As our uncertainty, however, continued over Hitler's intentions and Pétain's possible reaction, the President sent a further message, which Leahy handed the Premier on September 12, again urging that French sovereignty in the African colonies be preserved. Pétain replied he had no intention of ceding any bases in Africa to the Germans; but France was a conquered country and he could never know when the *Diktat* might come. He added that, so long as the British tolerated De Gaulle—whom he described as "a viper that he had warmed in his bosom"—there could be no better understanding between Britain and France.

I brought up the question of French Africa when Ambassador Henry-Haye stated to me on September 16 that his Government desired that the

United States, in any negotiations with Japan, should keep in mind the interests of Indo-China, and especially her desire to be completely independent of Japan when a settlement was reached in the Pacific.

This request, coming after Vichy France had given its legal sanction to Japan's invasion of Indo-China, struck me amidships, and I halted the Ambassador at that point.

"Regardless of where the truth lies," I said, "there is a real belief that during August, 1940, Japan requested Hitler to ask the Vichy Government not to be too demonstrative in opposing Japanese occupation of Indo-China and Indo-Chinese waters. There exists likewise the belief that the Vichy Government, notwithstanding the fact that such action went beyond the terms of the armistice, complied in an effort to placate Hitler."

I added that my Government was opposed alike to Japanese conquest and to German conquest and was contesting both in various ways. Also, we profoundly believed that Hitler's movement would mean utter ruin to France and Europe and finally to America unless he were stopped by force, and we intended to continue our opposition until he was stopped.

"The general attitude in America toward Japan's occupation of Indo-China has manifested itself in various ways," I pointed out, "because this occupation evidently is next to the final step in a possible military invasion of the South Seas area. In addition, we are fundamentally opposed to the invasion of small or helpless countries by a powerful country like Japan, and we have emphatically made this known to Japan in more ways than one."

I then tied in the question of French Africa with French Indo-China. "Your Government," I said, "comes to us with regard to Indo-China but says nothing about French Africa, especially the northern and western parts along the Atlantic coast. We have no selfish interests in that area whatever, but we do have a definite interest in opposing Hitler's seizing French Africa with its harbors on the Atlantic coast as part of his movement to get control of the seas and seriously threaten this hemisphere. The Vichy Government has not requested us to render aid to prevent such German occupation—on the contrary there are implied threats by some high French officials to deny to this Government the privilege of discouraging Hitler from going into North Africa.

"We've thanked the Vichy Government, of course, for such efforts as it has made to observe the terms of the armistice relating to French ports and French Africa. But we don't know from week to week when Hitler may press Darlan to make concessions which go entirely beyond the armistice terms, to the detriment of peaceful nations like the United States."

I finally said to Henry-Haye that, if our conversations with Japan reached the right stage, I would then hear representations from his Government with regard to Indo-China and would make appropriate comment.

The Free French National Committee was organized in London on September 24, and the British Government accorded it a considerable degree of practical recognition. To the President and me there came a renewed flood of demands that we do likewise. We could never, however, expect to recognize De Gaulle without breaking with the legal government of Pétain, who incidentally entertained a bitter hatred toward his former subordinate. The Vichy Government, and not De Gaulle, was in control of the population in unoccupied France.

A few weeks later, on November 11, we did, however, extend practical aid to De Gaulle when the President instructed E. R. Stettinius, Jr., Lend-Lease Administrator, to include any French territory under the control of the Free French within the scope of the Lend-Lease Act. I fully supported this move. We were already stationing consular representatives in such territories.

The distinction in our treatment of the Free French was thus clear. We would give them material assistance wherever necessary in their efforts to combat the Axis. We would keep in touch with them through our consular representatives. But we would not recognize them as a government.

During the autumn three developments began to shake the conviction of Darlan and his group that France's future lay with Germany. One was the fact that the resistance organization in occupied France, which had been steadily growing in importance during 1941, began to make itself felt through numerous acts of sabotage. The second was the cruel German reaction to this, marked by the wholesale shooting of hostages. And the third was the slowing down of the German invasion of Russia. Leahy reported to us that Darlan and some others of his ilk were beginning to lean toward our point of view, while awaiting the outcome of the campaign in Russia before finally making up their minds.

But the first tremors of Darlan's change of heart were not sufficient to alter his determination that Weygand must go. We knew that the Germans had been bringing pressure on the Vichy Government for some months to get the General out of the African picture. They did not trust him, they did not like his economic accord with the United States, and they feared that the accord would be followed by American military assistance. Darlan and his group detested Weygand because he had stood successfully against the agreement Darlan had reached with the Germans to make African bases available to them.

Pétain again summoned Weygand to Vichy, and on November 18 announced his dismissal. He sent Leahy a note on the same day, saying that German pressure had taken an imperative form that morning and he believed that, if he had not removed Weygand, German troop penetration into Africa would have been inevitable.

The following day Leahy cabled me that Pétain told him the decision had caused him great pain but he was helpless. "I am a prisoner," he repeated twice. The Germans, he said, had sent a "brutal ultimatum" threatening to occupy Vichy France and quarter a large army there so that the French would starve.

We were now faced with the need to decide whether to continue our economic accord with North Africa, since Weygand was no longer there to serve as the leader of all those resolved to oppose a German invasion. Was his dismissal a portent of worse to come?

Ambassador Leahy cabled on November 19 his suggestion that we might possibly suspend economic aid to North Africa and recall him for consultation. At almost the same time Robert Murphy recommended that no change be made in our policy, at least until we came into possession of the full facts of Weygand's dismissal.

Because I was engaged in the final phases of our negotiations with the Japanese—Pearl Harbor was less than three weeks away—I asked Welles to handle the matter, after conferring with the President. On November 19 Welles informed Ambassador Henry-Haye that Weygand's dismissal rendered necessary a complete change in the policy we had been carrying out toward France. On the following day the State Department announced that American policy toward France was being reviewed and all plans for economic assistance to French North Africa were suspended.

It was almost immediately apparent, however, that this decision was premature. The British had begun a strong advance into Libya against General Rommel on November 17 and were progressing well. It was possible that Hitler might seek to meet this threat by sending troops to North Africa through Italy and Tunisia or through Spain, and might demand the use of French bases for this purpose. Hitler's invasion of Russia was now beginning to bog down for the winter, and he might transfer troops from Russia to North Africa. We had pursued our policy toward Vichy to hinder these objectives. If we abandoned it now, we might well leave the Vichy Government and French North Africa no alternative but complete collaboration with the Axis.

Murphy sent us on November 21 a message from Weygand himself begging that we continue our existing policy. "Nothing is changed in French policy by my departure," he said. "Just suppose that I have passed to the other world. French Africa would continue to exist notwithstanding that unimportant normal accident. . . . How much do I count on the maintenance between our two countries of the union necessary for the near future of the world!"

We now began to receive a bevy of cables from Madrid and London that the Nazis had again asked Vichy for facilities at Bizerte, Mers-el-Kébir, and Dakar. Pétain, accompanied by Darlan and General Juin, the new commanding general of the French forces in North Africa, met with Göring at Saint-Florentin on December 1. We later learned that the interview had been most unpleasant, with Pétain accusing Hitler of having failed to maintain his many earlier promises to France to return prisoners of war, abolish the line of demarcation between occupied and unoccupied France, reduce economic demands, and permit some rearmament of France and North Africa. But at the time the meeting carried connotations of ominous German intentions toward Africa.

Lord Halifax came to my apartment on December 5 to give me reports from his Government that Vichy had agreed that Germany should use the railroad lines to Marseille, occupy the Rhone valley, and use naval and air bases in Africa. This, he said, meant that Germany was planning to send troops and supplies across the Mediterranean on a large scale.

On the following day we cabled Leahy to tell Pétain that, if he would renew his assurances regarding the fleet and the colonies and state that Weygand's dismissal meant no change in his North African policy, we would consider renewing our economic and relief program.

Leahy was unable to deliver this to Pétain and Darlan until December 11. They gave the desired assurances on the next day, and we thereupon resumed our previous policy. We were then at war with Japan, Germany, and Italy.

Eighteen months had passed between the fall of France and Pearl Harbor. During that time we pursued toward Vichy France one of the most difficult policies of the Roosevelt period. Events of that year and a half showed that a contrary policy might well have been disastrous.

On innumerable occasions it seemed that the French fleet was about to be consigned to Hitler, or French African bases were about to be made available to him. Frequently it seemed that Darlan or Laval and the groups that backed them were about to force the withdrawal of Pétain, take over, and cast France bodily into Germany's corner. But when the Japanese struck at Pearl Harbor none of these possibilities had come to pass. The Vichy Government had granted concessions in Syria and had agreed with Japan on Indo-China; but it had still not consented to outright collaboration with Germany, and North Africa was safe for the moment. Weygand was gone, but our tilling of the North African soil had been so effective that his successor, General Alphonse Juin, chosen by the Germans from among the prisoners of war, found himself surrounded by Weygand's anti-Axis assistants and continued virtually in his predecessor's footsteps.

Our policy toward Vichy had been firm throughout, and never wavered from our basic principles. We had not once appeased. By pressure, by protest, and occasionally by support, we had helped keep Pétain in the stirrups and North Africa free. Throughout that time our influence at Vichy was predominant over that of any other nation, with the possible— only the possible—exception of Germany. We were better informed on developments at Vichy and in French North Africa than any other nation. And we had done much toward laying the groundwork for our invasion of North Africa in the following year.

Had we broken relations with Vichy, we should have taken away some of the last props of Marshal Pétain. We should have encouraged Darlan, or perhaps Laval, to take over, and France undoubtedly would have reentered the war on a partial scale on Germany's side. We should have lost the posts in North Africa from which we could observe developments, seek to influence local authorities, and prepare the way for the landings of November, 1942.

The price we paid for these successes was comparatively infinitesimal. We had sacrificed no principles, we had made no political commitments.

We were disappointed at times in the results of our policy toward Vichy, but German sources after the war have revealed that Hitler was profoundly disappointed in Vichy France. He had expected much more than he received. Our policy toward Vichy was a major cause of his disillusionment.

76: Conflict in the Atlantic

THE ADVENT OF the Tojo militarist Cabinet in Japan in September, 1941, coincided with an embittering of our relations with Germany as Hitler intensified the Battle of the Atlantic. His submarines and planes sank or damaged a number of American-flag and American-owned vessels. It was evident that new orders had gone out from the German Navy to submarines and surface raiders to treat American ships as belligerents and sink them.

And it was equally evident that unless we took new steps to meet this threat we should be driven off the high seas.

One of the Administration's first moves was to redefine the term "United Kingdom," as used in the Neutrality Act proclamation, so as to permit American ships to carry arms to the overseas territories and possessions of the British Empire. We made this public on September 15, 1941.

Throughout the summer of 1941 a revision of the Neutrality Act so as to permit American ships to sail to the United Kingdom and to be armed had been under discussion. Toward the end of June, from White Sulphur Springs, I recommended to the President through Welles that he call in the appropriate leaders of the Senate and House and discuss with them the urgent desirability of amending the Act. It seemed to me ever more vitally necessary that the President obtain authority to permit American vessels to carry supplies to Britain.

Welles wrote me on June 30 that the President had agreed enthusiastically to this suggestion and had asked for a memorandum as to the nature of the amendments that should be sought; and he sent this to me for my comment. I approved it, but with a suggestion that, if the political situation might cause too much delay in Congress, legal opinions be obtained from the Attorney General and the Legal Adviser of the State Department on whether the Lend-Lease Act did not modify the provisions of the Neutrality Act we had in mind.

The President began his conferences with Congressional leaders. The first reaction was that a majority in both Houses would favor revision of the Act, but that the debate would be prolonged and the isolationist group might filibuster.

Early in September, however, Hitler forced the issue as his submarines sank or damaged American ships in quick succession. When the President returned to Washington from Hyde Park on the evening of the 10th, I met him at the station and gave him a résumé of the information concerning these attacks.

At the White House Secretaries Stimson and Knox joined in the discussion of what action to take. We agreed that the President, in a radio address the following evening, should make it emphatically plain that our naval vessels in the Atlantic would fire on any Axis submarines or surface warships seeking to intercept shipping in our defensive waters.

Accordingly, on the evening of September 11 the President declared: "The time for active defense is now . . . our patrolling vessels and planes will protect all merchant ships—not only American ships but ships of any flag—engaged in commerce in our defensive waters. . . . From now on, if German or Italian vessels of war enter the waters the protection of which is necesary for American defense they do so at their own peril."

He did not set any geographical limits to what he meant by "defensive waters." But it was clear that, as the defense of Britain was vital to our security, the waters between the United States and Britain were defensive waters. Consequently our armed protection would extend to the shipping lanes across the North Atlantic, as well as to the waters to the South.

During the last week in September I held several meetings with my principal advisers in the State Department to consider revising or repealing the Neutrality Act. We decided to recommend to the President several modifications in the Act rather than its outright repeal. We still desired to retain several sections in the Act, such as supervision of arms exports and imports and of the collection of charitable funds for belligerents.

We prepared three varying drafts of necessary legislation by September 24, together with a draft message for the President to send to Congress, if he wished. I took them to him that afternoon, and we went over them at length.

During conferences the following week with the President and with Congressional leaders agreement was reached to seek separately the repeal of Section 6 of the Act (prohibiting the arming of merchant ships) and of Sections 2 and 3 (prohibiting our ships from visiting belligerent ports and entering combat areas). It was our thought that, in view of the German sinking or damaging of some of our ships far from the combat zones, it would be easier to obtain repeal of Section 6 first.

On October 9 the President sent to Congress a message that we had drafted in the State Department, asking for the repeal of Section 6. Up to that time two American-flag merchantmen had been sunk, the United States destroyer *Greer* and another merchantman had been attacked and the latter damaged, and five American-owned vessels flying the Panamanian flag had been sunk.

During June, 1941, the President, acting on an opinion of the Attorney General, had authorized the arming in this country of foreign-flag vessels. The Navy Department thereupon made available one low-angle gun to be mounted on some eighty-three Panamanian-flag vessels, in most of which there was some degree of American ownership. Panama's laws did not prohibit the arming of merchantmen.

Early in October, however, the Government of Panama decided to prohibit the arming of merchant vessels flying the Panamanian flag. With the approval of the President, I wrote Admiral Land, chairman of the Maritime Commission, on October 8, notifying him of that Government's action. I stated that the State Department was of the opinion that any installation of armament now in progress on Panamanian-flag vessels owned by American interests should be discontinued, and that steps should be taken to remove any such armament already installed.

The situation was quickly reversed when Arnulfo Arias, President of Panama, whose action prohibiting the arming of merchant vessels seemed to have been taken under German pressure, was deposed on October 9. In violation of a provision of the Constitution of Panama that the President might not leave the country without the permission of the National Assembly or the Supreme Court, he had departed on a personal visit to Cuba on October 6. Ricardo Adolfo de la Guardia, the Vice President, became President on October 9, and on the following day the Panamanian Cabinet decided to cancel the former Government's action.

This was so clearly to our advantage that German propaganda immediately sought to make out that the United States Government had staged a putsch in Panama. I vigorously replied to its charge on October 16 with a public statement in which I said: "I state clearly and categorically for the record that the United States Government has had no connection, direct or indirect, with the recent governmental changes in the Republic of Panama."

I appeared before the House Foreign Affairs Committee on October 13 to argue for repeal of the section of the Neutrality Act that prohibited the arming of American merchant vessels. Basing my argument on self-defense, I said: "The Neutrality Acts did not remotely contemplate limiting the steps to be taken by this country in self-defense, especially were there to develop situations of serious and immediate danger to the United States and to this hemisphere. There was never any thought or intention to abandon to the slightest extent the full right of our necessary self-defense."

I pointed out that the prohibition against arming merchant vessels was not called for under international law, that our government in previous decades had often armed our merchantmen, and that "it is our right to arm our vessels for purposes of defense."

Outlining the dangerous extent of Hitler's broad movement of conquest, world-wide in its objectives, I said: "We cannot turn and walk away from the steadily spreading danger. Both the Congress and the Executive have recognized this change in the situation."

I stressed the point that Hitler's attempt at world conquest appeared so unusual and unprecedented that many people, especially in a peace-loving country like ours, did not at all perceive the danger to our country from such a movement. "This failure," I said, "to realize and comprehend the vastness of the plan and the savagery of its unlimited objectives has been, and still is, the greatest single source of peril to those free peoples who are yet unconquered and who still possess and enjoy their priceless institutions."

I concluded by stating my own judgment that Section 2 (our vessels not to visit belligerent ports) should also be repealed.

A few days before, on October 8, I had asked the opinion of Admiral Stark, Chief of Naval Operations, whether abolishing the combat zones around the British Isles and elsewhere would facilitate our getting aid to Britain; whether it would be possible for United States naval vessels to escort merchantmen all the way across the Atlantic; and also what were the risks involved. I was seeking an expert opinion on the military side before proceeding further with our campaign for neutrality revision.

Admiral Stark replied on the same day that it would be advantageous from the war-effort viewpoint if American-flag vessels, manned by American crews, could increase the shipping both to the British Isles and to other military areas. He thought that the greater speed of our cargo ships would decrease submarine losses. He considered it impracticable for ocean escorts based in North America to make the entire trip across the Atlantic.

He thought it probable that Germany would declare war on the United States. This would involve the possibility of Japan's entering the war. He believed that efforts to keep Japan out of the war would best be served by our continued strong stand against Japanese aggression. He also stated his opinion that Germany could not be defeated unless the United States were wholeheartedly in the war and made a strong military and naval effort wherever strategy dictated.

My own thought, as I expressed it to the Congressional committees, was that Hitler would not declare war as a result of any action of ours unless he felt it was to his own advantage. He had so acted toward all the countries he had attacked, whether their attitude was submissive or determined.

When I appeared before the Senate Committee on Foreign Relations on October 21, I drew attention to the repeated attacks made on American vessels in widely separated areas, and said that Hitler and his satellites were now trying to sever the sea lanes that linked the United States to the remaining free peoples.

"Hitler under his policy of intimidation and frightfulness," I said, "has in effect given notice that American lives and American ships, no less than the lives and ships of other nations, will be destroyed if they are found in most of the north Atlantic Ocean. In the presence of threats and acts by an outlaw nation, there arises the right, and there is imposed the duty, of prompt and determined defense. Our ships and men are legitimately sailing the seas. The outlaw who preaches and practices indiscriminate, terroristic attack in pursuit of world-conquest is estopped to invoke any law if law-abiding nations act to defend themselves."

On October 27 the President delivered a strong radio address in which he said:

"Our American merchant ships must be free to carry our American goods into the harbors of our friends.

"Our American merchant ships must be protected by our American Navy.

"It can never be doubted that the goods will be delivered by this Nation, whose Navy believes in the tradition of 'Damn the torpedoes; full speed ahead!' "

The Senate amended the House resolution to include repeal of Sections 2 and 3 as well as of 6. Opposition now developed in the House to the Senate amendments. Both the President and I addressed letters to the Speaker and to the Majority Leader of the House on November 13 urging favorable action on the resolution as amended. The same day the House passed the amended resolution, 212 to 194, and the President signed it on November 17. American ships could now be armed, and they could carry supplies to Britain.

Almost simultaneously we took another action to protect ourselves in the Caribbean area by sending an occupying force to Dutch Guiana, also known as Surinam. Since early in August we had been receiving reports of the activities of certain persons believed to be Nazis or Nazi-hired, along the Amazon River in Brazil, and of the clearing of savannas on the Brazilian border about two hundred and seventy miles from the bauxite mines at Paramaribo. The output of these mines, which furnished 60 per cent of the requirements of the United States aluminum industry, was vital to our national defense.

During the summer the President had had an exchange of messages with Queen Wilhelmina of the Netherlands, whose Government was in London. He had invited the Queen to visit Hyde Park, but she was unable to accept. I had an acknowledgment of the Queen's letter drafted at the State Department, and sent it to the President on September 1. In it we took the opportunity to indicate our anxiety with regard to the bauxite installations in Dutch Guiana, pointing out that any interruption in this supply of bauxite would seriously delay the production of aircraft so urgently needed by all nations resisting aggression. We said we were prepared to arrange for the immediate entry of troops into Dutch Guiana in keeping with the procedure established at the Havana Conference in 1940.

Two days previously, the Governor of Dutch Guiana had received information that a German surface raider was operating in waters of the Guianas. He immediately requested assistance from the Governor of Trinidad, and simultaneously we alerted our troops at Trinidad (one of the bases we had acquired from the British).

Queen Wilhelmina on September 5 agreed in general to the President's suggestion. We advised her, in the President's name, that we would first discuss the project with the Brazilian Government, since Brazil had a common border with Dutch Guiana, and we would ask Brazil to join in any military action involving the colony.

Brazil agreed without difficulty and arranged to maintain special vigilance in the frontier zone adjacent to Dutch Guiana and to send a mission to Paramaribo to cooperate with the United States and Netherlands forces.

While the President and I were working on the project of sending American merchant ships to Britain, former President Herbert Hoover had been bringing to a head his proposals for sending food to the children of Belgium. He specifically proposed that the United States Government persuade a small neutral country to negotiate agreements with the British and German Governments toward this end, whereby the United States would transport meats and fats to Belgium, and Germany would send a quantity of grain.

I had Hoover's proposals exhaustively studied in the State Department. While I personally got on well with Hoover and sympathized with his intentions, I was opposed to his ideas. Our commitments for the supply of food to England were considerable, and the shortage of shipping in the Atlantic was ever more acute. I further believed it was the duty of the occupying nation, Germany, and not the United States, to feed the conquered peoples. We could not afford to assist Hitler by relieving him of this obligation.

I stated this opinion to Congress with all the emphasis I could. I had already made my point clear in a letter on June 19, 1941, to Senator George, acting chairman of the Senate Foreign Relations Committee.

"It is clear," I said, "that the responsibility and manifest duty to supply relief rests with the occupying authorities, as it is well known that the German authorities have removed from the countries under occupation vast quantities of foodstuffs belonging to the peoples of those countries, and within those countries have diverted food supplies from children to persons working in behalf of the German military effort. . . .

"It is all the more difficult to understand why no demand has been made upon Germany to fulfill its obligations in this regard when the German Government has never put forth any claim to poverty of food for its own people and its huge armies which are striking at the roots of freedom and civilization wherever they can."

Congress took no action on relief proposals.

The Belgian Government itself concurred in the British Government's decision to let no food enter the occupied countries. I had several conversations on this point with the Belgian Ambassador, Count Robert van der Straten-Ponthoz. When I saw him on September 26 I inquired about the distress in his country due to lack of food. He said his people were suffering. I then inquired what the attitude of his Government (then in London) was. He said his Government was going along with the British blockade policy in order to cooperate to the fullest extent with the British in their efforts to defeat Hitler and restore liberty to conquered countries like Belgium. As to our attitude, I referred the Ambassador to my letter to Senator George, and we did not discuss the matter further.

The President and I, in the course of a conversation around November 18, agreed that I should make an address or public statement on the aims of our national policy. I had pointed out to him that in preceding months there had been certain divergencies in statements made by Administration leaders. With the aid of several of my associates at the State Department I began to work on a speech that would deal with freedom of the seas and control of the seas from the viewpoint of our national policy.

But the address was never completed. My attention now was claimed almost entirely by the mounting crisis in our relations with Japan.

77: Warlords Rule Japan

LITTLE GOOD as we had had to expect from the Konoye Cabinet, we had even less to expect from the Cabinet headed by Premier General Hideki Tojo after October 17. Tojo, who had been Minister of War, continued even as Premier to be an active Army officer. He was a typical Japanese officer, with a small-bore, straight-laced, one-track mind. He was stubborn and self-willed, rather stupid, hard-working, and possessed a quantity of drive.

The new Foreign Minister, Shigenori Togo, was a typical Japanese Foreign Office official, a good technician in his craft but also rather narrow in his views and unable to gain a broad perspective.

The new Cabinet almost immediately stated to us with emphasis, through Togo in Tokyo and Nomura in Washington, that they wanted to continue conversations with us and reach an agreement for peace in the Pacific. They sought to impress upon us that they supported the assurances of peaceful intentions so often conveyed to us by the Konoye Cabinet.

This was on the surface, of course. Other developments were ominous. Japanese military movements continued in Manchuria and Indo-China. The anti-American campaign went on in the Nipponese press. Navy and Army officers made inflammatory speeches. The director of the naval intelligence section of Imperial Headquarters said in a public address, "The Imperial Navy is itching for action, when needed." And Ambassador Grew cabled me on October 25 information from a reliable informant that it was only as a result of pressure from the Emperor that the Tojo Cabinet became committed to an attempt to conclude the conversations with us successfully.

No indication came from Tokyo that the Tojo Government was at all willing to modify Japan's position so as to reach a peaceful agreement on the basic principles of justice and equity we deemed essential to a lasting peace in the Pacific. On the contrary, it seemed to us that the Tojo Government was likely to insist on stiffer terms than the Konoye Cabinet.

At the same time I began to note a sense of urgency in Tojo's and Togo's attitude toward our conversations. Konoye had pressed us to move rapidly in accepting his terms; but one of his purposes had been to continue himself in office, with the help of an agreement with us. Tojo wanted something done quickly, but it was apparent that his purpose was different from Konoye's. If an agreement were not reached he was prepared, I believed, to take action that would mean war.

This sense of urgency, this almost frantic effort to push us into an agreement that would give Tokyo all it wanted, continued up to Pearl Harbor. We noted it a few days after Tojo came to power when the translation of an intercepted message from Togo to Nomura dated October 21 came to my desk. It said, in part: "Our country has said practically all she can say in the way of expressing of opinions and setting forth our stand. We feel that we have now reached a point where no further positive action can be taken by us except to urge the United States to reconsider her views. . . . We urge, therefore, that, choosing an opportune moment, either you or Wakasugi [Counselor of the Embassy] let it be known to the United States by indirection that our country is not in a position to spend much more time discussing this matter."

There were two prime elements in this message. One was that the Tojo Cabinet had no intention of receding from Japan's minimum demands: Japan to remain allied with the Axis and go to war with us if hostilities broke out between us and the Axis; Japanese troops to stay in China; Japan to enjoy a preferential commercial position in the Far East; and the United States to lift her economic restrictions against Japan, cease strengthening the Philippines, and desist from aiding China and the British and Dutch Far Eastern territories. The other element was that we had to accept these conditions within a short space of time—or else.

When Ambassador Nomura came on October 28 for his first real conversation since General Tojo had come to power, he said his Government was still anxious to reach an understanding with us. I said I was of course interested, and I emphasized the importance of patience on both sides as the only hope of improving relations.

"At the present moment," I commented, "the Japanese Government must know that in whatever direction they might make a rash move, whether south or north, this might well have immediate and incalculable consequences. On the other hand, there is no desire in Great Britain, and I think none in the United States, to pick trouble with Japan. The drawing together of all those who feel themselves threatened by Japanese policy is purely defensive. When there is so much gunpowder lying about, he would be a very rash man who dropped a match on it."

The President had delivered a strong speech the night before in which he further stated our determination to protect our shipping from German submarines. I asked Nomura what he anticipated would be Japan's reaction if, as seemed likely following that address, there were shooting between the Germans and ourselves. Nomura replied that Japan would be quite free to decide her own course of actions.

"The Japanese Government," I remarked, "would certainly be wise to consult Japanese interests and not German interests. You must realize that all Hitler's actions are dictated solely by regard for what he conceives to be German interests. I've never been able to understand what good Japan thought the Tripartite Pact could possibly do her, compared with an understanding with the United States and Great Britain, both of whom have effective interests in the Pacific."

On the following day Lord Halifax suggested to me that our two countries should notify Japan that we would fight if Japan blockaded Vladivostok or attacked Russia. I countered with the suggestion that the question be broadened. Instead of dealing specifically with this one area, Japan might be tactfully advised that her blockading of the Sea of Japan and parts of the Pacific coast of Russia would have to be treated by this country and by Great Britain as the beginning of an unlimited program of conquest by force. This approach would embrace the whole question of Japan's occupancy or domination of the entire South Seas area. Consequently the other interested Governments would be obliged, of course, to act to preserve their own interests and rights in all this area as well as in the area to the north. Halifax said he would take up this suggestion with his Government.

The impression of urgency on the part of the Tojo Government continued to heighten. Foreign Minister Togo on November 3 instructed Saburo Kurusu, former Japanese Ambassador to Germany, to come to Washington ostensibly to assist Nomura in his conversations with me. At the request of the Japanese Government we immediately took all the steps we possibly could to facilitate his trip by air across the Pacific.

On the same day Ambassador Grew cabled me his opinion that Japan might make a do-or-die attempt, if our conversations failed, actually risking national hara-kiri.

For the first time we now saw a dead line stated in the intercepts. In a message to Nomura on November 5, Togo said: "Because of various circumstances, it is absolutely necessary that all arrangements for the signing of this agreement be completed by the 25th of this month. I realize that this is a difficult order, but under the circumstances it is an unavoidable one. Please understand this thoroughly and tackle the problem of saving the Japanese-American relations from falling into a chaotic condition."

This, to us, could mean only one thing. Japan had already set in motion the wheels of her war machine, and she had decided not to stop short of war with the United States if by November 25 we had not agreed to her demands.

At about the time this intercept came to us I received a memorandum from the Chief of Staff, General Marshall, and the Chief of Naval Operations, Admiral Stark, analyzing the Far Eastern situation from our military point of view. This was in response to a request I had made of the War and Navy Departments that they study an appeal Chiang Kai-shek had addressed to us on October 30. Chiang had wanted us to send air units to China to counter what he believed would be a Japanese attack on Künming.

Marshall and Stark disapproved the sending of United States armed forces to China for intervention against Japan, but recommended the acceleration of material aid to China, including the maximum strengthening of the American Volunteer Group in China. They asked that no ultimatum be delivered to Japan.

I agreed thoroughly with their recommendations, and so informed the President. At the State Department we prepared a reply from the President to Chiang Kai-shek along the lines of the Marshall-Stark memorandum, which he sent on November 14.

From the tone of the intercepts, from the inflamed statements made in Tokyo, from the unyielding and drastic nature of the Japanese demands, and from constant reports of Japanese military activity, it was now obvious to me that Japan was rapidly veering toward further aggressive advances in the South Seas, including war with the United States if we did not sign the agreement she required.

On November 7 I therefore delivered at a regular Cabinet meeting a solemn warning of the dangers ahead. At this somber meeting the Far Eastern situation occupied the minds of all of us. The President customarily opened the Cabinet session by discussing a situation himself and then turning to the appropriate Cabinet officer for additional comment, or by asking the Cabinet member to give his estimate. On this occasion he turned directly to me and asked whether I had anything in mind.

I then spoke for about fifteen minutes and pointed out the dangers in the international situation as a whole. I went fully over the developments in our conversations with the Japanese.

"In my opinion," I concluded, "relations are extremely critical. We should be on the lookout for a military attack by Japan anywhere at any time."

There was a moment of silence. Then the President went around the Cabinet, asking each member his opinion. All concurred in my estimate of the dangers.

The Cabinet then agreed that the critical situation should be emphasized in speeches by high officials so as to prepare the country at large for such a development. During the next few days the President, Secretary Knox, and Under Secretary Welles delivered emphatic addresses along this line.

On the evening of the Cabinet meeting Ambassador Nomura came to my apartment and handed me a draft supposedly containing new Japanese proposals relating to Nipponese forces in China and in Indo-China and to the principle of nondiscrimination in commercial relations. The proposals, however, were merely rewordings of the previous Japanese points. They contained nothing basically new, nor did they offer any real concessions. Japanese troops would continue to be stationed in North China, Inner Mongolia, and the island of Hainan "for a certain required duration" following peace between Japan and China. Japanese forces in Indo-China would be withdrawn after settlement of the "China Affair." The principle of nondiscrimination would be applied to all the Pacific area provided it were applied to the rest of the world as well—a transparent loophole in view of the fact there could be no nondiscrimination in Hitler's Europe.

In discussing this document with Nomura an idea occurred to me which I stated to him.

"Suppose," I said, "the Chinese were now to say that they desired a real friendship with Japan and would do everything in their power to work together with Japan along peaceful ways. Would this not be a wonderful opportunity for Japan to launch forth on a real new order, an order in which Japan would gain real moral leadership in the Far East? At a time when Europe is threatened with anarchy, would not the adoption by Japan of a new policy of conciliation and friendship with China— not maintained at the sword's point—provide a real opportunity for progressive leadership in which she and the United States would cooperate to save the world?"

Nomura, who seemed to be much impressed with this suggestion, promised to refer it to his Government. He said he was personally convinced of the wisdom of the policies I had pursued and would use his influence, when he went back to Japan and retired, toward steering Japan away from outmoded ideas such as those calling for the retention of Japanese troops in China.

I pointed out again the advantages our Government had derived from renouncing its previous policy of stationing troops in certain Latin American countries, and mentioned the great increase in United States trade with those Republics. "If Japan would adopt a broad-gauge liberal policy toward China," I said, "she would derive incalculable advantages in the way of trade and prosperity."

From England two days later, November 9, came strong assurances from Winston Churchill of support of the United States in the Pacific. The Prime Minister, speaking at the Lord Mayor's banquet, said that, if the United States became involved in a war with Japan, Britain's declaration of war "will follow within the hour."

We had no agreement with Great Britain on this point. It was obvious, however, that war could not break out between Japan and one of the major English-speaking nations without the other becoming involved. The fate of Britain in Europe was inextricably interlinked with the fate of Britain in the Orient. And our policy of aiding Britain to resist Germany was not confined to Europe. Any weakening of Britain, as by a Japanese attack in the Orient which interfered with the supplies she needed from the Indian Ocean and Australia area for her struggle in Europe, would be indirectly an attack on us, and could not leave us indifferent.

I accompanied Nomura at his request to the White House on November 10 for a talk with the President. He read the President a long, written explanation of the Japanese view on three main questions separating us Japanese troops in China, the Tripartite Alliance, and the principle of nondiscrimination. He argued that Japan had made considerable concessions, and he pressed for a quick decision, saying that time was very precious under the present circumstances.

The President commented that, in his opinion, "nations must think one hundred years ahead, especially during the age through which the world is passing." We had consumed only six months, he said, in discussing a solution of our relations and those of other countries in the Pacific; patience was necessary, and we did not want a temporary agreement.

Two days later, on November 12, I handed Nomura a statement that recapitulated statements the Konoye Government had given us in regard to their position, and asked him to obtain assurances for us that the Tojo Government maintained the same views.

Nomura again pressed for haste, saying that the internal situation in Japan was difficult, people were becoming impatient, and a session of the Diet was impending. He hoped that an agreement could be reached within a week or ten days. Obviously he was thinking of the November 25 deadline.

I replied that we were working as rapidly as possible on the long explanation Nomura had read the President on November 10, and that as soon as we reached a good basis in our exploratory conversations we would approach the Chinese Government and sound out its attitude.

As we discussed again the Tripartite Alliance, I pointed to the growing distress of European populations, which raised the question how long Hitler could keep them crushed down.

"For this reason," I said, "the time is approaching for preparing a postwar program. This is a matter in which I feel that the Japanese Government must be interested. I feel sure that Japan will want to play a part in a constructive program to meet the after-war situation, and that, for this reason, Japan will probably not want to be tied in with Hitler."

Although Nomura continued to offer protestations of Japan's peaceful intentions, the intercepted messages that flowed to my desk told another story. One, dated November 14, from Tokyo to the Japanese representative in Hong Kong, described what would happen in China if our conversations failed to produce an agreement. "We will completely destroy British and American power in China," it read. "We will take over all enemy concessions and important enemy rights and interests (customs and minerals, etc.) in China."

I handed Nomura on November 15 the draft of a joint American-Japanese declaration on economic policy. This, if agreed to, would form one part of our general agreement.

Under this document the two Governments were to cooperate in urging all nations to reduce trade barriers, eliminate forms of discrimination, and work toward an equitable acquiring by all nations of the goods and commodities they needed. They were to take practicable measures as rapidly as possible to restore normal commercial relations. They were to begin discussions looking toward a reciprocal trade agreement. They were to permit the export to each other of desired commodities subject to restrictions necessitated by self-defense. They were to cooperate in restoring complete economic, financial, and monetary control to China. Neither was to seek preferential or monopolistic commercial or other economic rights in

China. They were to try to induce other Pacific countries to apply the same principles.

In general, under this draft declaration of economic policy Japan could have joined with the United States in leading the way toward a general application of economic practices that would have given her much of what her leaders professed to want.

In the discussion that ensued concerning this document, Nomura said he wanted to bring up the point that his Government considered we were now engaged in actual negotiations and not in merely exploratory conversations, as we contended.

Asking Minister-Counselor Wakasugi, who had accompanied Nomura to my apartment, to take accurate note of what I was about to say, I replied:

"If we are to work out a peaceful settlement in the Pacific area, I can do this only on the basis of carrying on exploratory conversations until we reach a stage where I can go to Great Britain, China, and The Netherlands and say to them that I believe that the attitudes of Japan and the United States are such as to afford a basis for negotiation. Otherwise they might read in the newspapers that I am negotiating with Japan on matters affecting them without their being consulted."

I asked Nomura whether, if we entered into an agreement with Japan, we could assume that the Tripartite Alliance, so far as Japan was concerned, would automatically become a dead letter.

"Suppose I were to go to the British and Dutch," I remarked, "and say that Japan is willing to enter on a peaceful program but at the same time desires to adhere to a fighting alliance with their enemy, Germany— what would the British and Dutch say? How could I make the British believe in Japan's peaceful intentions while Japan proclaims her adherence to a military alliance with Germany?

"It would be very difficult for me to make the people of this country and the people of all peaceful nations believe that Japan is pursuing a peaceful course so long as she is tied to an alliance with the most flagrant aggressor who has appeared on this planet in the last two thousand years."

Nomura commented that the public had so much confidence in me that they would accept a Japanese-American agreement if I recommended it.

"If we were to go into an agreement with Japan," I replied, "while Japan has an outstanding obligation to Germany that might call upon

Japan to go to war with us, it would cause so much turmoil in the country that I might well be lynched."

Pointing out that, notwithstanding the existence of a neutrality pact between Japan and Russia, large Japanese armies in Manchuria were facing Russian armies in Siberia, I said:

"What we have in mind is an agreement that will promote mutual trust and enable us to get away from the expansion of military preparations. What I want is a clear-cut unequivocal agreement which will remove doubts that Japan is trying to face two ways at the same time."

Neither in this nor in any conversation we had did Nomura give me a satisfactory reply on the question of Japan's commitments under the Tripartite Pact. He argued on several occasions that, if we signed an agreement with Japan, the psychological effect in his country would be such that the Japanese Government could not in future interpret the Axis alliance as requiring it to go to war with the United States. We could not accept a statement so vague and so at variance with the statements and actions of Japanese leaders. Moreover, we too had to consider the psychological effect of such an agreement as Japan wanted. Even supposing the effect might be good in Japan, it would be disastrous in the United States, in China, and throughout the Orient with the exception of Japan.

As Nomura and his Government continued to importune us for early action, I remarked to him on November 15: "The new Government in Japan seems to take the attitude that we must reply at once to their points. We do not feel we should be receiving ultimatums of such a character from the Japanese Government under circumstances where the United States has been pursuing peaceful courses throughout and the Japanese Government is the one that has been violating law and order."

That same day Ambassador Saburo Kurusu arrived in Washington, and on November 17 Nomura brought him to my office. Kurusu seemed to me the antithesis of Nomura. Neither his appearance nor his attitude commanded confidence or respect. I felt from the start that he was deceitful. Knowing what I did of Japan's intentions from the intercepts, from our regular information, and from my analysis of Japan's attitude during our previous conversations, it did not seem possible to me that Kurusu, when he left Japan, did not know the plans of his Government and the role he was intended to fill. The purpose in sending him to Washington was an alternative one. In the first place he was to use all pressure and persuasion possible to induce us to accept Japan's terms. In the second place, if that failed, he was to lull us with talk until the moment Japan got ready to strike.

Kurusu, as Japanese Ambassador to Berlin, had signed the Tripartite Pact with Germany and Italy. Previously, among other posts, he had been head of the economic section of the Foreign Office. He had been Ambassador to Belgium at the time of the Brussels Conference in 1937, which Japan had refused to attend, and had played the role of a too cunning eavesdropper. His only recommendation in my eyes was that he spoke excellent English, having married his American secretary. Nevertheless, I found that Nomura, despite his faulty English, understood the points I made much better than did Kurusu, whose mentality was such that he could not appreciate our views.

Nomura, on bringing Kurusu to me, handed me a statement from his Government which answered in the affirmative our request for confirmation by the Tojo Cabinet of a series of points already made by the Konoye Cabinet.

After a short conversation, during which Kurusu said that Premier Tojo, although a military man, was sincerely desirous of reaching an agreement with us, I accompanied both Ambassadors across the street to the White House for a conference with the President. The situation could not have been more tense. Only the previous day Nomura had received from Foreign Minister Togo a message confirming the dead line of November 25. I had it also through an intercept.

"In your opinion," it said, "we ought to wait and see what turn the war takes and remain patient. However, I am awfully sorry to say that the situation renders this out of the question. I set the dead line for the solution of these negotiations . . . and there will be no change. Please try to understand that. You see how short the time is; therefore do not allow the United States to sidetrack us and delay the negotiations any further. Press them for a solution on the basis of our proposals, and do your best to bring about an immediate solution."

It was therefore ever more a case of signing on the dotted line or taking the consequences.

President Roosevelt began the conversation by stating our desire to avoid war and to achieve a fair peace settlement in the Pacific. Nomura and Kurusu said this was also Japan's desire. Kurusu then made a specious attempt to explain away the Tripartite Alliance.

"Any kind of peace settlement for the Pacific," I commented, "with Japan still clinging to her Tripartite Pact with Germany, would cause the President and me to be violently denounced. Such a peace arrangement would not be taken seriously for a moment, and all the countries interested in the Pacific would redouble their efforts to arm against Japanese aggression.

"When Hitler started on a march of invasion across the earth with ten million soldiers and thirty thousand airplanes, and with an official announcement that he was out for unlimited invasion objectives, the United States from then on was in danger, and that danger has grown each week until this minute. This country has recognized the danger and has proceeded thus far to defend itself before it is too late. Yet the Government of Japan says it does not know whether this country is thus acting in self-defense or not. The United States feels the danger so acutely that she has committed herself to ten, twenty-five, or fifty billions of dollars expenditure for self-defense—but when Japan is asked whether this is self-defense she indicates she has no opinion on the subject."

Kurusu said Germany had not up to this time requested Japan to fight, and that Japan was serving a desirable purpose without doing so. He obviously meant that his country was keeping huge Russian forces and large portions of the American and British navies and air and ground forces diverted to the Pacific.

Kurusu sought to defend his Government's plan of not bringing its troops out of China. The President remarked that the question ought to be worked out in a fair way, and that, although Japan did not desire us to mediate, we might, if the other Pacific questions had been settled, introduce Japan and China to each other and ask them to proceed with the remaining adjustments.

Neither in that conversation nor in those that followed during the next three days among Nomura, Kurusu, and myself did the new envoy advance any new proposal. It was obvious to the President and me that he had come to Washington not for the purpose of stating any concessions to our point of view but to put backbone into Nomura's virtual demands that we accept Japan's terms.

When Nomura and Kurusu came to see me at the State Department on November 18 I sought to point out to them the fallacy of Japan's adhering to the Axis Pact.

"Our people do not trust Hitler," I said. "We feel that, if Hitler won out, he inevitably would get around to the Far East and double-cross Japan. After Germany concluded the Anti-Comintern Pact with Japan she later surprised Japan by entering into a nonaggression pact with

Russia, and finally she went back on the nonaggression pact by attacking Russia. I presume that Japan did not know in advance what Hitler's intentions were any more than we did."

I pointed out that we were giving the Philippines their independence in 1946 and we were now bringing our marines out of China. "In this way," I said, "we are trying to make a contribution to the establishment of a peaceful world based on law and order. This is what we want to work out with Japan. We have nothing to offer in the way of bargaining except our friendship."

I added that I frankly did not know whether anything could be done toward reaching a satisfactory agreement with Japan. "We can go so far," I said; "but rather than go beyond a certain point it would be better for us to stand and take the consequences."

Kurusu said he could not say that Japan would abrogate the Tripartite Pact; but Japan might do something which would "outshine" the Pact.

"Unless peacefully minded nations," I commented, "start their program of reconstruction now it will be impossible to get such a program started later on. The selfish elements would then get control of the situation and prevent materialization of a liberal policy. It is necessary to get the fundamental principles established now so that we may begin to enable the peaceful forces, which are now demoralized, to assert leadership."

Kurusu emphasized that Japan would not be a cat's-paw for Germany, that her purpose in entering into the Tripartite Alliance was to use it for her own ends, and that she had signed it because she felt isolated. I observed that it would be difficult to get public opinion in this country to understand the situation as he described it.

I then took up with Kurusu a point I had already sought to make clear to Nomura. For about a week, the Government at Tokyo had insisted that our conversations were now formal negotiations, while I insisted they were exploratory conversations.

"The reason," I said, "is that I cannot go to the British or the Chinese or other Governments involved without having first reached a real basis for negotiations, since those Governments have a rightful interest in these problems."

Kurusu retorted that under such circumstances American-Japanese relations would be at the mercy of Great Britain and China.

"I repeat," I said, "that we must have something substantial in the way of a basis for an agreement to take to those Governments, for otherwise there would be no point in talking to them."

Kurusu said that the situation was so pressing it might get beyond our control.

I agreed but pointed out that the fact that Japan's leaders kept announcing programs based on force added to our difficulties.

"I shall have to leave your relations with Hitler to your Government for its consideration," I said.

Turning to China, I asked Kurusu how many soldiers Japan wanted to retain in China, and for how long.

He replied that possibly 90 per cent would be withdrawn. He did not say how long the remainder would stay in China.

"Keeping Japanese troops in China," I said, "is a question in which there are many elements of trouble. American interests in China have suffered severely from the actions of Japanese forces. Yet we have exercised great patience. Extremists in Japan seem to be looking for trouble in this situation, and it is up to the Japanese Government to make an extra effort to take the situation by the collar. The United States and Japan have trusted each other in the past; but the present difficulty is one of Japan's own making, and it is up to the Japanese Government to find some way of getting itself out of the difficulty in which it has placed itself."

I added that the situation was now exceptionally advantageous for Japan to put her factories to work to produce goods needed by many peaceful countries, if only the Japanese people could get war and invasion out of mind.

Kurusu suggested that the United States had been responsible for delay in our conversations.

"We could more rightly accuse the Japanese of delays," I replied. "I've met with Ambassador Nomura promptly every time he has asked for a meeting, and I've discussed matters fully with him. Japan's movement into Indo-China last summer interrupted our conversations. It was then that I could no longer defend continued shipments of petroleum products to Japan, especially since I had been under severe criticism for the past year for not having cut them off."

Kurusu asked whether we wanted the status quo ante restored, or what we expected Japan to do.

I replied that if Japan could not do anything now on the three basic points separating us—troops in China, the Tripartite Pact and commercial policy—I could only leave to Japan to decide what she could do.

"Our desire," I added, "is to see Japan help furnish a world leadership for a peaceful program. I feel that Japan's long-swing interests are the same as our interests."

At this point the Japanese envoys turned the conversation toward the possibility of a modus vivendi, or short-term, partial agreement that would tide the situation over until a long-term basic agreement could be reached.

I asked Kurusu, "If there should be a relaxation of our freezing order, to what extent would that enable Japan to adopt peaceful policies? What I have in mind is something to enable the peaceful leaders in Japan to get control of the situation there and assert their influence."

Kurusu suggested the possibility of going back to the status existing before late July when, following Japan's move into southern Indo-China, we put our freezing measure into effect.

"If we modify our embargo," I commented, "on the strength of a step by Japan such as you mention, we don't know whether the troops you withdraw from Indo-China will be diverted to some equally objectionable movement elsewhere."

The envoy said what he had in mind was simply some move toward arresting the dangerous trend in our relations.

"It will be difficult for me," I replied, "to get this Government to go a long way in removing the embargo unless we believe Japan is definitely started on a peaceful course and has renounced purposes of conquest."

Kurusu remarked that Japan was tired of fighting China and would go as far as she could along a different course.

I said I would consult with the British and the Dutch to see what their attitude would be toward his suggestion

Later that day of November 18 I called Minister Campbell of the British Embassy to my office to inform him of the suggestion made by the Japanese envoys concerning a temporary arrangement, or modus vivendi. I said that the Japanese proposal meant that, while the United States and perhaps Great Britain and the Netherlands East Indies would somewhat relax embargoes on exports to Japan, Tokyo would correspondingly take steps toward a peaceful policy and toward educating its public opinion in support of such a policy during the next few months.

I also called in Chinese Ambassador Hu Shih and gave him the substance of my conversations with the Japanese envoys. I did not, however, refer to the suggestion for a temporary arrangement, since China would not be called upon to take action under it, and it was still in a nebulous stage.

Nomura, Kurusu, and I discussed this suggestion further the following day when the Ambassadors came to see me at my apartment. I asked Nomura whether, if the suggestion were carried out, our conversations would continue in order to iron out the important points on which we had been unable to agree. He replied, Yes. He added, however, that the Japanese Government had already expressed its intention to maintain peace in the Pacific, but that it could not abrogate the Tripartite Pact and was bound to carry out its obligations.

"One way you could be helpful," I suggested, "would be to let the Russian forces in the Far East and the British forces at Singapore go back to Europe. This illustrates how much Japan is hindering us. If Hitler were helping the world the situation would be different; but the fact is, he is injuring all of us."

Intercepted messages from Tokyo were now proving beyond all doubt that the crisis was at hand. Nomura received instructions concerning the evacuation of Japanese from the United States. He received a new code whereby, through listening to the daily Japanese language short-wave news broadcast, he would know, from a mention of the direction of the wind, whether diplomatic relations were about to be broken with the United States, Russia, or Britain. He was told to destroy all code and secret papers on hearing this message.

Then on November 20—Thanksgiving Day—Nomura and Kurusu handed me a new set of proposals from their Government which on their face were extreme. The intercepted message had apprised us of the fact that this was Japan's final proposition. It was an ultimatum.

78: Japan's Ultimatum

JAPAN'S LAST-WORD PROPOSAL, handed me by Ambassadors Nomura and Kurusu on November 20, in the nature of a temporary agreement or modus vivendi, was clearly unacceptable. In six points the Tokyo Government put conditions that would have assured Japan domination of the Pacific, placing us in serious danger for decades to come.

These were:

Japan and the United States to make no armed advance into any region in Southeast Asia and the Southwest Pacific area;

Japan to withdraw her troops from Indo-China when peace was restored between Japan and China or an equitable peace was established in the Pacific area;

Japan meantime to remove her troops from southern to northern Indo-China upon conclusion of the present agreement which would later be embodied in the final agreement;

Japan and the United States to cooperate toward acquiring goods and commodities that the two countries needed in the Netherlands East Indies.

Japan and the United States to restore their commercial relations to those prevailing prior to the freezing of assets, and the United States to supply Japan a required quantity of oil;

The United States to refrain from such measures and actions as would prejudice endeavors for the restoration of peace between Japan and China.

My associates and I subjected these points and their implications to minute study, but it required very little scrutiny to see that they were utterly unacceptable.

The commitments we should have to make were virtually a surrender. We on our part should have to supply Japan as much oil as she might require, suspend our freezing measures, and resume full commercial relations with Tokyo. We should have to discontinue aid to China and withdraw our moral and material support from the recognized Chinese Government of Chiang Kai-shek. We should have to help Japan obtain products of the Netherlands East Indies. We should have to cease augmenting our military forces in the western Pacific.

Japan, on her part, would still be free to continue her military operations in China, to attack the Soviet Union, and to keep her troops in northern Indo-China until peace was effected with China. There was no limit on the troops Japan could send into Indo-China. Her willingness to withdraw her troops from southern Indo-China to northern Indo-China was meaningless because those troops could return within a day or two. Japan thus clung to her vantage point in Indo-China which threatened countries to the south and vital trade routes.

The President and I could only conclude that agreeing to these proposals would mean condonement by the United States of Japan's past aggressions, assent to future courses of conquest by Japan, abandonment of the most essential principles of our foreign policy, betrayal of China and Russia, and acceptance of the role of silent partner aiding and abetting Japan in her effort to create a Japanese hegemony over the western Pacific and eastern Asia.

Acceptance of Japan's proposals would have placed her in a commanding position later to acquire control of the entire western Pacific area. It would have destroyed our chances of asserting and maintaining our rights and interests in the Pacific. It would have meant abject surrender of our position under intimidation. And, in final analysis, it would have meant a most serious threat to our national security.

Although Japan's proposals were of so preposterous a character that no responsible American official could ever have dreamed of accepting them, I felt I should not be too sharp in my reactions, and should avoid giving the Japanese any pretext to walk out of the conversations.

After Nomura read me Japan's proposals on November 20, I said I wanted to make a few comments but these were not directed specifically to the proposals, to which I would give sympathetic study. "Japan," I said, "has it in her power at any moment to put an end to the present situation by deciding upon an all-out peaceful course. At any moment Japan could bring to an end what she chooses to call encirclement. We should like to have Japan develop public opinion in favor of a peaceful course."

Kurusu said that, if we could alleviate the situation by accepting a proposal such as the Japanese Government had just made, it would help develop public opinion.

I asked the two Ambassadors what they thought would be the public reaction in the United States if we were to announce tomorrow that we had decided to discontinue aid to Great Britain. There was no reply. "In the minds of the American people," I continued, "the purposes underlying our aid to China are the same as the purposes underlying aid to Great Britain. The American people believe there is a partnership between Hitler and Japan aimed at enabling Hitler to take charge of one half of the world and Japan the other half. The fact of the Tripartite Alliance and the continual harping by Japanese leaders upon slogans of the Nazi type such as 'new order in East Asia' and 'co-prosperity sphere' serve to strengthen the public in their belief. What is therefore needed is a manifestation by Japan of a clear purpose to pursue peaceful courses."

The following day Ambassador Kurusu came alone to see me and handed me a formula that he said clarified Japan's obligations under the Tripartite Alliance. This merely recited Kurusu's personal interpretation, given from his viewpoint as the man who had signed the treaty for Japan. He declared that Japan herself could interpret her obligations under the Pact.

I asked him whether he or Nomura had anything more to offer on the whole subject of a peaceful settlement. He replied that he had not. I said I did not think the paper he had handed me would be of any particular help, and so dismissed it.

After this visit from Kurusu and his statement that he had nothing more to offer on the subject of a peaceful settlement, I redoubled, in conversations with individuals in authority in Washington—among them Admiral Stark—my warnings that Japan might attack at any time.

On the same day the Dutch Government informed us that a Japanese force had arrived near Palau, the nearest point in the Japanese Mandated Islands to the heart of the Netherlands East Indies. We had also received reports from our consuls at Hanoï and Saïgon concerning extensive new landings of Japanese troops and equipment in Indo-China. The zero hour was approaching.

Diplomatically the situation was virtually hopeless. We on our part, however, wanted to exhaust all means to find a peaceful solution and to avert or delay war. Secretary of War Stimson, Secretary of the Navy Knox, the Chief of Staff, General Marshall, and the Chief of Naval Operations, Admiral Stark, with whom I was in constant contact, pleaded for more time in which to prepare American resistance. On the other hand, Japan was calling for a showdown. We stood firmly for our principles; the Japanese were unyielding and intimidating in their demands.

As I went over the possibilities with the President and with my associates, following the presentation of the Japanese take-it-or-take-the-consequences proposal of November 20, it seemed to us we had one of three possible choices as a next step.

We might make no immediate reply, whereupon the Japanese war lords could convince their people that we would not offer any alternative.

Or we might reject the Japanese proposal, whereupon the same war lords could use this as a pretext for making war.

Or we might try to present a reasonable counter proposal.

We chose the third.

As we sought to prepare our counter proposals on November 21 and 22, we drafted a possible modus vivendi, or temporary agreement, to which would be attached the outline of a permanent agreement. The modus vivendi, to last for three months—the President originally wanted it for six months—would tide us over while conversations continued on the general agreement.

I realized that there was very little possibility that the Japanese would accept a modus vivendi except such as they had proposed on November 20. But even if they refused it our presentation of a modus vivendi would at least show our interest in peace to the last, and would further expose the Japanese determination to make war. On the other hand, if by some good chance they accepted it three more months would have been gained for the Army's and Navy's preparations in case Japan attacked at the expiration of the temporary agreement.

As it was finally drafted by our State Department experts and myself, the modus vivendi provided for mutual pledges by both countries that their policies would be directed toward lasting peace. Neither country would advance farther in the Pacific area by military force or threat of force.

Japan would withdraw her forces from southern Indo-China. She would reduce the total of her forces in northern Indo-China to 25,000—the number there on July 26, 1941. Here we reasserted that this provision did not prejudice our position that there should be no foreign troops in that area.

On our part, we would permit limited resumption of certain categories of trade with Japan. Imports from Japan would be freely permitted, the proceeds from which would go into a clearing account to be used for the purchase of exports from the United States. There could be exported from the United States raw cotton to the value of $600,000 per month; petroleum solely for civilian use, the amount to be determined after consultation with the British and Dutch; and food and medical supplies, subject to limitations on commodities in short supply in the United States. Japan would modify her existing freezing and export restrictions. Our exports could be increased, and further commodities added, by agreement between the two Governments if it appeared that the operation of the modus vivendi furthered the solution of their other problems.

The United States would urge Australia, Britain, and The Netherlands to take similar measures.

We also affirmed our fundamental position that any settlement between Japan and China should be based upon the principles of peace, law, order, and justice.

At the same time we worked on an outline of a ten-point peace settlement to accompany the modus vivendi. In general, my associates and I had reached a stage of clutching at straws to save the situation. We groped for anything that might offer any possibility for keeping serious conversations going. The Department's Far Eastern experts had drafted a proposed outline of settlement on November 11, which I went over word for word. This was drawn up with a view to keeping the conversations going—and thus gaining time—and also, if accepted, to serving as the basis for an eventual comprehensive settlement. Secretary Morgenthau sent me a further draft written in his Department. Although this was a further example of what seemed to me to be the Secretary of the Treasury's persistent inclination to try to function as a second Secretary of State, some of its points were good and were incorporated in our final draft.

I called in the British and Chinese Ambassadors and the Netherlands and Australian Ministers on November 22 and went over with them in detail the Japanese proposal of November 20 and our own proposed modus vivendi as a substitute therefor. The envoys were in general agreement that it was more desirable to submit a substitute proposal than to reply specifically to the Japanese proposal, section for section.

Each of the representatives seemed well pleased with our modus vivendi, except Hu Shih. He was somewhat disturbed, as he always was when anything concerning China arose not entirely to his way of thinking —which reaction was very natural. He was not seriously concerned, however, in view of the provision in our proposed modus vivendi which by limiting Japanese forces in Indo-China to 25,000 troops would preclude a Japanese attempt to seize the Burma Road.

Hu Shih inquired whether the modus vivendi would commit the Japanese not to invade China further during the coming three months. I replied in the negative, adding that this was a question to be decided under the permanent agreement to which we were giving attention.

I made it clear that there was probably not one chance in three that the Japanese would accept our modus vivendi, even though we provided that the temporary arrangement would constitute a part of the general conversations looking toward a basic agreement.

An intercepted message from Tokyo to Nomura and Kurusu on that day, November 22, confirmed my belief. This message extended the dead line from November 25 to 29. After that, war. "Stick to our fixed policy and do your very best," it said. "Spare no effort, and try to bring about the solution we desire. There are reasons beyond your ability to guess why we wanted to settle Japanese-American relations by the 25th; but if within the next three or four days you can finish your conversations with the Americans, if the signing can be completed by the 29th (let me write it out for you—twenty-ninth), if the pertinent notes can be exchanged, if we can get an understanding with Great Britain and The Netherlands, and in short if everything can be finished, we have decided to wait until that date. This time we mean it, that the dead line absolutely cannot be changed. After that things are automatically going to happen."

It was in the shadow of that phrase—"after that things are automatically going to happen"—that we labored desperately during the next two weeks, striving to the last for peace or at least more time.

A few hours after my conversation with the British, Chinese, Australian, and Dutch envoys, Nomura and Kurusu called at my apartment. It was almost unreal to see these representatives come to my home smiling, courteous, and outwardly friendly. It was a strain to talk to them in the same tone and on the same level, knowing what I did of Japan's nefarious plans from the intercepted messages, and knowing that Nomura and Kurusu had the same information. There they sat, bowing agreeably, Nomura sometimes giggling, Kurusu often showing his teeth in a grin, while through their minds must have raced again and again the thought that, if we did not say Yes to Japan's demands, their Government in a few days would launch new aggressions that sooner or later would inevitably bring war with the United States and death to thousands or millions of men.

I informed the Ambassadors of my conversation with the four envoys earlier in the day. I said the envoys had the same kind of misgivings that had troubled me in the course of my conversations with Nomura. I referred to the position in which the Japanese Government had left Nomura and me in July when it made its move into Indo-China. I referred also to the mounting oil purchases by Japan in the spring while our conversations were in progress, to the fact that I had endured public criticism for permitting those shipments because I did not wish to prejudice a successful outcome of our conversations, and to the fact that the oil was not used for normal civilian consumption.

"The Japanese press," I said, "which is adopting a threatening tone, gives me no encouragement. No Japanese statesmen are talking about a peaceful course, whereas in the American press advocacy of such a course can always get a hearing. Why doesn't some Japanese statesman back up you Ambassadors by preaching peace? If we and other countries should see Japan coming along a peaceful course there would be no question about Japan's obtaining all the materials she desired—and the Japanese Government knows that."

I told the Ambassadors that, while no decisions were reached that day on the Japanese proposals, I felt we would consider helping Japan out on oil for civilian requirements only when the Japanese Government asserted control in Japan over the policy of force and conquest.

Kurusu quoted a comment Foreign Minister Togo had made to Ambassador Grew, that we seemed to expect that all the concessions should be made by Japan.

"The United States," I remarked, "has remained from the first in the middle of the road. It is the Japanese who strayed away from the course of law and order, and they should not have to be paid to come back to a lawful course."

Kurusu said that our denunciation of the commercial treaty had placed Japan in a tight corner.

"Japan cornered herself," I commented. I reminded them we had been preaching for nine years that militarism was sapping everybody, and that if the world were to be plunged into another war there would not be much left of people anywhere. I recalled that I had told Japanese Ambassador Saito in 1934 that Japan was planning an overlordship in East Asia. I added that I had tried to persuade Hitler that his participation in a peaceful course would assure him of what he needed.

"It's a pity," I said, "that Japan cannot do just a few small peaceful things to help tide over the situation."

Kurusu asked what I meant.

"A peaceful movement could be started in thirty or forty days by moving gradually," I replied, "and yet Japan all at once pushes everything she wants into her proposal."

Nomura explained that Japan needed a quick settlement, and that its psychological value would be great.

I said I was discouraged, that I felt I had made a real contribution when I called in the four envoys, but that I could go only a certain distance. I pointed to the fact that Japan's demand that we cease aiding China would effectually prevent us from successfully extending our good offices for a peace settlement between Japan and China.

This was Saturday night. As Nomura and Kurusu pressed me for an answer to their document of November 20, I said that if Japan could not wait until Monday before getting my answer there was nothing I could do about it, since I was obliged to confer again with the representatives of the other Governments after they had consulted their Foreign Offices. Nomura said they would be quite ready to wait until Monday.

I called Lord Halifax, Dr. Hu Shih, Australian Minister Casey, and Dutch Minister Loudon back to my office on Monday November 24, and handed them copies of the latest draft of our proposed modus vivendi. They spent an hour reading it and taking notes to cable to their Governments.

Hu Shih objected to more than 5,000 Japanese troops being left in Indo-China. I said that General Marshall a few minutes before had expressed to me his opinion that 25,000 troops would be no menace.

"While my Government," I said, "does not recognize the right of Japan to keep a single soldier in Indo-China, we are striving to reach this proposed temporary agreement primarily because the heads of our Army and Navy often emphasize to me that time is the all-important question for them, and that they must be more fully prepared to deal effectively with a possible outbreak by Japan. It must be admitted that there are real possibilities that such an outbreak may soon occur—any day after this week—unless a temporary arrangement is effected that will cause the agitated state of public opinion to become more quiet and thereby make it more practicable to continue the conversations for a general settlement."

As Hu Shih continued to dwell on the possibility of reducing to 5,000 the 25,000 Japanese allowed to remain in Indo-China, I pointed out the great advantage it would be to our five countries to have Japan committed to a peaceful course for three months. Each of them would have additional time in which to make further preparations.

The envoys seemed gratified at the thought, but they seemed to be thinking of the advantages to be derived from the modus vivendi without being willing to make concessions in return.

Finally I discovered that none of their Governments except the Netherlands had given them instructions relative to the modus vivendi.

"Each of your Governments," I said bluntly, "has a more direct interest in the defense of that area of the world than this country; yet at the same time they expect this country, in case of a Japanese outbreak, to be ready to move in a military way and take the lead in defending the entire area. But your Governments, through some preoccupation in other directions, do not seem to know anything about this matter under discussion. I am definitely disappointed at this unexpected development, at their lack of interest and lack of disposition to cooperate."

They said nothing except the Netherlands Minister, who stated that his Government would support our modus vivendi. I then indicated I was not sure I would present it to Nomura without knowing anything about the views of the other Governments.

On that same day, November 24, an intercepted message from Togo to Nomura stated that the dead line of November 29 set in a previous message was in Tokyo time. The sword of Damocles that hung over our heads was therefore attached to a clockwork set to the hour.

That day, too, President Roosevelt cabled, through the State Department, a message to Prime Minister Churchill explaining our proposed modus vivendi and concluding: "I am not very hopeful, and we must all be prepared for real trouble, possibly soon."

The reaction to the modus vivendi from China was violent. Chiang Kai-shek himself sent cables of protest to Churchill and to his brother in-law in Washington, T. V. Soong, asking the latter to hand the message to Secretaries Stimson and Knox. In these cables he said that any relaxation of our economic restrictions against Japan would lead to a collapse of Chinese morale and the Chinese Army.

Dr. Hu Shih called on me on November 25 to hand me a note from Chinese Foreign Minister Quo Tai-chi. This said that Chiang Kai-shek showed "rather strong reaction" when given Hu Shih's cable recounting our conversation of November 22 concerning the modus vivendi. The Generalissimo got the impression, the note added, that the United States Government was putting the Chinese question to one side in its conversations with Japan, instead of seeking a solution, and was inclined to appease Japan at the expense of China.

Dr. Hu Shih virtually apologized as he handed me the note, saying that the Generalissimo was not so well acquainted with the broad international aspects of the Japanese conversations as they related to other countries; hence his opposition to the modus vivendi.

I pointed out to the Ambassador that the proposed modus vivendi was really a part and parcel of our efforts to carry forward our general conversations with Japan, and repeated the statement of our military heads that they needed more time to prepare their defenses in the Pacific.

I remarked that the Generalissimo and Madame Chiang Kai-shek had recently almost flooded Washington with long, strong cables telling us how extremely dangerous was the Japanese threat to attack the Burma Road through Indo-China and appealing loudly for aid.

"Practically the first thing this present proposal of the President and mine does," I said, "is to require the great majority of Japanese troops to be taken out of Indo-China and thereby to protect the Burma Road from what Chiang Kai-shek said was an imminent danger. Now Chiang Kai-shek ignores this situation, which we have taken care of for him, and inveighs loudly against another matter—the release of certain commodities to Japan corresponding to the progress made in our general conversations. He also overlooks the fact that our proposal would relieve for ninety days the menace of Japan in Indo-China to the whole South Pacific area, including Singapore, the Netherlands East Indies, Australia, the Philippines, and the rubber and tin trade routes."

I informed Hu Shih that one of our leading admirals had stated to me that the limited amount of more or less inferior oil products we might let Japan have during that period would not increase Japanese war and naval strength to any appreciable extent.

Hu Shih said he would give his Government a fuller explanation that he hoped might relieve the situation.

At about the same time Lord Halifax also called to hand me a memorandum containing his Government's lukewarm approval of the modus vivendi, with some exceptions. Foreign Secretary Eden said his Government had complete confidence in my handling of the negotiations, and I was in the best position to judge which tactics to follow. But he objected to letting Japan have any oil, and he wanted Japan to remove all her troops from Indo-China and to suspend operations in China.

"It's impossible," I commented to Halifax, "not to let the Japanese have some oil for strictly civilian use, if we, in turn, are to secure the tremendously valuable commitment by the Japanese not to move on any

aggressive course outside of China proper during the next three months."
I remarked to Halifax, as I had to Hu Shih, on the great advantage to
China in that our modus vivendi would obviate Japan's invading China
through Indo-China.

I also pointed out the utter impracticability of requesting a suspension of further military advances in China, in addition to the other assurances we were requesting.

When Halifax suggested that the upper limit of 25,000 we had placed
on the number of Japanese troops to remain in Indo-China be reduced
in our draft, I said we would do the best we could, but that our Army
and Navy experts felt that 25,000 Japanese soldiers in Northern Indo-
China would not be a menace to the Burma Road, and that even double
that number would not be a serious menace.

I delivered a warning to the War Council meeting at the White
House that day, November 25, emphasizing as fully as I could the imminent danger confronting us from Japan. The War Council consisted of the
President, the Secretaries of State, War, and Navy, the Chief of Staff,
and the Chief of Naval Operations. Convening once each week or at the
call of the President, who presided over it in his oval office, it was a sort
of clearinghouse for all the information and views we had under discussion
with our respective contacts and in our respective circles. It was one
further step in solidifying the top-level officials in these three Departments with the White House.

The War Council coordination was in addition to numerous other
activities of a similar nature, including frequent conferences among the
Secretaries of the three Departments held on Tuesday mornings in my
office, and among numerous groups of lower rank. We already were quickly
exchanging every item of pertinent information that came to any of our
respective Departments either individually or officially. This exchange was
taking place at called conferences among officials representing each Department, at regular meetings among them at frequent intervals, at meetings in our respective homes, and in the Cabinet sessions. There were likewise brief but important exchanges at dinners, receptions, and like occasions, even though we three Secretaries attended very few of them. In
consequence of this continuous interchange of information I did not secure
at the meetings of the War Council much information that seemed to be
new. Our meetings were mostly exchanges of views on the information
that was coming in to us.

At the meeting of November 25 I set forth that our relations with Japan were critical.

"There is practically no possibility of an agreement being achieved with Japan," I said. "It would be a mistake to assume that our conversations are going to go on.

"The Japanese are heavily armed, and they have been on this movement of conquest for a number of years, yoked hard and fast with Hitler most of the time. The Japanese are in control of the whole situation, we are not. We can only affect the movement of Japanese armies of invasion by surrendering the principles for which peace-loving nations, including ourselves, stand."

I then gave my opinion of what might happen.

"The Japanese," I said, "are likely to break out at any time with new acts of conquest by force. The question of safeguarding our national security lies in the hands of the Army and the Navy.

"With due deference to the chiefs of our Army and Navy, I must express my judgment that any plan for our military defense should include an assumption that the Japanese might make the element of surprise a central point in their strategy. They might attack at various points simultaneously with a view to demoralizing efforts of defense and of coordination for defense."

My statement that the question of safeguarding our national security lay in the hands of the Army and Navy did not imply that the State Department had relinquished its constitutional functions of continuing through diplomacy to try to preserve peace. I did not make, and could not have made in the light of what occurred, the statement later attributed to me that I had "washed my hands" of the matter. As long as there was the most microscopic possibility of peace, I intended to continue working toward that end, as the record shows.

That evening I continued discussing with my associates whether to submit the modus vivendi to the Japanese. I knew there was but a very slight chance of Japan's accepting it, but I was nevertheless very much in favor of presenting it because it would contribute to keeping the record clear. It would help emphasize for all time to come that we were doing everything we could to avoid war, and a Japanese rejection would serve more fully to expose their predetermined plan for conquest of the Orient. I was disappointed that the Chinese Government could not see this point of view, and that the British Government was only half-hearted in its support.

During the night a cable came in for the President from Mr. Churchill, commenting on our modus vivendi. Obviously influenced by Chiang Kai-shek's cable to him, the Prime Minister wondered whether the Generalissimo was not getting "rather meager rations" under the modus vivendi. China, he said, was the cause of his being anxious, and a Chinese collapse would hugely augment our common dangers.

After talking this over again with the Far Eastern experts of the State Department, I came to the conclusion that we should cancel out the modus vivendi. Instead, we should present to the Japanese solely the ten-point proposal for a general settlement to which originally the modus vivendi would have been in the nature of an introduction.

Although the modus vivendi proposal contained only a little "chicken feed" in the shape of cotton, oil, and a few other commodities in very limited quantities, as compared with the unlimited quantities the Japanese demanded, it was manifest that there would be widespread opposition from American public opinion to supplying Japan even limited quantities of oil. The Chinese were violently opposed, the other interested governments either unfavorable or lukewarm. Their cooperation would have been essential.

The slight prospect of Japan's agreeing to the modus vivendi therefore did not warrant assuming the risks involved in proceeding with it, especially the risk of collapse of Chinese morale and resistance, and even of disintegration in China.

The Japanese were charging us with encircling them. On the other hand, others were charging that we were about to "appease" Japan. It therefore seemed to me important to restate the fundamentals by handing Japan the ten-point draft of a basic agreement.

We could offer Japan once more what we offered all countries—a suggested program of collaboration along peaceful and mutually beneficial, progressive lines. It had always been open to Japan to accept that kind of program. She could still do so, if she wished. Our hope that she would so decide had been virtually extinguished, yet I felt it desirable to make this further effort, in the form of an outline for a broad but simple settlement to be worked out in future conversations. I believed that no effort, even as the clock moved toward zero hour, should be spared to test and exhaust every method of peaceful settlement.

Accordingly I prepared and signed a memorandum that I took to the President at the White House early on November 26, and read to him. Its conclusion was:

"In view of the opposition of the Chinese Government and either the half-hearted support or the actual opposition of the British, the Netherlands, and the Australian Governments, and in view of the wide publicity of the opposition and of the additional opposition that will naturally follow through utter lack of an understanding of the vast importance and value otherwise of the modus vivendi, without in any way departing from my views about the wisdom and the benefit of this step to all the countries opposed to the aggressor nations who are interested in the Pacific area, I desire very earnestly to recommend that at this time I call in the Japanese Ambassadors and hand them a copy of the comprehensive basic proposal for a general peaceful settlement, and at the same time withhold the modus vivendi proposal."

The President promptly agreed.

That afternoon Ambassadors Nomura and Kurusu called at the State Department, and I handed them copies of our basic proposal. Japan at that very time, as we knew later, had already put her naval forces in motion for the attack on Pearl Harbor.

79: Zero Hour

THE PROPOSAL I handed Ambassadors Nomura and Kurusu on November 26 was an honest effort to keep our conversations going, with the forlorn hope that even at this ultimate minute a little common sense might filter into the military minds in Tokyo.

It consisted of two documents. One contained our proposals, and the other explained them. The proposals document comprised two sections, the first of which outlined a mutual declaration of policy. This contained affirmations that the national policies of the United States and Japan were directed toward peace in the Pacific, that the two countries had no territorial or aggressive designs, and that they would base their foreign policies upon certain fundamental principles of peace. It also provided for mutual pledges to support liberal economic principles based upon non-discrimination in international commercial relations and upon equality of commercial opportunity and treatment.

In the second section we made ten proposals. Nine were for mutual commitments. These embraced:

A multilateral nonaggression pact among the Governments principally concerned in the Pacific;

An agreement among the principally interested Governments to respect the territorial integrity of Indo-China and equality of economic opportunity therein;

No support of any Government in China other than the National Government (Chiang Kai-shek);

Relinquishment of extraterritorial rights in China;

A trade agreement between the United States and Japan on liberal lines;

Removal of freezing measures;

Stabilization of the dollar-yen rate;

An agreement not to interpret any agreement which either country had concluded with any third Power or Powers in such a way as to conflict with the fundamental purpose of the proposed basic accord (this had reference to the Tripartite Pact);

The United States and Japan to use their influence to cause other Governments to accept and apply the principles set forth in our proposed agreement.

The one unilateral commitment was that Japan would withdraw her armed forces from China and Indo-China.

In the explanatory statement accompanying these proposals, I stated that the Japanese proposals of November 20 contained some features that would not be likely to contribute to the objective we had sought in our conversations. We therefore suggested that a further effort be made to resolve the divergencies between the two Governments, for which purpose we were offering the attached proposals.

The document I handed Nomura and Kurusu was essentially a restatement of principles that had long been basic in United States foreign policy. Our ten points embodied at least five that the Japanese would have found to their distinct benefit had they accepted them. Among these were the removal of all freezing measures, a trade agreement between the two countries, and the stabilization of the dollar-yen rate, which would have bolstered the slipping yen. There was nothing in the memorandum that any peaceful nation pursuing a peaceful course would not have been delighted to accept.

We offered this proposal to Japan as one practical example of a program to be discussed. It did not rule out other practical examples that either Government was free to offer. It did not foreclose further conversations, but on the contrary expressly invited them.

In view of Japan's refusal throughout our conversations to abandon her policy of conquest and domination, I felt there was scant likelihood of her accepting our plan. But I also felt it was the task of statesmanship to leave no possibility for peace unexplored, no matter how slight.

Later on, Japanese propaganda—especially after Japan had begun to suffer serious defeats—tried to distort our memorandum of November 26 by calling it an "ultimatum." This was in line with a well known Japanese characteristic of utilizing completely false pretexts to delude their people and gain their support for military depredations.

At the very moment I handed our proposals to the Japanese Ambassadors, the Tokyo Government's military preparations for launching widespread attacks throughout the Pacific were nearing completion. The Japanese fleet was already steaming toward Pearl Harbor. It was Tokyo that intended to attack if the negotiations failed—not Washington. We had no plans for an attack on Japan. Japan was prepared for war in the Pacific, we were not. We wanted peace. We wanted nothing to interrupt the flow of our aid to Britain, Russia, and other Allies resisting Hitlerism. It was Japan, not the United States, who took the offensive eleven days later and made war, not alone on the United States who, she said, had delivered an ultimatum, but also upon Great Britain, Australia, and The Netherlands.

Nomura and Kurusu themselves recognized that the responsibility for a rupture with us would be Japan's, and in a message to Tokyo on that same day, November 26, which our Army and Navy intercepted and decoded, suggested an attempt be made to shift that responsibility. "Should we," they said, "during the course of these conversations, deliberately enter into our scheduled operations, there is great danger that the responsibility for the rupture of negotiations will be cast upon us. There have been times in the past when she [the United States] could have considered discontinuing conversations because of our invasion of French Indo-China. Now, should we, without clarifying our intentions, force a rupture in our negotiations and suddenly enter upon independent operations, there is great fear that she may use such a thing as that as counter propaganda against us."

When I handed our proposals to Nomura and Kurusu at the State Department I remarked to them that our proposed agreement would make practical measures of financial cooperation possible. These, I said, had not been referred to in the outline for fear they might give rise to misunderstanding. What I had in mind was a loan to Japan that would render even more unreasonable any economic pressure excuse she might advance for going to war.

Kurusu spoke disparagingly of our proposals. He objected to our proposal for a multilateral nonaggression pact on the ground that the Japanese Government had had bitter experience with international organizations. He did not see how it could agree to "take off its hat to Chiang Kai-shek" and withdraw its troops from China.

I asked whether the matter could not be worked out.

Kurusu rejoined that when they reported our answer to their Government it would be likely "to throw up its hands."

I suggested that the Ambassadors study the documents carefully before discussing them further, and added that our proposal was as far as we could go.

Referring to the oil question, I said that public feeling was acutely opposed to permitting oil to go freely to Japan. "Japan," I remarked, "does not know what tremendous injury she is doing to us by keeping immobilized so many forces in countries neighboring Indo-China. Japanese troops in Indo-China, menacing the countries to the south and west, affect our direct interests."

Kurusu said it would be difficult for Japan to renounce her support of Wang Ching-wei, the puppet "ruler" at Nanking.

"Chiang Kai-shek," I replied, "has made an outstanding contribution in bringing out national spirit in China. The Nanking regime has not asserted itself in a way that would impress the world."

Kurusu agreed with what I had said about Chiang, but observed that the standing of the Nanking regime was a matter of opinion.

He said further that he felt that our response to their proposals of November 20 meant the end, and asked whether we were not interested in a modus vivendi.

I replied that we had explored that point.

Kurusu asked whether it was because the other powers would not agree.

I answered simply that I had done my best in the way of exploration.

The following day, November 27, I accompanied Nomura and Kurusu to the White House for a conference with the President. Previously I had gone over with Mr. Roosevelt what were likely to be the points of discussion.

Nomura said they were disappointed over the failure of an agreement on a modus vivendi.

The President said that we appreciated the efforts of the peace element in Japan, that most people in the United States wanted a peaceful solution in the Pacific, and that he did not give up yet, although the situation was serious and this fact should be recognized.

He then made three main points that we had sketched out in advance. The first was our disappointment that during the course of our important conversations Japanese leaders had continued to express opposition to the fundamental principles of peace and order that constituted the central spirit of the conversations.

The second was that we had been very patient in dealing with the whole Far Eastern situation and were prepared to continue to be patient if Japan's course of action permitted.

The third was our conviction that Japan's own best interests would not be served by following Hitlerism and courses of aggression.

I held a lengthy background press conference on that day, November 27, at which I comprehensively outlined to American correspondents the status of our discussions with the Japanese, in order to emphasize to the American public, through the press and radio, that the situation was dangerous. I said we were straining heaven and earth to work out understandings that might mitigate the situation before it got out of hand—in charge, as it substantially was, of Japanese military extremists. But I stressed the fact that Japanese reenforcements were pouring into Indo-China, and that a Japanese attack might come within a few days.

General Marshall and Admiral Stark sent a memorandum to the President that same day, with a copy to me, in which they pleaded for more time, particularly because of the reenforcements en route or destined for the Philippines. They recommended meantime that military counteraction be considered only if Japan attacked or directly threatened United States, British, or Dutch territory. I was again in full accord with their recommendations. Generally, the eight months of conversations we had held with the Japanese involved gaining time. There was no conflict between this objective and our intensive efforts to persuade the Japanese to pursue policies of peace. We wanted peace with Japan; but if we could not have peace, then we needed time.

At the War Council meeting on the following day I went over the November 26 proposal I had handed to the Japanese Ambassadors.

"There is practically no possibility of an agreement being achieved with Japan," I said.

I repeated what I had said at the War Council meeting three days before, that in my opinion the Japanese were likely to break out at any time with new acts of conquest, and that the matter of safeguarding our national security was in the hands of the Army and Navy. I reemphasized that our Army and Navy authorities should include in their calculations the assumption that the Japanese might make surprise attacks at various points simultaneously.

An ominous indication of what was coming appeared in an intercepted message from Foreign Minister Togo to Nomura and Kurusu that day. This said that the negotiations with us would be ruptured. "However," it went on, "I do not wish you to give the impression that the negotiations are broken off. Merely say to them that you are awaiting instructions, and that, although the opinions of your Government are not yet clear to you, to your own way of thinking the Imperial Government has always made just claims and has borne great sacrifices for the sake of peace in the Pacific."

In other words, the second phase of Kurusu's mission was at hand. The first had been to push us into accepting Japan's overlordship in the

Orient. That having failed, the second was to lull us with talk until the moment the Japanese military were ready to strike.

On November 28 the President left for Warm Springs, Georgia, for a rest.

To Lord Halifax, who came to see me on November 29, I stated for the benefit of his Government my view that the danger from Japan hung just over our heads.

"The diplomatic part of our relations with Japan," I said, "is virtually over. The matter will now go to the officials of the Army and Navy, with whom I have talked, and to whom I have given my views for whatever they are worth.

"It will be a serious mistake for our country and other countries interested in the Pacific situation to make plans of resistance without including the possibility that Japan may move suddenly and with every possible element of surprise. They must envisage that Japan will spread out over considerable areas and capture certain positions and posts before the peaceful countries interested in the Pacific have time to confer and formulate plans to meet these new conditions. My theory is that the Japanese recognize that their course of unlimited conquest, now renewed all along the line, probably is a desperate gamble and requires the utmost boldness and risk."

I remarked to the Ambassador that a calm, deliberate Japanese Government would more than ever desire to wait another thirty days to see whether the German Army was driven out of Russia by winter.

"But," I continued, "the extremist fire-eating elements in Japan, who have preached a general forward movement supported by the Army and Navy, have influenced a vast portion of the Japanese public to clamor for such a movement. They would probably take no serious notice of the Russian-German situation, but go forward in this desperate undertaking that they have advocated for some time.

"At least it would be a mistake not to consider this possibility as entirely real, rather than to assume that they would virtually halt and engage in some movements in Thailand and against the Burma Road while awaiting the results on the Russian front."

I think Halifax had his reservations on this last point.

He had come primarily to inquire as to the status of the proposed modus vivendi. This led me to remark that the mechanics for carrying on diplomatic relations among the Governments resisting aggression were so complicated that it was nearly impossible to conduct them in a manner at all systematic, safe, and sound.

I commented that Chiang Kai-shek had sent numerous hysterical cables to different Cabinet members outside the State Department, sometimes even ignoring the President, and had projected himself into a delicate situation without a complete understanding of the facts.

"When Churchill received Chiang's loud protest about our modus vivendi," I added, "it would have been better if he had sent Chiang a strong cable to brace up and fight with the same zeal as the Japanese and Germans were displaying. Instead, he passed the protest on to us without objection on his part, thereby virtually killing what we know were the individual views of the British Government toward these negotiations.

"And Chiang on his part gave the Chinese people to understand that all the friendly countries were now striving primarily to protect themselves and to force an agreement between China and Japan. Every Chinese should have been given to understand that the best possible course was being pursued, and that this called for resolute fighting until the undertaking was consummated by peace negotiations that Japan in due course would be obliged to enter into with China."

Australian Minister Casey also came to me on November 29 and suggested that Australia would be glad to act as mediator between the United States and Japan. I answered that the diplomatic stage was over, and that nothing would come of a move of that kind.

Later that day extracts were brought to me from explosive speeches Premier Tojo and Foreign Minister Togo were to deliver on November 30 under the sponsorship of the Imperial Rule Assistance Association and the "Great Japan East Asia League." Part of Tojo's text read:

"The fact that Chiang Kai-shek is dancing to the tune of Britain, America, and Communism at the expense of able-bodied and promising young men in his futile resistance against Japan is only due to the desire of Britain and the United States to fish in the troubled waters of East Asia by pitting the East Asiatic peoples against each other and to grasp the hegemony of East Asia. . . .

"For the honor and pride of mankind we must purge this sort of practice from East Asia with a vengeance."

After thinking this over, discussing it with our military authorities and our Far Eastern experts, and going over again the various reports we had been receiving on new Japanese movements in Indo-China, I telephoned the President at Warm Springs that night, November 29. I emphasized the imminent danger of a Japanese attack and advised him to advance the date of his return to Washington. Mr. Roosevelt agreed.

Lord Halifax came to me the following day, Sunday, with a memorandum from his Government telling us they had important information that Japan was about to attack Thailand, and that a Japanese sea-borne expedition would be sent to seize strategic points in the Kra Isthmus. The British were wondering whether to make a preventive occupation of the Kra Isthmus themselves. Halifax said he greatly desired to ascertain what the United States would do if the British should resist any Japanese attempt to establish a base on the Isthmus. I promised to take this up with the President upon his return.

Mr. Roosevelt reached Washington on Monday morning December 1. A short time before his arrival Nomura and Kurusu called on me at the State Department to ask why the President was returning to the Capital in advance of schedule. The Ambassadors obviously were worried over the probability that the President's rushing back to Washington conflicted with their instructions to keep us lulled with talk. I said that one of the reasons was the loud talk of the Japanese Prime Minister.

A long conversation followed, during which we went over again, without progress, many of the points we had had under discussion. I pointed out that my Government had no idea of trying to bluff Japan, and I saw no occasion for Japan's trying to bluff us. "There is a limit beyond which we cannot go," I emphasized, "and one of these days we may reach a point when we cannot keep on as we are."

Kurusu said his Government had directed him to inquire what was the ultimate aim of the United States in our conversations and to request us to make "deep reflection of this matter."

"The United States," I commented, "would be glad to give Japan all she wants in the way of materials if Japan's military leaders will only show that Japan intends to pursue a peaceful course. But we don't propose to go into partnership with these military leaders. I've not heard one whisper of peace from the Japanese military, only bluster and blood-curdling threats."

I emphasized again that we could not overlook Japan's digging herself into Indo-China, the effect of which was to create an increasing menace to us and our friends, that we could not continue to take chances on the situation, and that we would not allow ourselves to be kicked out of the Pacific.

Kurusu tried to make a lame apology for the direct military mind of the Japanese Army and commented that Premier Tojo was in position to control the situation.

"What possibility is there," I asked, "for peace-minded people in Japan coming out and expressing themselves? I doubt whether anybody in Japan would be free to speak unless he preached conquest."

Nomura commented that the Japanese people were not talking about conquest.

"We all understand," I said, "the implications of such terms as 'controlling influence,' 'new order in East Asia,' and 'co-prosperity sphere.' Hitler is using similar terms as synonyms for purposes of conquest."

Kurusu asserted there was no similarity between Japan's purposes and Hitler's purposes.

"There is no reason for conflict between the United States and Japan," I also commented. "There is no real clash of interests. Japan does not have to use a sword to gain for herself a seat at the head of the table. Equality of opportunity, in our opinion, is the key to the future peace and prosperity of all nations."

I saw the President at the White House at noon, following his return, and went over the situation with him. We both agreed that, from all indications, a Japanese attack was in the immediate offing. When I informed him of Halifax's inquiry about the Kra Isthmus, he agreed to see Halifax about it.

The President now had before him two draft messages, which I had sent him during his absence. One was a message to Congress, which Secretaries Stimson and Knox had helped me prepare, advising it of the imminent dangers in the situation. The other was a message to Emperor Hirohito of Japan, appealing for peace.

This second message had been under discussion since October among those of us concerned with the Far East.

In my memorandum to the President accompanying these drafts, I suggested: "If you should send this message to the Emperor it would be advisable to defer your message to Congress until we see whether the message to the Emperor effects any improvement in the situation. I think we agree that you will not send the message to Congress until the last stage of our relations, relating to actual hostility, has been reached."

I had two reasons for this last comment. One was that the message to Congress could contain very little that was new without giving the Japanese leaders material with which to arouse their people against us all the more. The other was that the powerful isolationist groups still existing in Congress and in the United States might use it to renew their oft repeated charges of "warmongering" and "dragging the nation into foreign wars." The Japanese military could then have played up the situation as evidencing disunity in the United States, thus encouraging the Japanese to support their plans for plunging ahead into war.

I also was not in favor of the message to the Emperor, except as a last-minute resort, and I so informed the President. I felt that the Emperor, in any event, was a figurehead under the control of the military Cabinet. A message direct to him would cause Tojo's Cabinet to feel that they were being short-circuited and would anger them. Besides, I knew that the Japanese themselves did not make use of such means as a direct Presidential message. Normally they did not shift from a bold front to one of pleading until the situation with them was desperate. They would therefore regard the message as our last recourse and a sign of weakness.

Since we were clutching at any means to give us more time, however, I placed both messages before the President to get his reaction.

The President also had on his desk a cable from Prime Minister Churchill, dated November 30, suggesting that the United States and Britain give Japan an additional warning "that any further act of aggression by Japan will lead immediately to the gravest consequences." We felt it best, however, to hold up any such warning until we saw what the reaction would be to the President's message to the Emperor, if he sent it. Warnings by the major English-speaking nations might furnish material for the Japanese militarists' propaganda about encirclement.

I had before me an intercepted message from Tokyo to Berlin, dated November 30, instructing the Japanese Ambassador in Berlin to see Hitler and Ribbentrop. "Say very secretly to them," it said, "that there is extreme danger that war may suddenly break out between the Anglo-Saxon nations and Japan through some clash of arms, and add that the time of the breaking out of this war may come quicker than anyone dreams."

On December 1 I was ill and had to remain in my apartment. On that day the President, through Welles, gave a memorandum to Nomura and Kurusu asking their Government for an explanation of the continued Japanese troop movements into Indo-China.

During the next two days I kept in close contact with the President and Secretaries Knox and Stimson, as well as with the Department's Far Eastern experts. Additional information kept coming to us concerning

Japanese fleet and troop movements. Then on December 5 Nomura and Kurusu called at the State Department and handed me their Government's reply to the President's inquiry with regard to Japanese troops in French Indo-China. This was a specious statement, unworthy of a child's intelligence, that Japanese reenforcements had been sent to Indo-China as a precaution against Chinese troops in neighboring China. "It seems," the reply stated, "that an exaggerated report has been made of these movements."

After reading this note, I remarked to the Ambassadors that I had understood that Japan had been putting forces into northern Indo-China for the purpose of attacking China from there. "I have never heard before," I added, "that Japan's troop movements into northern Indo-China were for defense against Chinese attack. This is the first time I've known that Japan is on the defensive in Indo-China."

Nomura commented that the United States Government blamed Japan for her move into Indo-China, but that if Indo-China were controlled by other powers it would be a menace to Japan.

"As you're aware," I replied, "we can solve matters without delay if only the Japanese Government will renounce courses of force and aggression. We are not looking for trouble, but at the same time we are not running away from menaces."

Later that day Lord Halifax came to my apartment to say he had had a message from Foreign Secretary Eden. This set forth the British view that the time had now come for immediate cooperation with the Dutch East Indies for self-defense against Japan. I expressed my appreciation of this view.

On the same day I wirelessed instructions to our diplomatic representatives in Tokyo and other points in the Far East concerning the destruction of codes, secret archives, passports, and the like, the closing of offices, and the severance of local employees, in the event of a sudden emergency cutting off communications with the Department.

During the following day, December 6, numerous reports came to us that a Japanese fleet of thirty-five transports, eight cruisers, and twenty destroyers was moving from Indo-China toward the Kra Peninsula. I was in frequent contact throughout the day with Secretaries Knox and Stimson, discussing these reports. It seemed manifest to us that the long threatened Japanese movement of expansion by force to the south was under way. We and our friends were in imminent danger.

In the President's opinion the moment had now come to send his message to the Emperor. He sent me a draft which mainly was the same as the one I had sent him the week before, but with some changes and additions of his own. I went over this with my associates and found several statements in it that seemed to require revision from the viewpoint of technical accuracy. These we changed, and sent the draft back to the White House. That evening Mr. Roosevelt sent it to me with no further changes, accompanied by this note:

DEAR CORDELL:
        Shoot this to Grew—I think it can go in gray code [our least secret code]—saves time—I don't mind if it gets picked up.   F. D. R.

I sent it forward to Tokyo at nine o'clock that night. In it the President said we had hoped that the peace of the Pacific could be consummated in such a way that many diverse peoples could exist side by side without fear of invasion, that unbearable burdens of armaments could be lifted, and that all peoples would resume commerce without discrimination against or in favor of any nation.

Saying that the concentration of such large Japanese armed forces in Indo-China created a reasonable doubt of its defensive character, the President continued that the peoples of the Philippines, the Netherlands Indies, Malaya, and Thailand could not sit indefinitely "on a keg of dynamite" (his own phrase). He concluded with the fervent hope that the Emperor might give thought to ways of dispelling the darkening clouds, and with the statement that both he and the Emperor had "a sacred duty to restore traditional amity and prevent further death and destruction in the world."

This message did not get to Ambassador Grew, or to the Emperor, before the Japanese struck at Pearl Harbor.

80: Japan Strikes

SUNDAY MORNING December 7, 1941, I went to my office, as I had done almost every Sunday since I entered the State Department in 1933. I first conferred with Far Eastern experts Hornbeck, Hamilton, and Ballantine, and then had a lengthy conference with Secretaries Stimson and Knox. The faces of my visitors were grim. From all our reports it appeared that zero hour was a matter of hours, perhaps minutes.

During the morning I received a series of decoded intercepts consisting of fourteen parts of a long telegram from Foreign Minister Togo to Nomura and Kurusu. This was the answer to our proposals of November 26. There was also a short message instructing the Ambassadors to present this to our Government, if possible to me, at one o'clock that afternoon. Here then was the zero hour.

The Japanese note was little more than an insult. It said that our proposal "ignores Japan's sacrifices in the four years of the China affair, menaces the Empire's existence itself, and disparages its honor and prestige." It accused us of conspiring with Great Britain and other countries "to obstruct Japan's efforts toward the establishment of peace through the creation of a new order in East Asia." It concluded by saying that, in view of the attitude of the American Government, the Japanese Government considered it impossible to reach an agreement through further negotiations.

The note did not declare war. Neither did it break off diplomatic relations. Japan struck without such preliminaries.

Toward noon Ambassador Nomura telephoned my office to ask for an appointment with me at one o'clock for himself and Kurusu. I granted his request.

A few minutes after one, Nomura telephoned again to ask that the appointment be postponed until 1:45. I agreed.

The Japanese envoys arrived at the Department at 2:05 and went to the diplomatic waiting room. At almost that moment the President telephoned me from the White House. His voice was steady but clipped.

He said, "There's a report that the Japanese have attacked Pearl Harbor."

"Has the report been confirmed?" I asked.

He said, "No."

While each of us indicated his belief that the report was probably true, I suggested that he have it confirmed, having in mind my appointment with the Japanese Ambassadors.

With me in my office were Green H. Hackworth, Legal Adviser, and Joseph W. Ballantine who had been with me during most of my conversations with the Japanese. I turned to them, saying:

"The President has an unconfirmed report that the Japanese have attacked Pearl Harbor. The Japanese Ambassadors are waiting to see me. I know what they want. They are going to turn us down on our note of November 26. Perhaps they want to tell us that war has been declared. I am rather inclined not to see them."

As I thought it over, however, I decided that, since the President's report had not been confirmed and there was one chance out of a hundred that it was not true, I would receive the envoys. After a brief discussion, Hackworth left the room, and Ballantine remained as I called for the Ambassadors.

Nomura and Kurusu came into my office at 2:20. I received them coldly and did not ask them to sit down.

Nomura diffidently said he had been instructed by his Government to deliver a document to me at one o'clock, but that difficulty in decoding the message had delayed him. He then handed me his Government's note.

I asked him why he had specified one o'clock in his first request for an interview.

He replied that he did not know, but that was his instruction.

I made a pretense of glancing through the note. I knew its contents already but naturally could give no indication of this fact.

After reading two or three pages, I asked Nomura whether he had presented the document under instructions from his Government.

He replied that he had.

When I finished skimming the pages, I turned to Nomura and put my eye on him.

"I must say," I said, "that in all my conversations with you during the last nine months I have never uttered one word of untruth. This is borne out absolutely by the record. In all my fifty years of public service I have never seen a document that was more crowded with infamous falsehoods and distortions—infamous falsehoods and distortions on a scale so huge that I never imagined until today that any Government on this planet was capable of uttering them."

Nomura seemed about to say something. His face was impassive, but

I felt he was under great emotional strain. I stopped him with a motion of my hand. I nodded toward the door. The Ambassadors turned without a word and walked out, their heads down.

I have seen it stated that I "cussed out" the Japanese envoys in rich Tennessee mountain language, but the fact is I told them exactly what I said above. No "cussing out" could have made it any stronger.

Ballantine took notes of what I said. The moment the Ambassadors left, I called in a stenographer and dictated from memory what I had told them. This is the statement as issued to the press.

Nomura's last meeting with me was in keeping with the ineptitude that had marked his handling of the discussions from the beginning. His Government's intention, in instructing him to ask for the meeting at one o'clock, had been to give us their note a few minutes in advance of the attack at Pearl Harbor. Nomura's Embassy had bungled this by its delay in decoding. Nevertheless, knowing the importance of a dead line set for a specific hour, Nomura should have come to see me precisely at one o'clock, even though he had in his hand only the first few lines of his note, leaving instructions with the Embassy to bring him the remainder as it became ready.

It was therefore without warning that the Japanese struck at Pearl Harbor, more than an hour before Nomura and Kurusu delivered their note.

I talked with the President on the telephone shortly after the Ambassadors left my office, and repeated to him what I had told them. He said he was pleased that I had spoken so strongly. By then he had received further reports on the attack at Pearl Harbor.

Shortly after three o'clock I went to the White House, where I talked with the President and others for forty minutes. Mr. Roosevelt was very solemn in demeanor and conversation. The magnitude of the surprise achieved by the Japanese at Pearl Harbor was already becoming evident. But neither he nor any of us lost faith for a moment in the ability of the United States to cope with the danger.

We had a general discussion preparatory to a conference that the President decided to hold that evening with Stimson, Knox, myself, General Marshall, Admiral Stark, and other principal advisers. We discussed in a tentative way the many different steps that would have to be taken, when and by whom. The President early determined to go to Congress with a message asking for a declaration of a state of war with Japan.

I returned to the State Department at four o'clock, and called a conference of my chief advisers which lasted until six o'clock. We were joined by Norman Davis.

We perfected a statement I intended to make regarding the Japanese reply handed to me by Nomura and Kurusu, and my reply to them. This we issued to the press shortly before six o'clock. Attached to it was the text of our proposals of November 26, and an accompanying statement in which I said:

"Japan has made a treacherous and utterly unprovoked attack upon the United States.

"At the very moment when representatives of the Japanese Government were discussing with representatives of this Government, at the request of the former, principles and courses of peace, the armed forces of Japan were preparing and assembling at various strategic points to launch new attacks and new aggressions upon nations and peoples with which Japan was professedly at peace, including the United States. . . .

"It is now apparent to the whole world that Japan in its recent professions of a desire for peace has been infamously false and fraudulent."

We then discussed a draft of a message for the President to deliver to Congress the following day. We decided that this should include a statement of the nature used by Woodrow Wilson on April 2, 1917, to the effect that the President requested Congress to declare the existence of a state of war that had been thrust upon the United States. While we were considering this, a press report came in announcing that Japan had declared war on us.

I requested my associates to watch our relations with the Vichy Government very closely in view of the Japanese attack.

We agreed that the other American Republics and the members of the British Commonwealth should immediately be notified officially of Japan's assault.

We decided that every American merchant vessel in the world should be advised of the existence of hostilities, since we feared that our merchantmen anywhere would be prey for German, Italian, or Japanese warships.

I emphatically expressed my disappointment that our armed forces in Hawaii had been taken so completely by surprise. I repeated to my assistants that during recent weeks I had time after time warned our military and naval officials with all the vigor at my command that there was constant danger of a treacherous attack by Japan anywhere, and in all probability at many places at the same time.

Nevertheless, it was the feeling of many of us that the Japanese, in their own interest, had been exceedingly unwise in attacking Pearl Harbor, thereby instantaneously and completely uniting the American people. However, as reports came in of the tremendous damage suffered at Hawaii, this feeling became somewhat diluted.

I spoke with contempt of the Japanese Ambassadors who had come in to see me a few hours before, and I mentioned their cowering attitude while they were in my office. On the other hand, I said I did not feel that they were aware, when they came to my office, that an attack had been made at Pearl Harbor. In fact, I am satisfied that they did not learn of the attack until they returned to their Embassy.

Appropriate officials of the State Department had already taken the necessary steps to see that absolute protection was given the Japanese official establishments and personnel within our jurisdiction. We notified Ambassador Grew of this action, with the hope that the Japanese Government would afford similar protection for our official personnel in Japan.

Several hours after the attack began at Pearl Harbor Japanese Foreign Minister Togo informed Grew that the Emperor regarded the note delivered to me by Nomura and Kurusu as his reply to the President's message to him. Togo made the further ironic statement that the Emperor also replied to the President to the effect that the establishment of peace "in the Pacific and consequently in the world has been the cherished desire of His Majesty for the realization of which he has hitherto made the Government to continue its earnest endeavors."

After having been at the State Department all that Sunday I went home to a somber dinner, and then to the White House at 8:30. A number of other Cabinet members and military officials were gathered about the President.

For three hours we discussed the various steps that would have to be taken now that war had come, steps in the military and diplomatic fields. We early agreed that the outbreak of war should not interfere with the flow of our supplies to Britain and Russia. We also discussed the main points of the message the President intended to deliver to Congress the following day.

There was some discussion of whether we should declare war on the other members of the Axis. We assumed, however, that it was inevitable that Germany would declare war on us. The intercepted Japanese messages passing back and forth between Berlin and Tokyo had given us to understand that there was a definite undertaking on this point between the two Governments. We therefore decided to wait and let Hitler and Mussolini issue their declarations first. Meantime we would take no chances and would act, for example in the Atlantic, on the assumption that we were at war with the European section of the Axis as well.

The President continued calm, although his face was grave and he made no effort to minimize the extent of the losses we had suffered at Pearl Harbor.

The next day, Monday, I went to the Capitol to hear the President deliver his message to Congress. The Senate and House quickly voted the declaration of a state of war.

Three days later, following declarations by Hitler and Mussolini, the Senate and House voted additional declarations of a state of war with Germany and Italy.

The voices of diplomacy were now submerged by the roar of the cannon.

* * *

We had had two objectives in mind in all our relations with Japan since the outbreak of war in Europe, and especially since the fall of France. One was peace. The other, if peace could not be had, was to gain time to ready our defenses.

We failed to win peace, but we gained invaluable time.

It was not until twenty-seven months after the invasion of Poland, not until eighteen months after the fall of France, that Japan struck. Although we still needed more time to complete our defenses, nevertheless we were comparatively far better prepared on December 7, 1941, than we had been on September 1, 1939, or on June 17, 1940.

Prime Minister Churchill put it ably in his speech on December 26, 1941, to a joint session of Congress in Washington, by saying: "We have, indeed, to be thankful that so much time has been granted to us. If Germany had tried to invade the British Isles after the French collapse in June, 1940, and if Japan had declared war on the British Empire and the United States at about the same date, no one can say what disaster and agonies might not have been our lot. But now, at the end of December, 1941, our transformation from easy-going peace to total war efficiency has made very great progress."

Throughout all this period we had been firm in our dealings with Japan, though we were careful not to push her toward war; at the same time we always made it clear that we could and should live at peace in the Pacific.

We wanted peace with Japan for the sake of the better development of the world and also because we needed it. I felt that peace in the Pacific was necessary if we were to make an adequate contribution to the defense of Britain and the defeat of Hitler which was vital to our own security. Events in the Far East seemed of double importance to me because they were so closely interlocked with events in Europe. If at any time after France fell, Japan, with surface and underwater warships, had cut Britain's line of supplies and reenforcements from Australia, New Zealand, India, and South Africa, it is doubtful that the United Kingdom could have survived. Virtually alone we should then have faced Germany in the Atlantic and Japan in the Pacific.

When I entered into conversations with the Japanese in April, 1941, I determined to do everything I could to bring about a peaceful and fair settlement of the situation in the Pacific. Even though I realized at the very outset that the chances for such an agreement were no bigger than a gnat, I still felt we had to make the effort. Not only was such effort in accordance with the traditional attitude of the United States, but it was also imperative for our over-all concept of world defense against Hitlerism.

In the negotiations from April to December I was forever conscious of the stupendous responsibilities that devolved upon me. A series of momentous decisions had to be made, and in many cases the initiative had to come from me. I am very happy that the President and I worked throughout in perfect harmony to avoid any misstep in our discussions with Japan.

In those discussions there were involved issues decisive for our national honor and destiny. The decisions that had to be made placed upon the President and me a responsibility almost unthinkable in its breadth and depth. We had to decide whether to enter into discussions with Japan in the first place on the basis of her proposals of May 12; whether to break off negotiations in July, after Japan invaded Indo-China; whether to apply freezing restrictions to Japan; and whether to agree to a meeting between the President and Premier Konoye. We had to make a fateful decision as to how to deal with Japan's ultimatum of November 20, and whether to present a modus vivendi.

I had the task of conducting almost all the discussions with the Japanese Ambassadors and of suggesting to the President in advance what he might say to the Japanese in the conferences in which he took part. I had to assume the responsibility of concluding that the diplomatic phase of the negotiations was finished and of stating that the task of safeguarding the nation had passed into the hands of the Army and the Navy.

I never had any thought that Japan was bluffing. Instead, I was convinced she had embarked on a steady, fixed course of conquest that would reach us in her own chosen time. I believed she was playing the role of an international desperado, and it is the business of a desperado—whether a nation or an individual—to fight.

During the period of our conversations Japan believed she was exceedingly well armed to achieve her intended conquests in the Pacific. She likewise knew we were by no means sufficiently armed to resist her attack successfully. Therefore, when Japan presented her successive and ever harsher demands, I was satisfied she was not bluffing but rather was giving us a last chance to yield our basic principles and thus enable her to continue her conquests without further risk of serious resistance.

Premier Konoye's memoirs confirm this view. He relates that on September 6, 1941, an Imperial Conference was held at which "the basic principles for the carrying out of the national policy of the Empire" were determined. Several "basic principles" were these:

"(1) The Empire shall perfect war preparations generally by the latter part of October with a determination to be prepared for war with America, England, and The Netherlands in order to assure its independent national existence and self-defense.

"(2) Parallel with the foregoing, diplomatic measures vis-à-vis the United States and Great Britain shall be exhausted toward obtaining fulfillment of our demands. . . .

"(3) In case there is no expectation of achievement of our demands by the aforesaid diplomatic measures within the first ten days of October, decision shall be made to go to war with the United States, Great Britain, and The Netherlands; policies other than those toward the southern regions shall be carried out in accordance with the already fixed decisions of the Government; and efforts shall be made to prevent a joint American-Soviet front against Japan from materializing."

Here was a cold-blooded determination to go to war—one of the most sinister episodes in history.

Japan's willingness to make war, plus the far greater state of her military preparedness, provide full explanation for our holding off as long as we did on applying embargoes on the shipment of petroleum, scrap iron, and other strategic materials to Japan. The President and I saw eye to eye on this policy. We felt that Japan might well retaliate in a military way if we cut off such shipments. Even if she did not attack us directly she might invade other areas, such as the Dutch East Indies, to obtain the products we denied her.

Prior to January, 1940, we had a commercial treaty with Japan, as with most all other countries, which obligated us to trade alike with each nation. Moreover, a strong segment of the American people stood adamantly for isolation and subjected any intimation of such a move as an embargo to a terrific bombardment of criticism. We could not but recall our failure in 1936 to induce Congress to enact a law that would have authorized us to impose embargoes on merely the export of materials above a normal peacetime level. This would have given legal effect to the moral embargo the President and I had instituted after the outbreak of the Italo-Ethiopian War. We could not but remember the fierce reaction to the President's "quarantine speech," one implication of which would have been the severance of commercial relations with Japan. We were assailed by other, contradictory critics, some even voicing violent threats, who one day shouted "Warmonger" if we made any suggestion to increase our military strength, and the next day demanded rigid embargoes against Japan. I often stated in reply that I did not believe in making a threat unless the nation was prepared to back up the Government; that if the Navy could accompany our policy in the Far East we would have no hesitation in embargoing Japan in any manner or at any time. But any half-informed person should have known that our Navy during those years of armament by the aggressor nations was not satisfactorily prepared to station itself for any time in the Far Eastern waters. Furthermore, at the very intimation that the Navy would be sent to the other side of the earth to back up what we knew was a threat that might lead to dangerous complications with Japan, a large section of the American public would have almost crucified the Government officials advocating such a policy.

The British and Dutch Governments saw the possibility of Japanese military reaction to embargoes as well as we. During the negotiations between Japan and the Netherlands East Indies, from September, 1940, until June, 1941, the British and Netherlands Governments urged that we refrain from taking drastic steps to curtail exports to Japan because they feared that such curtailment might result in an increase of Japanese pressure and enlarged demands for concessions from the Netherlands Indies.

The President said publicly on July 24, 1941, that it was very essential from our own selfish point of view of defense to prevent a war from starting in the South Pacific, and that such a conflict might have resulted from our embargoing exports of petroleum to Japan. We had already begun, in October, 1940, to refuse all licenses for shipment of iron and steel scrap of any kind to Japan, after having already placed restrictions on the export of numerous basic materials. After our freezing of Japanese credits in July, 1941, trade with Japan virtually ceased. We had adopted restrictions on the export of strategic materials to Japan as rapidly as we felt would be prudent, and by proceeding in this way we gained the time we needed so desperately.

It is my considered opinion that, if Japan had attacked us six months before Pearl Harbor, the whole aspect of the world war might have changed. In that event Hitler most likely would have promptly abandoned his plan to attack Russia. Feeling that Japan would tie the United States down in the Pacific and would cut off Britain from the assistance of Australia, New Zealand, India, and possibly South Africa, he might well have concentrated on the reduction of the United Kingdom by air and submarine warfare, and possibly invasion, leaving Russia to be dealt with later.

There were three methods to meet the danger from Japan. One was by a preventive attack. But democracies do not engage in preventive attacks except with greatest difficulty. Had I suggested to the President that he go to Congress and ask for a declaration of war against Japan at some time after the invasion of southern Indo-China, he could have made a good case concerning the dangers to us inherent in Japan's course of aggression. But, remembering the fact that on August 13, 1941, only three weeks after Japan invaded southern Indo-China, the House of Representatives sustained the Selective Service Act by a majority of just one vote, it seems most unlikely that the President could have obtained a declaration.

Nor would the military and naval authorities have been ready for a preventive attack. The fact that they pleaded for more time solely to prepare our defenses in the Pacific was proof in itself that they were not prepared to take the offensive.

A preventive attack, moreover, would have run counter to our determination to pursue the course of peace to the end, with the hope, however microscopic, that even at the last hour the Japanese might have a change of heart.

The second method to meet the danger was to agree to Japan's demands. This would have given us peace—that is, until Japan, after strengthening herself through the concessions we should have made, was ready to move again. But it would have denied all the principles of right living among nations which we had supported; it would have betrayed the countries that later became our allies; and it would have given us an infamous place in history.

When we realize that Japan was ruthlessly invading peaceful countries, that the United States had pleaded with her from the beginning to cease her course of military conquest in partnership with Hitler, and that all problems in the Pacific would have practically settled themselves if Japan had adopted a policy of peace, it is evident that Japan had no right to make demands upon us. Japan negotiated as if we, too, were an aggressor, as if both countries had to balance their aggressions. Japan had no more right to make demands upon us than an individual gangster has to make demands upon his intended victim.

The third method was simply to continue discussions with Japan, to convince to her that her aggressions cost her more than they were worth, to point out to her that her partnership with Hitler could be as dangerous to her as it was to the rest of the world, to lay before her proposal after proposal which in the long run would have given her in peace the prosperity her military leaders were seeking in conquest.

It was this third that we chose. Of the three, it was the only American method.

Part Six

DIPLOMACY IN WAR

(1942–1943)

81: United Nations Join for War

AFTER WAR CAME, the armed forces of the nation, under the direction of the President as Commander-in-Chief, moved to the forefront—but the diplomatic establishment became a significant factor in the conflict. Relations with the enemy countries ceased, but vastly augmented duties fell to our lot in relations with Allied and neutral nations.

During peacetime the State Department had been responsible, under the President, for the conduct of our international relations and also for making recommendations regarding movements of our military forces abroad, as, for instance, whether our troops in China should be increased or decreased. When war came the Department was no longer connected with military operations abroad, which became subject only to the command of the appropriate military authorities.

Almost immediately after Pearl Harbor I said to my associates that the role of the State Department from now on was to contribute to the war effort, and I wanted everyone in the Department to cooperate to the full with the War and Navy Departments and all war agencies, and to place at their disposal all our facilities.

I made it a practice not to let officials of the Department come to me with the statement that an official of the War or Navy Departments was doing something wrong. I said to them, in effect: "Remember, they are the fellows who are taking responsibility for the strategy and conduct of the war. They have a right to our fullest cooperation."

Prior to Pearl Harbor I had been a member of the War Council, composed of the President, the Secretaries of State, War, and the Navy, the Chief of Staff, and the Chief of Naval Operations, and I took part in its meetings. After Pearl Harbor I did not sit in on meetings concerned with military matters. This was because the President did not invite me to such meetings. I raised the question with him several times. It seemed manifest to me that, in numerous important instances, the Secretary of State should sit in on the President's war councils, particularly on those of a combined military and diplomatic nature, for it was obvious that scarcely any large-scale military operations could be undertaken that would not have diplomatic aspects.

I feel it is a serious mistake for a Secretary of State not to be present at important military meetings. I often had occasion to point out to the President that some development of a military character, which undoubtedly had been decided at one of these meetings, also had a strong foreign affairs angle of which I should have been informed at the time.

The President did not take me with him to the Casablanca, Cairo, or Tehran conferences, which were predominantly military meetings, nor did I take part in his military discussions with Prime Minister Churchill in Washington, some of which had widespread diplomatic repercussions. I said to him: "I'm not looking for increased responsibilities, but I do believe the Secretary of State should attend these meetings." I referred to the British practice whereunder Foreign Secretary Anthony Eden participated in all war councils.

The President's reply was that we had a different system here—which, I agreed, was true—in the sense that the British Cabinet constituted the Government, and Eden had stronger claims under their system than I would have under ours to participate in war councils, even though the diplomatic phases were vital factors for consideration.

I learned from other sources than the President what had occurred at the Casablanca, Cairo, and Tehran conferences. I had no special occasion to interrogate Mr. Roosevelt on developments at these conferences, but, if I asked him questions relating to his discussions, he was prompt, with few exceptions, to inform me frankly on the most secret matters.

One question of a military nature I did discuss with the President and his military assistants was the location of the second front. I agreed that our major effort should be made across the English Channel into France. The question of where the armies would land and what routes they would take across the Continent in the grand military movement to conquer Hitler was a subject never discussed with me by the President or any of his top military officials, although I was early informed of the decision reached.

I was not told about the atomic bomb. Occasionally someone gave me a veiled hint, but I did not press any questions. I did not really know about it until it was dropped and the announcement made. During the last months of its preparation, however, and when it was dropped, I was no longer Secretary of State, and consequently not likely to have any knowledge of it. Mr. Roosevelt deserves great credit for making the tremendous decision to go the length of spending $2,000,000,000 in developing the atomic bomb.

The President continued not to invite me to his military meetings.

He loved the military side of events, and liked to hold them in his own hand. Following Pearl Harbor, he preferred to be called Commander-in-Chief rather than President. He relished the title. He may have felt that this all-important position was now more essential than that of President.

At a Cabinet dinner, probably in 1942, where I was to propose the toast, the President asked me, before I rose to speak:

"Please try to address me as Commander-in-Chief, not as President."

It was impossible, of course, not to take up some military subjects in my conversations with ambassadors, particularly the representatives of our principal Allies. On December 8, 1941, during my first conversation with the new Soviet Ambassador, former Foreign Commissar Maxim Litvinov, with whom I had conducted the initial negotiations that resulted in the establishment of Soviet-American diplomatic relations in 1933, I raised the question of Russia's permitting us the use of air bases on Russian territory to facilitate the bombing of Japanese areas. We likewise discussed the question of getting supplies to Vladivostok in Russian ships, since Japan would obviously not permit American ships to carry them to Russia.

Three days later, when Litvinov called at my request, he said his Government had communicated to him that it was not then in position to cooperate with us against Japan. Russia, he said, was fighting on a huge scale against Germany and could not risk an attack by Japan.

I replied that I could appreciate Russia's position. Recalling to him the warnings we had given Russia earlier in the year of an impending German attack against her, I said I now had information that I deemed equally reliable, to the effect that Japan, notwithstanding the terms of the Russo-Japanese neutrality agreement, was under the strictest commitment to Germany to attack Russia and any other country fighting against Germany whenever Hitler demanded. This arrangement, I added, had contemplated that Japan would first attack the United States, in which assault Germany and Italy would join, and that later, when Germany demanded, Japan would invade Russia.

Although Stalin had thus early made up his mind not to join us against Japan at that time, I wanted to keep the question before him for some time in the future. I pointed out to Litvinov that we were fighting a world movement of international desperadoes who would not cease their movements of conquest voluntarily—somebody had to stop them.

"They will not be stopped," I said, "by our merely slowing down one phase of their world movement. If we are to deal effectively with this movement, we must consider it as a whole, and our movement of resistance must be carried on in each part of the world at the same time." Litvinov did not disagree.

I said that if our Government could get two air bases, one on the Kamchatka Peninsula and one around Vladivostok, our heavy bombers could get over Japanese home naval bases and the home fleet as well as over their cities.

Litvinov suggested that bombing cities was not necessarily decisive in view of experiences in Moscow, London, and elsewhere.

I reemphasized the world nature of the Axis movement of conquest and the extreme danger of more and more cooperation between Japan and Germany. "We must envisage the possibility," I said, "that the Japanese fleet might cut across the Indian Ocean to the Persian Gulf oil fields, to the mouth of the Suez Canal, and to the Cape of Good Hope. Then if Germany should be successful in her contemplated African invasion, Japan on the sea would meet her on the African coast. The effect of this on the whole British European situation would be terrific. Hitler and Japan would have a new lease on life, the effects of which would be terrible on all of us, including Russia."

Litvinov agreed as to these possibilities.

"If Russia," I remarked, "should refrain from cooperation with us in the Far East while we continued to aid her in Europe, there would be a constant flow of criticism as to why we were aiding Russia against a world movement involving all alike when Russia was not cooperating with us in the Orient." I reminded him that I had had to issue a statement that same day to allay some of this very kind of rising criticism, and that it would become an increasingly serious matter for both Governments.

Chiang Kai-shek had already, on December 9, informed us that he had cabled his brother-in-law, T. V. Soong, in Washington, and Ambassador Hu Shih, to see the President and the Soviet Ambassador and urge a simultaneous Soviet-Chinese declaration of war on Japan. The Generalissimo cited a Soviet view that, if Russia fought Japan, the United States might not concentrate her main effort in the Pacific, and Russia would be left to bear the major burden. He therefore suggested that, if the United States gave priority to the Pacific over the Atlantic until Japan was conquered, this undoubtedly would bring Russia in.

Russia persisted in her view, to which we could not but give sympathetic understanding, that she was too heavily engaged with Germany to court the chance of a Japanese attack in the Far East. It was not until the Moscow Conference of October, 1943, that I was able, during a personal talk with Stalin, to obtain assurances that Russia would make war on Japan.

I went over with the President and Secretary Stimson on December 12 the entire problem of unifying and coordinating the forces of all opposition to Japan in the Far East, with special reference to the South Seas area. I took this question up with British Ambassador Halifax the same day and with Chinese Ambassador Dr. Hu Shih the following day. I said to all of them that, in my opinion, the situation in the whole South Seas area was dangerous and called for emergency treatment to the fullest possible extent by all the countries concerned. I urged the importance of conference and collaboration on joint action at the earliest possible date. I suggested to Halifax that he begin conferences with the Canadian and Australian representatives.

The labors of the State Department changed or intensified in many ways following the outbreak of war. We had been representing in the Axis capitals the interests of the British, French, Canadians, South Africans, Norwegians, Dutch, Poles, Greeks, and Yugoslavs. Now we had to divest ourselves of this representation, and we also had to turn over the representation of our own interests to a neutral country. Switzerland agreed to undertake this vast work, and she carried it out with consummate skill.

We were likewise engaged in negotiations, which consumed many months, for the exchange of our diplomats and other civilians for Axis representatives and civilians. In the midst of a State Department conference on this subject a few days after Pearl Harbor, we received word from a highly reliable source that Japanese Ambassador Nomura and his Naval Attaché had received orders to commit hara-kiri in the Embassy, whereupon the Japanese Government would say that we had murdered them.

Our apprehension over what might happen to our officials in Japan if such a plan materialized was keen. We induced the Swiss Minister to go immediately to the Japanese Embassy, inform Nomura of the report we had received, and ascertain his intentions. They had a long conversation which did not entirely dissolve our fears because Nomura said the decision rested not with him but with higher authorities.

We were also faced with the problem of getting additional thousands of Americans out of Europe. Before and after the outbreak of war in

Europe on September 1, 1939, the State Department had given Americans living or traveling in Europe repeated warnings to come home if at all possible. Later we had given similar notice with regard to the Orient. Many hundreds had heeded the warning and had taken advantage of the special shipping and other arrangements we had made for their repatriation, but large groups of Americans were still in Europe and Asia at the time of Pearl Harbor.

My associates and I had been preparing a comprehensive summary of our relations with Japan, culminating in Pearl Harbor, which the President might wish to send to Congress. We completed this about December 10, and Mr. Roosevelt sent it as a message to Congress on December 15.

Further declarations of war against us were now reported from Bulgaria, Hungary, and Rumania. When I talked this fact over with the President on December 13, however, we agreed that, at least for the time being, we would not ask Congress for declarations of war against these satellites. We realized that their Governments were puppets of Hitler and had merely jumped when the strings were pulled.

I was then beginning to work, along with my associates at the State Department, on a far more important declaration—that which later was called the Declaration by United Nations. Almost immediately after Pearl Harbor I had begun to consider the form of unity the nations fighting against Hitler and Japan should take. By now, including the Latin American Republics that had accompanied us into war against the Axis, an imposing list of nearly thirty nations was arrayed against the Axis.

My first idea of the unity the Allied nations should take was based on the conferences at Lima and Havana, with regard to the Western Hemisphere. This was that, when danger developed, a united resistance must be organized. In my mind I extended that policy to the world situation for, from the Montevideo Conference on, I had often stated that our Pan American policies were capable of being applied to the world.

I asked my associates to go back over the period from 1938 on with regard to Latin America, to review what the President had said on the subject of unity among the nations fighting the Axis, and to scrutinize the procedures followed in the First World War, including the subject of unity of command and military alliances.

Then on Saturday December 13 I asked Maxwell M. Hamilton, Chief of the Division of Far Eastern Affairs, to draw up a draft of a declaration to be made by the nations fighting the Axis, which would bind them together until victory and would commit them to the basic principles that we upheld. The following morning, Sunday, exactly one week after Pearl Harbor, I met with a group of my associates to discuss this declaration and another declaration setting up a Supreme War Council.

Hamilton had prepared two alternative drafts of a declaration by the Allies. These differed only in that one brought in all the Allies, whereas the other consisted of two separate declarations, the first to be signed by all the Allies with the exception of Russia, who was not at war with Japan, and the latter to be signed by Russia. We quickly decided to discard the second draft, believing it would be far more effective to have Russia included with the rest of the Allies. After further exchanges of views, I requested Assistant Secretary Berle, Economic Adviser Feis, and Hamilton to go to another room, incorporate in the draft the changes suggested, and bring it back to the meeting. This they did, and returned in half an hour.

We now agreed on the main points of what became the Declaration by United Nations. The preamble first reasserted the principles agreed to by President Roosevelt and Prime Minister Churchill in the Atlantic Charter. It then stated that the nations fighting the Axis were "convinced that complete and world-wide victory of all of them is essential to defend and preserve life, liberty and independence, and to preserve human freedom and justice not only in their own lands but everywhere, and that the struggle in which they are now engaged is a common defense against savage and brutal forces seeking to subjugate the world."

Then followed the specific points of agreement, three in number. Each Government pledged itself, first, "to employ its full resources against the Government or Governments which signed the Tripartite Pact on September 27, 1940, with which it is or may be at war, and to continue such employment until that Government or those Governments have been finally defeated."

Second, "to cooperate with the others to the entire extent of its capacity to effect full coordination of military effort and use of resources against the common enemies or any of them."

Third, "not to cease hostilities against or conclude a separate armistice with the common enemies or any of them, except by common agreement."

Here, I felt, we were taking two long and helpful steps forward in comparison with our position during the First World War. First, we intended to try to bind all the nations fighting the Axis to the acceptance of certain principles already stated in the Atlantic Charter. These were the right of peoples to choose their own form of government; no aggrandizement; no territorial changes opposed by the peoples concerned; access to trade and raw materials; improved labor standards, economic advancement, and social security; international security; freedom of the seas; and disarmament.

Our Government, on entering the First World War, had not endeavored to bind the Allies to any war aims. Various secret accords had already been agreed to by the Allied Governments whereunder territorial changes would be made if they won the war. Wilson's Administration was subsequently criticized severely for not having tried to get the Allies into a common agreement on war aims. His problems at the peace conference were greatly complicated by the fact that no such agreement existed.

This time I felt that the Allies should all be committed in advance to certain principles, leaving details of boundary adjustments and the like to be settled later. If the principles were strongly enough proclaimed and adhered to, the details would find readier solution when the time came to solve them.

It was naturally necessary for us to know whether any secret agreements again existed among the Allies. When I had this question put to them they assured us that there were no such agreements.

Secondly, we were willing this time to join in a full alliance with the other nations fighting the Axis. During the First World War we had considered and called ourselves an "Associated Power," not an Ally. The Declaration we now prepared was in the nature of an alliance. It embraced the two main points of the usual military alliance; namely, a pledge of full support and cooperation in conducting the war against the common enemy, and a pledge not to cease hostilities against the common enemy except by mutual agreement.

From December 15 to December 19 my associates and I spent considerable time perfecting drafts of the document that became the United Nations Declaration. We also discussed another document that would have created a Supreme War Council composed of the heads or representatives of the Governments of the United Kingdom, the United States, China, and the U.S.S.R. The function of the War Council would be "to supervise and coordinate the general conduct of the war and to provide for its successful prosecution." The Council would determine theaters of war and provide for representation of any other Government actively engaged in war against a common enemy in such theaters. It would be responsible for coordinating the distribution of available resources of all categories between various theaters of war. It would be charged with effecting unified command in any theater of war determined by it. The Council would create a staff of representatives of their respective armed forces to carry out their orders.

In drawing up this second document, we considered and discussed thoroughly the creation, functioning, and achievements of the Supreme War Council set up during the latter stages of the First World War. During my years in the House of Representatives, I had made a study of the relations of the United States with the Allies and of the operation of their joint councils. I had given particular attention to the book on this subject by General Tasker H. Bliss, the United States Army Chief of Staff. It was now my thought that the Supreme War Council should be set up at once and not wait until a long period of war had passed, as was the case in the previous conflict.

I sent both papers to the President at the White House at one o'clock on December 19, along with a memorandum outlining the activities of the Supreme War Council of 1917-1918. Although a proposal to create a Supreme War Council was not strictly a function of the State Department, I felt impelled to make the suggestion to the President because of my belief that a close working together of the Allies was imperatively necessary, and that our diplomatic efforts toward that end would be immeasurably bolstered by an intimate working relationship in the military field. My own studies of the relations of the Allied and Associated Powers during the First World War were still so fresh in my mind that I wanted to communicate the results of these studies to the Commander-in-Chief, in so far as they might be of aid to him.

In an accompanying memorandum to the President I said: "The four chief nations now fighting together, as well as any others who will join with them, should forthwith sign a common declaration of principle, which should embody a pledge to employ their entire resources and their full military effort to defeat the common enemy, and should include a pledge to coordinate these efforts, and should include also a pledge by all of them not to cease hostilities nor conclude a separate armistice with the common enemies or any of them until these enemies are finally defeated."

As to the Supreme War Council document, I said: "Second, it seems essential to provide machinery which will effectively coordinate the use of resources and the military effort, making suitable allocation between theaters of war, keeping continuous check on the execution of war plans and, if possible, achieving unified command in theaters where this is feasible."

An hour later, at the Cabinet meeting presided over by the President, I went over both papers for the benefit of the Cabinet members. I pointed out the great advantages to all concerned in unifying all the nations fighting the Axis in a common determination to carry the fight through to victory by pledging all their resources in the common effort, and in an acceptance of the principles that should be applied when victory was attained.

I said that military alliances usually stipulated that the parties to them would not conclude peace except by mutual agreement, and that the Joint Declaration might be an improvement in that it provided that the signatories would not "cease hostilities against or conclude a separate armistice" except by common agreement.

As for the Supreme War Council, I said the one we had outlined would probably be far more effective than that of 1917–1918 because the United States would have political representation, whereas in the previous war our participation had been chiefly military. Furthermore, our plan called for representation on the Council's staff of army, naval, and air forces, whereas the plan of 1917 provided only for a permanent military representative.

One of the most important arguments in favor of our plan, I said, was that it would probably result in unified command in many theaters of the war. The creation of the Supreme War Council in 1917 had greatly assisted in bringing about a unified command on the Western Front. This unification was all the more necessary now, I concluded, inasmuch as the theaters of war were far more widely spread than they had been in the war of 1914–1918.

In the Cabinet discussion that followed, there seemed to be general approval of both documents. The President raised only one point about which he had any hesitancy. This concerned the constitutionality of the Joint Declaration, which later became known officially as the Declaration by United Nations. He brought up especially the question whether he had the constitutional right to sign an agreement that pledged the signatories not to conclude a separate armistice or cease hostilities.

When I returned to the State Department I called my advisers in for a discussion of this point. We generally felt that there was no real doubt as to the constitutionality of the provisions. I suggested, however, that the provision might well be taken from the Joint Declaration, which would be signed by many countries, and placed in the Supreme War Council agreement, which would be signed by four countries. We therefore prepared new drafts, also embodying two other minor changes, and I sent these to the White House that evening to be substituted for the two documents I had placed before the Cabinet.

December 22 I sent the President an eight-page opinion by Green H. Hackworth, Legal Adviser of the State Department, to the effect that there was not the slightest question about the constitutionality of the President's undertaking not to cease hostilities against or conclude a separate armistice with the common enemies or any of them except by common agreement. I wrote the President that, in my judgment, Hackworth's opinion "makes clear the legal and constitutional validity of this provision."

This opinion stated: "Both by the resolutions of Congress and by the Constitution the President is to be the judge as to how best to prosecute the war. Its successful termination may depend upon the ability of the President to make certain that Great Britain, Soviet Russia, and China shall continue the struggle until the enemies are defeated. The best way to be sure that this situation shall obtain is through a pledge by them not to cease fighting except by common agreement of all four Powers. The President could not obtain such a pledge from the other Powers without making one himself. He is justified in doing so by reason of his responsibility as Commander-in-Chief and his broad powers in the conduct of foreign relations."

The President thereupon agreed that this clause could well be reinserted in the Declaration.

That day I gave the President a further memorandum on the Supreme War Council my associates and I proposed. This outlined the organizations that might function under the Council. They included a Military Council, a Naval Council, an Aviation Council, a Shipping Council, and an Economic Council. The last body would be divided into Food, Munitions, Raw Materials, and Petroleum committees. I recommended that the seat of the Supreme War Council be Washington.

And on the same day Prime Minister Churchill arrived in Washington. During the next few days the President went over with the Prime Minister our texts of the proposed Joint Declaration and of the proposal for the Supreme War Council. Mr. Churchill or Ambassador Halifax communicated these to London for the War Cabinet's opinion.

The President sent me on December 27 his written comments on the two texts. Churchill had received recommendations from the War Cabinet on the Joint Declaration and the President said he had taken these into account.

"I think," he said, "every effort should be made to get religious freedom into that document. I believe Litvinov can be induced to agree to this."

He thought the language in the pledge to continue the fight against the Axis was difficult for the Russians. This was because they were not at war with Japan. He suggested a slight change in the wording so that the pledge would apply against the Axis forces of conquest with which the signatory was at war.

The President said he had been trying to think of a way to obviate the necessity of two different documents, the Joint Declaration and the Supreme War Council proposal.

He suggested that the list of countries mentioned in the opening paragraph of the Joint Declaration should embrace all the nations at war against the Axis, including the Latin American Republics. "It seems to me a distinct advantage," he said, "to have as long a list of small countries as possible in this Declaration."

The President believed that China and the U.S.S.R. should be lifted from the alphabetical listing and placed with the United States and Britain at the head of the list. "I have a feeling," he commented, "the U.S.S.R. would not be pleased to see their name following some of the countries which are realistically making a minor contribution."

He presumed it was up to the British to decide whether India should be included. "But," he said, "I don't understand why they don't include it. Perhaps you could prod them a little."

Further he suggested: "I feel that the Free French should not be included in this document."

In general he concluded: "I am anxious that the most careful thought be given to the language in this Declaration, which will supplement the Atlantic statement, particularly in reference to the real purpose for which we fight.

"As soon as you and Halifax have reached a meeting of minds on the Joint Declaration, I think we should have a prompt conference between yourself, Halifax, the Prime Minister, and me."

Later the President called a meeting of these four persons to be held at the White House at six o'clock that evening.

That afternoon I called Welles, Hackworth, and Carlton Savage to my office to consider the President's memorandum. We incorporated the President's suggestions in a new draft of the Joint Declaration. We further wrote in two additional statements, which were that:

(1) The signatories had determined that the effective prosecution of warfare against their enemies required the creation of a Supreme War Council;

(2) The Declaration might be adhered to by other nations which are or which may be rendering material assistance and contributions toward the defeat of the members of the Tripartite Pact.

The President's memorandum had made no direct comment on the proposed Supreme War Council. To meet his thought that there should not be two separate documents, we prepared a draft combining the Joint Declaration and the Supreme War Council proposal.

I now had ready three drafts to take to the White House—the new draft of the Joint Declaration, a copy of the December 19 draft on the Supreme War Council, and the amalgamated draft containing the Joint Declaration and the agreement on the Supreme War Council.

Lord Halifax joined in the later stages of the conference in my office. His principal comment was that the British Dominions probably would have to be given a status in the Supreme War Council similar to that given Britain. We explained to him that if the Council should comprise a large number of representatives it would become unwieldy and ineffective. We also pointed out that provision was made for *ad hoc* representation on the Council and its staff for Governments actively engaged against the common enemy in specific theaters of war.

Halifax and we agreed that the Soviet Government would be willing to subscribe to the principles contained in the Joint Declaration and to the formation of a Supreme War Council.

Halifax and I then went to the White House for our conference with the President and the Prime Minister. During the conference it was apparent that Mr. Roosevelt and Mr. Churchill were not yet in agreement that a Supreme War Council should be set up. Most of our discussion was devoted to this subject. We therefore agreed to adopt the new draft of the Joint Declaration, standing alone, leaving the Supreme War Council draft for further discussion.

Following the meeting the President called in Soviet Ambassador

Litvinov and handed him a copy to be sent immediately to his Government for comment.

Two days later Litvinov came to my office with three amendments suggested by his Government. Two were unimportant changes of wording. The third was that the phrase in the final paragraph "and contribution towards the defeat of members or adherents of the Tripartite Pact" should be changed to, "and contributions in the struggle for victory over Hitlerism."

I said to Litvinov that the Soviet amendments were unobjectionable with the possible exception of the one quoted, and that it would be almost impossible for us to omit Japan from the document should Hitler be mentioned. Litvinov agreed with me that we could work this out in some way that would be mutually satisfactory.

The Ambassador seemed surprised when I said that the proposed declaration had not been delivered to any other country for signature pending Soviet Russia's reaction. He had brought with him a separate declaration that Stalin planned to make upon the assumption that the Joint Declaration was already in circulation among other countries for signature. This declaration stated that the Government of the U.S.S.R. shared the general principles laid down in the Joint Declaration but was unable to sign it, not being at war with one of the states of the Tripartite Pact. "The Government of the U.S.S.R.," it said, "declares that it considers the chief enemy of freedom-loving peoples, and the center of the Axis, to be Hitlerite Germany, against which the Soviet Union is fighting and now bearing the brunt in the war against Hitlerite tyranny."

Litvinov and I agreed that it would be more effective for the Soviet Union to sign the Joint Declaration than to issue a separate Declaration.

I sent the Soviet amendments to the President later that day. I wrote in an accompanying memorandum: "The Soviet Ambassador tells me that the word 'Hitlerism' with his country includes Nazism, Fascism, and Japanism, and hence his Government may stick rather strongly for this word. I mention this so you will have the full background. I see no particular objection to the other proposals."

The President agreed to the incorporation of the Soviet amendments. I thereupon sent him a new draft which he returned on December 30 with a handwritten marginal note:

C. H.
    O. K. It is approved now by Russia and W. S. C. [Churchill] but not yet by China.   F. D. R.
    Let's get it out on January 1. That means speed.   F. D. R.

We transmitted the Joint Declaration immediately to the Governments listed in it. In accordance with the President's request, I asked the interested Governments to give an immediate response so that the document could be made public on January 1. I called in Chinese Ambassador Dr. Hu Shih and gave him personally a copy for his Government.

At the last moment Lord Halifax wanted to have a reference to "social security" inserted in the Declaration. Since the President and the Prime Minister, however, desired not to make any changes in the Declaration in view of the approval already given by the Soviet Government, Assistant Secretary Berle convinced Halifax that his Government should not press the suggestion.

Halifax had received a cable from the Foreign Office which agreed to the inclusion of India among the signatories but suggested the use of the words "high contracting parties" instead of "Governments signatory hereto" on the ground that much of India was composed of native states that could only be bound by the signature of the King. We replied that the words "high contracting parties" might raise difficulties on our side because of the moot question as to when a governmental agreement became a treaty. The words "high contracting parties" were customarily employed in treaties and, if this phrase were used, a demand might arise that the President submit the accord to the Senate as a treaty instead of dealing with it as an agreement based on his war-prosecution powers.

Halifax also wished to make a change at the end of the document to enable organizations such as the Free French to sign. I did not feel we could make any change without the President's approval—and from his memorandum of December 27 I already knew his sentiments on the particular point of the Free French signing the Declaration—hence nothing was done.

The following day, December 31, I sent the Joint Declaration in its final form to the President for signature by himself and the Prime Minister. I suggested that the President might desire to ask Ambassador Litvinov and T. V. Soong, who had just been made Foreign Minister of China, to attach their signatures at the White House.

By now the three points of agreement were combined into two, which read:

"(1) Each Government pledges itself to employ its full resources, military or economic, against those members of the Tripartite Pact and its adherents with which such Government is at war.

"(2) Each Government pledges itself to cooperate with the Governments signatory hereto and not to make a separate armistice or peace with the enemies."

Later I telephoned the President and suggested that since there would not be enough signatures on the document by the next day, January 1, it would be preferable to wait a few days before releasing it. The President and I agreed that the Joint Declaration should be dated January 1 and made public on January 2 or 3.

Over the telephone the President said, with respect to the memorandum on the creation of a Supreme War Council, that it seemed desirable to work on a regional basis for the time being, with the possibility that eventually it might be feasible to create an over-all Council. A Supreme War Council such as we at the State Department had suggested was not set up, but the President and the Prime Minister took a major step in that direction during Mr. Churchill's visit by creating the Combined Chiefs of Staff, with headquarters in Washington, to integrate the strategy of the two countries. They also established combined Anglo-American boards to deal with the assignment of munitions, the supply of raw materials, production and resources, shipping and food. Subsequently, unified commands were agreed upon for the Mediterranean, European, Southwest Pacific, and Southeast Asia theaters.

On the morning of December 31, while Prime Minister Churchill was having a bath in the White House, the President came to him and suggested that the Joint Declaration carry the title, "Declaration by United Nations." The distinguished bather agreed, and thus the term "United Nations" came into being. The President had our final draft recopied at the White House so as to bear the new title.

On the first day of the New Year, Roosevelt, Churchill, Litvinov, and Soong signed the historic document.

The following morning the President sent the Declaration to the State Department, where we placed it in the office of Assistant Secretary Berle for signature by the remaining twenty-two nations fighting the Axis. During the course of the day, representatives of those nations signed, some of them with obvious emotion. The Czech Minister, Vladimír Hurban, saying it was the most important document he had ever signed, was so nervous that he could not subscribe for some minutes after entering Berle's office. The Panamanian Minister got up from a sick bed to sign for his Government. The representative of India remarked that he was signing for 400,000,000 people.

While these signatures were being affixed, I issued a public statement, saying: "The Declaration by the United Nations joins together,
in the greatest common war effort in history, the purpose and will of
twenty-six free nations, representing the overwhelming majority of the
inhabitants of all six continents. This is a living proof that law-abiding and
peace-loving nations can unite in using the sword when necessary to preserve liberty and justice and the fundamental values of mankind. Against
this host we can be sure that the forces of barbaric savagery and organized
wickedness cannot and will not prevail."

For some days we had been discussing at the State Department and
with the President the possibility of adherence to the United Nations
Declaration by political groups representative of the peoples of countries
overrun by the Axis which had no governments functioning in exile. The
final paragraph of the Declaration had provided for the adherence of
"other nations" that contributed to the struggle against the Axis, in addition to the original twenty-six signatories, but nothing was said of "free
movements" and the like which purported to represent certain conquered
peoples and even peoples of Axis countries.

At the State Department we had sought in December to clarify our
position with regard to such movements by issuing a public statement on
December 10. In this we pointed out that the people of the United States
had a sympathetic interest in movements by aliens in this country who
desired to liberate their countries from Axis domination, although at the
same time we emphasized that we did not look with favor on any activities designed to divide the allegiance of any group of American residents
between the United States and any foreign government, in existence or in
prospect.

It was obvious that such "free movements" could not adhere to
the United Nations Declaration as such, which was signed by representatives of governments. But it might be possible for them to state their
adherence to the principles of the Declaration. The President favored some
such clause with the thought that it would give the Free French movement an opportunity to adhere to the Declaration's principles. I concurred in this thought with regard to the Free French, but I stated my fears
lest such a clause would produce a rush of conflicting adherences from a
variety of other groups, committees, movements, and the like, many at
loggerheads with each other, and that difficulties might arise with some
of our Allies over such adherences.

On January 4, after informing Britain, Russia and China of our purpose, we issued a statement, saying: "In order that liberty-loving peoples silenced by military forces may have an opportunity to support the principles of the Declaration by United Nations, the Government of the United States, as the depository for that Declaration, will receive statements of adherence to its principles from appropriate authorities which are not governments."

The Free French did not adhere under this offer because they wanted to come in as a government, but a flood of other adherences from committees allegedly representing the peoples of a dozen other countries' poured in. Many of these committees were at odds with one another, ranging from royalists to communists, and many hoped to obtain a degree of recognition by the fact of adherence. Several of our Allies, Russia in particular, objected to some of these groups. As a result, we simply filed the requests for adherence, and the statement of January 4 brought little but trouble.

The United Nations Declaration on the whole proved to be an inspiring link binding together the nations fighting against the Axis movement of world conquest. By it these Allies bound themselves to the basic principles of sound international relations, to full cooperation among themselves, and to the continuance of the fight against the Axis until the achievement of victory. As new nations joined the fight they were proud of the honor of signing the statement of common aims and purposes. Coalitions have historically been impermanent and difficult, and sharp disputes did arise between several of the United Nations, as for example between the Soviet Union and Poland, but the United Nations Declaration proved a standard around which right-minded peoples and governments could rally and advance. It was a powerful factor in achieving the surprising degree of unity that was reached.

82: Troubles Over France

DURING PRIME MINISTER CHURCHILL'S visit to the President before and after Christmas, 1941, the two leaders decided that an Anglo-American expeditionary force should be sent to North Africa. They agreed that General Weygand, then in retirement in Vichy France following his dismissal as Governor General in North Africa by Marshal Pétain, should be approached to learn whether he would return secretly to North Africa and cooperate with the Allied Army.

The President accordingly prepared a letter to Weygand, which was delivered on January 20. Weygand, however, absolutely declined to take any action. He said he was now a private citizen, completely loyal to Pétain, and would have to inform Pétain of the President's letter.

In any event the project of an expeditionary force to North Africa had to be abandoned until much later in the year because Japanese successes in the South Seas area diverted our strength to that arena.

At about the time of his letter to Weygand, the President also sent a special message to Admiral Leahy for Pétain or Weygand, or both. In this Mr. Roosevelt said that if Germany or Italy attacked unoccupied France or any of the French colonies, we could not regard acquiescence in such an attack as anything else than "playing the German game." On the other hand, he continued, resistance by the French would have the support "of every possible military and naval assistance we could bring to bear."

Leahy communicated this message to both Pétain and Darlan on January 27. Pétain, reading from a penciled memorandum, replied that he had made it very clear that his Government would resist invasion by British, De Gaullists, Germans, or Americans. He said that use of the French fleet or North African bases by the Germans was no longer a question. He added that he did not consider a German invasion of French North Africa at all imminent, but, if it occurred, he would accept American aid only if he himself requested it.

Following Pearl Harbor the President received from various sources outside the State Department suggestions that the United States should adopt strong-arm methods toward Vichy, should join with Britain in seizing portions of the French fleet or French bases, should break relations with Vichy or should establish full diplomatic relations with De

Gaulle and his movement. Fortunately, the President refused to let himself be swayed by advice so ill considered.

At that very moment our informal relations with De Gaulle were embittered by his unwarranted action in ordering the forcible occupation of the French islands of Saint-Pierre and Miquelon, off the Newfoundland coast, by Free French forces. The incident occurred on Christmas Eve while the President was entertaining Mr. Churchill at the White House.

These islands had been under the jurisdiction of Governor Robert at Martinique. We had already reached agreements with Admiral Robert, renewed a few days after Pearl Harbor, whereby our interest in maintaining the status quo of Saint-Pierre and Miquelon was safeguarded. We had also had negotiations with Canada during November and December concerning a powerful wireless station on Saint-Pierre which both Canada and we feared might serve as a guide to German submarines. We agreed that Canada should send operators to supervise messages transmitted by the station and that we would join Canada in economic pressure against the islands if the local governor refused to accede to Canada's move.

The Canadian Government had informed us on December 4 of a suggestion from the British Government that the islands be occupied by the Free French. This suggestion did not appeal either to the Canadians or to ourselves. For my part, I looked with something like horror on any action that would bring conflict between the Vichy French and the Free French or the British. Though our advice had not been asked, I had been strongly opposed to the British attack on the French fleet at Oran in 1940, and I had worked hard to bring Britain and Vichy France back into some degree of friendship.

At the end of November, De Gaulle had sent his "Minister of Marine," Admiral Muselier, to inspect the Free French corvettes operating with the British off Newfoundland and at the same time to undertake to rally the Saint-Pierre-Miquelon islands to his movement. Muselier went to Ottawa where he sought the opinion of the Canadian Government. The Canadian External Affairs Department would not give him permission.

On December 15 the British Foreign Office stated that Prime Minister Churchill felt it would be desirable for the Free French forces to land and control the radio station rather than for the Canadian Government to take action in what might be an embarrassing political situation. The Foreign Office said further that no action would be taken unless the consent of the American and Canadian Governments had been obtained.

Muselier saw our Minister in Ottawa, Pierrepont Moffat, that same day and asked for the opinion of the American Government as to a landing of Free French troops on the islands. The President read Moffat's telegram to this effect and said he did not favor any policy whereby the Free French were permitted to move in on the Saint-Pierre and Miquelon situation. This was telephoned to Moffat.

Moffat informed Muselier of our views on December 16. Muselier said to Moffat he felt we were making a mistake, but he would accept this decision.

The Counselor of the Canadian Legation in Washington, Mr. Hume Wrong, informed the State Department on December 22 that, since the British Government did not "go along" with the policy suggested in the American-Canadian discussions for action by Canada to supervise the radio station at Saint-Pierre, the Canadian Government was not going ahead with its proposed action. Wrong said, however, he could inform us that any action by the Free French forces had been called off.

Canadian Prime Minister Mackenzie King stated to Minister Moffat on the same day that he agreed with the decision of the United States and felt that any slight advantages of action by the Free French in occupying the islands would be outweighed by the bigger issue involved, which he said he understood.

Meantime, however, Muselier had communicated with De Gaulle, who ordered him to go ahead just the same.

Without previous warning to Canada or the United States, Admiral Muselier therefore landed a small force on the islands on Christmas Eve and took charge. Our Consul at Saint-Pierre, Maurice Pasquet, reported to us on December 26 that Muselier was much aroused against De Gaulle whom he accused of having acted as a dictator. Muselier said he intended to resign in protest against the unilateral order given him by De Gaulle without the prior approval of the United States and Canada. Sometime later Muselier did break with De Gaulle.

British Ambassador Halifax came to see me Christmas afternoon to inform me on behalf of the Foreign Office that the British Government disclaimed all responsibility for the Free French action and that Muselier had acted contrary to the instructions of the Foreign Office. Minister Moffat reported to me from Ottawa that the Canadian Government was "shocked and embarrassed" by the incident and regarded it as "so close to a breach of faith that it cannot fail to embarrass their future relations with the Free French."

On that Christmas Day I issued a statement, with the approval of the President, characterizing the incident by three "so-called Free French ships" as "an arbitrary action contrary to the agreement of all parties concerned and certainly without the prior knowledge or consent in any sense of the United States Government." I said we had inquired of the Canadian Government as to the steps Canada was prepared to take to restore the status quo of the islands.

Comparatively unimportant though the islands were, their forcible occupation by the Free French was greatly embarrassing to us for several reasons. It might seriously interfere with our relations with Marshal Pétain's Government. Only eleven days before the occupation the President had sent a message to Pétain, following Vichy's proclamation of neutrality, in which he gave "full recognition to the agreement reached by our two Governments involving the maintenance of the status quo of the French possessions in the Western Hemisphere."

Moreover, we had just renewed an agreement with Admiral Robert at Martinique on this subject. And, finally, the American Republics had agreed at the Havana Conference to oppose the transfer of sovereignty, possession or control of any territory in the Western Hemisphere held by European Powers.

Admiral Robert quickly informed us that in his opinion the United States was "obligated to obtain the reestablishment of French sovereignty over Saint-Pierre-Miquelon." And Admiral Leahy cabled me from Vichy that Admiral Darlan informed him that the Germans immediately used De Gaulle's seizure of the islands as an argument for the entry of Axis troops into French North Africa so that they might protect it against a similar invasion.

Unfortunately, many influential people, both in the United States and abroad, did not comprehend these broader issues, and unleashed a violent attack on the State Department and on me for having issued the statement I did on the seizure of the islands. Few actions that seemed so minor have ever aroused opposition that became so bitter. In the weeks that followed, the State Department, with myself as its chief, became the target of editorials, radio attacks, and representations from various organizations, although the President had given his full approval to our reaction.

A special offensive was launched against us because of the word "so-called" in the phrase "so-called Free French ships" in the statement. Our attackers thought that with this word we were questioning the existence of the Free French or the fact that they were free, whereas by the phrase we simply meant: three ships supposedly of the Free French.

I sought to work out with Lord Halifax and with French Ambassador Henry-Haye a speedy settlement of the controversy. To Halifax on December 26 I suggested it might well be possible to get an agreement with Governor Robert at Martinique, approved by Vichy, to allow three or four Canadian experts to supervise messages passing over the radio station at Saint-Pierre. Thereupon the British Government could request the Free French to withdraw from the islands; and Britain and Canada, in order to give De Gaulle a face-saving way out, could then praise very highly the part the Free French occupation had taken in securing the agreement for supervision.

Halifax argued that nothing should be done about the occupation by Britain, Canada, or the United States.

"According to you," I replied, "we should ratify the unlawful act of the Free French, taken in absolute violation of their pledges to Great Britain, which means that the United States would have to throw over the entire problem of Vichy and French Africa which we've been nursing for a considerable period. If we hadn't been nursing this problem, Germany would probably be in occupation of North or West Africa, or both, now and during most of the past twelve months. Your Government is perhaps more interested, if possible, in the Vichy angle of this matter than is the United States."

Halifax said he saw the force of this position. He agreed to my discussing with Canadian Prime Minister Mackenzie King a proposed agreement with Vichy France and to our then asking Prime Minister Churchill to request De Gaulle to remove his forces from the islands.

After I talked at length the following day with French Ambassador Henry-Haye, he said he would recommend earnestly to his Government and to Governor Robert a settlement that would either involve shutting down the wireless station at Saint-Pierre, with a Canadian guard over it, or permitting two or three Canadians, along with an American attached to the consulate, to supervise the operation of the station.

When I informed the Ambassador that the Governor of the islands had made himself personally offensive to Canada and to some of the people on the islands, and that it was desirable he should be replaced, Henry-Haye said he would undertake to see that this was done. Three days later he brought me the reply of his Government. Vichy left the settlement of the matter to Governor Robert, but stated with dramatic emphasis its claim to sovereignty over the islands. Henry-Haye himself launched into a loud monologue about French sovereignty and about France being a great country and having to be treated accordingly.

I interrupted him by saying: "At a moment when I'm being subjected to every sort of abuse, even in this country, as I try to safeguard the whole situation by friendly settlement, just and fair to all, the only reply I receive from you is a stump speech about the greatness of the French nation. Soon it will be too late to handle this matter on its merits and in a proper spirit because of its explosive possibilities."

Henry-Haye promised to take the question up with his Government again.

The previous day Lord Halifax had come to tell me that his Government was very fearful of injuring the De Gaulle movement in Africa if it should resist De Gaulle's desire to hold on to the islands.

I had a blunt conversation with Prime Minister Churchill at the White House on the whole question of our relations with Vichy France, with the seizure of the islands as a springboard. The President, who thoroughly agreed with my position, was present at this discussion, but he remained on the side lines while Mr. Churchill and I indulged in some plain speaking.

I pointedly accused De Gaulle of being a marplot acting directly contrary to the expressed wishes of Britain, Canada, and the United States, and I asked the Prime Minister to induce him to withdraw his troops from the Saint-Pierre and Miquelon islands, with Canadians and Americans assuming supervision over the radio station at Saint-Pierre.

Mr. Churchill said that if he insisted on such a request his relations with the Free French movement would be impaired.

I replied that the presence of the Free French on the islands, without our doing anything about it, jeopardized our relations with the Vichy Government. I reemphasized the importance of continuing those relations in that they enabled us to use our influence to keep the French fleet and bases from falling into German hands and to keep observers in Vichy France and in French North and West Africa. I said it was unthinkable to me that all these benefits to the British and American Governments should be junked and thrown overboard in order to gratify the desire of the De Gaulle leaders.

Mr. Churchill agreed that these relations with Vichy were important to Britain as well as to the United States.

I directly asked the Prime Minister whether he could not do something to prevent De Gaulle's movement from continuing its radio and press attacks on the American Government. I said that, since these attacks were made from London and continued unchecked, the impression was being created that Britain approved them or acquiesced in them.

When the Prime Minister wondered whether he would be in position to exercise any such censorship over De Gaulle, I said that De Gaulle's propaganda campaign against us was being financed by British funds, and De Gaulle could be quickly stopped dead in his tracks if Mr. Churchill threatened to withdraw Britain's subsidies.

Mr. Churchill agreed to consider the various points I had raised.

Matters were at this point when the Prime Minister went to Ottawa and there on December 30 delivered a violent diatribe against Vichy along with fulsome praise of De Gaulle. Coming at a moment when public agitation over the seizure of the Saint-Pierre and Miquelon islands and over our reaction to it was so rabid, it gave a popular impression that the Prime Minister was approving De Gaulle's action. At the same time it was an implied condemnation of our continued diplomatic relations with any Government so base and despicable as his description of the Vichy group.

And yet, only nineteen days before, on December 11, Mr. Churchill, as the "former naval person," had sent the President an important cable with a very different approach to the subject. Referring to reports that Admiral Leahy was leaving Vichy to return to the United States, he said he was most anxious to discuss with the President a project of offering Vichy "blessings or cursings," following a British victory in Libya, and he then added: "Trust your link with Pétain will not be broken meanwhile. We have no other worth-while connection."

The day after Mr. Churchill's speech, I sent the President a memorandum in which I said: "Our British friends seem to believe that the body of the entire people of France is strongly behind De Gaulle, whereas according to all my information and that of my associates, some 95 per cent of the entire French people are anti-Hitler, whereas more than 95 per cent of this latter number are not De Gaullists and would not follow him. This fact leads straight to our plans about North Africa and our omission of De Gaulle's cooperation in that connection."

Regarding this last point, the President had early determined that De Gaulle would not be included in any plans for an Anglo-American expedition to French North Africa, and he emphasized this determination to Mr. Churchill. He felt that inclusion of De Gaulle might prejudice the secrecy of the plans and would automatically produce resistance from the French in North Africa.

In the same memorandum I summed up the Free French seizure of the islands by saying: "It is a mess beyond question, and one for which this Government was in no remote sense responsible." I remarked that it might lead to "ominous and serious developments."

Mr. Churchill returned to Washington almost immediately after his Ottawa speech. I saw him at the White House on January 2 and did not hesitate to say that his remarks about Vichy and De Gaulle were "highly incendiary" and had brought far-reaching injury to me and to the State Department.

I pleaded with him that, since our relations with Vichy were of great value to Britain as well as to the United States, as he himself had repeatedly acknowledged to us, it would be of wonderful assistance to us if he could say "just a few little words" to the effect that, although Britain had not desired to maintain relations with Vichy, those maintained by the United States were worth while in the common cause. Otherwise, I said, the existing general impression that the United States was "appeasing" Vichy, in direct violation of British wishes, would continue and spread.

The Prime Minister was not cordial to the suggestion.

I then asked the President to bring his own personal influence with Churchill to bear to produce a straightening out of this anomalous situation. Mr. Roosevelt, however, said he had done what he could and he could not do anything further. These attitudes of the President and the Prime Minister were in striking contrast to their later attitudes when they both became bitterly hostile to De Gaulle, and remained so.

When I returned to the State Department I had several of my assistants draw up a draft statement that might be issued by the President and the Prime Minister. This I sent to the President the same day, with a memorandum in which I said it was designed "to quiet steadily spreading rumors and reports very damaging to the British-American situation."

I said I had just talked with the French Ambassador. "I went after him very strongly," I said, "about simply closing down the [Saint-Pierre] wireless station and agreeing for a Canadian citizen to be about the premises at all times to see that it is kept closed down, and also to change governors—all of this to be done if and as the Free French who are occupying the islands make their departure, thereby restoring the status quo." Henry-Haye, I added, agreed to arrange for his Government's concurrence. I said to the President that the question then remained whether the Prime Minister would cooperate with us to see that the Free French moved out, with the thanks of their interested friends.

The proposed statement I sent the President was a general one intended to be a prelude to a settlement such as I had outlined. Referring to the islands controversy, it said that the President and the Prime Minister were in entire agreement that an arrangement satisfactory to all concerned should not be difficult. It added that the matter was receiving further attention in the light of the United States' commitments under the 1940 Havana Treaty and other international policies and agreements of great importance to the conduct of the war. This referred to our policy of continuing diplomatic relations with Vichy. The statement finished with the thought that "there should be no occasion for confusion or misunderstanding since there is complete cooperation and understanding between the United States, Great Britain, and Canada in this as in other matters."

The President, however, did not press this statement upon his visitor, nor did Mr. Churchill agree to it.

I now drafted a proposed agreement I believed acceptable to the United States, Britain, and Canada which would make withdrawal of the Free French forces from the islands agreeable to De Gaulle. This provided that the United States, Britain, and Canada would exercise joint supervision over the islands, which would be neutralized and demilitarized. Canada and the United States would provide personnel to control the wireless station. The Governor would be withdrawn for the duration of the war, to be succeeded by a consultative council. All armed forces would be recalled, and the United States and Canada would provide economic assistance.

I sent this to the President at Hyde Park on January 8. On the same day I had a conversation with Minister Sir Ronald Campbell, Counselor of the British Embassy, in which I frankly criticized the British Government, as far as one could well go, for its conduct in fomenting against the United States for British benefit the bitter agitation against this country over the islands.

"This," I said, "was led off by the incendiary speech of the British Prime Minister in Canada, which gave trouble-making people a pretext to make it appear that the British were the only friends the Free French had, and, inferentially, that the United States was not their friend; that the British were violently opposed to any connection with Vichy, and that, inferentially, the United States was tied with Vichy to an extent that was damaging and subject to criticism."

I informed Campbell that throughout the week I had strongly pleaded with Mr. Churchill to say just a few words to correct these wrong impressions, which he could have done without in the slightest way affecting British relations with the Free French.

"I asked him to do this in simple fairness to the United States," I said, "so as to cause a cessation of the injurious propaganda being circulated in the name of the Prime Minister since his speech in Canada."

Speaking as I had seldom spoken to the representative of a friendly nation, I said: "I wonder whether the British are more interested in a dozen or so Free Frenchmen, who seized these islands, and the capital they can make out of it primarily at the expense of the United States Government, than they are in Singapore and in the World War situation itself. I have neither seen nor heard of anything from British spokesmen in the last few days that would indicate to me that there existed a World War compared with the Saint-Pierre-Miquelon situation."

What heightened our exasperation over the Saint-Pierre-Miquelon incident was this very fact that De Gaulle should have so recklessly plunged into an adventure eminently calculated to disturb relations among the United States, Britain, and Canada, and that Britain should have been so reluctant to redress the damage done at the precise moment when the Japanese were driving the Western Powers out of the Orient, slashing into Malaya, the Philippines, and the Dutch East Indies, threatening Australia, and inflicting defeat after defeat on the Occidental forces, while the wreckage of the American Navy listed at crazy angles in Pearl Harbor.

The President agreed to my proposed solution. We thereupon submitted it to Mr. Churchill. He accepted it on condition that De Gaulle agreed. Meantime the Pétain Government agreed to it. But De Gaulle rejected it. I was thereupon informed that Mr. Churchill, then in Ottawa, cabled De Gaulle in London that the United States would send warships to the islands to expel the Free French.

After Mr. Churchill returned to London he informed the President on January 23 that he had had a "severe conversation" with De Gaulle on January 22. Previously De Gaulle had said to Eden that he would agree to the issuance of a communiqué to straighten out the matter provided all parties agreed to three secret points that would not be mentioned in the communiqué. These were that the Free French administrator would remain on the islands but be merged in a consultative council, that the marines should remain on the islands, and that the council would be under the orders of the Free French National Committee.

The Prime Minister informed the President that De Gaulle agreed not to insist that his secret points be accepted. De Gaulle, however, never did consent to our proposed agreement which would have ironed out the dispute.

Mr. Churchill said in his cable to the President that he did hope that the solution for which he had worked "would be satisfactory to Mr. Hull and the State Department. I understood fully the difficulty in which they were placed."

Finally, as the turmoil over the incident declined, I felt that the wisest course would be to let the matter rest until the end of the war. I so recommended to the President in a memorandum on February 2, 1942. I repeated to him that I had been greatly preoccupied throughout the incident lest the Vichy Government should be outraged, for the simple but compelling reason that I still hoped to hold Vichy to its assurances concerning the French fleet, colonies, and bases.

The President agreed with my recommendation, and a matter that had threatened to become a whole chapter in history accordingly declined to a footnote.

Our relations with De Gaulle's movement were not helped by the incident. There was no doubt in the minds of the President or myself that De Gaulle personally was responsible for violating his commitment to Britain and for going directly contrary to the wishes of the United States and Canada. We regarded him as more ambitious for himself and less reliable than we had thought him before.

As for myself, the refusal of the President to bring more pressure on Mr. Churchill to clarify the relations between Great Britain and the United States with regard to De Gaulle and Vichy was one of several factors that almost caused me to resign as Secretary of State in January, 1942. I so seriously considered taking this step that I penciled out a note to the President tendering my resignation.

My principal reason for almost resigning was the state of my health. In this note I pointed out that I had to give serious attention to conserving my health. I recalled that during the first half of the previous year, 1941, I had been hopelessly overworked and had been obliged to take a long rest. "In no other possible circumstances," I wrote, "could I consider the step I feel constrained to take—that of leaving the service." I ended by praying that the President would have the health and strength to keep up his great fight against the Axis countries.

After thinking this over very intensively, I decided that I could not give up at this moment when disaster after disaster was overtaking the United Nations in the Far East, even if it meant the total collapse of my health. I put the letter to the President away in a drawer, and turned to the many problems facing me, including the unfortunate conduct of Under Secretary Welles at the Rio de Janeiro Conference, of which I write in the following chapter.

83: Neighbors and War

WHEN THE PEARL HARBOR attack occurred, and when Hitler and Mussolini declared war upon us, my heart was truly warmed during the early days of disaster by the immediate rallying of the Latin American nations to our support. Within a few hours or days after Japan attacked, nine Latin American Republics declared war on the Axis and three more severed diplomatic relations. The heads of the Latin American Republics sent us messages of support, and those that did not break with the Axis formally assured us they would not regard us as belligerents and therefore would not apply the laws of neutrality against us.

Here, almost eight years to the day after the Montevideo Conference, was a striking affirmation of the value of the Good Neighbor Policy. We were now to gather the fruits of patient cultivation at the conferences of Montevideo, Buenos Aires, Lima, Panama, and Havana, and of our innumerable measures to apply and solidify the doctrine of the Good Neighbor.

I could look back to the time of our entrance into the First World War and rejoice that our friendship with our neighbors to the south was now so firm. In 1917 we had had to maintain troops on the Mexican border, where we had intervened more than once since 1913. Now Mexico broke off relations with the Axis Powers almost at the moment of our declarations of war. Farther to the south suspicion of our power and motives had been rampant in many countries. Now we could count on the active aid of almost all of them.

In general, the Latin American Republics quickly put into effect one of the resolutions agreed to at the Havana Conference, which I had signed on behalf of the United States. This provided: "That any attempt on the part of a non-American State against the integrity or inviolability of the territory, the sovereignty or the political independence of an American State shall be considered as an act of aggression against the States which sign this declaration."

Our negotiations with the Latin American Republics during 1941 had intensified in various directions. We signed a series of agreements providing for the dispatch of military, naval, and air missions to Central and South America. Congress passed an Act in July authorizing the admission to the Annapolis Naval Academy of up to twenty persons at a time from the American Republics. In October we announced a plan for the training in the United States of up to five hundred Latin Americans as aviation pilots and technicians.

We reached an economic agreement with Brazil for the construction of a $45,000,000 steel mill in that country. Through negotiations with Britain and certain American Republics, we arranged for the release and use of Axis shipping tied up in Western Hemisphere ports.

We had signed a trade agreement with Argentina on October 14, 1941. This was a major step forward, especially in view of the fact that our negotiations with Argentina toward the same end in 1939 had failed. While I was attending the Havana Conference in 1940, the Argentines indicated to us that the war and blockade had upset their international commerce and they asked whether we would purchase a substantial quantity of their surpluses of linseed, wool, hides, and meat. There seemed therefore a possible basis for reopening negotiations.

At the State Department we studied these prospects for a number of months and had informal exchanges with Argentina on the subject. Then on March 14, 1941, I wrote the President that the question of an Argentine trade agreement had in the past provoked considerable political controversy in this country but that now an agreement would ease Argentina's position without involving concessions harmful to ourselves. I said that the time was particularly opportune to dispose of this long-standing, difficult matter. Our domestic producers were enjoying increased protection owing to Argentina's augmented shipping costs and other difficulties of exporting to the United States. And, furthermore, there was a growing realization by Americans that good trade relations with the other American Republics, notably Argentina, were essential to effective hemisphere cooperation.

The President agreed. This time the negotiations proceeded without undue obstructions from Argentina and opposition from American interests, and the signature took place in Buenos Aires. It was the first commercial accord negotiated between the two countries in ninety years.

Less than three weeks before Pearl Harbor, we reached an agreement with Mexico on November 19 to settle the controversy over Mexico's expropriation of American oil properties in 1938. We had been negotiating this difficult problem for three years. We had granted Mexico's right to expropriate, and Mexico had granted our claim to compensation. We asserted that this compensation should be "adequate, effective, and prompt," and here lay the kernel of the dispute.

By August, 1941, the United States and the Mexican Governments had approved a tentative formula of settlement. I held a meeting of American oil-company representatives in my office on September 27, 1941, and laid this proposed settlement before them. I sought to place it on a broader basis by outlining to them the world situation and the important role Mexico could play in cooperation with us. I stressed the Axis activities being conducted in Latin America and the help Mexico had already given us in preventing strategic materials from going to Japan. I pointed out that President Camacho of Mexico had adopted policies affording a timely opportunity to work out all problems harmoniously, and in this spirit I urged consideration of the oil settlement.

The company representatives objected to various points in our proposal, and asserted that we were sacrificing the principle of property rights. They said they would rather see the question remain unsettled, even with the result of losing the property, than see this principle sacrificed.

I had further meetings and exchanges of conversation with the oil-company heads in October and November without being able to bring them around to our point of view. Knowing what I did about the dangerous status of our negotiations with Japan, I felt, and the President with me, that we could not wait longer. On November 19, therefore, an exchange of notes took place with Mexican Ambassador Nájera, which covered a wide range of subjects.

Mexico agreed to pay $40,000,000 to settle the long-pending general and agrarian claims we had against her. Other provisions were: negotiation of a trade agreement; stabilization of the dollar-peso rate; the Treasury's purchase of newly mined Mexican silver; and assistance in financing Mexico's portion of the Pan American Highway. As to the oil properties, the two Governments agreed to appoint one expert each to determine the just compensation to be paid the American owners, and Mexico deposited $9,000,000 as the first payment.

At the moment of our exchange of notes, I issued a statement in which I said that the agreements not only concerned most of the principal problems that had long been pending between the two sister Republics, "but they mark a new milestone of great importance in the cause of increasingly closer collaboration and solidarity between the countries of the New World."

Although the American oil companies still did not agree to the petroleum settlement, they cooperated with the State Department in the preparation of data for the American expert. The advent of Pearl Harbor placed the dispute on its right footing as simply one of the elements in a perilous world situation, and eventually the companies agreed to a settlement. The experts arrived at a figure of $29,137,700.84 for compensation, including principal and interest, and the two Governments agreed to this sum on September 29, 1943.

The broad settlements reached with Mexico were a large factor in having our neighbor to the south in full accord with us at the moment of Pearl Harbor. A few months later Mexico declared war against the Axis.

Running parallel with the negotiations leading up to the settlement of November 19 were our efforts to restore relations between Britain and Mexico, which had been broken off in 1938 following Mexico's expropriation of British oil properties. We had had several conversations on this point with Mexico and Britain in 1940 and the first part of 1941, but Britain insisted that settlement of the oil dispute must precede resumption of relations.

This situation gave us serious concern, heightened by the fact that disputes had already risen between Britain and several Latin American countries, including Brazil and Mexico, over the enforcement of the British blockade. In 1941 Britain was seeking to induce us to agree to her warships intercepting neutral shipping in the Caribbean and to her establishing a naval control station in that sea.

The President and I saw the gravest objections to this proposal. Contraband in this hemisphere was not on a serious scale; British blockade activities would run counter to the principles we had asserted in proclaiming the Western Hemisphere neutrality zone; and undoubtedly opposition to Britain would flare up violently from Latin America at the very moment we were trying to calm the animosity that had already arisen, particularly in Brazil.

We believed we could work out the problem by inducing the American Republics to apply a system of export control of trade such as we ourselves were applying. We accordingly communicated with the American Republics and received from them a marked degree of cooperation.

After many exchanges on the subject of restoration of British-Mexican relations, Ambassador Winant in London cabled me on August 28, 1941, that Foreign Secretary Eden had instructed the British Embassy in Washington to take up the question with us. Eden said to Winant he hoped I would personally help him in working out the negotiations, since he wanted the situation cleared up as I had been urging.

I cabled Winant in reply the following day a suggestion from Mexican Ambassador Nájera that the most satisfactory solution, following preliminary discussions, would be merely to announce simultaneously the appointment of diplomatic representatives in London and Mexico City. The Mexican Government promised to assure British oil interests in Mexico as favorable treatment as that given American oil interests. We suggested to the British Chargé here, in the absence of Lord Halifax, that he contact the Mexican Ambassador directly.

Negotiations quickly followed, during which we constantly urged a prompt agreement, and on October 21 relations between Britain and Mexico were reestablished.

The following year Britain, then about to negotiate an oil settlement with Mexico, asked whether we would withhold from Mexico any assistance that might in any way tempt that Government to prolong the proposed negotiations or to refrain from agreeing upon a satisfactory basis for settlement, and whether we would press Mexico to reach a conclusion satisfactory to the British oil interests. The impossibility of this request was obvious. We could not undertake for the British oil interests what we had decidedly refused to undertake for the American oil interests.

Following Pearl Harbor our relations with Latin America crystallized in the Rio de Janeiro Conference opening on January 15 and closing on January 28, 1942. Two days after Pearl Harbor we sent notes to the other American Republics informing them of our desire to hold a consultative meeting of foreign ministers at the earliest possible moment. We referred to the resolution adopted at the Havana Conference in July, 1940, whereby the Republics agreed to consider as an act of aggression against them any attempt on the part of a non-American state against the integrity or inviolability of the territory, the sovereignty, or the political independence of an American state.

The many important problems pressing upon me after Pearl Harbor made it impossible for me to head the American delegation. The President and I agreed that Under Secretary Welles should go in my stead.

I held a meeting of the delegation in my office on January 7 just prior to their departure for Rio. After discussing the various projects that were likely to be presented to unify the whole of the hemisphere in the struggle against the Axis, we agreed that major emphasis should be placed on inducing all the Republics to sign a joint declaration to break off relations with the Axis Powers. We felt that, if they would take this step, all the other steps necessary to make the hemisphere a composite unit in opposition to the Axis would come more easily.

The majority of the Republics had already severed relations with the Axis; but it was soon apparent to us that Argentina would again be an obstacle, as she had been at other inter-American conferences.

Argentine Foreign Minister Ruiz Guinazu, for instance, had taken exception to the signing of the United Nations Declaration by nine American Republics which he said had entered into an alliance with non-American nations without previous consultation with the remaining American Republics. He thought this was not in accord with the Declaration of Lima of 1938 and other inter-American peace agreements. Nevertheless, Argentina's commitments at other Pan American conferences, most recently Havana, to consider an aggression from outside the hemisphere against any American Republic as an aggression against all the Republics, led us to hope that she too would cooperate.

Before our delegation left for Rio, we cabled to the Brazilian and Argentine Governments the text of a proposed declaration breaking off diplomatic relations with the Axis. After Welles reached Rio he cabled me on January 13 that the Argentine Foreign Minister had tried unsuccessfully to create a bloc composed of Chile, Peru, Uruguay, and Paraguay along with Argentina to oppose a joint declaration for the breaking of relations. Nevertheless some of the Republics, particularly those with exposed seacoasts, were hesitant because the Axis diplomats in their capitals hinted strongly that severance of diplomatic relations would be followed by war.

On the day the conference opened Assistant Secretary Berle sent Welles a cable on my behalf. This stated, in paraphrase:

"Messages obviously intended for you from some of your Argentine friends have been received by me. They urge earnestly that in the matter of breaking relations you make no compromise with the Argentine delegation. Compromise is considered impossible by them and they believe that were the Argentine position to prevail it would be disastrous for Argentina. That view is rather supported by the press here. In the Department from Secretary Hull down, the feeling is in accord on the belief that rather than a compromise formula a breach in unanimity would be preferable. The Argentines must accept this situation or go their own way, and in the latter event reliance may be placed upon the overwhelming public feeling in Argentina to supply the corrective."

This view of ours was a change from the view we had maintained at previous Pan American conferences when we believed that unanimity of decision was all-important. On several occasions we had had to compromise with Argentina in order to induce that Government to agree. We had had to dilute the strength of some of our resolutions or risk losing the signature of the Buenos Aires Government.

But now the issue had become crucial. It was time for the Argentine Government to choose. This was a life-and-death struggle, the result of which could only mean freedom and advancement for Latin America or domination and probably occupation by the Axis. During the course of that struggle, the presence of Axis diplomats and agents in any American Republic, which they would inevitably use as a headquarters for their subversive activities in other Republics, could not but be a danger to the whole hemisphere. Enjoying the full use of diplomatic codes and communications, they could make that Republic their message center, and from it they could communicate quickly and secretly information concerning ship movements, raw-materials purchases, defense activities, flights of planes, and the like. Argentina, or any other Republic, therefore had to decide whether to cut off this danger or to let it flourish.

In the face of this situation compromises were absurd.

Naturally, with the war raging through Europe and Asia and on most of the Seven Seas, the course we and our other American Allies wanted to pursue at Rio was to strive to the utmost to secure unanimous action. But, failing in this, there was literally no time in which to carry on protracted parleys with any one or two American Governments who were making it clear to us that they were backing out of their definite obligations to cooperate with us. The house was on fire, so to speak, and the one course of duty and self-preservation was for all the other American nations to rush forward with the prosecution of the war of resistance to the Axis. The recalcitrant country or countries could then be appealed to to meet the responsibilities they had voluntarily assumed. If possible, a further conference could be called later in an effort to prevail upon them to join with us.

President Vargas and Foreign Minister Aranha of Brazil were at one with us in this attitude, as were the Governments of almost all the other Republics.

Welles cabled me on January 16 that he completely shared my feeling that no effort should be spared to preserve unanimity but that Argentina should be allowed to proceed alone if the Argentine Government were unwilling to join in a continental declaration for a rupture of relations with the Axis Powers.

Three days later Welles cabled me again, following three long talks he had had with the Argentine Foreign Minister. He said that although other delegation chiefs and he would do everything possible to find an acceptable phraseology for an agreement, provided the necessary principles were not sacrificed, he believed the issue was one that could not be compromised.

When Soviet Ambassador Litvinov came to my office on January 21 and asked what influences were operating in Argentina against the proposals being made at Rio, I replied that the people of Argentina were overwhelmingly in favor of the objectives at the conference.

"Nevertheless," I said, "a small but powerful group in Argentina has for nearly two generations violently opposed the Monroe Doctrine, notwithstanding that the Doctrine has protected all Latin America for more than a century. Without this protection many or most of those countries, especially those comprising the lower half of the Continent, would have been seized and occupied by foreign governments long since. Furthermore, there are certain leaders there who always oppose what they call the upper end of the Continent. Finally, there is a powerful German fifth-column movement in South America which has had its effect."

That night, during the course of a long meeting in Rio of the Argentine, Brazilian, Chilean, and Peruvian foreign ministers and Welles, an agreement was reached on the text of a Declaration, which Welles cabled me the following day. This began with a good paragraph:

"The American Republics reaffirm their declaration to consider any act of aggression on the part of a non-American state against one of them as an act of aggression against all of them, constituting as it does an immediate threat to the liberty and independence of America."

Then followed another good paragraph: "The American Republics reaffirm their complete solidarity and their determination to cooperate as one for their mutual protection until the effects of the present aggression against the Continent have disappeared."

The third paragraph, however, was the crux of the Declaration. This read: "The American Republics consequently declare that in the exercise of their sovereignty and in conformity with their constitutional institutions and powers, provided the latter are in agreement, they cannot continue their diplomatic relations with Japan, Germany, and Italy since

Japan has attacked and the others have declared war upon a nation of the Continent."

In reading this paragraph, my associates and I wondered what interpretation should be given to the language "in the exercise of their sovereignty and in conformity with their constitutional institutions and powers, provided the latter are in agreement." This looked to us very much like one of the loopholes or watering-down phrases the Argentines had so frequently sought, sometimes successfully, to insert in Pan American resolutions.

While we were studying this phraseology, Ambassador Norman Armour in Buenos Aires informed us that the Acting President of Argentina, Dr. Ramón Castillo, had disavowed his Foreign Minister's agreement to the text. The previous day Castillo had stated to Ambassador Armour in Buenos Aires that Argentina would not agree to vote for a resolution breaking off relations with the Axis Powers because sentiment in Argentina would not tolerate the Government's taking such action. He expressed regret and added that in everything else his Government was determined to show its solidarity with the United States and the other American Republics and to cooperate fully to that end.

I cabled Welles on January 22, saying that Castillo's attitude had caused disappointment to all of us here as it must have to Welles. I asked him to let us know at once if there were any useful steps we could take here or elsewhere.

In the same cable I requested Welles to telegraph me what meaning should be attributed to the phraseology of the third paragraph of the Declaration. I also asked him to include in his telegram comment as to the course of action Argentina and Chile had agreed to take under this article. It seemed that Chile might follow whatever course Argentina adopted.

Welles cabled me the following day that the phrase on which I queried him had been inserted solely to satisfy the foreign ministers of Argentina and Chile, which confirmed my suspicion. These foreign ministers, Welles said, insisted they would have to request legislative approval in their respective Congresses for the breaking of relations, notwithstanding the provisions of their Constitutions.

Welles asked me to bear in mind that the rupture of diplomatic relations meant an almost immediate entry into war for the American Republics. I did not believe this was necessarily so, and considered it primarily an Axis threat. Actually the Axis did not declare war on the

Republics that severed diplomatic relations. On the other hand, the failure to rupture diplomatic relations did mean an almost immediate utilization of those Republics by Axis agents for their machinations in this hemisphere.

Furthermore, Article Three of the Declaration, if it contained loopholes, would be a terrific comedown and almost a contradiction following the first two articles. Article One branded an aggression on the part of a non-American state against any American Republic as an act of aggression against all American Republics. And Article Two stated the determination of all the Republics to cooperate jointly for their mutual protection until the effects of the present aggression against the Continent had disappeared. If therefore a specific Republic, such as Argentina, considered the attack at Pearl Harbor and Germany's and Italy's declarations of war as an aggression against herself, as she had to do by virtue of this language, and if she were determined to cooperate with other American Republics for their mutual protection, as she also had to do under this language, how could she possibly or logically insist on retaining diplomatic relations with the aggressor? How could we agree to the insertion of a back door through which any Republic could escape the responsibilities it had freely assumed?

Welles's cable reached the Department at five o'clock that afternoon, January 23. In it he said he was trying to find a new formula, but, if this were not acceptable to Argentina, the nineteen countries that favored the earlier text rejected by Castillo would sign it, leaving Argentina and Chile to take such course as they might see fit.

A few hours later, nothing more having come in from Welles, I was sitting in my apartment listening to a news broadcast. Suddenly the announcer stated that an agreement had been worked out at Rio and accepted by all the twenty-one American Republics, but that the United States had found herself obliged to surrender her principal position. The announcer said that the Argentines had secured a modified understanding by which they could leave the conference and return home without having committed themselves to cooperate against the Axis powers by breaking off diplomatic relations.

I telephoned the Department and learned that nothing had come in from Welles concerning the signing of an agreement. I then telephoned the President, and through the White House connection put in a call for Welles at Rio.

With Mr. Roosevelt listening in, Welles confirmed the signing of the agreement and gave me the substance of the crucial Article Three. I then spoke to him more sharply than I had ever spoken to anyone in the Department. I said I considered this a change in our policy, made without consulting me, and the equivalent of a surrender to Argentina. I added that it contained an escape clause that would permit the Argentines to return home with a straight face and thereafter move gradually over toward the camp of our Axis enemies and render the enemy aid and comfort, to our damage and even to the loss of life as the war progressed.

Welles said in reply that he had tried hard to secure agreement to the original proposal but had found it impossible, and therefore he had agreed to the modified arrangement.

Our conversation continued in this vein for several minutes, whereupon the President interrupted. Without going into the merits of the resolution agreed to at Rio, he said, a decision had already been reached, the conference was in the act of adjournment, and it would not be feasible to reconsider the action Welles had taken.

I was frankly very angry that Welles had acted as he had. He had not only acted without consulting me; worse, he had committed his Government to an unwise agreement. He had compromised the all-important issue despite the fact that we in the State Department and he from Rio had clearly stated in cables our determination that the issue was one that could not be compromised.

The crucial article of the Declaration in its final form stated:

"The American Republics, in accordance with the procedures established by their own laws and in conformity with the position and circumstances obtaining in each country in the existing continental conflict, recommend the breaking of their diplomatic relations with Japan, Germany, and Italy, since the first-mentioned State attacked and the other two declared war on an American country."

In addition to the loopholes of "procedures," "position," and "circumstances," the Declaration thus contained merely a recommendation that the Republics break off diplomatic relations with the Axis. The Argentines, who refused to agree to a declaration to break off relations, were willing to "recommend" to themselves to break off relations. They could now return to Buenos Aires content that they had not been isolated at Rio and were still perfectly free to continue relations with the Axis as long as they liked.

Welles sent the President a long telegram the following day to justify his position. He argued that if he had not agreed to the Declaration, the united American front would have been broken and Argentina and Chile undoubtedly would be turned into hotbeds for Axis activities.

The fact, however, was the opposite. The united American front had already been broken at Rio by Argentina's refusal to sign a real Declaration. The Declaration that was signed did not achieve the purpose we had in mind in going to Rio, namely, to obtain a complete break of the Western Hemisphere with the Axis. Argentina and Chile continued their diplomatic relations with the Axis, and Argentina did become a hotbed for Axis activities. We were to pay heavily in the future for this failure at Rio.

Although the political discussions revolving around the Declaration overshadowed the other work of the conference, the delegates achieved many important results. Among these were resolutions relating to the production of strategic materials, to the development of commercial relations and transportation facilities in the hemisphere, to measures to be taken to interdict commerce with the Axis, to the curbing of subversive activities, to postwar problems, and to the creation of an inter-American defense board. In the achieving of these resolutions Welles took one of the leading roles at the conference.

Axis propaganda, of course, made much of its claim that the United States had suffered a defeat at Rio. Partly to answer this propaganda and partly in sincere acknowledgment of the hard and generally fruitful work Welles had done at Rio, I cabled him on January 29 my heartiest congratulations on his part in the over-all success of the conference.

At this time my health became affected. This was partly because of the strain of the long negotiations with the Japanese, many of which I had conducted at night following a long day at the office; partly because of the intensive work that followed Pearl Harbor; and partly because of my deep disappointment at our partial failure at Rio. I had to leave my office on February 5 and rest at my apartment for two weeks. Then my doctor—Matthew W. Perry—ordered a longer rest away from Washington. I left Washington for Miami, Florida, on February 19. I delayed my departure for one day because Dr. Perry, who was to accompany me, lost his associate physician through death. The train I would have taken was wrecked, and from our train we saw the overturned locomotive and cars lying near the track.

It was not until some weeks later, on April 20, that I regained strength enough to return to my office in the State Department.

Before my departure I brought to a head two actions which were completed during my absence—a further amendment of the Neutrality Act, and a master Lend-Lease agreement with Great Britain.

I had sent the President a memorandum on January 28, 1942, enclosing for his consideration a draft message to Congress recommending that the Neutrality Act of 1939 be amended to provide that Section 7, relating to financial transactions with belligerents, should not be operative when the United States was at war. I said I was convinced that Congress never intended this section to operate during our belligerency as it now did to prevent essential transactions with cobelligerents.

I added that the proposed amendment had the approval of the Treasury and Justice Departments and the Federal Reserve. I said I would be glad, if the President approved, to obtain the reaction of the Congressional leaders before he transmitted the message formally to Congress.

The President returned the memorandum to me with his O.K. We thereupon communicated with Senate and House leaders, who concurred in our view. The President sent the message to Congress on February 9; the Senate and House soon approved; and Mr. Roosevelt signed the bill on February 21.

With regard to the master Lend-Lease agreement with Britain, we had had discussions with the British since July, 1941. As I have already mentioned, I had been disappointed in Article Four of the Atlantic Charter, relating to international trade after the war, because it contained Mr. Churchill's reservation intended to protect the British Empire preferential tariff system. Since the signing of the Charter I had had numerous exchanges with Britain on this subject, in connection with a proposed master Lend-Lease agreement, in the hope of getting Britain to commit herself to liberal trade policies following the war. Our discussions had dragged on largely because a few Tory members of the British Cabinet objected to any provision that would interfere with Empire preference. They regarded the Lend-Lease agreement I had in mind as an attempt to infringe on British imperial sovereignty.

I sent the President a memorandum on November 19, 1941, enclosing the redraft of a preliminary Lend-Lease agreement with Great Britain. I recalled that the State Department, with his approval, had given Britain informally a draft agreement in July. The purport of that draft was to carry out his instructions that the decision concerning the *quid pro quo* for our Lend-Lease supplies and facilities should be deferred until a final settlement were reached, and that it should then be framed within certain broad principles relating to world peace and international economic relations. We had stated these principles in Article VII of the agreement.

I informed the President that the British had now informally handed us a redraft that made no changes of substance in the agreement except in Article VII. These changes, I said, grew out of the fear in London that our draft would commit the British to a specific commercial policy that they could not carry out in the absence of action by the United States and other countries to make possible the payment for imports which Britain would need in the reconstruction period and after.

The Department having redrafted the British draft of Article VII, I sent this to the President and said that the Article recognized the need for agreed action between the nations, by international and domestic measures, to expand production, employment, and exchange and consumption of goods. Also the necessity for international agreement to eliminate all forms of discriminatory treatment in commerce and to reduce tariffs and trade barriers. Since British Empire preferential tariffs were discriminatory, they were automatically discarded in this last clause without being specifically mentioned.

The President was in agreement with this position. We informed British Ambassador Halifax on December 2 that we had expressed Article VII in general terms so as to avoid specific reference to preferential arrangements, which reference might cause political embarrassment to the British Government. We added that all such arrangements were included within the scope of our general provisions and that, if the agreement were published and we were asked to explain what did fall within its terms, we proposed to say it was all-inclusive.

During Prime Minister Churchill's visit to Washington late in December, I brought the pendency of this agreement to the President's attention with the thought that he might discuss it with Mr. Churchill. Halifax, at my suggestion, discussed it himself with Churchill.

Halifax came to see me on December 29 and informed me that Mr. Churchill said he was too preoccupied to take the matter up here and would be obliged to wait until his return to London. I said to the Ambassador that it was very important from our viewpoint that some action be taken without much delay, for the reason that another Lend-Lease appropriation bill would come up in Congress in January and we would be called upon to explain why Britain delayed signing the proposed agreement. Halifax seemed impressed. We agreed that I should speak to the

President before Mr. Churchill returned to Washington from Ottawa and Halifax would speak to the Prime Minister.

I brought up the question with the Prime Minister myself while sitting beside him at a dinner at the White House on January 12. He was categorical in saying he definitely refused to agree to giving up imperial tariff preferences and would not accept the inclusion of such a clause in the Lend-Lease agreement.

Mr. Churchill returned to London without having entered into a real discussion of the agreement. At the beginning of February the President, at my suggestion, cabled Mr. Churchill urging quick affirmative action. Ambassador Winant cabled us on February 9 that the British entertained a rather vague fear that they were bartering Empire sovereignty in settlement of a debt. The President sent another urgent message to the Prime Minister on February 11.

The British Cabinet shortly agreed, and the document was signed in Washington on February 23.

In its final form, Article VII stated that the determination of the benefits to be provided by Britain in exchange for Lend-Lease should be such as not to burden commerce between the two countries, but to promote mutually advantageous economic relations between them and the betterment of world-wide economic relations.

It provided that the two countries should agree to action, open to participation by all other countries of like mind, directed to the expansion, by appropriate international and domestic measures, of production, employment, and the exchange and consumption of goods, which were the material foundations of the liberty and welfare of all peoples; to the elimination of all forms of discriminatory treatment in international commerce, and to the reduction of tariffs and other trade barriers; and, in general, to the attainment of all the economic objectives set forth in the Atlantic Charter.

This article also set out that conversations would begin between the two Governments to determine the best means of attaining these objectives and of obtaining the participation of other like-minded Governments.

The agreement, a long step toward the fulfillment, after the war, of the economic principles for which I had been fighting for half a century, furnished the pattern for our agreements with other countries. Those nations likewise accepted the article pledging them to liberal international commerce when the conflict ended. The foundation was now laid for all our later postwar planning in the economic field.

84: Laval Versus De Gaulle

THREE ELEMENTS OF CRISIS immediately faced me when I returned to Washington on April 20, 1942. All required instant attention.

One was the fact that the President, by Executive order dated April 13, 1942, had conferred upon the Board of Economic Warfare, of which Vice President Henry Wallace was chairman, sweeping authority to deal directly with foreign Governments and to send representatives abroad for this purpose, thus virtually creating a second State Department.

The second was the ominous change wrought in the situation at Vichy through the return of Pierre Laval to the Government in the role of Premier.

The third was the fact that Britain was about to sign an agreement with Soviet Russia recognizing the incorporation of the Baltic States, Latvia, Lithuania, and Estonia, into the U.S.S.R., thereby running directly counter to the provisions of the Atlantic Charter.

At that moment the military situation was of the blackest. Japan had overrun the Philippines, Malaya, Burma, and the Dutch East Indies, and won the naval battle of the Java Sea. Germany was preparing a new campaign in Russia, and was inflicting appalling losses on our shipping in the Atlantic. Accordingly, on my first day back at the office, I issued a statement designed to strengthen public confidence in the outcome.

"I have observed with keen satisfaction," I said, "the splendid showing made in the whole war effort of the country during recent months, and particularly in the production of war supplies for the fighting fronts. . . . I am confident that our Nation and all those who are with us have only one watchword: to move forward today and not tomorrow. With this will to victory, free men the world over will triumph over the forces of barbarism."

That same day I had luncheon with the President at the White House, as invariably happened when either he or I returned from a trip. I took this occasion to go at once with him into the implications of his order on the Board of Economic Warfare.

In the preceding summer the President had set up the Economic Defense Board, with Henry Wallace as its chairman, which after Pearl Harbor became the Board of Economic Warfare. I had recommended to Mr. Roosevelt that he give this position to one of the most capable men in the nation, Vance C. McCormick, formerly chairman of the Democratic National Committee, who had filled a similar position during the First World War with great credit. But the President was unwilling to make the appointment. This board took over the function, which the State Department up to then had exercised, of controlling the export of a long list of products needed for our own defense. It was also to buy in other countries essential materials for ourselves or the Allies which otherwise would go to the Axis. Mr. Wallace, with his usual energy, began at once to make the BEW a strong agency capable of fulfilling its important task. We now had the situation, unprecedented in our history, of a Vice President performing administrative functions.

While I was absent from Washington, however, Wallace convinced the President that his agency did not have sufficient powers to conduct its work effectively. Hence the Executive order of April 13.

This order naturally aroused great concern in the State Department. The BEW was given the function of negotiating with foreign Governments on economic matters, which function had previously been performed by the State Department through its Foreign Service and through its contacts with the foreign diplomatic representatives in Washington. The BEW was empowered to send representatives abroad for this purpose, who would be responsible solely to it.

Of enormous importance to us at the State Department was the fact that the order could be interpreted—and undoubtedly would be interpreted—as giving the BEW the authority to conduct negotiations for a postwar economic settlement. Such negotiations involved delicate interrelations of the British Commonwealth, of the British with the Middle East, and of the American Republics with one another and with ourselves. They could cover the political and even military fields because the kind of postwar economic order we were seeking was inextricably interwoven with the new dispositions that would have to be made in other fields. The BEW alone would determine the terms and conditions under which the United Nations were to reciprocate for our Lend-Lease. As has already been noted in our negotiations with Britain for a master Lend-Lease agreement, these terms did not relate solely to reciprocal goods and services but also to the even more vital conditions under which international commercial relations would be conducted after the war.

The State Department was already bedeviled by the multiplicity of Departments and agencies speaking for the government in foreign relations, such as the Treasury, the Coordinator of Inter-American Affairs, the Coordinator of Information, the Petroleum Coordinator, and the Office of Lend-Lease Administration. Foreign diplomats were repeatedly coming to us to express their confusion at the number of agencies that approached them as the authorized representatives of the United States Government.

The State Department had been performing most of the functions in the foreign field being conferred on these new agencies. After war came to Europe on September 1, 1939, we immediately recognized the need to provide an added and diversified field staff to handle our scores of new duties abroad. We sent four hundred additional Foreign Service officers and clerks to the field for the duration of the war. These included economic analysts, agricultural economists, mineral and petroleum specialists, attachés to work on the proclaimed list of blocked nationals, on freezing regulations, on foreign requirements, and on export control. We had permitted the interested agencies to select many of these persons. We were also seeking more funds to make the necessary additions to this staff.

But throughout we insisted on one point; namely, that all our representatives abroad should be responsible to our ambassador or minister in the country of their assignment. Also, that they should work under him and report through him and the State Department. It was manifestly impossible to have representatives of various American agencies running about the world responsible only to their agencies in Washington many thousands of miles away. The President himself had agreed to this principle in 1939. My associates and I felt that only in this way could we maintain a coherent, effective foreign policy.

On my return to Washington I found that Welles had made a strong argument to the President that the Executive order of April 13 was exceedingly harmful. He was not able, however, to induce Mr. Roosevelt to change his mind.

Accordingly, I went over this problem with the President myself. I did not hesitate to tell him that the State Department could not function as it should if the Executive order were to stand.

The President seemed impressed. He asked me to talk to Wallace and then talk with him again. I conferred with Wallace the following morning, saw the President later in the morning, and again had luncheon with him the next day. During a meeting held in his office, attended by Wallace, myself, and several others, I saw the President become really angry. He turned to Wallace and said, in effect: "I was always told that the State Department knew about this transfer of authority and agreed to it.

Otherwise I would not have signed it." Wallace replied, in substance: "We knew that if you knew that the State Department had not agreed to it you would not sign it." Mr. Roosevelt glowered at him.

Shortly thereafter the President decided to change his order. He announced in his press conference on May 1 that there was no question but that the State Department was in charge of the foreign affairs of the United States. Some people had not quite realized that fact, he said, and some people in other departments of the Government wanted to run foreign affairs.

On May 20 he issued a "Clarification and Interpretation" of the April 13 order. This restored the situation to what it should logically be. We were to have difficulties later with the BEW, but at least our respective jurisdictions were now clear.

The second problem that faced me on my return—our relations with Vichy—had already reached a head during my absence. Marshal Pétain felt obliged on April 15 to call Laval back into the Government as Premier, with Admiral Darlan remaining as chief of the armed forces. The President decided on the following day to recall our Ambassador to Vichy, Admiral Leahy, for consultation.

The death of Mrs. Leahy delayed the Ambassador's return for several weeks. During that time both Pétain and Laval sought to reassure us, through Leahy, that the change in the Government did not mean French military assistance to the Germans. Laval's past conduct, however, had been so perfidious that we could place no trust in his assurances. After Leahy returned to the United States we had no thought of returning him to Vichy or of sending another ambassador in his stead. Nevertheless, there was still value to the United Nations in the continuance of our relations with Vichy, and we conducted these through our experienced, capable Chargé d'Affaires, H. Freeman Matthews.

When British Ambassador Halifax called at my office on April 25, 1942, I brought up with him the information I had received the day before to the effect that Foreign Secretary Eden had notified Canada that it was agreeable to Britain for Canada to cease diplomatic relations with Vichy and in substance had indicated there was no further occasion for diplomatic connections. I commented that it probably would have been very advisable to have had a prior conference or an exchange of views among the British, Canadian, and United States Governments on the whole Vichy and French situation with a view to salvaging whatever might be possible for the advantage of the United Nations.

"It will apparently not be possible for the United States Government long to keep up diplomatic contacts with Vichy," I said, "after Canada rebuffs that Government. This is especially so because British propaganda agencies are continuing their past policy of making it appear that the British Government is not only opposed to American diplomatic relations with Vichy but that in some respects those relations are of a sinister nature."

Halifax immediately began to urge that for various reasons we should not dissolve relations with the Vichy Government, but I repeated that we, of course, could not be left out on a limb by ourselves very long in these circumstances.

Canada limited her action to recalling her representative at Vichy for consultation, without severing diplomatic relations.

I had with Halifax, on May 4, a thorough thrashing out of our relations with Vichy. I said that, while maintaining relations with Vichy, this Government had bitterly opposed everything the Vichy Government stood for in the way of denial of the aspirations of the French people for the restoration of their freedom, free institutions, and their way of life. At the same time we had most strongly and consistently opposed everything the Vichy Government stood for that was of a pro-German or pro-Hitler nature. We had also uniformly asserted to the world that the Vichy Government did not represent the French people and the true interests of France.

"This Government," I continued, "has therefore continued relations with the Government at Vichy solely for the advantages derived from having representatives in Vichy France, French Africa, and elsewhere, affording channels for our insistent demands that the Vichy Government observe the rules of neutrality and not go beyond the terms of the armistice. This position is calculated to safeguard the French fleet and bases from being transferred to Hitler or Axis agencies. It is based solely on a policy of promoting to the fullest extent the military progress of the twenty-six United Nations."

As for the Free French, I said we were continuing to give them the fullest possible military cooperation but we did not contemplate their political recognition.

Halifax said that his Government, in his opinion, while supporting De Gaulle to an unlimited extent militarily, would likewise support him in dealing with any local situation arising in connection with the prosecution of the war, but that this was entirely different from political recognition in the broader sense, that is, recognition of the De Gaulle group as a political Government either now or in the postwar period.

Bearing in mind that the British dealings with the Free French were confined mainly to London, I inquired whether this course was practicable, especially in cases where it might be necessary for a military force to move rapidly and to work with any local officials who might be in control.

I further asked whether his Government would be disposed to urge the organization of a French political committee to work coordinately with the De Gaulle military committee in order to compose all angles of the situation. Halifax said he would query his Government on this point.

I should have liked to see created a Free French political committee headed by a noted Frenchman. One of the tragedies of the De Gaulle situation, however, was that De Gaulle had attracted to himself not a single eminent Frenchman. The very few who had gotten away from France distrusted him or could not work with him.

De Gaulle had the unhappy faculty of alienating most of those of any nationality with whom he came into contact, while at the same time undoubtedly inspiring millions of Frenchmen who were far removed from him. He delivered speeches in the spring of 1942 which in effect criticized both Britain and the United States. His followers quarreled with the British in Syria.

As I remarked to Halifax on May 4, De Gaulle was reported to be on not too good terms with most British officials except Prime Minister Churchill, and with most French officials except the Governor of Central Africa and the civil governor in New Caledonia.

On the day I had this conversation with Halifax, the British occupied the French island of Madagascar, off the east coast of Africa. We informed French Ambassador Henry-Haye that evening, along with our Embassy in Vichy, and made public, that "this occupation has the full approval and support of the Government of the United States. The island of Madagascar presents the definite danger to the United Nations of occupation or use by the Axis Powers, especially Japan."

We added that in view of the fact that Madagascar would be held in trust for France, any warlike act permitted by the French Government against the British or American Governments would have to be regarded by the United States Government as an attack upon the United Nations as a whole.

Vichy, of course, protested this action. But De Gaulle also protested to the British because, wishing to avoid a further spectacle of Frenchmen fighting Frenchmen, they had not included Free French troops in their expeditionary force against Madagascar.

I sent the President a memorandum on May 5 in which I gave him the State Department's latest views on De Gaulle and his group. "It is evident from numerous indications," we said, "that the Free French national commissioners who constitute the committee and who have undertaken the functions of ministers are now endeavoring to create the future Government of France, and a political character is being sought for the committee, whereas it is apparent that the main reason for its existence has been to preserve the symbol of French resistance. In this latter character it has secured the bulk of its adherents.

"It is questionable whether it would continue to command the support now manifest should it be given primarily a political character as seems intended, as evidenced, for example, by General de Gaulle's speech of April 1, 1942. This speech can only be interpreted as a demand for complete recognition by the United Nations of the Free French as the leaders and representatives of France of the future. It is, however, clearly evident that the French people who have rallied to General de Gaulle as the head of a military movement are not prepared to regard him as the future leader of France."

A few days later the President and I agreed to send a small mission to Martinique for direct negotiations with Governor Robert. Our purpose was to make it impossible for the French Caribbean possessions to furnish any aid to the Axis, especially to submarines that were appearing in that area. The mission was headed by Admiral John H. Hoover, who was accompanied by Samuel Reber, Assistant Chief of the State Department's Division of European Affairs. We publicly stated that the direct negotiations were necessitated by Laval's collaboration policy.

Vichy again objected, but so did De Gaulle. After many months of negotiation we were able, however, to arrive at a comprehensive agreement with Governor Robert.

French Ambassador Henry-Haye came to me on May 11 to attempt an elaborate apologia for Laval. He argued that Laval had a difficult and trying job, but that he would not hurt the United States; that he was not a tricky man as some thought, but that he did on occasion use words direct and even brutal.

I replied that, regardless of what he and certain others around Laval thought of him, every person in this country was convinced that he was associated with Hitler. This Government could not consider for a moment any negotiations with Laval with regard to the French Caribbean possessions. Laval was avowedly pro-Hitler in every possible sense and was very desirous of seeing Hitler win the war, whereas all Americans were unanimously of the view that Hitlerism personified everything that was inhuman and calculated, if Hitler succeeded, to inflict the greatest blow to the human race since the dawn of history.

What result we could have expected from any negotiations with the Pétain Government over Martinique was proved two months later when the President proposed to Marshal Pétain that the portion of the French fleet at Alexandria, Egypt, should be sent through the Suez Canal to some American or neutral port in the Western Hemisphere. Mr. Roosevelt guaranteed that the warships would not be used by the American or British Governments and would be returned to France at the end of the war. At that moment the ships were in danger of falling into German hands because of the disastrous British defeat in Libya which threw our Ally back almost to the Nile.

Laval, however, rejected this proposal, along with a further suggestion from the President that the warships should be sent to Martinique for demobilization until the end of the war. Laval proposed instead that the ships go to a near-by French port, where, of course, they also would be within seizing distance of the Germans.

Despite Laval's return to power, the President and I were resolved to differentiate between our policy toward Vichy and our policy toward French North Africa. Our relations with Vichy were on a basis of virtual hostility, but we still sought to keep our relations with North Africa as friendly as possible.

During my absence from Washington in April, the State Department had temporarily suspended our shipments of supplies to North Africa when Laval regained power. It was obvious, however, that after our entrance into the war, North Africa had become one of our most vital strategic areas. German occupation of the area would have brought the Nazis to West Africa and therefore to the South Atlantic, with all the prospects of threat and danger to the Western Hemisphere implicit in that position. We therefore had to keep French North Africa with us until we ourselves were able to take positive action there.

We knew that the Vichy Government had allowed supplies to go from Tunis to the German Army in Libya. We also knew that some strategic materials produced in North Africa were reaching Germany by way of Vichy France. But we knew as well that by continuing our close contact with French North Africa we could count on a large portion of the civil and military administration when the time came. And likewise, through the control officials we had been able to install in French North Africa to supervise the economic accord with that area, we were being closely and accurately informed on all developments relating to the colonies and to the Axis armistice commissions. The advantages of intimate contact with French North Africa clearly outweighed the disadvantages.

Contemplating resumption of our shipments of supplies to French North Africa, we requested opinions on the subject from Secretary of War Stimson and from the Coordinator of Information, William J. Donovan. Both of them wrote us that it would be of value to continue the shipments. With the President's approval, I thereupon announced on June 12, 1942, that shipments would be resumed.

The shipments we were able to make between then and our landing in North Africa on November 8 were small. We were confronted at every turn by the Board of Economic Warfare, which could see the situation only in the narrow light of keeping supplies from the enemy and could not envisage the broader aspects and potentialities of our contact with the French colonies. Although the President issued instructions on July 29 that the economic accord with North Africa was to be carried out without interruption or delay, the Board of Economic Warfare interfered incessantly.

In June, during the visit of Winston Churchill to Washington, the President and the Prime Minister agreed that an army should be sent to French North Africa toward the end of the year.

The President was still resolved that General de Gaulle should not be included in this expedition or even informed of it, for the reasons already stated. He knew, however, that this decision would inevitably arouse De Gaulle's irascibility. He therefore suggested to the British that De Gaulle might be invited to visit Washington. But both Foreign Secretary Eden and Ambassador Winant dissuaded him. Eden thought it would take more than an invitation to Washington to keep De Gaulle quiet if he got wind of what was afoot, and Winant pointed out that the invitation would make a bad impression on the French leaders in North Africa.

The British Government on July 3 recognized De Gaulle's French National Committee as the symbol of resistance to the Axis of French nationals who did not accept capitulation. It was apparent to us that larger segments of the French population were rallying to De Gaulle than before. The restoration of Laval had alienated thousands of Frenchmen who had clung to Pétain and who now, with nowhere else to turn, fastened their hopes on De Gaulle. We therefore offered to arrange for consultation and cooperation between our military authorities and those of the French National Committee.

After consulting with the President, I cabled Ambassador Winant to this effect on July 7, and on July 9 he handed De Gaulle a note that began by saying:

"The Government of the United States recognizes the contribution of General de Gaulle and the work of the French National Committee in keeping alive the spirit of French traditions and institutions and believes that the military aims necessary for an effective prosecution of the war, and hence the realization of our combined aims, are best advanced by lending all possible military assistance and support to the French National Committee as a symbol of French resistance in general against the Axis Powers."

We further said that we would continue to deal with the local Free French officials in effective control of their respective territories, but that we would centralize with the National Committee in London the discussion of those matters relating to the prosecution of the war, and we were therefore prepared to appoint representatives in London for this purpose.

De Gaulle accepted at once, and Admiral Harold R. Stark, formerly Chief of Naval Operations, and Brigadier General Charles L. Bolte were named the American representatives.

De Gaulle, however, quickly wanted this initiative to assume more significance than it carried. He wanted to be taken into the Anglo-American-Russian military discussions, and he still sought some form of recognition in the political sphere. Ambassador Winant reported to us in August that the Free French wanted to be asked to sign the United Nations Declaration because they felt that such adherence would make them appear as the French provisional Government. He added that the British Foreign Office supported this view with the thought that it would create greater unity among the French.

It was De Gaulle's constant insistence on political recognition, however, that excited so much suspicion against him. If he, as an Army general, had thrown himself wholeheartedly into the fight against the Axis in a military sense, if he had actually led French troops against the enemy wherever possible instead of spending most of his time in London, he could have rallied far more support to himself among the French and among the United Nations. Instead, his own dictatorial attitude, coupled with his adventures in the political field, inevitably inspired the thought that he was trying to develop a political standing that would make him the next ruler of France.

Meantime, however, other ambitions, those of Russia, had been giving us much work and more anxiety.

85: Stalin's Ambitions

ONE OF THE GREATEST preoccupations of the President and me during the first half of 1942 was Russia's suddenly revealed territorial aims in Europe, coupled with her determination to induce the Western Allies to guarantee them in advance.

This important and troublesome development came to light during British Foreign Secretary Eden's visit to Moscow in December, 1941.

Several months prior to this visit we began to learn from Ambassador Steinhardt in Moscow that relations between Britain and Russia were strained over the fact that Prime Minister Churchill had not acquiesced in Stalin's insistence that a British army be sent to Murmansk or Rostov to relieve pressure on the Red Army.

Then on December 4, 1941, Ambassador Winant in London cabled the President and me that Eden was leaving for Moscow on Sunday (Pearl Harbor Sunday). Stalin had cabled Churchill that an understanding should be reached not only on military matters but also on war aims and on plans for a postwar organization of the peace. Stalin, Winant said, seemed in a suspicious, even resentful mood.

The Soviet Ambassador in London, Ivan M. Maisky, according to Winant, had already indicated that his Government felt it should have been consulted beforehand regarding the Atlantic Charter, although Maisky in September announced his Government's agreement with the fundamental principles set forth therein. Russia, Winant reported, was suspicious that the British and ourselves aimed at excluding her from the peace and postwar settlement, and that we would not be prepared to take sufficiently harsh measures in that settlement to render Germany harmless.

When this telegram arrived I was intensely absorbed in the rush of events immediately preceding Pearl Harbor. I therefore asked Ray Atherton, Chief of the European Division, to draft a reply along lines we agreed to. I read this over, approved it and sent it and Winant's message to the President, who returned it with his O.K.

In this telegram, which we asked Winant to read to Eden personally, we said that, as proof of our policy of aid to Russia, we had recently sent representatives (the Harriman Mission) to the Soviet Union who had entered into an agreement with the Soviet Government on our furnishing of supplies.

We said it was our conviction that the test of our good faith with regard to the Soviet Union was the measure of our fulfillment of this agreement.

As for our postwar policies, we pointed out that these had been outlined in the Atlantic Charter which represented the attitude also of Great Britain and the Soviet Union.

We then concluded that it would be unfortunate were any of these three Governments to express any willingness to enter into commitments regarding specific terms of the postwar settlement. We would, of course, expect a continuation of discussions among the several Governments toward the fullest possible agreement on basic policies and toward later arrangements at the proper time and with full public knowledge. When Hitler was defeated, the Soviet Government would participate no less than Britain and the United States in an effort to restore peace and order. But no commitments as to individual countries should be entered into at this time lest they jeopardize the aims we all shared in common, looking toward an enduring peace. It would be unfortunate if we approached the peace conference thus hampered. Above all, there must be no secret accords.

Furthermore, we pointed out the constitutional limitation by which this Government was bound, meaning the necessity for Senate approval of treaties. We said it would be difficult if not impossible for us to implement the common understanding among the three big powers by a more detailed agreement at this time.

We assured Britain that our basic policy of aid to her was no less strong than our policy of aid to Russia. And we concluded that we were thus very frankly indicating our position on the eve of Eden's departure for Moscow so that he would have no misunderstanding on that score.

It was clear to us that Eden would be confronted at Moscow with specific territorial demands. Stalin did lay such demands before Eden in their first conversations. He wanted Britain's immediate agreement to the restoration of Russia's borders to what they were prior to Hitler's attack. Concretely, the Baltic States of Estonia, Latvia, and Lithuania, also portions of Finland, Poland, and Rumania would be incorporated in the U.S.S.R. The Polish border would be based on the "Curzon Line" which was approximately the Russo-German boundary following the partition of Poland in 1939. Rumania should also give Russia special facilities for bases, and in return receive certain Hungarian territory.

Stalin also proposed the restoration of Austria as an independent state; the detachment of the Rhineland from Germany as an independent state or protectorate; possibly the constitution of an independent state of Bavaria; the transfer of East Prussia to Poland; the return of the Sudetenland to Czechoslovakia; Yugoslavia should be restored and receive certain additional territory from Italy; Albania should be reconstituted as an independent state; Turkey should receive the Dodecanese islands, with possible readjustments of Aegean islands in favor of Greece; Turkey might also receive some territory from Bulgaria and in Northern Syria; Germany should pay reparations in kind, particularly in machine tools, but not in money.

Stalin said to Eden that the conclusion of any Anglo-Soviet agreement would depend on whether the two countries reached an agreement on the future Soviet frontiers, particularly the inclusion of the Baltic States and the restoration of the Finnish-Soviet frontier of 1940.

Stalin said he was willing to support any arrangements Britain might make for securing bases in the Western European countries, France, Belgium, The Netherlands, Norway, and Denmark.

Eden parried these demands by saying that for many reasons it was impossible for him to enter into a secret agreement, one of which was that he was pledged to the United States Government not to do so. Stalin and he agreed that Eden should take these provisions back to London for discussion with the British Cabinet, and they should be communicated to the United States.

When Eden returned to London he loaned his papers and notes to Ambassador Winant, who sent us a comprehensive account of the conversations in a series of cables.

At the State Department we gave intensive study to these cables. Two of our most capable officers, James C. Dunn, Political Adviser on European Affairs, and Ray Atherton, headed this study. Following several conversations, I requested them to draw up a full memorandum for the President along lines we agreed to.

I sent this to the President on February 4, 1942. In an accompanying letter I referred to the telegram I had sent Ambassador Winant on December 5, and said:

"I am inclined to the opinion that the policies which we outlined in our telegram to Ambassador Winant are sound and that a deviation therefrom would be unfortunate, particularly just now when we are endeavoring to unite all forces opposed to the Axis on the primary task of defeating the enemy.

"In that telegram we took the position that the test of our good faith with regard to the Soviet Union should not be our willingness to agree to the recognition of extended Soviet frontiers at this time, but rather the degree of determination which we show loyally to carry out our promises to aid the Soviet Government with equipment and supplies.

"I am sure that you will agree with me that by our actions we should make it clear to the Soviet Government in the future to an ever greater degree that we are doing our utmost to live up to our promises."

In the memorandum to the President we pointed out that Stalin had attached so much importance to the question of an immediate settlement of boundaries that Eden had indicated to Stalin he would endeavor to obtain a favorable decision from his Government. We therefore considered it likely that the British Government would approach our Government shortly and request that we state our position with regard to Britain's making certain territorial commitments to the Soviet Union or that we approve certain commitments which Britain might desire to make.

We recalled to the President that our Government thus far had not recognized as Soviet territory any of the areas that had been annexed to the Soviet Union since the outbreak of the European War. Our attitude had been predicated on our general policy not to recognize any territorial changes that had been made in European frontiers since the outbreak of the war and not to enter into any territorial commitments that might hamper the proceedings of the postwar peace conference.

"It is believed," we said, "that it would be unfortunate if, at the present time, an ally of the American Government of such standing as Great Britain, which also has thus far refused to make any commitments of a territorial nature on the European continent, should begin bargaining with the Soviet Union or any other continental country with regard to frontiers. There is little doubt that if the principle is once admitted that agreements relating to frontiers may be entered into prior to the peace conference, the association of nations opposed to the Axis, which thus far has been based upon the common aim of defeating the enemy, may be weakened by the introduction among its members of mutual suspicion and by efforts of various members to intrigue in order to obtain commitments with regard to territory at the expense of other members."

We further stated our belief that Britain's assent to Stalin's territorial demands would result in only temporary improvement in relations between Britain and Russia. "If the British Government," we said, "with the tacit or expressed approval of this Government, should abandon the principle of no territorial commitments prior to the peace conference, it would be placed in a difficult position to resist additional Soviet demands relating to frontiers, territory, or to spheres of influence which would almost certainly follow whenever the Soviet Government would find itself in a favorable bargaining position.

"There is no doubt that the Soviet Government has tremendous ambitions with regard to Europe and that at some time or other the United States and Great Britain will be forced to state that they cannot agree, at least in advance, to all of its demands. It would seem that it is preferable to take a firm attitude now, rather than to retreat and to be compelled to take a firm attitude later when our position had been weakened by the abandonment of the general principles referred to above."

We thought it likely that Stalin would make use of all the weapons at his disposal to attain immediate recognition of some territorial gains. He might refuse at least temporarily to cooperate with Britain and the United States. He might insinuate that he would make a separate peace with Germany. He would no doubt endeavor, through the Communist Parties in the United States and Britain, to bring pressure on the British and American Governments. But we warned that, if those Governments succumbed to such pressure, Stalin would be encouraged to resort to similar tactics later in order to obtain further and more far-reaching demands.

We pointed out that Stalin's insistence on obtaining at least certain territorial commitments at this time could be ascribed to three desires. One was to break down the principle of not making any territorial commitments prior to the peace conference. The second was to use such recognition as justification of the Soviet invasion of Poland and the Baltic States and the 1939–1940 war against Finland. The third was to have promises with regard to Soviet frontiers which might be useful to him at the peace conference in case the war should end with a weakened Soviet Union not occupying the territories he was demanding.

Our agreeing to Stalin's demands, we added, would have an unfortunate effect upon the attitude of small countries everywhere toward the United States and Britain and also of countries that were especially opposed to the spread of Communism. It might well be regarded by the Latin American Republics as a departure from the principles we had hitherto advocated. It would give concern to the Vatican. It would affect the integrity of the Atlantic Charter. (In the first two clauses of the Charter the signatories declared that they sought no aggrandizement, territorial or other, and that they desired to see no territorial changes that did not accord with the freely expressed wishes of the peoples concerned.) And it would afford a wonderful opportunity to German propaganda.

In handing this memorandum to the President, I hoped he would be able to discuss it with Prime Minister Churchill in the course of the direct exchanges they were constantly having on the progress of the war. It seemed to me we were in great danger of relapsing into the practice of the Allies during the First World War, when they concluded a series of secret treaties splitting up among themselves territories belonging to the Central Powers. These secret treaties had become one of the principal weapons of the isolationists in the United States in the period between the two wars. At least one of the provisions of the Atlantic Charter had been especially devised to prevent the same old device of power politics from being revived.

I could sympathize fully with Stalin's desire to protect his western borders from future attack. But I felt that this security could best be obtained through a strong postwar peace organization. And it certainly could be achieved without the necessity of absorbing the life of the Baltic peoples, who possessed a strong feeling of independence, into that of the U.S.S.R.

The President felt that the Soviet Union was legitimately entitled to obtain full security at the end of the war, but this security would necessarily depend on the solution of many problems still outstanding, one of which was the status of Germany. The security that the Soviet Union should rightly obtain would depend upon the type of Germany to be established after the war, and he recalled that the Atlantic Charter had clearly called for the disarmament of Germany.

Thus the matter stood when I became ill in February. After I returned to my office on April 20 I found that events had moved in the wrong direction. Prime Minister Churchill seemed reluctantly determined to go ahead with the accord, and Stalin continued to press for an immediate signature.

The President had accepted our view at the State Department that such an accord would be both dangerous and unwise. He had sent messages to Churchill and to Stalin strongly urging our point of view. To Stalin he expressed the willingness of the United States to support the

Soviet Union in seeking, in postwar adjustments, all legitimate measures necessary to ensure the security of the U.S.S.R. Stalin, in effect, refused to discuss the question with us, however, on the grounds that it was a matter between Russia and Britain. Churchill informed the President that his Government had finally determined to conclude the treaty.

The British could not help but remember that their own protracted discussions with the Russians in 1939 over these same Baltic States might have been one of the causes of Stalin's signing an agreement with Hitler instead of with Chamberlain. They did not want their relations with Russia to go sour again. They feared lest, in those circumstances, Stalin might negotiate a separate peace with Germany.

The only concession the British had felt able to make to our viewpoint was that the treaty would be public, not secret. The President informed Mr. Churchill that this Government would not indicate approval of the treaty either directly or indirectly.

Then, in the face of Churchill's belief that Britain had to sign, the President suggested a compromise. This was that Lithuanians, Latvians, Estonians, and Finns who did not wish to be incorporated into Russia should have the right to leave those territories with their properties. He thought this would be more in accord with the Atlantic Charter. Welles communicated this to British Ambassador Halifax on April 1, and the British passed it on to the Russians.

Generally my associates at the State Department, with the exception of Welles, opposed this suggestion, as did I, on several grounds, one being that it would result in untold hardships for the peoples who would be transferred, and another being that the fact of our making such a suggestion could be taken to signify our concurrence in the absorption of the Baltic Republics into Russia on condition that the suggestions were carried out.

Ambassador Winant was in Washington on leave when I got back to my office. I saw him on April 21 and 27 and made very emphatic our opposition to the proposed Anglo-Soviet treaty embracing territorial clauses. Several days after Winant returned to London, he cabled us on May 4 that Foreign Commissar Molotov was expected in London within forty-eight hours to complete the negotiations for the treaty, which would include British recognition of the Russian frontiers of June, 1941, with respect to the Baltic States and Finland. He said that, although Eden had pressed the President's suggestion upon the Russians, they had thus far failed to include it in their draft. Churchill and Eden said to Winant that

Stalin had made the Baltic States and Finland issue the basis of trust in Britain as a friendly ally, and they felt that if mutual confidence could be established with Russia this would mean much in the prosecution of the war and in building future peace.

Winant suggested to us that Molotov, after arriving in London and engaging in preliminary discussions concerning the treaty, could then go on to Washington for the visit that the President had invited him to make. Meantime the text could be communicated to Moscow and the final phraseology agreed upon, whereafter Molotov could return to London to sign it.

We rejected this idea on the grounds that the impression might thereby be created that Molotov had come to the United States to gain our consent to the treaty, that we had given it, and that he had then returned to affix his signature.

After some delay Molotov arrived in London on May 20 and the issue quickly rose to a climax. Winant cabled the President and me on May 21 that, during the first meeting held that morning, the Russians still stuck to their original demand for the Baltic States and the Finnish boundary of 1940. Eden explained to Molotov the strong opposition of the United States to agreeing to boundary settlements during the war, and the close relationship of Britain and the United States. Molotov replied that there was also Russian public opinion to be taken into account.

At this point I sent the President another memorandum, which was even stronger than the one of February 4. It bluntly expressed our belief that signature of the proposed Anglo-Soviet treaty, with the territorial clauses included, would be a terrible blow to the whole cause of the United Nations. We proposed that a final telegram along these lines be sent to Winant to be communicated to the British.

We indicated that, if the treaty in its proposed form were signed, we might not be able to remain silent since silence might give tacit consent. On the contrary we might have to issue a separate statement clearly stating that we did not subscribe to its principles and clauses. This would be a sharp break within the United Nations, on this point at least, but there was no other course we could logically pursue.

Our memorandum was so strong that we were in some fear lest the President disapprove it. Mr. Roosevelt, however, quickly returned it with his O.K., and we immediately sent Winant a cable repeating its substance.

The British position now began to veer toward our view. Winant cabled us on May 24 that up until noon of the day before, both the British and the Russians appeared to consider an agreement unlikely. Molotov had brought up the question of agreeing to Russia's possession of eastern Poland, which Eden rejected as being incompatible with the August 25, 1939, British-Polish agreement. Eden again advanced the President's suggestion to allow the Baltic peoples who wished to do so to emigrate elsewhere, but Molotov refused to accept it. Molotov also desired a secret agreement whereby the British would agree to support Russian claims relative to the Rumanian frontiers.

Eden at this point suggested a substitute treaty of alliance between Russia and Britain omitting all reference to frontiers.

By the evening of the 23rd the Russians began to give way, Winant informed us. They withdrew their demands relative to Poland. They agreed to a compromise on the clause permitting the withdrawal of Baltic peoples. They dropped their proposal for a secret agreement relating to Rumania and Finland, but proposed instead that a clause be inserted whereby Britain would recognize Russian special interests in those countries.

Winant saw Molotov at the Russian Embassy on the evening of May 24. He informed Molotov of telegrams the Department had sent him stating that we were preparing to discuss commercial policy with the Russians and were also attempting to evolve a relief program including Russia. Winant expressed our interest in a second front, which was the other of Molotov's two objectives in going to London. He emphasized to Molotov that the President and I were both opposed to introducing frontier problems at this time. He said that he had presented to the President and me the Soviet view on this point as best he could, but that both of us definitely opposed frontier agreements in an Anglo-Soviet treaty.

Molotov listened attentively and said that the President's views on this matter warranted serious consideration.

Molotov asked whether Winant had seen Eden's draft treaty omitting all reference to boundaries. Winant said he had because he had cooperated with Eden in trying to arrive at a treaty omitting this reference which the Russians might find satisfactory. Molotov said he would again consider Eden's draft and might delay making a decision until he had seen the President. This appeared to be a definite concession.

The following morning Molotov requested permission from Stalin to negotiate an agreement with Britain on the basis of Eden's draft. Stalin suggested minor modifications, to which the British agreed, tending to emphasize the alliance character of the treaty after the war.

The treaty, without any territorial provisions, was signed the next day, May 26. I was enormously relieved.

Within a week after the signing of the Anglo-Soviet alliance, Foreign Commissar Molotov was in Washington. Since his conversations were mainly military, they were conducted chiefly with the President and the President's military advisers. Molotov was pressing strongly for the creation of a second front in Europe in 1942. One phrase of the communiqué issued by the White House on June 11—"full understanding was reached with regard to the urgent tasks of creating a second front in Europe in 1942"—was to give us trouble with Russia later on.

I called on Molotov on June 3 and had with him an extended conversation during which we agreed that full cooperation between our two countries was essential not only for ourselves but also for the world. Then and during our numerous conversations at Moscow in 1943 I found Molotov to be a quiet-mannered, very agreeable man who confined his talk strictly to the serious emergency matters pending. At our first meeting in Washington he was not too easy to approach, and seemingly kept a reserved attitude, although at Moscow he became more affable. He early impressed me with his ability, shrewdness, and resourcefulness.

Recalling to Molotov the information concerning Hitler's plans to attack Russia which I had had Welles pass on to Ambassador Oumansky in January, 1941, I jokingly said that some day, when we had won the war and he and I and others were sitting around the peace table planning for world restoration on sound and healthy lines, I might then presume to inquire just when it dawned on the Soviet Government that Hitler would attack them. Molotov came right back by saying this conclusion had been reached in April or May, but that of course most of the Russian people did not believe it until after the war was actually on.

I brought up with Molotov the discouraging situation in China. The United Nations' series of defeats at the hands of the Japanese during the first half of 1942, plus the fact that the Japanese had cut the Burma Road and that China was now virtually isolated from her friends with the exception of Russia, had inflicted a serious blow to Chinese morale.

Early in the year I had prepared an appeal to Congress in support of a projected $500,000,000 loan to China, which Assistant Secretary Long read for me on February 3 to the House Foreign Affairs Committee. I pointed out the great sacrifices China had already made during nearly five years of war, and the importance of China in the common struggle against the Axis. Congress approved the loan, and the agreement was signed on March 21. The day before my talk with Molotov I signed with Chinese Foreign Minister T. V. Soong a master Lend-Lease agreement almost identical with that we had reached with Britain.

Nevertheless, I was forced to remark to Molotov that our dispatches from Chungking had been very disquieting. Chiang Kai-shek, believing that he was not receiving anything like adequate consideration and co-operation, especially from the United States, was greatly discouraged and in very low spirits. I said we had done everything we could to reassure the Generalissimo that we were as much interested in the success of China in the war as in the success of other allied nations. But because of our necessities on other fronts and because of the difficulties of transportation now that the Burma Road was closed to us, we had not been able to furnish China with all the supplies she insisted upon.

Molotov immediately emphasized Russia's preoccupation with the Western battle front.

I replied that I fully appreciated the situation and therefore made no request of the Soviet Government. But I added that I did not know but that the Soviet Government might still have some standing with Chiang Kai-shek and could extend its own verbal assurances to the Chinese Government even though the Russians were in no position to aid in any other way. Molotov agreed to consider this.

The day before my long talk with Molotov, the President had asked Congress for declarations of war against Hungary, Rumania, and Bulgaria. The first two were actively fighting Russia, and Bulgaria was serving as a German base of operations.

All three had declared war against us at the time of the German and Italian declarations, but by the President's wish we had held off asking for declarations of war against them. Mr. Roosevelt had sent me a note on December 12, 1941, which read:

"I see by tonight's bulletins that the Government of Slovakia has declared the existence of a state of war with the United States.

"Also that the Government of Hungary has done so, or is about to do the same thing.

"Other puppet Governments may join.

"It is my present thought that the United States should pay no attention to any of these declarations of war against us by puppet Governments."

On the following day he asked me to inform the Congressional leaders of this viewpoint, so that they would not press for declarations of war. This I did.

The President sent me a further note on January 31, 1942, saying:

"I think that for the record it would be a rather ingenuous thing to do if you were to send a letter to the Committee on Foreign Affairs and the Committee on Foreign Relations telling them that for their information Hungary and Rumania and Bulgaria and Siam have all declared war on the United States, giving the date of the action of each country. Then I would merely add that this is sent for the information of the Committees only and that in your judgment no action is necessary, either by the Congress or by the Executive Branch of the Government!

"F. D. R.

"P.S. If my boy Johnny were doing it he would add as a postscript, 'SO WHAT!' "

I accordingly wrote letters on February 7 to this effect to Senator Connally and Representative Bloom, chairmen of the committees mentioned.

Rumania, Hungary, and Bulgaria were giving Germany increasing assistance, however. On March 24, 1942, the State Department cabled our Legation in Bern to request Switzerland to inform those Governments that we had not declared war against them because they were vassals of Germany, but now that they were engaged in military activities directed against us and were planning to extend them we intended declaring war unless they gave prompt evidence of a definite character that they would not assist the Axis Powers. Switzerland agreed, but the move was without effect.

Since the three Governments were extending their military activities, the Department drew up a draft on April 16 of a message that the President might send to Congress to recommend the declaration of a state of war. We held this for some weeks in the hope that the threat of such a declaration might induce Rumania, Hungary, and Bulgaria to lessen their assistance to Germany. When this hope proved vain, I sent the draft to the President on June 1. He transmitted it to Congress the following day; appropriate resolutions declaring war were quickly passed; and the President signed them on June 5.

On June 11 I signed with Soviet Ambassador Litvinov a master Lend-Lease agreement identical in substance to those signed with Britain and China. Following the signing, Litvinov made a casual reference to the omission of the Baltic territorial question from the British-Russian agreement signed a fortnight before. I replied that, if I had been Stalin's chief adviser, I would have most earnestly advised him, from the viewpoint of Russia's own interest, against inserting the territorial provision in the treaty. I said that an infinite number of questions would come up at the end of the war, some of which might negate many matters of supposed importance and even urgency at this time.

By way of further assistance to Russia, we cancelled our consular representation in Finland in July, in the hope that this would bring additional pressure on Finland to desist from her war against the Soviet Union.

When July, 1942, arrived, I felt that the time had come for me to make a major public address on foreign policy. I had not spoken since Pearl Harbor, in fact since October 21, 1941, when I appeared before the Senate Foreign Relations Committee to speak in favor of amending the Neutrality Act. The United States position in the war required restatement.

I went over with my associates the principal points I had in mind, and we then set to work preparing many successive drafts until the speech was completed to our satisfaction. I took it to the President on July 21, and he went over it in detail. At his press conference that day he was good enough to call special attention to the address, scheduled for two days later. He said it was a very able and conclusive summary of the world situation and that its general subject would be the seriousness of the war, what the winning of the war meant, what victory meant to civilization not only in this country but throughout the world, what it meant to every man, woman, and child throughout the world. He successfully asked all the radio networks to carry the speech, although ordinarily all of them carried only his own speeches.

I delivered the address on the night of July 23. Devoting a large part of the speech to postwar considerations, I came out flatly for the creation of an international security organization, of which the United States of course must be a member. And I was willing that that organization should be able to use force to maintain the peace. This was the first time that I publicly stated my position on this point, although I had often expressed it in conversations with foreign ambassadors and, during the conferences leading up to the United Nations Declaration, with my associates.

"No nation," I said, "can make satisfactory progress while its citizens are in the grip of constant fear of external attack or interference.

It is plain that some international agency must be created which can—by force, if necessary—keep the peace among nations in the future. There must be international cooperative action to set up the mechanisms which can thus insure peace. This must include eventual adjustment of national armaments in such a manner that the rule of law cannot be successfully challenged and that the burden of armaments may be reduced to a minimum."

I advocated continuing surveillance by the United Nations over aggressor nations until such time as the latter demonstrated their willingness and ability to live at peace with other nations. "How long such surveillance will need to continue," I said, "must depend upon the rapidity with which the peoples of Germany, Japan, Italy, and their satellites give convincing proof that they have repudiated and abandoned the monstrous philosophy of superior race and conquest by force and have embraced loyally the basic principles of peaceful processes. During the formative period of the world organization, interruption by these aggressors must be rendered impossible."

One of the institutions that had to be established and given vitality, I suggested, was an international court of justice.

I inveighed against extreme nationalism. "All will agree," I said, "that nationalism and its spirit are essential to the healthy and normal political and economic life of a people, but when policies of nationalism— political, economic, social, and moral—are carried to such extremes as to exclude and prevent necessary policies of international cooperation, they become dangerous and deadly. Nationalism, run riot between the last war and this war, defeated all attempts to carry out indispensable measures of international economic and political action, encouraged and facilitated the rise of dictators, and drove the world straight toward the present war."

Excessive trade barriers had to be reduced in the postwar world, I said, and practices that imposed injuries on others and diverted trade from its natural economic course had to be avoided. National currencies had to be freely exchangeable for each other at stable rates of exchange. A system of financial relations had to be devised so that materials could be produced and ways found of moving them where there were markets created by human need.

I stressed the necessity for an informed public opinion. "This," I said, "is a task of intensive study, hard thinking, broad vision, and leadership—not for governments alone, but for parents, and teachers, and clergymen, and all those, within each nation, who provide spiritual, moral, and intellectual guidance. Never did so great and so compelling a duty in this respect devolve upon those who are in positions of responsibility, public and private."

Finally, lest undue concentration on postwar problems should deflect our thoughts from the main task in hand, the winning of the war, I concluded my speech with an appeal for the dedication of our utmost efforts toward that end.

There were now some elements for optimism in the military picture. The Battle of Midway had been won, and we were assuming the offensive in the Pacific. The President had established a European theater of operations for United States forces, with Major General Dwight D. Eisenhower in London as commanding general. In Africa, however, the scene was dark, the Germans having driven the British forces to El Alamein, seventy miles from Alexandria.

British Ambassador Halifax had come to me on June 18 to inform me that his Government had received peace feelers in the past few months from a number of persons claiming to represent the anti-Nazi groups in Germany. Britain suspected that these approaches emanated from the German secret service in an effort to create confusion or dissension among the United Nations, and asked whether we had received any such overtures. I replied that nothing of a tangible nature had come to us.

Far from peace coming, I realized, we had a hard, perhaps a long, fight ahead. Our course was clear; to exert ourselves to the utmost in the diplomatic field to aid the armed forces of the United Nations to win the war.

In August, 1942, when Prime Minister Churchill went to Moscow for his first meeting with Stalin, the President authorized W. Averell Harriman to accompany him and sit in on the conversations. The discussions were stormy, centering almost entirely on the question of a second front in Western Europe. Stalin bluntly accused Britain of being afraid to take risks. He took it for granted that Molotov had obtained definite promises in London and Washington that a second front would be started in Europe in 1942. When Churchill said it was impossible to organize a second front in Europe in 1942, Stalin complained bitterly that this inflicted a moral blow on the whole Soviet public, complicated the situation of the Red Army, and impaired the plans of the Soviet Command, which had been based on the creation of a second front.

He presented these complaints in a written memorandum to Churchill and Harriman on August 13. Churchill replied in detail, while Harriman limited himself to saying he had nothing to add to what the Prime Minister had said except to reaffirm his statement that no promises had been broken.

The question of the second front was outside my province, being handled exclusively by the President and his military assistants. Of particular importance to me, however, was the information conveyed to me on September 1 by our Ambassador to Russia, Admiral William H. Standley, that throughout the Stalin-Churchill-Harriman conversations the question of Soviet postwar frontiers had not been mentioned at any time.

The question was not raised in earnest again until the Roosevelt-Stalin-Churchill Conference at Yalta, which was after I resigned as Secretary of State.

86: Prelude to African Invasion

AFTER ALMOST A DECADE as Secretary of State, I was forced in 1942 to give up a practice I had followed since I entered the State Department in 1933. At my doctor's request I ceased going to my office every Sunday morning. This meant abandoning the informal Sunday morning gatherings I had held in my office with my chief associates.

These gatherings had proved uniformly useful. During the Sunday morning quiet, with our discussions on a friendly, informal footing, with the telephone for once reasonably silent, and with my associates feeling under no pressure to hasten back to their offices for appointments, we exchanged views and information, clarified our thoughts, and paved the way for the decisions of the coming week.

I gave in to my doctor's conviction that a man of seventy in questionable health should not work six and a half days a week. Nevertheless I still continued to take papers and memoranda home with me to read on Sundays.

Unfortunately, my official social life suddenly quadrupled. I had thus far been able to live up to the decision I reached in 1933, to limit my social activities to the bare official minimum, so as to have more time to study issues of foreign policy at home and to see diplomats, officials of the Department, and others at my office. It was a case either of seeing them in an ephemeral way at dinners and luncheons or of seeing them in a serious way in my office. I had chosen the latter, and the diplomatic corps seemed well content.

But with our entrance into the war, the heads of many Governments came to the United States to seek our special help, to coordinate their activities with ours, and to sound us out on our postwar views, with special reference to their own countries. During 1942 there were in Washington, in addition to Churchill (twice) and Molotov, the President of Peru, the President of the Philippines, the King of Greece, the King of Yugoslavia, the Queen of the Netherlands, the Grand Duchess of Luxemburg, the Prime Minister of New Zealand, the President of Ecuador, the President of Cuba, the Prime Minister of Poland and the President-elect of Colombia along with other distinguished visitors.

I usually went to the airport or the railroad station to welcome them, attended a dinner or luncheon at the White House in their honor, and myself gave a dinner for them at the Carlton Hotel. In this last function I had the able assistance of Mrs. Hull, in whose hands I left all arrangements. She managed to give a touch of home to the dinners by bringing down from our apartment decorations, silverware, rugs, and even furniture.

Further, I held long conversations with these visitors on many of the special problems troubling them. Although I was glad to talk with them and get their views, their visits took much time and energy.

There was one occasion, however, when I was very glad to be of help to many hundreds of "distinguished visitors" who came to United States territory in a body. The incident rose out of an agreement we had with the Canadians whereby, in the event of an invasion of the Aleutians by the Japanese, American air units in Alaska would move out to meet the threat, and Canadian air units would move in to take their place.

The agreement was carried out except that at the Yukon frontier in Alaska the Canadian airmen got into difficulties with the United States customs officer because he decided some of their equipment and supplies were dutiable. It being wartime, he should have looked the other way; but when he made his decision and referred it to the main United States customs office in the Treasury the situation became complicated.

Since Canada had brought the matter to our attention, I asked John D. Hickerson, Assistant Chief of the European Division, to check with the Treasury. The Treasury officials said they would have been glad to overlook the matter were it not for the fact that the Yukon customs officer had made a decision, and they had to uphold him. Hickerson, however, discovered a loophole. If the Secretary of State certified that a person was a distinguished visitor, he could enter the United States without customs examination.

I immediately agreed. I wrote a letter to the Treasury stating that the Canadian airmen, hundreds of them, were all distinguished visitors. I pointed out that they were the first foreign nationals to join with the United States in the common defense of our nation since the days of Lafayette.

There was no further trouble.

In August, 1942, the President agreed with the Republican presidential candidate of 1940, Wendell Willkie, that the latter should make a trip abroad, ostensibly to show to the world that the United States was unified in her foreign policy. I had first met Willkie at a Gridiron Club dinner in Washington some years before, at the conclusion of which he introduced himself and expressed his strong support of the trade agreements policy. My attention, which had been attracted to him when he was representing public utilities interests in Tennessee, increased as he became more active in politics and championed progressive policies. He possessed brilliancy of the first order and sincerely stood for a number of progressive ideas, including the trade agreements program. He had a pleasing personality and a presence sure to draw favorable attention from all groups in which he participated.

When Willkie wanted to make a trip around the world and felt out President Roosevelt to see to what extent the latter would sponsor it, the President, who talked his language of liberalism, took him right in and proposed to extend him every kind of diplomatic courtesy. He sent him to me with the request that I go over our foreign affairs with him. I talked with Willkie for about an hour and a half on all phases of foreign affairs I thought would be helpful to him. When I finished I asked him what he thought of our ideas, and he replied that, in his opinion, they were good.

The President and I thought that Willkie, in making his trip, would give expression to ideas somewhat in common with ours. I did not ask any assurances on this point, having left that up to the President. Willkie, however, caused us some difficulty because of his statements concerning Great Britain and Russia. When he returned, he was informed by some that an increasing number of Republicans, believing he was too close in with Mr. Roosevelt to function effectively as a Republican leader, were turning against him. Instead of reporting back to the President as a matter of courtesy, he began to criticize him. I was therefore, to some degree, disappointed with the results of the trip.

In the autumn of 1942 we entered into a period of diplomatic preparation and waiting for the Allied landing in North Africa on November 7. We brought various diplomatic developments to a head, but the dominant feeling in those months was one of suspense until the first major Anglo-American expedition in the Occident could be accomplished.

One of the negotiations that concerned us largely was a common agreement among the United Nations on the punishment for atrocities inflicted by the Germans. Even before we entered the war, the President, after consulting with us of the Department, issued a statement on October 25, 1941, strongly condemning Germany's practice of executing innocent hostages. Prime Minister Churchill made a similar statement and asserted that henceforth retribution for such crimes must be numbered among the major purposes of the war.

In January, 1942, representatives of nine countries occupied by the Nazis met in London, with United States Ambassador Biddle sitting in as an observer. They took note of the Roosevelt-Churchill statements, and placed among their war aims the punishment of war criminals through the channel of organized justice.

On receiving in June, 1942, reports of the German atrocities at Lidice, Czechoslovakia, I stated publicly that "this latest example of mass terrorization through wanton butchery of hostages and brutal torture of innocent women and children has shocked and outraged humanity." When Premier Sikorski of Poland sent the President a message later in the month urging various measures of retaliation for German atrocities the State Department drafted the President's reply, which thoroughly denounced such atrocities and recalled my statement on the occasion of the wiping out of Lidice. But we said we were not yet prepared to resort to measures of retaliation such as indiscriminate bombing of civilian populations in enemy countries or the punishment of innocent enemy aliens in the United States.

I saw the Dutch Ambassador, the Yugoslav Minister, and the Luxemburg Minister simultaneously on July 31, to receive from them a joint letter from the nine countries that had met in London in January. This suggested that the President amplify his statement of October 25, 1941, so as to make the enemy understand that the determination and power of the United States were a guarantee that the warning previously issued would be carried into effect.

I sent this letter to the President. He asked us for recommendations, and we drew up a statement that he issued on August 21, 1942. "The United Nations," he said, "are going to win this war. When victory has been achieved, it is the purpose of the Government of the United States, as I know it is the purpose of each of the United Nations, to make appropriate use of the information and evidence in respect to these barbaric crimes of the invaders, in Europe and in Asia. It seems only fair that they should have this warning that the time will come when they shall have to stand in courts of law in the very countries which they are now oppressing and answer for their acts."

The President had discussed this question with Mr. Churchill during the Prime Minister's visit to Washington in June, and particularly the creation of a United Nations commission on atrocities. When Churchill returned to London the War Cabinet appointed a committee to study the subject, and Ambassador Winant sat in on the committee meetings. After a number of exchanges with London, the Department prepared a statement for the President declaring that this Government was prepared to cooperate with the British and other Governments in establishing a United Nations Commission for the Investigation of War Crimes. At the President's request a sentence was included to the effect that neither this Government nor the Governments associated with us intended to indulge in mass reprisals and they sought only to punish the ringleaders responsible for atrocities. The President issued his statement on October 7, and the British Lord Chancellor made the British announcement in the House of Lords.

In the preparations for the landing in North Africa the State Department had nothing to do with the military angles, although the consuls and vice consuls we had stationed in North Africa by virtue of our economic accord with General Weygand, approved by Vichy, rendered invaluable assistance even in this field. They collected and sent information which was used by the War Department, and they maintained contact with the local French underground groups. They and the personnel of the Office of Strategic Services who were organizing the underground were under the local direction of our Foreign Service officer, Robert D. Murphy, who had been appointed by the President in September to be Adviser for Civil Affairs under General Eisenhower. We had also assigned H. Freeman Matthews, formerly Chargé d'Affaires in Vichy and now serving under Ambassador Winant in London, to work as political adviser on Eisenhower's staff.

North Africa was not the only portion of the Dark Continent that engaged our diplomatic efforts in 1942. One of our most fruitful achievements was in Liberia, on the west bulge of Africa, across the South Atlantic from Brazil. At this time fortunately our relations were of the best with the little country which a hundred years before had been founded by American freed slaves with the assistance of our Government. As I entered office in 1933, no formal diplomatic ties existed between the United States and Liberia. The United States, as well as Great Britain, had severed such relations in 1930 as a result of various abuses of power by Liberian officials.

In 1935 I had sent to Liberia my assistant, Harry McBride, who already had a first-hand knowledge of that country, and his conferences with President Edwin Barclay resulted in the resumption of diplomatic relations and the beginning of a new era of friendship. We signed a treaty of friendship, commerce, and navigation with Liberia in 1938, and a consular convention, an air navigation agreement and a treaty of conciliation in the following months. In 1939 Pan American Airways signed a contract with the Liberian Government for the operation of transatlantic service to Liberia.

Shortly after Pearl Harbor I again sent McBride to Liberia to induce that Government to coordinate its defenses with ours. It consented to the use by the United States Army Air Forces of the Pan American airports in Liberia, and Liberia became a vital link in the air route across the South Atlantic to the Near and the Far East. We formalized this arrangement on March 31, 1942, by signing an agreement providing for the defense of Liberia by the United States and giving us the right to establish defense areas in Liberia and to build military installations there. Three weeks before, at the Department's suggestion, President Roosevelt had opened Lend-Lease to Liberia. With Japan's occupation of the rubber producing areas in the Far East, Liberia became of greatly increased importance to us as one of the few remaining available sources of natural rubber.

Throughout the remainder of the war the United States contributed materially to developing Liberia by constructing a port, enlarging the airports, building roads, and providing the Liberian Government with technical assistants. Liberia declared war on the Axis, expelled Axis citizens, and signed the United Nations Declaration. Visits were exchanged between President Roosevelt and President Barclay and President-elect Tubman. We worked out a long-range policy toward Liberia designed to lift the standard of living of this traditional godchild of the United States and to strengthen our economic and political ties.

Our diplomatic preparations for the Anglo-American landing in North Africa embraced particularly an effort to see to it that Spain and Portugal were kept reassured as to our intentions, and that Spain would maintain her neutrality and prevent a German march through the Iberian peninsula to Gibraltar to attack our landing troops in the rear.

Although plans and preparations for the North African landing were in the top-secret category, both Spain and Portugal could readily guess that some such move was at least a logical possibility. Spain lay just across the Strait of Gibraltar from North Africa, and Portugal lay a little farther away. In October, 1942, we received cables from our new Ambassador to Madrid, Professor Carlton Hayes, and from our Minister to Lisbon, Bert Fish, indicating that formal assurances regarding the integrity of Spanish and Portuguese territory in the event of an Anglo-American landing in North Africa would be advisable.

With Spain our relations since the end of the Civil War in the spring of 1939 had been replete with difficulties of two kinds. On the one hand General Franco's Foreign Minister, his brother-in-law Ramón Serrano Suñer, lost no opportunity to show his dislike of the democracies and his head-over-heels commitment to the Axis cause. And on the other hand those segments of our own population who had passionately embraced the Loyalist cause during the Civil War continually urged us to break off diplomatic relations with Spain or to take other actions that assuredly would have brought Spain into the war on the Axis side.

We could not hope to swing Spain to an active support of the Allies; but we did feel there was a good possibility of keeping her neutral, which fact would be of great advantage to the Allied side.

When Spanish Ambassador Don Juan Francisco de Cárdenas came to me on September 13, 1941, just prior to returning to Spain for a visit, I spoke to him as bluntly as I had ever spoken to any diplomatic envoy. After telling him that the American people, including myself, had a warm friendliness toward the Spanish people, that we had sympathized deeply with them in their unfortunate experiences of recent years, and had been thoroughly disposed to offer them assistance in their very great distress, I said:

"While it's most disagreeable even to recall our experiences in dealing with the Spanish Government, I must state that in all the relations of this Government with the most backward and ignorant Governments in the world, it has not experienced such a lack of ordinary courtesy or consideration customarily prevailing between friendly nations as it has at the hands of the Spanish Government. Your Government's course has been one of aggravated discourtesy and contempt in the very face of our offers to be of aid.

"We could not think of embarrassing, not to say humiliating, ourselves by further approaches of this nature, bearing in mind the coarse and extremely offensive methods and conduct of Serrano Suñer in particular and in some instances of General Franco. When I think about the details of the conduct of the Spanish Government toward this Government, what has happened is really inconceivable."

I remarked that I had little hope that the Ambassador could make the slightest impression on Franco and Serrano Suñer since they were capable of adopting so unworthy and contemptible an attitude toward the United States Government without any cause whatever.

De Cárdenas did not undertake to defend the course of his Government except to say that there must be some misunderstanding between our Ambassador and Serrano Suñer. He said he would do his best to bring about better relations.

Five days after this interview, I cabled Ambassador Weddell on September 18 our conclusions on relations with Spain. I said that, in spite of this Government's constant disposition to cooperate in solving Spain's economic problems, and of the free access to the American market enjoyed by Spain, no wish to reciprocate had been shown by the Franco Government. That Government's policy had been to exclude American investment and enterprise and to restrict Spanish purchases here to an irreducible minimum. In the light of these facts, and of our continued disposition to consider sympathetically Spanish requirements in so far as these were compatible with our own defense needs and the limitations imposed by the war, the State Department would like to receive an immediate and detailed report on what contributions Spain was ready to make toward cooperating in this country's efforts to better our mutual relations.

Upon his arrival in Madrid, Ambassador de Cárdenas arranged a meeting on October 6 between General Franco and Weddell, the first time our Ambassador had been able to see the head of the Spanish Government for many months. Weddell stated our general position in the light of my cable of September 18, and received an affirmative reply from Franco when he asked whether the Spanish Government desired to look into the possibility of better commercial relations with the United States. Franco stressed Spain's urgent need for gasoline, wheat, and cotton.

The following day Weddell cabled, in reply to an inquiry from us, that British investigations in Spain did not substantiate the reports that gasoline and other petroleum products purchased by Spain in the United States were finding their way into Axis hands, except perhaps in isolated and clandestine instances.

I submitted to the President on October 10, 1941, a memorandum, which he approved, recommending that our petroleum exports to Spain be permitted to continue within the limitations of quantity imposed by the British, and of quality (meaning high-octane content) imposed by our own regulations.

After discussions with the British, we handed Ambassador de Cárdenas through Assistant Secretary of State Dean Acheson an *aide-mémoire* on November 29 in which we proposed to continue—subject to our own national defense demands—to supply Spain's requirements of most urgently needed products, including petroleum. This was subject to two conditions: first, that Spain accept the principle that these products could not be used in any way to benefit Italy or Germany or the countries occupied by them; second, that Spain agree to supply us in significant quantities with certain specified Spanish products such as mercury, tungsten, tin, zinc concentrates, lead, and olive oil.

We also proposed, in this *aide-mémoire*, to institute a system for controlling petroleum supplies in Spain "not only in the aggregate but as to the various types of petroleum products, their uses, and the inventories of these in the various zones of distribution in Spain," through American Government agents operating in Spanish territory.

During the few weeks following Pearl Harbor, we temporarily suspended our economic program toward Spain because of insistent reports that Hitler might, without particular opposition from Spain, send an army into the Iberian peninsula. The British Ambassador, Lord Halifax, called on me on December 29, however, and earnestly expressed the belief, based on information from Spain, that further cooperation of the United States with Britain by continuing our program of economic aid to Spain would be very helpful and very important, since this policy tended to discourage German movements in or through Spain and Spanish cooperation with Germany. I replied that I could understand the significance of what he said, and would be glad to take up the matter further.

After Spanish Ambassador de Cárdenas had expressed objections to certain phrases in our November *aide-mémoire*, particularly in connection with the proposed control system, we revised the document to substitute a regulatory system, to be established and operated by the United States, British, and Spanish Governments in consultation. This we sent Ambassador Weddell on January 8, 1942, and handed to Ambassador de Cárdenas on January 13. In this *aide-mémoire* we named Japan as one of the countries to which Spain might not reexport, and we placed great emphasis on our obtaining certain supplies from Spain and on supply conditions here so far as exports to Spain were concerned.

We cabled Ambassador Weddell on January 12 that, in making the substitution, we had been influenced primarily by the British Government's strong insistence that some petroleum and other products must be supplied to Spain, so as to keep her economy functioning sufficiently to supply products Britain badly needed and the strategic materials listed for this country. We did not, we said, regard as a major consideration the possible effect, if any, of our proposal on the Spanish Government's general policy, and we would consequently base our decisions regarding exports to Spain on whether a valuable and tangible *quid pro quo* could be obtained from Spain.

We added that we had insisted in our discussions with the British that, since we had to supply the petroleum products, we must have the final determination of the amounts to be exported. It had been our consistent belief that the quantities that could be sent would be much under the British recommendation. And, since our war needs and those of this hemisphere had to be met first, our discussions with respect to Spain would be restricted to minimum requirements.

In a memorandum dated January 28, 1942, from the Spanish Embassy, the Spanish Government accepted our proposals "in principle." Negotiations began which continued for several months and resulted in an agreement in May. We made every effort to live up to our commitments, even as did the Spanish Government in supplying us with strategic materials; and in general the agreement worked out to the over-all advantage of the United Nations.

In April, 1942, Ambassador Weddell retired because of illness. He was one of our finest representatives, and the bad relations that had developed between him and Foreign Minister Serrano Suñer were no fault of his. The President chose Professor Carlton Hayes, a noted historian, to succeed him, and I concurred.

Happily for us, General Franco became convinced of the unfortunate consequences of continuing his brother-in-law in the position of Foreign Minister, and replaced him by Count Jordana, who was far more reasonable.

Nine days before the Allied landing in North Africa, Ambassador Hayes reported to us that Jordana had informed him that the British had given General Franco and Jordana solemn assurances with regard to the integrity of Spanish soil in the event of an Allied invasion of North Africa, and that the Foreign Minister would like to receive similar assurances from the United States. Jordana referred to articles in the American press favoring the breaking of relations, and even war, with Spain, saying that while he himself did not think these articles reflected any official policy, he would very much like to have a definite statement of our position. He added that he would expect us to attach to such a statement a provision against Spain's giving military assistance to our enemies.

We accordingly cabled Hayes on the following day authorizing him to give the necessary assurances and to state that the articles in the Ameri--

can press to which Jordana had referred did not represent the official point of view.

Hayes cabled us a report on November 3 that Germany had asked Spain the previous week to allow her to send troops through the peninsula if the Allies conducted military operations in Morocco or the Canary Islands.

After consulting with the President, we cabled Hayes the following day authorizing him to make a further statement to Franco either directly or through Jordana. He was to refer to the assurances already given, in which we had fully recognized Spain's wish to stay out of war and declared our purpose to do all we could to see that she was not drawn into the war. He was then to add that the United States Government, recognizing her difficult position, planned immediately to consider increasing the scope of our economic arrangements with Spain so as to permit her to obtain more readily and in greater volume within the United States some of the supplies she needed. This increased economic assistance would be possible only so long as Spain stayed out of the war and did not allow the Axis to infringe upon her territory.

Hayes was to add that we had heard reports that Germany either thought of demanding or had demanded permission to move troops into Spanish territory. This Government was confident that the Spanish Government would resist any such demands. In the event such demands were made and were resisted, this Government, if the Spanish Government desired, would offer Spain as soon as possible all practical support.

When Hayes saw Jordana, the Foreign Minister denied that any demands had been made by Germany but said Spain might not be able to refuse German assistance if Allied forces invaded French Morocco or Oran, thereby affecting Spanish Morocco and making it necessary for Spain to take precautionary military measures. Hayes thought this was a threat to oppose us if we invaded North Africa, but was not necessarily indicative of Spain's readiness to carry out the threat.

Meantime messages from the President to General Franco, President Carmona of Portugal, Marshal Pétain, Governor General Yves Charles Chatel of Algeria, Admiral Jean Pierre Esteva, the Resident General at Tunis, and the Bey of Tunis, Sidi Moncef Pacha, were being drafted. In general terms, these messages emphasized that Germany and Italy were proposing to invade and occupy French North Africa in order to execute their schemes of domination and conquest over the whole of Africa; that a powerful American force was being landed in North Africa to cooperate with the Governments of Algeria, Tunisia, and French Morocco in fore-stalling this threat; and that we sought no new territories for ourselves. We emphatically assured Spain and Portugal that the presence of Ameri-can forces in French North Africa presaged no move whatever against their peoples, Governments, or territories, metropolitan or overseas.

These messages, bearing the President's name, went out in the most secret manner possible to our respective envoys. As our representatives presented them to the addressees during the night of November 7–8, Amer-ican and British forces were landing in strength along hundreds of miles of the North African coast, carrying out one of the greatest amphibian operations in history.

With the landing in North Africa, our policy toward Vichy France—which came in for perhaps the sharpest criticism of any foreign policy during the Roosevelt Administration—reached its end. The following day Pétain and Laval severed diplomatic relations with the United States.

At this point, therefore, a few comments may be in order in summing up the effects of our Vichy policy. It is unfortunate that that policy aroused so many emotions in the United States that even today some per-sons refuse to see anything in it but the most mournful black. Some of these persons are like those who throughout history have been drawn to the dramatic figure on horseback, who follow him blindly, who will see no fault in him, and who regard as bitter enemies all who refuse to admit his supremacy. Curiously, many Britons and Americans, looking upon De Gaulle as a newborn Joan of Arc, embraced him with more intensity than the average among his own French followers.

The first point is that President Roosevelt and I saw as one toward Vichy and toward De Gaulle. The Vichy policy was not that of either of us, but of both of us. The President needed no urging, and often he took the initiative himself.

The second point is that Prime Minister Churchill, and sometimes Eden, strongly supported to the President and me our maintenance of relations with Vichy, even though they themselves condemned Vichy and made those relations difficult.

The third point is that our relations with Vichy brought us proven advantages. They meant contacts in Vichy France and in French North Africa which would have been cut off completely had we broken with Vichy. They meant information. They meant having our own representa-tives on the spot to convince Frenchmen that the Allies would win, how-ever long it took, and that Vichy France should not collaborate with

Germany. They helped keep alive in the minds of the French people their basic concepts of freedom and the hope that France's free institutions would be restored. They were instrumental in preventing the cession of bases and materials to Germany in May, 1941.

These relations played a part in keeping the French fleet from passing into German hands. I do not claim that they were the sole or even the predominant factor. I feel that Pétain's and Darlan's realization of the abhorrence of the average Frenchman for any such betrayal was an important factor. But their realization of the basic patriotism of the French had not been sufficient in itself to prevent Darlan's deal with the Germans in May, 1941—stopped only by the pressure from General Weygand, whose friendship we had assured through our North African policy, and from Admiral Leahy.

The fourth point is that we had no preeminent French leader to turn to if we cut off Vichy entirely and perhaps pushed Pétain's government into Hitler's arms. To give De Gaulle full diplomatic recognition meant withdrawing diplomatic recognition from Vichy. The disadvantages to us obviously outweighed the advantages. Nevertheless, we did go as far as we could in giving him military assistance and in trying to build him up as what he should have been—a military leader and a general of the French armies who was willing to leave political considerations to a later date and to take the field and fight the Germans.

The fifth, and most important, point was that our relations with Vichy, which permitted us to maintain consuls in North Africa, paved the way and prepared the ground for the Anglo-American military expedition into the western Mediterranean area and for the movements supporting the British operations farther east. We should have paid a far higher toll of life for the landing in North Africa had we not maintained our representatives in Algeria, Tunisia, and French Morocco from June, 1940, on.

The landing in North Africa was not without bloodshed; but if we consider the length of the coast line involved, and if we compare our losses with the much greater ratio of losses of the British and the Free French in the invasion of Syria, our casualties could have been many times greater, and the task of sweeping the Axis out of North Africa could have dragged on far longer, without the thirty months of preparation of the terrain permitted us by the maintenance of our relations with Vichy France.

In general, no harm was done to any of our national interests by our

Vichy policy. Not only did it not harm our interests, but it had the beneficial effects I have mentioned.

The critics of our policy thought largely of ideologies, less of American interests. To them Vichy was fascist and collaborationist, and consequently every member of the Vichy Government, from high to low, was fascist and collaborationist. Fascist it was, and collaborationist it sometimes tried to be and was; but the critics failed to see that thousands of officials and Army and Navy officers operating under Vichy were Frenchmen first, and therefore anti-Nazi and anti-Axis. We fought Hitlerism at Vichy as strongly as we fought it anywhere.

During the period of intense criticism against our Vichy policy before the landing in North Africa, the President and I labored under the handicap of being unable to announce the advantages that were accruing to us from that policy. We could not expose the results of the contacts we were keeping in Vichy and in North Africa or of the economic accord with Weygand. Easy as it was to criticize, it was correspondingly hard to give the whole story. Publishing a balance sheet of our policy would have prejudiced the policy itself and incited the Germans to require Vichy to reduce or eliminate these contacts and negative their results. Consequently, the criticism accumulated with virtually no opposition until it solidified into a position that no doubt will endure for years.

The President and I felt strongly that our policy toward Vichy involved no sacrifice of principle, and that it did prevent the sacrifice of perhaps many thousands of American lives.

87: Aftermath of African Landing

THE FIRST REACTIONS in the diplomatic field to the landing in North Africa were a mixture of the favorable and the unfavorable.

At nearly midnight on November 8, our Chargé in Vichy, Pinckney Tuck, telephoned the State Department to inform us that Premier Laval had sent for him that evening and told him that, following a decision of the Cabinet, relations between France and the United States had been broken. On the same day Marshal Pétain sent the President a message in which he characterized the landing in North Africa as an act of aggression.

But from Spain and Portugal there came within the next few days messages assuring the President of their continued neutrality and friendship.

Our relations with Vichy severed, I sent the President on November 9 the draft of a proposed statement he might give to the press, saying I thought it would be well for him take this step. I said I was sending French Ambassador Henry-Haye his passports.

The President issued this statement the same day. In it he regretted Laval's action in severing relations, and said: "He is evidently still speaking the language prescribed by Hitler." The President said that no act of Hitler, or of any of his puppets, could sever relations between the American people and the people of France. We had not broken relations with them. We never would.

"This Government," he said, "will continue as heretofore to devote its thought, its sympathy, and its aid to the rescue of the forty-five million people of France from enslavement and from a permanent loss of their liberties and free institutions."

General de Gaulle's first reaction to the landing in North Africa was highly encouraging. The President had stuck to his determination, communicated to Prime Minister Churchill earlier in the year, that De Gaulle be not informed of the invasion until it had begun. Churchill had tried to get the President to agree at least to informing De Gaulle a day or so before the landing, but Mr. Roosevelt had stood firm.

British Ambassador Lord Halifax came to me on November 9 and handed me a telegram from Eden which stated that Churchill and Eden had seen De Gaulle on the morning of November 8. They informed him that the landing was occurring.

The telegram added that De Gaulle's attitude was eminently satisfactory. De Gaulle said that the interests of the French people must be the paramount consideration, and that it was essential to avoid the coexistence of two or more Free French movements—one looking to Britain and another to the United States—from which the Communists would be the only gainers. He thought General Giraud well fitted to play the role for which he had been chosen. If Giraud could bring over North Africa to the Allied cause De Gaulle would be ready to make an agreement with him, with Britain's assistance.

(General Eisenhower had brought General Henri H. Giraud from Vichy France to lead the French Army in North Africa. Giraud had escaped from a German prison camp in April, 1942, and had made his way to Vichy. The State Department had been kept informed concerning the efforts to get him to North Africa, but had not taken direct part in them, since this was a military project.)

Ambassador Halifax also showed me a copy of the radio address De Gaulle had delivered the night before, in the same spirit as the talk with Churchill and Eden. I thanked him and commented with satisfaction on the signs of practical judgment which both utterances of De Gaulle surprisingly revealed.

Halifax congratulated the State Department on its part in the work of establishing and carrying out our policy toward Vichy. I thanked him but remarked, "Your Government might well give an expression of approval after having concealed its position over all these months."

Halifax said he thought so too and would give the matter early attention.

Events that seemed moving so satisfactorily were, however, complicated by the presence of Admiral Darlan in Algiers at the time of the landing. General Eisenhower, through General Mark Clark, was now conducting the negotiations that resulted in Admiral Darlan's being made the supreme French leader in French North Africa. In these negotiations neither I nor the State Department had any part.

The President, after receiving a cable from Churchill to the effect that he felt obliged to see that De Gaulle got a fair deal, and that the formation of rival French Governments, one supported by Britain and the other by the United States, should be prevented at all costs, cabled the Prime Minister on November 11:

"In regard to De Gaulle, I have heretofore enjoyed a quiet satisfaction in leaving him in your hands. Apparently I have now acquired a similar problem in Brother Giraud. I wholly agree that we must prevent rivalry between the French émigré factions and I have no objection to a De Gaulle emissary visiting Giraud in Algiers. We must remember there is also a cat fight in progress between Giraud and Darlan, each claiming full military command of French forces in North and West Africa. The principal thought to be driven home to all three of these prima donnas is that the situation is today solely in the military field, and that any decision by any one of them, or by all of them, is subject to review and approval by Eisenhower."

Two days later we at the State Department wanted to send instructions to Robert Murphy in North Africa on three points—officials of the Vichy regime to be retained in office in Africa should not include those to whom well founded objection might be taken; any persons found imprisoned for having aided the United Nations should be released; and anti-Jewish measures imposed by the previous French authorities should be lifted. Our telegram was sent to General Marshall for clearance; but he observed that the first recommendation appeared to be directed at Darlan, the man to whom General Eisenhower had to look for immediate results in the Tunisian operation and in the matter of the French fleet. He agreed to forward the other two recommendations.

On November 14 I received two representatives of the French National Committee, André Philip and Adrien Tixier. I said to them that we were then in a full military situation, and that all our efforts at the moment had to be concentrated on assisting the military authorities. This was particularly true in North Africa, where happily there was French military cooperation.

M. Philip said he had received information from within France that the presence of American troops once more on French soil had given new hope to the French people. He hoped we were not accepting blindly offers of military assistance from Frenchmen who necessarily by their past record would never be accepted by the French people in the future as representing the true Free France. While the people gave full support to the Free French movement and to General Giraud they would never accept Admiral Darlan as other than a Vichy tool of Germany.

I replied that I was not even informed as to the activities of Admiral Darlan beyond reports appearing in the press. I then reviewed the policy we had pursued toward Vichy France and the purposes we had had in mind. I said I believed that our aims and the aims of the Free French movement were identical, but method was also something to be considered, and in method personalities figured importantly.

"I have been in politics fifty years," I remarked, "and I realize the full implications of everything you say. But France has a unique and glorious opportunity today to reconstruct herself very much as the United States reconstructed herself after the American Revolution, when perhaps nearly one-half our inhabitants were Tories. The reason that Americans of that period live in American history today is that they were big enough to overlook differences and convince all parties that the construction of America was a great common problem outweighing sectional, factional, or political differences."

That afternoon I had a long telephone conversation with the President, during which I informed him of the substance of my talk with the Free French representatives.

"The situation now presented in North Africa," I said, "is a very difficult one. I am very much afraid of the possibilities in view of the various French interests involved, including the Free French, General Giraud, Admiral Darlan, and others."

The President said his first idea of a solution would be to place Admiral Darlan, General Giraud, and a De Gaulle representative in one room alone and then give the government of the occupied territory to the man who came out.

I suggested to the President that he have General Eisenhower turn over the command of the local French military forces to General Giraud and of the French naval forces to Admiral Darlan, giving the latter as lofty a title as possible, perhaps second only to the Admiral commanding the Allied forces.

The President replied that, unfortunately, this solution was too late in view of the fact that an agreement had been made the day before among Admiral Darlan, General Giraud, and General Clark, as General Eisenhower's representative, whereby Admiral Darlan had been placed in charge of the civil functions of the local government and General Giraud in command of all of the French military and naval forces.

I said I also thought it was unfortunate that this agreement had already been made. I added that I was still very much afraid that trouble would be caused by the presence of Admiral Darlan in the picture.

The President stated that, with regard to giving Admiral Darlan a high rank and command of the French naval forces, the fact was that there was so small a part of the French Navy in the waters of French

North Africa that, if such an arrangement were made, Darlan would have practically no power at all.

He concluded by saying that he had another solution in mind that might be used if the situation did not clear up. This was to place Robert D. Murphy in control of the civil administration to the extent of having the power of veto over any act proposed by the local officials.

The President's statement to me over the telephone was the first news I received of the Eisenhower-Darlan agreement. Militarily, this agreement had every justification. Darlan's authority was sufficient to end the sporadic resistance from those few French military elements whose mistaken patriotism induced them to resist our landings. It soon succeeded in bringing French West Africa, with its strategic port of Dakar, to our side without the loss of a single life. It enabled our Army to proceed with the advance against the Germans in Tunisia unimpeded by any necessity to secure its lines of communication in Morocco and Algeria from a hostile army or population.

A number of reputable American military officials estimated to me that our agreement with Darlan resulted in a saving of more than 16,000 American and British lives, and that victory in North Africa had been moved up by sixty days.

But the agreement came in for the bitterest of attacks from many persons on ideological grounds. Darlan had so often voiced his antagonism to the cause of the Allies that he was popularly believed to be a man of Hitler. Critics, ignoring the saving of lives of our soldiers and the acceleration of the end of fighting in North Africa, devoted their whole efforts to a bitter assault against our Government over the Darlan episode.

In conversations with the President I earnestly suggested that he make our position toward Darlan thoroughly clear. We could not disavow General Eisenhower's agreement with Darlan without creating chaos in North Africa, where it had developed that the French were more disposed to recognize Darlan's authority than General Giraud's. But we could at least emphasize that the arrangement was a temporary one, primarily a military one, and was in no sense designed to lift Darlan into permanent political control.

We accordingly outlined a statement that he might issue. Late on November 17 he sent me this note:

"I got a telegram from Winston this afternoon and having to work in a hurry, and with the help of the statement okayed by you, the Secre-

tary of War, and Elmer Davis [Chief of the Office of War Information],
announced the enclosed at my Press Conference. I think it will 'take' all
right."

The "telegram from Winston," couched in the Prime Minister's usual
vigorous language, suggested that our two countries should not overlook
the serious political injury that might be done to our cause not only in
France but throughout Europe by the feeling that we were ready to make
terms with local Quislings. Darlan, he said, had an odious record, and it
was he who, by promoting his creatures to command, had inculcated in
the French Navy its malignant disposition. French sailors but yesterday
had been sent to their death against the American line of battle off Casablanca, and now Darlan was playing turncoat for the sake of power and
office.

The President's statement accepted General Eisenhower's arrangements made for the time being in North and West Africa. Mr. Roosevelt
said he thoroughly understood and approved the feeling in the United
States and Great Britain and among all the other United Nations that, in
view of the history of the past two years, no permanent arrangement
should be made with Admiral Darlan. The people of the United Nations
likewise would never understand the recognition or a reconstituting of the
Vichy Government in France or in any French territory.

The President added that no one in our Army had any authority to
discuss the future Government of France and the French Empire, and
that the present "temporary arrangement" in North and West Africa was
a "temporary expedient," justified solely by the stress of battle. That
arrangement had accomplished two military objectives—not only saving
American and British lives on the one hand and French lives on the other,
but also speeding up the attack on the Axis forces in Tunisia.

This statement did much to allay the resentment of those who opposed any dealings whatever with Admiral Darlan.

I had also had a thorough discussion with the President on the economic, political, and fiscal questions that were developing in North
Africa, and how these should be handled. Mr. Roosevelt wrote me a letter
on November 18 stating that the conduct of such affairs should lie in my
hands, and I was authorized to draw upon any of the other Departments
or agencies of the Government for assistance.

In accordance with this letter I communicated to General Eisenhower
through General Marshall a message stating my belief that civil matters
in North Africa should be turned over to the State Department gradually.

A transition period, I thought, might ensue during which the Allied commander-in-chief in North Africa might wish to transfer his civilian responsibilities, as military operations dictated, to the civilian group under Robert Murphy, who would return to the jurisdiction of the State Department. General Eisenhower agreed.

Eisenhower and Murphy jointly cabled me on December 9 that Darlan was considering Marcel Peyrouton, former Minister of the Interior under the Vichy Government, for Governor General of Algeria, or some other important post. Darlan recommended that we grant Peyrouton facilities for travel from Buenos Aires, where he was now, to Algiers. Both Eisenhower and Murphy said they saw no objection, and recommended that the Department extend the requested facilities.

I replied on December 11, saying that we naturally regarded the whole North African situation from the military point of view, and consequently civil questions were subordinate except as they contributed to military effectiveness. We should therefore consider Darlan's request for Peyrouton in this light. If General Eisenhower considered that failure to agree would result in friction or in any way impair our military chances, the State Department would place no obstacles in the way of Darlan's request. If General Eisenhower recommended, we would even facilitate Peyrouton's trip to North Africa. We felt, however, that in reaching any final judgment the political connotations involved in Peyrouton's arrival in North Africa should be evaluated, particularly in view of his former position as Vichy's Minister of the Interior.

General Eisenhower and Robert Murphy cabled General Marshall and me on December 13, recalling that, although Peyrouton had been associated with the Vichy regime in 1940, he was one of the key men who had caused the downfall of Laval because he disapproved thoroughly of Laval's policy of collaboration with the Axis. They said they had no doubt of his anti-Axis sentiments. Because he had once been Resident General in Tunis he could well qualify as either Resident General of Morocco or Governor General of Algeria.

We accordingly arranged travel facilities for Peyrouton, who arrived in Algiers on January 16, 1943, and was named by Darlan to be Governor General of Algeria. Instantly he became a focus for bitter attacks by the De Gaulle group, which lasted until pressure from De Gaulle forced him out six months later.

De Gaulle had been eager to negotiate an agreement with Giraud to unite all French anti-Axis elements into one movement, probably under his own control; but he refused to deal with Darlan, and he withdrew the representatives he had sent to talk to Giraud. To ease the situation, the President suggested to Churchill that a Briton and an American be appointed to whom would be given, not authority to administer civil functions, but a veto over French civil administrators and the power to direct them in rare instances to follow out certain policies. When Churchill agreed the President named Robert D. Murphy as his personal representative on General Eisenhower's staff, with the rank of Minister.

When Admiral d'Argenlieu, De Gaulle's representative in the Pacific, accompanied by the Free French representative Adrien Tixier, called on me on December 8 while passing through Washington en route to London, I took the opportunity to emphasize our views because I knew he would shortly see De Gaulle personally. I said that, although General Giraud had been at first the choice of American military leaders, even this great French General, on arriving in Africa, found he was unable to command the support of the French armed forces. Undoubtedly the reason for this was that for two years previously Admiral Darlan had been filling all places of importance with his own followers.

However, I went on, Giraud was a big enough man to realize that when he could not command the necessary support he should subordinate himself to Admiral Darlan. The latter had appeared on the scene entirely unexpectedly, but was able to prove that the fighting strength of the French in North Africa was under his orders. This military cooperation of Admiral Darlan had saved the lives of many American soldiers even in the first days of occupation; but when the lives saved by the cooperation of French West Africa were added as well, the total mounted into very impressive figures. Also, our military plans were advanced at least sixty days by French cooperation under Darlan, and thus we were sixty days nearer contact with the Germans, and sixty days nearer the winning of the war.

"If I were attacked by a thug on the street," I said, "and someone came to my assistance, I would welcome the assistance of this collaborator in destroying the would-be murderer. But I would not stop fighting to ask this unexpected collaborator to tell me his name and antecedents.

"In wartime one should be wary of politicians. I have been a politician myself all my life, and I know they have limitations in a purely military effort.

"However, I do think that a great deal of the alleged fear of Darlan as a menace to France at this particular moment is somewhat exaggerated. I cannot conceive that Darlan in North Africa, an unsettled area that at most has less than three million European inhabitants, can impose himself on the French nation of forty-five millions as a political figure if the French people do not wish it. I am quite sure in my own mind that the French people do not wish this. Therefore Admiral Darlan remains a military figure, and his only collaboration with the United States is purely a military arrangement. The British and American fleets are in control of the Mediterranean, and this in itself controls Darlan's approach to France."

I added that De Gaulle stood for something very special to all Americans, and it was their prayer that all Frenchmen who could contribute to a military victory that would restore France to her independence would give their fullest military cooperation in the war against Hitler, leaving all politics aside.

At the end of our talk M. Tixier said he had never had so clear a picture of our attitude toward the French situation. Admiral d'Argenlieu echoed this thought.

After a conversation with the President, I cabled our Legation at Cairo on December 14 to inform Admiral Godefroy, who commanded the French naval squadron tied up at Alexandria, that the President would be pleased to have his squadron come to America for repairs and refit to join with us against the common enemy under the same arrangements as had been made with other patriotic Frenchmen in Africa. Godefroy did not accept this invitation, but after a few months he joined his squadron to the naval forces of the French in North Africa, and the uncertainty that had persisted with regard to this unit since June, 1940, was at last resolved.

De Gaulle's propaganda machine in England, with its offshoots here, was now grinding out violent attacks against the French set-up in North Africa, with scarcely veiled assaults against us for being responsible for it. A new hair-trigger situation was fast developing.

When British Ambassador Halifax called on me on December 21, 1942, I reminded him that the President had made one or more worldwide appeals, and I had made two such appeals, for the unification of all United Nations military forces and all peoples behind the lines in support of those forces. I emphatically remarked that not one word had come from the British Government along the same line; instead, constant reports of a trouble-making nature relating to De Gaulle and the United States, De Gaulle and Darlan, or De Gaulle and some other disturbing factor had come to us from our Embassy in London and through the British press and radio.

"The war," I said, "is not yet won. It could be lost. The battle of Africa is not won, and it's not at all certain that the last word has been spoken in Spain. The situation behind the lines in Africa is as difficult and delicate as it can possibly be. In these circumstances, it seems to me that the British Government could serve the Allied cause very well by putting out to the world an earnest appeal for unity and teamwork among all the United Nations."

Halifax said he would present the matter to his Government.

During this conversation I brought up with the Ambassador the likelihood of conflict at Djibouti, French Somaliland, where the British were trying to induce the French Governor to permit them to occupy the colony. I said this Government was not disposed to interfere with British measures in the situation at Djibouti, provided the British did not get into a military clash with the French resulting in French blood being shed. Such a development, I said, would play havoc with our situation in North and West Africa and materially affect the prosecution of the African campaign, if not the war itself.

Halifax said he fully appreciated this view, with which he personally agreed, and would present it to London.

Three days later, as the situation at Djibouti continued dangerous, I suggested to Halifax that the British and American Governments between them select two individuals, who would, in turn, choose a suitable Frenchman not conspicuously identified with either the Darlan or the De Gaulle faction, to become head of French civil affairs at Djibouti. Halifax communicated this to his Government. Although this suggestion was not carried out, Britain followed our exhortation to handle the situation gently, and eventually French Somaliland came into the United Nations cause without bloodshed.

But on the day of my conversation with Halifax, Christmas Eve, Admiral Darlan was assassinated at Algiers.

I had never held any brief for Darlan's activities at Vichy. I had condemned them in the strongest words possible. But there was no blinking the fact that he had been of great assistance to our landing in North Africa.

Both the President and I excoriated the assassination. "The all-important consideration," I said to the press, "is that we be not diverted for a moment from the supreme objective of the United Nations in the present battle against the Axis forces for control of the African continent and the Mediterranean. This battle is still at a crucial and critical stage. The fullest measure of unified support is needed by General Eisenhower and his associates.

"Of Admiral Darlan, it may be repeated that the part he played in North Africa related primarily to the military situation and was of incalculable aid to the Allied armies in the battle which is still raging. His assassination was an odious and cowardly act."

The slaying of Admiral Darlan did nothing to moderate the savage warfare of propaganda, maneuvering, and pressure raging between the two major French factions, the De Gaullists and the anti-de Gaullists. Late in December and in January the De Gaullist press and radio attacks from British soil against the French administration in North Africa reached a new crescendo, and our Government found itself in the midst of the barrage. General Giraud had taken over the leadership of the French in North Africa, in agreement with General Eisenhower, and the De Gaullist propaganda artillery was now aimed at him.

I called to my office on December 31 British Minister Sir Ronald Campbell, in the absence of Halifax, to express the serious concern that many members of our Government and I felt over the course of what seemed to be British policy, more or less, to back up De Gaulle publicity aimed directly at this Government. I added that this propaganda was resented by many Americans. Our Government was doing all in its power to protect the British Government from attacks here, especially attacks on British policy with respect to India; but at the same time the British were more and more creating the impression that they were rather closely associated with De Gaulle's widespread propaganda which was constantly attacking this Government in the most sweeping fashion. I concluded that I did not see how matters could drift on in this manner much longer without unfortunate results.

De Gaulle made a radio broadcast and issued a general public statement on January 2, 1943, which constituted a wholly unjustified attack on the United States Government. Lord Halifax said to me on January 5 that Foreign Secretary Eden had communicated to him that he had tried to stop De Gaulle from making the broadcast and issuing the statement, but had failed.

"The public in this country," I commented, "is rapidly reaching the conclusion that De Gaulle is primarily interested not in winning the extremely crucial battle in Africa, but in dismissing the military side of the battle while negotiations are carried on to settle his demands for political supremacy in one form or another in the French Empire. It's reported here that the entire British press and radio and many British leaders of public thought devoted the better part of the two days following De Gaulle's broadcast to shouting their approval. And this was going on in Great Britain while the battle for most of Africa and the western Mediterranean area had become increasingly serious, and while the American and French generals in command had to give up their military emergency duties and go to the rear in an effort to calm a confused situation and discuss the political aspirations of De Gaulle when approached by his representatives there."

I concluded by saying that the impression spreading in the United States, that Britain was supporting De Gaulle in his movement for political preferment at the expense of the prosecution of the African battle, would soon create real differences between our two countries. No one, I knew, would regret such a development more than the Minister and myself.

Two days later Campbell came to my office with a memorandum containing views that Mr. Churchill and Eden wished to present to me. This was in answer to the strong representations I had made to Halifax and Campbell in preceding days. Mr. Churchill and Eden said they themselves had been ceaselessly exposed to "emotional views of little men on political matters," and to check this entirely would involve their Government in a direct attack on freedom of Parliament and press. There was a deep loathing in Britain, particularly strong among the working classes, against anything that savored of intrigues with Darlan and Vichy. There was almost a passion on the subject, they insisted; and if it broke loose it would certainly cause differences of opinion and controversy in the United States.

The Prime Minister and the Foreign Secretary said they had done their very best to help in the Darlan business and continued to do so with regard to Vichy contacts still being preserved in North Africa; but the general feeling was that a brilliant military episode had been tarnished and tainted.

After reading this memorandum, I remarked to Minister Campbell that I wished to correct any impression that we were urging rigid censorship of the British press and radio which was supporting in the loudest and most extravagant ways De Gaulle's desire for supreme political control of France. I added that when I was at the London Economic Conference in 1933 the British Government had only to indicate to the press the line of attack it desired made on some of the issues raised and the press promptly complied.

"I insist," I said, "that where there is a plain and palpable interference with the prosecution of the North African campaign by pure brazen politics it is high time, in my opinion, that this should receive the serious attention of the British Government."

Minister Campbell handed me a further memorandum which proposed a settlement between De Gaulle and Giraud. This called for the establishment at Algiers of a single French authority to take the place of both the French National Committee in London and Giraud's administration in North Africa. This authority would not be recognized as the Government or even the provisional Government of France; but it would maintain relations with foreign governments, it would be treated as an Allied Power and be formally admitted to the ranks of the United Nations.

As I talked over these developments with the President, he decided to make a personal effort to bring about an understanding between De Gaulle and Giraud. He and Prime Minister Churchill agreed in exchanges of messages to go to Casablanca, French Morocco, for a conference at which De Gaulle and Giraud would be brought together. He left for Casablanca at the beginning of January, 1943.

A few days after his arrival in Casablanca, I received a message from him on January 18, in which he said, in paraphrase:

"We produced the bridegroom, General Giraud, who cooperated very nicely on the proposed nuptials and was prepared to go through with it on our terms, I am sure. Our friends, however, could not produce De Gaulle, the temperamental bride. She has become quite high hat about the whole affair and doesn't wish to see either of us, and shows no intention of getting into the bed with Giraud. We intend to do the best we can under these circumstances, and I believe can turn out something fairly good from it all. Giraud seems to me to be a man who wants to fight, and is not greatly interested in civil matters."

The "temperamental bride" did make an appearance in the course of the next few days and conversed at length with the "bridegroom." No agreement as to political nuptials ensued, however, and De Gaulle returned to London to renew his attacks on all French elements that had not embraced his movement, showing particular venom toward Giraud.

After the President returned to Washington he became angered at these attacks. His feeling was all the more acute because he had made a genuine effort to bring the two French leaders together in effective cooperation.

Mr. Roosevelt recounted to me the difficulty he and Mr. Churchill had had in getting De Gaulle to go from London to Casablanca. Churchill, he said, had urgently communicated with De Gaulle in London, requesting his immediate presence for a conference at Casablanca with the President and himself. De Gaulle in effect ignored the request. Churchill made a second attempt, with the same result. Then the President, knowing that De Gaulle was totally dependent on British subsidies, insisted to Churchill that if the Prime Minister would send a message to London threatening in earnest to drop De Gaulle from his payroll, the Free French leader would probably change his mind. This Churchill did, with the result that De Gaulle appeared at Casablanca posthaste.

The President said also that De Gaulle, walking up to him rather stiffly, remarked, "I am Joan of Arc. I am Clemenceau." Mr. Roosevelt commented pointedly to me on the contrast between the two characters De Gaulle professed to embody.

From the time of the Casablanca Conference the President refused to warm up to General de Gaulle and his movement except to pursue the policy of giving him full military aid. On February 3, at his request, I cabled H. Freeman Matthews, our Chargé in London, asking him to deliver this message to Eden from me:

"The President has shown some annoyance at the continued propaganda emanating from the De Gaulle headquarters in London. The President labels their attitude as a continuing irritant. He knows that the Prime Minister would agree with him and hopes that you can take further steps to allay the irritation."

Our troubles did not stem entirely from De Gaulle; we had our difficulties with Giraud as well, but they were not nearly so thorny. On January 24 the President and Giraud had drawn up a memorandum whereby Mr. Roosevelt agreed that Giraud should be considered as the trustee for French interests in French North Africa. Mr. Churchill had gone on to Turkey from Casablanca, and when he returned to Algiers he thought the language of the memorandum too broad. Consequently Churchill, Giraud, and Robert Murphy drew up a new memorandum, which General Eisenhower approved. Murphy cabled this to me on February 6, 1943.

Article Three of this memorandum stated that the French nation and people were the only ones who could fix their representation and designate their Government. Because it was impossible for the French motherland to pronounce freely her will, France did not now possess a recognizable Government, and the question of the future Government of France was not capable now of final solution.

Article Four was the one relating to Giraud. This stated: "In the interests of the French people, in order to safeguard France's past, her present, and her future, the President of the United States of America and the British Prime Minister attribute to the French Commander-in-Chief, with his headquarters at Algiers, the right and duty of acting as a trustee for French interests, military, economic, and financial, in French territories, which are associated or which hereafter become associated with the movement of liberation now established in French North and West Africa. They bind themselves to aid him in this task by all means in their power."

Murphy quoted Giraud as saying to Mr. Churchill and to him that he had understood from his conversation with the President that Mr. Roosevelt favored Giraud's representation of French interests in the United States. He also said he hoped the British would support him in prevailing upon the French National Committee to cease its vindictive and personal radio campaign against certain Frenchmen in North Africa who were wholeheartedly and sincerely engaged in prosecuting the war against the Axis.

While we were analyzing this memorandum, we received a second cable from Murphy stating that General Giraud wished the President to confirm that he recognized the Commander-in-Chief residing in Algiers as the trustee of French interests in the United States as well as in other countries "of American influences." At the same time the American press carried an interview with Giraud's assistant, M. Gentil, announcing his intention of visiting Latin American countries to obtain their reaction "to the possibility of recognizing the North African Government as legal for all France."

My associates and I thereupon drew up a memorandum for the President, which I sent him on February 11. This attached Murphy's telegram of February 6, communicating the text of the new memorandum, and referred to his cable of February 9 and the Gentil interview.

"These reports," I said, "suggest the desirability of making our position on the subject entirely clear in order that there may be no doubt in the mind of anyone, including General Giraud and General de Gaulle, concerning our interpretation of Article Four."

I attached the draft of a cable that I proposed, if the President approved, to send to Murphy. Following Mr. Roosevelt's approval, this went out February 15. It stated that a number of circumstances made it desirable that there be no doubt in the mind of General Giraud concerning our interpretation of the memorandum. Our position, as determined by the President, was this:

The question of recognition of a French Government until the French people were free to express their will was disposed of by Article Three. This therefore disposed of the question of a French diplomatic or consular service.

We regarded Giraud as the trustee of French North African interests in the United States. We should welcome civilian representation from him on the French military mission in the United States. We did not recognize Giraud as a trustee of French interests in the United States not associated with his movement. Giraud was, of course, aware of our relationship with the French National Committee.

As for the question of representation in other countries, including the Latin American Republics, this was entirely between Giraud and the countries concerned. If they asked us for advice we would inform them of the position we had taken.

Within these limits Giraud could count on our full cooperation.

My thought was that it was better for Giraud and all concerned not to play into the hands of De Gaulle and his professional agitators. Without giving these agitators any new material to keep up their agitation, there would be little left for them to seize upon.

After further exchanges to clarify the memorandum, the President approved the agreement with Giraud on March 27.

It may thus be seen that the President and I had no intention to set up Giraud in opposition to De Gaulle as representing or heading a French Government fighting the Axis. We were opposed to setting up anyone in a capacity that would automatically make him a ruler of France when she should be liberated by the American and British armies. Our major interest was the protection of the right of the French people to make their own choice.

88: Churchill and Eden

IN THE MIDST of our numerous problems in foreign relations during the first half of 1943, another fight faced the Administration over whether the Trade Agreements Act was to be renewed. Since the beginning of the year my associates and I had prepared for our fourth struggle on behalf of the trade agreements policy, which began with the Act of 1934, and was extended for three years in 1937 and again for three years in 1940.

There persisted somewhat the same arguments in opposition that were made in 1940, when the battle against trade agreements was bitter; namely, that the advent of war had so dislocated trade as to render 'them useless. But the fact that the agreements during the ensuing three years had continued to operate effectively wherever it was possible for them to do so, rendered these arguments less efficacious, and the struggle to preserve the policy in 1943 was much less intense.

By this time we had trade agreements with twenty-seven countries. The war, however, with its special demands, had reduced the proportion of our foreign trade affected by the trade agreements program. Generally our trade was being conducted for the purpose of supplying the sinews of battle. On the other hand, the Lend-Lease program had enabled us to incorporate Article VII into the Lend-Lease agreements whereby the signatories agreed to the elimination of all forms of discriminatory treatment in international commerce and the reduction of tariff and other trade barriers after the war. Britain, China, the Soviet Union, Belgium, Poland, The Netherlands, Greece, Czechoslovakia, Norway, Yugoslavia, Australia, New Zealand, and Canada had accepted this clause.

I appeared before the House Ways and Means Committee on April 12, 1943, to argue for a three-year extension of the Trade Agreements Act. I pointed out that of the twenty-seven countries with which we had concluded trade agreements, only tragic Finland was then at war with any of our allies, and even she was not at war with us. Of the others, sixteen were now by our side, at war with our enemies. Six of the remaining ten had broken off relations with the Axis countries and were cooperating with us in many ways. The remaining four were neutral, and one of these, Switzerland, was representing American interests in the countries controlled by the enemy.

"The nations," I said, "which entered into trade agreements did so because they were peace-loving nations, seeking peaceful relations in all respects, economic and political. It is no accident, therefore, that in the searching test to which individuals and nations are being subjected in this war, those nations which have entered into a cooperative economic relationship with us through the conclusion of trade agreements are opposing rather than aiding the forces of aggression.

"As we look into the future, it is this theme of international cooperation that should be uppermost in our minds if we really want to make sure that another world conflict is not to be ahead of us after we win this war."

When victory came, I emphasized, we and other nations would have before us a choice of courses. Basically, that choice, even as it was in 1918, would be on the one hand between extreme nationalism, growing rivalries, jealousies, and hatreds—with the ultimate certainty of another and even more devastating war—and on the other hand increased international cooperation in a wide variety of fields, and at least the hope of secure peace for our children.

I pleaded for nonpartisan support of the trade agreements, saying that this was neither Republican nor Democratic doctrine, but American doctrine, and the greater the extent to which we could get it accepted by other nations, the better would be the prospect for our own future prosperity and peace.

I appeared before the Senate Finance Committee on May 17 to carry this argument still further.

The House of Representatives by a vote of 343 to 65, passed a resolution to extend the Act for two years instead of the three years we had asked for. The Representatives believed that within those two years the war would be over, and the issue could then be reviewed. The Senate on June 2 approved the resolution in this form by 59 to 23 votes, and the President signed it on June 7.

The Trade Agreements Act thus remained on the statute books during the difficult days of international trade in wartime. The trade agreements continued to exist to furnish, along with Article VII of the Lend-Lease master agreements, a sound basis on which to build economic relationships for the years to follow the war.

In the spring of 1943 Prime Minister Churchill and Foreign Secretary Eden paid separate visits to Washington, and their presence here furnished an excellent opportunity to thrash out a number of questions, some of which were disturbing our relations. Chief among them was France.

Before I left Washington on February 25 for a rest at Palm Beach I asked Eden by cable to postpone his visit for a few days. After I arrived in Florida, Welles informed me it was not convenient for Eden to delay his visit. He said that the President and he, Welles, thought it was all right for Eden to come on, that they would take care of our side of the conversations, and that I should remain in Florida to complete my rest.

I was on the train that night for Washington, cutting my vacation five days short, and arrived Sunday March 14.

Eden, with Ambassador Halifax, came in to see me the following day. We at once took up the Free French situation and its bearing on the relations between Britain and the United States. Eden did not seem to me to be familiar with the United States' side of the question. I therefore gave him a complete exposition of our policy toward Vichy, the Free French, and the French people as a whole, from the time of the fall of Paris on. I emphasized the fact that Mr. Churchill in 1941 had in writing strongly urged this Government to maintain its policy toward Vichy, and that on other occasions, including his two visits to this country, he personally had urged me to continue it by all means. Mr. Churchill had said, among other things, that, if the United States discontinued relations with Vichy, the French fleet would go over to the Germans, thus giving the balance of power in the Mediterranean to the enemy.

I said to Eden that De Gaulle had rarely ever approached this Government except for political recognition, and he had never engaged in serious discussion of the military situation. "This Government," I said, "not deeming it practical to become involved in French politics, consistently declined to join in the desires of De Gaulle for general and world-wide political recognition. And, so far as I know, that's the sum total of his grievance against us."

The American Government, I emphasized, had no ill will toward De Gaulle; but we regretted that he seemed to be so constituted, temperamentally at least, that he sought political preferment in the main. I quoted Mr. Churchill as saying to us that De Gaulle was a most difficult person to get along with and had given the British almost unlimited trouble. I concluded by saying that if there were other cases of temperament like De Gaulle's they would materially interfere with the military undertakings of our Government.

Eden made a mild effort to justify Great Britain's course by mentioning the aid that De Gaulle had given Britain in the war. I contended that the tremendous aid the United States had given Britain and the whole

Allied cause through its Vichy policy more than counterbalanced this assistance.

The following day Eden and Halifax called and handed me a statement Mr. Churchill proposed to make in the House of Commons on the
next day, and expressed a desire that we approve it and release one of our
own here at the same time. This statement backed up the speech General
Giraud had just made in which he abolished French legislation in North
Africa subsequent to June 22, 1940, thus removing all race distinction between native Moslems and Jews. Giraud declared that municipal assem-
blies and general councils would resume their traditional role with their
members elected by the people.

After telephoning the President, I prepared and released a statement
in which I said we were in the heartiest accord with the British Prime
Minister's timely and splendid statement and we found satisfaction in
strongly commending the further step toward French unity taken by
Giraud. I had already, on March 15, made a public statement heartily
praising Giraud's speech as making it possible "for all elements who desire the defeat of the Axis powers and the liberation of French territory
to unite in their will to rid French soil of the weight of the Axis yoke."

I again took up with Eden on March 22 the question of North Africa
and the position of the De Gaulle organization. I commented that De
Gaulle had apparently entrenched himself with the support of large British
newspapers, which at times he turned loose on us with bitter criticism of
certain attitudes and policies of this Government that did not please him.
This had the effect of confusing public opinion and diverting it from the
main purpose we were determined to accomplish in North Africa—the
defeat of the enemy and the liberation of that area from Axis domination.

"The people of this country," I said, "are now of course able to
see what we are driving at. They thoroughly understand that we consider
the fighting of the enemy our first aim, and that we have continually had
in mind and have never lost sight of the gradual liberalization of conditions in North Africa, promoting all such steps along these lines as might
be possible without interfering with the military situation."

I then remarked that, during the time so many attacks had been
directed against American policies, no statement had ever been made by
Mr. Churchill, Eden, or any official of the British Government. It would
be extremely helpful in promoting and sustaining good relationships between the British and American peoples for more public concurrence with
American policy to be expressed from time to time. I asked Eden point-

blank whether officials of the British Government could not occasionally drop some appropriate statement with respect to this as we went along.

Eden readily agreed that something might be done along these lines, but I did not gain the impression that either he or Halifax was convinced of the advisability of the British Government's taking action to indicate solidarity with the American viewpoint.

I said to Eden we had information that De Gaulle was making another drive for political power. In connection with the forthcoming conversations between his organization and the Giraud authorities in North Africa he fully expected to press for control, as political head, of whatever form of cooperation might result from the talks. I remarked that our own policy toward the French situation had always been that no supreme political power should be set up now to exercise control over the French people. No provisional Government should be created or recognized, and any political activities should be kept to the minimum dictated by necessity.

Eden said it was his understanding that De Gaulle did not want to set up either a Government or a provisional Government, but did want to establish a unified French authority that could deal with French questions all over the world. He asked whether there would be any objection on our part to the creation and recognition of some central authority of this kind.

I replied that it was our earnest desire to have the French factions settle these questions among themselves. Up to that time we had recognized the authority of each group with respect to the territory in which it was operating. We particularly desired to refrain from introducing political questions into our relations with different French factions. We had always stressed our desire that these French organizations should have a military character.

Eden then asked whether, assuming that the French got together and agreed on a unified authority that might deal with questions affecting all territories then under French control, such an arrangement would be satisfactory to this Government.

I said that it seemed to me perfectly possible for the French factions to agree on certain things, but that we must always consider the true relation of such a unified action. It would not be possible for them to be considered as having political authority with respect to the French people or the disposition of French territories before it became possible for the French people to reestablish their own Government by their own will.

Halifax then posed two questions. One: Was it desirable for Giraud and De Gaulle to get together? Two: In getting together and making it clear that the formation of their organization was purely temporary and did not prejudice any future authority for France, was it possible for them to form some organism comparable to the French National Committee in London?

I replied that if such a committee were formed it was absolutely essential to avoid the picture that was presented by some of the refugee Governments which would try to go back to their countries and carry on the authority that they had exercised while in exile. It was our opinion that some refugee Governments, which had experienced numerous changes of personnel, were no longer representative of the will of their peoples.

"Particularly in the case of France," I said, "which has no Government, it seems to me that it would be inadvisable for any political power to be assumed by such an organization."

Eden said his Government would say "No" to any question of a Government of France, even provisional, but did not object to a rather larger French National Committee composed of people from both French factions. The British Government would consider that these persons were not officials but merely place holders temporarily dealing with questions that might affect French interests everywhere.

Prime Minister Churchill came to the United States in May, 1943, at the moment when the last Axis resistance in North Africa ceased and the vast African continent passed wholly into the hands of the Allies.

At that moment, too, General de Gaulle was making almost frantic efforts to fly to Algiers for a conference with General Giraud, with the probable intention of bringing Giraud into his movement and himself taking charge in North Africa.

The President gave me on May 8 a memorandum he intended handing Mr. Churchill, and asked my comments. In it he said that the issue presented in the French situation had come to a head and we must take a definite position that would determine the future of the controversy.

I handed the President on May 10 a memorandum in which I agreed with his premise and added that if the controversy, although outwardly between two French factions, were permitted to continue it might involve both the British and the American Government in difficulties.

The issue at stake, I commented, was not only the success of our future military operations, but also the very future of France itself. I was in complete agreement with the statement in the President's memorandum that United Nations military forces must be on hand in France at the conclusion of hostilities to prevent anarchy and remain just as long a period as the French people in metropolitan France, unhampered and un-threatened, needed to formulate machinery to carry on a French Government.

"It is very evident," I said, "that the French National Committee is basing its whole policy on the idea that, when France is liberated from the Germans, organized elements under De Gaulle may be in control. At the moment, this policy is leading the De Gaullists to attack all French and other elements not with them. To obtain this control, De Gaulle has permitted to come under his umbrella all the most radical elements in France. Under their statement of April 1, the Communists in France, probably the most highly organized political group there today, have announced their insistence that De Gaulle be their leader."

My memorandum pointed out that the British Government had given its full financial and official weight to the De Gaulle movement. Thus the active propaganda carried on in the United States and in North Africa against all elements insisting on the free and untrammeled will of the French people to determine their own future had had more weight than would have been otherwise possible.

"Today, however, we face a situation," I said, "where De Gaulle's active political propaganda directed from London immediately threatens the military success against the Axis Powers to which we have dedicated our every effort. It cannot but be realized from your message of congratulation for the Allied victory in North Africa that the real French contribution was given by the French forces under General Giraud, while throughout the period of the battle De Gaulle, through his political agitation directed from London, caused nothing but disturbance and concern to our military commanders."

The remedy for this situation, I pointed out, was in our hands today, but might not be tomorrow. We therefore had to reach an agreement with the British on the fundamental question of the future of France and the manner in which the free expression of the French will as to their Government might be obtained.

If this agreement with the British could not be reached, I recommended that the President state candidly in his forthcoming conversation with Mr. Churchill: "Since General Giraud is fully cooperating and contributing to the military purposes we had in view, and his military aid in North Africa is an essential in our war effort, we intend to support him in every way as military head of the French Allied forces whose collaboration is not only essential to the British and Americans, but to the cause of the United Nations as well."

The President, after reading this memorandum, readily agreed with my various points, and said he would take them up with Mr. Churchill.

Mr. Roosevelt made little headway with the Prime Minister, however, and he therefore asked Mr. Churchill to talk to me on the subject. The distinguished visitor thereupon asked me to call upon him at the White House for a private talk, which I did on May 13.

He began the conversation by expressing his extreme gratification at the final and complete military victory in Africa.

I interjected to say, " 'Your' and our Vichy policy has been justified and vindicated 100 per cent."

He promptly replied with enthusiasm that it had been vindicated 140 per cent. It had been one of the greatest classical operations, perfect in every essential respect in that the air, land, and naval forces and the diplomatic activities of our Governments were all synchronized with great precision and thrown against the enemy with the most powerful effect.

The Prime Minister said that the United States had not received credit for the two years' work of paving the way for the African expedition under our Vichy policy.

"I must agree with you on that," I remarked, "but one of these days the full facts will come out."

Mr. Churchill said the President had suggested he might talk to me about De Gaulle. He was not pushing forward De Gaulle, he pointed out, although he had heard it reported that we felt that De Gaulle was receiving British financial support with which to do the things that were most objectionable to us. He and Eden found De Gaulle terrible to get on with, and he wanted it understood that they were not undertaking to build him up. He added that we on the other hand should not get behind Giraud and pit him against De Gaulle, one reason being that De Gaulle was considered a symbol of French resistance and the British just could not throw him overboard, notwithstanding his many very objectionable and difficult ways.

"The one big point in the situation," I said, "that should appeal to both our Governments alike is that if this De Gaulle matter is allowed to go forward as it has been, it will undoubtedly bring about serious friction between our two Governments. Large sections of people in this country will finally become aroused through false propaganda and constant agitations and machinations on the part of the De Gaulle organization, and in turn the two Governments will be subject to repercussions that will seriously affect the relations between them."

I said there was nothing personal implied in my remarks, but I wished to point out with emphasis the poisonous propaganda activities of the De Gaulle organization both in this country and in North Africa. In the latter area the purpose seemed to be to undermine and break down support of Giraud and then for De Gaulle to take charge politically from top to bottom and transplant this organization to metropolitan France.

De Gaullist agents were then trying to wean French sailors away from French ships touching at American ports and to induce them to become De Gaullists by offering them higher salaries. At the President's orders, following a request from the Giraud mission, the sailors who left their ships were treated by our immigration authorities as deserters. This was to prevent further desertions and the immobilization of the French ships. The De Gaulle group, of course, demanded their release.

I called these incidents to the Prime Minister's attention, saying that wherever a De Gaulle representative went he kept everything in an uproar. I then made very emphatic more than once the universal belief that the British were definitely behind such De Gaullist actions with money, the aid of their radio stations, and through other methods.

Mr. Churchill replied, first, that he personally was utterly disgusted with De Gaulle and, second, that the British were not aiding him as much as I seemed to think.

I suggested that there were numerous ways for the British to get away from their build-up of De Gaulle, rapidly or gradually, if the latter course should prove necessary.

I made no special impression on the Prime Minister concerning this point, since he continued to urge that this Government should not support Giraud to the point of engaging in a quarrel with De Gaulle and the British. I replied that this would be the inevitable outcome of the British policy in regard to De Gaulle.

Our conversation ended without any particular accord. On May 19, 1943, I sent the President a dispatch from Robert D. Murphy in Algiers quoting General Catroux, one of De Gaulle's principal lieutenants, in a very frank revelation of some of the machinations going on within the De Gaulle committee to get full control over all French elements. Catroux showed Murphy a long communication from De Gaulle expressing the greatest distrust of American policy, which he asserted was opposed to French unity and a strong France, and fear that the United States was

counting on an early Italian debacle and would make concessions to Italy
at the expense of France in order to arrive at an early armistice.

Catroux recommended that the British and American Governments
take a definite stand, making it clear that they supported fully the idea
of French unity but opposed De Gaulle's drive for personal power. He
pointed out that the British Government had ample means at its disposal
to insist on the termination of De Gaulle's present tactics.

In an accompanying memorandum, I said to the President: "I feel
that you and Prime Minister Churchill are becoming more and more
equally interested in disposing of this increasingly troublesome and serious, not to say dangerous problem."

Mr. Roosevelt was unable, however, to win Mr. Churchill to the full
and definite agreement both he and I desired.

At the end of May, De Gaulle, following numerous exchanges of messages with General Giraud, finally flew to Algiers for conferences with him.
He immediately exerted all the pressure he could command to obtain control in North Africa, and met with much success. Marcel Peyrouton, Governor General of Algeria, who was among the first on De Gaulle's black-
list, resigned to become an infantry captain.

Then on June 3 De Gaulle and Giraud announced the formation of
the French Committee of National Liberation, of which they were co-presi-
dents. They proclaimed the committee as the French central power, which
would direct the French war effort in all forms and in all places and
would exercise French sovereignty in all territories placed beyond the
enemies' power.

Regardless of the tactics of pressure used by De Gaulle to achieve
this end, the President and I, after consultation with Mr. Churchill and
Eden, decided to accept this development in the hope that it would end the
bitter fighting between French factions and bring them unity of action.
The committee, moreover, had announced that it would turn over its
powers to the provisional French Government that would be established
as soon as permitted by the liberation of metropolitan France.

On June 8 Henri Hoppenot, chief ad interim of the French Military
Purchasing Commission, and Philippe Baudet, delegate ad interim of the
French National Committee in the United States, called on me and handed
me a notice of the formation of the French Committee of National Liberation and the text of the declaration establishing it.

I said to them that, as was well known, this Government had con-
tinuously hoped for the unification of all French resistants in a common

effort against Axis aggression, wherever it might be found throughout the world. I therefore warmly welcomed the spirit in which the French Committee of National Liberation had been formed.

I concluded by expressing deep appreciation of the spirit of sacrifice that had made the union of true French interests possible, and added the conviction that the same spirit would continue to animate all Frenchmen in meeting the problems still to be faced for the liberation of continental France.

We made this statement public the following day, while Prime Minister Churchill communicated somewhat the same thought to the House of Commons.

The President's thoughts toward the French Committee, however, were clearly indicated in a memorandum he wrote following his receipt on June 6, of a memorandum from Robert Sherwood of the Office of War Information, who suggested that France be included among the United Nations in the celebration of United Nations Day on June 14, and that the President make a statement for the inauguration of a new radio station near Algiers on that day. Mr. Roosevelt's memorandum, addressed on June 8 to his executive secretary, Stephen T. Early, said: "Will you talk with Cordell about this? I have distinct doubts as to whether a United France should be included in the roster of the United Nations next Monday. I should say that was premature. Also I hesitate to make any statement."

Early sent this to me for my comment. I replied on June 10 that, while we had been notified that the French Committee of National Liberation had been formed, there were many unsettled questions as to the committee's future. Consequently we agreed with the President that any action at this time looking to the admission of the French into the United Nations would be premature. Furthermore, I concluded, it was our custom to consult certain other United Nations before admitting new members.

Despite our new note of friendship toward the French committee, there still remained two basic questions. One was our desire that General Giraud should be left in full command of the French military establishment in North Africa—for it was vital that no disturbance should cut athwart our lines of communication and supply. On June 19 the British and ourselves requested assurances from both De Gaulle and Giraud that there would be no important change in the French command in North Africa at present. Giraud continued as the French commander, at least for the time being.

Prime Minister Churchill was in full agreement with the President on this military question. He cabled on June 18 that it was imperative that the French Army in North Africa, especially on the eve of the great operation then pending (the invasion of Sicily) should be in loyal and trustworthy hands. He said he agreed with the President that no confidence could be placed in De Gaulle's friendship for the Allies, and he himself could not be responsible to the British nation whose armies had been placed under Eisenhower's command if the existence of a French Army under potentially hostile control, not properly subordinated to the Supreme Command, disturbed or endangered the Allied base and lines of communication. He expressed his pleasure at the clear instructions the President had given to General Eisenhower not to permit De Gaulle to direct, or to control through his partisans, the French Army in North Africa in the field of supplies, training, or operations.

The second question was the degree of official recognition to be given the new committee. Was it to be regarded as a provisional government or was it not? This question was to be partly settled at the First Quebec Conference, which was now in the offing.

The question that further troubled us was whether De Gaulle was going to be content with his apparent copartnership with Giraud, or whether he intended to maneuver within the new committee so as to obtain complete control. We had every reason to suspect the latter.

I now began to get a few indications that Prime Minister Churchill's attitude toward De Gaulle, despite the agreement between De Gaulle and Giraud in Algiers, was becoming more barbed. Eden, however, was not keeping pace with Mr. Churchill in this change.

British Ambassador Halifax called on June 17 to hand me an *aide-mémoire* from his Government which stated that British subsidies to De Gaulle's headquarters in London were being terminated, and any future payments would be made to the French Committee of National Liberation at Algiers.

Calculating the amount of the subsidy, as based on the June payment of £1,300,000, I estimated that the British had been paying De Gaulle's headquarters annually a minimum of $60,000,000. Unfortunately, some of this subsidy had financed De Gaulle's attacks on the United States Government.

On the same day Robert D. Murphy in Algiers cabled me the British press guidance that had come from the Prime Minister. This stated that Mr. Churchill was concerned at the apparent bias in favor of De Gaulle in press messages from Algiers and in their presentation in England. De Gaulle, the Prime Minister said, owed everything to British assistance and support; but he could not be considered a trustworthy friend of Britain. Wherever he had been he had left a trail of Anglophobia behind him. He had made many attempts to play Britain against the United States, and vice versa. He had done his utmost to cause friction between British and French in Syria. It was part of his strategy to gain prestige in France by showing how rough he could be with the British and French and now with the Americans. He had undoubtedly fascist and dictatorial tendencies. At one time he represented himself as a sole barrier against Communism; at another, as enjoying Communist support. The Prime Minister pointed out that President Roosevelt, the best and truest friend that Britain and Europe ever had had, maintained strong views on the subject of De Gaulle.

Within the lines of this dispatch I could detect some results of the emphatic talks the President and I had had with the Prime Minister concerning De Gaulle.

Lord Halifax called on June 24 to inform me, at Eden's request, that his Government would no longer support the publication in London of two Free French newspapers. Eden admitted that one of these, the paper and finances for which were furnished by the British Government, had spent most of its time in attacking the United States or General Giraud or in making general trouble for the British Government itself.

We made much progress at this time in settling another French problem—that of the French West Indies. Admiral Hoover and Samuel Reber, Assistant Chief of the Department's Division of European Affairs, whom we had sent to Martinique in May, 1942, had negotiated an agreement with Governor Robert very shortly after the Allied landings in North Africa in November, 1942. The agreement was to our satisfaction in that it gave us sufficient guarantees that the French islands should not be used in any way by the Axis.

Stiff-necked Governor Robert, however, who still thought his allegiance was to Marshal Pétain despite the German occupation of Vichy France, raised innumerable objections to carrying out the agreement. On April 26, 1943, I instructed our Consul General at Martinique, Marcel E. Malige, to return to this country, thus terminating the informal direct relations we had with the French West Indies.

After the creation by De Gaulle and Giraud of the Committee of National Liberation in Algiers, Governor Robert resigned. We thereupon agreed with the committee that Henri Hoppenot, Director of Civil Services of the French Military Mission in Washington, should be designated to assume authority over the French West Indies, also called the French Antilles, and to go to Martinique.

We worked out a statement to this effect with Hoppenot and the War and Navy Departments. I sent it to the President on July 13; he approved; and it was issued that day. In it we stated that Hoppenot had assured this Government that the facilities and resources of the French Antilles would be devoted to the fullest extent to the prosecution of the war against the Axis; that the military interests of the United States in the Caribbean were fully recognized; and that all immobilized French naval and merchant ships would be put to use. We would send relief supplies to Martinique and Guadeloupe, cooperate in the resumption of their economic life, and return Consul General Malige to his post.

Thus ended the question of Martinique and her sister island. In the face of Governor Robert's intransigence we had been extremely forbearing. Desiring to create no cause for conflict in the Caribbean, we had, as the President commented to me, "taken it on the chin" for many months. But by exercising what at times was almost superhuman patience and restraint, we had at last achieved our purpose without a direct struggle with the hardheaded and small-bore Governor.

Toward the middle of June, Eden had invited me to make a trip to London during which we could talk over our various problems. When Halifax presented the invitation I said I hoped I might be able to accept. Churchill, using his code name "Former Naval Person," cabled the President on June 22 with reference to Halifax's report of our conversation. "After all the visits we have inflicted upon you," he said, "I really think it is time we played the hosts; and, short of yourself, there is certainly no one whose visit would be more welcome to the public or more valuable to us than Mr. Hull."

The Prime Minister said he hoped very much that the President would give me any encouragement he might think I needed. The President sent the message to me with his comment: "I do hope that you can go this autumn. I honestly think it would do a great deal of good."

I thought hard over the invitation. I, too, thought that much good could be accomplished by going to London. On the other hand, it was probable that Mr. Churchill and Eden would soon again be on this side of the Atlantic, and there were problems coming to a head over here that had to be settled.

I replied to Eden on July 7 expressing my deep gratitude to the Prime Minister and to him for their invitation and saying I had delayed my final reply in violation of propriety in an anxious effort to see my way clear to accept. It was with the profoundest regret that I was unable to do so.

New cable exchanges were now taking place between President Roosevelt and Prime Minister Churchill on the broader subject of the relations of our two countries to the French Committee of National Liberation. Mr. Churchill had cabled on July 8 a suggested formula for accepting the committee and dealing with it as the organization acting for French interests in French territory which acknowledged its authority, subject always to the military requirements of the American and British forces.

After my associates and I had studied this in detail, I sent the President a memorandum on July 17 suggesting that for the present the committee should give further and more satisfactory evidence of its complete and genuine unity with the hitherto French factional elements in support of the single cause of the French Empire and of the United Nations. There continued visible signs of bitter propaganda against French elements by other French groups, and against the Allied Governments. There were appearances of unity on the surface, but only on the surface.

We drew up, however, a suggested formula for future relationship with the French Committee of National Liberation. This stated that the British and American Governments were prepared to treat with the committee as administering those parts of the French overseas empire that acknowledged its authority, and as acting as a trustee for French interests. The committee would afford such military and economic facilities as might be required by the United Nations for the prosecution of the war.

The President sent our formula to Mr. Churchill on July 22. At the same time he informed him that he objected to the use of the word "recognition" in any form.

Mr. Churchill replied on August 3, sending us a new Foreign Office formula. Despite the President's objection the British came right back with the word "recognition."

In a memorandum to the President on August 5 I pointed out the necessity, in our dealings with the French committee, to make a clear-cut distinction between military and other questions. The British had not made this clear.

It was perfectly plain to us that De Gaulle already was exerting every effort to make himself supreme in the committee and take over Giraud's position as commander-in-chief of the French Forces in North Africa. The French committee on July 31 had issued a new decree creating a Committee of National Defense under the chairmanship of De Gaulle. Giraud, interested only in military matters, was a babe in arms in dealing with De Gaulle on a political level. If De Gaulle, whose hostility to the United States was well known, assumed military control of North Africa, he would in all probability create innumerable difficulties for General Eisenhower.

In my memorandum to the President I said: "We have assumed that this Government has undertaken to equip a French Army of approximately 300,000 men to serve, in the first instance, under the direct orders of General Giraud and, in the final analysis, under the orders of the Allied Commander-in-Chief. We likewise assume that this undertaking on our part was predicated on the understanding that General Giraud would have the final word with respect to the French forces which we are arming, and that in military matters General Giraud would be the sole responsible French authority with whom the two Governments would deal with respect to the French armed forces."

I attached for the President a new draft of an Anglo-American agreement which sought to reconcile our various drafts with those of the British. This he sent to Mr. Churchill.

As their exchanges continued, the President and the Prime Minister agreed that they should meet, along with Eden and me, at Quebec, beginning August 11. I sent Mr. Roosevelt on August 11 the draft of a statement he might issue if he reached an agreement with Mr. Churchill on relations with the French committee. I asked him, if an agreement were concluded, to withhold publicity long enough for us to inform the Soviet Government prior to any announcement. The President and I had agreed that he should leave Washington before me, so as to begin his military talks with Mr. Churchill, and that I would join him in Quebec on August 20.

89: First Quebec Conference

BEFORE PRESIDENT ROOSEVELT LEFT for Quebec he requested Sumner Welles to resign as Under Secretary of State. He called Welles to his office at the White House and made this clear to him.

During the previous few weeks the President and I had talked more than once about the problem of Welles. We were in agreement that he should resign, be given a special appointment outside the country, and assume the new duties involved.

Some of the problems presented by Under Secretary Welles, which I will not enumerate at length since no purpose would be served by so doing, had been growing for two to three years. The Rio de Janeiro Conference in January, 1942, had demonstrated an attitude of his which was not new to me—his readiness to make major decisions from time to time without consulting me.

From our earliest association I had sought to give him reasonable latitude in carrying on his work. I had asked him to go directly to the President with matters on which he was working, especially when I was closely engaged at the Department. This was in line with my policy that my immediate associates, the Under Secretary, the Counselor, and the Assistant Secretaries, should see the President themselves on specified matters and with my knowledge. I felt that this occasional contact would give them more experience, greater prestige, and keener interest in their work, and also relieve me of some of the innumerable burdens thrust upon a Secretary of State, especially in the difficult times through which we were passing.

I found, however, that Welles abused this privilege by going to the President at times without my knowledge, and even attempting to secure a decision, again without my knowledge. There was perhaps some explanation for this tendency in the fact that Mr. Roosevelt and Welles were old family friends with the same social and school background.

During the period leading up to the outbreak of the war in Europe, when my duties in the Department were piling higher and higher each month, I authorized Welles to see many or most of the Ambassadors and Ministers desiring to call at the Department, especially in connection with routine matters and those of lesser importance. Naturally I would, in any event, see all foreign representatives desiring to see me, and also would keep in contact with them on matters of major importance. Also, Welles was expected to bring or send foreign representatives to me in connection with crucial questions. This last I soon discovered he was not doing in a number of instances, notwithstanding that I had made clear that I must insist on seeing representatives on such occasions, no matter how busy I was. Later, when a topflight Ambassador came to see me at my invitation and I asked him to come back again and resume our discussion, he immediately threw up his hands and said I would have to speak first with Mr. Welles. The foregoing practices gradually but steadily became more aggravated.

I began to note that Welles was carrying on personal correspondence with our diplomats and with officials of other Governments which should have been carried on through the official channels of the State Department. He was sending personal notes to them and inviting personal responses from them on matters calling for Department notes handled in the regular way. The adverse effect of this was that he was gathering into his own hands items of negotiation or discussion that should have been of more general knowledge to me and to the Department officers directly concerned.

In the late spring of 1942 Welles delivered two addresses on foreign affairs that tended to commit this Government to new lines of foreign policy. The more important was on Memorial Day at Arlington Cemetery, during the visit of Foreign Commissar Molotov, and dealt with our postwar plans. On neither occasion did he consult with me in advance as to these new pronouncements.

I called Welles to my office on June 20, 1942, and pointed out to him that no Under Secretary or Assistant Secretary had ever had the function of giving out new foreign policy to any extent, and this function did not in any sense exist now. Any attempt to have two leaders in the person of the Secretary and the Under Secretary both undertake it or to have the Under Secretary assume this role alone, I said, created a situation that I could not acquiesce in for a moment.

I added that, under the well defined rules of the State Department, no Under Secretary or Assistant Secretary should go direct to the President on any official matters except at the President's direction or with the knowledge and authority of the Secretary, and no one knew this better than Welles himself. I said that the unprecedented privilege I had given him of access to the White House might have been a mistake on my part, for it was a privilege that none of his predecessors, to my knowledge, had had.

Welles replied that he was not aware that he had been defining new foreign policy in his speeches. He then said that, in view of what I had said, he would cease making speeches altogether.

I responded that he made splendid speeches, and that I should like to see him make even a hundred speeches in support of the war; this single question of omitting new foreign policy from his speeches, unless we had agreed upon it, was the sole thing I had in mind.

To my surprise, Welles continued to the end of our conversation to confuse the two entirely different classes of speeches, and to insist that he would not make any more speeches at all. To my further surprise, he said that the President had remarked in a conversation that he himself did not expect to make any speech on postwar problems but it would be all right for other members of the Government to do so as trial balloons.

I replied that he had not told me about this talk with the President, nor was it in harmony with his first contention that he was not conscious of having referred to new foreign policy.

Our conversation had the effect of clearing the air for the time being. Subsequently Welles did make speeches on foreign affairs, but he consulted with me first. Nevertheless, he did not cease his practice of going to the President over my head. I could not repose the same confidence in him that I did in my other associates.

I felt that, notwithstanding his education and training in foreign affairs, he was narrower and less sound than my other associates on quite a number of major questions and policies. Before the war in Europe came we differed on armed intervention in Cuba and on our evaluation of the results of the Munich Conference. After war came, we differed on the Western Hemisphere Neutrality Zone and on the proposed ultimatum to Japan to which Roosevelt and Churchill agreed at the Atlantic Conference, and in the formulation of which he had been an adviser. I felt this would have brought on war with the Japanese at a time when we were less prepared than at the time of Pearl Harbor. After Pearl Harbor we differed on the handling of Argentina at the Rio Conference, on the nature of his speeches, and on the structure of the postwar international security organization with which I deal in Part Eight. These divergences were due at times to a difference of philosophy and at others to differences over the more practical and effective means of handling crucial questions and issues, to say nothing of Welles's frequent unwillingness to do teamwork with me. This situation was particularly acute during the later years of his service, and was a handicap to those of us who were working together as a unit.

For some years I had looked to him to supervise the administration of the State Department in the most efficient manner possible. This was the normal function of an Under Secretary, permitting the Secretary of State to devote more time to the formulation of policy. He seemed, however, to become engrossed with other matters, with the result that most of us in the Department in position to judge were keenly disappointed by the result of his administrative services. After Stettinius became Under Secretary I encharged him with a complete administrative reorganization of the Department.

The President himself had begun to appreciate the extent of Under Secretary Welles's disloyalty to me. He complained particularly and more than once about the Under Secretary's delivering the Arlington Cemetery speech without having consulted either of us, and told me of remonstrating later with him about the speech. On one occasion Welles had gone to him with a suggestion that he be sent on a given mission. Mr. Roosevelt did not mention the nature of the mission, but he was sharply critical of the fact that Welles had not consulted me before making the suggestion.

In early summer, 1943, the President himself realized that the situation in the State Department could not continue. He decided on his own that in the light of all existing circumstances the efficiency of the Department would be improved by Welles's retirement. We agreed that Welles's resignation should be rendered easier for him by the President's offer to send him to South America as roving Ambassador or to Russia on a special mission.

The President made this proposal to Welles when he requested his resignation, pointing out that he could thus leave the State Department without undue sensation.

Without giving the President a definite reply Welles came to my office immediately and indicated his belief that the President had acted at my instance. I gave him the full facts, including the one that the President had acted on his own deliberate judgment, after full investigation of the situation, regardless of whether or not he had acted as a result of any suggestion from me.

I then urged upon Welles the President's suggestion of a special mission, with particular reference to a conference at Moscow. In a tone of finality, he promptly said that nothing could be gotten out of that sort of trip. He soon got up, came over to my desk, shook hands, and then departed. I have not talked with him since.

I left shortly thereafter for the Quebec Conference. Welles went up to Maine. Instead of accepting the President's suggestion of a special mission, he wrote out his resignation and mailed it to the White House.

Meantime I had arrived in Quebec on August 20 to take part in what became known as the First Quebec Conference. Prior to my arrival President Roosevelt and Prime Minister Churchill had engaged in some days of intensive military discussions.

They had decided that an Anglo-American invasion of northern France should be made in the spring of 1944. Mr. Churchill had argued— and continued to argue up to the Tehran Conference—that the invasion of Europe by the Western Allies should be through the Balkans, the "soft underbelly of Europe." With the Gallipoli campaign, which he had fathered in the First World War, still in mind, he yearned to prove his theory that the war in Europe could be settled from the south. He repeatedly stated that an invasion across the English Channel might involve frightful casualties, and that Britain could not afford the loss of hundreds of thousands of lives such as at Passchendaele, Vimy Ridge, and Ypres during the previous war. He argued that a victory under such conditions would be barren for Britain; she could never recover from it and would be so weakened that the Soviet Union would inevitably dominate the European continent. He said that the southern European coast line was long and badly defended and offered huge tactical advantages, and he pointed to the fruitful North African campaign as an example. He also felt that an Anglo-American entry into the Balkans and southern Europe would prevent a Soviet rush into that area which would permanently establish the authority of the Soviet Union there, to the detriment of Britain and incidentally of the United States.

The President and his military advisers, however, argued that the invasion of southern Europe could be even more costly, and that the problem of supply and reenforcements across the length of the Mediterranean or around Africa and through the Red Sea was insurmountable. They felt that a decisive defeat could be inflicted more quickly on the Germans in France than in the Balkans. Since the United States would have to furnish the majority of the forces involved in an invasion of Europe, the President was able to prevail upon the Prime Minister at Quebec, although the question came up for discussion again at Tehran.

When I arrived at Quebec the President and the Prime Minister had also discussed the terms of surrender for Italy. Following Mussolini's resignation on July 25, the Italian surrender seemed imminent. They had likewise agreed that British forces should enter the Azores islands, with the concurrence of Portugal, to be followed by American forces two weeks later.

But they had not been able to agree on a joint Anglo-American declaration concerning relations with the French Committee of National Liberation, and this Eden and I took up at our first meeting on August 20 at the Citadel in Quebec. Eden was accompanied by Sir Alexander Cadogan, British Permanent Under Secretary of State for Foreign Affairs, and I by James C. Dunn, the State Department's Political Adviser on European Affairs, and by our Minister to Canada, Ray Atherton.

When Eden brought up the subject I made the point that at no time had the Prime Minister not fully agreed in his telegrams to the President with the policy of the American Government.

Eden remarked, however, that in 1940 De Gaulle had been their only friend. I promptly replied that Britain had had another friend, the United States, and I reminded him of our many forms of assistance, including our actions in preventing the French fleet and North African bases from falling into German hands, Admiral Leahy's work in keeping up the spirit and courage of the French people in Vichy France, and our naval support long before we got into the war.

Eden thereupon said he felt that Mr. Churchill could not accept any formula with regard to the French Committee of National Liberation which did not contain the word "recognition." My advisers and I argued that "recognition" was given only to a government or some form of government, whereas in this case we understood that both the British and the United States Governments had no intention whatever of considering the French Committee as a government.

Eden said it might therefore be necessary for the two Governments to adopt their own formulas and make their announcements in their own separate ways.

I remarked that such a procedure, even if done by both Governments simultaneously, would mean an obvious divergence of views.

Eden said he realized that any such policy would be so considered, and he regretted such a possibility.

I replied that I very much regretted the consideration of any such divergence of views, but that if the British could stand it, we could too.

I made a comprehensive exposition of our view that we had to consider the long-range future of France; but we reached no agreement and left the question open for further discussion. Eden remarked that the British public was against our view, and that this fact required consideration.

At some moments the conversation had become a trifle sharp, although Eden and I had more than enough respect and friendship for each other to keep our voices calm and our manners friendly. I remarked to Eden, with a smile, that he reminded me of a politician in my own country.

He rejoined, "Are you, Mr. Secretary, not a politician too?"

"Well," I replied, "I've been a politician during my long public service of nearly forty years." Then, in a humorous way I added, "But I retired from politics, and now I'm a statesman."

Eden asked: "If you are a statesman, what am I?"

"A statesman," I remarked, "is a retired politician like myself."

At the following day's session Eden and I and our advisers threshed out other questions. I asked him how his thoughts were running on the question of whether to leave Germany after the war as an entity or to dismember her.

He replied that while some members of the British Government felt that Germany should be dismembered, he himself—and he felt, in general, the Cabinet also—were not in favor of imposing dismemberment, largely because of the impracticability of carrying it out. He said it would be well to bring about a separation of the different states of Germany if it could be done voluntarily.

I said that those of us at the State Department who were studying this question seemed to be arriving at the same view as to the difficulties of imposing or maintaining a separation of the different sections of Germany. We thought that an imposed dismemberment of Germany might merely create a German national slogan for union. A German economy must exist for the support of the people of Germany, and toward this end such national systems as canals, railroads, post office, and telegraph must exist as units. But it was not impossible to consider an economic reorganization of Germany whereby in her own interests the decentralization of the country would unconsciously develop. Such a means might be found through providing special access to a Mediterranean port for southern

Germany so that those regions might look south for their outlet to the sea rather than be dependent on northern Germany. An area including Fiume and Trieste might be the proper solution.

I threw this out simply as a thought we had been discussing, not as a decision made or contemplated by our Government. Eden and Cadogan gave the idea considerable approval. The discussion indicated that the British, too, had been giving much thought to the possibility of bringing about, by natural forces, a separation of the German states, and specifically using the Adriatic ports as a southern German access to water.

Eden added that he had never been in favor of detaching Bavaria from Germany and setting it up as a separate state with Austria. His view was that it would be more advisable to restore, in general lines, the separate states of the old Austro-Hungarian Empire and form them into a Danubian group.

I then brought up with Eden a subject very close to my heart, one to which I had devoted many hours of work and study over a long period of time—dependent or colonial peoples and their eventual attainment of independence. At the conference with President Roosevelt which Eden and I had attended on March 27, during Eden's visit to Washington, the President had raised the question of the policy of trusteeship after the war. He said he had read the draft of a proposal on dependent peoples which I had handed him, and that it seemed to be all right with the exception of two or three minor points.

I remarked on that occasion that our draft contemplated international supervision over dependent peoples except in cases of parent governments and their colonies; and even in those cases we proposed that international agencies might observe the entire operations of the parent Government relating to each colony and make public any and all facts that it would have the public know.

At the State Department we had given intense thought to the subject of dependent peoples, and the draft I had given the President was the result of many months of study. It had been written, under my guidance, by Leo Pasvolsky with the help of Green Hackworth and Stanley Hornbeck.

We had agreed that a copy of the draft might be handed to the British, with the understanding that this was not intended to be our final word on the matter. I accordingly instructed Pasvolsky to give Eden a copy, which he promised to study and comment on in due course.

Since this was the seed of the trusteeship system set up by the United Nations organization after the war, and this was the first time we brought it up for international discussion, I give its substance here.

Our draft stated that it was the duty and purpose of those United Nations charged with responsibilities for the future of colonial areas to cooperate fully with the peoples of such areas in order that they might become qualified for independent national status. Toward this end such nations had to adopt five procedures.

First, they were to give their colonial peoples protection, encouragement, moral support, and material aid and to make continuous efforts toward their political, economic, social, and educational advancement.

Second, they were to make available to qualified persons among the colonial peoples, to the fullest possible extent, positions in the various branches of the local governmental organization.

Third, they were to grant progressively to the colonial peoples such measures of self-government as they were capable of maintaining in the light of the various stages of their development toward independence.

Fourth, they were to fix, at the earliest practicable moments, dates upon which the colonial peoples would be accorded the status of full independence within a system of general security.

Fifth, they were to pursue policies under which the natural resources of colonial territories would be developed, organized, and marketed in the interest of the peoples concerned and of the world as a whole.

We suggested that regional commissions should be set up with these ends in view. The commissions would be composed of nations directly responsible for the future of various colonial areas, and other nations which had substantial interests in the region. The colonial peoples would have appropriate opportunity to participate and to have or to achieve representation on the commissions.

As a result of the war, we believed, peoples in several areas still unprepared for full independence would be released from political ties with nations formerly responsible for them. We therefore suggested that the United Nations assume a special responsibility with regard to them, analogous to that of a trustee or fiduciary.

We accordingly proposed the establishment of an International Trusteeship Administration composed of representatives of the United Nations and of all other nations which would cooperate in carrying forward and applying the provisions of the Atlantic Charter. The Administration would operate through regional councils composed of representatives of the nations having major interests in the respective regions. The peoples of the territories held in trust would be given full opportunity to take part in the work of the appropriate regional council.

In general, the proposal was an effort to implement the pledges contained in the Atlantic Charter relating to the right of all peoples to choose the form of government under which they would live.

Eden had already given me, through Lord Halifax on February 4, the draft of a proposed joint declaration on colonial policy which went in the direction I had in mind, though not nearly so far.

We were even then well launched on one form of international co-operation leading toward the improvement of the conditions of dependent peoples—a utilization of the regional commission which was one of the suggestions in my draft. We had set up with the British on March 9, 1942, an advisory Anglo-American Caribbean Commission. The economic and social conditions of the peoples in the colonies and territories of the Caribbean were of keen interest to us because these lands lay in our strategic front yard. Affairs of the United States and Great Britain in the Caribbean had become "somewhat mixed up together," to use Mr. Churchill's phrase, when we acquired the lease of bases on some of the islands. Security reasons and an honest regard for the welfare of those peoples impelled us to suggest to Britain the creation of a commission that would work toward this end.

This commission was conceived by Charles W. Taussig, a broad-gauge, highly intelligent businessman with extensive knowledge of the Caribbean area, who in 1941, as the President's representative, made a survey of the British West Indies in connection with the bases we had leased from Britain. Mr. Roosevelt appointed him the United States Co-Chairman of the Commission, with Rexford G. Tugwell, Governor of Puerto Rico, and Coert duBois, Chief of the Caribbean Office of the State Department, as the other United States members. The United States section of the Commission became integrated into the State Department, and Taussig was later an adviser on trusteeship to the American delegation at the San Francisco Conference.

The terms of reference of the commission were broad, including matters of labor, agriculture, housing, health, education, social welfare, and economics. It was conceived as a peacetime organization, and its mandate clearly related to a world at peace, but it was immediately plunged into efforts to keep the Caribbean peoples from being starved out by the greater war demands in other areas.

The commission followed the principle of encouraging active participation by dependent peoples in shaping the policy in their area. Commissioners were drawn from the area, a Caribbean Research Council composed mostly of local scientists and technicians was formed, and arrangements were made for biennial meetings of the West India Conference, with delegates directly representing the people.

The British and United States members worked closely together and obtained great cooperation from the island administrations as well as from the Caribbean Republics of Cuba, Haiti, and the Dominican Republic. They early contemplated inviting France and The Netherlands, the other European nations possessing colonies in the Caribbean, to join in, which the latter did in 1946.

The commission provided an example that I felt and said could well be followed by other nations and in other parts of the world. The South Pacific Commission, formed in 1947, was modeled on the basis of the experience gained in the Caribbean.

Two days after the White House Conference on March 27, 1943, at which the President brought up the subject of dependent peoples, Eden said to me that he was much interested in our draft and asked whether he might in strict confidence show it to the Ministers of the British Dominions. I agreed, although emphasizing that this was not a final proposal but only a draft to which thought and attention might be given at this stage, with the understanding that the President might have further views when the recommendations came to be drawn up.

Now at Quebec in August I raised the subject with Eden again. In fact, I brought it up three times during the Quebec discussions in an effort to get his reactions. On the third occasion the Foreign Secretary said that, to be perfectly frank, he had to say he did not like our draft very much. He said it was the word "independence" that troubled him. He had to think of the British Empire system, which was built on the basis of Dominion and colonial status.

He pointed out that under the British Empire system there were varying degrees of self-government, running from the Dominions through the colonial establishments which had in some cases, like Malta, complete self-government, to backward areas that were never likely to have their own government. He added that Australia and New Zealand also had colonial possessions that they would be unwilling to remove from their supervisory jurisdiction.

I remarked that my thought in dealing with this problem had been to give encouragement to the peoples in dependent areas. This was not with any view to their being given, tomorrow or next week, complete independence as separate entities, but to offer them, at some time when they could prove they were capable of independence, the possibility of so conducting their political development that they might be able to hope for this achievement. I cited the example of the Philippines in that we had always held out independence to them as a possibility if and when they were able to assume the responsibilities that went with such status.

At the end of the long discussion that followed, Eden's position remained unchanged. His irremovable objection was to the word "independence." He felt this term could never have a satisfactory meaning that would cover what various governments might have in mind by it.

I believed the subject was too important for the long-range advancement of the world to let it drop. Digging my toes in for a lengthy struggle, I brought it up again and again with the British in the months that followed. Two months later I presented it for discussion at the Moscow Conference of Foreign Ministers in October. Eventually these discussions led to the establishment of a United Nations trusteeship system, a material improvement over the old mandates system of the League of Nations. The principles I set forth for the treatment of dependent peoples appear today in Chapter XI—"Declaration Regarding Non-Self-Governing Territories"—of the United Nations Charter. And the word "independence" appears in Chapter XII—"International Trusteeship System."

During this same session with Eden at Quebec on August 21, I showed him the draft of a Four-Nation Declaration that we had prepared at the State Department to bind Britain, the Soviet Union, China, and the United States together after the war. My associates and I had had numerous discussions in the course of preparing the declaration, and I had gone over its various points in detail with the President and obtained his approval.

By this declaration the four powers would agree to establish at the earliest practicable date a general international organization, based on the principle of the sovereign equality of all nations, and open to membership by all nations, large and small, for the maintenance of international peace and security.

Here, I hoped, would be the basis for the foundation of the international organization I had envisaged in my speech of July 23, 1942, to maintain the peace—by force if necessary.

The declaration also provided that, until the international organization was set up, the four powers would consult with a view to joint action for the maintenance of peace and security on behalf of the community of nations. They would establish a technical commission to advise them on the military problems involved, including the composition and strength of the forces available to meet a threat to the peace. They would cooperate toward reducing armaments. They would not employ their military forces within the territories of other states except for the purposes envisaged in the declaration and after joint consultation and agreement. They would act together in all matters relating to the surrender and disarmament of the enemy and the occupation of enemy or enemy-held territory. They would take all measures necessary to provide against a violation of the requirements imposed upon the enemy.

It seemed to me that it was all-important to bring Russia in on a common determination to set up an international organization after the war. If an agreement were reached on this point, the settlement of other problems would be easier. If Russia refused, all other problems would be magnified.

After Eden had read the draft he immediately said he liked it and asked for a copy, which I gave him. Without hesitation he said he thought the declaration offered a good basis for an approach to the Soviet Government. It would be a good idea, he thought, for the United States to transmit a copy to Moscow, saying at the same time that a copy had been given the British Government for its consideration.

Before the Quebec Conference ended we also discussed the draft with Mr. Churchill and obtained his concurrence. It was agreed that I should send it to the Soviet Government for Marshal Stalin's and Molotov's reaction.

Eden and I agreed at this same session that Allied military government should not be installed when Allied countries in Europe now occupied by the Axis were liberated by Allied armies. Eden brought up the subject by handing me a memorandum. He said it would be desirable to dissipate the impression which had arisen that the Allied Military Government system now in effect in Sicily would be carried over and put into effect in the liberated countries. While this system was perfectly appropriate for use in enemy countries, he thought there was general objection to the thought of imposing only military government on the populations of the liberated countries. These countries had constituted Governments which we had recognized, and which felt they should bear their share of responsibility for maintenance of order in the civilian administration as soon as possible and in such areas as were not actually under military operations.

I agreed with Eden's points. I said I had given this matter considerable thought myself, and had arrived at these same conclusions. We decided to discuss the whole question with the Combined Chiefs of Staff, for eventual decision by the President and the Prime Minister.

Mr. Roosevelt and Mr. Churchill took up this question the following day, August 22, in a conference attended by Eden and myself, Cadogan, Atherton, Harry Hopkins, and Dunn. I presented the text of a statement designed to remove apprehension as to putting military government into effect in friendly and Allied countries liberated by the military operations we would undertake against Germany on the Continent. After a few minor amendments the draft text was agreed to. We decided to communicate it to the Soviet and Chinese Governments and the refugee Governments concerned, with a view to eventual publication.

We discussed the attitude the British and American Governments should take toward the constituted refugee Governments. We decided, in general, that the two Governments should continue to support these Governments and regimes, as then recognized by us through the present period up to the defeat of the enemy. Then the peoples of the liberated countries should have the full right to choose their own Governments. I pointed out that this attitude was in line with the statement we had agreed to with respect to the administration of liberated areas.

In connection with this discussion, a message that King George of Greece had sent to the President and the Prime Minister was presented to the meeting. The King had asked advice from the President and the Prime Minister as to the action he should take in view of a request of certain Greek elements that he should not return to Greece until after a plebiscite on the subject of the monarchy had been held.

Roosevelt and Churchill agreed that the British Foreign Office should reply to the King, supporting his contention that he was prepared to return to Greece as soon as possible, and that he would then submit the question of the royal house to a plebiscite. The President said this Government would not take any different position.

Mr. Churchill volunteered that the British Government would instruct its agents working with Greek guerrilla groups to refrain from encouraging those elements to put forward political claims at this time as to the future form of government of Greece.

Although agreements on various subjects were arrived at without too much difficulty, the French Committee of National Liberation again furnished an insurmountable obstacle. Mr. Churchill said that all the liberal elements in the world, including the Governments-in-exile and the Soviet Government, were demanding an immediate decision granting full recognition to the committee.

The President took the view that we had to think of the future of France herself. He said this would be in no way advanced by turning over the whole control of the French liberation movement to the present group comprising the French committee.

The discussion surged back and forth for a long time, until the President suggested that he himself draft the form of a statement that he thought should be made. This was agreed to, and he said he would apply himself to it that evening.

On the following day, however, and at the last session, held on the morning of the 24th, it was still impossible to reach any agreement. The British held out for a strong form of recognition of the French committee. The President said he did not want to give De Gaulle a white horse on which he could ride into France and make himself the master of a government there. I was willing to deal with the French committee on all French territories over which the committee exercised control, but no further, and the President backed me up completely.

The President offered to wager Eden a dinner that before many months had run he would have quite a different view of the French committee from that he had now. Eden said he did not want to take the bet. After the conference was over the President said he thought he could have made much further headway with Churchill on the matter if it had not been for Eden. He laughed heartily when Ray Atherton told him privately of the exchange I had had with Eden on our being politicians.

It was finally agreed that the two Governments would issue separate statements. Each did the other the courtesy of showing the other its statement and accepting suggestions.

The President issued ours on August 26. In it we stated that: we proposed to cooperate with all patriotic Frenchmen; we welcomed the establishment of the French Committee of National Liberation; we expected the committee to function on the principle of collective responsibility of all its members for the active prosecution of the war; our relationship with the committee must be subject to Allied military requirements; and we noted with sympathy the desire of the committee to be regarded as the body qualified to insure the administration and defense of French interests, but the extent to which it might be possible to give effect to this desire had to be considered in each case as it arose.

On these understandings, the statement said, "the Government of the United States recognizes the French Committee of National Liberation as administering those French overseas territories which acknowledge its authority.

"This statement does not constitute recognition of a Government of France or of the French Empire by the Government of the United States.

"It does constitute recognition of the French Committee of National Liberation as functioning within specific limitations during the war. Later on the people of France, in a free and untrammeled manner, will proceed in due course to select their own Government and their own officials to administer it."

The British statement, issued on the same day, went further in granting the committee recognition and authority, but it too stated that it would be for the French people themselves to settle their own constitution and establish their own Government after they had had an opportunity to express themselves freely.

Immediately after my return to Washington on August 25 I began to work with my associates on a project we had had in mind for some time, the adherence of the French committee to the principles of the United Nations Declaration. I had prepared a memorandum for the President on August 12 stating that a public announcement by the American and British Governments concerning their future relationship with the French committee would be a propitious occasion for the two Governments to invite the committee to adhere.

I pointed out in the memorandum that such a step would not involve political recognition since it would be covered by the announcement the State Department made on January 5, 1942, stating that this Government, as the depository for the declaration, would receive statements of adherence to its principles from appropriate authorities that were not governments.

I recalled that the British during the previous summer had proposed that the French National Committee in London be invited to adhere. At our suggestion final decision had been postponed. At that time we felt that adherence by the French committee would give Laval an excuse to turn the French fleet at Alexandria over to the Germans if the German forces then pushing the British back to El Alamein should reach that port. But now that the new French committee had been set up in Algiers, and now that French forces had taken part in the Libyan and Tunisian campaigns and the French military contribution could be expected to increase in the future, the time had come to take the initiative.

Moreover, the memorandum concluded, the basis recommended for our relations with the French committee would probably fall far short of the committee's expectations, but the invitation to adhere to the principles of the United Nations Declaration would have the broadest kind of appeal to all Frenchmen. At the same time, it would be a concrete manifestation of our good will which would place at a disadvantage those who might be inclined to criticize our formula as not going far enough along the road to political recognition.

The President having agreed to proceed, I sent him a further memorandum on August 30 attaching for his consideration a draft telegram to London, Moscow, and Chungking to obtain their consent to the invitation to the French committee. This he approved. Moscow and Chungking were agreeable, but London objected that the French committee would not be content to adhere to the principles of the declaration and wanted to adhere to the declaration itself by virtue of the final paragraph of that document which stated that "other nations" rendering material assistance and contributions in the struggle for victory over Hitlerism might adhere.

I had also cabled Robert Murphy in Algiers to inform him of our telegrams to our three major Allies. Murphy cabled me on September 16 that the French committee wanted to know if adherence to the declaration would make it a member of the United Nations. I replied on September 16 that adherence would not affect its status so far as we were concerned.

Our initiative, therefore, did not bear fruit. The French committee, at De Gaulle's urging, wanted to be considered a government or a nation or a member of the United Nations. To this, in consideration for the French people themselves, the President and I could not agree. The French did not adhere to the United Nations Declaration until January 1, 1945.

I had a conference on French and other matters with the President at the White House on October 5. Mr. Roosevelt decided that French representation on the politicomilitary commission being set up at Algiers should be restricted to matters other than the military occupation of Italy and to matters on which Britain, Russia, and the United States decided that France had a direct interest. The French were not to function as full members.

The President on October 6 gave his approval to the draft of a plan that I took to him embracing the administration of liberated France. The British and we intended to present this at the Moscow Conference, then in the offing.

By the terms of this draft, Britain and we agreed that the ultimate aim of the Allies should be the free and untrammeled choice by the French people of the form of government under which they wished to live. Until that stage should be reached, the largest measure of personal and political liberty compatible with military security should be restored to the French; there should be freedom of speech, of opinion, of the press and of correspondence; and the French flag should be used on French public buildings.

In all liberated areas, however, the Supreme Allied Command would have supreme authority so long as and so far as military necessity required. The civil administration under the Supreme Allied Commander should be conducted by French citizens as far as possible. The Director of Civil Affairs would be a French officer appointed by the Supreme Allied Commander from the French contingent or French Liaison Mission with the military operations in France.

Military control of civil affairs would be as short as practicable. If circumstances permitted, the transfer of civil responsibility to French hands would be progressive.

The Supreme Allied Commander, in order to achieve the eventual aim of full freedom of choice by the French people of the form of government they wished, would do his best to hold the scales even between all French political groups sympathetic to the Allied cause. One of his first tasks would be to establish relations with resistance groups within France and to secure their cooperation in civil matters. He would have no dealings with the Vichy regime except to liquidate it. He would not employ anyone who had collaborated with the enemy.

We made a further gesture of friendship toward the French Committee of National Liberation in November when the President designated Edwin C. Wilson as the United States representative to the committee, with the personal rank of Ambassador.

Mr. Roosevelt and I, however, continued throughout 1943 to resent De Gaulle's ambitions and the pressure and propaganda methods he utilized to fulfill them. Even as we had feared, he soon forced Giraud into the discard. Giraud resigned as co-president of the committee on November 9, and the reshuffling of positions that followed left De Gaulle with full power.

The President, and we at the State Department too, took full note of De Gaulle's high-handed overthrow of the independent Lebanese Government in the Near East on November 11, 1943, and the imprisonment of the President and Ministers of the Lebanese Republic. Two weeks later De Gaulle, as a result of strong pressure from the British and American Governments, was required to abrogate his decrees suspending the Lebanese Constitution, dissolving the Lebanese Parliament, and naming a "Chief of Government." He had to release and restore the President and Ministers to their offices.

From Cairo the President cabled me on November 27 that he was convinced no final decisions or plans concerning civil affairs for France should be made at this time.

"The entire North African situation is complicated," he said in paraphrase, "but the Lebanon affair illustrates the general attitude of the committee and especially De Gaulle. The latter now claims the right to speak for all France and talks openly of plans to set up his Government in France as soon as the Allies get in.

"The thought that the occupation when it occurs should be wholly military is one to which I am increasingly inclined."

The President said he would discuss this informally with Stalin and Churchill, but he hoped we could hold up the entire matter.

After his return to Washington, I sent him in late December a memorandum informing him of the position of the French committee's representative on the Allied Commission for Italy. He sent me on December 31, 1943, a copy of a memorandum he had dispatched to Churchill, attaching my memorandum. In this he said:

"When you and I look back eleven months we realize that De Gaulle and his committee have most decidedly moved forward by 'the process of infiltration'—in other words, here a little, there a little.

"This is another example. This puts France on to the Allied Commission for Italy, even though the memorandum says that the French representative will not have anything to say about it. However, he will still be a member of the commission.

"For the life of me I cannot see why France is entitled to anybody on the Allied Control Commission for Italy. His presence there will, we know from experience, cause controversy and more trouble with the

French Committee. . . . I wish you and I could run this Italian business. We would not need any help or advice."

In the latter part of 1943, however, our attention became concentrated on problems of a more important nature, relating to a larger nation and a full-fledged ally, the Union of Soviet Socialist Republics.

90: Stalin the Sphinx

RUSSIA OFFERED to the United States and to all the United Nations in 1943 the most puzzling problem in international relations. What could be expected of her in the postwar world? Would she cooperate with the Western nations and with China? Would she join an international organization to maintain the peace? Would she insist on territorial expansion at the expense of her smaller neighbors? Would she go to the opposite extreme, give up all ambitions and retire to strict isolation within her old borders?

At the beginning of 1943 Russia was a complete sphinx to all the other nations of the world, except that she stood there fighting heroically.

We knew what Stalin's territorial ambitions were, as expressed to Eden in December, 1941; but we also knew that Stalin had reluctantly acquiesced in Britain's last-minute refusal to agree to them in May, 1942. We realized that friction, sometimes sharp, had risen between the U.S.S.R. and the Western Allies over the second front; we recalled the intemperate language Stalin had used toward Churchill in August, 1942. But we knew that military preparations were under way that should more than satisfy Stalin on this point. We had also seen the bitterness of the Polish-Russian dispute.

In every important Foreign Office in the world interest in Russia was rapidly developing. Allied statesmen were urging that somehow the intentions of the Soviet Union should be ascertained so that the United Nations might know how to plan the world that would exist after the peace.

The enigma of Russia came very much to the fore in my series of conferences with Eden in March, 1943. We agreed on the extreme importance of ascertaining Russia's probable future course with respect to Europe and the world. I asked Eden whether he thought Stalin had any other choice than these two alternatives: one, isolation after lopping off certain territory along Russia's boundaries, accompanied by the maintenance of heavy armaments; two, become part of the world and meet all Russia's responsibilities under a sane, practical policy of international cooperation. Eden said he knew of no other choice.

I discussed at some length the question of Britain and the United States making earnest, friendly representation to the Soviet Government to the end that the Soviet Union should broaden its perspective and show some interest in the postwar world by working more closely with Great Britain, China, and this country.

"Many people here," I said, "are stating that Russia is saying almost nothing about her future plans and purposes, and that, at the end of the war, Russia will do as she pleases, take what she pleases, and confer with nobody. The same people add that this Government is spending many billions of dollars in supplying Russia and Britain with immense military supplies, and that unless Russia shows some appreciation and speaks out in a spirit of teamwork and cooperation more fully both now and especially after the war, it will be difficult, if hostilities continue for some time, to prevail on the American people to continue to furnish supplies to Russia."

Eden said that Russia in the meantime was destroying Germans.

"We all know this, of course," I replied. "But those people who are dissatisfied with the failure of Russia to show any interest or concern about future joint efforts to promote peace and economic rehabilitation based on liberal commercial policies find that nothing would be gained thereby except that Russia and Great Britain will have succeeded in eliminating Germany."

(At a dinner during Eden's visit I proposed a toast to the effect that there were terrific difficulties ahead in the world, that the three great nations working together might not solve all of them, but that any one or two of these nations alone would not solve a single one of them.)

Eden agreed with me that the Governments of Britain, Russia, China, and the United States should tighten up their policies in regard to preventing criticisms of one another by their respective citizens, especially those coming under governmental control.

When Prime Minister Churchill came to Washington in May, 1943, I brought up with him the need for a more complete understanding with Russia on the part of Great Britain and the United States, and repeated what I had told Eden on this point.

"It's extremely important," I said, "that our two countries should proceed systematically through carefully selected persons to talk Mr. Stalin out of his shell, so to speak, away from his aloofness, secretiveness, and suspiciousness until he broadens his views, visualizes a more practical international cooperation in the future, and indicates Russia's intentions both in the East and in the West."

The Prime Minister said he thought Russia would help fight Japan when the war in the West was over.

I replied that, so far as I knew, there was no evidence or intimation of any kind to what Russia would do in this respect.

"It's my opinion," I said, "that if Russia should eventually come into the war in the Pacific, it will probably be two or three weeks before victory, during which time she can spread out over Manchuria and other large areas and then be assured of sitting in at the peace conference. She may come into the war in the East, but the point I am emphasizing is that I cannot get any intimation as to her future plans except in regard to certain territorial matters on her borders in Europe."

For well over a year the President had hoped that, through a personal meeting with Stalin, he might iron out the problems that existed between Russia on the one hand and virtually all the United Nations on the other. He had been much impressed by the head-on clash between Stalin and Churchill; but he thought that through the force of his own personality, and with the terrific power behind him that the United States was now demonstrating in the Pacific and in Europe, he could succeed where the Prime Minister had failed. He was eager to meet Stalin, whether alone or in company with Churchill.

In the spring of 1942 he had begun to prospect a meeting with Stalin; but the Marshal, preoccupied with preparing Russia's second summer of resistance, declined. The President sent him a message on April 11, through the Russian Embassy, saying it was unfortunate that topographical distance made it practically impossible for them to meet at this time. "Perhaps next summer," he said, "you and I could spend a few days together near our common border off Alaska. I have in mind a very important military proposal involving the utilization of our armed forces in a manner to relieve your critical western front. This objective carries great weight with me." Mr. Roosevelt proposed that Stalin consider sending to Washington Foreign Commissar Molotov and a general upon whom he relied, so that this could be talked over.

What the President had in mind was the Anglo-American landing in North Africa. Molotov, as I have narrated, came to Washington in May and June, 1942.

At the time of the Casablanca Conference in January, 1943, the President tried to induce Stalin to meet him and the Prime Minister. Stalin, still engrossed in his military command, and suspicious of what he considered an Anglo-American line-up that was refusing to open a major second front in Europe, declined.

Mr. Roosevelt tried a third time when he sent Joseph E. Davies, former Ambassador to Russia, on a special mission to Moscow in May, 1943. Davies suggested on the President's behalf that, if Stalin and he and Molotov and myself could get together, all questions could be settled. Stalin replied that he wondered whether this really was true. He finally inclined toward a personal meeting with the President; but when Churchill suggested that he too should be present Stalin pulled back. He was less disinclined to see a meeting of the Foreign Ministers.

In that same month of May I went thoroughly into American-Soviet relations with Soviet Ambassador Litvinov, seeing him on the 8th shortly before his departure for Moscow on leave. I emphasized that self-preservation was the foundation of international cooperation for the purpose of winning this war against the worst desperadoes in history. This, I said, was secondary in importance only to the purpose of preserving the peace by the same international cooperation after the war.

In other words, I said, the common interest of self-preservation caused this country and others to fly instantly to the side of Russia when she was attacked by Germany, and all to fight jointly for the common purpose of defeating the Axis aggressors. Good social relations between peoples and countries were fine; good friendly relations were better; but, desirable as such relations were, the real basic foundation of close political and economic relations between Governments and peoples in these modern times rested on the doctrine of self-preservation.

I recalled that for sixty years prior to the First World War the peoples of Russia and the United States knew both collectively and individually that they were friendly toward each other. That friendship had become traditional. And there was no reason whatever why we could not continue that same true friendship, together with a common interest in the future peace and stability of the world.

"Of course," I said, "Russia or the United States could isolate itself and ward off outside attacks for a few years. But the inevitable result would be a considerable drain on the economic strength of the country pursuing such a policy. And in time a more or less chaotic world, led by unscrupulous dictators, as at present, would get out of hand."

I emphasized and reemphasized my opinion that the Russian people were intelligent, agreeable, and capable, and that they made a good impression on others. The American people likewise had these same qualities. It would therefore be entirely natural for friendly relations, which had existed for long years between our two countries, to be continued and strengthened even though the clearing up of misunderstandings and suspicion might require a little effort on the part of the leaders and officials of each country.

I stressed the disastrous alternative to this course, and expressed the hope more than once that Litvinov would bring these ideas home to his Government when he arrived in Moscow.

Litvinov expressed some skepticism about the state of mind in the United States regarding isolation, and also thought there was some feeling on the part of many Americans directed against Russia and the Russian people because of some alleged discrimination or accusation.

I went again over some of the points I had made, and said that one step that would improve our relations would be the avoidance of precipitate action such as Russia recently had taken in severing diplomatic relations with Poland without notice to any of the United Nations.

Two weeks after this conversation we were encouraged by the official dissolution of the Communist International, or Comintern, in Moscow, announced on May 22, 1943. The activities of this organization, which directed the Communist movement throughout the world, had long given our Government much concern. The Soviet Union had formally promised, at the time we established diplomatic relations with her in 1933, that she would restrain all organizations under her direct or indirect control from any agitation or propaganda designed to bring about by force a change in the political or social order in the United States. But this promise had been evaded on the specious ground that the Comintern did not come under the direct or indirect control of the Soviet Government. The continued activity of the Comintern, and its connections with the Communist Party in the United States, had been one of the principal causes for our inability to achieve the close and friendly working relations with the Soviet Government from 1933 to 1941 which the President and I desired.

Mr. Roosevelt and I could logically believe that Stalin's dissolution of the Comintern was due in large part to the representations our Government had made over and over again to the Russian Government. We had never left Stalin, Litvinov, and Molotov in any doubt as to our attitude that the existence of the Comintern, and the obvious connection between it and the Russian Government despite all Moscow's statements to the contrary, were keeping our two countries from achieving the cooperation we wished and needed. From the time we sent Ambassador Bullitt to Moscow we had never ceased to insist on the Russian Government's observing its pledges to abandon its support of subversive activities in the United States. The Russians had insisted that they had, in fact, carried

out their pledge; but Bullitt in Moscow and I in Washington kept replying, in effect, "You know that we know better." We strongly reemphasized
our position at the time of the world Comintern meeting in Moscow in the
summer of 1935, to which American Communists had been invited. We
had not yielded our ground during the years that followed but kept our
position alive and encouraged other countries to maintain a like stand.
After war came to Russia and the United States, we pressed upon the
Russians the doctrines of cooperation contained in the Atlantic Charter
and the United Nations Declaration, and made it clear that such cooperation was incompatible with any sort of support of subversive activities
within any of the United Nations.

What the dissolution of the Comintern now portended, neither Mr.
Roosevelt nor I could definitely say. Whether its activities would still
be continued under some other guise remained to be seen. It was at least
a gesture of friendship in the direction of the Western Allies, and the
President and I were prepared to hail it in that sense. I made a public
statement on May 24 in which I said:

"The dissolution of the Communist International is welcome news.
The elimination of that organization from international life and the cessation of the type of activity in which that organization has in the past
engaged is certain to promote a greater degree of trust among the United
Nations and to contribute very greatly to the wholehearted cooperation
necessary for the winning of the war and for successful postwar undertakings."

The President made his fourth unsuccessful attempt to meet with
Stalin at the time of the Quebec Conference in August, 1943. He had
hoped to induce the Soviet leader to attend that meeting.

At about the time of the Quebec Conference, a portion of the Soviet
press suddenly put forth the idea that, although a meeting of the chiefs
of the American, British, and Russian Governments was impossible because of Stalin's preoccupation with directing the stupendous battle in
the east against Germany, a meeting of the Foreign Ministers could well
and fruitfully be held.

The President and Churchill both took up this suggestion concur-
rently and asked Stalin whether he shared the opinion that a meeting of
the Foreign Ministers of the three powers in the near future would be
expedient. Stalin replied to both on August 24, stating that he was in
accord. He added that the meeting should not be of a narrow exploratory
character but should be a practical preparation leading to definite deci-

sions by the three Governments. He suggested that the range of questions to be discussed should be determined in advance.

At that moment one or two columnists who on various occasions in the past had taken fierce delight in attacking me, unleashed a particularly virulent campaign to the effect that I was intensely anti-Russian, and that my real objective was to see Germany and Russia fight each other to the death, with Russia bled white and the United States holding aloof.

On August 27 I issued a public statement designed to combat the evil effects of this publicity, which I said lent aid and comfort to the enemy. On the same day I called the Soviet Chargé d'Affaires, Andrei A. Gromyko, to my office and said to him that the absolute falsity of this publicity should, of course, be well known to Soviet officials just as it was to American officials, but I feared lest it should injuriously affect the state of mind of uninformed persons in Russia, in the United States, and in other countries.

Gromyko agreed that I, along with other officials of this Government, was doing everything possible to promote and preserve the friendly relations now existing between our two Governments and to carry forward on this basis the fullest cooperation in the prosecution of the war.

When I saw Molotov at Moscow in October I spoke in warm praise of Gromyko, saying that he was proving himself very capable. In numerous conversations in 1943 and 1944 Gromyko, who soon became Ambassador to the United States, impressed me most favorably by his practical judgment and efficiency.

I was gratified to receive from Gromyko on September 3, 1943, a communication in which Russia joined with the United States and Great Britain in agreeing that Iran should be permitted to sign the United Nations Declaration. This meant a further assurance that Russia would respect the independence of Iran after the war.

Following exchanges of views with Churchill, the President sent Stalin a further message on September 6, in which he said that both Churchill and he were pleased with the idea of a political and military meeting on the Foreign Minister level. Although the Prime Minister had suggested London or another city in England as the meeting place, the President said he thought a more remote spot would be better. He mentioned Casablanca or Tunis, or even Sicily. He said he wanted to send me to the meeting but did not want me to undertake so long a journey, hence he would send Under Secretary Welles.

Two days later Stalin suggested Moscow as the place and the beginning of October as the time, and on September 11 the President agreed.

I delivered on September 12 a radio address over a national network to sum up our latest views on foreign policy and to convince our people that it was to the highest interest of the nation to take our full share in postwar cooperation with other nations.

"It is abundantly clear," I said, "that a system of organized international cooperation for the maintenance of peace must be based upon the willingness of the cooperating nations to use force, if necessary, to keep the peace. There must be certainty that adequate and appropriate means are available and will be used for this purpose. Readiness to use force, if necessary, for the maintenance of peace is indispensable if effective substitutes for war are to be found."

I suggested three postulates for organized international cooperation after the war.

The first was that each nation should maintain a stable government. Each nation would be free to decide for itself the forms and details of its governmental organization—so long as it conducted its affairs in such a way as not to menace the peace and security of other nations.

The second was that each nation should conduct its economic affairs in such a way as to promote the most effective utilization of its human and material resources. Although each nation should be free to decide· for itself the forms of its internal economic and social organization, it should conduct its affairs in such a way as to respect the rights of others and to play its necessary part in a system of sound international economic relations.

The third was that each nation should be willing to submit differences arising between it and other nations to processes of peaceful settlement, and be prepared to carry out other obligations that might devolve upon it in an effective system of organized peace.

At this time Welles was still in Maine, and I had reliable information that he was writing numerous letters to friends in Washington that he had been the victim of ill treatment.

After a certain amount of this had accumulated, I went to the President. I recalled to him that he and I had agreed to Welles's making the trip to Moscow as the best means of getting him out of the Department without a public sensation, but that now conditions were different. Welles had not seen fit to join in with our plans but had gone off to Maine, whence he was writing many persons and apparently endeavoring to martyrize himself. I also recalled Welles's remark when I had brought up with him our plan to send him to Moscow; namely, that nothing could be gotten out of such a trip. I said I now would oppose his being given recognition by the State Department unless he retracted some of the harsh criticism attributed to him and declared his loyalty to the Department and the Administration.

Welles did nothing of the sort, but continued his long-distance criticism of me and the Department generally. As the campaign by one or two newspaper critics went on, to the effect that I was Russia's enemy and wanted to see her bled white, I went to the President and said I would strenuously oppose Welles's going to Moscow.

I said to the President that, wherever the conference might be held —anywhere between here and Chungking—I would be there myself.

The President immediately expressed his gratification that I would go, and he repeated it two or three times with emphasis. He was also surprised. He knew I had not been feeling well, that I was no longer young— I was then on the eve of seventy-two—and that I had never before been in an airplane.

He did not know another fact—I suffered somewhat from claustrophobia. One hot night some years before, while on a railroad sleeping car with the windows open which was passing through a long tunnel, I awakened and became conscious of apparently suffocating from carbon or other gases. I thought the train had been obstructed in the tunnel. Ever since then I had had a horror of being in cramped, enclosed places. I had that feeling about airplanes, and consequently had never flown before.

Nevertheless I now decided I had to fly to the diplomatic engagement at Moscow just as an officer has to take his unit into battle whether he wants to or not.

I made my decision on my own, without consulting my doctor or Mrs. Hull.

The President cabled Stalin on September 24, saying that on further consideration he was most anxious that I attend in person the meeting with Mr. Molotov and Mr. Eden. He said I would find the long flight to Moscow extremely difficult for physical reasons, and could the conference therefore not be held in England? He believed it would be a great advantage to all of us if I could personally attend the conference. He felt sure the British would be willing to make the change. He suggested October 15 for the opening session.

Stalin replied that he must reluctantly insist on Moscow as the meeting place. I accordingly said to the President I would go to Moscow. My health was less important than the conference.

The President on September 25 announced Welles's resignation as Under Secretary of State and his replacement by Edward R. Stettinius, Jr. I had a high regard for Stettinius on account of his extensive business experience, his fine character, and his belief in the principles and policies President Roosevelt and I were supporting. He made a splendid showing as Under Secretary. Had he continued in the Department during the years following he would have correspondingly increased his prestige and capacity as a top-ranking official in our foreign relations.

Intensive exchanges of cables were taking place among the State Department, the British Foreign Office, and the Kremlin on the topics to be considered at the conference. These included the postwar treatment of Germany, Italy, and Austria; the scope of the politicomilitary commission in Algiers to handle Mediterranean problems; the attitude of the three powers toward the French Committee of National Liberation, toward Turkey, toward Iran, toward the resistance movement in Yugoslavia, and toward the liberated areas; and relations between Russia and Poland.

The economic topics included cooperation in rehabilitation of war damage in the U.S.S.R.; joint action for assistance to other countries; collaboration on such matters as food and agriculture, transport and communications, finance and trade, and the International Labor Office; and reparations.

I had hoped to get our Four-Nation Declaration on postwar agreements, including the establishment of an international organization to maintain the peace, which Mr. Churchill and Eden had approved at the Quebec Conference, included as possibly the principal point on the agenda. Immediately after the Quebec meeting I had sent the full text to Moscow, with the hope that the Soviet Government would give it favorable consideration.

My disappointment was sharp indeed, therefore, when Foreign Commissar Molotov informed us that Russia could not accept the declaration. Her principal objection seemed to be that we had included China. Russia felt that China had no interest in European matters and consequently should be left out.

The President and I believed, on the contrary, that China had a rightful place in such a declaration. She was not nearly so powerful militarily as the other three nations; but her population was larger than those of the other three put together, she had vast potentialities if her people could be united, she had been fighting against the major Pacific enemy for more than six years, and after the defeat of Japan she would be the principal strictly Asiatic Power.

I felt it would be a bad blow to China psychologically to be excluded from the Four-Nation Declaration. Her long war with Japan had been a terrible strain on her resources and morale, and any such exclusion might plunge her into the depths of defeatism and resentment. It would also be easier to influence China's development internationally and internally if she were on the inside of any special relationship among the big Powers than if she were on the outside.

Of keen interest to us were the relations between Russia and China, who had the longest common boundary of any two nations in the world, longer even than the Canadian-American boundary. These relations would be better if Russia and China were on an equal footing in a four-nation arrangement. I was convinced that Russian cooperation would be of great assistance to us in rehabilitating and unifying China after the war. Russia would have moral influence on the Chinese Communists, even though their type of Communism was not exactly the same as the Russians. We did not put any specific proposal to Russia on this score during my period of service; but we repeatedly talked with her, as we did with other countries, to emphasize the interest of all nations in China's rehabilitation, and hence the need of their active aid for this purpose.

Britain had adopted our view that the Four-Nation Declaration was of vital necessity, though she was not so convinced as ourselves that China should be one of the signatories.

At the beginning of the year our Government, to improve the status of China, had taken an important step—the relinquishment of our extraterritorial rights in that country. As early as 1934 the President had expressed our willingness to negotiate this project with China when conditions were favorable. I had been on the point of proceeding with such negotiations in 1937 when the Japanese invasion of China rendered them impossible.

British Ambassador Halifax called on me on April 25, 1942, to hand me an *aide-mémoire* from his Government suggesting that negotiations should begin. This referred to a memorandum we had given the British Foreign Office on March 30, 1937, making the same suggestion.

Numerous exchanges took place between the British and ourselves to arrive at a common agreement. The Foreign Office wanted to make a special issue of the International Settlement at Shanghai. They also felt it necessary to consult the Dominions. I stated that what we had in mind was the complete wiping out of all rights of a special character. Any hold-over from the existing anomalies would be a further problem and the cause of continuing friction. Britain agreed.

Finally, on October 9, 1942, the British and we notified China of our willingness to begin negotiations. Our decision was made public on October 10, the Chinese national holiday, and occasioned a stirring exchange of friendly messages between the President and Chiang Kai-shek.

I handed the draft of our proposed treaty to Chinese Ambassador Dr. Wei Tao-ming on October 24. In a press statement I said the step we were taking was one of special personal gratification because we had long desired to take it in practical application of the fundamental principles of our foreign policy.

The negotiations on the basis of this draft were shortly concluded, and I signed the treaty with Dr. Wei Tao-ming on January 11, 1943. The treaty provided for the relinquishment by the United States of extra-territorial and other special rights in China and stipulated that Americans in China would be subject to the jurisdiction of the Chinese Government in accordance with the principles and practice of international law. It also provided that negotiations would be entered into at a suitable time to conclude a comprehensive modern treaty of friendship, commerce, navigation, and consular rights.

The Senate unanimously voted its approval, and the President ratified the treaty on May 4, 1943. Thus we gave up special rights, some of which dated from the American-Chinese treaty of Wanghia of July 3, 1844, and China could now hope to see herself at the war's end in complete possession of full sovereignty. In due course a number of other countries followed the example set by Britain and the United States.

My discouragement at the Soviet Government's rejection of the Four-Nation Declaration was counterbalanced by the encouragement I received from the overwhelming passage by the House of Representatives on September 21 of the Fulbright Resolution. This committed the House to "favoring the creation of appropriate international machinery with power adequate to establish and to maintain a just and lasting peace, among the nations of the world, and as favoring participation by the United States therein."

At almost the same time a conference of Republican leaders at Mackinac Island, Michigan, went on record as approving United States participation in an international cooperative organization following the war. I had had several conversations with Will Hays shortly before this conference, and he had communicated to the Republican leaders my strong belief that the two major parties should adopt a common, nonpartisan attitude supporting an international organization to maintain the peace.

Here, I felt, was strong backing for the issue of an international organization which I expected to press at Moscow. It was also ripe fruit from the tree of nonpartisan foreign policy which I had been cultivating. It was a far cry from 1919 and 1920 when the Senate rejected the League of Nations, and from 1935 when the Senate rejected our participation in the World Court. Now at long last Congress was coming to support the view I and others in the minority had fought for during two decades and a half, that a world organization was necessary, and that it could not function effectively unless the United States were a member.

For some months I had been in close contact with leading members of the major parties in both Houses of Congress, to work with them in developing a resolution that would pledge Congressional support of United States membership in a world organization. I felt that such Congressional action would be of great help when I approached other nations, particularly Britain and Russia, in an endeavor to agree on the creation of such an organization. They would be more willing to work with us toward that end if they were reasonably certain that the United States would be a member.

I seldom lost an opportunity to hammer home again and again to Senators and Representatives, whether Democratic or Republican, two main points. One was that a world organization to maintain the peace, by force if necessary, was absolutely imperative, and the United States had to be one of its principal members. The other was that our policy in this respect should be entirely nonpartisan, with both Republicans and Democrats joining in its support. I had frequently invited Senators and Representatives to visit my office so that I might go over these thoughts with them in detail.

Throughout my career in the State Department I had never ceased to insist that internal politics should be entirely divorced from our foreign policy. There could always be honest differences of opinion regarding this policy, but there should not be purely partisan differences. And this principle, bearing on foreign policy in general, I particularly emphasized in relation to the postwar organization and the necessity for our prominent participation in it.

Representative Sol Bloom, chairman of the House Committee on Foreign Affairs, had written me on February 3, 1943, asking for my comment on a resolution advising that the President enter into agreements with the United Nations and other nations to secure and maintain law, order, and peace among the covenanted countries. Replying on February 16, I said:

"What action the Congress wishes to take on this resolution is, of course, a matter for its own discretion. I may say, however, that the spirit of the resolution is entirely in accord with the foreign policy of this Administration, which has consistently endeavored to secure and maintain law, order, and peace by the conclusion of international agreements, by keeping alive and maintaining the principles which underlie wholesome and peaceful relations, many of which have been repudiated and abandoned by a number of countries during recent years, as well as by every other means within its power. The Administration is firmly determined to press forward this policy, in cooperation with Congress, as rapidly as events make further progress possible."

During the series of talks I had with Foreign Secretary Eden the following month he seemed much interested in the state of opinion in Congress and throughout this country with reference to United States participation in international cooperation following the war. He was undoubtedly wondering whether the United States would again take the course Woodrow Wilson's antagonists had followed—isolation and refusal to join a world organization.

When he brought up the subject on March 15 I said that a suitable expression by Congress on the United States' taking part in a world organization would have a splendid effect abroad, including Russia. The whole question of establishing and preserving close and sympathetic working relations between the Legislative and Executive branches of the Government, I added, called for close attention at all times during the war and the postwar period. Thorough understanding had to be maintained between the two branches to the end that each might function as effectively as possible within its own sphere. And this was the only way to avoid controversy and deadlocks, with their deadly effects on our international situation.

"The Executive Branch," I said, "charged of course under the Constitution with the conduct of foreign relations, is at least impliedly charged with the initiation of foreign policy. In order to avoid misunderstanding and apparent conflict between the Executive and Legislative branches, especially the Senate, it is very important that neither should bestow on the other functions or privileges or other authority that might result later in efforts of one to veto the plans or objectives of the other. The Senate can undertake on its own initiative to define its views on any phase of foreign policy, present or future, without any surrender by the Executive Branch of its legitimate functions under the Constitution. And such expression by the Senate is most desirable, assuming that the situation is first carefully canvassed to make sure that any such proposal will receive an overwhelming vote—in any event more than two-thirds of the vote."

The task before us, therefore, I said, was to get detailed discussion with all the Senators favorably inclined. We carefully had to work out during the next few weeks an agreement on every essential phase, so that there would be understanding and unity when the Senate took action. This preliminary step of full and detailed conference was an indispensable prerequisite to any successful action by the Senate on a proposed resolution.

I also added that it was all-important to keep public opinion educated and stabilized up to date with respect to the hitherto controversial questions in foreign affairs. Otherwise Congress could not be expected to maintain any position that it might take in the event public opinion should lapse or swerve in the wrong direction.

I talked on March 19 with Senator Gillette of Iowa, who had introduced one of the resolutions to put the Senate on record as favoring participation by the United States in an international peace agency. I said that what was needed was an advance agreement among the Senators as to what sort of resolution could pass the Senate overwhelmingly. I communicated the same thought to Senator Lucas of Illinois, who was acting President pro tem of the Senate. Lucas had asked the Department to prepare a resolution that it could recommend.

At the Department we prepared a brief resolution. During this preparation, I cautioned my associates that such a resolution had great importance and also great dangers. There were still some elements in our population who might run away from this proposition like a horse at the rustle of a leaf; and if we were not careful they would get away as fast as a wild stallion.

The resolution consisted of two paragraphs. The first called for the full and relentless prosecution of the war until the complete defeat of the Axis. The second declared that the Senate "advocates participation by the United States in the creation and maintenance of an international organization to insure permanent peace."

I went over the whole proposition with Republican Senator McNary, Minority Leader, who promised me complete cooperation. I held a conference on March 22 with Senators Connally, George, Vandenberg, and Gillette and read them the text of our proposed resolution.

We had no pride of authorship in the resolution, however. I stated to a press conference that day that the Government was convinced that some international agency must be created to keep the peace among nations in the future, and it therefore followed that the Executive Branch favored the broad principles of the various resolutions introduced in Congress with this purpose in view.

I read our resolution that same day to Eden and Halifax. I said I now felt that, with careful management and by taking the matter up with Senators individually, we had every assurance that a resolution would come through the Senate. The matter, however, had to be handled with extreme care and delicacy, lest it revive old controversies, including the discussions on isolationism and even more ancient bones of contention.

The following day I held a meeting on the same subject with Senators Ball, Burton, Hatch, and Hill.

During the summer I kept in close touch with Senators and Representatives to urge unceasingly that Congress begin to align itself behind an international organization, in which the United States would play a prominent part.

The President wrote me on June 28, 1943, about the Fulbright Resolution: "What do you think of pushing the resolution of the Foreign Affairs Committee of the House? It seems to me pretty good, and if we can get it through the House it might work in the Senate also. I do not think it can do any harm. Will you talk with me about this. But you had better talk to Connally first."

I wrote to the President the same day that I had called the Speaker of the House some days before and said I was for the resolution and it was an excellent first step. The Speaker had replied that he also was for it, that recently Jim Wadsworth (Republican Representative from New York) came to him and said there would not be more than fifty Republican votes against it at that time, but that if a few weeks could be had in which to give attention to them there would not be over ten or twelve unfavorable Republican votes. The Speaker then said he had called a meeting of Fulbright, Wadsworth, and the Floor Leader, and it was agreed that the resolution would be taken up when the House reconvened in September.

"Naturally," I said, "the Senate is very jealous of its prerogatives on foreign policy, with the result that we are obliged to be discreet in working with the two Houses in connection with these subjects. I think likewise that we should watch every opportunity to advance the utterances on postwar policy which embrace the principles contained in the Fulbright, the Ball, and any other resolutions that may be offered."

Perhaps partly as a result of my insistence on thorough organization in the Senate and House so as to secure an overwhelming vote, the resolutions did not come to a head until some months later—but when they did they were handled in such a manner and passed with so stupendous a majority as to be eminently satisfactory.

I felt that the passage of the Fulbright Resolution on September 21 would give me a real advantage in Moscow because it would show Molotov and Eden that the people of the United States, at least through their Representatives in the House, wanted their country to take its full share in an international organization.

I was also much encouraged at this time of preparation for the Moscow Conference by a communication Soviet Chargé Andrei A. Gromyko handed me on September 16 from his Government, flatly rejecting a Japanese attempt to bring about a separate peace between Germany and Russia. Japan was then becoming alarmed over the progress of the United Nations in the Pacific. She wanted to see Germany's might released from the East so as completely to confront the Allies in the West and thus force us to divert much of our strength from the Pacific. Naturally such a peace with Russia would be solely one of expediency, and when the Axis powers had defeated the Western Allies they could then deal with Russia at their leisure.

The Soviet Government informed us that on September 10 the Japanese Government had proposed to send a high official with various assistants to Moscow for talks with the Soviet Government. They would then go on to Germany and other countries for conferences and later return to Moscow for further talks. Molotov replied on the 13th that the Soviet Government had no doubt that the purpose of this mission would be an attempt at mediation between Russia and the countries which were at war with her. The Soviet Government considered that any armistice or peace with Hitlerite Germany and her European satellites was absolutely out of the question, and therefore declined the Japanese proposal.

When Gromyko read me this communication, I thanked him profusely. I said that, even before he concluded his reading, I felt sure in my own mind what Molotov's answer would be, and when he concluded his statement my judgment was confirmed.

I felt that the Soviet Union's decisively adverse reaction to Japan's approach, coupled with the prompt and full information she furnished us concerning it, was a happy augury for the forthcoming conference.

During the pre-conference exchanges among Moscow, London, and Washington, Stalin placed considerable emphasis on military discussions centering on the second front in Europe. He specifically requested a landing in France. He sent the President several messages on this point, and Mr. Roosevelt replied on October 4 that, at Stalin's request, he would welcome the fullest exchange during the Moscow meeting, even though he did not consider the conference as one that would plan or recommend military strategy. He felt sure the conference would find a meeting of minds for the important decisions that had to be made; and if difficulties developed he would still have every confidence that they could be reconciled when Stalin, Churchill, and himself met.

I foresaw trouble in connection with Stalin's determination to discuss military strategy during the conference. It was apparent that we should have to reassure Stalin completely on this point before we could induce him to come in with us on the political decisions.

My preference, of course, was to leave military discussions for the meeting of Roosevelt, Stalin, and Churchill, whenever that should be. It was now generally understood among Washington, Moscow, and London that such a meeting would take place some time after the Moscow Conference; but no decision had been definitely reached, and there was nothing agreed as to time and place. I expected to take up this subject with Stalin in Moscow.

91: Russia Versus Poland

PRIOR TO MY DEPARTURE for Moscow, I had conferences with the President on October 4 and 5 and luncheon with him on the 6th to go over the various projects likely to come up at Moscow. On the 5th I took Stettinius, Hackworth, Dunn, Matthews, and Pasvolsky with me to the White House for a comprehensive discussion with the President in which Admiral Leahy also took part.

We agreed at this conference that we should make every effort to secure both British and Russian agreement to China's participation in a four-power arrangement. Two three-power arrangements, we felt, would not be nearly so good as one four-power agreement. We thought the four-power concept should be preserved, even at the cost of getting no agreement at this time. China was too important a factor, both now and in the future, both because of herself and of her influence in British India, to be alienated.

As for Germany, the President said categorically he favored the partition of that country into three or more states, completely sovereign but joined by a network of postal arrangements, communications, railroads, customs, and perhaps electric power, although he thought power arrangements should be made on a continental basis. The new German states, he went on, should be deprived of all military activities, including training, and of armament industries. East Prussia should be detached from Germany, and all dangerous elements of the population forcibly removed.

The President took up the argument others of us advanced, that partition would have many undesirable results and that the customs union arrangement either would prove to be unworkable or would become a powerful instrument for the reunification of Germany. He said we were inclined to exaggerate these effects. He said he had traveled and studied in Germany, could speak German, and thought he knew Germany better than we did. He insisted that partition was the solution. The conversation shifted to other topics, but after a considerable time the President suddenly brought it back to Germany by saying that, after all, it was many years ago that he had become acquainted with Germany and perhaps he didn't know so much about her as he thought. He then said that the whole transitional period would have to be one of trial and error, and that it might well happen that we would discover that partition, undertaken immediately after the war, would have to be abandoned. He thought that reparations should be exacted in man power and equipment.

Mr. Roosevelt said there was not likely to be any trouble over the restoration of Holland or the Scandinavian countries, but that Belgium was likely to present difficulties. Apart, he said, from the equivocal position of King Leopold, then a prisoner of the Germans, who had British support because Churchill believed in the restoration of monarchies but who might cause trouble with regard to the Belgian Government-in-exile, Belgium was an artificial, bilingual state with the Walloons and Flemings traditionally at odds with each other. The President mentioned, in this connection, a German study made in 1940 proposing a federal union of Alsace, Lorraine, Luxemburg, and the two parts of Belgium.

As for Poland and the Baltic States, the President said that, when he should meet with Stalin, he intended to appeal to him on grounds of high morality. He would say to him that neither Britain nor we would fight Russia over the Baltic States, but that in Russia's own interest, from the viewpoint of her position in the world, it would be a good thing for her to say that she would be willing, two years or so after the war, to hold a second plebiscite in the Baltic countries. While Russia was satisfied that the plebiscite she had already held was conclusive, he commented, the rest of the world did not seem to think so. He thought that the same idea might be applied to eastern Poland, but that the new boundary in any event should be somewhat east of the so-called Curzon Line, with Lemberg (Lwów) going to Poland, and that a plebiscite should be held after the shell shock of war had subsided.

Mr. Roosevelt felt that the Baltic passages—Kiel and the Straits— might each be set up as a free zone under international trustees, and that a similar zone might be arranged for Russia to the Persian Gulf.

The following day I received Polish Ambassador Jan Ciechanowski to discuss with him the painful state of Polish-Soviet relations on the eve of my departure for Moscow, where the subject was certain to be discussed. These relations had greatly disturbed us and Britain for a number of months, particularly since the Soviet Government severed all diplomatic ties with the Polish Government in London on April 25, 1943. The future of Poland was naturally of keen interest to us. At the end of the last war, the United States Government had taken an active part in setting up a free and independent Poland, which was one of Wilson's Fourteen Points. We had continued to recognize the Polish Government after Germany and the Soviet Union had divided Poland between them in September, 1939, and we had refused to recognize that partition.

Hitler's invasion of the Soviet Union on June 22, 1941, had resulted in a marked betterment of relations between the Polish and Soviet Governments, signalized by their Joint Declaration of Friendship and Mutual Aid of December 4, 1941. Nevertheless, numerous difficulties persisted, centering principally in the boundary question and the release of Poles who had been taken prisoners of war by the Russians. In 1943, as the Russians approached the Polish borders, these difficulties sharpened.

Then in April, 1943, the Germans broadcast allegations that 10,000 Polish officers had been killed by the Russians two years earlier at Smolensk and buried in a huge pit recently discovered by the Germans. The Polish Embassy informed us of these charges on April 14. While acknowledging that the story might well be a fabrication on the part of the Germans, the Embassy said the Polish Government could not fail to take note of the allegations since it had been trying for over a year and a half to ascertain without success from the Soviet authorities the whereabouts of approximately 8,000 Polish officers known to have been captured by the Red Army in 1939.

The Polish Government did take up the allegations. It requested the International Red Cross to make an investigation on the spot. Tension between the Polish and Soviet Governments thereupon rapidly heightened toward an explosion.

British Ambassador Halifax handed me an *aide-mémoire* on April 21, 1943, which indicated that because of the grave deterioration in Polish-Soviet relations there was danger of serious trouble among the Polish armed forces abroad, particularly those in the Middle East. The *aide-mémoire* informed us that Prime Minister Churchill was considering sending a message to Stalin, the draft of which would be communicated to us shortly with a view to seeing whether this Government would wish to make an equivalent approach to Moscow.

I told Halifax that the President might be prepared within a week or two to make a direct approach. (He was then away from Washington.) In my opinion, I said, approaches would have to be made by the President and the Prime Minister to Stalin directly, if they were to have any effect.

Soviet Ambassador Litvinov sent me on April 24 a message from Stalin to the President, dated April 21, indicating that the Soviet Government was breaking relations with the Polish Government in London.

The message was a fiery condemnation of the Sikorski Government. It said that that Government, far from taking a stand against a vile German slander of the Soviet Union, had not even seen fit to ask the Soviet Government for information or explanation but had engaged in an investigation farce under the stage management of Hitler. I had this wirelessed to the President that evening.

The President cabled me with reference to Stalin's message, suggesting we send an immediate message to Stalin in his name, requesting the Soviet leader not to create a formal rupture of relations with Poland. I dispatched this message to Moscow on the morning of April 26. Unfortunately, the Moscow radio shortly thereafter announced that the Soviet Government had severed diplomatic relations with the Polish Government. The text of the Soviet communiqué was similar in content to the message Stalin had sent the President.

The rupture between Russia and Poland was now an accomplished fact, and it was easy to foresee the enormous damage it would inflict on the unity of the United Nations that was so essential if we were to win the war and assure the peace. It was an ominous omen for the future.

On April 28 the Union of Polish Patriots in the U.S.S.R., an organization of Polish Communists encouraged by the Soviet Government and cherishing ambitions toward ruling in postwar Poland, came to the fore with a declaration against the Polish Government in London. Here appeared the beginnings of a second Polish Government under the influence of Moscow.

On that same day Prime Minister Churchill cabled the President, attaching for his information a cable he had just sent to Stalin. At the State Department we prepared an answer, and I took this myself on April 20 to the President, who meantime had returned to Washington.

This stated to Mr. Churchill that the President approved everything the Prime Minister had said to Stalin, particularly his statement that we would not recognize another Polish Government set up in the Soviet Union or anywhere else. The setting up of a rival Polish Government by the Soviet Government constituted in our opinion the chief danger at that time and should be avoided at all costs. We shared Mr. Churchill's view that General Sikorski, Premier of the Polish Government, was the most helpful Polish leader whom we or the Russians were likely to find for the purposes of the common cause.

The President's cable noted with gratification that Churchill did not mention the underlying territorial dispute between the Poles and the

Russians, since attempts to solve it would not add to the unity of the United Nations at this time. The President was glad that Churchill's approach to Stalin was based primarily upon the obvious necessity of creating the most favorable conditions for bringing the full armed weight of the United Nations to bear upon the common enemy. Unless the other Allied nations could prevail upon Russia and Poland to adopt a course of collaboration with all members of the United Nations and to declare a truce with regard to all controversial questions likely to impede the prosecution of the war, our whole war effort would be jeopardized.

We left to the British the initiative in the effort to restore relations between Poland and Russia. This was for the reason that the Polish Government was located in London, that Britain had a special alliance relationship with Poland, and that Britain had been the intermediary in bringing Russia and Poland together in 1941.

Lord Halifax gave me an *aide-mémoire* from his Government on May 3 urging us to agree to look after the interests of Poland at Moscow pending the reestablishment of diplomatic relations between the two Governments. The Ambassador read the note, and when he reached the end of the first paragraph, in which the British Government said it was not in a position to perform this function, I said that this likewise well expressed the situation of the United States.

"Both our Governments," I said, "should be in a position at all times to exert their best efforts and influence to restore relations between Russia and Poland. But this influence is likely to be impaired, as the British *aide-mémoire* well states, if one of our Governments agrees to represent the interests of Poland at Moscow. The Russians, being a very suspicious people, are not favorably disposed toward this policy in any respect; and it would be easy for either the British or this Government to jeopardize its good standing with Russia, which is all-important to maintain for the present and the future as well."

Our two Governments, I continued, could do much more for Poland and for the United Nations' cause by exercising our fullest influence, not only to restore relations between Russia and Poland, but also to persuade Russia that she simply had to desist from this sort of flare-up from time to time in the future.

The Polish-Russian diplomatic break, I added, had done great injury to the Allied cause. To avoid a repetition of it was the most important problem now presented. If Russia could be persuaded to see these broader aspects of the situation, the more or less personal matters between Poland

and Russia would almost automatically iron themselves out. I concluded that the United States Government, like that of Great Britain, was most desirous of being of every feasible service to the Poles both as a Government and a people, and expected to see a new Poland reconstituted at the end of the war.

I promised Halifax I would confer with the President and let him know the President's views. When I brought this up with the President, he said at once he agreed with the views I had expressed. I so informed Halifax, who did not argue against our position.

I brought up the subject of Soviet-Polish relations several times with Soviet Ambassador Litvinov and with Chargé d'Affaires Gromyko, emphasizing the necessity of an agreement, while Ambassador Standley did likewise with Molotov in Moscow.

Most unfortunately, General Sikorski was killed in an airplane accident off Gibraltar on July 4, 1943. This was doubly tragic because we believed that Sikorski was not only a splendid leader of the Poles, but probably the only member of the Polish Government capable of bringing about a rapprochement with Russia. The President, after we had discussed this development, issued a statement urging all Poles to continue to follow Sikorski's policies.

Since March, 1942, at Sikorski's personal request to the President, we had been giving Poland a special credit of $12,500,000 annually, the major portion of which was for the development of the Polish underground and the remainder to pay the expenses of Polish diplomatic missions in the Western Hemisphere. Following a visit from Polish Ambassador Ciechanowski on July 21, 1943, I took to the President a request for a credit advance, under this arrangement, to the new Government of Stanislaw Mikolajczyk, to which Mr. Roosevelt agreed.

Britain's efforts and our own informal attempts to bring about a reconciliation between Russia and Poland having failed, the President and I sought in July and August to make a comprehensive, formal approach to the problem. After consultation with the British Government, I cabled Ambassador Standley in Moscow on July 17 an outline of a proposed agreement between the Soviet Union and Poland which he, together with British Ambassador Kerr, might present directly to Stalin. This stated that, in the opinion of this Government, the absence of friendly relations between the Polish and Soviet Governments was injurious to the common war effort in that it disrupted the unity of the United Nations, it lent encouragement to the endeavors of the enemy to create and intensify differences among the United Nations, it tended to strengthen those forces throughout the world which contended that prolonged cooperation among the United Nations during and after the war period was impossible, and it distracted the minds of millions of persons who should be concentrating all their energies upon the winning of the war.

We then made six proposals. All racial Poles in Russia who were domiciled in Poland on September 1, 1939, would be immediately recognized as Polish citizens by the Soviet Government. The Polish and Soviet Governments would permit all nonracial Poles in Russia who were living in Poland on September 1, 1939, to opt for Polish or Soviet citizenship. Those who opted for Polish citizenship and had close relatives abroad, would be permitted to leave Russia. Polish children would be evacuated from Russia. The Polish Government would agree to permit relief and welfare work among Poles in Russia to be carried on by Soviet organizations, Polish citizens to receive treatment no less favorable than that given Soviet citizens. The Soviet Government would permit the Polish Government to establish consulates in those areas in Russia where large numbers of Polish citizens were located.

We pointed out that our proposals did not in any way involve the question of frontiers, which was a matter we felt was not subject to discussion at that time and was not germane to the principal questions involved—the legitimate rights of individuals and the restoration of United Nations unity.

We likewise sent the same proposal to the Polish Government in London. The American and British Ambassadors saw Stalin on August 11 and presented our suggestions. The Soviet Government, delaying their reply until September 27, turned down our attempt to arrange a settlement. They argued that the disruption of diplomatic relations with Poland was not directly connected with the questions we had raised but with the hostile direction of Polish policy expressed in the Polish Government's attitude toward the German allegations concerning the 10,000 Polish officers reportedly buried at Smolensk.

Thus the matter rested when Polish Ambassador Ciechanowski came to my office the day before my departure for Moscow. Knowing that the subject would be discussed by the three Foreign Ministers at Moscow, he handed me a long memorandum outlining Poland's position. This, among other points, asked the American and British Governments to guarantee Poland's independence, integrity, and security, and to assure Polish par-

ticipation in the occupation of Germany and in the work of the Mediterranean Commission. It deemed undesirable either temporary or partial
occupation of Polish territories by the Russians. If such occupation were
unavoidably to take place as a result of military operations against Germany, it had to be dependent upon a previous Polish-Soviet understanding based on the reestablishment of mutual relations. It asked that British
and American troops be stationed in Poland to prevent Polish-Soviet
friction and to protect the population. It stated that the Polish Government could not be indifferent to the Soviet occupation of Rumania, Hungary, and Slovakia, because this would mean the encirclement of Poland
by countries under Soviet control. It expressed reservations against a
projected alliance of Czechoslovakia and the Soviet Union.

Nevertheless, the Polish Government was ready to take part in a
general security pact which, in addition to the directly interested countries of eastern Europe, would comprise Russia, Britain, and the United
States.

Ambassador Ciechanowski went over this memorandum with me
point by point. I said we would give it our fullest attention.

In connection with the Polish-Russian dispute then and later, and in
connection with other questions between us and Russia, a suggestion was
advanced from time to time that all we had to do to bring about a settlement was to threaten Russia that we would cut off the Lend-Lease assistance we were sending her. Neither the President nor I seriously entertained this suggestion for a moment. Russia, Britain, and the United
States were in the same boat, which would float or sink depending on
their abilities in jointly fighting the common enemy. Our Lend-Lease
supplies to Russia were helping to pin down or eliminate enemy armed
forces on the Eastern Front which otherwise we would have had to fight
on the Western Front.

The very making of such a threat would have engendered bad feeling
between Moscow on the one hand and London and Washington on the
other. Russia could always argue, moreover, as we ourselves had done,
that the sending of aid to her was in our own best interests. If we made
the threat and Russia still refused to accede to our demands, we would
then have faced a dilemma. Would we cut off military aid and thereby
hurt ourselves militarily? Or would we continue it, thereby proving that
our threat had been an empty one? And if we did cut it off, and let
Moscow go its own way, could we then have the slightest hope of reaching
a general postwar agreement with the Soviet Government?

On the other hand, if Stalin bowed to such a threat—and we had not the slightest assurance he would do so—what valid hope could we cherish that an agreement negotiated under a virtual ultimatum would be carried out when the Axis Powers were defeated and Russia no longer needed our military help?

We wanted to see normal diplomatic relations restored between Russia and Poland; and we wanted the Soviet Government to agree to broad principles of international cooperation after the war, centered around the creation of an organization to maintain the peace. But we did not intend to insist on a wartime settlement of specific questions such as the determination of the future boundary between Poland and Russia. Raising this question, at the insistence of the Polish Government or of anyone else, would have reopened the whole question of numerous other boundaries of interest to Russia—a Pandora's box of infinite trouble—which we had successfully postponed for the time being by the strong stand we had emphatically taken when the British-Soviet agreement of May 26, 1942, was under negotiation.

As I left for the capital of the U.S.S.R. I had made no promises to do more than urge the Soviet Government, with all the earnestness possible, to agree to a restoration of diplomatic relations with Poland.

92: Moscow Conference Begins

AT NOON ON THE SUNSHINY DAY of October 7 I went to the Washington airport and boarded an airplane for Moscow—the first time I had ever put foot in one.

Accompanying me were James C. Dunn, the Department's Political Adviser on European Affairs; Green H. Hackworth, Legal Adviser; Michael J. McDermott, Chief of the Division of Current Information; Cecil Gray, Assistant to the Secretary of State; Colonels Charles W. McCarthy and Harry A. McBride, War Department liaison officers; Dr. Matthew W. Perry; Lieutenant Commander Frank Myers, who was sent by the Navy to supervise the oxygen on the plane, and Henry Thomas, agent. The chief pilot was Major Alexis Klotz. He and his two co-pilots had previously flown into Russia.

The plane, a four-engined transport, was followed by two similar planes largely containing Army and Navy personnel.

After I boarded the plane, Commander Myers pointed out to me the emergency exits to use in case the craft had to "ditch" on water. The fact of several exits, I said, reminded me of the story of the old gentleman in Tennessee who kept three cats. A friend, visiting him one day, noticed three large semicircular holes cut in the bottom of the front door.

"What are those for?" he asked.

"To let my cats out," was the reply.

"But why won't one hole do them?"

"Because," the old gentleman retorted emphatically, "when I say 'Scat!' I mean 'Scat!' "

Our first lap was to West Palm Beach. Over Georgia the plane had to go up to 10,000 feet and at 8,000 feet I was asked to wear an oxygen mask. Elderly men do not react well to high flying altitudes, which are prone to bring on heart attacks, but I experienced no discomfort.

The next lap, the following morning, was to San Juan, Puerto Rico. There we boarded the cruiser *Phoenix* to make the Atlantic crossing to North Africa. Those in charge of arrangements believed that the sea crossing would give me a rest.

We put to sea almost immediately, escorted by two destroyers. Captain Noble, who was in command, kindly showed me around the ship, explaining her marvelous equipment, including radar. About halfway across I watched the cruiser refuel the destroyers, during which operation a seaman was thrown into the sea when a line broke, but was rescued by one of the destroyers.

At two o'clock of one morning, as we approached the Azores, the cruiser veered so suddenly I was nearly thrown from my bunk; "General quarters" sounded through the loud speaker system, and the crew were ordered to battle stations. I learned that the radar had picked up a submarine just as it surfaced about two thousand yards ahead of us. The destroyers rushed in, but the submarine immediately submerged and was not located.

Later in the day one of the four planes the cruiser carried sighted a supposed submarine and dropped a smoke bomb at the spot. Again "General quarters" sounded, and the destroyers dashed in. But the "submarine" turned out to be a whale.

The Azores were a danger point at which German "cow" submarines were known to meet and refuel other Axis underwater craft. At almost the time we were passing the Azores, however, announcement was made in London that Portugal had agreed to permit the United Nations to use the Azores for convoy protection. This was the result of the combined pressure Britain and we had been exerting in Lisbon toward this end.

We landed at Casablanca. There I sadly viewed the wreckage of the French warships, including the 35,000-ton battleship *Jean Bart,* which had sought to oppose the Allied landing the previous November. It was a tragic sight, one that would have aroused painful reflections on the frequent inability of human beings to think straight, if I had had time for such speculation. But I was met by Robert Murphy, our Foreign Service officer who was handling our political affairs in North Africa, and taken immediately to the airport. There we boarded our plane which meantime had flown the Atlantic.

Murphy accompanied us on the next stage of the flight, which was to Algiers, and gave me a summary of his latest impressions on the situation in North Africa and Italy. At Algiers I dined with General Eisenhower, who came from Italy for the occasion and whose personality and confidence impressed me greatly. I also received a visit from General de Gaulle. We had a long, reasonably frank conversation without reaching any decisions. De Gaulle was more friendly than I thought would be the case.

At that point I sent the President a message suggesting that he propose to the Soviet Government that China, Brazil, Yugoslavia, and Greece be invited to limited representation on the politicomilitary commission at

Algiers. I said I would like very much to have the question of French representation on the commission cleared up before I arrived in Moscow. I emphasized that the military functions of the commander-in-chief in the Mediterranean should not be interfered with.

From Algiers we made a night flight to Cairo. I slept fairly well in a berth. At the airport we were met by Alexander Kirk, our Minister to Egypt, by General Patrick Hurley, and by Richard Casey, Australian Minister to the United States at the time of Pearl Harbor, who was now British representative in the Middle East. During the afternoon Kirk took me to his home near the Pyramids, where King Faruq of Egypt, a handsome bearded man in his early twenties, King George of Greece, and the boy King Peter of Yugoslavia called on me.

The following morning we took off for Tehran, Iran. I saw the Suez Canal with long lines of freighters passing through. We then flew over land of which I had so often read in the Bible, and sighted Bethlehem and the Tigris and Euphrates rivers.

A surge of memory swept over me as the Holy Land flowed past me. I could see my mother reading the Bible to us night after night. I could see my brothers and me handing the book from one to another. I could hear us reciting verse after verse.

I was talking with a little group when one of the pilots came over and, pointing to a city up yonder about ten miles off, said: "Do you see that city? That's Beersheba."

"Oh, yes," I said, "and where is Dan?"

He studied a bit, then threw up his head and asked, "Dan who?"

We had a good laugh and I told him Dan was a biblical city in Palestine, the farthest removed from Beersheba.

Later a member of the party spoke up and said he wanted to know where Sodom and Gomorrah were.

"You ought to remember that," I said jocosely. "They were at the foot of Mount Vesuvius and were destroyed there between A.D. 6 and 7."

"Oh yes," he exclaimed, "I remember that now."

We again laughed as I said: "We're flying over Sodom and Gomorrah now." We were then passing over the Dead Sea, which covers the site of the ancient twin cities. He asked no further questions.

Approaching Tehran we flew past mountain peaks that towered up to 20,000 feet. Our pilot followed the passes and did not go above 13,000 feet, which meant, however, that for some time I had to wear an oxygen mask. From the plane and on the ground we saw much evidence of the vital role Iran was playing as a transportation route for American supplies going to Russia.

In Tehran I paid a courtesy visit to the Shah of Iran in his alabaster palace. I plied our Minister to Iran, Louis G. Dreyfus, Jr., with questions not only on our political relations in that area, but also on the biblical background of the region. Since there were many of these latter he could not answer, I said I would return in a couple of weeks and would appreciate the answers then. He must have crammed in the meantime, for when I next saw him he had all the information I wanted.

British Foreign Secretary Eden had cabled me suggesting he and I meet for a preliminary conference at Cairo before going on to Moscow. I replied that our Russian friends were rather suspicious generally, and that it might look as if Britain and the United States were forming a common policy in advance of discussing it with Russia. However, when I reached Tehran, Eden, following his own schedule, arrived at somewhat the same time. We thereupon met to exchange a few greetings and casual observations without entering into any real discussion.

At Tehran two Russian navigators came aboard. We were also joined by W. Averell Harriman, our new Ambassador to Russia, who continued on with us.

We arrived in Moscow late in the afternoon of a cold October day, the 18th, just as the sun was setting. Molotov and Litvinov, as well as Donald Nelson, Chief of our War Production Board, and a large crowd of other officials were at the airport to meet us. Molotov and Litvinov greeted me warmly. I then drove to the American Embassy.

We had purchased this building, known as Spaso House, from the Russians after we had established diplomatic relations in 1933. I was told that this had been the home of a wealthy Russian merchant who had done much to develop the mineral wealth of Russia. A few weeks after he moved into it, he was murdered there by his own son who came home drunk and wanted money. The house subsequently had been used by officials of the early Soviet revolutionary period, who were all executed later on. At Spaso House a Chinese boy named Gin was assigned to look after me. Brought into Russia by an American newspaperman, he had married a Russian woman and had two children; but he wanted to leave Russia and go to America.

I had little opportunity to draw conclusions from the past story of our Embassy, for a preliminary conference of the three foreign ministers was scheduled for that very evening.

The three foreign ministers met in the Kremlin the evening of October 18, with every appearance of cordiality and cooperation, and a strict attendance to business. We quickly agreed on no speechmaking, on the advisers who would sit in with us, on the meeting place, and on the first communiqué to be issued.

When I returned to the Embassy I found a telegram from the State Department referring to a message Mr. Churchill had sent the President on October 12 proposing a joint statement by the chiefs of the three Governments on the punishment of Germans guilty of atrocities. The cable said the President would like me to consider the text of some such statement to be issued at the close of the Moscow Conference. It suggested that, without prejudice to any action we might take against past offenders, the warning should refer specifically to present and future atrocities; this was to avoid driving German offenders to desperation and inducing them to take the same action as cornered rats in past history who had murdered their helpless victims.

Prior to the first formal meeting scheduled for the afternoon of the 19th I received separate visits at Spaso House from Eden and Molotov.

I suggested to Eden it would be well to give the Russians every indication possible that both the American and the British delegations were ready separately to discuss any matters with them. I considered it important to avoid a feeling of suspicion on the part of the Russians that the British and American groups were conferring without giving the Russians the benefit of their discussions. Eden agreed.

British Ambassador Sir Archibald Clark Kerr, who accompanied Eden (he later became British Ambassador to Washington), brought up the desire of the Russians to have military discussions, particularly with reference to the second front. I indicated I would state the United States' determination to prosecute the war to its conclusion and to give full assistance to her allies. We agreed that we should give the Soviet Government full information on our plans, the reasons for our decisions, and the results obtained, and receive any suggestions they might wish to make, but that it should be made clear that no military negotiations could be carried on at the conference.

With Molotov I first brought up the question of the Russian censorship. American correspondents had not been permitted to send human interest stories concerning the arrival of the American delegation. I asked whether such stories concerning the conference generally, which did not touch upon the official business of the meetings, could not be permitted.

Molotov exclaimed over the "stupidity" of the censor, and said he would see to it.

I then said I wanted to tell Molotov what I had already told Eden, that I envisaged cooperation among the three countries on an entirely equal footing and that there should therefore be no secrets between any two of us. Molotov heartily agreed.

Since I was convinced our three countries could engage in close cooperative action not only during the war but in the postwar period as well, I said it was important that misunderstandings or suspicions that might exist between our peoples should be steadily and progressively broken down, and I was prepared to devote the closing period of my life to facilitating such collaboration. Molotov said he was prepared to do everything he could toward the same end.

At our first regular meeting, held October 19 in Spiridonovka Palace, a fine old Czarist mansion tiled with marble and heavily ornamented in gold, Molotov distributed copies of the draft agenda, and drew attention to one omission—our proposal regarding the Four-Nation Declaration. He said it had not been included because it was not clear to his Government from the correspondence with the British and American Governments whether it was to be omitted or not, and, if we desired, this point could receive further consideration.

I immediately said that, while I appreciated the reasons why the Four-Nation Declaration (which had constituted Point One in the agenda previously circulated) had not been included, I was glad that Molotov had expressed willingness to put this point back on the agenda. I added that the Declaration affected so many mutual interests of the three countries at the conference that I proposed it be made Point Two on the agenda, immediately following the Soviet proposal for the consideration of measures to shorten the duration of the war against Germany and her European allies. Molotov and Eden agreed.

Molotov then handed us a written proposal for Item One—measures to shorten the war. This contained three points. The first asked whether the assurances given by Churchill and Roosevelt at the beginning of June, 1943, to the effect that Anglo-American forces would invade northern France in the spring of 1944, remained in force. The second point was that the three Powers propose to the Turkish Government that Turkey immediately enter the war. The third was that the three Powers propose to Sweden that she provide the allies with air bases for the struggle against Germany.

I said I would like to submit the proposals concerning Turkey and Sweden immediately to the President, to which Molotov agreed.

At this meeting I was accompanied by Ambassador W. Averell Harriman, Major General John R. Deane, our military attaché in Moscow; Green H. Hackworth, James Clement Dunn and Charles E. Bohlen, the last-mentioned being a Foreign Service officer very familiar with Russia, who interpreted for me. He later rose to high position in the State Department.

Our next session, on October 20, was devoted entirely to military discussions centering around the second front. British Lieutenant General Ismay and General Deane stated in some detail the Anglo-American plans for launching a major offensive across the English Channel in the spring of 1944. These plans were subject to two conditions, one being a reduction in the German air fighter force in northwestern Europe, the other being that the German land forces then able to resist the assault should not exceed certain totals.

Eden and I gave an affirmative reply to Molotov's formal question whether the Roosevelt-Churchill statement of June, 1943, that an invasion of northern France would be carried out in the spring of 1944, still remained in effect. We said that that decision had been reaffirmed at the recent Quebec Conference, subject to the conditions just stated, and preparations to carry out the operation were being pressed forward as rapidly as possible.

Molotov said his Government took note of these statements, as well as those made by Ismay and Deane, and expressed the hope that the plan of invasion would be carried out on time.

The Four-Nation Declaration came up for discussion at the third meeting, on October 21. I said we were now at a stage when the cooperation of all the United Nations, based primarily on self-interest, must be considered in the light of the period that would follow our final victory. It was clear there were overwhelming common interests that were a close second to the first task of winning the war.

"We have many interests in common," I said. "Among them is a mutual interest in the preservation of peace and the establishment of international security which we regard as the only means of assuring the political, economic, and social welfare of every people in the world. The welfare of our peoples depends not only upon the measures taken internally by each Government, but also upon the establishment of a world power under law that will at all times preserve peace and guarantee to the peoples of the world the possibility of continuing their progress. We feel that the basic principles of this international policy are those set forth in the Atlantic Charter and in the subsequent declarations of the United Nations, and that only worth-while nations will be interested in the preservation and extension of those principles."

In all the United Nations, I said, there was a growing desire to obtain leadership and guidance from the great powers, particularly concerning the future course of international affairs. They wanted to know whether the great nations would revert to isolation and its suicidal consequences or whether, in the interest of self-preservation, they would adopt the path of cooperation.

I emphasized that democratic countries in general required a considerable period of time to formulate their international policies. Public opinion in those countries moved slowly, and the people desired to see clearly the direction in which their governments were moving. For this reason we regarded it as important that the peace-loving Governments of the world take, even during the war, such steps as would hasten this process and set forth the principles that pointed the way to international cooperation.

I added that, since I always wished to speak with clarity and frankness, I wanted to inform the conference that we had sent the draft of the Four-Nation Declaration to the Chinese Government, as well as to the British and Soviet Governments, for their consideration and comment.

Eden strongly supported my arguments. Molotov, too, said his Government was very favorably disposed toward the principles set forth in the Declaration and therefore welcomed it. However, he immediately brought up the question of China, and objected that, if she were included it would probably be impossible to get her adherence in time to sign the document during the conference.

I informed Molotov that I had learned from the Chinese Ambassador to Moscow that his Government had approved the draft of the Four-Nation Declaration I sent them and merely desired to be informed of any changes that might be made in the text.

Molotov suggested that the conference consider a declaration by three, and not four, Powers, but if it proved possible to obtain the consent of the Chinese Government before the end of the conference it could then be transformed into a Four-Nation Declaration.

I pointed out the importance of the psychological situation of all nations participating in one form or another on our side in the war. I felt that if one of the great nations that was making an important contribution to the war should be excluded, the psychological effect would be most harmful for the unity of the United Nations.

The discussion went on for some time, until Molotov proposed a recess. During the conference a recess was customarily called about midway through each session, and tea was served. This consisted of a seemingly infinite variety of delicacies and wines in addition to the usual tea. Many days the weather was so fine that during the recess we walked in the garden of the palace. I was then often able to have a private and fruitful conversation with Molotov.

The Foreign Commissar who, during our first meeting in Washington, had seemed to maintain a reserved attitude, was becoming increasingly pleasant and communicative in Moscow as I saw and conversed with him from day to day. Our conversations were becoming freer and more outspoken. In all my contacts with him in the course of the conference proceedings, I was more and more impressed with his broad grasp of the questions entering into the discussions.

Now during this intermission I took up very earnestly with Molotov his objections to including China in the Declaration.

"The American Government," I said, "is doing everything and has done everything possible with respect to the Chinese situation. In my judgment it would be impossible to omit China from the Four-Nation Declaration. My Government believes that China has been in the world picture as one of the Big Four for the prosecution of the war. For her now to be dumped out on her face by Russia, Great Britain, and the United States in connection with the Declaration would create in all probability the most terrific repercussions, both political and military, in the Pacific area.

"This might call for all sorts of readjustments by my Government to keep the political and military situation in the Pacific properly stabilized. Great Britain would probably be likewise affected. Furthermore, public opinion in my own country would be hopelessly rent by the news that my Government had joined with the Soviet Government to throw China out of the war picture, as the public would probably interpret her exclusion from the Declaration."

Molotov appeared to recognize the reasonableness of what I had said. Immediately after the conference resumed he indicated he was willing to leave open the question of Chinese participation, and to proceed with discussion of the clauses of the Declaration.

Numerous suggestions were then advanced and agreed to for changes in phraseology. Molotov encountered difficulty in accepting the clause setting up a technical military commission. He said that, while he could say in strict confidence that the Soviet Government and people would welcome it when the Allies had defeated Japan, nevertheless to include China in a technical military commission might lead to complications in Russia's relations with Japan, which it would be better to avoid. I proposed, out of consideration for Molotov's views, that the article be omitted. This was agreed to.

At the fourth meeting of the foreign ministers, on October 22, Eden advanced the proposal that a European Advisory Commission be set up, with headquarters in London, to consider all problems that would come up affecting the three Powers. I had proposed that such problems be considered at meetings called in the respective capitals, presided over by the respective foreign minister, with the other two countries represented by their ambassadors. However, I stated my willingness to agree to Eden's proposal. Molotov was also in agreement.

When the question of Italy arose, Molotov stated that his Government had been very happy at the unconditional surrender of Italy, and, while realizing the predominant part played in this by the British and American armies, he felt that, although far away, the Soviet armed forces had also contributed their part. Since Italy was the first country to surrender to the Allies, he added, new problems in this connection were arising which affected very directly the cooperation among the three Powers. The Soviet Union was greatly interested in receiving accurate information on Italy, including the manner in which the terms of surrender were being carried out, and this was impossible in the absence of a Soviet representative on the spot.

Eden promised full information, and said that Molotov's suggestion concerning a Soviet representative was taken care of by the proposal Eden had made that the three Powers appoint high commissioners to an Inter-Allied Advisory Council, to be set up to deal with Italy.

Molotov then presented a paper containing seven measures that the U.S.S.R. desired to see introduced in Italy largely to assure the "defascistization" of the country. Eden observed that most of the measures proposed were already in effect.

I promised that Eden and I, jointly or separately, would submit to the conference a chronological and detailed list of the policies that our two Governments had followed in Italy since the invasion of Sicily.

Molotov stressed the great necessity for a public statement by the three powers concerning Italy which would include the Soviet suggestions. This was subsequently agreed to, as was also Eden's proposal for an Advisory Council for Italy. The Council was to be composed of representatives of the three nations, plus the French Committee of National Liberation, with Greece and Yugoslavia to come in later. The Council was to have the particular duty of watching the operation of the machinery of control in Italy which would be enforcing the terms of surrender.

The Declaration regarding Italy stated the agreement of the three nations that Fascism should be utterly destroyed in Italy and that the Italian people should be given every opportunity to establish governmental and other institutions based upon democratic principles. The measures suggested by Molotov toward this end were included.

Molotov, at the October 22 meeting, proposed that, since Italy's participation in the war against Russia had wrought great damage to the Soviet economy, particularly to the Navy and merchant fleet, there be turned over to the Soviet Union immediately one Italian battleship, one cruiser, eight destroyers, four submarines, and 40,000 tons of merchant shipping.

Eden and I said we would submit this request to our Governments, and I said I would urge the President to give it sympathetic consideration on a fair and equitable basis.

I presented to the conference on the following day, October 23, our draft of a proposal for the postwar treatment of Germany. This we had evolved at the State Department during frequent consultations among ourselves and with other interested Departments and following a number of conversations I had had with the President. It represented the first comprehensive statement of the thoughts of the American Government on what we considered should be done with and in Germany.

About March 20, 1943, I had had a long discussion with the President at the White House on the subject of the postwar treatment of Germany. We both felt it was not too soon to begin a serious study of the question.

Mr. Roosevelt sent me a note on March 23 in which he said: "Apropos of our conversation the other afternoon, I wish you would explore, with the British, the question of what our plan is to be in Germany and Italy during the first few months after Germany's collapse.

"I think you had better confer with Stimson about it too.

"My thought is, if we get a substantial meeting of the minds with the British, that we should then take it up with the Russians."

During the following months we discussed the subject intensively at the State Department, with the British, and with Secretary Stimson until we perfected the project I now presented at Moscow.

As was my usual custom, I handed this very informally to my Russian and British colleagues. When I was together with Molotov, I drew the document out of my pocket and gave it to him saying: "This is not a formal United States proposal but something to show a slant of mind. It is just a personal suggestion you and I can talk about. Then, if you like, we can talk to Eden about it and see what he thinks. I can make the proposal mine, or you can make it yours."

Molotov said he would like to take the document and study it. The next day he came back, his face radiant. "I have shown this to Stalin," he said in effect, "and he is enthusiastic. It expresses Russia's thoughts about Germany exactly as if we had expressed them. We have had those thoughts but have not been able to express them. Stalin would like to make this a Russian suggestion." I agreed.

Our proposal, calling for the unconditional surrender of Germany, provided for the signing of an instrument by an authorized agent of whatever German Government exercised legal or actual power and by an authorized agent of the military authorities. This document would contain an admission of the total defeat of Germany; empower the United Nations to exercise all the rights of an occupying power throughout Germany; bind the German Government to deliver up all prisoners of war and other detained nationals of the United Nations; empower the United Nations to regulate the demobilization of German armed forces; stipulate the release of political prisoners, abandonment of concentration camps and delivery of war criminals; bind the German Government to the continued maintenance of all agencies of economic control together with their staffs, complete records, and other equipment, for subsequent disposition by the United Nations; empower the United Nations to supervise the economic activities of Germany; and require the German Government to deliver up all arms and armaments, other military and naval stores, and stocks of raw materials.

We recommended that, during the armistice period, an Inter-Allied Control Commission be set up to carry out the terms of surrender. Germany would be occupied by British, Soviet, and American forces. There would be minimum interference with local government, but all Nazi officials would be promptly removed and every vestige of the Nazi regime uprooted. The Nazi Party would be dissolved. Germany would pay reparations for the physical damage inflicted upon the U.S.S.R. and other Allied and occupied countries, such reparations to be determined through a Commission on German Reparations consisting initially of representatives of the three Powers. Germany would be totally disarmed.

As measures of permanent control of Germany's military potential, we suggested that Germany be denied a standing army, the German General Staff be disbanded, the military caste system be eliminated, arms manufacturing facilities be dismantled, importation and manufacture of arms, ammunition, implements of war, and materials essential to their manufacture, including all types of aircraft, be prohibited; and a permanent audit and inspection system be established and maintained under supervision of the United Nations.

We made several observations and suggestions concerning the permanent political status of Germany. As for the problem of German political unity, we said, there was then no indication whether the effect of defeat would be to strengthen the trend toward political unity within Germany, or whether the reaction against the defeated Hitler regime would lead to the emergence of a spontaneous movement for the creation of several separate states. The question was still under study.

We did state our view, however, that the potential threat of Germany to general security might be lessened through decentralization of the German political structure. This might be accomplished by assigning to the state units control over a wide range of administrative functions, and by encouraging any movement that might emerge within Germany in favor of the diminution of Prussian domination over the Reich.

We also stated our belief that, in the long run, the most desirable form of government for Germany would be a broadly based democracy operating under a bill of rights to safeguard the civil and political liberties of the individual. For democracy to work in Germany there had to be: a tolerable standard of living; restriction of measures of control to the requirements of general security; and harmony of policy and purpose among the British, Soviet, and American Governments.

We pointed out that, since the administration of Germany would be controlled by the inter-Allied mechanisms during the armistice period, it was during that period that the bases of a democratic regime should be laid. Early steps should be taken to restore freedom of speech, religion, and of the press, freedom to organize political parties other than of Nazi-

Fascist doctrine, cultural associations, and trade unions. When conditions permitted, preparations should be made for the holding of free elections for the creation of a central German Government to which the occupation authorities would gradually transfer their responsibility for the internal administration of the country.

As for frontiers, we simply said this was a matter that should come within the purview of the general settlement with Germany.

Detailed discussion of this plan at later sessions revealed an identity of views on the major points. In the session on October 25, Eden said his Government would not like to see a united Germany remain but would prefer to see her divided into separate states, particularly a separate Prussia. He said his Government would therefore encourage any separatist tendencies within Germany, but that it was divided in its opinion on the desirability of attempting to impose the dismemberment of Germany by forcible means.

Molotov said the Soviet Union gave its full approval to all measures that would render Germany harmless in the future.

I remarked that my Government had been struck by the widely divergent views among Allied Governments on the subject of the dismemberment of Germany. In high quarters in the United States, I added, when the study of this problem had begun there had been a general disposition to favor the dismemberment of Germany. But, as the discussions progressed and conflicting and often very convincing arguments were advanced for or against, there was an increasing disposition to keep an open mind on this point and to explore it more fully before determining upon our final attitude—although dismemberment was still in favor.

I myself had been opposed to dismemberment from the beginning.

Molotov added that his Government was somewhat behind in its study of the postwar treatment of Germany due to the preoccupation of its leaders with the war. He said that to the United States and to me in particular belonged the honor of setting forth the first definite expression of an attitude toward Germany. The plan we had prepared corresponded to the Soviet Government's ideas, but this should be regarded as a minimum and not a maximum proposal.

We all agreed that Germany should be made to give up all her conquests and return to her pre-1938 borders, and that East Prussia should be separated from Germany.

We later decided to refer the plan for detailed study to the European Advisory Commission in London which we were setting up. Many of its points were incorporated in later Allied agreements for the postwar treatment of Germany.

Prior to this meeting on October 23, I had an hour's conversation with Molotov during which I strongly urged that certain bases for postwar settlement be laid now, particularly an agreement on a world organization to maintain the peace and on economic principles. I said that, if such problems were left until the end of the war, it would be very difficult to get unified support of public opinion in many democratic countries.

"The end of the war," I said, "will probably be followed by many divisions of opinion within the various countries concerned. The peoples of the United Nations will not be so united as they are now. It is very important for us now to take advantage of the unity brought on by the war, in order to apply that unity to the solution of postwar problems."

Molotov agreed.

I remarked that at the end of the last war there had been great changes in a number of important countries. In my opinion, at the end of the present war there would be from ten to fifteen countries going through the same process, many without adequate food and in no condition to guide themselves along the proper channels. I had participated in some of the discussions with President Wilson at the end of the last war and I had seen how catastrophically events had developed.

"I have been tempted to convey to the British," I said, "my belief that this time the United States is prepared to play her part in the postwar world. But I have waited until I was reasonably certain that this was true. Now I am reasonably certain, and I can convey this belief both to the British and Soviet Government at this conference."

Molotov said he warmly welcomed these views. He also agreed to my statement that the closest relations and confidence between our two countries were of vast importance, and that, if we could emphasize to both our peoples that they were in fact allies and comrades in the common struggle, nothing could prevent their becoming fast friends.

I added that our two peoples had many things in common. They shared in large measure the same tastes, the same jokes, and in general were very congenial. I went on that, speaking frankly as must be the case between friends, one of our difficulties had come from the efforts to promote Communism in the United States from abroad and also from the question of freedom of religion in the Soviet Union. Happily, steps had been taken in recent months to improve this situation.

Molotov smiled and said he did not see why the United States had any reason to fear the forcible imposition of Communism. As for religion, he commented that the widespread opinion with regard to religious matters in the Soviet Union was different from what actually existed in fact.

I replied that certain religious groups in the United States might put the wrong interpretation on religious events in the Soviet Union, and this was one reason why I felt that the exchange of full information between our two countries was so important. "You are right in your observation," I said, "that there is little danger that Communism will be established in the United States, but what I was really referring to is the extreme opposition of the American people to what they regard as attempts from the outside to interfere in the internal affairs of the United States."

I urged Molotov to send delegates to Washington to take part with the British and ourselves in the discussions we were holding on postwar economic problems. Both Eden and I had sent him various documents concerning these discussions. Molotov limited himself to saying that his Government was studying the various points at issue.

Just before we went to the conference meeting, Molotov said he had discussed with Marshal Stalin the proposed declaration sent me by the President regarding German atrocities. With a few minor changes, Stalin agreed to it.

In the conference discussions we were having on atrocities, the Russians took a strong stand. They had suffered severely at the hands of the Germans, and they wanted to administer stern, swift justice to the German officials responsible for the wholesale murder of Soviet citizens.

Eden argued that all the legal forms should be observed.

When it came around to me to state my opinion, I said:

"If I had my way, I would take Hitler and Mussolini and Tojo and their archaccomplices and bring them before a drumhead court-martial. And at sunrise on the following day there would occur an historic incident."

As this was translated, Molotov and his entire delegation broke into loud exclamations of approval, and for a minute the calm of the conference was shattered.

The main point I had in mind at Moscow in this connection was to emphasize further that the world had to deal in drastic fashion with a state of affairs wherein powerful dictators had arisen with plans of world-wide conquest, enslavement, and vicious methods of barbarism and savagery. I felt that this class of world desperadoes should be summarily dealt with just as they were summarily dealing with the innocent peoples of the world. This speedy action would make certain the prompt disposition of world gangsters who were worse in their methods and purposes than a million mad dogs let loose on every center of population.

I assumed that, when we captured the chiefs of the three Axis Powers and their ringleaders, we would also secure their secret papers and handle this evidence somewhat as we would if we were carrying out the forms of an international law trial. But I did not want this process to disturb the prompt disposition of those bandit chieftains.

I had submitted this view to President Roosevelt and to Prime Minister Churchill and Eden during their visits to the United States. I had also mentioned it a number of times at Cabinet meetings. I said bluntly I thought that the instigators of the war, German, Japanese, and Italian, should all be hanged.

I argued that since all ranks in the army, from general to private, were dealt with by court-martial, I did not see why the Axis ringleaders should be given preference in a fancy trial. Such a trial, among other disadvantages, would enable the archcriminals to manufacture a vast network of claims and pretenses embodied in a false and fraudulent defense. This, carefully thought out and prepared, would be passed on to the German, Italian, and Japanese populations to be taught them as gospel truth and so to shape their future course.

Besides, I felt that a summary trial would provide a more striking example to other would-be aggressor dictators in the future than a long drawn-out formal trial.

I was mindful, too, of the important fact that international lawyers in the past had set forth the opinion that persons like Napoleon could rightfully be summarily executed. Also, that international law was an outgrowth of treaties and of accepted customs, and the United Nations could therefore, by treaty, agree among themselves to the execution of the Axis outlaws.

The point that weighed most heavily in my mind was that the world was making a hairbreadth escape from being conquered and enslaved under the worst methods of savagery. This was not a mere local or regional war but one which, if successful for the Axis, would involve the utter destruction of everything worth while that the human race possessed. The conquerors, in their efforts to succeed, were literally torturing and crucifying tens of millions of innocent persons. Therefore, every consideration of self-preservation required that these ringleaders be summarily executed, just as military personnel down the line could be so executed following court-martial.

To my mind it was most important, not only that these savage men should be executed, but also that they should be executed summarily.

When I presented these arguments to the President, Churchill, and Eden, their general reaction was more in the direction of a formal trial under some form of international law. Nevertheless, no decision was reached, and I was still free at Moscow to express my personal opinion.

As long as I was at the State Department, my idea was not definitely rejected. It was changed in favor of a formal trial after I resigned as Secretary of State.

I do not want, however, to be understood as being opposed to the Nuremberg trial. I heartily supported that course when it was later decided upon. My thought has only to do with the difference in the form of trial.

The Declaration on German Atrocities, as finally agreed on at Moscow, and issued over the signatures of Roosevelt, Stalin, and Churchill, stated that Germans guilty of atrocities would be sent for judgment and punishment to the countries in which they had committed their deeds. Major criminals, whose offenses had no particular geographical localization, would be punished by the joint decision of the Allied Governments.

The Declaration ended with a warning whose language had almost a biblical resonance: "Let those who have hitherto not imbrued their hands with innocent blood beware lest they join the ranks of the guilty, for most assuredly the three Allied Powers will pursue them to the uttermost ends of the earth and will deliver them to their accusers in order that justice may be done." Prime Minister Churchill was its author.

93: Birth of the United Nations Organization

AFTER HAVING BEEN IN MOSCOW nearly a week, I remarked to Molotov that I did not know what the protocol was with regard to an audience with Marshal Stalin; I did not know how long to wait or whether I had waited too long; but in any event I would be honored if I could see his "boss" and I would leave the matter to Molotov.

Eden had seen Stalin briefly soon after getting to Moscow, but he had made arrangements in advance for the audience. I had made no such arrangements. My theory was that I should do business with Molotov and not let him think I wished to go over his head to Stalin.

In very short order Molotov informed me that Stalin would see me at the Kremlin at three o'clock, October 25.

One of the foremost topics of our conversation, I knew, would be the proposed meeting of Roosevelt, Stalin, and Churchill. Considerable difficulties, however, had arisen. Before and after my arrival in Moscow, the President was exchanging cables with Stalin relating to the meeting. The conference was agreed to in principle, but an insurmountable obstacle appeared to have risen over the place of the meeting.

In a cable on October 14 the President suggested Bagdad, capital of Iraq, or Asmara, capital of Italian Eritrea in East Africa, now occupied by British troops, or Ankara, capital of Turkey. Stalin had already proposed Tehran. The President suggested November 20 or 25 as the date.

On October 19 Stalin replied that he could not accept any of the places proposed by the President in lieu of Tehran. He said it was not a question of protection, which did not worry him, but a question of maintaining close contact with the Soviet Army during its present offensive operations. He said his colleagues considered that these operations demanded his personal contact with the High Command. Such contact could be assured at Tehran because of the existence of direct telegraph and telephone connections with Moscow.

The President sent me a long telegram on October 21 saying that Tehran, as he had learned from careful check of the time risk involved and his own constitutional obligations, was impossible for him. He meant he could not be in a place so isolated as physically to prevent his receiving legislation from Congress and returning it within ten days. Tehran was difficult of approach by airplane because of high mountains, and planes might have to wait several days before getting in or getting out.

The President said that Stalin had shown no realization of Mr. Roosevelt's obligations in his reply to the President's several messages. He therefore asked me to give Stalin a message from him and explain to him orally the definite and plain reasons for not wanting to go to Tehran, which were not based on personal desire but were fixed constitutionally. This was not a matter of theory, he commented, but a question of fact.

In his message to Stalin, the President said he was deeply disappointed over the Marshal's cable. He appreciated Stalin's desire for daily contact with the Supreme Command, but he asked Stalin to appreciate his own obligations, which he outlined in detail. He said he could not go to Tehran, and the Cabinet and legislative leaders were in agreement with him on this point.

He therefore suggested Basra, Iraq, instead. Stalin could run a special telephone wire from Tehran to Basra which would be controlled by Russians and would still give him direct contact with Moscow.

The President emphasized the fact that he was willing to go all the way from the United States to within six hundred miles of Russian territory. He had to carry on a constitutional Government more than one hundred fifty years old. Were it not for this fact he would gladly go ten times the distance to meet Stalin. Future generations, he concluded, would look upon it as a tragedy if a few hundred miles caused Stalin, Churchill, and himself to fail of meeting.

I went over all these points with Stalin when I sat across a great beige table from him in the Kremlin on the afternoon of October 25. Ambassador Harriman and Charles E. Bohlen were with me, while Molotov and an interpreter flanked Stalin.

As I entered the Marshal's large office, he entered from another door, met me halfway and shook hands. He was very cordial and affable. He escorted me to my seat at the table, and then sat opposite me, with his back to the wall.

Our conversation began on personal notes. We exchanged views on how to plant wheat. I told Stalin about planting wheat six inches deep in Tennessee, which seemed something new to him. We discussed rafting. I described how we had bound logs into rafts in Tennessee, using hickory walings. Stalin described how his people had bound rafts together with vines.

I told Stalin of my pleasure at being in Moscow, which was in fulfillment of a long-held desire to visit his country. I said I had attended many international conferences in my life, but at none had I received greater hospitality and consideration than we had from our hosts, the Soviet Government, and particularly Molotov. Stalin replied that he had not expected to hear this comment.

I remarked that one of the most important functions of the present conference was to lay the groundwork for a meeting between himself, President Roosevelt, and Prime Minister Churchill, in which all my people and indeed all the peoples of the world who were engaged in the fight against Nazism and Fascism were most vitally interested. I then handed Stalin the President's communication concerning the place of meeting.

Stalin, after reading the Russian translation, handed it to Molotov with the remark that it would be necessary to think about it and consult with his colleagues. The Foreign Commissar, after perusing it, said that important military operations were then in progress and that all the top civil and military authorities of the Soviet Government were of the unanimous opinion that Stalin should not absent himself at all, but in any event only to a place where direct and certain daily communications could be maintained.

Stalin then suggested it might be best to postpone the meeting until spring, at which time Fairbanks, Alaska, would be an appropriate place.

I said that both the President and I felt very profoundly that the international situation called for this meeting, and its failure to occur would cause profound disappointment among all the Allied peoples since its effect would be to unify our three nations in ever increasing cooperation for the prosecution of the war and for collaboration in the postwar period.

"If we should wait until the end of the war," I said, "to formulate a basic foundation for a postwar international program, peoples in all the democracies will be scattered in every direction under every sort of discordant influence by various elements, groups, societies, and individuals. As a result, nothing will be more impossible at that belated stage than for a country like mine to pursue a suitable postwar program and rally and unite all essential forces in support of it. This makes it all-important that we should realize the disastrous nature of the opposite course of postponing everything until the military decision has been reached. If an official in my country should now announce that he was opposed to formulating the fundamental policies for a postwar world until after the war is over, he would be thrown out of power overnight."

I added, however, that while both the President and I felt that the situation called for serious consideration, we did not mean that it should take precedence over the proper conduct of the war. I said I had felt a sense of relief when Stalin, after having read the President's communication, stated it was a matter calling for deliberate consideration. I told him we were prepared to send to Basra qualified engineers to look after the practical arrangements, particularly communications.

Stalin replied that there were very important military operations in progress in the Soviet Union, and that the Soviet summer campaign was merging with the plans for the winter campaign. He said that from the military point of view it was an opportunity that might occur only once in fifty years to inflict a decisive defeat on the German Army, which at that time possessed very few reserves while the Soviet armies had ample reserves for a year's operations. He said that obviously the Soviet Union could not expect to fight Germany every ten years. It was therefore impossible to let anything interfere with their taking advantage of this present opportunity which, he repeated, might occur only once in fifty years. He again said he would have to confer with his colleagues.

I answered that I fully agreed with him as to the military situation but felt it would be possible from the Soviet viewpoint to ensure just as good communications between Basra and Moscow as between Tehran and Moscow, so as not to impair his direction of military operations. I said that I ventured to suggest that, on the information I had, all the Governments and peoples of the Allied nations were awaiting this meeting with the keenest of expectation as an example of close cooperation among the Soviet Union, Great Britain, and the United States. I added that if it were possible, in addition to the announcement of such agreements as we might reach at the present conference, to indicate a disposition on the part of the three heads of Government to meet within a reasonable time, these two announcements would electrify the peoples of all the United Nations and correspondingly dishearten their enemies.

Stalin interjected that he was not against the meeting in principle.

I replied that I realized he was thinking merely of the immediate plans we were discussing.

He emphasized that on his part there was no question of stubbornness or prestige, but he was unable to understand why a delay of two days in the delivery of state papers should be so vital a matter, whereas a false step in military operations was not a grammatical error that could be subsequently corrected, but might cost tens of thousands of lives. So far as he was concerned, the difficulties at Basra related entirely to physical arrangements, particularly communications.

Stalin observed that he was not at all worried on the subject of protection. He made this remark after Ambassador Harriman said that the heads of state could stay each in his own camp in the hills back of Basra, guarded by troops of his own nationality, and thus be assured of complete privacy and protection.

Our conversation having lasted an hour—effectively a half-hour because of the necessity for translation—and because the hour of the conference was approaching, I informed Stalin that, since I was a pupil of Molotov's, it was now time to go to class. The Marshal smiled and wished us luck.

As the discussion ended, he rose and came around the table, shook hands, and said something in Russian. His interpreter was still sitting at the table finishing his notes, and Stalin's words went out into thin air. The Marshal turned upon the interpreter and spoke sharply to him, saying (Bohlen told me later) that an interpreter's duty was to be always at his elbow. I then learned that Stalin had been expressing his great pleasure in having seen me.

I immediately informed the President of the substance of our conversation.

During a recess in the conference session that followed my meeting with Stalin, I buttonholed Molotov and reemphasized the arguments I had presented to Stalin for a meeting of the three chiefs of state at Basra. Molotov asked me what were the programs of international cooperation I had said I thought should be settled now.

I repeated to him the numerous proposals I had more than once stated to him since arriving in Moscow. These were: cooperation to preserve the peace permanently and to provide for the maximum of economic advantages and benefits to each country for the equal enjoyment of their respective peoples; to preserve world order under law so as to avoid international anarchy; to provide for relief against starvation in many nations immediately following as well as during the war; to provide for the postwar German situation; to deal with dependent peoples; and to deal with currency stabilization as a basis for suitable international trade and financial relations.

Molotov said that an agreement should be reached on these programs. After some thought, he suddenly remarked:

"Isolation was almost your country's undoing, was it not, Mr. Secretary?"

"Yes," I replied, "it was. And isolation was almost your country's undoing, was it not, Mr. Secretary?"

Molotov smiled and admitted it was.

"After the war," I said, "you can follow isolationism if you want, and gobble up your neighbors. But that will be your undoing. When I was young I knew a bully in Tennessee. He used to get a few things his way by being a bully and bluffing other fellows. But he ended up by not having a friend in the world."

In the course of our conversation, Molotov brought up the question of Turkey's entering the war. He made it very clear that Russia's proposal was that the three Powers should "suggest" to Turkey that she come into the war, but that this meant to suggest peremptorily—in other words, to command. I replied that this was a purely military matter that came within the province of the President and the chiefs of staff.

At the session that afternoon we agreed on a declaration concerning Austria which had been introduced by Eden. This stated that the three Powers regarded the annexation imposed upon Austria by Germany on March 15, 1938, as null and void, and that they did not consider themselves bound by any changes effected in Austria since that date. Austria should be reestablished as a free and independent country, and the way thereby opened for the Austrian people themselves, as well as those neighboring states that would be faced with similar problems, to find that political and economic security which was the only basis for lasting peace.

Austria was reminded, however, that she had a responsibility that she could not evade for participation in the war on the side of Hitlerite Germany, and that in the final settlement account would inevitably be taken of her own contribution to her liberation.

We next agreed to inform one another immediately of any peace feelers that any of us might receive from the Government of or any groups or individuals in a country with which any of us were at war. We also agreed that the three Governments would consult together so as to concert their action in regard to such approaches.

Molotov interrupted this session to announce the Soviet Army's capture of Dnepropetrovsk. The great Russian counteroffensive of the autumn of 1943 was now in full swing, and from time to time Molotov dramatically communicated to us new successes of the Red Army.

The question of confederation of the smaller European nations, with particular reference to the Danubian area, came up for discussion at the following session, October 26, on the basis of a proposal sanctioning such confederations, submitted by Eden. The British had previously submitted this to us, but we had refused to go along with their view. The question was a concrete one in view of the efforts of some of the small United Nations to join together, politically or economically, after the war.

I said at the session that my Government believed that the first step we should take was to agree upon a broad set of principles capable of world-wide application which would then guide our three countries in our consideration of separate and specific questions, of which the British proposal was one. I had in mind the Pan American principles of cooperation applied on a world-wide scale. My Government, I added, had not sought to select any particular area or problem for special consideration before the general principles were agreed on, and I personally felt very strongly that the only orderly and reasonable approach to the entire topic of international collaboration and the creation of a stable and lasting basis for world peace was to take the general questions first.

Connected with this issue was another proposal on the agenda, also introduced by Eden, that the three Governments state their opinion in favor of joint responsibility for Europe as against separate areas of responsibility.

On this point I said that my Government very much hoped that no decision would be taken at this conference in favor of separate areas of responsibility or zones of influence.

Eden likewise opposed the principle of separate areas of responsibility.

Molotov said he knew of no reason to believe that the Soviet Government would be interested in separate zones or spheres of influence, and he could guarantee that there was no disposition on the part of his Government to divide Europe into such separate zones.

Molotov read a statement that emphatically criticized the idea of planning federations of small nations at this time. His Government considered the active consideration or encouragement of such schemes as premature and even harmful, not only to the interests of the small countries but also to the general question of European stability. Some of the plans for federations, he said, reminded the Soviet people of the policy of the "cordon sanitaire" directed in previous years against the Soviet Union.

Eden said it was hardly necessary to state that his Government was not interested in creating a "cordon sanitaire" against the Soviet Union but was very much interested in creating one against Germany. There was great force in Molotov's statement, he added, and he would not therefore insist.

I said that my Government had for some years consistently upheld the right of small nations to take such measures as they considered desirable for the welfare of their people, particularly in the economic sphere, provided such measures did not affect the larger questions of peace and security.

The Four-Nation Declaration, agreeing upon the establishment of a world organization after the war, came up for further discussion at this session, and I again brought up the question of China, which had been left open.

Molotov now said he had no objection to the inclusion of China as an original signatory, but, since he was most anxious to have the Declaration announced before the conference broke up, he doubted whether the Chinese Ambassador here could receive the necessary powers in time. I had been wrestling with Russia for some days over this question, and I felt that she was really against the admission of China and therefore sought to postpone any action.

I volunteered to communicate the text of the Declaration as it now stood to the Chinese Government, saying I was convinced that the necessary powers would be forthcoming to the Chinese Ambassador before the end of the conference. The conference thereupon authorized me to do so.

Molotov wanted clarification of the clause in the Declaration providing that none of the signatories would use its armed forces within the territory of another state except for the purposes envisaged by the Declaration. I replied that this article was in the nature of a self-denying act on the part of the large nations to allay the suspicions of the smaller countries in regard to the use of superior force.

Molotov inquired whether this would apply to the establishment of naval and air bases that might result from agreements between one of the signatories and smaller states.

Eden said his Government believed it inconceivable that any of the powers represented at the conference would use their armed forces or establish bases in the territory of other states except for the purposes envisaged by the Declaration.

Molotov inquired whether this article would require prior consultation among the signatories before one of them could conclude an agreement with any other country for the establishment of bases within the territory of the latter.

I asked Molotov what he had in mind precisely in regard to the article.

Molotov replied he wanted to be sure that, in connection with this clause, no obstacles to the future collaboration of our three Governments might result from agreements that one of the three might have with other countries for mutual assistance and the establishment of bases.

I said I thought that this article could not be taken apart from the rest of the Declaration. The purpose of the Declaration was clearly set forth in all its articles. It was designed to ensure that the signatories would act together in matters relating to the surrender and disarmament of our respective enemies. Such measures would be taken as might be necessary to ensure observance of the terms of surrender and the other aims set forth in the Declaration. In addition the Declaration consisted of a general set of principles dealing with the whole approach to the question of international collaboration and every consideration was sufficiently taken care of in the text.

Molotov said he was satisfied with this explanation.

Later on he proposed that a resolution be adopted that the three powers appoint representatives to a committee that would work out jointly the preliminary questions connected with the establishment of the general international organization called for by the Declaration. This committee could meet in any one of the three capitals and, if necessary, other members of the United Nations could be invited to participate.

I immediately replied that this was a very practical step. I thought that the best results, however, would be obtained by having the work of the committee informal and by not associating other members of the United Nations with it in the early stages since that might lead only to rivalries and jealousies.

Eventually we agreed that a commission such as Molotov proposed might give rise to difficulties. It would attract undue publicity, and dissension might follow the inevitable efforts of other nations and groups to secure representation on it. We felt that the same results could be achieved by less formal methods. We agreed that exchanges of views be carried on through representatives of the three powers, in the first instance in Washington and also in London and Moscow.

Immediately after the meeting of October 26, I communicated the text of the Four-Nation Declaration to the Chinese Ambassador in Moscow, Foo Ping-sheung. I told him pretty strongly that his Government should immediately seize this opportunity which my insistence had made available to them, and give a quick reply so that he could sign the Declaration before the conference ended. Knowing that the Ambassador's communications with his capital were slow, I cabled full information to the State Department with instructions to forward it to our Ambassador at Chungking, Clarence E. Gauss, so that he would take it up with the Chinese Government and let me have their reaction.

After some discussion of the memorandum which the British and ourselves presented on the subject of civil affairs in France when that country should be invaded, the conference decided to refer this to the European Advisory Commission for further study. This was the memorandum approved by the President on October 6, which I outlined in a previous chapter.

I communicated to the conference on October 28 the President's reply to Molotov's proposals concerning Turkey and Sweden. The answer, to which Britain also agreed, was in the negative on both points.

We said we did not consider it advisable at this time to induce Turkey to declare war. We were straining our resources for building up the invasion of northern France and supporting the Italian offensive. We proposed, as an alternative, that inquiries be made of the Turkish Government for the lease of air bases and transportation facilities.

As for Sweden, we felt that a system of air bases should not be requested at this time because this would require Allied defending forces that we could not afford to divert from the cross-Channel operation. We recognized that the use of Swedish facilities would be valuable for the emergency landing and refueling of planes that penetrated deep into northeast Germany and German-held territory. We therefore suggested that we give consideration, at a later date, to seeking this privilege which could then be expanded as circumstances permitted.

The conference agreed that the three countries should continue to study the problem of Turkey and Sweden.

On the same day I presented the President's reply to Molotov's request for Italian warships and merchantmen. Mr. Roosevelt had previously sent me a cable stating his willingness to hand over to the Russians one-third of all the Italian ships. I did not feel, however, that the situation had been made clear to him, and held up presenting this cable until I could have further confirmation. It seemed to us that giving the Russians one-third of the Italian ships at this time would be hopelessly discouraging to whatever Italian effort was now to be made on our side in the war, and, moreover, the Italian ships were now being usefully employed in the Mediterranean under American and British direction, with Italian crews, and might later be useful in the Pacific. The President quickly appreciated this view and cabled me accordingly.

I informed Molotov that the President had advised me of his desire that the Italian naval and merchant vessels in the hands of the Allies should be utilized where they could be most effectively employed in the Allied cause, without final transfer of title to any of us at the present time. Further discussion should be held between the staffs of our three Governments, or perhaps by the heads of the Governments. I said I would present the Soviet views in detail to the President on my return to Washington.

Molotov expressed some resentment at this answer, which reaction I communicated to the President. He replied on October 30 that the ships should be used to prosecute the war against our enemies, and the final determination of what would become of them should be made at the Peace Conference.

The American delegation, through Major General Deane, had made three proposals of a military nature to the conference. One was that the U.S.S.R. should make bases available for British and American aircraft so that shuttle bombing of industrial Germany could be carried out. A second was that more effective mutual interchange of weather information be agreed to, and, toward this end, communication facilities between the United States and the Soviet Union should be strengthened. The third was that air communication between the two countries be improved. I took up this last point myself with Molotov with much vigor.

Molotov informed us that the U.S.S.R. agreed to our proposals in principle, and that the appropriate Soviet authorities would be given instructions to work them out.

The President cabled me on October 28: "I am made very happy by your splendid achievement in putting things through. I know the China part of it was due to your personal insistence."

The President informed me he expected to "turn up" in North Africa shortly and would have to leave Washington by November 9. (This was for his meeting with Churchill and Chiang Kai-shek at Cairo.) He said he hoped I could maintain my original schedule of getting back by November 7 because it was imperative that he and I should talk before he left.

He suggested that, if Stalin found it impossible to meet him, the Marshal should fly as far as Basra even for one day. This was of supreme importance. The rest of the time, the President hoped, Stalin would let Molotov sit in with Churchill and him.

I replied to the President on the following day that I had been kept in Moscow longer than I expected, and would be glad to meet him on the Eastern side of the Atlantic. I said there were increasing indications that Stalin would not go beyond Tehran, and I doubted seriously whether Molotov, not being a military man, would be sent as a substitute.

Two days later I was forced to cable the President that four members of my party had contracted malignant malaria on the way to Moscow and could not return, and I did not think it advisable for me to be exposed to malaria, dysentery, and the like while waiting for him in North Africa because I had had no vaccinations or immunizations. The President agreed to postpone his departure and meet me in the United States. I thereupon cabled that I would fly the South Atlantic rather than take the cruiser.

The conference on October 29 took up a series of economic recommendations I had distributed to Molotov and Eden several days before. These concerned cooperation in the repair of damage in the U.S.S.R.; joint action for assistance to other countries; collaboration on matters such as food and agriculture, transport and communications, finance and trade, and the International Labor Office; and the question of reparations.

On the first point, damage in the U.S.S.R., we suggested that conversations begin between the Soviet Government and the American Embassy in Moscow to work out the magnitude and character of the material and equipment needed by the Russians to repair the ravage caused by the Germans. This was agreed to.

On the second point, aid to other countries, we suggested the setting up of an international lending agency to supplement private and governmental lending facilities. This was held for further study.

As the third point, we presented a long summary of our thinking on international economics. I made it clear that this was not to be taken as a formal proposal but as the basis for further thought and discussion. I remarked that I recalled very clearly the insufficient preparation on economic matters at the time of the Versailles Conference and the incalculable harm the world suffered as a result of the inadequate treatment of economic problems after the last war. I wished to ensure that this time these questions should be considered in good time.

We proposed an international agreement to lay down the rules and principles that should govern trade relations between nations. The nations would abandon preferences and discriminations, reduce trade barriers and refrain from export dumping practices. The agreement would be so drawn as to enable a state (like Russia) whose trade was conducted by the Government, to adhere on an equitable basis.

We proposed the orderly regulation, and ultimately the elimination, of arrangements, public or private, to restrict production and trade in individual commodities. This included international cartels.

We suggested the establishment of an international commission to develop the work that had been well carried on by the International Labor Organization toward the improvement of labor standards and conditions.

The conference agreed that the three Governments would consider these suggestions and exchange ideas among themselves. Molotov said he could state that his Government viewed these principles with favor.

On the point of reparations, we stated certain principles. Reparations should be imposed on Germany to the extent that they might contribute to strengthening the postwar world economic and political order. They should be in terms of goods and services, not money. They should be distributed in proportion to the losses of nonmilitary property suffered through German action. They should be limited to a period coinciding with the time required for the first stage of European reconstruction. They should not be relied on as a major instrument of control over Germany's military power. A Commission on German Reparations should be created, composed initially of representatives of the three Powers, with provision for the representation of other interested Governments.

The conference decided that this document should be further discussed by the three Governments.

I now brought up for discussion the proposed Declaration by the United Nations dealing with dependent peoples—the inhabitants of colonies and mandates—and proclaiming the necessity to lead them gradually to a condition of independence. This was the document we had prepared at the State Department and had given Eden at the time of his visit to the United States in March.

In the conference my associates and I and Admiral Leahy had with the President on October 6, just prior to my departure for Moscow, Mr.

Roosevelt had said we ought to lay great stress on the possibilities of the trusteeship idea and apply it widely to all sorts of situations. The areas he mentioned ranged from the Baltic to Ascension Island in the South Atlantic and to Hong Kong. He said the draft declaration we had prepared offered great possibilities, especially as concerned its inspection and publicity features, which would be powerful means of inducing colonial powers to develop their colonies for the good of the dependent peoples themselves and of the world.

Eden, however, had written me a note saying that, in general, his Government could not agree with our document. Nevertheless I distributed it at the conference solely to give the conferees an idea of our position.

When I brought this before the conference on October 29, I said it was what we considered desirable policy, but I realized there was not sufficient time for the conference to consider it.

Eden said he was not prepared to discuss the question, but he could state that his Government was not in agreement with the views set forth in my paper.

Molotov said he felt that the question of dependent peoples should receive further study and that his Government attached great importance to it.

Although nothing was done at the Moscow Conference about the declaration on dependent peoples, nevertheless the discussions among the three Governments concerning it continued, and the bases were laid for what later became the trusteeship system under the United Nations.

Relations between the Soviet Union and Poland came up for discussion at this session. Eden had come to see me on October 24 to request my support in bringing pressure on Molotov to restore diplomatic relations between the U.S.S.R. and Poland. I said I considered this more of a British problem because of Britain's treaty relationships with Poland, but I agreed that, when Eden opened the discussion by indicating that the break in relations between the Soviet and Polish Governments was a breach in United Nations solidarity, I would take the floor to explain that friendly relations existed between the United States and the Polish Governments, paralleling similar relations with the Soviet Government, and to express the strong hope that the Soviet Government would reestablish relations.

Eden made an ample statement when the question came up at the conference. I said that, when two neighbors fell out, the other neighbors, without going into the causes or merits of the dispute, were entitled to express the hope that these differences could be patched up.

Molotov said that the Soviet Government desired to see an independent Poland and was prepared to help it, provided there was a Polish Government friendly to the Soviet Union. Considerable discussion followed, with Eden and myself warmly urging a resumption of diplomatic relations, but no agreement was reached.

Molotov came to my room at the Embassy that evening during the course of a reception given by Ambassador Harriman which, in keeping with my desire to shun social events during the conference, I did not attend. I brought up with him two points that I felt might continue to disturb relations between our two countries.

One was the terrific campaign conducted by a portion of the Russian and American press over the second front. This campaign had begun in 1942, and, regardless of our degree of preparation or of the plans of the combined chiefs of staff, its proponents insisted on an immediate second front so as to relieve the pressure on Russia. I said this was calculated to create serious friction between our countries in the future and might handicap the fine movement launched at this conference.

Molotov seemed interested in my views and did not undertake to argue in a contrary direction.

The second point was that the public of other countries was steadily getting the impression that Stalin did not desire to go to meetings away from home but preferred to remain at home as in the past. I suggested that if the Marshal could see his way clear at the end of the conference strongly to approve its work and at the same time to say he was thoroughly agreeable to meeting Churchill and Roosevelt at points abroad—and if he could then go to the Roosevelt-Churchill meeting—the effect of this, combined with the Moscow Conference, would be world-wide and tremendous.

Molotov again emphasized the view that most people, including ourselves, did not give Stalin full credit for the true significance of the military emergencies and their effect on his own movements.

At the last session of the conference, held the following day, October 30, we three foreign ministers and the Chinese Ambassador signed the Four-Nation Declaration. Ambassador Foo Ping-sheung had received his full powers in good time. The State Department had forwarded to me on October 28 a message from Ambassador Gauss stating that the Chinese Foreign Office was telegraphing full powers to the Chinese Ambassador to sign and to "express the thanks of the Chinese Government to Mr. Hull for what he had done for China in this connection."

I was truly thrilled as I saw the signatures affixed. Now there was no longer any doubt that an international organization to keep the peace, by force if necessary, would be set up after the war. As I signed, I could not but recall my long personal battles on behalf of the old League of Nations. Now it was probable that the United States would be a member of a new security organization. It was equally probable that the Soviet Union would be one of the principal members. And China, too, would be one of the charter members by virtue of her signature of the Four-Nation Declaration. Had I not persisted in the effort to get China in as one of the original signatories, her claim to permanent membership on the Security Council of the United Nations would not have been so solid.

As Soviet newsreel cameramen took motion pictures of the signing of the Four-Nation Declaration, I could not help feeling that they were recording an historic event.

94: Stalin Against Japan

THE CATHERINE THE GREAT HALL of the Kremlin was the scene of a banquet given to the delegations by Marshal Stalin on the night of the last day of the conference, October 30. This was the first social event of the conference I attended. Immediately on arriving in Moscow, I had told Molotov that in my state of health I could not combine social activity and work. At the beginning he did not seem to believe me and pressed upon me invitations to the theater and to other gala functions. When I persisted in my refusal he seemed impressed, and I was later told that this emphasized to him the intensity of purpose I had in traveling all the way to Moscow in my uncertain health so as to help lay the foundations for a better postwar world.

I was seated at Stalin's right. This gave me a wonderful opportunity to talk to him during the long dinner and the entertainment that followed. I utilized it to the utmost in an effort to discuss our relations and future, knowing this would be the last chance I would have before leaving Moscow. I approached him somewhat in circles to draw him out.

Stalin was in a most agreeable state of mind. No matter what subject was discussed, he seemed to overlook nothing that might make clearer my understanding of his situation, present and prospective. He opened the conversation by saying: "You have had a successful conference." I at once replied that the credit was entirely his, that he had authorized his great country to take the decisive step of joining with Great Britain and the United States in a world program based on cooperation. This seemed to please him. Throughout the conversation he expressed himself as unqualifiedly for a broad program of international cooperation—military, political, and economic—for peace.

In the strongest way possible I presented to Stalin all the considerations calling for his joining in personal cooperation and leadership with the President and the Prime Minister. As for meeting them at Basra, however, he definitely stated his conclusion that he could not leave his military-emergency situation at present. He said we should give him credit for being sincere in this regard.

He then said he would send Molotov in his stead, since under the Soviet law Molotov was his duly constituted second-ranking man in the

Government, designated to take 'his place when he himself might be absent. He asked what I thought of this idea.

I promptly replied that, of course, if he should find it absolutely impossible to go, Molotov would make a good representative. But in the minds of the President and myself, the main point was that, if Stalin himself were to go, it would have a tremendous psychological effect that would extend throughout the world. I said I desired still to plead with him to go himself if at all possible.

I got nowhere with this. His conclusion seemed to be final. I inferred that he had talked this over with his advisers and they felt that the time had not yet come when either the military situation or the necessity for a conference was such as to warrant his leaving. I decided to press the point no further, since to do so might hurt rather than help our purposes.

But I did say that he and the people of Russia had a tremendous prestige in many parts of the world, and there was an extremely compelling need for leadership such as he, in conjunction with President Roosevelt and Prime Minister Churchill, could offer. I remarked that he had no idea how great was his prestige in the world and therefore how necessary it was for him to exert leadership without delay, and that failure to do so would be serious and damaging.

"Through all past history," I said, "more than three-fourths of the human race until very recently have simply had to have leadership. Real leaders appear in the world only every one or two centuries. You yourself have demonstrated that leadership both at home and abroad, and you have a responsibility to exercise it in this stage of the gravest possible world crisis by immediately appearing out in the world in close conjunction with President Roosevelt and Prime Minister Churchill."

He agreed that I was correct about the course of human affairs in the past and about the need for leadership now, but made no further response about meeting Roosevelt and Churchill.

Then, however, he did make a statement of transcendent importance. He astonished and delighted me by saying clearly and unequivocally that, when the Allies succeeded in defeating Germany, the Soviet Union would then join in defeating Japan.

Stalin had brought up this subject entirely on his own, although he may have had in mind the conversations I had had on this subject with Ambassador Litvinov. He finished by saying that I could inform President Roosevelt of this in the strictest confidence. I thanked him heartily.

The Marshal's statement of his decision was forthright. He made it emphatically, it was entirely unsolicited, and he asked nothing in return.

At the Yalta Conference in February, 1945, Stalin made this same promise to the President in writing, but then only as a result of the President's agreement to numerous territorial concessions to the Soviet Union in Asia, including the Kurile Islands and part of Sakhalin Island. I had resigned in November, 1944, hence do not know what changed situation might have rendered these concessions necessary—but when Stalin made his promise to me, for transmission to the President, it had no strings attached to it.

Later in the evening Stalin said the Soviet Union was not for isolation. I emphasized the soundness of that view by pointing out that isolation had almost ruined my country and his.

The Marshal stressed the necessity for collaboration and cooperation between the United States and Russia in the most sympathetic manner. I replied that this was a wonderful program to be carried out, that our two peoples were very much alike in many respects, that each was a great people, and that there need be no serious difficulty at all in promoting close understanding, trust and friendship—and, based on these, a spirit of cooperation—to all of which he agreed.

I concluded that patience on the part of both countries, and especially of their leaders in key positions, would be necessary in dealing with a mistake made here and there, and with intemperate individuals who would try to give trouble in both countries.

During the dinner innumerable toasts were drunk. Stalin and I drank them in red wine, though many of the guests preferred vodka. General Deane stole the show when, in answer to Stalin's toast to the American armed forces, he offered a toast to the day when American and British forces would meet Russian forces in Berlin. Stalin rose from his chair beside me and paid Deane alone the high honor of walking around the table to clink glasses with him.

When we left the dinner table Stalin led me and two or three others to an adjoining room for a few minutes before going to another room for a motion picture. He proceeded on his own initiative to speak in the most sarcastic terms about reports circulated in the past that the Soviet Union and Germany might agree on a separate peace. I remarked that any person who knew the Russian people and their relation to Germany in this war knew they would not make a separate peace with Germany. To this he heartily subscribed.

Our hosts then exhibited to us a motion picture depicting the bitter fight of Red partisans against the treacherous Japanese in Siberia during the revolutionary period of 1918. The film had been produced in 1938, and, when publicly shown in Moscow, had evoked a strong protest from the Japanese Ambassador. There was now no attempt to conceal from us the purpose behind the selection of this film. Coming so shortly after Stalin's statement to me that the Soviet Union would join in the fight against Japan, it had double significance.

A concert followed the movie, and I stayed to the end, which was around two o'clock in the morning—this despite the fact that we were due to take off for home at five in the morning. Stalin seemed pleased that I remained for the concert, given by the most celebrated Russian musicians.

I had an impressive experience with Stalin as we parted. After the usual expressions of leave-taking, he shook hands with me and said "Goodbye" in Russian. Then after walking three or four steps away from me, he suddenly turned and walked back and shook hands a second time to a rather protracted extent, but without saying a word. Then, with serious demeanor, he turned and walked away. I thought to myself that any American having Stalin's personality and approach might well reach high public office in my own country.

After I returned to the Embassy I sent the President two messages. The information Stalin had given me on his decision regarding Japan I regarded as so secret that I sent one-half of it to the President over the Navy code and the other half over the Army code. Believing that the British Foreign Office was more disposed to give out important information than I sometimes thought wise, I left to the President the matter of passing this information on to Churchill alone.

As for the projected Roosevelt-Stalin-Churchill meeting, I informed the President that Stalin acted and talked apparently 100 per cent in favor of the new forward movement of international cooperation in every way which the Four-Nation Declaration proclaimed, yet at the same time he was at present unyielding about attending a meeting with the President and the Prime Minister at any place beyond Tehran. As the deadlock between the President and Stalin continued, I sought by implication to get Mr. Roosevelt's mind turned a little more favorably toward Tehran since I had become convinced that Stalin would not go to Basra. In due course the President agreed.

Weather conditions prevented our taking off, as planned, at dawn on

October 31, and actually it was not until November 3 that we were able to get away. Even then the Russians were averse to our leaving, but our pilots thought it could be done.

During this period Eden came to me twice on the question of getting air bases in Turkey. The British had landed forces on the Italian island of Leros, one of the Dodecanese group, but were endangered by German counterattacks. Bases in Turkey would help. Also, Churchill wanted the Turks to allow British submarines and merchant vessels to pass through the Dardanelles. Eden wanted my concurrence to his taking the question up with Molotov, which I gave.

Molotov at first objected because he felt this was a mild move and he wanted the three powers to go all out in bringing pressure on Turkey to come into the war as a full-scale belligerent. They compromised, however, on an agreement that Eden would make a request of Turkey for the immediate use of air bases, while Britain and Russia would join at a later date in requesting Turkey's entry into the war before the end of the year.

Molotov asked Eden to discuss with me whether the United States would make this a tripartite agreement, to be listed as one of the understandings of the conference. I replied that I was not authorized to discuss military matters and therefore could not take this step. Eden said he was sure Molotov would be satisfied with the bilateral agreement between Russia and Britain. The agreement was duly signed November 1. Eden was to see the Turkish Government on his way back to London.

When the Chinese Ambassador to the Soviet Union called on me on November 1 to thank me again for what our Government had done for China during the conference, I made it clear to him that neither my associates nor I had intimated anything to the press about China's difficulties in being permitted to become one of the original signatories of the Four-Nation Declaration. The Ambassador said he had cautioned his Government to say nothing about it, although he had given Chiang Kai-shek the facts as to just what had occurred.

I said to the Ambassador that throughout the conference all Russian officials had been exceedingly cordial and that, when matters of difference were under discussion, they had talked them out with us in a thoroughly agreeable spirit.

"This," I said, "is a splendid state of mind with which to launch our great forward movement of international cooperation, with Russia for the first time a full-fledged member of it without reservations of any kind. All signs indicate that Mr. Stalin and his Government are opposed to isolation

and are wholeheartedly in favor of the movement of international cooperation launched by this conference, with Russia as a full partner with the
United States, Great Britain, and China."

As I boarded the plane for home, I felt very strongly that great things
had been accomplished at Moscow. We had agreed on the creation of the
international organization that became the United Nations. Russia agreed
to be a member of that organization and to work closely with the Western
Powers in many other respects. We had agreed on a policy toward Italy
and toward Austria. We had created the European Advisory Commission
and the Advisory Council for Italy. We had exchanged numerous ideas on
the postwar treatment of Germany, on our attitudes toward France, and
on the economic policies to pursue after the war. And, apart from the
conference, Stalin had agreed to enter the war against Japan, once Hitler
was defeated.

Russia, moreover, never once raised the question that had disturbed
us the previous year; namely, the settlement at this time of postwar
frontiers.

Our flight home, by way of Tehran, Cairo, Algiers, Marrakesh,
Dakar, Fortaleza (Brazil), and Puerto Rico, was without incident. As we
neared Brazil we ran into a tropical front and had two hours of very rough
flying which embarrassed some of the party but did not seem to affect me.
At various stops I exchanged cables with the President and learned with
delight his decision to meet with Stalin at Tehran. He arranged a White
House conference between us on the morning of November 11, the day
after my scheduled arrival. The State Department sent me long cables
containing splendid press reaction to the achievements of the Moscow
Conference, which meantime had been announced through a joint communiqué issued at the close of the conference.

When we arrived at the Washington airport on November 10, there
to meet us was the President. With him was a delegation from Congress.

Both on the way to the White House and in our conversation the
following morning, I ran over the high lights of the Moscow Conference
for the President. There was really little to tell him, however, in addition
to the ample information I had cabled him as the conference progressed.
He was more interested in discussing the forthcoming conferences at Cairo
and at Tehran. He was looking forward to his meeting with Stalin with
the enthusiasm of a boy, and he was particularly anxious to get my personal impressions of the Marshal. A few hours later the President was on
his way to these historic meetings.

On my arrival in Washington, I was gratified to see the text of the speech Prime Minister Churchill made at the Lord Mayor's banquet in London the day before, in which he said:

"There is no doubt that the full and frank discussion between the three Foreign Ministers, Mr. Molotov, Mr. Eden, and that gallant old eagle Mr. Hull, who flew far on strong wings, has had the effect of making our Russian friends feel as they have never felt before, that it is the heartfelt wish of the British and American nations to fight the war out with them in loyal alliance and afterward to work with them on the basis of mutual respect and faithful comradeship in the resettlement and rebuilding of this distracted, tormented world."

I was invited by both Houses of Congress to address them in joint session and state the results of the Moscow Conference in relation to the world situation. This was the first time in our history that a Secretary of State addressed a joint session of Congress.

Already Congress had put itself formally and emphatically on record as favoring United States participation in a world organization to maintain the peace. While I was en route home from Moscow, the Senate, on November 5, passed the Connally resolution. This resolved "that the United States, acting through its constitutional processes, join with free and sovereign nations in the establishment and maintenance of international authority with power to prevent aggression and to preserve the peace of the world." Coming a few weeks after the passage of the Fulbright resolution in the House of Representatives, it solidified Congress behind the decisions we had taken at Moscow. Knowing the importance of this resolution, I had had the Department keep me daily informed of the debate on it in the Senate.

I had never felt in better voice than when I spoke to the joint session of Congress on November 18. Attention seemed rapt.

"From the outset," I said, "the dominant thought at the conference was that, after the attainment of victory, cooperation among peace-loving nations in support of certain paramount mutual interests will be almost as compelling in importance and necessity as it is today in support of the war effort." I pointed out that, although we reached important agreements, there were no secret agreements and none had been suggested.

Analyzing the achievements of the conference, particularly the Four-Nation Declaration, I said: "As the provisions of the Four-Nation Declaration are carried into effect, there will no longer be need for spheres of influence, for alliances, for balance of power, or any other of the special arrangements through which, in the unhappy past, the nations strove to safeguard their security or to promote their interests."

The question of boundaries, I said, had, by its very nature, to be left in abeyance until the termination of hostilities. This was in accordance with the position maintained for some time by our Government.

"Of supreme importance," I pointed out, "is the fact that at the conference the whole spirit of international cooperation, now and after the war, was revitalized and given practical expression. The conference thus launched a forward movement which, I am firmly convinced, will steadily extend in scope and effectiveness. Within the framework of that movement, in the atmosphere of mutual understanding and confidence which made possible its beginning in Moscow, many of the problems which are difficult today will, as time goes on, undoubtedly become more possible of satisfactory solution through frank and friendly discussion."

I paid warm tribute to the thorough cooperation and high abilities of Molotov and Eden. Of Stalin I said: "I found in Marshal Stalin a remarkable personality, one of the great statesmen and leaders of this age."

I likewise paid heartfelt tribute to Congress's having put itself on record as favoring our participation in a world organization, saying that, as an American, I was proud of the breadth and height of vision and statesmanship that Congress had thereby demonstrated.

Amid the heartening acclaim over the results of the Moscow Conference, I had one disappointment—the antagonism of the Polish press in the United States and Britain over the fact that Eden and I had not required Molotov to come to an agreement with Poland. We had gone to Moscow primarily to reach an agreement with Russia and ourselves, not an agreement between Russia and Poland, but a large segment of the Polish press thought the Moscow Conference a failure because we had not succeeded on the point that seemed to interest it most.

I took this up with Polish Ambassador Ciechanowski when he came to see me on the day following my address to Congress. Before giving him a chance to talk, I said in a friendly manner that, on my return I deeply regretted learning of Polish attacks on the Four-Nation Declaration. This Declaration, I said, meant everything to Poland in the future, and I brought this out clearly by reciting the provisions of the Declaration.

"At Moscow," I said, "I emphasized and reemphasized my friendly and earnest interest in Poland and urged Molotov to find a basis for reestablishing diplomatic relations between the two countries. It is only through this course of friendly discussion and conference that we can possibly get Polish and Russian difficulties worked out."

Ambassador Ciechanowski handed me a telegram from Polish Premier Stanislaw Mikolajczyk to the President stating that he was anxious to submit to Mr. Roosevelt personally and verbally certain suggestions, and was ready to undertake the necessary journey at any time and in complete secrecy. In presenting this to me, Ambassador Ciechanowski indicated that President Mikolajczyk wished to join the President and Churchill, who were then in North Africa prior to the Tehran meeting.

The Ambassador also gave me a memorandum appealing to the President to intervene with Stalin to restore Polish-Soviet relations and expressing the desire of the Polish Government to return to Poland when Soviet troops entered that country. The Polish Government said it could not consider giving up its eastern territories to Russia even though Poland were to receive East Prussia, Danzig, Oppeln, and Silesia. It threatened that, if Soviet troops entered Polish territory without previous resumption of Polish-Soviet relations, the Polish Government would undertake political action against this violation of Polish sovereignty, while the Polish local administration and army in Poland would have to continue to work underground. On the other hand, the Polish Government was planning a rising in Poland against Germany to break out at a moment mutually agreed upon with its Allies either before or at the very moment of the entry of Soviet troops into Poland.

I transmitted to the President the substance of these documents and of my conversation with Ciechanowski. I also informed him of a message from Ambassador Biddle on November 20 stating that Mikolajczyk and Polish Foreign Minister Romer insisted they be consulted in advance concerning any decisions that might be taken involving Polish interests. The Poles indicated that decisions taken without full consultation with the Polish Government upon which the underground in Poland staked its hopes would undoubtedly lead to a serious crisis in that quarter, would create a crisis in Polish circles in England and the Middle East, and might have serious repercussions among Americans of Polish origin.

I informed the President that, on the basis of the documents I had communicated to him, and the extremely agitated state of mind of the Polish Ambassador, it was apparent that the Polish Government felt itself in a desperate position. This might well lead to unfortunate public outbursts. I said to him that we were making every effort here and through Biddle in London to convince the Poles, official and unofficial, that they should take a calmer outlook and not prejudice their case by undue public agitation regarding our policies.

With the approach of the Red Army to former Polish territory, I pointed out, it would appear that we should take every friendly opportunity to bring about a resumption of Polish-Soviet relations. If this were not possible at the moment, I believed we should exert all our influence to persuade the Polish Government to instruct its underground army to launch a full-fledged attack on the Germans behind their lines at the opportune moment and assist the Red Army in its battle. The Polish Government, I commented, should realize that if this were achieved, the British and ourselves would be in a better position to convince the Soviet Government of the Polish Government's desire to make a material contribution to the shortening of the war and to collaborate with the other United Nations after the war in working for the establishment of an international organization to maintain the peace.

The President did not invite President Mikolajczyk to visit him in North Africa. The conversations at Tehran concerning Poland were conducted largely between Stalin and Churchill, and had no concrete results.

Our work at the Moscow Conference did not stop with my address to Congress. We proceeded at once to begin to give flesh and blood to its decisions. Even while en route from Moscow to Washington, I cabled the President suggesting that Robert Murphy, the Foreign Service officer who had rendered so effective assistance in North Africa, be appointed the United States member on the Advisory Council for Italy with the rank of Ambassador. Mr. Roosevelt replied on November 4 saying he was in full accord.

After the President arrived in the Middle East for the Cairo and Tehran conferences, I cabled him on December 3 recommending that Ambassador Winant in London head the American representation on the European Advisory Commission with headquarters in that capital. Mr. Roosevelt replied on December 4, agreeing to this, and suggesting that I make the announcement.

In the same message the President said he had had a very satisfactory conference with Chiang Kai-shek and liked him; the Generalissimo was delighted with the results of the Moscow Conference.

The President also said that things went on the whole very well in Tehran and better than he had expected. Stalin and he worked together toward what turned out to be very similar objectives. The Tehran Conference confirmed the decision reached at the Moscow Conference to found an international security organization.

Most important of all, we at the State Department began at once to work on plans for implementing the Four-Nation Declaration with regard to the creation of such an organization. We decided that another conference would have to be held for this purpose.

Here were the beginnings of the Dumbarton Oaks Conference, held ten months later, which set the general outlines for the Charter of the United Nations.

Part Seven

THE LAST YEAR

(1944)

95: Prologue to 1944

AS 1944, my last year as Secretary of State, edged across the horizon, our foreign policy became strengthened by the growing might of the United Nations forces throughout the world. During the first few months of the year substantial victories were won on widely separated fronts. The Red Armies crossed into old Poland, cleared the Ukraine of virtually all German forces, and entered Rumania. American forces invaded the Marshall Islands and also attacked Truk, Japan's Pearl Harbor of the Pacific. In the Atlantic, losses from German underwater, surface, and aerial craft declined appreciably. The round-the-clock aerial bombing of Germany had begun. Everywhere the United Nations were on the offensive. And the Axis as well as the United Nations knew that somewhere in the West a gigantic new offensive was in preparation of which the only secret was its time and place.

Our greater strength and brighter prospects opened up new avenues for the development of our foreign policy, and at the same time presented added problems for solution. It enabled us to proceed more resolutely toward the neutrals, such as Spain, Portugal, Sweden, Turkey, Switzerland, Eire, and Argentina. It required us to hasten the clarification of our position toward France. It necessitated an intensification of our planning for the postwar treatment of the Axis and for the establishment of an international organization to maintain the peace.

I made a comprehensive statement of our foreign policy as of the spring of 1944 in a radio address on April 9, which the President approved in advance. I delivered it against the background of brighter military fortunes, with final victory in Europe appearing a possibility even for 1944 and a probability in 1945. This transformation from relative weakness at the outbreak of the war in Europe to real strength I cited as one of the three outstanding lessons of our recent history. The second was the fact that we in the United States had moved from a deep-seated tendency toward separate action to the knowledge and conviction that only through unity of action could results be achieved which were essential for the continuance of free peoples. The third was that we had moved from a careless tolerance of evil institutions to the conviction that free Governments and Nazi and Fascist Governments could not exist together in this world.

As for our relations with the neutral countries, I said that in the two years following Pearl Harbor, while we were mustering our strength and helping to restore that of our Allies, our relations with the neutrals and their attitude toward our enemies were conditioned by the position in which we found ourselves. We had constantly sought to keep before them what they, of course, knew—that upon our victory hung their very existence and freedom as independent nations. We had sought in every way to reduce the aid that their trade with the enemy gave him and to increase the strength that we might draw from them. But our power was limited. They and we had continually been forced to accept compromises that we certainly would not have chosen.

"That period, I believe, is rapidly drawing to a close," I continued. "It is clear to all that our strength and that of our Allies now makes only one outcome of this war possible. That strength now makes it clear that we are not asking these neutral nations to expose themselves to certain destruction when we ask them not to prolong the war, with its consequences of suffering and death, by sending aid to the enemy.

"We can no longer acquiesce in these nations' drawing upon the resources of the Allied world when they at the same time contribute to the death of troops whose sacrifice contributes to their salvation as well as ours. We have scrupulously respected the sovereignty of these nations; and we have not coerced, nor shall we coerce, any nation to join us in the fight. We have said to these countries that it is no longer necessary for them to purchase protection against aggression by furnishing aid to our enemy—whether it be by permitting official German agents to carry on their activities of espionage against the Allies within neutral borders, or by sending to Germany the essential ingredients of the steel which kills our soldiers, or by permitting highly skilled workers and factories to supply products which can no longer issue from the smoking ruins of German factories. We ask them only, but with insistence, to cease aiding our enemy."

As for our Allies, the other United Nations, I said that, after two years of intensive study, the basis upon which our policy must be founded was soundly established. Action could not be separate, but must be agreed, united action. The free nations had been brought to the very brink of destruction by allowing themselves to be separated and divided. If any lesson had ever been hammered home with blood and suffering, that one had been.

"However difficult the road may be," I said, "there is no hope of turning victory into enduring peace unless the real interests of this country, the British Commonwealth, the Soviet Union, and China are harmonized and unless they agree and act together. This is the solid framework upon which all future policy and international organization must be built."

But I emphasized that the other United Nations also had their role to play. "This essential understanding and unity of action among the four nations," I said, "is not in substitution or derogation of unity among the United Nations. . . . Nor do I suggest that any conclusions of these four nations can or should be without the participation of the other United Nations. I am stating what I believe the common sense of my fellow countrymen and all men will recognize—that for these powers to become divided in their aims and fail to recognize and harmonize their basic interests can produce only disaster, and that no machinery, as such, can produce this essential harmony and unity."

Although it could hardly be supposed that all the more than thirty boundary questions in Europe could be settled while the fighting was still in progress, I pointed out that certain questions in the meantime could be solved by friendly conference and agreement. We were at all times ready to further an understanding and settlement of questions that might arise between our Allies, as was exemplified by our offer to be of such service to Poland and the Soviet Union. That offer was still open.

As for our policy toward our enemies, I emphasized that there could be no compromise with Fascism and Nazism. Those doctrines had to be eliminated everywhere. Their leaders, institutions, and the power that supported them had to go. They could expect no negotiated peace, no compromise, no opportunity to return. I said that the European Advisory Commission in London, which had been established at the Moscow Conference in October, 1943, was working on plans for the treatment of Germany.

In succeeding chapters I take up the major countries and problems with which we had to deal, and define our policies concerning them as of the effective date of my resignation, November 30, 1944. Our foreign policy in this my final year in office falls into three natural categories—that toward the neutrals, that toward our Allies, and that toward our enemies. The chapters also follow this sequence, dealing first with the European neutrals and with Argentina; next with our major Allies in Europe; and finally with the Orient and with Germany.

96: Iberia and the War

ONE OF OUR MOST difficult approaches in foreign policy from Pearl Harbor until my resignation was that toward the European neutrals—Spain, Portugal, Sweden, Switzerland, Turkey, and Eire. The geographical position of the first five enabled raw materials and other goods to flow from them to Germany or German-occupied territory in quantities disturbing to ourselves. All six were dependent to some extent on imports from overseas which the Axis could not supply. Some of them had bases or other facilities that we needed.

Hitler could have occupied any one of the first five from adjoining territory dominated by himself, but he had obviously calculated that the economic advantages he could obtain from them at peace outweighed the military advantages he might gain from occupation.

All six countries were classified as European neutrals, but they differed considerably one from another, and our policy toward them had to take these differences into account. Sweden and Switzerland were neutral "islands" surrounded by Germany and German-controlled areas. Turkey and Portugal had treaties of alliance with Britain. Spain, ideologically tied to the Axis, was neither an "island" nor an ally. Eire was not touched by German territory; theoretically she was a member of the British Commonwealth, but evinced a centuries-old antagonism to the United Kingdom.

After Pearl Harbor the United States became a partner in the economic warfare system established by the British in 1939. Britain had negotiated war trade agreements with most of the European neutrals to establish blockade quotas for goods received from overseas and to prevent reexport of such goods to Germany. We began to adapt our economic controls to the British blockade system and to cooperate with the British in preclusive buying operations in certain neutral countries.

The degree of pressure we could bring against the neutrals to reduce their economic and other aid to the Axis depended partly on the neutrals' nearness to the Axis and partly on their conception of the United Nations' military strength and prospects. In the first two years of the war, when our armed strength was at a low ebb, the gauge of our pressure stood at a low mark too. As our strength grew we could apply more pressure. It was our military successes that made possible the new bluntness with which I stated our attitude toward the neutrals in my address of April 9, 1944.

In dealing with the neutrals, we naturally had to coordinate our policy with that of Britain, and at times with that of Russia. Some differences of opinion, occasionally sharp, rose between Britain and us over the degree of pressure to apply and the approach to adopt toward the neutrals. In general we were inclined to take a stronger attitude than was Britain. Some differences also rose between the State Department and other Departments or agencies of the Government as to the degree of pressure and the scope of demands to be made on the neutrals. Other Departments often wanted us to leap ahead with unilateral action, whereas my associates and I realized that we had to coordinate our plans and actions with those of our major Allies.

Spain comes first in this discussion of the neutrals because of her own importance in the war situation, and because of the range and delicacy of our relations with her. Our policy toward Spain was dominated by three factors. First, we had to keep her neutral. Second, we had to get her strategic materials for ourselves and keep them from the enemy. Third, we wanted to obtain from her a series of facilities.

To achieve these objectives we had to be willing to supply Spain with certain products she vitally needed, such as petroleum, but we also had to be alert to see that no portion of such imports went on to the Axis.

Just after our landing in North Africa, Ambassador Hayes in Madrid, in accordance with my instructions, informed Spanish Foreign Minister Count Jordana that we were prepared immediately to consider expanding our economic arrangements with Spain. Jordana replied that Spain foresaw closer ties with the United States and greater economic dependence upon us. Hayes reported to us his belief that Jordana, and probably General Franco, were looking forward to an eventual United Nations victory and we could therefore regard them as potential friends rather than as enemies.

In a letter to Secretary of War Stimson on December 22 I outlined our program of trade relations with Spain and Portugal. I suggested, moreover, that we increase the number of our observers in Spain and Portugal to see that our exports were consumed there and not reexported to the Axis. The Joint Chiefs of Staff replied on January 14, 1943, that they agreed with the program. They also concurred in the increase in observers, provided nothing were done to arouse unduly the hostility of the Spanish and Portuguese Governments. The Combined Chiefs of Staff

(American and British) to whom the Joint Chiefs had referred my letter because of the British interest in the situation, wrote me on January 23:

"In order to assist in maintaining Spanish neutrality in the interest of Allied strategy, such quantities of oil, raw materials, and other supplies as are necessary to maintain a reasonable wartime economy should be made available to Spain, subject to all proper safeguards."

In March, 1943, Ambassador Hayes cabled a request from Foreign Minister Jordana that we promptly make available moderate amounts of aviation gasoline for Spain's civil air lines, which had been forced to suspend all services, leaving Axis air lines the only ones operating in Spain. The Combined Chiefs of Staff, to whom we referred this request, agreed on April 3, but no further action was taken until the military situation in Tunisia became clarified.

We then cabled Hayes on June 26, setting forth our conditions. These were that nothing higher than 87-octane gasoline would be supplied; this would come from the Netherlands West Indies, be carried in Spanish ships, and be used for civilian purposes only by the Iberia Air Line. We also stipulated that our Petroleum Attaché in Madrid should check the distribution and stocks of aviation gasoline, that German holdings in the Iberia Air Line should not be increased, and that operations of the air line should not be influenced by the Germans or Italians.

In addition I instructed Hayes to attempt to get the Spanish to agree not to carry enemy nationals on the Iberia Air Line to Spanish Morocco or Tangier without our express consent; to establish a direct Spanish or Swiss-controlled air line to Switzerland; and to grant landing rights in Spain for our commercial air lines.

Count Jordana received our proposals favorably, and, after some negotiation, the Spanish Foreign Office formally accepted an amended draft of these conditions. Previously Jordana informed Hayes that an agreement had been concluded that would eliminate German participation in Iberia Air Line ownership. The question of landing rights in Spain for American commercial air lines was left for further discussion, but Jordana informed Hayes on November 18 that our request had been approved by the Council of Ministers. The formal agreement was concluded a year later on December 2, 1944.

The importation of petroleum itself was even more important to Spain. My letter to Secretary Stimson on December 22, 1942, had envisaged petroleum imports into Spain at an annual rate of 541,000 tons. Petroleum receipts in Spain during the last quarter of 1942, however, had been only about 100,000 tons, and we believed this ratio had sustained Spain's economy, although at a level substantially below a peacetime normal. The Iberian Peninsula Operating Committee, embracing representatives of the State Department, the Board of Economic Warfare, and the British Embassy, which met in the State Department, agreed that Spain's imports should be kept to this quarterly figure. The Joint Chiefs of Staff also agreed to this figure after I informed them on April 24 of our decision.

Ambassador Hayes immediately sent a series of telegrams violently protesting against our figure as too low. He had also authorized the sailing of five Spanish tankers, and he said he was willing to justify this to the President because our petroleum program was related to our entire Spanish policy, which had been proving of inestimable benefit to the war effort. Hayes, filling his first diplomatic post, was at times inclined to take the bit in his own teeth.

I thereupon informed Hayes that, from my reading of his recent telegrams, it occurred to me that he was failing fully to weigh the importance of public opinion here, which I thought would take a most unfavorable view of any increase in oil shipments to Spain above the highest quarterly shipment in 1942. I pointed out that there was more criticism of our program permitting Spain to import oil than of any other foreign policy matter under my direction, in spite of the care we were taking in the matter.

When Hayes continued to protest, I cabled him on May 22 that our petroleum program for Spain was governed by two basic limitations. First, we would not provide Spain with petroleum beyond her minimum essential needs, and we were not interested at present in assisting Spanish production since this would certainly increase the supplies at the disposition of the Axis. Second, we did not want excessive stocks to be built up in Spain, regardless of in whose hands they were.

Hayes sent me a letter on June 7 saying he had had no intention of acting contrary to our instructions, but urging that we should not underestimate the strength of our petroleum weapon.

Public opposition to our Spanish oil program rose partly from the oil shortages in the United States. Many Americans, not realizing the broader aspects of our policy, did not want to see oil going to Spain when there was not enough to go around in our own country. They also did not appreciate the fact—although we made it clear on several occasions—that this oil came from the Dutch West Indies and was carried in Spanish tankers, and therefore had no effect whatever on the United States' supply. They likewise failed to understand that, unless we furnished Spain with certain products, we could not get from her the concessions we desired.

Foremost among these concessions was a restriction or total embargo on the export of wolfram to Germany. Spain and Portugal provided Germany with almost her total requirements of this vital element in the making of high-grade steel.

While I was returning from the Moscow Conference, Acting Secretary Stettinius on November 6, 1943, instructed Ambassador Hayes to seek from the Spanish Government an immediate embargo on wolfram exports and the removal of German agents from Tangier. The Department had suggested to Hayes on October 15 the possibility of obtaining a wolfram embargo in exchange for shipments of wheat from the United States. Meantime, however, there had occurred the so-called Laurel incident. The Spanish Foreign Office, replying to a telegram from José P. Laurel, a Philippine collaborationist whom the Japanese had made President of their puppet Philippine Government, had addressed him as President of the Philippines. The Spanish Foreign Office, embarrassed at having acknowledged Laurel's message, expressed its regret and hastened to explain that this did not constitute recognition of his Government in any sense. Nevertheless, Axis propaganda was utilizing the episode to the utmost, and American public opinion likewise was aroused. Consequently the Department dropped the idea of a *quid* for the *quo* of a Spanish embargo on wolfram to the Axis, and requested it outright. We also pressed for other concessions, among which were landing rights in Spain for our commercial air lines, which was still under discussion, and the release of Italian warships and merchant ships in Spanish ports. (We had recently signed an armistice with Italy.) Count Jordana assured Hayes his Government would give sympathetic consideration to these requests. We later requested the recall of the so-called Spanish Blue Division, consisting of volunteers sent to assist the Germans on the Russian front.

After my return from Moscow we cabled Ambassador Hayes on November 12 that, while we did not think any satisfactory explanation could be offered for Jordana's message to Laurel, the Ambassador could say to Jordana that we were prepared to let the matter stand, being convinced that the Spanish explanations had been given in good faith and desiring to believe that the Spanish Government had not intended to disturb relations with the United States or to imply recognition of the puppet Philippine Government. We added, however, that the incident had created an extremely unfavorable impression on the public mind here, which only acts of such character as to restore confidence could correct.

When I saw Spanish Ambassador de Cárdenas on November 22, I said to him that the Laurel incident, which no one here could understand, had seriously undermined the favorable atmosphere existing between our two Governments. "The American people," I remarked, "have so implacable a hatred of the barbarous conduct of the Japanese in murdering or mistreating American prisoners that they cannot understand why a country like Spain would engage in such an action as its reply to Laurel. It is therefore extremely important for the Spanish Government at once to act favorably on the requests we have made." De Cárdenas agreed to this, but said his Government could move only so fast.

The Spanish Government did not move fast on the most important of our requests, the wolfram embargo. Hayes himself having recommended that, in case Franco's Government did not agree, we should interrupt petroleum shipments to Spain, we suspended shipments at the end of January, 1944, after clearance with the Joint Chiefs of Staff.

The British, because of their own supply problem, particularly their need for food imports from Spain, were not prepared to support any drastic action to obtain a wolfram embargo. Instead, they advocated a compromise that would permit limited wolfram exports to Germany.

The Department accordingly drafted a message on February 12 for President Roosevelt to send to Prime Minister Churchill. This stated the belief that, as a result of our suspension of tanker loadings, the Spanish situation was developing satisfactorily, and that, if both our Governments held firm, we could obtain a complete and permanent Spanish embargo on wolfram. Our information indicated that the Germans were very short of wolfram and that supplies obtained at this time could be directly translated into terms of British and American casualties. We had had indications of a disposition on the part of the British Ambassador and ours in Madrid to accept some compromise short of a complete embargo. We did not consider this satisfactory and saw no danger that our joint insistence upon a complete embargo before resuming loadings of Spanish tankers would produce any serious reaction against us in Spain.

The British Embassy gave us an *aide-mémoire* from its Government, dated February 21, suggesting that to obtain the concessions we desired from the Spanish Government with regard to stopping German espionage activities, releasing Italian merchant vessels, and recalling the Spanish Blue Division from the Russian front, we should accept a compromise solution which in practice would result in an actual stoppage of exports of Spanish wolfram to Germany over the next six months. The President approved this suggestion, which had also been made to him direct by the Prime Minister.

Negotiations with the Spaniards, however, continued through March without result. On March 31 the President sent me a message he had received from Mr. Churchill and asked me to prepare a reply. The Prime Minister suggested a further compromise whereby a limited quantity of wolfram could still go to Germany.

The President having reluctantly agreed to the Prime Minister's proposal, I cabled Ambassador Hayes on April 13, informing him that we were ready to recede from our demand for a total wolfram embargo in the interests of complete Anglo-American agreement on the approach to the Spanish Government and out of respect for the direct request received by the President from the Prime Minister.

The Spanish refused, however, to accept our stipulation that the temporary wolfram embargo instituted early in February should continue at least through June. On April 10 the British urged us to accept the latest Spanish offer of maximum exports of three hundred tons for the remainder of 1944, including twenty tons each for April, May, and June.

I thereupon asked British Ambassador Halifax to see me on April 17. "It seems almost impossible," I said to him, "for us to agree to the shipment of oil to Spain as part of an agreement whereby wolfram will still go to Germany. There is the worst possible dynamite in the British proposal, especially in view of the long continued propaganda activities by critics of our Government, running back to the Spanish Civil War in 1937."

The same day I cabled Ambassador Winant and Under Secretary Stettinius, who was in London for a round of conferences with the British, that public opinion here sharply opposed arrangements with neutrals whereby we agreed to permit them to ship war materials to our enemies resulting in the killing of our troops. I concluded that I saw no alternative to our opposition to agreeing that neutrals might supply the enemy with important war materials.

At this time the President was resting at Bernard Baruch's estate in South Carolina. I received a memorandum from the White House on April 18 enclosing a message from Prime Minister Churchill to the President, and asking me to prepare a reply to the request it contained—that the President give personal consideration to the possibility of agreeing to the latest Spanish proposal.

Along with my draft of a reply, I sent the President a memorandum on April 20 in which I pointed out that our discussions with the British had reached a most difficult point. I recalled that we had been willing to agree to resume oil shipments in exchange for a total suspension of wolfram shipments until July 1, with only three hundred tons to go to Germany during the remainder of the year, but the Spanish now insisted they must have the right to ship sixty tons of this total before July 1, and this Prime Minister Churchill wished us to agree to.

"I believe," I said, "that this concession would have the most disastrous results. Our position in insisting upon suspension of shipments until July 1 is based on the belief that in view of pending military operations [the landing in Normandy] we must do everything in our power to prevent shipments from neutrals to the enemy of essential war materials until such time as the success of our military operations [separating Spain from contact with Germany] may render shipments impossible. Upon our success in maintaining this position will depend, I believe, our ability to eliminate or drastically reduce ball-bearing shipments from Sweden, chrome shipments from Turkey, and also our success in negotiations with Switzerland and Portugal to reduce their contribution to the enemy."

I also pointed to the widespread approval my statements on April 9 with regard to the neutrals had received in the United States. I said that this position represented the unanimous attitude of the American people, and to act in any way counter to it would weaken the widespread support of our foreign policy which had become increasingly manifest.

A memorandum from the White House on April 22 informed me that the President had sent our draft message without change to the Prime Minister on April 21.

The following day I received another memorandum from the White House enclosing a second message from Prime Minister Churchill to the President, dated April 22, to which the President requested I draft a reply. Mr. Churchill again argued strongly for the British position, saying that he himself would accept the entire responsibility.

The Prime Minister's cable was so insistent that I telegraphed the President on April 23, stating that I believed, and the Foreign Economic Administration concurred, that the wisest course was to agree to the latest Spanish offer, which the British had espoused. We all feared, I said, that to announce that the British were going ahead alone would result in repercussions detrimental to our united front toward the neutrals. The President agreed.

Accordingly, I cabled Ambassador Hayes on April 25, informing him of the Prime Minister's statement that he himself would accept the entire responsibility, but I said that in this event it would obviously be necessary for me to issue a press statement which could not but clearly indicate a break in the united front of the United States and Great Britain which was so essential in carrying on the general war effort. Therefore, I continued, I was reluctantly willing to authorize the Ambassador to proceed with the British Ambassador in Madrid, Sir Samuel Hoare, in arriving at an agreement with the Spanish for a maximum export of 280 tons of wolfram to Germany for the remainder of 1944 on condition that Spain immediately fulfill her promises with respect to our other demands.

An agreement with the Spanish Government was quickly reached on this basis. We issued a press release announcing it on May 2. Spain agreed to expel Axis agents from Tangier, Spanish Morocco, and Spain and to close the German Consulate and other Axis agencies in Tangier; to release Italian merchantmen in Spanish ports; to submit to arbitration the question of releasing Italian warships in Spanish ports; and to withdraw all Spanish military forces from the Eastern Front.

On our part we agreed to monthly exports of twenty tons of wolfram to Germany for May and June and forty tons per month for the remainder of the year if, as a practical matter, they could be made. We said in our press release that it was improbable that any of this could be utilized in military products during that year. "Although agreement was reached on a basis less than a total embargo of wolfram shipments," we stated, "this action was taken to obtain immediate settlement on the urgent request of the British Government."

Permission, we said, would now be given for the renewal of petroleum loadings for Spain.

Ambassador Hayes, to whom I had sent a text of this press release several days before, protested against it on April 29 on the ground that, by stressing British responsibility, it would minimize the "diplomatic victory" we had achieved in Spain. In reply I said I did not wish in any way to detract from the Ambassador's achievement in Spain, but it was known by the public here that we had pressed for a total embargo, and, while we had gained much without wholehearted British support, I was convinced that with full British support we could have achieved our objective. A large section of the public here, I added, might well have the same impression. Spain, I went on, was not popular with the American press; public and press alike would regard anything less than the complete attainment of our objective as a compromise; no compromise with Spain would be well received; and all criticism would not be allayed simply because the compromise might be in our favor.

In June, 1944, following Portugal's decision to place a complete embargo on the export of wolfram, the British and we sought similar action by the Spaniards. The Spanish Government agreed to suspend wolfram exports for June, and subsequently suspended the July and August quotas. Although we were never able to obtain from the Spanish Government a definite commitment with respect to a complete embargo, wolfram shipments to Germany were never resumed. The advance of the American and British armies into France and the disruption of rail transportation in France rounded out our diplomatic action, and Spain's economic contact with the Axis came to an end.

I summed up the results of our policy toward Spain in a letter to General Marshall, Chief of Staff, on August 19, 1944. "The degree of pressure which could be exercised," I said, "has been influenced by the progress of the war, and also we have borne in mind the earlier expressed desire of the Chiefs of Staff of the continued neutrality of Spain and to avoid the creation of any situation in Spain capable of interfering with our military operations. We feel that the policy we have pursued has been productive of results beneficial to our general political and military objectives."

I outlined eighteen concrete results that had been obtained. The Spanish censorship had been relaxed. Restrictions on our propaganda work had been removed. The Spanish press had adjusted itself to a neutral tone. Many thousands of refugees had been evacuated through Spain with the full cooperation of the Spanish Government. These included some 25,000 Frenchmen of military age moving to North Africa even while the battle of Tunisia was in progress.

About one thousand escaped American airmen who had entered Spain through the Pyrenees were evacuated through Spain to Gibraltar. The Spanish permitted the establishment of a French North African mission in Madrid, eclipsing the Vichy Embassy. They sharply limited enemy access to sources of strategic materials. They enforced a virtual embargo on wolfram beginning in February, 1944, incidentally effecting a saving for us of about $80,000,000, the amount we probably would have spent in 1944 on preclusive buying of wolfram in Spain.

The Spaniards released the Italian merchantmen interned in their ports. They closed the German Consulate General in Tangier. They expelled Axis agents. They placed a ban on the travel of Axis nationals on the Iberia Air Lines between Spain and Tangier. They gave us landing rights in Spain for American commercial airlines. They reoriented their foreign policy in a sense distinctly favorable to the United Nations. They liquidated the Blue Division. They undertook not to fire on American military planes even when over Spanish territorial waters. They permitted the extension of intelligence activities by our Army and Navy and the Office of Strategic Services into France from Spain. They supplied certain vital British economic requirements.

Ambassador Hayes in Madrid and we in Washington had worked ceaselessly to obtain these various concessions from Spain. When it is recalled that at the time most of them were granted the Germans were still in full occupation of France, and Nazi armed might touched the Pyrenees, the extent of the facilities we received and the importance of our diplomatic success in Spain become yet more significant. Contrast this, too, with the fear entertained almost generally in 1940, though not by the State Department, that General Franco would at any time cast Spain into the war on the side of the Axis.

Such was the situation with regard to Spain when I resigned. At that point, as victory by the United Nations came ever closer, our policy was one of desiring a restoration of a liberal form of government in Spain; but we were not disposed to intervene directly in Spain's internal situation and preferred to await developments. We fully realized that disorder in Spain would only operate against our own and the United Nations' interests, as well as against the interests of the Spanish people. Spanish groups outside Spain were pressing for the overthrow of General Franco and the establishment of some other form of government. But, as I left office, they were not unified, and their leaders were generally at odds with one another.

Our objectives in the case of Spain at the end of 1944 were the complete cessation of all forms of Spanish aid to Germany, the weakening of the Falange or Fascist Party, the orderly restoration of liberal forms of government, the utilization of Spanish resources for relief and rehabilitation in liberated territories, and the defense and promotion of American trade interests.

We were never friends of the Franco regime, and I felt that that regime was bad for Spain and the world. At no time prior to my resignation was the question raised as to Spain's membership in the United Nations organization. I would not have favored such membership.

Toward Portugal our policy from 1942 until my resignation resembled that toward Spain, but there were additional factors of importance. Portugal had an alliance with Great Britain, the oldest in the world, dating back to 1373. She had islands far out in the Atlantic which could be of great value to us in our hands or a great danger to us in enemy hands. And she had interests in the Far East, centered in her island colony of Timor, which the Japanese had occupied.

After the fall of France we supported Great Britain's objective of keeping Portugal out of the war. Although Portugal was an ancient ally of Britain, we had to recognize the community of interests existing between Portugal and Spain along with the fact that Spain had a close relationship with the Axis. All we could hope for in the darker years of the war was to keep Portugal neutral, and we felt that neutrality in the circumstances then existing was more valuable than belligerency.

In 1942 we began an intensive program to obtain from Portugal, through the Board of Economic Warfare, the strategic materials we needed, such as cork, and to keep from Germany the strategic materials she needed, particularly wolfram of which Portugal was a larger producer than Spain. Our success was considerable, but curiously we encountered more resistance in Portugal than in Spain. The Prime Minister of Portugal, Dr. Antonio de Oliveira Salazar, realized and valorized his strong bargaining power, derived from such factors as his control over the Lisbon terminal of Pan American Airways and the strategic position of the Azores, a way station of the air-clipper route and an important cable center.

We concluded a supply-purchase agreement on November 23, 1942, following tripartite negotiations between ourselves and the British on one hand and the Portuguese on the other. We agreed to sell Portugal various materials, including petroleum, iron and steel products, and fertilizers, and Portugal agreed to sell Britain and the United States portions of her output of strategic materials which were much larger than she would sell to the Axis.

Just as in the case of Spain, however, wolfram was at the same time the most important and the most difficult point to negotiate. It was the most vitally needed strategic material that Germany imported from Iberia, and consequently the Nazis were exerting the utmost pressure to get it.

Britain and the United States had on August 24, 1942, made the most satisfactory wolfram arrangement with Portugal they could, considering that their military fortunes were at ebb tide and German troops were at the Pyrenees. It permitted the United Kingdom and the United States to export the production of the British and American owned or controlled mines, and the Germans to export the production of mines owned or controlled by them. Of the wolfram from all other mines, 75 per cent was to go to Germany, 25 per cent to the United Kingdom and the United States. It was clearly understood that when this agreement ended on February 28, 1943, Britain's and our share would be increased.

When new negotiations began, following the expiration of this agreement, we suddenly found that the Portuguese Government, without consulting either London or Washington, had signed a new agreement with the Germans. Nevertheless, following vigorous protests by the British and ourselves, Dr. Salazar agreed to an interim arrangement whereby the Allies' portion of the production of free mines was increased from 25 to 50 per cent.

Later in the year we determined to bring more pressure on Portugal. We believed that the amount of wolfram going to Germany might directly affect the duration of the war. On September 10, in an aerogram to Ambassador Caffery in Rio de Janeiro, we asked the Brazilian Government, which had close ties with the mother country, Portugal, to come to our assistance. We pointed out that if German acquisitions of wolfram in Portugal could be kept to a minimum, there was little doubt that German reserves might be completely exhausted at the end of the year and that German production of armor-piercing ammunition would be very seriously impeded.

Brazilian Foreign Minister Aranha, who had always been a tower of strength to us when we needed help in Latin America, responded with the prompt support I knew we could count upon. He cabled the Brazilian Ambassador in Lisbon to work closely with our Minister there, Bert Fish, and give him Brazil's full backing in his negotiations with the Portuguese Government.

After our new Minister to Portugal, R. Henry Norweb, arrived at his post, he and the British Ambassador began new negotiations in January, 1944, with the Portuguese toward a total embargo on wolfram to Germany. Salazar's attitude, however, was unfavorable.

We cabled Norweb on January 17 suggesting that, if Salazar would not consent to embargo wolfram shipments to Germany alone, we were prepared, if necessary, to agree to a complete embargo on wolfram shipments to all countries even though we would be penalized quantitatively more than the Germans. We would also be prepared, should this result in German exports to Portugal being cut off, to do everything possible to make available the materials that Portugal would have received from Germany, and we and the British would increase our purchases of other Portuguese exports so as to alleviate possible unemployment resulting from cessation of wolfram production.

Should Salazar insist on continuing to export some wolfram to Germany, we added, we would be willing to see a quota system instituted for six months starting March 1, 1944, limiting exports to the United Nations and to Germany to a 250-ton maximum per quarter for each, with Portugal reserving the right to terminate the arrangement with Germany at the end of the first quarter.

In the negotiations that followed with the British Ambassador and Norweb, the Portuguese engaged in delaying tactics so as to await the outcome of our wolfram negotiations with Spain. We cabled Norweb on March 20 that Prime Minister Churchill had sent Salazar a letter expressing concern that continued Portuguese wolfram exports to Germany would affect Anglo-Portuguese relations and provide a bad example for the Spanish. Norweb reported to us on March 25, however, that Salazar, after receiving Churchill's letter, had remained adamant against the imposition of an embargo on wolfram exports to Germany.

We thereupon sought again the assistance of the Brazilian Government, and Brazil came resolutely to our aid. As a result of instructions from Foreign Minister Aranha, the Brazilian Ambassador in Lisbon requested Dr. Salazar to suspend wolfram exports to Germany. The Portuguese Premier, while insisting that he could not embargo exports to Germany completely and did not consider a complete wolfram embargo to all countries fair, agreed to take the Brazilian request under consideration.

In April we raised our Legation in Lisbon to the rank of an Embassy to give recognition to the increased importance of our relations with Portugal. On May 10 Dr. Salazar presented to Ambassador Norweb and the British Ambassador a proposal that the Germans and the Allies should continue to export the wolfram produced from their respective mines, and that the so-called neutral mines should be closed, or their production given the Allies for export or be stored in Portugal for American or British purchase after the war.

Ambassador Winant in London cabled me on the same day, urging that any compromise settlement in Portugal such as had been reached in Spain would constitute a failure in that the greater proportion of Germany's wolfram supplies came from Portugal, and nothing less than a complete embargo on Portuguese wolfram exports to Germany would have a decisive effect on Nazi war production. He called our attention to articles appearing in the British press which indicated that the British public was being prepared for a compromise settlement in Portugal.

I cabled Winant on May 14 that we were entirely in agreement with his views and intended to press rapidly and firmly for a total embargo on Portuguese wolfram exports. I asked him urgently to emphasize our views in London so as to leave the British Government in no doubt as to our position. I said it was essential that at all costs we avoid having a situation develop similar to that through which the achievement of our full purpose in Spain had been defeated.

At the same time I cabled Ambassador Norweb to inform Salazar as soon as possible that his proposal was entirely unsatisfactory and that we were interested in an immediate, total suppression of wolfram exports to the Axis. I expressed our conviction that the Portuguese Government would be entirely within its sovereign rights in instituting a complete wolfram embargo as a step in Portugal's national interest. That Government, I added, would thereby improve immeasurably Portugal's international position and give much satisfaction to public opinion throughout the United Nations. Any hesitation would arouse public feeling and seriously impair relations so far maintained on a most cordial basis.

At this point we received from the British Embassy on May 16 an *aide-mémoire* arguing in favor of a compromise permitting the export of certain limited quantities of wolfram to Germany. We replied in two days, arguing strongly against any compromise. We recalled the Spanish case and our contention then that any compromise would have far-reaching effects on negotiations between the British and American Governments and other neutrals. "As our negotiations with the neutrals have progressed," we said, "our prediction as to the unfortunate consequences which would flow from a compromise of our demands on Spain has unhappily proved to be entirely correct. In Turkey and Switzerland, in Sweden and Portugal we are met by the argument that demands made upon those Governments are more stringent than the settlement which we were willing to accept with Spain. We particularly directed to the attention of the British Government the likelihood of this argument being made by Portugal, upon whose wolfram exports Germany is now almost entirely dependent."

We pointed out that a compromise would be a major mistake and was not required by any exigencies of the situation. Portugal was entirely dependent for petroleum and other important products upon imports controlled by the British and American Governments. She was bound by the most solemn treaty obligations to the British Government. She could not seriously believe that her security was imperiled by acquiescing in the demands we were now making.

The British at this time indicated to us that they contemplated recommending a declaration of war by Portugal against Germany and Japan on the basis of the ancient Anglo-Portuguese alliance, but they dropped this idea and, after further exchanges between London and Washington, they resolutely pursued, along with us, the plan of obtaining a complete wolfram embargo. While the negotiations with Portugal were under way, a German U-boat stopped the Portuguese ship *Serpa Pinto* in mid-Atlantic and forced passengers and crew to abandon ship, with some resultant loss of life. This caused an unfavorable reaction in Portugal, and finally, after some further backing and filling, Salazar agreed unconditionally on June 5, 1944, to the immediate imposition of a complete embargo on wolfram and a total cessation of all wolfram operations.

Equally as important as the wolfram negotiations and equally as difficult were our negotiations with Lisbon for the use of Atlantic island bases. The Azores Islands, belonging to Portugal, offered the only mid-Atlantic stopping place for Allied planes. In German hands they could also afford strategic anchorage and refueling for Nazi submarines.

In the early months of 1943, President Roosevelt had formulated a plan with regard to the Azores. He believed that the flower of the Portuguese Army was in the Azores, which fact would invite and facilitate a German invasion of Portugal. He therefore proposed that an arrangement should be secretly agreed to between Brazil and Portugal whereby the Portuguese Government would withdraw to Portugal its troops in the Azores on the understanding that, should Germany invade Portugal, Brazil, with United States and British assistance, would immediately send the necessary Brazilian troops to garrison the Azores and other Portuguese islands. When this suggestion was presented to the British Government, however, the latter stated they did not wish Brazil to undertake any negotiations until they themselves had talked with the Portuguese Government.

Ambassador Winant in London cabled us on June 29, 1943, the text of a message from Mr. Churchill to the President informing him that the

British were ready to negotiate with the Portuguese for bases and facilities in the Azores, but that, except for fueling facilities for United Nations merchant ships and warships, Salazar was not prepared to give other than British forces access to these facilities unless Portugal were to enter the war. In connection with assurances the British had given relative to maintaining Portugal's sovereignty over all her colonies, Churchill said, the Portuguese Government would be happy to obtain a similar guarantee from the United States. The Prime Minister hoped the President would authorize him to say to the Portuguese that, if the forthcoming Anglo-Portuguese negotiations were successful, the United States Government was prepared to give these assurances.

Mr. Churchill also said he thought it would be possible later on, if this became necessary, to obtain Portuguese consent to the use of the Azores facilities by other United Nations forces. But he hoped the President would agree, since the Anglo-Portuguese alliance had served as the basis of the British approach to Portugal, that the British should conclude their agreement for access to the Azores facilities by British forces only.

After due consideration of this proposal, I sent the President a memorandum on August 10 suggesting that we should undertake to respect—not to maintain—Portuguese sovereignty over all Portuguese colonies.

The President approved, and I cabled Ambassador Winant accordingly. But I added that our Joint Chiefs of Staff had indicated, with the approval of the President, to the British Chiefs of Staff, that we found unacceptable any agreement that would restrict the Azores facilities to British aircraft. I pointed to the opinion of our Joint Chiefs that it was vitally important that our military operations, transport, and air ferry services should have facilities in the Azores.

The President and Prime Minister Churchill discussed this question at the first Quebec Conference later that month, and Eden and I also took it up. It was our understanding that we should ride into the Azores in the wake of the British.

The British signed their agreement with the Portuguese on August 17, 1943, the date of execution to be October 8.

On October 6 I sent Ambassador Caffery at Rio a message from the President to be communicated orally to President Vargas. Mr. Roosevelt, informing Vargas of the Anglo-Portuguese agreement, said it was based on the ancient Anglo-Portuguese alliance and that, while Vargas and he naturally would have preferred to see an arrangement whereby Portugal would have assisted the United Nations as a whole in their fight against the Axis, Dr. Salazar apparently was only willing to accept a bilateral arrangement. Reminding Vargas of their conversation the previous January (when Mr. Roosevelt was returning from the Casablanca Conference) regarding the Azores' strategic importance in the antisubmarine campaign, the President said he was confident that the British would now be able to take steps that would be of the utmost help in driving Axis submarines from the Middle and South Atlantic.

On October 4 I instructed our Chargé in Lisbon, George F. Kennan, if Salazar asked for such assurances, to say to him that this Government agreed to respect the sovereignty of Portugal in all her colonies. After we had informed London of this fact, a telegram from Churchill to Roosevelt suggested that these assurances might be of possible use as a bargaining point in connection with our desire for bases in the Azores. However, when the Portuguese Foreign Office took up with Kennan the question of our assurances, Kennan formally gave them on October 25. He believed that, since the Foreign Office had raised the question, any further delay would destroy their value.

While I was at the Moscow Conference, Acting Secretary Stettinius cabled me on October 22 that the President, following correspondence with Mr. Churchill, had directed him on October 16 to take up with Portugal our desire for Azores air facilities similar to those the British had obtained. Mr. Churchill had assured the President he would give us his fullest support.

Kennan suggested in reply that Salazar would refuse our requests outright if we presented them in the comprehensive form proposed by the Department Called home for consultation, Kennan returned to Lisbon early in November, carrying a letter from the President to Salazar devoted to the Azores. The President, at the suggestion of the Department, also cabled Prime Minister Churchill, informing him that Kennan was en route to Lisbon to open negotiations with Salazar, and asking him to support our approach. Mr. Churchill agreed.

Following my return from the Moscow Conference, I sent a memorandum on December 4 to the President, then in the Middle East for the Cairo and Tehran conferences, informing him that Salazar was willing to go the limit to extend us immediate use of existing British facilities if an appearance could be maintained of adherence to the agreement with Britain. He was unwilling to give the British further facilities for their own or our use unless he could be shown that the general military situation had diminished the German menace to Portugal as compared with last August.

Salazar seemed inclined to favor our proposal to construct an airport for Portugal on Santa Maria Island of the Azores, with a view to Anglo-American use when completed. He raised virtually no objection to our plans for sharing in antisubmarine patrol activity with the British at Terceira, the Azores.

I informed the President that Salazar and Kennan had further discussed a suggestion the Portuguese Premier had first advanced to the British; namely, that we should agree that Portuguese forces would take part in liberating their East Indies colony of Timor from the Japanese.

The same day I congratulated Norweb and Kennan by cable on the substantial and rapid progress they had made in their negotiations.

Following receipt of a memorandum from the Joint Chiefs of Staff, whom we were keeping minutely informed of the negotiations in Lisbon, we cabled Norweb that the Joint Chiefs desired that authority be secured to construct for the Portuguese Government a major airfield in the Azores, either on Santa Maria or on some other suitable island, which would be for our use. They also stated the desirability of obtaining most-favored-nation commercial rights in the airfield and continuing rights after the war for our military to supply outlying posts by air.

Salazar eventually agreed to invite the Pan American Airways to make a survey of the Azores to pick a location for a major airfield. He refused, however, to accept our plan to station a naval air squadron at Lagens Field, the Azores, in connection with the British antisubmarine campaign, even though the squadron was to be on loan to the British and under British command. Both we and the British continued to make strong representations on this point, but it was not until July, 1944, that we obtained Portugal's consent.

Our negotiations for the construction and use of the Santa Maria air base dragged on for several months more. We were increasingly anxious to obtain these facilities in the belief that the Azores would be a highly important station on our aerial highway to the Orient for the defeat of Japan. The President sent another message to Salazar, presented to the Premier on July 22 by Ambassador Norweb and by Paul Culbertson, Assistant Chief of the Division of European Affairs, who carried it to Lisbon, earnestly requesting authorization for the immediate sending to Santa Maria of the materials to construct the airbase. Salazar agreed, but postponed a decision on the question of our use of the base.

On October 6 I sent the President a memorandum in which I said we were now confronted with an attempt on Dr. Salazar's part to engage us in detailed commitments covering a wide range of supplies and services in the strategic shipping and economic fields, and I did not believe this Government was in a position so to commit itself, even should this seem desirable.

I enclosed the draft of a proposed message to Salazar. In this we stated that the Portuguese Government had expressed its desire to participate in an eventual expedition for the liberation of Timor, toward which end staff conversations were in progress in Lisbon. We had pointed out, however, that the greatest contribution Portugal could make toward the prosecution of the war in the Pacific, including the liberation of Timor, was to make available to the United States the facilities we required on the island of Santa Maria. This view had been confirmed by the Combined British and American Chiefs of Staff.

Our message went on to say that we were surprised and disappointed over the hesitancy of the Portuguese Government to make available the necessary lands and to permit construction to begin, and we could only interpret this as a lack of complete cooperation, as a grave obstruction to the prosecution of the war in the Pacific, and as an important aid to Japan. We therefore stated that, unless the Portuguese Government immediately authorized all necessary land expropriations and the completion of the air base on Santa Maria, we would be obliged to discontinue the staff conversations at once, to decline to engage in any negotiations with Portugal concerning economic or other matters, and immediately to curtail the economic aid we were furnishing her.

The President having approved, this message was conveyed to Salazar by Ambassador Norweb. It led within a few weeks to an agreement, signed November 28, 1944, for the construction and use of the Santa Maria air base. Portugal agreed that we should have complete use and control of the air base for the duration of the war and six months thereafter. On our part we gave the Portuguese assurances that their forces should take part in the liberation of Timor.

In summation, our negotiations with Portugal both for bases and in connection with strategic materials were often disappointingly long drawn-out. But it must be remembered that we and the British were exerting our pressure from a great distance, while the Germans, until the summer of 1944, were within overnight striking range along the Pyrenees. We received, moreover, a far greater supply of strategic materials from Portugal than was going to the Axis. Finally, we must recognize that the wolfram embargo meant the cessation of an industry that had been netting Portugal something like $100,000,000 annually. When these factors are taken into consideration, the success of our diplomatic efforts toward Portugal may be seen to have been considerable.

97: Sweden, Switzerland, Eire

SWEDEN, one of the most important of the European neutrals, became in the early 1940's a focal point for a portion of our diplomacy designed to support the military conduct of the war. Hitler's occupation of Norway and Denmark in 1940 had complicated our relations with Sweden in many ways. The Swedes' location behind the British and German blockades cut drastically into our commerce with them, while at the same time rendering it more difficult for Sweden to resist German economic and military demands. We were greatly concerned over the Swedish Government's continuing to permit German troops and supplies to cross Sweden to and from Norway. Sweden offered us both a valuable point of observation for northern Europe and Germany, and a source of anxiety because of the valuable supplies such as iron ore and ball bearings which were going to Germany.

At the beginning of 1943 I set forth our position at length in a telegram to our Legation in Stockholm on January 7, to be communicated to the Swedish Foreign Office. In this I said that the determining factor in American-Swedish relations during the war must be the extent of Sweden's resistance to Axis demands that were contrary to her rights as a neutral state and a democratic, independent nation. We entirely understood, I said, that in the past, military and other events had made it appear expedient for Sweden temporarily to acquiesce in Germany's imposition of certain servitudes; for example, the movement of German troops and armaments through Swedish territory.

But, I went on, Sweden need not expect that we could continue indefinitely to accept excuses of force and expediency for giving in to Germany. We thought Sweden's present position was strong enough to permit her to assert her rights in relation to Germany and to assume all her obligations to us as a neutral and sovereign state. We based our confidence in the present strength of Sweden not solely on the Swedish people's sturdy independence and the willingness they had shown to carry the heavy burden of maintaining strong armed forces for defense, but also on the powerful weapons Sweden had at her disposal to force Germany to respect Swedish rights; for example, her ability to refuse important supplies of iron ore to Germany.

I then said it was our intention, if Sweden concretely evidenced her determination to defend her rights against German pressure, to recognize that she had established a moral claim to have a share in the pool of supplies available to the Allies.

In the spring of 1943, triangular negotiations began in London among the British, the Swedes, and ourselves, which resulted in an agreement initialed on September 23. This had the effect of appreciably cutting down Swedish trade and shipping going to Germany. The Swedish Government also informed Germany that the transport of German troops and war materials across Sweden would no longer be permitted. We on our side agreed to supply Sweden, among other things, with a limited quantity of petroleum.

Sharp disputes arose between us at the State Department on the one hand and Secretary of War Stimson and Secretary of Navy Knox on the other over permitting shipments of petroleum to Sweden. Stimson and Knox argued that petroleum sent to Sweden might flow into German hands; that we ourselves might soon be short of petroleum; that, by continuing to assist Swedish overseas trade we helped the Axis since Swedish exports and concessions to Germany continued; and that we received no commensurate benefits from our policy.

I conferred with Stimson and Knox and their representatives and had written exchanges of views with the Joint Chiefs of Staff. I stated our position that there was nothing in our past experience to indicate that petroleum shipped to Sweden might reach the Germans, that we had a Board of Economic Warfare representative as Petroleum Attaché at Stockholm to report any such diversions, and that the Swedes in their own self-interest could not permit deliveries of oil to the Germans since they knew we would thereupon immediately cut off their supplies. I emphasized that the oil so far shipped to Sweden had been in accordance with directives already given by the President in November, 1942, and that, in return, we had already obtained substantial concessions from the Swedes. I added that, since the oil was to come from the Caribbean and Gulf areas where there was no shortage of oil of the types being shipped, and was to be transported in Swedish ships, there was consequently no drain upon our supply of oil or on our tankers. Neither the Department nor the staff of the Board of Economic Warfare, I pointed out, agreed that the continuance of trade with Sweden was of large aid to the enemy; rather we felt that it would permit us to effect a substantial reduction in Sweden's economic assistance to the enemy. I stressed the fact that officials of our

armed forces had repeatedly urged upon the Department the military importance of stopping the German transit traffic across Sweden.

In general the Board of Economic Warfare supported the Department's views, although in the previous year its chairman, Vice President
Wallace, had opposed us. The Board approved in principle the agreement
reached in London.

The opposition of Stimson's and Knox's Departments, however, was
so strong that I had to take the question to the President for settlement.
He decided in favor of the State Department.

During 1944 we concentrated largely on inducing the Swedish Government to reduce or eliminate Swedish shipments of ball bearings to
Germany. The Anglo-American strategic air forces had been seeking to
knock out the German ball-bearing factories, and Swedish shipments of
this vital product assumed greater importance to us than ever. The Joint
Chiefs of Staff, in a letter to me on March 23, expressed their deep concern over the military aid thus being rendered to Germany by Sweden.

In our negotiations with Sweden, however, we encountered opposition
arising from the fact that Sweden still had a lingering fear of German
armed reprisals, despite the growing strength and successes of the United
Nations. I said in a letter to the Joint Chiefs on May 19: "No matter how
unrealistic it may appear to us here, the factor which in the final analysis
will control the Swedish Government's decision . . . is its conviction that
full compliance with our demands will almost certainly expose Sweden to
German military attack. . . . This conviction is so strong that the Swedes,
in their disbelief that their present bearing exports to Germany are as
important as we say they are, strongly suspect that our real purpose in
pressing them on this matter is not to obtain a reduction in ball bearings
but to involve them in war with Germany."

We were able to conclude a direct agreement on June 12 with the
Swedish ball-bearing company, SKF, for a drastic reduction in the export
of bearing parts and machinery during the critical period of the next four
months—the period when Anglo-American armies were to push across
France. The War and Navy Departments, however, objected that the
reduction was not sufficient.

After numerous exchanges of views with the British Government,
including messages between the President and the Prime Minister, Foreign Secretary Eden and I agreed on joint representations to the Swedish
Government, made on August 24, stating that nothing short of cessation
of all trade relations with the Axis and of a radical change in Sweden's

German policy would meet our demands. At the same time the Soviet Government, whose support we had requested, made similar representations.

Swedish Foreign Minister Dr. Günther rejected our request on September 4. I informed the President in a memorandum on September 15, however, that the Swedes had usually turned down formal demands by the belligerent Powers although actually yielding to informal pressure. Since July, I said, we had, through informal pressure, secured from Sweden the cancellation of all insurance on Swedish vessels operating between Swedish and German ports, thereby reducing the tonnage in this trade by two-thirds; formal statements that Sweden would not grant refuge to war criminals or war loot, and the cessation of all transit traffic by way of Sweden between Germany and Norway.

I recommended that, unless Sweden immediately ended her trade with Germany, we should take over the control of various Swedish subsidiaries in this country. I further proposed that, if the British and Russians concurred, we should jointly inform Sweden that our attitude toward the release of supplies she required from Allied-controlled sources after the collapse of Germany would depend on her reply to this request.

While these suggestions were under study, we continued to bring strong pressure on the Swedish Government. On September 22 our Minister in Stockholm, Herschel V. Johnson, reported that the Swedish Government had decided to close all the Swedish ports on the Baltic to German shipping. This enabled me to send the President on September 28 a memorandum in which, after referring to this action, I said: "According to high Swedish officials, these steps reduce Swedish exports to Germany by approximately 98 per cent." I added that we were continuing our efforts to secure a completely effective embargo. I concluded that I did not consider it any longer necessary to proceed with the plans we had in mind with regard to Sweden.

A few days later the SKF company agreed to stop all exports of ball bearings and related parts to Germany as of October 12. And in November the Swedish Government agreed that all exports to Germany would cease. We were also able to obtain from Sweden the release of interned American airmen and permission for the Air Transport Command planes to maintain service.

Toward Switzerland, the other neutral "island" surrounded by German-controlled territory, our policy differed somewhat from that which we practiced toward other neutrals. We felt it essential, in presenting our demands and in exercising pressure to reduce Swiss exports of strategic manufactured goods to Germany, to avoid pushing Switzerland into a diplomatic rupture, or worse, with Germany. This was for the reason that Switzerland, representing us diplomatically in enemy countries, was our sole link with them. We had to depend upon her representatives to ensure the welfare of American prisoners of war. We were keenly gratified by the conscientious manner in which Switzerland had endeavored to fulfill this task, even though her efforts in the Japanese area had been largely ineffective because of the uncooperative attitude of the Japanese military authorities and the barbarism of many of them toward prisoners of war. The British agreed with us that our approach to Switzerland, while strong, should not be of such nature as to destroy our only channel for representations to the Axis.

After Pearl Harbor we supported the British economic warfare objective to limit Swiss exports to the Axis, particularly of war commodities, and to obtain from Switzerland strategic products including precision instruments. But the successes of Hitler's army, coupled with the fact that Switzerland was completely surrounded by the Axis and dependent upon them for raw materials, negated our efforts to obtain real concessions during 1942 and the first half of 1943. Swiss exports to the Axis, particularly of war materials, increased considerably during this period.

Our Minister in Bern, Leland Harrison, cabled us on April 9, 1943, that the Swiss were about to negotiate a new trade agreement with Germany. Swiss officials assured Harrison that they would do everything possible to bring about a satisfactory reduction in what we considered undesirable exports to the Axis.

I cabled Minister Harrison on April 27 a comprehensive outline of our position to be presented to the Swiss Foreign Office. I said to Harrison that the State Department, the Board of Economic Warfare, and the British were all agreed that the Swiss must be deterred, by fear of our taking unfavorable action, from making concessions desired by the Germans. He was to say to the Swiss that, pending clarification of Switzerland's position, we would suspend, with certain exceptions, all export licenses and navicerts covering Swiss imports.

As a result of this *démarche*, made simultaneously by ourselves and the British, Anglo-American negotiations with Switzerland were entered into which resulted in the signature of an agreement in London on December 19, 1943, whereby the Swiss would reduce their export of arms, ammunition, and machinery to the Axis by 45 per cent. The export of the most strategic manufactures, such as ball bearings, arms, fuses, and precision tools, was even more drastically reduced—60 per cent under that of 1942. The Swiss further agreed to prevent concentration of these exports in the early months of 1944, to send no such exports to Italy, to reduce exports proportionately whenever any part of Axis territory was liberated, and to make no credit commitments to the Axis without first consulting Britain and the United States. In return for these concessions, we restored the food and fodder export quotas to Switzerland as they existed prior to April, 1943, but coupled their restoration with a prohibition against the export of dairy products. In these negotiations we worked closely with the Board of Economic Warfare.

In February, 1944, the British and ourselves reopened negotiations with the Swiss to obtain still further reductions in their exports to Germany. The Swiss Government, however, strongly resisted all our efforts and engaged in delaying tactics.

With these negotiations still in course, I called in the Swiss Minister, Charles Bruggmann, on July 14. After emphasizing the traditional and inherently friendly relations between our peoples and Governments, I said I had already discovered that some of the countries listed as neutral did not seem clearly to appreciate the serious situation of countries like the United States. We, I pointed out, were losing thousands of lives, we had 8,000,000 armed men fighting on all battle fronts, we were spending $200,000,000,000, and we were supplying Great Britain and Russia to an enormous extent.

"It's not unnatural," I said, "that Swiss businessmen should ask the intercession of their Government with ours so as to retain as much trade with the Axis as possible. I saw this happen to a great extent during the First World War, and I've seen it happen in this war. The Swedes pleaded with tears in their eyes for some time against what they regarded as excessive requests of the Allied nations to limit ever more the Swedish exports to Germany. Their main argument was the possible loss of coal from Germany, whereupon we suddenly discovered that they had coal on hand to keep them supplied for a year.

"When the United States is losing lives right and left and is spending enormous sums of money because of neutral aid to the enemy primarily in order to gratify some businessmen, the question becomes most serious to this country."

We therefore earnestly requested Minister Bruggmann to take this matter up with his Government so as to arrive at once at a satisfactory agreement.

I asked British Foreign Secretary Eden if he would call in the Swiss Minister to the United Kingdom and make to him statements similar to those I had made to Minister Bruggmann, which he did. The American and British ministers in Bern also made representations. As a result of these approaches, combined with the effect of our military victories in France, Switzerland agreed to make further very considerable reductions in exports to Germany.

Following the Allied landings in southern France and the rapid progress of this new campaign toward the Swiss border, the British and ourselves made new demands on the Swiss on September 18, 1944, this time to embargo all exports to Germany of certain specified strategic commodities, and to reduce to a prewar level the transit traffic between Germany and Italy. In return, we offered Switzerland certain immediate and long-term economic concessions.

The Swiss agreed to prohibit as of October 1 the export of arms, ammunition, explosives, airplanes and parts, and bearings. Since this did not cover all the commodities we had specified, our negotiations continued but did not reach a satisfactory conclusion until March, 1945, four months after my resignation.

With a further neutral, Eire, our relations during the war years were complicated by a number of factors. These included the presence of American troops in Northern Ireland; the desire of our military chiefs for Irish bases; the desire of Eire for American ships; and the continuance of Axis diplomatic representation in Dublin. All these were colored by an often evinced anti-British feeling on the part of Eire's leaders.

During the period of the European War, Eire benefited by the program of the American Government and people to aid the British Commonwealth as a whole. After the fall of France we made available 20,000 rifles to the Irish Army.

I wrote the President on May 21, 1940, informing him of a telegram I had received three days before from our Minister in Dublin, David Gray, an uncle of Mrs. Roosevelt. Irish Prime Minister Eamon de Valera had inquired whether the United States Government could proclaim Irish status quo vital to American interests in view of Eire's strategic position commanding Atlantic air and sea traffic. Mr. de Valera thought such a statement would greatly strengthen his leadership in the face of a difficult and uncertain situation in Ireland.

I attached to my letter to the President a draft telegram that I proposed to send in reply if it met with his approval. He wrote his O.K. at the top of my letter and initialed the proposed telegram. In this I requested Minister Gray to inform Mr. de Valera that, although we should be pleased to assist Eire, we could not take the action he suggested because it would imply that this Government was departing from its traditional policies with respect to European affairs and it inevitably would lead to confusion and misunderstanding both abroad and in the United States.

In March, 1941, the Irish Minister for Defense, General Frank Aiken, arrived in the United States with letters of introduction from Mr. de Valera to the President and to me, for the purpose of purchasing arms, munitions, and ships. In his conversations with leading members of our Government, Aiken showed himself to be strongly anti-British.

Minister Gray reported to us from Dublin on April 8 that the Aiken mission was being exploited by the Irish Government to arouse anti-British sentiment and to indicate American approval of Irish policy. He suggested that the time had come for us to adopt a firmer attitude and demand from Mr. de Valera a definite clarification of his position.

I agreed. We authorized Gray on April 10 to take up with the Irish Prime Minister certain statements De Valera had broadcast to this country to the effect that Britain was blockading Eire as much as Germany and implying that Britain was fighting an imperialist war rather than defending democratic liberties. We requested Minister Gray to lose no opportunity generally to impress on the Irish the United States Government's determination and the scope of its effort in carrying out its policy of opposition to the forces of aggression. He was also to emphasize the President's profound belief, which had the backing of public opinion here, that the democratic forces throughout the world would win through to final victory.

The following day, April 11, Minister of Defense Aiken called upon me to present his letter from Mr. de Valera. He proceeded to talk for some minutes about the difficulties between Ireland and Great Britain for many years, extending down to the present, and about how impossible it was to get Britain to do the proper thing, and the like—all of which, I thought, related very little to the realities of the present situation.

In reply, I spoke very highly of Ireland and of the interest of the American Government and people in her present and future welfare. But I added: "There is another tremendously important angle to the present situation, which is imperatively claiming constant attention and effort on our part—and this relates to the world movement of conquest by force on the part of Berlin and Tokyo." I then made a long exposition of our policy from 1933 on, as we warned again and again of the impending danger and sought to gather together thirty-five or forty countries behind a broad, sound program for commercial and economic rehabilitation with a joint pledge to Germany and Italy of absolute equality of opportunity and of access to raw materials.

"All countries alike," I concluded, "are now in danger from Hitler, whether they are peaceful or otherwise. Hitler has no friends and is not a friend of anybody, and he would sacrifice any of his most loyal followers or sympathizers just as quickly as he would an enemy, if it would serve any small purpose for him to do so."

General Aiken had practically no comment to make.

On April 25 I cabled Minister Gray our reply, drafted by Under Secretary Welles, to the Irish request for arms, munitions, and shipping. I instructed Gray to say to Prime Minister de Valera that we sympathized with the fact that the reduction in shipping had brought about a food shortage in Ireland, and that we were willing to negotiate for the transfer of two freighters to transport food from the United States to Ireland.

I instructed Gray to make this offer directly to Mr. de Valera and to say that this Government had observed with regret, from General Aiken's conversation with various officials here, that the latter's attitude toward the British appeared to be that of blind hostility. This point of view, I said, seemed to be utterly lacking in any appreciation of the fact, which appeared completely clear to this Government, that Ireland's future security and safety inevitably depended on Britain's triumph. I continued that the United States Government, as the Irish Prime Minister fully realized, believed that the future security of liberty and democracy in the world rested on an ultimate victory of the British and of the other nations resisting aggression, and that this Government was pledged, in conformity with its declared policy, to do everything practicable to help those nations in their struggle. Any Irish policy that was contrary to this United States objective naturally would provide no basis for fruitful and helpful cooperation between Ireland and the United States.

I further requested Gray to state very definitely to Mr. de Valera that, in accordance with our policy, we would continue to make available to Britain and the Empire and to other countries resisting aggression all our production of military and naval matériel not required for our own rearmament program. We could not therefore make it available to Eire until that Government was ready to show a more cooperative attitude toward the war efforts of those nations. This Government, I concluded, did not question the determination or the right of the Irish people to maintain their neutrality, but between a policy of this character and one which potentially at least gave real encouragement to Germany there was a clear distinction.

An exchange of notes with the Irish Government followed, during which that Government stated its determination to defend itself if attacked by Germany. Eire continued to request arms and munitions, and we continued to refuse. In September, 1941, however, despite the growing shortage of shipping, we made available two merchant ships to carry foodstuffs and other necessary goods. Subsequently these were sunk, presumably by Axis submarines.

In 1941 some hundreds of American technicians and workmen went to Northern Ireland to help the British construct bases there. The Government of Eire asked us in October and again in November the purpose of these activities and what the intentions of the American Government were. We wrote Irish Minister Robert Brennan on November 18 saying that this had been taken up with the President and we were authorized to say that Eire's inquiry related to territory recognized by this Government as part of the United Kingdom, and to suggest that the Irish Government address its inquiry to the United Kingdom Government.

After Pearl Harbor Minister Brennan sent me a note on December 16 transmitting extracts from a speech made two days previously by Mr. de Valera who, after expressing Ireland's special sympathy with the United States by reason of our involvement in the war, declared that Irish policy would remain unchanged, and that Ireland could only be a friendly neutral because of the circumstances of her history and the fact of the partition of Ireland—meaning the division of the island into Eire and Northern Ireland.

At the State Department we had been considering for some days the advisability of a message from the President to Prime Minister de Valera. This seemed the appropriate moment to send it. The President agreeing, I dispatched a note to Minister Brennan on December 22, attaching the message with which, I said, I also desired to associate myself. In this the President said, in part:

"The policy of the American Government now as in the past contemplates the hope that all the free institutions, liberties, and independence which the Irish people now enjoy may be preserved for the full enjoyment of the future. If freedom and liberty are to be preserved, they must now be defended by the human and material resources of all free nations. Your freedom too is at stake. No longer can it be doubted that the policy of Hitler and his Axis associates is the conquest of the entire world and the enslavement of all mankind.

"I have every confidence that the Irish Government and the Irish people, who love liberty and freedom as dearly as we, will know how to meet their responsibilities in the present situation."

American troops landed in Northern Ireland on January 26, 1942, and the following day Prime Minister de Valera made a statement declaring that he had not been consulted by either the British or American Governments and that this move could have no effect on "the Irish people's claim for the union of the whole national territory and for supreme jurisdiction over it." He added that "the maintenance of the partition of Ireland is as indefensible as aggressions against small nations elsewhere which it is the avowed purpose of Great Britain and the United States in this war to bring to an end."

Irish Minister Brennan handed Under Secretary Welles on February 6, while I was absent from Washington, an official text of Mr. de Valera's statement and said that the Irish Government and people regarded our landing of troops in Northern Ireland as an official sanction by the United States of the partition of Ireland and increasingly believed that these troops were going to be used to attack Irish forces. Welles sought to reassure him.

The President sent further reassurances to Prime Minister de Valera on February 26.

Mr. de Valera thanked the President on April 20 for his assurances, and then reiterated his objection to the landing of American troops from the viewpoint of the partition question and asked that Ireland be allowed to purchase necessary military equipment in this country without delay.

The President commented on this in a memorandum to Welles suggesting that no reply be sent and then saying:

"If he would only come out of the clouds and quit talking about the quarter of a million Irishmen ready to fight if they had the weapons, we would all have higher regard for him. Personally I do not believe there are more than one thousand trained soldiers in the whole of the Free State. Even they are probably efficient only in the use of rifles and shotguns."

In 1943 we faced two major questions in the development of our relations with Eire. One concerned the possibility of our obtaining Irish bases, the other the possibility of inducing the Irish Government to demand the recall of Axis diplomats who, we had good reason to suspect, were passing on to their Governments vital information they were able to obtain by virtue of being stationed so close to the shipping lanes and to Britain.

On June 3, 1943, I wrote the President a memorandum enclosing suggestions along this line from Minister Gray in Dublin, who thought that a refusal of these requests should be met by a progressive shutting off by Britain and the United States of raw materials for Irish industries. The President wrote me on June 15:

"I have read David Gray's outline of views on American policy toward Ireland. What do you think we should do in regard to action?

"In the matter of asking for the use of ports, I think we might consider asking for a lease of the ports in a manner similar to the lease of the eight bases from Great Britain in 1940. However, the period could well be cut from ninety-nine years to the duration of the war.

"I think Mr. Gray is right in his desire to put De Valera on record. We shall undoubtedly be turned down. I think the strongest fact is that we are losing many American and British lives and many ships in carrying various supplies to Ireland without receiving anything in return, and without so much as 'Thank you.' "

I replied to the President that it appeared to me that without question air and naval facilities in Ireland would be of considerable usefulness to the United Nations' war effort. I added that a high officer of the War Department had informally advised us that these facilities would be enormously useful from a military standpoint. Prime Minister de Valera, however, I pointed out, had repeatedly declared that "there can be no question of leasing these ports" or "of handing them over on any condition whatsoever," and that any attempt by any of the belligerents to bring pressure to bear on the Irish Government to turn them over "could only lead to bloodshed." In making these statements, I said, Mr. de Valera no doubt had had principally in mind possible approaches from the British Government. Since our entry into the war, however, suggestions had been made that Ireland might be disposed to lease naval and air facilities to the United States.

"The Irish and the British," I said to the President, "have fought one another for seven hundred years. They suspect and distrust one another. Each tries on suitable occasions to obtain the support of the American people and Government against the other. We must be careful, therefore, to be sure that any action which we take in this regard has a sound military basis in the opinion of our own Chiefs of Staff. It seems to me that this is of fundamental importance to make it impossible for anyone to maintain that we took sides with the British against the Irish and 'pulled British chestnuts out of the fire.' "

I suggested that, since Ireland was at the back door of the United Kingdom and happenings inside Ireland were therefore of more immediate and direct interest to the United Kingdom than to the United States, we should first obtain the approval of the British Government.

I attached a draft letter for the President's signature, requesting the views of the Joint Chiefs of Staff on the military aspects of the question. Representatives of the War and Navy Departments designated by the Joint Chiefs of Staff advised us that they did not consider it possible at that time to foresee whether, with the progress of the war, we would actually desire bases in Ireland or exactly what military value such bases might have; but they did think it would prove of real help now in our strategic planning if we could be sure we would have the use of them if they were needed.

President Roosevelt and Prime Minister Churchill discussed the question of an approach to Ireland with regard to the bases at the time of the first Quebec Conference and later in the year at the Cairo Conference. Meantime I was in contact with Foreign Secretary Eden on the subject.

Finally on December 22, 1943, Eden gave us his Government's reply. He thought that Mr. de Valera would avoid a direct negative reply to any approach on the question of air and naval bases and would seek to cloud the issue by reiterating his grievances in regard to partition. Eden therefore believed that our proposed approach would be likely to give rise to acute difficulties and that it would be wiser to postpone it.

In a memorandum to the President on December 29 I said that, in view of this attitude by the British Government, I would let the matter rest unless he wished to discuss it further with Prime Minister Churchill.

The question of Irish bases was not taken up again.

In December, 1943, I received from Irish Minister Brennan two notes asking my support for Irish efforts to purchase two ships to replace those obtained from this country in 1941 and subsequently sunk. After consulting with Minister Gray in Dublin, I sent the President a memorandum on December 27 in which I suggested that we should refuse the Irish request

on the grounds that our Government had previously chartered two merchant ships to Ireland, and that the Irish Government had permitted them
to be sunk by Nazi submarines without offering the slightest word of
protest to the German Government. Mr. Roosevelt approved.

In 1944 we took up actively with the Irish Government the question
of the Axis diplomatic missions in Eire. On February 21, after coordinating our action with Britain, we made a formal request for their removal.
We pointed out that Eire's neutrality was operating in favor of the Axis.
One reason for this was the opportunity afforded to the Axis for highly
organized espionage because of Ireland's geographical position.

"Situated as you are," we said, "in close proximity to Britain, divided
only by an intangible boundary from Northern Ireland, where are situated
important American bases, with continuous traffic to and from both countries, Axis agents enjoy almost unrestricted opportunity for bringing military information of vital importance from Great Britain and Northern
Ireland into Ireland and from there transmitting it by various routes and
methods to Germany. No opportunity corresponding to this is open to the
United Nations, for the Axis has no military dispositions which may be
observed from Ireland."

All this was of particular importance to us at that time because the
United Nations preparations for the invasion of Normandy from Britain
were approaching the climax and we were making every effort to keep
them secret.

Nevertheless, Prime Minister de Valera, in a note transmitted to us
on March 7, refused our request. He reasserted Eire's right to remain neutral, and he sought to prove that we had been misinformed in believing
that Axis diplomats and agents were able to obtain and send from Ireland
vital information concerning United Nations military activities.

One week later I cabled Ambassador Winant in London that we were
considering a further message to Mr. de Valera. This would reaffirm the
position we had taken in our original message and state that the American
Government and people would inevitably hold the Irish Government
responsible for actions against our forces and military operations taken by
the Axis representatives in Eire. We felt, I said, that, without disclosing to
the Irish Government whether we contemplated any further action, we
should try to keep the question open. While we did not consider the use
of economic sanctions advisable, I said I did not think we should commit
ourselves, at least for the time being, not to use them, as both Minister
Gray and the British representative in Dublin had suggested. However, I

added, since Ireland obtained most of her supplies from Britain, this question was primarily a British one, and I requested Winant to obtain the views of the British Government.

The White House sent me on March 20 Britain's reply in the form of a message from Prime Minister Churchill to the President. Mr. Churchill, referring to my cable to Winant on the 14th, said that in his opinion it would be much better to keep the Irish "guessing for a while" than to offer them any immediate reassurances. He said he thought we should "let fear work its healthy process," and thereby we would get behind the scenes a continued stiffening up of Irish measures, which even then were not so bad, to prevent leakages of information.

Mr. Churchill said that, while Britain did not intend to stop necessary trade between England and Ireland, she did intend to prevent ships and airplanes from leaving Ireland for Spain, Portugal, and other foreign ports and to restrict all communications to the utmost until the invasion of France had been launched. This was purely from the viewpoint of protecting American and British soldiers' lives and our military plans.

I sent the President on March 31 the reply which he had requested me to prepare. This stated his belief that Mr. Churchill was pursuing the right line in taking the security measures without, however, adopting measures of coercion designed only to harm Ireland. We wondered, however, if measures forbidding Irish ships to go to all foreign ports from Ireland might not be interpreted as economic sanctions, and suggested they be permitted to continue to come to North America to carry wheat and other essential supplies to Ireland.

Mr. Churchill agreed.

We now planned to send a further note to Prime Minister de Valera concerning Axis representatives in Eire, and the President approved the text. The Irish Government, however, offered through our intelligence services to adopt whatever security safeguards we and the British desired in Ireland, and Mr. Churchill told us he thought our first note had done great good and had prompted Irish authorities to strengthen their security measures but that a second note was not necessary. I sent the President a memorandum on May 17 proposing that we let the matter rest, to which he agreed.

One week previously I sent the President a memorandum to give him my opinion on the question he had raised with us on May 9 as to whether two ships should be made available to the Irish Government. "We believe," I said, "that our request of the Irish Government that they expel the Axis representatives was a reasonable one with which they should have complied. We believe that public opinion in this country supported this request and in fact would be disposed to support pressure to cause Ireland to comply. The editorial reaction to this throughout the country was favorable. We believe that public opinion would find it difficult to understand our now making available two ships to get supplies to Ireland in view of the attitude which Ireland has taken toward us and the war."

I added that to make ships available to Ireland in the present circumstances might well retard the progress we had made in putting pressure on other neutral countries to reduce trade with Germany. The President agreed with this position.

During this period various Irish-American organizations urged the United States Government to use its influence with Great Britain to bring an end to partition between Eire and Northern Ireland, meaning that Northern Ireland would become a part of Eire. A resolution to this effect was introduced in Congress. I adopted an attitude of complete impartiality on this issue, however, and Under Secretary Stettinius stated our position on June 7, 1944, in a letter to Senator Danaher, as follows:

"The constitutional relationship between Northern Ireland and the Irish Free State is, of course, a matter for the proper authorities within the British Commonwealth to determine. The American Government could only take the position that the altering of political boundaries between the Irish Free State and Northern Ireland was not a matter in which it might properly intervene. International law and comity would permit no other course."

The possibility that neutral countries might give asylum to Axis leaders and war criminals who fled to escape the fate awaiting them entered into many diplomatic exchanges we had with the European neutrals, including the Vatican, and with Argentina, in 1943 and 1944. As the outlines of our victory became ever clearer, the President and I were resolved that the easy flight of the Kaiser into Holland in 1918 should not be duplicated by the Nazi, Fascist, and Japanese leaders responsible for the war and the criminals responsible for atrocities.

While we recognized the right of nations to grant asylum to political refugees, and were ourselves among the foremost in supporting this right, we refused to grant that the Axis leaders and criminals could come within this category. They had been responsible for a war costing the lives of untold millions of people and the destruction of uncountable treasure;

they were guilty of murder thousands of times over; and they had no more right than a murderer to obtain asylum in another country.

My view was that here was a bigger, broader question than the narrow one of the right of asylum as it had been interpreted toward the close of local or regional wars. We had seen a terrific attack on the people of the world, on world order and civilization, and an attempt to enslave all peoples. With these mad dogs of aggression let loose, it would be idiocy for neutral nations to harbor them, for they might later get out and do to the countries that sheltered them what Hitler had done, for example, to Norway. The Axis had violated all the rules of neutrality and war, and we did not feel that the neutrals had the right to prevent our making a lasting example of those ambitious men who had brought the world to the precipice of destruction.

The question first came to the fore officially a few days after the ousting of Benito Mussolini. On July 29, 1943, the British Government sent us a note stating it was concerned that Mussolini and other prominent Fascists might seek refuge in neutral countries. It therefore proposed to request the Governments of Switzerland, Spain, Portugal, Sweden, Turkey, the Vatican, and Argentina to refuse refuge to such war criminals. It would declare that any shelter, assistance, or protection given such persons would be regarded "as a violation of the principles for which the United Nations are fighting and which they are determined to carry into effect by every means in their power." The British asked us to make similar representations.

Since I was having luncheon with the President that day, I discussed this with him during the course of the meal. We agreed that he should issue a public statement the next day, and that this should be telegraphed to the Governments mentioned by the British. In this statement the President said: "I can only say that the Government of the United States would regard the action by a neutral Government in affording asylum to Axis leaders or their tools as inconsistent with the principles for which the United Nations are fighting and that the United States Government hopes that no neutral Government will permit its territory to be used as a place of refuge or otherwise assist such persons in any effort to escape their just deserts."

Only Turkey, Switzerland, the Vatican, and Argentina replied to our communication, and their replies gave us no assurances. They asserted, rather, their intention to follow the accepted principles of international law when the occasion arose for them to make decisions on the matter of asylum.

The question rested at that point for more than a year. Then, in August, 1944, when Allied forces were pouring across France and it seemed that the moment might be coming for Axis leaders to attempt to seek shelter, I raised it once more in a series of telegrams to Bern, Stockholm, Lisbon, and Madrid on August 23. I asked whether those Governments were ready to give assurances that they would refuse to admit Axis leaders and war criminals, whom they undoubtedly would regard in any event as undesirable aliens whose presence on their territory was not to their interests even if those persons were not wanted by the United Nations for eventual trial.

The wheels of justice, I said, were turning fast, and the neutrals might be faced at any moment with the need to make a decision in this matter. I therefore strongly urged that they give the desired assurances now. I pointed out that practically every individual in this country had been affected by the war, that our people knew that a small group of individuals in the Axis countries had played the leading role in plunging the world into this ghastly war, and they would not therefore understand neutral countries' extending protection or asylum to those responsible. The American people's feeling that adequate steps must be taken to hold the Axis leaders and their followers strictly accountable for their crimes against civilization was being intensified by the steadily growing casualty lists.

I said to our representatives in the neutral capitals that I did not want them to make any threats, but that I did feel they would be less than candid if they failed to make known to the appropriate officials our conviction that the admission of the Axis leaders and their followers would have an adverse effect on relations with this country for many years. I added that we were confident that the other United and Associated Nations shared our views, which were also shared, we did not doubt, by substantial sections of public opinion in the neutral countries.

We informed the British and Soviet Governments of this *démarche*, which we took independently to save time because of the possibility that, with our troops about to reach the Siegfried Line, some of the Nazi and Fascist leaders might attempt in the near future to take refuge in neutral countries. In response the British Government gave instructions to its diplomatic representatives in the four neutral capitals to support our stand. Soviet Ambassador Gromyko sent me a note on September 4 stating that his Government shared our views.

On August 30 Minister Johnson in Stockholm reported that Foreign Minister Günther believed his Government would decide to declare that Sweden would give no asylum to war criminals. On the following day the President sent me a memorandum, saying: "I note in the news that Sweden is taking action to announce that it will not harbor any war criminals. Don't you think that we might approach the Swiss to make a similar declaration? None of us want to send an Allied army into Switzerland to grab Hitler, etc., and if they make a declaration now it may keep some of the Nazis out or give them a chance later to hand over war criminals."

I informed the President that the Swedish reaction was the result of our urgent representations to Sweden of August 23, which representations had also been made to Spain, Portugal, and Switzerland.

The Swedish Government officially confirmed to us on September 3 that Sweden would not grant asylum to any category of war criminals. In the course of the next few weeks both Spain and Portugal gave us less satisfactory assurances which were not so categorical as those from Sweden. Switzerland gave definite assurances on November 14. The Argentine Government stated independently that Argentina would not grant refuge to war criminals or permit them to deposit capital or acquire property in Argentina.

We had more difficulty with Eire, whom we approached on September 21. Prime Minister de Valera replied on October 9 that the Irish Government was unable to give assurances that would make it impossible for it to exercise its right to grant asylum should justice, charity, or the honor or interest of the nation so require. At the same time the Irish note declared that that Government did not intend to alter its practice of not admitting any aliens whose presence in Ireland would be contrary to Irish neutrality, detrimental to the Irish people's interests, or inconsistent with their desire to avoid harming the interests of friendly nations, and of deporting as soon as possible to their countries of origin any such aliens who might land.

We did not consider this reply satisfactory. On October 23 we pointed out to the Irish Government that we failed to understand how that Government could feel that charity, justice, or the interest or honor of Ireland could make necessary the admission of war criminals. We did not, however, obtain better assurances.

In any event the result of our numerous diplomatic exchanges with the neutrals was that, when the war ended, we found no neutral disposed to welcome those infamous men responsible for the war and for atrocities. Almost without exception those men fell into our hands for the just punishment which should serve as an example to halt the ambitions of similar desperadoes of the future.

98: Turkey on the Edge of War

PRESIDENT ROOSEVELT and Prime Minister Churchill agreed at the Casablanca Conference in January, 1943, that Mr. Churchill should "play the cards" (one of his favorite phrases) in Turkey for both countries so far as military matters were concerned. This agreement inevitably led the United States to take in Turkey a role secondary to that of Britain, but Turkey none the less occupied a considerable corner in our foreign policy planning.

Following the Casablanca agreement, Mr. Churchill requested President Inönü of Turkey to confer with him, making the request in the name also of President Roosevelt. President Inönü sent Mr. Roosevelt a personal message on January 26, through Ambassador Steinhardt in Ankara, informing him of his acceptance and expressing warmest thanks for the President's support of the suggested meeting. Steinhardt reported that the President's support had been an important factor in President Inönü's decision to accept the invitation.

Meeting with President Inönü at Adana, Turkey, the Prime Minister assured him that arms and munitions would be supplied to Turkey by both Britain and the United States, but that pressure to enter the war would not be brought upon Turkey at that time.

Mr. Roosevelt's acquiescence in the thought that Britain should "play the cards" in Turkey was in line with his original thinking, even before Pearl Harbor, that Britain should take the lead in the Near East. When in March, 1941, we were discussing whether to send Lend-Lease aid to Turkey, Ambassador Halifax informed me on the 7th that he had happened to see the President, who had indicated that it would probably be preferable for us to aid Turkey through Great Britain.

Halifax handed me on October 22, 1941, a memorandum setting forth Britain's strategic interest in Turkish resistance in the event of an Axis attack or a German demand to be allowed passage through Turkey, and stressing the need therefore to maintain the Turkish will to resist and to build up her capacity to resist. I assured Halifax that our policy was based on the general proposition that we would take such steps as would give the British the maximum of weight in regard to Turkey if and when a Turkish-German crisis threatened. I suggested that a conference be held to work out the question of which Government should supply military implements and other materials to Turkey, keeping in mind our wish to build up British influence to the maximum.

Subsequently, the Lend-Lease Administration, in cooperation with the State Department and the British, worked out a procedure whereby Turkey obtained direct Lend-Lease aid from the United States and also indirect Lend-Lease aid by retransfer from the British.

Shortly after the President's return to the United States from the Casablanca Conference, Prime Minister Churchill sent him a message on February 2, 1943, saying that the highest security for Turkey in the postwar world would be found by her taking her place as a victorious belligerent and ally at the side of Great Britain and the United States and Russia. In this way, he said, a start would be made in all friendliness and confidence, and a new instrument would grow around the good will and comradeship of those who had been in the field together, with powerful armies.

Mr. Churchill surveyed in this message the possibility of Turkey's becoming a full belligerent and of her armies' advancing into the Balkans side by side with the Russians in the north and the British in the south. (This was in conformity with the Prime Minister's determination at that time that the major Anglo-American drive into Europe should be through the Balkans, a plan he later reluctantly gave up at the insistence of the President and the United States Joint Chiefs of Staff in favor of the invasion of Europe through Normandy.) He said it would be right for Turkey, before incurring additional risks, to seek precise guarantees as to her territorial rights after the war. Britain would be willing to give these guarantees in a treaty or join with Russia in giving them, and he thought Russia would be willing to make such a treaty. He said he was certain that the President would gladly associate himself with this treaty and that the whole weight of the United States would be used in the peace settlement to that end, although he recognized the difficulties interposed by the United States Constitution against prolonged European commitments. These treaties and assurances would naturally fall within the ambit of the world instrument to protect all countries from wrongdoing.

Two months after the Casablanca Conference, Foreign Secretary Eden came to Washington in March, 1943, for a series of conferences with the President and me. At that time we got the impression that the British were interpreting the President's agreement with Prime Minister Churchill, that the British should "play the cards" with Turkey in a military way, to mean that the British should handle all our relations in the political and economic spheres as well.

After Eden returned to London, the British Embassy informed me that the British Deputy Under Secretary of the Foreign Office had looked up the Casablanca agreement and, in order that the position might be perfectly clear, had asked the Embassy to state to us that the President had given the Prime Minister primary responsibility for "playing the cards" with Turkey.

Since this phrase was capable of very wide interpretation, I took the matter up with the President. Unfortunately, Mr. Roosevelt had not communicated to me the decisions reached at Casablanca. As I have said before, he did not include me in the conferences he held then and later with Churchill, Stalin, and Chiang Kai-shek on the ground that they were military discussions and did not concern the State Department. We had asked Admiral Leahy for a copy of the Casablanca agreement but had been told that no copy was available for us.

I sent the President a memorandum prepared by Wallace Murray, Chief of the Division of Near Eastern Affairs, in which we said we felt confident that the President, in the military agreements reached at Casablanca, had had no intention of limiting our independence of action in the political or economic spheres with regard to Turkey. We stated our belief that, if any question of a limitation on our freedom of action toward Turkey in favor of Great Britain arose, it would not be in the interests of the United States or of the United Nations cause for us to concede. "Even the military concession regarding Turkey made at Casablanca," we concluded, "while doubtless reached for valid considerations, has nevertheless caused very great consternation on the part of Turkish officials who are not allowed to handle direct with us their own requests for American Lend-Lease supplies."

This was a good illustration of the contention I advanced to the President on many occasions, though unsuccessfully, that fundamental military decisions often had diplomatic angles and reflections, and that I should therefore know about them.

I also sent the President the draft of a note I intended sending on the subject of Turkey and the Casablanca agreement to British Ambassador Halifax.

The President approving, I wrote Halifax on July 10:

"In view of a possible misapprehension of some of the British authorities in regard to this matter, I think I should point out clearly that, notwithstanding any military understanding reached, I am not aware of any commitment made by the President at Casablanca which relates in any way to the surrender by the United States of its full independence of action with regard to relations between the United States and Turkey in either the political or the economic sphere, either during the war or after. I hardly need assure you that this Government has every desire and intention of continuing the closest collaboration with the British Government in our mutual relations with Turkey, and that I have no apprehension whatever of difficulties in this regard. I feel it advisable, however, to clarify the situation by the present statement."

Subsequently, on July 16, I received a letter from Admiral Leahy giving us extracts from the Casablanca minutes relating to Turkey and stating that the decisions quoted were intended to be exclusively on our combined war effort. The decisions related to the equipping and supplying of Turkey, which should be undertaken through Britain. The President had concurred in Mr. Churchill's request that, since the troops involved in reenforcing Turkey would be primarily British, "the British be allowed to play the Turkish hand, just as the United States is now handling the situation with reference to China."

I wrote Admiral Leahy on July 22, saying: "The minutes confirm the Department's understanding . . . that nothing agreed upon at Casablanca limits in any way the full independence of action of the American Government in its political and economic relations with Turkey."

The President and the Prime Minister again discussed the subject of Turkey when they met at the first Quebec Conference in August, 1943. Again I had to write Admiral Leahy, on September 23, for information regarding policy decisions concerning Turkey taken at Quebec by the combined Chiefs of Staff "in view of the political implications which the British authorities attach to them." Leahy replied the following day that the President, the Prime Minister, and the Combined Chiefs had decided at Quebec that from a military point of view the time was not right for Turkey to enter the war on our side. He made available to me an extract from the record indicating that it had been decided that we should continue our efforts to equip Turkey and increase her military effectiveness while attempting to reduce her assistance to Germany, with particular reference to stopping the passage of all German shipping of military value through the Dardanelles and the supplying of Turkish chrome to Germany.

I have already recounted how, at the Moscow Conference, Molotov proposed to Eden and me that the three Governments should bring united, strong pressure on Turkey to enter the war. My own thought was that Turkey should come into the war as a full belligerent as soon as this was militarily feasible. Turkey in 1942 and 1943 had been fearful of the postwar strength of a victorious Russia, and I felt that the position of a Turkey that had taken a large and active share in the war would be stronger with regard to Russia than it would be if she had drifted through the war as a neutral. But, as the conference ended, I had gone no further, since Molotov's proposal was a military matter, than to inform the President about it. While I was en route home, Mr. Roosevelt agreed with the British and the Russians that Britain should take the lead, with the United States' support, in negotiations with Turkey to bring her into the war.

On Eden's way home from the Moscow Conference, he met with Turkish Foreign Minister Numan Menemencioglu at Cairo and raised the questions of Turkey's immediately making air bases available to the Allies and entering the war. Ambassador Steinhardt in Ankara reported to us that Turkey rejected the first proposal on the grounds that it would inevitably involve her in war with Germany. As to the second, Turkey replied that she could not yet make an effective contribution as a participant in the war since her defenses were still inadequate.

After the President reached North Africa late in November, 1943, en route to the Tehran Conference, I acted as intermediary between him and President Inönü of Turkey to arrange a meeting in Cairo between Inönü and Roosevelt, Churchill and a Soviet representative. President Inönü replied that he would go to Cairo so long as he was not being invited merely to be told of decisions already reached at Tehran affecting Turkey, but was being asked to participate in "a free discussion as between equals."

Actually at Tehran the three statesmen confirmed the agreement reached immediately after the Moscow Conference that the three Governments should request Turkey to enter the war, and agreed upon February 15, 1944, as the date of such entry.

On behalf of the President I cabled Ambassador Steinhardt on December 2 to inform President Inönü that on the morning of December 4 transport planes would be at Adana to take him to Cairo, and that Mr. Roosevelt was particularly happy to have this chance to talk to the Turkish President who was being asked, he assured him, to "a free discussion as between equals."

An episode of friendly rivalry between Mr. Roosevelt and Prime

Minister Churchill came to light the following day when I forwarded to Ambassador Steinhardt a message received from Harry Hopkins by the White House. This stated that Major John Boettiger, the President's son-in-law, was accompanying the President's plane to Adana in order to extend the President's greetings to President Inönü upon his arrival and to accompany him on the trip. The Prime Minister's plane, the message stated, had been dispatched with Randolph Churchill, the Prime Minister's son, for a similar purpose. It would please the President, the message concluded, to have Inönü ride in the American plane. Mr. Roosevelt won.

At Cairo President Inönü agreed "in principle" to Turkey's entrance into the war but made it clear that this could not be until Turkey's deficiencies in equipment, supplies, and transport had been made up so that she would be in position to defend herself.

In January, 1944, Anglo-Turkish military conversations began in Ankara to implement the Turkish decision "in principle" to enter the war. I sent the President a memorandum on January 8 informing him that the British Government had stated to us it had learned that the Turkish authorities considered the United States to be much less insistent on Turkey's entering the war than the British were and that Britain alone was putting pressure on Turkey in this regard. The British had requested us to authorize Ambassador Steinhardt to "back up any representations that the British Ambassador in Ankara may make" in order to dispel the Turkish impression.

I asked the President whether I was correct in assuming that, while he would not wish us to authorize Steinhardt to back up *any* representations the British Ambassador might make, he would like Steinhardt to make it clear to the Turks that we as well as the British would welcome Turkey's contribution to the common victory by active participation in the war. The President approving this position, I sent appropriate instructions to Steinhardt on January 11.

Nevertheless, the Anglo-Turkish negotiations made little if any progress. Steinhardt reported to us on January 24 that the British seemed to suspect the Turks of demanding an amount of war materials that would take sufficiently long to deliver to allow the Turks to remain neutral until the period of their usefulness to our cause had passed. On the other hand, he said, the Turks apparently suspected that the British had given commitments to the Greeks and the Russians with respect to the Aegean and the Balkans, respectively, and for this reason were unwilling to allow the Turks sufficient war materials to permit them to participate actively in military operations.

On February 4 I sent the President a telegram from the British Foreign Office reporting that the military conversations at Ankara had reached a stalemate. The British therefore proposed, I said, to withdraw, without notice or explanation, the head of their military mission in Ankara, to suspend shipments of military supplies, and to instruct their Ambassador to avoid contact with members of the Turkish Government until further notice.

I informed the President that the British requested our cooperation to the extent of instructing Steinhardt to "cool off" in his relations with the Turks for the time being. I said I believed we should meet this request. The President wrote his O.K. on my memorandum, and I sent appropriate instructions to Steinhardt on February 7. British and American arms shipments to Turkey ceased early in February.

At this time we were discussing means of cutting off Turkish shipments to Germany of chrome ore, vitally important in the manufacture of high-grade steel. Turkey was a prime source of this strategic product. In previous negotiations with the Turks, and through the Board of Economic Warfare's preemptive buying program, we had succeeded in reducing these shipments, but they still continued in disturbing quantities.

The President desired to send a personal letter to President Inönü requesting him to deny the Germans further access to Turkish chrome ore. This was dispatched in March, 1944, to Churchill and Stalin for their comment, and also by air pouch to Steinhardt. Ambassador Winant in London cabled on the 19th that Mr. Churchill was very pleased to approve the letter, but the following day the President sent me a message to him from the Prime Minister and asked:

Could I get this straightened out as Churchill has asked me not to send my proposed message to Inönü? Did the latter go? What shall I say to Churchill? F. D. R.

Mr. Churchill stated that, after consultation with Eden, he suggested that the President's letter be held in reserve lest the Turks interpret "so friendly a message" as a sign of weakening on the part of the Allies.

I replied to the President on March 22 stating that we had telegraphed Steinhardt not to deliver the letter until instructed to do so. I also informed the President that Steinhardt and the British Ambassador in Ankara had been recommending for some time that one or both of the railroad bridges across the Maritsa River dividing Turkey from Bulgaria be destroyed by bombing or sabotage, which would stop some 85 per cent of Turkish chrome ore deliveries to the Germans.

German negotiators had now reached Ankara to arrange the renewal of the Turkish-German trade agreement expiring April 30, and the British proposed to us a strong joint statement by our two Ambassadors warning the Turks that further strategic material shipments to the Axis would lead to blockade measures much like those applied to other neutrals. I recommended to the President on April 4 that he suspend indefinitely the delivery of his friendly letter to President Inönü. He agreed.

Ambassador Steinhardt and British Ambassador Sir Hughe Knatchbull-Hugessen presented identical notes on April 14 warning the Turks that if they made arrangements to furnish the Axis with essential war materials which we mentioned, including chrome ore, copper, iron, and steel, we would apply to Turkey blockade measures similar to those we had applied to other neutrals during the war.

Six days later the Turkish Government announced its decision to embargo at once all exports of chrome to the Axis. Subsequent negotiations resulted in a Turkish decision, reported to us by Steinhardt on June 16, to reduce immediately by 50 per cent the export to the Axis of the other commodities mentioned and to consult with the British and American representatives in Ankara regarding transactions under the other 50 per cent, with a view to reducing such exports still further where the Allies could provide the essential imports that Turkey would otherwise obtain from the Axis.

We next turned our attention to inducing Turkey to sever diplomatic relations with the Axis. British Ambassador Halifax sent me an *aide-mémoire* dated June 23, 1944, stating that, in Eden's opinion, the time had come, in view of the opening of a Western Front, to press Turkey to increase her assistance to the Allies by breaking off political and economic relations with Germany. Eden requested our support of such a move.

I cabled Steinhardt on June 28, authorizing him to support British representations to the Turkish Government for the severance of relations with Germany. Steinhardt reported on July 3 that Turkish Prime Minister Saracoglu informed him that the Turkish Government was prepared immediately to accede to this request but would like to receive British and American assurances that Turkey would be treated as a full Ally by Britain and would receive such assistance as was possible from the United

States and Britain with respect to war materials and to the disposition of surplus Turkish exports and the provision of essential Turkish imports.

At this moment, however, a new factor entered the situation in the form of Russia. Ambassador Harriman cabled us from Moscow on June 28 that Molotov had sent for him that evening and said that the proposed British request of Turkey, which Britain had communicated to the Soviet Government on June 25 with a request for Soviet support, was not in conformity with the Moscow Conference decisions in that it did not include Turkey's entrance into the war.

On July 10, the Soviet Chargé, Alexander N. Kapustin, left with me an *aide-mémoire* from his Government. This took the position that the British, in their request to Turkey, had departed from the agreement reached immediately after the Moscow Conference and confirmed at the Tehran Conference whereby the three Powers would work jointly to bring Turkey into the war, and that the British had acted without Moscow's concurrence.

This *aide-mémoire* informed us of diplomatic exchanges between Turkey and Russia in May and June as a result of a Turkish proposal that an agreement between the two countries be signed for closer political cooperation, including security guarantees in the Balkans. The Soviet Government had replied that the only way such an accord could be reached was for Turkey to enter the war against Germany.

The Turkish Government meantime had drawn up draft notes to exchange with Britain providing for severance of diplomatic and commercial relations with Germany and for the assurances Turkey wanted to receive, and recognizing Turkey's right, as a full Ally, to participate as an equal partner in the peace settlement.

I cabled Ambassador Winant in London on July 11, asking for an immediate report on the British reaction to this proposed exchange. I said that undue delay in accepting the Turkish proposal might give rise to Turkish criticism that the British and we had not been sincere in requesting the severance of relations, and would be even harder for the Soviet Government to understand since it thought that the request made of Turkey fell short of the Moscow and Tehran decisions.

I authorized Winant to inform the Foreign Office that, contingent on the advice of the military authorities, we agreed in principle with the views of the Soviet Government; but that the Turkish Government, by making its severance of relations with Germany a preliminary step toward entrance into the war very shortly, was in a position to bring about a quicker end to the war; and that, if the Turks clearly understood, as Prime Minister Saracoglu himself had said, that the severance of relations was a first step toward active belligerency, there should be no question relative to the Moscow and Tehran decisions. I added that, from a long-term view, it appeared probable that a useful friend might be found in a Turkey that had earned her participation in the peace negotiations.

Unless an unequivocal and forthright reply to the Turkish proposal, worked out between the British and Russians along the lines of the general views I had outlined, was made without further delay, the Turks, I concluded, might be led, on their own, to sever relations and enter the war, thereby turning toward the East and pushing the Anglo-Turkish alliance into the background.

On the following day the British Embassy handed Under Secretary Stettinius an *aide-mémoire* stating that the British Government did not favor the exchange of notes proposed by the Turks or a request to Turkey at that time to enter the war. Instead, they proposed to accept the Turkish agreement to sever relations and to give certain general assurances with respect to economic and military aid and Turkey's position at the peace settlement. They asked our cooperation.

The British *aide-mémoire* argued that the request for severance of relations could be acted upon without delay, involved us in no military commitments, and would have nearly the same moral effect on Germany and in the Balkans as would a declaration of war, while providing a useful first step toward a declaration of war if this later became desirable. A request for a declaration of war, on the other hand, would involve long discussions relative to military supplies, possibly extending beyond the period when Turkish belligerency would be of any use to the Allies. The British objected to the Turkish notes on the ground that they were too detailed and far-reaching.

I sent this *aide-mémoire* to Admiral Leahy on July 13, 1944, to obtain the opinion of the Joint Chiefs of Staff. I said that on political grounds the State Department was inclined to accept the British plan provided it was made clear to both the Turks and the Russians that the severance of relations between Turkey and Germany was regarded as only a first step toward active belligerency.

Immediate military returns, I pointed out, could be expected from the severance of relations. These included: high altitude flights over Turkey en route to Russia; expulsion from Turkey of some two thousand

Germans and other Axis agents; and the possible use of Turkish airfields as bases for strategic bombing and of Turkish harbors for naval operations.

General Marshall replied for the Joint Chiefs on July 19, stating that from a military point of view it was desirable that Turkey sever relations as soon as practicable. With respect to the proviso that such action be regarded as only a first step toward active belligerency, however, the Joint Chiefs' concurrence was subject to the reservation that, in taking this position, the United States should inform Turkey and our Allies that the United States was not thereby committed to military, naval, or air support of any campaign in the Balkans. The Joint Chiefs were also opposed to the diversion of any resources from the approved operations in Italy and the western Mediterranean.

Upon receipt of this letter, I replied to the British *aide-mémoire* of July 12, agreeing with the British plan provided it was "made clear to the Turks that the severance of relations between Turkey and Germany is regarded as only a first step towards active belligerency." We quoted the provisos set forth by the Joint Chiefs.

On the same day, July 20, I cabled our Embassy at Ankara to this effect. I also authorized the Embassy to inform the Turks that we would do all we could within reason to alleviate the economic disturbances that a break in relations might produce.

Two days later we replied to the Soviet note of July 10, saying that we considered the request to Turkey to break relations with Germany "only a first step toward active Turkish belligerency" and had so informed the British and Turkish Governments. We outlined the opinions expressed by the Joint Chiefs of Staff. We added that we did not regard the request to Turkey to break relations with Germany as a departure from our former position since we expected such action to be followed by Turkey's entry into the war, "a development which this Government would welcome." We thought that bringing Turkey into the war in this manner had definite practical advantages which would inure to the benefit of the Allies. We said we would not, of course, regard Turkey as an Ally until she was in a state of war with Germany and that, should Turkey then express a desire to adhere to the United Nations Declaration, we would seek the views of the Soviet Government before taking any action.

I instructed Ambassador Harriman in Moscow on July 25 to make it absolutely clear to Soviet officials that we wished in every way to abide by the decisions taken at Moscow and Tehran, and the only question, so far as we were concerned, was how Turkey might most advantageously be brought into the war. I suggested that, if the Russians regarded our support of the step-by-step approach to active Turkish belligerency as a departure from the Moscow and Tehran decision to bring Turkey into the war as soon as possible, it might be well for Harriman to raise with Molotov the advisability of Anglo-Soviet-American discussions relative to the best way of implementing the earlier decision.

The Soviet Government replied on July 27 to our *aide-mémoire* of July 22, stating its view that the Turkish Government's proposed action relative to Germany came much too late and was unsatisfactory. It added that there was no essential significance to the discussion of half-measures, and that the Soviet Government therefore found it necessary to leave the Turkish Government to its own devices and to discontinue pressure on it.

We cabled Ambassador Harriman on the same day, saying that, in view of this latest indication of Russian dissatisfaction with recent Turkish developments, it appeared all the more opportune to suggest to Molotov the advisability of a frank Anglo-Soviet-American discussion.

Harriman reported on July 30 that he had raised this question with Vice Foreign Commissar Víshinski, whose reaction had not been encouraging. Harriman recommended that any further approach be postponed. He pointed out that, as things stood, the U.S.S.R. would share in any benefits from the Turkish action without having assumed any obligations toward Turkey in connection with the peace settlement, and that the Soviet Union had used the Anglo-American action without Soviet concurrence to free herself from the obligation taken at Moscow to act with the United States and Great Britain in matters pertaining to Turkey. Harriman added, however, that he had no indication of any specific Soviet plans relative to Turkey that would create difficulties between us.

The British and American representations at Ankara had the desired effect. On August 2, 1944, the Turkish Government broke off all political and commercial relations with Germany. Following the severance of relations, the American Government made every effort to fulfill all its obligations toward the Turks. We had in mind the fact that Turkey had long been a steadying influence in the Balkans and that a strong Turkey was likely to be a useful friend when Balkan matters came up for discussion in postwar conferences. It was not, however, until after the Yalta Conference in 1945 that Turkey entered the war and became eligible for original United Nations membership.

99: The Bad Neighbor

THROUGHOUT OUR PREOCCUPATIONS concerning relations with Russia, with France, with the European neutrals; throughout our efforts to make diplomacy the right-hand partner of our armed forces; and throughout our work toward laying the bases for a postwar organization to keep the peace, we were incessantly plagued by the dangerous, devious course of the Argentine Government. I have waited until reaching 1944 in this narrative in order to deal with this thorny situation as a whole.

What I had foreseen when I roundly berated Under Secretary Welles over the long-distance telephone to Rio de Janeiro in January, 1942, came to pass, despite Welles's belief that everything would turn out all right. After the Argentine delegation went back to Buenos Aires from Rio, the Argentine Government, which never had any intention of severing relations with the Axis, continued those relations. Argentina inevitably became a haven for Nazi representatives and spies, a center for their finance and plans.

To me the tragedy of this situation lay in the fact, as I saw it, that the overwhelming majority of the Argentine people were wholeheartedly democratic, opposed the Axis at least in thought, and wanted no part of their country utilized by Axis agents to bring harm to the United Nations. But over them was a Government determined to rule by any methods in dictatorial fashion. I admired and respected President Dr. Roberto M. Ortiz, who on several occasions had shown a desire to work with us toward hemispheric solidarity. But very unfortunately for the whole hemisphere, Dr. Ortiz had become so ill that he had relinquished his office in 1941, for an indefinite period, and Dr. Ramón S. Castillo, the Vice President, a man of different character, became Acting President. Dr. Castillo had aroused the uneasiness of most of the American Republics by his efforts seemingly to make his power supreme.

During the spring of 1942 we received numerous reports of Axis propaganda and general activity in Argentina. On April 3, the State Department sent a list of these reports to Ambassador Norman Armour in Buenos Aires, with instructions, if he thought well to do so, to express orally to Foreign Minister Enrique Ruiz Guinazu our Government's concern over the effect a continuation of such rumors might have. Armour was one of the most capable, yet unpretentious, diplomats I found in our Foreign Service. Having character and firmness, he was exceptionally well equipped to fill any high position in that service.

An Argentine military mission had arrived in the United States in December, 1941, to obtain military matériel, and was conducting negotiations with the War and Navy Departments. Prompted by us at the State Department, our military officials gave the Argentines to understand that preferential treatment in the furnishing of naval and military matériel would be given only to those who exposed themselves in adopting an out-and-out policy of solidarity with the United States—this, moreover, because we did not have matériel enough to satisfy all the American Republics.

The Navy Department wanted to maintain close relations with the Argentine Navy. If the Panama Canal were blocked, we would need passage through the Straits of Magellan. Also, the Argentine Navy, if friendly, might balance what was regarded as a generally antagonistic Argentine Army. This latter was imbued with German methods and many of its officers hero-worshipped the successful Wehrmacht leaders.

We at the State Department suggested the insertion of clauses in the Navy agreement whereby the Argentines would aid in protecting shipping in the Atlantic between Argentina and the United States through a system of convoys. Late in April Foreign Minister Guinazu informed Ambassador Armour that this proposal implied the creation of a situation of belligerency which Argentina did not desire and for which she was not prepared. It was obvious that the Argentine Government wanted all the advantages from an association with the United States without assuming any of the responsibilities.

We sent the Argentine Government a strong note on May 13 in which we sincerely regretted that that Government was not disposed to collaborate effectively to further the cause in which nineteen of the American Republics (Chile likewise had not broken with the Axis) were actively cooperating. We disagreed with Argentina's conclusion that the proposal implied creating a state of belligerency, saying that the history of the last few years offered many instances of naval action taken by a neutral country in protection of its shipping that did not result in a state of belligerency. We cited the example of the United States in that our Government for many months prior to the declaration of war by Germany and Italy had been taking daily naval action to assure that its ships arrived safely in many distant ports, and we had not become a belligerent as a result of that action.

If our proposal, we continued, appeared like an exclusively Argentine obligation, it was because the nineteen other American Republics had already taken steps of far greater consequence and risk. Ten of them were at war with the Axis countries, and nine more had broken off diplomatic relations. In the absence of either action by Argentina, we said, this Government had hoped for some positive measures by Argentina that would persuade the other Republics that she was making her contribution to the maintenance of hemispheric solidarity, and therefore was entitled to share in the distribution of the armament available for the other Republics.

Shortly thereafter Foreign Minister Guinazu disclosed the contents of this note to the Chamber of Deputies with the hope that the Chamber would support the intransigent position maintained by Dr. Castillo. His maneuver was without effect.

At that moment the situation was almost upset entirely by a sudden move of Secretary of the Treasury Morgenthau and his advisers. Morgenthau often interfered in foreign affairs, and sometimes took steps directly at variance with those of the State Department. Since there was frequently a connection between foreign and financial affairs, he had in his hands monetary weapons which he brandished in the foreign field from time to time, often without consulting the State Department. In this practice he ran a close race with Vice President Henry Wallace, formerly head of the Board of Economic Warfare.

Morgenthau was particularly avid on the subject of freezing the credits of foreign countries in the United States. Now I suddenly became aware that he was proposing to freeze Argentina's funds in the United States, reported to amount to $500,000,000. Early in May the Treasury Department sent the Board of Economic Warfare a memorandum making this proposal. When a copy of it came to my hand, I sent it to the President on May 14 with an accompanying note in which I said:

"You will readily see that this proposes a complete reversal of the Good Neighbor Policy and a substitution of our old discredited policy of coercion and domination of South American countries by big stick methods. Naturally, I am greatly surprised that this view would be seriously presented by any other governmental agency, for two reasons. One is that this raises purely a question of foreign policy, and the other is that it would wipe out our Good Neighbor Policy, as stated, and substitute the big stick."

I urged the President to intervene at the earliest practicable time, especially in view of the fact that if this proposal became public it would have terrific repercussions all over South America. And I added that, from the type of some of the persons who were dealing with it, it was liable to become public at any time.

The President did effectively intervene and prevent this drastic move. Morgenthau, however, did not give up the idea.

We made another effort in June to induce the Argentine Government to work with us. The attitude of that Government had been further illustrated on June 8, when it sent us a long protest against our black list warning American citizens against dealing with certain firms in Latin America known to have connections with the Axis. By way of reply, we instructed Ambassador Armour on June 12 to seek an early interview with Vice President Castillo and lay before him quite candidly the serious problems resulting from the attitude of his Government. Far from breaking off diplomatic relations with the Axis, as the Rio Conference had recommended, the Argentine Government had just accepted a new Ambassador from Japan.

Our note recited numerous instances of Argentine territory being used as a base for Axis operations. The Argentine Government had failed to prevent group or individual activities detrimental to the security and welfare of the American Republics. Axis agents were openly engaged in espionage and other work to defeat our war effort. Other agents of the Axis were working to undermine democratic institutions. Newspapers, radio stations, and publishing houses were disseminating totalitarian propaganda. Argentina had become a communications center for the Axis nations. Each message and even each word, we said, that the Argentine Government permitted to be transmitted to Axis nations, either directly or indirectly, might mean the loss of valuable material needed for the prosecution of the war, and, what was more, the loss of precious lives of citizens of the American Republics now engaged in defending the hemisphere.

That same month, however, Castillo became President, the Argentine Congress having accepted the resignation of Dr. Ortiz.

Since the Argentine Ambassador, Don Felipe A. Espil, was going to Buenos Aires on leave, I had a lengthy conversation with him on August 13, 1942, with the hope that he would present my views to his Government. I recalled to him the numerous statements I had made in the past to the effect that Hitler and Mussolini intended to become the overlords of Europe, and Tojo of Asia, and that these statements had come true. "All the countries of this hemisphere," I added, "are in the same boat, and consequently common defense against military attacks or invasion is imperative. International guerrillas or bandits, such as Hitler, Mussolini, and Tojo, like individual bandits, never voluntarily abandon their occupation. As for international bandits or desperadoes, who are backed by armies and navies and impelled by visions of personal glory, there is much less likelihood of their halting, to say nothing of abandoning, their policy of world conquest, which they have boldly avowed and conclusively proven both by words and acts."

The Argentine Chamber of Deputies on September 28 approved a resolution recommending a break in diplomatic relations with the Axis, but President Castillo forthwith informed the President of the Chamber that the conduct of foreign affairs rested with the Executive.

When Ambassador Espil returned from Argentina, he came to see me on October 21, 1942, and gave me his conclusion that the people in Argentina were not war-minded and were continuing in their normal thoughts and actions. President Castillo, he thought, did not visualize the situation in its broader aspects.

I commented that he, I, and others had been laboring for ten years to bring Argentina more closely into the Pan American family, but that all our work might now go for nought. "During our Civil War," I recalled, "there were only two sides recognized by almost all people, and for fifty years after that war, when candidates ran for office, the public immediately demanded to know where they had stood in the war. If a person served on one side or the other, that was one thing, but those who were considered as having got rich by staying out of the war were carefully omitted in all elections."

Sooner or later, I added, it would dawn on the people of Argentina, including the present high Government officials, that this was a world movement of conquest, that there were only two sides, and that from the viewpoint of enlightened self-interest every country like Argentina would realize the vital importance of having fallen into line at a proper stage. I emphasized that it was now reasonably certain that the Axis Powers could not and would not win.

Ambassador Espil said that many of the people in Argentina did not know which way the war was going, and they were therefore wholly inactive and more or less indifferent. The Argentine high officials were also in doubt as to the outcome and therefore were proceeding on the theory that it was as likely to go one way as the other, hence their course of inaction.

It was a great tragedy, I said, that those statesmen did not look ahead just as we did during 1940, when we announced a policy of aiding Great Britain and the other countries attacked by the Axis, thereby defending ourselves before it was too late.

During the first few days of November, 1942, we sent a series of memoranda to the Argentine Government giving it further information that had come to us with regard to Nazi espionage and propaganda activities centering in Buenos Aires. Ambassador Espil came to me on November 9 to request, on behalf of his Government, that these memoranda be not published.

I replied that the Argentine Government was evidently derelict in stamping out subversive activities and now was complaining at this late date when my Government was attempting to give facts and figures that would help it wipe out such activities. The United States owed an obligation to the other American Republics to let them know what was occurring in Argentina in this respect. The present situation in Argentina, I concluded, had grown up under the rather peculiar policies of the Argentine Government, which was not in a good position to raise questions of publicity of facts and information such as we had gathered and turned over to it.

Finally, Ambassador Espil said this was a very small matter and he hoped we could give it further attention. To this I replied that, since it was indeed a very small matter, the Argentine Government should not have raised the question in the first place and certainly should not press it further.

The Argentine Government did follow up our memoranda to a degree by arresting a number of the Axis agents we named. Nevertheless, despite the detailed evidence gathered from such agents, which confirmed our memoranda in many points, the Argentine Government neglected to make the complete investigation we felt necessary in order to eliminate the subversive activities against which we were complaining.

Accordingly, on January 13, 1943, I sent a circular to certain of our diplomatic missions in other American Republics, informing them of this situation, and stating that the dangerous activities we had brought to the attention of the Argentine Government were continuing. I said that the

United States Government would be failing in its duties to the other Governments of this hemisphere if it did not apprise them of the information in its possession with regard to the activities carried on by Axis agents on Argentine soil. We also sent copies to the Inter-American Emergency Advisory Committee for Political Defense which had been set up in Montevideo.

We waited a few days before presenting this memorandum to the other American Republics in order to take full advantage of the fact that, on January 20, Chile broke diplomatic relations with Germany and Japan. The memorandum was handed to the Emergency Advisory Committee and to the Argentine Government on the following day. Two days later the Argentine Foreign Office issued a communiqué reciting what had been done by the judicial authorities in Argentina, calling attention to the pending departure of the Naval Attaché of the German Embassy in Buenos Aires, and declaring that the publication of our memorandum was considered "prejudicial and redundant."

But there was no blinking the fact that, with Chile's rupture of relations with the Axis, Argentina was now the only Latin American Republic which continued its ties with our enemies and thereby afforded them the opportunity and territory to carry on their espionage, subversive activities, and the dispatch by wireless code of information concerning shipping in the Atlantic.

Without bringing any pressure on Chile, we had earnestly sought to induce that country to sever relations with the Axis, while appreciating to the full the fears of the Chilean Government that its long coastline on the Pacific rendered it vulnerable to Axis naval attack.

Unfortunately, our relations with Chile had had a setback in October, 1942, as a result of a speech delivered by Under Secretary Welles in Boston in which he coupled Chile and Argentina together and urged them not to permit their brothers and neighbors in the Americas to be stabbed in the back by Axis emissaries operating in the territory of the two countries. At that moment President Ríos of Chile had been planning a visit to the United States in consequence of an invitation sent him by President Roosevelt on August 13. He immediately wrote the President postponing his visit.

Ambassador Claude Bowers reported to us from Santiago, Chile, that the general reaction there was one of indignation, that our friends there considered the allusions inopportune psychologically, with Ríos about to leave for the United States, and that all sections of opinion would rally to the support of the Chilean President. In Washington Chilean Ambassador Michels called on President Roosevelt and read to him a message protesting against Welles's address as offending the dignity of Chile. The President replied that he still hoped very much that President Ríos would make the visit so that they could sit down like brothers together and discuss all the problems in which our two countries were interested.

President Roosevelt's friendly attitude and our diplomatic efforts bridged this tense moment, as was evidenced by Chile's severance of diplomatic relations with the Axis on January 20. We resumed discussions with the Chilean Government for President Ríos's visit, but in 1943 plans were canceled because of new developments in Argentina, and again in 1944 because of Ríos's illness.

Chile's cutting off of relations with the Axis had no apparent effect on Argentina. That Government continued to act in negligent fashion toward the ever dangerous activities of Axis representatives, open and hidden. Then suddenly on June 4, 1943, a military revolutionary committee overturned the Castillo Government, and General Pedro Ramírez, Minister of War in the Castillo Cabinet, became President, with Admiral Segundo Storni as Foreign Minister. We recognized the new Government on June 11.

In conversations with Ambassador Armour, Ramírez and Storni indicated that, given a comparatively short time in which to prepare the country, the new Government intended to break relations with the Axis. Ramírez thought this would be done by August 15 at the latest. The Argentine Government, they said, intended to implement a policy of close inter-American cooperation based upon the inter-American pacts in force.

Taking up this last phrase, we outlined to Ambassador Armour on June 18 some of the steps we thought the new Argentine Government should take if it meant to offer convincing evidence of its sincerity. These were: to break diplomatic relations with the Axis; to take additional steps to prohibit the use of code for radio communications; to control effectively subversive activities; to stop leaks of funds and strategic materials to the Axis; to control clandestine radio stations within Argentina; to control press and radio propaganda within Argentina along with newsprint to Axis organs; to supervise carefully both civil and commercial aviation; to control foreign funds; to cooperate more effectively with regard to our black list of Axis-connected firms; to cut off financial and commercial relations with the Axis; to cooperate more generally with respect to shipping; to complete pending oil negotiations so that Argentine oil would be made available to Uruguay, Paraguay, and southern Brazil; to cooperate with respect to the export of fats and oils and the use of northbound tankers; to reduce sharply the amount of pesos then being made available to the Axis Embassies.

All these steps could be justified on the basis of inter-American accords which Argentina had signed but had never really carried out. The fact that we had to list so many indicated the extent to which Argentina was still maintaining relations of all kinds with the Axis.

It was not long, however, before we saw that the new Argentine Government was not likely to prove any more friendly and cooperative than its predecessor. The Argentine Minister of Finance said to Ambassador Armour on July 18 that President Ramírez was upset over information that the United States Government was no longer interested in seeing Argentina break relations with the Axis because it was too late to do any good. Armour pointed out to him the inconsistency between Ramírez's feeling upset at our reported indifference and the insistence both by Ramírez and by Foreign Minister Storni that there must be no evidence of pressure on our part. Armour added that, if the report that Ramírez received had any basis in fact, then surely this was the best evidence that the United States was not exerting pressure. I cabled Armour on July 23 that we thoroughly approved of the way he had handled this point.

Armour cabled on July 22 that those elements in Argentina opposed to a break of relations with the Axis were using as an argument in favor of their position the Allied bombing of railroad yards in Rome, and were stressing that United States and British armies would be used as a bulwark against Communism in Europe and that Argentina was already doing her share toward the cause by suppressing Communism in her territory. Armour suggested that, if the break in relations with the Axis did not come shortly in accordance with the assurances given him by Ramírez and Storni, he should ask for his return to Washington.

I cabled Armour on July 27, suggesting that he leave for Washington within a fortnight, depending on local circumstances. The President and I had become increasingly concerned by the trend of developments in Argentina; we desired to reexamine the whole question of our relations with Argentina, and we felt that Armour's presence in Washington would be invaluable for this purpose.

When Armour saw Foreign Minister Storni on July 29 to inform him that he had been requested to go to Washington for consultation, he asked Storni for a clear statement of Argentina's position, preferably in writing, before he left. He reminded Storni of Ramírez's promise of a break with the Axis by August 15. He also pointed out to Storni that Ramírez's and Storni's promises of cooperation against the Axis had not been put into effect, and he called attention to the action the Ramírez Government was taking against pro-democratic organizations in Argentina on the alleged ground of Communist affiliation.

Storni replied that Ramírez had decided, in view of soundings he had made among army officers, that he could not break relations with the Axis without serious repercussions. Mussolini having resigned a few days before, Storni said the Italian collapse had now made a break with the Axis impossible, that it was too late, that Argentina had missed the bus, and that to break now would be a cowardly act.

Armour gave us his opinion that the pro-Axis elements in the army had secured control, that the Government was gradually weeding out the anti-Axis officers in the army, and that the decision not to break relations with the Axis had been made before the fall of Mussolini.

Foreign Minister Storni now wrote me a letter on August 5, explaining Argentina's position. This arrived the middle of the month, at a time when we were receiving reports that the Argentine Government was sending military emissaries to Uruguay, Bolivia, and Chile in an endeavor to win over the armies in those countries to the Argentine point of view. Prolixly Storni explained why Argentina could not break with the Axis. Indicative of the type of thinking going on in the Argentine Government was his statement that the Argentine conscience could not be forced with a view to leading it coldly and without any immediate motive to the breaking of relations with the Axis. With the Axis inexorably facing defeat, he said, this unexpected rupture would put Argentine chivalry to a hard test. And he recalled the judgment that Italy merited when, in a similar situation, it took its position against defeated France.

Storni denied that the Ramírez Administration was totalitarian or sympathetic to the Axis. He emphasized that Argentina was aiding the United Nations by exporting supplies to them.

In my reply on August 30 I contested each of Storni's contentions. I quoted the text of the Declaration at Rio, which Argentina had signed, recommending the breaking of relations with the Axis, and reminded him that, with the exception of Argentina, all the American Republics had severed diplomatic relations with Japan, Germany, and Italy, and thirteen of them were at war with the Axis.

I mentioned that Resolution XVII adopted at Rio provided for a concerted effort to discover and combat subversive activities, but that it was notorious that Axis agents in Argentina had been and were engaging in systematic espionage which had cost the United Nations ships and lives.

I cited Resolution XL adopted at Rio which recommended that each American Republic close all radiotelephone and radiotelegraph communication with the Axis, except for official communications of the American Governments. Argentina, I pointed out, was the only one of the twenty-one American Republics now permitting radiotelephone and radiotelegraph communications with Japan, Germany, and Italy.

I expressed my astonishment at Storni's statement that for the Argentine Government to fulfill these obligations would afford grounds for the belief that such action was taken under the pressure or threat of foreign agents. The obligations in question, I said, were freely entered into by all the American Republics and had been carried out by all except Argentina.

Admitting that the products of Argentine agriculture and mining had been of the greatest value to the cause of the United Nations, I commented that equitable prices had been paid for them. The United Nations, I said, had consistently refused to take advantage of the fact that, thanks to their military and naval efficiency, they were the only major markets open to Argentina.

Taking up Storni's suggestion that the United States should supply airplanes, replacement parts, armaments, and machinery in order to restore Argentina to a position of equilibrium with respect to other South American countries, I said: "I must point out emphatically that questions of military and naval equilibrium as between American Republics are surely inconsistent with the inter-American doctrine of the peaceful settlement of international disputes to which so many practical contributions have been made by Argentine statesmen."

I concluded that, since Argentina, both by words and actions, had indicated clearly that Argentine armed forces would not be used to forward the cause of the security of the New World, and thereby the vital war interests of the United States, it would be impossible for the President to furnish arms and munitions to Argentina under the Lend-Lease Act.

Finally, I regretted that Argentina's failure to comply with her inter-

American commitments was depriving her of the opportunity to participate in the postwar studies of the United Nations.

While I was at the Moscow Conference, Secretary of the Treasury Morgenthau made another effort to block Argentine credits in the United States. Ambassador Armour was likewise recommending the same step, although in a modified form. Under Secretary Stettinius cabled me that the Department opposed this move on the grounds that the proposal had a political objective, namely, the upsetting of the Argentine Government, rather than an economic-warfare purpose, and that it was likely that it would have the opposite effect. It would strengthen the Argentine Government because of the supersensitivity of the Argentines to any suggestion of outside pressure. It would have a bad effect in other American countries, it probably would not have British support, and it might produce retaliatory action that would affect our imports of vitally needed materials from Argentina. Stettinius said that the Treasury was pressing the proposal vigorously, but the Department recommended that the Argentine Government be allowed to stew in its own juice for the time being.

I cabled Stettinius from Moscow on October 28 that I agreed with his position and reasoning on the question. The President decided that the blocking proposal should be tabled for the time being but reviewed every week or so.

A few weeks after my return from Moscow, a new complication was suddenly added to the Argentine situation when a revolution in Bolivia overturned the Government of President Peñaranda on December 20 and installed Major Gualberto Villarroel as President. There were substantial indications that the revolution had been engineered with German money and by Nazi and Argentine agents operating from bases in Argentina.

The new Bolivian Government on December 21 issued a statement that Bolivia would remain aligned with the United Nations and would faithfully carry out her inter-American commitments. On the following day, however, I stated the attitude of the United States Government by saying that considerations for the security of the hemisphere and for the war effort of the United Nations had first importance in any matter of this character. I raised the question whether outside influence unfriendly to the Allied cause played any part in the revolution, and said: "It must never be forgotten that the hemisphere is at present under sinister and subversive attack by the Axis, assisted by some elements from within the hemisphere itself."

A few days after the Bolivian revolt, the Inter-American Emergency

Advisory Committee for Political Defense at Montevideo agreed upon a declaration that recognition should be withheld from any new American Government that was brought into being by force during wartime until consultations had been held among the American Republics to determine whether the new Government was complying with the inter-American undertakings for the defense of the continent. I agreed on January 6 to this procedure. On the following day I stated that the information now available increasingly strengthened the belief that forces outside Bolivia and unfriendly to the defense of the American Republics had inspired and aided the Bolivian revolution.

The revolt in Bolivia now led to the next major development in Argentina—the severance of relations with the Axis—which in turn led to the overthrow of the Ramírez Government and the installation of one still more dangerous.

100: Break with Argentina

AS EVIDENCE ACCUMULATED that Argentine officials had been implicated in the overthrow of the Bolivian Government, my associates and I drew up and sent the President a memorandum on January 8, 1944, saying:

"The recent revolution in Bolivia has produced deep anxiety among the other South American countries because of their belief that it had the sympathy and support of the Argentine Government. They are fearful that Argentina may have plans to encourage similar revolutions elsewhere.

"I share this concern and believe that we should take all proper and effective steps to support these countries, some of which have declared war and others broken relations with the Axis. The Good Neighbor Policy and our war effort might be seriously jeopardized otherwise."

I suggested that a step that would have a most healthy psychological effect would be to provide Brazil with certain additional arms and equipment. This would show the Brazilian Government and people that we were standing behind them in a realistic way and would permit Brazil to move forward with her preparations to send an expeditionary force overseas.

"The effect in neighboring countries," I continued, "would be salutary. In particular, Paraguay and Uruguay, both of which border on both Argentina and Brazil, would feel reassured.

"The present military gang in control of Argentina would understand at once the import of this action."

I concluded by recommending that he strongly urge the Munitions Assignment Board to assign to Brazil such additional arms and equipment as the War Department might feel it could spare without impairment to combat operational requirements.

The President sent this back to me with his O.K. written on it. Then on January 12 he sent me a memorandum which he began by saying:

"During the last two or three days, I have had several conversations in regard to Argentina, Bolivia, and neighbors which make me more disturbed in regard to the future. It is not yet proved in the sense that we have full documentary evidence, but I believe that the plot is more widespread than most people believe; that it has direct ramifications in

Paraguay and that a great deal of preliminary work has been done in Uruguay, Chile, and Peru.

"Therefore, I am in hearty accord with the thought that this trend should be nipped in the bud and that we should proceed with the Argentine in strong ways."

At the same time, he said, he thought it essential that we make a move at once to build up Brazil's strength. "This," he added, "should cover American arms and munitions and possibly more Army instructors, so as to give Brazil an effective fighting force near the Argentine border such as two or three divisions of motorized regiments."

He also suggested that we let Brazil have some Lend-Lease cargo ships to take the place of the many Brazilian ships that had been sunk.

"It would be possible," he concluded, "to pursue one of two courses —either announce the whole thing publicly, or let it leak out—which would occur in a very short time."

I thereupon sent Secretary of War Stimson and Admiral Emory S. Land, Administrator of the War Shipping Administration, copies of the President's and my memoranda so that action could be taken to carry out Mr. Roosevelt's wishes.

The Argentine Government of General Ramírez was shaken, as 1944 began, by two facts. One was the knowledge that we had detailed information connecting Argentine nationalists with the revolution in Bolivia. The other was the scandalous revelations that came out in the case of a German agent, Osmar Hellmuth, arrested at Trinidad by the British. Hellmuth was serving as a go-between from members of the Argentine Government to the German Government as the Ramírez Cabinet sought to obtain arms and technicians from Germany.

Ramírez's new Foreign Minister, General Alberto Gilbert, saw Ambassador Armour on January 24 and commented that the Hellmuth case was proof that the German Government had broken a promise it had made to the Argentine Government that it would not abuse Argentine hospitality by engaging in espionage or subversive activities. Consequently, he said, the Argentine Government had definitely decided to break relations with Germany within a few days, and also with Japan if it were shown that Japan had taken part in espionage. Gilbert asked that no action be taken in the meantime by our Government giving rise to any interpretation that pressure was being applied.

Ambassador Armour informed Gilbert that we had planned to make a declaration against recognizing the Bolivian Junta and that this would include references to Argentina's having been the focal point not only against Bolivia but also against other neighboring countries. Gilbert pleaded that this be stopped in view of his promise of an early break of relations with Germany. Armour pointed out our disappointment over a similar promise made by President Ramírez and Gilbert's predecessor, Admiral Storni, the previous July.

Armour stressed to the Foreign Minister that he must realize that our Government knew of the participation of Argentine nationalists and others in pro-Axis subversive activities in neighboring countries, and that just breaking relations with Germany would mean little without stern action against Nazi collaborationists. Gilbert insisted that automatically with the rupture of relations his Government would take stern measures against all those guilty of subversive activities.

When Armour's telegram reached me I took it at once to the President. Mr. Roosevelt had already agreed with me on issuing the statement publicly declaring that Argentina was the base for hostile subversive groups which were trying to create disturbances within the governments of other American Republics. We now agreed, however, that, in view of Gilbert's promise of a rupture of relations with the Axis, we should delete this reference to Argentina and confine ourselves solely to nonrecognition of the Bolivian regime.

I cabled Armour immediately, and he informed Gilbert of our decision later in the day. Gilbert appeared much relieved. Armour again said to him, however, that a break of relations with Germany, unless accompanied by stern action against Nazi agents and Argentine nationalists, would not be sufficient. Gilbert insisted that his Government would proceed vigorously against all those implicated in the Hellmuth case and against Axis spies. He said their investigations proved us right and them wrong: that Nazi espionage was going on in the Argentine, and they proposed to admit it. Armour pointed out that, serious as this phase was, the plotting of the Argentine nationalists was equally serious and must be stopped to convince us of the Argentine Government's cooperation in defending the hemisphere.

I cabled Armour on January 25 that his action had the Department's complete approval. I said we welcomed the forthcoming rupture because we thought it of considerable military value in that it would afford Germany one fewer means of conducting espionage, sabotage, and subversive activities in the Americas. For this reason we were deferring the publication of the statement we had had in mind.

In the cable I pointed out that Argentina's contemplated action did not fulfill all her inter-American promises, although it was a belated indication of her realization of the dangerous nature of Axis activities, which had made necessary the adoption and carrying out of these commitments by all the American Republics. We expected, I said, to continue our program to hinder pro-Axis activities in Argentina and discourage anti-Allied movements in neighboring countries, with Argentine and Axis support, unless the Argentine Government completely reoriented its policy toward the Axis and identified its policy with that of the other American Republics.

We therefore stated that Argentina's change of heart could be demonstrated only by taking certain steps. These were: to make available to our intelligence services and those of our Allies the full results of Argentine investigations into the recently discovered spy ring, because we believed that a full disclosure would implicate persons high in the Argentine Government; to prevent Axis diplomats and officials from carrying on their activities while awaiting exchange; to close all channels which might be utilized by the Axis after the closing of the Axis diplomatic missions; to sever completely telecommunications with Germany and Japan; to implement fully the Rio and Washington conference agreements on financial and economic controls; to stop the activities of Argentine individuals and groups who had been cooperating closely with the Axis.

We were particularly concerned over the information that influential persons and groups within the Government were stimulating and assisting movements to overthrow the Governments of their neighbors who were friendly to the Allied cause and to replace them with Governments which had Axis support. We instructed Ambassador Armour to make certain that our attitude was immediately understood, particularly by President Ramírez, so as to avoid misunderstandings after the rupture of relations with the Axis had taken place.

Foreign Minister Gilbert cabled me on January 26, 1944, that the Argentine Government that day had issued a decree severing diplomatic relations with Germany and Japan, as a result of having proved the existence of a system of espionage for the benefit of those two countries that threatened Argentina's national sovereignty and the security of the Continent.

I cabled Gilbert on the same day that it was particularly gratifying to learn of this important step toward preserving the security and solidarity of the American nations. I said I was equally confident that it would result in an ever increasing collaboration and unity between our respective countries.

When, however, I received the Argentine Chargé d'Affaires, Don Rodolfo García Arias, the following day, after saying I was most pleased to learn from him what our Ambassador had been told in Buenos Aires to the effect that there would be a complete housecleaning, I added that if the important actions should be too long delayed the reaction in this country would be highly unfavorable, especially in view of the fact that his Government had been known to be pro-Axis in many vital respects. I stressed the extreme importance of making the housecleaning as thorough and expeditious as possible so as to leave no chance for misunderstanding in this and other Allied countries.

When the new Argentine Ambassador, Adrian Escobar, made his first call upon me on February 3, I tried to leave no doubt in his mind that, while I felt that Argentina was definitely progressing in the right direction, her position was by no means as yet identical with that of the other Republics. I expressed delight at Argentina's breaking off relations with the Axis and full confidence that the Argentine Government would proceed to a complete housecleaning and the elimination of all Axis influences. I added that with such a background of the situation the Ambassador would surely understand that in our press and public opinion skepticism regarding the intentions of his Government was bound to continue, but I hoped that these expressions of skepticism would in no way discourage the Argentine Government from pursuing the course to which Ambassador Escobar said it was now committed.

The Ambassador denied that the Argentine Government had any desire to intervene in the affairs of its neighbors; but he commented that in many Governments, and particularly in one situated as the Argentine Government was, there were likely to be persons who, while not in a position of authority, acted as if they possessed both influence and authority. He said these persons were liable to be eliminated soon either from natural causes or through drastic action by the authorities.

The drastic action, however, came from another direction. A group of comparatively junior army officers in Buenos Aires took possession of the Foreign Ministry on February 15, ousted President Ramírez and installed General Edelmiro Farrell as "Vice President in exercise of the Executive power." The coup d'état was the work of a military clique reputed to be more pro-Axis and anti-American than the Ramírez administration. These officers, headed by a group of colonels, of whom Juan Domingo Perón was one, were angered by Ramírez's rupture of relations with the Axis and feared that he might go still further and declare war against Germany and Japan. General Farrell formally assumed the office of President on March 10.

The overthrow of the Ramírez Government faced us at once with the question whether to recognize the new Government. In accordance with the procedure recommended by the Emergency Advisory Committee for Political Defense, with headquarters at Montevideo, it was of course necessary for the American Republics to consult with one another before granting recognition to a new Government created by force. While these consultations were under way, Acting Secretary Stettinius announced on March 4—I was out of the city at the time—that Ambassador Armour had been instructed to refrain from entering into official relations with the new regime pending developments. By "developments" we meant actions that would show the true attitude of the Farrell regime toward suppressing Axis activities in Argentina. It was unlikely that General Farrell would undertake to resume the relations with Germany and Japan which had been broken by his predecessor, but it seemed equally unlikely that he would carry out Ramírez's promises of stern action against Axis agents in Argentina and Argentine nationalists who were stirring up trouble in neighboring countries.

Some weeks of careful watching of the situation in Argentina followed. We had an Ambassador in Buenos Aires, but no formal relations with the new Farrell regime. During this time we maintained close contact with the other American Republics to arrive at a common viewpoint. Bolivia, Paraguay, and Chile, who were all close to Argentina, decided to continue relations with the new regime on the ground that, since Farrell had been Vice President under Ramírez, his was really not a new government. But all the other Republics held aloof from the Farrell regime.

Indicative of the confusion and fear into which the known designs and efforts of the Argentine Government had thrown neighboring countries was a conversation I had with the Uruguayan Ambassador, Dr. Juan Carlos Blanco, on March 20, 1944. Dr. Blanco said his Government desired to send an expert to investigate the River Plate section from a military viewpoint. He had in mind defense against a possible invasion from Argentina. He also earnestly requested more ships for Uruguay.

I took up with Dr. Blanco the argument being advanced in Buenos

Aires that refusal to recognize the Farrell regime constituted intervention in Argentina.

"No Government," I said, "known to be sympathetic to the Axis which has come into power by forcing out a preceding Government likewise known to have had Axis sympathies has the remotest right to invoke the doctrine of nonintervention to protect a seething mass of German intrigue and plotting within its boundaries, and to some extent within the Government. It's a travesty on the doctrine of nonintervention for any Government or a group of military officials who are the real power behind it to deny all their sister nations the right of self-defense by attempting to shield behind the doctrine of nonintervention a notorious state of pro-Axis activities within their boundaries."

I remarked that the British Government had completely blocked off Ireland from the world on account of the possibility—I emphasized "possibility"—of German espionage occurring within its borders. This, I said, was in striking contrast to the situation in the Argentine, where there existed in fact a notorious and confessed hotbed of German intrigue in support of the Axis Powers and against the Allied nations. While this element, I concluded, was seeking the complete protection of the Allies, it was also helping the Axis Powers by pretending to invoke the doctrine of nonintervention and expecting the other nations to extend full diplomatic recognition or run the risk of being charged with intervention.

Dr. Blanco said he agreed completely with this view.

During the spring of 1944, as we carefully watched developments in the Farrell regime, we were more and more alarmed by their characteristics of antagonism to the United States and most of the other American Republics and of sympathy and aid for the Axis. The new Foreign Minister insisted to Ambassador Armour that recognition had to be accorded to this regime before it would carry out the promises made by the Ramírez Government that the break with the Axis would be implemented. The Farrell regime gave Axis diplomats the run of the country; it set at liberty Axis spies and agents arrested by the Ramírez Government following the breaking of relations; it gave large official contracts to Axis firms and requisitioned critical materials from firms friendly to the Allies; it supported a string of pro-Axis newspapers. In all possible ways the Farrell regime sought to install a Fascist dictatorship in Argentina by controlling the press, courts, schools, and key institutions, and nullifying or impairing basic civil rights. It bent all efforts toward military rearmament, and the Minister of War indicated publicly that military power would be coupled with diplomacy to achieve the Argentine Government's political objectives. Bad as had been the Castillo and Ramírez Governments, the Farrell regime was worse.

In the face of these developments we could not remain inactive. Silence gave a species of acquiescence in the dangerous course of the Farrell regime, and we had no intention to acquiesce.

After consulting with the President, who readily gave his approval, I had a comprehensive summary prepared of all developments in Argentina since the Farrell regime had come into power. This we sent to the other American Republics (except Argentina and Bolivia) and to Great Britain on June 22.

In this memorandum we said that the time had come to break the impasse over Argentina, and as a first step we had decided to recall our Ambassador from Buenos Aires. Shortly thereafter, we said, we intended to begin an exchange of views through diplomatic channels to arrive at future common action. We instructed our Chiefs of Mission to see the President and Foreign Minister of the country to which they were accredited and, in advising them of our position, to state that in our opinion, if all the Chiefs of Mission remaining in Buenos Aires were to be brought home within the next two weeks, a most forceful reaction would be impressed on the Argentine regime.

On the same day we recalled Ambassador Armour from Buenos Aires.

The other American Republics expressed unqualified agreement with our memorandum. Taking similar action to ours, they, and Britain, recalled their Ambassadors in Buenos Aires for consultation.

During the following days I talked to a number of the Latin American Ambassadors to emphasize the points we had made in the memorandum of June 22. To Mexican Ambassador Dr. Don Francisco Castillo Nájera and Brazilian Ambassador Carlos Martins I said on June 23 that, if the American nations complied with the Argentine Government's request for recognition, they would give encouragement, prestige, and strength to that Government in its sympathetic and more dangerous relations with the Axis Powers. They would, in effect, be ratifying its acts, both in deserting its sister nations and in aligning itself more or less with the enemy. I had spoken in a similar vein to Colombian Ambassador Dr. Don Gabriel Turbay three days before.

The day after our circular telegram of June 22 and our recall of Ambassador Armour, Argentina's isolation was rendered still more marked by the recognition of the new Government of Bolivia by the other nine-teen Republics.

Six months had passed since the revolution in Bolivia had over-thrown the Government of General Peñaranda and installed that of General Villarroel. Throughout that time we were in constant consultation with the other American Republics. These had taken the same step we had in withholding recognition from Villarroel. Naturally the Argentine Government had recognized the Villarroel Government very soon after it came into being with the aid of extreme Argentine nationalists and Nazi agents.

These six months were a remarkable demonstration of the solidarity of the American Republics, with the exception of Argentina. Nineteen Republics held fast together in refusing to recognize the new Bolivian Government. That Government knew what it had to do to obtain recog-nition, and in view of the impressive demonstration of unanimity on the part of the other Republics, it gradually proceeded to do it.

Villarroel rid his administration of the known Nazi sympathizers who had helped boost him to power. His Government expropriated Axis business firms and arranged to expel the most active Axis nationals. He called a national election for July. He publicly made known his sympathies with the United Nations (Bolivia was legally at war with the Axis), and he took positive steps to show it, such as increasing the production of strategic materials and making them available for the general war effort.

At the beginning of May, with the President's approval, I requested Avra Warren, who was on his way to Panama City as Ambassador to Panama, to proceed to La Paz, Bolivia, and make a special report on the situation there to see whether we might be warranted in extending recog-nition.

In a telegram to the other American Republics—except Argentina— I said that they would be informed of Warren's estimate of the situation, but that our position remained what it had been; namely, that no change should be made without full exchange of views with all the other Repub-lics except Argentina. Mexico and Cuba now sent special representatives of their own to La Paz to make a survey on the spot.

Warren made an extensive report recommending recognition. I sent copies of the full report to the eighteen other Republics on June 2.

Brazilian Foreign Minister Aranha had been disturbed at my sending Warren to Bolivia. Since Bolivia was a next-door neighbor, he felt Brazil should have had some part in such a mission. But like the broad-gauged, farseeing statesman he was he continued his wholehearted cooperation with us.

After a number of diplomatic exchanges, nineteen American Republics, including the United States, agreed to recognize the Bolivian Government on June 23, a date proposed by Mexico.

I suggested to them in telegrams on June 17 that, to accent the united character of the action of the interested Governments, we should all incorporate in public announcements a statement that our decision followed upon full consultations with the other interested Republics in accord with the pertinent recommendations of the Committee for Political Defense at Montevideo. This was accordingly done.

Throughout the six months of debate over the Bolivian regime, our only criterion in considering whether to recognize it or not was whether it was a danger or a help to the security of the hemisphere. When it came into power with Argentine and Axis assistance, it was a danger. After the Villarroel administration took a series of positive steps, it became a help.

But the question of Argentina still remained.

101: An Unworthy Member

RECOGNITION OF the Bolivian Government did not affect our position and that of the other American Republics toward Argentina. The Government of General Farrell still had associated with it prominent Nazi sympathizers and collaborators. It still had taken no real steps to purge the country of Axis influence and to make Argentina a positive factor in hemispheric defense.

The reaction of the Farrell regime to our circular telegram of June 22 and the recall of the American Republics' and Britain's Ambassadors from Buenos Aires was in keeping with its previous attitude and acts. It delivered to us, through the Chilean Chargé in Washington, two memoranda to outline the steps taken by the Castillo, Ramírez, and Farrell Governments ostensibly to aid the United Nations and to implement the break in relations with the Axis. The memoranda were pitiful arguments because in themselves they tended to prove that the Farrell regime had done little or nothing to implement the action taken by the Ramírez Government.

Having received a suggestion from Paraguay that that Government and other American Governments might mediate between Argentina and the United States, I cabled Asunción on July 21 that the issue, arising from the desertion of the Allied cause by Argentina, involved all the Americas and was not one between the United States and Argentina alone. As between the United States Government and the regime in Argentina, I said, there could be no mediation.

The previous day I had sent out another circular telegram to our diplomatic missions in Latin America, except Buenos Aires, further outlining our position toward the Argentine regime. The President and I now decided that we should incorporate this and the circular telegram of June 22 in a full and public statement of our views regarding the Argentine regime. This we did on July 26, 1944.

Pointing out the enormous sacrifices the United States was making in the common American cause, and the full and wholehearted support of that cause by the other American Republics, we said:

"At this most critical moment in the history of the American Republics, the Government of one great Republic, Argentina, has seen fit to take two steps which have resulted in tremendous injury to the Allied cause, to wit: (1) it has deliberately violated the pledge taken jointly with its sister Republics to cooperate in support of the war against the Axis powers, and in thus deserting the Allied cause has struck a powerful blow at the whole system of hemispheric cooperation; (2) it has openly and notoriously been giving affirmative assistance to the declared enemies of the United Nations."

After comprehensively expounding the basis for these charges and refuting Argentina's claims of cooperation based on sporadic and superficial acts, we referred to the suggestion that the recent gestures made by the Farrell regime offered a basis on which to negotiate, and said:

"Bargaining or negotiating with regard to action which Argentina has long since agreed to take would be a serious error. The principles for which the free nations of the world are today contributing the full measure of their human and material resources cannot be the subject of a bargain. The controlling issue is support in good faith of the Allied cause.

"The injury to the solidarity of the Continent and to the war effort of the United Nations by the continuing acts and utterances of the Farrell regime is abundantly clear. It is the judgment of this Government that the American Republics and their associates among the United Nations should firmly adhere to the present policy of nonrecognition of the Farrell regime until by unequivocal acts it is conclusively demonstrated that there has been a fundamental change of Argentine policy in favor of the cause against the Axis and in support of inter-American unity and common action."

Some persons in this country and in other American Republics argued that we should automatically recognize the Argentine Government, whatever its alignment. They based their argument on the Estrada Doctrine (named after a former Mexican Foreign Minister) that once a new government had been established it should be recognized forthwith: recognition or nonrecognition should not constitute a policy.

My associates and I felt that in times of peace this argument might have validity. During peacetime our policy to recognize was based on certain criteria, such as the stability of the new government, the lack of substantial resistance to its authority, and its ability and willingness to observe international obligations.

But when the United States was at war, these criteria were not sufficient. We had to consider the further question whether recognition of the regime would be in our best interests. We had to determine whether the new government was friendly or unfriendly to our war purposes. It would be ridiculous for this Government to recognize and open formal diplomatic relations with a regime known to be working at cross purposes with our war effort. To strengthen the hand of a foreign government sympathetic with the cause of our enemies would be to close our eyes to the realities of the situation and to our own best interests.

It was significant that the American Republics, among whom the Estrada Doctrine was particularly popular, took the action they did at the Inter-American Emergency Advisory Committee for Political Defense at Montevideo, in December, 1943, when they decided that recognition should be withheld from a new government achieved by force during wartime until the American Republics had consulted among themselves. This consultation was for the stated purpose of determining whether the new government was complying with the inter-American undertakings for the defense of the continent. This decision in itself was a definite modification of the Estrada Doctrine, and recognized the existence of a new state of facts prevailing in wartime which did not prevail in peacetime. It came to be known as the Guani Doctrine, after Alberto Guani, the able Foreign Minister of Uruguay, who presented it.

Throughout the summer of 1944 the Farrell regime refused to take the steps most of the American Republics and Great Britain deemed necessary before considering recognition. Following publication of our July 26 statement it recalled the Argentine Ambassador from Washington. We on our part froze all remaining stocks of gold on deposit in Washington, including Argentina's, and ceased permitting American ships to go to Argentine ports.

The Farrell regime now put out a steady stream of propaganda, strenuously seconded by similar propaganda from Germany, that the United States was at loggerheads with Britain and with other American Republics over recognizing the Farrell regime, that the President and I were at loggerheads, and that I was at loggerheads with some officers of the Department.

Accordingly I sent the President a memorandum on September 28, saying:

"There has been a growing feeling among all of us alike in the Department, dealing with such matters, that the time has come when it would be worth much to our foreign policy in this hemisphere if your position were clarified in certain important respects, revolving around the Argentine situation. You may or may not know that according to reports your name has been used in such localities as Washington, London, and Argentina in ways calculated to confuse and injure our foreign policy interests, and during a pivotal period."

I attached a draft of a proposed statement and suggested that, if he could see his way clear to give out some such statement, it would be very helpful at this stage. I also stated my hope that he could keep the Argentine question before Prime Minister Churchill in a sufficiently strong way to secure results.

The President approved the statement without change and issued it on September 30. "I have been following closely and with increasing concern," he said, "the development of the Argentine situation in recent months. This situation presents the extraordinary paradox of Nazi-Fascist influence and the increasing application of Nazi-Fascist methods in a country of this hemisphere, at the very time that those forces of oppression and aggression are drawing ever closer to the hour of final defeat and judgment in Europe and elsewhere in the world. The paradox is accentuated by the fact, of which we are all quite aware, that the vast majority of the people of Argentina have remained steadfast in their faith in their own, free, democratic traditions and in their support of the nations and peoples who have been making such great sacrifices in the fight against the Nazis and Fascists."

Pointing to the Argentine Government's repudiation of solemn inter-American obligations, he said: "Unless we now demonstrate a capacity to develop a tradition of respect for such obligations among civilized nations, there can be little hope for a system of international security."

The President said he subscribed wholeheartedly to the words of Prime Minister Churchill, spoken before the House of Commons on August 2, 1944: "This is not like some small wars in the past where all could be forgotten and forgiven. Nations must be judged by the part they play. Not only belligerents but neutrals will find that their position in the world cannot remain entirely unaffected by the part that they have chosen to play in the crisis of the war."

On October 27, while I was still officially Secretary of State, though seriously ill in the hospital, the Argentine Ambassador on behalf of his Government addressed a note to me as chairman of the Governing Board of the Pan American Union, requesting the board to convoke a meeting of the foreign ministers of the Republics to discuss the situation existing between Argentina and other American nations.

This subject of a conference of foreign ministers was not a new one.

Mexican Foreign Minister Dr. Ezequiel Padilla had been proposing it to me since January, 1944. My thought was that a meeting then ran the risk of engendering division among the American Republics. The Argentine Foreign Minister, if he attended, and Argentina's few friends could inject all types of issues into the sessions. They would use the meeting as a sounding board; they would gladly adhere to its general agreements in hope of thereby obtaining diplomatic recognition; and they would use their participation in it as a cloak of legality and sanction for their existence as a Government. At some time in the not too distant future, I believed, a meeting of the United Nations would be held to establish a postwar organization, and it would be most unfortunate for the American Republics to enter that conference torn and rent by the Argentine question.

When Dr. Padilla had visited Washington I said to him on July 11 that no other meetings had been so enjoyable and interesting to me as those of the American Republics. Nevertheless we here, I added, faced so many problems, including the forthcoming Dumbarton Oaks Conference, that we should be in a most difficult situation if we were to participate in a meeting of foreign ministers at this time.

After Dr. Padilla returned to Mexico City he again presented his proposal to us, in the form of a memorandum dated November 6. He suggested that the foreign ministers of the American Republics which had cooperated in the war effort should meet to discuss urgent war and postwar problems. By this time I had been absent from the Department for more than a month because of illness. A formidable array of interests was now combining to bring every possible influence to bear on Acting Secretary Stettinius and other officials of the State Department to agree to holding a meeting of the foreign ministers. These groups embraced various business interests engaged in trade with Argentina, some Americans in Argentina, some friends in the United States of the fascist government at Buenos Aires, together with some malcontents here and there. They made the idea of a conference appear plausible, and in certain instances beneficial, though in reality it could not but be disruptive of the policies of President Roosevelt and myself toward Argentina.

Acting Secretary Stettinius replied on November 12, agreeing to Dr. Padilla's proposal for a meeting of the foreign ministers. He likewise agreed that the question of Argentina might be discussed, and that a representative of that country might appear to state its case following the close of the regular meeting of the ministers. Reviewing the Farrell regime's record of active assistance to the Axis, however, he made it clear that this Government did not consider that the regime was entitled to a hearing.

After my resignation the policy of President Roosevelt and myself toward Argentina was bequeathed to my successors and their associates. There was also on hand, however, an incipient, quietly conducted movement on the part of a few business interests, politicians, and marplots in this and other countries of the hemisphere to restore Argentina to full fellowship and diplomatic relations with the other American Republics, regardless of whether the Argentine Government changed its pro-Axis course sufficiently to justify such a step, even while the war was still being fought.

At the Mexico City Conference the Farrell regime obtained, as I feared it would, an entering wedge into the United Nations organization. As a condition thereof, the other American Republics agreed that Argentina should accept the common policy pursued by the Republics and make full use of her resources in the war against the Axis. This was easy enough for the Farrell regime to agree to, for the war against the Axis was now virtually over, and the victorious Axis star to which the Castillo, Ramírez, and Farrell Governments had hoped to hitch Argentine hegemony of South America was now falling.

Although I did not attend the United Nations Conference at San Francisco, I was a member of the American delegation, of which Secretary Stettinius was chairman. From my hospital bed I talked frequently over the telephone with Stettinius at San Francisco and kept alive my original contention that Argentina had not yet made herself worthy of being a member of the organization by complying with the requirements set out at Mexico City.

My position was that Argentina, before being admitted to the United Nations and hence to the San Francisco Conference, should make full apology for having deserted the cause of the American Republics to the support of which she had pledged herself in writing and for having assisted the Axis nations in waging the war. Moreover, she should in fact have complied with the specific requirements set out by the conference of sixteen American Ambassadors at the Blair House, Washington, in March, 1945. It was not enough that she should merely promise to comply with these requirements.

I felt that the only opposition to a general forward movement of the American Republics in resistance to the Axis Powers had come from the deliberate and open withdrawal of Argentina from her twenty American associates, and by the brazen act of Argentine officials in associating themselves with Germany and Japan and giving them notorious support— contrary, I knew, to the wishes of the great body of the Argentine people. While the fighting part of the war continued, it was the view of the United States and most of the other American Governments that it would be absurd for twenty American Republics battling for their existence to go out in search of the deserting Argentine Government officials in order to embrace them and assure them that we wanted to let "bygones be by- gones." The whole moral foundation and the splendid structure of hemi- spheric cooperation had been undermined and seriously impaired by Argentina's desertion. Some of the principles of Western Hemisphere cooperation had been vitiated. While I was in office, the general attitude of our Government had been to keep aloof from the Argentine Government as the fighting went on, and while that Government was engaged in aid- ing Germany and Japan fight us and our Allies. My position was that there would be suitable time and occasion, after the war ended, for the Argentine Government to find the most satisfactory way possible to bring about a reconciliation of a new attitude on its part with the basic policies of the other twenty American Republics. I assumed that after the conflict terminated, programs designed to revitalize and carry forward in a broad way our whole set of Pan American policies which had served the United Nations so well during the war would be worked out on lines fair and honorable to each country alike and satisfactory to the loyal friends of the Pan American ideals, so that the prewar unity of the Americas might be restored.

I should add that I was always prepared to see our Government recognize the Farrell Government and to approve that Government's admission to the United Nations organization when it had given proof of its compliance with the requirements laid down by the other American Republics and had wholeheartedly and actively placed itself on the side of the United Nations. We had been as prepared to recognize a reoriented Argentine Government as we had been to recognize the reoriented Bolivian Government.

Early in 1945, however, the leaders of the opposition to these ideas were riding a high horse, and they succeeded by devious methods in secur- ing the admission of Argentina to the San Francisco Conference. During that conference I felt that our own delegation as a whole earnestly favored the objectives I had in mind; but at the same time I was under the definite impression that there were well organized influences at work whose controlling purpose was to secure the admission of the Argentine delegation, and that they did not at all fully disclose the circumstances governing the situation, particularly the factual extent of Argentina's compliance— or rather lack of compliance—with the purposes of the United Nations.

I was separated by a continent from the American delegation at San Francisco, and it was never suggested that I should vote on any project at the conference. Had I been present and voting on the question of admitting Argentina at that time to the United Nations organization, I would have voted against it.

The report has been persistently circulated that President Roosevelt gave his approval to the admission of the Argentine Government to the United Nations organization shortly before his death. Actually what happened was that he wrote his "O.K." on the "Memorandum on Resolution LIX Regarding Argentina," which memorandum had been agreed upon on March 16, 1945, at a meeting at the Blair House, Washington, attended by sixteen ambassadors of the American Republics, along with State Department representatives, and presided over by Brazilian Foreign Minister Velloso, who was in the United States on a brief visit.

Resolution LIX had been agreed to at the Mexico City Conference in March, 1945, and concerned Argentina. Among other things it declared that "the Conference hopes that the Argentine nation will cooperate with the other American nations, identifying itself with the common policy these nations are pursuing, and orienting its own policy so that it may achieve its incorporation into the United Nations as a signatory to the Joint Declaration entered into by them."

The memorandum of March 16 stated that it should be acknowledged that the Argentine nation had accepted the invitation implied in the Mexico City resolution when, among other requirements, it had "expressed conformity with the principles and declarations of the Final Act [of the Mexico City Conference] and complied with such principles and declarations." The Argentine nation would then be recognized by the Governments of the American Republics; and the United States, as the depository of the Declaration by United Nations, would request that Argentina be invited to sign that Declaration.

In the above quotation I underline the word "complied." President Roosevelt had therefore given his approval to the recognition of the Argentine Government and to that Government's adherence to the United Nations Declaration on the express condition that the Government should first have complied with the principles and declarations of the Final Act of the Mexico City Conference. A mere promise to do so was not enough. Not many people knew at that time that the Argentine Government had notoriously failed to comply with the requirements for admission to the United Nations. In the quiet but intensive campaign between the Mexico City Conference and the San Francisco Conference to secure the admission of the Argentine Government to membership in the United Nations organization, the most powerful and persuasive plea was that that Government had fully complied with the specific and extremely important requirements for admission to such membership. These representations, which had a wide effect on the delegates at San Francisco, were known by many to be false at the time they were circulated, and their falsity has since become known to everyone.

The O.K. by President Roosevelt, therefore, should not be distorted into any interpretation that he would have supported the admission to membership in the United Nations organization of an Argentine Government that had not complied with the requirements set forth by the other Republics. It is inconceivable that he would have reversed himself for no reason whatever, especially when such an action would have been in direct contradiction to all his previous acts and utterances on this question. He had stood unequivocally and aggressively for the policy of the United States and the policy also of almost all the American Republics in opposition to the group in charge of the Argentine Government.

Toward the end of the San Francisco Conference, Harry Hopkins called on me at the hospital and stated that President Roosevelt—he had died in April—had been against the admission of this particular Government of Argentina into the United Nations. Hopkins said he had heard President Roosevelt at the Yalta Conference in February promise Marshal Stalin twice that he would not support such action on behalf of the Argentine Government.

To me, the hasty recognition of the Farrell regime through the establishment of diplomatic relations, and the admission of that regime to an organization of the very United Nations for whose defeat it had hoped and worked—compliance with the requirements of the other Republics being still unproved—was the most colossal injury done to the Pan American movement in all its history.

102: Britain and Argentina

THROUGHOUT the three troublesome years of our relations with Argentina while I was in office, 1942–1944, the attitude of Great Britain toward Argentina was of great importance to us and eventually became one of the major stumbling blocks in our solution of the problem. I have waited until this point to discuss this angle of the situation so as to deal with it consecutively.

Britain's economic ties with Argentina were appreciably stronger than ours. Her annual purchases of Argentine products were almost double ours. Furthermore, British subjects had made large investments in Argentina over a period of several generations, and the British colony in Buenos Aires enjoyed considerable prominence. After the European War broke out, and especially after the German conquest of most of Western Europe, Britain's dependence upon Argentina for food and other supplies became yet more acute.

At various times in 1942 Ambassador Armour cabled us that the Argentine Government was attempting to justify its position to its people by the argument that the British Government, in contrast with the United States, was entirely reconciled to the Argentine policy of neutrality and complete relations with the Axis. In December, Armour suggested that a member of the British Government make a public statement to overcome this argument. We knew that the British Embassy in Buenos Aires had made the position of its Government clear to the Argentine Foreign Ministry, yet we could not expect the Argentine Government to make this known since it was to their interest to convey the opposite impression.

Under Secretary Welles urged Armour's suggestion on British Ambassador Halifax on December 26. He remarked that, notwithstanding the official statements made by the British Government to the Argentine Government, many of the most important commercial and financial figures in the British colony in Argentina were consistently and publicly stating that Argentina should not break relations with the Axis, and that British interests favored the Argentine position of "neutrality."

The British Foreign Office received this suggestion favorably. It issued a statement to the effect that it wished to make it clear that both Britain and America were as one in regretting that Argentina had not yet moved forward in line with almost all other South American countries.

The British stated that the Argentine Government had arrested one or two more German spies, but still procrastinated in stopping Axis communications. The British Ambassador had therefore pointed out to President Castillo that, unless his Government could find a solution which would preclude U-boats from picking up such messages, the scarcity of shipping, and particularly of refrigerator ships, would make it impossible for Britain to go on receiving Argentine products.

Early in 1943 we took up with the British through Ambassador Halifax here and through Ambassador Winant in London our desire for greater coordination of the relations of Great Britain and the United States on the one hand, with Argentina on the other. We said to Britain that we were delighted that the recent British statement, together with Chile's probable break with the Axis, was making a good impression which it was to our advantage to increase. Since Britain and Argentina were then negotiating an agreement for the purchase of Argentine meat, we suggested that the signing be delayed until we could induce Argentina to prohibit the transmission of radio code messages from that country and to take more vigorous action toward Axis espionage and subversive activities. We urged that if these questions were injected into the meat negotiations, the hands of our friends in Argentina would be greatly strengthened. But at the same time we made clear we did not wish to interfere with Britain's procurement program, since we appreciated that the interests of the United Nations might be injured if meat shipments to Britain were interrupted.

The British Foreign Office went along with us in this suggestion, and their action, plus our own, had at least the effect of persuading the Argentine Government to prohibit the use of radio code messages.

Throughout 1943, however, British relations with Argentina continued close and reasonably cordial. It seemed to me absolutely essential, if we were to swing Argentina away from her dangerous connections with the Axis countries, that a combined British-American movement should be organized. We had close relations with the other American Republics, enhanced by Lend-Lease operations, and we could join with them in bringing pressure to bear on the Argentine Government; but Britain, because of her valuable economic relations with Argentina, was in position to bring still more effective pressure.

I went into this aspect of the question on two occasions with British Ambassador Halifax at the end of 1943. On December 27 I elaborated on the statement I had made to him the previous week when I earnestly urged the British Government to see to what extent it could cooperate with us in a general embargo against Argentina. Although I had opposed the blocking of Argentine funds in the United States because I believed it would have the opposite effect of that intended, it seemed to me that a joint British-American move along economic lines would produce the desired result.

I now suggested to Halifax, for transmission to his Government: "The British Government might determine whether it could go against the Argentine Government with a battering ram, so to speak. It could strenuously insist that that Government desist from all acts helpful to Germany and refrain from giving aid to movements calculated to bring on revolutions in neighboring countries. If the British and the United States Governments should at the same time make a pressing demand that this be done, this—probably within thirty days—would greatly change the attitude of the Argentine Government."

It would be of no use, however, I added, unless the British Government were willing to approach the Argentine Government most strongly. I pointed to the evidence we had that German money, with Argentine Nazi agents cooperating, was being used in Bolivia, and that these same agents reportedly were threatening to install in three or four other South American countries hard-boiled pro-Nazi military Governments similar to that in the Argentine. Such activities, if successful in other countries, would do the Allied cause serious harm.

"In the end," I said, "the vast British investment in Argentina would greatly suffer, and hence the very real interest the British should have in the proposal I'm suggesting. The British could let the Argentines know that they can get all the meat they need from other parts of the world as soon as the fighting ends, and that for the next twelve months they can hold out without serious suffering by using such supplies as are available."

Ambassador Halifax said he felt this was worth considering, and he would get it before his Government at once.

I pursued my argument further with Halifax when he came to see me on January 5, 1944, and stated my conclusion that the Argentine Government was an important factor in bringing about the revolution in Bolivia. I also said we had indications that there was a general movement of totalitarian and pro-Axis forces centered in the Argentine to overthrow the Governments of such countries as Uruguay, Chile, Peru, and Paraguay.

"Part of the propaganda being disseminated inside and outside of the Argentine," I said, "is that Great Britain is showing no concern about this movement. It is being said, on the contrary, that Britain is secretly pleased to see the United States in this trouble, especially with Argentina, for the reason that the British expect to buy meat and other foodstuffs during the war and then will have very little competition in trade and finance in Argentina after the war."

I made clear to Halifax that I was merely trying to state the attitude of the opposition and show how it might spread until Britain would be seriously concerned. The outlook, I added, was serious, and the time had come for the United States and Great Britain to make a frank, strong statement vigorously condemning the totalitarian influences that were conducting these subversive activities.

Halifax seemed much impressed and agreed that something should be done jointly by our two Governments. He said he would present a full picture to the Foreign Office at once.

Two weeks later, however, he indicated to me that his Government apparently did not intend to give the cooperation I had suggested. I pointed out that at least it could issue a strong statement simultaneously with one we were contemplating, to expose the pro-Axis movement with its base in Argentina and to warn all the other American Republics of the increasing dangers to them. I added that we also contemplated recalling our Ambassador in Buenos Aires for consultation. I asked Halifax to check again with the Foreign Office, saying that a statement by his Government would have a splendid effect on the pro-Axis authorities in the Argentine Government.

Britain's reply to this appeal came in the form of a message from Prime Minister Churchill to President Roosevelt, a copy of which, dated January 23, Halifax handed me on that day. Mr. Churchill stated that Britain would help all she could, and above all would avoid any public divergence with us in regard to Argentina. However, he begged the President to look into the formidable consequences that would follow Britain's losing Argentina's hides, meat, and other supplies. Saying that Britain received one-third of her meat supply from the Argentine, he asked how, if this supply were cut off, the British were to feed themselves plus the American Army being marshaled in Britain for the invasion of northern France. Cessation of Argentine supplies would disrupt military operations on the scale planned for this year. Before we leaped, he said, we really had to look; we could always pay the Argentines back when our hands were clear. He said he must inject his solemn warning of the gravity of the situation that would follow if the Argentine supplies were interrupted. To recall our Ambassadors meant only that the field would be left open for the Germans. These Argentine rascals, he concluded, knew the hold they had over us for the time being, and had calculated very carefully.

After Halifax made an argument in support of the Prime Minister's position, I remarked that the British were interested primarily in one situation in Argentina—meat supplies—while the United States was interested primarily in breaking up the ever-increasing pro-Axis elements based in the Argentine and steadily moving up the continent with the idea of overthrowing other Governments and setting up pro-Axis Governments as in Bolivia. I added that this movement was spreading and becoming increasingly dangerous.

"If my Government," I said, "should hesitate or falter at this time in carrying forward its known program of penalties against the Argentine, as has been thoroughly agreed and planned, the effect on the subversive movements in South America would be terrible. Apart from its resultant injury to the prosecution of the war and the security of South American countries, the United States would be discredited in the eyes of all countries interested in the war, especially the other South American countries."

I added that my Government must, without fail, go forward with the action we intended to take the following day, January 24; namely, the publication of a statement formally linking Argentina with the overthrow of the Bolivian Government. I suggested that the British Foreign Office might call in the Argentine Ambassador and strongly protest the pro-Axis attitude of the Argentine Government and insist on a break with the Axis Powers and a general housecleaning.

As I have already stated, we did not publish the statement we had in mind because the Argentine Government of General Ramírez broke diplomatic relations with the Axis. Foreign Secretary Anthony Eden nevertheless adopted the suggestion I had made, called in the Argentine Ambassador to Great Britain and counseled the Argentine Government to continue its program of housecleaning. When Ambassador Halifax on January 28 read me extracts from Eden's conversation with the Argentine Ambassador, I expressed much appreciation for his Government's cooperation.

During the next few months we kept in close touch with the British on all aspects of the Argentine situation. It was obvious, however, that our viewpoints, much as we both wanted to keep them identical, differed.

We desired a consistently strong attitude toward the Argentine Government, including refusal to recognize the Farrell regime. The British, fearful of an interruption in their meat supply, wanted to reach an agreement with the Farrell regime and to recognize it.

As the situation came to a head, I asked Ambassador Halifax to come to my office on June 23 and said that the Argentine situation was becoming worse from the Allied point of view, that the Army men constituting the Government at Buenos Aires were tough and hard-boiled and had been aiding the Axis from time to time to a considerable extent. I then informed him that we were withdrawing Ambassador Armour for consultation, and I expressed the hope that the British Government would take similar action with respect to their Ambassador at Buenos Aires, Sir Davis Kelly.

Halifax came back to see me three days later. Evidently having received his Government's reaction to my suggestion concerning the recall of its Ambassador in Buenos Aires, he proceeded with a line of talk about amicably working out the whole matter with the Argentine Government. He suggested that Ambassador Kelly might approach the Argentine Government, bring up its failures to meet the Allied Governments in this hemisphere halfway, refer to the seriousness of the situation from everybody's point of view, especially that of Argentina, and propose some acts of a pro-Allied nature that the Argentine Government should perform as a condition previous to recognition. Halifax emphasized Britain's difficulties in withdrawing her Ambassador, particularly because his Government within another two months would have to renew its meat contract with the Argentines.

"The British," I argued, "don't have to worry about Argentina cutting off their meat supply. Argentina has a huge surplus piled up, and has to sell her meat. Britain, being in the buyer's seat, has an advantage over the seller, especially since the Argentines cannot sell that portion of their meat elsewhere. The Argentines want a four-year contract with the British at a certain price. I suggest that Britain make contracts on a thirty-day or sixty-day basis, renewing them every month or two. This will bring the Argentine Government to reason and send it running after the British."

As for an approach by Ambassador Kelly to the Argentine Government, I said that Kelly was supposed already to have been saying all the things to the Argentine regime which it was now suggested he should say. I added that my Government had also put forth every kind of proposal about pro-Allied acts that might be performed by the Argentine Government to precede further conversations looking toward a settlement, but that the Argentine officials were becoming more indifferent and, in fact, unfriendly and more disposed to maintain friendly relations with pro-Axis elements. Now, I said, they had reached a stage of practically demanding recognition as a condition precedent to their doing anything to aid the Allied cause and to cut loose from their Axis contacts.

Most of the ambassadors at Buenos Aires, I added, had already left, but the Argentine Government was strenuously giving out the impression everywhere abroad and at home that the position of the nonrecognizing countries had broken down, and that recognition was only a question of days. This crisis, I concluded, had made it necessary for us to act at once; hence the action we had taken of recalling our Ambassador.

When Ambassador Halifax called on June 29 to say goodbye before going to London on leave, I said to him that the solution in Argentina at an early date depended on the attitude of the British Government. It was not necessary, I pointed out, to get into a name-calling match or a quarrel of any sort with the Argentines. But Britain should approach them firmly and state that the Argentine regime was getting into such friendly cooperation with the Axis enemies that it was creating a thoroughly unpleasant situation for the British as well as for the other nations. The British Government, I said, should with firmness and candor let Argentina understand that this course could not be carried on without upsetting the conduct of the war by Britain and the United States and their relations toward Argentina, that the Argentines were forcing a choice, and that they would be hurt worse than any other country if they continued their efforts to play up the Axis and to antagonize and undermine the Allies in this hemisphere.

When it seemed evident to me that the British Government did not intend to go along with us in our stronger policy toward Argentina, I went to the President and asked his intervention. I had no difficulty in obtaining it, for his thoughts on the Argentine situation dovetailed with mine.

The President thereupon sent a fervent personal message to Prime Minister Churchill on June 30, appealing to him to take a common stand with us and recall the British Ambassador in Argentina. Mr. Roosevelt said he was informed that the importance which we attributed to the proposal that the British Ambassador to Argentina be called home for consultation was fully known to the Foreign Office. The announcement of the recall of Ambassador Armour had been made, he added, and nearly all the other Republics were taking parallel action. It was clear, however, that if the British Ambassador remained in Buenos Aires the collective effect of this action would be seriously weakened.

The Prime Minister very reluctantly, and almost angrily, agreed with the President. In a message to Mr. Roosevelt on July 1, he said he had discussed the matter with Eden and had reached a decision to act as the President wished. A message had been sent to the British Ambassador in Buenos Aires recalling him for consultation.

The Prime Minister said they had taken this decision in response to the President's appeal for a common stand. In the War Cabinet and the Foreign Office, he continued, there was a good deal of anxiety. He did not see what we expected to get out of the Argentines by this method, and he did not himself see where this policy was leading. He only hoped that our vital interests and our war effort would not be affected adversely.

Finally he remarked that he hoped the President would not mind his saying, as was his duty, that this American decision had placed Britain in an invidious position, having been taken without consultation, and that Britain had been faced with a fait accompli.

The President sent me this message with a request that I prepare a reply. I sent this to him on July 4. In it we stated that the Prime Minister's decision to recall Ambassador Kelly, taken in conjunction with identical action by us and others, had already produced significant, concrete results. The immediate reaction, we pointed out, had been prompt, conciliatory, and definitely in the right direction, with a complete absence of irritation or threats toward any country. If we continued to stand firm, letting the Farrell regime understand, in a tone not necessarily unfriendly, that it should not, in violation of its pledge of hemispheric unity and solidarity, support the Axis in opposition to its sister nations, there was a good chance that the entire matter could soon be cleared up. It was everywhere recognized, we pointed out, that the issue at stake in Argentina was the same as that which was involved in the war against the Axis. The President was therefore confident that there was no risk in pursuing a firm and forthright policy toward the Farrell regime.

I held a conference in my office on July 17 with Ambassador Kelly, who was returning home via Washington, with Ambassador Armour, and with British Minister Sir Ronald Campbell. Kelly said he wished to make clear that his Government and certainly he himself held the same opinion of the present Argentine Government that we held, and that, if any difference of opinion existed, it was only as to the best procedure to follow to force that Government to change its policy into one of cooperation and support of the United Nations. He said he personally felt we should present the Farrell regime with specific conditions, strict compliance with which might be calculated to bring recognition.

I replied that I felt that Farrell and his Government must certainly know what was expected of them. I added, however, that, after Argentina's desertion of the other American Republics, followed by the aid that the Argentine Government and those around it had given to the enemy, it would be impossible, without abandoning our principles, to go to Argentina and say that all would be forgiven, and that we would be willing to enter into official relations with her.

Kelly then asked whether this meant that our Government would not be disposed to recognize the present Argentine regime under any circumstances. In that case, he said, we might have to be prepared for a long wait, since he did not see any opposition sufficiently strong to throw out the Farrell regime. He also wondered whether we should be able to hold the other American Republics with us.

Successive Argentine Governments, I replied, had found no difficulty in making clear their adherence to the Axis side, and I could not see that they required any suggestions as to how to proceed if they now wished to come over to our side. I said we had information that Axis subversive activities were continuing in Argentina, and that important intelligence of value to the enemy was still being sent from that country through clandestine radio stations.

I then repeated that I felt that the desertion by the Argentine Government of the American nations and the Allied cause in the most critical juncture in history, and the comfort it had given and was still giving to the enemy, called for a firm attitude on the part of all of us. I hoped, I said, that the British Government would be prepared to take this stand.

Minister Campbell remarked that it would be useful to Churchill and Eden to give Kelly a message as to how I felt the British Government could best use its influence at this time.

I said I felt that both Churchill and Eden had been inclined to minimize the serious nature of the Argentine situation, to overlook the principles at stake and the grave underlying issues involved, and to view the matter largely as a question only of meat and Britain's war requirements of certain Argentine supplies. This was not a question, I added, of future—and I stressed "future"—continental unity but an immediate threat to the whole unity of the continent and the prosecution of the war.

I said I did not ask the British to do anything that might jeopardize their sources of supply in Argentina. Furthermore, I did not believe that withholding of recognition would bring retaliation by the Argentine Government through an embargo on exports of meat to England. I recalled that for many years the United States Government had refused to recognize the Soviet Government, but this had in no way affected commerce between the two countries. In other words, the political and economic aspects could be kept separate.

In view of all we were doing and spending, I concluded, it was not too much to expect that the other Governments, including the British Government, should approach this whole question from the larger aspect rather than on a basis of whether or not the Argentine Government had complied, or would be willing to comply, with this or that point. The fact was that the line-up of the Argentine Government and the whole atmosphere in Argentina was bad and was a menace to the Allied cause, and I felt that the only way to handle it and perhaps bring that Government to reason would be for all the nations to continue in their policy of nonrecognition.

At the time of my conversation with the British Ambassador, the war was being waged with increasing intensity; Allied forces were battling desperately with the Germans in northern France, and fighting ferociously to drive the Japanese from island to island in the Pacific. Argentina, I felt, could rejoin her former allies and aid us in the conflict; but, if she refused, it would be monstrous for the Allies to forgive a deserter who had not requested forgiveness but instead was continuing actively to aid the enemy.

The summer went by, however, without Britain's bringing the pressure to bear upon the Argentine Government which I seriously believed she could and should. The gesture in grudgingly recalling Ambassador Kelly was obviously as far as Mr. Churchill intended to go. The Farrell regime was fully aware of this situation, believed it held all the cards in the form of invoices for meat and could successfully defy the United States and most of the other American Republics.

We argued with Britain—and the President and the Prime Minister had an exchange of cables on the subject—that the British had a sufficient surplus of meat on hand to do without Argentine meat for a time or at least to deal with Argentina on a month-to-month basis. The British, on the other hand, wanted to accede to the Argentine Government's request that they sign a four-year contract. We sought to prove that the buyer, Britain, was in the driver's seat in a situation where Argentina, because of the blockade, could sell nowhere else the meat that would go to Britain. The British thought that the seller, Argentina, was in the driver's seat because they were obliged to get the majority of their meat from her.

In one of my last conversations with Ambassador Halifax, prior to my resignation, I read to him on September 16, 1944, extracts from economic memoranda prepared in the State Department showing clearly that the British could aid us to the extent necessary without endangering their meat situation. I remarked that President Roosevelt, at an early stage when conditions were very different from what they were now, had said something to the effect that we, of course, wanted Britain to get all the meat she desired. The President, I said, had in mind that Britain could cooperate fully with us without in the least endangering the meat situation and could exercise powerful influence as the controller of the buyers' market, which would be acquiesced in by the sellers. However, I remarked, it seemed that the British officials were far more fearful about the risk than the President, myself, and other members of this Government, and we were basing our views on the most elaborate and careful examination of all the facts and circumstances.

"Argentina," I said, "under the control of the Fascist lawless government, is the refuge and headquarters in this hemisphere of the Fascist movement. That movement, entrenched in Argentina under the protection of a Fascist Government, is dangerous. If the United States and most of the other American nations should become seriously handicapped in their efforts to resist this movement and should fail because of the British attitude, the repercussions would be very loud throughout the hemisphere. This Government would then be obliged to state the full facts as it found them, for the reason that the whole future of Pan Americanism is measurably at stake."

Such were our relations with Great Britain over Argentina at the moment of my resignation. I believe that, if Britain and the United States had brought common economic, diplomatic, and moral pressure to bear upon the Argentine Government, with the backing of most of the American Republics, we could have induced that Government to cease being an active friend of our active enemies. There was no other way to do it.

103: The Good Neighbors

IN SUMMING UP our policy toward Argentina in the years 1942 to 1944, I feel that Prime Minister Churchill and Foreign Secretary Eden, along with some others in Britain, the United States, and Latin America, failed to realize the depth and danger of the relationship between Germany and members of the Argentine Government, beginning with Castillo and continuing to Ramírez and Farrell.

These persons did not fully grasp the fact that in 1942, when Japan had overrun the Southwest Pacific, when Germany, already in possession of most of Western Europe, had pushed deep into the Caucasus, and when Nazi U-boats were sinking masses of Allied shipping in the Atlantic, many influential Argentines in and out of the Government concluded that the Axis would win. They therefore determined to be on the winning side, and, with Axis assistance, make Argentina the leading, and perhaps the ruling country in Latin America, the capital of a Latin American federation pointed at the United States. Believing, at least at first, in a German victory, they were anxious to do what they could to assist in its early arrival or at least to do nothing to endanger Argentina's relations with the probable victors.

Some persons failed to see that the danger to the Allied cause lay not only in the Nazi spying, subversive, and propaganda activities in Argentina, but also, and even more importantly, in the designs and efforts of many of the principal members of the successive Argentine Governments to overthrow other South American Governments and bring the new regimes into virtual alliance with Buenos Aires, into friendship with the Axis, and into opposition to the United States.

They did not sufficiently appreciate the fact that the Argentine Government had deserted every basic principle of Pan Americanism, the foundation of which was peace and nonintervention. That Government had, in place of Pan American principles, installed the doctrines of Nazism and Fascism; namely, internally to destroy the party system of government and make the entire nation subservient to one ruling clique, and externally to dominate all neighboring countries and achieve the headship of a continent.

The strong policy we adopted toward Argentina did not bring Argentina to the United Nations side. Only a strong policy backed equally by

Great Britain, the United States and the other American Republics could have achieved that end.

Could a weak policy—that is, one of appeasement—have succeeded where the strong policy failed? It would naturally have succeeded in reestablishing diplomatic relations between ourselves and Argentina. Had we sought a settlement with the Argentine Government we doubtless could have reached one. But it would have been an agreement which in effect condoned the Argentine Government's desertion in the past and ignored its present and future connivance with the Axis.

We could not on the one hand sacrifice hundreds of thousands of our finest youth and immense quantities of treasure in fighting to overcome Nazism in the Old World, and on the other hand pay the lip service of diplomatic recognition to a transplanting of exactly the same poisonous plant to our own garden in the New World.

But our strong policy did succeed in one all-important respect. It effectually thwarted the ambitions of the extreme Argentine nationalists to upset one Government after another in South America, beginning with the Republics adjacent to Argentina, and to replace them with Governments subservient to the pro-Nazi program embraced by these nationalists. Those ambitions had their first expression in the revolution in Bolivia— the initial page of a book of blueprints.

If at that point we had adopted a policy of appeasement; if we had indicated by our actions that we would not oppose this march up the Continent; if we had not banded together with the other American Republics to stop this movement before it was too late, we should have found ourselves confronted not with one question over Bolivia but with four or five questions over other Republics upon whom the Argentine nationalists had fixed their designs. We then should have found ourselves in serious difficulty, to say nothing of danger. We should have had to divert some of our attention from the conflict in Europe and Asia, and the prosecution of the war would have suffered.

In that respect our policy succeeded. As between a policy that would restore a friendly relationship with Argentina and a policy that would prevent the formation of a bloc of Governments in South America antago- nistic to the United States and the United Nations, there was only one choice to make.

Our growing military might, our victories in the Pacific in 1942 and 1943, and our landings in North Africa, Italy, and finally in Normandy were a powerful backing for our policy. Had there been defeats instead of victories, the hands of the Argentine nationalists would have been greatly strengthened. The military successes we achieved in Europe, Africa, and the Pacific, however, tended to obscure in many minds the potential dangers we faced in Latin America through a combination of Argentine nationalists and Axis representatives. A moment's reflection brings easily into focus the dangers that would have confronted us in the southern part of South America had we been defeated in Europe and Asia, or had the war ended in a negotiated peace.

As I bring these observations on our policy toward Argentina to a close I wish to say again that I do not for an instant associate the great mass of Argentine citizens with the aid to the Axis rendered by the Castillo, Ramírez, and Farrell Governments. Large numbers of Argentine individuals did all they could to aid the United Nations cause. In my condemnations of successive Argentine Governments I constantly recognized that the majority of Argentine citizens favored the United Nations and opposed the Axis leanings of these Governments in so far as they were aware of them. Our quarrel was not with the Argentine people but with the Government at Buenos Aires.

It is a matter of real regret to me that the writing of some portions of these memoirs has had to follow the principle of relative importance of news as exemplified by headlines. Conflicts, whether personal, national, or international, crimes, disasters, and depressions naturally attract attention; whereas the daily progress and the doings and sayings of the man of peace go almost unnoticed. I find I have devoted considerable space to this discussion of the actions of Argentina, which were a crime against democracy, whereas I should greatly have preferred to give this space to an acknowledgment of the splendid relations we enjoyed throughout this period with the other American Republics and to the truly wonderful assistance they gave us in the prosecution of the war.

Despite the discouragement induced by the course of the successive Argentine Governments, I drew daily encouragement from the cooperation of the other American Republics even in the most trying days of the war. Thirteen of them declared war on the Axis, and six broke off diplomatic relations. All of them made a valid contribution to the winning of the victory. In general, the help of all kinds we received from Latin America during the Second World War was incomparably greater than that received in the First.

The assistance they gave us took many forms. Some of them, such as Brazil, Mexico, Ecuador, and Peru, gave us the use of naval or air bases.

When it is recalled that for many decades a number of the Latin American Republics feared armed intervention by the United States, their willingness to welcome armed forces of this country within their borders assumes added significance.

Without the air bases Brazil permitted us to construct on her territory victory either in Europe or in Asia could not have come so soon. These bases, jutting far out into the South Atlantic, permitted us to fly war planes across that ocean in waves to West Africa and thence to the theaters of operation in Europe or on to the Far East. Had it not been for these Brazilian bases we could not have got so much help to the British in Egypt as we did at the crucial moment of the Battle of El Alamein.

From Brazil, too, we received valuable diplomatic assistance in our negotiations with her mother country, Portugal. That farsighted statesman, Oswaldo Aranha, Brazil's Foreign Minister, never wavered from the cause of the Allies, and neglected no opportunity to give us his backing. In this he had the full support of President Getulio Vargas. Even in the dark days of the first half of 1942 they were willing to assume all the risks that aid to the United Nations comported.

Brazil sent an expeditionary force to Europe. Her small navy played its share in patrolling the Atlantic. She lost an appreciable portion of her merchant marine in the effort to transport supplies to the United States. She assisted us in keeping an eye on Dutch and French Guiana.

Mexico offered another outstanding example of helpful cooperation. Even before Pearl Harbor, Mexico reached agreements with us for the reciprocal transit of military aircraft, delivery of strategic materials, and the construction on her soil by the United States of a chain of landing fields. She embargoed oil and scrap iron to Japan when we did. She helped us overcome our labor shortage by permitting the temporary emigration to the United States of about 150,000 agricultural and railroad workers up to the time I left office. When President Roosevelt visited Mexico in 1943 he was given a memorable welcome.

All the American Republics, except Argentina, gave us some form of direct economic assistance. They adopted economic programs to increase their production of strategic materials for us and other United Nations. They cooperated in economic warfare to keep supplies from going to the Axis. They mutually agreed with us upon prices. Many Republics took over the Axis business houses which we had placed on our so-called Proclaimed List. The Republics instituted controls over financial transactions involving Axis interests. They took measures to prevent clandestine trade in industrial diamonds, platinum, and the like which the Axis was doing its utmost to obtain. Those Republics having shipping defied the German U-boats and delivered materials to the United States, some of them losing a number of ships.

It is true, of course, that we ourselves were of great help to the American Republics economically, and that we furnished them Lend-Lease supplies as liberally as we could. It is also true that, if we had not begun in 1940 to adopt the wide range of steps we did to absorb Latin American surpluses, bolster their finances, and maintain sea communications with them, economic chaos might well have resulted. This does not, however, diminish either the value or the spirit of the economic assistance which those Republics rendered us.

All the American Republics, except Argentina, took the necessary steps to rid their territories of Axis agents, including many wealthy and influential persons with strong political connections. They closed down Axis propaganda agencies, while giving open support to the efforts of the United Nations to disseminate propaganda in Latin America. They cut off communications with the Axis, and many Republics permitted United States censorship experts to help them establish satisfactory censorship over mails.

It must not be forgotten that all these steps required considerable courage, especially in those Republics farthest removed from our military and naval protection. The disastrous turn of events in the first half of 1942 which convinced the Argentine Government that the Axis would win, and that it should plan accordingly, was also in the minds of the other Republics. But their appreciation of the risks involved did not deter them from aligning themselves with the United States and the other United Nations, for better or for worse.

I appreciated the courage many Latin American Republics showed in helping to develop and in supporting the policy the President and I maintained toward Argentina. It was not an easy matter for the close neighbors of Argentina, such as Uruguay, Paraguay, and Chile, to join with us in common actions including the recall of ambassadors from Buenos Aires, the refusal to recognize the Farrell regime, and the refusal to recognize the Villarroel regime in Bolivia until it had stripped itself of Axis ties. Since they stood to suffer from economic and other reprisals by Argentina, their cooperation with us was of even greater moral value in emphasizing their condemnation of the course of that Government. It likewise was a striking confirmation of their belief in the efficacy of our policy—not only in its objective of bringing home to the Argentine Government the gravity of its desertion of the United Nations cause, but also in its major objective of preventing the spread of the Argentine nationalist movement to other countries.

As long as I was at the Department, we made it a point not to urge any American Republic to declare war upon the Axis. We did repeatedly state our opinion that all the Republics should sever relations with the Axis, since the continuance of such relations constituted an actual physical danger to us, and since the American Republics had agreed in successive inter-American conferences that an attack upon one American nation would be considered an attack upon them all. Nevertheless, we determined to leave the question of a declaration of war entirely to the American Republics themselves, and we so stated in numerous dispatches to our envoys in South America.

When I left office, six Republics—Uruguay, Chile, Peru, Paraguay, Venezuela, and Ecuador—had not declared war on the Axis. I was determined not to draw any distinction between them and the Republics which had declared war. Some of these six were rendering us far more assistance than some of the Republics at war. Ecuador and Peru gave us the use of bases we vitally needed, and Uruguay was a stalwart outpost against the intrigues of the Argentine nationalists. When we sent out invitations to the United Nations Food Conference at Hot Springs, Virginia, in the spring of 1943, we included the associated as well as the allied Republics.

Shortly before I left office the question began to be raised as to whether the associated Republics should be initial members of the proposed international organization. I believed that they should, without being required to declare war. Russia, however, took the position that only those countries that were actually at war with the Axis should receive initial membership.

The question was still pending when I left the Department. Shortly thereafter the State Department informed the associated Republics of its concern lest the fact that they were not full members of the United Nations prejudice their opportunity to participate in plans for an international security organization. The Department pointed out that it fully recognized the contributions made by those Republics to the war. Nevertheless, it called attention to the advantages to be gained by formalizing their status through a declaration of war against Germany and Japan, although the decision of course remained exclusively in their hands.

In summation, the attitude of the Latin American Republics during the war, with the exception of Argentina, was a striking justification of the Good Neighbor Policy. It fully rewarded the many thousands of hours my associates and I, with the President's approval, had devoted to it in the course of twelve years. It demonstrated that the United States and the Latin American Republics, despite differences in language and origin, have many fundamental interests in common. It made clear that the Good Neighbor Policy must be one of the major tenets of United States foreign policy in the future. The desertion by Argentina does not disprove the rule.

I felt that it was all-important for the American Republics in the future to restore and revitalize the principles on which the great structure of Pan American unity and cooperation had been built up in every way from 1933 to 1943. This effort would embrace the further development of all essential projects designed to improve the mutual welfare of the twenty-one Republics in the political, economic, and cultural fields.

104: France Regained

HAVING CONCLUDED this exposition of our relations with the neutrals as of the time of my resignation, I now pass to a discussion of our relations with our Allies, particularly Britain, Russia, and France, taking up the last-named first.

As the time approached for the Allied landing in northern France, across the English Channel, it had become urgently necessary to reach an agreement with the British and with the French committee of General de Gaulle concerning the civil administration of France as that country was liberated by the Allied armies. The President on March 15, 1944, signed a proposed directive to General Eisenhower on the administration of civil affairs in France, which he sent to Prime Minister Churchill.

Mr. Roosevelt had carried into 1944 the deep-seated suspicions he and I entertained regarding De Gaulle, which he stated as late as November 27, 1943, in his cable to me from Cairo (Chapter 89). His directive to Eisenhower, composed by the interested Government Departments, left it to the General to determine whether he should deal only with representatives of the French Committee of National Liberation or also with other French groups that might be in existence—always excepting the Vichy regime. Our thought was that not until we actually landed in France could we know for certain what percentage of the French people would support De Gaulle as chief of their Government, and the President did not wish to tie Eisenhower's hands to the extent of requiring him to maintain the French committee with American arms if it should prove unacceptable to the French people.

Mr. Roosevelt's feelings toward De Gaulle were not improved when, in an address on March 26, De Gaulle referred to the French committee as the "Provisional Government of the French Republic" and said that that Government need listen only to the French nation, implying that he could ignore his allies.

A few days previously, on March 21, we at the State Department were forced to take cognizance of apparently inspired reports and rumors which periodically issued from French North Africa that the United States Government, upon the liberation of France, intended to deal with the Vichy regime or certain of its members. We pointed out in a public statement that the fact that our Government had kept representatives at Vichy prior to the landing in North Africa for such vital purposes as combating Nazi designs, keeping the French fleet from German hands, and preventing the Nazi occupation of French Africa or the establishment of military bases there, had been falsely represented as founded upon a sympathetic relationship between the American Government and pro-Axis supporters at Vichy.

"No loyal supporter of the Allied cause," we said, "would make the ridiculous charge that the United States Government, while sending its military forces and vast military supplies to the most distant battlefields to prosecute the war against the Axis Powers, would at the same time have any dealings or relations with the Vichy regime except for the purpose of abolishing it."

The President and I agreed to send a special mission to London, headed by Under Secretary of State Stettinius, to explore all existing problems with the British, including the French question. The mission consisted also of Dr. Isaiah Bowman, vice chairman of the Department's Advisory Council on Postwar Foreign Policy; John L. Pratt, Consultant on Commercial Affairs; Wallace Murray, Director of the Office of Near Eastern and African Affairs; and H. Freeman Matthews, Deputy Director of the Office of European Affairs. It left the United States on March 30 and arrived in London on April 7.

Two days later I gave prominent position to France in my address of April 9. I prefaced my remarks by saying we looked with hope and deep faith to a period of great democratic accomplishment in Europe following liberation from the German yoke. "It is important to our national interest," I said, "to encourage the establishment in Europe of strong and progressive popular governments, dedicated like our own to improving the social welfare of the people as a whole—governments which will join the common effort of nations in creating the conditions of lasting peace and in promoting the expansion of production, employment, and the exchange and consumption of goods, which are the material foundations of the liberty and welfare of all peoples."

As for France, I said it was hard to imagine a stable Europe if there were instability in its component parts, of which France was one of the most important.

"Our first concern," I made it clear, "is to defeat the enemy, drive him from French territory and the territory of all the adjacent countries which he has overrun. To do this the supreme military commander must have unfettered authority. But we have no purpose or wish to govern

France or to administer any affairs save those which are necessary for military operations against the enemy. It is of the utmost importance that civil authority in France should be exercised by Frenchmen, should be swiftly established, and should operate in accordance with advanced planning as fully as military operations will permit. It is essential that the material foundations of the life of French people be at once restored or resumed. Only in this way can stability be achieved."

It had always been our thought, I said, that we should look to Frenchmen to undertake civil administration and should assist them in that task without compromising in any way the right of the French people to choose the ultimate form and personnel of the Government which they might wish to establish. That had to be left to the free and untrammeled choice of the French people.

"The President and I are clear, therefore," I said, "as to the need, from the outset, of French civil administration—and democratic French administration—in France. We are disposed to see the French Committee of National Liberation exercise leadership to establish law and order under the supervision of the Allied Commander-in-Chief. The committee has given public assurance that it does not propose to perpetuate its authority. On the contrary, it has given assurance that it wishes at the earliest possible date to have the French people exercise their own sovereign will in accordance with French constitutional processes."

I pointed out, however, that the committee was not the Government of France, and we could not recognize it as such. Nevertheless, the committee would have every opportunity to undertake civil administration and would have our cooperation and help in every practicable way in making this successful. The committee, I added, had been a symbol of the spirit of France and of French resistance. We had fully cooperated with it in all the military phases of the war effort, including the furnishing of arms and equipment to the French armed forces. Our central and abiding purpose, I concluded, was to aid the French people, our oldest friends, in providing a democratic, competent, and French administration of liberated French territory.

Under Secretary Stettinius reported to me in a series of telegrams from London that he had found the President's proposed directive of March 15 to General Eisenhower on civil administration in France still on the Prime Minister's desk. Mr. Churchill indicated that he did not want to bother the President about it at this time; but he seemed unwilling to authorize its acceptance or to have it discussed in the combined United States and British Civil Affairs Committee in London.

The British seemed delighted with the references I had made to France in my address on April 9, but thought they did not entirely coincide with the President's directive. Actually, my speech, which as I have mentioned was read and approved by the President, was a little more strongly in favor of the French committee in that it stated we were disposed to see the committee exercise leadership to establish law and order under the supervision of the Allied Commander-in-Chief.

Stettinius explained to the British that in practice General Eisenhower would deal with the French committee in all his pre-invasion planning and, wherever possible, after the landing in France. Moreover, neither the State Department nor Eisenhower had any intention of encouraging any rival group that might emerge in France. Nevertheless we did not feel that Eisenhower should be forced to maintain the committee in France with American bayonets should the French people refuse to accept it.

Eden said he could not accept the President's directive unless its second article were amended so as to make Eisenhower's dealings with the committee mandatory by changing the word "may" to "should."

In response to this suggestion, which I forwarded to the President, then at Georgetown, South Carolina, he sent me a message on April 15 saying that, in view of the fact that circumstances would differ so much in different areas, General Eisenhower should have complete discretion in the matter of civil government. He therefore disapproved of the substitution of "should" for "may."

The President, after having approved my speech of April 9, had backed away from my statement that we were disposed to see the French committee exercise leadership to establish law and order under the supervision of the Allied Commander-in-Chief. His resentment against De Gaulle was still lively.

The British, Stettinius further reported to me, seemed to want to give to the French committee the fullest possible support and did not wish to approve any document which implied that they contemplated dealing under any circumstances with any group other than the committee. They also indicated that it was contrary to their conception of government to permit important political decisions to be taken by a military commander.

Stettinius said there was much suspicion on the part of the British that after we got into France General Eisenhower might make a deal similar to that made with Admiral Darlan at the time of our landing in North Africa. The British had never more than grudgingly admitted that, however unfortunate the Darlan arrangements might have been from the political point of view, they nevertheless saved many thousands of lives and helped materially to shorten the African campaign. They feared that, for strictly military reasons, Eisenhower might again take some action under the President's flexible directive which would run counter to their determination to give full, undivided support to the French committee.

The British believed that all Frenchmen would rally to the support of De Gaulle and the committee and accept their dictates without question. We on the other hand, while not denying this possibility, thought that it was necessary not to take it for granted, and that it was also possible that, as France was liberated, a period of some confusion and disorder might follow. The British, in any event, stated they did not plan to recognize De Gaulle and the committee as a provisional government until they were established in metropolitan France.

During succeeding days, Prime Minister Churchill requested the President to modify his directive, but the President stood firm. Cables from our Embassy in London then indicated that the British were proposing to write a new formula based on my April 9 address. I spoke strongly on this point to British Ambassador Lord Halifax on May 4, saying that this was dangerous from the viewpoint of working relations between the President and Mr. Churchill, and that it was, in effect, going over the President's head and using my speech as a substitute formula without the President's expressed agreement. Further exchanges between the President and the Prime Minister left the question unsettled on the eve of the invasion.

At a Cabinet meeting about May 20, the President said that Ambassador Winant had raised with him the question of dealing with De Gaulle. He added that he had told Winant that if anyone could give him a certificate proving that De Gaulle was a representative of the French people he would deal with him, but that otherwise he had no idea of changing his mind.

We were now receiving suggestions from London that General de Gaulle should come to Washington to see the President personally, with the hope that his visit would facilitate an agreement. Exactly one week before the landing in Normandy, the President cabled the Prime Minister, on May 31, saying that he would like to make the matter of De Gaulle clear from his point of view beyond peradventure of a doubt. As for the visit to Washington, the President said he had told French Admiral Fénard, who was on the way to Algiers to see De Gaulle, that he had been hoping that the General would send him a message asking if a visit would be welcome. The President, if such a message were received, would answer in the affirmative immediately and cordially.

Mr. Roosevelt said he had explained to Fénard, as he thought he had made his stand clear to many people before, that he, as head of the Government and head of the state, could not well invite De Gaulle, who was not the head of the French Government or the French state, but only the head of a committee.

In general, he said we must of course do everything we possibly could to encourage French national spirit and get it working immediately with us at top speed. What the state of this French spirit was, he observed, we did not definitely know; we should not know until we got to France, but we hoped for the best.

The President informed Prime Minister Churchill, who was about to confer with De Gaulle, that General Marshall would be in London about four days after D-Day, but that we could not give him plenary powers to negotiate with the Prime Minister and De Gaulle jointly, or with De Gaulle singly, since the matter was wholly in the political and not in the military field. He said he could not send anyone to represent him at the conversations with De Gaulle.

In response to Churchill's suggestion that he go to London, the President replied that he hoped at a later date to accept "Dr. Churchill's advice to make a sea voyage"; but conditions here would not permit it shortly after D-Day plus fourteen, as the Prime Minister suggested. (The Democratic Convention of 1944 was now in the offing, and the Presidential campaign would soon get under way.)

Such was the situation when the American and British landing began in Normandy on June 6. General Eisenhower had reached an agreement on the military level with the French committee, but the committee's share in the civil administration of France still remained to be decided.

From the moment of the landing, we carefully scrutinized all developments in France to ascertain as best we could the sentiments of the French people toward the French Committee of National Liberation. It soon became evident that the French were willing to accept the committee as a provisional authority until they could, through popular vote, express their wishes with regard to their future government.

Accordingly, the President approving, my associates at the State

Department began discussions with the War Department and with representatives in Washington of the French committee to perfect arrangements for the administration of civil affairs in France by Frenchmen to be named by the committee.

General de Gaulle, having exchanged with the President the messages the latter desired, arrived in Washington on July 6. I attended a reception for him at the White House that day, and gave a dinner for him that evening at the Carlton Hotel.

I found that De Gaulle was now in a much more reasonable frame of mind. He had visited the Allied bridgehead in Normandy and was filled with admiration for the thoroughness of the invasion preparations and their magnificent execution, and for the fighting qualities of the American troops. His visit to Normandy and his conversations with French leaders there also convinced him that Britain and the United States were far more popular in France than he had thought, and that the old Parliamentary parties in France still had considerable strength. By now he was confident that the Allies would not deal with any group in France other than the French Committee of National Liberation. At any rate, he went out of his way to make himself agreeable to the President, to me, and to other members of the Government, and to assure us emphatically and repeatedly that he had no intention of forcing himself or his committee upon France as her future government.

The President therefore decided, and I concurred, that we should recognize the French Committee of National Liberation as the de facto authority in the civil administration of France. The announcement was made on July 11.

Our negotiations with the French representatives in Washington continued and reached a successful conclusion, which was incorporated in an exchange of letters in London, between General Eisenhower and General Koenig, representing the French committee. This the War and State Departments released jointly on August 24.

Our arrangements embraced civil administration and jurisdiction, currency, captured war matériel and property, publicity, and the distribution of civilian relief supplies. General Eisenhower was authorized to deal with the French committee, whose headquarters were at Algiers, as the de facto authority in France "so long as they continued to receive the support of the majority of Frenchmen who are fighting for the defeat of Germany and the liberation of France." We emphasized that this authorization was based on the understanding that, as Supreme Allied Commander, General Eisenhower had to receive whatever authority he considered necessary for the unimpeded conduct of military operations, and that, as soon as the military situation permitted, the French people would be given an opportunity freely to exercise their will in the choice of a Government.

Following the freeing of Paris, we reestablished our diplomatic mission in the French capital on September 8, 1944.

During the military operations throughout the summer of 1944, as American, British, French, and Canadian troops drove the Germans back to the Siegfried Line, the arrangements we had made with the French committee worked out to our entire satisfaction. As province after province fell into Allied hands, it was clearly proven to us that the great majority of the French people, at least for the period of the emergency, freely accepted the leadership of General de Gaulle and the administration that he had set up on French soil. The French people themselves, particularly the resistance elements of the French Forces of the Interior, made a real contribution to the Allied victory.

By October the military situation made possible the establishment of most of France, including Paris, as a "Zone of the Interior" in which, as our arrangements called for, the conduct of civil affairs became entirely the responsibility of the French authorities. Accordingly, after we had consulted with the British and Soviet Governments, we decided that the French de facto authority established in Paris under the leadership of General de Gaulle should be recognized as the Provisional Government of the French Republic. We announced this decision on October 23, and Britain, the Soviet Union, and other United Nations made similar announcements. With the approval of the French Provisional Government, the President named Jefferson Caffery, who had been our Ambassador in Rio de Janeiro, as Ambassador to France.

The French Foreign Minister, Georges Bidault, sent me a note on November 4, inviting the President and me to visit Paris. I had already left the State Department, however, because of my health and was soon to resign, and the President also was unable to accept.

A week later we, along with the British and Soviet Governments, invited the Provisional Government of the French Republic to full membership on the European Advisory Commission in London. One of the principal questions before the commission was the surrender terms to be imposed on Germany and the postwar treatment of Germany.

Meantime we joined with the British, Soviet, and Chinese Governments at the Dumbarton Oaks conversations beginning in August, 1944, in agreeing that France should be accepted in due course as a fifth permanent member of the Security Council in the proposed international organization for the maintenance of peace.

Thus stood our relations with France at the time of my resignation as Secretary of State. As I left office our policy toward France was based on two primary considerations. The first was to seek to increase France's contribution to the war in every possible way. The second was to assist France to resume her former position of influence and thus assume larger responsibility for maintaining the peace throughout the world following the defeat of the Axis.

In the course of many preceding chapters I have been forced to give considerable attention to General de Gaulle—an attention that sometimes may have seemed disproportionate to the importance of the man himself. The significance of the De Gaulle issue, however, was not limited to the General. It involved relations between the United States and Britain, and between the United States and the Vichy Government and French North Africa. It embraced the basic belief of the President and me that the future of France should not be mortgaged to or by any one man or group, unless the French people themselves so elected.

Not until we occupied large sections of France could we be sure that the French people would accept De Gaulle. The Free French had shown us numerous reports that they said came from the French underground, showing a great majority support for De Gaulle; but we had had other reports from inside France to the opposite effect.

Our military support of De Gaulle had begun early and had never wavered. This was because we were quickly convinced that the Free French could lend some military assistance to the Allies. They were among the first to receive Lend-Lease aid, which was granted them on November 11, 1941.

Our political support lagged behind our military support partly because of De Gaulle's actions in striving to impose himself as the governmental leader of all French elements opposed to the Nazis and of his propaganda which sought to play off Britain and the United States against each other, and the Anglo-Saxon nations against the Russians, and partly because of our uncertainty that he had the approval of a majority of the French people. Once this last point appeared assured, our political backing became cordial and wholehearted.

105: Question of Russia

RELATIONS BETWEEN the United States and Russia, as 1944 began, were closer than they had ever been. Through the Moscow and Tehran Conferences we had brought Russia into a program of real cooperation for the remainder of the war and, we hoped, for the future.

Throughout 1944, my last year in office, our relations continued good on the whole, with Russia joining wholeheartedly in the preparations for the postwar organization to keep the peace. It was obvious, however, that as Germany collapsed and Russia moved in to fill the vacuum in Eastern Europe, problems of a delicate nature would arise. It also was obvious that certain problems already existed that had not been settled.

For one, Russia and another of the United Nations, Poland, were at daggers' points. They maintained no diplomatic relations with each other, and constant recriminations were passing back and forth between Moscow and the Polish Government at London, sharply disturbing to the harmony of the United Nations.

Our submission in August, 1943, of our good offices for the settlement of their dispute had not been accepted; but we tried again in January, 1944, although in general we let the British Government take the lead in endeavors to resolve the dispute. This last was for the reasons that the Polish Government-in-exile was located in London, and that Britain had treaties of alliance both with Poland and with Russia. On January 14 the Polish Government announced its willingness to discuss all outstanding questions with the Soviet Union and indicated that it was approaching the United States and British Governments with a view to their acting as intermediaries.

The President and I quickly agreed to the Polish request. On January 15 I cabled Ambassador Harriman to remind the Soviet Government that, as that Government well knew, we were pledged to the principle of settling disputes by peaceful accord. Without regard to the merits of the case, we hoped that the Soviet Government would give most favorable consideration to the Polish offer to discuss outstanding questions, on the basis presumably of the renewal of official relations between the Governments of Poland and the Soviet Union.

A refusal by the Soviet Government, or any show of hesitancy in this regard at the present time, we added, would adversely affect the cause of general international cooperation. On the other hand, far-reaching beneficial effects on world public opinion would be brought about by a solution of the Polish-Soviet differences in conformity with the basic principles of international cooperation. We likewise pointed to the very considerable advantages to our war effort which would come from the restoration of unity in the ranks of the United Nations.

We informed the Soviet Government that, if it found it agreeable and desirable, we should be glad to extend our good offices toward initiating discussions between the Polish and Soviet Governments, with a view to the resumption of official relations between them.

In the cable to Ambassador Harriman I stated for his information that our proposal was intended primarily as an earnest, friendly effort to help Russia reach a settlement of this difficult problem. The Soviet newspaper *Pravda* had published a bitter reply to an article by Wendell Willkie dealing in part with Russia's supposed intentions concerning the political integrity of states around her borders, Finland, Poland, the Baltic and Balkan countries. This reply, I said, had had a far-reaching effect on public opinion here because it was interpreted as an indication that the Soviet Government proposed to follow a course of unilateral action. Important elements here, I added, viewed the Soviet Government's attitude and actions with regard to the Polish boundary question as a test of the reality of friendly international cooperation and respect for the rights of nations. The Moscow and Tehran Conferences had produced encouraging results in the United States, I concluded, but we frankly pointed out the danger to the cause of cooperation in an international security system which an arbitrary treatment of the Polish-Soviet difficulties would produce.

A week later, on January 24, Soviet Ambassador Gromyko transmitted to me a reply from Molotov stating in effect that conditions were not yet ripe for mediation. Molotov said it was clear that the Polish Government's aim, in turning to the Governments of the United States and Great Britain for mediation, was not to achieve agreement with the Soviet Government but to deepen the conflict and involve the Allies therein. It seemed to him that the exclusion of all pro-Fascist imperialist elements from the Polish Government and the inclusion of democratic elements would be a fundamental improvement and would create a favorable ground for the reestablishment of Soviet-Polish relations and the settlement of the border question between them, as well as for fruitful mediation.

Polish Ambassador Jan Ciechanowski called on me on January 26 and handed me a note from Premier Mikolajczyk to the President. This stated that Prime Minister Churchill had suggested a five-point solution which he would propose to Stalin if the Premier agreed. The five points were:

First, the Polish Government to accept the Curzon Line (roughly equivalent to the limit of Polish territory occupied by the Russians in 1939—this area contained a large percentage of Russians) as a basis for negotiations concerning its eastern frontier. Second, Poland to receive East Prussia, Danzig, and Upper Silesia as far as the Oder River. Third, Poles on the Soviet side of the Curzon Line to have the right to remove to the west of that line. Fourth, all Germans to be removed from the new Poland. Fifth, Britain, Russia, and the United States to guarantee this settlement.

Mikolajczyk asked the President in his note whether the United States Government considered it advisable to enter now upon a final settlement of European territorial problems; whether it would participate in bringing about and guaranteeing a settlement; and whether it supported Churchill's proposals.

I promised Ambassador Ciechanowski I would transmit the note to the President.

The President and I, in talking this over on January 31, agreed that we should not support any definite frontier recommendations during the course of the war. This was in line with the position I had stated on several occasions—namely, that new frontiers should not be fixed during the progress of hostilities except with the free consent of the countries directly concerned. There were more than thirty boundary questions in Europe alone, and an outside attempt to settle any of them would only result in raising all of them, to the detriment of the aggressive prosecution of the war.

We did not believe it possible to give a United States guarantee of the new Poland that might be constituted along the lines of Prime Minister Churchill's suggestions. We felt that all the guarantees necessary would be contained within the new international security organization to which the Russians, British, Chinese, and we had agreed at the Moscow Conference, and that the United Nations organization would get off to a better start if it were not embarrassed by individual arrangements of guarantee.

Accordingly, the State Department drew up answers to the three questions submitted by Premier Mikolajczyk. Mr. Roosevelt approved the answers, and we handed them to the Polish Ambassador.

On the first question—the advisability of entering now upon a final settlement of European territorial problems—the President pointed to the well known basic position of the United States Government that general discussions of European frontier problems during the progress of the war ran the risk of creating confusion and diverting attention from the principal objective of defeating Germany. This attitude, however, did not preclude direct settlement by mutual accord between any two countries that had mutual territorial problems. As for the Russo-Polish problem, the United States recognized that recent developments (Russian troops had crossed the old Polish frontier) might render it desirable for the Government of Poland to reach a solution without delay.

On the second question—participation by the United States in bringing about a settlement and guaranteeing it—the President said this Government would be prepared through the offer of good offices to the Polish and Soviet Governments to assist the Polish Government in freely reaching a settlement of its territorial problems. Although this Government would welcome a friendly solution of the outstanding questions between Poland and the Soviet Union, it was not in a position to guarantee any territorial settlement.

On the third question—supporting Churchill's proposals—the President said the United States was prepared to support the Prime Minister's endeavors to bring about the reestablishment of relations between the Soviet and Polish Governments on the basis of a friendly solution of all outstanding difficulties.

I cabled Ambassador Harriman on February 7 a message from the President to Stalin, which we had prepared in the State Department. Mr. Roosevelt said to Stalin that, in communicating with him on the basis of the conversations they had had at Tehran, he wanted to make it plain that he neither desired nor intended to suggest, much less to advise him in any way, where Russia's interests lay with regard to Poland, since he fully realized that Russia's future security was rightly Stalin's primary concern. He added, however, that the broad principles subscribed to at the Moscow and Tehran Conferences had been enthusiastically welcomed by the overwhelming majority of our people and Congress, and he knew Stalin would agree with him that it was highly important that faith in these understandings should not be questioned. He said he was sure a solution could be found that would fully protect Russia's interests and satisfy Stalin's desire to see a friendly, independent Poland and at the same time not affect the cooperation which the Moscow and Tehran Conferences had so splendidly established.

Foreign Commissar Molotov had stated to Ambassador Harriman on January 18 that it was impossible for the Soviet Government to have any dealings with the Polish Government in London in its existing form, and had suggested that the Polish Government should be reconstituted by including Poles at present in the United States, Great Britain, and the Soviet Union.

Referring to Molotov's statements, the President said to Stalin he fully appreciated the Marshal's desire to deal only with a Polish Government in which he had confidence, and which could be counted upon to establish friendly, permanent relations with the Soviet Union. Nevertheless, he earnestly hoped that, while this problem remained unsolved, neither party, by hasty word or unilateral act, would transform this particular question into one that would adversely affect future international collaboration. He said it was especially necessary to avoid any action that might appear to counteract the achievement of our long-range objectives at a moment when public opinion was forming in support of international collaboration.

The President mentioned that Churchill had informed him that he was urging Premier Mikolajczyk to accept the territorial changes proposed by Russia (the Curzon Line, more or less, in the east, with Poland to move farther west into former German territory). He then asked Stalin whether it was not possible on that basis to leave it to Mikolajczyk to make such changes in his Government as might be necessary without any evidence that a foreign country was pressing or dictating them.

Here Mr. Roosevelt added another paragraph in his own hand stating his opinion that the first consideration at that time should be that Polish guerrillas would work with and not against Stalin's advancing troops.

On the following day, February 8, I sent Ambassador Winant in London a message from the President to Prime Minister Churchill which also had been prepared in the State Department. This was by way of comment on a message that Churchill had sent to Stalin outlining his suggestions for a settlement of the Polish-Russian dispute. The President asked whether the Prime Minister's message might not give "U. J." (the President and the Prime Minister occasionally used this designation, abbreviation for "Uncle Joe," in referring to Stalin) the impression that Mr. Churchill was wedded to the present members of the Polish Government in London and was determined to see them become the future Government of Poland. Stalin, he thought, might interpret this as evidence of a wish on Mr. Churchill's part to see a Government set up along Russian borders which the Russians rightly or wrongly regarded as containing elements irrevocably hostile to them.

The President said he knew that this was not Mr. Churchill's wish, and that the Prime Minister was interested only in preserving the principle of the right of all countries to chose their governments without interference and also in avoiding the creation by the Soviet Government of a rival Polish Government. He suggested that this be made clear to "U. J." by referring to the possibility that, if a real solution of the frontier and other questions with Russia was near, the Polish Government of its own accord would accept the resignation of its members known to be particularly objectionable to Russia.

Mr. Roosevelt sent the Prime Minister a copy of the cable he had dispatched to Stalin.

Nothing came of these exchanges. Premier Mikolajczyk's Government would not accept the Curzon Line as a basis for negotiation with Russia. Stalin on his part said that before Polish-Soviet relations could be resumed, the Polish Government must publicly announce its recognition of the Curzon Line as its eastern frontier; but he added that he wished to have nothing to do with the present Polish Government in London, which, he said, was full of reactionaries who opposed good relations with Russia.

Premier Mikolajczyk had for some time been urging the President to invite him to Washington for a discussion of the Polish situation. Mr. Roosevelt felt, however, and I agreed, that a personal discussion with the Premier would not resolve the difficulty with Russia. We knew the opposition that existed within the Polish Government to any cession of eastern Poland to Russia, however valuable might be the German territory that Poland would receive; and we also knew that Russia would consent to no agreement with Poland that did not involve the reacquisition of eastern Poland which Russia regarded as her own. There was the further objection that a personal conference between Roosevelt and Mikolajczyk, with all the publicity it would naturally receive, might give rise to the impression that the United States had embraced Poland's position versus Russia.

Spring of 1944 was the period of preparation for the greatest military campaign in American history—the landing in Normandy. That landing had to be coordinated with Russian military movements in the east so that the Germans could not draw off too large a portion of their forces to meet us in the west. We could not afford to become partisan in the Polish question to the extent of alienating Russia at that crucial moment.

The President therefore desired to postpone Mikolajczyk's visit. When the Premier wrote him a long letter that Ambassador Ciechanowski sent to the State Department on March 25, stating Poland's position and emphasizing his desire to see the President personally, Mr. Roosevelt, replying on April 3, pleaded the state of his health and other commitments as reasons for postponing the visit at least until May.

The Polish question was now further complicated by the obvious Russian efforts to set up a rival Polish Government in Russia or in that Polish territory which, since the beginning of the year, they had occupied. Soviet Ambassador Gromyko came in on May 27 to inform me that a group of representatives of what was called the National Council of Poland had gone from Warsaw to Russia. They stated that the council was fighting Germans, it needed arms to continue such fighting, it would be willing to work with the Polish Government in London, although it disliked some members of that Government, and it desired to establish relations with the Soviet, British, and American Governments.

When I asked what kind of relations they wanted, Gromyko replied he did not know; but he assumed they meant some sort of political relations short of diplomatic relations.

The President and I had no desire, however, to give any encouragement to the creation of a second Polish Government. We maintained diplomatic relations in London with the Polish Government-in-exile. And we felt, as we did in the case of De Gaulle and the French, that the Poles should be left entirely free, when their country was liberated, to choose their own Government.

In pursuance of the thought Molotov had expressed on January 18 that the Polish Government should be reconstituted by including Poles in the United States, Britain, and Russia, Stalin sent the President a message at the beginning of March asking him to allow two American citizens of Polish descent to go to Moscow for discussions with Soviet officials. These were Professor Oscar Lange (at this writing Poland's delegate to the United Nations) and a Catholic priest, the Reverend Stanislaw Orlemanski, both of whom were known for their pro-Russian views.

Under Secretary Stettinius, who was acting for me during a brief absence from Washington, sent the President, after consulting with me, a memorandum on March 8 in which we opposed Stalin's request. The memorandum stated that Stalin's request raised very serious questions of policy. Orlemanski and Lange represented a heavily slanted view on the Polish-Soviet question which, according to our information, was not shared by American citizens of Polish descent or by American public opinion as a whole. We might become directly involved in the dispute if they went to Russia by our tacit consent and assistance. Their visit would be widely interpreted as the first step in this Government's abandonment of the legal Government of Poland. It was possible that their activities might bring them under the Logan Act, which prohibited American citizens from having any dealings with a foreign Government to defeat the measures of this Government. On the other hand, we concluded, it might be undesirable if not impossible to refuse two American citizens permission to accept an invitation tendered by the Soviet Government.

Despite these objections, the President thought he should accede to Stalin's request. I sent Ambassador Harriman on March 24 a cable for Stalin from the President, which had been drafted in the State Department, saying that Lange and Orlemanski would be given passports in accordance with the Marshal's request. The telegram suggested that the Soviet Union should furnish transportation facilities for the two visitors because of the military crowding of our own transportation facilities. It stated that our Government assumed no responsibility for their activities, and that, if their journey became the subject of public comment, we might find it necessary to emphasize this point.

The visit of the two Polish-Americans to Moscow did arouse, as we knew it would, considerable adverse comment and agitation in the United States. Polish Ambassador Ciechanowski protested on behalf of his Government.

When Soviet Ambassador Gromyko called on me on May 1 I said that this incident had caused great injury to both our Governments so far as public opinion here was concerned.

"I've been spending a large portion of my time," I said, "defending Russia against the attacks made on her mainly on account of these small incidents which in themselves amount to little but which for propaganda purposes of those unfriendly to this Government and to Russia are far-reaching in their damaging effects. If we are to go forward with the movement of international cooperation to preserve peace after the war, it's highly important that we should understand each other's situation and psychology better, so that we can diminish these small incidents."

I added that I would continue in a friendly way to do all possible to clear up these matters, but that frankly I could not do all this work myself.

Ambassador Gromyko said that he thought the criticism would be temporary, and that the matter of Orlemanski and Lange involved fundamental policy of his Government.

I replied that I could scarcely see the force of his last statement.

In any event, Orlemanski's and Lange's visit to Moscow had no effect on the disinclination of the President and me to see the Russians attempt to create a rival Polish Government.

Polish Premier Mikolajczyk's visit was at length arranged, and he arrived in June. He had long conferences with the President, and he came to see me at his request on June 12, along with Ambassador Ciechanowski. As our conversation began, I mentioned that I had happened to sit a little on the inside of the councils during the Wilson Administration, and that Poland had been a constant topic of discussion. I said that every person with whom I came in contact seemed to be consumed with a desire to see Poland once more become a free and independent nation, and that Mikolajczyk would find the American people inherently friendly toward the people of Poland.

"I repeat," I added, "what I have said both to the Russians and to the Poles . . . when two neighbors discontinue speaking terms, the neighbors of each unanimously desire to urge them to find a way to get back on speaking relations. The interests and welfare of each country equally require that they live on friendly terms. There is no way to settle differences that have arisen, and will inevitably arise, between nations hitherto friendly, except by persuasion, reason, remonstrance, and other methods of appealing to another government when it is considered in the wrong."

The Premier said he appreciated these points. He spoke, however, of the difficulties of getting along with Russia. He then brought up the question of credits for Poland, which he had presented to Under Secretary Stettinius several days before. I promised we would give his request every consideration.

As the Premier was about to leave, I said that if it were possible for appropriate Polish and Russian representatives to meet on a conversational basis, it would be of tremendous importance. It would probably mean a discussion in an increasingly friendly spirit of the differences between the two Governments and a solution that each Government would feel was reasonably fair.

"It's true," I commented, "that no country desires to have an unfriendly country living by its side. We Allies feel keenly the unfriendly pro-Axis attitude of the Argentine Government located 7,000 miles away. While it is not essential, though it is preferable, for a next-door neighbor to be thoroughly friendly, yet the purpose of the future welfare of each country is served if one country is not unfriendly toward the other."

The Premier agreed.

The Polish and Russian Governments, I said, had a serious argument over the attempted dictation by the Soviet Government regarding some of the personnel of the Polish Government at London. The Polish Government's resistance to that dictation was based on a sound position. On the other hand, Russia was not required to recognize the Government of any other country, and even then was not required to give any reason for doing so or for not doing so. These two opposing views, each sound, approached each other within a given distance, at which point arose the controversy. Some of these days, I concluded, when both Governments decided to make an equal contribution toward working out such deadlocks as this, they would find ways to do so.

Premier Mikolajczyk smiled and indicated his acquiescence.

In line with this thought that high officials of the two Governments in dispute should meet and talk things over, President Roosevelt communicated to Stalin that Mikolajczyk would be willing to go to Moscow to make a sincere effort to reestablish relations with the Soviet Union. He indicated his interest that Stalin should receive the Polish Premier.

Stalin did not acquiesce in the President's suggestion. Some weeks later, however, at the insistence of Prime Minister Churchill, he consented to receive Mikolajczyk in Moscow, and the visit took place in August, though without concrete results.

In the same month, August, 1944, we had a number of diplomatic exchanges with the Soviet Government in an effort to help the Polish resistance forces in Warsaw who had risen against the Germans as the Russian Army drew near that capital. We sought to obtain permission from the Russians for a shuttle mission of American bombers to drop arms to the Poles in Warsaw who were fighting desperately to hold their capital until the Russian forces could arrive.

On August 15 the Soviet Government refused our request of the 14th, saying that the Warsaw uprising was a "purely adventurist affair" and the Soviet Government would not lend its hand to it, and that, as Stalin had pointed out to Churchill on August 5, it was unimaginable that a few Polish detachments of the so-called National Army could have captured

Warsaw when the Nazis were defending the capital with four tank divisions.

I thereupon sent the President a memorandum on August 16, saying: "I believe for a number of considerations that it is impossible for us or the British to abandon to their fate the Polish underground forces which are actively fighting the Nazi invaders of their country simply because such action might not accord with Soviet political aims."

I attached the draft of a telegram to Ambassador Harriman whereby the President authorized him to associate himself with the British Ambassador in making representations to Stalin, or, if Stalin could not be seen, to Molotov, urging the Soviet Government to reconsider its attitude. The British had already asked our assistance toward this end.

After the President had given his approval, the telegram went out on August 17. We pointed out that, while we sincerely hoped that the Soviet Government would cooperate with us and the British in furnishing assistance to the Polish underground forces and would itself furnish such as might be practicable, the American forces intended, in any case, in so far as militarily feasible, to continue to furnish aid to the Polish underground inside German-occupied Poland. This Government, we concluded, saw no reason to depart from its consistent policy of furnishing all possible aid to any force of the United Nations engaged in fighting our common enemy.

The President himself was keenly interested in this project. From what we could learn, the Poles had gained control of a large part of Warsaw and were valiantly holding out against the Germans. We thought it would be highly advantageous to the general war effort for their resistance to continue until the Russians, who were only a comparatively short distance away, reached the city.

Before this telegram arrived Ambassador Harriman conferred with Foreign Commissar Molotov on August 17, and presented arguments similar to those we had stated. Molotov admitted that Stalin had promised Mikolajczyk, during his visit to Moscow earlier in the month, to give aid to the Poles resisting the Germans in Warsaw. He explained, however, that because of statements emanating from the Polish Government in London, it had become evident by August 12 that the movement in Warsaw was inspired by men antagonistic to the Soviet Union, and therefore the Soviet Government could no longer countenance any association with the uprising. He further said that his Government could not object to British or American planes dropping arms in the region of Warsaw, but they objected to the planes landing in Soviet territory since the Soviet Government did not wish, either directly or indirectly, to associate itself with "the Warsaw adventure."

The President and Prime Minister Churchill made a joint, direct appeal to Stalin on August 20. They said in substance that they were thinking of world opinion if the anti-Nazis in Warsaw were, in effect, abandoned. They expressed the belief that Russia, Britain, and the United States should do their utmost to save as many of the patriots in Warsaw as possible. They hoped that the Soviet authorities would immediately drop supplies and munitions to the Poles or agree to assist our planes in doing so. They stressed the extreme importance of the time element.

The Germans were then bringing overwhelming force to bear against the beleaguered Poles, and it seemed doubtful that the resistance forces could hold out much longer without help.

Stalin finally gave permission for one shuttle flight which was carried out successfully on September 18. He also gave permission for another flight, which, for operational reasons, was not made. The resistance in Warsaw ended on October 2 with the surrender of those Poles who had survived the incessant German attacks.

When Prime Minister Churchill went to Moscow in October for another effort to solve the Polish-Russian dispute, he induced Stalin to receive Mikolajczyk again. The Polish Premier, following his return to London from his second trip to Moscow, tried to persuade the members of his Cabinet to accept the Soviet proposal to use the Curzon Line as the basis for the Polish-Soviet frontier. Encountering difficulties from his colleagues, he appealed to President Roosevelt on October 26 to send a message to Stalin asking the Soviet leader to include the city of Lwów and the oil fields south of that city within Poland's future boundaries.

The President was looking forward at that time to another meeting with Stalin and Churchill within the near future. Consequently he decided not to send the message, preferring to talk the matter over with Stalin personally.

On November 15, after it had become evident that the meeting would be put off—it did not eventuate until February, 1945, at Yalta—the President addressed a letter to Polish Premier Mikolajczyk, which the State Department drew up. This contained four main points.

The first was that the United States Government stood for a strong, free, and independent Polish state in which the Polish people should have the right to order their internal existence as they saw fit.

The second was that we should have no objection to any frontier settlement that was reached in agreement among the Polish, Soviet, and British Governments, but that we could give no guarantee of any specific frontiers.

The third was that, if the Polish Government should desire to transfer population to and from Polish territory, the United States Government would have no objection and would facilitate such transfers as far as practicable.

The final point was that the United States Government, subject to legislative authority, would assist in the postwar economic reconstruction of Poland in so far as practicable.

Ambassador Harriman, who took the letter from Washington to London, was also instructed to discuss Lwów with the Polish Premier and to say that, if the Premier desired him to make a strong appeal to Stalin to have that district included in the future Poland, he would do so.

Premier Mikolajczyk said to Harriman on November 23, however, that he had already decided to resign, since he could not persuade his Cabinet to accept the Russian proposals regarding the eastern frontier. He said he regretted asking the President to take up the question of Lwów because, even if Stalin had agreed, his colleagues still would not have accepted the boundary. As I was in process of resigning, Mikolajczyk himself resigned on November 24.

When I left office, the Polish-Russian dispute was no nearer solution. I have no intention to go into the merits of that dispute. The policy of the President and me was to refrain from stretching the United States upon a bed of nettles. In our diplomatic exchanges with both sides and in our offers of good offices, we repeatedly stated we were not entering into the merits of the differences between Poland and Russia.

We certainly brought all the pressure we logically could on both sides to compose their quarrel. But our broader view of the interests of the United Nations would not permit us to accept the suggestion often advanced that we should cut off Lend-Lease supplies to Russia unless she made a settlement with Poland. Nor could we push our diplomatic approaches to either side to an extent that would injure our relations with the other side. We made it repeatedly clear that we wanted a strong, free Poland; but we were not going to say at that point that Poland's frontiers should be such and such a line, for to have done so would have sprung a Pandora's box of dozens of other frontier questions. We were already helping both Poland and Russia, through Lend-Lease, to the full extent of our ability, and we were willing to go much further in helping Poland transfer

Polish people from one area to another in furtherance of an agreement with Russia.

Poland was only one of a number of countries that entered into the channel of our policy toward Russia. Our relations with Russia were in one sense similar to our relations with Britain, in that there were few diplomatic moves we took toward other countries that did not have some reference to Russia and require consultation with her. I insisted again and again to the President and to my associates in the State Department that we could not have friendly ties with the Soviet Union unless we consulted her on any point or decision that was even remotely of interest to her.

On the other hand, Russia occasionally took a step without consulting us, and friction inevitably arose. Such a step was her sudden establishment of diplomatic relations with the Italian Government on March 13, 1944, without prior notice to us. This move was a stride further than the relations the British and ourselves had established with the new Italian Government. Public opinion naturally resented such a unilateral action; and, for some days following, Russia came in for a bad press in Britain and the United States.

Diplomatic exchanges between ourselves and the Russians straightened the matter out, but when Soviet Ambassador Gromyko came to me on April 13 to give me a second memorandum from his Government explaining its position, I remarked, in thanking him: "This has presented a relatively small question; but in my opinion the handling of this matter publicly has resulted in one hundred times more harm than good to Russia, both in connection with the international movement of cooperation and with public opinion in the United States. I earnestly hope that in future Russia will undertake to talk such matters out, as each of the three great nations should do, rather than go into the press with premature and unilateral decisions."

For three years the United States Government had tried to help Russia by exerting every possible pressure to induce Finland to withdraw from the war. In 1944, as in the preceding three years, we made the strongest of diplomatic representations to Helsinki, pointing out that it was to Finland's best interests to retire, while she still could, and warning her that the responsibility for her continuing in a state of war with Allies of the United States must be borne solely by the Finnish Government.

Finland's aid to Germany was economic as well as military in that Germany received from Finland nickel, cobalt, molybdenum, timber, newsprint, and other products which she needed. The President sent me on May 22, 1944, a memorandum he had received from Leo Crowley, Administrator of the Foreign Economics Administration, pointing out the desirability of cutting off Finnish ferroalloy supplies to Germany; and he asked me to prepare a reply for his signature.

I sent him a draft reply on May 27 in which we pointed out the long efforts we had made to get Finland out of the war, in order to bring to an end the very substantial military and economic aid she had been giving Germany. Apparently, I said, the only practical way to stop Finnish exports to Germany would be through military measures; and I was sure that Britain and the Soviet Union, which were at war with Finland, had this very much in mind. I added, however, that we were considering the early blacklisting of Finnish firms which traded with Germany, and we hoped this would have some effect. We announced the blacklisting of these firms on June 3.

On June 16 the State Department requested Finnish Minister Hjalmar Procopé and three counselors of his Legation to leave the United States because of propaganda activities they were carrying on inimical to our interests. We nevertheless pointed out that this did not constitute a rupture of diplomatic relations with Finland.

The rupture, however, occurred two weeks later, following a visit of German Foreign Minister Ribbentrop to Helsinki and an announcement by the Finnish Government indicating a complete comradeship in arms between the two countries. After consultation with the President, I sent the Finnish Chargé a note on June 30 breaking off relations.

In this we stated that we were not unaware of the fact that the infiltration of German troops into Finland and of Germans into the councils of the Finnish Government had deprived that Government of liberty of action. Nevertheless we had taken every opportunity, publicly and through diplomatic representations, to warn the Finnish Government of the inevitable consequences of its association with Nazi Germany. These warnings had been ignored, and the partnership was now complete.

"The Government of the United States," we said, "must take into account the fact that at this decisive stage in the combined operations of the military, naval, and air forces of the United States and the other United Nations, the Finnish operations have a direct bearing on the success of the Allied effort."

Finland, however, formed only a minor part of our relations with Russia. We were then giving greater attention to the Balkans as Soviet troops advanced into that trouble spot of Europe.

106: Russia—Conclusions

WHEN THE RUSSIAN ARMY began to push into Rumania in April, 1944, the relationship between the Soviet Union and the Balkans came to the forefront of our diplomacy. What were Russia's political intentions in the Balkans? Would she seek to set up a domain of her own in the Balkans? Would she retire completely after victory? Would she work with the other major Allies in solving Balkan questions?

Soviet Ambassador Gromyko came in on April 1 to hand me a statement from his Government relating to the advance into Rumania. This asserted that the offensive was the beginning of a full reestablishment of the border delineated in 1940 by treaty between the Soviet Union and Rumania. At the same time it promised that the Soviet Union did not aim at acquiring any part of Rumanian territory or at changing Rumania's social regime.

In effect, the statement was a reiteration of the position already announced with regard to territorial aims in eastern and southeastern Europe; namely, that the U.S.S.R. would restore its western boundaries as they had existed on June 22, 1941, when Germany attacked Russia. (This stand had been modified slightly when the Soviet Union proposed to establish the frontier with Poland on the basis of the Curzon Line, which in certain parts was a little to the east of the 1941 frontier.) The statement meant that Russia intended to reincorporate all of Bessarabia and all of Bucovina into the U.S.S.R. Bessarabia had formed part of the Russian Empire from 1812 until the end of the First World War. Bucovina had never formed part of the Russian Empire and was incorporated into the Soviet Union only in 1940, at the time Bessarabia was taken over. Its annexation would give the Soviet Union a common frontier with the eastern tip of Czechoslovakia.

A stir of speculation now arose in the press of many countries as to whether Russia's aim was liberation or acquisition. Suddenly British Ambassador Halifax inquired of me on May 30, 1944, how this Government would feel about an arrangement between the British and Russians whereby Russia would have a controlling influence in Rumania, and Britain a controlling influence in Greece. He said that difficulties had risen between Russia and Britain over the Balkans, especially with regard to Rumania.

He handed me a written communication from his Government asking whether we had any objection to an agreement between Britain and Russia whereby, in the main, Rumanian affairs should be the concern of the Soviet Government and Greek affairs the concern of the United Kingdom. This British-Russian understanding would apply only to war conditions and would not affect the rights and responsibilities which each of the three great Powers would have to exercise at the peace settlement.

The British Foreign Office said that the United Kingdom Government was fully alive to the importance of avoiding even the appearance of carving up the Balkans into spheres of influence. A temporary agreement such as they suggested seemed to them the best chance of amicable cooperation between the Allies in the countries concerned during the military period.

After telling Halifax that I would give this serious consideration, I said point-blank:

"At first blush, in view of the many charges and countercharges now rising—and which will certainly rise in the future—about encroachments first by one Government and then by another on the economic, political, military, or other internal affairs of the Balkans and other European countries, it would be a doubtful course to abandon our broad basic declarations of policy, principles, and practice. If these are departed from in one or two important instances, such as you propose, then neither of the two countries parties to such an act will have any precedent to stand on, or any stable rules by which to be governed and to insist that other Governments be governed."

I concluded by saying that, in my opinion, this fact should be carefully studied by all concerned before any definite departures took place. Halifax said he appreciated this thought.

I was, in fact, flatly opposed to any division of Europe or sections of Europe into spheres of influence. I had argued against this strongly at the Moscow Conference. It seemed to me that any creation of zones of influence would inevitably sow the seeds of future conflict. I felt that zones of influence could not but derogate from the over-all authority of the international security organization which I expected would come into being.

I was not, and am not, a believer in the idea of balance of power or spheres of influence as a means of keeping the peace. During the First World War I had made an intensive study of the system of spheres of influence and balance of power, and I was grounded to the taproots in their iniquitous consequences. The conclusions I then formed in total opposition to this system stayed with me.

On the following day, May 31, Prime Minister Churchill, to whom Halifax's cable reporting my remarks was undoubtedly communicated, sent the President a telegram direct in which he argued strongly for our approval of the proposed agreement. He emphasized that Britain did not wish to cut up the Balkans into areas of influence, that the arrangement would apply only to war conditions, and that there would be no change in the present collaboration between the American and British Governments in formulating and executing the policy of the Allies toward Greece and Rumania.

His telegram contained two additional items of information. One was that it was the British Government which had suggested the agreement to Russian Ambassador Gousev in London. The second was that the Russians had informed the British on May 18 that they were in agreement with the suggestion, but before they could give any final assurances they would like to know whether the United States Government had been consulted, and whether we were in agreement with the arrangement.

The Prime Minister said he hoped the President would feel able to give his blessing to the proposal.

Mr. Roosevelt sent this telegram to me for consideration and for the drafting of a reply.

My associates at the State Department agreed with the original attitude I had taken with Lord Halifax; namely, that we could not lend our support to any such agreement and, in fact, should do what we could to discourage it. While we could understand Britain's natural desire to strengthen herself in the Mediterranean through a position of influence in Greece, and to avoid causes of friction with the Russians in the Balkans, we felt that any such arrangement as that proposed, no matter how temporary it might be made to appear, would inevitably conduce to the establishment of zones of influence against which we had been stoutly fighting, and against which I had spoken out at the Moscow Conference.

While this reply was being prepared in the Department, Halifax handed us on June 8 another message from the Prime Minister—this one addressed to him. Mr. Churchill again said there was no question of spheres of influence being involved. But he added that, although we all had to act together, someone must "play the hand." It seemed reasonable to him that the Russians should deal with the Rumanians and Bulgarians, and that Britain should deal with the Greeks, who were in Britain's theater of operations and were Britain's old allies, for whom she had sacrificed 40,000 men in 1941. The same, he added, was true of Yugoslavia.

Mr. Churchill commented that he had kept the President constantly informed, but that Britain had been playing the hand in Greece and had to be very careful to play it agreeably to the Russians. Events, he remarked, moved very rapidly in the Balkans.

Britain, he said, followed the lead of the United States in South America as far as possible, so long as it was not a question of her beef and mutton, on which naturally she held strong views because of the "little folk."

This telegram was important in that it brought in two countries not hitherto mentioned by the British—Bulgaria to be dealt with by Russia, and Yugoslavia to be dealt with by Britain. It therefore seemed more urgent even than before to oppose the arrangement which would bring one set of countries under Russia and another set under Britain.

The President sent our reply to the Prime Minister on June 10. This recalled my conversation with Halifax on May 30 when I communicated to the Ambassador reasons why this Government was unwilling to give its approval. The President acknowledged in his reply that the Government responsible for military actions in any country—Britain was militarily responsible for Greece, and Russia for Rumania—would inevitably make decisions which military developments necessitated. But we were convinced that the natural tendency for such decisions to extend into the political and economic fields would be strengthened by the agreement proposed by the British. The President stated our opinion that this would surely lead to the persistence of differences between Britain and Russia and to the division of the Balkans into spheres of influence, regardless of Mr. Churchill's statement that the agreement would be limited to military matters.

The President concluded that we should prefer to see consultative machinery set up for the Balkans to resolve misunderstandings and to prevent the development of exclusive zones of influence.

The Prime Minister came back the following day, June 11, with a long, forceful telegram saying that the President's message had given him much concern. Action would be paralyzed, he said, if everybody had to consult everybody else before taking action. Events in the Balkans always outstripped the changing situations. Consequently a committee for consultation such as the President had indicated would merely obstruct action and, in emergencies, would always be overridden by direct interchanges between the President and the Prime Minister, or between Stalin and either of them.

Mr. Churchill advanced two examples in which direct action by himself had resolved situations—the mutiny of Greek troops at Easter, and a prospect of trouble in Egypt. If Britain had had to consult other Powers and a system of triangular or quadrangular cables had got under way, chaos or impotence might have resulted.

In the Greek crisis, he commented, the President's telegrams to him had worked wonders. His agreement with the President had been complete, and the result had been entirely satisfactory. He asked why all this efficient direction should be broken up into a committee of mediocre officials such as were being littered throughout the world. He further asked why he and the President could not keep this in their own hands, considering how they saw eye to eye about so much of it.

The Prime Minister finally suggested that the arrangement he had proposed should have a three months' trial, following which it would be reviewed by the three Powers.

When this telegram arrived, I was resting for a few days at Hershey, Pennsylvania. The President, without consulting me or the State Department, replied the following day accepting the Prime Minister's three months' proposal, but adding that care should be exercised to make it clear that no postwar spheres of influence were being established.

The President did not inform the State Department of this action.

I returned to Washington at this juncture. On the day of my return, June 12, not knowing of the President's telegram to the Prime Minister, we sent the British Embassy a memorandum which the President had previously approved in which we outlined our arguments against the proposed Anglo-Russian agreement. In particular, we said it would be preferable to give attention to proposals to establish adequate machinery for frank consultation regarding the Balkan region and thus direct the policies of the Allied Governments along lines of collaboration rather than independent action. We added that we attached particular importance to this policy at the present time when special efforts were being made for concerted action in laying the foundations of a broader system of general security in which all countries great and small would have their part. An arrangement suggestive of spheres of influence, we concluded, could not but militate against the establishment and effective functioning of such a broader system.

Still not knowing of the President's telegram of June 12 to the Prime

Minister, I sent him a letter on June 17, in which I pointed out that Mr. Churchill openly applied his proposition to the entire Balkan region by mentioning Bulgaria and Yugoslavia, in addition to Rumania and Greece, and that he advanced our position in South America as an analogy.

"Mr. Churchill's further exposition of the British case," I said, "did not overcome our objections or seem to us to warrant any change in our views toward this dangerous proposal."

I also called attention to what I termed an "extremely disturbing aspect of this matter"—namely, that the British had not discussed a proposal of this nature with us until after it had been put up to the Russians and the latter inquired whether we had been consulted.

The British Foreign Office had suggested that the whole proposal arose out of a chance remark by Eden to Ambassador Gousev, whereas Mr. Churchill's frank telegram of May 31 said plainly that Britain had suggested to the Russian Ambassador that Britain and Russia should agree between themselves as to Rumania and Greece. The Prime Minister's telegram, I said, "indicated that this Government would have been faced with a concluded spheres-of-influence agreement between the British and Russians if the latter had simply agreed without raising the question of our position."

I suggested that the President might want to call this to Mr. Churchill's attention, and accordingly I attached the proposed draft of a message from the President to the Prime Minister.

Our Ambassador to Greece, Lincoln MacVeagh, whose Embassy was at Cairo, cabled us on June 26 that his British colleague had informed him that the American Government had agreed to the proposal, with the provision that it should be subject to review after three months. This cable was the first intimation we had of the President's decision on June 12.

I wrote the President a letter, enclosing a copy of Ambassador MacVeagh's telegram, and asking him whether any changes had been made in our position.

The President replied on June 30, simply enclosing paraphrases or extracts of the messages which had been exchanged between himself and Mr. Churchill. These included his message of acceptance of June 12, to which Mr. Churchill had replied two days later expressing his deep gratitude and stating that he had asked Eden to convey the information to Molotov and make clear that the three months' limitation had been agreed to so that there would be no prejudgment of the question of establishing postwar spheres of influence.

Also among the enclosures was the message to Mr. Churchill which we had drafted in the Department and I had sent the President on June 17. He had dispatched this to the Prime Minister on June 22. In it he said that he was a bit worried, and so was the State Department, concerning the Balkans. He said that frankly we were disturbed that the British took the matter up with us only after they had presented it to the Russians and the latter had asked whether we were agreeable to it. He said that in future he hoped matters of this importance could be prevented from developing in this way.

The Prime Minister replied on the following day, June 23, that he could not admit that he had done anything wrong. Three people in different parts of the world, he remarked, could not work together effectively if each had to keep the third informed of any suggestion to either of the others. He cited as an example the President's message about his conversations with Premier Mikolajczyk of Poland, sent to "U. J." without informing Churchill about it.

In Yugoslavia and Greece, the Prime Minister said, he was struggling to bring order out of chaos and concentrating all efforts against the enemy. With regard to those two countries and to Turkey, he stated, he had been keeping the President constantly informed, and he hoped to have the President's confidence and help in the spheres of action in which Britain had been assigned the initiative.

Mr. Roosevelt replied to this on June 26 by saying that it would seem to him that each of them had inadvertently taken independent steps in a direction which they both now agreed was for the time being expedient. He emphasized that it was essential that they should always be in accord on questions bearing on the Allied war effort. He forthwith sent Mr. Churchill a duplicate of the message he had sent Stalin concerning his conversation with Premier Mikolajczyk.

The Soviet Union now made a direct approach to us to learn our views on Greece and Rumania. On July 1 Ambassador Gromyko sent me an *aide-mémoire* in which he outlined the situation to date, beginning with the initial conversation on May 5 between Eden and Ambassador Gousev and the Soviet reply on May 18.

We replied to this on July 15, after the President had approved our draft. We confirmed the fact that this Government had agreed to the arrangement, for a trial period of three months, our assent having been given in consideration of the present war strategy. Except for this overriding consideration, we pointed out, this Government would wish to make known its apprehension lest the proposed agreement might, by the natural tendency of such arrangements, lead to the division in fact of the Balkan region into spheres of influence.

We said it would be unfortunate if any temporary arrangement should be so conceived as to appear to be a departure from the principle adopted by the three Governments at the Moscow Conference definitely rejecting the spheres-of-influence idea. Consequently, this Government hoped that no projected measures would be allowed to prejudice the efforts toward directing the policies of the Allied Governments along lines of collaboration rather than independent action, since any arrangement suggestive of spheres of influence could not but militate against the establishment and effective functioning of a broader system of general security in which all countries would have their part.

We added that we supposed that the three months' trial period would enable the British and Soviet Governments to determine whether such an arrangement was practicable and efficacious as applying to war conditions only, without in any way affecting the rights and responsibilities which each of the three principal Allied nations would have to exercise during the period of the reestablishment of peace, and afterwards, in regard to the whole of Europe.

Finally we assumed that the arrangement would have neither direct nor indirect validity as affecting the interests of this Government, or of other Governments associated with the three principal Allies.

Events fully justified the apprehensions we entertained over this Anglo-Russian arrangement, which duly entered into effect following the President's acquiescence. When Prime Minister Churchill and Foreign Secretary Eden went to Moscow in October, 1944, to see Stalin and Molotov, they extended the arrangement still further, even reducing to percentages the relative degree of influence which Britain and Russia individually should have in specified Balkan countries. Cables from our Embassies in Moscow and Ankara mentioned that Russia would have a 75/25 or 80/20 predominance in Bulgaria, Hungary, and Rumania, while Britain and Russia would share influence in Yugoslavia 50/50. Later the Russians took it for granted that by the agreement of June, 1944, Britain and the United States had assigned them a certain portion of the Balkans including Rumania and Bulgaria, as their sphere of influence. This assumption had its untoward effect at the Yalta Conference in February, 1945.

Had we made such a determined fight against the Anglo-Russian agreement as we had made successfully against the proposed territorial clauses of the Anglo-Russian alliance in May, 1942 (Chapter 85), it is possible that some of our later difficulties in the Balkans might not have arisen.

As autumn, 1944, approached, my associates and I began to wonder whether Marshal Stalin and his Government were commencing to veer away from the policy of cooperation to which they had agreed at the Moscow Conference, and which, with a few exceptions, they had followed since then. We were beginning to get indications that the Russians were about to drive hard bargains in their armistice agreements with Hungary, Bulgaria, and Rumania, which would give them something in the nature of control over those countries. At the same time we had just been forced to take notice of Russia's strong attitude on the voting question in the United Nations Security Council—which will be taken up in Part Eight.

Accordingly I cabled Ambassador Harriman in Moscow on September 18. Mentioning the voting question that had risen at the Dumbarton Oaks Conference, I said that this, along with other recent developments that he had reported, raised most serious doubts with regard to future long-range Soviet policy. I added that I had begun to wonder whether Stalin and the Kremlin had determined to reverse their policy decided upon at Moscow and Tehran and to pursue a contrary course. I therefore asked Harriman's estimate of the present trend of Soviet policy so that we might decide how to meet this possible change in Russian attitude.

I stated to Harriman that I should find particularly helpful his views as to the causes that had brought about this change in Soviet policy toward the United States and hardening of attitude toward Great Britain. I asked whether he felt that Russia's adverse decisions at Dumbarton Oaks could be ascribed to the fact that her two Allies, Britain and the United States, had just met at the Second Quebec Conference, without Russia being present. I concluded by saying that I need not tell him that questions of the highest import to the future peace of the world were involved.

Harriman replied the following day giving a number of instances of Russia's unilateral actions or apparent unwillingness to collaborate with Britain and the United States. He said we had sufficient evidence to foresee that, if a world organization were established requiring agreement of all permanent members for the consideration of any dispute, regardless of whether or not one of them was involved, the Soviet Government would ruthlessly block consideration by the Council of any question that it considered affected its interests. The Soviet Government would also insist that such a matter be settled by the Soviet Union with the other country or countries involved, particularly any disputes with her neighbors.

Harriman stated his conviction that Stalin and his principal advisers placed the highest importance on the association of the Soviet Union in a major way with the three great Powers, but that they expected their political and military strength would enable them to dictate the conditions. There was no doubt, he said, that the Russian people craved peace and had been led to believe that the intimate relationship developed with Britain and the United States during the war would continue after the war and guarantee a lasting peace.

The Ambassador did not believe that Stalin could forgo the material as well as the psychological value of this association without causing grave concern among the Russian people. Nevertheless, there were powerful elements close to Stalin who were unwilling to give up the right of independent action where Russia's interests were affected or to see Russia depend for her security solely on an untried world organization with associates whom they did not fully trust. Stalin, he thought, liked to have two strings to his bow, and it did not appear inconsistent to the Marshal to pursue simultaneously these two methods to obtain security for his country and to promote its national interests as he envisaged them.

In a later telegram, Ambassador Harriman said he did not believe that the Anglo-American meeting at Quebec without Soviet participation had affected the Russian attitude. He said it was difficult to put one's finger on the causes for the change in the Soviet attitude toward the United States and Great Britain. He thought, however, that when the Russians saw victory in sight they began to put into practice the policies they intended to follow in peace.

In general, he said, Stalin and his principal advisers placed the greatest importance and reliance on the newly won relationship with the British and ourselves, and desired above all else to take a leading role in international affairs. But they were fearful of the antagonism of the world against them and were always conscious of the fact that they were a backward country materially and culturally. Hence they were unduly sensitive and suspicious of our motives and actions. Harriman suggested that we should be understanding of their sensitivity, meet them much more than halfway, encourage them and support them wherever we could, and yet oppose them promptly with the greatest of firmness where we saw them going wrong. He said there was no doubt that the overwhelming majority of the Russian people wanted friendship with us, and he felt that the principal men in the Government held the same view.

In October, 1944, we protested, in numerous diplomatic cables to Russia and Britain, over the nature of the armistice terms Russia was arranging with Rumania, Bulgaria (against whom she had just recently declared war), and Hungary. Prime Minister Churchill and Foreign Secretary Eden, who had gone to Moscow, were carrying on negotiations with the Russians concerning these armistices, and we likewise objected to this fact, stating that the armistice terms should be agreed upon through the European Advisory Commission rather than bilaterally between Russia and Britain. We stated our objection to Russia's inclusion of specific reparation sums in the armistice agreements, since we believed that the reparation settlements with all enemy countries should be decided jointly, after discussion and deliberation, by the United States, the United Kingdom, the Soviet Union, and other interested countries rather than unilaterally, and should be treated as parts of one broad problem.

We further expressed our view that the reparations demanded by Russia of Hungary, $400,000,000, were clearly excessive, from the point of view both of Hungarian capacity to pay and of legitimate Russian claims on Hungary. Furthermore, collection by Russia of the amount demanded might make it impossible for other United Nations that had claims against Hungary to obtain reparations.

We likewise stated our objection to the nature and functions of the Allied Control Commissions for the Axis satellites as outlined by the Russians. We felt that the Control Councils should act under instructions of the Soviet High Command only during the military period, which would come to an end with the termination of hostilities against Germany. Between that time and the conclusion of peace with the satellites, we felt that the three Allied Governments should have equal participation in the work of the commissions, and that their representatives should be able to report directly to their respective Governments.

When I left office the question of our future relations with the satellite countries was still under discussion.

In the summer of 1944 we had begun to receive reports that the Soviet authorities were transferring Lend-Lease supplies or similar goods to third countries, particularly Iran, Yugoslavia, Finland, Poland, and Bulgaria. When the American Embassy in Moscow made inquiries, the Vice Commissar for Foreign Trade denied that American equipment or supplies had been transferred by the Red Army to third parties. He admitted that trucks, grains, and other supplies had been turned over to authorities in liberated areas, but explained that such goods generally were of Soviet origin.

We sent the Soviet Government an *aide-mémoire* on July 6 requesting that this Government be consulted prior to transfers of equipment similar to Lend-Lease. The Russians delayed replying to this request, and at the time I left the State Department in November we had not received the assurances we requested.

In many other instances, however, the Soviet Government kept us fully informed of negotiations in which it was engaged. Soviet Ambassador Gromyko paid me a series of visits to hand me the successive notes his Government was sending to the Finnish Government seeking a basis for peace, and also the Finnish replies.

Gromyko came to me on April 13, 1944, to hand me a note informing us that the Japanese Government had approached his Government with an implied offer to bring about peace between Germany and Russia. Gromyko's note stated that his Government had replied in the negative.

In one of his last visits to me, on September 23, 1944, Gromyko brought me a further note along the same line. The Russians informed us that the Japanese Government had proposed to send a special mission to Moscow to discuss Soviet-Japanese relations. The Soviet Government, believing that the mission had as its aim not so much the relations between Japan and the U.S.S.R. as the possibility of concluding a separate peace between Germany and Russia, had rejected the Japanese proposal.

Our diplomatic exchanges with Russia on postwar subjects leading up to the Dumbarton Oaks Conference were friendly, with the exception of our failure to agree on the inclusion of China in the first phase of the conversations. Some differences of opinion—several of them acute—naturally rose between us during that conference, but in general we were seeing eye to eye.

Patience was the keynote of my attitude toward Russia, but it was a patience fortified and surrounded by principles we were determined to uphold, and activated by a constant effort to understand the Russians and induce them to try to understand us. On several occasions during 1944, when I had basic conversations with Soviet Ambassador Gromyko, I sought to clarify this attitude.

When I saw him on March 19, I said I had remarked to Molotov a number of times that our two peoples differed in many ways in their customs, habits, and psychology. "It will take time," I said, "for them to become really acquainted with each other in all these respects to enable them to function more harmoniously in the part each must play in helping carry forward the organized movement of international cooperation."

Small or temporary mistakes, I added, would often be made by both Governments, and by Great Britain. But we should be patient with each other, and in a friendly spirit discuss and work out amicable solutions of these small incidents.

"Soviet Russia," I said, "has been considerably injured by some small occurrences that have been magnified out of all proportion by persons either unfriendly to this Government or unfriendly to Russia, or by some who were precipitant in concluding that a small incident appeared to determine the whole future course of world cooperation."

When Gromyko mentioned Russia's unilateral establishment of diplomatic relations with the Italian Government under Marshal Badoglio, without prior consultation with us and Britain, and said he would send me a statement on this question the following day, I remarked that this was a case illustrating what I had just said. "It is these small matters involving a combustible psychology," I commented, "which enable trouble-makers and sinister influences to expand them like balloons and create a surprising amount of coolness toward Russia among people here and in Europe."

I therefore proposed that Russia should reiterate fairly often her interest in the Four-Nation Declaration of the Moscow Conference and in carrying forward her full participation in the movement of international cooperation. This, I concluded, would help to clear the air and protect both the United States and the Russian Governments from excessive criticism over minor matters.

Gromyko said he agreed with this and would communicate it to Molotov.

Ten days later he came back to me and said that Molotov had agreed that this would be a fine and timely thing to do, but had suggested that, instead of Russia making the statement herself, she should join with the United States and Great Britain in a joint statement reiterating their interest in and support of the Four-Nation Declaration.

We took this under advisement. Actions took the place of words in succeeding weeks in that we began preparing for the Dumbarton Oaks Conference to carry out the agreement we had reached in the Four-Nation Declaration to assist in creating an international organization to maintain the peace.

During 1944 I held a number of off-the-record conferences with members of the House and Senate and with groups of editors and clergymen, in which Russia was naturally a prominent subject of comment and questioning. In general, my remarks pursued the following theme, which I give here because it expressed my thoughts as to Russia at the moment I left office:

In the summer of 1943 it became increasingly necessary to ascertain Russia's views on some most important international questions: Would she make a separate peace with Germany? Would she drive the enemy to Russian borders and stop, leaving the Allies to finish the job? What was her attitude toward Japan? Would she cooperate with China? Would she abandon isolationism and cooperate internationally?

On these questions Russia was like a "closed book," "a complete sphinx."

At the beginning of the Moscow Conference Russia was interested only in discussing measures for shortening the war—that is, a second front in the west. But the time had come when the three powerful nations had to indicate what they would do in the future.

Russia held a deciding vote on whether the world would take the road to destruction or the road toward security and human welfare. Although the three most powerful nations might not be able to settle all major international questions if they acted together, no one or two of them, acting alone, could hope to resolve these fundamental problems.

In the end, Russia did put her name to the Four-Nation Declaration.

Some time after the Moscow Conference, difficulties appeared. Russian habits, customs, and manners are as inexplicable to us as ours are to them. It takes time to get acquainted.

We must remember that the Russians were locked up and isolated for a quarter of a century. During that time, whenever they heard somebody on the outside say something about Russia, it was generally a violent epithet. They became very seclusive and more suspicious than usual, and vituperative in return. They got into the habit of slashing back at anybody who attacked them, and sometimes much more savagely than the offense justified. Such sudden, sporadic acts and utterances became part of the Russian custom.

Nevertheless, I believe that the Russians are peacefully inclined people. I believe also that the attitude of the Soviet Government on religion is softening. We must not forget that the Russians have many qualities similar to our own. I believe that in a reasonable time they will work together with other nations in the projected international organization, but that it will take time for them to get into step internationally.

We must not let Russian unilateral action—for example, her recognition of Badoglio without previously consulting Britain and the United States—be magnified out of proportion to its importance. Narrow-minded people may continue to irritate Russia to a point where she will draw back into extreme isolationism and nationalism. Then we should have to arm to the teeth.

We must be patient and forbearing. We cannot settle questions with Russia by threats. We must use friendly methods. We are constantly conferring with the Russians in a friendly way.

When I was a boy I had to handle a number of mules in plowing on my father's farm in Tennessee. One of them could outkick any three mules. When he did I would lay my whip on him. That just gave him fuel, and he would kick all the more. I therefore had to give up and let him cool off. Then I would start quietly moving forward in the plow, whereupon he agreed to work. But whenever he kicked and I fought him with the whip he kicked all the more.

We must ever remember that by the Russians' heroic struggle against the Germans they probably saved the Allies from a negotiated peace with Germany. Such a peace would have humiliated the Allies and would have left the world open to another Thirty Years War.

As I left office, the policy I advocated toward Russia rested on two bases. The first was: Continue in constant, friendly discussion with the Russians. Consult them at every point. Engage in no "cussin' matches" with them. Explain to them, again and again if necessary, the principles upon which we felt peaceful international relations would prosper. Show them as clearly as possible the superior advantages to Russia of wholehearted cooperation with other nations as compared with the minor advantages of predominance in neighboring states. Make it clear to them that we did not object to a nation's preaching the merits of its form of government, whether Communism or Democracy, but that we did object to a nation's interfering in the internal affairs of other nations.

On many occasions I had made our policy on nonintervention clear to Russian representatives—including Molotov and the four Ambassadors who represented Russia to the United States during my tenure of office—right from the time of our establishment of diplomatic relations in 1933. I had said that if Russia after the war adopted a policy of relying for security on interfering with her neighbors she would not have a friend on earth. I reemphasized again and again the significance of the Four-Nation Declaration, which precluded policies of intervention. This stated specifically that the four nations would not employ their troops in other countries except for the purpose of carrying out the objectives of the Declaration.

I strongly stated to the Russians our policy toward the liberated areas, as I had presented it at the First Quebec Conference. This was that, as our Allied Governments liberated territory from the enemy, we would keep military supervision during the continuance of the war, and we would preach democracy to the people. When it became possible for the people to assume control of their Government we would authorize them to hold an election to choose their own form of government.

I repeatedly made clear to the Russians the nature of our policies in the Pan American field, where we had given up the thought of intervention, and where our little neighbors like Haiti and Salvador enjoyed parity, equality, and security with the larger countries. It was my plan, with regard to the Russians, to stand definitely on this policy of noninterference, and to show them that there was nothing more absurd than the pretension of any nation to a right to prowl about over the world and stick its nose into the affairs of other nations. I hoped, if my health permitted me to remain in office, to persuade Russia to adopt the policy of cooperation and nonintervention that prevailed in the Western Hemisphere, and to make this a solid world policy to which all nations subscribed. Under this Pan American policy transplanted to Europe, Russia could have the friendliest political relations and the liveliest economic exchanges with her neighbors while refraining from interference in their internal affairs.

The second premise of our policy toward Russia was: By our own actions give Russia a concrete example of how we thought she should act. Therefore I opposed the view of our Joint Chiefs of Staff that the Pacific islands we would take from Japan should become United States property. I felt strongly that there should be no exception to my view that all the colonial territories wrested from the Axis should be placed under a United Nations trusteeship system. It was not hard to see that Russia would not oppose our outright acquisition of these islands, but it also was not hard to see that Russia would thereupon use this acquisition as an example and precedent for similar acquisitions by herself. Our acquisition of these islands estopped us from objecting to similar acquisitions by other nations.

Therefore I likewise opposed the project later put through in the Act of Chapultepec at the Mexico City Conference in March, 1945, after my resignation, whereby the American Republics agreed in effect to intervene militarily in any one of them in certain circumstances. Once we had agreed to this new position on intervention, Russia had more excuse to intervene in neighboring states, and we had less reason to oppose her doing so.

President Roosevelt and I saw alike with regard to Russia. We both realized that the path of our relations would not be a carpet of flowers, but we also felt we could work with Russia. There was no difference of opinion between us that I can recall on the basic premise that we must and could get along with the Soviet Government.

The President did not confer with me regarding any phase of his Yalta Conference with Stalin and Churchill, nor did I know of the concessions made there to Russia until they were published. Yalta was the only international conference attended by Mr. Roosevelt when I was not in office. My views relating to the questions arising among the major nations were fully set forth in the State Department record of conferences and conversations. As I left office I was still opposed to any change in the vote to be given Russia, any more than the vote for our own country. My view was that each major country possessed such powerful prestige and influence generally that it would have little difficulty in securing a full representation of its rights and interests at all times, without any need to have more than one vote.

On the occasions when the President came to see me at the hospital after my resignation, including his last visit only a few days before his death, he said nothing about any fears he might have that Russia would abandon our cooperative movement for peace or would block or destroy it.

It might be said that the President and I were taken in by Russia's promises and written pledges, that we should have realized it was impossible to do business with Soviet Russia, that we should have come to the conclusion that the democratic United States could not be friendly with a Government founded on Communism, and consequently that we should have adopted the policy of the mailed fist toward Russia right from the beginning.

But as we went back over our relations with Moscow I felt, and President Roosevelt did too, that there was ample reason for the policy of friendship that we adopted. Since 1917 Russia had been wrestling with many nations that had refused to recognize her, more or less on account of her policy of conducting subversive activities from Moscow. By constant effort, she had gradually increased the number of recognitions—being obliged in connection with virtually all acts of recognition to agree not to practice subversive activities against the countries establishing relations wth her.

That she did not abandon these activities completely is a matter of record; but it was our view that the other governments, by steadily organizing and building up and strengthening world opinion against such activities, would make as nearly certain as possible Russia's abandonment of interference in the affairs of other countries. It is of record that the President and I had been hammer and tongs at the Russian Government many times during the years from the recognition in 1933 until we approached the Moscow Conference in 1943. I never lost an occasion to point out to the Russians the advantage to themselves of abandoning their thorny policy of intervention.

Before I went to Moscow I naturally looked backward and scrutinized to the utmost possible extent the Soviets' course, attitude, and utterances, together with their implications. This survey of the preceding years revealed Russia as having sought and secured admission to the League of Nations, and as having established herself as a reasonable and working factor at Geneva in promoting peace and suitable international relations for an improved state of affairs among the different peoples and nations of the world. There also stood out the fact that the Soviet Government and other leading governments raised no question about the inability of nations with basic differences in their forms of government to function in the League. All other governments proceeded to function along with a Russia that was apparently making conspicuous peace efforts during the years from her admission to the League in 1934 until her expulsion in 1939 following her invasion of Finland.

It was in the light of these facts and conditions that I proceeded in my conversations with the Russians to revive talk of a postwar peace organization. It seemed to me that, if Soviet Russia could function in the League of Nations, she could also function in the new international security organization which we hoped to create. But even as I sought to bring Russia into that organization, I made every effort to keep the situation entirely clear by pointing out to the Russians that international cooperation would necessitate the abandonment of interference in the internal affairs of other nations. The Russians, in turn, gave me their solemn assurances that they had abandoned this practice.

During the later years prior to the Moscow Conference in 1943 I began to emphasize my belief that, on account of the great difference in customs and habits and the entire lack of understanding between countries like my own and Russia, much time, patience, and education would be required for developing the trust and friendliness necessary to make effective a world organization, which would be based especially on the more powerful nations such as the United States, Russia, Great Britain, and China. When I returned from Moscow I continued to keep the American people reminded of the absolute necessity for such patience, education, and understanding.

When it was agreed among the four big nations to call a conference at Dumbarton Oaks, the favorable and cooperative attitude of each of them, including Russia, was encouraging. It was not until the meeting at Dumbarton Oaks, when the deadlock rose between us and the Russians over the voting procedure in the council and when the Russians confidentially made known to us that they desired sixteen votes in the organization, representing as many Soviet Republics, that any question developed in the minds of the President and myself about Russia's failing to go forward as a cooperative and working member of the proposed United Nations organization. Nevertheless, Russia had agreed on virtually all other important points with us, and it should be made clear that our difference was not over the veto as such, to which the United States was as much committed as Russia, but over the question whether a member of the Security Council concerned with a dispute should be permitted to vote in a balloting on the dispute.

My associates and I further reminded the American people, along with the representatives of other countries, that our own Constitution and the other great documents of liberty or those relating to more effective cooperation among nations had always been more or less imperfect or inadequate at the beginning. We were convinced that we had prepared the first draft of the postwar peace organization on a basis as broad and comprehensive as we could possibly prevail on all the nations to subscribe to. We depended on additions, amendments, and further developments, as time went on, to perfect it.

The President and I were convinced that it was eminently to the self-interest of Russia to be a full-fledged member of the United Nations security organization and to cooperate wholeheartedly with it, and that the Russian leaders would recognize this fact. We believed, as I believe today, that the United Nations would ultimately evolve into a unified, effective organization thoroughly adequate to maintain the peace. We recognized that there would be difficulties, that some of these would come from Russia, and that the United Nations would have to pass through uncertain, delicate periods; but we were certain by the end of 1944 that we and the nations working with us had laid the basis for a projected organization within which Russia and the United States could work together.

In our relations with Russia, the President and I also had constantly before us the emphatic advice of our military leaders, given on several occasions, that friendship with Russia after the war was vitally essential from their military point of view. On one occasion, May 16, 1944, the Joint Chiefs of Staff sent me a memorandum, replying to my request for their views on British informal proposals for the disposition of Italian overseas territory, in which they pointed out that such proposals might lead to conflict between Britain and Russia. They then said: "From the point of view of national and world-wide security, our basic national policy in postwar settlements of this kind should seek to maintain the solidarity of the three great powers and in all other respects to establish conditions calculated to assure a long period of peace, during which, it may be hoped, arrangements will be perfected for the prevention of future world conflicts. The cardinal importance of this national policy is emphasized by a consideration of fundamental and revolutionary changes in relative national military strengths that are being brought about in Europe as a result of the war."

During the Dumbarton Oaks Conference our military advisers held strongly to the same view, and were willing to go farther than many of the political advisers in agreeing to Russia's position that the veto should be applied without exception.

When I left office in November, 1944, we had had a promise from Stalin that Russia would enter the war against Japan as soon as the war against Germany ended. We had given him no promises of territory and made him no concessions in return. We had agreed to no Russian acquisition of territory by reason of the war. We had unfortunately agreed, through the President and over the opposition of the State Department, to a temporary delineation of military spheres of influence in the Balkans between Russia and Britain, proposed by the latter. We had induced Russia to cooperate in the future development and administration of the world security organization. We had rejected the Russians' claim, made at Dumbarton Oaks, to more than one vote in that organization. The Soviet Government had dissolved the Communist International encharged with the promotion of Communism in other countries.

As 1944 approached its close, it was easily apparent that many difficulties would inevitably rise between Russia and ourselves in the future. But it was also apparent that, with good will and understanding on both sides, and with the support of other nations, these difficulties could be solved and an era of fruitful working together come to pass.

107: Working with Britain

AS I COME TO WRITE a final chapter on our relations with Britain during my tenure as Secretary of State, and as I look back over those relations, I am struck by the fact that there was scarcely any point of our contact with the outside world at which we were not talking and working along with the British. Whether we were dealing with Spain or Russia, the Far East, the Middle East, or Latin America, Britain almost always entered into the ken of our negotiations and conclusions.

This was true before the outbreak of war in Europe; it intensified after the historic date of September 1, 1939; and it rose to its climax after Pearl Harbor.

I have devoted fewer chapters to our direct relations with Britain than to our relations with several other countries for the simple reason that Britain appears prominently in all those chapters. We were in constant discussion with the British, but the major portion of our discussions related to other countries.

From Pearl Harbor until my resignation, our policy toward Britain embraced three objectives. First, to arrive at the maximum cooperation in the prosecution of the war. Second, to work closely with the United Kingdom, the Soviet Union, China, and other countries toward creating institutions to deal with problems arising from the war and problems that would face us after the war. Third, to solve specific Anglo-American postwar problems by direct negotiation before the end of hostilities.

On the military side, the efforts of the two countries were integrated to a degree probably never previously reached by any two great allies in history. This was owing in large measure to the operation of the Combined Chiefs of Staff, the unified commands, and the combined boards for the allocation and distribution of munitions, certain strategic materials, and shipping. It was also owing to the close personal relations and frequent, friendly contact between President Roosevelt and Prime Minister Churchill. There were at times basic differences of opinion, as, for example, the President's desire to invade northern France and Churchill's to invade the Balkans; but they were ironed out with good will.

On the diplomatic side, it is probably true that never before in history have two great powers tried to coordinate so closely their policies toward all other countries. In this effort toward a virtual unification of

our foreign policies, so as to present a common front to encourage our
Allies and dishearten the enemy, it was inevitable that we should have
to solve problems of unprecedented magnitude. We did not always succeed to the degree we both should have liked, but it is a fact that we
reconciled to an astonishing extent our diverging interests, some of which
were based on geographic and national grounds.

Relations with Britain during the war period meant, to a considerable
degree, relations with Winston Churchill. In my opinion Mr. Churchill,
while a strong Conservative or Tory, showed great vision and sound statesmanship on many critical occasions. I had heard him crying out for armaments almost alone while Hitler was strenuously rearming Germany. I had
heard him inveigh against isolation after the disarmament movement
failed in the years 1934 and 1935. He had been in the forefront of every
movement to warn and arouse the people of Great Britain to the dangers
ahead from Germany.

After the war came and after he became Prime Minister, he promptly
went forward with every kind of leadership called for. When the supreme
crisis arrived during the Dunkirk period, involving life or death to Britain,
Churchill's was the one single voice that could be heard above the din
at home and abroad, instilling into every man, woman, and child in Britain a determination to resist German invasion to the last breath.

After Pearl Harbor I naturally saw Mr. Churchill many times in
connection with developments of joint or individual interest to our respective countries. He seemed to me to be one of the most approachable
of men, entirely agreeable in conversation even when we were discussing
points at acute issue between us. He could use the harshest language, but
in a tone and manner that disarmed any umbrage that might otherwise
be taken.

In a large sense he was the modern British Tory at his best. Nevertheless, in reviewing modern British statesmen, I found myself in the
opposite camp embracing the views of the Gladstone Liberals.

Numerous important points of difference rose between us—Mr.
Churchill on the one hand and the President and me on the other; for in
all these clashes of ideas with the Prime Minister, except the question
of spheres of influence in the Balkans, the President and I thought alike.
We differed with the Prime Minister over De Gaulle and the future of
France; over the extent of pressure to be brought upon European neutrals
to prevent their assisting Germany; over Italy and the Italian King; over

the treatment of dependent peoples; over India; and over the continuance of imperial tariff preferences.

The President and I considered social welfare to be a general policy. Wherever a situation presented itself for practicing sane and practical liberalism in our foreign relations we sought to apply it as conditions called for it. Mr. Churchill's conservatism, on the other hand, seemed to constitute a sort of cleavage between us.

I was in constant contact with Mr. Churchill's thought by reason of the fact that the President was, in general, accustomed to sending me the telegrams and messages he received from the Prime Minister on subjects involving foreign relations rather than military affairs. He asked me to prepare and recommend to him suitable replies, or to reply direct for him. This he did at almost all times in the case of messages to him from the chiefs of other governments as well, or when he wished to originate a message to a foreign statesman.

With Foreign Secretary Eden my relations were in general most satisfactory. He possessed an agreeable personality and a high order of intelligence. He was always on the alert when any matter pertaining to Great Britain or peace was involved. In a few instances, as in the case of De Gaulle, we had more opposition from him than from Mr. Churchill; but we could usually count on his understanding, and at the Moscow Conference I found him thoroughly cooperative and broad-minded. I considered Eden a person of unusual promise in the political field, barring the changes of fortune implicit in politics.

In all the differences with Britain our policy was based primarily on our desire that the war should be prosecuted in the most effective way possible, that the peoples of the countries occupied by Germany should have the full right, when liberated, freely to choose their own form of government and their leaders, and that the future peace should not be endangered by the development of rival spheres of influence in Europe.

Britain's policy, while motivated to a great degree by these same considerations, also took into account her greater preoccupation with her future political and commercial relations with the western European countries, her strategic and political position in the Mediterranean, and her wish to restore her prestige and reduced power relative to the Soviet Union and the United States.

Despite these diverging viewpoints, we were nevertheless able to achieve substantial coordination.

We differed with Britain over policy toward Argentina during my last two years in the State Department. Britain's dependence on Argentine meat and her desire to maintain her influence and commercial ties with Argentina made her reluctant to recognize as fully as we thought necessary the prime interest we and the other American Republics had in preventing the growth of Nazi ideology and methods in this hemisphere. Even in this sphere, however, Britain went along with us to a degree, though not nearly so far as the President and I felt the situation called for.

In another area of the Western Hemisphere, the Caribbean, we achieved a high and fruitful degree of cooperation with the British through the Anglo-American Caribbean Commission of which Charles W. Taussig was the United States co-chairman.

In the Far East Britain cooperated with us militarily to the full extent that she could spare her forces from the battle for Europe; and in that area we received wholehearted and valuable assistance from her Dominions, Australia and New Zealand. The British Government permitted us to occupy needed bases in British islands such as the Fijis. Prior to the outbreak of the European War, when transoceanic aviation increased the importance of Pacific islands, we asserted our claim to a number of such islands, and Britain vigorously contested some of these claims. We continued to press our position until the fall of France, but we then, at Britain's request, set the entire subject aside without prejudice until after the war, while agreeing with Britain on the joint use of some of the islands.

We declined to permit American Civil Affairs officers to serve under Lord Mountbatten in the Southeast Asia Command, because we wished to dissociate ourselves from British colonial policy as much as we could.

With regard to China, we were more determined than Britain in striving to treat that country as a great nation, bring her into the councils and agreements of the big three Western nations, and persuade Russia to adopt the same policy; but at moments of decision the British gave us valuable support.

In the Near East, to which the British for many generations have paid special attention, we had excellent cooperation with Great Britain on questions directly related to the war. Nevertheless, we had to take account of a somewhat contradictory attitude on the part of Britain in that she did not wish us to seek a predominant postwar position in any part of that area, while, on the other hand, she did not want us to lose interest there entirely.

We received the closest possible cooperation from Britain in working out the bases for international institutions to handle problems arising out of the war and the peace, including the United Nations organization. We at the State Department were careful, however, to work with the Governments of the United Kingdom, the Soviet Union, and China rather than separately with any one of them. All the ideas we developed and all the moves we took with regard to the United Nations were meticulously coordinated with these three Governments, rather than with the British alone. This was my approach during the preparations for the Moscow Conference and at the conference itself, and similarly in preparations for the Dumbarton Oaks Conference and at the conference itself.

In addition to these general discussions for postwar institutions, scarcely a week passed during my last years in office that we were not talking with the British toward laying a broad basis for continuing sound and friendly Anglo-American relations after the war. We engaged in technical conversations on such subjects as petroleum, double taxation, rubber, and commercial policy. The operation of the Lend-Lease policy, which Winston Churchill called "the most unsordid act in history," even though it too had its difficulties, brought our economic relations with Britain as close as they had ever been in our history.

But commercial policy was one of our most delicate meeting grounds with the British. After long negotiation we had induced the British to sign the Lend-Lease Agreement of 1942, of which Article VII pledged them in effect to give up preferential arrangements in the British Empire after the end of the war. Thereafter, however, it frequently became apparent to me that Prime Minister Churchill, despite this pledge, was determined to hold on to imperial preference.

I brought this subject up with Ambassador Halifax on May 4, 1944, when I complimented him on a speech he had recently made. "As I view it," I said, "your speech was quite in contrast with recent utterances of Mr. Churchill which give the impression that he favors the preservation intact of Empire preferences, while at the same time preaching closer relations among the three large Western nations and advocating a tightening up of the British Commonwealth. All of this, taken together, has discouraged many people in this country and many small nations which are growing more fearful that the three large nations in the West will come closer and closer together and practice the worst forms of imperialism, while neglecting the small nations."

I added that I was merely stating a situation which it seemed to me Mr. Churchill was overlooking. I repeated what we had done to keep alive our formula relating to future international commercial policy and economic cooperation and added that, unless we could have more cooperation now from the British, the future would become dangerous. I said that the President and I had made a fight in this country for more liberal commercial policy against overwhelming odds and that if we had faltered, as Mr. Churchill seemed to be faltering, we should have gotten exactly nowhere.

Richard Law, British Parliamentary Under Secretary of State for Foreign Affairs, came to me on July 20, 1944, to make a special request that further discussions of commercial policy based on Article VII of our Lend-Lease Agreement of 1942 be postponed until the autumn because of British economic difficulties and preoccupation with the war.

I said I could appreciate the situation of his Government and country, but I stressed the indispensable necessity for a broader and more liberal commercial policy after the war if we were to increase and broaden production and consumption. I emphasized that this course would require Herculean efforts such as Britain had put forth during the years following the British-French commercial treaty in the 1860's.

"Unless the business people in our two countries," I said, "recognize that we have to turn over a new page in economic affairs and go forward as resolutely as Britain did at that time, there will simply be no foundation for any stable peace structure in the future. On the contrary, there will be the inevitable seeds of future wars in the form of vast unemployment and hunger throughout the world."

I added that if we postponed such a tremendous undertaking, many of its supporters would take entirely too much for granted and would become inactive—which would be fatal. I suggested that Britain should now start a real revival and awakening in support of the long-view program of liberal commercial policy. The British Government and the majority of the British people, I said, might be submerged by high-pressure selfish or prejudiced minorities unless that Government organized and fought for such a program as we had fought for here through the trade agreements to make the first serious inroads on international economic isolation.

We had definite ideas with respect to the future of the British colonial empire, on which we differed with the British. It might be said that the future of that Empire was no business of ours; but we felt that unless dependent peoples were assisted toward ultimate self-government and were given it when, as we said, they were "worthy of it and ready for it," they would provide kernels of conflict.

Both the United States and Great Britain became committed, in the course of our conversations, to the progressive development of dependent peoples toward self-government, including their political, economic, social, and educational advancement. We both recognized, moreover, that other countries than the parent or administering country might have political, economic, or strategic interests in certain dependent areas, and that the economic development of such areas should be in the interests of the world as a whole.

The American Government advocated the eventual self-government of all colonial peoples. Both the President and I repeatedly said we considered the Atlantic Charter applicable to all such peoples throughout the world. The British Government, on the other hand, made it clear that self-government in British colonial areas should be achieved within the British Commonwealth. Prime Minister Churchill repeatedly maintained that Point Three of the Atlantic Charter (the right of self-determination) applied only to the occupied countries of Europe.

In my conversation with Richard Law on July 20 I remarked—in no spirit of criticism but in illustration of what I thought was a drifting policy in Great Britain—that for some time we had seen the two opposite extremes of thought in Britain badgering each other about dependent peoples. The leftists would go their own distance and take charge of colonies and supervise the treatment of their populations by the parent governments. On the other hand, Prime Minister Churchill merely stood on the policy that the British Empire, including India, would not be dismembered while he was in office.

"If all nations having special relations with backward peoples," I said, "would proceed simultaneously with an awakening and a general forward movement to give them more opportunities, more facilities, more encouragement, and any other feasible material cooperation to help all dependent peoples make greatly increased efforts to improve their levels of existence, this would be a wonderful thing in the end for all. It would increase production, employment, and purchasing power for surplus-producing countries. The United States' policy toward the Philippines is a case in point."

I concluded by saying it would be very hazardous to wait until the war was over, when political chaos set in and emotions got out of control, to undertake this great task and that of establishing liberal economic relationships.

In summation, our policy toward the United Kingdom had this primary objective, to work out the closest possible coordination of the material and political strength of the two countries so as to secure and maintain a just and lasting peace. Militarily, this meant the integration of strategy, forces, and resources. Economically, it meant the joint stimulation of the maximum flow of international trade, transportation, and communications. Politically, it meant the maintenance of friendly relations between us and also the coordination, wherever possible, of our policies toward all other countries.

As I have pointed out throughout these memoirs, we had numerous problems and difficulties with the British in my nearly twelve years as Secretary of State. But, had we not approached each other in the spirit of friendship sustained at a high level during all those years, our differences would have magnified in number and size. Napoleon said, in effect, "Give me a coalition to fight," because he knew how fragile such temporary alliances had proven. But the coalition of which the United States and Great Britain were a part proved it could not only stick together for the duration of a victorious war but also plan for the future.

In my efforts toward this end I was fully aided by the spirit of understanding and friendship unfailingly demonstrated by British Foreign Secretary Anthony Eden and by British Ambassadors Lothian and Halifax as well as by the efforts of Ambassador Winant in London. Both countries, too, were immeasurably aided by the British Dominions, in particular Canada, who had a fundamental interest in seeing that the two major English-speaking nations moved forward in the same way toward the same goal.

Throughout my twelve years at the State Department no sector of our foreign policy gave me more satisfaction or brought more fruitful results than our relations with Canada. In 1933 cooperation between the two countries had sagged to a low point; the depression, the Smoot-Hawley Tariff Act, and the Ottawa agreements had slashed their trade; and there was no adequate expression of the natural identity of the two countries, especially in the strategic and economic spheres. As I left office, we had built a solid economic relationship through two trade agreements and a truly wonderful industrial cooperation during the war; we had assured the strategic interdependence of the two countries through the establishment of the Permanent Joint Board of Defense; and our relations in general had increased in extent and importance. They offered to the world the highest example of nations, bordering on each other and cherishing the same free institutions, working together for their mutual advantage.

The masterly leadership and sincere friendship of Canada's true statesman, Prime Minister Mackenzie King, contributed enormously to revitalizing the relations between the two countries. Canada is one of the few countries that have practiced in a model way the rules governing the right living together of nations.

As I left office Canada flourished as an independent entity, fourth in industrial and military power among the United Nations, enjoying representation on an equal basis with the United States and the United Kingdom on certain of the key war boards and international agencies. We willingly agreed to the "functional policy" stated by Prime Minister Mackenzie King providing that small nations should be represented along with the great powers in those fields in which they could make a major contribution. In November, 1943, we recognized Canada's heightened stature by increasing the rank of our representative Ray Atherton from Minister to Ambassador, while thoroughly capable Minister Leighton McCarthy became Canada's Ambassador to the United States.

Before I left office we had already begun to take up problems of postwar reconversion, such as the orderly disposition of defense projects in Canada, and the removal of wartime barriers such as our visa requirements for Canadian visitors, Canadian labor exit and foreign exchange controls, and Canadian and American export and import controls. We appreciated the fact that the unique relationship between the two countries stemmed largely from the traditional free movement of people and ideas across our border, and therefore that the wartime restrictions should not continue into the peace.

Throughout, we had been careful to recognize Canada as a completely sovereign and independent nation, while at the same time taking no position that would affect her special ties with the United Kingdom and the other British Dominions. The question of Canada's becoming a member of the Pan American movement of cooperation was not much discussed or specially urged either by Canada or by the United States, both having in mind the fact that, although Canada is free to make her own decisions, she gets in and fights alongside the British when the United Kingdom becomes involved in war. This did not prevent virtually the same close-in relations and cooperation to every practical extent in the Western Hemisphere as would have occurred had Canada been a member of the Pan American system. Further steps should and doubtless will be taken to extend and strengthen these thoroughgoing cooperative relations.

108: Independence for India

WHEN JAPAN STRUCK at Pearl Harbor, the importance of India in the pattern of the war suddenly increased many times. The Japanese soon overran Burma and stood at the borders of the subcontinent. Tension between the Indians and Britain, and tension among the religions and factions in India, offered Japan an opportunity if she were able to use it. India was on the highroad to what I considered the most fateful possibility of the war—a juncture of German and Japanese forces in the Indian Ocean, severing the United Kingdom from the Middle East and the Pacific Dominions. That great peninsula, with a population of 400,000,000, was a source of materials essential to our own defense and our aid to Britain. Working wholeheartedly with the British, it could be of immense assistance in Britain's defense. Working against the British, it could be a frightful danger.

The President and I, both before and after Pearl Harbor, were convinced that the Indians would cooperate better with the British if they were assured of independence, at least after the war. We at the State Department were already working on our proposal for positive steps to raise dependent peoples to political and economic levels where they could begin to govern themselves, after the manner of our policy toward the Philippines. The people of India were among those we had in mind.

Nevertheless, we recognized that any change in India's constitutional status could be brought about only if Great Britain were in agreement, and we realized full well that, with Britain fighting for her life, we should take no step and utter no words that would impede her struggle. We also knew that the British Government, and Prime Minister Churchill in particular, considered India their own problem, and that an attempt by the United States to bring pressure to solve it might give rise to controversy between our two Governments and peoples. It was therefore a delicate question how far we could go in any representations to the British to grant independence, or in any actions that might encourage the Indians to demand it immediately.

At the same time there was a danger that doing nothing would have unfavorable repercussions both on the general war effort and on ourselves. After Pearl Harbor we felt that failure to solve the Indian problem would hamper military operations in the Far East and might later constitute a threat to peace when the war was over. And we also felt that our own position among the Asiatic peoples would be adversely affected by a belief on their part that we were helping Great Britain maintain her imperial policy in the Orient.

With these two viewpoints in mind, we had to keep our discussions with Britain on the subject of Indian independence on as informal a basis as possible. In publicly stating our conviction that subject peoples should be assisted toward self-government and eventual independence, we kept our statements general, without making specific reference to India. But in private conversations the President talked very bluntly about India with Prime Minister Churchill just as I was talking with British Ambassador Halifax. The President was entirely of the same mind as myself. While for the sake of good relations with Britain we could not tell the country what we were saying privately, we were saying everything that the most enthusiastic supporter of India's freedom could have expected, and we were convinced that the American people were with us.

Even before Pearl Harbor we had begun to see the need for more direct ties with India. Following a proposal delivered to me by Halifax on April 18, 1941, that an Indian official with the rank of Minister be attached to the British Embassy, we reached an agreement that a quasi-diplomatic American Mission should be established in New Delhi, and an Indian Agency General in Washington. Previously we had been represented in India by consuls rather than by diplomatic officers. The American mission was set up in October. Halifax presented to me the first Indian Agent General, Sir Girja Shankar Bajpai, on November 25, a fortnight before Pearl Harbor.

In 1941 we held discussions for a treaty of commerce and navigation with the Government of India. Early in 1942, however, the British indicated that they preferred that discussions on the treaty be suspended until after the war; and we accordingly left it in abeyance.

As early as the spring of 1941 I raised the question of Indian independence with Ambassador Halifax, when I saw him on May 7. I simply asked, in a general way, whether the British found it feasible to consider further acts of liberalizing the relations of the United Kingdom to India. Nothing came of this approach.

Ambassador Winant advocated in a cable of August 1 that our Government suggest to the British that they reach an agreement on Dominion status for India. Assistant Secretary Berle and Wallace Murray, Chief of the Near Eastern Division, supported this recommendation, but Under

Secretary Welles, in a memorandum to me on August 6, took the position that our Government was not warranted in suggesting officially to the British Government what the status of India should be, and that, if the President wished to raise the question, he could discuss it in a very personal, confidential way directly with Prime Minister Churchill. I agreed with Welles's view.

A few days later the President and the Prime Minister held their historic meeting on the Atlantic and agreed to the Atlantic Charter, Article 3 of which said: "Third, they respect the right of all peoples to choose the form of government under which they will live; and they wish to see sovereign rights and self-government restored to those who have been forcibly deprived of them."

Mr. Churchill, however, in an address to the House of Commons on September 9, specifically excluded India and Burma from the application of the Atlantic Charter. He said that Article 3 applied only to European nations under Nazi occupation and had no effect on British policy as previously enunciated relative to the development of constitutional government in India, Burma, and other parts of the Empire.

Ambassador Winant had tried to persuade the Prime Minister to eliminate this passage from his speech—without success. Mr. Churchill took the position that this was a question of internal British policy, and that the passage had the support of the Cabinet.

Although neither the President nor I and my associates accepted this interpretation, we had no desire to engage in an altercation with the British. Nevertheless then and in succeeding years we took appropriate occasions to state to the public and to the British Government our position that the Atlantic Charter applied to all peoples alike seeking independence in every part of the world.

In my radio address of July 23, 1942, I had India in mind, among other peoples, when I said:

"We have always believed—and we believe today—that all peoples, without distinction of race, color, or religion, who are prepared and willing to accept the responsibilities of liberty, are entitled to its enjoyment. We have always sought—and we seek today—to encourage and aid all who aspire to freedom to establish their right to it by preparing themselves to assume its obligations. We have striven to meet squarely our own responsibility in this respect—in Cuba, in the Philippines, and wherever else it has devolved upon us. It has been our purpose in the past—and will remain our purpose in the future—to use the full measure of our influence to support attainment of freedom by all peoples who, by their acts, show themselves worthy of it and ready for it."

On August 8, 1942, in connection with an Office of War Information suggestion for an exchange of messages between the President and the Prime Minister on the anniversary of the signing of the Atlantic Charter, British Minister Sir Ronald Campbell wrote me saying that Foreign Secretary Eden hoped that any such messages, if they were to deal with the interpretation of the Charter, would be carefully concerted, and that any reference to India or Burma in the messages or in any public statements by this Government would be consistent with the Prime Minister's statement of September 9, 1941.

While the anniversary message sent by the President to the Prime Minister on August 14, 1942, and published, did not go into the question of interpretation of the Charter, I discussed this point-blank with Ambassador Halifax on August 24. I said to him that, according to my idea of the Charter's proper construction and practical application, it should be universally applied to all nations and peoples—to all peoples, whatsoever their condition, and whatsoever shade of independence and freedom they might aspire to.

Halifax replied that some high officials of his Government were in the act of preparing an interpretation and application of the Atlantic Charter as it would relate to the British Empire.

I commented that, while it was not my business except in a general sense, in my judgment the application of the Charter should be made universal, and the British Empire would probably run into constant difficulties if it should seek to have the Atlantic Charter applied in separate compartments, so to speak.

Some of the hesitation we had in taking up with the British the subject of independence for India vanished after the Japanese attacked at Pearl Harbor and began to overrun the Far East. Prior to that time India could be considered a purely British object of concern. From then on India became an object of concern to us as well, from the viewpoint of winning the war. We were rendered more uneasy by the fact that the political situation in India seemed to be deteriorating.

President Roosevelt discussed India with Prime Minister Churchill during his visit to Washington in December, 1941, but no conclusions were arrived at. The President sent Ambassador Winant in London a telegram on February 25, 1942, saying that the situation in India gave him some concern, particularly in view of the possible necessity of retiring slowly from Burma to India. He said he gathered that the people of India would not give sufficiently enthusiastic support to the British defense. He therefore requested the Ambassador—or W. Averell Harriman, who was then in London on an official mission—to give him a "slant" on what Prime Minister Churchill thought relative to new Anglo-Indian relationships. The President concluded that he was hesitant to send the Prime Minister a direct message because it was not, strictly, our business; but, from the viewpoint of the conduct of the war, it was nevertheless of great interest to us.

Harriman replied on the following day that the Prime Minister told him the picture with regard to India was not yet definite, and that the Prime Minister intended to cable the President himself within a few days. A fortnight later Mr. Churchill announced the mission of Sir Stafford Cripps to India to lay before Indian leaders proposals of the Cabinet looking toward the eventual attainment of self-government. During Cripps's stay in India the President made every possible effort to prevent the negotiations from failing. I thought the British proposals were a far-reaching step in the right direction, but the Indian leaders turned them down. Mr. Roosevelt still sought to keep matters from reaching an open break by persuading Mr. Churchill to delay Cripps's return to Britain; but without success. Colonel Louis Johnson, formerly Assistant Secretary of War, whom the President had appointed his personal representative to India, had arrived in New Delhi during the stay of the Cripps mission, and he also had made earnest efforts to facilitate a satisfactory settlement.

The situation in India worsened instead of improving, and on June 3, 1942, I asked Ambassador Halifax to come to see me and discuss it. I said we had received disquieting news from India that explosive conditions might make their appearance during coming weeks and months. Halifax asked whether, in my opinion, an impartial commission should be sent to India to investigate and report. I said I was not sufficiently informed to discuss this definitely.

To Indian Agent General Bajpai, who came to see me on June 15, I said that Mahatma Gandhi to all intents and purposes was playing into the hands of the Japanese by preaching nonresistance, and that no practical steps of resistance were being advocated by the other leaders, including Nehru. When the Agent General replied that Gandhi's influence was strong only when he went to certain cities and called upon the people to adopt his nonresistance policy, I commented that Gandhi could go within a short time to many populous areas and get deadly results by his preaching.

Ambassador Halifax called again on June 18 to give me the substance of a telegram from the British Secretary of State for India, Leopold S. Amery. This suggested that Halifax might think it desirable to let me, or also the President, know that the British Government would be forced to take "drastic measures" against Mahatma Gandhi and the Indian Congress Party if the civil disobedience movement were launched which Gandhi was apparently contemplating to hasten Britain's withdrawal from India.

I asked Halifax whether he had any further thoughts on the impartial commission he had suggested at our previous meeting. He said Amery's opinion was that a mission of one or more persons sent by an American university to India to investigate and report on India's constitutional future, with suggestions as to a solution, might be beneficial in an educational way to America and might also have some advantageous effect on the Indian situation. He himself, however, did not think such a mission could have any effect on the immediate situation in India.

Chiang Kai-shek had cabled the President, asking our help in an effort to solve the Indian problem. My associates and I assisted in preparing the President's reply, which was given to the Chinese Ambassador on August 13:

"I think," said Mr. Roosevelt, "your position and mine should be to make it clear to the British Government and to Mr. Gandhi and his followers that we have not the moral right to force ourselves upon the British or the Congress Party; but that we should make it clear to both sides that you and I stand in the position of friends who will gladly help if we are called on by both sides.

"At the same time I think we should intimate to both sides that because both of them and China and the United States and all the other United Nations are in a struggle for existence, the assistance of India is vital to the common cause, including the cause of the people of India themselves."

The President remarked that he had delivered the same opinion at a meeting of the Pacific War Council the day before. He cited the thirteen American colonies in 1775 as an example for India, saying: "Each Colony was a separate sovereignty. They set up differing republican forms of government. They had a loose Confederation, but when their independence was acknowledged in 1783 they realized they must have a breathing spell before they could set up a permanent constitutional form of federal government. They, therefore, went through a six-year period of trial and error and discussion. Finally, they adopted a Federal Constitution which is in existence today—one hundred and fifty-three years later."

British Minister Sir Ronald Campbell gave me on August 8 a copy of a message to the President from Clement Attlee, in Mr. Churchill's absence, stating the British Government's intention to arrest Gandhi and certain other Indian leaders if the program for civil disobedience went into effect. This would be done to render the movement abortive by removing and detaining its leaders and to prevent widespread demonstrations and disorders. Mr. Attlee expressed the confidence of his Government that the President would agree that there was no other course open to them either from the viewpoint of the war effort or from that of orderly political advance in India itself.

I inquired of the Minister with some emphasis whether his Government had prepared a succinct statement showing the essential conditions and preparations necessary to enable India to set up the complete structure of an independent Government if independence should be granted at once. This might also show equally clearly the difficulties the Indians would experience in an attempt immediately to establish and carry into successful operation an entirely independent government—if not the impossibility of their doing so.

Sir Ronald seemed very much interested in the point I had raised interrogatively, especially in its psychological aspect in both the Empire and in other parts of the world.

The President on August 13 sent me the Attlee message along with a short memorandum saying: "This came in five days ago from Attlee in the absence of his chief. Frankly, I think it is best not to reply to it. What is your view?"

Answering on August 15, I said: "You and other officials of this Government during past months earnestly laid before Prime Minister Churchill and other British officials the unequivocal attitude of yourself in favor of an adjustment on a basis that could and should be mutually agreed upon in the relations between the home Government of Great Britain and either officials or certain political leaders headed by Mr. Gandhi in India."

Referring also to my conversations with Halifax and the efforts made by Colonel Johnson, I said our attitude had not been one of partisanship toward either contender, and in these circumstances there was scarcely more to add in relation to the Attlee message. I concluded, however, with the following suggestion:

"It would seem that if the British Government would repeat with full emphasis its proposal of independence to India at the end of the war, and accompany it by a statement of the adjustments to be made prior to the announcement of independence, including some reference to the equal interest of India with the twenty-eight nations in resisting the Axis Powers, it would clarify public opinion and might lead to the resumption of discussions between Great Britain and the Indian leaders. In any event, it ought to have the effect of reducing the feeling of tension in India."

We were now preoccupied with an additional development, of direct concern to ourselves. As part of the United States' operations in support of China, American military units, particularly air and supply forces, had been sent to India. Disturbing indications reached us that Congress Party supporters were tending to believe that American forces were in India for the purpose of supporting British rule. A telegram from Lauchlin Currie, special envoy of the President, prompted a memorandum which I sent the President on August 12, after consulting the War Department, with a draft of appropriate instructions to be sent the American forces in India and to be published.

The President having approved the draft of instructions I attached, we made these public on the following day, August 12. We stated that the sole purpose of the American forces in India was to prosecute the war of the United Nations against the Axis Powers, primarily to aid China. American forces were not to indulge to the slightest degree in any other activities unless India should be attacked by the Axis Powers, in which event they would aid in defending India. They were to exercise scrupulous care to avoid the slightest participation in India's internal political problems, or even the appearance of participating. In the event of internal disturbances they were to resort to defensive measures only if their own personal safety or that of other American citizens was threatened or if American military supplies and equipment required protection.

Meantime the President had received an appeal for assistance from Gandhi, to which he asked me to prepare a reply. Our response stated in effect that this Government had consistently striven for and supported policies of fair dealing and fair play and all related principles looking toward the creation of harmonious relations between nations. Nevertheless, now that war had come as a result of Axis dreams of world conquest and enslavement, we, together with many other nations, were making a supreme effort to defeat the enemies of mankind. The letter concluded with the hope that "our common interest in democracy and righteousness will enable your countrymen and mine to make common cause against a common enemy." It attached a copy of my address of July 23.

This letter went forward to our Mission in New Delhi on August 5 for delivery to Gandhi. By the time it arrived, however, Gandhi had been put in jail. We then faced a decision as to whether to ask the British to deliver it to Gandhi, whether to deliver it to the only Congress Party leader not then in prison, who was antagonistic to Gandhi, or to retain it in the Mission's files until it could be delivered to Gandhi directly. I recommended the third choice to the President, who agreed. The letter could not be delivered until two years later.

With the unleashing of the campaign of civil disobedience, and with the arrest of the Indian leaders, India now became a scene of violence and unrest. The President and I were keenly perturbed lest this situation promote Japanese conquest and Chinese discouragement.

I raised the question of India with Ambassador Halifax on September 17, 1942, and asked if there were any prospect of a resumption of conversations between the United Kingdom and the Indian leaders. Halifax replied that this would have to wait until Indian violence and resistance had ceased. I thereupon remarked that during this deadlock there was in prospect in the United States a general movement of agitation against Great Britain and in favor of independence for India which might create complications later on.

Prime Minister Churchill and Mr. Amery, the Secretary of State for India, having made strong speeches concerning India a few days before, I said I was wondering if speeches adequately firm to meet resistance, but at the same time expressing sympathy for India and calling attention to the British policy which gave such former colonies as Canada, Australia, New Zealand, and South Africa the equivalent of independence and to the continuance of this policy looking toward independence for India, might not be preferable to speeches of a blunt nature.

"More moderate and sympathetic speeches," I said, "could make it clear that the British Government desires to resume its course of going forward with its program for Indian independence just as quickly as this movement of violence ceases, and at the same time remove any impression that the British Government is being moved by undue pressure or threats. If the British could reach a point where they could announce that Indian resistance had definitely terminated, and that the British Government was therefore moving back to the resumption of further consideration of its original plans for granting independence to India, and if this step soon could be followed by conferences between even one person representing Great Britain and one person representing India, so as to make it appear that the situation was on the move in the right direction, this, in my judgment, would have a most wholesome psychological effect on the public opinion of other nations and India as well."

The Ambassador did not take issue with my views.

The Indian situation, however, grew more bitter as Gandhi and the other leaders stayed in jail and the passive resistance movement went on.

At that juncture I recommended to the President that he send William Phillips, former Under Secretary of State and Ambassador to Italy, one of our most competent diplomats, to India as his personal representative. (Colonel Johnson had returned to the United States.) The President agreed.

I cabled Phillips, then in London with the Office of Strategic Services, comprehensive instructions on November 20, 1942, which the President had approved. I said that the President and I and the entire Government earnestly favored freedom for all dependent peoples at the earliest date practicable. Our course in dealing with the Philippines offered, I thought, a perfect example of how a nation should treat a colony or a dependency in cooperating with it to make all necessary preparations for freedom. We offered this as a strong example to all other countries and their dependencies.

The President and I had not become partisans of either Great Britain or India, I added, and to do so would seriously handicap us in dealing with the other side. We had sought fellowship freely and in a thoroughly friendly way with both British and Indian peoples, especially their leaders, without making ourselves partisans in our acts and utterances to the extent of generating friction and ill feeling.

Therefore, I went on, we could not bring pressure to bear on the British, but we could in a friendly spirit talk bluntly and earnestly to appropriate British officials so long as they understood that it was our purpose to treat them in a thoroughly friendly way. Objectionable pressure upon either side would probably result not in progress but only in exasperation and, with the British, in a possible disturbance of our unity of command and of cooperation both during and after the war.

I concluded that the settlement of the Indian problem had an added interest for us by reason of its relation to the war. This fact probably gave us an opportunity to speak more freely and earnestly than we otherwise could, so long as we made it clear that we were speaking from a genuine friendship and will to cooperate both during the war and after it.

Shortly after Phillips arrived in New Delhi he found India confronting a dangerous situation. Gandhi, who had been in jail for some months, was apparently on the verge of death as a result of his prolonged fast. It seemed likely that, if Gandhi died in jail, India would explode in a revolution that would require extraordinary efforts to contain it and might invite the Japanese to invade the subcontinent.

Phillips cabled on February 16 asking whether, if he learned that Gandhi's death was imminent, the President and I would approve of his informally approaching the Viceroy of India, Lord Linlithgow, to express the deep concern we felt over the political crisis in India. The following day I cabled Phillips that the President and I concurred in his suggestion, and that he might also, at his discretion, express our hope that a way might be found to avoid the deterioration in the Indian situation which was almost sure to follow the death of Gandhi.

On the day I received Phillip's cable, February 16, I said to Ambassador Halifax that I had a feeling that if Gandhi should die during his fast acute conditions might arise which it would be important to foresee and prepare against. He said his Government was giving this the closest attention.

I then raised with him the question whether the British might find it possible and advisable to consider certain additions to the Cripps proposals made to the Indian leaders. I emphasized this possibility by again expressing my fear of the dangers which might arise from the sudden death of Gandhi.

Four days later, February 20, I saw Halifax again, and this time said that the President desired me to take up the matter of Gandhi's fast and express his view that Gandhi should not be allowed to die in prison.

Halifax said his Government was very desirous that Phillips should avoid any public reference to the Gandhi matter at this time.

I replied that Phillips was in a very difficult and unsatisfactory situation in this connection, and that the Viceroy of India had forbidden him to call on him just then on the ground that it would be exceedingly dangerous to the British-Indian situation. I referred again to Phillips's instructions from the President and myself to the effect that he would not be expected to remain absolutely quiet and nonvocal, and said that the

President now went much further and emphasized his position that the British should not allow Gandhi to die in prison.

"A vital question for the British to consider from their standpoint," I said, "would seem to be whether they cannot deal more effectively with the situation with Gandhi alive than if he were dead and his supporters were claiming martyrdom."

The Ambassador said he would get this message to his Government without delay.

Two days later he brought to Under Secretary Welles, in my temporary absence, a telegram from Prime Minister Churchill asking Halifax to make it clear to me and to his contacts that the British Government would not in any circumstances alter the course it was pursuing about Gandhi. Therefore great embarrassment between the British and American Governments would be created by any American intervention. Mr. Churchill earnestly hoped that Britain's difficulties would not be added to at so critical a moment, and said the Ambassador could be sure there would be no weakness in London. He asked Halifax to lay the whole matter before Harry Hopkins.

Welles communicated the matter to President Roosevelt, who replied that the United States Government would say nothing further now, but that, in the event that Gandhi died, he would have some statement to make. The President also suggested, that, in that event, I make clear the fact that this Government had expressed its concern over the possibility of Gandhi's death and its belief that the difficulties in the Indian situation would be less great if he were alive than if he were permitted to die.

The following month, during the visit of Foreign Secretary Eden to Washington, I pointed out to him on March 22 that we had made a real effort to keep down anti-British sentiment in this country growing out of the situation in India, and that we had done our best to prevent the question from becoming a matter of serious contention.

The President asked Phillips to return to the United States by the end of April or the beginning of May for a month's visit to report to us on the situation in India. Developments in India during Phillips's visit here were such that he did not return to New Delhi; another important post was awaiting him, on the staff of General Eisenhower in London. His appointment as the President's personal representative in India, however, continued in effect.

On April 19, 1943, Phillips sent me a copy of a letter to the President summing up his impressions on the situation in India. He said in his covering letter that the impressions did not make very pleasant reading, but nevertheless he felt he ought to send them to the President and me for whatever they were worth. He said India was in a state of inertia, prostration, divided counsels, and helplessness, with growing distrust and dislike for the British, and disappointment and disillusion with regard to Americans. The British had been completely successful in their policy of "keeping the lid on" and suppressing any movement among the Indians that might be interpreted as being toward independence. British armies dominated the picture; twenty thousand Congress leaders remained in jail without trial.

Phillips said it was hard to discover, either in New Delhi or in other parts of India, any pronounced war spirit against Japan, even on the part of the British. Rather, the British seemed to feel that their responsibility lay on the Indian side of the Burma-Assam frontier. Unless the present atmosphere changed for the better, we Americans should have to bear the burden of the coming campaign in that part of the world and could not count on more than token assistance from the British in British India.

Our inability to influence British policy in India, coupled with the presence of our troops in that area, gradually gave rise toward the end of 1943 to considerable anti-American feeling among the Indians, who felt that we were buttressing the British Empire. The President, seeing this in numerous dispatches, sent me a memorandum on January 17, 1944, saying: "What would you think of my telling the press something like the enclosed if I am asked? I think it would clear up a good deal of anti-American feeling in India."

I replied two days later, after consulting with my associates, saying that I thought the proposed statement would be very helpful, and suggesting two changes in wording proposed by Wallace Murray, Chief of the Near Eastern Division. The President made the statement on February 1. "The American objectives in India or elsewhere in continental Asia," he said, "are to expel and defeat the Japanese, in the closest collaboration with our British, Chinese, and other Allies in that theater. . . . No matter what individual or individuals command in given areas, the purpose is the same. . . . Nobody in India or anywhere else in Asia will misunderstand the presence there of American armed forces if they will believe, as we do at home, that their job is to assure the defeat of Japan, without which there can be no opportunity for any of us to enjoy and expand the freedoms for which we fight."

We took all steps we could to dissociate our activities in India, which merely served as a base for our operations in aid of China, from those of the British. We likewise took care to keep all American propaganda work based in India, other than that of a purely psychological warfare nature directed against the enemy, completely separate from similar work by the British.

In the summer of 1944 an unexpected and serious issue rose between us and the British when an American columnist published a large portion of the previously mentioned letter which Phillips had written to the President on April 19, 1943. This publication created excitement in the United States and resentment in Britain. Beginning with a visit to me by British Minister Campbell on the day of publication, July 25, 1944, the British repeatedly protested and requested our Government to issue a statement dissociating ourselves from the views expressed in the letter.

On August 15, however, we sent the President a memorandum stating: "It is the Department's feeling that it would be impossible to issue a statement satisfactory to the British inasmuch as we share in general the views expressed in the Ambassador's letter. Unless you feel that we should comply with the British request, I would appreciate having your permission to tell the British that we consider it preferable to make no public statement on the subject." The President went along with this view.

The question received considerable airing in Congress, particularly when Phillips's resignation from Eisenhower's staff was announced. We made a statement, however, to Representative Sol Bloom, chairman of the House Committee of Foreign Affairs, showing that there was no connection between Phillips's resignation, given on July 19, and the publication of the letter, made on July 25.

The British did not easily let the matter drop. Ambassador Halifax called on me on September 8 and very pressingly urged that the President at an early press conference refer to the Phillips letter without mentioning it and speak well of the Indian military forces, and then correct any impression that the British were not aiding in the war against Japan.

I talked this over with the President, who said he could and would make such a statement. He did not make it; but he joined with Prime Minister Churchill a week later in making a joint statement at the Quebec Conference that all the nations concerned with the war in the Orient were "ardent" to engage against the Japanese the massive forces which they were marshaling.

Throughout these years of political disturbance, we gave India what economic assistance we could. In March, 1942, the President appointed Henry F. Grady, former Assistant Secretary of State, to head an economic mission to India to study the subcontinent's needs. The mission proposed a program of assistance which, however, could be implemented only in small part because of the shortage of shipping.

When a serious famine developed in Bengal in 1943, we made efforts to secure from the all too inadequate rice stocks in the Western Hemisphere an allocation of rice for India. The British representatives on the Combined Food Board in Washington insisted, however, that the responsibility for Indian food requirements be left to Britain, and we perforce had to agree.

When I left the State Department at the end of November, 1944, the situation in India was still acute. The United Nations' military progress in the Pacific had largely removed the danger of a Japanese attack; but the danger of internal explosions was still ever present. We had taken every occasion we legitimately could to make clear our view that India should receive independence, but we had also proceeded with great caution so as not to antagonize either the British or the Indians. India continued to be one of the principal foci of our general policy on dependent peoples. And we had the conviction that, soon after the war ended, India must, and would, be granted independence.

Toward India's neighbor to the north, Afghanistan, our policy assumed a new importance with our entry into the war and with the manifest plans of the Germans to penetrate into western Asia en route to India. The mountain country's strategic position on the northwest frontier of India, the hostility of its people to both the British and the Russians, and the pro-German sentiment existing there, made it imperative for us to develop our relations with the Afghans. In February, 1942, we assigned a Foreign Service officer to Kabul, their capital, with instructions to open a Legation; and the President on May 2 appointed Cornelius Van H. Engert our Minister to Afghanistan. In June, 1943, the Afghans opened a Legation in Washington.

We forthwith lent what assistance we could in both a cultural and an economic way. Grants-in-aid were given to American teachers accepting posts in Afghanistan's higher schools. Assistance was given the Government in employing American engineers to develop irrigation projects. We tried to support the country's economy by continuing the importation into the United States of karakuls and other Afghan produce, and facilitating the export of manufactured articles to Afghanistan.

Toward the end of my years at the State Department, when it became apparent that the Germans could no longer carry out their plans of driving into the Middle East and effecting a juncture with the Japanese, we nevertheless continued our policy of cooperation with Afghanistan. We had in mind the possibility that a breakdown in Afghanistan's internal economy might lead to serious political disorders along the northwest frontier of India which would tie down a number of Allied troops. We also believed that the prestige we might acquire in Afghanistan would favorably affect our position in other Moslem areas in the Middle East. And we thought that, if it ever became economically feasible to develop oil and mineral resources in Afghanistan, a friendly attitude there toward the United States would be helpful.

On only one occasion did we take political action with regard to Afghanistan. This was in May, 1943, when we received reports that the British and Russians might be planning a joint demand on the Afghan Government that it expel the German and Italian diplomatic staffs. We felt that the Government's compliance with this demand might result in its overthrow by the tribes and in the creation of disorder. We accordingly informed the British Government that if any such demand were made the United States Government would openly disassociate itself from the *démarche*. The British replied that they had no present intention of asking for the expulsion of the Axis representatives, and that a request they had made for a reduction in the number of such representatives was not in the form of a demand. The Afghan Government brought about the departure of a few Axis representatives and arrested certain Axis agents.

Partly as a result of our efforts, Afghanistan throughout the war presented no element of trouble. The northwest frontier of India was secured against becoming a sore spot of disorder and a base for propaganda and other operations by the Axis.

109: The Near East Looms Big

THE NEAR EAST, in which our Government had evinced only a slight interest for a century and a half, became through the demands of World War II a vital area in the conduct of our foreign relations. Those legendary and, to the average American, somewhat shadowy countries of Asia Minor, whose names were linked with Bible lore and ancient history, suddenly presented us with concrete problems of the moment, requiring almost daily decisions and affecting our ties with other major nations. Iran (once known to us as Persia), Iraq, Saudi Arabia, Lebanon, and Syria began to appear more and more in American print, not as lands of the ancients but as cogs in the machine of war. Palestine, already known not only as the Holy Land but also as the goal of the Zionists and the kernel of the struggle between Jews and Arabs, took on new significance because of the war. The cities of Tehran, Bagdad, Beirut, and Damascus, which had heard the tread of armies of long-past centuries, now quivered under the roar of tanks or bombers.

Prior to June, 1941, when Hitler became engrossed in his struggle with Russia, the Near East was one of the immediate points of German ambition. British and Free French troops had to invade Syria in 1941 to prevent the Germans, with Vichy France acquiescing, from using it as a base to penetrate into the Middle East and support a rebellion in Iraq. In my eyes the Near East offered the greatest danger of the war, the possible juncture of German and Japanese forces, effectively cutting the world in two.

After the Nazi invasion of the U.S.S.R., the Near East became to the British and us a corridor for sending supplies to the embattled Russians, Iran being our major highway. We had to negotiate with Iran and other Near Eastern countries, and with Britain and Russia, for this purpose. At the same time we were in frequent diplomatic contact with Moscow and London to prevent dissension from rising between them over the Near East, and to forestall any thought on their part of dividing that region into spheres of influence.

Our policy was predicated on our belief that all the countries of the Near East should eventually be fully independent. Toward that end we furthered the legitimate aspirations of the Arab states toward an Arab federation, and we fought the attempt of General de Gaulle's committee to prevent the peoples of Syria and of Lebanon from achieving independence. We also worked hard to bring the Near Eastern states into the United Nations.

We likewise had our own interests to protect, principally the vast oil concessions in Saudi Arabia, held exclusively by American companies, as well as our large oil interests in Iraq and Kuwait, held jointly with citizens of other countries.

In pursuit of all these objectives we had to be ready to lend financial and other assistance to the countries of the Near East, including the sending of economic, military, and other missions, to establish closer diplomatic relations with them, and to exert our diplomatic influence, when necessary, upon them or upon our major Allies.

President Roosevelt and I agreed, in August, 1942, on a plan of procedure in the Near East and on a basic statement of our policy in that region, after the State Department and the Joint Chiefs of Staff had carefully studied the whole situation. I thereupon cabled Ambassador Winant in London to show our plan to the British and obtain their concurrence.

In support of our proposed plan we stressed the serious consequences the loss of the Near East would have for the United Nations, and we emphasized that every possible political and military effort had to be made to retain that vital area. The United States, we said, continued to have a unique position in the area, where our influence and prestige were still high because the Near Eastern peoples realized that we had no vested political or territorial interests there. This widespread good will toward us had developed into a deep-seated belief to this effect among the Near Eastern peoples, principally as a result of a century of American philanthropic, educational, and missionary efforts that no material interests or motives had ever tarnished. Such a position was occupied by none of the other United Nations.

We suggested therefore that we take specific steps with regard to the Near East: the appointment to Syria and Lebanon of a diplomatic agent; the issuance of a policy declaration by our Government with respect to the Near East; and the sending of an American mission, partly economic, partly military, to that area, although we recognized that the military responsibility for the region continued to be primarily British.

Finally we proposed that the American mission should use four main arguments in its approach to the Near East: first, the United Nations' military power and potentialities; second, the inevitable political and economic enslavement that the Near Eastern peoples would suffer, as had those in all the occupied countries, in the event of an Axis victory; third, the Near Eastern peoples' own interest and their better prospects for economic and political development in a United Nations victory; fourth, the assurance of this country's support, after the war, for their aspirations toward independence if, in line with the Atlantic Charter and American foreign policy, the peoples of the Near East actively assisted in winning the war.

I likewise sent Winant the text of the proposed basic statement of policy, built around and quoting my radio address of July 23, 1942, when I said: "It has been our purpose in the past—and will remain our purpose in the future—to use the full measure of our influence to support attainment of freedom by all peoples who, by their acts, show themselves worthy of it and ready for it."

The British reaction was more unfavorable than favorable. Eden welcomed our proposal to appoint a diplomatic agent to Syria and Lebanon, but Mr. Churchill opposed the wording of our proposed declaration. The British, in an *aide-mémoire,* saw "considerable dangers" in it; they thought the emphasis on "freedom" and "liberty" inappropriate in so far as the independent countries of the Near East were concerned, and apt to have dangerous repercussions in so far as Palestine and the Levantine states—Syria and Lebanon—were concerned. The *aide-mémoire* also deprecated the dispatch of an American mission of the character outlined, but indicated that the assignment of American specialized personnel to work with the British in those fields would be welcomed.

In consequence of this reaction, we did not pursue our proposal for a declaration of policy, and we did not take up the matter with the French National Committee, as we had intended. We did not, however, drop the idea of greater American participation in the affairs of the Near East, but took numerous steps relating to the countries of that region.

Iran probably attracted more of our attention than any other country in the Near East. With the British and the Russians occupying portions of that country, and with Americans using Iranian routes for the dispatch of supplies to Russia, Iran became the only common meeting place of the three major nations where they might work out a plan for the treatment and development of small nations. This was particularly important because Iran for more than a century had been a diplomatic battleground for predominance between Britain and Russia. The President believed, and I with him, that Iran, possibly because of the very difficulties inherent in the problem, offered us a unique opportunity to see what an unselfish American policy could do in raising the status of her national life.

Prior to the war our relations with Iran had never been of great importance. Iranian foreign relations had been oriented toward Russia and Britain. In the 1920's German technicians entered Iran by the hundreds, and Germany flooded the country with cheap goods. This German penetration later proved unfortunate for Iran, since it caused the British and Russians to invade her in 1941. The Iranian Government, under the hardheaded, ultrasensitive dictator, Shah Reza Pahlavi, from 1925 to 1941, had itself been an obstacle in the way of better American-Iranian relations. Reza Pahlavi, while trying to shut the door to any foreign influence, periodically complained to other Governments against any comment in the foreign press he considered injurious to Iran. He closed the Iranian Legation in Washington in 1936 because his Minister was unfortunately arrested in a traffic incident in Maryland, and opened it again only after a personal visit to Tehran in 1938 by Wallace Murray, Chief of the Division of Near Eastern Affairs.

At the time the British occupied southern Iran and the Russians northern Iran in August, 1941, both the British and the Iranian Government requested our support. The British wanted us to back the Anglo-Soviet representations to Tehran demanding the expulsion of most of the large German colony in Iran, which seemed to be a danger to the Allies particularly because Iran lay just to the south of the Russian oil fields toward which the Germans were then driving hard. Though refusing to associate our Government with these joint representations, I instructed Minister Dreyfus at Tehran to express to the Iranians our sincere hope that all the requisite measures were being taken by the Iranian Government to prevent Nazi activities from spreading—a development that would inevitably be disastrous to it.

The Iranian Minister, Mohammed Shayesteh, on the other hand, called on me on August 22 to ask on behalf of his Government what we should be disposed to do to prevent the threatened British invasion. I emphasized to him then and in later conversations the global nature of the conflict with the Axis and my belief that Iran should take all possible steps to avoid being of any assistance to the Axis and to aid the Allies.

Shah Reza Pahlavi, however, blindly pursuing a narrow policy of neutrality and nationalism, and refusing to heed our friendly advice to look at the war from a broader viewpoint, temporized until it was too late. The British and Russians invaded his country on August 25. The

Shah thereupon cabled President Roosevelt, asking for his intervention "to put an end to these acts of aggression." The President sent this to me on August 30 for a reply. Our response, which went out on September 2, followed the line of my conversations with the Iranian Minister, placing the Anglo-Soviet-Iranian dispute in its true light as one small element in the vast effort to stop Hitler's ambition of world conquest. The President also informed the Shah that we had noted the British and Russian statements to Iran that they had no designs on the independence or territorial integrity of that country. He added that we had already sought information from the British and Soviet Governments as to their immediate as well as long-range plans and intentions in Iran, and had suggested to them the advisability of a public statement to all free peoples of the world reiterating their assurances cencerning Iran's independence.

I had made these approaches in conferring on August 27 with Soviet Ambassador Oumansky and British Chargé d'Affaires Campbell, and I took this suggestion up again in cables to London and Moscow on September 4. A fortnight later, the stubborn Shah Reza Pahlavi abdicated and was succeeded by the Crown Prince, Mohammed Reza Pahlavi, who was more disposed to cooperate with the Allies. Although the British and Russians did not at that time issue the declaration of assurances I had suggested, they did, in the Anglo-Soviet-Iranian Treaty signed on January 29, 1942, undertake to respect the territorial integrity, sovereignty, and political independence of Iran and to withdraw their troops not later than six months after the end of hostilities.

Prior to the signature of this treaty our Legation in Tehran had reported that the Soviets were said to be giving at least sympathy to separatist movements in their zone in northern Iran. I had this report taken up strongly with the Russians, and Soviet Deputy Foreign Commissar Vishinski denied any knowledge on the part of his Government of political or propaganda activities in northern Iran looking toward separatist movements.

Nevertheless, alarmed by continuing reports of Soviet separatist activities in northern Iran, the Iranian Government asked us to become a joint signatory to the treaty of January 29. We contented ourselves, however, with taking note of the Anglo-Soviet assurances contained in the treaty, in a telegram from the President to the new Shah on February 6.

In the spring of 1942 Iran's strategic position became of great importance to all the United Nations because of a threatened German attack in the Near East and Japanese successes in the Far East. Iran was also providing the major supply route for the U.S.S.R. Despite the Anglo-Soviet-Iranian treaty, continuing anti-British and anti-Soviet sentiment in Iran prevented any wholehearted support of the United Nations' war effort. The Iranian Government appeared extremely apprehensive over Soviet objectives in northern Iran and resentful of British interference in Iranian internal affairs. The war had cut off Iran's export trade and made it difficult for her to obtain essential imports, while the continued presence of British and Soviet troops had produced internal difficulties both political and economical.

The Iranians, disliking the British, fearing the Russians, resentful against both because of their occupation of Iran, and looking upon the United States as the only disinterested large nation able to help them, turned to us for aid.

The President accordingly declared Iran eligible for Lend-Lease supplies on March 11, 1942. We likewise began to send economic, military, and other advisers to Iran, always at her own request. At the time I left office we had some seventy-five Americans in these advisory missions, to which the Iranian Government had granted a considerable degree of authority. The largest mission was of an economic and financial nature, headed by Dr. Arthur C. Millspaugh, with an authorized strength of sixty Americans. The Iranian Parliament granted these missions plenary powers to supervise and direct such vital activities as finance, internal revenue, customs, price stabilization, rationing, distribution, collection of harvests, public domains, and road transport. A military mission headed by Major General Clarence S. Ridley worked toward the reorganization of the Quartermaster Corps of the Iranian Army. Another military mission under Colonel H. Norman Schwarzkopf reorganized and administered the Iranian rural police.

The work of these missions was attended with many difficulties. Sharp disputes rose between some of the advisers, particularly Dr. Millspaugh, and some Iranian officials, and the latter interfered from time to time with the work of the advisers. We had to iron out the difficulties through diplomatic representations to the Iranian Government and through counseling the advisers; we had to keep Britain and Russia assured that we were not attempting to take control of the Iranian Government; and we had to keep in frequent contact with other Departments and agencies of our own Government in order to obtain their cooperation.

I recommended to the President on August 16, 1943, that the United States should adopt "a policy of positive action" in Iran, so as to facilitate not only the United Nations' war operations in that country but also a sound postwar development. In the memorandum I sent him, which was prepared in the Near Eastern Division under Wallace Murray, I said: "We should take the lead, wherever possible, in remedying internal difficulties, working as much as possible through American administrators freely employed by the Iranian Government. We should further endeavor to lend timely diplomatic support to Iran, to prevent the development of a situation in which an open threat to Iranian integrity might be presented."

We pointed out that the success of this proposed course of action was favored by the exceptionally high regard in which the United States was held by the Iranian people. We also had reason to believe that the British Government would acquiesce, or even lend its active support. The attitude of the Soviet Government was doubtful, but we felt we should be in a position to exert considerable influence on that Government if the occasion arose. We stated that the safeguarding of legitimate British and Soviet economic interests in Iran ought to be a basic principle of American action.

Our recommendations, we said, were rendered necessary by the deterioration of the political and economic situation in Iran. We felt that the geographical, political, and economic bases of the century-old ambitions of Britain and Russia in Iran still remained unchanged. The attitudes of the British and Soviet Governments gave us strong reason to fear that their rivalry would break out again as soon as the military situation eased. This danger was greatly increased by the economic and political weakness of the Iranian Government and the presence of British and Soviet armed forces on Iranian soil. If events were allowed to run their course unchecked, it seemed likely that either Russia or Britain, or both, would take action that would seriously abridge, if not destroy, effective Iranian independence. The best hope of avoiding such action, we believed, lay in strengthening Iran to a point where she could stand on her own feet, without foreign control or "protection," and in calling upon Britain and Russia, when necessary, to respect their general commitments under the Atlantic Charter and their specific commitments to Iran under the Treaty of Alliance of 1942.

The President was in agreement with the policy we suggested. The War Department joined with us in its implementation.

Iraq, one of Iran's neighbors, having declared war on the Axis, had been admitted to the ranks of the United Nations in January, 1943. Immediately the Iranian Government sought a like status. After exchanges of views the London, Moscow, and Chungking Governments joined with us in stating to the Iranian Government that when Iran entered the war against one or more of the Axis nations she would become eligible. Iran declared war on Germany on September 9, 1943, and adhered on the following day to the United Nations Declaration through an exchange of notes between the Iranian Minister and myself.

At the Moscow Conference in October, 1943, Eden, Molotov, and I discussed the question of a declaration by the three major nations concerning Iran. Eden had taken up with us the substance of such a declaration prior to the Moscow Conference, and I was in general agreement with it. This pronouncement stated that, so long as Iran complied with her obligations under the Anglo-Soviet-Iranian Treaty of Alliance and gave the Allies the aid they desired in the economic and financial fields, they had a moral obligation, in making use of Iranian facilities, to do the least possible harm to Iran's economy and to do all possible to safeguard the Iranian people against the privations that war must inevitably bring.

During one of my conferences with Eden in Moscow, I suggested on October 24 that the declaration be expanded to include a promise of support for the foreign advisers and domestic agencies working to improve conditions in Iran, and that separate declarations be made stating the intentions of the three Powers to withdraw their armed forces from Iran after the cessation of hostilities.

Eden agreed, and throughout our subsequent discussions at the conference the British and we were in substantial agreement. Molotov and his assistants, however, opposed the issuance of any declaration asserting that the assurances and undertakings involved were already covered in the Anglo-Soviet-Iranian Treaty and in a draft agreement we had drawn up relative to American troops in Iran, and that a reiteration of them might alarm rather than reassure the Iranians.

At that time we were discussing with the Iranian Government a draft agreement relative to American troops already in Iran. Following the establishment of the Persian Gulf Command in Iran late in November, 1942, and the arrival of American technical troops to superintend the transport of supplies to Russia, the Iranian Government had proposed that the United States become a party to the Anglo-Soviet-Iranian Treaty to clarify the status of our troops there. Not considering it feasible to become a party to a treaty of alliance with Iran, we proposed to the Iranians a separate agreement to cover the presence of our troops on their territory.

In our draft we undertook to "respect, in the future as in the past, the territorial integrity, sovereignty, and political independence of Iran." The Iranians, however, desired still broader guarantees, and difficulties also rose over certain of the economic clauses in the agreement. These negotiations were suspended by the Iranian Government in December, 1943.

The proposed three-Power declaration on Iran which Eden and I were supporting at Moscow ran aground on the rocks of Soviet opposition. Eden, Molotov, and I thereupon agreed to recommend that the declaration be further considered at the forthcoming Roosevelt-Stalin-Churchill meeting, although Eden and I should have preferred to continue the discussions at Moscow.

While returning to Washington from Moscow, I stopped at Tehran and received a visit from the Iranian Prime Minister, Ali Soheily, and the Foreign Minister, Mohammed Saed, who expressed their Government's desire for the early withdrawal of the British and Soviet troops in Iran, even before the end of the war. They contended that Iran's situation had radically changed since the Anglo-Soviet-Iranian Treaty of 1942; the Germans were no longer a threat; the Axis agent problem had been disposed of, and, most important, Iran was now at war with the Axis and a member of the United Nations.

The War Department, however, indicated to us on December 21, 1943, that it did not wish to see the British and Soviet troops leave Iran at that time, principally for manpower reasons. Our Chargé at Tehran, Richard Ford, also opposed the proposal on the grounds that it was highly unlikely that all Axis agents had been eliminated from Iran, that the presence of foreign troops exercised a deterrent influence on the unruly tribes that continued to menace the security of the supply line to Russia, and that the Persian Gulf Command and the American advisers to the Iranian Army desired to see the existing arrangement continued, with the British responsible for security in the south and the Russians in the north. We accordingly did not support the Iranian request.

Meantime the President, Marshal Stalin, and Prime Minister Churchill had signed at Tehran, on December 1, a declaration on Iran. This was prepared by our Legation at Tehran with the assistance of General Patrick J. Hurley, whom the President had sent on a special mission to the Near East, and was presented by Mr. Roosevelt. The declaration acknowledged Iran's contribution to the common war effort, recognized the special economic problems created for Iran by the war, pledged such economic assistance to Iran as might be possible, promised consideration of Iran's economic problems in the postwar period, and expressed a desire for the maintenance of Iran's independence, sovereignty, and territorial integrity.

This declaration was of the highest importance to Iran because, in addition to the pledges it contained of economic assistance, it gave the Iranians what they had so much wanted; namely, a formal expression of American desire for the maintenance of Iran's sovereignty and territorial integrity, and a renewal of the assurances previously given by Russia and Britain.

After the President returned to Washington from the Tehran Conference, I recommended to him on December 22 that we raise our Legation at Tehran to an Embassy. Mr. Roosevelt agreed and, on the Department's recommendation, appointed Leland B. Morris, then our Minister to Iceland, to be our first Ambassador in Tehran.

The President's personal interest in Iran was keen. He had sent General Hurley on one mission to the Near East and on another to Iran, and had closely read Hurley's reports and recommendations, in addition to numerous State Department dispatches and memoranda. On January 12, 1944, in a memorandum to me about a very interesting letter from Hurley, he wrote:

"Iran is definitely a very, very backward nation. It consists really of a series of tribes, and 99 per cent of the population is, in effect, in bondage to the other 1 per cent. The 99 per cent do not own their land and cannot keep their own production or convert it into money or property.

"I was rather thrilled with the idea of using Iran as an example of what we could do by an unselfish American policy. We could not take on a more difficult nation than Iran. I should like, however, to have a try at it. The real difficulty is to get the right kind of American experts who would be loyal to their ideals, not fight among themselves and be absolutely honest financially.

"If we could get this policy started, it would become permanent if it succeeded as we hope during the first five or ten years. And incidentally, the whole experiment need cost the taxpayers of the United States very little money."

Hurley was critical of British policy in Iran, which he considered imperialistic, and one of his recommendations was that the Lend-Lease Administration should take complete control of the distribution of our own Lend-Lease supplies in the Near East. These had been distributed largely through a British agency, primarily because of the difficulty of recruiting and transporting American personnel for the purpose. This recommendation, among others, was approved by the President and was gradually carried out, except in a very few cases where it proved impracticable.

In 1944 our assistance of all kinds to Iran increased. Nevertheless dissension intensified between some Iranian officials and a few of our advisers. Iranian officials at times resented or objected to the projects and procedures recommended by some of the advisers, and on the part of the latter, absorbed as they were in their specialized fields, there was often an inadequate realization of the need for diplomacy in conducting their relations with the Iranian Government.

When Mr. Abol Hassan Ebtehaj, governor of the National Bank of Iran, who according to our Embassy in Tehran was in "open warfare" with Dr. Millspaugh, visited the United States in June, 1944, he expressed great dissatisfaction with the trend of American-Iranian relations, basing his position on a series of minor incidents. I suggested to him that his chief complaints, about which he had allowed himself to become so much exercised, could well be brushed aside in the face of the more important questions and policies that our two peoples and Governments had to solve. I said that the United States Government was making an immense contribution toward bringing defeat to the Axis Powers, all of which protected the liberty of Iran. I was told later that this conversation had the effect of placating the irate governor.

Iran being one of the great oil-bearing countries of the Near East, one facet of our diplomacy consisted in supporting the efforts of American companies to obtain petroleum concessions there. The War and Navy Departments, alarmed by statistics tending to prove the depletion of the United States oil fields, and feeling that the oil of the Near East, because it lay closer to the Far East than the Western Hemisphere fields, might be vitally necessary in the war against Japan, strongly urged that the Near Eastern potentialities be developed.

When the Standard-Vacuum Oil Company asked the Department's views on its desire to enter into an arrangement with the Iranian Government to produce petroleum in Iran, we replied that we favored the development of all possible sources of petroleum because of the importance of the product both for war purposes and from the long-range point of view, and saw no objection to the company's undertaking negotiations with the Iranian Government. I approved this reply at a meeting with my associates on November 15, 1943. The British already had extensive oil concessions in Iran, but I said that, since we had no agreement with the British not to seek oil concessions there, I saw no reason why the company should not go ahead with its plans. We cabled our Legation in Tehran accordingly.

The Standard-Vacuum Company sent a representative to Tehran early in 1944, and the Sinclair oil interests did likewise. At the same time a representative of a British oil company was in Tehran trying to obtain further oil concessions. Then on February 28 Chargé Ford in Tehran reported that the Soviet Embassy had stated to the press that the U.S.S.R. had prior rights to the exploitation of any oil in northern Iran, a claim apparently based on an old concession never approved by the Iranian Parliament.

The negotiations of the American and British oil interests with the Iranian Government continued satisfactorily through the summer of 1944 until, in September, a Soviet delegation arrived in Tehran and requested the immediate concession to the Russian Government of exclusive rights for a five-year period to explore for petroleum and other minerals in an area of 200,000 square kilometers in northern Iran. All other foreigners were to be excluded from such exploitation.

Iranian Prime Minister Saed, therefore, informed Ambassador Morris on October 9 that his Government had decided to postpone all oil negotiations until after the war. We cabled Morris on October 16 to inform the Iranian Government that we had taken note of its decision; that, although the two American firms involved were naturally disappointed at its decision, we were confident that the Iranian Government had acted in good faith in carrying on the previous negotiations; that we should naturally expect, when and if the Iranian Government was ready to consider applications for oil concessions, that the applications received from Americans would be given no less favorable treatment than those received from the Government or nationals of any other country; and that we should also expect the Iranian Government to inform us or the American companies concerned as soon as it was ready to consider such applications.

The British took a similar position, but the Soviet reaction was quite different. The Russian press immediately began a campaign against the Saed Government, and the Soviet officials in Tehran expressed their displeasure. Ambassador Harriman in Moscow, acting on our instructions, thereupon informed the Soviet Foreign Office of our instructions to Ambassador Morris on October 16 and said that these were based on our recognition of an independent nation's sovereign right to withhold or grant commercial concessions on a nondiscriminatory basis. We called attention to the Tehran Declaration on Iran and said we could not agree to any action constituting undue interference in Iranian internal affairs.

Nevertheless, Soviet pressure brought about the fall of the Saed Government on November 9, three weeks before my resignation. While Soviet demands for the desired oil concession thereafter relaxed somewhat, this was a basic question involved in the crisis in Soviet-Iranian relations in 1946.

110: Near East and Oil

OIL LUBRICATED THE DIPLOMACY of the major nations toward the Near East. When it became apparent in the twenties and thirties that the petroleum deposits in that area represented one of the greatest reserves in the world, the attention of the larger nations turned toward the Near Eastern production of a commodity whose importance to industry and transport was becoming ever more marked.

In Saudi Arabia the element of oil entered into United States diplomacy to a greater extent than in the case of any other Near Eastern country. With that comparatively unknown land, consisting largely of Arabian desert, under the rule of King Ibn Saud, the greatest single influence among the Arabs, we had had only unimportant relations in the years before the war. In 1933 we had signed with Saudi Arabia a provisional agreement for diplomatic and consular representatives, juridical protection, commerce, and navigation. In the same year the Standard Oil Company of California obtained a concession to develop the Saudi Arabian oil fields, which it began to do, in conjunction with the Texas Company, through a jointly owned subsidiary, later called the Arabian American Oil Company. The company had obtained the concession on its own initiative, in competition with various foreign interests. King Ibn Saud, suspicious of governmental diplomatic processes, had preferred to deal directly with company officials.

During the next few years the company did not require our diplomatic protection and, in view of Ibn Saud's attitude toward diplomacy, we felt it better to remain in the background. Later, as tests revealed the Saudi Arabian oil fields to be among the most important in the world and as many more American technicians went to Saudi Arabia, we thought it advisable to establish diplomatic relations with the King. In 1939 Minister Bert Fish, already accredited to Egypt, was accredited also to Saudi Arabia.

Following the outbreak of the European War, King Ibn Saud began to experience serious financial difficulties primarily owing to the curtailment of the pilgrim traffic to Mecca and Medina as a result of the war. In June, 1941, he requested a $10,000,000 credit from the United States Government. The President agreed but found there were legal difficulties in the way. The British Government having recommended payment of cash and goods subsidies to Saudi Arabia, the President also felt that there was more reason for the British, with their greater strategic and political interests in the Near East, to attend to Ibn Saud's financial needs.

After our entry into the war, however, the preservation of law and order in the Near East became of great concern to us. The planning and carrying out of the campaign in North Africa, where the Arab population predominated, and the establishment of important American supply lines to Russia through the Near East, showed the necessity for stability in the Near East, toward which end stability in Saudi Arabia was essential.

In January, 1942, we took up with the President and with Secretaries Ickes of Interior and Wickard of Agriculture a request from the Saudi Arabian Government for the services of American experts in irrigation and agriculture, and obtained their approval. A mission, headed by Mr. K. S. Twitchell, who had acted in the United States as an informal representative of King Ibn Saud, went to Saudi Arabia in May, 1942, remained until December, and received the commendation of Ibn Saud in a letter to the President.

We opened an American Legation on May 1, 1942, at Jidda under a Chargé d'Affaires, who, in July, 1943, was appointed Minister Resident. Early in January, 1943, the State Department recommended that Saudi Arabia be made eligible for Lend-Lease assistance, and the President so declared on February 18, 1943.

These steps were taken in recognition of the importance of King Ibn Saud and Saudi Arabia to the United Nations' war effort. Ibn Saud had granted our air forces fly-over privileges, and the War Department had evinced an interest in obtaining aircraft landing rights there. Both the War and Navy Departments were interested in securing oil reserves in Saudi Arabian ground. Furthermore, King Ibn Saud exerted great influence upon the Arab countries of the Near East, where American troops were stationed.

The President himself was drawn to the powerful personality of King Ibn Saud, and looked forward eagerly to making his personal acquaintance. We drafted for him in July, 1943, a message to the King inviting him to visit the United States in the near future, or, if he were unable to come, to designate a member of the Royal Family to make the visit on his behalf. The King accepted the latter part of the invitation, designating his son, Amir Faisal, Foreign Minister of Saudi Arabia, to represent him. The news of the invitation and acceptance leaked out and became twisted to indicate that Ibn Saud's son was coming to the United States for propaganda purposes in connection with the Jewish problem in Palestine. The President sent me a tart note on August 15, attributing the leak to the State Department, and adding: "Of course, I have no sympathy with those Jews who object to my seeing the son of Ibn Saud any more than I have any sympathy with those Arabs who are starting anti-Semitic prejudices in this country."

I replied to the President three days later, saying I did not believe any leak had occurred in the State Department. I remarked that a member of the British Embassy had called on an officer of the Department about the time the invitation was sent to Ibn Saud and said he had learned through Zionist contacts in New York that an invitation was to be extended. So far as Arab propaganda activities in the United States were concerned, I added, our Minister Resident at Jidda had reported that the British Legation there had advised the Saudi Arabian Government to undertake such propaganda to counteract Zionist propaganda in the United States.

The Arab princes, Faisal and his brother Khalid, arrived in Washington in the autumn of 1943 and, during my absence at the Moscow Conference, held a series of conferences with officers of the Department on economic aid for Saudi Arabia, development of Saudi Arabian petroleum resources, and American policy in the Near East generally.

Meantime, by arrangement between the State and Treasury Departments, a Treasury representative, John W. Gunter, had gone to Saudi Arabia to explore with that Government the Saudi Arabian financial situation. As a result of this visit, we signed an agreement on October 3, 1943, to loan Saudi Arabia over 5,000,000 ounces of silver. At the end of the year an American military mission, headed by Major General Ralph Royce, visited Saudi Arabia, at King Ibn Saud's invitation, to survey Saudi Arabian military requirements, and in the spring of 1944 a small United States Army training mission went to the desert kingdom.

Rivalry with Britain in Saudi Arabia sharply disturbed us in the first half of 1944. Although the British Government, in an *aide-mémoire* of October 30, 1943, had expressed to us their anxiety to coordinate their policy in the Middle East with that of this Government and their hope for close collaboration with us in that area; although they had accepted, early in 1944, our proposal for discussion of Saudi Arabian fiscal and currency problems; and although British Ambassador Halifax had called on me on March 20, 1944, to characterize as entirely erroneous a statement attributed to General Hurley that the British were opposed to American development of oil interests in Saudi Arabia, the State Department, in March and April of 1944, received reports of increasing British activity in Saudi Arabia potentially prejudicial to American interests there.

I could credit the British Government with acting in good faith and friendship, but there was no blinking the fact that they had at Jidda an overzealous Minister, S. R. Jordan, who was working in numerous ways to supplant American interests in Saudi Arabia by British interests. Britain had been subsidizing King Ibn Saud for several years, and Minister Jordan was making full use of this fact to exalt British prestige by lowering our own.

Our Minister in Jidda, James S. Moose, Jr., informed us on March 31, 1944, of reports that Jordan had persuaded King Ibn Saud to remove certain key officials known to be friendly to the United States and to agree to appoint a British economic adviser and possibly a British petroleum adviser as well. He had also reported that Jordan, without consulting him, had arranged for certain road work in Saudi Arabia to be undertaken under the supervision of the British military, although General Royce, during his visit to Saudi Arabia in December, 1943, had discussed the construction of two military roads with King Ibn Saud, and the King had given his permission for United States military forces to make a survey toward this end.

It seemed to my associates and me that we should meet these developments in two ways. One was to increase our own economic assistance to King Ibn Saud so that he would not lean too heavily on Britain for aid. The other was to talk the situation over frankly with the British and reach an arrangement with them whereby our national interest in the petroleum resources of Saudi Arabia would be protected and Ibn Saud would not have an opportunity to play Britain and the United States off against each other with respect to the granting of help.

I outlined the situation to the President in a memorandum on April 3, 1944, stating our belief that we should extend additional financial and economic assistance to Saudi Arabia so as to safeguard our national interest in her petroleum resources. Pointing out that the Government of Saudi Arabia had relied principally upon British subsidies during the previous few years, I informed the President that we had now ascertained that the British Government proposed in 1944 to subsidize Saudi Arabia to the extent of nearly $12,000,000, which was approximately six times the value of Lend-Lease aid our Government contemplated extending in 1944.

After citing the activities of the British Minister in Jidda, I said: "If Saudi Arabia is permitted to lean too heavily upon the British, there is always the danger that the British will request a *quid pro quo* in oil. To obviate this danger, it is recommended that this Government share the subsidy on an over-all equal basis with the British."

The President wrote his O.K. on this memorandum, and we entered into negotiations with the British. These were conducted by Wallace Murray, Chief of the Office of Near Eastern Affairs, who had accompanied Under Secretary Stettinius on a special mission to London. The British assured us there had never been any intention on their part to undermine or to prejudice American oil rights in Saudi Arabia, and they agreed to investigate the possibility of an Anglo-American goods subsidy program for Saudi Arabia on as nearly an equal basis as possible.

The British proposed that a joint Anglo-American military mission, headed by a British officer, should be sent to Saudi Arabia. After obtaining the concurrence of the War Department, we agreed to this proposal since we recognized that the primary military responsibility in the Near East was British. We made our approval contingent, however, upon the Foreign Office's agreeing that an American should head any economic or financial mission sent to Saudi Arabia at Ibn Saud's request in view of the preponderant United States economic interests in that country.

The Foreign Office hedged on this reservation, saying that the leadership of an economic and financial mission should be determined according to which country had the preponderant interest in Saudi Arabian economy and finance at the time the mission were sent. We rejected this idea, saying that our proposal was based on the fact that the preponderant interest in the economy of Saudi Arabia was without any question American and presumably would continue to be so for a long time to come since the Saudi Arabian economy would be based on the oil produced by reason of substantial American capital investments. The British came back with the assertion that our claim to a preponderant American interest in Saudi Arabian economy was based on a "misconception of the facts" and stated that they would be very willing to reconsider the position when oil production had increased and Saudi Arabia no longer depended primarily on her economic relations with sterling-area countries.

We could reach no agreement. We were willing to agree that the British should head the joint military mission, but they sought to keep open the possibility of heading the joint economic mission as well, which we could not accept.

In July, 1944, however, we did agree to participate during 1944 equally in a joint supply program for Saudi Arabia which would make up the difference between inadequate imports and consumption. King Ibn Saud had appealed in June to both countries for assistance in alleviating a very grave economic situation in Saudi Arabia, and this agreement was a major step in putting the relations of Britain and the United States toward Saudi Arabia on a better footing.

Although our relations with Britain in regard to Saudi Arabia were now on a better basis, the activities of British Minister Jordan in Jidda continued in what we regarded as a definitely anti-American direction. On June 26 I had asked British Ambassador Halifax to call in order to raise with him the question of Jordan. I said to him that our officials in the Middle East were convinced beyond peradventure of doubt that Jordan was doing his level best to injure the United States Government's relations with King Ibn Saud, and was endeavoring in other ways to undermine our position in Saudi Arabia, and that we just could not put up with these activities without making constant and louder complaint to the British Government.

I cabled our Legation at Jidda on July 12 that the joint supply and financial program of aid to Saudi Arabia agreed upon between the British and American Governments was to be considered as expressing a single combined policy toward Saudi Arabia in this field. I instructed Minister Moose to treat all proposals relative to financial and supply aid to Saudi Arabia jointly with the British Minister, cooperating with him closely and wholeheartedly and making all approaches to the Government of Saudi Arabia on such matters jointly with him. I added that similar instructions were being sent by the British Government to Minister Jordan.

We continued to receive from our Legation at Jidda, however, dispatches showing that Minister Jordan refused to cooperate. We therefore informed the British Embassy that the continuance of Mr. Jordan in Saudi Arabia was unacceptable so far as we were concerned. Eventually, some time after my resignation, Jordan was transferred.

Saudi Arabia and her vast oil deposits provided one of the reasons for the negotiations we undertook with the British in 1944 for a world-wide agreement to cover the production and distribution of oil, in which other nations subsequently would be invited to join.

Throughout most of 1943 we at the State Department had been giving intensive study to the problem of oil reserves outside the United States. We had before us the statements of many experts that reserves inside the United States were dwindling and that the demands for oil during the war and the postwar period would be greatly augmented. I had set up a Committee on International Petroleum Policy within the State Department, with Economic Adviser Herbert Feis as its chairman, and had created the position of Petroleum Adviser. On Dr. Feis's recommendation, I appointed Max W. Thornburg to it. When we later learned, however, that Thornburg still was connected with an American oil company, I immediately requested his resignation, and in December, 1943, named as his successor Charles Rayner, who had been an independent petroleum producer for twenty-five years and had had no connection with a major oil company during that time. Rayner carried out his functions with marked efficiency.

Dr. Feis's committee submitted a report to me on March 22, 1943, saying that both Secretary of the Navy Knox and Secretary of the Interior Ickes had repeatedly indicated to the committee their eagerness that some action be taken to safeguard our petroleum reserve situation. After two meetings with the committee to consider their report, I sent copies of it on March 31 to Secretaries Stimson, Knox, and Ickes and suggested that they and I meet to discuss the situation. The report proceeded on the assumption that the future American demand for oil, both for defense and for essential economic requirements, would be in excess of production within the United States. It added: "Unless our ability to derive required supplies from abroad at all times (tranquil, overshadowed, or critical) is safeguarded, the United States will be in hazard (a) of having to pay an economic or political toll to secure the oil, or (b) actually fail to secure it."

The committee therefore recommended that, while continuing to study the possibility of concluding an international petroleum agreement, our Government should organize a Petroleum Reserves Corporation. This corporation would negotiate option contracts with companies (American or foreign, privately or publicly owned), holding petroleum concessions in foreign countries. The contracts would give the Government the right to procure specified amounts of petroleum for delivery to it at times to be agreed upon. They would be negotiated only with the consent of the Government in whose territory lay the reserves. The board of directors of the corporation might be composed of representatives of the State, War,

Navy, and Interior Departments, with the State Department representative as chairman.

We now began exchanges of views with those Departments. Stimson, Knox, and Ickes were of the opinion that the United States Government should become part owner, probably majority owner, of the American company producing Saudi Arabian oil. Admiral Leahy sent me a memorandum dated June 11, 1943, recommending that our Government should make immediate efforts to obtain from Saudi Arabia oil concessions for the United States Government for the purpose of establishing a naval oil-fuel reserve similar to those then existing in the United States. The Joint Chiefs of Staff, in a memorandum to the President, had emphasized the crisis in oil and proposed that the Reconstruction Finance Corporation be directed to organize a corporation specifically for the purpose of acquiring proven foreign petroleum reserves, including the immediate acquisition of a controlling interest by the United States Government in Saudi Arabian oil concessions. The President had directed Leahy to take up these recommendations with me personally.

During a series of meetings presided over by James F. Byrnes, Director of War Mobilization, the interested Government Departments reached the conclusion that a Petroleum Reserves Corporation should be set up.

A clear-cut difference of opinion developed during the conversations we were having with other Government Departments. Ickes believed, as he stated in a letter to the President, that the Government should purchase a controlling stock interest from the two parent companies in the American company developing oil in Saudi Arabia. The Joint Chiefs of Staff recommended the negotiation of a new oil concession with Ibn Saud by our Government. My associates and I, on the other hand, believed that the Government should not itself enter the oil business; it should merely contract with the American company owning the oil concessions in Saudi Arabia—ultimately known as the Arabian American Oil Company—for the creation of oil reserves to be delivered when called for. Moreover, we considered the problem of oil a delicate element in the more important question of our over-all foreign relations.

Accordingly, I sent the President a memorandum on June 14, 1943, which Feis, at my direction, had prepared. After stating our attitude that the task of proceeding in the petroleum field with the development and construction needed for war purposes was primarily one for the War and Navy Departments, the Petroleum Administrator for War (Ickes), and other interested Government agencies, with such cooperation as the State Department had given in many previous cases, we said:

"Experience clearly shows that the acquisition and maintenance of foreign concessions requires carefully directed negotiations with foreign Governments, and these negotiations are always closely connected with other questions in the political and economic field being dealt with at the same time.

"In each and every negotiation the Department has had to reckon with many and variable factors such as (a) the frequent tendency for foreign governments to seize control of oil resources or restrict their development to their own nationals; (b) rival efforts on the part of foreign countries and governments; (c) fears of imperialism; (d) the interplay of diplomatic bargaining."

We added that the principles on which our Government based its efforts to obtain control of petroleum reserves, and the use of such reserves, would affect every phase of our relations with foreign governments in the postwar period—including territorial settlements and matters affecting international political relations.

"It will be recalled," we said, "that in many conferences after the last war the atmosphere and smell of oil was almost stifling. It is essential that our own efforts in the period ahead be so directed as to achieve our ends without stimulating new restrictive moves on the part of other countries and creating intense new disputes."

We therefore thought the State Department should occupy an important place in the Petroleum Reserves Corporation and have prime responsibility for its negotiations with foreign governments.

As for Ickes's recommendation that the United States Government acquire controlling interest in the American company developing oil in Saudi Arabia, we stated our belief that, if it were approved, it would be necessary to notify King Ibn Saud of this intention and that it was not known what attitude he might take toward the entrance of the American Government into the business of developing oil reserves located within his domain. We also referred to a provision in the agreements between the company and Ibn Saud prohibiting the company, without the consent of the Saudi Arabian Government, from assigning to anyone its rights and obligations under its contract.

As to the Joint Chiefs of Staff recommendation that the United States Government negotiate with King Ibn Saud for oil concessions for itself, we pointed out that the most promising oil-bearing land in Saudi Arabia was already included within the concessions held by the American company. We added that any negotiations that disturbed the present concession might have adverse results and possibly lead to new demands either upon the company or upon our Government under penalty of reducing the present concession or of admitting representatives of other countries.

Representatives of the State, War, Navy, and Interior Departments next held a series of meetings in the office of Under Secretary of War Patterson to reconcile the views of the several Departments. This group drew up a report which I sent to the President on June 26, with a letter signed by Stimson, Ickes, Acting Secretary of the Navy Forrestal, and myself. This first recommended the establishment by the Reconstruction Finance Corporation of a Petroleum Reserves Corporation. It then submitted to the President the two conflicting views as to the method of obtaining Saudi Arabian oil for the Government—Ickes's proposal that our Government acquire 100 per cent of the stock of the company owning the oil concessions in Saudi Arabia, and the State Department's proposal that the Government contract with the company for the purchase of oil. The report stipulated that the Petroleum Reserves Corporation should not embark on any major projects without receiving the prior approval of the Secretary of State and that all major negotiations with foreign Governments should be conducted through or under the supervision of the State Department.

The President seemed to lean toward the recommendation that the Government acquire 100 per cent of the company's stock.

The Petroleum Reserves Corporation was set up. I stated I did not want to be chairman of it, and Feis, on my behalf, said he thought the logical choice should be Ickes, who was, in fact, elected president of the Board of Directors on August 9, 1943.

Under Ickes's impetuous leadership, the Corporation began to develop sweeping plans for the injection of the Government into oil fields not only in Saudi Arabia but in other areas as well. It drew up projects for expanding the operations of the Anglo-Iranian Oil Company, a wholly British-owned concern, for a new pipeline to the Mediterranean from the British-controlled Iraq oil fields, and for a refinery in British India. At the same time Ickes began negotiations with the Standard Oil Company of California and the Texas Company to purchase 100 per cent of the stock of the company—Arabian American—they had set up to produce oil in Saudi Arabia. The two companies, however, refused to permit the Petroleum Reserves Corporation to acquire 100 per cent of the company's stock, a controlling share, or even one-third.

As new reports began to be published about the failure of these negotiations, and about the ambitious plans of the corporation, I wrote Ickes, its president, on November 13, 1943, pointing out that its activities were already causing us embarrassment in the Near East, and might well weaken in the eyes of King Ibn Saud the position of the American company which held the oil concession in Saudi Arabia since there was now no assurance that its holdings would be substantially developed in the near future.

"This Department," I said, "believes that there should be a full realization of the fact that the oil of Saudi Arabia constitutes one of the world's greatest prizes, and that it is extremely shortsighted to take any step which would tend to discredit the American interest therein, whether that interest be of a public or private character."

We also objected to the corporation's seeking to aid the expansion of British oil interests, and pointed out that the expansion of American facilities should have priority over any further expansion of British facilities in the Near East area. "We believe," my letter stated, "that strong criticism will develop if British petroleum facilities in the Middle East are further expanded for American purposes and with American materials, for to do so will retard the development of American enterprises, jeopardize their holdings, and so tend to make this country dependent on British oil in the future."

We in the State Department had, in fact, been considering for some months a possible agreement between the United States and British Governments with respect to Near Eastern oil reserves. On December 2, 1943, I addressed a note to British Ambassador Halifax proposing that informal and preliminary oil discussions be undertaken between the two Governments. I sent the President a memorandum on the 8th reemphasizing that the full development of Near Eastern oil resources was of tremendous wartime and long-range importance. "Because of the complex problems involved," I said, "those resources, which are held to a substantial extent jointly by American and British interests, cannot be adequately developed unless the United States and British Governments reach an agreement providing for close cooperation." I suggested that, in view of the delicate political situation in the Near East and the close connection between foreign oil questions and the general conduct of our foreign relations, it was extremely desirable that any conversations with the British on oil be under the clear supervision and guidance of the State Department.

Ickes, however, wrote the President a letter—of which Mr. Roosevelt sent me a copy on December 29—stating, "This is my baby," and insisting that he himself be one of the negotiators. We in the State Department thought the negotiations should be begun by experts of the State and Interior Departments, but Ickes contended that they should be on a Cabinet level, and would not name a representative to sit for him.

We also suggested that any further negotiations with American oil companies whereby the Government would obtain an interest in the American company in Saudi Arabia should be postponed until it was seen what direction the negotiations with Britain would take, but Ickes objected. The President, in a memorandum to Ickes and me on January 10, adopted Ickes's position. "It is, of course, true," he said, "that the State Department should handle, in general, matters relating to foreign affairs—but at the present time I think it vital that we should go ahead with some speed in negotiating with the American companies, in order to find out just where the United States stands before we take the matter up with the British. . . . I feel that time is important—because after the war the American position will be greatly weaker than it is today. Can't we agree on a policy and on the method of putting it into effect?"

Ickes continued his negotiations with the American oil companies and reached an agreement late in January, 1944, for government construction of a pipeline from the Persian Gulf to some point on the eastern Mediterranean and for the establishment of a billion-barrel oil reserve in Saudi Arabia and in the sheikdom of Kuwait for the use of our armed forces. The President approved this agreement. I acquiesced in it with reservations. I did not want to see government ownership of the pipeline. I was willing to go along to the extent of government ownership during the period of the war, after which it would revert to private companies; Ickes on the other hand wanted permanent government ownership. Nor did I want to see the pipeline operated by the Government. Ickes compromised to the extent of agreeing that the pipeline should be privately operated and that at the end of the war the question of ownership should be reviewed.

Ickes, however, still wanted personally to conduct the negotiations with the British Government. During my brief absence from Washington early in February, he induced the President to make him chairman of the negotiating group, with the Under Secretaries of State, War, and Navy, and Charles E. Wilson, vice chairman of the War Production Board, as the other members. Under Secretary Stettinius, after telephoning me, informed the President of my view that it would be a great mistake to deprive the State Department of leadership in the negotiations, and that the discussions should be conducted on a working level with technical and political experts who could devote full time to the many intricate problems involved. I had already advised the British, with the President's approval, that the conversations would be conducted at the working level with the American group headed by Charles Rayner, Petroleum Adviser of the State Department, the other members being Paul Alling, Deputy Director of the Office of Near Eastern and African Affairs, and a representative of Secretary Ickes. I had likewise so advised the American petroleum industry.

The President thereupon, on February 15, suggested a compromise solution, whereby I would be chairman of the group, and Ickes vice chairman, the other members being the Under Secretaries of War and Navy and Wilson and Rayner.

The British, however, immediately protested this decision. They said it would be impossible to send representatives of Cabinet rank to Washington at that time in view of the coming invasion (of Normandy).

The President's reaction, which Stettinius communicated to Ambassador Halifax, was that the whole matter of mutual agreement on petroleum problems was of such extreme importance to both countries and to international security that high ranking representatives of both Governments should constitute the negotiating groups.

Thereupon Prime Minister Churchill cabled the President on February 20, stating that certain British quarters were apprehensive that this country wished to deprive the British of their Near Eastern oil interests. He added that any announcement of a conference on Near Eastern oil, with the American delegation led by the Secretary of State, was sure to raise questions in Parliament which the Prime Minister would be unable to answer with an assurance that no transfer of property was involved— although he himself was sure there was no ground for such suspicions so far as the United States Government was concerned.

President Roosevelt replied to this message two days later, saying he had particularly noted the Prime Minister's concern that a wrangle over oil between the two Governments be avoided. While the Prime Minister, the President said, had pointed to British apprehensions with respect to United States aims in the Near East, he himself was concerned over a rumored British desire to "horn in" on the oil reserves of Saudi Arabia. Mr. Roosevelt said that questions and problems that occasioned apprehensions and rumors of this kind clearly showed the great need for a basic Anglo-American understanding relative to the oil of the Middle East, from which should develop oil agreements more extensive in scope. He insisted on the negotiators being of Cabinet rank because of the importance of the negotiations, and said that he himself wished to preside at the first meeting of the joint discussion group, which would be held in the Cabinet room in the White House.

Following further exchanges of messages between the President and the Prime Minister, involving primarily an exchange of assurances with respect to British oil interests in Iran and Iraq and American interests in Saudi Arabia, they agreed that an announcement should be made of the forthcoming discussions, first on a technical, then on a higher, or Cabinet level. The President was very anxious to have this announcement made—it was issued March 7, 1944—because of press intimations of Anglo-American discord on oil.

The President was also concerned over opposition that had risen in the Senate following Ickes's announcements at the beginning of February concerning the pipeline agreement he had reached and his big oil expansion program throughout the Near East. This opposition in general stemmed from anxiety, on the one hand, over the extent—as indicated by Ickes's announcements—to which the Government was becoming involved in the oil business, and, on the other, over the extent of the major oil companies' control of government policy in this field. The implications with respect to our future foreign policy also aroused apprehension.

Following the passage of a resolution on March 13, the Senate established a special Committee to Investigate Petroleum Resources. After discussions between members of this committee and the State and Interior Departments, we informed our Legation at Jidda on June 27 that there was within our Government an informal understanding that no further action would be taken on the pipeline as a government project until after the British and American Cabinet-level discussions to take place shortly, and such public hearings as the Senate special committee might wish to hold subsequently. The plan for a government-constructed pipeline was not revived while I remained in office. When an Arabian American Company reconnaissance group desired to go to Saudi Arabia in the autumn of 1944 to survey a pipeline to be constructed by the company itself, the Department cabled our Legation at Jidda on October 16 that, if the question were raised by King Ibn Saud or officials of his Government, the position to be taken was that this was solely an Arabian American Company matter not involving this Government, although we had no objections to the company's plans of which we were fully informed. Subsequently, the company was successful in obtaining from certain of the governments directly concerned permission for the construction of the pipeline through their territories.

Meantime preliminary conversations on a technical level had been held in Washington between the British and ourselves, looking toward an Anglo-American oil agreement that subsequently would be joined by other nations. The British committee of Cabinet rank, headed by Lord Beaverbrook, arrived in Washington in July to conclude the discussions. I presided over the first meeting on July 25 and thereafter turned the meetings over to Ickes as vice chairman. An Anglo-American petroleum agreement was reached following a series of conferences, and was announced on August 8, 1944.

This agreement embraced five principles of cooperation between Britain and the United States with regard to international trade in petroleum. These were:

(1) Adequate petroleum supplies should be made available to the nationals of all peaceable countries at fair prices and on a nondiscriminatory basis, subject to such collective security arrangements as might be established.

(2) Petroleum resources should be developed in such a way as to encourage the sound economic advancement of the countries in which the petroleum deposits lay.

(3) There should be equal opportunity to acquire exploration or development rights in areas not already under concession.

(4) There should be respect for valid concession contracts and lawfully acquired rights. (This was designed to put an end to the suspicion that had beclouded Anglo-American relations in the Near East for many years.)

(5) The operations of the petroleum industry should not be hampered by restrictions inconsistent with the purpose of the agreement. (This principle restated the basic purpose of the agreement; namely, that the international petroleum trade should be conducted in an orderly manner on a world-wide basis so that ample oil supplies would become available in international trade to meet the economic needs of all coun-

tries, subject always to considerations of military security and to the provisions of international security arrangements.)

The Anglo-American agreement also provided for the establishment of an International Petroleum Commission. This would prepare long-term estimates of world petroleum demand and suggest how this demand might best be satisfied by production equitably distributed among the various producing countries. It would analyze short-term problems. It would make reports and recommendations to the two Governments.

The agreement was intended to be voluntary in nature, with no executive authority vested either in it or in the International Petroleum Commission to be established under it. It was preliminary to the negotiation of an international agreement to which the Governments of all producing and consuming countries interested in the international petroleum trade would become parties and which would establish a permanent International Petroleum Council.

I sent this agreement to the President on August 22, and he transmitted it to the Senate two days later.

Much adverse reaction followed the publication of the agreement. The American petroleum industry felt that the accord was so worded that it could be construed to cover operations of the domestic petroleum industry, and they were already apprehensive that Secretary Ickes was seeking to control these operations. It thought the agreement gave mandatory powers to the proposed International Petroleum Commission.

Such was the situation when I resigned at the end of November, 1944. In January, 1945, the President, at the suggestion of the State Department, asked the Senate to return the agreement for revision. Subsequently certain provisions were reworded so as clearly to limit its scope to the international and not the domestic trade in petroleum, and further to define the functions of the International Petroleum Commission as advisory and recommendatory only. Ickes went to London, obtained British approval of the revised agreement, and it was again submitted to the Senate, where it lies at this writing. The agreement in its final form embraced all the principles contained in the original agreement.

I continue to believe, as I have consistently advocated, that the United States Government should confine itself to the role of negotiator and mediator in the international petroleum field, and should not itself enter into the business of producing, transporting, or selling oil. It was from this viewpoint that I advocated an international agreement on petroleum.

Oil has become so important a commodity in international trade; it has so often in the past provided the spark for disputes between nations; it will continue so strong a temptation for the domination of small countries by strong nations, that I strongly believe that an international accord such as we negotiated is all-essential. For many years I have seen the problems of oil assume greater and greater importance in our foreign relations until I am convinced that an acceptable international understanding on the principles by which so vital a commodity is to be handled in world commerce has become an essential factor in the establishment and preservation of lasting peace.

111: The Problem of Jews and Arabs

FEW PROBLEMS of a more delicate nature faced us during the war than the question of the Jewish National Home in Palestine. On the one hand we had the burning aspirations of a great percentage of the Jews to establish a state for their people in Palestine, coupled with the fact that the barbaric Nazi persecution was forcing the Jews to flee the charnel house of Central Europe. On the other hand we had the fierce opposition of the Arabs to the establishment of a Jewish state in Palestine and to the continued immigration of Jews into Palestine, plus the fact that the decision in the case was the function of the British Government, not ours. We were constantly being pressed for action by the nearly five million Jews in the United States, while at the same time our representatives in the Near Eastern Arab countries, plus our own military officials here, were informing us of the danger of antagonizing the sixty million Arabs there at a moment when their help in a strategic area of the war was so vital.

Our own relations to Palestine rested on the American-British Mandate Treaty of December 3, 1924, whereby the United States had recognized Britain's mandate over Palestine confided to her by the League of Nations. This provided for nondiscriminatory treatment in matters of commerce; nonimpairment of vested American property rights; permission for Americans to establish and maintain educational, philanthropic, and religious institutions in Palestine; safeguards with respect to the judiciary; and, in general, equality of treatment with all other foreign nationals. We had no right to prevent the modification of the terms of the mandate, but we could refuse to recognize the validity of any modification as it affected American interests.

The Roosevelt Administration's diplomatic interest in Palestine began during the first term. A conflict having broken out in Palestine between Jews and Arabs in the spring of 1936, an investigation of the situation by the British Government gave rise to reports that Jewish immigration into Palestine might be suspended, severely curtailed, or completely eliminated. On July 27, 1936, I cabled Ambassador Bingham in London that influential Jewish groups here had informed the President that Britain was thinking of suspending Jewish immigration into Palestine. Saying that Jewish leaders here feared that such action might prove hard to revoke and might close the German and Polish Jews' only avenue of escape, I asked Bingham to mention this entirely unofficially and personally to Foreign Secretary Eden.

The following year, on April 27, I sent Bingham another telegram of similar tenor. I added that Bingham might mention to Eden that large groups of Jews here were of the opinion that, because of their experience under certain European Governments, Jews throughout the world had logically become the supporters of democratic institutions and looked naturally to the democratic Governments to give them equitable and fair treatment.

Then on October 12, 1938, shortly before the British Government's Palestine Partition Commission was due to report, I cabled Ambassador Kennedy, who had succeeded Bingham, to inform Eden's successor, Lord Halifax, that the White House and the State Department had received thousands of letters and telegrams of protest from all over the country. These messages inveighed against the British Government's alleged intention to eliminate or curtail Jewish immigration and thereby jeopardize the policy that the Balfour Declaration of 1917, with respect to the Jewish National Home in Palestine, had established.

In each of these telegrams to London, however, I instructed our Ambassador to make it entirely clear to the British that we were not in any way questioning Britain's responsibility for Palestine's administration or presuming to interfere in that administration.

Two days later we issued a long public statement of our position toward Palestine. In this we said: "As is well known, the American people have for many years taken a close interest in the development of the Jewish National Home in Palestine. Beginning with President Wilson, each succeeding President has on one or more occasions expressed his own interest in the idea of a National Home and his pleasure at the progress made in its establishment." I also referred to the joint resolution of Congress on September 21, 1922, of the same nature.

Finally the British Government, in May, 1939, released its White Paper on Palestine. Among other provisions, this eliminated immigration into Palestine after March 31, 1944, unless the Arabs agreed to its continuance. I had an analysis made of this document and sent it to the President.

Mr. Roosevelt strongly objected to the British White Paper in a memorandum he sent me on May 17, saying: "I have read with interest and a good deal of dismay the decisions of the British Government regarding its Palestine policy." He continued:

"Frankly, I do not believe that the British are wholly correct in saying that the framers of the Palestine Mandate 'could not have intended that Palestine should be converted into a Jewish state against the will of the Arab population of the country.'

"My recollection is that this way of putting it is deceptive for the reason that while the Palestine Mandate undoubtedly did not intend to take away the right of citizenship and of taking part in the Government on the part of the Arab population, it nevertheless did intend to convert Palestine into a Jewish home which might very possibly become preponderantly Jewish within a comparatively short time. Certainly that was the impression that was given to the whole world at the time of the Mandate. The statement on your Page 6, Paragraph 2, quoting the White Paper of 1933, bears out my contention."

The President, after noting that the new White Paper admitted that the British Mandate was "to secure the development of self-governing institutions," said: "Frankly, I do not see how the British Government reads into the original Mandate or into the White Paper of 1922 any policy that would limit Jewish immigration.

"My offhand thought is that while there are some good ideas in regard to actual administration of government in this new White Paper, it is something that we cannot give approval to by the United States.

"My snap judgment is that the British plan for administration can well be the basis of an administration to be set up and to carry on during the next five years; that during the next five years the 75,000 additional Jews should be allowed to go into Palestine and settle; and at the end of five years the whole problem could be resurveyed and at that time either continued on a temporary basis for another five years or permanently settled if that is then possible. I believe that the Arabs could be brought to accept this because it seems clear that 75,000 additional immigrants can be successfully settled on the land, and because also the Arab immigration into Palestine since 1921 has vastly exceeded the total Jewish immigration during this whole period."

This memorandum coincided also with the thoughts of the State Department. The President, however, did not want it communicated to the British Government, and we limited ourselves to a cable to Kennedy on May 23, 1939, instructing him to mention informally and orally to Foreign Secretary Halifax that disappointment here, especially in Zionist circles, over certain of the White Paper's provisions was rather wide-spread, particularly over those that foreshadowed a marked reduction eventually in Jewish immigration into Palestine. A flood of protests was, in fact, pouring into the State Department.

War came to Europe only three months later. Following the outbreak of fighting, Zionist agitation in this country lay comparatively dormant for a period, although several delegations of Zionists and also Dr. Chaim Weizmann, president of the World Zionist Organization, called on me during 1940 and discussed the development of Palestine as a Jewish refuge after the war.

In the spring of 1941, however, the American Palestine Committee was organized under the chairmanship of Senators Wagner and McNary and with Cabinet members Ickes, Wickard, and Jackson, along with prominent members of Congress and other public figures, as members. The British Embassy thereupon made several representations to us to the effect that if speeches were made in the United States by persons high in the Government advocating the immediate opening up of Palestine to Jewish resettlement planners in the event of a British victory, very great unrest would be created in the Arab world, particularly in Iraq, where a highly critical situation already existed. A rebellion had broken out in Iraq, which the British later had to quell.

I took the occasion of the twenty-fifth anniversary of the Balfour Declaration of 1917 to make a public statement relating to Palestine on October 31, 1942. A group of rabbis having presented to me a memorandum on Palestine, I pointed to the fact that the United States had followed with interest and sympathy the work that had been done under the Balfour Declaration, in which work American citizens had played a useful part.

"Of all the inhuman and tyrannical acts of Hitler and his Nazi lieutenants," I said, "their systematic persecution of the Jewish people—men, women, and children—is the most debased." But I put the solution of the Jewish problem on a broader basis than merely that of the National Home in Palestine. "The Jews," I said, "have long sought a refuge. I believe that we must have an even wider objective; we must have a world in which Jews, like every other race, are free to abide in peace and in honor."

The continuing Zionist agitation in the United States began to have increasingly serious repercussions among the Arab states in the Near East, according to reports we were receiving in the State Department late in

1942 and early in 1943. The Prime Minister of Iraq, Nuri Pasha, protested to our Minister at Bagdad about the pro-Zionist statements emanating from the United States. The heir to the Egyptian throne, Prince Mohammed Ali, raised the same point with Minister Kirk in Cairo.

Lieutenant Colonel Harold B. Hoskins, who, speaking Arabic fluently and knowing the Near East well, had been sent to that area in the autumn of 1942 on a mission for the Joint Chiefs of Staff, reported to us from Cairo on January 23, 1943, his fears that unless some action were taken to reduce the tension, Arab-Jewish conflict might soon break out again in Palestine, even before the end of the war, and throw all the Arab Near East into turmoil. Egyptian Minister Mahmoud Hassan Bey called on me on February 3, 1943, to hand me an *aide-mémoire* from his Government calling attention to "the deplorable effect on the Arab and Mohammedan world" of the Zionist activities, and to their possible repercussions with respect to this Government and the Allied war effort.

King Ibn Saud of Saudi Arabia sent President Roosevelt a message in April and a letter in May. He expressed his personal interest, as an Arab and Moslem leader, in the Arab question, with particular reference to Palestine and Syria. He said, however, that, although urged to make representations to the United States Government respecting Palestine, he had refrained from doing so only because of his desire not to embarrass the United States at this time or to prejudice the United Nations cause by taking a step likely to increase Arab-Jewish antagonisms. He wanted to know whether the President approved of his attitude of silence and, if so, whether he would be advised in advance of any steps of an affirmative character contemplated by the American Government with respect to Palestine.

On May 26, 1943, I sent to Cairo for delivery to the King a message from the President voicing his appreciation of the King's helpful cooperation and sympathetic understanding. He expressed his complete agreement with the King's policy of silence as being most helpful to the United Nations. If, however, the President said, a friendly understanding on Palestine should be reached by the interested Jews and Arabs through their own efforts before the end of the war, a development of that nature would be highly desirable. In any event, he assured the King, it was our Government's view that no decision altering the basic situation of Palestine should be reached without fully consulting with both Jews and Arabs.

The President felt strongly that, if the Arab and Jewish leaders could be brought together for friendly conversations, they might be able to settle their basic differences. In a further message to Ibn Saud in June, Mr. Roosevelt said: "It appears to me highly desirable that the Arabs and Jews interested in the question should come to a friendly understanding with respect to matters affecting Palestine through their own efforts prior to the termination of the war."

The following month I instructed Colonel Hoskins, at the President's direction, to pay a personal visit to King Ibn Saud and ask him whether he would enter into discussions with Dr. Chaim Weizmann or some representative selected by the Jewish agency. The President had already talked this project over with Dr. Weizmann. The King, whom Hoskins saw in August, 1943, refused to see Weizmann, giving as one of several reasons that, despite his position of leadership in the Arab world, he could not, without prior consultation, speak for Palestine, much less "deliver" Palestine to the Jews, even if he were willing for even an instant to consider such a proposal.

In this connection the President had already invited Ibn Saud to come to the United States, hoping that, among other objectives, they might be able in personal conversation to solve some of the problems connected with Palestine.

During the spring and summer of 1943, we discussed with the British a suggestion by Colonel Hoskins that a joint declaration be issued by the United Nations stating that no final decisions regarding Palestine would be taken until after the war, and that any postwar decisions would be taken only after full consultation with both Arabs and Jews. To these points we added another; namely, that, if the interested Jews and Arabs found it possible to arrive at a friendly understanding through efforts of their own prior to the war's end, such a development would be extremely desirable. The President approved this text, and the British did likewise. As a result of objections from the War Department, however, the issuance of the statement was postponed, and President Roosevelt and Prime Minister Churchill decided at the First Quebec Conference, on August 22, 1943, that the question of the statement should be held in abeyance and be discussed further between the two Governments from month to month.

When Colonel Hoskins returned to the United States from his mission to King Ibn Saud, and saw the President on September 27, 1943, Mr. Roosevelt said to him that his own thinking leaned toward a wider use of the idea of trusteeship for Palestine. He thought Palestine should be made a real Holy Land for all three religions, with a Jew, a Christian, and a Moslem as the three responsible trustees. While I was at the Moscow Conference, the State Department gave serious study to this idea; but the impossibility of bringing the Jews and Arabs together on a common, friendly ground at that time, and the danger of stirring the sands of the Near East by a premature attempt to settle the question of Palestine made it wiser to postpone action until a more propitious time.

Beginning with a conversation I had with British Ambassador Halifax on December 13, 1943, we made numerous efforts to induce the British to relax the decision they had made in 1939 to terminate immigration of the Jews into Palestine after March 31, 1944. On that occasion I said to Halifax, who had called at my request, that the United States Government had been exerting itself in every possible way to render all aid and relief to the persecuted Jewish people. "The President and I and other officials of this Government," I said, "in the light of our international interest in the Jewish situation, are in earnest sympathy with the Jews' proposal that immigration into Palestine be extended by the British Government beyond March 31 and that in every other possible way relief and aid be given to the Jewish people." I mentioned that the only question in my mind was how I could best define the attitude of our Government publicly without seriously embarrassing the British in dealing with the military situation in the Near East.

Following several further conversations I had with Halifax, during which he assured me that Eden was giving urgent consideration to my suggestion, the British stated their intention of continuing immigration into Palestine for a certain period after March 31, 1944, inasmuch as the immigration quota for the preceding five years lacked being filled by about 30,000 immigrants.

Early in 1944 we were suddenly confronted by an alarming situation developing in the Near East as a result of resolutions introduced in the Senate and House of Representatives stating that "the United States shall use its good offices and take appropriate measures to the end that the doors of Palestine shall be opened for free entry of Jews into that country, and that there shall be full opportunity for colonization so that the Jewish people may ultimately reconstitute Palestine as a free and democratic Jewish commonwealth."

At the State Department we felt that the passage of these resolutions, although not binding on the Executive, might precipitate conflict in Palestine and other parts of the Arab world, endangering American troops and requiring the diversion of forces from European and other combat areas.

It might prejudice or shatter pending negotiations with Ibn Saud for the construction of a pipeline across Saudi Arabia, which our military leaders felt was of utmost importance to our security. And it would stimulate other special interests to press for the introduction of similar resolutions regarding controversial territorial issues relating to areas such as Poland and Italy.

The reaction in the Near East to the mere introduction of the resolutions had been, as we feared, sharply antagonistic. We received protests from the Governments of Iraq, Egypt, and Lebanon, from King Ibn Saud and from Imam Yahya of Yemen. We assured them that the resolutions, even if passed, were not binding on the Executive. The President on March 13 renewed his previous assurances to the King that it was our Government's view that no decision should be reached changing Palestine's status without full consultation with both Jews and Arabs. The Department sent assurances along the same line to the Egyptian Government and to Imam Yahya.

In the latter notes the Department said: "Although Palestine is primarily a British responsibility, it is the view of the Government of the United States that no decision altering the basic situation of Palestine should be taken until an appropriate time is reached, and that at such a time the Governments responsible for the establishment of peace and the maintenance of law and justice in the world should come to an equitable settlement of all the questions involved, in full consultation with both Arabs and Jews." This continued to be our position throughout the remainder of my period in office.

We were also considering what steps we could take to induce both Houses of Congress not to consider the resolutions. At my request, Assistant Secretary Breckinridge Long met with a group of Senators in Senator Connally's office and orally expressed the Department's views. I had a memorandum drawn up which I intended to give the President to be sent to Congress. At that point, however, Secretary of War Stimson wrote a letter to Senator Connally in the latter's capacity as chairman of the Senate Committee on Foreign Relations. Stimson forthrightly pointed out that the Senate resolution was a matter of deep military concern to the War Department since its passage, or even public hearings on it, would be apt to provoke dangerous repercussions in areas where we had many vital military interests. General Marshall testified in identical vein before the Senate Foreign Relations Committee in executive session. In consequence of the position taken by the State and War Departments, the resolutions were not then reported out of the Senate or House committees.

The apprehensions of the Arabs, however, were further aroused when the President gave two Jewish leaders, Dr. Stephen S. Wise and Dr. Abba H. Silver, an interview on March 9, 1943. The press reported the President as having authorized them to announce that "when future decisions are reached full justice will be done to those who seek a Jewish National Home," that this Government "has never given its approval to the White Paper of 1939," and that the President was "happy that the doors of Palestine are today open to Jewish refugees."

Two days later Minister Kirk in Cairo reported that he had received an inquiry from the Egyptian Prime Minister, Nahas Pasha, regarding this reportedly authorized statement. On March 14 I sent the President for his approval two proposed replies, one to Kirk in Cairo, the other to Minister Loy Henderson in Bagdad. The President approving, these went out to Kirk and Henderson, informing them that the Zionist leaders' statements had in fact been authorized by the President substantially as reported in the Near East. The Ministers were to point out that a Jewish National Home, rather than the Jewish commonwealth referred to in the Congressional resolutions, was mentioned in this statement and that, although the American Government, it was true, had never approved the White Paper, our Government, it was also true, had never taken a position relative to it. Our Ministers were also to renew assurances that it was our Government's view that no decision changing Palestine's basic situation should be arrived at without full consultation with both Jews and Arabs.

Prime Minister Nahas Pasha replied that the Arabs were reassured, although not entirely, by the clarification of the President's statement to the Zionists.

In general the President at times talked both ways to Zionists and Arabs, besieged as he was by each camp. Rabbis Wise and Silver believed that the President had made pledges to them. The State Department made no pledges.

When Under Secretary Stettinius went to London on a survey mission in the spring of 1944, I sent Wallace Murray, Chief of the Office of Near Eastern and African Affairs, with him to discuss Palestine, among other problems, with the British Foreign Office. Murray took with him the draft of a possible joint statement on Palestine by the two Governments similar to that we had prepared the year before. In London it was agreed, however, that the draft should be held in reserve.

During the Republican and the Democratic conventions in 1944, planks were inserted in both platforms urging free immigration into Palestine and the creation there of a Jewish state. The Iraq Government forthwith expressed its deep concern. I sent the President a memorandum on July 26, 1944, saying: "I believe that it would be advisable for leaders of both parties to refrain from making statements on Palestine during the campaign that might tend to arouse the Arabs or upset the precarious balance of forces in Palestine itself."

Fortunately Palestine did not become an issue in the 1944 campaign.

As I left office our policy toward Palestine was one of constantly being on the alert to prevent that explosive area from touching the match to the powder train of the Near East. We could not resolve the questions of the relationship of the Jews to the Arabs, the immigration of the Jews into Palestine, and the creation of a Jewish state in Palestine since these were primarily the responsibility of the British. We had, however, made clear our interest in the solution of the Palestine question; we had induced the British to relax their decision to cut off Jewish immigration into Palestine, and we had made serious, albeit unsuccessful, efforts to bring the Arabs and Jews together for friendly discussion of their differences.

At the same time we had been eminently successful, through unremitting diplomacy, in preventing the already dangerous issue of Palestine from embroiling the whole of the Near East and from stirring up the Moslems in India. The strategic Near East continued to furnish the British and ourselves with much needed oil and to serve as the southern gateway for supplies to Russia without requiring the dispatch of any troops to that area from the vital combat zones in Europe and Africa. It is easy to see the serious consequences to the United Nations cause that might have followed from any diversion of Allied troops to the Near East because of Palestine when the British were thrown back to El Alamein or when we and the British were grappling with the Germans in North Africa. The effect of such German machinations as led to the uprising in Iraq and the British and Free French invasion of Syria would have been multiplied had fighting broken out between Jews and Arabs.

Palestine was but one facet of the unremitting effort of the State Department for over a decade to assist the Jews caught by the unspeakable Nazi persecution. In the 1930's we had made innumerable representations to the Germans and taken concrete steps to evince our condemnation of this persecution and to induce the Nazis to desist. We had likewise brought every possible influence to bear on countries adjacent to Germany to receive, feed, and clothe the Jews of Germany, and on other countries to afford them refuge. This Government took the initiative in creating the Inter-Governmental Refugee Committee, of which Myron C. Taylor became president. In the State Department we began to fill the German, Austrian, and later Czech immigration quotas almost entirely with Jews, and in addition we issued scores of thousands of visitors' visas to Jews in the hope that after coming to this country they could find refuge in other countries or could eventually be received here permanently.

From 1933, when Hitler's persecution of the Jews began, until I resigned at the end of November, 1944, we took into the United States from Germany and Nazi-occupied Europe approximately 600,000 persons, mostly refugees from persecution for racial, political, or religious reasons. In one year alone, that ending in June, 1941, we granted enough visas to save 135,000 refugees. We had made special efforts to get out rabbis, professors and students in rabbinical colleges, Jewish writers, and others who were the light of the Jewish Church. Many came out through Russia and went to Japan, where we issued visas for them.

After the closing of our consulates in Germany and German-occupied areas in June, 1941, our efforts to save the Jews became much more difficult, and the difficulties increased after Pearl Harbor. We could no longer send Americans into Germany to try to induce the Nazi officials to permit the Jews to leave. Shipping was much harder to obtain. Finding it impossible to issue visas to Jews in German-held countries, we concentrated on granting visas to Jews who escaped from that area into adjacent countries.

In 1942 however, we and people throughout the world were horrified to learn that Hitler and his Nazis were inflicting on the Jews the most fiendish outrage that savages or demons could commit against human beings—their inconceivable effort to exterminate utterly the entire Jewish race within their reach. As these menacing developments gradually revealed themselves, the American Government and people, especially the Jewish people, gave the most serious attention to the problem of thwarting Hitler's designs. We exhausted all efforts authorized by law to grant visas or in any feasible way to aid in securing the exit of Jews or to assist their escape from the Hitler area of savagery. And we officially and emphatically, along with Britain and Russia, called to the attention of the

Nazi authorities the condign punishment that would await any of them guilty of such atrocities.

During the war, with the cooperation of the British, Portuguese, and Spanish Governments, and the French National Committee of Liberation in North Africa, we got out of Spain some 30,000 refugees who had trickled over the Pyrenees to that country. We sought places of refuge for them ranging from Madagascar, Cyrenaica, Palestine, and French North Africa, to the Dominican Republic and Ecuador.

President Roosevelt and I had many conferences on the subject of Hitler's attempt to exterminate the Jews. We eagerly studied all ideas and information that might be in the least helpful in relieving their inconceivable situation.

The inescapable fact was, however, that Jews could not leave German-occupied Europe unless they escaped across borders into neutral Spain, Switzerland, or Sweden, or unless the German authorities permitted them to leave. And the Germans permitted Jews to leave only when they were amply paid to do so. We were reluctant to deposit sums of money to the credit of the Nazis, even though the deposits were to be made in Switzerland, were to be liquidated only after the end of the war, and apparently could not be used by the Nazi leaders. Moreover, the State Department did not have the large amounts of money and the personnel needed to carry out a plan of reaching and bribing the German officials in charge of the extermination program.

We also found that the Nazi authorities were sending out intelligence agents in the guise of refugees, and the Federal Bureau of Investigation was called upon to handle a number of such cases. We accordingly set up a control commission in the Department to screen refugee applications, consisting of representatives of the State, War, Navy, and Justice Departments, and the President appointed a little group to serve as an appeals board from this commission.

In 1944 the President created the War Refugee Board to handle the work of aiding refugees, and the State Department fully cooperated in its institution and administration.

Naturally the more extreme sympathizers in this country, especially among the Jews, and some in high positions such as Secretary of the Treasury Morgenthau, found grievous fault with the State Department and especially with every official handling the refugee problem. It was but natural that, in their anguish over the projected extermination of their race in Europe, they should feel that even the strenuous efforts we were making were inadequate. Nevertheless, it can be safely said that the results accomplished by the State Department, up to the time of the creation of the War Refugee Board, at least equalled those of all other countries combined, and that some hundreds of thousands of Jews are now alive who probably would have fallen victim to Hitler's insane enmity had not the Department begun so early and so comprehensively to deal with the refugee problem. President Roosevelt at no time complained to me that the Department had not done enough.

Our interest in the establishment of a Jewish national home in Palestine was paralleled, especially during the war years, by our interest in seeing that independence should eventually come to all the Arab countries and also by our sympathy with the aspirations of Arab leaders toward the creation of an Arab federation. The Arab national movement had begun in the nineteenth century in an effort to achieve independence from Turkey, and it had been no little encouraged by the liberal ideas imparted by American educators in the Near East. Woodrow Wilson expressed the sympathy of this country toward Arab national aspirations by stating in the twelfth of his Fourteen Points that "the other nationalities which are now under Turkish rule should be assured an undoubted security of life and an absolutely unmolested opportunity of autonomous development."

After the First World War, however, the League mandates granted to Britain and France in the Near East seemed to the Arabs a negation of their hopes for the independent Arab empire they believed had been promised them. Their primary objective in the postwar period became the termination of French and British control. They felt that until the Arabs both in the mandated areas and in the nominally independent states could achieve complete independence, any movement toward unity among the various Arab countries was impossible.

After Iraq became independent in 1932, the Arabs concentrated on obtaining independence for the Levantine states of Syria and Lebanon, which were under French mandate. France agreed in 1936 to grant independence to these two mandates, but did not carry out her agreement.

Syria became of keen concern to us in June, 1941, when the British and Free French were forced to invade the mandate after finding that the Germans, with acquiescence of the Vichy Government, were using it as an air base. At that time both the French and the British promised independence to Syria and Lebanon. At the conclusion of the fighting, the British expressed their disinterest in the Levant states and acknowledged the "predominant" French position there. The Free French General Catroux proclaimed Syria independent with certain conditions. We were asked to take a position on this question when the British, after officially recognizing Syrian independence on October 28, 1941, informally urged us to do likewise on the ground that such action would bring greater stability to the Near East and would also strengthen the position of the Allies in the Arab countries.

We demurred, however, on the grounds that recognition without the negotiation of a new treaty might jeopardize the rights we had under the 1924 treaty with France, guaranteeing us nondiscriminatory treatment in Syria and Lebanon; that we were still maintaining relations with the Vichy Government; and that the British acknowledgment of France's "predominant" position and an assertion made by General de Gaulle that France had a "preeminent and privileged position" raised serious complications. We also suggested that our delay in recognizing the independence of Syria might well support British policy since the United States would remain in a position to insist on clarification of the special privileges sought by the French, whereas the British were precluded from doing so by the fact that they had already acknowledged these special privileges.

General Catroux, the Free French Delegate to the Levant states, proclaimed Lebanon independent on November 26, 1941, but emphasized that France did not renounce her "tutelary friendship" or privileged position acquired over the centuries. We thereupon issued a public statement on November 29, 1941, expressing the sympathy of our Government and people with the natural and legitimate aspirations of the peoples of Syria and Lebanon, including the full enjoyment of sovereign independence, which we had endorsed in principle in the treaty with France in 1924 consenting to the French mandate. We added that this treaty guaranteeing American rights must be regarded as continuing in effect until a new treaty could be concluded.

This statement was welcomed by the Syrian and Lebanese authorities, but they, along with the British and Free French, continued to press for formal recognition. We thought it wiser, however, to hold such recognition in abeyance for the time being, to see how the declarations of independence were being implemented. This attitude was amply justified in the spring of 1942 when a serious conflict developed between the French and the British as a result of the latter's insistence that elections be held in Syria and in Lebanon to choose representatives to replace the handpicked appointees placed in power by the French at the time of their "independence" proclamations. Relations between General Spears, the British Minister to the Levant states, who was a personal friend of Prime Minister Churchill, and General Catroux, the Free French Delegate, deteriorated.

We sent instructions on April 24 to our Consul General at Beirut, Cornelius Van H. Engert, to say to the local British and French commanders, Generals Spears and Catroux, that our Government would be very glad to assist in any way we could to achieve a better understanding among the French, the British, and the peoples of the Levant states. As the situation worsened, we took the question up with the British Foreign Office.

General de Gaulle, by agreement with Foreign Secretary Eden, went to Beirut in August in an effort to clarify the situation. We immediately began to receive reports, however, that his presence in the area was having exactly the opposite effect. De Gaulle emphatically and repeatedly told our Consul at Beirut, William M. Gwynn, who was then in charge, that he was determined to bring about an immediate showdown with the British in the Levant. He complained that, through General Spears's intervention in Levantine internal affairs, the British had broken their promises to acknowledge the predominance of the Free French. He said that if the British did not agree to remove Spears all collaboration would end. De Gaulle was apparently convinced that the British intended to eliminate the French from Syria and Lebanon. He told Gwynn that France would, when possible, grant independence to the Levant states, but that this could not be done until the peoples were ready for it, which might not be for many years.

I cabled this information to Ambassador Winant in London on August 21, 1942, instructing him to discuss the situation with Eden again. I authorized Winant to say that we were unable to support in their entirety either the Free French or the British positions, but we could not remain indifferent to a dispute that had an important effect on the common war effort. I said we thought that De Gaulle's statement that the Levant states might not be ready for independence for many years was not in harmony with the statements made by the Free French and the British just before they occupied Syria when, primarily for its propaganda value with the Arabs, they had announced that the Allies were bringing independence to the two areas, or with the later proclamations by General Catroux that the two Levant states had begun an independent existence. On the other hand, I said, General Spears seemed to be exceeding the functions of a foreign diplomatic representative.

I cabled Consul Gwynn at Beirut on the same day to point out to

General de Gaulle our concern, as a country participating in the common war effort, that there be scrupulous fulfillment of the assurances that had been given the Levant states. If this were not so, we said, the Arab world and all peoples asked to believe in our sincerity would feel justifiable doubts relative to the assurances given by any of the Allied nations or groups.

We ourselves made a gesture toward encouraging the peoples of Syria and Lebanon when, on the recommendation of the State Department, the President approved of our giving our Consul General in Beirut the additional rank of Diplomatic Agent, a designation reserved for representation in semi-sovereign states. Mr. Roosevelt named George Wadsworth, a Foreign Service officer, to the new office, the appointment being announced on October 2, 1942.

The British and Free French continued to quarrel over British insistence that the French live up to the assurances they had given with regard to the independence of the Levant states, although relations became temporarily less strained following an exchange of correspondence between Prime Minister Churchill and De Gaulle in the autumn of 1942. Finally the French gave in on the question of holding elections, which were conducted in July and August, 1943, in Syria and Lebanon, respectively. Nationalist regimes were elected in both states, and a crisis was soon precipitated as the new Governments indicated their intention to secure control of the governing powers still exercised by the French.

In view of the potential gravity of the situation the British handed us an *aide-mémoire*, dated September 10, in which they reiterated their willingness to recognize France's "predominant position" in the Levant states. They added, moreover, that they would not oppose treaties between the Free French authorities and the Syrian and Lebanese authorities if such treaties, defining their relationship, were desired by both parties.

In our reply on October 25 we made it clear that our Government "was not a party to the agreements concluded prior to the invasion of the Levant states by British and Free French forces in 1941, and is not prepared to admit that France should enjoy a 'preeminent and privileged position' in Syria and the Lebanon." However, we added, should the French and the Levant states desire to enter into free and voluntary negotiations, we were in substantial agreement with the British provided that the interests of the local populations and of the United States were adequately safeguarded and that the treaties would only be applied provisionally pending formal ratification.

As it became apparent that the situation was mounting to a climax in Lebanon, we instructed Counselor Robert D. Murphy at Algiers on November 9, 1943, to advise the appropriate French authorities that the United States Government was of the opinion that practical steps should be taken to implement the "independence" promised Syria and Lebanon. Failure to do so, we said, would cast doubt on the announced principles of the United Nations.

Before Murphy could act on these instructions, however, the French on November 11 arrested the President of Lebanon, Sheik al-Khuri, and the Cabinet, and installed a government of their own choosing. Riots broke out in Beirut.

We immediately sent out two cables, one to Diplomatic Agent Wadsworth in Beirut, the other to Murphy in Algiers. We instructed Wadsworth to have no official relations with the regime just set up by the French. We instructed Murphy urgently to inform the French National Committee in Algiers that our Government had learned with surprise of the repressive action taken by their authorities in Lebanon. We said it was "difficult to understand how the French, whose country is now groaning under the heel of the invader, can be unmindful of the aspirations toward independence of another people"; that the French action in Lebanon "must cast the gravest doubt upon the sincerity of the avowed declarations of all the United Nations"; and that the United States Government could not "permit itself to be associated in any way with such acts of repression."

We further said that unless the French National Committee took "prompt steps to restore the duly elected Government of the Lebanese Republic and to implement the solemn promises of independence given to the Lebanese people" in 1941 in the name of the French National Committee, our Government would be "obliged publicly to announce its complete disapproval of the acts of the French authorities in the Lebanese Republic and to take such further steps as may appear appropriate." We added that we would take such action with the utmost reluctance but that we felt "it would be less detrimental to the united war effort than for us by silence to appear to accept a situation which is contrary to the aims and principles for which the liberty-loving nations are fighting."

We repeated this telegram to London, Beirut, and Cairo, for the information of the appropriate authorities, and used it as the basis of our replies to protests over the French action we received from the Egyptian, Iraq, Syrian, and Saudi Arabian Governments.

I kept President Roosevelt, who was on his way to Cairo, informed of the situation, and he discussed it with Prime Minister Churchill, whose Government was taking a strong position similar to ours. I received a message from the President on November 20 saying: "I think we should back up the British position in Lebanon and try to make it even more positive."

The British, who commanded the defense forces in Lebanon, informed the French National Committee that they would declare martial law unless the duly elected Lebanese Government were reinstated by November 22. The French at first tried to compromise by reinstating only the President and not the Cabinet, but the British and we continued to insist on the reinstatement of the entire Lebanese Government. The French thereupon gave in, and the crisis—a crisis not only for the Near East, but for relations with the French National Committee and for the principles of the United Nations—ended. We issued a press release on November 26 noting with approval the remedial action taken by the French National Committee and expressing "the earnest hope of this Government that friendly negotiations can now proceed in an atmosphere of good will on both sides for the solution of the underlying issue of the independence of the Levant states."

In December, 1943, General Catroux concluded a series of informal accords with the Syrian and Lebanese Governments providing for the transfer to them of the powers formerly exercised by the French in their joint behalf. In succeeding months these accords were gradually given practical application, and in August, 1944, we concluded that the Governments of Syria and Lebanon could now be considered representative, effectively independent, and in a position satisfactorily to fulfill their international obligations and responsibilities. Thereupon, with the President's approval, we informed the Governments of Lebanon and Syria on September 7, 1944, that we were prepared to extend full and unconditional recognition of their independence and to exchange Ministers with them upon receipt from them of written assurances that the existing rights of the United States and its nationals (embracing nondiscriminatory treatment) would be fully recognized. The Syrian and Lebanese Governments having given these assurances, the President nominated George Wadsworth as our first Minister to those countries. In a public statement on September 19, 1944, I said:

"I am confident that the free nations of Syria and Lebanon will play a helpful part in the cooperative task of international peace and progress which lies before us."

At that moment the French were pressing the Levant Governments for the conclusion of treaties of alliance with France. We received reports that the French desired that recognition be given to a "special position" for France in Syria and Lebanon, and that the Syrian and Lebanese Governments were resisting this pressure. We accordingly informed the French National Committee, in a memorandum of October 5, 1944, that our Government could "not agree that France or French nationals should enjoy discriminatory privileges in independent Syria and Lebanon." Subsequently in a telegram to Wadsworth we took the position that, while we would not approve a treaty under which France or her nationals obtained discriminatory privileges, we were of the opinion that it would be well for those Governments to consider seriously the arguments the British had made in favor of negotiations between them and France, particularly the desirability of obtaining formal and clear confirmation by the French of the independence of Syria and Lebanon before the withdrawal of British forces by reason of the favorable progress of the war.

As Syria and Lebanon took long but troubled steps toward independence, the movement toward a Pan Arab Federation in the Near East gathered impetus. Foreign Secretary Eden had declared to the House of Commons on February 24, 1943, that the British Government would view with sympathy any move among the Arabs to promote their economic, cultural, or political unity. Eden said, however, that the initiative would clearly have to come from the Arabs themselves, and that, so far as he was aware, no such scheme which would command general approval had yet been worked out.

This declaration induced Nuri Pasha, Prime Minister of Iraq, to write Nahas Pasha, Prime Minister of Egypt, urging the latter to take the initiative in calling an Arab congress. Nahas Pasha soon began a series of individual conferences with representatives of Iraq, Trans-Jordan, Saudi Arabia, Syria, Lebanon, and the Yemen, regarding an Arab union, preliminary to convening an Arab congress.

It was during this series of conferences that our Government stated its sympathetic attitude toward the formation of an Arab union or federation. The Saudi Arabian representative, while conferring with Prime Minister Nahas Pasha, addressed a query to Minister Kirk in Cairo to learn the attitude of the United States Government toward an Arab union.

On October 26, 1943, the Department (I was then in Moscow) replied, in paraphrase:

"This Government desires to see the independent countries of the Near East retain their freedom and strengthen their economic and social condition, and fully sympathizes with the aspirations of other Near Eastern countries for complete liberty.

"If the peoples of the Near East should find it advantageous to unite of their own free will, it naturally follows from this Government's basic attitude that such a development would be viewed with sympathy, always on the understanding that it should take place in accordance with the principles of the Atlantic Charter and in harmony with the declarations of Secretary Hull, notably those of July 23, 1942, and September 12, 1943.

"It is realized that the countries concerned will shape their own decision, but it seems to this Government that the events and problems of the war years have shown that the Near Eastern countries need greater strength in the economic, social, and cultural domains, and that first steps toward unity might well have these ends in view."

We repeated this reply to our diplomatic missions in the Arabic-speaking countries for their information.

Our attitude, therefore, was that we fully favored the concept of an Arab federation, but we took the realistic view that the Near Eastern countries should move toward this objective gradually and should take the first steps in the economic, social, and cultural fields before proceeding to political federation.

When the convening of a preliminary Arab conference was under discussion in July, 1944, the Saudi Arabian Government again sought our Government's views. We replied in substantially the same terms as in October, 1943. We also referred, however, to the position we had taken on the Palestine question in March since this question obviously would have to be solved before any true Arab unity could be achieved.

As I left office, I entertained the strong hope that the Arab states of the Near East would soon begin to take the economic, social, and cultural steps we believed necessary as an approach toward political unity, that they would be able to compose the conflicting ambitions of various of their leaders, and that, not too many years after the conclusion of the war, they would be able to bring stability, unity, and economic development to that historic corner of the world.

112: Italy: Enemy and Friend

PRESIDENT ROOSEVELT and I believed almost from the time of Mussolini's declaration of war against the United States, four days after Pearl Harbor, that we should draw a distinction between the Italians on the one hand and the Germans and Japanese on the other. In the discussions I had with the President on this subject in 1942 we reached two conclusions. The first was that Americans had always been friendly with the Italians, despite our opposition to the Fascist regime, and that Mussolini had led the people of Italy into an unpopular war without in the slightest consulting them. The other was that it might be possible to withdraw Italy from the war before the surrender of Germany and Japan, and that this withdrawal would in fact hasten that surrender. Italy's retirement, we felt, would be accelerated if we were to adopt an attitude toward the Italians different from that toward the Germans and the Japanese.

In consequence of this position, Attorney General Biddle announced on Columbus Day, October 12, 1942, that Italian aliens in the United States would no longer be classed as "alien enemies." The following day Assistant Secretary of State Berle, recalling in a public address the pledge in the Atlantic Charter that all peoples had the right to choose the form of government under which they would live, said that this pledge would be redeemed when Italy had rid herself of her Fascist government. He said that no punitive peace for Italy was envisaged, and that Americans did not desire to destroy Italy as a nation.

Three years of war, punctuated by defeat after defeat, which reached a climax with the Western Allies in full possession of Italy's African possessions and Sicily and about to put foot on the Italian mainland, brought the Italians to the end of their resistance. After exchanges of telegrams, in which the State Department took part, President Roosevelt and Prime Minister Churchill agreed on a joint message to the Italian people which they made public on July 16, 1943. In this they stated: "The sole hope for Italy's survival lies in honorable capitulation to the overwhelming power of the military forces of the United Nations. If you continue to tolerate the Fascist regime which serves the evil power of the Nazis, you must suffer the consequences of your own choice."

Nine days later Mussolini resigned, and King Victor Emmanuel III entrusted the Government to Marshal Pietro Badoglio. On July 31 I sent the President a memorandum suggesting that, since it was obvious that the Soviet Government was becoming concerned over the Italian situation, a joint Anglo-American message should, be sent to that Government informing it of developments and asking for any suggestions the Russians might care to offer. I attached a draft of a message which stated that this Government continued to share the view that it was essential that the United States, British, and Soviet Governments keep one another fully informed regarding military and political developments in the various areas in which their respective armed forces were operating.

The President agreed to this approach.

During the following weeks negotiations for surrender were conducted in Lisbon between representatives of the Anglo-American Combined Chiefs of Staff and representatives of Marshal Badoglio. The State Department had little share in these discussions, which were of a military nature. We saw to it that the Russians were kept informed of the terms of surrender, and the British did likewise. On August 28 Admiral Standley, our Ambassador in Moscow, cabled us that the Soviet Government approved the terms and empowered General Eisenhower to sign on their behalf, a special representative of the Soviet Government not being required in this instance.

On the same day I sent the full draft instrument of surrender and a summary outline to the Governments of Russia, the British Dominions, Brazil, Ethiopia, Greece, and Yugoslavia and to the French Committee of National Liberation. The Greek Government had informed us of its interest in two regions then occupied by Italian forces—Epirus and the Dodecanese Islands—but, with the approval of the President, I informed Greek Ambassador Cimon P. Diamantopoulos on September 15 that it was the policy of this Government that territorial questions be left for settlement until after the war.

A plenipotentiary of Marshal Badoglio signed the terms of surrender in Sicily on September 3, and Eisenhower and Badoglio announced them on September 8, the day they became effective. Two days later President Roosevelt and Prime Minister Churchill sent a joint message to Marshal Badoglio and the Italian people urging them to strike hard alongside their American and British friends to drive the Germans out of Italy.

During the discussions between the British and ourselves on the terms of surrender for Italy, which were drawn up by the Combined Civil

Affairs Committee of the Anglo-American Combined Chiefs of Staff in Washington, a basic cleavage of opinion had developed over the status of the Italian Crown and the Badoglio Government. The British had strenuously objected to American proposals to limit the scope and duration of authority of the Badoglio Government and to suspend the power of the Crown in Italy. This cleavage later became deeper and more pronounced.

I myself was not at all sympathetic to the idea of keeping King Victor Emmanuel on the throne. He had, to all intents and purposes, gone along with Mussolini. We had hoped that the King would keep Mussolini from going to war, but he had done nothing, possibly because he could do nothing. In any event, his name had been associated with that of Mussolini in aligning Italy militarily with Germany against Britain and France, and later against Russia, and still later with Germany and Japan against the United States. I felt that Italy was virtually without a chief of state after the King had diminished himself and his position to such an extent.

As for Badoglio, he was the appointee of a King with whom we had no sympathy. He was adequate for the purpose of signing the terms of surrender, but I did not consider him adequate for the purpose of governing Italy. I felt that, as soon as feasible, the people of Italy, represented by the parties in opposition to Fascism, should be permitted to express their choice of the form and personnel of the Government they wanted.

As I talked over these ideas with the President, I found he was fully of the same opinion.

The British, on the other hand, and Prime Minister Churchill in particular, would have been glad to see the Italian royal family continue its rule. They wanted the royal family kept in power at least temporarily, but with the idea in mind that during this temporary period the King could strengthen his position and render his rule or that of his family permanent.

I sent a telegram on September 22 to Robert D. Murphy, the State Department representative on General Eisenhower's staff, giving him and Eisenhower the President's and my thoughts on the policy he should carry out with respect to Italy and the Italian Government. This stated that Eisenhower should make recommendations from time to time to lighten the provisions of the Italian armistice in order to permit the Italians to wage war against Germany within the limit of their capacities. If the then Government of Italy declared war on Germany it would be permitted to carry on as the Government of Italy and treated as a cobelligerent. It had to be clearly understood, however, that these concessions were not in any way to prejudice the untrammeled right of the Italian people to decide on the form of government they would eventually have. And no final form of government for Italy would be decided upon until the Germans were driven from Italian territory. Finally, Eisenhower should encourage the vigorous use of Italian armed forces against Germany.

On October 13, 1943, the Italian Government declared war on Germany. Badoglio's proclamation to this effect, in the name of the King, stated that the Government he headed would shortly be completed, and that representatives of every political party would be asked to participate so that it might be a truly democratic Government. This arrangement, he said, would in no way impair the untrammeled right of the Italian people to choose their own form of democratic government when peace was restored. On the same day, Roosevelt, Churchill, and Stalin issued a joint statement accepting Italy as a cobelligerent.

At that time I was en route to the Moscow Conference. I have already recounted how, at that conference, Molotov, Eden, and I agreed upon a policy to restore democratic institutions and practices in Italy. We likewise agreed to establish the Advisory Council for Italy, consisting of representatives of the Governments of Great Britain, the United States, the Soviet Union, Greece, and Yugoslavia, and the French Committee of National Liberation. The Council provided a channel for the expression of United Nations policy toward Italy, and made recommendations concerning this policy to the Allied Commander-in-Chief in Italy, General Sir Henry Maitland Wilson. Those United Nations who were not actively taking part in the fighting in Italy but who had an interest in Italian affairs were allowed a voice in Allied policy in Italy through the Advisory Council.

As I returned from the Moscow Conference on November 10, Marshal Badoglio was having difficulty incorporating the other political parties into his Government as he had promised in his October 13 proclamation. Generally they did not relish serving under the King; they thought he should abdicate; and they did not consider Badoglio himself a shining emblem of democracy.

The center of this opposition to the King was Carlo Sforza, who had been Italian Foreign Minister prior to the advent of Mussolini to power. He had spent some years in the United States lecturing and writing, and was the acknowledged leader of Italian anti-Fascists in North and South America. Sforza came to see me on August 16 and expressed his desire to return to Italy. Following an exchange of letters he had with Assistant Secretary of State Berle, in which he agreed to support Marshal Badoglio or any other Italian Government acceptable to the United Nations in fighting against Germany, our Government aided his return to Italy. Passing through London en route to Italy, Sforza had luncheon with Prime Minister Churchill and repeated to him the same promise.

After Sforza returned to Italy and consulted other anti-Fascist leaders, he balked at the prospect of entering an Italian Government as long as Victor Emmanuel remained on the throne. Both the King and Badoglio sought personally to induce him to enter their Government, but he refused. He drew up papers of abdication for the King's signature, naming the Prince of Naples, the King's grandson, as his successor, with Badoglio as Regent. These would have passed over the King's son, Prince Humbert of Piedmont, who seemed as unacceptable as his father to the anti-Fascist parties. The King refused to sign.

Generally we in Washington thought Sforza's formula a happy solution. The British, however, thought otherwise. We took a less serious view of the consequences of abdication than the British, who felt that so fundamental a decision should not be made at that time.

In November, 1943, when the Italian political situation was critical, General Eisenhower recommended a compromise solution to which the President agreed. This was that, if the King failed to form a liberal Government but refused to abdicate, the existing arrangement with the King and Badoglio should continue until Rome was in Allied hands. Eisenhower made this recommendation, believing that the occupation of Rome was imminent.

Following the Allied landing at Anzio, I cabled the acting American representative on the Advisory Council for Italy, G. Frederick Reinhardt, on January 25, 1944, the thoughts of the President, my associates, and myself concerning the Italian situation. I said that the State Department had concluded that there should be no further delay in reorganizing the Italian Government on a broad political basis, and that liberal forces in Italy should be allowed to proceed at once to set up a representative Italian regime to function until the full liberation of the country.

We had also concluded, I said, that no political reconstruction under King Victor Emmanuel was possible. We believed he would never abdicate of his own free will, and that the longer his abdication was postponed the more difficult it would be to bring it about. We were definitely opposed to the King's return to Rome, believing that his arrival there would strengthen his determination to remain on the throne. Nevertheless, I said, it was not our intention to go into the constitutional question of the monarchy as an institution and form of government; in line with our announced policy, that question should be left to the determination of the Italian people when Italy was freed of the Germans.

We had also communicated this position to the British. Mr. Churchill, however, did not like it. On January 23 he cabled the President urging that we should hold on to Badoglio and the King until we could be sure of something better and more effective for our purpose, and do nothing to weaken them in the interval. On the contrary, he said, should we become masters of Rome in the near future the early return of Badoglio and the King to the capital would be beneficial. He thought that, after Rome was occupied, we could at leisure survey the scene and see what other alternatives were in sight.

The same month the British and we stated there was no objection on our part to the return from Russia to Italy of Palmiro Togliatti, alias Ercole Ercoli, the leading Italian Communist who had spent many years in Russia and had risen to a high position in the Communist International. We stated, however, that this had to be agreeable to the Italian Government and to Allied Forces Headquarters at Algiers. Togliatti went to Italy soon thereafter.

The expectation of Allied military authorities that Rome would soon be occupied proved vain. The Germans established a strong defensive line between Naples and Rome and also contained our landing at Anzio. Moreover, Allied troops were already being diverted from the Mediterranean theater to the British Isles for the landing in Normandy.

At the beginning of February, Mr. Churchill cabled the President that he was much concerned at any attempt to work with Sforza and the Italian Junta at this critical moment in the battle. He accused Sforza of having completely broken his undertaking to support the Badoglio Government, and asked that no decisions be taken without Britain being consulted and without the President and the Prime Minister trying to reach agreement. He believed we were in for a very heavy struggle on the Italian front.

I talked the situation over with British Ambassador Lord Halifax on February 9 and informed him that, when the State Department recommended that the King not be permitted to go to Rome but that consideration be given to other elements in the political situation, it appeared that the Allied Armies would be in Rome within a few days, whereas it now appeared that they would not be there for some time to come. I said that the application of our attitude toward the King was not of the same urgency as it had appeared a short time before.

Later in the day I discussed the matter with the President in the same vein. Accordingly he sent me a memorandum on February 10, saying: "Please take such action as is necessary and feasible in the Department of State to insure that no effort is made by the United States Government to effect any change in the existing Government of Italy at the present time, and until our military situation in the Italian campaign is sufficiently improved to warrant risking disaffection of those Italians who are now assisting the Allied Armies."

I had left Washington that morning for a short vacation, and Stettinius communicated this to our representatives in Italy.

The Executive Junta of the six opposition parties in Italy, however, formally requested Allied support for its program of obtaining the King's abdication and preparing the formation of a Government with full powers to govern until general elections could be held after the liberation of all Italy. The Supreme Allied Commander for the Mediterranean theater, General Wilson, recommended support of this program.

American concurrence in this recommendation was submitted to the British members of the Combined Civil Affairs Committee of the Combined Chiefs of Staff on February 23. Our agreed position was that General Wilson should be authorized to inform the Junta that their program would have Allied support; to confirm that support to the King if necessary; and so to inform the members of the Advisory Council.

British concurrence, however, was never given. A few days later, on February 29, Prime Minister Churchill publicly stated to the House of Commons that Britain opposed any change in the Italian Government at present. This statement received an adverse reaction from all the anti-Fascist parties in Italy and was construed by them as a negative Allied reply to the Junta's proposal. We hastened to state to our representatives in Italy on March 2 that the Prime Minister's statement was not to be considered as a reply to the Junta, that the subject was still being considered by the Combined Chiefs of Staff, and that only from them could come any agreed Allied reply.

We had already stated our attitude directly to Marshal Badoglio in a letter from the President dated February 21, which was drafted in the State Department. This answered a letter to the President from Badoglio in which the latter pleaded that Italy be given full status as an ally. The

President rejected this appeal "until the Government of Italy can also include the articulate political groups of anti-Fascist liberal elements." He referred to the existing plan "for the reconstruction of the Italian Government on a broad political basis as soon as the present critical military situation will permit and not later than the liberation of Rome."

That same day the King, up to that moment stubbornly determined to prolong himself on the throne regardless of the political turmoil his decision was producing, weakened. He informed British General MacFarlane, chief of the Allied Control Commission for Italy, that, since his position had become almost untenable "because the Allies had permitted him to be openly discredited and attacked through the Psychological Warfare Board and lax censorship," he proposed to nominate Crown Prince Humbert as his lieutenant with full powers as soon as Rome was reached, and to make an announcement to that effect immediately. He did not, however, carry out this latter intention.

During March the President and Prime Minister Churchill exchanged numerous cables seeking in vain to compose the divergent American and British viewpoints. On March 7 the President reiterated to Mr. Churchill our view that liberal groups must be brought into the Italian Government at the earliest opportunity. The following day the Prime Minister gave the President his opinion that it would be a serious mistake "to yield to agitation, especially when accompanied by threats on the part of groups of politicians who are seeking office," and that action should be postponed until the battle had been gained, or, best of all, until Rome had been taken.

The political situation in Italy was deteriorating, however, to the disadvantage of the Allied war effort, and the President cabled the Prime Minister on March 8 asking for his suggestions as to how it could be remedied in a way acceptable to the British. Five days later the President cabled again, urging action on the basis of the plan approved both here and by the Allied commander in Italy and his British and American advisers. The Prime Minister replied on March 15 that the six anti-Fascist parties were not representative of Italy or Italian democracy and that they could not now replace the existing Italian Government, which had "loyally and effectively" worked in our interests, but that the question of timing would, of course, have to be reviewed if the capture of Rome were unduly delayed. He said the War Cabinet felt that nothing could be worse for our joint interests and for the future of Italy than to set up a weak democratic Government which "flopped."

In his cables the Prime Minister pointed out that Britain had suffered 232,000 casualties in her war with Italy which had lasted since June, 1940, as well as extensive ship losses. He therefore felt that his views toward Italy should receive the President's consideration. He pleaded that the divergence which had risen between the two Governments be kept quiet.

The President cabled Mr. Churchill on March 17, agreeing that the divergence of views should not be divulged "particularly at this time," but saying that the situation should be carefully watched and the matter be kept continually before the Advisory Council for Italy.

Suddenly, while these numerous exchanges of cables between the President and the Prime Minister were occurring, the Soviet Government out of a clear sky announced that it was exchanging diplomatic representatives with the Badoglio Government. Simultaneously the Communist Party in Italy deserted the six-party front and declared its support of the King and Badoglio.

This unilateral action, taken without advance consultation with the British or ourselves, was highly disconcerting. It tended to undermine the authority of the Advisory Council for Italy through which the United Nations carried on relations with the Badoglio Government. Neither the British nor ourselves had diplomatic representatives accredited to that Government.

I instructed Ambassador Harriman in Moscow on March 16 to see Molotov and explain to him that all the complicated machinery of control for Allied government in Italy was designed to support and secure the supreme authority of the Allied Command, and that any development outside the established machinery of control over Italian administration, economy, and resources must be brought into relationship with the Allied military authorities responsible for that major theater of operations.

I added that at the Moscow Conference the United States and Great Britain, in accordance with Soviet desires, had welcomed and agreed to full Soviet participation in all matters of policy with regard to Italy. The Moscow Conference had thus established the principle of Allied as against individual approach to particular questions in the liberated areas of Italy, including relations with the Italian Government. Up to the present time, I said, the Soviet Government had given us no indication that these arrangements were in any way unsatisfactory, and it was a fact that the Soviet representatives on the Advisory Council and on the Control Commission were afforded means of contact with the Italian authorities identical to those enjoyed by the British and American representatives.

In conclusion I pointed out that the supreme responsibility for matters relating to the Italian theater continued to be vested in the Allied Commander-in-Chief, and that no special arrangement between the Italian Government and one of the Allied Governments could modify in the slightest degree that responsibility.

We informed Badoglio, moreover, that the Italian Government was not entitled to make any arrangements with any foreign Power, whether Allied or neutral, without the consent of the Supreme Allied Commander.

Molotov sought to justify the Soviet action on the ground that Russia had not been sufficiently consulted concerning developments in Italy—this despite the fact that we had made every effort to keep Russia thoroughly informed.

I instructed Ambassador Harriman on March 24 to say to Molotov that we expected that, during the period of our active military operations against Germany, any further developments in the relations of the Soviet Union with Italy would be referred to the Advisory Council for consideration and appropriate action.

The President and Prime Minister Churchill had agreed in their early discussions concerning Italy that, the Mediterranean being in general a British theater of operations, Britain should have the major degree of control in Italy. This applied to the command of the military operations there and also to the conduct of the Allied Control Commission and Allied Military Government. The British occupied most of the key posts in the military command and in civil affairs.

Nevertheless, when Badoglio, in a conversation with Samuel Reber, our political adviser on the Allied Control Commission, expressed his regret on March 22, 1944, at what seemed to him a decision by the United States Government to "pull out of" the Mediterranean, both politically and militarily, leaving the dominant role to others, I took sharp exception to his statement. I cabled Reber on April 3 that, if any suggestion came up that we were "pulling out," he should state that the policy of this Government had undergone no change whatever from the time we undertook the campaign in Italy with the Anglo-American landing in Sicily. We had, I added, just as much interest as before in the Italian situation, and we had just as much hope that Italy would be restored to the family of nations and that the Italian people would, as soon as military exigencies permitted, be free to choose their own leaders and Government.

Since the President and the Prime Minister were unable in their exchanges of telegrams to resolve the differences between our two Governments over whether and when the Italian Government should change or the King go out, I instructed the acting American representative on the Advisory Council, G. Frederick Reinhardt, on March 24, to place the question on the Council's agenda to be worked out by that body.

The British Embassy had left with us an *aide-mémoire* on March 6 containing Eden's suggestion that both Governments watch developments without declaring for any solution, and that the Combined Chiefs of Staff inform General Wilson to this effect. In reply we referred to a statement by the President in his telegram to Mr. Churchill on March 13 when he said he had not at any time intended to convey to the Prime Minister his agreement that all political decisions should be postponed until after Rome had been taken. We stated that this Government favored the proposal presented by the Junta of the Italian anti-Fascist parties involving the abdication of the King and the delegation of all or some of the royal powers to a lieutenant. We desired an immediate solution along these lines. The mere policy of preserving the status quo until after the liberation of Rome favored the position of one group, and we could not avoid the responsibility of supporting one of the various solutions. We said we were opposed to a policy calculated to suppress normal political activity in those areas of Italy restored to Italian administration.

As a result of our initiative, the Advisory Council began a discussion of the question of the Italian Government. Since the King's stubborn determination to keep his throne still seemed to be the major obstacle, the American representative, Robert D. Murphy, obtained the agreement of his British colleagues that he should inform the King personally and unequivocally that the time had come for him to retire.

Murphy saw the King on April 10 and demanded his acceptance by the following day. Apparently relying on the support of the Italian Communist Party, the King refused to go further than announce his intention to withdraw in favor of Crown Prince Humbert after Rome was occupied. The British representative would not agree to press the matter further, and Murphy therefore consented to the formula which the King announced on April 12. The Soviet representative had no part in this *démarche*, but he was kept fully informed, and the Soviet Government went along with it.

The Executive Junta of the opposition parties decided on April 16 to accept the King's plan and to enter immediately a new Government composed almost entirely of the representatives of the six anti-Fascist parties. The new broad-based Government under the premiership of Badoglio was announced on April 21, and for the first time in two decades that part of Italy which had been liberated from German and Fascist domination had a truly representative Government.

At this time Marshal Badoglio sent the President a personal letter asking for "a full reexamination of the very harsh terms made to us six months ago" with a view to Italy's transition from cobelligerency to alliance. He made the same request of the British.

For three months we had been exchanging cables with the British on the subject of an Italian Government request of December 27, 1943, that it be permitted to make formal announcement of its desire to adhere to the principles of the Atlantic Charter. We saw no objection to this wish, but the British were opposed. Finally, British Ambassador Halifax came to see me on March 31 and handed me a memorandum from his Government sustaining the British position and pointing out that it would be most inexpedient to take any action that would give even the appearance of creating an obligation to maintain Italian territories intact. The matter rested in abeyance.

The British now made known to us on April 20 their views concerning Italy's plea for the status of an ally. The British felt that, while Italy's position as a cobelligerent entitled her to better treatment than as merely a defeated enemy, she must not forget her position as a defeated enemy nor claim the privileges of an ally. The greater the concessions now made, they thought, the more difficult would it be to impose such sanctions as the Allies might wish when all Italy had been freed, and at the end of the war. The British said they planned to seek Soviet agreement to a positive stand that Allied status for Italy could not be considered at the time, but before drafting the note they asked that we coordinate our views.

We agreed with this position, and so informed the British. I cabled Murphy on April 29 that, should the matter be raised in the Advisory Council, he should make it clear that the Department had no intention of agreeing to Allied status for Italy.

Since agitation for Allied status continued, I cabled Murphy again on May 16, stating that the plight of Italy had the full sympathy of the Department and that this Government should take with the Allies all feasible steps to strengthen the new Italian Government and assure its position until Rome was reached. Nevertheless, I added, the Department considered it premature to raise the question of Allied status. This was not only because of the far-reaching consequences this would have toward breaking down the entire machinery of the Allied Control Commission and the armistice terms far in advance of the date when Italy, as a defeated Power, would inevitably sign a peace treaty, but also because of the unfavorable impact it would have on the Yugoslavs, the Greeks, and the French, sufferers from Italy's aggression.

The Allied armies were now in full campaign to capture Rome. For eighteen months the question of whether Rome might be preserved from bombing had been a subject for diplomatic exchanges among ourselves, the British, and the Vatican. The British, whose capital, London, had been bombed by Italian planes, did not wish to renounce the possibility of bombing the Italian capital.

Myron Taylor, the President's representative to the Vatican, had suggested to Mr. Roosevelt on November 30, 1942, that this Government adopt an independent course. The President asked me the following day to prepare a reply. I sent the President a memorandum on December 3, stating my own view that it would be inadvisable for us to adopt an independent course from that of our principal associate in the war. "It seems to me," I said, "that if we disagree with the policy of the British Government in regard to the bombing in Italy, we should communicate with them and endeavor to reach a meeting of minds and a common policy."

The President replied to Taylor in this sense.

The Apostolic Delegate in the United States, Archbishop Cicognani, left a memorandum with Assistant Secretary Berle on December 4, requesting this Government to use its good offices so that the Pope might be assured, at least informally and confidentially, that Vatican City and the city of Rome might be spared the horrors of aerial bombardment. Taylor sent the President on December 17 a further message from the Vatican stating that the Vatican had undertaken negotiations with the Italian Government to remove Axis military installations from the Eternal City, and that the Italian Government had given on December 13 oral assurances that the Supreme Command and the General Staff, together with Premier Mussolini, were about to leave Rome.

The day following this memorandum from Taylor to the President, Mr. Roosevelt sent me a note, dated December 18, in which he said:

"I really think that England and the United States could agree not to bomb Rome on condition that the city itself, outside of the Vatican, be not used in any shape, manner, or form either by the Germans or the Italians for war purposes.

"I understand that today most of the Italian Departments have left Rome with their civil and military personnel, but that Germans, who are of course all military, are using Rome as central headquarters.

"I should think that we might consider that it is up to the Vatican itself to propose that Rome be demilitarized. If that is accomplished, there is no reason for us to bomb it."

British Ambassador Halifax took up with me on December 21 the question of stating certain conditions which, if carried out, would relieve Rome of the risk of being bombed. These included the removal of the Italian Government and all German organizations from the Rome area within a certain time limit, the removal to be verified by Swiss officials.

"This Government," I replied, "has been approaching the matter the other way around, so to speak. Instead of presenting what is really an ultimatum as to the evacuation from Rome of all military agencies, including the King, the German officials and others, this Government feels, and has so indicated to the Vatican and others, that we do not want to bomb Rome or see it bombed. At the same time we have inquired why Italians and those at the Vatican who do not want Rome bombed are not proceeding to cause objectionable military agencies, properties, and interests to be cleared out of Rome before making pointed and unqualified requests that Rome be not bombed."

I said we were also calling attention to the fact that many of the United Nations, like Britain, had been and were being bombed to the limit of endurance in the most inhuman, uncivilized, and unauthorized manner.

"Instead of an ultimatum in effect," I concluded, "this Government prefers to keep alive all its rights with respect to the possible bombing of Rome and in the meantime from week to week inquire of those opposing such bombing why they are not more fully and actively paving the way for their objective by causing a removal from Rome of objectionable interests and agencies."

I also had the British Embassy informed, through Ray Atherton, Chief of the Division of European Affairs, that we doubted whether the Italians had the power to agree to an ultimatum and to force the Germans to leave Rome. If the ultimatum were not accepted, we should then be in a position either of having made an empty threat or of being forced to bomb Rome. The implications of the latter step and its effect on the war effort might be serious in the extreme.

The President, having received a further letter from Myron Taylor, urging that we take some action, sent it to me with a notation: "What do we do about this next?" I replied on January 5, 1943, stating that we were awaiting the reaction of the British to our negative position on a possible ultimatum, and suggesting that we continue to wait for it.

"The memorandum from the Apostolic Delegate," I said, "indicates that the military objectives, both Italian and German, are actually being transferred from Rome and that the initiative for this action has been taken by the Holy See. This confirms the position which we took with respect to the British proposals, that is, that those officials, both Vatican and Italian, interested in saving Rome from bombardment should more fully and actively pave the way for their objective by causing the removal from Rome of the objectionable military agencies, properties, and interests."

Ambassador Halifax sent me a memorandum on January 12 stating that his Government had decided, somewhat reluctantly, to abandon its idea, partly as a result of our attitude. The British also felt it would be well to keep the Italian Government and the Vatican guessing about our policy toward the bombardment of Rome. Moreover, the British Government had promised Egypt that Rome would be bombed if Cairo were bombed by the Axis.

Harold H. Tittmann, Jr., who represented us at the Vatican in the absence of Myron Taylor, cabled us on January 12 that he was stating to questioners that he had received no instructions from his Government on the subject of the bombing of Rome, and that we must be reserving our right to bomb should the military situation require it. Tittmann asked our approval of this position, which I gave. The War Department also agreed with this attitude.

This continued to be our policy until the taking of Rome. The initial effort of the Italians to remove their military installations from Rome was not followed by the Germans. Following a statement by Pope Pius XII appealing again for the safety of Rome, I stated publicly on March 13, 1944, that the Allied military authorities in Italy were dealing primarily with considerations of military necessity forced on them by the activities and attitude of the German military forces. Naturally, I added, we were as much interested as any Government or any individual in the preservation of religious shrines, historic structures, and human lives. "If the

Germans," I concluded, "were not entrenched in these places or were they as interested as we are in protecting religious shrines and monuments and in preserving the lives of innocent civilians and refugees, no question would arise."

The President the following day stated to the press that the Germans were using the Holy City of Rome as a military center, whereas we had tried scrupulously—often at considerable sacrifice—to spare religious and cultural monuments, and we would continue to do so.

After receiving an appeal from Irish Prime Minister de Valera on April 3, the President replied on April 19 that, if the German forces were not entrenched in Rome, no question would arise concerning the city's preservation.

The center of Rome was, in fact, not bombed, although Allied planes dropped bombs on the city's railroad yards. The Allied advance on Rome was carried out so as to encircle the city and force the Germans to retire without contesting the capital street by street, which would have wrought great destruction. When the Allies reached Rome they found the city comparatively untouched, with the exception of the fact that the Germans, on leaving, had crippled its water supply.

On June 5, the day after the fall of Rome, King Victor Emmanuel carried out his promise and transferred his powers to Crown Prince Humbert. The King had wanted to go to Rome, but I cabled Kirk and Murphy on May 31 that we felt that under no circumstances should he be permitted to return to Rome at that time.

Crown Prince Humbert entrusted Badoglio with the task of forming a new Government, but the latter was unable to do so. A new Cabinet was then constituted, with Ivanoe Bonomi, a prominent anti Fascist leader, who had been in hiding in Rome during the German occupation, as premier.

Almost immediately difficulties rose between us and the British over the new Government. General MacFarlane, head of the Allied Control Commission, insisted to Bonomi that Count Sforza should not be appointed Foreign Minister. Since he undertook to speak in the name of the British and American Governments, we instantly protested to the British that MacFarlane had no right to speak in our name on a matter of this nature; and we requested General Wilson, the Allied commander, to inform Bonomi that MacFarlane's position did not represent the views of the United States Government since the appointment of Sforza would be entirely agreeable to this Government.

More basically, Prime Minister Churchill objected to the formation of the Bonomi Government itself. In an irate telegram to the President on June 10, 1944, he gave his opinion that Badoglio's replacement by "this group of aged and hungry politicians" was a great disaster. He said Badoglio, from the time he had safely delivered the fleet into our hands, had been a useful instrument, and he added that he had thought it was understood that Badoglio was to carry on, at least until the democratic north could be brought in and a thoroughly sound Italian Government could be formed. He objected that the Advisory Council for Italy had not been consulted. He said he was not aware that we had given the Italians, who had cost us so dearly in life and material, the right to form any government they chose without reference to the victorious powers.

The President sent me this cable for the preparation of a reply. I sent him a preliminary memorandum on June 13, suggesting that we should not be unduly influenced by Mr. Churchill's precipitate action, that the latter's alarm might be unwarranted, and that his attitude toward the political developments in Rome did not appear to accord with American policy. I indicated further that, pending the liberation of all Italy, no better indication of the popular will had appeared than that expressed through the parties of the Italian Committee of National Liberation. I said our policy had been to welcome political solutions worked out by the Italian people themselves, that such a solution seemed to lie in the present Italian Government, and that its anti-Fascist and democratic character should be welcomed and supported by this Government and the other democracies. I concluded that any interference on our part at this time to change the complexion of a Government which we had every reason to believe was friendly to the Allies and bitterly anti-Fascist and anti-Nazi would appear to be contrary to the Moscow Declaration and to our general policy of encouraging the development of a truly democratic, representative Government, and would be generally misunderstood.

After obtaining the views of the Advisory Council for Italy and General Wilson, we prepared the President's reply to the Prime Minister, which he duly sent. In this Mr. Roosevelt said he had reached the conclusion that it would be a grave mistake not to permit the prompt installation of the Bonomi Cabinet. Badoglio's withdrawal, while regretted, might be of distinct advantage, allaying criticism at home and abroad and pointing to the implementation of our proclaimed policy. The surrender terms, hitherto associated with Badoglio's person, would become the obligation of the most representative men today available in Italy, forming a Cabinet regarded as 100 per cent anti-Fascist. The intention to broaden the Government when Rome was reached, the President continued, had long been foreseen, and negotiations were held, following the fall of Rome, with the approval of and in constant consultation with the Allied Control Commission. The parties represented in the Rome Committee of National Liberation, which seemed to be the best available channel existing in Italy for the expression of the popular will, had chosen Bonomi unanimously, while they were divided on Badoglio. Interference on our part at this late moment, the President feared, would have serious repercussions both at home and in Italy, to the detriment of the military situation, and would directly violate our announced policy to let the Italian people choose their own Government.

Prime Minister Churchill now agreed to the installation of the Bonomi Cabinet without delay. Later, arriving in Rome in August for an inspection, he stated to Ambassador Alexander Kirk, then the American representative on the Advisory Council for Italy, that some mark of confidence should be given to the Bonomi Government short of a "preliminary peace" with Italy.

Premier Bonomi soon sent a series of messages to our Government outlining the numerous difficulties that confronted Italy in the economic and political field during her period of cobelligerency, and asking for alleviation of the armistice conditions. I dispatched a comprehensive reply to Rome on August 23, 1944. I said our Government would be glad to receive any specific proposals for revision of the armistice terms, but I reminded Bonomi that those terms were applied by the Allies solely to further our common primary objective of Germany's total defeat. We understood and appreciated, I added, Italy's wish to participate more actively in the war, and, within the limits of military needs and supply possibilities, would continue to give sympathetic consideration to this wish. I likewise expressed our full sympathy with Italy's desire to participate in international organizations.

"Patience, understanding, and hard work will be needed," I said, "to overcome the crimes Fascism committed in Italy's name, but any efforts in this direction will meet with this Government's sympathy and support." We were continuing to give constant, careful study, I added, to Italy's economic problems. Until victory was won, the Allied theater commander must retain full authority, but the recent return of seven provinces in central Italy to the authority of the Bonomi Government was proof of the Allied desire to restore liberated areas to Italian administration when military conditions permitted. Italy's aims, I concluded, were in harmony with ours, and our friendship and cooperation in achieving them could be counted on.

I had a number of cable exchanges with Kirk in September on the subject of Italian diplomatic representation abroad. On September 16 I stated our willingness to receive unofficially a technical Italian representation in the United States. I added that I did not favor continuance of Italian relations with the Argentine Government, the only American Government which had not severed its relations with Fascist Italy; that Italian prestige would not be enhanced if Italy continued to maintain diplomatic relations with the one American Government which had isolated itself from the United Nations; and that I favored unofficial Italian representation to the United Nations. I concluded that the Italian Foreign Office should make careful choice of its representatives abroad, especially in the Western Hemisphere, so that they would have clear records as regarded Fascism.

A few weeks later Mr. Churchill discussed the question of Italy with the President at Hyde Park, following the Second Quebec Conference. They announced on September 26 that an increasing measure of control would be gradually handed over to the Italian Administration, and that, to mark the change, the Allied Control Commission would be renamed "the Allied Commission." The British High Commissioner in Italy would assume the additional title of Ambassador, which the United States representative (Kirk) already held. The Italian Government would be invited to appoint direct representatives to Washington and London.

The Roosevelt-Churchill statement devoted much attention to the economic rehabilitation of Italy. In doing so it took account of exchanges of views we had been having with the British, which revealed another divergence of opinion between us. We had proposed that the dollar equivalent of the lire issued as pay to American troops in Italy be credited to the Italian Government to enable the latter to finance the procurement of relief and rehabilitation supplies. Generally we had proposed a more generous treatment of Italy in the field of supply policy than had hitherto been the agreed Anglo-American practice.

British Ambassador Halifax gave me on August 22, 1944, an *aide-mémoire* from his Government maintaining that to depart from the minimum standard agreed to and to embark on a program of general rehabilitation for Italian industry would be most difficult to justify to the Allies still subject to Axis domination, and especially difficult to justify to the victims of Italian aggression. The British thought that any concessions now made to Italy would bring requests from our Allies for more favorable treatment than that given to this ex-enemy.

Believing that the situation in Italy was serious, however, we went ahead with our plan to give the Italian Government the dollar credit we had in mind, which would amount to about $100,000,000 as of September 30.

At Hyde Park the President and the Prime Minister agreed that the first steps should be taken toward the reconstruction of an Italian economy, but that they should be taken primarily as military measures to put the full resources of Italy into the struggle to defeat Germany and Japan.

The day before the issuance of the Roosevelt-Churchill statement, I sent a circular message on September 25 to our diplomatic missions in all the other American Republics except Argentina, telling them of the new decisions reached. I said we were considering the establishment of full diplomatic relations with the Italian Government as being of material aid in the successful conclusion of the war and the reestablishment of democratic government. I requested the opinion of the foreign ministers as to the attitude of their Governments.

The American Republics forthwith stated their desire to resume diplomatic relations with Italy, and agreed to make an announcement to that effect along with us on October 26.

The Soviet Union reached the same decision, but the British, with whom we had disagreed more than once on the subject of Italy, took a different position. The British Embassy handed us a telegram of October 20 from the Foreign Office stating that British public opinion would react most unfavorably to an announcement at that stage of the war of any intention to resume full diplomatic relations with the Italian Government. The Foreign Office stated that it would not be clear how "full-blown" diplomatic relations between the Allies and Italy were compatible with the continued existence of an armistice regime, and also that the British public would consider it derogatory to the dignity of the King if he were to address a letter to the head of a state with whom he was still legally at war. It would be curious, to say the least, they commented, to accredit Ambassadors to Italy while refusing to accredit Ambassadors to the French Government in Paris. The Italian precedent would give rise to claims from Bulgaria, Rumania, and so on, for similar exchanges of diplomatic representatives.

We nevertheless went ahead on our own, along with the American

Republics and the Soviet Union, and announced on October 26 that full diplomatic relations with the Italian Government would be resumed. The President submitted to the Senate the nomination of Alexander Kirk as American Ambassador to Italy.

Basically we felt that, while the British arguments were cogent, the need to encourage the Italians to evolve a democratic form of government was a still more cogent argument. We pointed out that the resumption of diplomatic relations with Italy did not reestablish peace, nor did it settle the many questions that would have to be settled before a formal state of peace was declared—which required Senate consent. But it was intended to facilitate our return to a state of peace, which was an objective of our Italian policy. And it was designed to recognize the efforts of the Italian people during the preceding year to establish a healthy political basis for government and to cooperate with the Allies in the struggle against the common enemy.

Understandably, the British, and particularly Prime Minister Churchill, looked at Italy with different eyes. It was not easy for the British to be lenient toward Italy, for they had suffered far more casualties and damage in a much longer war against Italy than had we. Moreover, the British did not have among them millions of citizens of Italian origin, as we had, whose natural sympathy for their distant friends and relatives could not but affect our thinking.

As I left office at the end of November, 1944, the Bonomi Government was plunged into another Cabinet crisis. Again the State Department was forced to protest to Great Britain over the fact that the Foreign Office had once more vetoed the appointment of Count Sforza as Foreign Minister. We expressed our regret that the Foreign Office, without prior consultation with us, felt it necessary to intervene in an internal political crisis in Italy, and we stated our position that the composition of the Cabinet was a purely Italian problem, and that any objection made by the Supreme Allied Commander had to be based solely on important military reasons.

The policy we had pursued toward Italy from the time of the Italian armistice until my resignation assisted in bringing about a natural evolution toward democratic forms of government, as against the possibility of a revolution marked by civil war and chaos. King Victor Emmanuel, tainted with his long years of association and concurrence with Mussolini, left his throne. Marshal Badoglio, who had no democratic affiliations, remained in office for a period of emergency, and then gave way to a

Government with a broader base. The Bonomi Government, with the exception of a few émigrés, embraced men who had lived and suffered under Fascism and then Nazism, who represented varying political parties, from Right to Left.

We opposed King Victor Emmanuel, but we did not seek to influence the Italians relative to the institution of the monarchy itself. We considered that to be their own concern. The Italian Government undertook to call a constituent assembly when all Italians had been liberated and to postpone a decision on the monarchy until then. That decision has since been rendered through a plebiscite, which decided against the retention of the monarchy.

In addition to supporting the development of a representative Government in Italy, we took many steps to restore self-respect to Italy. We assumed the lead in trying to modify the prisoner-of-war status in which large numbers of Italian soldiers continued to be held in United Nations territory. We suggested inviting the Italian Government to send a representative to the Bretton Woods Financial and Monetary Conference, although the suggestion failed of implementation because of strong British and French opposition. We early agreed to receive an Italian technical mission to discuss economic and financial problems of concern to Italy.

Bearing in mind the terrific demands for shipping to support our Army in France and our armed forces in the Pacific, we sent all the relief we possibly could to Italy. From the time of the armistice until my resignation, Allied military authorities had spent about $158,000,000 for civilian supplies for Italy, of which the United States' share was $120,-000,000.

At the time I left office, the President and I felt that Italy, after more than two decades of Fascist domination, had made gratifying progress toward embracing the concepts and forms of democracy. We had no illusions that the task would be easy in a country economically prostrate, but we did have hopes that the basic good sense of the Italians, plus the lesson of the terrible catastrophe into which Fascism had plunged them, would keep them headed in the right direction. During the three years that have followed, Italy has made excellent advances toward improving her internal conditions as well as toward achieving political stability on democratic lines.

Having concluded this exposition of our policies toward our Allies, plus Italy, I turn now to our policies toward our enemies, particularly Germany and Japan.

113: Unconditional Surrender

THE PRINCIPLE of unconditional surrender overshadowed our policy toward the Axis and their satellites and our planning for their future.

Originally this principle had not formed part of the State Department's thinking. We were as much surprised as Mr. Churchill when, for the first time, the President, in the Prime Minister's presence, stated it suddenly to a press conference during the Casablanca Conference in January, 1943. I was told that the Prime Minister was dumbfounded.

Basically, I was opposed to the principle for two reasons, as were many of my associates. One was that it might prolong the war by solidifying Axis resistance into one of desperation. The people of the Axis countries, by believing they had nothing to look forward to but unconditional surrender to the will of their conquerors, might go on fighting long after calmer judgment had convinced them that their fight was hopeless.

The President himself had qualified his unconditional surrender phrase by stating at Casablanca that this did not mean the destruction of the people of Germany, Japan, and Italy, but the ending of a philosophy based on the conquest and subjugation of other peoples. Nevertheless the phrase itself spread more widely than the qualification, and it became a weapon in the hands of Nazi propagandists.

The second reason was that the principle logically required the victor nations to be ready to take over every phase of the national and local Governments of the conquered countries, and to operate all governmental activities and properties. We and our Allies were in no way prepared to undertake this vast obligation.

I thought that our principle of surrender should be flexible. In some cases the most severe terms should be imposed. I had Germany and Japan in mind in this connection. In other cases we would have preliminary informal conversations that would result in substantial adjustments away from the terms of unconditional surrender. Here I had in mind Italy and the Axis satellite states, Rumania, Hungary, Bulgaria, and Finland.

In our postwar planning discussions in the State Department, which had begun more than three years prior to the Casablanca Conference, we had not embraced the idea of unconditional surrender. In the United Nations Declaration of January 1, 1942, each Government simply pledged itself not to make a separate armistice or peace with the enemies. Nevertheless, after the President had stated the principle so emphatically at Casablanca, there was nothing we could do except to follow it at least in form. It was to rise on numerous occasions to plague us and to require explanation.

The President became aware of this after his return to the United States from Casablanca. His first statement on the subject, made in the course of his address to the White House Correspondents Association, February 12, 1943, was still strong as he said: "The only terms on which we shall deal with any Axis Government or any Axis factions are the terms proclaimed at Casablanca: 'unconditional surrender.' In our uncompromising policy we mean no harm to the common people of the Axis nations. But we do mean to impose punishment and retribution in full upon their guilty, barbaric leaders."

He softened this somewhat a few months later when, in his message to Congress on August 25, 1943, transmitting a report on Lend-Lease operations, he said: "Except for the responsible fascist leaders, the people of the Axis need not fear unconditional surrender to the United Nations. . . . The people of Axis-controlled areas may be assured that when they agree to unconditional surrender they will not be trading Axis despotism for ruin under the United Nations. The goal of the United Nations is to permit liberated peoples to create a free political life of their own choosing and to attain economic security."

In line with this thought, the surrender of Italy the following month, although ostensibly on an unconditional basis, was actually, as I have previously mentioned, a negotiated surrender, and the terms of the armistice were agreed to in discussions in Lisbon, Portugal, between representatives of the Anglo-American Combined Chiefs of Staff and Marshal Badoglio.

With the President's definition in mind, Molotov, Eden, and I used the term "unconditional surrender" in the preamble to the Four-Nation Declaration we agreed to at the Moscow Conference in October. This had been approved by the President in advance of my departure for Moscow. The four nations declared their determination to continue hostilities against those Axis powers with which they respectively were at war until such powers had laid down their arms on the basis of unconditional surrender.

Following the Tehran Conference, I received a cable on December 17, 1943, from William Phillips in London, who was then a member of

General Eisenhower's staff, stating that it seemed that at the Tehran Conference Marshal Stalin had objected to the principle of unconditional surrender, and that Prime Minister Churchill had agreed with him. Phillips said there appeared to be no record of what the President thought, although it was reported in London that he had not dissented from Stalin's view.

Phillips informed us that the British Foreign Office had suggested that the term "unconditional surrender" be avoided until a final decision was reached, and that meanwhile the phrase "prompt surrender" be used.

The British Embassy handed us an *aide-mémoire* on December 22, 1943, which stated that the Tehran Conference had considered the question of a joint declaration to the German people on the basis of unconditional surrender. Marshal Stalin, it added, informed President Roosevelt on November 29 that he thought this would be bad tactics toward Germany and suggested instead that the Allied Governments concerned should work out terms together and make them generally known to the German people.

Foreign Secretary Eden suggested to us that the matter be dealt with as soon as possible by the European Advisory Commission. He hoped we would send appropriate instructions in this sense to our representative on the commission.

I sent the President a memorandum on December 22, informing him of the contents of this *aide-mémoire*, and adding: "As I have no information on this question of a joint declaration, and as I have not been under the impression that the European Advisory Commission would undertake political discussions of this character, I would be glad to know what your views are with regard to avoiding the use of the term 'unconditional surrender.' "

The President replied that this matter had not been brought up in any way at Tehran in his presence, and he felt that Ambassador Winant in London should take the matter up with Churchill as soon as the Prime Minister returned to London. I so cabled Winant on December 24.

That night, Christmas Eve, the President delivered a radio address in the preparation of which the State Department assisted. He said: "The United Nations have no intention to enslave the German people. We wish them to have a normal chance to develop, in peace, as useful and respectable members of the European family. But we most certainly emphasize that word 'respectable'—for we intend to rid them once and for all of

Nazism and Prussian militarism and the fantastic and disastrous notion that they constitute the 'master race.' "

At the end of December the British Embassy handed us an *aide-mémoire* informing us that peace feelers had come to the British Government through Sweden from a prominent member of the German Foreign Office and from Heinrich Himmler, Hitler's police chief. The feelers were in the nature of a statement that Himmler was ready to send an army officer and a Nazi Party official to meet British representatives to obtain a definition of "unconditional surrender." The British informed us that their plan was to reply only that the United Nations demanded unconditional surrender of Germany, without further interpretation. We assented to this reply.

Unconditional surrender was next raised with us by the Russians during a conversation between Molotov and Ambassador Harriman on December 31. In consequence of this approach, and after discussing it with my associates, I sent the President a memorandum on January 14, 1944, informing him that Molotov on his own initiative had brought up with Harriman the definition of "unconditional surrender" and had inquired as to the attitude of this Government.

"It is my understanding," I said, "that the Soviet interest in this matter is not based on any desire to weaken the principle of unconditional surrender or to offer milder terms to enemy countries but rather on the belief that the present undefined term 'unconditional surrender' affords enemy propaganda an opportunity to play on the natural fear of the unknown in the minds of their people and consequently stiffens their will to fight.

"As I understand it, the Soviet Government believes that some definition, however general and severe, of the conditions of surrender which will be imposed on the enemy countries would deprive the enemy of this propaganda advantage and consequently weaken the morale of their armed forces and people. In view of the Soviet interest in this matter, do you approve of discussions with the Soviet and British Governments to explore the desirability of some public definition for propaganda exploitation of the terms of unconditional surrender to be imposed on the respective enemy countries?"

Three days later the President, on January 17, sent me a memorandum in reply which he began by saying:

"Frankly, I do not like the idea of conversation to define the term 'unconditional surrender.' Russia, Britain, and the United States have agreed not to make any peace without consultation with each other. I think each case should stand on its own merits in that way."

He then continued:

"The German people can have dinned into their ears what I said in my Christmas Eve speech—in effect, that we have no thought of destroying the German people and that we want them to live through the generations like other European peoples on condition, of course, that they get rid of their present philosophy of conquest. I forget my exact words but you can have them looked up.

"Secondly, the German people and Russia should also be told the best definition of what 'unconditional surrender' really means. The story of Lee's surrender to Grant is the best illustration. Lee wanted to talk about all kinds of conditions. Grant said that Lee must put his confidence in his [Grant's] fairness. Then Lee surrendered. Immediately Lee brought up the question of the Confederate officers' horses, which belonged to them personally in most cases, and Grant settled that item by telling Lee that they should take their horses home as they would be needed in the spring plowing."

(The President had a comprehensive knowledge of American history, which he had studied thoroughly and intensively. It was not at Appomattox, however, that Grant demanded unconditional surrender, but at Fort Donelson in 1862, when he received the surrender of General S. B. Buckner.)

"A few little incidents like the above," the President concluded, "will have more effect on the Germans than lots of conversations between the Russians, British, and ourselves trying to define 'unconditional surrender.' Whatever words we might agree on would probably have to be modified or changed the first time some nation wanted to surrender."

I communicated the substance of this memorandum to Ambassador Harriman in Moscow on January 25. I added that Harriman might inform Molotov that our Government would rather deal with the case of each individual enemy country as it arose because we did not consider it wise to attempt at this time to make any general public definition of "unconditional surrender."

A few weeks later the Russians were themselves modifying the principle of unconditional surrender in their discussions with the Finns directed toward reaching a peace. Instead of demanding unconditional surrender from Finland, they offered to negotiate on certain specified subjects. As to Germany, Marshal Stalin had already stated that Russia had no desire to destroy that country but only Hitlerism.

Foreign Secretary Eden made the Russian approach to Finland the basis of a proposal to us to soften the principle of unconditional surrender so far as the minor Axis states as a whole were concerned. On March 20, 1944, British Ambassador Halifax handed me a telegram from Eden to this effect, dated March 17, 1944.

Eden suggested that, while it might be desirable to continue to apply unconditional surrender to Germany and Japan, we could achieve better results by dropping it either tacitly or openly with regard to the minor Axis states. Rigid application of the principle, he argued, was likely to hinder our desire to get them out of the war as soon as possible. We might wish to give them some assurance that their desertion of Germany and any contribution they might make toward hastening Germany's defeat would earn them some reward. Also, we would want to be able to discuss with them such questions as military cooperation, future frontier claims, or the possibility of our giving them assistance against the Germans.

Five days later I recommended to the President that we follow the British suggestion in order to obtain more flexibility with regard to the Axis satellites. In a memorandum of March 25 to Mr. Roosevelt, attaching the note from Eden, I said:

"While the British telegram correctly points out that the Soviet terms to Finland definitely do not impose unconditional surrender, such terms are not required under the joint Four-Nation Declaration for the reason that Finland is not a member of the Axis, whereas the other satellites are. Although the premise of the British reasoning may not be strictly correct, I recommend, however, that we concur in the proposal in order to obtain more flexibility vis-à-vis the Axis satellite states.

"The events of the past few days make it unlikely that the question of surrender terms for Hungary and Rumania will have any immediate importance. [This referred to Russia's advance into Rumania and Germany's occupation of Hungary.] Furthermore, Mr. Molotov has indicated that he is not yet prepared to discuss Bulgarian surrender terms in the European Advisory Commission currently meeting in London. Nevertheless, for the purpose of handling either propaganda or peace feelers, I think it would be advantageous now to free ourselves from the Moscow decision on the unconditional surrender of Axis satellite states."

While I was awaiting the President's response to this recommendation, I received a memorandum from Soviet Ambassador Gromyko indicating that his Government was in agreement with the position the British Government and the State Department were taking; namely, that the principle of unconditional surrender should be modified. This stated that the Soviet Government had received a communication on the subject from the British—this was Eden's telegram of March 17—and that it had replied on March 29 that under certain circumstances it considered it possible not to apply the principle to the satellites of Germany. To apply unconditional surrender, the memorandum said, might strengthen rather than weaken the bonds of the satellite countries with Germany. The principle would still be preserved to the full extent with regard to Germany. The Soviet Government asked our views.

Before I had a chance to communicate this to the President I received his reply, dated April 1, to my recommendation of March 25.

"I think this should be handled differently," he said. "It would be a mistake, in my judgment, to abandon or make an exception in the case of the words 'unconditional surrender.' As a matter of fact, whom do we mean those words to apply to? Evidently our enemies.

"In August, 1941, at the time of the Atlantic Charter, and in January, 1943, at the time of Casablanca, Hungary, Bulgaria, Rumania, and Finland were the Axis satellites. But they were not our enemies in the same sense that Germany and Italy were. These four little satellite states were enemies under the duress of Germany and Italy.

"I think it a mistake to make exceptions. Italy surrendered unconditionally but was at the same time given many privileges. This should be so in the event of the surrender of Bulgaria or Rumania or Hungary or Finland. Lee surrendered unconditionally to Grant but immediately Grant told him that his officers should take their horses home for the spring plowing. That is the spirit I want to see abroad—but it does not apply to Germany. Germany understands only one kind of language."

On the copy of Eden's March 17 telegram, which the President returned to me, he had written: "No—the British Foreign Office has always been part of this and it is N.G.—F. D. R."

Following the receipt of the President's response, various of my associates strongly recommended in memoranda to me that I take the matter up with Mr. Roosevelt again. After some discussion, I sent the President a letter on April 4 saying: "Upon further reflection, I am very much afraid that the Soviets will not understand our refusal to accede to the desire of both the British and Soviet Governments on this point.

Since the Soviet Government itself has to some extent laid down without objection from us definite conditions in the case of Finland, I am sure they will not understand why there should be any objection to doing the same in the case of Rumania and Hungary as in their opinion there is a definite military advantage to be gained. We might find ourselves in the position of being accused of having rendered more difficult the Soviet military task."

I asked the President to let me have his views in the light of these considerations and said that meantime I would withhold replying to the British and Soviet Ambassadors.

The President at this time was confined to bed in the White House with a severe attack of bronchitis, and it was not possible to talk to him personally; hence the series of written messages. He replied the following day.

"I understand the problem thoroughly," he said, "but I want at all costs to prevent it from being said that the unconditional surrender principle has been abandoned. There is real danger if we start making exceptions to the general principle before a specific case arises.

"We all know that this would happen if we were to make any exceptions to the principle which would thereafter apply in all cases.

"I understand perfectly well that from time to time there will have to be exceptions not to the surrender principle but to the application of it in specific cases. That is a very different thing from changing the principle.

"If the Soviet and British Governments will advise us of any case of this kind, I am quite sure that we will agree with them. This should be made clear to both of these Governments. Then they cannot accuse us of having rendered more difficult the Soviet military task."

In consequence of this note, I replied to both the British and the Soviet Embassies on April 11 saying that this Government had come to the conclusion that it was undesirable to make any general departure from the doctrine of unconditional surrender. Such a departure might serve as a precedent for all future cases. We would prefer that the general principle of unconditional surrender be retained intact, and that consideration be given to any modification on the basis of specific cases. We concluded that, rather than abandon the principle with respect to the satellite countries as a group, we were prepared to give favorable consideration to modifying the principle in the specific case of any one satellite when either the British or the Soviet Government believed it would be advantageous to the common cause to do so.

The question, however, would not die. Only two days later it was strongly raised from another quarter, the military. On April 13, 1944, I received a cable from Under Secretary Stettinius, who was then in London, conveying recommendations made to him by General Eisenhower and General Bedell Smith, Eisenhower's Chief of Staff. Stettinius said both generals had brought up the question with him and expressed their considered opinion that the term "unconditional surrender" should be clarified by announcing the principles on which the treatment of a defeated Germany would be based. He said this seemed highly desirable to them because of the accumulated evidence that German propaganda was interpreting the words "unconditional surrender" to strengthen the morale of the German Army and people.

The generals thought it was necessary to create certain conditions through our own propaganda to offset this. One condition to be created was a mood of acceptance of unconditional surrender in the German Army such as would make possible a collapse of resistance similar to that in Tunisia. The other was a mood in the German General Staff whereby a German Badoglio would undertake the necessary political steps for unconditional surrender.

Toward this end Eisenhower and Smith suggested that an American-Anglo-Russian statement be issued to define unconditional surrender and to guarantee the promotion of law and order. They likewise suggested that, once an Allied bridgehead were established in France, the Commander-in-Chief should make a statement calling for surrender and at the same time recapitulate the terms of other declarations clarifying unconditional surrender.

General Smith, Stettinius reported, felt that, in default of such statements, it would be impossible to exploit the crisis in the German Army to which a successful Allied landing in France would undoubtedly give rise.

Stettinius stated that William Phillips, the American political adviser to General Eisenhower, was in hearty accord with these views, and that the British political officer corresponding to Phillips had been asked to express the same views to the Foreign Office.

I sent this cable on to the President, who was then resting from his recent illness at the estate of Bernard M. Baruch at Georgetown, South Carolina. On April 15 I cabled Phillips stating that the President held very strongly to the maintenance of the principle of unconditional surrender for Germany, as Phillips knew. I said I felt that the case for action should be given every consideration, but before going further I suggested that it should be ascertained whether the European Advisory Commission had progressed in its work to arrive at a tripartite declaration upon a military government for Germany. I also questioned whether we should proceed on this subject by other means than through the European Advisory Commission unless the British and Russian Governments were willing to do so.

Later in the day I received a brief message from the President which, referring to Stettinius's cable of April 13, said: "Any reply thereto should have my approval before being sent."

I cabled Phillips on April 17 asking him to inform all concerned that the President wished that the subject be given no further consideration without his approval.

I telegraphed the President on the same day that, since Stettinius's cable had raised the question of a tripartite statement to define unconditional surrender, I had thought it well to send a message immediately to the effect that the President was holding very strongly to the principle of unconditional surrender for Germany. I also informed him of the further points we had raised with Phillips and of the second message just sent him on April 17.

The British and Russian Governments continued strongly to press the point that some modification of unconditional surrender, at least in the case of the Axis satellites, should be made. Since March we at the State Department had been working on the draft of a proposed statement to the satellites which the British, Russian, and American Governments might issue.

The President having returned to Washington on May 7, I sent him a memorandum on the subject three days later. I said the State Department had been informed by the British Embassy that the British Government considered it important that Allied propaganda to the satellite states should be reenforced. With special reference to Hungary and Bulgaria this propaganda should henceforth omit use of the term "unconditional surrender" in order to attain the maximum military advantage in strengthening resistance to Germany. Abandonment of the general principle would be avoided.

After referring to my letter of April 4 to the President and his reply directing that the general principle of unconditional surrender be retained, though exceptions might be made in its application in specific cases, I said:

"In making this proposal, the British Embassy has pointed out that the Soviet Government had not applied the principle to Finland, and the same could be said for Rumania, if the Rumanians should come to terms along the lines proposed for their surrender. It is supposed that the propaganda agencies will take these considerations into account in preparing their directives. As for Hungary and Bulgaria, the Department thinks that advantages can in fact be gained from energetic action at this time in propaganda operations, and I should therefore be grateful if you would indicate whether you would approve our taking parallel action with the British and the Russians in authorizing a degree of latitude for propaganda purposes, having it clearly understood that the exception is authorized to enable the propaganda services to omit reference to the term, though of course there would be no public recantation of the principle as applicable to these countries."

The President sent this back to me with his O.K. written on it.

As a result of further diplomatic exchanges among London, Moscow, and Washington, we agreed upon a joint statement which the three Governments made simultaneously on May 12, 1944. In this we stated that Hungary, Rumania, Bulgaria, and Finland "still have it within their power, by withdrawing from the war and ceasing their collaboration with Germany and by resisting the forces of Nazism by every possible means, to shorten the European struggle, diminish their own ultimate sacrifices, and contribute to the Allied victory."

We gathered some fruits of this position several months later, when Rumania, Finland, and Bulgaria asked for and obtained an armistice. Hungary was in the hands of the Germans.

As for Germany, we now sought to concentrate on a statement that Roosevelt, Stalin, and Churchill might issue addressed to the German Army, designed to weaken the German will to resist, especially at a moment when that Army felt the impact of the Anglo-American invasion in northern France. In May the President agreed to the extent of submitting a draft to Churchill, stressing the inevitability of the German defeat, the stupidity of the Germans continuing the struggle, and the wisdom of their throwing overboard the philosophy of their leaders. Churchill and his War Cabinet, however, did not like the draft.

The Department accordingly sent the President a new draft in June, and then on July 11 I sent him a later and shorter draft. This recited the overwhelming power of the United Nations and stated that every German life lost was a needless loss. Germany's only hope lay in unconditional surrender, but the draft went on to say that, while we promised nothing, the Allied leaders—Stalin, Churchill, and Roosevelt—had made it abundantly clear that they did not seek the destruction of the German people.

The President wrote me, however, on July 17, 1944: "It does not appear to me that Allied progress on all the fronts has yet been sufficiently impressive to promise the best results that might be obtained from such a tripartite statement. Later, when our combined attack shall have made further and more impressive advances, an approach to Churchill and Stalin suggesting a tripartite statement may give better promise of agreement and more prospect of advantage to our attack."

The following month, on August 21, I sent the President a further memorandum on the subject. I attached this to a letter to me from Admiral Leahy, transmitting a telegram the Supreme Headquarters, Allied Expeditionary Forces had sent to the Combined Chiefs of Staff to recommend the issuance of synchronized orders of the day by General Eisenhower, Marshal Stalin, and General Wilson, addressed in effect to the German Army. SHAEF said the psychological climax of the war was approaching and that a decisive demonstration of military unity between the Western, Eastern, and Southern Fronts might rapidly demoralize the already flagging German morale. They thought this could be true not only of the German home front but of the German Army which recently had shown significant signs of slackening in its relatively high fighting morale.

In my memorandum, I said: "I see no objection to this proposal from the political point of view and consider it primarily a military matter. If you approve the proposal, you will no doubt wish to take it up with Churchill and Stalin."

Three days later, however, Admiral Leahy wrote me that he had been directed by the President to tell me that Mr. Roosevelt did not consider the time appropriate for issuing such a statement.

The public statements made at different times by the leaders of the three major Allies to soften the interpretation of unconditional surrender did not conduce to the early surrender of Germany. The Nazi propaganda machine continued until the last to stress its drastic interpretation of unconditional surrender. The police hold by Hitler and his Nazis over the German people was too strong to permit of any successful reaction, and Germany went on fighting needlessly and hopelessly until her total collapse in May, 1945. Whether the Germans would have surrendered at an earlier date had there been no enunciation of the principle of unconditional surrender or had easier terms been agreed upon and stated by the United Nations will remain a question.

In any event, the continued application of unconditional surrender to Germany did have this effect, that no future propaganda machine in Germany could ever claim, as did the Nazis during the twenties and thirties, that the German armies had not been defeated and that Germany surrendered because of the weakness of the civilian government and people behind the lines.

As for our Oriental enemy, Japan surrendered three months later when she perceived that the principle of unconditional surrender could be applied conditionally.

114: Toward Victory in the Orient

OUR DIPLOMATIC EFFORTS directed toward Europe during the last years of my period at the State Department were naturally of greater intensity than those directed toward Asia. There were more nations to deal with in Europe, whereas in the Orient, with Japan an enemy, there was only one major nation left, China. Nevertheless, a large part of the attention of my associates and myself centered on the Far East, as we attempted to solve problems of real magnitude.

Toward China we had two objectives. The first was an effective joint prosecution of the war. The second was the recognition and building up of China as a major power entitled to equal rank with the three big Western Allies, Russia, Britain, and the United States, during and after the war, both for the preparation of a postwar organization and for the establishment of stability and prosperity in the Orient.

In 1943 we had taken three major steps to demonstrate our recognition of China as a great power. I signed on January 11, 1943, the treaty relinquishing our extraterritorial rights in China. At the Moscow Conference I was successful in introducing China as one of the signatories of the Four-Nation Declaration which called for the creation of an international organization to maintain the peace. On December 17 Congress, at the suggestion of the Administration, passed an Act repealing the Chinese Exclusion Laws and permitting Chinese citizens to enter the United States as immigrants. This last had been one of my projects for a number of years, just as it had been in the case of the Japanese. Believing it unwise and unfair to exclude Chinese and Japanese as immigrants, I felt they could be placed under a quota system like citizens of other nations, and I considered repeal of the Exclusion Laws necessary as one means of improving our relations with the Orient. The quota for Chinese immigrants, worked out on the same proportional basis as that assigned to other countries, would be very small indeed, but the principle was important. Especially after Pearl Harbor it seemed anomalous to strive for complete cooperation with our Chinese Ally while barring her citizens from our shores. When the matter came before Congress, I repeatedly conferred with members of both Houses to urge their support of repeal. Following the enactment, the President on February 8, 1944, set a quota of 105 Chinese immigrants annually.

As our military pressure on Japan became ever stronger in 1943, the Japanese overlords sought to make a separate peace with China so as to free themselves for the major conflict in the Southwest Pacific. The Government of Chiang Kai-shek, however, although sorely tried by China's growing exhaustion after six years of unremitting resistance to the invader, repulsed all such attempts. I cabled the President in Cairo on November 29, 1943, that our Embassy at Chungking had informed us that Japan was continuing to make peace offers to the Chinese Government, but without success.

President Roosevelt and Chiang Kai-shek made great progress in friendship and cooperation at the Cairo Conference. There the President agreed that all territory taken from China by Japan should be returned, including Manchuria, Formosa, and the Pescadores Islands.

The President did not consult with me before this agreement; nor did he consult with me before agreeing with Chiang Kai-shek and Prime Minister Churchill on a statement that independence would be restored to Korea "in due course." I considered this statement unwise for several reasons. One was that the Koreans wanted their independence immediately Korea was liberated, and not in due course. They did not welcome the Cairo Declaration, and they feared that their country would be placed under the control of China. Another reason was that the Soviet Union should have been consulted first. Although Russia was not at war with Japan, she was our Ally in Europe, and she had an interest in Korea.

The United States supplied China with every possible military assistance considering the enormous difficulties of transportation and our immense commitments elsewhere. This help ranged from the establishment of an air force of American volunteers in China and an air transport service into China to the operation of a staff school for higher Chinese officers.

Nevertheless, we encountered a feeling from time to time on the part of the Chinese Government that we were not giving it sufficient representation in our Allied military councils. This was the burden of a conversation I had with Chinese Foreign Minister Dr. T. V. Soong when he called on me September 22, 1943, shortly before returning to Chungking. He said his Government had one matter most strongly in mind; namely, more recognition in connection with the work of the Combined Chiefs of Staff. Dr. Soong had already taken this up with the President directly.

I told Dr. Soong that the President was a great friend of China, as everyone knew, and that I was sure he desired to do the proper thing.

The United States did, in fact, make every effort to give China adequate representation in Allied military deliberations.

On the economic side, this Government took many steps—in addition to Lend-Lease, which was for direct military purposes—to assist China's economy, endangered by the long-continued strain of war. The assistance ranged from a credit of $500,000,000 and the facilitation of China's import and export trade, to technical advice in organizing a Chinese War Production Board under the direction of the President's representative, Donald M. Nelson.

We lost no opportunity to bolster China's own consciousness of her position as a major Power. In addition to her recognition at the Moscow Conference, to our relinquishment of extraterritorial rights, and to our admission of Chinese immigrants, China was encouraged to play a prominent part in the United Nations Relief and Rehabilitation Administration, in the Bretton Woods Monetary Conference, and finally in the Dumbarton Oaks Conference for the establishment of the United Nations organization.

At the same time, we took every opportunity we could to state to China that we felt justified in expressing our expectation that she would solve her internal problems and achieve political stability. The tense relations between the Chinese Communist organization in the north, and the Kuomintang Party in Chungking were of persistent concern to us. We decidedly wanted China to assume a position of influence alongside the three big Western powers, but we knew this was impossible if China were torn by internal strife.

Vice President Wallace went to China in 1944 with the idea of converting both parties to this point of view. This was his own idea, and when I became aware of it I sent Joseph W. Ballantine, one of the Department's Far Eastern experts, to try to dissuade him from it. It seemed to me that a special mission of this nature might harm instead of help the situation.

I never at any time favored excursions into foreign affairs by Wallace, especially through trips abroad such as he made to Latin America in 1943 and to China in 1944. A network of questions and conditions existed in our international affairs, especially during the war period, which necessarily had to be handled with extreme care and delicacy. I was convinced that no person outside the State Department and the White House could break into these affairs without serious risk of running amuck, so to speak, and causing hurtful complications. For this reason I always opposed suggestions that raw materials, as I called them, should be recruited from the outside to go abroad and undertake seriously to handle important phases of our foreign affairs.

But when Ballantine saw Wallace the latter had already got to the President and secured his permission. Ballantine had to present the points I had given him as pitfalls to be avoided rather than as arguments to dissuade him from the trip. So far as I could see, Wallace's trip was without beneficial effect.

When Lord Beaverbrook, British Minister of Production, came to see me on July 24, 1944, we discussed the Chinese situation, and I remarked that it sometimes worried us. "I myself believe," I said, "that China has only a fifty-fifty chance to reestablish herself as a great power. But if she's rebuffed now by the other major Allies even that chance might be lost, and the Chinese Government would tend to dissolve. In that case it's quite likely that the Soviets might have to assume responsibility for the whole situation—if they would."

There had been some thought, I said, in certain business circles here that the Pacific situation could be stabilized by agreement among London, Washington, and Tokyo, and some Britishers shared this view. But by now, I concluded, it was plain that Japan was out of it, and if China went out too there was no stabilizing means at all.

Beaverbrook agreed. He said there was, however, a feeling in Britain that the Government of Chiang Kai-shek was not a real fighting Government but was "something plastered on top of China like a button on a coat."

Chiang Kai-shek, in my opinion, had followed faithfully in the footsteps of Sun Yat-sen in attempting the task that many considered next to impossible, the creation of a real Republic out of the innumerable divisions and subdivisions composing the vast territory of China. He was wise and patriotic. He knew the Chinese people.

Nevertheless, we had great difficulty in our relations with China during my last years in office because of the loose procedure followed by Chiang Kai-shek in dealing most irregularly with our Government through the Treasury, War, and Navy Departments, and other agencies of the Government. He sent numerous cables direct to different officials of this Government, taking up political subjects that should have been handled through the State Department. His brothers-in-law, H. H. Kung and T. V. Soong, were in Washington dealing on political matters with officers, for example, of the Treasury, War, and Navy Departments. They were circumventing the State Department and our Ambassador in China. The President unfortunately permitted this condition to continue.

I felt rather strongly that if the State Department had been permitted to hold a stiff rein on the Chinese situation, and require the Chinese Government to deal directly with it alone, it might have induced that Government to rely far more on itself and to pursue a stable, resolute course instead of bumping along expecting aid of all sorts from other countries, particularly the United States.

I felt that American aid to China could not be effective by itself without the cooperation of the Chinese Government. That Government was dominated by the reactionary groups in the Kuomintang, which were devoted to their own selfish interests and were afflicted with much corruption and little efficiency. I felt we could have had more military cooperation. Chiang Kai-shek kept some of his best divisions near himself, traffic continued between the Chinese and Japanese zones, and the Government seemed more interested in the blockade against the Communists than against Japan.

Nevertheless, I never faltered in my belief that we should do everything in our power to assist China to become strong and stable. It was obvious to me that Japan would disappear as a great Oriental power for a long time to come. Therefore, the only major strictly Oriental power would be China. The United States, Britain, and Russia were also Pacific powers, but the greater interests of each were elsewhere. Consequently, if there was ever to be stability in the Far East, it had to be assured with China at the center of any arrangement that was made.

At this point I should say that, after my resignation, President Roosevelt gave me not the slightest hint of his plans for the Yalta Conference, at which he made decisions of great concern to China. The day before his departure for Yalta, the President came to the hospital to see me. He had hardly sat down when I began to state the thoughts I had in mind. I restated the most pertinent doctrines and policies we had been standing for, which more and more had become part of our postwar policies. These policies would have negated some later developments, such as a few decisions at Yalta. After talking with Mr. Roosevelt thirty-five minutes, I apologized for taking so much of his time. He said he was glad to hear my views; but he did not indicate what he would take up at Yalta, nor did he seek my views on such points.

Toward China's neighbor to the south, Thailand (Siam), our policy after Pearl Harbor revolved around the fact that we refused to consider her as an enemy, regardless of the fact that the Thai Government had declared war against us on January 25, 1942. We did not declare war, but took the position that the Government at Bangkok, under the domination of the Japanese, did not represent the desires of its people; and we continued to recognize the Thai Minister in Washington as the Minister of his country.

Our desire being to see Thailand restored as an independent nation, we held discussions on this point with the British Government in 1944. The British, however, stated that they regarded Thailand as an enemy country which had to work its passage toward independence. Foreign Secretary Eden assured us that Britain desired the ultimate restoration of Thai sovereignty, but he made reservations with regard to security and economic collaboration by Thailand and to strategic guarantees in the Kra Isthmus which cuts across Thailand.

We on our part agreed that the new territories Thailand had acquired through Japanese "mediation," principally from French Indo-China, should be restored to their former owners, although this was to be without prejudice to eventual adjustments or transfers of territories by orderly, peaceful processes.

The President requested the Department on November 3, 1944, to instruct American representatives and to inform the British, French, and Dutch Governments, that the United States expected to be consulted on any arrangements as to the future of Southeast Asia. This included Thailand.

As I left office, our policy with regard to Thailand was to favor its restoration as a sovereign country, with an independent Government representing the free will of the people. We did not recognize the Government then existing. We were sympathetic to the "Free Thai Movement" which had been started here and in other countries, but we did not intend to make any political commitment to it, since we desired to leave the choice of government to the Thai people themselves.

With regard to Japan, the work of the State Department during my last years in office followed three main lines. The first was an unceasing effort to obtain humane treatment for prisoners of war and civilian internees in Japanese hands and to hasten the repatriation of these civilians. The second was a constant use of diplomacy to concert with our Allies all efforts toward prosecuting the war in the Orient to victory. The third was to prepare a plan for the postwar treatment of Japan.

Through the Swiss Government, which ably represented our interests toward Japan, we made literally scores of representations to Japan to induce her to accord proper treatment to Americans in her hands. Right after Pearl Harbor we took care to give the Japanese in our hands humane treatment, hoping that the Japanese Government might follow our example. Although Japan was not a signatory of the Geneva Prisoners of War Convention, we obtained from that Government a commitment to apply the provisions of the convention to American prisoners of war and, so far as adaptable, to civilian internees.

When, however, the first group of Americans repatriated from Japan, including Ambassador Grew, arrived on the first exchange voyage of the *Gripsholm*, they told stories of outrageous treatment by the Japanese. We made their accounts the basis of a vigorous, comprehensive protest to Japan.

As succeeding reports came in, it was obvious that Japan was flagrantly violating its commitment to carry out the provisions of the Geneva Convention. The hideous treatment of many American prisoners of war and civilian internees revealed a barbarism among the Japanese military which shocked the civilized world.

This mistreatment reached one of many climaxes when the Japanese executed the American aviators who fell into their hands after General James Doolittle's raid over Tokyo. We made this the subject of a vigorous protest on April 12, 1943. Calling again upon Japan to carry out its agreement to observe the Geneva Convention, we bluntly warned that the United States Government would punish all Japanese officers who participated in such atrocities.

I wish I could say that the many steps we took, and the valid support we received from the Swiss, had some effect. It did not seem that they had; Japanese barbarism was too deeply rooted; and our protests were still continuing when I left office. We were able, however, to build up a vast record of substantial evidence against individual Japanese which was of later aid in bringing these criminals to the punishment they amply deserved.

In 1943, and particularly in 1944, my associates and I devoted much time to the subject of the future treatment of Japan as a whole. We had frequent discussions among ourselves and with the War Department. In May, 1944, we in the State Department arrived at certain basic conclusions which we submitted to the War Department.

One was that Japan should be treated as a whole; it should not be partitioned, although the territories it had wrested from other nations should be returned to them.

Another was that the Japanese Government as a unit should be suspended during the period of armed occupation. That is, its policy-making functions should cease. The Privy Council, the Cabinet, the Diet, the Board of Field Marshals and Fleet Admirals, and the Supreme Military Council should go. The Ministries of War, Navy, Munitions, and Greater East Asia Affairs should be liquidated; routine administrative functions of the Ministry of Foreign Affairs should be performed under the direction of Allied Civil Affairs officers, with policy matters referred to the State Department.

Administrative Departments, such as the Ministries of Home Affairs, Finance, Justice, Transportation and Communications, Agriculture and Commerce, Education and Welfare, could continue under Civil Affairs officers in the top policy-making positions. We also believed that the municipal and prefectural administrative machinery could be retained, at first under Civil Affairs supervision.

A third point in our thinking was that all the principally interested United Nations who had taken part in the war against Japan, should participate in the occupation and control of Japan. We felt it was undesirable to assume the sole onus for future Japanese resentment. We believed it more effective to show the Japanese people, through the presence of other nationalities in the forces of occupation and control, that the condemnation of Japanese aggression was world-wide. We wished to see the presence in Japan of the armed forces of other nations, even if only token forces, and we were particularly anxious to have forces of other Asiatic peoples in evidence, such as Chinese, Indians, and Filipinos, so as to impress the Japanese with the fact that this had been not merely a white man's war against them.

We divided our thinking with regard to Japan into three postwar periods. During the first, comparatively short, period, Japan should be deprived of her prewar colonial empire and be completely demilitarized.

During the second, and longer, period, we proposed the establishment of permanent bases from which Japan could be militarily policed so as to prevent a revival of Japanese aggression; the establishment of control systems to prevent Japanese rearmament and the development of a war potential; the encouragement of democratic thought, with the help of Japanese moderate elements; the elimination of ultranationalistic organizations; and Japan's gradual participation in world economy.

During the third period, of indefinite duration, we proposed the establishment of a Japanese Government that would carry out its proper functions in a peaceful manner.

The Emperor of Japan and his future naturally occupied a considerable portion of our thinking. Should the institution of the Emperor, hallowed in Japanese history, be continued, or should it be abolished? The opinion of the State Department on this point was requested at various times by the War and Navy Departments. It proved to be one of our most difficult questions to answer, because it was impossible at the time to prophesy accurately the effects of an attempt by the United Nations to eliminate the institution of the Emperor.

We summed up our conclusions, however, and gave our recommendations in a memorandum on May 9, 1944. In this we pointed out that, since the Japanese then showed an almost fanatical devotion to the Emperor, an attempt from the outside to abolish the institution of the Emperor would probably be ineffective. The mere dethronement of the Emperor would not abolish the Emperorship if the Japanese were determined to maintain it, and an indefinite military occupation of Japan might be necessary if the United Nations wished to prevent its revival. We called attention to the unique position of the Japanese Emperor in that he was considered as the source, sacred and inviolable, from which all authority emanated.

Accepted governmental procedure had allowed the Emperorship to be made an instrument of the Japanese military, we pointed out; and accordingly this close relationship would probably have to be severed if we were to wipe out militarism in Japan. In any event, the supreme authority in Japan must be the Allied military Government.

If the Emperor were retained, we said, there were three choices— redelegate to him none, all, or only some of his functions. We argued against the first in that it might create a difficult situation for the occupation authorities. Japanese functionaries considered the throne as the source of their authority, and they might refuse to serve under foreign masters if the Emperor were deprived of his rights of sovereignty. We questioned whether a sufficient number of Allied Civil Affairs personnel could ever be trained to operate by themselves the entire administration of Japanese government and the essential functions of Japanese economy.

We argued against the second on the grounds that it might infringe too much on the authority of the occupation forces, it might imply that the latter were supporting the continuance of the throne, and it would probably encounter the opposition of American public opinion.

We felt that the third choice, to redelegate to the Emperor some of his functions, offered the best possibilities. The Allied governor would permit the Emperor to exercise only those functions that related to the assignment of administrative duties to subordinate officials. Without impairing the essential authority of the theater commander, this would tend to assure the good behavior of the Japanese people and to keep in office the maximum number of Japanese officials willing to serve directly under the supervision of Civil Affairs officers.

We did not think the Japanese would interpret this procedure as support of the Emperorship and its symbolic value, in view of the fact that foreign military forces would have apprehended the imperial family and would be using some of the Emperor's functions for their own ends. Moreover, the Japanese would be uncertain as to the eventual disposition of the Emperor.

It might well be possible, we thought, for the Civil Affairs administration to diminish even the limited use it might make of the institution of the Emperor as the administrative machinery of military government functioned more effectively. We considered this desirable politically. And, if a substantial movement developed among the Japanese people to abolish the imperial institution, the Allied military authorities should take no action against that movement, except to maintain law and order, and should cease to utilize the Emperor as a political instrument.

Generally, we recommended that the Allied military authorities adopt as flexible a course as possible. If they decided to permit the Emperor to exercise certain limited functions, we then made five recommendations.

The first was that the Emperor should be kept in seclusion, after being removed from the Imperial Palace and taken to a location which was comparatively easy to guard. But his personal advisers should have reasonable access to him, and he should be accorded normal courtesies. The Japanese people could therefore be assured of the Emperor's safety and welfare and of the fact that he was under surveillance.

The second was that the authority and responsibility of the theater commander should supersede that of all officials and organs in the occupied territory. The military governor would permit only those functions of the Emperor to be exercised which related to the assignment of administrative duties to subordinate officials. He should suspend those functions of the Emperor relating to the enactment of laws and to the armed forces. This would show to the Japanese people that the authority of the occupation government was superior to that of the Emperor.

The third was that, if retaining the Emperorship did not facilitate the use of Japanese personnel under the supervision of Civil Affairs officers, it might become advantageous to suspend all the functions of the Emperor, but the occupation authorities would have to be prepared to take charge of the actual operation of all Japanese governmental activities. We requested that, before such action were taken, the State Department be given an opportunity to express its opinion.

The fourth was that, if a portion of Japan were occupied for any length of time prior to unconditional surrender of the entire country, the occupation authorities should be prepared to operate directly most of the functions of government in the occupied area. This for the reason that it would probably be difficult to obtain the services of any Japanese officials of significance in that area.

The fifth was that the occupation authorities, in all their treatment of and contact with the Emperor, should refrain from any action that would imply recognition of or support for the Japanese concept that the Emperor was different from and superior to other temporal rulers, that he was of divine origin and capacities, that he was sacrosanct, and that he was indispensable. They should permit absolute freedom of discussion of political as well as other subjects, except where there might be incitement to breaches of the peace.

In general, we felt we should not make advance commitments that would prejudice the situation in favor of the Emperor institution or against it. We did not want to come out against the institution lest this give the Japanese militarists live coals to blow upon and bring up a flame of last-man resistance. Nor did we wish to come out for the institution lest this discourage whatever popular movement there might be in Japan to erase it.

Just before Secretary of State Byrnes left for the Potsdam Conference in July, 1945, he telephoned me at my apartment and gave me the substance of a draft statement which he said President Truman had given him. This proposed statement, for issue by the United States, Britain, and Russia at the Potsdam Conference, contained a declaration by the Allies to Japan that the Emperor institution would be preserved if Japan would make peace. Byrnes asked my opinion. He said that high officials of the State, War, and Navy Departments had approved it.

I replied that, since he was leaving in a few minutes, there was no time to write anything for him, but that the statement seemed too much like appeasement of Japan, especially after the resolute stand we had maintained on unconditional surrender. I pointed out that, as it was worded, it seemed to guarantee continuance not only of the Emperor but also of the feudal privileges of a ruling caste under the Emperor. I said that the Emperor and the ruling class must be stripped of all extraordinary privileges and placed on a level before the law with everybody else.

I then sent Byrnes a cable on July 16, through the courtesy of Under Secretary Grew, to outline my thoughts in further detail. I said that the support of the statement by the chief people in the State, War, and Navy Departments called for the most serious consideration. Nevertheless I pointed out that the central point calculated to create serious difference was in the paragraph relating to a proposed declaration by the Allies now—I underlined "now"—that the Emperor and his monarchy would be preserved in the event of an Allied victory. The proponents of this promise, I added, believed that somehow the influences and persons who paid allegiance to the Emperor and his religious status would fight and resist less hard and so save Allied lives and shorten the war.

The other side, however, I concluded, was that no person knew how the proposal would work out. The militarists would try hard to interfere. Also, should it fail, the Japanese would be encouraged and terrible political repercussions would follow in the United States. I therefore asked whether it would be well first to await the climax of Allied bombing and Russia's entry into the war.

The following day I received a message from Secretary Byrnes agreeing that the statement should be delayed, and that, when it was issued, it should not contain this commitment with regard to the Emperor.

When the Potsdam Declaration concerning Japan was issued, it contained no commitment with regard to the Emperor. The Japanese Government stated it would accept the Potsdam Declaration provided the right of the Emperor to rule were accepted. In line with the conclusions we had previously reached at the State Department, however, President Truman and Secretary Byrnes agreed to retain the Emperor only if his right to rule were subject to the Allied Command in carrying out the terms of surrender agreed to at Potsdam. The Japanese agreed.

The Potsdam agreement differed from the State Department recommendations made under me in that it permitted the continuance of the Japanese Government as such. We had recommended that certain sections of that Government be retained for administrative purposes; but at Potsdam it was agreed that the Government as a whole should continue along with its policy-making functions. Our recommendation that Allied Civil Affairs officers be stationed in all Government Departments likewise was not followed.

Concerning the vast area of the Southwest Pacific, my associates and I had been doing considerable thinking and, along with the President, had arrived at certain conclusions during my last years in office. This area embraced such important territories as the Dutch East Indies and the Philippines, and could be taken to include Malaya and French Indo-China.

These enormous lands entered into the intensive discussions we had been holding on the subject of dependent peoples. Without being specifically mentioned, they were included in the projects I had presented to the British and Russians under that heading.

We believed that the time had come when all parent countries should begin to plan and prepare for the self-government of these peoples, to be given them when they were ready for and worthy of it. Before us we always had the example of the Philippines, whom the United States had been preparing for independence almost since the day of our acquisition of the islands, and for whom an independence date had been formally set by national legislation in the Tydings-McDuffie Act of 1934.

The President was in thorough agreement with our proposals. He himself entertained strong views on independence for French Indo-China. That French dependency stuck in his mind as having been the springboard for the Japanese attack on the Philippines, Malaya, and the Dutch East Indies. He could not but remember the devious conduct of the Vichy Government in granting Japan the right to station troops there, without any consultation with us but with an effort to make the world believe we approved.

From time to time the President had stated forthrightly to me and to others his view that French Indo-China should be placed under international trusteeship shortly after the end of the war, with a view to its receiving full independence as soon as possible.

When British Foreign Secretary Eden came to the United States in March, 1943, he and I attended a conference with the President at the White House on March 27. William Strang (Assistant Under Secretary of State in the British Foreign Office), Harry Hopkins, Welles, British Ambassador Halifax, and Ambassador Winant, who was here on leave from London, were also present.

One of the first subjects brought up was whether China was to be one of the four controlling powers after the war, and whether the British and ourselves were in agreement on this point. The consensus was Yes on both points.

Another question related to our postwar policies regarding Manchuria, Korea, Formosa, and Indo-China. The President suggested that a trusteeship be set up for Indo-China, that Manchuria and Formosa be returned to China, and that Korea might be placed under an international trusteeship, with China, the United States, and one or two other countries participating.

He said that the Japanese mandated islands should be internationalized for the purpose of keeping the peace. Eden indicated he was favorably impressed with this proposal.

The President went over this subject again in the conference my associates, Admiral Leahy, and I had with him at the White House on October 5, 1943, two days prior to my departure for the Moscow Conference. On that occasion he said the British might, as a gesture of generosity, return Hong Kong to China while China might, in return, immediately declare Hong Kong a free port under international trusteeship.

He added that Indo-China and the Japanese mandated islands in the Pacific might be placed under international trustees, along with security points in many parts of the world. He mentioned Truk, the Bonin Islands, the Kurile Islands (although he thought the Kuriles should really go to Russia), Rabaul or some point in the Solomons, appropriate points in the Dutch East Indies, Ascension Island in the South Atlantic, Dakar, and some point in Liberia.

Ambassador Halifax came to me on January 3, 1944, and remarked that information had come to him from the Foreign Office that the President, during his visit to the Near East for the Cairo and Tehran Conferences, had rather definitely stated to the Turks, Egyptians, and perhaps others his views to the effect that Indo-China should be taken away from the French and put under an international trusteeship. Halifax said he had heard the President make remarks like this during the past year or more, but it was important to know whether his utterances represented final conclusions, in view of the fact that they would soon get back to the French.

I replied that I knew no more about the matter than the Ambassador. I said I had heard the President make these remarks occasionally just about as he had heard them. I added that, in my judgment, the President and Prime Minister Churchill would find it desirable to talk the question over fully, deliberately, and perhaps finally at some future stage.

I informed the President of this conversation in a note to him on January 14. I enclosed two brief memoranda citing the more important public statements or commitments we and the British had already made with regard to the future of French territory after the war. These were: the August 2, 1941, statement relative to the French-Japanese agreement; the President's letter to Pétain in December, 1941; a statement on New Caledonia made on March 2, 1942; a note to the French Ambassador on April 13, 1942; the President's statements and messages at the time of the invasion of North Africa; a letter from Robert D. Murphy to Giraud on November 2, 1942; and the Clark-Darlan agreement of November 22, 1942. Generally these looked toward the restoration of French territories after the war.

Ten days later the President sent me a memorandum, dated January 24, which began by saying: "I saw Halifax last week and told him quite frankly that it was perfectly true that I had, for over a year, expressed the opinion that Indo-China should not go back to France but that it should be administered by an international trusteeship. France has had the country—thirty million inhabitants—for nearly one hundred years, and the people are worse off than they were at the beginning."

He then went on: "As a matter of interest, I am wholeheartedly supported in this view by Generalissimo Chiang Kai-shek and by Marshal Stalin. I see no reason to play in with the British Foreign Office in this matter. The only reason they seem to oppose it is that they fear the effect it would have on their own possessions and those of the Dutch. They have never liked the idea of trusteeship because it is, in some instances, aimed at future independence. This is true in the case of Indo-China.

"Each case must, of course, stand on its own feet, but the case of Indo-China is perfectly clear. France has milked it for one hundred years. The people of Indo-China are entitled to something better than that."

In August, 1944, the British, in an *aide-mémoire*, raised with us the question of a French role in military operations in the Far East, with particular reference to Indo-China. They requested our concurrence in steps looking toward French participation in the liberation of Indo-China and in the war against Japan, for which the French had requested British approval. I sent this to the President on August 26, and commented, in a memorandum that, while these steps were "ostensibly military in character, they have wide implications and for this reason they are being referred to you for decision."

The President informed me orally that he planned to discuss these French proposals with Mr. Churchill at Quebec, where he was shortly going. He and the Prime Minister were unable, however, to reach any agreement. We subsequently received reports that the British were going ahead with the proposal to attach a French military mission to the Southeast Asia Command headquarters, though the mission, in the absence of American agreement, would at first be "ostensibly unofficial."

After learning that a French military mission had gone to Kandy to consult with the Southeast Asia Command regarding military operations affecting Indo-China, the President on November 3, 1944, gave instructions that American approval must not be given to any French military mission being accredited to the Southeast Asia Command, and that no American representatives in the Far East, whether civilian or military, were authorized to make any "decisions on political questions with the French mission or anyone else."

When we sent Mr. Roosevelt another memorandum on October 13 relative to an Office of Strategic Services proposal to assist resistance groups in Indo-China, he sent me a memorandum three days later, saying: "In regard to the Indo-China matter, it is my judgment on this date that we should do nothing in regard to resistance groups or in any other way in relation to Indo-China. You might bring it up to me a little later when things are a little clearer."

The President's opposition to the return of Indo-China to France continued at the time of my resignation the following month.

My own thought was that Indo-China should fall within the general category of dependent peoples, to whom the mother countries should be pledged to grant eventual independence. I favored this method rather than placing Indo-China under a trusteeship. Though the Vichy Government had betrayed Indo-China to Japan, I felt that an international agency would have great difficulty handling so large an area and population unless it were exceptionally well equipped. If France were prepared to restore her own popular institutions and to deal properly with the colonies, I favored the return of Indo-China, with France's pledge of eventual independence as soon as the colony became qualified for it, along the lines of our pledge to the Philippines. If France were not prepared to do full justice to Indo-China in accordance with this example, then it would be necessary to look to an international trusteeship; but I did not underestimate the terrific undertaking that administration by a trusteeship would represent, both in service and in money.

Our prime difficulty generally with regard to Asiatic colonial possessions, of course, was to induce the colonial Powers—principally Britain, France, and The Netherlands—to adopt our ideas with regard to dependent peoples. Britain had refused to go along with us on the idea of eventual independence for her colonies, believing instead that they should in time achieve self-government within the Empire. We had frequent conversations with these parent countries, but we could not press them too far with regard to the Southwest Pacific in view of the fact that we were seeking the closest possible cooperation with them in Europe. We could not alienate them in the Orient and expect to work with them in Europe.

At no time did we press Britain, France, or The Netherlands for an immediate grant of self-government to their colonies. Our thought was that it would come after an adequate period of years, short or long depending on the state of development of respective colonial peoples, during which these peoples would be trained to govern themselves. Our cause was harmed, not helped, by some vociferous persons in the United States, including Vice President Wallace, who argued for an immediate grant of independence or for the total separation of colonies from their mother countries.

These persons disregarded the magnitude of the problem that would thereupon face all nations. When a certain Texan argued with me along the line of separating all colonies from their mother countries and particularly urged that Britain should return Hong Kong to China, I retorted that Hong Kong had been British longer than Texas had belonged to the United States, and I did not think anyone would welcome a move to turn Texas back to Mexico.

We also encountered resistance from our own War and Navy Departments, which felt that our ideas conflicted with their desire to acquire sovereignty of Japanese islands in the Pacific for use as United States bases. We were accordingly not able to bring before the Dumbarton Oaks Conference our dependent peoples project, embraced within a plan for a trusteeship system to be set up under the United Nations organization. To me this was a keen disappointment.

As Allied, principally American, forces began the reconquest of the Southwest Pacific islands, we summed up our thinking with regard to the Netherlands Indies in a letter of February 28, 1944, to the Director of the Civil Affairs Division of the War Department. We began this by saying that arrangements for the civil administration of liberated Netherlands Indies territory should be predicated on the assumption that the exercise of all attributes of sovereignty would be resumed by the Netherlands Government as soon as the situation, in the judgment of the Supreme Commander of the Allied Expeditionary Force (General Douglas MacArthur) permitted. We then said:

"However, in any military agreement of the nature under consideration no commitments should be made which would prejudice the right of the Government of the United States to bring up either prior to or after the resumption of sovereign rights by the Netherlands Government certain proposals for discussion and agreement of a general character which it may believe to be of rightful concern to the United States Government and to all Governments which have subscribed to the principles of the Atlantic Charter, and to the Four-Nation Declaration at Moscow, and certain particular proposals which may be of special mutual concern to the people of the Netherlands Empire and the people of the United States."

In brief, we did not want agreements made between our military commander and Netherlands authorities which would militate against our presentation of proposals relating to the eventual independence of the Netherlands Indies.

We summarized our thoughts on colonial areas in Southeast Asia generally in a Department memorandum which I sent to the President on September 8, 1944. In this we suggested the value of "early, dramatic, and concerted announcements by the nations concerned making definite commitments as to the future of the regions of Southeast Asia." We added:

"It would be especially helpful if such concerted announcements could include (1) specific dates when independence or complete (dominion) self-government will be accorded, (2) specific steps to be taken to develop native capacity for self-rule, and (3) a pledge of economic autonomy and equality of economic treatment toward other nations.

"Such announcements might well be accompanied by ·. . . a pledge to establish a regional commission. . . . The value of such concerted announcements would be still further enhanced if each of the colonial powers concerned would pledge a formal declaration of trusteeship under an international organization for the period of tutelage; but it might be unwise for the United States to attempt to insist upon such a declaration of trusteeship by one country if similar declarations could not be secured from the others. In addition to their great value as psychological warfare, such announcements would appear to be directly in line with American postwar interests."

The President warmly approved these ideas. He subsequently directed that instructions be sent to American officers at home and abroad, and that the British, Dutch, and French Governments be informed as well, that the United States expected to be consulted on any arrangements as to the future of Southeast Asia.

Such was our policy toward the Southwest Pacific as I left office. It might be thought that we were presumptuous in seeking to present our ideas to the British, French, and Dutch Governments as to what they should do with their own Pacific possessions. We had, however, two rights to take such action. One was the fact that the liberation of those possessions would not have been achieved—and possibly never could have been—except by United States forces. The other was our interest in seeing that peace in the Pacific, restored by our forces, should continue. And we could not help believing that the indefinite continuance of the British, Dutch, and French possessions in the Orient in a state of dependence provided a number of foci for future trouble and perhaps war. Permanent peace could not be assured unless these possessions were started on the road to independence, after the example of the Philippines. We believed that we were taking the long-range view, and that a lasting peace in the Pacific was of greater ultimate benefit to Britain, France, and The Netherlands—as well as to the whole world—than the possible immediate benefits of holding on to colonies.

115: Plan for Germany

WHEN THE PRESIDENT decided to meet with Prime Minister Churchill for the Second Quebec Conference, in September, 1944, he asked me whether I wished to accompany him. The conference, however, was intended to be largely military. I was not well, the Dumbarton Oaks Conference was in progress, and I told him I preferred to remain in Washington but would be available if he needed me.

Shortly before the conference was to assemble, the President was prevailed upon to permit Secretary of the Treasury Morgenthau to attend the meeting. Morgenthau and his friends had been working for some time on a drastic plan for the postwar treatment of Germany, and the leaders of groups who had been justly wrought up by German outrages requested the President to invite him to go to Quebec primarily to present his plan for Germany.

My associates and I at the State Department had spent hundreds of hours working on a plan for Germany. We had had frequent conferences on the subject with the War Department. I had presented a preliminary plan, which had the full approval of the President, at the Moscow Conference. There it received the general approval of Eden and Molotov, and was referred to the European Advisory Commission in London to be worked out in detail. That Commission had done considerable work in setting up arrangements for the postwar government and control of Germany, and numerous exchanges of views had taken place among the United States, Britain, and Russia.

To Morgenthau, however, our plan (which I have outlined in Chapter 92 on the Moscow Conference) was too mild. He insisted to the President that Germany should be stripped of all industries and converted into an agricultural country.

The President himself leaned to the idea that the German people as a whole should be given a lesson they would remember. On August 26, 1944, he had sent a long memorandum to Secretary of War Stimson, a copy of which was sent to me, protesting against the handbook drawn up for the guidance of military government officials in Germany.

"It gives the impression," he said, "that Germany is to be restored just as much as The Netherlands or Belgium, and the people of Germany brought back as quickly as possible to their prewar estate.

"It is of the utmost importance that every person in Germany should realize that this time Germany is a defeated nation. I do not want them to starve to death, but, as an example, if they need food to keep body and soul together beyond what they have, they should be fed three times a day with soup from Army soup kitchens. That will keep them perfectly healthy, and they will remember that experience all their lives. The fact that they are a defeated nation, collectively and individually, must be so impressed upon them that they will hesitate to start any new war."

After quoting from several of the handbook's pages to which he particularly objected, he concluded:

"There exists a school of thought both in London and here which would, in effect, do for Germany what this Government did for its own citizens in 1933 when they were flat on their backs. I see no reason for starting a WPA, PWA, or CCC for Germany when we go in with our army of occupation.

"Too many people here and in England hold to the view that the German people as a whole are not responsible for what has taken place— that only a few Nazi leaders are responsible. That unfortunately is not based on fact. The German people as a whole must have it driven home to them that the whole nation has been engaged in a lawless conspiracy against the decencies of modern civilization."

With regard to the disposition of the German Navy, the President advanced a new idea. The Joint Chiefs of Staff wrote me on September 4, 1944, stating that they wanted the complete destruction of the German fleet except for a limited number of ships that could be retained for experimental purposes. If no agreement could be reached with the Russians and British on this basis, they said, the United States should press for either a one-third share in each category of vessel, or an agreement that all capital ships, such as battleships, pocket battleships, heavy cruisers, and submarines, be destroyed, while smaller craft would be shared equally by the United States, Russia, and Great Britain.

After I sent this letter to the President, he wrote me a memorandum on October 13 in which he accepted the views of the Joint Chiefs of Staff with regard to the complete destruction of the German fleet, but had one amendment to make.

"Destruction in the past," he said, "has meant taking the ships to sea and sinking them. I think that in some cases surrendered ships have been destroyed by converting them into scrap metal. I do not like the idea of complete destruction by the sinking of thousands of tons of steel.

"Recently a new use for such ships has been discovered. We have used sunken ships as breakwaters for the formation of new harbors. This has been done in Italy, and it has been done on the coast of Normandy. It is a relatively cheap way to build a breakwater. I think that the United Nations should be in a position to pass on applications by Allied nations for these ships for the definite and specific purpose of sinking them as breakwaters to improve or create safe anchorages. It is rather a nice thought to use them for such peaceful purposes.

"In any such cases, the ships should be sunk at a designated place as quickly as possible and under the eyes of a United Nations Committee. Once sunk it would be practically impossible to raise them and restore them to war purposes."

We cabled Ambassador Winant in London on October 19 instructing him to guide himself according to the President's memorandum in the discussions of the European Advisory Commission.

Harry Hopkins came to me on September 1, 1944, and informed me of the President's desire to establish a "Cabinet Committee on Germany." He said the President had asked him to give his undivided attention to this matter in the next few weeks. Hopkins at this time also explained Morgenthau's interest in the question, arising from his disagreement with certain sections of the plans for Germany which already had been prepared.

My associates at the State Department, particularly H. Freeman Matthews and James W. Riddleberger, went over with Hopkins in detail the studies concerning postwar Germany made at the State Department and by the European Advisory Commission in London. They prepared a memorandum, which I approved, explaining the work that already had been done and setting forth the State Department's views on the treatment of Germany. This Matthews and Riddleberger presented at a meeting of representatives of the State, Treasury, and War Departments called by Hopkins in his office at the White House on September 2.

Morgenthau's, or the Treasury's, plan was presented at this session by Dr. Harry White. This plan proposed, among other things, that parts of Germany should be given to neighboring countries and the remainder split into three units.

Poland should get southern Silesia and that part of East Prussia which did not go to Russia. France should get the Saar and the adjacent territories bounded by the Rhine and Moselle rivers. Denmark should get territories north of the Kiel Canal, between her present borders and an International Zone.

This International Zone would be one of the three units into which Germany would be partitioned. It would contain the Ruhr and the surrounding industrial areas and the Kiel Canal, and would be run by the proposed United Nations organization. The remaining portion of Germany would be divided into two autonomous, independent states—a South German state comprising Bavaria, Württemberg, Baden, and some smaller areas, and a North German state comprising a large part of the old state of Prussia, Saxony, Thuringia, and several smaller states. There would be a customs union between the new South German state and Austria, the latter to be restored to her pre-1938 borders.

Industrial plants and equipment situated within the International Zone and the North and South German states would be removed and distributed among devastated countries. Forced German labor would be used in such countries.

Dr. White explained that no trade would be permitted between the International Zone and the remainder of Germany. He emphasized that the productivity of this zone would in no way be permitted to contribute to German economy.

Later the Treasury inserted in its plan this paragraph with regard to the Ruhr and surrounding industrial areas:

"This area should not only be stripped of all presently existing industries but so weakened and controlled that it cannot in the foreseeable future become an industrial area—all industrial plants and equipment not destroyed by military action shall either be completely dismantled or removed from the area or completely destroyed, all equipment should be removed from the mines and the mines shall be thoroughly wrecked."

The Treasury plan stated that the United States would have military and civilian representation on whatever international commission might be established to carry out the German program, but that the primary responsibility for the policing of Germany and for civil administration in Germany would be assumed by the military forces of Germany's continental neighbors, specifically Russia, France, Poland, Czechoslovakia, Greece, Yugoslavia, Norway, The Netherlands, and Belgium. United States troops could be withdrawn within "a relatively short time."

It was obvious on its face that this plan was drastic. It would leave Germany with practically no industry, and would force the population to live entirely on the land, regardless of the fact that there was not enough land on which the large German population could live.

Essentially, this was a plan of blind vengeance. It was blind because it failed to see that, in striking at Germany, it was striking at all of Europe. By completely wrecking German industry it could not but partly wreck Europe's economy, which had depended for generations on certain raw materials that Germany produced.

The Treasury recommendation that the German mines be ruined was almost breath-taking in its implications for all Europe, because various other countries relied upon German coal for their industries. After the Allied occupation of Germany began, the Allied authorities there did, in fact, have to bend every effort to restore German mines to the fullest production so as to improve Europe's economy generally.

At the State Department we had drawn up on September 1 a memorandum to emphasize our views on this point. "If a far-reaching program of industrial destruction or dismantlement is agreed upon," we stated, "it is apparent that, if put into effect, it will bring about extensive and important changes in European economy as a whole.

"Germany is a deficit country in foodstuffs, and it is doubtful if a plan of making Germany predominantly agricultural can be put into effect without the liquidation or emigration of X millions of Germans.

"Germany is furthermore an important producer of certain raw materials—namely, coal and bauxite—for Europe as a whole, not to speak of the vast amount of industrial goods which Germany normally exports. If we advocate a 'wrecking program' as the best means of assuring our security, we may face considerable European opposition on account of its effect on European economy; and if we desire continuing reparations out of Germany, we shall eliminate any such program by a policy of destruction of German industry."

We were also agreed at the State Department to oppose Morgenthau's ideas of a partition of Germany. We stated in our memorandum:

"The State Department is, in general, opposed to the forcible partition of Germany into two or more separate states as has been advocated as a practical means of forestalling any renewal of German aggression. Such a measure, however drastic in itself, would not offset the necessity of imposing and enforcing far-reaching security controls upon Germany for an indeterminate period, whether Germany is left united or is divided. Moreover, because of the high degree of economic, political, and cultural integration of Germany, it must be anticipated that partition would not only have to be enforced but also maintained by force.

"The victor powers, by imposing partition, would take on themselves a burdensome and never-ending task of preventing surreptitious collaboration between the partite states and of restraining the nationalistic determination to reunite, which would, in all probability, be the response of the German people. Finally, the disruption of German economic unity would carry with it grave dangers for the economic stability of Europe as a whole, and not merely to Germany."

On the other hand, we said that we should not oppose any spontaneous German movement for partition.

We recommended that, in place of partition, every effort be made to promote a federal system of government in Germany, and a division of Prussia into a number of medium-sized states. We pointed out that Prussia in 1938 included five-eighths of the area and two-thirds of the population of Germany, and it might well be that in reaction to the Nazi overcentralization many Germans would want to return to a considerable degree of federal decentralization, including the break-up of Prussia.

The War Department representatives at the meeting on September 2, Assistant Secretary McCloy and General Hilldring, pointed out the difficulties that would arise for the Army under any such plan as that advanced by the Treasury.

Following the presentation of the Treasury plan, Matthews and Riddleberger presented the State Department views and explained how they fitted into British and Russian ideas in so far as these had been communicated to us. The conferees thereupon requested Riddleberger to draw up a further memorandum attempting to reconcile the views of the three Departments, which the Secretaries of State, Treasury, and War might be willing to sign and submit to the President as their recommendation.

After Assistant Secretary of War McCloy said it was essential that General Eisenhower be given an interim directive for the treatment of Germany, Hopkins thought it most important that this directive be prepared as soon as possible, and urged McCloy to hasten the work. McCloy said that the State and War Departments had both been working on this directive, and that there were only minor differences between them which could easily be adjusted, but that the Treasury memorandum obviously ran counter to some major provisions of the directive. It was thereupon decided that a meeting be held, in which Treasury representatives would participate, to hasten the completion of the directive.

Harry Hopkins met on September 3 with James C. Dunn, the State Department's Political Adviser on European Affairs, Matthews, and Riddleberger, on which occasion Dunn emphasized to Hopkins the supreme importance of working with our Allies, particularly Britain and Russia, on the whole question of the postwar treatment of Germany. He pointed out the impossibility of obtaining the concurrence of Russia and Britain to some of the provisions advocated by the Treasury. He explained the tripartite control of Germany envisaged in proposals submitted to the European Advisory Commission by the United States and Britain, which would have to be modified extensively if the Treasury's ideas were accepted. Hopkins seemed to realize the validity of these contentions, and remarked that in his opinion it was essential that the President and the Secretary of State keep in step on all plans that might be developed for Germany.

I held the first meeting of the "Cabinet Committee" in my office on September 5, with Hopkins, Morgenthau, and Stimson attending. I laid before them a memorandum my associates and I had prepared, dated September 4, containing suggested recommendations the Cabinet Committee might present to the President.

This suggested the appointment, as soon as possible, of an American High Commissioner for Germany, who would meet with equivalent representatives of Britain and Russia immediately upon the occupation of Germany. We proposed the complete demilitarization of Germany, the dissolution of the Nazi Party and all affiliated organizations, the maintenance of extensive controls over communications, press and propaganda, and education, and the breaking up of the great Junker estates. These proposals had appeared in our previous plans and also in the Treasury plan.

We differed with the Treasury, however, on the partition of Germany. We said that no decision should be taken on this point, as distinguished from territorial cessions to neighboring countries, until we saw what the internal situation in Germany and what the attitude of our principal Allies would be. We should, however, encourage a decentralization of the German governmental structure, and, if any tendencies toward spontaneous partition arose they should not be discouraged.

We differed also on making Germany an agricultural country. In this connection we said that the American Government had no direct interest in obtaining reparations from Germany and consequently no interest in building up German economy in order to collect continuing reparations. However, the United Kingdom and the U.S.S.R., along with a number of small states, might have claims on German production which they would require for purposes of reconstruction. Consequently, we should not take a fixed position on reparations at this time but await the views of Governments more directly interested.

We stated three primary objectives of our economic policy in Germany. The first was that the standard of living of the population should be held down to subsistence levels. The second was that Germany's economic position of power in Europe must be eliminated. The last was that German economic capacity must be converted in such a manner that it would be so dependent on imports and exports that the country could not by its own devices reconvert to war production.

Secretary Stimson agreed with virtually all this memorandum, except the point that the standard of living of the German population should be held down to subsistence levels. Secretary Morgenthau also seemed to agree with large sections of the memorandum, but he would not commit himself to it. Harry Hopkins sent me a note on September 5 in which he said that, with minor reservations about language which did not affect the content of the document, he approved it.

On the following day our little group met with the President at the White House. I presented our memorandum of September 4, with the statement that it had not been agreed to by the other members of the committee, but might serve as a basis for discussion. Stimson presented a War Department memorandum that was very largely in line with our memorandum. Morgenthau, however, presented the original drastic Treasury memorandum.

The discussion that followed was inconclusive. The distance between the views of the State and War Departments on the one hand and of the Treasury on the other was so great that no meeting of minds ensued.

Secretary of War Stimson sent me a copy of a memorandum he addressed to the President on September 9. In this, after citing Morgenthau's proposal that industrial plants and equipment in the Ruhr and surrounding areas be dismantled, removed, or completely destroyed and the mines thoroughly wrecked, he said he was unalterably opposed to such a program. These resources, he said, constituted a natural and necessary asset for the productivity of Europe. In a period when the world was suffering from destruction and from want of production, the concept of the total obliteration of these values was to his mind wholly wrong. His insistence was that these assets be conserved and made available for the profit of the whole of Europe, including Great Britain particularly.

Stimson recommended that the President accept a program generally in accord with the memorandum I had submitted on September 5. He added suggestions for several modifications, and canceled out our provision that the standard of living of the German population be held down to subsistence levels.

Thus the matter stood when the Quebec Conference met on September 11. We had been able to achieve no further reconciliation of views. As I have already stated, the President was induced to permit Morgenthau to attend the conference, at which the latter intended to advocate his extreme plan before the President and the Prime Minister. I requested Ray Atherton, our Ambassador to Canada, to represent us at the meetings.

Four days after the conference began, I was astonished to receive from the President a memorandum addressed to me, dated September 15, which indicated that he and Churchill had largely embraced Morgenthau's ideas. The memorandum set forth that the President and the Prime Minister felt that an essential feature of the best measures to prevent renewed rearmament by Germany was the future disposition of the Ruhr and the Saar. The ease with which the metallurgical, chemical, and electric industries in Germany could be converted from peace to war had already been impressed upon us by bitter experience. It had also to be remembered that the Germans had devastated a large portion of the industries of Russia and of other neighboring Allies, and it was only just that these injured countries should be entitled to remove the machinery they required in order to repair the losses they had suffered.

The memorandum then stated:

"The industries referred to in the Ruhr and in the Saar would therefore be necessarily put out of action and closed down. It was felt that the two districts should be put under somebody under the World Organization which would supervise the dismantling of these industries and make sure that they were not started up again by some subterfuge.

"This program for eliminating the war-making industries in the Ruhr and in the Saar is looking forward to converting Germany into a country primarily agricultural and pastoral in its character.

"The Prime Minister and the President were in agreement upon this program."

In his note to me introducing this memorandum, the President said this seemed eminently satisfactory to him, and he thought I would approve the general idea of not rehabilitating the Ruhr, Saar, and so on.

I could not, however, approve any program "looking forward to converting Germany into a country primarily agricultural and pastoral in its character." Seventy million Germans could not live on the land within Germany. They would either starve or become a charge upon other nations. This was a scheme that would arouse the eternal resentment of the Germans. It would punish all of them and future generations too for the crimes of a portion of them. It would punish not only Germany but also most of Europe.

The President also said in his note to me that he thought he had worked out the locations of the occupying forces in Germany. He had been hoping to get the northwestern portion of Germany as the American zone of occupation, but finally agreed with Churchill that Britain should have it, while the United States would have most of southern Germany, including Bavaria.

Thus was settled a difference of opinion between the President and the Prime Minister which had remained unsolved for some seven months. The original plan of the Combined Chiefs of Staff had been to make the British sphere of occupation (if occupation were necessary in all these areas) northwestern Germany, Norway, Belgium, Luxemburg, Holland, and Denmark; the United States' sphere southern Germany, France, and possibly Austria; Russia's sphere the area to the east of the British. After the United States Chiefs of Staff, however, proposed that the British and American spheres be exactly reversed, Mr. Churchill cabled the President in February, 1944, strongly urging that the original plan continue. He said Britain was better equipped and situated to ensure the naval disarmament of Germany; close liaison had already been established between the Royal Air Force and the Norwegian and Netherlands Air Forces which the British had trained, and it was desirable to continue this liaison after the war, which would be difficult if Norway and the Netherlands were outside the British zone. The United States, on the other hand, had had major responsibility for reequipping French forces. Mr. Churchill further argued that the plans for the invasion of Normandy had already been agreed to, placing the British on the left flank going toward Germany, with bases in the Havre-Cherbourg area, and American forces on the right flank, with bases in the Brittany ports. A reversal of the spheres would involve crossing the lines of communication, and it was obviously too late to replan the invasion so as to reverse the British and American forces.

The President, who had the whole matter much at heart, sent a memorandum on February 21, 1944, to Under Secretary Stettinius, while I was briefly absent from Washington, strongly stating his own arguments. "I do not want the United States," he said, "to have the postwar burden of reconstituting France, Italy, and the Balkans. This is not our natural task at a distance of 3,500 miles or more. It is definitely a British task in which the British are far more vitally interested than we are."

Our principal object, he pointed out, was not to take part in the internal problems in southern Europe "but is rather to take part in eliminating Germany at a possible and even probable cost of a third World War." He said the British argument about the difficulties of transferring our forces from a French front to a northern German front—what was called "leap-frogging"—was "specious" because, no matter where British and American troops were on the day of Germany's surrender, it was physically easy for them to go anywhere, north, east, or south.

"I have had to consider also," he said, "the ease of maintaining American troops in some part of Germany. All things considered, and remembering that all supplies have to come 3,500 miles or more by sea, the United States should use the ports of northern Germany—Hamburg and Bremen—and the ports of The Netherlands for this long-range operation."

He therefore thought that the American policy should be to occupy northwestern Germany, the British to occupy the area from the Rhine south and also be responsible for the policing of France and Italy if this should become necessary.

As for the long-range security of Britain against Germany, he commented, this was not a part of the first occupation period, and the British would have plenty of time to work that out, including Helgoland, airfields, and the like. "The Americans by that time," he said, "will be only too glad to retire all their military forces from Europe."

He concluded by saying: "If anything further is needed to justify this disagreement with the British lines of demarcation, I can only add that political considerations in the United States make my decision conclusive."

These arguments were duly communicated to the British, but without visible effect, the President and the Prime Minister continuing at opposite poles on the subject.

After Under Secretary Stettinius went to London in April, he cabled me on April 14 that General Eisenhower was deeply convinced that the British and American zones in Germany should be combined in one Anglo-American zone of occupation. Eisenhower argued to Stettinius that it would be very difficult from a military point of view to split up in two distinct occupation commands, after Germany surrendered, what amounted to a unified combined Anglo-American command. Various combined Anglo-American boards were slated to direct shipping and supply for western Germany; and to set up each zone with its own transportation and supply programs in separate American and British zones would be very confusing administratively. Eisenhower's suggestion, however, had possible political implications that negatived its acceptance.

In August the question of the zones again came to a head when the Russians indicated that they did not wish to continue discussions concerning the Allied zones of control in Germany until we and the British had settled the location of our respective zones.

On August 3, 1944, the President, who was on a trip to Hawaii, the Aleutians, and Alaska, cabled the Department asking us to inform Ambassador Winant in London that he was awaiting an agreement by the Prime Minister that American troops would police northwestern Germany and would not police southern Europe. "It is essential," he said, "that American troops of occupation will have no responsibility in southern Europe and will be withdrawn from there at the earliest practicable date. . . . No possible difficulty with England is foreseeable in regard to her naval problems in northwestern Germany. They can march hand in hand with the supply of our troops; but in consideration of our 3,000 miles of transport I want to be able to carry this out through Holland and Hamburg and Bremen."

We cabled Winant accordingly, but it remained for the personal meeting of the President and the Prime Minister at Quebec to iron out their differences. The President accepted the southern section of Germany as the American zone of occupation, but his insistence on having the use of northern ports was met by assigning an enclave to us which included Bremen.

On the same day, September 15, that the President sent me the memorandum embracing the Morgenthau plan and the decision on the zones of occupation, he sent me another memorandum which informed me that Morgenthau had presented at Quebec, in conjunction with his plan for Germany, a proposal of credits to Britain totaling six and a half billion dollars. This might suggest to some the *quid pro quo* with which

the Secretary of the Treasury was able to get Mr. Churchill's adherence
to his cataclysmic plan for Germany.

The President said in his memorandum that he had agreed that, after
the defeat of Germany and while the war against Japan went on, Britain
should continue to receive munitions assistance from us to the extent of
$3,500,000,000 and other assistance of $3,000,000,000. He concurred in
Churchill's statement that if the United Kingdom were once more to pay
her way it was essential that her export trade, which had shrunk to a
very small fraction, should be reestablished. Naturally no articles obtained
on Lend-Lease or identical thereto would be exported or sold for profit;
but it was essential that the United States should not attach any conditions to supplies delivered to Britain on Lend-Lease which would jeopardize the recovery of her export trade.

This struck me amidships. It tended to shatter negotiations we had
been conducting with the British for three years. It derogated from Article VII of our basic Lend-Lease agreement with Britain, signed in 1942,
which provided that Britain would adopt a nondiscriminatory commercial
policy after the war, meaning that she would give up imperial tariff
preferences.

This whole development at Quebec, I believe, angered me as much as
anything that had happened during my career as Secretary of State. If
the Morgenthau plan leaked out, as it inevitably would—and shortly did
—it might well mean a bitter-end German resistance that could cause the
loss of thousands of American lives.

Morgenthau returned to Washington from Quebec, while the President went first to Hyde Park, where Prime Minister Churchill paid him a
visit. Morgenthau was wildly enthusiastic over what he had accomplished,
and came rushing to Stimson and me and others with the latest copies of
his plans.

I held a meeting of the Cabinet Committee in my office on September
20 to go over these developments, with Morgenthau and Stimson, Harry
White of the Treasury, Assistant Secretary of War McCloy, and H.
Freeman Matthews of the State Department. I made no effort to hide my
stupefaction at what the President and Mr. Churchill, at Morgenthau's
insistence, had agreed to at Quebec. I considered it a tragedy for all
concerned. I emphasized that I did not regard the matter as closed.

Morgenthau said that the President's invitation to him to go to
Quebec had been a complete surprise to him, and he did not want people
to think he had engineered it. He then went into a long explanation of

what had happened at Quebec. He said that Mr. Churchill had at first been violently opposed to the Morgenthau policy toward Germany. The Prime Minister had bluntly inquired whether he had been brought over to Quebec to discuss a scheme that would mean "England's being chained to a dead body."

Morgenthau turned to Stimson and said, in effect, "He was even more angry than you, Harry." Stimson had been as angered as I was over Morgenthau's high-handed procedure in conducting negotiations at Quebec on a matter of primary concern to the State and War Departments, without consultation with us; and he made no effort to conceal the fact.

Morgenthau said he then took up the subject with Lord Cherwell, personal assistant to the Prime Minister, and apparently convinced him. Cherwell discussed it with Churchill and won him over. The proposal apparently appealed to the Prime Minister on the ground that Britain would thus acquire many of Germany's iron and steel markets and eliminate a dangerous competitor. Morgenthau said they then made several attempts to put the understanding on paper, none of which pleased the Prime Minister, who thereupon called in his secretary and dictated his understanding of what had been agreed to. This was the document initialed by the President and the Prime Minister and dispatched to me on September 15. Morgenthau said it was drafted entirely by Mr. Churchill.

Stimson asked Morgenthau point-blank whether there had been any connection between Churchill's acceptance of this policy and his eagerness to obtain the credits that Morgenthau was offering him. Morgenthau answered No, but he said that the credits were clearly the Prime Minister's principal nonmilitary objective at Quebec.

The following day, Morgenthau said, Foreign Secretary Eden arrived at Quebec and became very much upset at the agreement reached by the President and the Prime Minister concerning Germany. Eden had a heated discussion with Mr. Churchill, who instructed him not to take it up in the War Cabinet until the Prime Minister returned, for he was bent on pushing it through.

Morgenthau said he was surprised at Eden's opposition, since he had gained a contrary impression when he talked with Eden in London a short time before. This statement disclosed to us that the Secretary of the Treasury, even prior to Quebec, had been discussing with British officials a matter of primary concern to the State and War Departments.

As for the credits side of the picture, Morgenthau said he had found the President prepared to accept the Prime Minister's views without question, but that he, Morgenthau, had insisted that a committee be set up to work out the project. Morgenthau himself did not seem to feel that the committee would be any too effective in obtaining British cooperation toward liberal economic policy, but he felt that at least it gave us a foot in the door. He said that the President had not raised any question as to what economic policy the British should pursue in return for our assistance.

Without cushioning my words, I said I was acutely shocked at the way such vital matters had been settled without any consultation with the appropriate experts of our Government and without any regard for the policy we had been trying to pursue in the past.

While awaiting the President's final ruling on the decisions reached at Quebec, representatives of the State, Treasury, and War Departments met in the War Department on September 22 to draw up an interim directive for Germany. After an all-day session they agreed tentatively on a directive, to which I gave my formal approval a few days later. During this meeting the Treasury representatives made it plain that they expected to be consulted henceforth not only on financial matters relating to Germany but on all other questions as well. They said this was the purpose behind the establishment of the Cabinet Committee, and they also indicated that the views set forth in the original Treasury memorandum on Germany had received the President's approval.

I sent the President a memorandum on September 25 suggesting that we should have the firm agreement of the British and Soviet Governments to the policy he had outlined in his memorandum of September 15 before going any further. "We have thus far," I said, "acted on the basis that every action followed with respect to Germany, particularly in the post-hostilities period, would be on an agreed tripartite basis. It has also been our understanding that the Soviet Government has also acted on this general assumption, and of course the European Advisory Commission, established by the Moscow Conference, was set up for the purpose of working out the problems of the treatment of Germany. We must realize that the adoption of any other basis of procedure would enormously increase the difficulties and responsibilities not only of our soldiers in the immediate military occupation period but also of our officials in the control period following."

I concluded by saying: "Our information up to the present has been to the effect that the British Government no doubt has ideas of its own with respect to the application of economic controls to Germany, and we have not yet had any indication that the British Government would be in favor of complete eradication of German industrial productive capacity in the Ruhr and Saar. We have no ideas as yet what the Soviet Government has in mind. Would it not be well at this time for the State Department to sound out the British and Russian views on the treatment of German industry either through the European Advisory Commission or otherwise?"

Shortly after the President returned to Washington I went to see him at the White House. I took his memorandum of September 15 and the Morgenthau plan with me.

I said bluntly to the President that Morgenthau's plan was out of all reason, and that no experts, no appropriate officials of our Government or the President, and no other Governments had had anything to do with its preparation. Morgenthau's plan, I added, would wipe out everything in Germany except land, and the Germans would have to live on the land. This meant that only 60 per cent of the German population could support themselves on German land, and the other 40 per cent would die.

I remarked that with regard to the postwar treatment of Germany I would bear in mind two controlling points. The first was that Germany should be kept under military control for twenty-five or fifty years, as necessity might require, until she experienced an absolute change of heart away from all theories and notions of Nazism and the absurd idea that Germans were a superior race and had a right to govern other races. The second was that the standard of living of the German population should be kept below the average of neighboring populations but should be raised gradually in proportion to the rate of change on their part away from Nazism, racial superiority, and the like, toward ideas of human rights, individual liberty, freedom, and peace.

I concluded that I was satisfied that the British at Quebec had joined in on this extreme starvation plan in order to get Morgenthau's help in obtaining the six-and-a-half-billion-dollar credit proposed by the Secretary of the Treasury. I particularly inveighed against this credit.

For one reason, I said, negotiations with Britain should be conducted primarily through the State Department, the organ of the Administration set up to negotiate with foreign Governments. For another reason, Morgenthau's proposal had attached to it no conditions whatever. There were numerous questions pending between us and Great Britain on which we should seek settlement or action, and the credits would be needed as a part of our bargaining position with her. Morgenthau had brushed aside or ignored these considerations, and made an unconditional offer of six and a half billion dollars without consulting any appropriate official of the Government either in the State Department or in Congress.

I concluded that, apart from all the other serious objections, if Morgenthau's proposals became known and the President were connected with them, it would greatly injure him politically. He was then in the midst of the 1944 Presidential campaign.

The President said very little during this conversation except to indicate that he had not actually committed himself to Morgenthau's proposals. In fact, he did not seem to realize the devastating nature of the memorandum of September 15 to which he had put his "O.K.—F.D.R."

I now asked my associates at the State Department to assist me in preparing a further memorandum for the President. This, dated September 29, I handed to him personally on October 1, and went over its major points with him.

"The Cabinet Committee," the memorandum said, "has not been able to agree upon a statement of American policy for the postwar treatment of Germany. The memorandum presented by the Secretary of the Treasury is decidedly at variance with the views developed in the State Department. In the meantime, I have received your memorandum of September 15, with the statements of views respecting the Ruhr, Saar, etc., and the conversion of Germany into an agricultural and pastoral country, which was formulated at Quebec. This memorandum seems to reflect largely the opinions of the Secretary of the Treasury in the treatment to be accorded Germany. I feel that I should therefore submit to you the line of thought that has been developing in the State Department on this matter."

We pointed out that the instrument of unconditional surrender of Germany had been recommended by the European Advisory Commission and had been formally approved by this Government, and we expected that British and Russian approval would be forthcoming. The European Advisory Commission, we continued, was going ahead on plans for tripartite control machinery and military government for Germany during the occupation period. All three Governments had submitted similar proposals. Our proposal contemplated a Supreme Authority consisting of the three commanding generals of the United States, United Kingdom, and U.S.S.R., which would coordinate Allied control of Germany and supervise the centralized governmental functions and economic activities they deemed essential. A Control Council, composed of representatives in equal numbers from the three Allied Governments, would be established by the Supreme Allied Authority. It would coordinate the administration of military government throughout Germany, including detailed planning for the execution of directives received from the three Governments.

We then set forth the objectives we had stated in the memorandum of September 4, such as demilitarization of Germany, dissolution of the Nazi Party, and control of communications, press and propaganda, and education. No decision should be taken on the possible partition of Germany, but we should encourage a decentralization of the German governmental structure, and if any tendencies toward spontaneous partition of Germany arose they should not be discouraged.

We stated our economic objectives to be, first, to render Germany incapable of waging war, and, second, to eliminate permanently German economic domination of Europe. A shorter-term objective was to require the performance by Germany of acts of restitution and reparation for injuries done to the United Nations.

We made five specific recommendations to achieve the first two objectives. First, destroy all factories incapable of conversion to peaceful purposes and prevent their reconstruction. Second, enforce the conversion of all other plants to peaceful manufacture. Third, eliminate self-sufficiency by imposing reforms that would make Germany dependent upon world markets (that is, annul the Nazi plan of economic autarchy or self-sufficiency). Fourth, establish controls over foreign trade and key industries for the purpose of preventing German rearmament. Fifth, eliminate the position of power of large industrialists and landowners.

We concluded the memorandum by stating: "It is of the highest importance that the standard of living of the German people in the early years be such as to bring home to them that they have lost the war and to impress on them that they must abandon all their pretentious theories that they are a superior race created to govern the world. Through lack of luxuries we may teach them that war does not pay."

The following day I received from the President a memorandum he had written me on September 29, that is, before my talk with him on October 1. This was by way of reply to my memorandum to him on September 25, and it clearly revealed that he had not realized the extent to which, at Morgenthau's urging, he had committed himself at Quebec.

"I do not think," he wrote, "that in the present stage any good purpose would be served by having the State Department or any other Department sound out the British and Russian views on the treatment of German industry. Most certainly it should not be taken up with the

European Advisory Commission which, in a case like this, is on a tertiary and not even a secondary level.

"The real nub of the situation is to keep Britain from going into complete bankruptcy at the end of the war." This last sentence he emphasized by inking a double line alongside it.

The press during the last week had come out with a number of articles indicating the drastic nature of the postwar treatment of Germany discussed at Quebec. This furnished Nazi propaganda agencies with wonderful ammunition to spur the Germans on to fight to the end.

"Somebody," the President said in his memorandum, "has been talking not only out of turn to the papers or [sic] on facts which are not fundamentally true.

"No one wants to make Germany a wholly agricultural nation again, and yet somebody down the line has handed this out to the press. I wish we could catch and chastise him."

(Secretary Stimson later informed me that the President thought the news leak had occurred in the State Department. By showing the President the article of the columnist who first came out with the story, and who was in close contact with certain officials in the Treasury, Stimson said he convinced the President that the leak had not occurred in the State or War Department.)

"You know," the President continued, "that before the war Germany was not only building up war manufacture, but was also building up enough of a foreign trade to finance rearming sufficiently and still maintain enough international credit to keep out of international bankruptcy.

"I just cannot go along with the idea of seeing the British Empire collapse financially, and Germany at the same time building up a potential rearmament machine to make another war possible in twenty years. Mere inspection of plants will not prevent that.

"But no one wants 'complete eradication of German industrial productive capacity in the Ruhr and Saar.'

"It is possible, however, in those two particular areas to enforce rather complete controls. Also, it must not be forgotten that outside of the Ruhr and Saar, Germany has many *other* areas and facilities for turning out large exports."

Turning to Russia, apropos of my insistence that the Soviet Government must be consulted regarding any plan for Germany, he said:

"In regard to the Soviet Government, it is true that we have no idea as yet what they have in mind, but we have to remember that in their occupied territory they will do more or less as they wish. We cannot afford to get into a position of merely recording protests on our part unless there is some chance of some of the protests being heeded.

"I do not intend by this to break off or delay negotiations with the Soviet Government over Lend-Lease either on the control basis or on the proposed Fourth Protocol basis. This, however, does not immediately concern the German industrial future."

My conversation with the President on October 1 had obviated the need to take any action on his memorandum. This latter showed me, however, the line of thought he had been pursuing. In his mind the future of Britain was linked inversely with the future of Germany. Britain needed to get back her export trade after the war, but he felt that she could not do so if Germany were permitted to develop an extensive export trade in competition. Therefore he embraced Morgenthau's plan. But he forgot, despite Churchill's initialing of the agreement, that the British Government was the last to desire the conversion of Germany into a pastoral country, because Britain's livelihood would be impaired if Europe's economy collapsed because of a wrecked Germany.

The President's memorandum also showed plainly that he had not understood the meaning of what he had agreed to at Quebec. At about this time Secretary Stimson had a talk with the President, from which Stimson drew the same conclusion. He informed me that he had thereupon read to the President several sentences from the President's memorandum of September 15, concluding with the phrase "looking forward to converting Germany into a country primarily agricultural and pastoral in its character."

Stimson informed me that the President was frankly staggered at hearing these sentences and said that he had no idea how he could have initialed the memorandum, and that he had evidently done so without much thought.

In any event, the President, after my conversation with him, ceased to embrace Morgenthau's ideas on Germany. Three weeks after my memorandum of September 29 he sent me a reply dated October 20 which he began by saying: "I think it is all very well for us to make all kinds of preparations for the treatment of Germany, but there are some matters in regard to such treatment that lead me to believe that speed on these matters is not an essential at the present moment. It may be in a week, or it may be in a month, or it may be several months hence. I dislike making detailed plans for a country which we do not yet occupy."

He said he agreed with our proposals for the demilitarization of Germany and suggested they include everything having to do with aircraft. He was "in hearty agreement" with our proposals for the dissolution of the Nazi Party and its affiliated organizations, and for extensive controls over communications, press, and propaganda. He agreed with our suggestion that no decision should be taken on the possible partition of Germany. With regard to our section on economic objectives, he said: "I should like to discuss this with the State Department in regard to some of the language. I agree with it in principle, but I do not know what part of it means. Much of this subhead is dependent on what we and the Allies find when we get into Germany—and we are not there yet."

Such was the situation when I left office. The American, British, and Soviet Governments had approved an instrument of unconditional surrender for Germany. They had also agreed to the plan for tripartite control machinery and military government of Germany. The President had appointed Robert D. Murphy as Political Adviser for Germany to General Eisenhower, with the rank of Ambassador. Work had been completed on a directive outlining the policies to be followed in German territory during the period prior to surrender or the collapse of armed resistance. An interim directive was in preparation covering the post-hostilities period.

The ideas my associates and I had stated in the memoranda of September 4 and 29, to which the War Department generally subscribed, and to which Britain and Russia later agreed, became to some degree those that were carried out when Germany was occupied. Nevertheless, Morgenthau did not cease to press his philosophy of crushing Germany to the dust, and his ideas had an adverse effect on the Allied program for that country, resulting in a more drastic plan than what we had in mind at the State Department prior to my resignation. The experience of several years' occupation of Germany, however, coupled with a realization of the validity of our argument that Germany's economy was interconnected with that of Europe, eventually required the American and British Governments to move away from Morgenthau's vengeful philosophy.

My talk with the President on October 1 was my last important item of business in his office. I was now on the verge of the collapse that necessitated my resignation.

Part Eight

PEACE AND AFTER

(1939–1945)

116: We Begin to Plan

THE SIX AND A HALF YEARS of my tenure as Secretary of State up to the outbreak of war in Europe on September 1, 1939, had been a spectacle of the futility of existing methods for maintaining the peace, whether by the League of Nations or by the efforts of individual nations working singly or together. War had come despite all the earnest endeavors of many nations to prevent it. And policies of neutrality had not served to keep nation after nation from being drawn into the vortex.

From the moment when Hitler's invasion of Poland revealed the bankruptcy of all existing methods to preserve the peace, it became evident to us in the State Department that we must begin almost immediately to plan the creation of a new system. This, profiting by the failures of the past, had to erect a viable and practical structure by which the peace of the world could be successfully maintained. Thus it was that, in an address on which we in the State Department had worked with him, the President at the very outset stated on September 3, 1939, the night of the day Britain and France declared war on Germany:

"It seems to me clear, even at the outbreak of this great war, that the influence of America should be consistent in seeking for humanity a final peace which will eliminate, as far as it is possible to do so, the continued use of force between nations."

The United States was thus committed from the very moment when chaos descended upon Europe to devote her influence toward developing a postwar world in which peace could be assured.

In this country and elsewhere in the world, the horror aroused by the advent of the war almost immediately produced thoughts along the same line. The Council on Foreign Relations in New York proposed on September 12 to amplify its studies and make them available to the State Department. We forthwith accepted. The Federal Council of Churches of Christ in America and a number of other organizations made similar offers of help. To each we stated we should be glad to receive its views.

From Europe we also began to garner indications that nations there, likewise spurred by the thought that the holocaust must not be permitted to occur again, were dedicating some of their energies to postwar studies. The British Foreign Office early organized a group of experts toward this end, and Pope Pius XII on October 20, 1939, advocated the necessity of founding a stable international organization after the war.

President Roosevelt's exchanges of messages with the Pope, the President of the Federal Council of Churches, and the President of the Jewish Theological Seminary of America on December 23, 1939, were a step in the direction of enlisting the assistance of the churches in parallel endeavors for a righteous peace.

Immediately after Hitler's invasion of Poland, I asked my principal associates in the Department to begin giving attention to long-range problems, and the Department's actual work on postwar questions may be said to have begun about that time. In connection with this work I asked Leo Pasvolsky, an economist and specialist in international affairs, to return to the State Department and resume his position as Special Assistant to the Secretary of State, from which he had retired some time before. His capacities were splendid, his service exceedingly valuable. I requested him specifically to work on long-range problems bearing on the postwar future.

Late in December, 1939, after consultation with my principal associates, I decided to organize postwar preparations within the State Department and to establish a Department committee for this purpose. In formulating this decision, the importance of which was manifest, I called to my office on December 27 Welles, R. Walton Moore (Counselor of the Department), Assistant Secretaries of State Berle, Messersmith, and Grady, Legal Adviser Hackworth, Leo Pasvolsky, Economic Adviser Feis, Political Adviser Hornbeck, and Chief of the European Division Moffat, to discuss the question with them.

We agreed upon a memorandum outlining the work we would undertake. At that time I had also thought to create a special division within the Department to study the problems of peace and reconstruction and to assemble and analyze information and views with regard to international economic relations, territorial, political, and armaments problems, neutral rights and duties, and the whole machinery of international cooperation. This, however, would have required a staff of Department officers, and our personnel were even then working night and day because of the many problems the war had thrust upon us.

The committee we set up was divided into three subcommittees. One was to handle political problems, chiefly the organization of peace. Another was to deal with the limitation and reduction of armaments. The third was to embrace economic problems. I stated my thought that the committee should make recommendations on immediate problems arising from the war as well as analyze postwar questions.

We publicly announced, on January 8, 1940, the creation of this committee, called the Advisory Committee on Problems of Foreign Relations, of which I named Welles chairman and Hugh Wilson, formerly Ambassador to Germany, vice chairman. The other members, in addition to those who had met with me on December 27, were Assistant Secretary of State Breckinridge Long, Political Adviser James C. Dunn, Norman Davis (who had so often assisted me in many valuable ways in the past), and George Rublee, director of the Inter-Governmental Committee on Political Refugees. The chairmen of the three subcommittees were: George Rublee for political problems; R. Walton Moore for armaments; Pasvolsky for economic problems.

The Advisory Committee had fifteen members in all. With the exception of Davis and Rublee, it was composed entirely of Department officials. Because of Rublee's illness, Welles carried on most of the work of presiding over the subcommittee for political problems.

The President stated in his message to Congress on January 3, 1940, the aim with which we began to work when he said, "We can strive with other nations to encourage the kind of peace that will lighten the troubles of the world."

The committee undertook to study means whereby the war might be limited and possibly ended, the foundations of a peaceful world order laid, and the defense of the Western Hemisphere strengthened. The three subcommittees began to work intensively despite the fact that their members were largely Department officers already heavily engaged in other duties. The work in the beginning had to be informal and exploratory. Individual members presented papers outlining their views. The respective subcommittees considered these views and, if agreement were reached, sought to state them in the form of recommendations, which were considered by the Advisory Committee as a whole and were then communicated to me.

During the spring of 1940 the political subcommittee began to consider the organization of world order after the war. Naturally it had to make its views tentative, because so much depended on the outcome of the war. Should the United States be a member of a world organization, or should we advocate regional organizations? Should the League of Nations be retained, should we join it, or should a new organization be set up?

As early as January 15, 1940, the economic subcommittee outlined the bases for an economic settlement that we hoped might be presented at a conference of neutral nations which we then had in mind. The subcommittee had to take into consideration the probability that, however the war in Europe ended, its conclusion would find many countries in desperate economic need. Should such needs be neglected, recovery in all countries might be retarded and social upheavals might follow that would seriously impair postwar reconstruction.

On February 9 and 10 we began diplomatic conversations with forty-seven neutral Governments looking toward an exchange of views on "two basic problems connected with the establishment of a sound foundation for a lasting world peace; namely, the establishment of the bases of a sound international economic system, and the limitation and reduction of armaments." We specified that our conversations would not involve present problems arising from the war.

Our purpose in proposing this exchange was to obtain, before the advent of a peace conference, as definite commitments and understandings as possible with other nations on the basic principles of a stable international relationship after the war.

More than two-thirds of the replies we received promised full cooperation. The others were reserved, particularly as to disarmament. Many asked that we set forth our ideas as a basis for discussion.

The economic and disarmament subcommittees accordingly worked hard to prepare a comprehensive memorandum stating the views of this Government on postwar economic relations and disarmament, to be presented at a conference of neutrals. Since the field of their inquiry extended to questions of interest to other Government Departments, especially Treasury, Commerce, and Agriculture, and to the Tariff Commission and the Export-Import Bank, those Departments and agencies were duly consulted. But when Hitler invaded Scandinavia in April and the Low Countries and France in May, further action along these lines became impracticable.

After Welles returned from his trip to Europe in 1940, he informed the President and me that, important as were the territorial, political, and economic problems, security was the basic problem. He thought there might be a slight chance to restore peace if the United States and other neutrals prepared a practical plan of security and disarmament upon which the major powers of Europe would agree. I myself placed not the slightest faith in this recommendation, believing that Hitler was already determined to test the might of his war machine against his ancient enemy, France.

Hitler's overwhelming victories in western Europe forced the Advisory Committee to consider the effects of a peace imposed by the Nazis, with the German system of economic autarchy extended to most of Europe and possibly to other continents as well. Such a peace would confront the United States with postwar economic problems of a totally different nature from those that had been discussed up to that time. To debate this and other issues, the economic subcommittee was thereupon constituted into what became known as the Inter-Departmental Group to Consider Post-war Economic Problems and Policies, under the chairmanship of Leo Pasvolsky, composed initially of representatives of the State, Treasury, Commerce, and Agriculture Departments.

The political subcommittee on May 31, 1940, began to consider what we might have to do if Germany were victorious. It emphasized the possibility that one or more Latin American Republics might find themselves becoming politically dependent upon Germany because of economic necessity as Hitler organized Europe into an economic bloc. To prevent this the subcommittee believed the United States would have to grant export subsidies to the Republics thus threatened.

The subcommittee also considered the possibility that Germany would demand the transfer to her of the Western Hemisphere possessions of the European countries she had conquered. The President and I had already approved the draft of a proposed joint resolution for immediate submission to Congress dealing with this point, and Congress passed such a resolution on June 18, 1940.

The subcommittee finally dealt with the possibility that Japan might move into the Dutch East Indies as a result of the German victory, and recommended that all possible preparations should be made for adequate defense beyond the Western Hemisphere. It also recommended that existing legislation should be changed to enable the Allies to obtain credits in this country and to purchase the needed military supplies.

The work of the political subcommittee regarding the Western Hemisphere was now merged with the work of the American delegation to the Havana Conference (July, 1940) which I headed. At Havana, formal inter-American arrangements (described in Chapter 59) were made for the eventuality of an Axis claim for the transfer of European possessions in the Western Hemisphere to Germany. The Inter-Departmental Group on Economic Problems and Policies, the principal members of which accompanied me to Havana, had meantime prepared the economic proposals that we put forward at the conference, embraced in a resolution on current and postwar economic policies and in a plan for economic assistance to the Latin American countries to enable them to meet the difficulties caused by the war. This resolution, unanimously adopted by the twenty-one American Republics, was in fact the earliest official declaration by any group of nations with regard to postwar commercial policy. It reaffirmed the adherence of the Republics to liberal principles of international trade and stressed the desirability of conducting trade "with the entire world in accordance with these principles as soon as the non-American nations are prepared to do likewise."

Upon our return from Havana, the Inter-Departmental Group resumed its work on a broad scale.

Early in 1941 our consideration of postwar problems intensified. To forward our work in this field I created a Division of Special Research in the State Department, on February 3, 1941, with Leo Pasvolsky as its chief, and Harley Notter and Julian Wadleigh as his principal assistants. When the President dramatically stated the Four Freedoms in his annual message to Congress on January 6, 1941, the promotion of these human freedoms became the basis for our consideration of a future world order.

I was able to state publicly, in an address on April 24, 1941, that the Department was working "at the task of creating ultimate conditions of peace and justice." And again, in a radio address on May 18, I said: "It is none too early to lay down at least some of the principles by which policies must be guided at the conclusion of the war, to press for a broad program of world economic reconstruction, and to consider tentative plans for the application of those policies." I added that: "In the final reckoning, the problem becomes one of establishing the foundations of an international order in which independent nations cooperate freely with each other for their mutual gain—of a world order, not new but renewed, which liberates rather than enslaves."

Congress was likewise displaying interest in postwar organization. Senator Elbert D. Thomas (Democrat of Utah) introduced a resolution to authorize the Committee on Foreign Relations to make a full study of all matters pertaining to the establishment of a lasting peace throughout the world. I wrote Senator Walter F. George, acting chairman of the committee, on June 7, 1941, telling him of the State Department's work in that direction.

The Atlantic Charter agreed to by President Roosevelt and Prime

Minister Churchill in August provided us a further basis on which to build our structure for a postwar world.

Meantime the Department's Division of Special Research was making headway in its exploratory and preparatory work, although by the end of 1941 there was only a handful of officers in the Division. I recognized that this was too small a number for the vast array of problems to be explored, but the demands of war upon the personnel of the Department made a larger organization still impossible. The Division undertook, among many other tasks, the compilation and analysis of all official views and policy commitments with regard to postwar questions, as expressed by the Allied and neutral Governments. Studies made by outside organizations were now beginning to come to the State Department and were carefully analyzed and considered.

Other governments now began to approach us to learn something of our postwar planning. Australia informed us of the efforts she was making. The British Government in October, 1941, asked whether we desired to take part with the Allied Governments in a joint study concerning a future international juridical organization. At that time we could only reply that we were interested in receiving further information, but that, in our work, we were considering the creation of an international court of justice in connection with a world organization rather than as a problem by itself.

Early in 1941, in connection with the establishment of the Division of Special Research, we had begun to consider the possibility of creating a broad-gauge committee on postwar problems consisting of State Department officials, officials of other Departments, Members of Congress, and distinguished private citizens. While this project was under discussion, we began to note numerous indications that other agencies of the Government were reaching out to assume responsibility for postwar planning, which we considered should be the function of the State Department working with other Departments and agencies of the Government. This was particularly true of the Board of Economic Defense, established on July 30, 1941. One of its functions was stated to be the rendering of advice to the President on the relationship of defense measures to postwar economic reconstruction and on steps to expedite the establishment of sound, peacetime international economic relationships.

In October, 1941, Welles and I talked over with the President the whole problem of arrangements for postwar planning, and obtained his oral approval for the creation by his authority of an advisory committee on postwar foreign policy, with the Secretary of State as chairman and the Under Secretary of State as vice chairman, along the lines of our plan considered earlier in the year. Under our proposal, the Division of Special Research, other appropriate divisions of the Department, other Departments and agencies and cooperating nongovernment agencies would prepare research studies and draft memoranda on postwar planning under the aegis of this Advisory Committee, and the committee's recommendations to the President would be made through its chairman. Basically, this was a proposal to draw together the resources of the whole Government and of interested outside organizations toward one end. The mounting crisis in the Far East, however, forced us to suspend action on the plan for the time being. The Japanese attack was approaching.

Within a few days after Pearl Harbor, I initiated the preparation of the Declaration by United Nations. Dated January 1, 1942, and adhered to at once by twenty-six nations, it bound the United Nations together in a common determination to win the fight against the Axis, and support the principles of the Atlantic Charter, thereby providing a foundation for the union we hoped would come to pass after the war was over. At the time we were preparing this Declaration in the State Department I wrote a letter to the President on December 22, 1941, recalling to him the conversation Welles and I had had with him in October. I enclosed a list of proposed members of the committee, which would be known as the Advisory Committee on Postwar Foreign Policy, consisting of several officials of the Government and of several prominent persons from outside the Government with special qualifications for contributing to this work.

The new committee, I said, would maintain close contact with all appropriate Departments and agencies of the Government and with such nongovernmental agencies as might be in position to contribute to an all-around consideration of the problems involved. I then stated that, since it was his further desire that all recommendations regarding postwar problems of international relations from all Departments and agencies of the Government be submitted to him through the Secretary of State, and that all conversations or negotiations with foreign Governments bearing on postwar problems be conducted, under his authority, by or through the Department of State, I should appreciate it if he would cause the heads of the various Departments and agencies concerned to be apprised of his views.

The list of proposed members I transmitted to the President consisted of: myself as chairman; Welles as vice chairman; Norman H.

Davis, president of the Council on Foreign Relations and chairman of the American Red Cross; Myron C. Taylor, the President's personal representative to the Pope; Dean Acheson, Assistant Secretary of State; Hamilton Fish Armstrong, editor of the quarterly *Foreign Affairs;* Adolf A. Berle, Jr., Assistant Secretary of State; Isaiah Bowman, president of Johns Hopkins University; Benjamin V. Cohen, general counsel, National Power Policy Committee; Herbert Feis, State Department Adviser on International Economic Relations; Green H. Hackworth, Legal Adviser; Harry C. Hawkins, Chief of the Division of Commercial Policy; Mrs. Anne O'Hare McCormick, editorial staff, the New York *Times;* and Leo Pasvolsky, Special Assistant to the Secretary of State and Chief of the Division of Special Research.

Within a week the President sent this letter back to me after having written on it: "I heartily approve.—F. D. R."

We were now launched on our postwar work with a definite and prominent committee organized under Presidential authority. Our jurisdiction was clear, and the field was open for truly constructive achievement.

117: Roosevelt-Churchill Ideas

WHEN THE Advisory Committee on Postwar Foreign Policy began its work in 1942, the United States was at war, the entire population was intensely concerned with the outcome, and virtually every American had already begun to think in terms of avoiding a recurrence of such bankruptcy in international relations.

Even as a neutral we had been convinced that we would have an important role to play in the eventual peace conference. But as one of the mightiest of the belligerents, we now knew that we could strongly influence the creation of any international organization to maintain the peace. And because of this increased influence we recognized that our responsibilities for adequate, wise, and careful planning for the postwar world were correspondingly greater. Moreover, the war had by now become so destructive and so vast in its extent, embracing almost the whole world, that we realized that the work of building anew after it was over would be immeasurably augmented.

The Advisory Committee first met in the office of Under Secretary Welles on February 12. It decided that it should not merely provide the President with information on postwar problems, but also submit definite recommendations to him, since his time was so taken up with grave war problems. Because the first months after Pearl Harbor were black with defeat and retreat in the Far East, the committee decided to keep its existence secret for the time being lest publicity on our postwar studies tend to impair the public's realization that a long, hard fight would be necessary before victory could be won. The committee discussed whether its work should be confined to the postwar field or should also cover problems connected with the war. I later decided that the committee should devote itself entirely to postwar problems, leaving current questions to the State and other Departments.

The committee agreed to set up six regular and three special subcommittees, in political, security, and economic fields, and one to coordinate the work and maintain contact with private organizations engaged in postwar studies. The Advisory Committee itself would deliberate on the recommendations prepared by the subcommittees and then would submit its views to me. Usually I would transmit views to the President. The work of the subcommittees would be coordinated through Leo Pasvolsky, who was made Executive Officer of the Advisory Committee and its Director of Research.

There was a subcommittee on political problems, under Welles first and later myself; one on security presided over by Norman Davis; one on territorial problems under Isaiah Bowman; and two economic subcommittees under Dean Acheson and Adolf Berle, which later were combined into a single committee on postwar foreign economic policy headed by Myron C. Taylor. There was also a special subcommittee on international organization under Welles; one on legal problems under Green Hackworth, and one, under Hamilton Fish Armstrong, to consider problems of possible European federation.

Shortly after the establishment of the Advisory Committee we began to increase the number of its members to obtain the benefit of additional ability and to give representation to major points of view, particularly political points of view. Eventually the Advisory Committee itself included forty-five members enlisted from the public, the Senate and the House of Representatives, the State, War, Navy, and other Departments, the White House staff, the Library of Congress, and other Government agencies.

My first concern was to make the membership of the committee absolutely nonpartisan, and to give Republicans as well as Democrats adequate representation. Right from the beginning I was determined that the mistakes made in 1919–1920, which led to the United States' holding aloof from the League of Nations, should not recur. I resolved to do all that I could to get the Republican Party as well as the Democratic Party 100 per cent behind the creation of an international organization to maintain the peace, in which the United States would be a full-fledged member.

The first of the invitations I sent out to new members, after consultation with the President, were addressed on May 27, 1942, to Senator Tom Connally, Democrat of Texas, and Senator Warren R. Austin, Republican of Vermont, respectively the chairman and a minority member of the Senate Committee on Foreign Relations. Austin later became the United States Representative to the United Nations organization.

Later I invited Senators Walter F. George, Democrat of Georgia, Elbert D. Thomas, Democrat of Utah, and Wallace H. White, Republican of Maine, to join. I sent invitations likewise to a number of Representatives of both parties: Sol Bloom, Democrat of New York; Charles A. Eaton, Republican of New Jersey; and Luther A. Johnson, Democrat of Texas. Still later, Senators Scott W. Lucas and Claude Pepper, and Representatives Schuyler Otis Bland, J. Hardin Peterson, Richard J. Welch, Alfred Bulwinkle, and Charles A. Wolverton were invited to take part in the work of special committees set up under the Advisory Committee.

By agreement with the President, I invited many other eminent Americans to join the Advisory Committee. Among them were James T. Shotwell of the Carnegie Endowment for International Peace; Brooks Emeny, director of the Foreign Affairs Council, Cleveland, Ohio; William Green, president of the American Federation of Labor; Philip Murray, president of the Congress of Industrial Organizations; Walter Reuther, United Automobile Workers; and Eric Johnston, president of the United States Chamber of Commerce.

Harry White of the Treasury, Major General George V. Strong, and Admiral Arthur J. Hepburn, representing respectively Secretaries Morgenthau, Stimson, and Knox, shortly became members. Two members of the President's staff, David K. Niles and Lauchlin Currie, were included, along with Archibald MacLeish, Librarian of Congress.

I rigidly kept down the number of State Department officials who were members of the committee, since this was designed to be a national committee advisory to the President through the Secretary of State. Various officers of the Department, however, were constantly assisting the committee and its subcommittees in their work. Many other officials of various Departments and agencies of the Government also took part in specialized discussions. In general, the whole resources of the Government were at our disposal, and we made full use of them.

An enormous amount of extremely valuable work was done by the various subcommittees. The one on territorial problems explored meticulously and comprehensively every aspect we could imagine of postwar territorial problems and adjustments, as well as problems of regionalism and dependent areas. The economic committee formulated far-reaching plans for postwar economic policies and for the creation of international agencies in the field of economic and social problems. The security committee canvassed thoroughly the various phases of postwar security arrangements such as the regulation of armaments. The political committee, in addition to much other work, was the principal one devoting attention to plans for the establishment of a postwar world organization for the maintenance of peace and security and for the promotion of general cooperation among nations.

Since the only phase of our postwar planning that actually came to full fruition before I retired from the Department was that which related to an international organization, I shall devote most of my attention to that problem, which in my thinking was always the central and decisive problem of the postwar future.

Within two months after the Advisory Committee, with Welles presiding, began to meet, it had considered the creation of an interim international political organization during the war, without waiting for the peace, so that, in contrast with what occurred in the First World War, we should have machinery ready before hostilities ceased. This body, to be known as the United Nations Authority, would consist of representatives not only of the four major powers—the United States, Great Britain, Russia, and China—but, in some manner, of all the other United Nations, so that all nations would feel they had a voice in the organization.

The committee likewise considered the creation of an International Relief Council, composed of representatives of the United Nations, the head of which would be an American. The committee believed that, while it was true that the United States would have to bear the main burden of relief, it should do so on an international basis, in cooperation with other nations. It was thought that early action toward the creation of this Council would contribute to the war effort by giving greater substance to the concept of the United Nations and might serve as an experiment with regard to the organization of a United Nations Authority.

The committee disapproved the idea of using relief for political purposes. It agreed that for reasons of morale the peoples of the occupied countries should be informed as soon as possible that the United Nations were conferring on how to extend them relief. It was accordingly agreed that the United States should take the initiative toward the formation of the International Relief Council as soon as possible.

When I met with the Advisory Committee on May 21, 1942, I expressed anxiety over the influences that inevitably would bring their forces to bear against the constructive views for the peace settlement and world improvement contemplated by the committee.

"Such special interest groups and influences," I said, "constitute perhaps the greatest threat that the committee faces, and undoubtedly the best program the committee can devise will be attacked. We need to make better preparation for world peace than was made at the close of the First World War. Even then the chances are only about one to two or three that a sound peace can be carried to fruition. It is of the utmost importance to have the informed support of the American public behind us."

Two months later I publicly stated the gist of our postwar thinking when, in my radio address of July 23, 1942, I said: "It is plain that some international agency must be created which can—by force, if necessary—keep the peace among nations in the future. There must be international cooperative action to set up the mechanisms which can thus insure peace. This must include eventual adjustment of national armaments in such a manner that the rule of law cannot be successfully challenged, and that the burden of armaments may be reduced to a minimum."

Having laid out the general framework for its studies, the Advisory Committee ceased to meet as a whole. Its work of reviewing the findings of the subcommittees then largely devolved upon the Subcommittee on Political Problems, of which Welles was chairman. He continued as its chairman until January 30, 1943, when I took it over. Though I had not been participating in this subcommittee's meetings, I had kept in close touch with its work from the beginning and had had numerous conferences with its individual members. The whole war and possible postwar situation apeared to me such that a stage had been reached where we should begin to arrive at definite decisions, and that I should therefore take charge.

In the same month, we decided to expand the research staff and reorganize the Division of Special Research into a Division of Political Studies, with Harley Notter as Chief, and a Division of Economic Studies, with Leroy Steinbower as Chief, both functioning under the direction of Leo Pasvolsky.

The Political Subcommittee and the special subcommittees continued intensive studies throughout the spring of 1943. Their considerations ranged from the preparation of an international bill of rights and the creation of a war crimes commission, to the future organization of the Southwest Pacific, a plan of international trusteeship for dependent peoples, and the creation of a general international organization.

On the question of trusteeship, the Political Subcommittee first suggested that a trusteeship plan should be drawn up to include all colonial territories. Subsequently, for obvious reasons of political feasibility, it concluded that a trusteeship system should be set up under the international organization to include only the Axis dependencies and the territories mandated by the League of Nations. The subcommittee recommended that regional councils for dependent areas be created, under the general international organization. The dependent areas would be administered, under the supervision of a regional council, either by international agencies or by individual trustee states. It agreed that the United States should restrict her trusteeship responsibilities mainly to the Western Hemisphere and the Pacific.

The Political Subcommittee believed that the United States should not fix a minimum postwar program but should rather set forth a maximum program of sound international relations. We sought to plan an ideal settlement which we should try to attain with other nations as fully as possible. Our discussions were based upon our belief in absolute victory by the United Nations and in cooperation by the United Nations after the war. Although we considered international security our supreme objective, we also maintained that its attainment must dovetail with principles of justice so that it would last. We believed that the American people would support whatever American participation was needed to maintain international peace and security. We further believed that Russian cooperation on the principal international problems was essential and could be obtained.

Our discussions were marked by informality, and I made it clear that the members were not required to make commitments, nor were they bound by any views they might express. This particularly was the case with members of the Senate and House of Representatives from both political parties who were members of the committee.

We kept the President informed of the progress of our discussions at all times. Welles or I frequently saw him in this connection, and we sent him many drafts, particularly those in the fields of an international organization, trusteeship, and the treatment of Germany. In turn we passed on to the committee the President's views expressed to us.

In the spring and summer of 1943 the Political Subcommittee resolved a number of basic questions that still remained. As to whether to revive the League of Nations or set up a new international organization, we decided in favor of the latter. The Political Subcommittee had appointed a Special Subcommittee on International Organization, with Welles as chairman, which concentrated on working out the prospective bases for such an organization. This work began on October 23, 1942, and resulted in the preparation by March 26, 1943, of a draft of a proposed charter for an international organization.

While this draft contained many good features it leaned rather strongly in the direction of regionalism by providing that the Executive

Council of the proposed organization would consist of eleven members, of whom only the four major powers, as permanent members, would be represented as individual nations. The other seven members would each represent a region of the world rather than any individual nation. In this respect the draft reflected Welles's influence, since he was a convinced advocate of regional organization.

When these plans were brought to my attention in the Political Subcommittee, I could not go along with the regional feature; hence I started the subcommittee upon a detailed consideration of international organization in the spring of 1943 on the basis of fundamental issues rather than on the special subcommittee's draft. The subcommittee, after thorough discussion, expressed itself as being overwhelmingly in favor of a universal rather than a regional basis for an international organization.

With respect to regionalism, Welles echoed the ideas of President Roosevelt and Prime Minister Churchill. In the spring of 1943 both the President and the Prime Minister were convinced that after the war the world should be organized on a regional basis. The nations in certain geographical regions would band together to maintain the peace in those areas. There might be an international organization, but it would do little more than coordinate the work of the regional organizations. I, along with most of my associates in and out of the State Department, except Welles, argued on the other side; namely, that we should have a strong world organization which would be supreme over any regional associations, and that the latter should not be constituted in such a way as to interfere with the authority or work of the general organization.

Mr. Churchill stated his ideas to the President in a long message dated February 2, 1943, which he entitled "Morning Thoughts: Note on Post-War Security." Mr. Roosevelt gave me a copy.

After commenting that it was the intention of the chiefs of the United Nations to create a world organization for the preservation of peace based upon the concepts of freedom and justice and the revival of prosperity, the Prime Minister came at once to his own idea. As part of this organization, he said, an instrument of European Government would be established embodying the spirit of the League of Nations but not subject to its weaknesses. The units forming this body would be not only the great nations of Europe and Asia Minor; there was obvious need also for a Scandinavian bloc, a Danubian bloc, and a Balkan bloc.

A similar instrument, Mr. Churchill went on, would be formed in the Far East with different membership, and the whole would be held together by the fact that the victorious Powers continued fully armed, especially in the air, while imposing complete disarmament upon the guilty.

No one, he said, could predict with certainty that the victors would never quarrel amongst themselves, or that the United States might not again retire from Europe; but after the experiences which all had gone through, and their sufferings and the certainty that a third struggle would destroy all that was left of the culture, wealth, and civilization of mankind and reduce us to the level almost of wild beasts, the most intense effort would be made by the leading powers to prolong their honorable association and win for themselves a glorious name in human annals by their sacrifice and self-restraint.

Great Britain, he concluded, would certainly do her utmost to organize a coalition of resistance to any act of aggression committed by any power. He believed that the United States would cooperate with Britain and even possibly take the lead of the world, on account of her numbers and strength, in the good work of preventing such tendencies to aggression before they broke out in open war.

During Foreign Secretary Eden's visit to Washington in the latter half of March, 1943, Mr. Churchill made a radio address in which he came out publicly for regional organizations in Europe and the Far East, while assigning only a vague and secondary role to an over-all world organization.

When Mr. Churchill came to the United States in May, 1943, he presented these ideas earnestly to the President and to other members of the Government. Saying that the first preoccupation in discussions of a postwar structure should be to prevent future aggression by Germany and Japan, he contemplated an association of the United States, Great Britain, and Russia. If the United States wanted to include China he was perfectly willing, although China was not comparable to the other three.

Subordinate to this world council, he believed, there should be three regional councils, one each for Europe, the Orient, and the American hemisphere. The European council, he thought, might consist of some twelve states or confederations. He wanted a strong France re-created because the prospect of having no strong country on the map of Europe between England and Russia was not attractive. The European council would have its own high court and armed forces.

In the regional council for the Americas, Mr. Churchill thought Canada would naturally be a member and would represent the British Commonwealth.

In the regional council for the Pacific he supposed Russia would participate. He thought it possible that Russia, when the pressure on her western frontiers had been relieved, would turn her attention to the Far East.

Mr. Churchill's view was that the regional councils would be subordinate to the world council, and that members of the world council would sit on the regional councils in which they were directly interested. He hoped that the United States, in addition to being represented on the American and Pacific regional councils, would also be represented on the European council.

He added that to the four Powers on the world council there should be added other members by election in rotation from the regional councils. His central idea of the international structure was that of a three-legged stool—the world council resting on three regional councils.

He concluded that he attached great importance to the regional principle, because it was only the countries whose interests were directly affected by a dispute that could be expected to apply themselves with sufficient vigor to secure a settlement. Only vapid and academic discussion would result from calling in countries remote from a dispute.

In July, 1943, the British Government proposed to us and to the Soviet Government the creation of a European commission to coordinate the execution of surrender or armistice terms imposed on the enemy and also to assume far-reaching functions with regard to long-range European arrangements in the fields of security and economic integration. After giving this considerable study in the State Department and after conferring with the President, I replied that we could agree to the creation of such a body for dealing with the terms to be imposed on the enemy, but we opposed entrusting to such a body long-range peacetime functions. We took this up at the Moscow Conference in October and agreed to create the European Advisory Commission with functions limited to the formulation of terms of surrender and plans for their execution.

President Roosevelt agreed in general with the Prime Minister's regional ideas. During the spring of 1943 I found there was a basic cleavage between him and me on the very nature of the postwar organization.

The President favored a four-power establishment that would police the world with the forces of the United States, Britain, Russia, and China. All other nations, including France, were to be disarmed. He felt that the four nations had functioned well together during the war, and he wanted this relationship to continue. He believed in the efficacy of direct personal contact between Churchill, Stalin, Chiang Kai-shek, and himself, and he thought that this direct relationship among the chiefs of the four nations would result in efficient future management of the world.

At that time he did not want an over-all world organization. He did favor the creation of regional organizations, but it was the four big powers that would handle all security questions.

On the economic side he favored the creation of entirely separate functional agencies. It was on this basis that, at his insistence, a plan was developed early in 1943 for the convocation of the Hot Springs, Virginia, conference on food and agriculture, and for the holding of similar conferences on other economic matters with a view to creating a series of uncoordinated functional agencies. While I favored the creation of such specialized agencies, I differed with the President in that I thought it was also necessary to have some sort of over-all agency of coordination in the whole field of economic and social cooperation, such as the United Nations Economic and Social Council which later came into being.

When I called on the President to discuss questions concerning the international organization, I frequently took to the White House some of the men who were working with me on these matters, particularly Myron C. Taylor, Isaiah Bowman, Norman Davis, James C. Dunn, Green Hackworth, and Leo Pasvolsky. We argued with the President to induce him to change his ideas, but for some time without avail.

On one occasion we asked: "Aren't you at least in favor of a world secretariat? We'll need some such organization to handle international conferences."

He laughed as he said: "I'll give you the Pentagon or the Empire State Building. You can put the world secretariat there."

As this trend toward regionalism seemed to me to be assuming a strength that might imperil the future postwar organization, I asked our postwar political subcommittee to give it special study. In the conversations that ensued among us we fully agreed on the necessity of a universal international organization, as opposed to regional organizations, although regional associations of the Pan American type should of course continue and be brought into a proper relationship with the world organization.

We admitted that regional organizations had certain advantages. They could facilitate peaceful adjustments locally. If their members accepted certain principles, the regional organization might be in advantageous position to apply them. Such an organization would provide political, economic, and legal buffers between the nations and the universal organization to absorb the shock of various local controversies. It would give the universal organization greater freedom to carry out its wider functions. And, if a great power crippled the universal organization by leaving it, the regional organizations would offer something to fall back upon.

But it seemed to us that their disadvantages far outweighed their advantages. We argued that regional organizations such as Mr. Churchill proposed would profoundly change the functions of the universal organization. The latter might then have to deal with groups of nations rather than with individual nations.

As regional organizations became solidified, we thought, it might be possible that conflicts would spring up, not between nations but between regions. And the universal organization might find itself incapable of dealing with such conflicts. It would be easier for the proposed United Nations organization to deal with a nation alone than with a nation tied into and supported by a region.

We felt that a regional organization by its very nature set up a special relationship between the one or two great powers and the small states in that region. In the United States' relationship with the American Republics in the Pan American system we, at least under the Roosevelt Administration, had exercised economic and other self-restraint; we had not sought to set up preferential arrangements in the Western Hemisphere or to dominate the economies of the other Republics. But such self-restraint might not be exercised by a great power in another region, and there might develop, in consequence, closed trade areas or discriminatory systems. These would defy the universal organization, induce the creation of similar systems in other regions, and produce serious interregional economic conflicts, with dangerous political repercussions.

From the particular point of view of the United States we could see many objections to international organization on a regional basis. If we participated in the European and Pacific councils we might have thrust upon us the undesirable role of mediating between the other dominating powers in those regions, or we might be used by one against another.

If we were represented on the European council, the Latin American Republics might feel that we were representing them in Europe without having been so chosen.

Further, would we, who had not looked with favor on the participation of European nations in the Pan American Conferences even as observers, be content to see European or Asiatic powers participating in a Western Hemisphere council?

We questioned, too, whether the Latin American Republics would want to see the creation of a council of the Americas, in which the United States might officially have to act as the dominant member.

We did not think that the people of the United States would support this country's participation in a European council and a Pacific council, in addition to a Western Hemisphere council, and also in a universal organization. We felt that the American people were more ready to take responsibilities in a world organization than in any regional plan except perhaps one embracing this hemisphere. Moreover, the latter alternative would be a haven for the isolationists, who could advocate all-out United States cooperation in a Western Hemisphere council on condition that we did not participate in a European or Pacific council.

In general, however, we did not oppose regional and other special arrangements supplementary to the general international organization so long as these did not infringe on the powers we thought should reside in the world-wide association of nations. We recognized the freedom of action of small nations to make such regional arrangements among themselves as might be to their mutual advantage. As an example, we viewed with sympathy the plans for an Arab union, particularly in the economic and social field. We had made clear our desire to see the Pan American system of cooperation continued and strengthened in the postwar period as part of the general plan for international cooperation.

It was my view that, subordinate to the world organization and within its framework, groups of nations located in a given area might with entire consistency carry forward the policies we had adopted in our structure of Pan American cooperation, provided they did not go further than the Pan American system. The American Republics had agreed to consider any danger or threatened danger to any American nation from outside the hemisphere as a danger to all of them, and to cooperate in meeting it. Under a continuance of this policy after the creation of a world organization, the American Republics would proceed to deal with such danger locally, while simultaneously bringing the matter before the council of the universal organization, and cooperating within the framework of that body. When a house catches fire, the nearest neighbors hasten there with the common objective of putting out or preventing the spread of the fire until the Fire Department, which has been instantly notified, can arrive on the scene.

I could see no reason for a clash between the council of the world organization and a regional system of the Pan American type in these circumstances. Both the council and the local organization would have common purposes, the maintenance of peace. The world organization would in the end be supreme.

I recalled the simultaneous efforts made by the League of Nations and the Pan American Conference at Montevideo and also by groups of American Republics to stop the Chaco War. The American Republics nearest the Chaco conflict, and also the United States, made earnest efforts to halt the fighting. Meantime the world organization at Geneva had sent a commission posthaste to the site of the war to exercise its influence and cooperative efforts toward the same end. The Montevideo Conference and the League Commission cooperated fully, understandingly, and in the most effective way possible to find means of ending the conflict. There was complete harmony of purpose and effort on the part of the world organization at Geneva and the American nations, and there was no interference and no need for interference with the supremacy of the world organization.

The more advanced regional ideas of President Roosevelt and Prime Minister Churchill, however, might lead to questions of balance of power, and regional organizations of the type they envisaged might deal arbitrarily with one another and in the internal affairs of their members, whether by military force or economic pressure or their equivalent. This would open the door to abuses and the exercise of undue privileges by greedy, grasping nations possessing great military and economic strength.

In various meetings at the White House, my associates and I presented these arguments to the President with all the force we could. As summer arrived he began to turn toward our point of view.

He thereupon agreed with our draft of the Four-Nation Declaration which I handed Eden at the first Quebec Conference and then presented and had adopted at the Moscow Conference in October, 1943. Despite his earlier views, Mr. Churchill did not object to the Four-Nation Declaration. This expressed the agreement of the four major nations on the necessity of establishing at the earliest practicable date "a general international organization, based on the principle of the sovereign equality of all peace-loving states, and open to membership by all such states, large and small, for the maintenance of international peace and security."

We had originally couched this declaration in the form of a treaty, but changed over to the declaration form for obvious reasons. A treaty would require ratification by the signatory governments. A declaration required no ratification, would come into effect at once, and would have the immediate result of convincing the peace-loving nations that the governments of the four major powers were in agreement among themselves that a general international security organization should be created.

The emphasis was now on a general international organization. Nothing was said of regional security organizations in the declaration, and in the discussions at Moscow I argued strongly against them.

In July, 1943, I approved the setting up within the Department of a drafting group for the United Nations Charter under the direction of Leo Pasvolsky, to work out a new draft charter based on the views of the Political Subcommittee that there should be a universal rather than a regional basis for the world organization. The group, composed of a dozen staff experts, made extensive studies of the experience of the League of Nations and of other international agencies. During the first part of August this group completed a "tentative Draft Text of the Charter of the United Nations" and seven fundamental policy analyses, each dealing with a basic function of an international organization. At their heart lay the same broad basic ideas that were contained in the Four-Nation Declaration I presented at Moscow. This draft and the seven analyses formed the foundation for our proposals presented at Dumbarton Oaks.

In a radio address on September 12, 1943, I gave public indication of the extent of our postwar studies. "The form and functions of the international agencies of the future," I said, "the extent to which the existing court of international justice may or may not need to be remodeled, the scope and character of the means for making international action effective in the maintenance of peace, the nature of international economic institutions and arrangements that may be desirable and feasible—all these are among the problems which are receiving attention and which will need to be determined by agreement among governments, subject, of course, to approval by their respective peoples. They are being studied intensively by this Government and by other governments. They are gradually being made subjects of consultation between and among governments. They are being studied and discussed by the people of this country and the peoples of other countries. In the final analysis, it is the will of the people of the world that decides the all-embracing issues of peace and of human welfare."

It was on the basis of acceptance by the four signatories of the Four-Nation Declaration that, in my address to the joint session of Congress on November 18, 1943, following my return from Moscow, I declared that when the provisions of the Declaration were carried into effect there would no longer be any need "for spheres of influence, for alliances, for balance of power or any other of the special arrangements through which, in the unhappy past, the nations strove to safeguard their security or to promote their interests."

We were now free to work wholeheartedly toward the single goal of establishing the United Nations organization.

118: Planning Intensifies

FOLLOWING THE MOSCOW CONFERENCE, and after President Roosevelt's return from the Tehran Conference, our preparatory work on the United Nations organization intensified. The passage of the Connally Resolution in the Senate during my trip back from Moscow, following the previous passage of the Fulbright Resolution in the House, had cleared the path at home, while the Four-Nation Declaration of Moscow had cleared the path abroad.

I had luncheon with the President on December 21, 1943, directly after his return from Tehran, to discuss with him the steps that should next be taken. Three days previously the British Embassy had handed us a paper from the Foreign Office which suddenly raised the old question of regional organizations. It argued in favor of regional security police arrangements. The nations in a given region would supply armed forces, naval ports, and air bases which would function under a regional supreme commander. Not long afterwards, however, several of my associates were informed that the thinking in London had shifted from regional to worldwide security police arrangements.

The President and I agreed that our postwar planning experts should draw up our latest ideas on the international organization for Mr. Roosevelt's consideration. During the next two days we worked late at the State Department composing this paper. It was completed and dated December 23, and took into account all of the work that had been done up to that time.

On the following day the President stated in a radio broadcast that the four nations "are agreed that if force is necessary to keep international peace, international force will be applied—for as long as it may be necessary."

I sent Mr. Roosevelt on December 29 our memorandum containing the basic ideas that might be embodied in the constitution of an international organization. On February 3 he gave me formal clearance to go ahead with our planning for the United Nations organization on the basis of the draft I had sent him on December 29. Practically all the points contained in this draft were later embodied in the proposals we submitted to the Dumbarton Oaks Conference.

In the State Department we undertook, early in 1944, a general reorganization of our work. The war had brought to the Department a vast increase not only in the number but also in the kind of activities it was called upon to perform. This was particularly true in the economic and social fields. Moreover, the progress of the war itself was making the problems of the peace settlement and of the organization of the postwar world of much greater urgency. We gave these developments formal recognition in the administrative structure of the Department through the reorganization announced on January 15, which was planned primarily by Under Secretary Stettinius.

This reorganization brought together all the Department's functions in the economic and social fields, both of a current and of a postwar character, under two Assistant Secretaries of State. It placed the work on postwar political problems on a par with, though organized separately from, the Department's other operations, and provided for the integration of these activities with the other work of the Department in the formulation of policy. As part of this reorganization we created the Committee on Postwar Programs, of which I was chairman, Under Secretary Stettinius vice chairman, and Leo Pasvolsky executive director.

At the Moscow Conference, Eden, Molotov, and I had agreed that exchanges of views should take place among our Governments, in Washington in the first instance, with regard to the establishment of the international organization which we had envisaged in the Four-Nation Declaration. Not long after the conference, Eden began pressing me to start this exchange of views. On February 8 I requested James C. Dunn and Leo Pasvolsky to inform the British and Soviet Embassies that we should like to proceed with an exchange of documents setting forth the tentative views of each Government as to the nature and functions of the projected organization.

We stated to the British and Russians that we would keep the Chinese Government informed, but that we did not ask at that time that that Government be brought into the discussions, although we might raise the question later. We took this position at the request of the President, who thought we should wait until our discussions with the British and the Russians had proceeded further, at which point he might send someone from the State Department to China to take the matter up directly with Chiang Kai-shek, thus obviating the possibility that our proposals would be discussed by too many persons and become publicly known.

On February 17 we handed the British and Soviet Embassies a list of topics on which we were preparing studies in connection with the proposed organization. We had received a similar list from the British the day before. The Russians were not yet ready, but on April 5 they agreed to use the American and British lists as a basis for discussion.

I devoted considerable attention in my address of April 9, 1944, to an international organization to maintain peace and prevent aggression. "Such an organization," I said, "must be based upon firm and binding obligations that the member nations will not use force against each other and against any other nation except in accordance with the arrangements made. It must provide for the maintenance of adequate forces to preserve peace and it must provide the institutions and procedures for calling this force into action to preserve peace. . . . It must provide for an international court for the development and application of law to the settlement of international controversies which fall within the realm of law, for the development of machinery for adjusting controversies to which the field of law has not yet been extended, and for other institutions for the development of new rules to keep abreast of a changing world with new problems and new interests."

I emphasized that there was no hope of turning victory into enduring peace unless the United States, the British Commonwealth, the Soviet Union, and China agreed to act together. "This," I said, "is the solid framework upon which all future policy and international organization must be built. It offers the fullest opportunity for the development of institutions in which all free nations may participate democratically, through which a reign of law and morality may arise, and through which the material interests of all may be advanced. But without an enduring understanding between these four nations upon their fundamental purposes, interests, and obligations to one another, all organizations to preserve peace are creations on paper and the path is wide open again for the rise of a new aggressor."

There was no suggestion, however, I pointed out, that the conclusions of these four nations could or should be arrived at without the participation of the other United Nations.

Our experts in postwar problems were now discussing with me the method of initiating the establishment of the international security organization. On April 12, 1944, they submitted to me a series of recommendations toward this end. They suggested that the four major nations take immediate steps to reach a consensus in principle on the fundamental features of a plan for the organization. When this consensus had been reached, the four nations would further agree upon the draft of a charter. This would then be transmitted jointly by the four Governments to the Governments of the United Nations, the nations associated with them, and such other nations as the United Nations might determine.

When a general consensus had been reached on essential features of the charter, the four nations would jointly convene a general conference for final consideration, approval, and signature of a general agreement embodying the charter. This conference would establish a provisional United Nations Council consisting of the four major nations and four others elected by the conference. The Council would act on behalf of all the signatories of the general agreement until the first meeting of the General Assembly following the ratification of the charter by fifteen nations including the four major ones.

In April, Under Secretary Stettinius was in London discussing the postwar organization, among other topics, with Prime Minister Churchill and Foreign Secretary Eden. Eden proposed that Moscow be the site of the meeting that would have to be held to reach an agreement on the tentative charter for the international organization. He thought that holding the conference in the Russian capital would overcome Russian suspicions of Britain and the United States. He also proposed that he, Molotov and I meet at a place to be designated by me.

I replied on April 17 that I would give consideration to Moscow as the meeting place for the exchange of views on the international organization. Molotov had, however, agreed along with Eden and me at Moscow that exchanges of views should take place in Washington in the first instance, and it was but natural that Washington became the eventual choice for the conference.

We now drew up an outline of the provisions to be contained in a proposed charter, which, dated April 24, 1944, embodied the conclusions upon which we had been able to agree up to that point. We suggested an Executive Council consisting of the four major nations and four others elected by the General Assembly for annual terms, to have primary responsibility for the maintenance of international security and peace.

This draft recommended that the Council should make decisions by a majority vote—including the concurring votes of all permanent members—on four categories of questions. These were: the final terms of settlement of disputes; the regulation of armaments and armed forces; the determination of threats to the peace, of breaches of the peace, and of acts obstructing measures for the maintenance of security and peace; and the institution and application of measures of enforcement.

Other decisions would be taken by a simple majority vote. In this respect we were resolved to avoid the unhappy experience of the League of Nations, whose decisions required a unanimous vote of all members. Any member of the Council had the right in our plan to abstain from voting, but that nation would still be bound by the decision.

In previous drafts we had provided that the vote of a member of the Council directly involved in a dispute would not be counted, but this we dropped in our draft of April 24, leaving the whole question open. Our experts differed on this point, some maintaining that the veto power should not be impaired and others that the ends of justice would not be served by permitting a nation to vote in a case to which it was a party. We decided to leave the question for future consideration.

To maintain security, our draft stipulated that the members of the international organization should undertake to supply forces and facilities when needed, at the call of the Executive Council. An agreement governing the number and kind of forces and facilities to be supplied would be concluded among the member states at the earliest possible moment after the organization came into existence.

Our draft assigned a wide range of important duties to the General Assembly. Among other functions, this body would, on its own initiative or on request of a member state, make reports on and recommendations for the peaceful adjustment of any situation or controversy which it deemed likely to impair the general welfare. It would assist the Executive Council, upon the latter's request, in enlisting the cooperation of all states in questions of peace and security. It would elect the nonpermanent members of the Executive Council and judges of the International Court of Justice.

We made provision in the draft for economic and social activities by the organization and for a possible system of trusteeship.

A president of the general international organization was also provided for by this draft, although the drafters had reservations as to the advisability of the provision. The president of the organization—"a person of widely recognized eminence"—would be elected by the General Assembly, on the nomination of the Executive Council. He would serve for two years, would act as chairman of the Executive Council, and would be free to take part in the deliberations as representing the general interests and purposes of the organization, though without the right to vote. He would open each new session of the General Assembly and preside until the election of its president.

We likewise provided for a director general of the organization, who would be its chief administrative officer. He would be elected by the General Assembly with the concurrence of the Executive Council.

I now submitted this draft in great confidence to three of the ablest men in America, and probably among the best qualified to pass on the questions involved. They were Charles Evans Hughes, former Chief Justice of the United States, who had been the Republican candidate for the Presidency in 1916 and later served as Secretary of State; John W. Davis, Democratic candidate for the Presidency in 1924, and Nathan L. Miller, formerly Republican Governor of New York State. They were all eminent broad-gauge lawyers. Myron C. Taylor acted as intermediary between us.

After they had studied the document, I had two long conferences with Mr. Hughes, and had luncheon with Mr. Davis and Mr. Miller together. All three signified their approval of the draft while making some useful suggestions.

By this time we had held three international conferences on collateral problems and another was in course of preparation. These were the Food and Agriculture Conference at Hot Springs, Virginia, in May and June, 1943; the Relief and Rehabilitation Conference at Atlantic City in November and December, 1943; the International Labor Conference at Philadelphia in April, 1944; and the Monetary and Financial Conference at Bretton Woods scheduled for July, 1944.

The State Department was not the leading department in these conferences, but we of necessity had to negotiate with other nations for their organization and operation, and many officials of the Department took part in them. The conducting of these conferences was in the hands of the chiefs of other departments, along with their associates and the delegates of other governments. Miss Frances Perkins, Secretary of Labor, conferred with me at length before the Philadelphia Labor Conference, and we agreed on policy and procedure.

These conferences arrived at valuable decisions on food supply, on relief, on the improvement of labor standards, and on the creation of an international monetary fund and an international bank. To us at the State Department they had the additional value of serving as a barometer of the degree of cooperation we could expect from the other United Nations in the establishment of the postwar security organization. They were a rehearsal for the later, much more important conference on the United Nations organization itself.

It seemed to us wise to hold these conferences in advance of the conferences that would determine the structure of the United Nations organization. In general, they embraced concrete problems such as food, relief, and money on which the United States individually was in position to be of great material assistance. These propositions were less controversial than some of those involved in the establishment of an international security organization. I realized that we had to prove to the people of the occupied areas that the major nations were taking steps regarding the postwar world and the handling of the immediate problems of relief, reconstruction, and credits. I felt that we had to convince them that we meant to implement the Four-Nation Declaration, that we were advance proponents for an orderly postwar world to the degree that programs could be developed during the war itself, and that cooperation among the United Nations did not rest solely on winning the war but also on planning for the postwar.

These preliminary conferences served to bring the United Nations together in detailed discussion, to show them the possibilities of working out problems through mutual debate and concession, and to get them accustomed to working with one another.

The discussions concerning the formation of a United Nations security organization, however, embraced security problems which involved special responsibilities on the part of the four major powers that would have to provide the force to keep the peace. It was not therefore possible to envisage a general conference of the United Nations on this objective until a basis of agreement had been reached among the four major nations.

The time had now come for us to approach the three others, Russia, Britain, and China, so that concrete steps could be taken toward the creation of the new organization. But before going to the houses of others we had to make sure that our own house was in order. We first had to be certain that Congress was with us, lest the tragedy of the League of Nations occur again.

119: Nonpartisan Policy

JUST AT THE TIME when our formative work in preparing for a United Nations organization was forging ahead in 1944, this nation was thrown again into a presidential campaign. After years of striving to maintain our foreign policy on a nonpartisan basis, it seemed to me imperative to concentrate during this presidential year on an effort to keep the discussions concerning the postwar organization out of politics. If that organization became a political issue it might well suffer the fate of the League of Nations in the Senate in 1919.

As a member of the Executive Committee of the Democratic National Committee during the years prior to 1928, I had made a special effort to observe the efficacy of various peace arrangements. This underlined to me the crucifying consequences of injecting partisan politics into any peace movement.

As a result, ever since my entry into the State Department in 1933, I had taken numerous steps to prevent politics from coming into the Department and our foreign policies. My endeavors to achieve nonpartisanship in foreign affairs went along two lines. The first was to keep foreign relations from becoming a battleground of politics. The second was to keep related domestic issues that dovetailed with foreign affairs from being dragged onto the same battleground. This was particularly true of the trade agreements program, where I sought the support of both parties, and where both assistance and opposition to the program frequently departed from party lines.

I had also gone out of my way to maintain friendly relations with the Legislative Branch of the Government, to consult with Senators, Representatives, and other leading members of both major parties, as well as with editors and writers, and to keep them as fully informed as possible. Following the outbreak of war in Europe on September 1, 1939, I intensified this practice, and I heightened it still more following Pearl Harbor. I made Assistant Secretary of State Breckinridge Long the liaison officer between the State Department and Congress, with the task of keeping in touch with Republican as well as Democratic Senators and Representatives. His broad political experience of several decades was of great value to us. Then in 1944 I determined to bring our nonpartisan practice to a head.

The President was fully behind me in my efforts to maintain cordial relations with the House and Senate, particularly their committees dealing with foreign affairs, but he was skeptical that I could achieve a nonpartisan agreement with the Republicans which they would keep. He had expressed this skepticism to me when I began calling in Republican Congressional leaders and going over our foreign policy with them in detail. When I made the agreement of August, 1944, with the Republican leaders that the world organization and the necessity for United States participation in it should not form a battleground of the 1944 campaign, as I shall narrate later, he again said he was skeptical. I asked why. He said in effect: "You'll see. They won't keep the agreement. They'll make a campaign out of foreign affairs."

Nevertheless, he was not opposed to my making the nonpartisan approach, and I accordingly went ahead.

I was trying strongly to keep Congress, and the country as well, fully in the picture in international agreements. I had spoken to a joint session of Congress following my return from the Moscow Conference. In the autumn of 1943, after the United Nations Relief and Rehabilitation Agreement was reached with forty-three other nations, members of the Senate objected to the accord being promulgated as an executive agreement rather than as a treaty. My associates thereupon met with a subcommittee of the Senate Committee on Foreign Relations to rewrite the agreement so that it could be submitted to both branches of Congress as part of a joint resolution of authority for appropriations.

On January 30, 1944, I appeared on a radio program with Senators Connally and Vandenberg, Speaker Sam Rayburn and Long, with Richard Harkness representing the public. I was then able to say that Rayburn, Connally, Vandenberg, and I were in complete agreement that effective cooperation in foreign affairs between the Executive and Legislative branches of the government was indispensable.

Two months later our close contact with the Senate acquired a more specific character. On March 22 I made a two-hour appearance before the Senate Committee on Foreign Relations in executive session. Senator Tom Connally, chairman of the committee, and fourteen other Senators were present. With them I went very frankly through the whole gamut of our foreign relations, from Russia to Argentina.

I concluded by saying that the State Department had been working on postwar plans for more than two years, and it was now ready to confer further with the committee on a number of these topics, especially an international organization to maintain peace and security. I suggested that the committee name two or three Democrats and two or three Republicans to discuss these matters informally at the State Department. I emphasized the need for cooperation between the Legislative and Executive Branches in dealing with important problems relating to the war and the peace to come, and I remarked that in some respects I had had to work harder toward maintaining harmony within our nation than toward maintaining harmony between nations.

The committee accepted my invitation and named four Democratic and four Republican members as a special committee to confer with me from time to time. They were Senators Connally, Barkley, George, Gillette, Vandenberg, La Follette, White, and Austin. Connally and Vandenberg both gave powerful support to an international movement to preserve peace, and each was to render immense service toward the future United Nations organization. Generally it was a notable group of Senators and Congressional leaders with whom I conferred from time to time during this period. Outstanding in ability, they backed the creation of a security organization in the most enthusiastic spirit.

We held our first meeting, in my office, on April 25. I made it clear at the outset that this was an entirely informal meeting, and each one present could feel entirely free and easy, and no one would be requested to express an opinion, much less assume obligations, unless he wished. I then set forth the main points in our draft of the proposed postwar security organization. I emphasized that for nearly two years the work of study and preparation, and finally of drawing up first drafts, had been carried forward by the State Department under the leadership of the President, and that outstanding persons and officials in the Government, in the two Houses of Congress, and in the country, had been fully consulted on each important question under examination. I mentioned the names of Senators White, Austin, Connally, George, and Thomas, and Congressmen Bloom and Eaton, among other Members of Congress, who had sat in on meetings with us for nearly a year and had contributed their impressions and slants of opinion.

"The United States," I added, "has a tremendous responsibility both of leadership and of preparing a plan that will be workable. Therefore we are obliged to proceed in a spirit of mutual concession and avoid long drawn-out consideration especially of details and controversies. Otherwise Russia, Great Britain, and other countries will soon decide that we are not able to function any more than we did in 1920."

I thereupon handed each Senator, in strict confidence, a copy of our draft for a United Nations organization, along with related documents. I suggested that we meet soon again to exchange views so that, if we could get sufficient agreement, we might then in confidence give copies to the British, Russians, and Chinese, and thus our proposal, along with our proffered leadership, would be safeguarded, and delay avoided. The Senators agreed to meet with me the following Tuesday.

I informed them that I had given this document to three men whom I described as being among the ablest and best qualified in America to pass on the plan advanced. I did not give their names, but they were the three I mentioned in the preceding chapter. Two of them were Republicans.

During our discussion, I said that unless the large nations such as Russia, Great Britain, China, and the United States promptly assumed broad responsibilities as we came to them, it would be easy to delay until it was too late to organize peoples and governments behind a suitable postwar program. This was especially true if we waited until chaotic conditions arose among peoples at the conclusion of the fighting.

I stressed the necessity for unity especially among the United States, Russia, and Great Britain, if this postwar international undertaking were to succeed. Malcontents in this country, I pointed out, were doing their best to drive Russia out of the international movement by constant attacks and criticisms largely about minor incidents or acts. Unless it was possible to prevail upon newspapers, commentators, and columnists to refrain from this line of activity which during the past two months had greatly confused the mind of the public with regard to the more essential phases of the postwar situation, it would be difficult for any international undertaking, such as that offered by us, to succeed. I was also appealing to all Russian officials with whom I came into contact to refrain from similar activities against us from their side.

We faced three pivotal questions, I said. The first was to keep Russia solidly in the international movement. The second was to develop an alert and informed public opinion in support of the program proposed. And the third was to keep the entire undertaking out of domestic politics.

That evening I telegraphed the President, who was resting in South Carolina, and summarized the meeting for him. I said that the Senators seemed intensely interested, and that at the end of the meeting the atmosphere was good.

When the eight Senators met with me again, on May 2, they had read and digested the draft for the United Nations organization. I said I had done most of the talking at the previous meeting, and now wondered if they had any comments to make.

A major point was quickly raised, as one of the Senators said he desired to know whether we should have a good or a bad peace agreement before he could commit himself finally to an agency to keep the peace.

Knowing that this was an important question probably on the minds of others as well, I commented that the Senate would of course pass on the peace treaties and therefore would itself have much to do with the adoption of a good or a bad peace. I then asked what we should do if the peace agreement were not quite to our notion. Would we abandon all idea of an organization to keep the peace, or would we proceed with determination—as the statesmen did in bringing about the adoption of the Constitution amidst every difficulty—to perfect the peace and, if necessary, to develop further and perfect further the proposed organization to keep the peace? What would have happened, I inquired, if our Revolutionary statesmen had become discouraged because the outlook ahead for the preservation of freedom was not just what they desired, and if, in consequence, they had failed to establish the Government—which effort had, in fact, almost failed?

Later in the discussion I asked the Senator if he were opposed to perfecting the present postwar organization proposal until he first ascertained whether we were to have a good or a bad peace. He instantly said that not for a moment would he fail to cooperate to perfect the document.

Another Senator wondered about the necessity for some organization to keep the peace before the final peace agreement. I replied that originally we had discussed the creation of a temporary peace organization not very different from the proposed postwar organization, but that for numerous reasons this had not been practical. Moreover, under the Four-Nation Declaration of Moscow, the four major nations—Russia, Great Britain, China, and the United States—were already committed to consult with one another and, as occasion required, with any other nations that might be necessary, with a view to joint action for the maintenance of peace and security until the permanent peace organization was finally established and became a going concern, irrespective of when the peace treaties might be concluded.

When we met again, on May 12, the view was again expressed that it would be unjust to the American people to commit them to supporting a peace that to them might be odious, and that it therefore would be well to see more fully the nature of the peace before any final commitments were made on the proposed postwar organization.

I argued that, if we should halt our forward movement in support of the postwar organization proposal, the remainder of the world would promptly conclude that we had surrendered our leadership in the situation. The small nations, which were looking mainly to us for leadership and for the championship of the basic principles involved, would at once become utterly discouraged. We should also run the grave risk in this country of bringing about a schism between the two great political parties on the question whether we should halt our forward movement to develop and secure tentative approval first from Members of Congress, next from the three other large nations, and finally from the smaller nations.

"A good peace," I continued, "will be much facilitated by keeping alive the beneficial and softening doctrines and policies contained in the Atlantic Charter, the Moscow Four-Nation Declaration, and the Connally Resolution. Otherwise, when the fighting is over, there will be no program halfway perfected even tentatively; our leadership will be gone; and each country will already be preparing to hoe its own row in the future. This Government, however, acting through the Senate, can probably prevent a bad peace, and, failing that, will have nothing to do with it. We will not fail for the reason that we shall be supported by the small nations and probably by most of the large nations."

One of the Senators, strongly supporting my position, emphasized that we were concerned about furnishing leadership and basic programs that would include the preservation of peace and world order under law, and would be most helpful in avoiding what some of the other Senators called a possible bad peace. He added that, if the peace should prove bad, we would not stand for it for a moment, and that naturally and inevitably both the peace treaty and the organization now proposed to keep the peace would all go down in a crash together. I added, "And automatically."

But another Senator argued on the other side, saying that at this time it would be impossible to get ratification by the Senate of our document without some definite assurance that it would not be used to protect and perpetuate a bad peace.

I replied that, by going forward and advocating our proposal, along with the Atlantic Charter, the Four-Nation Declaration, and the Connally Resolution—this Government furnishing the leadership—we should greatly facilitate the working out of a good peace rather than a bad peace.

This question of obtaining a good peace before founding the international organization seemed rivaled in importance to the Senators by the question of the veto power of the major nations on the Council. The question rose when a Senator said he thought it would be a serious defect to let any one of the major nations kill a righteous proposal by interposing its veto.

"The veto power," I replied, "is in the document primarily on account of the United States. It is a necessary safeguard in dealing with a new and untried world arrangement. Without it the United States would not have anywhere near the popular support for the postwar organization as with it in, any more so perhaps than in 1920. We might as well recognize that this is about the best that can be done as a beginning, and that it would be inadvisable to throw out this veto power for each of the four large nations, and especially the United States. We should not forget that this veto power is chiefly for the benefit of the United States in the light of the world situation and of our own public opinion. We cannot move any faster than an alert public opinion in perfecting a permanent peace organization, but we should not be deterred for an instant from pursuing the sole course that is open, the alternative being international chaos such as we have had heretofore."

I said that from the very outset of our work to develop a basic plan for permanent world peace and order we had faced at every turn the realization that it would be unavoidably necessary at the beginning to rely chiefly on the three or four major nations. This meant, in the light of our disastrous experience with the peace movement following the First World War, that we had to adopt provisions of a world organization acceptable to these nations.

As for our own country, we recalled the insistent demand made in Woodrow Wilson's period for veto privileges in the League of Nations. Bitter opposition had been raised to the United States' entry into the League on the basis of erroneous assumptions that, if we became a member of the League, the Covenant allowed an agency of the League to give orders to our military forces in preserving peace. The biggest stumbling block that sent the Wilson movement in support of the League to utter destruction in 1920 was the argument over this point, and no other political controversy during our time had been accompanied by more deep-seated antagonism. The hint in 1919—however false it was—that we were in any sense surrendering or impairing Congress's prerogative to declare war or the President's prerogative to direct the movements of our armed forces proved fatal. I had not forgotten this fact.

My associates and I had carefully sounded out opinion on this question as it related to our own world organization proposal. We readily discovered that on this particular point there was not a chance for us to make any advance with a large number of leading members of both Houses of Congress and with many influential groups and persons in the country. We felt that real time would be necessary to improve and perfect a completed world peace structure that would function effectively and satisfactorily to all. The veto, which had been held up by some as a kind of scarecrow, could unquestionably in our opinion be later placed on a milder basis, becoming less and less an impediment as time went on. We considered time and patience to be absolutely necessary.

In all the discussions with my associates in postwar planning, two important conditions had been understood and repeatedly stated in connection with the veto. The first was that none of the permanent members of the Council would exercise its right of veto capriciously or arbitrarily. It would call this power forth only on a matter of the gravest concern to itself, never on secondary matters and never in a way to prevent thorough discussion of any issue. The veto would be exercised in the same broad, cooperative spirit that pervaded the preparatory efforts of the major nations leading toward the creation of the United Nations. It is obvious that the provision was universally intended to aid and facilitate the maintenance of permanent peace by the security organization. Naturally the entire spirit of any such qualification, intended to be liberalized as rapidly as public opinion would permit, in no sense contemplated the exercise of the privilege except in instances of first importance.

The second condition was that we were thinking largely of the application of the veto power to military or other means of compulsion. We recalled that this had been the chief bone of contention in connection with the League Covenant. In conferring upon the proposed Council the authority to control and direct at least some of the military forces of member nations to any point where the Council believed the exercise of force was required, we also had to give the major nations that would furnish such force the right of veto. It was our thought, therefore, that the main focus of the veto would be military and other means of exercising force, such as economic sanctions, and not the numerous other issues that were certain to come before the Council.

What we were proposing was a substantial advance over the League system, in which every nation had veto powers both in the Assembly and in the Council. Under our proposal the veto requirement would be completely eliminated from the work of the Assembly and would be retained in the Council for the major nations in connection with the discharge of their special responsibility to keep the peace.

A Senator expressed his deep concern over the veto power in the hands of the four major nations on the Council. This, he said, constituted a weakness and also a discrimination against the small nations.

I commented that these four nations would not take on all the responsibilities of keeping the peace if the smaller nations which made but small contributions were given practical control over the administration of policy in connection with the use of force. There was no possible way, I said, to initiate this organization except by each of the large nations on the Council retaining the veto power in connection with the use of force or sanctions. I added that France, too, might be given a seat on the Council with the veto power. But, no matter how many additions might be made to the Council, both with and without the veto power, our Government would not remain there for a day without retaining its veto power. The beginning had to be made on this rather narrow basis, with the hope and expectation that, as time went on and the merits and benefits of this organization revealed themselves, the base of the organization could be broadened in many desirable ways and by unanimous consent.

In our discussions both on the question of a good and a bad peace and on the veto power, it was obvious that some of the Senators were worried over the position Russia would occupy after the war.

"Inevitably," I said, "we all have to recognize that no great world movement sufficient to preserve law and order in international affairs can be set on foot fully developed at the outset. Nations will make mistakes, and we have to reason and plead with each other to refrain from such mistakes and undertake to educate each other toward that end. It would be unspeakably disastrous if we became discouraged at the outset over every little error, or even a single large mistake of some one country, and abandoned the whole peace and welfare of the world. This is a problem that will test the ability, patience, unity, and determination of the peaceful nations and their peoples, both jointly and severally."

One Senator inquired pointedly whether Russia really desired to go forward with us and the other United Nations in the proposed movement of international cooperation. I replied that not only while I was in Moscow, but at all times up to this day, Marshal Stalin and Molotov and their associates had quickly made clear to any inquirer their unqualified desire to become full-fledged associates in the international cooperation movement.

"Our customs and manners," I said, "are about as mysterious to Russia as hers are to us. Time and patience are indispensable if our peoples are to become acquainted and learn to understand each other. Such understanding is absolutely necessary if we are to avoid acts and utterances on the part of both Governments which in themselves constitute errors. We simply must not quarrel with each other, but we must patiently point out the full facts and circumstances and their significance and plead with each other to abandon any acts or utterances not entirely in harmony with the basic principles of the international cooperation movement. All these principles and policies are so beneficial and appealing to the sense of justice, of right, and of the well-being of free peoples everywhere that in the course of a few years the entire international machinery should be working fairly satisfactorily. Of course, some years will be necessary to perfect and broaden and otherwise develop such a political, economic, and peace structure."

The Senators were of course keenly interested in the respective jurisdictions and authorities of Congress and the Executive in relation to the proposed United Nations organization. My view was asked on Congressional and Executive authority in relation to a major use of force. I replied that I felt that the President alone should have the authority to deal with minor breaches of the peace or threatened breaches, keeping Congress fully informed at every stage. No other course, I thought, was practical, because there were threatened breaches of the peace almost every week of the year in some part of the world or other. My position was that major breaches of the peace meant war rather than police action, in which event the prerogative of Congress to declare war would be completely safeguarded.

A question was then asked whether the proposed treaty, whereby each member of the organization would allocate armed forces to keep the peace, would be submitted to the Senate for its advice and consent. I replied in the affirmative, which seemed to satisfy the group.

A Senator remarked that he was under the impression that our proposal was to complete a document as quickly as possible, and then secure unconditional and unqualified ratification by the Senate before the war ended.

I recalled to him that it required more than a year to negotiate the supposedly simple UNRRA agreement with some thirty-five nations, although that was a mere proposal to distribute money for nothing and most of it was to come from this Government. Judging from this, I went on, we need not assume that we could go forward with these tentative plans for informal discussions, first with Congress, then with the three other major nations, and finally with the more than thirty smaller nations, and get the document ready for a final draft without much delay. Our main purpose, I added, had not been so much to complete and ratify the proposal within a given time, as to carry forward the whole undertaking with the idea that, as time went on, there might occur a gradual evolution in its terms that would prove suitable for final approval by all the nations.

I also remarked that, from time to time, persons came to my office to suggest the vital importance of postponing consideration of the postwar organization document until after the November election, since it was so essential that it be kept out of domestic politics. To this I was replying that, much as we all desired to keep it out of politics, I considered it impossible to postpone consideration until after election. One reason was that such a step would itself be calculated to get the whole matter into politics, thereby causing demands to go up all over this country and in other countries to know what we were fighting for, and especially what plans and agencies we had in mind, if any, to preserve peace and world order under law in the postwar world. And such demands could not be resisted.

A Senator, recalling that our Revolutionary statesmen provided that the Constitution should take effect when nine States had ratified it, asked how the peace organization proposal would go into effect.

I replied that there was literally no way to institute this international movement of cooperation to keep the peace except under the leadership and on the initiative of the four large nations which were of necessity virtually fighting the war alone and would furnish almost all the force to keep the peace. Therefore, this movement depended on the ability and willingness of the four chief nations to work together. No two of the three great powers—Russia, Great Britain, and the United States—I concluded, would undertake another world peace organization with one of them omitted, after the failure of the League of Nations when one of the great countries was missing.

An inquiry was then made whether it would not be wise to have regional organizations each select a member of the Council of the United Nations organization, along with the five other members to be selected by the Assembly. I replied that we were not quite in harmony with Mr. Churchill's suggested regional federation idea, which would build a world structure in the form of regional organizations, with a common head at the top.

We felt, I said, that it would be more practical for the nations resident in given areas to agree in advance to join with their sister nations in the same region just as soon as they discovered a breach or threatened breach of the peace, at the same time keeping in close touch with the Executive Council and notifying it of their efforts to ward off breaches of or threats to the peace. This would be their function, I pointed out, rather than the erection of regional structures clothed with jurisdiction and authority that would extend into the very head office of the organization; namely, the Executive Council. The Assembly would no doubt select its nominees for the Council on a geographical basis.

I informed the Senators at our meeting on May 12 that the three eminent jurists to whom I had submitted the document for their opinion had all three approved it in its essentials as practical and workable and as representing a good approach to the conditions to be dealt with.

The Senators all agreed at this meeting that we should go forward with our postwar proposal. Generally they said they looked with favor on our postwar organization draft as a document calculated to meet the views of the American public, and were strongly in favor of carrying it forward. They said they were willing for me to bring it now to the attention of the other large nations.

As the meeting ended, they said they would confer among themselves with regard to their issuing a statement that our document was suitable from their viewpoint and to my taking early steps to get it before the three other governments. But when we met again, on May 29, they were forced to say that, although they had tried to agree on a statement that might be addressed to me and given to the press, it had been impossible to reach an agreement on the wording.

Knowing that the prime difficulty in arriving at that agreement was the continued anxiety of a couple of them over the possibility that a bad peace treaty would be signed which the international organization would have to uphold and administer, I reopened the question. I said I felt that no rational person in any civilized country would for a moment favor preserving a peace that was not worth preserving. There were numerous advantages, however, I added, in not fixing at this time an inflexible date, tied in with the peace treaty, for the going into effect of the postwar security organization. That organization, if perfected in advance, would be of great help in bringing about a better peace than might otherwise be the case, and hence in avoiding a bad peace.

The fighting, I went on, might continue in some parts of the world for one, two, or four years, during which time it might be desirable to put the security organization into operation. Repeating that there was a tremendous demand on the part of peoples to know what their respective governments were planning to do to preserve peace after the war, I said that to announce a broad condition dependent upon the conclusion of a peace treaty would seriously handicap the whole movement.

I therefore suggested that we might state in an announcement that we were all unanimously against establishing and preserving a bad peace. We could state further that the present draft plan would be presented to other governments and that, when an informal plan had been completed and tentatively and informally agreed upon, the Senators, the President, and I and others would confer as to when and in what circumstances the postwar security plans would be put into effect.

A Senator thereupon restated a belief he had expressed before, which he said had been accentuated by reading several articles in a national magazine; namely, that secret agreements existed between the President and the heads of other large nations. The peace organization, he said, was so tied in with the peace treaty itself that it could not be considered separately. Any further consideration of the security organization should be accompanied by a reservation on the part of the Senators to the effect that they should await the full development of the peace terms to see whether they were good or bad.

Another Senator asked me whether reports were true that regional federations had been secretly agreed to for Europe by the President, Stalin, and Churchill.

I replied that I knew of no such agreements.

I then informed the Senators that I must forthwith issue a statement telling of our intention to proceed with discussions with foreign Governments. The President and I had agreed that my conversations with the Senators had brought us enough agreement and support to permit us to take the next step—to set in motion a direct exchange of views among the United States, Russia, Britain, and China. I accordingly read to the Senators the statement, which I released later in the day. This said:

"The first phase of the informal conversations with the eight Senators has been concluded. We had frank and fruitful discussions on the general principles, questions, and plans relating to the establishment of an international peace and security organization in accordance with the principles contained in the Moscow Four-Nation Declaration, the Connally Resolution, and other similar declarations made in this country. I am definitely encouraged and am ready to proceed, with the approval of the President, with informal discussions on this subject with Great Britain, Russia, and China, and then with governments of other United Nations."

The statement added that meanwhile I would also have discussions with leaders of both parties in Congress, and with others. The door of nonpartisanship, I said, would continue to be wide open at the State Department, especially when any phase of the planning for a postwar security organization was under consideration.

Thus ended the first chapter of my conversation with the Senators. I did not accomplish all I had hoped for, but we had achieved much. The Senators were in agreement on the necessity for an international organization to keep the peace, on the importance of the United States' becoming a member thereof, on the general lines of the draft of the organization which we had prepared, and on the advisability of going ahead to perfect the draft and of placing it before the other major nations. Furthermore, the Senators were convinced of my sincerity in wishing to keep the United Nations organization out of domestic politics, and generally they appeared willing to adopt the same position. They also seemed impressed by our willingness to give them all the information in our possession on the full breadth of our foreign policy and on our thoughts with regard to the postwar organization. Only one difficulty, which could still become serious, remained—the insistence of two Senators on a reservation concerning a good peace treaty. The other points that seemed principally to interest the Senators were the questions of sovereignty, involving the veto; of the Executive's authority in connection with the international organization; of avoiding the creation of a superstate; and of the role of small nations in the organization.

I held a meeting of leading Representatives of both parties in my office on June 2. Attending were Speaker Sam Rayburn, John W. McCormack, Majority Leader; Joseph W. Martin, Jr., Minority Leader; Sol Bloom, chairman of the House Committee on Foreign Affairs; Charles A. Eaton, ranking Republican member of the committee; Robert Ramspeck, and Leslie C. Arends. I handed each one a copy of our draft of the proposed United Nations organization, and I covered with them virtually the same ground as during my first conference with the eight Senators. With the Representatives the discussion did not become as involved as with the Senators.

Senators Ball, Burton, Hatch, and Hill having asked for a meeting with me to obtain information concerning the proposed postwar organization, I met with them in my office on June 22. Although I did not give them copies of our draft of the organization, I went over with them generally the points that had been discussed during my meetings with the eight Senators from the Committee on Foreign Relations.

Meantime Assistant Secretary of State Breckinridge Long, working on my behalf, was conducting a quiet campaign to induce the Democratic and Republican national conventions to adopt planks favoring the international organization. He was materially assisted by Secretaries Stimson and Knox, by Myron Taylor, Will Hays, and the Senators with whom I had been conferring. When the platforms of both major parties came out with planks supporting the creation of an international organization to maintain the peace, of which the United States would be a member, I felt greatly encouraged.

As a result of all my discussions with Senators and Representatives, and of the action taken at the conventions, I now had more than a reasonable assurance that the presidential campaign of 1944, however bitterly it might be fought on domestic issues, would not make the postwar organization a gage of battle.

120: Dumbarton Oaks

MY EXCHANGES OF VIEWS with the Senators having achieved sufficiently satisfactory results, I was ready to proceed with an approach to Britain, Russia, and China. Accordingly I asked British Ambassador Halifax and Russian Ambassador Gromyko to come to my office on Memorial Day, May 30, 1944. It was a fitting occasion on which to begin a further stage of the movement to prevent another war.

I informed them in detail of the conversations I had been having with the Senators and outlined our attitude toward the postwar security problem. I said I was now ready to proceed with informal talks with the British and the Russians. I asked them to request their Governments to fix a date, as early as convenient, for these conferences to begin. I said we would be ready as soon as they were.

I then made, through them, a very earnest appeal to their Governments to let China take part in the conferences. I used very much the same arguments I had employed at the Moscow Conference when I struggled to have China become a signatory to the Four-Nation Declaration. They promised to present this matter fully to their respective Governments.

I did not give the Ambassadors our tentative draft for the proposed security organization. Instead I suggested that each of the Governments should prepare its respective draft for consideration at the opening of the informal conference.

That same day I also saw Chinese Ambassador Dr. Wei Tao-ming and made similar statements to him. Seemingly depressed over the general situation, the Ambassador said Russia was undertaking to secure more power and control of the Far East than anyone imagined, and mentioned recent diplomatic exchanges that had taken place between Russia and Japan. I sought in a general way to disabuse his mind as to the significance of this latter development. I was convinced that Russia would go to war against Japan when the time came, and Stalin's words to that effect were still to the forefront of my memory. In any event, I said we would handle the discussions on the international organization so as to take care of China's prestige in every way possible, and I knew this was the President's feeling as well as mine.

I foresaw that Russia, still not at war with Japan, might object to having China present at a conference, just as she had objected with regard to the Four-Nation Declaration. Accordingly, on the following day I telephoned British Minister Sir Ronald Campbell, in the absence of Ambassador Halifax, to make a new suggestion. I said that, if the Soviet Government should not agree to China's sitting in on the conference, I most earnestly hoped that the British Government would be willing to sit in with the United States and China, and, at another time, with Russia and the United States—the procedure followed in the successive Cairo and Tehran Conferences in 1943. I made the same suggestion to Soviet Ambassador Gromyko and to Chinese Ambassador Wei Tao-ming.

Generalissimo Chiang Kai-shek cabled the President on June 2 expressing his gratification that we had proposed that China be included in the discussions.

British Ambassador Halifax informed me on June 12 that the British would participate in the Washington discussions and that the permanent Under Secretary for Foreign Affairs, Sir Alexander Cadogan, would represent Britain. After thanking him, I remarked that we had heard nothing from his Government about China sitting in with us, and that it would be calamitous if the project of bringing in the Chinese should fail. He agreed to take this up with his Government again.

Halifax informed me on June 15 of the contents of a telegram from Eden in which the latter, repeating that he was sending Under Secretary Cadogan to head the United Kingdom delegation, said he hoped I would be on hand, and Halifax for Britain, to follow the discussions generally and take up any necessary points.

As weeks went by without an answer from the Soviet Government to the invitation I extended on May 30, we instructed our Embassy in Moscow to urge Molotov to reply as soon as possible.

The Soviet Chargé, Alexander N. Kapustin, brought me on July 9 an *aide-mémoire* from his Government stating its readiness to take part in negotiations in Washington on the basis of my suggestion of Anglo-American-Soviet negotiations and Anglo-American-Chinese negotiations separately. The Soviet Government was ready to start the negotiations without preliminary exchanges of documents between the Soviet, American, and British Governments; it suggested the beginning of August for the conference, and said Ambassador Gromyko would be the Soviet representative.

In this note, however, the Soviet Government sought to limit the scope of the negotiations. Referring to an exchange of letters it had had

with the British Government, the Russians wanted to postpone discussion
on two subject headings suggested by the British. One concerned the relations to be established between the economic organs and the main organization. The other concerned the processes of peaceful settlement of disputes. The Soviets were willing to begin discussions on the other points,
including the scope and character of the international organization and
the procedure for establishing it; safety measures through which threats
to peace and violations of peace could be prevented; and plans of combined actions.

We replied to the Soviet *aide-mémoire* on July 12, expressing our
pleasure at the Soviet Government's readiness to take part in the discussions in Washington, and suggesting the date of August 2 for the opening
meeting. We opposed, however, any idea of limiting the scope of the discussions. We said that procedures for a peaceful adjustment of disputes
must necessarily constitute an integral part of any effective scheme for an
international organization, and we expected to state fully our own views
during the forthcoming discussions. We also said we expected fully to
express our views on possible arrangements for territorial trusteeship and
on the relationship of specialized economic and social agencies to the
general organization.

As a result of further exchanges of cables with London, Moscow, and
Chungking, we secured British agreement to a two-phase arrangement
for the conversations, and Russian agreement not to limit the scope of
the discussion. Accordingly, on July 17 I publicly announced that conversations among the four Governments signatory to the Declaration of
Moscow would begin in Washington probably early in August on the
subject of an international security organization. I stated that the first
phase of the conversations would be among the United Kingdom, the
United States, and the Soviet Union, and that conversations among the
United States, the United Kingdom, and China would be carried on either
at the same time or shortly thereafter.

Two days later I announced that the conversations would be held
at Dumbarton Oaks, the former home of Robert Woods Bliss, one of my
Special Assistants who had once been our Ambassador to Argentina. He
had conveyed Dumbarton Oaks to Harvard University, which, by arrangement with Under Secretary Stettinius, had made it available to us.

By July 18 we had drawn up a new tentative draft for a proposed
general international organization. On that day I asked British Chargé
Campbell and Russian Chargé Kapustin to come to my office and handed

them each a copy. I informed them that we were also sending a copy for each of their Governments to our Ambassadors in their respective capitals. Our thought, I said, was that each of the three Governments might have some weeks in which to consider these suggestions before the meeting opened in Washington. I added that we would be glad to have copies in return of any similar draft proposals that they might offer. Since our own communications with Chungking were better than those enjoyed by the Chinese Ambassador, we wirelessed a further copy direct to the Chinese capital, in addition to handing one to the envoy here.

The draft I handed the envoys was essentially that which I had discussed with the Senators, with one or two noteworthy changes. We now provided that the Executive Council should consist of eleven members instead of eight. We stated that to the four permanent members already mentioned France should be added when the Council found that a Government freely chosen by the French people had been established and was in effective control of the territory of the French Republic.

Another change was the dropping of the office of President of the United Nations. We had had numerous reservations ourselves on this provision in the April draft, and additional objections had been raised during our discussions following its circulation. Our chief thought was that an undesirable competition might ensue among leaders of nations for the position, and that the post might become the goal of overly ambitious men.

The draft specifically left open the question of voting procedure in the case of parties to a dispute by suggesting that provisions would need to be worked out to take care of cases where one or more of the permanent members of the council were directly involved.

Soviet Chargé Kapustin brought me on July 20 an *aide-mémoire* from his Government in reply to mine of July 12. The Russians said they did not consider it necessary to start an exchange of views with the presentation of written drafts. (This note was written before the Russians received our draft of July 18.) The Soviet Government thought it desirable in the beginning to have a more flexible basis for discussion. It felt that oral exchanges of views might better conduce to working out drafts of an international organization which in turn would serve as the basis for a joint draft by the three Governments.

The Russians proposed that the Anglo-American-Russian discussions and the Anglo-American-Chinese discussions should be conducted not simultaneously but at different times, and said they would agree to any sequence of these cycles.

The date of August 14 was agreed upon for the opening session with the Russians. Later, however, they informed us that they had not had available for study a translation of our proposals until August 4; they had not intended to make an advance exchange of documents and, now that they had received ours, they wished to have more time to study it. We accordingly consented to postponement to August 21.

The President and I agreed that Under Secretary Stettinius should head the American delegation and be assisted by those men in and out of the Government who had taken a principal share in the work of postwar planning. These were: Isaiah Bowman, Benjamin V. Cohen, James C. Dunn, Henry P. Fletcher, Joseph C. Grew, Green H. Hackworth, Stanley K. Hornbeck, Breckinridge Long, Leo Pasvolsky, Edwin C. Wilson, Lieutenant General Stanley D. Embick, Major General George V. Strong, Major General Muir S. Fairchild, Admiral Arthur J. Hepburn, Vice Admiral Russell Willson, and Rear Admiral Harold C. Train. Myron C. Taylor was not included, being then at the Vatican. The delegates were aided by the outstanding staff of experts who had been working on every phase of the postwar planning in the State Department under Pasvolsky's direction, including Alger Hiss, Harley Notter, Benjamin Gerig, and Durward Sandifer. This staff functioned as the international secretariat at the conference, serving not only the American delegation but the British, Russian, and Chinese delegations as well.

When the British Delegation, headed by Under Secretary Cadogan, paid a courtesy call on me on August 14, Cadogan and Ambassador Halifax remained behind for a conversation. I brought up with them the suggestion Eden had made that the Foreign Ministers of the United States, Britain, and Russia should meet to discuss international matters. I remarked that before we met, and especially before any formal agreement were reached on the postwar organization, it would be very important first to discuss steps toward conferring with the small nations. I said that if the four major nations should go on until they turned out to the world a completed document and then sent copies to the small nations in a "take it or leave it" manner, as this would be construed, it would be difficult to avoid serious attacks by demagogues, politicians, and uninformed persons.

Cadogan and Halifax said they could see the importance of this suggestion, and they would take it up with Eden.

Both the British and the Soviet Governments handed us their draft proposals for an international organization, the former dated July 22 and

the latter August 12. Fortunately so many exchanges of ideas had occurred among us that we were already thinking along the same basic
lines. As we studied the British and Russian drafts we felt that their
ideas paralleled ours in many respects.

On August 15 I telephoned Senators Connally and Vandenberg and
informed them that the British had in general accepted the principles
contained in the document which I had gone over with the eight Senators. I explained that the conversations at Dumbarton Oaks would be
on a technical or expert level. Neither Connally nor Vandenberg expressed
any desire to be present at the conference, but I told them I would get in
touch with them in case any new fundamental principles arose, and in
any event I or one of my associates would keep them abreast of day-to-
day developments. I telephoned the same information to Speaker of the
House Sam Rayburn, with the request that he pass it on to the Representatives who had met with me on June 2.

Secretary of the Treasury Morgenthau insisted that the Treasury
should have an observer at the conference. I took this up with the President who sent word to Morgenthau that this would not be possible.

I opened the Dumbarton Oaks Conference on August 21 with an
address in which I said it was the sacred duty of the governments of all
peace-loving nations to make sure that international machinery be fash-
ioned through which the peoples could build the peace they so deeply
desired.

"It is generally agreed," I said, "that any peace and security organization would surely fail unless backed by force to be used ultimately
in case of failure of all other means for the maintenance of peace. That
force must be available promptly, in adequate measure, and with certainty. The nations of the world should maintain, according to their
capacities, sufficient forces available for joint action when necessary to
prevent breaches of the peace."

I said it was the intention of the United States Government, following the Dumbarton Oaks Conference, that the conclusions reached should
be communicated to the Governments of all the United Nations and of
other peace-loving nations and made available to the peoples of all countries for public study and debate.

"The people of this country," I said, "are now united as never before
in their determination that the tragedy which today is sweeping the earth
shall not recur."

The first several days of discussion at Dumbarton Oaks revealed that there was a very large area of agreement among the three countries on the basic principles involved and also on a number of matters of important detail.

The most important difference that developed at this time was whether the scope of the projected organization should include international cooperation in the economic and social fields. The British and we favored the lodging of these important functions in the General Assembly and in an economic and social council under its authority. We argued that economic and social cooperation was essential to the creation of conditions necessary to maintain security and peace. The Russians, while fully recognizing the need for economic and social cooperation, believed that these functions should be assigned to a separate organization rather than to a security organization.

The tentative drafts which the British and Russians had given us in advance of the conference seemed to assign a relatively unimportant role to the Assembly, in contrast to our position that the Assembly, comprising all member states, should be given real functions. This was especially true of the Soviet proposals. In the first few days of discussion the British and the Russians substantially accepted our viewpoint.

As the conference got under way I arranged that Under Secretary Stettinius should take up with the President directly, as well as with myself, questions that required decisions on high levels. Two days after the conference opened, the President gave his approval to several important decisions I had made at a meeting with my associates in my office on August 19, two days before the Dumbarton Oaks Conference opened. One was that at this stage the Executive Council should not be given the right to impose the terms of settlement of a dispute. This provision had seemed unacceptable to the British and the Russians. The Council's functions, we agreed, should be to promote peaceful settlement, to make recommendations to the parties to a dispute, and to settle disputes only on the request of those parties.

The President also gave his approval to our new position that the votes of the nations involved in cases before the Council, including the great powers, should not be counted in the Council's decisions on such cases. I had decided this point on the basis of five possible methods of procedure which my associates had submitted to me. In the April 24 draft handed to the Senators and in the July 18 draft submitted to Britain, Russia, and China, this point had been left open. The British, however, had consistently argued that the votes of parties to a dispute should not be counted.

We believed that all the rules of civil justice provided that a person involved in a dispute should not be able to cast a vote in the decision relating to the dispute. He should not be one of the judges or a member of the jury. There was still some difference of opinion among us, however, as to whether this abstention from voting should apply only to the pacific settlement of disputes in which one or more of the major nations were involved, or should apply also to enforcement action.

The President further agreed that we should accept a general provision for a two-thirds, rather than a simple majority, vote in the Council, except for procedural decisions. This was very strongly urged by the British.

The President likewise agreed that France should be given a permanent seat on the Council when she had a Government that was recognized (he said he would like to see another word than this) by the four major powers, and meantime have provisional representation without the prerogatives of a permanent member.

We felt we should also raise at this time the question of giving Brazil a permanent seat. I myself felt strongly on this point, believing that Brazil's size, population, and resources, along with her prospect of a great future and the outstanding assistance she had rendered her sister United Nations, would warrant her receiving permanent membership. The President was fully of the same opinion. During the following days, however, both the British and the Russians emphatically opposed our view.

Yet another point in which Mr. Roosevelt concurred was that we should oppose the inclusion of provisions for the withdrawal or suspension of members of the organization.

An entirely new and startling proposal was injected into the discussions by the Soviet representative, Ambassador Gromyko, as the second week of the conference opened on August 28. The discussion in the steering committee of the conference was revolving around the question of what nations should be initial members of the organization. Both the Russians and ourselves said that the members should be the United Nations and the associated nations. However, there emerged a basic difference of interpretation. We meant that the members should be all the signatories to the United Nations Declaration, together with eight other nations that had not declared war against the Axis but had been materially helping the Allies in the prosecution of the war—helping more, in fact, than some of the Allies themselves. These were six Latin American Republics, Iceland, and Egypt. The Russians said the members should be the twenty-six original signatories to the United Nations Declaration, and they defined "associated nations" as being those that had signed the Declaration subsequently. They did not wish to include the eight nations we mentioned. Our discussion on this latter point was proving inconclusive, and, in fact, the conference ended with it still unsolved.

Suddenly, in the midst of this discussion, Ambassador Gromyko said to the steering committee that all sixteen Republics composing the Union of Soviet Socialist Republics should be made initial members of the United Nations organization. Russia would therefore have sixteen votes. He left Stettinius and Cadogan breathless, but they lost no time in telling him that his proposal would raise great difficulties.

When Stettinius reported this to the President, Mr. Roosevelt said emphatically that the United States could under no conditions accept such a proposal. He instructed Stettinius to explain to Gromyko that it would present untold complications, and that it was just as logical for us to ask for the admission of the forty-eight states of the Union as it was to agree to admit the sixteen Soviet Republics.

When Stettinius reported it to me, I said I was amazed that such a proposal had been made. I added that no such question had ever entered the minds of any of us in the American group who had been working on postwar planning. I concluded by saying I would oppose it with all my strength.

On August 29 Stettinius reported to Gromyko the substance of his conversations with the President and me and stated that it was our opinion that the suggestion was out of order, and that to press it at this time might jeopardize the success of the conference. He appealed to Gromyko to withdraw his suggestion and said that, if the Soviet Government had such a thing in mind, it should more properly present it to the Council of the United Nations organization after the latter's creation.

Gromyko proved most cooperative. He said he had raised the point merely to advise us and the British that his Government had the matter in mind. He agreed that there should be no further reference to it during the conference. Nevertheless, he indicated that on some other occasion his Government would probably raise the question again.

The fact that the Soviet Government had such a question of multiple membership in mind was disturbing. I accordingly asked Ambassador Gromyko to come to see me on August 31, at which time I stated to him as plainly as possible the manifold objections I saw to the suggestion he had raised on behalf of his Government.

I said to him, in effect, that this proposal would "blow off the roof." The large nations, I commented, that would have to furnish leadership and the military force for the organization would have no difficulty in getting their views listened to, whether they had one vote or many votes. The United States, I added, did not think to have more than one vote, and we nevertheless felt that our influence would enable us at all times to assert ourselves.

We prepared at the State Department that same day a message on the subject to be sent by the President to Stalin. The President approved it, with the addition of a sentence saying that our position did not prejudice later discussion of the question after the organization had been formed, at which time it would have full authority to deal with the matter.

· This question of plural Russian membership was mentioned once more by Gromyko toward the end of the conference, and thereafter was not again raised prior to my resignation in November, 1944. At no time did the Soviets take up with me their later request for the admission of the White Russian and Ukrainian Republics, to which President Roosevelt agreed at the Yalta Conference. Had they done so, I would have opposed it.

In all our discussions we strove to keep this proposal absolutely secret. Even in our own memoranda we referred to it as the "X matter." It seemed to me so explosive an issue that, if it got out, it would inevitably be dramatized by forces of opposition everywhere and do injury to Russia's situation as well as to that of the conference.

In my conversation with Ambassador Gromyko on August 31 I took up another question that was disturbing us—the Russian attitude toward the provision we were advocating that a member of the Council should not vote in a case in which it was involved. The British held this same view, but in the Dumbarton Oaks discussions the Russians took exactly the opposite position and held to it strongly.

I presented to Gromyko all the arguments I possibly could to support our contention, and he promised to transmit them to his Government.

During the same conversation I strongly emphasized the great importance of an elaborate discussion of economic problems. The Russians were contending that economic and social problems should be handled by a separate organization apart from the international security organization, which should be concerned with peace and security questions only. I argued to Gromyko that peace and security were inextricably linked with economics, because a world in economic chaos would be forever a breeding ground for trouble and war.

I concluded the conversation by complimenting Gromyko very highly on his excellent showing as head of his delegation. I expressed this compliment in all sincerity, for the Russians had in general shown an admirable cooperation from the first day of the conference.

Stettinius and I met with the President at the White House on September 6 to discuss the principal outstanding points at issue at Dumbarton Oaks. Mr. Roosevelt first brought up the question of the location of the new organization. His view was that the various organs of the organization should meet at various spots around the globe.

He thought that the Secretariat of the organization might be established at Geneva, but that neither the Council nor the Assembly meetings should be held there. He believed that the Assembly should meet in a different city each year, and that the Council should have perhaps two regular meeting places, one being in the Azores in the middle of the Atlantic and the other on an island in the Hawaiian group in the middle of the Pacific. He felt that the International Court of Justice should return to The Hague.

The President was serious in stating these ideas, and he said he was planning to discuss them with Prime Minister Churchill, whom he was to meet at Quebec for the Second Quebec Conference later in the month. The State Department prepared maps and memoranda on the suggested locations in the Azores and on the island of Niihau, Hawaii, and the President expected to take them to Quebec with him.

Mr. Roosevelt had given much thought to the location of the United Nations, and this was not the first time he had mentioned his ideas to me. He felt that locating the Council in the Azores or the Hawaiian Islands would bring the benefit of detachment from the world. Being at heart a naval man, he liked the perspective obtained from surveying the world from an island out at sea. He had been eager, in the later thirties, to promote a meeting of the heads of nations on a battleship or on such an island as Niihau. He felt that, far out at sea, the Council would not be subject to the pressure of any country. He recalled the Paris Peace Conference and the pressures to which it had been subjected in that great capital. He felt that the League of Nations had been subjected to pressure in London before being moved to Geneva.

In essence, he said, he wanted to establish something in the nature of an international District of Columbia. (I often found the President stating his views on foreign events in terms of situations in the United States. The most striking example was contained in his speeches in 1940 and 1941 when he compared Axis planes, in the ease with which they could fly from Dakar to Brazil, with planes flying from city to city in the United States.)

It was illogical, however, thus to scatter the international organization throughout the world, and we never seriously pressed these ideas at the Dumbarton Oaks Conference. In any event, it was a question to be decided not by the four major nations but by the full membership of the future organization.

We also discussed with the President a Russian proposal that an international air force be constituted under the United Nations organization and commanded by the Council. Stettinius and I explained the position of the American delegation that we should oppose an international air force, and advanced our proposal of having air-force contingents of the different nations available for service on a combined basis at a moment's notice. This was in line with a statement the President had made on June 15 (Chapter 121) that an international police force would not be set up. The President agreed that we should adhere to our position. Stettinius indicated to Mr. Roosevelt that this question might be raised with him at Quebec by Prime Minister Churchill, because we had heard that Mr. Churchill had been somewhat impressed by the Soviet proposal.

We likewise discussed a Soviet proposal that small countries which were unable to contribute armed forces to the security organizations should be required to contribute territory for bases. Both the President and I strongly objected to this provision as being an infringement on the sovereign rights of smaller countries. We felt that all action of this type should be voluntary, and that smaller nations should not be compelled to provide bases. Russia's idea, however, was given some recognition in the provision in the Dumbarton Oaks proposals calling for special agreements to place at the disposal of the Security Council "facilities" as well as armed forces and other assistance.

In view of the fact that the conference was unable to agree on the question whether voting in the Council should be by a simple majority rather than by a two-thirds vote, we agreed that our position should be that we were prepared to accept either the British position that the majority should be two-thirds or the Russian position that it should be a simple majority. We ourselves had originally proposed a simple majority, but at one time expressed our willingness to go along with the British proposal if the Russians agreed. This point could not be resolved at Dumbarton Oaks, and was left open.

The question whether a member of the Council involved in a dispute should vote on that dispute hung heavily over us. The President and I authorized Stettinius to maintain our position, which the British also maintained, that such a vote should not be counted.

Aside from this, there was no question in our minds, however, that the vote of the permanent members of the Council should be unanimous on questions involving security. This was the so-called veto power. We were no less resolute than the Russians in adhering to this principle, with the exception of our view that the vote of a Security Council member involved in a dispute should not be counted. We felt that only if the United States retained the right to veto a proposal that force or other sanctions be applied, which would naturally include American action, could we hope to obtain Congressional approval of United States membership in the international organization. We had debated various substitutes but agreed on none.

Although the President and I had previously felt that the Charter of the new organization should not contain any reference to the suspension or expulsion of members (Britain had proposed the former, Russia the latter), we now agreed that the American delegation might act at its own discretion on this question, giving in, if necessary, in compensation for a concession on some other point made by the others.

By this time we were frequently referring to the new organization as "the United Nations." We had long since used this title in some of our drafts. The President felt this should be its name, and we agreed that the name under which twoscore nations were fighting the war to a successful conclusion was a happy title under which to work together following their victory. When Stettinius proposed this to the conference, however, we met with unexpected opposition from both the Russians and the British. Gromyko tentatively suggested the name "World Union." Cadogan said he believed his Government did not particularly like the title "United Nations" and had thought at one time of proposing a title including the word "Union."

On September 8 Ambassador Gromyko withdrew the Soviet objection to the inclusion of an economic and social council under the Assembly as part of the international organization.

By September 10, after three weeks of discussion, the British, Russian, and American delegations had achieved a gratifying amount of agreement—enough for the conference to settle upon a proposed final draft of proposals for a United Nations Charter. All the essential points in the tentative draft I had handed to the British and Soviet Chargés and cabled to Chungking on July 18 were incorporated in the draft now accepted by the conference, with the addition of a few new points. Since the basic ideas of the three Governments were remarkably similar right from the beginning of the conference, the new draft was not dissimilar from the original views of the British and Russians either.

This new draft gave the General Assembly greater powers. The Assembly had the right, on its own initiative, to consider the general principles of cooperation in the maintenance of peace and security, including regulation of armaments, and to make recommendations, although action on such questions was still the function of the Council. The latter now carried the name "Security Council," in preference to our former name of "Executive Council" to emphasize its principal role.

The new draft proposed that the agreement or agreements governing the provision of armed forces and facilities should be subject to the approval of the Council as well as to ratification by the signatories through their constitutional processes. This addition was designed to make more certain that all countries would contribute forces and facilities to maintain peace and security. The Security and Armaments Commission originally proposed by us was renamed Military Staff Committee, and the draft proposed that it should consist of military representatives of the permanent members of the Council and that similar representatives of other members of the organization should be brought in when necessary.

The British and Soviet delegations cabled the text of the new draft to their Governments for comment. During the next two days Soviet Ambassador Gromyko informed us of a series of decisions by his Government which enabled the conference to reach a still further degree of agreement. He withdrew the Soviet proposal that countries having insufficient armed forces should make territory available for the establishment of bases. He also withdrew his proposal to establish an international air force. Finally he withdrew his previous opposition to our proposal that the Military Staff Committee should be responsible under the Security Council for the strategic direction of armed forces placed at the disposal of the Council. He also accepted United Nations as the title of the new organization. The British had already accepted it.

Ambassador Gromyko gave us concern, however, when he stated that his Government did not agree to our suggestion that the four major powers should join in communicating to the other United Nations the recommendations agreed upon at Dumbarton Oaks. The Soviet Government preferred a three-nation communication, leaving out China.

On September 13, Ambassador Gromyko gave us still greater concern when he informed the conference that he had received instructions on the question of voting in the Council, and that his Government maintained its position that the principle of the unanimity of the four great powers was inviolable. Russia could not agree that the vote of a permanent member of the Council, even if that country were involved in the dispute being voted upon, should not be counted. He said he had made a number of other concessions, but it was impossible for him to give in on this point.

The conference now resolved itself into a strenuous discussion to break this deadlock with a compromise formula. I leave the conference temporarily at this point to go back a little and deal with our effort to insert the keystone in the arch of our nonpartisan policy to keep the United Nations organization out of politics.

121: Hands Off United Nations

THE REASONABLE ASSURANCE I had that the presidential campaign of 1944 would not make the proposed postwar security organization a puck of politics was suddenly shattered on August 16. Late on that sultry day Governor Thomas E. Dewey, the Republican candidate for the Presidency, issued a statement in which he said he was deeply disturbed by some of the recent reports concerning the forthcoming Dumbarton Oaks Conference. "These indicate," he said, "that it is planned to subject the nations of the world, great and small, permanently to the coercive power of the four nations holding this conference."

When this statement, part of a much longer press release, was issued, I had already left the State Department for home. After I was informed of it I asked some of my principal associates—Stettinius, Long, Hackworth, Dunn, Pasvolsky, McDermott, and Savage—to come to my apartment.

There I expressed to them my concern that Governor Dewey's statement might throw the postwar organization into the political campaign, with disastrous consequences.

Actually, I had already taken several steps to emphasize that the small nations would be given adequate consideration in the postwar organization. I believed that the preliminary plans for the organization should be made, at least tentatively, by the four great nations, Russia, Britain, China, and the United States, because they were the ones primarily conducting the war, and because it would be difficult for a huge conference consisting of representatives of twoscore nations to sit down and begin from scratch to formulate the constitution of a postwar organization. But I had made it clear, I thought, that the smaller nations would be duly consulted and their opinions given full consideration, before any constitution was finally decided upon.

In my address to the joint session of Congress on November 18, 1943, following my return from the Moscow Conference, I had stated: "The principle of sovereign equality of all peace-loving states, irrespective of size and strength, as partners in a future system of general security will be the foundation stone upon which the future international organization will be constructed."

On the same day I had sent telegrams to London, Moscow, and

Chungking, asking the concurrence of those Governments in a formula that we quoted whereby other nations could adhere to Paragraph 4 of the Four-Nation Declaration of Moscow which expressed the agreement that a postwar security organization should be established. This initiative failed through an objection by the British Government. The Foreign Office informed us on December 2 that, while fully understanding the importance of associating other governments with the establishment of the international organization, they thought preliminary conversations should first take place among the United States, the United Kingdom, and the Soviet Union. Otherwise a number of questions might be presented relative to the nature of the organization which it would be awkward to dispose of.

In the spring of 1944 some objections were raised here and abroad that the small nations were not being given sufficient voice in postwar planning discussions. To try to combat this impression I made a public statement on June 1 in which I said: "As far as this Government is concerned, whenever I have said anything on this subject, it has always emphasized the all-inclusive nature of the world situation and our disposition and purpose to see that all nations, especially the small nations, are kept on a position of equality with all others and that, in every practicable way, there will be cooperation."

During the night of June 13 I awakened and, unable to return to sleep, sat up and thought over this situation. Some Republican orators, probably in preparation for the forthcoming campaign, had been continuing their attacks to the effect that we were neglecting the small nations and working toward a rule of the world by the four large nations. Others had been attacking us with the charge that we were attempting to create a superstate. And still others asserted their right to discuss any phase of foreign policy during the campaign, including the proposed postwar organization, in the hope of making political capital. With the exception of my statement of June 1, the Administration had not come out with any statement on postwar plans. I now felt that the President, who had remained quiet on this subject for a long time, should himself say something, and say it emphatically.

As soon as I reached my office in the morning I called in Leo Pasvolsky and asked him to begin preparation of a statement on this point which the President might issue. The following morning I called him again to my office, along with several others of my associates. I handed them the draft of a statement I had dictated, which could be worked into the one they were preparing. They forthwith began to get together a final draft.

Meantime I had communicated with the President, who asked me to see him that morning. Taking Stettinius, Norman Davis, Isaiah Bowman, and Pasvolsky, I had to leave for the appointment before the draft could be typed in final form. Fortunately, we had to wait for the President, and meantime an official arrived from the Department with the text.

The President, as frequently happened, spent the first few minutes talking generally and telling an amusing story. When he paused to light a cigarette, I placed the statement before him and said that the need for such a statement was dictated by the increasing confusion in public discussion of the proposed organization, the possibility of leaks concerning our proposals, the fact that statements had recently been made by Churchill and Eden concerning an international organization, and the approach of the Democratic and Republican National Conventions, at which the organization, and United States participation in it, would undoubtedly be discussed. Bowman suggested, as an additional reason, the increasing number of rumors that the President and I were not in accord with regard to the future organization.

Mr. Roosevelt immediately agreed that a statement should be issued. He read our text aloud and then exclaimed that it was "awfully good." He wanted one or two minor changes made in the text, which we wrote in. The statement was issued at the White House that afternoon, June 15.

It first emphasized the nonpartisan nature of the discussions we had been having on the postwar organization, and then said:

"The maintenance of peace and security must be the joint task of all peace-loving nations. We have, therefore, sought to develop plans for an international organization comprising all such nations. . . . It is our thought that the organization would be a fully representative body with broad responsibilities for promoting and facilitating international cooperation. . . . It is our further thought that the organization would provide for a council, elected annually by the fully representative body of all nations, which would include the four major nations and a suitable number of other nations."

The statement made clear: "We are not thinking of a superstate with its own police forces and other paraphernalia of coercive power. We are seeking effective agreement and arrangements through which the nations would maintain, according to their capacities, adequate forces to meet the needs of preventing war and of making impossible deliberate preparation for war and to have such forces available for joint action when necessary. . . . The hope of a peaceful and advancing world will rest upon the willingness and ability of the peace-loving nations, large and small, bearing responsibility commensurate with their individual capacities, to work together for the maintenance of peace and security."

The President's statement calmed the clamor over the small nations for a time, but Governor Dewey's statement showed that it was still an issue that could easily be magnified into a major campaign conflict. When my associates met with me at my apartment on the evening of August 16, I said I felt I should immediately answer Governor Dewey's charge. I accordingly requested several of them to return to the State Department and begin to prepare a response. They brought it to me later that evening. After approving it, I read it over the telephone to Senator Connally, who concurred in it. It was issued the following morning.

"Governor Dewey," I said, "can rest assured that the fears which he expressed in his statement are utterly and completely unfounded. No arrangement such as described by him, which would involve a military alliance of the four major nations permanently to coerce the rest of the world, is contemplated or has ever been contemplated by this Government or, as far as we know, by any of the other governments. . . . The meeting at Dumbarton Oaks is for the purpose of a discussion among the signatories of the Moscow declaration as to the most feasible and desirable methods of establishing the kind of organization envisaged in that declaration and in the Senate [Connally] resolution, preliminary to similar discussion and early conference among all the United Nations and other peace-loving nations, large and small."

This controversy had aroused considerable excitement, and my press conference later that morning was crowded. In response to questions, I said I should welcome a conference with Governor Dewey to straighten out any points connected with the postwar organization and a nonpartisan approach to it.

On the afternoon of August 18 I received a telegram from Governor Dewey accepting the proposal I made at the press conference and designating John Foster Dulles, a well known lawyer who was his adviser on foreign affairs, to confer with me for him. Dewey said he was convinced that every effort to organize both temporarily and permanently for the establishment of lasting peace should be accelerated and he was happy to extend his fullest cooperation to the end that the result should be wholly bipartisan and have the united support of the American people.

This message arrived while I was attending a Cabinet meeting at the White House and was sent me there. The President agreed that I should send a reply agreeing to confer with Dulles, although he continued skeptical of any nonpartisan agreement with the leading Republicans. My telegram, in which I said I was immensely gratified to receive Governor Dewey's assurance of bipartisan cooperation in the effort to establish lasting peace, went off that afternoon.

Dulles came to Washington the following week, after putting out several statements giving his views on foreign affairs. When he arrived he consulted with Wendell Willkie and with Republican Senators, among others. The Senators, especially those on the Foreign Relations Committee, told him they had agreed with me on keeping the postwar organization on a nonpartisan basis, and advised him that Governor Dewey should follow the same course.

Our conversations began in my office on August 23. At the outset I handed Dulles a copy of our latest draft on the postwar security organization, dated July 18, and a copy of a four-page summary of its major provisions. One page of this summary dealt with the position of small countries in the United Nations organization, and contained six references to the draft of the United Nations Charter showing that the participation of the small nations was fully provided for.

I said to Dulles that the word "nonpartisan" rather than "bipartisan" should be used to describe the correct approach to the problem of keeping the United Nations organization out of domestic politics. "Bipartisan," I explained, meant that both parties would be involved on a political basis in policy toward the United Nations organization. "Nonpartisan" meant that neither party would be involved in that policy on a political basis.

Dulles argued warmly for "bipartisan." His thought apparently was that his party would thereby be recognized as being equally involved in the formulation of the United Nations agreement and could obtain some political advantage thereby.

I maintained, however, that, under our constitutional structure, we could not have both parties sharing the responsibility. The party in power had the responsibility for the execution of foreign policy. This responsibility could not be delegated. The opposition party, in my opinion, had the moral responsibility not to base its opposition, if any, to our proposals for the United Nations organization on partisan grounds.

I went to a dictionary and studied the definitions of the two words. "Nonpartisan" seemed to me ever more right. I called Dulles's attention to the fact that "bipartisan" referred to two parties, and there might come a time in American history, as there had come in the past, when three parties would have to be considered.

I did not believe it possible to have a nonpartisan approach to foreign policy on all current issues. All I insisted on was that both parties should approach postwar problems, especially the United Nations organization, on a nonpartisan basis, and that they should be agreed on this point.

I emphasized to Dulles that Governor Dewey was in a position where he might destroy the movement under way to get a postwar security organization, if he wanted to do so. I added that Dulles had a real opportunity to help put over this project which meant so much to mankind.

After a discussion literally of some hours over the words "nonpartisan" and "bipartisan" and all the potentialities of their meanings, Dulles agreed with me to adopt "nonpartisan."

When he came back for our second discussion, on August 24, Dulles said he had studied the draft of the proposed United Nations Charter and the four-page memorandum I had given him, and he considered the draft excellent. He appeared to think that it amply took care of the small nations. In this connection I emphasized the interdependence of nations, large and small, saying that they were all interconnected, and we could not consider large nations in one compartment and small nations in another.

The memorandum I had handed Dulles explained the position the small nations would occupy in the United Nations organization, citing chapter and verse of the draft Charter. The organization was open to membership of all peace-loving nations, large and small, on the basis of their sovereign equality. All members were equally represented in the Assembly and voted as equals except that on budgetary questions they would vote proportionately to their contributions (this last clause was later dropped). All small nations were equally eligible to membership on the Executive Council and would participate in the election of Council members. There were more small nations than large nations on the Council. No decisions of the Council on security matters could be made without the concurrence of at least some of the small-nation members of the Council; thus the large nations, although having the veto power in the use of force, could not by themselves undertake any coercive action. Finally, all members of the organization, large and small, would share in the application of measures not involving the use of armed force and also would contribute armed forces and facilities for joint action in accordance with their respective capacities and on the basis of agreements entered into by them. Dulles appeared satisfied with this exposition.

I went over with Dulles virtually every aspect of our foreign policy and our relations with any nations in which there was any particular interest. I doubt that any real point of our foreign affairs was left untouched.

During our discussions of the proposed United Nations Charter, it developed that there was an omission relating to the ratification of agreements for the use of armed force to assure peace and security. I immediately had a sentence inserted providing that the agreement would be subject to ratification by each country in accordance with its constitutional processes.

During the second meeting and during our third and final meeting on August 25, I went over with Dulles successive drafts of a statement we might issue. On the morning of the third day Dulles came to my office and said, in a tone of much satisfaction, that Dewey and he—meaning all the Republicans for whom Dewey was speaking, therefore the Republicans generally—were prepared to go the entire distance with me. We had been talking out differences very earnestly for two days, and we were both immensely pleased at this outcome. I was particularly gratified because at about the time of our conferences some leading Republicans close to Dewey had asserted their right to discuss during the campaign any foreign policy, including the postwar organization.

In the midst of our final meeting, Dulles telephoned Governor Dewey to talk over our proposed statement with him. I left my office so that he might have complete privacy, and, when I returned, found that Dewey had approved it with the insertion of one word—"full"—before the phrase "public nonpartisan discussion."

The statement, which was issued on August 25, read that Dulles and I had had an exchange of views on the various problems connected with the establishment of an international peace and security organization, and "there was agreement of views on numerous aspects of this subject." It went on:

"Secretary Hull and Mr. Dulles expect to continue to confer about developments as they arise.

"The Secretary maintained the position that the American people consider the subject of future peace as a nonpartisan subject which must be kept entirely out of politics.

"Mr. Dulles, on behalf of Governor Dewey, stated that the Governor shared this view on the understanding, however, that it did not preclude full public nonpartisan discussion of the means of attaining a lasting peace.

"The question of whether there will be complete agreement on these two respective views and their carrying out will depend on future developments."

I felt that our agreement was of much aid in uniting the Republican leaders in support of the policy I was both practicing and urging others to practice. Be it said to the credit of Governor Dewey that from the date of this agreement he uniformly rendered excellent service to the nonpartisan approach toward the United Nations.

A number of Democratic leaders and advisers of the President had communicated with me just before and during my conversations with Dulles, and had criticized the nonpartisan policy I was undertaking to follow. Their theory, like that of the President, was that the Republicans would not observe the obligation they had undertaken to give nonpartisan treatment to the postwar organization problems, and they continued to retain their doubts until the last. Some other Democratic leaders had felt that the international organization could not be kept out of politics. Nevertheless, once the agreement with Dewey was reached, they too were scrupulous to observe it.

I have seldom worked harder on any project than on the preparation for and conduct of the conversations with John Foster Dulles. I was convinced that, if I did not reach a satisfactory agreement with him, successful American participation in an international security organization might be seriously jeopardized. During the three days of our conversations I held repeated conferences with my associates to get their views and to communicate to them the observations being made by Dulles.

Governor Dewey wrote me on August 25 expressing his deep gratification at the result of the discussions. They constituted, he said, a new attitude toward the problem of peace. I replied on September 4, after submitting my letter to the President for his approval, that these conversations and his letter constituted a heartening manifestation of national unity on the problem of establishing an international peace and security organization.

I also wrote Governor Dewey suggesting that our exchange of letters be made public so that there might be fuller public understanding of our common ground on this important subject. He telephoned me on September 6 and said he would be delighted to have our letters given to the press.

He volunteered to send me shortly two or three suggestions in connection with the Dumbarton Oaks meeting, and added that he hoped he and I could carry on as we had done, regardless of the result of the election.

Two days later I received from Governor Dewey a memorandum suggesting several changes in the proposed Charter of the United Nations. One was that the right to bring a question to the attention of the General Assembly or the Executive Council ought to be extended to any state, and not limited to member states. Another was that the subject matter that might be brought to the attention of the Assembly or the Council should include treaty conditions.

We felt that the powers given to the Security Council and the Assembly to consider and make recommendations on any situation likely to endanger international security or peace took ample care of any need for recommendations by the United Nations relating to existing treaties. Nevertheless, I immediately sent Dewey's suggestions to Under Secretary Stettinius at Dumbarton Oaks, with the request that, if possible, they should be incorporated in the joint document then being formulated. The American delegation agreed that the suggestions should be inserted if there were no objection from the other two Governments concerned. The Russian and British delegations offered no objection, and the suggestions were written into the joint draft.

The Republican leaders wholeheartedly maintained their agreement to keep the postwar security organization out of the presidential campaign. In only one or two minor instances did I find any cause for complaint. As one example, Governor Dewey had begun to make references to the nonpartisan agreement and to infer that his party had taken the initiative in reaching it, and thus should have the credit for it. I finally drew up a statement that the President made public, calling attention to the origin of the agreement and the role I had played in it.

As another example, Governor Dewey made a strong attack on what he regarded as the secrecy being maintained at the Dumbarton Oaks Conference. I asked Hugh Wilson, our former Ambassador to Berlin, who was now seeing me on behalf of Dewey and Dulles, to convey to them my regret that the Governor should have made a remark that was destructive in effect, instead of one that might have been constructive.

I continued, however, to remain in contact with Dewey and Dulles through Wilson, and to keep them informed in detail of developments at Dumbarton Oaks. On September 11 I handed Wilson a five-page memorandum stating the principal changes, additions, and omissions that had been made by the conference to date in the original draft of July 18 which I had handed to Dulles.

At the same time I asked Wilson to inform Dewey and Dulles of the movement under way to call for Congressional approval of all specific applications of force under the security organization. I said that this movement might endanger the whole peace program if it were not nipped in the bud, and that it was up to the Republican leaders to do something about it before it was too late.

Dulles telephoned me the following day, September 12, to express his pleasure over the progress being made at Dumbarton Oaks. I told him the suggestions Governor Dewey had made for changes in the original document had gone through all right. I said that I was talking with Republicans and Democrats alike to get the question of Congressional approval disposed of. The difficulty, I said, was that if we got into a lively controversy over it, the Russians and the British would be scared off, believing that we would not be in position to implement an agreement on an international organization. I commented that we had enough ticklish questions with the Russians already.

Meantime I had continued my conversations with the special committee of eight Senators. On the morning of my last conference with Dulles, August 25, I met in my office with Senators Connally, Austin, George, La Follette, Vandenberg, White, and Thomas. The last-mentioned, Elbert D. Thomas of Utah, was added to the group because he had participated during the previous two years in the work of postwar committees in the State Department and had been out of town when the Senators conferred with me during the spring. Senators Barkley and Gillette were away from Washington.

Two days before our meeting I had sent these Senators a copy of our latest outline of the United Nations organization. During the meeting I called to their attention a number of changes that had been made since I first gave them a copy of the draft in April. These were based on my discussions with Congressional leaders and others.

Among them was a new paragraph providing for the encouragement of the use of local or regional procedures to settle local disputes through peaceful means. Another was a provision for the eventual addition of France to the permanent members of the Council. A third called attention to the fact that in the event of a dispute in which one of the nations on the Council was involved, the vote of that nation would not be counted in the Council's decision. Another was the dropping of the provision for an office of President of the organization, while retaining an office of Director General.

During our conversation the question was asked whether the Executive or Legislative Branch of the Government, or both, should decide upon the application of force under the postwar organization. Two Senators took the position that there must be Congressional sanction of the use of force in some instances.

I replied that the only practicable way to make the security organization work would be to leave to the Executive the decision as to the use of force. I added, however, that I presumed that the President would consult Congressional leaders in important instances before taking action. I urged that we go forward with our plans for the organization and that, when the Senate received the agreement for the application of force under the organization, it would have an opportunity to deal with the subject, which was really domestic.

I had a similar conference with Senators Ball, Burton, Hatch, and Hill on August 28. I then met in my office on the following day with Representatives Arends, Bloom, Martin, McCormack, Ramspeck, and Rayburn. Representative Eaton was absent from Washington. From neither of these two meetings came any objection to our plan and procedure for establishing the security organization.

Senator Vandenberg, however, wrote me a long letter on August 29, in which he stated that, if the American delegate to the security organization voted in favor of the use of force, this was tantamount to a declaration of war and therefore conflicted with the exclusive power to declare war lodged in Congress by the Constitution. He said he might be willing to see the President and his delegate to the international organization act in the Western Hemisphere without Congressional reference, but if an aggressor arose who could not be curbed except through another worldwide war, he did not see how we could escape the necessity for Congressional consent.

Two days later, however, Green H. Hackworth, Legal Adviser of the State Department, gave me a memorandum in which he held that, when the Senate approved the treaty stipulating the American military forces to be made available, in conjunction with other members of the United Nations, for use in maintaining peace and security, the President would have the right to use those armed forces for this purpose without further recourse to Congress. I had this circulated among the Senate Foreign Relations group and in due course, Senator Vandenberg's objections on this score ceased.

I met with the Senatorial committee again on September 12, present being Senators Barkley, Connally, George, Gillette, Vandenberg, and White. I brought them up to date on the progress of the Dumbarton Oaks meetings, and they indicated their satisfaction.

Several Senators raised objections to the proposal on which we had been working for many months calling for economic and social cooperation with regard to dependent peoples. They were greatly afraid of extreme views being advanced which they said were very unpopular in the United States.

I replied that I sympathized 100 per cent with their apprehension, and that no one was more opposed than I to the drastic views that had been expressed on some phases of this question by Henry Wallace and Wendell Willkie. I explained the more practical view we maintained, as exemplified by our course toward the Philippines, politically and economically. With one-half of the world's population lying on its back and living on the lowest levels of existence, I contended, if we should pass up an opportunity to exert our best efforts for an awakening throughout the world with respect to dependent peoples and their welfare and progress and instead leave them to be exhausted by their parent, reactionary governments, it would be a world calamity that would greatly impair the prestige of our peace organization. No special issue was taken with my views, although various Senators held out against extreme attitudes.

We spent some time discussing the question previously raised by Senator Vandenberg about the right of Congress to participate in directing the forces of this Government allotted to the keeping of the peace in conjunction with those of other members of the security organization.

I said to the Senators that we were approaching the most critical stage of our peace undertaking, and that there was, as they had indicated, a serious situation in the United States because of the question posed by Senator Vandenberg. Russia, I pointed out, was watching closely to see whether the American people were strongly behind our document or whether they were showing prime interest in this question and forgetting the whole question of future peace. Russia would want to know with reasonable assurance that this Government would not adopt a plan which, by allowing Congress to direct our military forces under the security organization, might not function as promptly as a threat to the peace called for.

Bringing up again the proposition that a good peace should be assured before the security organization entered into effect, I said there should be no issue betwen us on this point. I informed the Senators that we hoped soon to see our conferences with the three other large nations concluded, and then our work, with tentative reservations, would go straight to the other United Nations. I hoped to see a full-dress conference called to meet, probably in this country, in the fore part of November. When that conference concluded its work and the agreement on an international organization was ratified and put into effect, the appropriate nations would then proceed to investigate and analyze carefully the whole situation of the world with a view to synchronizing the steps to be taken in reference to the coming peace treaties. I should then hope to see the existence of the security organization made a powerful lever to promote the most satisfactory peace settlement in all respects, thereby insuring the best possible treaty to accompany the operation of the peace organization agreement.

As the meeting ended, the Senators seemed fully conscious of the extreme danger ahead for the peace movement if the United States became greatly aroused over this question, with the probable result of running Russia out of the picture.

The following day, September 13, I met with the leaders of both parties in the House of Representatives, Rayburn, McCormack, Bloom, Eaton, Ramspeck, and Arends, and went over the same ground with them. The next day I covered the same ground with Senators Ball, Hatch, and Hill.

As a result of all these penetrating discussions of the constitutional problem involved, in the course of which it had become so clear that immediate American participation, if necessary, in enforcing peace had to be assured, the American delegation at the Dumbarton Oaks Conference proposed a specific method which happily proved acceptable to all concerned. This took the form of the provision that all members of the international organization should undertake to make armed forces, facilities, and assistance available to the Security Council in accordance with "a special agreement or agreements," and that these special agreements should in each case be subject to ratification by the signatory states in accordance with their constitutional processes.

As I have already remarked, I had scarcely ever devoted so much concentrated effort and attention to any one project as to the nonpartisan policy toward the United Nations organization. I made detailed preparations for each meeting with the leaders of the two major parties. When we met, I had before me memoranda of the latest developments in our postwar planning, so that I could keep the party leaders accurately and minutely informed. Previously I held meetings with my associates in the State Department so that I might have the benefit of their advice. I have never argued more strenuously for any objective than I argued, not only with Republicans but also with Democrats, for keeping the United Nations organization planning completely out of politics.

The result of nearly twelve years' striving to lift foreign policies out of partisan politics was all that I could have hoped for. The United Nations did not become a campaign issue in 1944. The nation was not split over this question so vital to its future, as it had been over the League of Nations in 1919 and 1920. When the elections of 1944 were over, the nation was as resolved as before, and both major political parties were as resolved as before, that a United Nations organization should be founded to keep the peace, by force if necessary, and that the United States should not only be part of it, but also take her share of the leadership in creating and maintaining it, with all the responsibilities such leadership entailed.

122: Cornerstone of United Nations

THE MID-SEPTEMBER DEADLOCK at Dumbarton Oaks over voting procedure in the Council would not resolve itself. I kept in close touch with the President and with Under Secretary Stettinius and the American delegation as we labored night and day to compose the difference and bring the first phase of the conference to an end.

In accordance with our suggestion, the President had sent a message direct to Stalin appealing to him to authorize Ambassador Gromyko to agree to the British and American position that the vote of a member of the Council involved in a dispute should not be counted. Mr. Roosevelt sent this telegram after Stettinius, by agreement with the President and myself, had taken Gromyko to the White House at seven-thirty in the morning—a most impressive time—for a bedside conference.

The President and Gromyko talked for more than an hour. Mr. Roosevelt pointed out that when husband and wife fell out with each other they stated their case to a judge and abided by his ruling; they did not vote in the case. This principle, that any party to a dispute could be heard but could not vote, he said, had been imbedded by our forefathers in American law. He added that the idea of a member of the Council voting in a dispute involving itself would be unacceptable to the small nations, most of whom would not be members of the Council.

He sought and obtained Gromyko's consent to his sending a telegram direct to Stalin to put the case up to the Marshal. The President said this had to be settled at Dumbarton Oaks because if it were not it would be necessary for the British and American Governments to state publicly— five minutes after debate opened—that they were in agreement on this point, in contrast to Russia.

To the President's cable Stalin replied in the negative on September 15. He emphasized the importance which his Government attached to the preservation of the principle of unanimity among the four great powers in the organization on all questions, even those involving one or several of these powers. Returning to the suggestion we had made in our July 18 draft that a special procedure for voting in the Council be worked out for disputes in which one or more of the major nations were involved, he said that in his opinion this was the correct approach. But he pointed out that any departure from the principle of unanimity of the leading powers in establishing the international organization would be a deviation from the understanding reached on this point at Tehran.

The Marshal, saying that unanimity among the great powers presupposed the absence of mutual suspicion between them, remarked that the Soviet Union had to take account of the existence of what he called certain ridiculous prejudices which frequently hampered an objective view toward the Soviet Union. He said that other nations of the world should consider the consequences that would ensue if the leading powers failed to preserve their unanimity.

He hoped that the President would appreciate the importance which he, Stalin, attached to the question of unanimity, and that a satisfactory solution would be found.

The experts of the British, Russian, and American delegations now worked out a compromise formula as a basis for discussion and without any commitment on the delegations' part, for submission to their respective Governments. Under this formula the Security Council would act on a dispute, without the vote of the parties to the dispute being counted, even if those parties were permanent members of the Council, so long as enforcement action was not involved. On the other hand, consideration of and decisions as to enforcement action of any kind would require the unanimous consent of all the permanent members of the Council, whether or not one of them were involved. I regarded this formula as a substantial concession to the Soviet point of view and the absolute minimum of what we could accept.

When Stettinius, after consulting with me, telegraphed this solution to the President, who was now at Quebec for his conference with Prime Minister Churchill, Mr. Roosevelt replied that neither he nor the Prime Minister was inclined to approve it. He thought that the compromise proposal should merely be mentioned in the final Dumbarton Oaks draft as having been discussed but without a decision having been reached, so that it could be left up to a meeting of the full United Nations. He said that Mr. Churchill, however, was afraid that this last suggestion would be unacceptable to the Russians, since they would know that they would be overwhelmingly defeated in a United Nations meeting and might "get sore" and try to take it out on the other major nations on some other issue. I had the impression that the President and the Prime Minister were so busy with their discussions at Quebec that they simply did not take the time to give the question the serious consideration it deserved.

I thereupon suggested to Stettinius that he go to Hyde Park, New

York, where the President had gone from the Quebec Conference, and discuss the question with him personally. When Stettinius telephoned the President at Hyde Park on September 17 to make the appointment, Mr. Roosevelt said that Mr. Churchill was arriving the following morning, he himself was tired, he did not see how he could work in a discussion with Stettinius, and he asked Stettinius to tell me he hoped to be in Washington the following Wednesday, at which time he would be delighted to talk over the whole problem with me. He added that he had tried to get Mr. Churchill interested in the subject, but that the Prime Minister took the position that he had not studied the papers and did not have the time to get into it.

The British and we informed the Russians that the compromise formula was not acceptable to either of us, and Ambassador Gromyko stated that, although he had not heard from Moscow, his Government probably would not accept it either.

I asked Stettinius to see Gromyko and emphasize to him, on my behalf, the very serious consequences, both for the creation of an international organization and for the Soviet Union, which might result from ending the Dumbarton Oaks Conference without an agreement on voting procedure in the Council. Stettinius did so and asked Gromyko whether his Government would be willing to reconsider our position or discuss some new formula. Gromyko replied that his Government's position was final, and that continuing the conversations for a week or for a year would not change it. He said emphatically that the Soviet Government would never consider joining an organization in which a major power involved in a dispute did not vote. He added that he did not think his Government would agree to the holding of a conference of the United Nations before agreement had been reached among the four powers on this vital question.

Sir Alexander Cadogan likewise stated that his Government could not accept a plan to bring the draft proposals before a United Nations conference prior to agreement by the four major nations on all basic issues.

A difference of opinion now developed in the American delegation. One group favored proposing additional compromises to the Russians and, if the Russians did not accept, agreeing to the Russian position. It felt that continuance of the disagreement would prejudice the holding of a successful United Nations Conference, would impair the military cooperation among the three large Western powers in bringing the war to a victorious conclusion, and would adversely affect the prospect of Russia's entering the war against Japan. Some of them also felt that the Russian position was essentially sound.

The other group insisted that the effect of a lack of agreement on the voting arrangements was being overemphasized. A quick compromise on the Russian terms, they thought, might conceivably imperil the creation of the United Nations organization because it might be rejected by the British Dominions, the Latin American Republics, and other countries. They thought that most of what we could expect to achieve at Dumbarton Oaks had been agreed upon, and that the vital issue of voting might be referred for discussion at a higher level; namely, the chiefs of state. They therefore suggested that the Russian phase of the discussions be brought to a close and Ambassador Gromyko informed that the voting question had been referred to the heads of state.

Meantime both groups proposed that the President send a further personal appeal to Stalin, although each suggested different phraseology.

At that point I called the entire delegation to my office on September 19 to canvass the whole situation. I remarked that all who had seen the recent motion picture, *Wilson,* were probably impressed, as I had been, by the remarkable similarity between the conditions that confronted American leaders at that time and those that now confronted us. It was instructive to see, I said, that American statesmen then had done their best, often in the face of difficulties and obstacles, to arrive at agreement on ways to preserve the peace.

With regard to the present conversations, I suggested the need of patience and of taking a friendly attitude in dealing with our friends from the Soviet Union.

"In my judgment," I said, "which I formed at Moscow and have had confirmed in the months of the remarkably substantial progress since then, the Soviet Union has made up its mind to follow the course of international cooperation. All Russia's interests caused her to take this course. It is only through international cooperation that she can advance her general economic interests, her industrial development, her social welfare—all of her permanent interests. Like some other nations at various times and under various circumstances, the Soviet Union might get off the line, but if this happens she would have to come back into line in time because she would discover that any course other than cooperation was against her own interests."

I remarked that we had made so much progress already, and everything seemed to have gone off so well, that sometimes we who were in the midst of this effort were likely to forget that in any great endeavor such as this to establish an international organization, there would be hitches now and then. I said we could not expect to attain rapidly all our objectives, including this big objective.

It had been my thought for some time, I said, that the international organization might not actually be established as soon as some people thought desirable. As one of our problems I mentioned the view presented to me that we should wait to establish the organization until it could be seen whether we were to have a good peace or a bad peace. Another problem was our effort to bring into the organization the nations associated with the United Nations which had broken off relations with but had not declared war against the Axis. I had particularly in mind the six Latin American Republics in this category, not including Argentina.

"I have thought for some time," I added, "that it might be desirable to take all the necessary steps to perfect the lines on which the United Nations organization should be established and then to halt, in order to survey the political and economic conditions and settlements before deciding when we should actually establish the organization and set it in motion."

I again emphasized that it would be unwise to let ourselves think of rushing through with our task. The movement for an international organization to maintain peace and security had already taken four hundred years, I commented, going back in our country as far as William Penn. Moreover, the public might require time to get a clear understanding, particularly of new proposals. And the very process of getting agreement on points demanded patience. For example, it was necessary to explain certain things to the Russians that they did not understand; then there had to be time for discussion among the Russians themselves at Dumbarton Oaks; and finally there had to be time for the Soviet Government to discuss the issues. I concluded by saying we would discuss the points in suspense with the President in the next day or two.

When the meeting was over, I felt that my talk with the delegation had stimulated them to return to the conference with the determination to bring it to as successful a conclusion as possible. The two segments of the delegation—one urging in effect an agreement on Russia's terms and the other urging adjournment of the conference followed by a discussion among the chiefs of state—withdrew the separate memoranda they had presented, and redoubled their efforts to agree on a common program.

When Stettinius and I talked over the conference situation with the President on September 21, being later joined by James C. Dunn and Leo Pasvolsky of the State Department and Vice Admiral Willson and Lieutenant General Embick, the President said he felt that the only course to pursue was to recess the Dumbarton Oaks Conference with the Russians as quickly as possible. He thought that the voting question should be left for the future.

General Embick stated the view of the Joint Chiefs of Staff that, whatever course was followed, it should be worked out in a harmonious way so as not to endanger our relations with the Soviet Union. He and Admiral Willson agreed with the plan of postponing a settlement of the pending questions.

The proposed further message from the President to Stalin was left in abeyance. The President was then looking forward to another personal meeting with Stalin and Churchill in a matter of weeks, at which he could take up the voting question with Stalin personally. This meeting, however, was delayed from week to week because of Stalin's refusal to go to any city far removed from his general headquarters—the same situation that had arisen prior to the Tehran Conference. The President and the Prime Minister finally had to give in, and the meeting was held at Yalta, on the Black Sea, in February, 1945.

There the three statesmen, although each had previously rejected it, agreed to a voting formula almost identical with the compromise formula worked out at Dumbarton Oaks, to the effect that in the pacific settlement of a dispute the vote of a party to the dispute, even if a permanent member of the Council, would not be counted, whereas it would be counted in balloting on enforcement action. The voting formula actually adopted at Yalta had been worked out by State Department experts in the interval between the Dumbarton Oaks and the Yalta Conferences, and accepted by the President. He proposed it at Yalta.

To return to the Dumbarton Oaks Conference, Ambassador Gromyko on September 27, after receiving final instructions from his Government concerning the latest draft of the proposed United Nations Charter, communicated to the conference a series of concessions. His Government accepted the chapter on amendments. It agreed to the insertion of a provision that the American delegation had proposed relating to the promotion of human rights and fundamental freedoms. It consented to the paragraph proposed by the British to the effect that the section on pacific settlement of disputes should not apply to matters of domestic jurisdiction.

The conference agreed to insert in the text of the proposed Charter a statement that the question of voting procedure in the Council was still under consideration.

Gromyko took the edge off his concessions by stating that he wanted to make it plain that his Government's agreement to a general conference of the United Nations depended upon two conditions. The first was that the British and American Governments should meet the Soviet proposals as to voting in the Council. Gromyko reemphasized his Government's contention that the principle of the unanimity of the four great powers had to be applied unconditionally. The second was that those Governments should agree that the sixteen Soviet Republics would be initial members of the United Nations organization.

The President and I both felt that some agreement could be reached on Russia's first condition, but we thought Stalin's desire to include the sixteen Soviet Republics as members of the United Nations an insurmountable obstacle, and resolutely opposed it.

There were now five questions concerning the United Nations organization left unsettled, for future decision. These were: voting in the Council; statute of the International Court of Justice (the creation of the Court as a part of the United Nations organization had been agreed to); initial membership; trusteeships; and liquidation of the League of Nations.

To my great disappointment, the project of trusteeships under the United Nations, to replace and liberalize the old system of mandates under the League of Nations, had not been brought up at the conference. This had been a project conceived and elaborated in the State Department by my associates and me and enthusiastically concurred in by the President. We had not brought it up at the Dumbarton Oaks Conference, however, because of the specific and insistent request of the United States Joint Chiefs of Staff.

The Joint Chiefs felt that a discussion of the trusteeship system would inevitably embrace concrete questions of who should be trustee over what territories, and that dissension might therefore arise among the major Allies.

Furthermore, they were anxious to keep the whole matter open pending a determination within our own Government of a definite policy with regard to the subsequent disposal of some of the Japanese islands in the Pacific, including those held by Japan under mandate. It was their view that complete control of these islands by the United States for military purposes was necessary to our national security, and they felt that this could perhaps best be achieved through outright annexation rather than through a trusteeship system.

My associates and I, on the other hand, were convinced that the security interests of the United States in the Pacific, including the attainment of the specific objective of United States control of the islands for military purposes, could be fully secured through a system of trusteeship. Such a system was eventually worked out at San Francisco. While we agreed to the omission of this subject from the Dumbarton Oaks discussions, we did not intend to let the project die and hoped to bring it up again at the general meeting of the United Nations.

The Russian phase of the Dumbarton Oaks Conference ended on September 28, and the Chinese phase began at once. In opening this second stage, I said to the delegates that I was fully convinced that the excellent work already done, and that which we were about to undertake, would carry us a long way toward complete understanding among our Governments and toward the wider understanding which the peace-loving peoples of the world so ardently desired.

I added that the joint recommendations to be made by the representatives of our Governments would, upon the conclusion of the second phase of the conversations, be made available to the peoples of all peace-loving nations for full public discussion. "The strength of the organization which we propose to establish," I remarked, "can be no greater than the support given to it by an informed public opinion throughout the world."

It was also our hope, I said, that a full United Nations conference might be convened at an early date to bring to fruition the work already done.

The conversations with the Chinese delegation, headed by the eminent and very able statesman, Dr. Wellington Koo, offered no particular difficulties. The Chinese delegation had been currently informed of the developments in the first phase. Moreover, in general, they were already of our way of thinking. They offered a number of cogent observations, but they were willing to go along on the basis of the draft already agreed to and to bring up their further views at the general conference.

At the end of the Chinese phase of the conference the British, Chinese, and Americans agreed in two documents on changes in wording of the proposed Charter, for submission to the full conference of all the United Nations. In the first document we agreed that the Charter should provide specifically for settlement of disputes "with due regard for principles of justice and international law." In the second, relating to the economic and social council, we agreed that the council should provide for the promotion of educational and other forms of cultural cooperation.

The three delegations felt that all three of these concepts—justice, international law, and cultural cooperation—were already imbedded in the text of the proposed Charter as agreed upon during the first phase of the Dumbarton Oaks conversations. They were perfectly willing, however, in order to avoid any misunderstanding, to see them introduced textually into the draft. It seemed too late at that point to discuss the matter with the Russians, particularly since to open up this issue might entail long delays because of the need to exchange communications with Moscow, and might therefore retard the publication of the text already agreed upon. The British, the Chinese, and ourselves therefore decided that the understanding reached would be brought to the attention of the Soviet Government after the publication of the Dumbarton Oaks text with a view to securing their approval to having it presented to the full conference in the name of the four Governments. In the meantime these supplementary documents were not to be made public. The Soviet approval of this understanding was obtained shortly after the opening of the San Francisco Conference, and the points contained in the understanding were then presented to the San Francisco Conference as a proposed amendment by the four major nations.

As the Anglo-American-Chinese conversations neared their close, British Foreign Secretary Eden suggested to me through Ambassador Winant on October 4 that a follow-up meeting should be held by the foreign ministers of the four nations to accept the conclusions of the Dumbarton Oaks Conference and to sign documents. He suggested a meeting place in Africa. The illness that was now overtaking me did not permit my accepting his proposal.

Prior to the release of the Dumbarton Oaks draft to the press I sent copies to John Foster Dulles for Governor Dewey. I had previously telephoned him on September 23 to inform him that the first phase of the Dumbarton Oaks Conference had resulted in practical agreement, and that we and the British would shortly go into conference with the Chinese. Dulles wrote me on October 13 that Governer Dewey and he highly appreciated the proposals agreed to at Dumbarton Oaks. Although there were many imperfections and inadequacies, he added, the main thing was to get started, and the proposals brought that within the realm of early possibility. "For this," he continued, "the world owes you much."

Also prior to the release of the proposals we sent copies to our diplomatic missions in Latin America to be handed to the Governments of the American Republics. Throughout the conference we had kept the representatives of those Republics as fully informed of developments as we possibly could. A few of the statesmen of Latin America nevertheless had felt that they were not being sufficiently consulted on postwar planning.

It was impossible, however, to bring the American Republics into a preliminary conference such as Dumbarton Oaks without bringing in all the other United Nations. It was obvious that the most effective way to prepare the Charter was for the four major nations to reach tentative agreement first among themselves, always with the thought that their conclusions were not fixed and final but were subject to modification after discussion with the other United Nations. A full-scale conference among the United Nations at this point might have led to innumerable difficulties and differences of opinion and to great delay. Meantime the Latin American Republics, as well as all United Nations, had had full representation at the other conferences, such as the United Nations Food Conference, the International Labor Organization Conference, the Monetary and Financial Conference, and the United Nations Relief and Rehabilitation Administration Conference.

Prior to and during the Dumbarton Oaks Conference I had made every effort to keep the Latin American Republics, except Argentina, as fully informed as possible. On June 26 I had called the Ambassadors of the Central American Republics—Costa Rica, El Salvador, Guatemala, Honduras, Nicaragua, and Panama—to my office and had given them in comprehensive background report of our efforts to date.

I had sent a circular telegram to all our diplomatic missions in Latin America, except Argentina, on July 11 instructing them to inform those Governments that we were about to initiate exchanges of views with the United Kingdom, the U.S.S.R., and China on a postwar organization, and that as soon as possible thereafter exchanges of views would be held with other United Nations and associated nations.

In our studies, I said, we had devoted particular attention to the special relationship that existed between the United States and the other American Republics. I invited their attention to the President's statement of June 15 and asked their comments.

I said there was no inconsistency between what I had described in my June 1 statement as "our disposition and purpose to see that all nations, especially the small nations, are kept on a position of equality with all others" and the fact that our first conversations were to be held only with the United Kingdom, the Soviet Union, and China. Since these three nations and the United States, I pointed out, inevitably had to bear the major responsibility for the maintenance of peace in the postwar years, there was no possibility of the successful establishment of a general international organization unless all these nations were prepared to support it.

As the Dumbarton Oaks Conference neared its conclusion, I had two long conferences with Latin American representatives to give them all information possible on the conversations. On September 15 I called in the representatives of Brazil, Chile, Colombia, Mexico, Peru, Uruguay, and Venezuela, and on the following day the representatives of Bolivia, Costa Rica, Cuba, the Dominican Republic, Ecuador, Guatemala, Haiti, Honduras, Nicaragua, Panama, and El Salvador. I pointed out that in the Dumbarton Oaks talks we had insisted on certain principles already established in the inter-American community—for example, nonintervention and nondiscrimination. I added that we had also insisted on the observance of the rights of middle- and small-sized nations, that we recognized that the large and small nations were interdependent, and that we had sought in every way to increase the functions of the United Nations Assembly, in which every nation would be represented.

On October 9 we released to the press the proposals for the establishment of a general international organization agreed upon at Dumbarton Oaks. The President, Stettinius, and I made statements expressing our satisfaction with the work thus far accomplished but emphasizing that the task of planning the United Nations organization still required constant effort along with an unfailing determination that the sacrifices of the war should not be in vain. Mr. Roosevelt, referring to his extreme satisfaction and even surprise that so much could have been accomplished on so difficult a subject in so short a time, stated: "This achievement was largely due to the long and thorough preparations which were made by the Governments represented, and, in our case, was the result of the untiring devotion and care which the Secretary of State has personally given to this work for more than two and a half years—indeed for many years."

Three days later, on Columbus Day, Under Secretary Stettinius represented me at a reception given at Blair House for the chiefs of diplomatic missions from the other American Republics and talked with them further about the achievements of the conference. On my behalf, he assured them that he and I, as well as other officials in the Department, would welcome all opportunities to discuss postwar questions with them. A series of discussions between Latin American diplomats and Department officials followed.

After the Dumbarton Oaks Conference adjourned, a temporary lull came in the series of meetings on postwar planning I had held during six months with Congressional leaders. I took that occasion to send each of them a letter thanking him for his extremely valuable service as we moved forward in a spirit of nonpartisanship toward the creation of machinery for a just and lasting peace.

One of my last acts in office was to request Under Secretary Stettinius to set up a committee within the State Department to give continuing attention to keeping the security organization out of politics. Stettinius sent me a memorandum on October 19, the day before I left my bed at home for the hospital, saying he had instituted such a committee. Political Adviser James C. Dunn would keep in touch with Hugh Wilson so that Governor Dewey would be kept informed of steps taken to carry forward the work begun at Dumbarton Oaks. Stettinius also talked with Benjamin V. Cohen, one of the President's advisers, to ask that he do what he could at the White House to continue scrupulous adherence to the nonpartisan agreement I had reached with Dulles.

I likewise gave my hearty endorsement to a proposal Stettinius took up with me that the Department, because of the enormous stake of our people in a successful general international organization to keep the peace, should undertake off-the-record conversations in all sections of the nation to discuss with the people everywhere the meaning and limitations of the proposed organization and our expectations concerning it. In this way not only was the public informed and taken into our confidence, but also the responsible officials of the Government received the benefit of the thinking and indeed the prayers of the American people as a whole. These talks also revealed that Americans in overwhelming majority, as well as the leaders of the political parties, regarded the question of the future peace and security of the world as above any partisan consideration.

During October, Myron C. Taylor, who had returned to the Vatican as the President's personal representative, had a long audience with Pope Pius XII. Without expressing a final determination as to Vatican policy, the Pope raised the question of possible Vatican membership in the

United Nations, and sought information as to the terms under which a small state such as Vatican City would be admitted.

After studying this question, however, we did not believe it advisable to encourage Vatican membership. While recognizing the world-wide and beneficent influence of the Vatican, we concluded that Vatican City was too small to be able to undertake the responsibilities, such as participation in measures of force to preserve or restore the peace, which every member of the United Nations had to incur. We recalled that the League of Nations had similarly discouraged the admission of very small states.

In the same month Prime Minister Churchill had an exchange of messages with the President prior to his going to Moscow, in which he said in effect that he knew the President's mind so well that he thought he could speak for both countries and take up with Marshal Stalin the questions left unsettled at Dumbarton Oaks. Mr. Roosevelt replied, however, that he preferred to wait until the three of them could meet, and Mr. Churchill agreed.

The Dumbarton Oaks proposals were now before the peoples of the peace-loving nations for discussion. Before I resigned the following month I had the satisfaction of seeing these proposals meet with reasonable approval. Naturally there were criticisms, some of which were well taken. And admittedly the question of voting procedure in the Council still had to be ironed out.

Nevertheless, we had now laid a basis on solid rock for the formation of the United Nations organization, in agreement with the other major nations having the same aspirations as ours.

The San Francisco Conference in April, May, and June, 1945, worked on the basis of the Dumbarton Oaks proposals. These were supplemented and amended by suggestions put forward by the various delegations, including those of the four nations that had participated in the Dumbarton Oaks meeting. The final results were embodied in a formal legal text accepted unanimously, without reservations, and signed by representatives of fifty nations on June 26.

The San Francisco Conference is entitled to great credit for the immense services it rendered. No one would be disposed, however, to question the general opinion of those participating in the Dumbarton Oaks Conference and later the San Francisco Conference that the chief foundations of the world organization, including its basic principles and machinery, grew out of the five years' study and preparation that culminated in the meeting at Dumbarton Oaks, the results of which, in turn, became the chief foundation for the San Francisco Conference. In fact, if out of the Charter of the United Nations that emerged from San Francisco one were to take the Dumbarton Oaks proposals, the remainder would in a large sense resemble a tree without a trunk or roots.

123: Fourth Term and Resignation

SOME TIME BEFORE Franklin D. Roosevelt was nominated at Chicago on July 20, 1944, for a fourth term, he again proposed to me at the White House my nomination as Vice President. He said he knew I could have the nomination if I would take it.

The President knew I would not take it, however, because the war was still on and I was thoroughly involved in foreign affairs. I felt as I had in 1940, when I repeatedly refused an identical suggestion; namely, that I could serve better, in the circumstances, as Secretary of State than as Vice President. I expressed my appreciation to the President, but said I was deeply engaged in foreign policy and did not feel I could leave it.

The fourth term seemed more natural to the general public, including myself, than the third term. The tradition had already been shattered, and in 1944 we were at war, which had not been the case in 1940. The President felt the situation was difficult, we were in so deep, he was at the helm, and therefore he should yield to the widespread demands that he stand for election again.

I took no part in the campaign that followed. I was thoroughly absorbed in working for the creation of the United Nations organization and in solidifying a nonpartisan policy approach to it. I particularly wanted to keep free of politics while engaged in this work, which I believed to be above party.

The President sent me a memorandum dated September 29, 1944, in which he said: "I hope much that, in making your plans, you will arrange to go on the air about twice between now and election day. The country needs some of your clear thinking and needs to have it kept up to date."

He then said it was his thought that he would make one speech between then and election day on foreign policy, and he would be "eternally grateful" if I would have prepared for him a draft of a speech containing six points. These were:

"(1) What we have done in the past to promote peace in the world.

"(2) What we have done to promote international trade.

"(3) How we tried to keep our own peace after Poland was attacked, and before Pearl Harbor.

"(4) Some of the specific steps taken by the Republican leaders to block our efforts in all these things.

"(5) The steps we have taken for the future peace of the world in the past two years.

"(6) The prospects of a permanent international peace in the future."

The President concluded his memorandum by saying: "It is my thought that if you could outline what you would say in your two speeches and what you suggest I should say, the three of them will not conflict. It seems to me that this is a practical way of going about it, and I need not tell you that what you say will have very great weight both in the later peace proceedings and in our own election."

When I received this memorandum I had already planned to call on the President at the White House the following Sunday and inform him of my forthcoming resignation. I made the call as planned and told him, with a feeling of the keenest disappointment, that I had been overexerting myself for some time and now found myself in such physical condition that I should have to resign. I said I was leaving my office within another day or two to go straight to bed, where I must remain for an indefinite period.

The President did not seem to want to believe me. We had a rather casual conversation before I left his office. The question of preparing a speech for him and of my making two campaign speeches was not mentioned by us then or thereafter, although the Department later assisted the President in preparing his major foreign policy address of the campaign.

Three days later, on October 2, my seventy-third birthday, I left the State Department a very ill man. I spent eighteen days at my apartment trying vainly to recover, during which I carried on my work to some degree, and was then taken to the Naval Medical Center at Bethesda, Maryland, where I remained for about seven months, at times in very grave condition. The terrific strain of nearly twelve years in the State Department—half again longer than anyone else in our history—during one of the most crucial periods in the life of our nation, had utterly exhausted me.

Soon after I arrived at the hospital, the President sent the White House physician, Vice Admiral Ross T. McIntire, to reassure me about my condition and to convince me that I would recover sufficiently to resume my duties within a reasonable time. Then the President visited me for an hour and a half during which he urged upon me the wisdom of not resigning. He assured me I could take some leave and, after a reasonable period, return to my office at the State Department.

I did not hesitate but promptly declined to withhold my resignation. I said it was next to taking my life to be compelled to resign, with the tremendous plans to which I had been giving my chief attention not yet adopted. But, I added, I had almost utterly exhausted my strength in undertaking to carry forward these gigantic efforts, and I had swung down to the lowest rung on the physical ladder; I could not possibly retain my office with its terrific responsibilities and at the same time make a recovery.

The President then urged very insistently that I not resign until the end of his present term, January 20, 1945. I replied that personally I should be extremely glad to take this course; but I pointed out that if I did so critics would begin almost in no time to emphasize the tremendous responsibilities resting on me and the State Department and, while expressing sympathy for me in my illness, they would soon begin to insist that the critical nature of conditions required a Secretary of State on close watch at the Department, with the result that they would soon be criticizing the President.

Mr. Roosevelt then asked that I withhold my resignation at least until after the election. To this I agreed.

On October 26, a fortnight before the elections, I issued a personal statement praising President Roosevelt's leadership and characterizing him as a statesman equipped by nature and experience to meet the enormous problems confronting the nation.

A fortnight after the election I dictated a letter to the President, tendering my resignation. Happily, the war was now largely won. Allied forces occupied virtually all of France and Belgium, part of Holland, and the Italian peninsula up to Florence. American forces had landed in the Philippines. The menace of German submarines and raiders in the Atlantic had been largely overcome. Bulgaria, Rumania, and Finland had surrendered.

"It is a matter of special satisfaction to me," I said in my letter of November 21, "that throughout my almost twelve years at the Department of State, our personal relations have been uniformly and invariably agreeable, and that, by our joint efforts, many difficult tasks growing out of the foreign relations of this country before and during this war have been brought to partial or full completion; many great questions have been faced successfully; and many forward movements of surpassing importance to friendly relations among nations have been instituted."

Looking ahead, I continued: "As the war draws to a close there remains a vast area of complex and difficult conditions and problems which must be dealt with in the months and years immediately ahead. It is a supreme tragedy to me personally that I am unable to continue making my full contribution to such great international undertakings as the creation of the postwar peace organization, the solution of the many other problems involved in the promotion of international cooperation, and the final development of a full and complete structure of a world order under law."

I concluded by saying that when I recovered my health I should be always at his service in every possible way.

The President that same day wrote me a splendid letter, which he began by saying that my letter had hit him "between wind and water." "It has been very sad," he went on, "for me even to contemplate the ending of our close relationship during all these twelve years. It is not merely that our personal relations have been so uniformly and invariably agreeable, or that our joint work has borne true success in so many fields, as it is the personal feeling of not being able to lean on you for aid and intimate interchange of thought.

"This is especially true because we have come so far along the road of friendly relations among nations that I have counted so much on your help in carrying this work through the final stage of complex and difficult conditions which still face us.

"Your health is honestly my first thought, and I am really confident that you will be on your feet again in a relatively short time, even though you are limited to special tasks and avoid the daily routine of Department work. As of today, therefore, you must devote all your thought to getting back on your feet and on this all your friends will join in helping."

He then repeated his suggestion that I continue in office until the beginning of the fourth term, saying:

"I will, of course, accept your resignation as Secretary of State if you want me to do so. But I wish you would, as an alternative, allow me to accept it as of January twentieth, which is the end of our Third Term. Perhaps sentiment enters into this suggestion a little bit, but it would give me great satisfaction if we should round out the three terms. That means two months more, and during that time I could see you from time to time and get your advice on some of the things that will come before us."

The President then made a suggestion which would have been dear indeed to my heart had I been able to accept it. "Incidentally," he said, "when the organization of the United Nations is set up, I shall continue to pray that you as the Father of the United Nations may preside over its first session. That has nothing to do with whether you are Secretary of State or not at the time, but should go to you as the one person in all the world who has done the most to make this great plan for peace an effective fact. In so many different ways you have contributed to friendly relations among nations that even though you may not remain in a position of executive administration, you will continue to help the world with your moral guidance."

The President's appeal was so heartfelt and affected me so greatly that I had an earnest talk with the doctors who were treating me. Their answer was that I could not possibly return to my office for a long time to come. I did not think it fair either to the Government or to myself, therefore, to accept the President's suggestion that I remain in office until January 20. I felt it was only just that a new Secretary of State should be named to take over. And I felt that, as titular head of the State Department, I would be held responsible for foreign policies in the formulation of which I had no active part.

I therefore replied to the President on November 23, telling him I was deeply moved by his letter and eternally grateful for his kind solicitude about my health and his generous references to our close personal and official relationship of twelve years. After repeating that it was a personal tragedy to me that my state of health made it impossible to continue in the public service, and after stating that I would always cherish the ties between us of friendship and affection, I said:

"With all my heart I wish that I could meet your desire that my resignation as Secretary of State become effective on January 20 rather than now. I have consulted again with my physicians. The speed of my recovery is definitely connected with the extent to which I can be free from all worry and responsibility. You can well understand that, at a time like this, it is impossible for me to lay aside the heavy responsibilities of the Secretaryship of State so long as I remain in that office. In fairness to the cause for which you and I have worked so long together, to the country, to you, and to myself, I feel that my resignation must become effective now."

I repeated that, as soon as I recovered my health, I would be entirely at his service with whatever contribution I could make individually to the solution of the tremendous and crucial problems that lay ahead.

The President now accepted my resignation, and announced it on November 27. He named the Under Secretary of State, Edward R. Stettinius, Jr., to succeed me. My tenure ended officially on November 30, 1944.

In the days that followed I received messages of regret from foreign ministers and leading statesmen and citizens throughout the world, including Churchill, Molotov, and Eden. Mr. Churchill assured me of his "admiration for your long service in such exacting times" and hoped I should "soon be restored to health and able once more to bring to our counsels the great weight of your experience and wisdom in international affairs." Molotov, sending me Marshal Stalin's regards and wishes for good health, said he hoped that "your knowledge and experience will continue to serve the cause of collaboration between the United States and the Soviet Union as well as between other United Nations for the achievement and cementing of our common victory." I regarded all these messages as tributes to the principles I had long been advocating rather than to myself.

The President came to see me at the hospital several times. On one occasion, looking tired and worn—he was then only a few weeks from death—he said to me as I lay in bed, "I ought to be there where you are."

During the seven long months in the hospital I was frequently heartened by signs that, though I was out of office, my work was not forgotten. On November 24, 1944, the Variety Clubs of America conferred upon me their Humanitarian Award for 1943. On December 29 the personnel of the Department of State and the Foreign Service presented a bust of me to the Department. The United States Senate, on January 3, 1945, established a precedent when it accepted a bust of me for placement in the Capitol. The bust, sculptured at the initiative of the *Evening Times* and *Sunday Times* of Cumberland, Maryland, was presented by Senator Millard Tydings and accepted by Vice President Wallace, presiding over the Senate. A motion permitting its acceptance had been·made by Senator Kenneth D. McKellar of Tennessee and passed by the Senate and the House.

The Tennessee State Legislature also unveiled a bust of me in the State Capitol at Nashville on January 9, 1945. The State Senate passed a joint resolution, the House concurring, paying me many compliments and also, to my delight, specifically praising Mrs. Hull. The resolution resolved "that Tennessee, through this means, voices the State's grateful acknowledgments to Mrs. Hull, not only for her devoted and unremitting attentions to her illustrious husband during his illness, but for the intelligent support she has uniformly given him in his efforts to fulfill his responsibilities to his office, to his Country and to all mankind."

President Roosevelt wrote me on February 10, 1945, from the Yalta Conference that I was his and Secretary Stettinius's first choice as chairman of the American delegation to the United Nations Conference. He added that Admiral McIntire, his physician, felt, however, that in my own best interests I should not be asked to assume this arduous task. The President therefore requested me to be a member of the American delegation and senior adviser to it.

Also from the Yalta Conference I received a cable signed by Roosevelt, Stalin, Churchill, Molotov, Eden, and Stettinius, saying: "We have missed you at this conference and send to you our affectionate greetings. We wish for you a speedy recovery in order that all of us may have the benefit of association with you again."

I should state at this point that I was not consulted by the President or anyone else on policy issues prior to or during the Yalta Conference. The President visited me at the hospital just before departing for Yalta, but he did not take up any of the topics he expected to discuss with Stalin and Churchill or the decisions he might make. Nor was I informed beforehand of the purposes of this Government at any other important conference subsequently, except that at San Francisco.

I should say, in fairness to others, that since my resignation I have not taken part in the conduct of our foreign policy. I have followed in a general way from the sidelines the course of world affairs, commenting in public statements now and then on basic questions and talking informally with both private citizens and officials, but referring mainly to our policies in operation while I was at the State Department. On account of my health I have been obliged to refrain from any role of consultant or adviser to officials of the Government on foreign affairs, with the exception that, as a delegate, I offered some long-distance advice during the San Francisco Conference, and that I made one suggestion to Secretary of State Byrnes with regard to the Emperor institution in Japan, which I have related in the last chapter on the Far East. In conversations with officials who called to see me I sought only to repeat and emphasize the principles to which this Government had adhered up to the time of my resignation. It is not the province of these Memoirs to take up our foreign relations since the date of my resignation.

Two months after the Yalta Conference I was stunned on April 12 by President Roosevelt's sudden death. He had come to see me the day before leaving for Hyde Park and then for Warm Springs, where he died a few days later. On the occasion of his visit I admonished him about his health, saying he should take more rest. He said he was leaving the following day for this purpose. On the day of his death I issued a statement saying: "No greater tragedy could have befallen our country and the world at this time. His inspiring vision, his high statesmanship, and his superb leadership were factors without which the United Nations could not have come to the present phase of the war with victory just in sight. That leadership is gone, but his vision and the spirit of his statesmanship must continue to inspire us for the crucial task which even now is before us, the task of building a world peace. Mankind will be vastly poorer because of his passing."

President Roosevelt, in my opinion, was one of the greatest social reformers in our modern history, even though many persons might disagree with certain of his reforms. As Commander-in-Chief, his achievements were outstanding among those of other commanders-in-chief. In my opinion he had no contemporary rival in political skill. As long as I knew him he was always an earnest follower of individual liberty, freedom, and other basic rights and privileges necessary for the welfare of the private citizen. These included the ideals of justice, law, and order. He was a strong and consistent, and oftentimes an extreme, liberal in his views. The steps he took in the military field which led straight toward victory meant everything to us in the diplomatic field by giving to the force of our diplomacy the indispensable backing of military success.

When the President died I was composing a letter on trade agreements, which had formed one of the cornerstones of the foreign policy of his Administration. This I sent on April 14, 1945, to Representative Doughton, chairman of the House Ways and Means Committee, to urge strongly the passage of a resolution to extend the Trade Agreements Act, which otherwise would expire June 12, 1945. I was later gratified to see the Act extended.

Prior to his death, President Roosevelt had appointed me, as he had suggested from Yalta, a member of the American delegation to the San Francisco Conference and its senior adviser, with Secretary of State Stettinius as chairman. Being still in the Naval Hospital, I was unable to take a large share in the proceedings at San Francisco.

In a letter to Stettinius on April 20 telling him that I should be unable to attend the opening of the conference, although I hoped to attend its later stages, I said: "What happens at San Francisco will be an acid test of whether mankind has suffered enough and has learned enough to have acquired the vision and the resolution to build a structure of organized international relations, through which order under law can be established and maintained.

"I have profound faith that, whatever the difficulties, the labors of the conference will be crowned with success. I shall follow its work from afar with absorbing interest. So far as my strength may permit, I shall endeavor to make whatever contribution I can to its successful outcome."

Stettinius sent a daily telegram on the proceedings at San Francisco to Under Secretary Joseph C. Grew, addressed to the President and me, and I followed developments with close attention. Several times Stettinius telephoned me directly. I gave advice when I thought it would be helpful. Carlton Savage, who had been one of my associates at the State Department, was designated by Stettinius to keep me informed of the developments at San Francisco and telephoned me almost daily.

To Secretary Stettinius over the telephone I spoke as strongly as I could against admitting Argentina to the San Francisco Conference. I said that the American delegation had to regain the leadership in the Argentine question that the United States had lost at the Mexico City Conference.

I said it was evident that other delegations had outmaneuvered the United States on the Argentine question, and that consequently irreparable harm had been done. As I have already mentioned in Chapter 101 on Argentina, I would have voted against the admission of Argentina to the United Nations had I been called upon to vote. I was suddenly informed, however, that our delegation had already voted unanimously to admit her.

I also said to Stettinius that if the American delegation were not careful we should get Russia into such a state of mind that she might decide that the United Nations organization was not going to furnish adequate security to her in the future. Thereupon, I added, she might decide that, while giving lip service to the organization and keeping up her membership and paying her dues, she ought at the same time to go back home and establish outposts, bases, and warm-water harbors in many areas and add buffer territory and otherwise prepare her own outward defenses just as fully as if the United Nations were not in existence.

When Stettinius telephoned me to discuss the problem of regional security I commented that, if we could not check the trend of nations to rely on national and regional self-protective measures, the United Nations would gradually fade away.

On another occasion I warned against the great danger of military preparations as an alternative to international organization. I said that such programs were a question that concerned both Russia and the United States, and that if these two countries did not agree soon on the limitation of military preparations Russia might enlarge her activities for building up a federation of nations close to her. I added that if we were not careful the United States would create enough precedents to estop us from protesting against Russia's activities taken in the name of self-defense.

When Secretary Stettinius explained over the telephone Russia's attitude on the veto by permanent members of the Security Council, I said I felt that the Russian position would definitely narrow the base of the United Nations organization and that we must continue, with great patience—I emphasized this last phrase—to press the Russians to modify their attitude.

In general, aside from my disappointment over the admission of Argentina, I felt that the results achieved at San Francisco were highly satisfactory. I sent Secretary Stettinius on June 26 my warmest congratulations on the successful conclusion of the conference and the adoption of the United Nations Charter.

In a public statement on the same day I said: "We now have, at long last, a Charter of a world organization capable of fulfilling the hopes of mankind. It is a human rather than a perfect instrument. It has within it ample flexibility for growth and development, for dynamic adaptation to changing conditions.

"The Charter will work, and grow, and improve, if our nation and all nations devoted to peace maintain the spirit in which they have created it and remain eternally vigilant in support and defense of the great ideals on which it is founded."

Secretary Stettinius was good enough to write me on June 23 a letter from San Francisco in which he said: "Your many years of leadership in the preparation for this conference, including your historic achievement at Moscow in 1943, have paid rich dividends during our work here. The evidences of your wise statesmanship have ever been apparent. Your outstanding contributions to this great cause merit more than ever Franklin Delano Roosevelt's designation of you as the 'Father of the United Nations.'"

It was with keen pleasure that I personally signed the Charter. As

I affixed my signature, I felt that the many years I had devoted, ever since the First World War, to the study and then to the preparation of an international security organization had reached fruition. The task was now in other hands, but I was confident that with reasonable understanding among the nations, particularly the major ones, the organization could move forward with the grace of God to the task of keeping the peace.

By now I had been able to return from the Naval Hospital to my apartment to complete my recovery there. I issued a statement on the occasion of VJ day to mark our victory over Japan, and went to the White House at the invitation of President Truman to observe this historic event. At about this time I began to work on a long exposition of our policy toward Japan up to the time of Pearl Harbor, to be made to the Joint Committee of Congress on the Investigation of the Pearl Harbor Attack. I was assisted by Joseph W. Ballantine and Maxwell M. Hamilton, who had aided me in the negotiations with the Japanese. I personally presented this statement, about 25,000 words long, to the committee on November 23. That afternoon and again on November 26 and 27 I answered questions addressed to me by the committee.

At the end of 1945 I received the Nobel Peace Prize, awarded me by the Nobel Committee of the Storting (Parliament) of Norway, on December 10, 1945. I had been recommended for this award a number of times in my twelve years as Secretary of State. The first time was in 1934. I had then been occupying the office of Secretary of State only a year and a half, but some persons and organizations, whose identity I do not know, thought fit to suggest my candidacy for the prize to the Nobel Committee. The basis for their friendly suggestion was my work for trade agreements as a means toward obtaining peace.

In 1936 I championed the candidacy of Dr. Saavedra Lamas, the Argentina Foreign Minister. This was successful.

The following year, he proposed my candidacy, and other kind persons made similar recommendations. The Governments of Argentina, Uruguay, Peru, Nicaragua, Panama, Chile, Honduras, Bolivia, Belgium, and Greece formally nominated me. I then became aware that President Roosevelt had also been proposed. In April I made a full appraisal of the claims of the President in contrast with any claims I might have. My conclusion was that he was really more entitled to this recognition than I might be.

Accordingly I wrote strongly to the Nobel Prize Committee at Oslo, emphasizing the claims of the President and earnestly supporting his nomination. Simultaneously I requested and insisted that my name be withdrawn from consideration. I also notified Dr. Saavedra Lamas to this effect, along with others who I knew had transmitted to Oslo their recommendations in my behalf.

At the same time, however—and unknown to me—the President endorsed my candidacy. Later I was informed that the Nobel Committee had been distressed at my withdrawal and had decided to continue their deliberations as if they had not received it.

In 1938 President Roosevelt again proposed me. Dr. Saavedra Lamas did likewise. On December 27, 1939, the President wrote me: "I have been careful for a number of years not to let you know that I have been recommending and re-recommending you for the Nobel Peace Prize. Just for your own family records I think you may care to have copies of my previous letters and of this year's letter to the Nobel Committee. I do not need to tell you that I hope, before I am through, this very just and well earned award will be made to you."

In his letter of January 13, 1938, to the Nobel Committee the President wrote: "Since the spring of 1933, Mr. Hull has been largely instrumental in establishing on a firm footing among the twenty-one American Republics the so-called principle of 'The Good Neighbor.'" Also: "In the world field, largely through Mr. Hull's efforts, trade barriers have at least been lowered on the principle of the most favored nations' clause, thus making it possible for nations voluntarily to join in the reduction of economic barriers which have been so greatly responsible for isolation and, therefore, for hostile actions."

In 1939 Mr. Roosevelt based his proposal of my candidacy on my work on behalf of the Good Neighbor Policy. "It is my belief," he wrote, "that what has been accomplished in the American Hemisphere has been of great moral influence in other parts of the world, for it has furnished an example of what can be accomplished by such leadership."

In 1940 I again proposed Mr. Roosevelt as a candidate for the prize. But in April of 1940 Nazi troops invaded Norway, and six years were to pass before another Nobel Prize was awarded.

When I was informed in December, 1945, that I had been awarded the Nobel Prize for 1945 I was unfortunately in too poor health to make the trip to Oslo to receive the award in person. In response to a kind address by Gunnar Jahn, chairman of the Nobel Committee, outlining and evaluating my work, our Ambassador to Norway, Lithgow Osborne, read a message from me. Stating that "peace has become as essential to civilized existence as the air we breathe is to life itself," I noted that the first

General Assembly of the United Nations would meet the following month in London.

"I fully realize," I said, "that the new organization is a human rather than a perfect instrumentality for the attainment of its great objective. As time goes on it will, I am sure, be improved. The Charter is sufficiently flexible to provide for growth and development, in the light of experience and performance, but I am firmly convinced that with all its imperfections the United Nations organization offers the peace-loving nations of the world, now, a fully workable mechanism which will give them peace, if they want peace. To be sure, no piece of social machinery, however well constructed, can be effective unless there is back of it a will and a determination to make it work."

When I was notified I was to receive the Nobel Peace Prize, I promptly said to my wife that she had been so helpful to me in innumerable ways indispensable to the success of my work that she was richly entitled to one-half of the award. I meant that she was entitled to equal credit for whatever achievements I was able to bring to pass during the nearly three decades of my public service that followed our marriage. When the award arrived, I divided it between us.

I began the new year, 1946, by starting in January to work on my Memoirs. I had long had these in mind, but there had been no time during my arduous twelve years in the State Department to do more than think about them, and during the thirteen months since my resignation I had not had the strength to undertake them. I decided to begin them after I obtained the assistance of Lieutenant Colonel Andrew Berding, an old friend, a veteran newspaper correspondent and writer, with an education, including Oxford University, in modern history, who was then about to leave the United States Army after a long period of overseas service.

Our work on the Memoirs was somewhat hindered in the spring of 1946 by my receipt of 169 interrogatories submitted by Senator Homer Ferguson, Republican member of the Congressional Joint Committee on the Investigation of the Pearl Harbor Attack. Although my health was still precarious and I wanted to concentrate on these Memoirs, I spent some weeks, with the help of Joseph Ballantine, in preparing complete responses, and sent these to Senator Alben W. Barkley, chairman of the committee, on May 16, 1946.

I wrote a long letter on July 12, 1946, for publication, to Speaker Sam Rayburn of the House of Representatives, advocating passage of the resolution under discussion to extend a $3,750,000,000 credit to Great Britain.

On July 30 I went to the Canadian Embassy to receive the Canadian Club of New York Award Medal in recognition of efforts toward furthering friendship and understanding between the United States and Canada, and delivered a short address to point to the admirable relations between the two countries as an example to the rest of the world.

At the end of July, 1946, I was gratified by the issuance of the report of the Congressional Joint Committee on the Investigation of the Pearl Harbor Attack. The majority report, in which two Republicans joined, found: "The diplomatic policies and actions of the United States provided no justifiable provocation whatever for the attack by Japan on this Nation. The Secretary of State fully informed both the War and Navy Departments of diplomatic developments and, in a timely and forceful manner, clearly pointed out to these Departments that relations between the United States and Japan had passed beyond the stage of diplomacy and were in the hands of the military."

In September my doctor, sensing a coming relapse in my health, had me return to the Naval Hospital at Bethesda. There I prepared a statement to be issued on my seventy-fifth birthday, in which I pleaded for more cooperation among the large nations, without which the United Nations could not function effectively. But before my birthday arrived I had a collapse, and throughout that day I was unconscious.

Since then my return to health has been slow, but, with the assistance of Colonel Berding, I have gone on working on these Memoirs, convinced that the principles of sound international relations for which I fought deserve a full exposition.

In April, 1947, I was delighted to receive a visit at the hospital from President Harry S. Truman, who conferred upon me the Medal for Merit, with oak leaf cluster in lieu of a second medal. He read from one citation: "With a high order of statesmanship based on deep loyalty to his country, Mr. Hull served with great distinction and selfless devotion during the years of crises and difficulties. . . . He endeavored to prepare the United States to meet the rising dangers from abroad. He contributed immensely to the Good Neighbor Policy, which was to bear rich fruit in a tragic hour for the United States and the entire Western Hemisphere."

Then the President read from the second citation: "He made diplomacy a powerful weapon in support of our armed strength. He made diplomacy also a potent instrument in laying the foundations of a stable and peaceful world order in the postwar era. As a tribute to his effective work in bringing about the establishment of an international organization, he is now known as the 'Father of the United Nations.' "

124: What of the Future?

MY STORY BEGAN among the hills of Tennessee in the troubled aftermath of the greatest war the United States had fought up to that time; it comes to an end in the difficult epilogue of the greatest war the United States has ever fought. In the three-quarters century of my life I have seen this nation grow from a continental to a world power, with interests in every corner of the globe. As a boy I felt the effects of the war that solidified the nation so that it could forge ahead as a unit. I took part in the war that projected us into the Orient. I was in Congress during the war that taught us the interrelationship of the continents, though the lesson went unheeded. I conducted our foreign relations, under the President, in the war that proved to us all the need for a world organization to prevent further wars.

We are today powerful in arms and powerful in the cause of peace and humanity. But with our great strength have come great responsibilities. The heaviest of these, which we have accepted in the light of our power and duties, is that of providing our full share of leadership toward cooperation among nations for peace, justice, freedom, and progress.

It has been a popular view in the past, supported by tradition, that the United States has nothing to fear, that the future is assured, that our great resources and organizing ability guarantee our destiny, and that our institutions will endure forever. No belief could be more dangerous.

We have, in fact, reached the time when we should stop, look, and listen. We should analyze ourselves and our position in the world with sharp introspection.

· Are the people of this generation better off than their predecessors of former generations? Science and invention have given us many more of the desirable items of enjoyment, and in this respect we are undoubtedly much better off. We have all sorts of new things to eat and wear, and amusements to follow, compared with the limited possessions and means to enjoy life in the past. But in certain other respects we are worse off. We suffer from a striking lack of a broad education and of devotion to the spirit of liberty and law, and we fail to maintain the deep interest and keen alertness necessary for the proper conduct of public affairs.

Organized society during the past generation has, in my opinion, deteriorated. Behind the broad world policy I have outlined lies a first duty of civilized people everywhere to restore and preserve intact the precious ideas and ideals on which organized society must always be based. This goes to the very heart and foundation of world civilization and peace.

We have seen a striking deterioration of the whole political international structure, with threats of destruction of the entire international economic structure. In political and economic affairs the human race has suffered a steady decline, and it will not do to put everyone to sleep by singing of our progress in science and invention. Unless the citizens of our own and other countries keep themselves informed and give something of the same degree of thought and attention to public affairs that they do to their private businesses, we are going to fail signally in dealing with our own internal affairs and the problems of peace, greatly augmented by the invention of the atomic bomb.

Liberty and democracy in the world were more seriously in danger a few years ago than at any time since they were overwhelmed in the last days of the Athenian democracy. Our whole modern democratic civilization twice hung by a thread during the recent war—once during the summer of 1940 after Dunkirk and the fall of France, when Britain even with her Navy might have failed to repulse a full-scale German attack across the Channel, and again during 1942, when German submarines were sinking three Allied merchant vessels for every one constructed, and when almost every sea lane in the Pacific was blocked by the Japanese. I shudder to look back on those hairbreadth escapes. Civilization was brought to the edge of the precipice by the failure of many peoples, including ourselves, to understand and be alert to world conditions.

I cannot overemphasize that, unless there is a greater awakening, more intelligence, and more alertness on the part of the people everywhere, especially with respect to international affairs, and a greater understanding of what Government officials are trying to do, liberty and democracy are destined to a more dangerous and uncertain existence than that which they have recently so painfully experienced.

Democracy is not a static structure, like a cathedral or a skyscraper. Once erected, it cannot be expected to stand by itself from generation to generation. It is a living organism, and therefore must be cared for, guarded, nurtured, and guided.

We cannot rest on past achievements and present possessions. All the liberties we have today came from resistance to tyranny, either domestic or foreign; and most of them were won by blood and iron. Liberty came through the efforts of those men and women who were willing to die for it. We are their heirs, and must be vigilant to guard our heritage.

We Americans should return again and again to the fountainhead of our national greatness, the founding fathers. Their thinking, their struggles to obtain cooperation among the thirteen states, are magnificent prototypes for the thinking and struggles we must undertake today to bring cooperation among the nations. Like Antaeus who gained renewed strength each time he touched the earth, we can renew our faith and fortitude each time we study the writings and actions of the fathers of the Republic.

The founding fathers were familiar with all that human experience had taught about government; but, being mindful of the natural ambitions of man and the danger of too great a centralization of authority, they formed a government of checks and balances. They did know the meaning of human liberty, and hence it was the Bill of Rights and a series of restrictions rather than the powers conferred upon the Government that made the Constitution a charter of liberty. In the widest and deepest sense, however, our American history does not begin with the Constitution and the Declaration of Independence, but centuries ago in England.

The capacity for self-government is something inherent in the people themselves. It can be developed by education, but it cannot be created by arbitrary law. Elihu Root defined it as organized self-control. Men must be trained to self-government over many generations. The generations that founded the American Government derived their training from the Anglo-Saxons. With the growth of the country, other nationalities have been melted in and have fought for these same ideas.

Our form of government has proved itself in the past; it has brought us greatness and prosperity; it has preserved us comparatively untouched by foreign invasion. It has been able to function under the rapidly changing social, political, and economic conditions of the nineteenth and twentieth centuries. It must be preserved; but we shall not preserve it unless we are willing to defend it, support it, and give it every contribution of which we are able.

Our people should know that their own enlightened interest in their Government is the greatest safeguard of their liberties. They should realize that study and attention to public affairs demand real time, sacrifice, and effort on their part—day by day, week by week, year by year, and not just during a Presidential or a Congressional campaign. In the early days of the Republic, when two Americans met on the road they discussed the Government. They felt they were a part of the Government and the Government was a part of them. In these days, when two Americans meet they are more likely to discuss the motion picture they saw the night before. Government, of course, has become more complicated than in the days of Washington, Jefferson, Jackson, and Lincoln, but its interest for the citizen is none the less compelling.

The future of mankind rests upon the ability of statesmen and peoples to recognize that all are living in a brand-new world, and that the salvation of those who love liberty and civilization renders imperative a genuine awakening and a far more consistent and broader performance of their duties to the Government, to world order under law, and to organized society itself. We love liberty more than life; life must mean liberty, or it is death; and, under the modern methods of waging war, peace means both life and liberty.

Public opinion is an instrument the strength of which the public itself often ignores. A Minister of Louis XVI defined public opinion as "an invisible power which, without treasury, guards, or an army, ruled Paris and the Court—yes, the very palace of the King."

There are people throughout the world who make their living by creating confusion. Disaster to the peoples will follow if they are led astray and fail to rededicate themselves to an active, vigilant discharge of the imperative duty of keeping themselves informed and manifesting their considered opinions on events of national and world importance.

We, who are but a few generations removed from those who fought and conquered the wilderness, still have with us today the frontiers of endeavor. We still have to conquer the wilderness of want, oppression, ignorance, and fear. Has civilization finished its task—with poverty, despair, conflict, and even barbarism existing in some parts of the world? Our ancestors were without material comforts and aids to life as they pushed back the frontier. Each helped the other in time of trouble, and out of this mutual aid there developed in our people a growing concern for the welfare of their neighbors which characterizes the modern American in his attitude toward the rest of the world. This American is imbued with a disposition to help his fellow man less fortunate than himself. Hence his altruism, his philanthropy, and his idealistic schemes to help others. Let that spirit not weaken but expand in helpfulness toward other nations less richly endowed. It is one harvest that cannot fail.

Let us choose for our leaders men who know the needs of the people. Some of our leaders, like Jefferson, went into public life to promote democratic doctrines and to give the people their benefits. Jefferson cared not for power, still less for place or patronage for its own sake, and even tried to substitute Madison for himself as a candidate for the Presidency. Surely we have men today imbued with the same exalted spirit.

We have a desperate need for more religion and morality as the background for Government. The religious and moral foundations for thought and conduct require strengthening here, as well as throughout the world. There is no higher civilizing influence than religious and moral concepts. Corruption and tyranny can be driven out of Government only when these concepts give men the faculty to recognize such evils and the strength to eliminate them.

The States should exercise ceaseless vigilance to protect the civil rights of their citizens. The right of all citizens freely to vote should be guarded, and their pathway to the voting booth should not be obstructed.

Congress should deal with national problems from a national viewpoint. If what would bring an immediate benefit to a few States would ultimately redound to the disadvantage of the nation, the welfare of the nation must predominate.

The utmost cooperation must prevail between Congress and the Executive. The separation of powers of the Government ordained by the founding fathers makes such cooperation essential. Unlike the British Cabinet, which grows out of Parliament and is directly responsible to it, the American Executive Branch is an individual entity, responsible directly to the electorate. The Executive Branch must take Congress as fully as possible into its confidence.

I believe it vitally necessary that Congress and the Executive observe strict economy in government, and that the States, counties, and cities do likewise. In this modern world there is little regard for either public or private economy on the part of an increasing number of officials and individuals. There is great need today for more definite and stable rules and policies that will afford the fullest practicable measure of comfort and social satisfaction to the people, along with the fullest measure of wholesome economy in government consistent with efficiency. There is no practice more pernicious or contagious than indiscriminate spending by governments. And the most effective sinking fund for the retirement of national debt is economy of expenditure.

Let us adhere, as closely as developing conditions permit, to our time-honored policy of individual initiative and free enterprise. Government has an essential role of supervision and inspection to fill, to ensure that free enterprise is truly free and fair and that the people as a whole are protected; but it must not kill the spirit that made our nation great.

Congress and the Executive have an inescapable responsibilty to keep our foreign policy on a nonpartisan basis. Partisan considerations have no place in foreign policy, for there the welfare and perhaps the future of the whole nation are at stake. It is always licit to criticize foreign policy, provided the critic honestly bases his argument on his conception of our national interests; but it is inadmissible to inject advantages of party or of person into foreign policy. Attempts to do so weaken the influence of our Government abroad by presenting to foreign and possibly hostile governments a picture of divided councils, confusion, and lack of popular support of this Government's position toward the world.

I continue to believe that the two-thirds requirement for Senate consent to the ratification of treaties should be changed by Constitutional amendment to a simple majority.

The American people, Congress, and the Executive must keep sharp watch lest the United States return again to the dangerous policy of isolation. Two major wars within a generation should have convinced all Americans that we are an important part of the world, that conflict abroad cannot but affect us, and that our welfare, peace, and security are tied to those of other nations. We have a responsibility for leadership and co-operation which we cannot avoid, if we would.

There will inevitably be disputes and quarrels, disappointments and disillusionment in our relations with other nations, just as there are among individuals. But let these not support the argument that, if we mind our own business and have no ties with other nations, we can be safe and prosperous. For we cannot.

Few things are more certain than that during the 1930's peace-loving nations, had they not been hamstrung by isolationist forces in and out of governments, could have armed adequately in time, and by joint representation could have demanded a showdown with the aggressors, Germany, Italy, and Japan, and averted the recent World War. In the same way they could have prevented its predecessor. The age-old experience that free peoples are always slow to arm adequately for self-defense asserted itself disastrously throughout the period from 1930 to 1939.

Isolationism is not merely political. It can also be economic and social. It is an interesting fact that the American people, however much they adhered to political and economic isolationism until recent years, have never hewn to social isolationism. They have cooperated with other nations to the utmost and have had the most fruitful exchanges in the fields of science, medicine, education, philanthropy, and social services. They are the world's most numerous tourists. Had our cooperation in the political and economic fields attained the same high level, the world today would be a better place in which to live.

In the past, until 1934, perhaps our most flagrant violation of our duty to the world was economic isolationism. Ages of civilization have taught us that international commerce promotes material welfare, peace, and advancement. Intellectual and social progress in the Ancient World, the Middle Ages, and the Modern Era was the result in large part of the reciprocal influence of nations on one another. But we Americans have not fully learned this lesson. We showed the world a true example of the right way from 1934 until the end of the war by embracing a policy of liberal commerce, tariff reduction, and nondiscrimination, but since the end of the war there has been evidence of tendencies to return the United States to the disastrous course of the twenties and early thirties. High tariffs do not bring us prosperity. They do bring us unsalable surpluses at home and the resentment of other nations abroad. If each nation could have profitably exchanged its surpluses from 1922 on, there would have been no economic collapse in 1929.

The people of the States in which special interests demand high tariffs of an embargo nature should understand this. They should know that one successful attempt to put a stone on the high-tariff wall in favor of one product inevitably leads to similar attempts to put many more stones on the wall in favor of other products. Let them realize that high tariffs affect them in their daily life through higher prices, and let them, as consumers, keep their Congressmen advised that the interests of the people at large are superior to those of the comparatively few industrial and agricultural interests that clamor for "protection."

And let the Members of Congress appreciate the still higher issue involved—our cooperation with other nations. We cannot erect high-tariff walls around our nation and expect to cooperate, politically or economically, with the rest of the world.

The people, Congress, and the Executive must recognize the imperative need to bury isolationism as an American tradition. It should no longer be a part of American life any more than is the covered wagon. When President Washington said that Europe's primary interests were different from ours, there was then no steamship, no railroad, no wireless, no telephone, no telegraph, no internal combustion engine, no airplane anywhere—and no atomic bomb. The United States was then isolated geographically as well as politically from the world. The geography has not changed, but its significance has altered. Our language and customs may be different from those of the rest of the world, but we have the same interest in public welfare, peace, and international trade. Sarajevo was an unknown town to us until June, 1914; but what happened there was the first step that brought us into the First World War. What happened in the thirties in China, Ethiopia, Austria, Czechoslovakia, and Poland—all far removed from us geographically—was a cumulative series of steps that led unerringly to our involvement in the Second World War.

President Washington spoke against permanent alliances with other nations, although he countenanced temporary alliances. We are now, however, a member of the United Nations, which is in the nature of an alliance against aggression. Let none of us be shocked by this fact of an alliance. It is not an alliance against a combination of other nations but against any aggressor. It is an alliance not for war but for peace.

The creation of the United Nations organization, embracing all the peace-loving nations, was in my opinion a turning point in the political development of the world. The United Nations came into being after elaborate, painstaking study over a period of years by experts of many countries. At San Francisco fifty nations formulated and unanimously accepted its Charter as the beginning of a great, solid world structure of peace, able to defy any and all forces or influences calculated to weaken or undermine it. No one before or since has suggested any other mutually acceptable plan that was as good, much less better.

Let us not, however, expect the United Nations to perform a miracle. Its Charter is a human instrument, not a perfect one. The organization requires time, patience, and a spirit of cooperation among nations if it is to function effectively.

Major wars are generally followed by a widespread feeling of uneasiness, impatience, unrest, and suspicion. Our people and leaders and the peoples and leaders of other nations must be willing to overcome this feeling. They must examine with sympathy and patience the views of others. They must try to ascertain the true facts in any situation. They must avoid assuming adamant positions. They must refrain from exaggerating and overemphasizing their own claims and from appealing to prejudice.

The new spirit of understanding can find its most fruitful expression in the United Nations. The success of that organization requires that the frequent conferences of representatives of the nations made possible by the provisions of the Charter should be grounded on the broad patriotism of world peace and human progress.

The United Nations deserves and must have the unwavering support of the American people. Let us not be discouraged over the dissensions voiced in the initial councils of the new organization. Let us not on the one hand insist that the United Nations cannot work and we must there-fore return to nationalism and isolation, nor on the other hand urge that the United Nations is inadequate and we must therefore replace it with a world government. Restless persons, agitators, and even well-meaning persons will offer plans and projects for new organizations, the sole effect of which will be to obstruct the peace movement. We can do the cause of peace no greater service than by working at all times possible with and within the United Nations, and neglecting no opportunity to promote its prestige and the prompt acceptance of its conclusions.

It would be impossible to exaggerate the importance to nations and peoples of maintaining at all times a spirit of peace and of cooperation to maintain peace—by force if necessary. This common world undertaking must contemplate the availability of armed forces at all times sufficient to prevent the use of any kind of military force or any kind of weapon capable of undermining, materially injuring, or destroying the world structure of peace based on world order under law.

We should strive, however, to promote the idea of universal reduction of armaments, with complete United Nations inspection in all countries to make sure it is carried out. A wild race of armaments, economic and military, is an indictment of civilization. Proponents of heavy armaments are playing with the lives and property of tens of millions of men, women, and children. But disarmament must be comparative, and we must never again permit the United States to decline to a level of relative military helplessness. Other nations, in looking at us as we explain our foreign policies, must still be able to see over our shoulder the symbols of our power, sufficient at all times to preserve our security.

We Americans need to practice moderation in our expressions of opin-ion concerning other nations. As a people we are too prone to condemn other nations and rulers, to apply epithets, to caricature, to ridicule. We forget that our sharp words are not buried in newspaper columns or lost on the rostrum or radio. They come to the knowledge of the governments and peoples they anathematize; they are reproduced and commented upon by the press and radio of those countries, which may not understand our freedom of criticism; and they hamper the conduct of our foreign relations. To the old rule that one should count ten before berating another individual I would add a new rule that we should count ten hours or ten days before berating another nation, and meantime we should try to ascertain the true and full facts of the event that seems to call for condemnation.

This rule I would call to the particular attention of the minority groups in the United States, whether racial, national, or religious. The Constitution was designed to protect all the people, but especially minorities. Nevertheless, in recent years some of these groups, aided by the improvement of methods for diffusing information and propaganda, have raised a voice and exerted a pressure in foreign affairs far out of proportion to their numbers. These interfering minorities are generally composed of or influenced by left-wing or reactionary extremists and also by persons who have immigrated in recent years and are chronic agitators and advocates of ideas calculated to undermine both our political and our economic structure. On many critical occasions, when the international relations of our Government require the most delicate and careful handling and the support of a unanimous and aggressive public opinion, some of these groups scatter poison or otherwise play havoc with them. Men and women who have left other countries and chosen the United States as their home should think of foreign policy not in terms of the land they left behind them but in terms of the land that is giving them refuge and sustenance. And at the same time the majority of our citizens, while scrupulously guarding and protecting all the rights of minorities, should be consistently on the alert to prevent the confusion, misunderstanding, and misrepresentation, with steadily increasing bitterness and hatred, that inevitably result from widespread, violent, and troublemaking propaganda on the part of minorities.

Our great nation should stand always for the progressive attainment of self-government and eventual independence by dependent peoples when they are ready for it, in accordance with our example in the Philippines. But let our policy in this respect not be limited to one of exhortation only but also embrace active economic help to raise the level of life of such peoples.

Let us stand, too, for the free play of public opinion in the world. Today there is, generally, no free press or radio around the globe. Perhaps half the nations suppress, filter, or color information. Not until the thoughts of peoples can be fully and freely communicated from one to another can we hope for the attainment of the real understanding that will make wars impossible.

We must recognize and be willing to assume our commitments regarding our former enemies, Germany and Japan. If it is necessary to maintain surveillance, military and otherwise, over them for decades to come, then we should be willing to maintain it. There should be no thought among us of quick withdrawal from Europe or Asia. We cannot withdraw, for where can we go? The world is with us, here and now, and all about us. It is in our front yard, in our back yard, at our side porch. To withdraw from Europe and Asia is to pull Europe and Asia in upon us.

In the Western Hemisphere let us continue to develop and expand the Good Neighbor Policy in all possible ways. The fruit we have gathered from that policy is sufficient warrant for the planting of further seed. In our time of need our friends to the South, with one exception, became our friends indeed. Let the Good Neighbor Policy become a permanent foundation of our foreign policy. In sowing a crop of cooperation in our own garden we can give the world an example of the highest type of political harvest.

We should maintain forever the friendliest relations and the closest cooperation with the United Kingdom and the British Dominions, but with the proviso that this be not exclusive. Let us not be persuaded that a union of the English-speaking peoples is the cure-all for the ills of the world. Let us consult with other interested nations whenever we consult with Britain.

Despite the dangerous conduct of the Soviet Union in the last several years, let us follow in respect to it a policy of patience, combined with firmness, inspired by calm strength, and rooted in an unswerving determination that, so far as lies in our power, mankind shall at long last attain a just and peaceful world order. In dealing with the Soviet Union we must never waver in this determination, or give any evidence of weakness, or cease to insist that, though the Soviet Union is entitled to freedom from intervention in its domestic affairs by any other nation, its government has no right to force Communism on other nations or to intervene in their domestic affairs in any other way.

During my years as Secretary of State we consistently pursued the broad policy of nonintervention, and we lost no opportunity to condemn and oppose all practices in violation of that precious doctrine, whether such practices were conducted by Germany or Japan or the Soviet Union or any other country. We repeatedly emphasized to the Soviet Government that its idea of penetrating into other countries by promoting within them subversive movements designed to supplant their established forms of government with Communist systems like its own, while at the same time claiming for the Soviet Union immunity from such intervention, was a hopelessly unsound and hazardous theory of international relations. No nation that had once dedicated itself to popular forms of government could tolerate indefinitely the enforced substitution for its free institutions of a system of tyranny, destitution, and lowering of all moral standards that are the inevitable concomitants of a police state. We repeatedly stressed our hope that the Soviet leaders would themselves in due course recognize this.

The sovereign equality of all peaceful nations, large and small, and the right of each of them to freedom from intervention in its internal affairs are among the cardinal principles of the United Nations, to which the Soviet Union, together with the United States and more than fifty other nations, has pledged its solemn adherence. The faithful observance of these principles constitutes an indispensable foundation for international cooperation without which no nation can progress or feel secure. Much time, perhaps many years, of unremitting effort may be necessary before the Soviet leaders come to understand fully that the ways of cooperation with other nations are to their country's benefit as well as to ours. However difficult and hopeless the task may on occasion appear to be, let us take this time, employing neither denunciation nor threats, but a friendly, honest, stalwart approach. Every feasible opportunity should be used to converse with the Soviet leaders, within the United Nations or wherever possible.

It may be that our efforts will fail and the leaders of Soviet Russia will fall into the same tragic error that has brought to their doom so many ancient and modern masters of police states. If that utter calamity should come to pass, let it not be said that the United States had neglected any honorable means to avert it. While keeping ourselves strong to face any eventuality, let us work unceasingly toward the end that the leaders of the Russian people and we may ultimately see eye to eye on the values of human freedom and on the preciousness of enduring peace based on justice and fair dealing.

My twelve years as Secretary of State were a difficult period in which to live. It was an epoch filled with conflicts, tragedies, and seeming impossibilities. One could not come through it, however, without feeling its vibrant pulsations. And it has left the nations of the world with an opportunity for advancement such as they have never had before, such as they may never have again.

But our nation and all nations, including especially our major allies in the recent death struggle against the forces of tyranny, would merely deceive themselves if they failed to realize that they are facing the supreme crisis of all ages. If they resolve that the forces of peace, order, and civilization shall proceed unceasingly with the task of restoring their economic health and solidifying their political and moral strength, they will thereby become powerful enough to preserve the peace, freedom, and culture of the world. On the other hand, if some nations or peoples persist in destructive policies and methods calculated seriously to cripple or shatter this great world undertaking, the human race may yet be dragged down to unimaginably low levels of barbarism.

All peace-seeking nations should make every effort without ceasing to prevail on one another to do teamwork, on a basis of fair dealing, equality, mutual respect, and nonintervention in one another's affairs— with understanding and trust but without favoritism or appeasement— toward the attainment of the basic principles of international relations to which they committed themselves in accepting the Charter of the United Nations. The one inescapable duty and responsibility of all nations and peoples is to maintain and develop the United Nations as an international organization capable of establishing real peace and keeping such peace permanently. It is well-nigh axiomatic that all countries will receive equal and incalculable benefits from a faithful performance of their United Nations duties, but a bottomless pit is liable to open in the pathway of nations failing in such performance. It is beyond any doubt to the best interest of each and all to join together in perpetuating the world organization and in making it truly effective.

The experience of the League of Nations proved conclusively that a world security organization could not function effectively toward this all-important end unless all major nations were members and were cooperating. The same is true of the United Nations organization. If any of the major nations should choose the course of noncooperation, the others, willing to support this great world movement, must nevertheless carry it forward with all their strength. They must resolutely resist in every legitimate way any acts calculated to impede or undermine the organization. But the door should always remain open to all nations, including those that are temporarily misled into recalcitrant noncooperation, once they had demonstrated their willingness to follow the principles embodied in the United Nations Charter.

I am firmly convinced that in the world of today all nations will be forced to the conclusion that cooperation for law, justice, and peace is the only alternative to a constant race in armaments—including atomic armaments—and to other disruptive practices that will bring the nations participating in them on either side to a common ruin, the equivalent of universal suicide.

I conclude these Memoirs with the abiding faith that our destiny as a nation is still before us, not behind us. We have reached maturity, but at the same time we are a youthful nation in vigor and resource, and one of the oldest of the nations in the unbroken span of our form of government. The skill, the energy, the strength of purpose, and the natural wealth that made the United States great are still with us, augmented and heightened. If we are willing from time to time to stop and appreciate our past, appraise our present and prepare for our future, I am convinced that the horizons of achievement still stretch before us like the unending Plains. And no achievement can be higher than that of working in harmony with other nations so that the lash of war may be lifted from our backs and a peace of lasting friendship descend upon us.

THE END

Index

[Roosevelt, Churchill, Stalin, De Gaulle, Mussolini, and Hitler are so closely identified with the policies of their respective countries that, in order to avoid repetition, entries under their names have been limited to personal matters, with policies indexed under country and by subject. Entries for the author have been treated in the same manner.]

Abe, Nobuyuki, 717, 728
Abetz, Otto, 958, 959, 962
Abyssinia. See Ethiopia
Acheson, Dean, 1633, 1635
Adams, John Quincy, 292
Adana, Turkey, 1365
Addis Ababa, Ethiopia, 468–469, 579
Addresses by CH, preparation, 392–393; see also subject
Adler, Cyrus, 714–715
Advisory Committee on the Far East, League of Nations, 272
Advisory Council for Italy, Inter-Allied, 1283–1284, 1317, 1551, 1552, 1556, 1557, 1558, 1559, 1564, 1565
Afghanistan, 1496–1497
Africa, North. See North Africa
Africa, West. See Dakar
African Exploration and Development Corporation, 423–425
Aggressor, definition of, 227
Agricultural Adjustment Administration, 248, 321, 353
Agricultural mission to Saudi Arabia, 1512
Agriculture Conference (1943), 1643, 1654–1655
Aiken, Frank, 1352–1354
Air bases. See Bases
Aircraft production, U.S., CH recommendation for increase in, 767, 910
Airplanes, new, at Martinique, 818, 820, 907
Albania, occupation by Italy, 618–619; U.S. nonrecognition and closing of Legation in Tirana, 619; freezing of assets in U.S., 945
Aldrich, Nelson W., 60–61, 70; see also Payne-Aldrich tariff
Alexander, De Alva Stanwood, 220
Alfieri, Dino, 844–845

Algeria, 1191–1192, 1201, 1220
Aliens in U.S., Italian, 1548
Al-Khuri, Sheik, 1544
Allen, Henry, 663
Allied Control Commissions, for Italy, 1245–1246, 1555, 1557, 1560, 1563, 1565, 1566; for Germany, 1285, 1618–1619; for Axis satellites, 1461
Alling, Paul, 1523
Amau, Eiji, 279, 284
Ambassadors. See Foreign Service
American-British Mandate Treaty (1924), 1528
American Federation of Labor, 545
American Palestine Committee, 1531
American Principles, Declaration of (1938), 609–610
American republics, trade with U.S., 308; exemption from U.S. Neutrality Act, 466; U.S. nonintervention policy, 484; Axis activities in, by 1936, 495–496; by 1938, 601–602 (see also Argentina) ; solidarity, 608, 1398; joint protest on invasion of Low Countries, 764; economic effects of World War II, 827–828; U.S. naval and air bases in, 833, 841–842, 1422–1423; appeal to Spain not to enter war, 941; agreements with U.S. for military, naval, and air missions, 1139; admission of citizens of to U.S. Naval Academy, 1139; training of aviation technicians in U.S., 1140; Ambassadors' conference at Washington (1945), 1405, 1407; efforts by Argentina to overthrow other governments, 1388–1389, 1420, 1421; support of U.S. during war, 1139, 1422–1426; diplomatic relations with Italy, 1567–1568; informed on developments at Dumbarton Oaks, 1709–1711; see also

American republics—*Continued*
Good Neighbor policy; Buenos Aires, Havana, Lima, Mexico City, Montevideo, Panama, Rio de Janeiro Conferences; *and individual countries*
American Society of International Law, 764, 941
American Volunteer Group in China, 983, 1057
American Zeppelin Transport Co., 597–598
Americans. *See* Citizens, U.S.
Amery, Leopold S., 1487, 1490
Amtorg, Russian trading organization in New York, 293, 296
Anglo-American Caribbean Commission, 1236–1237, 1475
Antarctic claims, U.S., development, 758–759
Anti-Comintern Pact (1936), 488, 489, 556, 634, 639, 717, 908, 980
Antigua, U.S.-British agreement for lease of bases, 831–843
Antiwar pacts. *See* Kellogg-Briand Pact; Saavedra Lamas Antiwar Pact
Anzio, Italy, 1552, 1553
Arab-Jewish question, propaganda in U.S., 1513; U.S. relations with Palestine, 1528; British suspension of Jewish immigration to Palestine, 1528–1530; Zionist agitation in U.S. against suspension, 1531; Arab repercussions, 1531–1532; U.S. efforts toward settlement, 1532–1534; British suspension relaxed, 1534; U.S. Congressional resolutions introduced favoring Jewish national home, 1534–1535; Arab protests against resolution, 1535; FDR statement to Jewish leaders, 1536; summary of U.S. Palestine policy, 1537
Arab states, federation, 1498, 1540, 1546–1547, 1645
Arabia. *See* Saudi Arabia
Arabian American Oil Co., 1511, 1518, 1519, 1520–1521, 1524
Aranha, Oswaldo, 499, 604, 1145, 1336, 1337, 1398, 1423
Arbitration, of international disputes, 153, 172, 422–423, 443, 500, 622, 1254, 1436–1442, 1447–1449; as means for peace, 174; inter-American convention

Arbitration—*Continued*
(1929), 322, 328, 332; Brussels Conference (1937), 550–556
Arctic claims, U.S., development, 758–759
Arends, Leslie C., 1670, 1696, 1698
Argenlieu, Georges Thierry d', 1202–1203
Argentina, in Cuban situation, 314, 316; Antiwar Pact, 309, 322, 328, 332, 344, 469; efforts to end Chaco War, 336, 337, 347; CH visit to, 339–340; in Italo-Ethiopian situation, 469; nonratification of Pan American agreements, 609; U.N. Declaration, 1144; implication in Bolivian revolt, 1389–1390, 1391–1392, 1413; relations with Italy, 1566;
policy toward Axis activities, 1150, 1360, 1361, 1363, 1377, 1380, 1382–1383, 1384–1385, 1386–1387, 1396, 1410; severance of diplomatic relations with Germany and Japan, 1391–1392, 1393 (*see also* Rio de Janeiro Conference);
participation in international conferences: Havana, (1928) 308, (1940), 791–792, 816, 821–830; Montevideo, 317, 318, 326–329, 331, 332, 334–336; Buenos Aires, 494–503; Lima, 602–608; Rio de Janeiro, 1144–1149; Mexico City, 1403–1405; San Francisco, 1405–1406, 1407–1408, 1722, 1723;
relations with U.S.: Nye Committee allegations, 400; trade agreement with U.S., 1140; opposition to Monroe Doctrine, 1146; military mission to U.S., 1378–1379; propaganda against U.S., 1402–1403;
U.S. policy: efforts to combat pro-Axis activities, 1379–1380, 1382–1383, 1388, 1397, 1400–1401, 1410–1413, 1419; question of recognition of Farrell regime, 1395, 1401–1402; recall of U.S. Ambassador, 1397; consultations with British, 1414–1418;
British policy: on Axis activities, 1409–1410; agreement for meat purchases, 1410; question of recognition of Farrell regime, 1414; recall of British Ambassador, 1416; divergencies from U.S. policy, 1474–1475
Arias, Arnulfo, 1048

Arias, Rodolfo García, 1394
Arita, Hachiro, 628, 718, 888–895
Armaments, 284, 286–290, 1285, 1286; see also Arms; Disarmament; Munitions; Rearmament
Armistice (1918), 98
Armistice, German-French (1940), 791, 793, 795, 804, 849, 851, 960
Armour, Norman, CH appraisal, 1377–1378; U.S. Ambassador to Argentina, 1377, 1380, 1384, 1385, 1386, 1388, 1391, 1392, 1395, 1396, 1409; recalled, 1397, 1414, 1416
Arms, ammunition, and implements of war, international supervision of manufacture and trade in, 228, 231–233; U.S. disapproval of export to Germany (1934), 233; Nye Committee investigations, 380, 398–404; control of traffic in, 405, 411, 414, 416, 509, 597, 679, 697; suspension of arms shpiments to Turkey, 1371; see also Armaments; Embargo; Neutrality policy
Arms and Munitions Control, Office of, State Department, 416, 902
Armstrong, Hamilton Fish, 1633, 1635
Army, U.S., 774, 845, 910, 998; see also Joint Chiefs of Staff; National defense; Rearmament; War Department
Arosemena, Juan, 691, 692
Aruba, 814, 816, 891, 893
Ascension, trusteeship, 1596
Ashton-Gwatkin, F., 735
Assets. See Credits
Asylum to political refugees in neutral countries, 1360–1364
Athenia, torpedoing, 677
Atherton, Ray, 883–884, 1167–1170, 1232, 1240, 1241, 1480
Atlantic, Battle of the, Western Hemisphere neutrality zone, 689–692, 945; defense of Greenland, 935; U.S. plans for possible German occupation of Azores, 940; CH and FDR addresses, 941–942; U.S. shipping to Britain, 942; sinking of Robin Moor and other ships, 944, 1046–1050; U.S. patrol in, 945; U.S. forces to Iceland, 946–947; use by U.S. and Britain of Azores bases, 1339–1344
Atlantic Charter, protection of British Empire tariff preferences, 975–976,

Atlantic Charter—Continued
1151; Soviet attitude toward, 1165, 1166, 1170, 1171; implementation, 1236, 1252, 1281, 1547, 1600, 1630–1631, 1632, 1661; interpretations of point three, 1478, 1484–1485; see also United Nations Declaration
Atlantic Conference (1941), 974–976, 1017–1020; see also Atlantic Charter
Atom bomb, development, 1110
Atrocities, German, 1183–1185, 1278, 1289–1291, 1538
Attlee, Clement, 1488
Augusta, bombing, 540
Austin, Warren R., 649, 1635, 1658, 1695
Australia, harmful effects of U.S. neutrality legislation, 692–693; fear of officials of British defeat, 775; desire for U.S. declaration of war, 775–776; preservation of status quo in Netherlands East Indies, 891; proposals for handling Japanese demands, 897–899; plans for unified defense in the Pacific, 906–907, 909, 912, 914, 1113; views on Japanese proposals (Nov. 20, 1941) and U.S. substitute proposals, 1073, 1076, 1077, 1082; mediation offer to U.S. and Japan, 1089; cooperation with U.S. in war, 1475; postwar planning, 1631
Austria, assassination of Chancellor Dollfuss, 242; as German objective, 244; German invasion, 575; German refusal to assume debts, 575–576; freezing of assets in U.S., 945; Declaration on, 1297
Avenol, Joseph, 274, 432
Aviation, abandonment of plans for loans to Latin America for improvements, 332; air communication between U.S. and U.S.S.R., 1302; see also Bases
Aviation gasoline, embargo on export to Japan of materials for production of, 729–730; Spanish request of U.S. for, 1326
Axis, Rome-Berlin accord (1936), 488; Anti-Comintern Pact (1936), 488, 489, 634, 639, 717, 908, 980; U.S. relations in 1941, 926–927; U.S. efforts to solidify resistance of Balkan countries, 928–933; shipping in U.S. ports,

Axis—*Continued*
927, 928, 942–943; U.S. request for removal of diplomatic missions in Eire, 1358; asylum to Axis leaders in neutral countries, 1360–1364; U.S. objections to Allied Control Commissions for satellites, 1461; Allied unconditional surrender policy, 1570–1582;
in South America, subversive activities, 495–496, 601–602, 813–814, 820–821, 827, 1146, 1148, 1150; subversive activities in Argentina, 1377, 1380, 1382, 1383, 1384–1385, 1386–1387, 1391–1392, 1393, 1396–1397, 1410, 1412, 1413, 1419; condemnation by Lima Conference, 609; diplomatic relations severed by Argentina, 1381, 1384, 1385, 1386, 1391–1392, 1393; by Chile, 1383;
Tripartite Pact (1940), 489, 627–628, 908–909, 932, 1002, 1006–1007, 1010, 1021, 1059, 1061, 1062, 1063, 1064, 1071, 1083;
see also Germany, Italy, Japan
Ayres, William, 132, 151
Azores, possible occupation by Germany, 940–941; use of bases and facilities by Britain and U.S., 1232, 1339–1343; use by Allies for convoy protection, 1275; proposed meeting place for U.N. Council, 1681

Badoglio government in Italy, 1449, 1463, 1550–1559, 1564–1565, 1568
Bahamas, 831–843
Bailey, Joseph W., 60
Bailey, Josiah W., 699
Bajpai, Sir Girja Shankar, 1483, 1487
Baker, Newton D., 335
Balance of power, 86, 1314, 1452
Baldwin, Stanley, 379, 384
Balfour, Arthur J., 403–404
Balfour Declaration, 1529, 1531
Balkans, U.S. efforts to solidify resistance to Axis (early 1941), 928–933; Churchill plan for major Anglo-American drive into Europe through, 1366; Soviet-British arrangement for military spheres of influence in (1944), 1451–1459; see also individual countries

Ball, Joseph H., 1262, 1670, 1696, 1698
Ball-bearings exports from Sweden to Germany, 1347, 1348
Ballantine, Joseph W., 671, 672, 895, 1585–1586, 1724, 1726; participation in U.S.-Japanese conversations (1941), 988, 989, 996, 1003, 1030, 1031, 1095, 1096, 1097
Baltic States, 701, 1266, 1348; see also Estonia, Finland, Latvia, Lithuania, and Sweden
Bankhead, William B., 109, 564, 643
Barclay, Edwin, 1185, 1186
Barkley, Alben W., 217, 649, 861, 1658, 1695, 1697, 1726
Barr Shipping Corp., 468
Barter trade agreements, 371–374
Baruch, Bernard M., 114, 457, 1330, 1578
Bases, on British territory, 193, 212, 831–843, 1475; in Greenland, 935, 936; in U.S.S.R., 1111–1112, 1302; in Azores, 1232, 1339–1343; in Sweden, 1279–1280, 1301; in Turkey, 1301, 1312; in American Republics, 1422, 1423
Batista, Fulgencio, 315
Battle of the Atlantic. See Atlantic, Battle of the
Baudet, Philippe, 1220
Baudouin, Paul, 791, 793, 795
Bauxite mines at Paramaribo, 1051
Beaman, Middleton, 80
Beard, Edward E., 27
Beaverbrook, Lord, 910, 1525, 1586
Beck, Josef, 596
Beigbeder y Atienza, Juan, 875, 876
Belgium, World Congress of the International Chamber of Commerce at Brussels (1925), 125; trade agreement with U.S., 361, 375; Brussels Conference (1937), 550–556; concern over effect of U.S. arms embargo, 647; peace appeal of King, 663; Belgian-Dutch peace move, 712; invasion by Germany, 712, 761, 764; application of U.S. Neutrality Act, 761, 763; freezing of credits in U.S., 763; surrender of army to Germans, 773; U.S. relief plans, 804; policy on relief to occupied countries, 1052; as a postwar problem, 1266

Belligerents, regulations on travel of U.S. citizens on ships of, 428, 430, 432, 433, 471, 507, 679, 697, 785; regulations on credits to, 679, 681, 697; regulations on contributions for relief, 679, 697; financial transactions with, 1151; trade with (see Trade, U.S.)

Benavides, Oscar, 340, 611

Beneš, Eduard, 582–583, 590–591, 592

Bennett, Richard, 246, 260, 263, 264, 265

Benton, J. Webb, 652

Berding, Andrew, 1726, 1727

Berle, Adolf A., Jr., 179, 591, 596, 671, 672, 1115, 1123, 1483, 1548; delegate to international conferences, 494, 603, 822; CH appraisal of, 495; postwar planning, 1626–1627, 1633, 1635

Bermuda, U.S.-British agreement for lease of bases, 831–843

Bessarabia, 300, 807, 810, 1451

Beveridge, Albert J., 108

Bidault, Georges, 1434

Biddle, Anthony J. Drexel, 596, 662, 677–678, 685–686, 789, 791–793, 805, 1184, 1548

Bingham, Robert W., 182, 512

Blacklists, 734, 1380

Blaine, James G., 83

Blair, Henry W., 18, 197

Blanco, Juan Carlos, 1395–1396

Bland, Schuyler Otis, 1636

Blechingberg, Einar, 937

Bliss, Robert Woods, 1673

Bliss, Tasker H., 1117

Blockade, U.S.-British disagreement over blockade of German ports, 733–736; British, in Western Hemisphere, 1142

Bloom, Sol, 218, 643–646, 1495, 1658, 1669, 1696, 1698

Blum, Léon, 476, 482

Board of Economic Warfare, 204, 1154–1157, 1162, 1346–1347, 1350

Boettiger, John, 1370

Bohlen, Charles E., 1280, 1293

Boisson, Pierre, 949, 961

Bolivia, German attempts to intimidate, 821; expropriation of foreign-owned oil properties in, 610; revolution instigated by Nazi and Argentine agents (1943), 1388–1389; memoranda by

Bolivia—Continued
FDR and CH on, 1390–1391; recognition of Villarroel regime, 1392, 1397–1398, 1398–1399; war with Paraguay (see Chaco)

Bolshevism. See Communism

Bolte, Charles L., 1163

Bombing of civilian populations, in China by Japanese, 558, 559, 569, 632–634, 729–730, 1031; in Poland, 672, 674, 677–678; proposal of Herbert Hoover for commission to investigate, 678; FDR's appeal to refrain from, 672, 674, 678; by U.S.S.R., 706–707, 709, 744

Bonds, Government, as means of defraying Government war expenditures, 90–91, 100

Bonin Islands, trusteeship, 1596

Bonnet, Georges, 263, 586, 588, 589, 592, 646, 652, 661

Bonomi, Ivanoe, 1563–1565, 1568–1569

Borah, William E., 59, 60, 102, 215, 216, 465, 649–653

Boström, W., 702

Bowers, Claude G., 128, 182, 475, 485, 504, 616, 1383

Bowling Green normal school, 18–19

Bowman, Isaiah, 1428, 1633, 1635, 1643, 1675, 1688

Boycott, German protests against U.S., 236, 240, 241

Braden, Spruille, 319

Brandegee, Frank B., 102, 216

Brandt, George L., 674

Brazil, on Leticia dispute, 311; in Cuban situation, 314, 316; CH visit to, 323; efforts to end Chaco War, 336, 337, 347; concern over U.S.-Argentine friendship, 349; German-instigated revolution against Vargas, 601; increased military strength to offset Argentine activities, 1390–1391; question of permanent seat on U.N. Council, 1678;

participation in inter-American conferences: Montevideo, 317; Buenos Aires, 499; Lima, 609–610; Rio de Janeiro, 1143–1150;

relations with U.S.: trade agreement, 375, 520; economic agreement, 1140; Warren mission to Bolivia,

Brazil—*Continued*
  1398; assistance to U.S. during war,
  1422, 1423;
    in the war: plans for possible Ger-
  man occupation of the Azores, 941,
  1339; joint protection with U.S. of
  bauxite mines in Paramaribo, 1051;
  politicomilitary commission in Algiers, 1275; efforts for Portuguese
  embargo on wolfram to Germany,
  1336, 1337; expeditionary force to
  Europe, 1423
Breckinridge, Sophonisba P., 319
Brennan, Robert, 1354, 1355
British Guiana, U.S.-British agree-
  ment for lease of bases, 831–843
British Imperial Conference (1937),
  528–529
British West Indies, U.S. lease of bases,
  193, 212, 831–843
Brock, William E., 134
Brown, Aaron S., 663
Brown University, 473
Bruce, S. M., 775
Bruggmann, Charles, 1350
Brussels Conference (1937), 550–556
Bryan, William Jennings, 33, 37, 53, 67–
  68, 71, 87, 114, 117, 121, 180, 182,
  270
Buchanan, John P., 25
Buckner, S. B., 1574
Buenos Aires, CH visit to, 339; FDR
  visit to, 495, 497
Buenos Aires Conference (1936), prepa-
  rations and purpose, 493–494; U.S.
  delegation, 494; FDR address at
  opening, 495; CH's "Eight Pillars of
  Peace," 498; agreements, 499–501;
  question of Spanish observer, 501;
  CH's closing address, 502; CH's summary of achievements, 503; U.S. ratification of agreements, 503
Bukovina, Soviet occupation, 810, 1451
Bulgaria, German occupation, 926, 931;
  signs Tripartite Pact, 931; U.S. efforts
  to solidify resistance to Axis, 928–
  929; credits in U.S. frozen, 931; attack on Greece and Yugoslavia, 933;
  declaration of war against U.S., 1114;
  U.S. declaration of war, 1175–1176;
  Soviet sphere of influence in, 1453,
  1454; U.S. protests on Soviet armi-

Bulgaria—*Continued*
  stice terms with, 1461; nonapplication
  of unconditional-surrender policy to,
  1570, 1575–1577, 1579–1580
Bullitt, William C., European mission
  (1933), 160; practice of communicating directly with FDR, 200, 790; adviser, London Economic Conference,
  262; proponent of U.S. recognition of
  U.S.S.R., 296; participant in discussions *re* U.S.S.R. prior to U.S. recognition, 300, 301–302, 303; U.S. Ambassador to U.S.S.R., 182, 302, 418;
    U.S. Ambassador to France: urges
  peace appeal in German-Czech crisis,
  590, 591, 593; commendation, 596;
  receives assurance *re* obligations of
  Franco government, 616, 617; suggests appeal to Hitler and Mussolini
  to guarantee independence of other
  nations, 620; reports French reaction
  to U.S. arms embargo, 646, 647, 693;
  reports imminence of war in Europe,
  652, 653; of German attack on Poland, 655, 656, 657, 660–665 *passim;*
  of Soviet attack on Poland, 685; on
  Finland, 705; urges appeal against
  bombing civilian populations, 671–
  672; urges stand against U.S.S.R. in
  League, 709–710; warns of French
  vulnerability, 762–763; request for aid
  for France, 766, 772; conversations
  with French officials on U.S. aid to
  France, 767–770; on preservation of
  French fleet, 771, 772; fear of British
  surrender, 774; reports likelihood of
  French surrender, 776; suggestions for
  coercive measures against Italy, 781;
  decision to remain in Paris after Ger-
  man occupation, 789–791; return to
  U.S., 805
Bulwinkle, Alfred, 1636
Burleson, Albert S., 58
Burma Road, 722, 897–899, 900, 901,
  911, 916, 1078, 1079, 1174, 1175
Burton, Harold H., 1262, 1670, 1696
Butler, M. G., 42–43
Butler, N. M., 811, 985, 1007
Buttrick, George A., 714
Byrd, Harry, 141
Byrd, Richard E., 758–759

Byrnes, James F., 1518, 1593, 1594, 1720
Byrns, Joseph W., 64, 109, 135, 357

Cabinet Committee on Germany, 1604, 1608, 1614, 1616, 1618
Cabinet of FDR, 167, 203–210, 902, 1057–1058
Cadogan, Sir Alexander, 1232, 1233, 1240, 1672, 1675, 1679, 1683, 1702
Caffery, Jefferson, 341, 1336, 1337, 1434
Cairo Conference (FDR, Churchill, and Chiang Kai-shek, 1943), 1110, 1302–1303, 1313, 1317, 1357, 1584
Cairo meeting (FDR, Churchill, and Turkish President Inönü 1943), 1369–1370
Calderón, Luis, 478
Campbell, Sir Ronald, 979, 1029, 1416–1418, 1488
Canada, preparatory meetings for London Economic Conference, 246; plans for unified defense in Pacific, 1113; policy toward Free French occupation of Saint-Pierre and Miquelon, 1128–1137; recall of diplomatic representative at Vichy for consultation, 1157–1158; relations with U.S., 1479–1481; tariff-reciprocity agreement with U.S. rejected (1911), 65; U.S. claims for alleged nonpayment of excise taxes, 206–207; Ogdensburg defense agreement (1940), 212, 834; assistance in Anglo-American relations, 385; trade with U.S., 355, 375, 529–530; economic discussions with U.S., 526–528; Queens University address of FDR (1938), 587–588; effects of U.S. neutrality legislation on, 678–679; waiver of U.S. customs for airmen, 1182
Canadian Club Award Medal to CH, 1727
Canadian Society of New York, CH address on "four pillars of peace," 234
Cannon, Joseph, 50, 54–55, 56–57, 57–58, 62
Cantilo, José María, 602–608, 703
Capps, John A., 14
Cárdenas, Juan Francisco de, 617–618, 696, 1187–1188, 1189, 1329
Cárdenas, Lázaro, 610

"Career" appointments in Foreign Service, CH policy, 181–183
Caribbean, Anglo-American Commission, 1236–1237, 1475
Carlock, L. H., 27–29
Carmona, Antonio Oscar de Fragoso, 1191–1192
Carol of Rumania, 686–687
Carr, Wilbur J., 161, 183, 590, 596
Cartels, international, 1304
Casablanca Conference (1943), nonattendance by CH, 1110; attempts to settle Giraud-De Gaulle controversy, 1207–1208; policy decision on Turkey, 1365; CH views on agreement, 1367–1368; FDR statement of unconditional-surrender policy, 1570
Casey, Richard, 775–776, 891, 896, 898, 912, 914, 996, 1089, 1276
Castillo, Ramón S., 1147, 1377, 1380–1384
Castillo Nájera, Francisco, 1141
Castle, William, 202
Catroux, Georges, 1219–1220, 1540, 1541, 1542, 1545
Cayenne, French Guiana, U.S. consulate, 820
Censorship, mails, by Britain, 733, 734, 735; press, by U.S.S.R., 1278–1279
Cerda, Aguirre, 845
Cespedes, Carlos de, 314, 317
Chaco War, 468; Montevideo Conference efforts to end, 193, 322, 323, 328, 336–338, 1646; League of Nations efforts to end, 336–337, 346–347, 386, 1646; mediation by neighboring countries, 336, 337, 347
Chadbourne, Thomas L., 114
Chamber of Commerce, International, 125; CH address, 390
Chamber of Commerce, U.S., CH address, 377, 391
Chamberlain, Neville, participation in London Economic Conference, 260, 263, 264, 266; statement on nonintervention in Spain, 482–483; observations on world situation, 532–534; CH appraisal, 531, 595; suggested meeting with FDR, 548–549; appeasement of Germany and Italy, 573, 579, 581, 591; peace efforts in Czech crisis, 586, 589, 590, 592, 593; Munich

Chamberlain, Neville—*Continued*
agreement, 595; change of policy, 614, 615, 623; certainty of war in Europe, 662
Chapultepec, Act of, 1467
Charter, Atlantic. *See* Atlantic Charter
Charter of United Nations. *See* United Nations
Chatel, Yves Charles, 1191–1192
Chautauqua, N.Y., FDR address on foreign policy, 479
Chauvel, Jean, 908
Cherwell, Lord, 1615
Chiang Kai-shek, views on ending hostilities with Japan, 539; requests for U.S. aid, 567, 1057; views on Japanese objectives as to British rights in China, 631; proposal for conference on Far Eastern situation, 723–724; protests on proposed U.S. *modus vivendi* with Japan, 1077, 1078, 1081, 1088–1089; urges Soviet-Chinese declaration of war on Japan, 1112; concern over lack of Allied cooperation, 1175; on U.S. extraterritoriality in China, 1258; at Cairo Conference, 1302–1303, 1317, 1584; message to FDR on Indian problem, 1487; task in China, 1586; habit of circumventing State Department, 1586–1587; favors trusteeship for Indo-China, 1597; represented at Dumbarton Oaks Conference, 1672
Chicago "quarantine" speech of FDR, 544–546
Chile, consultation in Cuban situation, 314, 316; proposal to postpone Montevideo Conference, 317; efforts to end Chaco War, 336, 337, 347; CH visit to, 340; partial support of Argentine stand at Lima Conference, 606; proposal for peace move, 845; opposition at Rio Conference to declaration to break relations with Axis, 1146–1150; diplomatic relations with Axis severed, 1383; relations with U.S. following address by Welles (1942), 1383–1384
China, as world power and stabilizer in the Orient, 444–445, 1583, 1585, 1586–1587, 1595–1596; preparatory meetings for London Economic Conference, 246; signatory to U.N. Declara-

China—*Continued*
tion, 1120, 1123–1124; Four-Nation Declaration, 1238–1239, 1256–1257, 1265, 1279, 1281, 1282, 1299, 1301, 1302, 1306–1307, 1312; representation on Allied military councils, 1275, 1584–1585; Cairo Conference, 1302–1303, 1317, 1584; Yalta decisions *re*, 1587; Dumbarton Oaks Conference, 1641, 1650, 1671–1674, 1685, 1707; treaty rights of foreign nations, 279–280, 291, 532–533, 565–566, 727; violation by Japanese, 569, 627, 630–631, 632–633, 634, 635–638, 640, 723, 912; relinquishment, 565–566, 717–722, 901, 1257–1258, 1583; Japanese efforts to obtain special position in, 117, 270, 271, 279, 284, 635, 1008, 1035;
U.S. policy: open-door policy, 117, 270, 271, 290, 569; silver-purchase policy, 446; aid to China, 401, 567, 639, 907, 914–915, 983, 997, 1057, 1174–1175, 1584, 1585; neutrality, 229, 556–558, 638, 641, 696; withdrawal of troops from, 568, 1065; relinquishment of extraterritoriality, 565–566, 1257–1258, 1583; unified defense in Pacific, 1113; cooperation with British in, 1475; repeal of U.S. exclusion laws, 1583; Wallace mission, 1585–1586; postwar disposition of territory taken from China, 1584, 1596, 1599;
Japanese military operations: invasion of Manchuria, 160, 170, 270–276, 379, 539, 639; North China, 440, 445–446, 534, 538, 541, 542, 557, 639, 930, 1004–1005, 1010, 1022, 1032, 1035, 1058, 1059, 1064, 1066, 1083; injuring, killing, etc., of U.S. citizens, 540–541, 559, 569, 627, 632–634, 639, 914; injuries, etc., to other foreign citizens, 561, 630–631, 632–633, 635; bombings of civilians in, 558–559, 569, 632–634, 729–730, 1031; Hainan, 628, 634; puppet government in Nanking, 724–725, 894, 914, 1086; Burma Road, 722, 897–899, 900, 901, 911, 916, 1078, 1079, 1174, 1175; Hong Kong, 897, 900; suggested Soviet-Chinese

China—*Continued*
declaration of war, 1112; Chinese morale, 1174–1175; efforts to end war with Japan: request for U.S. mediation, 535, 542; U.S.-British efforts, 538–540, 555, 897–899; League policy, 542, 543–544; Brussels Conference, 550–556; Chiang's proposal for conference on, 723–724; U.S.-Japanese conversations (1941), 992, 1000, 1002, 1004, 1005–1006, 1009, 1022, 1026, 1028, 1031, 1033, 1058, 1067, 1073–1089 *passim;* Japanese attempts for a separate peace (1943), 1584

Christian, King of Denmark, 937–939

Christian Foreign Service Convocation, FDR address, 739

Christie, Loring, 694, 755–756

Chrome ore, Turkish embargo to Germany, 1371–1372

Chungking, Japanese bombing of, 632–633

Churchill, Randolph, 1370

Churchill, Winston (*for nonpersonal items, see* Great Britain *or subject*), practice of using code name, 691; becomes British Prime Minister, 764; visits to U.S., 798, 1100, 1119, 1132, 1152–1153, 1248, 1614, 1702; CH admiration, 870, 1473; address before joint session of U.S. Congress, 1100; naming of "Declaration by United Nations," 1124; relations with FDR and CH, 1473–1474; personal messages to CH, 1719, 1720

Ciano, Count Galeazzo, 779–780, 783

Cicognani, Archbishop, 1560, 1562

Ciechanowski, Jan, 1271–1272, 1316, 1438, 1443, 1444

Cincar-Markovic, Alexander, 928–929

Citizens, U.S., German financial obligations to, 237–240; rights to trade with belligerents, 463; enlistments in Spanish Loyalist Army, 505; extraterritorial rights in China, 565–566; protection, abroad, 189, 192; in Germany, 236, 240, 241; in U.S.S.R., 292, 294, 297, 299, 300, 301, 658; in China, 540–541, 559, 627, 632–634, 639; in Spain, 616, 617; in Japan, 569, 718, 719, 722, 1588–1589;

Citizens, U.S.—*Continued*
travel restrictions, 428, 430, 432, 433, 471, 507, 675–676, 679, 697, 785; repatriation: plans for, upon outbreak of war in Europe, 663–664, 673–674; from Europe, 475, 480, 752, 760, 770, 1113–1114; from Far East, 914, 1114, 1588–1589

City of Flint, capture and release, 704–705, 709

Civilian internees, treatment by Japan, 1589

Claims, Mixed Claims Commission, U.S. and Germany, 239; Spanish, of U.S. citizens, 880; U.S. against Mexico, 1140–1142

Clark, Bennett Champ, 217, 465

Clark, Champ, 58, 60, 63, 64, 67–69, 104, 109, 111

Clark, J. Reuben, Jr., 319

Clark, Mark, 1196, 1198

Claudel, Paul, 160

Clayton Antitrust Act (1914), 73

Cleveland, Grover, 29–30

Cleveland-Harrison campaign (1888), 21–22

Close, Ralph W., 694–695

Clouse, Wynne, 105

Coast Guard, dispatch of cutters to Greenland, 756, 757; custody of foreign shipping, 927, 942, 959

Cockran, Bourke, 108, 220

Cohen, Benjamin V., 1633, 1636, 1675, 1711

Cohen, John S., 141

Cole, Felix, 854

Colijn, Hendrikus, 263, 266

Colombia, Leticia border dispute with Peru, 170–171, 309, 310–311; proposal to postpone Montevideo Conference, 317; efforts to end Chaco War, 337; CH visit to, 340; trade with U.S., 354, 375

Colonial peoples. *See* Dependent peoples

Colonial preferential tariff. *See* Empire

Colonies. *See* European possessions; *see also name of colony*

Colonna, Prince Ascanio, 777, 785, 927

Combat areas. *See* Neutrality

Combined Chiefs of Staff, 1124, 1325, 1549, 1550, 1571, 1584–1585, 1611–1613

Comintern, anti-Comintern policy of Axis, 488, 489, 634, 639, 908, 980; dissolution, 1251–1252

Commerce, International Chamber of, 125; CH address, 390

Commerce, U.S. Chamber of, CH address, 377, 391

Commercial Policy, Executive Committee on, 353, 354, 356

Commercial policy, U.S. For policy toward individual countries, see country; see also Embargo; Tariff; Trade, international; Trade, U.S.; and Trade agreements

Commercial treaty, U.S. and Japan (1911), 636–638, 725–729

Communications, 1302, 1303

Communism, propaganda in U.S., 292, 294, 305, 1288–1289; opposition by U.S., 634–635, 978; in China, 990; doctrine forced by U.S.S.R. on other nations, 1739–1740

Communist International. See Comintern

Concentration camps, German, 1285

Concha, Carlos, 602, 605–606

Conciliation, Inter-American Convention, 322, 328, 332

Confederations, Soviet objection to, 1298–1299

Conference of Seaport Cities on International Trade, CH address, 391

Conferences, international. See name of conference

Congress, general appraisal of members, 46; salaries, 47; press notices on new members, 53; special session to consider tariff agreement with Canada, 65; military service for Members of Congress, World War I, 89; CH opposition to adjournment (1918), 95–97; opposition to Woodrow Wilson, 98, 102–104; CH appraisal of, 107–109; CH relations with as Secretary of State, 178, 211, 214–215, 1656–1658; relations with Executive branch, 211–214, 1260–1261, 1665, 1696, 1733–1734; question of Congressional jurisdiction in foreign affairs, 211–214; Supreme Court decision on right to delegate authority to Executive to embargo arms, 468; Churchill address

Congress—Continued
before joint session, 1100; CH address before joint session, 1314–1315, 1657; nonpartisan support of U.N., 1259–1263, 1314, 1315, 1630, 1635, 1639, 1655, 1656, 1657–1670, 1695–1698, 1711; effect of U.N. on power to declare war, 1665, 1669, 1695–1696; placement of bust of CH in Capitol, 1719; Joint Committee on Investigation of Pearl Harbor Attack, 1724, 1726, 1727; isolationists in (see Isolationism); for legislation, see acts under title or subject;

Senate: direct election of Senators by people (17th amendment), 66–67; CH appraisal, 108; CH campaign and election, 134–139; CH familiarity with, 146; CH resignation, 162; treaty jurisdiction, 192, 211–213, 252–253, 354; majority as opposed to two-thirds vote for treaty approval, 212, 1734; Nye Committee, 380, 398–404; Committee to Investigate Petroleum Resources, 1524; Foreign Relations Committee, CH discussion of U.N., 1657–1669, 1676, 1695–1698;

House of Representatives: CH election to 60th Congress, 43–44; CH pursuit of broad national objectives rather than local, 46, 51; domination of House by Joe Cannon, 50–51, 54–55; CH maiden speech, 51–53; CH election to 61st Cong., 53, 55; powers of Speaker curtailed, 57–58, 62–63; CH committee memberships, 63–64; achievements of 62d Cong., 66–67; admission of draftsmen, 80; Democratic control (1916), 87; Republican control (1918), 99; CH retirement (1921), 104, 107; CH appraisal of members, 107–109; CH self-appraisal as member, 109–111, 124; CH election to 68th Cong., 115; desire to share in Senate treaty jurisdiction, 212

Connally, Tom, 1262, 1635, 1657, 1658, 1676, 1689, 1695, 1697

Connally resolution on world organization, 1314, 1649, 1661, 1669

Constitution, U.S., amendments, income tax (16th), 48, 59, 60–61, 66,

Constitution, U.S.—*Continued*
70; election of Senators (17th), 66–67
Consular and diplomatic officers, restriction of political activities, 827
Contraband, in World War I, 409; British practices in World War II, 679–681, 733–736
Control Commissions, Allied, for Italy, 1245–1246, 1555, 1557, 1560, 1563, 1565, 1566; for Germany, 1285, 1618–1619; for Axis satellites, 1461
Cookeville, Tenn., bill to establish U.S. Court branch, 53–55
Coolidge, Calvin, 123, 127, 387
Cooper, Jere, 357
Cordell, John M., 6
"Cordon sanitaire," 1299
Corporation excise-tax bill, preparation, 80
Costa Rica, trade agreement with U.S., 375; German attempts to intimidate, 821
Costigan, E. P., 156
Coughlin, Father Charles Edward, 389
Council on Foreign Relations, CH's address, 503
Court, Customs, 107
Court, Federal, branch at Cookeville, Tenn., 53–55
Court, World. *See* World Court
Couzens, James, 249
Cox, James M., 104, 105, 142, 220, 249, 258, 259, 262
Cox, Oscar S., 873
Craig, Hiram, 11
Credits, from U.S., to Italy, 427; Spanish request for, 875, 876, 880, 881, 882; to U.S.S.R., 976–977; to Britain, 1613–1614, 1615, 1616, 1617–1618, 1726–1727;
freezing by U.S., Norwegian, 752; Danish, 752, 754; Belgian, Netherlands, Luxemburg, 763; French, 791, 795; Estonian, Latvian, Lithuanian, 811; Axis and Axis-occupied countries, 931, 932, 945; Argentine, proposed, 1379–1380, 1388
Cretzianu, Mr., 687
Crimes, war, 1183–1185, 1278, 1289–1291, 1538, 1589
Cripps, Sir Stafford, 811, 1486

Crowley, Carl, 154
Crowley, Leo, 1450
Crump, Ed, 134, 135, 138
Cuba, administrative and social plight under Spain, 34–35; ouster of Machado, 309, 312, 314; rise and fall of de Cespedes government, 314, 317; Batista revolution, 315; Grau San Martin as President, 317, 342; U.S. recognition of Mendieta, 341, 342–343; criticism of U.S. at Montevideo Conference, 333; trade with U.S., 313, 344, 359, 368; U.S. modification of 1903 treaty, 317, 334, 343; U.S. arms embargo, 344; U.S. economic assistance, 344; cooperation with Anglo-American Caribbean Commission, 1237; Havana Conference (*see* Havana Conference)
Cudahy, John, 761, 762, 763, 773
Cuevas, Emilio del Toro, 603
Culbertson, Paul, 1342
Cultural Relations, Division in State Department, 610
Cumberland (Md.) *Evening Times* and *Sunday Times*, presentation of bust of CH to Senate, 1719
Cumberland River Valley, efforts toward improvement of, 43–44
Cumberland University, CH address, 245
Cumberland University Law School, Lebanon, Tenn., 26–27
Cumming, Hugh S., 302, 758
Cummings, Homer S., 98–99, 198, 209, 303, 405
Cummins, Albert B., 59, 60
Curaçao, British occupation, 814–816, 891, 893
Currency, stabilization, 91, 246, 248, 250, 260–266, 378–379, 522; charge of manipulations by Germany, 472–473
Currie, Lauchlin, 1489, 1636
Curtiss-Wright Export Corp., 468
Curzon Line, 1166, 1266, 1438, 1441, 1447
Customs, U.S., waived for Canadian airmen, 1182
Customs Court, CH offered nomination as Chief Justice of, 107
Cvetkovic, Dragisha, 928

Czechoslovakia, German objective, 244; German preparation for conquest, 582–583; crisis ending in Munich agreement (1938), 586–597, 614–615, 623; Polish and Hungarian demands on, 592, 596, 614; German conquest (1939), 614–615; U.S. nonrecognition and other actions, 615, 945; Anglo-French policy, 615, 623; signing of U.N. Declaration, 1124; German atrocities at Lidice, 1184

Dakar, French West Africa, U.S. consulate reopened, 852; British and Free French attempt to capture, 852; U.S. efforts to prevent establishment of German bases at, 962–963, 1038–1045; Allied occupation, 1199; trusteeship, 1596
Daladier, Edouard, 227, 586, 592–593, 595, 615, 652, 656, 660–661, 662, 693, 765, 770, 781
Danaher, John A., 1360
Daniels, Josephus, 162, 170, 182, 316, 610
Danzig, freezing of assets in U.S., 945
Darlan, Jean François, Minister of Marine, 791; policy re French fleet, 793, 799; becomes Vice Premier, Foreign Minister, and Minister of Interior, 949; collaboration with Hitler, 948, 949, 952, 953, 955, 956, 958–963, 1038, 1039, 1042, 1043; made supreme French leader in North Africa, 1196–1198; civil functions in North Africa, 1198, 1201; U.S. position re, 1199–1200, 1202–1203; assassination, 1204–1205
Daugherty, Harry M., 127
Davies, Joseph E., 200, 547, 647, 710, 712, 1249–1250
Davis, Elmer, 1200
Davis, John K., 685
Davis, John W., 122, 123, 142, 215
Davis, Norman H., address, 120; urges CH to accept office of Secretary of State, 157; CH appraisal, 224; U.S. delegate to Disarmament Conference at Geneva, 224–231, 273; endeavors to reconcile British-French viewpoints, 382; statement re League sanctions, 407; chairman of U.S. delegation to

Davis, Norman H.—*Continued*
London Naval Conference, 446; conversation with CH on world situation (1936), 455; suggestion for Presidential power to distinguish "right and wrong" in aggressive warfare, 466; preparation of "quarantine" speech for FDR, 544; suggestion for Chamberlain-FDR meeting (1937), 548–549; U.S. delegate to Brussels Conference, 552, 553, 554, 556; conference with CH on European peace moves, 711; participation in CH conference following Pearl Harbor attack, 1098; postwar planning, 1626–1627, 1632–1633, 1635, 1643, 1688
Dawson, William, 822
Deane, John R., 1280, 1302, 1310
Debt, U.S. national, 89–93, 94–100
Debts, cessation of payment by Germany on external debt, 237–238; repudiation by U.S.S.R. of obligations of Czarist government, 292, 294, 303–304; settlement a prerequisite to U.S. recognition of U.S.S.R., 294, 295, 297, 301; failure of U.S. and U.S.S.R. to reach agreement, 303–304; Mexican resolution at Montevideo Conference, 335–336; German nonassumption of Austrian debts to U.S. after *anschluss*, 575–576; *see also* War debts
Debuchi, Katsuji, 272, 273–274
Declaration by United Nations. *See* United Nations Declaration
Declaration of American Principles, 609–610
Declaration of Lima, 603–609
Declaration of Neutrality, General, 689
Declaration of Panama, 689–692, 774
Defense, Permanent Joint Board of, 834, 1479
Defense Board, Inter-American, 1150
De Gaulle, Charles (*for nonpersonal items, see* France, Free French, *or subject*), character, 961–962, 1040, 1159, 1208, 1213, 1218, 1223; political aspirations, 1160, 1163–1164, 1205–1206, 1206–1207, 1213, 1215, 1217, 1219, 1222, 1225–1226, 1241, 1244, 1245, 1433, 1435; meeting with CH, 1275; visit to U.S., 1431, 1433

De Laboulaye, Andre, 385–386, 420
Democracies, western, relations during
1933–35, 378–386
Democracy, "world safe for" (Wilson),
118; slump in, 127, 136; CH's analysis, 383, 1730
Democratic Party, 21–22, 52, 62, 67–
69, 113–114, 117–123, 138, 140, 352;
in Tennessee, 24–26, 77–79, 134, 135,
138; Smith-Raskob attempt to control party, 140–145; FDR decision
on third term (1940), 859–860, 861,
868; CH proposed for President
(1940), 749–750, 855–859; CH proposed for Vice President (1940 and
1944), 860–861, 1714; support of international organization (see Nonpartisan foreign policy);
    National conventions and platforms,
(1908) 59, 60; (1920) 104; (1924)
25–26, 122–123, 130; (1928) 129–131;
(1932) 25–26, 140–145, 149, 150–151,
153–154, 183, 228, 310, 330, 352, 387,
477; (1936) 485–488; (1940) 861, 862,
864; (1944) 1537, 1714;
    National Committee: CH as mem-
ber, 74; CH as member of executive
committee, 86, 1656; CH as chairman,
104, 113, 116, 122, 132; financial rehabilitation, 114, 116, 122–123; Raskob as chairman, 140–145
Denmark, protests discriminations in
pending U.S. neutrality bill, 695;
alarm over Soviet advance in Baltic,
702; German invasion, 751, 753; freezing of credits in U.S., 752, 754; nonapplication of U.S. Neutrality Act,
752; U.S. continued recognition of
government, 753; disposition of shipping, 759–760; ships in U.S. ports,
927, 943; authority of Danish Minister in Washington following Greenland agreement with U.S., 936–939;
see also Greenland; Iceland
Dependent peoples, 1234–1238, 1304–
1305, 1477–1478, 1482, 1484, 1491,
1496, 1498, 1500, 1595, 1598–1601,
1638–1639, 1697, 1738
Destroyers, U.S., exchange with British
for bases in Western Hemisphere, 193,
212, 831–843
Deutschland, bombing, 506

De Valera, Eamon, 872, 1351–1363
passim, 1563
Dewey, Thomas E., 174, 1686, 1689–
1695, 1708, 1711
Diamantopoulos, Cimon P., 1549
Dieckhoff, Hans, 572–573, 575, 583–585,
594, 599–600
Dingley Law, 52
Diplomatic Corps, 176, 177–178, 187–
188
Diplomatic representatives, U.S. and
Axis, repatriation, 1113
Diplomatic Service, U.S. See Foreign
Service
Disarmament, CH views on, 116, 155,
172, 455, 1737; in Democratic Party
platform (1932), 153; Hoover suggestion for committee to consider,
160; international supervision of trade
in arms, 228, 231–233, 379–380; FDR
appeal to heads of nations (1933),
273, 293; Soviet policy, 292–293, 304,
306; in Four-Nation Declaration,
1239; in postwar planning, 732, 1627,
1628, 1636, 1638;
    Conferences, Washington Conference,
116, 222, 271; Geneva Conference,
171, 222–233, 386; London Economic
Conference, 246; London Naval Conference, 444–455; conference of neutrals, 738, 1628; see also Armaments;
Arms
Djalal, Ghaffar Khan, 232
Djibouti, French Somaliland, 1204
Dodd, William E., 182, 244–245, 527,
572
Dollfuss, Engelbert, 242
Dolliver, Jonathan, 108
Domestic affairs, necessity for reforms
(1907), 45–46; CH policy of keeping
foreign affairs separate, 174; CH non-
participation in as Secretary of State,
196, 198–199, 204, 218; CH attitude
toward FDR domestic policy, 196–
199
Dominican Republic, 1237
Donovan, William J., 200, 928, 1162
Doolittle, James, 1589
Dooman, Eugene H., 635
Doughton, Robert L., 357, 1721
Doyle, Michael Francis, 494
Dreyfus, Louis G., Jr., 1277, 1501

Drought, Father, 984, 985, 989, 991, 1003
Drummond, Sir Eric, 272
du Bois, Coert, 1236
Duggan, Laurence, 822
Dulles, John Foster, 174, 1689–1693, 1694, 1695, 1708
Dumbarton Oaks Conference (1944), preparation, 1318, 1652; arrangements for Chinese participation, 1671, 1672, 1673, 1674; agenda, 1671, 1672–1675, 1675–1676; delegations, 1672, 1675; discussions, 1676–1685, 1700–1707; purpose, 1689; unsettled questions, 1706; Latin American republics kept informed, 1709–1711; proposals a basis for San Francisco United Nations Conference, 1712–1713; see also San Francisco; United Nations
Dundas, H., 423–424
Dunn, James Clement, 181, 755–756, 811; CH appraisal, 523; on Czech crisis, 596; conference with CH following outbreak of European war, 671, 672; attacks on, 857; memorandum on Soviet territorial demands, 1167–1170; at First Quebec Conference, 1232, 1240; Moscow Conference, 1265, 1274, 1280; postwar planning, 1608, 1626–1627, 1643, 1650; Dumbarton Oaks Conference, 1675, 1686, 1705, 1711
Dutch East Indies. See Netherlands East Indies
Dutch Guiana, 1051; see also Netherlands
Duties, countervailing, against German exports to U.S., 472–473, 615; see also Tariff; Trade agreements

Early, Stephen T., 1221
East Indies. See Netherlands East Indies
Eaton, Charles A., 218, 1635, 1658, 1669, 1696, 1698
Ebtehaj, Abol Hassan, 1508
Economic agreement with Brazil, 1140
Economic Conference at London (1933). See Monetary and Economic Conference
Economic conferences, world, 146, 155, 160

Economic conversations of neutrals, 738, 1628
Economic Defense Board, 1631
Economic mission to Iran, 1503, 1508
Economic nationalism, abandonment. See Trade agreements
Economic policy in French North Africa, 853–854, 949–952, 955, 961, 963, 966, 1039–1040, 1043–1044, 1161–1162
Economic problems, postwar. See United Nations
Economic relations, effect on political relations, 364
Economic Studies Division, State Department, 1638
Economic Warfare, Board of, 204, 1154–1157, 1162, 1346–1347, 1350
Economic warfare, U.S. coordination with British, 1324
Ecuador, CH visit to, 340; U.S. bases in, 1422, 1425
Eden, Anthony, British Lord Privy Seal, 384; British Secretary for League of Nations Affairs, 385, 419, 432; British Foreign Secretary, 443, 581; at London Naval Conference, 454; Brussels Conference, 550; Moscow Conference (see Moscow Conference, passim); invites CH to London, 1224–1225; visits U.S., 1366, 1595; CH appraisal, 1474, 1479; personal messages to CH, 1719, 1720;
  as British Foreign Secretary, views, discussions, and actions on: U.S. arms embargo against Germany and Italy, 512; trusteeship system, 1234, 1237–1238; Four-Nation Declaration, 1238–1239; governments of liberated countries, 1239–1240; world organization, 1260–1261, 1708; Swiss exports to Germany, 1351; Atlantic Charter, 1485; unconditional surrender principle, 1575, 1576; Argentina, 1413, 1417, 1420; Azores, 1340; Eire, 1357; Far East, 553; Free French, 1195, 1213–1216, 1222, 1232–1233, 1241–1242, 1430; Germany, 1233–1234, 1615; India, 1493; Japan, 1078, 1093; Mexico, 1142; Palestine, 1534, 1546; Spain, 482; Turkey, 1369, 1372;
  visit to Moscow, 1165–1167; negotiations for Anglo-Soviet treaty, 1167–

Eden, Anthony—*Continued*
1174; discussions with CH on Soviet postwar intentions, 1247–1248
Edison, Charles, 208
Education, State, Federal aid to, 18, 197
Egypt, concern over Arab-Jewish question, 1532, 1535, 1536; Arab Congress, 1546–1547; *see also* Cairo
"Eight Pillars of Peace," CH's address at Buenos Aires Conference (1936), 498, 535
Eire, 125; war policy in 1941, 922; Churchill views on possible union with Northern Ireland, 922; relations with U.S. during war, 1351–1360; asylum to war criminals, 1363
Eisenhower, Dwight D., commanding general, European theater, 1179; command in North Africa, 1196–1202, 1205, 1208, 1222; dines with CH, 1275; civil affairs in France, 1427, 1429, 1433; dealings with French Committee of National Liberation, 1430, 1432, 1433; Italian surrender, 1549; recommendation *re* Italian political situation, 1552; for clarification of term "unconditional surrender," 1578; conviction that British and American zones in Germany should be combined, 1613
Ellsworth, Lincoln, 758–759
El Salvador, German attempts to intimidate, 821
Embargo, U.S., on exports to Japan, 636–638, 897; on essential materials, 802, 807–809, 901, 907, 912–914, 915; arms, ammunition, and implements of war: CH efforts to secure legislation on embargo to aggressors, 228–229, 407; inflexibility of embargo clause in Neutrality Acts, 412–416, 460, 461–465, 508; Supreme Court decision, 468; elimination of embargo clause (*see* Neutrality policy); embargo on exports to Cuban insurgents, 344; to Bolivia and Paraguay, 346–347; to Italy and Ethiopia, 411–412, 414, 419, 428–433, 471; to Spain, 491, 505–506, 509, 513–514, 516–517, 615; to nations engaged in civil strife, 507; to Germany and Italy, 510–513; moral embargo: on exports to Italy

Embargo, U.S.—*Continued*
in Ethiopian war, 192–193, 425, 426, 430–442, 460–461, 467, 471, 809; to Spain, 478, 480–481, 483, 490; to U.S.S.R. in Finnish war, 706–707, 744, 969; to Japan, 636, 729–730, 901–902;
see also Rearmament
Embargo by neutrals on strategic materials to Axis. *See* Strategic materials
Embassy building, U.S., in Moscow, 1277
Embick, Stanley D., 1675, 1705
Emeny, Brooks, 1636
Emperor of Japan, treatment by occupation authorities, 1591–1593; Potsdam Conference, 1593–1595
Empire preferential tariff, 85, 101, 355, 519, 526, 530; retention by Atlantic Charter, 975–976; elimination from lend-lease agreements, 976, 1151–1153, 1211, 1476–1477, 1614
Engert, Cornelius Van H., 469, 579–580, 965, 1496
England. *See* Great Britain
Ercoli, Ercole, 1553
Ertegün, Mehmet Münir, 715–716, 932
Escobar, Adrian, 1394
Espil, Felipe A., 322, 469, 1381, 1382, 1383
Estate taxes, 77, 80–81
Esteva, Jean Pierre, 1191–1192
Estonia, Soviet pressure, 701; Soviet occupation, 810, 812; freezing of assets in U.S., 811; Soviet territorial aims, 1166, 1167, 1171, 1172, 1173
Estrada doctrine of recognition of new governments, 1401, 1402
Ethiopia, petroleum concession to U.S. company, 423–424;
war with Italy, 410; efforts to avert, 418–427; U.S. moral embargo, 192–193, 425, 426, 430–442, 460–461, 467, 471, 809; U.S. neutrality with respect to, 411–412, 414, 417, 419, 428–433, 467, 468, 471; Italian occupation of Addis Ababa, 468; Hoare-Laval plan to cede territory to Italy, 443; U.S. nonrecognition of Italian possession of, 469–470; British recognition, 579–582; FDR's statement on resistance to aggression, 930

European Advisory Commission, creation, 1283, 1642; consideration of postwar treatment of Germany, 1287, 1602, 1604, 1608, 1617, 1618; of civil affairs in France, 1301; French membership, 1434; problem of unconditional surrender, 1572, 1579

European possessions in the Western Hemisphere, 791, 804, 814–817, 822–826, 1629–1630; in the Far East, 888–895; *see also name of possession*

Evans, H. Clay, 31–33

Evian, France, conference on refugees (1938), 578

Excess-profits tax, 81, 92–93, 110

Excise-tax legislation, 66, 80

Excise taxes, U.S. claims against Canada for alleged nonpayment, 206–207

Exclusion Laws, Chinese, repeal, 1583

Executive, relations with Secretary of State, 191–210; relations with Congress, 211–214, 1260–1261, 1665, 1696, 1733–1734; power to negotiate treaties and executive agreements, 211–213; question of authority in neutrality matters, 415–416, 464, 468, 516, 517; assumption of emergency powers, 910; effect of U.N. on power to direct U.S. armed forces, 1665, 1669, 1695–1696

Executive agreements, negotiation of, compared to treaty-making process, 211–213; preferred, rather than treaties, for trade agreements, 354–355; *see also subject of agreement*

Executive Committee on Commercial Policy, 353, 354, 356, 472

Export Control, Office of, creation, 902

Export-Import Banks, incorporation, 303; refusal of extension of credit to U.S.S.R., 303–304; aid to Cuba, 344; loan to Finland, 707, 741; to China, 914–915

Export surpluses in Western Hemisphere, 827, 828

Exports, German, subsidized, 238–239, 472–473, 615

Exports, U.S. See Embargo; Trade, U.S.; Trade agreements; *and specific commodity*

Expropriation of oil properties in Mexico, 610, 1140–1143

Extraterritorial rights in China, U.S. and British relinquishment, 565–566, 1257–1258, 1583

Ezima, Lieut. Comdr., 1012

Fairchild, Muir S., 1675

Faisal, Amir, 1512–1513

Fall, Albert B., 102, 114, 127

Far East, League of Nations' Advisory Committee, 272; Japanese proposal for spheres of influence, 281–285, 894; Grew report on outlook in 1936, 456; review of situation in early 1941, 986; plans for unified defense in, 1113; U.S. policy, 448, 911–912, 995, 1029, 1083–1084; U.S. rights and interests in, 291, 634, 635, 640, 899 (*see also* China); U.S. destruction of official codes and papers in event of war, 1093; evacuation of U.S. citizens, 1113–1114; cooperation with British, 1475; *see also individual countries*

Farley, James A., 116, 143, 154, 208–209, 564, 861

Farm Bureau Federation, CH address, 747

Farmers Alliance, 25–26, 49

Farmers Free List Bill, 64–65

Farmers' tariff bill (1921), 106, 126

Farrell, Edelmiro, regime in Argentina, 1394–1408

Faruq I, of Egypt, 1276

Federal Bureau of Investigation, arrest of Japanese espionage agents, 1011–1012

Federal Council of Churches, peace studies, 1625, 1626

Federal Reserve, 72–73, 151

Federal Trade Commission Act (1914), 73

Feis, Herbert, 181, 671, 672; program to build up reserves of strategic materials, 457, 625–626, 1517, 1518–1519; operation of navicert system, 680–681; draft of United Nations Declaration, 1115; postwar planning, 1626–1627, 1633

Fénard, Raymond, 1431–1432

Fenwick, Charles G., 494, 603

Ferguson, Homer, 1726

Finance. See Credits; War debts

Financial and Economic Advisory Committee, 692, 827

Financial transactions with belligerents, 1151

Financing, Government, World War I, 89–93, 94–100, 124–125; CH attitude toward FDR policy, 196

Finland, trade agreement with U.S., 375; war debts, 382, 707; protests discrimination of U.S. neutrality bill, 695; suggestion for U.S. peace move in Europe, 711;
  war with U.S.S.R. (1939): Soviet demands on Finland, 702–703, 705; efforts of neutrals to avert war, 702–704; offer of U.S. good offices, 705–706, 809; Soviet attack, 706; FDR statement and appeals to refrain from bombing civilian populations, 706–707, 709, 744; U.S. moral embargo against U.S.S.R., 706–707, 744, 969; nonapplication of Neutrality Act to U.S.S.R., 707; aid to Finland, 707, 740–741; U.S.S.R. expulsion from League, 709–710; Finnish request for U.S. good offices, 741–742; end of war, 740; peace negotiations, 742–743, 1462; territory regained, 978; Soviet territorial aims, 1166, 1167, 1171, 1172, 1173; nonapplication of unconditional surrender policy to Finland, 1570, 1574, 1575–1577, 1579–1580;
  alliance with Germany (1941): U.S. pressure on Finland to cease aid to Germany, 977–980, 1449–1450; signature of Anti-Comintern Pact by Finland and British declaration of war, 980; withdrawal of U.S. consuls, 1177; rupture of relations with U.S., 1450

Fish, Bert, 940, 1186, 1336, 1511

Fish, Hamilton, 218, 545

Flandin, Pierre Étienne, 882

Fleet. See Navy

Fletcher, Henry P., 1675

Flynn, Edward J., 867

Foley, E. H., 873

Folk, Joseph W., 67, 68

Foo Ping-sheung, 1301, 1306, 1312

Food and Agriculture Conference (1943), 1643, 1654–1655

Food relief. See Relief

Ford, Richard, 1506

Fordney, Joseph W., 95

Fordney-McCumber Tariff Act (1922), 114, 126, 363, 364

Foreign-exchange restrictions, removal of, 250

Foreign Ministers conferences. See Havana Conference; Mexico City Conference; Panama Conference; and Rio de Janeiro Conference

Foreign policy, U.S., increase in publicity on, 219–220; CH basic principles of international conduct (July 16, 1937), 535–537; summarization in addresses and statements by CH, (Apr. 13, 1927) 128, (Feb. 24, 1933) 159, (Sept. 15, 1936) 487, (Mar. 17, 1938) 576–577, (Oct. 26, 1940) 864–866, (July 23, 1942) 1177–1179, 1500, (Sept. 12, 1943) 1254, (Apr. 9, 1944) 1321–1323; nonpartisan approach (see Nonpartisan foreign policy); see also specific subject

Foreign Relations, Council on, peace studies, 1625

Foreign Relations, State Department Advisory Committee on Problems of, 1626–1630

Foreign Relations Committee of Senate, CH discussion of U.N., 1657–1669, 1676, 1695–1698

"Foreign Relations of the United States," volumes on diplomatic history, 219–220

Foreign Service, U.S., CH address before (1933), 172–173, 174–175; retrenchment, 183; close relationship of field service and Department, 188–189; duties, 188–189; CH appraisal, 189; habit of envoys of corresponding directly with President, 200; method of appointing envoys, 200–201; restrictions on, by U.S.S.R., 708–709; restriction of officers' political activities, 827; increase in, 1156; withdrawal of consuls from Finland, 1177; assistance in preparations for African landing, 1185, 1193; presentation of bust of CH to State Department, 1719; see also State Department

Foreign Trade Council, CH address, 391

"Forgotten man" phrase, use of, 147–148

Formosa, 1584, 1596

Forrestal, James A., 208

Fort-de-France, Martinique, U.S. consulate, 820

Fotitch, Constantin, 929, 930

Four Freedoms, 195, 920, 1630

Four-Nation Declaration, need for, 1280–1281; draft, 1238–1239, 1283, 1299–1300, 1646–1647; Soviet objection to China's inclusion, 1256–1257, 1265, 1279, 1281, 1282, 1299, 1301, 1302, 1312; signature, 1306–1307; implementation, 1314, 1318, 1463, 1600, 1647–1648, 1655, 1661, 1669; Polish attack on, 1315; use of term "unconditional surrender," 1571, 1575; as substitute for temporary peace organization, 1660; question of adherence of other nations, 1687

"Four pillars of peace," CH's address on, 234

Four-Power Treaty (1921), 277, 289, 889

Fourth term of FDR, 1714

France, prewar:

CH trip to, 125; disarmament, 222, 224, 230, 231; German violation of Versailles Treaty, 243; participation in London Economic Conference, 246, 253; in London Naval Conference, 444, 452; in Brussels Conference, 552; trade agreement with U.S., 375, 385; relations with U.S. (1933), 378; with Britain, 382–383; war debts, 385; position on Ethiopia, 421; nonintervention in Spanish War, 476–477, 481–482, 489–490, 512; currency stabilization agreements with U.S. and Britain, 522; Munich agreement on Czechoslovakia, 586, 588, 589, 590, 592, 593, 595; reaction to German conquest of Czechoslovakia, 615, 623; recognition of Franco government, 616, 617; assistance guaranty to Poland, 623; Japanese occupation of Hainan and Spratly Islands, 628–629, 634; effects of U.S. arms embargo, 642–643, 646, 647, 648–649, 651, 653, 683–684, 693; imminence of war in Eu-

France, prewar—Continued
rope, 652, 656, 660–661, 662, 664; preparations for war, 665;

France at war:

reply to FDR's bombing appeal, 674; declaration of war on Germany (1939), 675; rumors of peace moves, 710–712, 844–845; withdrawal of troops from China, 718–722; futile efforts to aid Finland, 740–741; wartime trade restrictions and discriminations, 748; mining of Norwegian waters, 751–752; U.S. assistance in arming, 763, 766; German advances, 765, 770, 773, 776, 787; appeals for British aid, 765, 774, 776; for U.S. declaration of war, 767–770, 787–788; for U.S. fleet in Europe, 773–774; safety of French fleet, 771, 772, 787; removal of gold to U.S. for safekeeping, 772; likelihood of French surrender, 776;

attempts to prevent Italy's entry into war, 780, 781–782, 784; declaration of war by Italy, 784–785; FDR's "stab-in-the-back" address, 784–785; German occupation of Paris, 789; Bullitt's decision to remain in Paris, 789–791; question of withdrawal of Government to North Africa, 787, 789, 793–794; German armistice (June 22, 1940), 791, 793, 795, 804, 849, 851, 960;

France, Vichy:

formation of Pétain government, 791, 799; assets in U.S. frozen, 791, 795; British and U.S. concern over safety of French fleet, 791, 792–793, 795, 796–797, 804, 846–848, 849, 850, 871, 884, 952, 956, 1158, 1161, 1193, 1203, 1224; British destruction of fleet at Oran, 798–799, 800; diplomatic relations with Britain severed, 798–799; U.S. relief to unoccupied France, 804, 879, 881, 882, 884, 885, 949, 952–955, 957, 963; British opposition to relief, 879, 881, 884, 885, 952–955, 957; suggested move to influence Soviet in favor of Allies, 806; Hitler meeting with Pétain, 849; U.S. and British efforts to limit collaboration with Germany, 849–852; dismissal of Laval, 882–883; Darlan-Abetz agree-

France, Vichy—*Continued*
ment for concessions to Germany, 958–961, 962–966; ships in U.S. ports, 959, 960; resistance movement, 1042, 1434; meeting between Göring and Pétain, 1044; appointment of Laval as Premier, 1157, 1160–1161; recall of U.S. and Canadian diplomatic representatives for consultation, 1157–1158; British occupation of Madagascar, 1159; diplomatic relations with U.S. severed, 1192–1195;

  U.S. policy toward Vichy, 804–805, 883–884, 948–949, 963–964, 965, 1038, 1044–1045, 1158, 1192–1194; British relations with Vichy, 796, 798, 804, 846–847, 848, 849, 851, 852, 884, 948, 949, 950, 952–954, 959, 964, 971, 1133–1134; British attitude toward U.S. Vichy policy, 805, 948, 965, 1132, 1133, 1134, 1135–1136, 1192, 1196, 1213, 1218;

  in North Africa (*see* North Africa);
  in the Far East: policy of *status quo* in Netherlands East Indies, 892, 893; agreements with Japan *re* transit of goods through Indo-China, special rights in China, and currency arrangements, 896; *re* passage of Japanese troops through Indo-China, 903–904, 905, 1595; recognition of predominant interest of Japan in Far East, 904; Japanese occupation of Indo-China, 906–908, 1038, 1039, 1041, 1042; trusteeship for Indo-China favored by FDR, 1595–1598;

  in the Western Hemisphere: U.S. and inter-American policy toward European possessions in, 791, 804, 814–817, 822–826; occupation of Aruba by French troops, 814, 816, 891, 893; U.S. efforts to avoid British-French trouble at Martinique, 818–820; Vichy reaction to Free French occupation of Saint-Pierre and Miquelon, 1130, 1134–1135, 1136, 1137; U.S. mission to Martinique, 1160;
France, Free French:
  French National Committee: recognition of De Gaulle as leader of Free French by British, 806; by French colonies, 852; formation of Commit-

France, Free French—*Continued*
tee, 1042; attacks on U.S., 961, 1132–1133, 1159, 1205–1206, 1208, 1214, 1219, 1222, 1223; recognition by U.S. and Britain as "symbol of resistance to Axis," 1162–1163; U.S. unwillingness to give political recognition, 961–962, 1158, 1160, 1193, 1213, 1215; North African policy (*see* North Africa);

  French Committee of National Liberation: formation, 1220; U.S.-British formulas for relations with, 1225–1226, 1232, 1233, 1241–1242; U.S. representative to, 1244; recognition as *de facto* authority in civil administration of France, 1434;

  U.S. cooperation with, 1042, 1158, 1163, 1193, 1435; U.S. efforts toward solidarity with British on French policy, 1132–1137, 1158–1159, 1200, 1203–1204, 1205–1207, 1208, 1213–1220, 1221, 1222–1223, 1225–1226, 1232–1233;

  military activities in Dakar, 852; in Syria, 964–965, 1498, 1540; in Saint-Pierre and Miquelon, 1128–1137; in Far East, 1597–1598; independence of Syria, 1540–1541; efforts to establish "special position" in Syria, 1541–1546; overthrow of Lebanese government, 1245, 1544–1545;

  participation in Allied activities: question of inclusion in United Nations, 1120, 1123, 1125, 1126, 1163, 1221, 1242–1243; membership on Politicomilitary Commission in Algiers, 1243, 1276; on Control Commission for Italy, 1245–1246; on Advisory Council for Italy, 1284, 1551; aid to Jewish refugees, 1539;
  see also De Gaulle;
France, postwar:
  government of, 1160, 1200, 1208–1209, 1210, 1215–1216, 1216–1217, 1242, 1244, 1245, 1301; U.S. recognition of French Committee of National Liberation as *de facto* authority, 1427–1433; as Provisional Government of France, 1434; membership on European Advisory Commission,

France, postwar—*Continued*
1434; on U.N. Security Council, 1434–
1435, 1674, 1678; notified of U.S.
Southeast Asia policy, 1599–1601
Franco, Francisco, U.S. recognition of
government in Spain, 616–618; appeal
for localization of European conflict,
701; desire to remain neutral, 770; refusal to enter war, 849; assurances *re*
U.S. conditions for food shipments to
Spain, 876, 877, 879; attitude toward
U.S., 1187, 1188; message from FDR
on African landing, 1191–1192; *see
also* Spain
Frazier, James B., 38
"Free list" imports, definition, 359
Freedom. *See* Human rights
Freedom of the seas, change in traditional U.S. attitude, 224, 228; disagreements with Britain, 733–736; *see
also* Neutrality policy
French Indo-China, 552; Japanese demands to cease transit of goods to
China, 896; Japanese granted passage
of troops through, 903–904, 905, 1595;
U.S. opposition to Japanese advances,
904–905, 906, 907, 911–912, 914, 915–
916; Japanese occupation of, 906–
908, 1013–1014; Vichy efforts to obtain planes and munitions for, 907;
evacuation of U.S. citizens, 914; border dispute with Thailand, 985, 991;
FDR proposal for neutralization,
1014; Japanese use as base of operations, 1031, 1071, 1078, 1087, 1090,
1092, 1093, 1094; Vichy approval of
Japanese occupation, 1038, 1039,
1041, 1042; negotiations for reduction
or withdrawal of Japanese troops,
1014, 1016, 1021, 1031, 1058, 1069,
1070, 1076, 1079, 1083, 1085; U.S.
proposal for guarantee of territorial
integrity, 1083; trusteeship favored by
FDR, 1595–1598; resistance groups,
1598
French North Africa. *See* North Africa
French West Indies, *See* Martinique
Fulbright resolution, 1258–1263, 1314,
1649
Furstner, Admiral, 652

Gamelin, Maurice, 693, 770
Gandhi, Mohandas K., civil disobedience
movement, 1486–1487, 1488, 1490,
1491, 1492; appeal for U.S. assistance,
1489–1490; imprisonment, 1490, 1491,
1492, 1493
Garay, Narciso, 764
Gardenhire, J. M., 855
Garner, John N., 133, 153–154, 217, 357,
398, 567, 649
Garrett, Finis J., 64, 79
Gasoline, restrictions on U.S. export to
Spain, 875
Gaulle, Charles de. *See* De Gaulle
Gauss, Clarence E., 1027, 1301, 1306
Geneva, Switzerland, Disarmament Con-
ference, 171, 222–233, 386; proposed
location for U.N. Secretariat, 1681
Geneva Prisoners of War Convention,
1589
Gentil, M., 1209
George, Walter, 944, 1262, 1630, 1635,
1658, 1695, 1697
George II, of Greece, 1276
George V, of England, 256, 258
George VI, of England, 595, 623–624
Gerig, Benjamin, 1675
German Atrocities, Declaration on,
1278, 1289–1291
German Reparations Commission, 1286,
1304
German Zeppelin Co., contract for he-
lium from U.S., 597–598
Germany, prewar:
   U.S. declaration of war (1917), 87–
88; Versailles treaty, 103, 233, 243;
CH trip to, 125; Nazi elections, 170;
persecution of Jews, 170, 236–237,
240–241, 578, 599, 1537–1540 (*see also*
Atrocities); rearmament, 222, 230,
233, 235–245, 527, 531; fraudulent financial transactions, 237–240; withdrawal from League, 241; purge of
June 30, 1934, 242; death of von
Hindenburg, 243; possible secret alliance with Japan, 244–245; preparatory meetings for London Economic
Conference, 246; trade methods, 374–
375, 615–616; French and British inaction *re* during 1930's, 383; Air
Force, 384, 590; naval limitation, 452;
   occupation of Rhineland (1936),

Germany, prewar—*Continued*

452; participation in Spanish war, 484, 485, 489–490, 506, 511, 512, 513; Anti-Comintern Pact (1936), 488, 489, 556, 634, 639, 717, 908, 980; Nazi penetrations in Latin America by 1936, 495–496; by 1938, 601–602; absence from Brussels Conference, 553; invasion of Austria, 575–576; invasion of Czechoslovakia, and Munich agreement, 582–583, 586, 589–593, 595–597, 614–615, 623; Hitler exchanges with FDR on independence of other nations, 620–623; reported naval maneuvers off Morocco, 620; as benefactor of U.S. arms embargo, 642, 643, 646, 647, 648–649, 651, 653;

U.S. relations with: recall of U.S. Ambassador Wilson, 170, 599; appointment of U.S. Ambassador Dodd, 182; U.S. export of arms to, 233; maltreatment of U.S. citizens, 236, 240, 241; trade, 371–372, 472–473, 527, 615–616; nonapplication of U.S. arms embargo, 510–513; protest against speech of former U.S. ambassador on Hitler, 572–573; relations with U.S. (1938), 583–585; helium transactions, 597–598; recall of respective ambassadors, 599; propaganda against U.S. in Latin America, 601;

Germany at war:

Tripartite Pact (1940), 489, 627–628, 908–909; war crimes, 1183–1185, 1278, 1289–1291, 1538; asylum to Axis leaders, 1360–1364; penetration in Afghanistan, 1497; application of unconditional surrender principle to, 1570–1582;

attack on Poland (*see* Poland: German attack);

invasion of France (*see* France at war; *and* France, Vichy); moves on Africa (*see* North Africa; *and* Dakar);

war with Britain (*see* Great Britain, at war);

invasion of Norway, 751, 752; declaration of war on Norway, 752; invasion of Denmark, 751, 753, 936–937; activities near Iceland, 754; near Greenland, 758; invasion of Belgium,

Germany at war—*Continued*

761, 764, 773; of Netherlands, 761, 762, 763, 765; of Luxemburg, 761, 763; occupation of Bulgaria, 926, 931; invasion of Yugoslavia and Greece, 928; possible occupation of Azores, 940; Finnish aid to, 977–980, 1449–1450;

invasion of U.S.S.R. (*see* U.S.S.R.);

maritime warfare: torpedoing of *Athenia*, 677; German protest against attempts of U.S. ships to avoid stoppage and search, 682; capture of *City of Flint*, 704–705; German ships in U.S. ports, 927, 942–943; sinking of *Robin Moor*, 944–945; attacks on other ships, 1046–1050; pressure on Panama to prohibit arming of merchant ships, 1048;

policy in Western Hemisphere: scuttling of *Graf von Spee*, 690, 691–692; U.S. and inter-American policy toward European possessions in, 791, 804, 816–817, 822–826, 1629–1630; economic and political penetration in South America, 813–814, 820–821, 1146, 1148, 1150; subversive activities in Argentina, 1377, 1380, 1382, 1383, 1391–1392, 1393, 1396–1397, 1402, 1412; distorted interpretation of Monroe Doctrine, 817–818; political activity by embassy and consular staffs, 827;

war with U.S.: assets in U.S. frozen, 945; closing of consulates in U.S., 945; U.S. policy of self-defense, 1002, 1012; pressure on Japan to take measures against U.S., 1022, 1034; declaration of war on U.S. and by U.S., 1100; Swiss representation of U.S. interests, 1113, 1349; U.S. measures to reduce imports of strategic materials, 1328–1333, 1335–1339, 1346–1351, 1371–1372, 1449–1450;

Southeastern Europe: U.S. efforts to solidify resistance to Axis in Balkans, 928–932; concessions in Syria, 958, 960, 962, 964–965, 1540; Turkish embargo on strategic materials to Germany, 1371–1372; Turkish severance of diplomatic relations, 1372–1376; Turkish entry into war, 1279–1280,

Germany at war—*Continued*
1297, 1301, 1312, 1368–1369, 1370,
1371, 1373, 1375–1376; penetration in
Iran, 1501, 1506; Iranian declaration
of war on Germany, 1505;
    relations with European neutrals:
German plans for troops movements
through Spain, 1191; imports of strategic materials from Spain, 1328–
1333; from Portugal, 1333, 1335–
1339; from Sweden, 1346–1348; from
Switzerland, 1349–1351; from Turkey, 1371–1372; from Finland, 1449–
1450; German U-boat attack on Portuguese ship, 1339; Swedish ports
closed to German shipping, 1348;
    Italian declaration of war on, 1550–
1551; entrenchment in and near
Rome, 1553, 1561, 1562–1563;
Germany, postwar:
    partitioning, 1233–1234, 1265, 1287,
1604–1605, 1606–1607, 1608, 1622;
reparations, 1266, 1286, 1304, 1609;
Inter-Allied Control Commission,
1285, 1618–1619; surrender terms,
1285, 1618, 1622; FDR views, 1602–
1603; destruction of fleet, 1603–1604;
    State Department plan for postwar
treatment, presented at Moscow,
1284–1287; challenged by Morgenthau, 1602, 1604, 1607, 1618–1619;
    Morgenthau plan, 207–208, 1602,
1604–1605, 1622; State Department
opposition, 1605–1607, 1608; War Department opposition, 1607, 1609–1610;
efforts toward reconciliation of views,
1608–1610; agreed to by FDR and
Churchill, 1610–1611, 1614–1615; Morgenthau's offer of credit to Britain a
quid pro quo for approval of plan,
1613–1614, 1615, 1616, 1617–1618;
Eden's opposition, 1615; CH's protest
to FDR and restatement of views,
1616–1618; FDR's replies, 1618–1622;
question of British and Soviet participation, 1607, 1608, 1609, 1616–1617,
1618, 1619, 1620–1621, 1622; interim
directive to Eisenhower, 1607–1608,
1616, 1622; location of Allied zones of
control, 1611–1613; military surveillance by U.S., 1739
Gibson, Henry R., 33

Gibson, Hugh S., 182, 183, 223–224, 347
Gilbert, Alberto, 1391–1393
Gillett, Frederick H., 109
Gillette, Guy M., 1261, 1262, 1658, 1695,
1697
Giraud, Henri H., command of French
military and naval forces in North
Africa, 1196–1199, 1201–1202, 1221,
1226; De Gaulle resentment against,
1205, 1207, 1209, 1219, 1223; trustee
for French interests in North Africa,
1208–1210, 1214, 1217; co-president,
French Committee of National Lib-
eration, 1220; forced out by De
Gaulle, 1216, 1220, 1225–1226, 1244–
1245
Giraudy, Angel, 333
Glass, Carter, 72–73, 124, 151
Godefroy, Admiral, 1203
Golikov, Filip I., 974
Good Neighbor League, CH address, 487
Good Neighbor policy, proclaimed by
FDR, 167; inheritance of ill will in
Latin America, 308–309, 324;
    nonintervention, 310, 339–340, 477;
in Haiti, 312, 320; in Cuba, 312–317,
334, 340–341, 342–344;
    consultation with other nations in
settling disputes in Leticia, 310–311;
in Cuba, 314; in the Chaco, 346–347;
    removal of points of friction: revi-
sion of treaty with Cuba, 317, 334,
343; withdrawal of Marines from
Haiti, 312, 320, 345; revision of treaty
with Panama, 344–345; settlement of
U.S. claims against Mexico, 348–349;
economic assistance to Cuba, 313,
344; transportation and communications, 319, 332, 348;
    advancement at Montevideo Con-
ference, 317, 319–320, 325–330, 340,
349–351, 477;
    value of, upon entry into war, 1139;
cornerstone of U.S. foreign policy,
1426, 1739; awards to CH for work
in behalf of, 1725, 1727
Good offices, in Soviet-Finnish dispute,
706, 741–742, 809; Swedish offer to
Germany and Britain, 845; in Soviet-
Polish boundary dispute, 1268–1271,
1305–1306, 1436, 1437; *see also* Mediation

Gordon, George A., 647, 761–762, 763
Gore, John J., 37–38, 106
Gore, M. L., 37
Gore, Thomas P., 81
Göring, Hermann, 590, 1044
Gousev, Ambassador, 1453, 1456
Grady, Henry F., 366, 1496, 1626–1627
Graf von Spee, scuttling, 690, 691–692
Grant, Ulysses S., 1574, 1576
Grau San Martin, Ramon, 317, 342
Gray, Cecil W., 184, 1274
Gray, David, 1351–1353, 1356, 1357
Graziani, Rodolfo, 579
Great Britain, Empire preferential tariff, 85, 101, 355, 519, 526, 530, 975–976, 1151–1153, 1474, 1476–1477, 1614; CH trip to, 125; disarmament, 225, 227, 379–380; German violation of Versailles treaty, 243; Ottawa agreements, 355; foreign policy in 1937, 531–534; Brussels Conference, 550–556; Munich agreement on Czechoslovakia, 586, 589–593, 595–597, 614–615, 623; assistance guaranty to Poland, 623; imminence of war in Europe, 652, 662; preparations for war, 652, 665; Churchill becomes Prime Minister, 764; death of Lord Lothian, 874;
at war: declaration of war on Germany (1939), 672, 675; reply to FDR bombing appeal, 674; rumors of German peace moves, 710–712, 844–845, 1573; futile efforts to aid Finland, 740–741; wartime trade restrictions and discriminations, 748–749; mining of Norwegian waters, 751–752; landing of troops in Iceland, 754, 946–947; discussion of status of Greenland, 755; controversy over Danish shipping, 759–760; U.S. assistance in arming, 763, 766, 775; determination to resist Germany, 765–766, 775; safety of fleet, 193, 766, 771–772, 774, 796–797, 837–838, 838–839, 840–841; suggestions for U.S. aid, 770; withdrawal of army from Dunkirk, 773; refusal of further aid to France, 774, 776; attempts to prevent Italy's entry into war, 778–779, 782; declaration of war by Italy, 784–785; Churchill message on German advance into France,

Great Britain—*Continued*
and British needs, 787; proposal for military staff conferences with U.S., 796, 797–798;
perilous position in June 1940, 801–803; opposition to relief in occupied countries, 803–804; export surpluses, 828; German air assaults, 844; attempt to capture Dakar, 852; CH admiration of British, 870; need for U.S. financial assistance, 871–873;
military position and needs for 1941, 920–922; encouragement of Yugoslav-Turkish resistance to Axis, 928, 931; shipping losses, 935; agreement on U.S. occupation of Azores in event of German move, 941; U.S. aid in Libya, 944; aid from U.S. accelerated, 944–945; participation in Atlantic Conference, 974–976, 1017–1020 (*see also* Atlantic Charter); declaration of war on Finland, 980; signatory to United Nations Declaration, 1119–1124; Allied invasion of Africa, 952, 1127, 1133, 1162, 1183, 1185, 1186, 1190–1191, 1191–1192, 1216, 1218, 1275; plans for European invasion, 1231–1232; policy on unconditional surrender, 1570–1581;
cooperation with U.S. on policy toward neutrals, 1324–1325; measures for reduction of exports of strategic materials to Germany by Spain, 1329–1333; by Portugal, 1336–1339; by Sweden, 1346–1348; by Switzerland, 1349–1351; by Turkey, 1371–1372; supply-purchase agreement with Portugal, 1335; agreement with Portugal for use of Azores bases, 1339–1340; position on U.S. lease of bases in Eire, 1357; on economic sanctions against Eire, 1359; position on asylum to Axis leaders, 1362–1363; policy decision with U.S. on joint efforts in Turkey, 1365–1368; urges Turkish entrance into war, 1366, 1369, 1370–1371; urges Turkish severance of relations with Germany, 1372–1376; U.S. special mission to explore existing problems (1944), 1428; aid to Jewish refugees, 1539;
relations with U.S.: concern over

Great Britain—*Continued*

U.S. naval building, 287–288; relations with U.S. (1933–35), 378–382, 384–385; Nye Committee allegations, 380, 400, 402; war debts, 381; negotiations *re* strategic materials, 457, 624, 625–626; trade agreement with U.S., 519–530; currency stabilization agreement, 522; U.S. unwillingness to supplant in world trade, 594; visit of King and Queen to U.S. (1939), 595, 623–624, 643–644; harmful effects of U.S. arms embargo, 642–643, 646, 647, 648–649, 651, 653, 683–684, 693; navicert system in U.S., 680–681, 735–736; protests discrimination in U.S. neutrality bill, 695; delay in placing armament orders in U.S., 700; disagreements with U.S. over neutral rights, 733–736; exchange of bases for U.S. destroyers, 187, 193, 212, 831–843, 946; U.S. lend-lease, 873–874, 976, 1151–1153, 1476–1477, 1614; Anglo-American war boards, 1124; U.S. special mission to London to explore existing problems (1944), 1428–1430; summary of U.S.-British policy, 1472–1479; negotiations for Anglo-American oil agreement (1944), 1521, 1522–1523, 1524, 1525–1526; U.S. loan, 1613–1614, 1615, 1616, 1617–1618, 1726–1727; CH views on relations with U.S., 1739; proposals *re* U.S. fleet transfers (*see* Navy, U.S.); *for relations with U.S. concerning third parties, see country, area, or subject involved;*

Western Hemisphere relations: position on Hemisphere neutrality zone, 691; occupation of Curaçao, 814–816, 891, 893; desire to send troops to Aruba, 816; U.S. and inter-American policy toward European possessions in Western Hemisphere, 814–817, 822–826; U.S. efforts to avoid British-French trouble at Martinique, 818–820; bases leased to U.S., 193, 212, 831–843, 946, 1475; relations with Mexico, 1142–1143; cooperation in the Caribbean, 1236–1237, 1475; relations with Argentina, 1409–1419, 1420, 1474–1475;

Great Britain—*Continued*

relations with Spain: nonintervention in civil war, 481–482, 489–490; recognition of Franco government, 616, 617; food relief, 878–879, 880, 881, 882; suggests joint appeal against alliance with Germany, 941; urges economic aid to, 1189; position on export of strategic materials to Germany, 1329–1333;

relations with France (*see* France);

relations with Italy: position on war with Ethiopia, 420, 421, 426–427, 433, 441, 579–582; appeasement policy toward, 573, 579, 581; attempts to prevent Italy's entry into war, 778–779, 781, 782; declaration of war by Italy, 784–785; plans for Italian surrender terms, 1232; member, Advisory Council for Italy, 1283–1284, 1551; Churchill messages *re* Italian capitulation, 1548–1549; opposition to U.S. policy *re* status of crown and Badoglio government, 1550–1558; opposition to status of ally for Italy, 1559; position on bombing of Rome, 1560–1563; opposition to Bonomi government, 1563–1565, 1568; position on economic aid to Italy, 1566–1567; on resumption of diplomatic relations with Italy, 1567–1568;

relations with U.S.S.R.: efforts to bring about Soviet shift in favor of Allies, 806, 811; suggests U.S. embargo on exports to U.S.S.R., 970–971; improvement of relations, 971, 1247–1250, 1252; assurances *re* aid to U.S.S.R., 973, 974; Eden's visit to Moscow (Dec. 1941), 1165–1167; Anglo-Soviet treaty, 1167–1174; pressure on U.S. and Great Britain for second front, 1173, 1174, 1179–1180, 1249, 1264, 1278, 1279, 1280, 1306; efforts to effect Soviet-Polish reconciliation, 1267–1271, 1305–1306, 1315–1317; efforts to settle Soviet-Polish boundary dispute, 1436–1442, 1445, 1447–1449; spheres of influence in Balkans, 1451–1459; negotiations *re* armistices with Rumania, Bulgaria, and Hungary, 1461;

Near Eastern relations: general pol-

Great Britain—*Continued*
icy in, 1475; reaction to U.S. proposed declaration of policy on, 1500; relations with Afghanistan, 1497; with Iran (*see* Iran); with Iraq (*see* Iraq); with Saudi Arabia (*see* Saudi Arabia); invasion of Syria (*see* Syria); *see also* Arab-Jewish question;

Far Eastern relations: position on rights and obligations in China, 279–280; policy in 1937, 531, 532, 553; efforts to end hostilities in Sino-Japanese war, 538–540, 555, 897–899; Tientsin incident, 630–631, 632–633, 635;

recognition of Japanese "special requirements" in China, 635; apprehension over war with Japan (1939), 717, 719–720, 721–722, 727; withdrawal of troops from China, 718–722; policy of *status quo* in Netherlands East Indies, 815–816, 890–891, 892, 893; concessions to Japan, 896–897; proposal for sending U.S. fleet to Singapore, 897, 911, 914; closing of Burma Road and Hong Kong frontier, 897–899, 900, 901; withdrawal of troops from Shanghai, 901; aid to Indo-China, 906;

plans for unified defense in the Pacific, 906–907, 909, 912, 1113; end of appeasement of Japan, 910–911; reopening of Burma Road, 911, 916; request for U.S. aid to Thailand, 985, 991, 997; concern over Japanese aggression, 986; report on Japanese plan to attack Malaya, 996; joint defense of Netherlands East Indies, 1007, 1017, 1093; joint Anglo-American warnings to Japan, 1017–1020, 1023, 1056, 1059, 1092; reaction to U.S.-Japanese peace proposals for the Pacific, 1067, 1073, 1076–1077, 1078–1079, 1080, 1081, 1088–1089; report on imminent Japanese attack on Thailand and Kra Isthmus, 1090; summary of U.S.-British relations, 1475; postwar disposition of Thailand, 1588; divergence with U.S. on Indo-China policy, 1596–1598;

postwar policies: punishment of war crimes, 1183, 1278; on trusteeship sys-

Great Britain—*Continued*
tem, 1234–1238, 1599–1601; administration of liberated countries, 1239–1240, 1244; postwar disposition of Thailand, 1588; divergence with U.S. on Indo-China policy, 1596–1598; reaction to U.S. dependent peoples policy, 1599–1601; postwar treatment of Germany, 1233–1234, 1607, 1608, 1609, 1610–1611, 1615, 1616–1617, 1618, 1619, 1621, 1622; disagreement with U.S. on Allied zones of occupation in Germany, 1611–1613; postwar studies, 1625, 1631; advocacy of regional basis for international organization, 1640–1647, 1649, 1667, 1668; exchange of views with U.S. and U.S.S.R. on international organization, 1260, 1650–1651; participation in Dumbarton Oaks Conference, 1671–1685, 1700–1708, 1712;

see also Cairo Conferences; Four-Nation Declaration; India; Monetary and Economic Conference; Moscow Conference; Naval Conferences; Quebec Conferences; Tehran Conference; Yalta Conference; *and the dominions*
Greece, Italian invasion, 839, 885–886; application of U.S. Neutrality Act, 886; U.S. aid to, 886; German invasion, 928; resistance to aggression, 930; question of plebiscite on monarchy, 1240; representation on Politicomilitary Commission in Algiers, 1275; on Advisory Council for Italy, 1284, 1551; British wartime sphere of influence in, 1451–1459; territorial interests, 1549
Greek Orthodox Church, 715–716
Green, Joseph C., 400, 402, 416, 506, 569, 775, 857
Green, Nathan, 27
Green, William, 1636
Greenland, inclusion under Monroe Doctrine, 753, 755; U.S. opposition to landing of British or Canadian forces, 755–756; U.S. refusal of protectorate, 756; U.S. aid in strengthening defenses, 756, 757; landing of U.S. troops, 757–758; establishment of consular relations with U.S., 756–757; defense of, 935–939; agreement for U.S.

Greenland—*Continued*
lease of airfields, 935, 936; question of
Danish Minister's authority, 936–939
Greenslade, John W., 820
Greer, attack on, 1048
Grew, Joseph C., views and reports as
Ambassador to Japan: on war psychology in Japan, 273; good-will mission to U.S., 275; outlook in Far East
in 1936, 456; Japanese-German alliance, 489, 627–628; Japanese reaction
to Brussels Conference, 551, 555; Japanese reaction to U.S. Neutrality Act,
558; stability in Far East, 723; urging
U.S. policy of firmness, 904–905; on
planned Japanese surprise attack on
Pearl Harbor, 984; proposed FDR-
Konoye meeting, 1025; Tojo support
of U.S.-Japanese conversations (1941),
1054; Japanese action in event of failure of conversations, 1056; Emperor's
reply to FDR message, 1099;
exchanges with Japanese officials: on
U.S. offer of good offices in Sino-Japanese hostilities, 539; bombing of open
cities, 558; *Panay* incident, 559–560,
561; Japanese naval construction,
568; U.S. position on "new order in
East Asia," 569–570; to improve U.S.-
Japanese relations (1940), 893–895;
imminent Japanese southern advance,
1002; U.S. basic principles in Far
East, 1029; U.S.-Japanese conversations, 1030;
participation in Dumbarton Oaks
Conference, 1675
Griggs, James M., 55
Gromyko, Andrei A., 1253, 1363, 1437,
1442, 1443, 1444, 1449, 1451, 1462; at
Dumbarton Oaks Conference, 1671,
1672, 1678–1685, 1700, 1702, 1705–
1706
Grotius, Hugo, 175, 407–408
Grundy, Joseph R., 132
Guam, 289
Guani doctrine of recognition of new
American governments in wartime,
1402
Guardia, Ricardo Adolfo de la, 1048
Guatemala, trade agreement with U.S.,
375; German attempts to intimidate,
821

Guinazu, Enrique Ruiz, 1144, 1146, 1377,
1378, 1379
Gunter, John W., 1513
Günther, Christian E., 1348, 1363
Gunther, Franklin Mott, 686–687, 807,
810
Gustav V, of Sweden, 703–704
Gustav Adolf, of Sweden, 702–703
Gwynn, William M., 1542

Haakon VII of Norway, 752–753
Hackworth, Green H., 181, 671, 1096,
1686;
opinions and memoranda on U.S.
claims against Canada, 206; on seizure of U.S. property en route to neutrals, 507; on Danish-Icelandic relationships, 753; on Neutrality Act,
872; on U.N. Declaration, 1119, 1121;
on operation of U.N. security organization, 1696;
delegate to international conferences, 603, 822, 1265, 1274, 1280, 1675;
drafts of destroyer-bases agreement,
837, 838, 840; on proposal on dependent peoples, 1234;
participation in postwar planning,
1626–1627, 1633, 1635, 1643
Hague Convention (1907), 842, 872
Haile Selassie, Emperor of Ethiopia, 418,
419, 423, 424
Hainan, Japanese occupation, 628, 634
Haiphong, Japanese occupation, 906, 907
Haiti, 312, 333, 1237; withdrawal of
U.S. Marines, 170, 312, 320, 345; removal of U.S. financial controls, 170,
345–346; trade agreement with U.S.,
375
Hale, Nathan W., 54–55
Halifax, Lord, British Foreign Secretary, views and discussions on: U.S.
peace efforts in Europe, 588, 623; German aggression, 615; U.S. fleet in Pacific, 630; imminence of war, 652, 662;
Czechoslovakia, 815–816; Dutch possessions, 586; Ethiopia, 581;
British Ambassador to U.S., 926;
views and discussions on: Empire tariff preferences, 976, 1476–1477, 1479;
U.N. Declaration, 1119–1123; Dumbarton Oaks Conference, 1671, 1672,
1675; Argentina, 1410–1412, 1413,

Halifax, Lord—*Continued*
1414–1415, 1419; Balkans, 928, 1452, 1453; Far East, 996, 1003, 1017, 1056, 1088–1089, 1090, 1091, 1113, 1595, 1596–1597; Finland, 980; France, 949–957 *passim,* 959, 962, 1129, 1131, 1132, 1158–1159, 1196; Iceland, 946; India, 1483, 1485, 1486, 1487, 1490, 1492, 1495; Italy, 1561; Palestine, 1534; Spain, 941, 1189, 1330; Turkey, 928, 931, 1365, 1367–1368; U.S.S.R., 970–971
Hamaguchi, Yuko, 287
Hamilton, Maxwell M., 895, 989, 1003, 1031, 1114–1115, 1724
Hampton, John, 24
Hankey, Sir Maurice, 266–267
Hanna, Margaret M., 181
Hanoi, Japanese occupation, 906, 907
Harding, Warren G., 104, 114, 127, 387
Harkness, Richard, 1657
Harmon, Judson, 67, 68, 104
Harriman, Mrs. J. Borden, 183, 752, 760
Harriman, W. Averell, 200; mission to U.S.S.R., 977, 981, 1165–1166; accompanies Churchill to Moscow, 1179–1180, 1486;
U.S. Ambassador to U.S.S.R.: at Moscow Conference, 1277, 1280, 1293, 1296, 1306; views and discussions on Turkey, 1373, 1375–1376; Polish-Soviet dispute, 1436, 1437, 1439, 1440, 1443, 1446, 1448; Soviet foreign policy, 1459–1461
Harris, Isham G., 33
Harris, Miss Will, 47
Harrison, Leland, 543–544, 648, 1349
Harrison, Pat, 217, 357
Harrison-Cleveland campaign (1888), 21–22
Harvard University, 794, 1673
Harvey, George, 67
Hassan Bey, Mahmoud, 1532
Hatch, Carl A., 1262, 1670, 1696, 1698
Havana Conference (1928), 308
Havana Conference of Foreign Ministers (1940), invitation, 791–792; date of convening, 816; German and Italian propaganda against, 821; U.S. delegation, 822; CH's opening address, 823, 827; efforts of CH to bring about accord on collective trusteeship for Eu-

Havana Conference—*Continued*
ropean possessions, 823–826, 1629–1630; Act of Havana, 826; agreements to curb subversive activities, 827; arrangements to combat economic effects of war, 827–828; resolution regarding aggressive acts of non-American states, 1139, 1143; summation of results, 829
Hawaii, Japanese espionage activities in, 1011; Japanese attack on Pearl Harbor, 984, 1095, 1096, 1098; proposed meeting place for U.N. Council, 1681
Hawkins, Harry C., 366, 1633
Hawley-Smoot Act (1930), 132, 152, 355, 357, 358, 359, 363
Hay, James, 62
Hay, John, 271
Hayes, Carlton, 1190, 1191, 1326–1332 *passim*
Hays, Will, 1259, 1670
Hearst, William Randolph, 67, 68, 150, 389
Heath, Donald R., 844
Heiskell, Samuel G., 31
Helium, 597–598
Hellmuth case in Argentina, 1391, 1392
Henry-Haye, Gaston, appointment as French Ambassador to U.S., 847; views and discussions on Vichy policies, 848, 851, 1039; relief for unoccupied France, 952, 954; French ships in U.S. ports, 960; Syria, 960, 964; Laval, 1160–1161; St. Pierre-Miquelon, 1131–1132;
recall, 1195
Hepburn, Arthur J., 1636, 1675
Herriot, Edouard, 246
Hickerson, John, 206, 1182
Hill, Ebenezer J., 83, 358
Hill, Lister, 1262, 1670, 1696, 1698
Hilldring, John H., 1607
Himmler, Heinrich, 1573
Hindenburg, Paul von, 243
Hindenburg, German dirigible, 597
Hiranuma, Baron K., 627, 631–632, 633, 717
Hirohito, 1091–1092, 1093–1094, 1099, 1591–1595
Hirota, Koki, views and discussions on good relations with U.S., 275, 555; Sino-Japanese war, 539, 542, 558; *Pa-*

Hirota, Koki—*Continued*
  nay incident, 560, 561, 562; naval limitations, 568–569
Hiss, Alger, 1675
Hitchcock, Gilbert Monell, 152
·Hitler, Adolf (*for nonpersonal items, see* Germany *or subject*), 226, 227; speech of former Ambassador Dodd concerning, 572–573; meetings with Chamberlain, 589, 590, 595; Franco, 849; Pétain, 849; speech on peace with Britain, 844; *see also* Germany
Hoare, Sir Samuel, 384, 443, 1332
Hoey, Clyde R., 856
Holbrook, Alfred, 22
Holland. *See* Netherlands
Honduras, 375, 821
Hong Kong, 897, 900, 1596, 1599
Hoover, Herbert, policies as President, 131, 140, 148, 160, 223, 226, 228, 309, 387; relations with FDR, 183, 202; activities in World War II, 678, 804, 1052
Hoover, J. Edgar, 968
Hoover, John H., 1160, 1223
Hopkins, Harry, relations with FDR, 195, 205, 873; missions abroad, 200, 922, 973; at First Quebec Conference, 1240; participation in foreign affairs, 862, 923, 976–977, 1370, 1408, 1493, 1595, 1604, 1607, 1608, 1609
Hoppenot, Henri, 1220, 1224
Hore-Belisha, Leslie, 693
Horinouchi, Kensuke, 628–639 *passim,* 719, 721, 724, 729–730, 889–893, 912–914
Hornbeck, Stanley K., 181, 552, 671, 672, 895, 988, 1031, 1095, 1234, 1626–1627, 1675
Horton, Henry H., 134
Hoskins, Harold B., 1532, 1533
House, Edward, 121–122
House of Representatives, U.S. *See* Congress
Houston, William C., 64
Howe, Louis, 132, 149, 154, 319
Hu Shih, 685, 1006, 1026, 1033, 1067, 1073–1074, 1076, 1077, 1078, 1079, 1082, 1112, 1113
Hughes, Charles Evans, 116, 148, 167, 308, 318, 360
Hughes, William, 62

Hull, Allen B., 3, 22
Hull, Cordell (*for nonpersonal items, see subject*), birth, 3, 5–6;
  family: grandparents, 3, 22; father (*see* Hull, William); mother, 5, 7–8, 42; brothers, 5–6, 10–11, 12, 14–19, 22–23, 115–116; wife (*see* Hull, Frances Witz);
  childhood and early youth, 6–23; locale, 6–9, 10, 13; employment, 10–11, 12, 14, 19–21; education, 11, 14–19, 21, 22–23, 26–27; debating successes, 14–15, 27–28;
  health, 13, 19, 23, 24, 30, 122, 129, 134, 1137–1138, 1150, 1255, 1303, 1308, 1715–1719, 1720, 1721;
  legal and judicial career, 19, 24, 26, 27, 29, 33, 37–42, 107, 113;
  military service: Spanish-American War, 34–36; offer of services in World War I, 69–70, 333;
  congressional career (*see* Congress); social life, 36, 47–48, 177–178, 179, 199, 675, 1181–1182, 1306, 1308, 1311; marriage, 93–94; religion, 94; smoking habit, 111, 129; European visit (1925), 125;
  potential candidate for President, (1924) 122, 130; (1928) 129–130; (1932) 149; (1940) 749–750, 855–859; for Vice President, (1940) 860–861, (1944) 1714;
  appointment as Secretary of State, 156–158; appraisal and commendations of FDR, 122–123, 185, 191, 194–200, 205–206, 208, 249, 267, 285, 340, 440;
  honors and awards: designation by FDR as "Father of United Nations," 1718, 1723, 1728; Nobel Peace Prize (1945), 1724–1726; other honors and awards, 1719, 1727;
  resignation as Secretary of State, 1137–1138, 1323, 1715–1719; visits from FDR in hospital, 1719, 1720, 1721; commencement of *Memoirs,* 1726; views on U.S. affairs and the future, 1729–1742; *see also* Secretary of State
Hull, Elizabeth Riley, 5, 7–8, 42
Hull, Frances Witz (Mrs. Cordell), marriage to CH, 93–94; assistance in so-

Hull, Frances Witz—*Continued*
cial and official functions, 178–179,
856, 1182; attendance at international
conferences, 125, 258, 339; gift to
FDR, 451; praise by Tennessee State
Legislature, 1719–1720

Hull, Orestes (Ress), birth, 5–6; education, 11, 14–19, 22–23; work, 10–11,
12, 14; death, 116

Hull, Roy, 5–6, 10–11, 12, 14, 116

Hull, Senadius Selwin (Nade), birth,
5–6; education, 11, 15–18; work, 10–
11, 12, 13, 14; later life, 115–116

Hull, Serena Maynard, 3

Hull, William, description and early
life, 3–4, 10; politics, 7–8; logging,
10, 11, 12, 13, 19–21; business, 12,
13–14, 19; education of children, 11,
14–19, 22–23; removal to Carthage,
Tenn., 111; death, 115–116

Hull, Wyoming, 5–6, 10–11, 12, 14, 116

Human rights, CH views on, 16–17, 25,
37, 128, 136, 175, 187–188

Humbert, Crown Prince of Italy, 1552,
1555, 1558, 1563

Hungary, demands in Czech crisis, 592,
596, 614; attack on Yugoslavia, 933;
war with U.S., 1114, 1175–1176; Soviet armistice terms, 1461; nonapplication of unconditional surrender
policy to, 1570, 1575–1577, 1579–1580

Hurban, Vladimír, 615, 1124

Hurley, Patrick J., 200, 1276, 1506,
1507, 1514

Iberia. *See* Spain *and* Portugal

Iberia Air Line, 1326

Iberian Peninsula Operating Committee, 1327

Ibn Saud, King of Saudi Arabia, 1511,
1512, 1513, 1532–1533, 1535

Iceland, 753, 754, 946–947

Ickes, Harold L., 207, 1512, 1531; CH
appraisal, 209; refusal to sell helium
to Germany, 597–598; views on safeguarding U.S. oil reserves, 1517, 1518,
1519, 1520; president of Board of Directors of Petroleum Reserves Corp.,
1520–1521, 1522, 1524; participation
in Anglo-American oil discussions,
1522–1523, 1525, 1526

Immigration, Jewish, to Palestine (*see*
Arab-Jewish question); Jewish, to
U.S., 1538–1540; repeal of U.S. laws
excluding Chinese, 1583

Imports, U.S. *See* Tariff; Trade, U.S.;
Trade agreements; *and specific commodity*

Income tax, efforts by CH to secure
legislation (1907–11), 48–50, 52, 58–
61, 66; amendment to Constitution
ratified, 70; legislation drafted by
CH, 70–71, 73–74; enacted (1913),
71, 76; amended (1916), 77, 80–81,
89

India, inclusion in U.N. Declaration,
1120, 1123, 1124; strategic importance
in World War II, 1482, 1485, 1487;
U.S. advocacy of independence, 1482–
1483, 1488–1489, 1490–1491, 1496;
establishment of diplomatic relations
with U.S., 1483; exclusion from provisions of Atlantic Charter, 1484–
1485; Cripps mission, 1486, 1492; activities of personal representatives of
U.S. President, 1486, 1488, 1489, 1491,
1492–1494, 1495; civil disobedience
movement, 1486–1487, 1488, 1490,
1491, 1492; proposal for U.S. fact-
finding commission, 1486, 1487; role
of U.S. forces in, 1489, 1494; U.S.
economic mission, 1496

Indo-China. *See* French Indo-China

Inheritance and estate taxes, 77, 80–81

Inönü, Ismet, 1365, 1369–1370, 1371–
1372

Inter-American conferences. *See* Buenos
Aires; Havana; Lima; Mexico City;
Montevideo, Panama; *and* Rio de
Janeiro

Inter-American Defense Board, 1150

Inter-American Emergency Advisory
Committee for Political Defense, 1383,
1388–1389, 1399

Interdepartmental Committee for Reciprocity Information, 366

Intergovernmental Committee on Political Refugees, 578

Interior Department, 597–598

International conferences. *See name of
conference*

International cooperation, policy of,
CH urges, 123, 124, 126–127, 138, 157,

International cooperation—*Continued*
159, 173–174, 211, 230, 1212, 1254,
1735, 1740, 1742; Democratic Party
on, 134, 153; FDR "quarantine"
speech, 544–546; opposition of isolationists (*see* Isolationism); discussed
at Moscow, 1279, 1280–1281, 1296,
1297, 1308, 1310, 1311, 1312–1313,
1314, 1315
International Court of Justice, 1178, 1631,
1647, 1651, 1653, 1681; *see also* Permanent Court
International Labor Conference (1944),
1654–1655
International Labor Organization, 177
International Law, American Society of,
764, 941
International Nonintervention Committee, 481, 482, 489, 504, 512
International organization for peace.
See United Nations
International Petroleum Commission,
1526
International Petroleum Policy, Com-
mittee on, 1517
Inukai, Tsuyoshi, 276, 287
Iran, 1277; question of sovereignty in
Persian Gulf, 232; occupation by
Britain and U.S.S.R., 976, 1500, 1501–
1502, 1506; signs U.N. Declaration,
1253, 1505; use as supply route to
U.S.S.R., 1498, 1500, 1502–1503, 1506;
German influence in, 1501, 1506; U.S.
interest in preserving independence,
1501, 1502, 1504, 1507; Anglo-Soviet-
Iranian treaty, 1502, 1505, 1506;
changes in government, 1502, 1510;
U.S. lend-lease aid, 1503, 1507; U.S.
economic and military missions, 1503,
1505, 1506, 1507, 1508; declaration of
war on Germany, 1505; U.S. troops
in, 1505–1506; three-power declaration at Tehran, 1505, 1506–1507, 1510;
FDR views on, 1507; establishment
of U.S. Embassy, 1507; competition
for oil concessions, 1508–1510; *see
also* Tehran Conference
Iraq, uprising against British, 958, 964,
965; U.S. oil interests in, 1499; declaration of war on Axis and admission
to U.N., 1504; protests U.S. pro-

Iraq—*Continued*
Zionism, 1532, 1535, 1537; Arab
Congress, 1546–1547
Ireland. *See* Eire
Iron and steel scrap and products, export control, 907, 912–914, 915
Ishii, Viscount Kikujiro, 246, 265, 274,
285, 635–636
Ismay, Sir Hastings Lionel, 1280
Isolationism, in the 20's, 112, 123, 127,
134, 157; CH opposition to, 112, 176–
177, 187, 211, 246, 256, 666–667, 1734–
1735; isolationists in Congress during
FDR administration, 215–218; opposition to international cooperation, 279,
304, 397, 409, 425, 429, 431, 464, 465,
588, 1297; to effective prosecution of
World War II, 288, 573–574, 641–
653, 684, 803, 863, 943, 960, 1104;
Nye Committee, 399–400, 404; Ludlow resolution, 563–564; in U.S.S.R.,
1297, 1310, 1313; *see also* International cooperation; *and* Neutrality
policy
Italy, 171, 243, 246; London Naval
Conference, 444, 452; Axis accord
with Germany (1936), 488; Anti-
Comintern Pact, 489, 556, 634, 639,
908; nonsupport of mediation offer
for Spain, 489–490; subversive activities in Latin America, 495; aid to
Franco Government in Spain, 482,
510–513; Brussels Conference, 553,
556; Munich agreement, 595; occupation of Albania, 618–619; reaction to
U.S. arms embargo, 647, 693; war
debts, 785;
war with Ethiopia: international
efforts to avert, 418–427; U.S. moral
embargo, 192–193, 425, 426, 430–442,
460–461, 467, 471, 809; U.S. neutrality, 411–412, 414, 417, 419, 428–433,
467, 468, 471; occupation of Addis
Ababa, 468; Hoare-Laval plan, 443;
U.S. nonrecognition of possession of
Ethiopia, 469–470; British recognition, 579–582;
World War II: FDR message to
King urging peace appeal, 655, 661,
662, 664; Mussolini's proposal for
five-power conference, 664; FDR's
bombing appeal, 672, 674; rumor of

Italy—*Continued*
peace move by Mussolini, 712–713;
U.S., British, French, and Vatican
efforts to prevent Italy's entry into
war, 620–622, 777–784; declaration of
war on Britain and France, 784–785;
FDR's stab-in-the-back address, 784–
785; U.S. neutrality (1939), 785; U.S.
and inter-American policy on European possessions in Western Hemisphere, 791, 804, 816–817, 822–826;
propaganda against Havana Conference, 821; political activity by embassy and consular staffs, 827; invasion of Greece, 839, 885–886; Tripartite Pact (1940), 489, 627–628,
908–909; closing of consulates in U.S.,
926, 945; shipping in U.S. ports, 927,
942; freezing of assets in U.S., 945;
declaration of war on U.S. and by
U.S., 1100; Allied Control Commission for Italy, 1245–1246, 1555, 1557,
1560, 1563, 1565, 1566; Inter-Allied
Advisory Council for Italy, 1283–
1284, 1317, 1551, 1552, 1556, 1557,
1558, 1559, 1564, 1565; Declaration *re*
Italy, 1283–1284; Soviet request for
Italian war vessels, 1284, 1301–1302;
Swiss exports to, 1349–1351; U.S.
distinctive treatment, 1548; surrender,
1232, 1549, 1570, 1571, 1575–1577,
1579–1580;
Badoglio government, 1550–1559,
1564–1565, 1568; declaration of war
on Germany and acceptance as cobelligerent, 1550–1551; Sforza's participation, 1551–1552, 1553; diplomatic relations with U.S.S.R., 1449,
1463, 1556–1557; new government
formed, 1558–1559; status of ally refused, 1554–1555, 1559–1560; bombing
of Rome, 1560–1563;
Bonomi government, 1563–1569;
Sforza's participation, 1563, 1568;
British objections, 1563–1565; Italian
Committee for National Liberation,
1564, 1565; economic relief, 1565,
1566–1567, 1569; establishment of
diplomatic relations abroad, 1566,
1567–1568; King's abdication, 1568–
1569

Iwakuro, Hideo, 1003, 1004, 1005, 1009,
1014

Jackson, Andrew, 17, 121
Jackson, Robert H., 209, 835, 841, 943,
1531
Jackson, Thomas J. (Stonewall), 219
Jahn, Gunnar, 1725
Jamaica, 831–843
James, Ollie M., 81
Japan, preparatory meetings for London Economic Conference, 246; military and liberal elements in, 276, 286,
290, 727, 728, 1003, 1034, 1089; demands for naval parity, 223, 286–290,
384, 444–450, 455; subversive activities in Latin America, 495;
policy of aggression: record of aggressive actions, 117, 170, 270–271,
1036; League of Nations' actions *re*,
160, 170, 270, 272, 386, 542–544, 559;
possible secret alliance with Germany
(1934), 244; avowals of peaceful intentions, 273, 279, 281, 284, 989, 990,
1009, 1011, 1021, 1060, 1063; efforts
to consolidate acquisitions through
diplomatic agreements, 277–278, 631;
Amau statement on Japanese sole responsibility in East Asia, 279, 284;
reported naval construction, 568–569;
Tripartite Pact, 489, 627–628, 908–
909, 991, 1002, 1006–1007, 1010, 1011,
1021, 1028, 1035, 1059, 1060, 1061,
1062, 1063–1064, 1066, 1071, 1083;
claim to Spratly Islands, 628–629; demands on France and Britain (1940),
896; military activities following Imperial conference (1941), 1012;
in Southeast Asia: Thailand, 985,
991, 997, 1090; Malaya, 996, 1002;
Kra Isthmus, 1090, 1091, 1093; *see
also* French Indo-China;
in China (*see* China);
in Manchuria (*see* Manchuria);
see also Netherlands East Indies
relations with U.S.: anti-U.S. sentiment, 272–274, 639, 1023, 1054, 1075;
friendly overtures, 274, 278, 556;
false concept of Monroe Doctrine,
281–282, 890, 892–893, 1032; proposal
for U.S.-Japanese spheres of influence, 281–285, 894; bombing of

Japan—*Continued*

U.S.S. *Panay,* 559–563; U.S. position
on "new order in East Asia," 569–570,
982; Saito ashes returned on U.S.
warship, 629; proposal for joint action to avert European war, 631–632,
633; good-will missions to U.S. discouraged, 275, 629, 630; Grew-Arita
conversations to improve relations
(1940), 893–895; proposed nonaggression pact with U.S., 997, 1014;
U.S. interception of Japanese official
code messages, 998; espionage activities in U.S. and Hawaii, 1011–1012;
freezing of assets in U.S., 1014; German pressure to rupture Japanese-
U.S. relations, 1022, 1034; instructions
for evacuating Japanese in U.S., 1068;
CH's warnings of imminent danger to
U.S. (1941), 203, 1057–1058, 1079–
1080, 1087, 1088, 1098;

conversations with U.S. to avert
war (1941), 187, 193, 985, 989; unofficial Japanese proposals (Apr. 9)
re Tripartite Pact, peace with China,
mutual trade relations, 991–993; U.S.
principles prerequisite to negotiations,
994, 995, 1029; submission to Tokyo
for approval, 996–998; official Japanese proposals (May 12) *re* same,
999–1007; U.S. proposals (May 31)
on Tripartite Pact and China, 1007–
1008; U.S. oral statement on divergencies of view, 1008–1010; Japanese
draft on, 1010–1011; U.S. decision to
close conversations upon Japanese invasion of Indo-China, 1013–1015,
1066; resumption of conversations,
and Japanese proposals *re* special position in Indo-China, 1016–1017, 1021;
U.S. warning against further Japanese
aggression, 1017–1020, 1027; Japanese
propose FDR-Konoye meeting, 992,
1020–1036 *passim;* Japanese proposals (Sept. 6) on main points of difference, 1028–1029, 1031–1032; technical difficulties, 1030–1031; U.S.
statement on progressive narrowing
of Japanese position, 1033, 1035; CH
reviews six months' developments under Konoye Cabinet, 1035–1037; Tojo
Cabinet's attitude on conversations,

Japan—*Continued*

1054–1055, 1056, 1059, 1062, 1063;
Japanese deadline for agreement,
1056–1057, 1063, 1068, 1074, 1077;
reworded Japanese proposals (Nov.
7) on three main points, 1058–1059;
U.S. proposal for joint declaration on
economic policy, 1060–1061; discussions on points of difference, 1061–
1068; Japanese ultimatum (Nov. 20),
1068–1070; possible U.S. counterpro-
posals, 1072–1079, 1080–1082, 1088–
1089; U.S. ten-point basic proposals
for mutual commitments (Nov. 26),
1083–1086, 1090–1091; Australian mediation offer, 1089; FDR message to
Hirohito, 1091–1092, 1093–1094, 1099;
U.S. inquiry on Japanese troops in
Indo-China, 1092, 1093; Japanese reply to Nov. 26 proposals (Dec. 7),
1095–1097, 1098; CH reviews conversations, 1100–1105;

trade with U.S.: Japanese exports
(1934), 286; following U.S. abroga-
tion of 1911 commercial treaty, 636–
638, 725–730, 894; U.S. embargoes on
strategic materials, 229, 636–639, 641,
729–730, 901–902, 912–914, 983, 990,
1014, 1067, 1102–1103; question of
U.S. embargo on petroleum, 983,
1066, 1075, 1078, 1081, 1085, 1102–
1103, 1104; U.S.-Japanese conversations on mutual trade relations, 992,
1007, 1014, 1022, 1029, 1036, 1058,
1059, 1060–1061, 1066, 1069, 1072,
1083;

war with U.S.: attack on Pearl
Harbor, 983, 1095, 1096, 1724, 1726,
1727; U.S. declaration of war against,
1097, 1098, 1100; U.S. destruction of
codes and papers in U.S. official establishments in Japan, 1093; Japanese
establishments and personnel in U.S.
protected, 1099; Swiss representation
of U.S. interests, 1113, 1349; unified
defense in Pacific against Japan, 1113;
application of unconditional surrender policy to Japan, 1570–1582; treatment of U.S. prisoners of war and
civilian internees, 1589;

postwar treatment: disposition of
mandated islands, 1466, 1596, 1599,

Japan—*Continued*
1706–1707; Korean independence, 1584, 1596; State Department proposal, 1589–1593; Potsdam agreement, 1593–1595; CH recommendation, 1739; relations with U.S.S.R., 293, 295, 298, 302, 552, 627, 628, 634–635, 639, 977, 1012, 1462; concern over U.S. recognition of U.S.S.R., 276–277; Anti-Comintern Pact with Germany, 488, 489, 634, 639, 717, 908, 980; resentment over German-Soviet nonaggression pact, 717, 720–721; Outer Mongolia border dispute with U.S.S.R., 720, 811; nonaggression treaty with U.S.S.R., 969, 993, 1020; protests on U.S. oil shipments to U.S.S.R. via Vladivostok, 1017–1018; efforts for separate German-Soviet peace, 1263–1264, 1462; Soviet reluctance to antagonize, 1111–1113; Soviet declaration of war on, 1249, 1309–1310, 1311, 1470

Jefferson, Thomas, 24–25, 37, 169, 173, 197, 860

Jewish Theological Seminary, 1626

Jews, 207; in Germany, 170, 236–237, 240–241, 578, 579, 599; in North Africa, 1197, 1214; in Palestine (*see* Arab-Jewish question); refugees, 1528, 1529, 1531, 1534, 1537–1540; *see also* Atrocities

Johnson, Andrew, 21

Johnson, Herschel V., 181, 1348

Johnson, Hiram, 217, 465, 573–574

Johnson, Hugh, 242

Johnson, Louis, 208, 1486, 1488, 1491

Johnson, Luther A., 218, 1635

Johnson, Nelson T., 539, 631

Johnson Act (1934), 303, 381–382, 427

Johnston, Eric, 1636

Joint Chiefs of Staff, views on trade with Spain and Portugal, 1325; U.S. bases in Eire, 1357; Turkish severance of relations with Germany, 1374–1375; disposition of Pacific islands, 1466; postwar friendship with U.S.S.R., 1470; oil concessions in Saudi Arabia, 1518, 1519; Dumbarton Oaks Conference, 1705, 1706

Jones, Grosvenor M., 822

Jones, Jesse H., 204, 210, 861

Jones, W. A., 278

Jordan, R. S., 1514–1515, 1516

Jordana y Souza, Count Francisco Gómez, 617, 1190, 1191, 1326

Judicial career of CH, 38–42

Juin, Alphonse, 1045

Jung, Guido, 246, 263

Justice, International Court of, 1178, 1631, 1647, 1651, 1653, 1681; *see also* Permanent Court

Justo, Agustín P., 497, 499

Kalinin, Mikhail, 293, 297–298, 703

Kane, U.S.S., 480

Kauffmann, Henrik de, 753, 756, 759, 927, 935, 936–939

Keifer, Joseph W., 54–55

Kelchner, Warren, 351

Kelley, Robert F., 181, 299, 302

Kellogg, Frank B., 333

Kellogg-Briand Pact (1928), 128, 153, 304, 309, 322, 328, 332, 418, 419, 420, 421, 427, 433, 583, 588

Kelly, Sir David, 1415, 1416–1418

Kennan, George F., 1341, 1342

Kennedy, Joseph P., relations with FDR, 200; chairman, U.S. Maritime Commission, 558; reports and views as U.S. Ambassador to Britain, 586, 588, 589, 590, 592, 596, 623, 652, 662, 663, 671, 672, 675, 677, 693, 763, 765–766; resignation, 926

Kerr, Sir Archibald Clark, 1270–1271, 1278

King, William H., 232, 315

Kirk, Alexander, 647–648, 651, 655, 710–711, 712, 761, 762, 1276, 1568

"Kitchen" cabinet, FDR, 204–205

Kitchin, Claude, 63, 92, 95, 96

Kleffens, E. N. van, 1007

Klotz, Alexis, 1274

Knatchbull-Hugessen, Sir Hughe, 1372

Knox, Frank, 208, 838, 839, 910, 935–936, 943, 1047, 1058, 1071, 1077, 1091, 1092, 1093, 1095, 1097, 1346, 1347, 1517, 1518, 1670

Knudsen, William S., 910

Koenig, General, 1433

Konitza, Faik, 619

Konoye, Prince Fumimaro, 286, 542, 556, 627, 630, 902, 977, 997, 1002, 1012, 1019–1037 passim, 1102
Koo, Wellington, 1707
Korea, 270, 1584, 1596
Kra Isthmus, 1090, 1091, 1093, 1588
Kung, H. H., 1586
Kuniholm, Bertel E., 946
Kurile Islands, 1596
Kurusu, Saburo, 276, 1034, 1056; conversations with CH, 1062–1067, 1068, 1074–1076, 1082, 1085–1086, 1087–1088, 1090–1091, 1092, 1093, 1095–1097; CH appraisal, 1062–1063; conversations with FDR, 1063–1064, 1086

Labor, CH views on, 52, 196, 197; labor conditions discussed at Moscow Conference, 1303, 1304
Labor, American Federation of, 545
Labor Conference, International (1944), 1654–1655
Labor Organization, International, 177
Ladybird, British gunboat, 561
La Follette, Philip F., 335
La Follette, Robert M., 108
La Follette, Robert M., Jr., 1658, 1695
Lais, Alberto, 927
Land, Emory S., 698, 1391
Landon, Alfred M., 603, 611
Lane, Arthur Bliss, 618, 928–932 passim
Lange, Oscar, 1442–1443, 1444
Lansing, Robert, 82, 285, 403–404, 635–636
Latin America. See American republics; and individual countries
Latvia, Soviet pressure, 701; Soviet occupation, 810, 812; assets in U.S. frozen, 811; Soviet territorial aims, 1166, 1167, 1171, 1172, 1173
Laurel, José P., 1328
Laval, Pierre, 432, 854; role in Italo-Ethiopian war, 419, 442, 443; CH appraisal, 441; collaboration with Germany, 791, 804, 848–849, 850, 851, 852, 884–885, 908, 949, 952, 953, 1039, 1157, 1160–1161, 1195
Law, Richard, 1477, 1478
Lea, Luke, 77–79, 134, 135, 138
League of Nations, 497, 499; U.S. refusal to join, 102–104, 112–113, 124, 150, 212, 216, 222, 386, 387, 1307,

League of Nations—Continued
1662–1663; Japan's withdrawal, 170, 270; German withdrawal, 241, 386; sponsorship of London Economic Conference, 246, 386; admission of U.S.S.R., 304; expulsion of U.S.S.R., 709–710; mandates, 1528, 1540; action in Japanese aggressions, 160, 170, 270, 272, 386, 542–544, 559; Leticia dispute, 170–171, 310–311; Chaco War, 336–337, 346–347; Italo-Ethiopian War, 418–420, 425–435, 440–442, 469–470, 471; Russo-Finnish War, 709–710;
U.S. cooperation, 182, 386–387; in Far East, 160, 272, 274, 311, 386, 542–544, 559; in Leticia dispute, 170–171, 310–311, 386; in Chaco War, 336–337, 346–347, 386, 1646; U.S. independent action in Italo-Ethiopian War, 418–420, 425–435, 440–442, 469–470, 471; in Russo-Finnish War, 709–710; U.S. decision not to revive, 1627, 1639
Leahy, William D., U.S. Ambassador to France, 201, 883–884, 948–957, 958, 963, 1038, 1040, 1043, 1044, 1157; Chief of Staff to the President, 1265, 1304, 1367, 1368, 1518, 1581
Lebanon, 1245, 1535, 1540, 1544–1547
Lee, Robert E., 1574, 1576
Leffingwell, Russell C., 92
Legal and judicial career of CH, 19, 24, 26, 27, 29, 33, 37–42, 113
Léger, Alexis, 646, 652, 664, 693, 712–713, 767–768, 806
Leith-Ross, Sir Frederick, 260, 529
Leitner, Rudolf, 240, 242, 496
Lend-lease, passage of legislation, 873–874, 922, 923–925; inclusion of nondiscriminatory clauses in agreements, 976, 1151–1153, 1211, 1212, 1476–1477, 1614; aid to China, 997, 1175; Free French, 1042, 1435; Great Britain, 976, 1151–1153, 1476–1477, 1614; Iran, 1503; Liberia, 1186; Saudi Arabia, 1512; Turkey, 1366; U.S.S.R., 981, 1176, 1272–1273, 1461–1462
Leopold III, of Belgium, 663, 710, 712, 762, 764, 773, 1266
Leticia border dispute, Colombia and Peru, 170–171, 309, 310–311

Levant states. *See* Syria *and* Lebanon
Lewis, Kathryn, 603
Liberated areas, policy on administration, 1239–1240, 1244, 1466; *see also countries liberated*
Liberia, 1185–1186
Lidice, Czechoslovakia, 1184
Lima, Peru, CH visit to, 340
Lima Conference (1938), 601–611; U.S. delegation, 603; Declaration of Lima, 603–609; resolutions regarding Axis, 609; Declaration of American Principles, 609–610; other resolutions, 610; CH addresses, 605, 610–611
Limitation of armament. *See* Disarmament
Lincoln, Abraham, 173
Lindbergh, Charles A., 590, 925
Lindsay, Sir Ronald, 160, 593–594; CH appraisal, 380; conversations with CH, on war debts, 381; on Johnson bill, 382; on unauthorized publication of British correspondence by Nye Committee, 402; on Italo-Ethiopian war, 420, 441; on delivery of British tin to U.S., 457; on trade policies, 520–523, 526; on British recognition of Italian possession of Ethiopia, 580–581
Linlithgow, Lord, 1492
Lithuania, Soviet pressure, 701; Soviet occupation, 810, 812; assets in U.S. frozen, 811; Soviet territorial aims, 1166, 1167, 1171, 1172, 1173
Little America, U.S. expeditions to, 758–759
Litvinov, Maxim, CII appraisal, 294; replaced as Soviet Foreign Commissar, 656; appointed Soviet Ambassador to U.S., 981; meets CH in Moscow, 1277;
views, discussions, or actions: London Economic Conference, 294; U.S. recognition of U.S.S.R., 299–302, 303; disarmament, 304; Soviet policy toward Japan at Brussels Conference, 552; Soviet desire to check aggression, 658; Soviet cooperation with U.S. against Japan, 1111–1112; United Nations Declaration, 1121–1124; lend-lease agreement with U.S., 1176; U.S.-Soviet relations, 1250–1251

Loans, U.S., effect of Johnson Act, 303; efforts of U.S.S.R. to obtain loans, 294, 295, 300, 301, 303–304; loans to China, 907, 914–915, 1174–1175, 1585; Poland, 1270
Lobbyists, 72
Lodge, Henry Cabot, 86, 102, 216
London Economic Conference. *See* Monetary and Economic Conference
London naval treaty (1930), 289, 447
London naval treaty (1936), 453–455, 568–569
London Naval Conference (1930), 223; discussions (1934), 288, 384;
London Naval Conference (1935–36). *See* Naval Conference
Long, Breckinridge, U.S. Ambassador to Italy, 182, 418, 425, 426, 461, 470; supervision over Special Division of State Department, 674; Assistant Secretary of State, 861, 968, 1535, 1627, 1656, 1657, 1670, 1675, 1686
Longworth, Nicholas, 109, 358
Lorrimer, William, 56
Lothian (Philip Kerr), Lord, visit to U.S., 384; CH appraisal, 674, 874, 1479; death, 874;
British Ambassador to U.S., views and discussions on: destroyers-bases agreement, 187, 831–843; Far Eastern situation, 721–722, 727, 897–899, 900–901, 906, 911, 912; U.S. opinion of Britain, 734–735; Welles' mission to Europe, 740; British wartime trade restrictions, 748–749; Iceland, 754; Greenland, 754–755; suggestions for U.S. aid to Britain, 770, 871; U.S.-British military staff conferences, 796, 797–798; Curaçao and Aruba occupations, 815–816; Martinique situation, 819; foodstuffs for Spain, 876, 878–879
Loudon, Alexander, 712, 765
Loveless, Mrs., 3–4
Lowden, Frank, 335
Lowell, Abbott Lawrence, 86
Lucas, Scott W., 1261, 1635
Ludlow, Louis, 563–564, 574
Luther, Hans, as German Ambassador to U.S., views and discussions on: German rearmament, 230, 231; persecution of Jews, 236–237; U.S. boycott

Luther, Hans—*Continued*
    of German goods, 236, 241; German
    peaceful intentions, 244; trade rela-
    tions, 374
Luxemburg, 761, 763
Lwów, 1447, 1448

McAdoo, William Gibbs, 74, 92, 122,
    153–154
MacArthur, Douglas, 1600
McBride, Harry, 179, 184, 219, 1185–
    1186, 1274
McCarthy, Charles W., 1274
McCarthy, Leighton, 1480
McCloy, John J., 1607, 1614
McCormack, John W., 217, 1669, 1696,
    1698
McCormick, Anne O'Hare, 1633
McCormick, Vance C., 86, 95, 150,
    1154–1155
McDermott, Michael J., 181, 596, 1274,
    1686
MacDonald, Ramsay, plan for disarma-
    ment, 171, 225, 227; discussion of war
    debts, 247; at London Economic
    Conference, 246, 256, 259, 260–261,
    264–266; CH appraisal, 260; attitude
    toward U.S., 378–379, 384
MacEachran, Clinton E., 181
Macedo Soares, José Carlo de, 499
MacFarlane, General, 1555, 1563
McGinness, H. B., 47
Machado, Gerardo, 309, 312, 314
McIntire, Ross T., 1715, 1720
McKellar, Kenneth D., 79, 218, 1719
Mackenzie King, W. L., 385, 623, 624,
    679, 756, 1129; signs Ogdensburg
    agreement, 212, 834; CH appraisal,
    526, 1480; discussions with CH on
    trade policies, 527–528
MacLeish, Archibald, 1636
McMillin, Benton, 15, 26, 29–30, 33, 42,
    48–49, 112
McMillin, Joe S., 15
McMillin, John H., 15, 24, 26
MacMurray, John Van A., 929
McNary, Charles, 217, 388, 649, 651,
    1262, 1531
McReynolds, Sam D., 156, 217, 229,
    249, 412, 462, 507, 564
MacVeagh, Lincoln, 715
Madagascar, British occupation, 1159

Maglione, Cardinal Luigi, 777, 778
Mails, U.S., British censorship, 733–735
Maisky, Ivan M., 1165
Malaya, reported Japanese plan to at-
    tack, 996, 1002; postwar plans for,
    1595
Malige, Marcel E., 1223, 1224
Manchukuo, Japanese puppet regime,
    271, 275–276; nonrecognition by
    League and U.S., 274; *see also* Man-
    churia
Manchuria, Japanese economic penetra-
    tion, 117; Japanese invasion, 160, 170,
    270–276, 379, 539, 639; Japanese-
    Soviet Outer Mongolian border dis-
    pute, 720, 811; evacuation of U.S.
    citizens, 914; postwar plans for, 1584,
    1596
Mandate Treaty, Palestine, American-
    British (1924), 1528
Mann, James R., 54–55, 108
Mannerheim, Baron Carl Gustaf Emil,
    978
Marines, U.S., withdrawal from Nica-
    ragua, 309; withdrawal from Haiti,
    312, 320, 345; sent to Shanghai, 540;
    withdrawn, 568
Maritime Commission, 697–700
Maritime warfare, World War I, 87;
    World War II, 87, 540, 677, 682, 704–
    705, 944–945, 1046–1050, 1275, 1378;
    see also Shipping
Marler, Herbert, 589–590
Marquez Sterling, Manuel, 343
Marshall, George C., 1333, 1432, 1535;
    views on Far Eastern situation, 1057,
    1071, 1076, 1087, 1097; on Turkish
    severance of relations with Germany,
    1375
Martha, Crown Princess of Norway, 760
Martin, Andrew B., 27
Martin, Joseph W., Jr., 217, 1669, 1696
Martin Co., Glenn L., 478
Martinique, U.S. efforts to avoid trou-
    ble between France and Britain over,
    818–820; U.S. agreement with Gov-
    ernor Robert, 1160, 1223; Laval's re-
    fusal to demobilize French fleet at,
    1161; relations with U.S. under Hop-
    penot, 1223–1224
Martins, Carlos, 886–887

Matsuoka, Yosuke, 270, 272–273; pro-Axis and bellicose statements and actions as Japanese Foreign Minister, 902, 969, 983, 990, 991, 993, 997–998, 1002, 1007, 1011, 1013, 1014

Matthews, H. Freeman, as Chargé in Vichy, 850, 1157; political adviser on Eisenhower's staff, 1185; discussions on Moscow Conference, 1265; plan for postwar Germany, 1604, 1607, 1608, 1614; special mission to London, 1428

Maxwell, Russell L., 902

Medal for Merit, with oak leaf cluster, to CH, 1727–1728

Mediation, in Cuba, 313; Chaco war, 347; Italo-Ethiopian war, 425; Spanish war, 489, 490; Sino-Japanese war, 535, 542; Australian offer to U.S., 1089; see also Good offices

Mello Franco, Alfranio de, 329, 349, 605, 607

Mellon, Andrew, 149

Melo, Leopoldo, 823–827

Memel, German objective, 244

Memoirs of CH, 1726, 1727

Memorial Day address of Sumner Welles, 1228, 1230

Mendieta, Carlos, 342–343

Menemencioglu, Numan, 1369

Menzies, R. G., 693

Merchant marine. See Atlantic, Battle of; and Shipping

Messersmith, George, 236, 241, 596, 599, 671, 672, 673, 708–709, 1626–1627

"Methods short of war" policy, 612, 614, 615–616

Mexico, Josephus Daniels as U.S. Ambassador, 70, 182; position on Cuban situation, 314, 316; debt resolution at Montevideo Conference, 335–336; efforts to end Chaco War, 337; claims of U.S. citizens, 348–349; Nye Committee allegations, 400; inquiry re arms shipments to Spain, 480–481; expropriations of American and British oil properties, 610, 1140–1143; Pan American highway, 1141; declaration of war against Axis, 1142; U.S. use of bases in, 1422, 1423; agreements with U.S. for delivery of strate-

Mexico—Continued
gic materials and embargo on oil and scrap iron to Japan, 1423

Mexico City Conference of Foreign Ministers (1945), 1403–1405; resolution LIX re Argentina, 1407–1408; Act of Chapultepec, 1467

Michels, Rodolfo, 1384

Michelson, Charles, 144

Mikolajczyk, Stanislaw, becomes Polish Premier, 1270; efforts toward settlement of boundary dispute with U.S.S.R., 1316, 1317, 1438, 1439, 1441, 1447–1448; visit to U.S., 1441–1442, 1444–1445; visits to Moscow, 1445, 1447; resignation, 1448

Military conferences, CH nonparticipant, 1109–1111, 1367

Military equipment, export control, 901

Military missions to American Republics, U.S., 1139; to Iran, 1503, 1505, 1506, 1507; to Saudi Arabia, 1513

Miller, Hunter, 181

Miller, James T., 42–43, 53

Millspaugh, Arthur C., 1503, 1508

Minority groups in U.S., CH's observations regarding, 1738

Mississippi Valley improvement, efforts toward, 43–44

Mixed Claims Commission, U.S. and Germany, 239

Moffat, Jay Pierrepont, 181, 552, 596, 671, 672, 739, 754, 1626–1627

Mohammed Ali, Prince, of Egypt, 1532

Mohammedans, question of U.S. special mission, 715–716

Molev, Raymond, appointment as Assistant Secretary of State, 161; interest in war debts, 247; denial of interest in Secretary of Stateship, 247; speech condemning tariff program, 249, 353; fiasco in London, 259–262, 268; transfer from State Department, 268

Molotov, Vyacheslav, appointment as Soviet Foreign Commissar, 656; visit to Berlin (1940), 969; CH appraisal, 1174, 1282; personal messages to CH, 1719, 1720;
    views, discussions, or actions on: U.S. recognition of U.S.S.R., 293; Soviet bombings, 706; U.S. trade discriminations, 807, 809; Anglo-Soviet

Molotov, Vyacheslav—*Continued*
treaty, 1171–1174; second front, 1173, 1174, 1179–1180, 1249; Four-Nation Declaration, 1256–1257, 1463; Turkish entrance into war, 1368–1369, 1373, 1376; Polish-Soviet border dispute, 1437; Polish government in London, 1440; Polish underground, 1446–1447; Declaration on Iran, 1505; participation in U.N., 1665;
see also Moscow Conference *and* U.S.S.R.

Monetary and Economic Conference (1933), preparatory meetings, 171, 225, 246, 247; objectives, 246, 247, 250; state of confusion, 247–248, 253; American delegation, 249; instructions to American delegation, 249–250; lack of definite program on tariff revision, 248–249, 250–252, 353; CH's opening address delayed, 256; organization of conference, 258; King George's reception for delegates, 258; CH's Pilgrims luncheon address, 259–260; the Moley episode, 259–261, 268, 350; results of FDR's rejection of Moley's stabilization agreement, 262–266, 378; CH's efforts to save FDR from blame for failure of conference, 262–266; collapse of conference, 267, 386; CH's closing address, 267; CH's report to FDR, 268; results of conference, 268, 354

Monetary and Financial Conference (1944), 1654–1655

Monroe Doctrine, Japanese distortion of, 281–282, 890, 892–893, 1032; CH and FDR views on, 310, 311; considered in provisions of 1936 Neutrality Act, 466; participation of Latin America in enforcing provisions of, 500; inclusion of Iceland and Greenland in scope of, 753, 755; German distortion of, 817–818; Latin American opposition to, 824, 1146; proposed expansion to include part of Africa, 959–960

Montevideo, Uruguay, as center of Nazi subversive activity, 820

Montevideo Conference (1933), 300; consideration of postponement, 317; CH economic proposal, 317, 320–322, 328, 329, 331, 347–348, 353; U.S. dele-

Montevideo Conference—*Continued*
gation, 319; proposal for ratification of peace agreements, 322, 328–329, 344; discussion of U.S. nonintervention policy, 323, 333–335, 477; moves to end Chaco War, 193, 322, 323, 328, 336–338, 386, 1646; CH cultivation of Latin American statesmen, 323–330, 349; transportation and communications questions, 319, 332, 348; debts resolution, 335–336; CH visits en route, 323, 339–340

Montvale Institute, Celina, Tenn., attended by CH, 15–16, 17–18

Moon, John A., 64

Moore, R. Walton, CH appraisal, 301; jurisdiction over arms control, 416; controversy with Welles over Undersecretaryship, 509–510; appointment as Counselor, 510; views or discussions on Soviet recognition, 301–302, 303; World Court, 388; neutrality, 404, 462; Spanish war, 490; neutral rights, 507; postwar policies, 732, 1626–1627

Moose, James S., Jr., 1514, 1516

Moral embargo. *See* Embargo

Morality in foreign affairs, 40, 46, 49, 128, 173, 187–188, 536–537, 1733

Moreland, William D., Jr., 663

Morgenthau, Henry, complaints against State Department official, 207; habit of interfering in foreign policy, 207–208, 902, 1073, 1379, 1676; member, National Munitions Control Board, 416; CH appraisal, 472; attendance at Second Quebec Conference, 1602, 1610, 1614; plan for postwar Germany (*see* Germany, postwar); views or discussions on excise claims against Canada, 206–207; Soviet recognition by U.S., 300; lend-lease, 872–873, 923; refugee problem, 1539; freezing of Argentine credits, 1379–1380, 1388

Morocco, 620, 853, 880

Morris, Leland B., 1507, 1509

Morrison, Ralph W., 249

Moscicki, Joseph, peace appeal of FDR, 662–663, 664, 665, 675; telegram to FDR on German bombing of Polish cities, 678; internment in Rumania,

Moscicki, Joseph—*Continued*
686; offer of refuge in U.S., 686–687;
refuge in Switzerland, 687
Moscow Conference of Foreign Ministers (1943), date and place, 1252–1253, 1253–1254, 1255–1256; U.S. delegation, 1253, 1254–1255, 1274; agenda, 1256–1257, 1264, 1265, 1279; U.S. preliminary discussions, 1265–1266; CH's trip across, 1274–1277; Soviet press censorship, 1278–1279;
declarations: on German atrocities, 1278, 1289–1291; on Italy, 1283–1284; on Austria, 1297; on Iran, proposed, 1505, 1506; Four-Nation Declaration (*see* Four-Nation Declaration);
inter-Allied bodies: creation of European Advisory Commission, 1283, 1287, 1301, 1642; of Advisory Council for Italy, 1283–1284, 1551; of Control Commission for Germany, 1285;
other actions and discussions: second front, 1278, 1279, 1280, 1306; postwar cooperation, 1279, 1280–1281, 1288, 1294–1295, 1308; question of Turkey's entering war or leasing air bases, 1279–1280, 1297, 1301, 1312, 1368–1369, 1373–1376; Swedish bases, 1279–1280, 1301; Soviet request for Italian war vessels, 1284, 1301–1302; postwar treatment of Germany, 1284–1287, 1304; U.S.-Soviet relations, 1288–1289, 1310; projected meeting of FDR, Churchill, and Stalin, 1292–1293, 1294–1296, 1303, 1306, 1308–1309, 1311, 1313; peace feelers, 1297; federation of small nations, 1298–1299; spheres of influence, 1298; civil affairs in France, 1301; military proposals, 1302; repairs to war damage in U.S.S.R., 1303; aid to other countries, 1303; economic recommendations, 1303–1304; dependent peoples, 1238, 1304–1305; Soviet-Polish relations, 1305–1306, 1315–1317; social events, 1306, 1308, 1311; Stalin's statement *re* declaration of war on Japan, 1309–1310, 1311;
return of U.S. delegation, 1311–1312, 1313; summary of achievements, 1313, 1314; Churchill's statement,

Moscow Conference—*Continued*
1314; CH's address to joint session of Congress, 1314–1315, 1647–1648
Moslems, question of U.S. special mission, 715–716; *see also* Arab-Jewish question
Most-favored-nation principle. *See under* Trade, international
Mountbatten, Lord Louis, 1475
Mountcastle, R. E. L., 74
Munich agreement, 586, 589–593, 595–597, 614–615, 623
Munitions. *See* Armaments; Arms; Embargo; Neutrality policy
Munthe de Morgenstierne, Wilhelm, 751–752
Murphy, Robert D., economic mission to French North Africa, 854, 949–950, 951, 961, 1039, 1043, 1044; Adviser for Civil Affairs on Gen. Eisenhower's staff in North Africa, 1185, 1197, 1199, 1201; personal representative of President on Gen. Eisenhower's staff, 1202, 1208, 1209, 1219, 1222, 1243, 1275; U.S. member, Advisory Council for Italy, 1317, 1558; Political Adviser for Germany to Gen. Eisenhower, 1622
Murray, Philip, 1636
Murray, Wallace, 181, 419, 423, 443, 1428, 1483, 1494, 1501, 1504, 1515, 1536
Muselier, Admiral, 1128–1129
Musser, Elise F., 494, 603
Mussolini, Benito (*for nonpersonal items, see* Italy *or subject*), 227, 419, 546, 664; resignation, 1232, 1548, 1560; possible refuge in neutral countries, 1361–1362
Myers, Frank, 1274

Nahas Pasha, 1536, 1546
Naples, Prince of, 1552
Nashville, Tenn., 19–21
National City Bank, 346
National defense, U.S., destroyer-bases agreement with Britain, 193, 212, 831–843; Ogdensburg Agreement with Canada, 212, 834; naval increase to treaty strength, 287, 288, 456, 457; promoted by CH, 456, 458, 667, 910, 929; construction of two-ocean navy,

National defense, U.S.—*Continued*
568–569, 573–574, 845–846; proclamation of national emergency, 679; appropriations, 767, 774, 845–846; National Guard, 774, 845; embargo on essential materials, 802, 807–809, 901, 907, 912–914, 915; National Defense Act, 832, 833; Permanent Joint Board of Defense (U.S.-Canada), 834, 1479; Selective Service Act, 845, 943, 1104; plans for unified defense in the Pacific, 906–907, 909, 912, 1007, 1017, 1113; proclamation of unlimited national emergency, 942; *see also* Atlantic, Battle of; Army, U.S.; Joint Chiefs of Staff; Navy, U.S.; Navy Department; Rearmament; War Department
National Foreign Trade Council, 391
National Guard, U.S., 774, 845
National Munitions Control Board, 405, 411, 416, 597, 697
National Normal University, Lebanon, Ohio, 22–23
National Press Club, 350, 576–577, 864, 865–866
National Recovery Administration, 248, 321, 353
Naval Academy, U.S., 1139
Naval and air bases. *See* Bases
Naval armaments. *See* Armaments
Naval Conference, London (1930), 223; naval discussions, London (1934), 288, 384
Naval Conference, London (1935–36), 444–445; U.S. delegation, 446; U.S. policies, 447–448; Japanese and British proposals, 448–450; Japan's withdrawal, 450; treaty provisions, 453–455
Naval Disarmament Conference, Geneva (1927), 223
Naval missions to American republics, U.S., 1139
Naval parity, Japanese demands for, 223, 286–290, 384, 444–450, 455
Naval treaty, London (1930), 289, 447
Naval treaty, London (1936), 453–455, 568–569
Naval treaty, Washington (1922), 288–290, 444, 447, 448
Navicert system, 680–681, 735–736

Navy, British, safety of, 193, 766, 771–772, 774, 796–797, 837–839, 840–841
Navy, French, movements, 620; British and U.S. efforts to insure safety, 771, 772, 787, 790–793, 795, 796–797, 804, 846, 847–848, 849, 850, 871, 884, 952, 956, 1158, 1161, 1193, 1203, 1224; destruction at Oran, 798–799, 800; at Casablanca, 1275
Navy, German, scuttling of *Graf von Spee,* 690, 691–692; postwar destruction, 1603–1604
Navy, U.S., increase to treaty strength, 287, 288, 456, 457; transfer of fleet from Pacific and back, 288, 630; dispatch of units to Cuba, 314, 315; bombing of *Kane, Augusta* and *Panay,* 480, 540, 559–563; construction of two-ocean navy, 568–569, 573–574, 845–846; intended employment of, 573–574; survey of Spratly Islands, 628; dispatch of units to Greenland, 756, 757; to Martinique, 819; proposals for transfer of fleet to Atlantic, 768, 769, 772, 773–774, 781; visit of units to Buenos Aires and Montevideo, 821; bases from Britain, 193, 212, 831–843; proposals for transfer of fleet to Singapore, 897, 911, 914; patrol activities in Atlantic, 945; deciphering of Japanese code, 998; convoys, 1047, 1049, 1050, 1275, 1378; attack on *Greer,* 1048; *see also* Atlantic, Battle of; Joint Chiefs of Staff; National defense; Navy Department; Rearmament
Navy Department, objection to international supervision of arms, 233; informed of international situation, 864–865, 866; warned of Japanese attacks, 984, 1080, 1087; membership on War Council, 1109; relations with Argentine Navy, 1378; *see also* Joint Chiefs of Staff; Knox, Frank; National defense; Navy, U.S.
Nazi Party, in Germany, 170, 588, 1286; in Latin America, 495–496, 601–602; *see also* Germany
Near East, U.S. policy toward, 1498–1500 (*see also* Arab-Jewish question; *and individual countries*)
Nehru, Pandit Jawaharlal, 1486

Nelson, Donald M., 1277, 1585
Netherlands, CH trip to, 125; trade agreement with U.S., 375; recognition of Franco Government in Spain, 616; concern over effect of U.S. arms embargo, 647, 652; Belgian-Dutch peace move, 712; invasion by Germany, 761, 762, 763; application of U.S. Neutrality Act, 761, 763; freezing of credits in U.S., 763; cessation of organized resistance, 765; U.S. and inter-American policy toward European possessions in Western Hemisphere, 791, 804, 814–817, 822–826, 1629–1630; U.S. relief plans, 804; reaction to U.S.-Japanese peace proposals for the Pacific, 1073, 1076, 1077, 1082; joins Anglo-American Caribbean Commission, 1237; see also Netherlands East Indies; Netherlands Guiana; Netherlands West Indies
Netherlands East Indies, preservation of status quo in, 815–816, 888–895; Japanese economic penetration, 895–896, 916; plans for defense against Japan, 906–907, 909, 912, 1007, 1017, 1071, 1093; postwar plans for, 1595, 1596, 1599–1601; see also Netherlands
Netherlands Guiana, U.S. protection of bauxite mines at Paramaribo, 1051; see also Netherlands
Netherlands West Indies, British and French occupation of Curaçao and Aruba, 814–817, 891, 893; provision of aviation gasoline to Spain, 1326; see also Netherlands
Neurath, Konstantin von, 327
Neutral rights, in World War I, 409, 463; in World War II, 679–682, 733–736
Neutrality, General Declaration of, 689
Neutrality pact, Japan-U.S.S.R. (1941), 969, 993, 1020
Neutrality policy, U.S., concept of, 224, 228, 406–409, 514–515, 865–866, 919, 1002, 1012; U.S. action independent of League, 426, 429, 432–433, 436; restrictions on travel of U.S. citizens, 428, 430, 432, 433, 471, 507, 675–676, 679, 697, 785; FDR address, 479; creation of Interdepartmental Neutrality Committee, 654–655;

Neutrality policy, U.S.—Continued
act of 1935: effect of Nye Committee hearings on legislation, 404, 410; study of legislation, 404–406; Nye-Clarke proposed legislation, 410; State Department draft rejected, 410–411; enactment of Pittman Resolution, 412–413; weaknesses, 413–417;
act of 1936: drafting, 460–466; enactment, 466–467; CH views, 467–468; application to Italy and Ethiopia, 467; nonapplication to Spain, 478;
act of Jan. 8, 1937: embargo on arms to Spain, 491, 505–506, 509, 513–514, 516–517, 615;
act of May 1, 1937: enactment, 507–509, 532; pressure for application to Germany and Italy, 510–513; attempts to amend or repeal, 515–516; nonapplication in Sino-Japanese conflict, 556–558; efforts of FDR and CH to eliminate arms embargo clause (1939), 612–614, 641–646, reaction abroad to House bill, 646–648; failure of Senate to act, 648–653; decision of FDR to call special session to revise (1939), 673, 675; issuance of proclamations and regulations, 675–676, 678–679; FDR's message to Congress urging revision, 682–684, 713, 714; question of breach of U.S. neutrality by revising act after outbreak of war, 684, 696; British, French, and Australian concern over embargo clause, 692–693;
act of 1939: Pittman bill lifting embargo but restricting shipping, 693–696; protests of foreign governments, 694–696; bill amended and enacted, 697; effect of City of Flint incident on pending legislation, 705; nonapplication to Russo-Finnish conflict, 707; to U.S.S.R., 973; to Denmark, 752; application to Norway, 752–753; to Belgium, Netherlands, and Luxemburg, 761, 763; to Italy, 785; to Greece, 886; modifying as to Red Sea, 944; repeal of sections on arming of merchant ships and on ships' entering belligerent ports, 802, 1046–1050; question of repeal (early 1941), 943, 944;

Neutrality policy, U.S.—*Continued*
amendment relating to financial transactions with belligerents, 1151; *see
also* Embargo
Neutrality zone, Western Hemisphere,
689–692, 945
Neutrals, U.S. policy toward, 1321–1322;
see also individual countries
Neville, Edwin L., 276
New Dealers, 857, 858, 860
New York *Times,* 96–97, 219
New Zealand, plans for unified defense
in the Pacific, 906–907, 909, 912; co-
operation with U.S. in war, 1475
Newfoundland, U.S.-British agreement
for lease of bases, 831–843, 946
Nicaragua, withdrawal of U.S. Marines,
309; trade agreement with U.S., 375
Niihau, Hawaii, proposed meeting place
for U.N. Council, 1681
Niles, David K., 1636
Nine-Power Treaty (1922), 223, 271;
Japanese violation of, 270, 277, 637;
U.S. observance of, 447, 533; Brussels
Conference on Japanese violation, 550–
556; Congressional resolution for embargo against violators of, 638, 641
Nobel Peace Prize (1936), CH nomina-
tion of Saavedra Lamas for, 329,
1724; (1945) awarded to CH, 1724–
1726
Noble, Captain, 1274
Nomura, Kichisaburo, as Japanese Foreign Minister, 723, 725; as Japanese
Ambassador to U.S., 985, 987, 988,
1113; *for participation in pre-Pearl
Harbor conversations with CH and
FDR to avert war, see* Japan: conversations with U.S. to avert war
Nonaggression pacts, Soviet-Japanese,
969, 993, 1020; proposed U.S.-Japa-
nese, 997
Nonintervention, CH adherence to principle of, 174, 308, 310, 477, 1465–
1466, 1467, 1739–1740; U.S. policy in
Haiti, 312, 320; U.S. policy in Cuba,
312–317, 334, 340–341, 342–344; convention adopted at Montevideo Conference, 323, 333–335, 500; FDR statement on, 339–340; French and British
policy in Spain, 476–477, 479, 481,
482, 483, 484, 489; U.S. policy in

Nonintervention—*Continued*
Spain, 477–479, 480, 481–485, 491–
492, 504–505, 513–514; International
Nonintervention Committee, 481, 482,
489, 504, 512
Nonpartisan foreign policy on trade
agreements program, 1212, 1656; on
U.N. organization, 1258–1263, 1314,
1315, 1630, 1635, 1639, 1655–1670,
1676, 1686–1699, 1711; CH's views
on, 1734
Norris, George W., 57–58, 62, 156
North Africa, French, question of withdrawal of French Government to,
787, 789, 793–794; Weygand named
Delegate-General, 853; U.S. economic
policy toward, 853–854, 949–952, 955,
961, 963, 966, 1039–1040, 1043–1044,
1161–1162; German agents in, 951,
953, 954, 956; German negotiations
with Darlan for bases, 962–964; U.S.
efforts to prevent establishment of
German bases, 1038–1045; Weygand's
dismissal, 1038, 1042–1043; territorial
integrity and neutrality of Spain and
Portugal prior to Allied African landings, 1186–1191, 1195; Allied invasion,
952, 1127, 1133, 1162, 1183, 1185,
1186, 1190–1191, 1191–1192, 1216,
1218, 1275;
post-invasion period: De Gaulle reaction to African landings, 1133–1134,
1162, 1195–1196; Darlan assignments,
1196–1203; Free French distrust of
Darlan, 1197–1198, 1201–1203; assassination of Darlan, 1204–1205; Giraud
assignments, 1196–1199, 1201–1202,
1208–1210, 1214, 1217, 1221, 1226;
political prisoners released, 1197; anti-
Jewish measures lifted, 1197, 1214;
State Dept. jurisdiction over civil
matters, 1200–1201; Peyrouton Governor General of Algeria, 1201, 1220;
Free French attacks on Giraud and
French administration in North Africa, 1201, 1203–1204, 1205, 1207,
1209, 1217, 1219, 1223; U.S.-British
attempts to settle Giraud-De Gaulle
controversy, 1207–1208, 1210; formation by Giraud and De Gaulle of
French Committee of National Liberation, 1220; ousting of Giraud by De

North Africa, French—*Continued*
Gaulle, 1201–1202, 1216, 1220, 1225–1226, 1244–1245
Northern Ireland, Churchill views on possible union with Eire, 922; objections by Eire to British bases and U.S. troops in, 1354, 1355
Norway, reduction in whale oil exports to U.S., 376; protests discriminations against foreign shipping in U.S. neutrality bill, 695; alarm over Soviet advance in Baltic, 702; German invasion, 751, 752; mining of territorial waters by British and French, 751–752; application of U.S. Neutrality Act, 752–753; freezing of credits in U.S., 752; U.S. continued recognition of Haakon Government, 752–753; disposition of shipping, 759; refuge in U.S. for Crown Princess, 760; U.S. determination to restore independence, 930
Norweb, R. Henry, 603, 1336–1339 *passim*, 1342, 1343
Notter, Harley, 1630, 1638, 1675
Nuremberg trial, 1291
Nuri Pasha, 1532, 1546
Nye, Gerald, investigation of campaign expenditures in Tennessee, 139; isolationist effects of Senate committee on manufacture and sale of arms and munitions, 216, 217, 380, 398–405, 410; other isolationist moves, 464, 510–511, 516, 649

Ochs, Adolph, 219
O'Connor, John, 462
Office of Strategic Services, underground in North Africa, 1185
Ogdensburg Agreement (1940), 212, 834
O'Hara, John F., 603
Oil. *See* Petroleum
Okada, Lt. Comdr., 1012
Open-door policy in China, 117, 270, 271, 290, 569
Oran, Algeria, British destruction of French warships, 798–799, 800
Orlemanski, Stanislaw, 1442–1443, 1444
Ortiz, Roberto M., 607–608, 826, 1377, 1380
Osborne, F. D. G., 287
Osborne, Lithgow, 1725–1726

Ottawa agreements of 1932, 355, 1479
Oumansky, Constantine, CH appraisal, 743, 807; Soviet grievances against U.S., 708–709, 744–745, 807–810; conferences with U.S. officials, 968, 970, 971–972, 973, 974, 976–977
Outer Mongolia border dispute between Japan and U.S.S.R., 720, 811
Owen, Robert L., 73
Owen, Ruth Bryan, 183

Pacific War Council meeting, views of FDR on India, 1487
Padgett, Lemuel P., 64
Padilla, Ezequiel, 1404
Pahlavi, Mohammed Reza, 1503
Pahlavi, Shah Reza, 1501–1502, 1503
Palestine. *See* Arab-Jewish question
Palestine Partition Commission, 1529
Palmer, A. Mitchell, 70, 86, 150–151, 352, 387
Panama, CH visit to, 340, 345; revision of treaty of 1903, 344–345; registry of U.S. ships, 697–698; prohibition on arming of merchant ships, 1048; signing of United Nations Declaration, 1124
Panama Canal, acquisition of naval and air bases a protective measure, 841; possible blocking, 1378
Panama Conference of Foreign Ministers (1939), objectives, 688; agenda, 688; CH address on, 689; proposals of U.S. delegation, 689; General Declaration of Neutrality, 689; Declaration of Panama, 689–692; Inter-American Financial and Economic Advisory Committee, 692
Pan American Airways, service to Liberia, 1186; air survey in Azores, 1342
Pan American conferences. *See* Buenos Aires; Havana; Lima; Mexico City; Montevideo; Panama; *and* Rio de Janeiro
Pan American Day, FDR address (1933), 311; FDR address (1939), 620–621; CH address, 689
Pan American highway, 319, 332, 348, 1141
Pan American Scientific Congress, Eighth, FDR address to, 763

Pan American Union, 311–312, 391, 1403

Pan Arab Federation, 1540, 1546–1547, 1645

Panay, U.S.S., bombing, 559–563

Panic of 1929–32, 126, 148, 155, 161, 172, 257

Paraguay, suggestion for mediation between U.S. and Argentina, 1400; *see also* Chaco War

Paramaribo, U.S. protection of bauxite mines, 1051

Paris, Pact of (1928), 128, 153, 304, 309, 322, 328, 332, 418, 419, 420, 421, 427, 433, 583, 588

Paris Peace Conference (1919), 101–102, 382–383

Pasquet, Maurice, 1129

Pasvolsky, Leo, U.S. delegate to Havana Conference, 822; White House discussions on Moscow Conference, 1265; postwar planning, 732, 1234, 1626–1627, 1629, 1630, 1633, 1634, 1638, 1643, 1647, 1650, 1675, 1686, 1687, 1688, 1705

Paternalism, CH opposition to, 52, 136, 147, 197

Patterson, Josiah, 25

Patterson, Malcolm, 77, 79

Paul, Prince Regent of Yugoslavia, 928–931, 933

Payne, Sereno, 54–55

Payne-Aldrich Tariff Act (1909), 59–61, 62, 65, 66, 83–84

Peabody, Dr., 167

Peace, freer trade a factor in, 81, 84, 85, 101, 157, 522–523, 525 (*see also* Trade agreements); peace through disarmament, 222, 227, 234, 455 (*see also* Disarmament); CH address on "four pillars of peace," 234; CH warnings of threats to (1933–35), 390–394; CH's "Eight Pillars of Peace" for the Americas, 498 (*see also* Good Neighbor policy; Buenos Aires, Havana, Lima, Montevideo, Panama, Rio de Janeiro conferences); observance of principles of international conduct essential to, 535–537; Welles' proposal for international meeting at White House (1937), 546–549; Chamberlain's efforts for "peace in our time," 573,

Peace—*Continued*
579, 581, 586, 589–595; peace rumors as result of Welles' special mission to Europe (1940), 737–740; FDR and CH efforts to maintain peace in Europe, 537, 591–593, 620–623, 655, 661–667, 675, 777–784; U.S.-Japanese pre-Pearl Harbor conversations (*see* Japan: conversations with U.S. to avert war); German peace moves and feelers during World War II, 710–711, 844–845, 1179, 1297, 1573; postwar preservation of, 1322–1323, 1470, 1737, 1741, 1742 (*see also* United Nations)

Peace, League to Enforce, advocate of association of nations, 86

"Peace and War," volume on pre-Pearl Harbor foreign policy, 219

Peace Conference, Paris (1919), 101–102, 382–383

Peace Prize, Nobel (1945), to CH, 1724–1726

Peace treaties, Versailles, 103, 112–113, 127, 223, 230, 233, 243; Kellogg-Briand Pact (1928), 128, 153, 304, 309, 322, 328, 332, 418, 419, 420, 421, 427, 433, 583, 588; Argentine (Saavedra Lamas) Antiwar Pact (1933), 309, 322, 328, 332, 344, 469; Inter-American Peace Treaty (1923), 322, 328, 332; Inter-American Conciliation Convention (1929), 322, 328, 332; Inter-American Arbitration Convention (1929), 322, 328, 332

Peaceful settlement of disputes. See Arbitration

Pearl Harbor, Japanese attack on, 984, 1095, 1096, 1724, 1726, 1727

Peay, Austin, 122

Peek, George N., 353–354, 356, 357, 370–374

Pelényi, John, 589–590

Peñaranda del Castillo, Enrique, 1388

Penfield, James K., 757, 936

Pennsylvania Military College, CH address, 391

Pepper, Claude, 1635

Perkins, Frances, 198, 210, 1654

Perkins, Mahlon F., 936–939 *passim*

Permanent Court of International Justice, 153, 177, 212, 215, 387–389; see also International Court of Justice

Permanent Joint Board of Defense (U.S. and Canada), 834, 1479
Perón, Juan Domingo, 1395
Perry, Matthew W., 1150, 1274
Pershing, John J., 883
Persia. *See* Iran
Peru, Leticia border dispute with Colombia, 170–171, 309, 310–311; efforts to end Chaco War, 336, 337, 347; CH visit to, 340; Lima Conference (1938), 601–611; U.S. bases in, 1422, 1425
Pescadores Islands, disposition after the war, 1584
Pétain, Henri Philippe, appointment as French Vice Premier, 770; advocacy of armistice with Germany, 776, 791; forms new French Cabinet, 791; denounces British attack on fleet at Oran, 799; respected in France, 805; forced collaboration with Hitler, 849–850, 871, 948, 949, 955, 956, 1039, 1043, 1044; congratulates FDR upon reelection, 854; assurances *re* safety of French fleet, 871; *re* bases in Africa, 1040; dismissal of Laval, 882–883; hatred for Laval, 949; stand on Darlan agreement with Germany, 958, 963–965; dismissal of Weygand, 1038, 1042–1043; hatred for De Gaulle, 1040; meeting with Göring, 1044; on invasion of North Africa, 1127, 1191–1192, 1195; appointment of Laval as Premier, 1157; *see also* France, Vichy
Peter II, of Yugoslavia, 933, 1276
Peters, Andrew, 70
Peterson, J. Hardin, 1636
Petroleum, proposed control of Industry by Manchukuo Government, 275–276; Ethiopian concession to U.S. company, 423–425; U.S. moral embargo to Italy, 435, 441, 442, 471; Mexican expropriation of U.S. properties, 610, 1140–1142; of British properties, 1142–1143; exports to Spain, 875, 1188–1190, 1326–1333; question of U.S. embargo to Japan, 983, 1066, 1075, 1078, 1085, 1102–1103, 1104; to Sweden from U.S. in exchange for certain concessions, 1346; U.S. interests in Iraq and Saudi Arabia, 1499; U.S. and British efforts for concessions in Iran,

Petroleum—*Continued*
1508–1509; Allied supplies endangered by Palestine trouble, 1535, 1537; U.S. reserves: study, 1517, 1518; CH's views, 1518–1519, 1526–1527; creation and activities of Petroleum Reserves Corp., 1520–1521, 1522, 1524; preliminary Anglo-American discussions, 1521, 1522–1523, 1524, 1525; special Senate Committee to Investigate Petroleum Resources, 1524; Anglo-American agreement (1944), 1525–1526; reaction of U.S. petroleum industry, 1526
Petroleum Commission, International, proposed, 1526
Petroleum Policy, International, Committee on, 1517
Petroleum Reserves Corp., 1517, 1518, 1519, 1520–1521, 1522, 1524
Pettus, Edmund W., 108
Peyrouton, Marcel, 1201, 1220
Philip, André, 1197
Philippines, independence, 278, 1065, 1238, 1595; U.S. agreement not to fortify, 289; U.S. naval reinforcements, 915; "Laurel incident" (1944), 1328
Phillips, Sir Frederick, 873, 923–924
Phillips, William, as Under Secretary of State, 160, 184, 273, 300, 301, 353, 373–374, 404, 446; as U.S. Ambassador to Italy, 470, 509, 546, 618–619, 647, 655, 713–715, 777, 779–780, 782, 783, 886, 926; as FDR's personal representative to India, 1491–1492, 1493–1494, 1495; as political adviser to Eisenhower, 1493, 1495, 1571–1572, 1578–1579
Pittman, Key, 215–216, 249, 254, 266, 388, 398, 405, 573–574; on neutrality legislation, 229–230, 412, 413, 462, 491, 507, 613–614, 638, 641–649, 693–697
Pittman-Bloom Act (June 15, 1940), 874
Pitts and Meeks law office, 24
Platt Amendment, FDR and CH decision not to invoke, 312–313
"Plow-under" doctrine, CH opposition to, 146–147
Poland, Nye Committee allegations *re* munitions contract with British firm, 380, 400; demands in Czech crisis, 592, 596, 614; freezing of assets in

Poland—*Continued*
U.S., 945; death of Sikorsky and appointment of Mikolajczyk as Premier, 1270; U.S. credit, 1270; visit of Mikolajczyk to U.S., 1441–1442, 1444–1445; resignation of Mikolajczyk, 1448;

German attack (1939): French and British guaranty of assistance, 623; imminence of attack, 647, 651, 652, 653, 655, 661–662, 663, 664; peace appeal of FDR, 662–663, 664, 665, 675; entry of German troops, 665, 671; bombing of civilian populations, 672, 674, 677–678; resistance of Polish underground, 1270, 1316, 1317, 1445–1447;

Soviet attack (1939), 685; evacuation of U.S. Foreign Service staff, 685; successor to President Moscicki, 685–686; nonrecognition of new government by U.S., 686; U.S. offer of refuge to Moscicki, 686–687; Soviet territorial demands, 1166, 1173; Joint Declaration of Friendship and Mutual Aid with U.S.S.R., 1267; investigation of deaths of 10,000 Polish officers, 1267; U.S.S.R. breaks relations with, 1267–1268; U.S.-British efforts to effect reconciliation (1943), 1267–1271, 1305–1306, 1315–1317; outline of Polish position, 1271–1273; Polish disappointment over results of Moscow Conference, 1315–1316; U.S.-British efforts to effect reconciliation (1944), 1436–1442, 1447–1449; Soviet efforts to establish rival Polish government, 1268, 1442–1444; visit of Mikolajczyk to Moscow, 1445, 1447; Soviet opposition to aid for Polish underground, 1445–1447; visit of two Polish-Americans to Moscow for discussions at Stalin's request, 1442–1443, 1444

Political Studies Division, State Department, 1638

Politicomilitary Commission in Algiers, 1243–1244, 1256, 1276–1277

Poll tax, 31–32

Pollack case (1895), 48, 66

Pope Pius XII, 713–715, 778, 1626, 1711–1712; *see also* Vatican

Populist Party, 25–26

Portugal, nonsupport of mediation proposal for Spain, 489–490; reaction to U.S. foreign-policy statement (1937), 536; neutrality in the war, 770, 1195, 1335; U.S. reassurances at time of African landing *re* integrity, 1186, 1191–1192; wolfram exports to Germany, 1333, 1335–1339; supply-purchase agreement with U.S. and Britain, 1335; forced abandonment of *Serpa Pinto* by German submarine, 1339; liberation of Timor from Japanese, 1342, 1343; assurances on asylum for war criminals, 1363; aid to Jewish refugees, 1539;

Azores: exchange of views with U.S. *re* possible German occupation, 941; agreement for use for Allied convoy protection, 1275; agreements for use of bases and facilities by Britain, 1232, 1339–1340; by U.S., 1340–1343

Postwar economic problems, interdepartmental group to consider, 1629

Postwar Foreign Policy, Advisory Committee on, 1631–1639

Postwar planning, economic conversations with neutrals, 738, 1628; with Britain (1943), 1289; Welles' Memorial Day address on, 1228, 1230; for an international organization (*see* United Nations)

Postwar Programs Committee, State Department, 1650

Potocki, Count Jerzy, 596, 597, 652, 672, 686

Potsdam Declaration, 1593–1595

Pou, Edward, 63

Pramoj, Mom Rajawongse Seni, 985

Pratt, John L., 1428

Pravda reply to article by Wendell Willkie, 1437

Presidency, CH as potential candidate for, (1924) 122, 130; (1928) 129–130; (1932) 149; (1940) 749–750, 855–859

President. *See* Executive

President Hoover, liner bombed, 540

Press, 53, 62, 65, 96–97; CH daily press conferences, 218–219; attacks on State Department, 220–221; responsibilities to public, 220; attacks on CH as anti-Russian, 1253, 1255; censorship in U.S.S.R., 1278–1279

Prisoners of war, German, 1285; treatment by Japan, 1589
Procopé, Hjalmar, 702, 978–980, 1450
Production Management for Defense, Office of, 910
Progressive Party, 67
Prohibition, campaign issue (1932), 140, 141, 142, 144, 145, 151, 152
Protective Bondholders Committee, 335–336
Public information, 219–220, 1178–1179, 1261
Public opinion, U.S., effects of Nye Committee investigations and approach of Italo-Ethiopian War, 399–400, 404, 410; trend away from peace efforts through collective action, 473–474; reactions to FDR's "quarantine" speech in Chicago, 545; education through Brussels Conference, 552; state in 1937, 563, 564; on U.S. oil program with Spain, 1327, 1330; on Soviet attitude toward political integrity of neighboring states, 1437; Soviet establishment of diplomatic relations with Italy, 1449; importance in U.S., 1732; to world, 1738
Puig Casauranc, José Manuel, 335–336

"Quarantine" speech of FDR at Chicago, 544–546
Quebec Conferences,
First (1943): Stalin's refusal to attend, 1252; discussions on European invasion plans, 1231–1232; Italian surrender terms, 1232; Free French problem, 1232–1233, 1241; German dismemberment, 1233–1234; trusteeship system for dependent peoples, 1234–1238; draft of Four-Nation Declaration, 1238–1239; administration of liberated countries, 1239–1240; U.S. naval bases in Eire, 1357; policy on Turkey, 1368; Palestine, 1534;
Second (1944): preparations for, 1681, 1682; Morgenthau's attendance, 1602, 1610, 1614; approval of Morgenthau plan for postwar Germany, 1610–1611, 1615; agreement on U.S.-British occupation zones in Germany, 1611–1613; Morgenthau proposal for loan to Britain, 208, 1613–1614, 1615, 1616,

Quebec Conferences—*Continued*
1617–1618; discussion of voting procedure in U.N. Council, 1701–1702
Queens University (Canada), address by FDR, 587–588
Quo Tai-chi, 1077

Rabaul, trusteeship, 1596
Raczkiewicz, Wladyslaw, 685–686
Raeder, Erich, explanation of sinking of *Athenia,* 677
Rainey, Henry T., 109, 132, 151, 357
Ralston, Samuel M., 122
Ramírez, Pedro, 1384–1394
Ramspeck, Robert, 1669, 1696, 1698
Raskob, John J., 140–145, 352
Raushenbush, Stephen, 399, 405
Rayburn, Sam, 109, 154, 217, 643, 1657, 1669, 1676, 1696, 1698, 1727
Rayner, Charles, 1517, 1523
Rearmament, U.S., difficulties facing program, 287–288, 573; naval increase to treaty strength, 287, 288, 456, 457; rearmament urged by FDR and CH, 456, 457, 458, 459, 576, 667, 766–767, 866, 885; construction of two-ocean navy, 568–569, 573–574, 845–846; appropriations, 767, 774, 845–846; embargo on essential materials, 802, 807–809, 901, 907, 912–914, 915; *see also* Embargo; National defense
Reber, Samuel, 1160, 1223, 1557
Reciprocity Information, Interdepartmental Committee for, 366
Recognition, of new governments set up in wartime, inter-American declaration, 1388–1389; Estrada Doctrine, 1401, 1402; Guani Doctrine, 1402
Reconstruction Finance Corporation, 828, 977
Red Cross, American, 504, 622, 876–882, 884, 949, 955
Red Cross, International, 504, 505, 1267
Reed, James A., 68, 102, 216
Reforms, domestic, need for (1907), 45–46; CH attitude toward FDR policy, 196–199
Refugees, 578, 713–715, 1528, 1529, 1531, 1534, 1537–1540
Reinhardt, G. Frederick, 1552, 1558
Relief, to Spain, 504–505, 875–882; to occupied countries, 803–804, 1052; to un-

Relief—*Continued*
occupied France, 879, 881, 882, 884, 885,
  949, 952–955, 957, 963; to Greece, 886;
  to Belgium, 1051–1052; contributions
  for, 509, 679, 697, 785; postwar, 1296,
  1637
Relief and Rehabilitation Conference
  (1943), 1654–1655
Religious freedom, a prerequisite to U.S.
  recognition of U.S.S.R., 292, 294, 297,
  299, 300, 301, 1288–1289; in United Nations Declaration, 1120
Reparations, German, 1266, 1286, 1304,
  1609; Hungarian, 1461
Reparations Commission (1927), 129
Repatriation of U.S. citizens. *See* Citizens,
  U.S.
Representation of interests of other governments by U.S., 674, 1113; of U.S. interests by Switzerland, 1113, 1349
Republican Party, 45, 48, 55, 56–57, 59,
  67, 99, 104, 105–106, 114, 352, 864; Palestine plank, 1537; support of international organization (*see* Nonpartisan
  foreign policy)
Reuther, Walter, 1636
Revenue Act (1917), 91–92; (1918), 98
Reynaud, Paul, appeals for British aid to
  France, 765, 774; for U.S. declaration of
  war, 767–770, 787–788; for U.S. fleet in
  Europe, 773–774; determination to pre-
  serve French fleet, 772; consternation
  over war with Italy, 780; overtures to
  Italy to avoid war, 782, 784; opposition
  to armistice with Germany, 791; resig-
  nation from French Cabinet, 791; mes-
  sage to FDR, 793; request to U.S. for
  destroyers, 831, 832
Rhineland, occupation by Germany, 452
Ribbentrop, Joachim von, 646, 653, 817–
  818
Rickett, Francis, 423
Riddleberger, James W., 1604, 1607, 1608
Ridley, Clarence S., 1503
Riley, Isaac, 5
Riley, James, 5
Riley, Lucy Flowers, 5
Rio de Janeiro, CH visit to, 323
Rio de Janeiro Conference of Foreign
  Ministers (1942), invitations, 1143;
  Sumner Welles as delegate, 1143; ef-
  forts to secure joint declaration to

Rio de Janeiro Conference—*Continued*
  break diplomatic relations with Axis,
  1143–1149; Argentine opposition, 1146–
  1148; Welles' capitulation, 1148–1150;
  achievements, 1150
Ríos, Fernando de los, 484, 501, 513, 617
Ríos Morales, Juan Antonio, 1383
Rist, Charles, 735
Robert, Georges, 818–820, 1128, 1130,
  1131, 1160, 1223, 1224
Robin Moor, sinking by Germany, 944–
  945
Robinson, Joseph T., 141, 217, 357, 388
Rogers, Will, 389
Röhm, Ernst, execution, 242
Rome, Italy, bombing, 1560–1563
Romer, Tadeusz, 1316
Rommel, Erwin, 958
Roosevelt, Eleanor (Mrs. Franklin D.),
  199
Roosevelt, Franklin D. (*for nonpersonal
  items, see subject*), early associations
  with CH, 94, 131–132; appraisal and
  commendations of CH, 122–123, 185,
  194–200, 205–206, 208, 249, 267, 285,
  340, 440; break with Alfred E. Smith,
  141, 143–145; use of "forgotten man"
  phrase, 147–148; offer of Secretary of
  Stateship to CH, 156; visit to Tennessee Valley Authority area, 156; attempt
  on life, 158; working relations with CH,
  158–159, 191–210; inauguration as
  President (1933), 167–168; domestic
  policy, 167, 196–199; Cabinet, 167, 203–
  210, 902, 1057–1058; attitude toward
  Herbert Hoover, 183, 202; CH appraisal of FDR, 191, 194–196, 1716,
  1721; attitude toward State Department, 202–203; anecdote *re* habit of
  talking, 205; preference for communicating directly with heads of states,
  297–298; technical knowledge of naval
  affairs, 451; reelection (1936), 485–488;
  Christmas greetings to CH at Buenos
  Aires, 502–503; conviction that U.S.
  must stay out of war, 665–667, 672,
  675, 676–677, 867, 885; urges CH to become Presidential candidate, 855, 856,
  858; to become Vice Presidential candidate, 860–861, 1714; decision to accept third term, 858–860; nomination,
  861; advantages of continuity of lead-

Roosevelt, Franklin D.—*Continued*
ership, 861–862, 866, 868; reelection (1940), 854, 861, 868; preference for title of "Commander-in-Chief," 1111; reelection (1944), 1714; attitude on resignation of CH as Secretary of State, 1715–1718; visits CH in hospital, 1719; messages to CH from Yalta, 1720; proposes CH for Nobel Peace Prize, 1725; death, 1721; *see also* Executive
Roosevelt, Sara Delano, 199
Roosevelt, Theodore, 45, 49, 52, 53, 56–57, 67, 70, 86, 197
Root, Elihu, 50, 102, 271, 1731
Roper, Daniel C., 65, 92, 151, 153–154, 162, 182, 416, 431
Rosenman, Samuel, 683
Rosso, Augusto, 419, 420, 436–440
Roux, Charles, 806
Rowe, Leo S., 351
Royce, Ralph, 1513, 1514
Rubber, reserve stocks, 624–626; Liberia as a source, 1186
Rublee, George, 1626–1627
Ruhr, postwar, 1605, 1606, 1610, 1611, 1617, 1618, 1620
Ruiz Moreno, Isidoro, 604–607 *passim*
Rumania, interest in peace move in Europe, 710; Soviet occupation of Bessarabia and Bukovina, 300, 807, 810, 1451; support of aggression against Yugoslavia, 933; war with U.S.S.R., 977, 978; declaration of war against U.S., 1114; Soviet territorial aims, 1166, 1167, 1173; U.S. declaration of war, 1175–1176; Soviet advance into, 1451; Soviet wartime sphere of influence in, 1451–1459; U.S. protests over nature of Soviet armistice terms with, 1461; nonapplication of unconditional surrender policy to, 1570, 1575–1577, 1579–1580
Runciman, Walter, 524–526, 586
Russia. *See* U.S.S.R.
Russo-Finnish War. *See* Finland: war with U.S.S.R.
Russo-Japanese war, 270
Rye, Tom, 77, 78
Ryti, Risto, 741–742

Saar, postwar, 1610, 1611, 1617, 1618, 1620·

Saavedra Lamas, Carlos, 317, 322–323, 602; Antiwar Pact, 309, 322, 328, 332, 344, 469; CH collaboration with at Montevideo Conference, 327–329, 331, 332, 334–336; policies at Buenos Aires Conference, 497, 499, 501; recipient of Nobel Peace Prize, 329, 1724; proposed CH for Nobel Prize, 1725
Sabotage of Axis shipping in U.S. and Latin American ports, 927, 928
Saed, Mohammed, 1506, 1509–1510
St. Lucia, U.S.-British agreement for lease of bases, 831–843
Saint-Pierre and Miquelon, U.S. consulate, 820; occupation by Free French, 1128–1137
Saint-Quentin, Count René de, 586, 589, 590, 796, 819–820, 846–847
Saito, Hirosi, 277, 281–285, 534, 560–561, 629, 1075
Salazar, Antonio de Oliveira, 770, 941, 1335, 1336–1343
Sales tax, 80, 110
San Francisco United Nations Conference (1945), based on Dumbarton Oaks proposals, 1712–1713; CH views on admission of Argentina, 1405–1406, 1408, 1722; CH as senior adviser and member of U.S. delegation, 1405, 1720, 1721, 1722–1723; *see also* Dumbarton Oaks Conference; United Nations
Sanctions, U.S. policy at Geneva Disarmament Conference, 223, 226, 227–228, 234; against aggressors, 408–409; against Italy, 426, 431–432, 434, 435, 436, 471; against Japan, 550, 551, 570–571
Sandifer, Durward, 1675
Sandler, Rickard, 703
Santa Maria Island, Azores, U.S. air base, 1342–1343
Santos, CH visit to, 323
São Paulo, CH visit to, 323
Saracoglu Shukru, Bey, 1372, 1374
Saudi Arabia, concern over Arab-Jewish question, 1532–1533, 1535; Arab Congress, 1546–1547;
relations with U.S.: U.S. minister to, 1511; U.S. credit and lend-lease aid to, 1511–1512, 1513; U.S. economic and military missions to, 1512,

Saudi Arabia—*Continued*
1513; visit of princes to U.S., 1512–1513;
oil interests of U.S., 1499, 1511, 1516, 1518, 1519, 1520–1522, 1523, 1524; British interests, 1513–1514; efforts for joint U.S.-British program in, 1515–1516
Saugstad, Jesse, 927
Savage, Carlton, 219, 645, 671, 672, 1121, 1686, 1722
Sayre, Francis B., 356, 357, 366, 388
Scavenius, Eric, 936–939
Schacht, Hjalmar, 226, 237–238, 246, 374, 527, 547, 712
Schleicher, Kurt von, 242
Schwarzkopf, H. Norman, 1503
Scientific Congress, Eighth Pan American, 763
Scotland, CH trip to (1925), 125
Seaport Cities Conference on International Trade, CH address before, 391
Second Front, 1110, 1173, 1174, 1179–1180, 1249, 1264, 1278, 1279, 1280, 1306
Secrecy in conduct of foreign affairs, 213–214
Secret agreements between FDR and foreign nations, allegation, 1668
Secretary of State, CH as: Secretary of Stateship offered to CH, 156–158; first public statement as, 159; first speech as, 172–173, 174–175; background in foreign affairs, 162–163; duties and responsibilities, 158–159, 192–194; problems confronting (Mar. 1933), 170–172; daily schedule, 183–189; working relations with President, 191–210; relations with Congress (*see also* Nonpartisan foreign policy), 211–214; press conferences, 218–219; election as chairman of Governing Board of Pan American Union, 311–312; preparation of addresses, 392–393; campaign reports (1940) *re* selection of CH for, 863–864; membership on War Council, 1109–1110; exclusion from military discussions, 1109–1111, 1367; address to joint session of Congress, 1314; resignation as, 1137–1138, 1323, 1715–1719; *for policy matters, see subject*

Selective Service Act, 845, 943, 1104
Selective Service system, World War I, 89
Self-defense policy, U.S., 514–515, 865–866, 919, 1002, 1012; *see also* National defense; Neutrality policy
Senate, U.S. *See* Congress
Serpa Pinto, Portuguese ship, 1339
Serrano Suñer, Ramón, 876–877, 878, 879, 880, 1187, 1188, 1190
Sforza, Carlo, efforts to establish Italian Government, 1551–1552, 1553, 1563, 1568
Shackleford, Dorsey, 62
Shanghai, international efforts to eliminate hostilities in, 539–540; U.S. withdrawal of marines, 568; British withdrawal of troops, 901
Shayesteh, Mohammed, 1501
Sherman, Lawrence Y., 102–103
Sherman Anti-Trust Act (1890), 45
Sherwood, Robert, 1221
Shipley, Ruth B., 181
Shipping, foreign, admission of armed ships to U.S. ports, 676, 695, 697; sinking, 677, 921, 935; U.S. discrimination against, 695–696; taken into protective custody in U.S. and Latin American ports, 759–760, 927, 928, 959, 960; British shipping needs, 921; U.S. requisitioning of seized vessels, 927, 942–943; arming of foreign ships in U.S. ports, 1048; Soviet request for seized Italian ships, 1284, 1301–1302; exclusion of German ships from Swedish Baltic ports, 1348
Shipping, U.S., CH advocates expansion, 85–86, 106, 699; arming and protection, 87, 507–508, 697, 943, 1046–1051; damage or sinking, 87, 480, 540, 944, 1046–1050; detention and release, 676, 679–680, 682, 704–705, 709, 733–736; interdepartmental committee on merchant marine, 681–682; transfer to foreign registry, 697–700; convoys, 1047, 1049, 1050, 1275, 1378; *see also* Atlantic, Battle of; Neutrality policy
Shipstead, Henrik, 217
Shiras, George, Jr., 49
Shotwell, James T., 1636
Shouse, Jouett, 143–144
Siam. *See* Thailand

Siberia, 117, 271, 299
Sicily, military government, 1239
Sidi Moncef Pacha, 1191–1192
Sidwell, M. C., 27
Sikorski, Wladyslaw, 1184, 1268, 1270
Silver, Abba H., 1536
Silver purchase policy of U.S., effect on China, 446
Simmons, Furnifold M., 95, 129
Simmons, John Farr, 181
Simon, Sir John, 280, 293, 379, 384, 539
Simovic, T. Dushan, 933
Sims, Thetus W., 64, 79
Sinclair oil interests, negotiations with Iran for concessions, 1509
Singapore, availability to U.S. fleet, 897, 911, 914; imminence of Japanese attack, 914, 1017
Sinking-fund, 99–100, 125
Sino-Japanese war. See China
Skinner, Robert P., 182
Skvirsky, Boris, 293, 296
Smathers, William H., 565
Smiljanic, Mr., 932
Smith, Alfred E., 122, 129–131, 140–145, 152, 154
Smith, Walter Bedell, 1578
Smith, James, 67
Smith, W. T., 38
Smith-Raskob group in Democratic Party, 140–145, 352
Smoot-Hawley Act (1930), 132, 152, 355, 357, 358, 359, 363
Smuts, Jan Christian, 694
Smyth, Robert L., 811
Soheily, Ali, 1506
Solidarity of the American Republics, 608, 1398
Somaliland, 1204
Soong, T. V., 246, 1077, 1112, 1123, 1124, 1175, 1584–1585, 1586
South Africa, Union of, concern over U.S. neutrality bill, 694, 694–695
South Pacific, plans for unified defense in, 906–907, 909, 912, 1007, 1017, 1113
South Pacific Commission, 1237
Southeast Asia. See also French Indo-China; Kra Isthmus; Malaya; Thailand
Southwest Pacific, U.S. policies, 1599–1601; see also Netherlands East Indies; Philippines

Soviet Union. See U.S.S.R.
Spain, participation in League of Nations commission on Leticia dispute, 311;
civil war (1936–39): U.S. nonintervention, 476, 477, 478, 481–483, 513–514; European agreement on nonintervention, 476, 481, 482, 489; mediation proposals, 480, 489–490; intervention by other countries, 482, 511, 512, 513; evacuation of U.S. citizens, 475, 480; U.S. moral embargo, 478, 480–481, 483, 490–491; U.S. arms embargo, 491, 505–506, 509, 513–514, 516–517, 615; question of U.S. commercial dealings with Insurgents, 504; U.S. relief operations, 504, 509; Loyalists favored by Ambassador Bowers, 485; U.S. volunteers in Loyalist army, 505; Loyalist dispute with Germany over bombing of *Deutschland*, 506; collapse of Loyalist Government, 616; recognition of Franco Government by Germany and Italy, 513; by U.S., Britain, and France, 616–618;
neutrality in World War II: Franco's appeal for localizing European conflict, 701; U.S., British, and Latin American efforts to insure neutrality, 770, 874–881, 941, 1186–1191, 1191–1192; Franco's assurance of continued neutrality, 1195; U.S. petroleum exports to, 874, 1188–1190, 1326–1333; U.S. aviation gasoline to, 874, 1326; U.S. food relief, 875–882; request for U.S. credit, 875, 876, 880, 881, 882; Serrano Suñer becomes Foreign Minister, 876; political refugees, 878; British credit arrangements, 878–879, 880, 881; occupation of Tangier, 620, 880; U.S. citizens in, 880; embargo on wolfram exports to Germany, 1328–1334; U.S. requests for airlines privileges, 1326, 1328, 1334; U.S. requests for recall of Blue Division and release of Italian warships in Spanish ports, 1328, 1334; U.S. policy toward Falange, 1334; removal of German agents in, 1328, 1332; assurances *re* asylum for war criminals, 1363; aid to Jewish refugees, 1539

Spanish-American War, 34–36, 69–70, 333

Spaulding, E. Wilder, 219

Spears, General, 1541, 1542

Special Research Division, State Department, 1630, 1631, 1632, 1638

Speeches and public statements of CH, preparation, 392–393; see also subject

Spellman, Francis J., 714

Spheres of influence, 1298, 1452

Spratly Islands, Japanese claim to, 628–629

Stabilization of currency, 91, 246, 248, 250, 260–266, 378–379, 522

Stahlman, James, 78

Staley, Newton, 11

Stalin, Josef (for nonpersonal items, see U.S.S.R., or subject), refusals to meet with FDR, 1249–1250, 1252; insistence on Tehran as meeting place of heads of states, 1292–1293, 1294–1296, 1303, 1306, 1308–1309, 1311, 1313; meeting at Tehran, 1317–1318, 1506, 1572; statements re declarations of war on Japan, 1309–1310, 1311, 1313; Yalta Conference, 1310, 1458, 1467, 1587, 1680, 1705, 1720; CH audience with, 1292–1296; CH appraisal, 1293, 1311, 1315; banquet during Moscow Conference, 1308–1311; personal messages to CH, 1719, 1720

Standard Oil Co., 559, 1511, 1520–1521

Standard-Vacuum Oil Co., 423–425, 1508–1509

Standley, William H., 288, 446, 476, 1180, 1270–1271

Standpatters, 45, 53, 58, 65, 67

Stark, Harold R., 824, 838, 839, 840, 940, 1049, 1163; on Far Eastern situation, 1057, 1071, 1087, 1097

State Department, policy attacked by Cabinet members, 205; relations with Congress (see also Nonpartisan foreign policy), 211–218; question of secrecy in conduct of foreign relations, 213–214; increase in volume of information made public, 219–220; attacked by press, 220–221; unauthorized publication of documents by Nye Committee, 400–401, 403–404; attacked as result of Saint-Pierre–Miquelon incident, 1130;

State Department—Continued
personnel: Secretary of State (see Secretary of State); Undersecretary, 160, 184, 187, 509–510, 1230; Assistant Secretary, 161; nonpartisan basis for selection, 179–180; praised by CH, 180–181, 596; interest of FDR in high appointments, 200–201; attacks on by Cabinet members, 207; repatriation of diplomatic representatives in Axis countries, 1113; increase in field staff, 1156;

organization and functions: reorganizations in times of stress, 161; economy, 183; administration by Undersecretary, 187, 1230; close working relations with field service, 188–189; infringement on duties by other agencies, 204, 207–208, 209, 902, 1154–1157, 1631; annual report to Congress not required, 213; Office of Arms and Munitions Control, 416, 902; Office of Cultural Relations, 610; night watch, 663; relief and repatriation of U.S. citizens, 663–664, 673–674, 1113–1114; representation of interests of other governments, 674, 1113; committee for postwar planning, 732; destruction of codes by diplomatic missions in Far East in event of emergency (Dec. 5, 1941), 1093; wartime functions, 1109; exclusion from military discussions, 1109–1111, 1367; jurisdiction over civil affairs in North Africa, 1200–1201; Petroleum Adviser, 1517; Committee on International Petroleum Policy, 1517; Advisory Committee on Problems of Foreign Relations, 1626–1630; Division of Special Research, 1630, 1631, 1632, 1638; Divisions of Political and Economic Studies, 1638; drafting group for U.N. Charter, 1647; Department reorganization (1944), 1649–1650; Committee on Postwar Programs, 1650; committee on nonpartisan policy toward U.N. organization, 1711

building and offices: offices of the Secretary, 168–169; architecture, 169; visit of FDR to building, 202; bust of CH presented to Department, 1719; see also Foreign Service

States' rights, 18, 52, 140, 151, 197

Stefánsson, Stefán Jóhan, 946

Steinhardt, Laurence, U.S. delegate to Lima Conference, 603; CH appraisal, 603–604; actions as U.S. Ambassador to Moscow, 656, 685, 704–705, 708–709, 741, 810, 973, 993; as Ambassador to Turkey, 1365, 1369, 1370–1372

Stepp, Mr., attack on William Hull and death, 3–4

Sterling, Frederick A., 703

Stettinius, Edward R., Jr., as Lend-Lease Administrator, 1042;
Under Secretary of State: appointment, 184, 1230, 1256; views, proposals, etc., on Moscow Conference, 1265; Spanish wolfram exports to Germany, 1328, 1330; U.S. air bases in Azores, 1341; U.S. impartiality on Irish question, 1360; Argentina, 1388, 1395; proposed meeting of American foreign ministers, 1404; visit of Polish Americans to Moscow, 1442; negotiations for oil agreement with British, 1523; nationwide discussions on U.N., 1711; head of special mission to London (1944), 1428–1430; reorganization of State Department, 1649–1650; at Dumbarton Oaks Conference, 1673, 1677, 1679, 1681, 1682, 1683, 1686, 1688, 1694, 1700, 1701, 1702, 1705, 1710–1711;
appointment as Secretary of State, 1719, 1720; as chairman of U.S. delegation to San Francisco Conference, 1405, 1721–1723

Stimson, Henry L., 179, 202; CH appraisal, 160, 208; views or actions on disarmament, 223, 226; Japanese acquisition of Manchuria, 270, 271; Latin America, 309; neutrality, 408, 943; destroyers-bases agreement, 838; national defense measures, 910; convoys, 1047; Far East, 1071, 1077, 1091, 1092, 1093, 1095, 1097; South Seas defense, 1113; economic accord with North Africa, 1162; postwar treatment of Germany, 1284, 1285, 1602, 1608, 1609–1610, 1614, 1615, 1620, 1621; trade with Spain and Portugal, 1325, 1326; oil program with Sweden, 1346, 1347; Brazilian

Stimson, Henry L.—Continued
military strength, 1391; U.S. oil reserves, 1517, 1518; pro-Zionist Congressional resolution, 1535; United Nations, 1670

Stinebower, Leroy, 1638

Stockholm conference on rights of northern neutrals, 703–704

Stockpiles. See Strategic materials

Storni, Segundo, 1384–1387 passim

Story, Ephraim, 29

Strang, William, 1595

Strategic materials, U.S. efforts to build up reserves, 457, 624–626, 1189, 1190, 1517, 1518–1519 (see also Embargo, U.S.); export by Netherlands East Indies to Japan, 895; agreements reached at Rio de Janeiro, 1150; embargo on exports to Axis, by Spain, 1328–1334; by Portugal, 1333, 1335–1339; by Sweden, 1346–1348; by Switzerland, 1349–1351; by Turkey, 1371–1372

Straten-Ponthoz, Count Robert van der, 1052

Straus, Jesse Isidor, 461

Strong, George V., 1636, 1675

Submarine warfare. See Maritime warfare

Subsidies, 52, 85, 101; German export subsidies, 238–239

Sudetenland, 615

Sulzer, William, 63

Sumner, William G., 147

Supreme Allied Command, 1244

Supreme Court decisions, on income-tax law of 1894, 48, 59, 66; on arms embargo, 468

Supreme War Council, CH concept of, 1115, 1116; presentation of memorandum on to President and Cabinet, 1117–1118, 1119; consideration by President, 1120–1121; decision to create Combined Chiefs of Staff, 1124

Surinam, U.S. protection of bauxite mines at Paramaribo, 1051

Surpluses, 133, 257; CH opposition to "plow under" doctrine, 146–147; export surpluses in Western Hemisphere, 827, 828

Suvich, Fulvio, 470

Swanson, Claude, 72, 141, 208, 287, 405, 416
Sweden, trade agreement with U.S., 375; protest over pending U.S. neutrality bill, 695; alarm over Soviet advance in Baltic, 702–703; refuses passage to Anglo-French forces, 740–741; offer of good offices to Britain and Germany, 845; Soviet desire for air bases in, 1279–1280, 1301; U.S. and British efforts to reduce shipments of strategic materials to Germany, 1346–1348; petroleum from U.S., 1346; closing of Baltic ports to German shipping, 1348; declaration against granting asylum to war criminals, 1363; medium of peace feelers, 1573
Switzerland, trade with U.S., 355, 375; concern over effect of U.S. arms embargo, 648; representation of U.S. interests, 1113, 1349; Anglo-American efforts to eliminate trade with Axis, 1349–1351; assurances re asylum for war criminals, 1363
Syria, Vichy French concessions to Germany in, 958, 960, 962–963, 964; British and Free French invasion, 964–965, 1498, 1540; independence, 1540–1541; U.S. position, 1499, 1500, 1541, 1543, 1544, 1546; French efforts to establish "special position" in, 1541–1546; U.S. recognition, 1545; Arab Congress, 1546–1547

Tachibana, Lt. Comdr., 1011–1012
Taft, William Howard, 55, 62, 65, 86, 102
Tanaka, General, 271
Tangier, Spanish occupation, 620, 880; Spanish removal of German agents in, 1328, 1332
Tangku Truce between China and Japan, 274
Tanner, Väinö Alfred, 742
Tariff, CH's early interest in, 21–22; CH's ideas on become international in scope (1916), 81, 83, 84, 101; reciprocity agreement with Canada (1911), 65; Empire preferential, 85, 101, 355, 519, 526, 530, 975–976, 1151–1153, 1476–1477, 1614; truce and reduction

Tariff—Continued
proposed by CH, 155; inability of U.S. delegation to discuss at London Economic Conference, 248–249, 250–252, 257; truce at London Economic Conference, 354, 356; FDR attitude, 132, 352, 353, 357, 372, 374, 747, 750; multilateral and bilateral methods of reduction, 356; tariff plank in Democratic platform (1936), 486; reduction in lend-lease agreements, 1151–1153, 1211;
high tariff: protective championed by Theodore Roosevelt, 52; CH attacks in maiden address to Congress (1908), 52, 352; on wood pulp, 62, 65; CH's continued fight against, 81–82, 84, 101, 106–107, 123, 124, 126, 128, 146, 352, 353, 356–358; accepted in Democratic platform (1928), 130–131; condemned in Democratic platform (1932), 140–145, 152–153, 352; effect on Latin America, 308; efforts at Montevideo Conference to lower, 320–322, 328, 329, 331–332, 347–348; George N. Peek advocate of, 354, 370–372; retaliation of foreign governments against U.S., 355; effect on war debts, 381;
acts and bills: Wilson (1894), 48, 66; Payne-Aldrich (1909), 59–61, 62, 65, 66, 83–84; "pop-gun" tariff-reduction bills, 64–65; Underwood (1913), 70–72, 73–74, 75–76, 84, 91, 352, 358; Farmers' (1921), 106, 126; Fordney-McCumber (1922), 114, 126, 363, 364; Smoot-Hawley (1930), 130, 152, 355, 357, 358, 359, 363;
see also Most-favored-nation; Trade, international; Trade agreements; and under individual country
Taussig, Charles W., 1236, 1475
Tax Advisers, Board of Excess Profits, 93
Taxation, as means of defraying war expenditures, 89–93, 94–100
Taxes, income tax (see Income tax); excise tax, 66, 80, 206–207; estate tax, 77, 80–81; sales tax, 80, 110; excess-profits tax, 81, 92–93, 110
Taylor, Andrew J., 18

Taylor, Myron C., 578, 714-715, 777-779, 1538, 1560-1562, 1633, 1635, 1643, 1670, 1675, 1711
Teapot Dome investigation, 114-115
Tehran Conference (1943), Stalin's insistence on Tehran as meeting place of heads of states, 1292-1293, 1294-1296, 1303, 1306, 1308-1309, 1311, 1313; meeting, 1110, 1317-1318; Declaration on Iran, 1505, 1506-1507; discussions on unconditional surrender, 1572
Tennessee, terrain and people of Kentucky border area in 1871, 6-9; "Volunteer State," 17, 89; poll tax in 1890's, 31-32; CH as judge of 5th judicial circuit (1898, 1903-7), 38-42; nomination and election of CH to State Legislature (1892), 27-29, 36; activities of CH as member of Legislature (1893-97), 29-33; CH declines nomination for 3d term in Legislature, 33; CH elected to Congress from 4th district, 43-44; his first efforts toward State improvement, 43-44; delegation in 62d Congress, 63-64; political regime of Luke Lea, 77-79, 134, 135, 138; State Library at Nashville custodian of CH's Cabinet and State Department desk and chairs, 204; State Legislature honors CH, 1719
Tennessee Valley Authority, 156
Terra, Gabriel, 325, 336, 337-339, 347
Texas Co. oil concession in Saudi Arabia, 1511; negotiations with Petroleum Reserves Corp., 1520-1521
Thailand, Japanese control of, 985, 991, 997, 1090; FDR proposal for neutralization, 1014; postwar plans for, 1587-1588
Third term, FDR's decision to accept, 858-860; CH views on, 861; nomination and election of FDR, 861, 868
Thomas, Elbert D., 1630, 1635, 1658, 1695
Thomas, Henry, 1274
Thomsen, Hans, 927, 943
Thornburg, Max W., 1517
Thurston, Walter, 807, 811
Tientsin incident, 630-631, 632-633, 635
Timor, Portuguese participation in liberating, 1342, 1343

Tin reserves, U.S. efforts to acquire, 457, 624-626
Tinkham, George H., 545
Tipton, John A., 31
Tirana, Albania, closing of American Legation, 619
Tittmann, Harold H., Jr., 1562
Tixier, Adrien, 1197, 1202, 1203
Tobacco, American, removal of British ban on purchases, 748-749
Todd, A. L., 135-139
Togliatti, Palmiro, 1553
Togo, Shigenori, 1054, 1055, 1075, 1087, 1095, 1099
Tojo, Hideki, 1054, 1089
Townsend, Judge, 837, 838
Toyoda, Teijiro, 1014, 1029, 1030, 1032, 1034
Tracy, Dan W., 603
Trade, German, in South America, 813-814, 820-821, 828
Trade, international, removal of barriers and restrictions, 81-84, 101, 126, 155, 257, 286, 353, 356, 368-369; removal of barriers from lend-lease agreements, 976, 1151-1153, 1211, 1476-1477, 1614; FDR's views on international trade, 167, 191, 248, 249, 250-251, 319, 331-332, 353, 354, 357, 372, 374, 521-522, 747, 750; effect of economic relations on political relations, 355, 363-365; U.S.-British discussions on rehabilitation, 520-523, 524-526; provision in Atlantic Charter, 975-976; postwar trade, 1153, 1178, 1477;
  most-favored-nation principle, conditional, 360; unconditional, definition, 84, 248, 359; CH advocate of, 84, 101, 146, 155, 172; application, 356, 359-363; extension to U.S.S.R., 304-305; in economic resolutions at Montevideo Conference, 320-322, 328, 329, 331-332, 347-348;
  international conference developments: London Economic, 248, 249, 250-254, 257-258; Montevideo, 320-322, 328, 329, 331-332, 347-348; Buenos Aires, 498, 501; British Imperial, 528-529; Lima, 610; Moscow, 1303-1304;

Trade—*Continued*
  see also Embargo; Tariff; Trade
  agreements; *and specific commodity
  of trade*
Trade, interstate, Federal Trade Commission Act (1914), 73
Trade, Japan–Netherlands East Indies,
  895–896
Trade, U.S., decline (1929–33), 354,
  357; during World War II with belligerents (*see also* Embargo; Neutrality policy), 414–415, 431–432, 435,
  442, 461, 463, 464, 698–699; with
  neutrals, 680–682, 733–736; *see also*
  Tariff; Trade agreements; *and country and specific commodity*
Trade agreements program, CH early
  views on, 81–84, 101, 126, 146, 155,
  172; attempts of CH to secure legislation in 1933, 156, 248, 249, 250–254;
  opposition of Key Pittman to program, 215; of George N. Peek, 353–
  354, 370–374; FDR attitude, 248, 249,
  250–254, 353, 357, 372, 374, 521–522,
  747, 750; CH efforts to enlist support
  of other nations at London, 266; at
  Montevideo, 320–322, 328, 329, 331–
  332, 347–348; CH appointment of
  Francis B. Sayre to head program,
  356; effect of Italo-Ethiopian war on,
  440; campaign issue (1936), 486; CH
  promotion of nonpartisan support,
  1212, 1656;
    act of 1934: drafting, 354, 356, 357;
  passage, 357–358; operation, 358–366;
  machinery for negotiation of agreements, 366–367; procedure, 367–368;
  difficulties encountered, 368–374, 376–
  377; results by 1936, 375–377;
    renewal (1937), 518–519; renewal
  (1940), 746–750; renewal (1943),
  1211–1212; renewal (1945), 1721; *see
  also* Trade, international; *and individual country*
Train, Harold C., 1675
Transfer of territory from one European nation to another, U.S. and
  inter-American policy, 791, 804, 814–
  817, 822–826
Trans-Jordan, Arab Congress, 1546

Treasury Department, 92–93, 472–473,
  615, 1182, 1676; plan for postwar
  Germany (*see* Germany: postwar)
Treaties, observance of, 153, 159, 172,
  174, 243, 270, 271, 284, 290; method
  of negotiating, 192; treaty-making
  process compared to negotiation of
  Executive agreements, 211–213, 252–
  253, 354; Senate approval by majority rather than two-thirds vote,
  212, 1734; *see also* Peace treaties
Trinidad, U.S.-British agreement for
  lease of bases, 831–843
Tripartite Pact (1940), 489, 627–628;
  signing, 908–909; adherence of Bulgaria, 931; adherence of Yugoslavia,
  932; discussions of Japanese commitments under, 991, 1002, 1006–1007,
  1010, 1011, 1021, 1028, 1035, 1059,
  1060, 1061, 1062, 1063–1064, 1066,
  1071, 1083
Troyanovsky, Alexander A., 302–303,
  657–660
Truk, trusteeship, 1596
Truman, Harry S., 699, 1593–1594, 1727–
  1728
Trusteeship system for dependent peo-
  ples, 1234–1238, 1304–1305, 1466, 1599,
  1600, 1638–1639, 1653, 1706–1707;
    favored by FDR for French Indo-
  China, 1595–1598; for Korea and
  Japanese mandated islands, 1596; *see
  also* Dependent peoples
Trusts, 45, 52, 73
Tubman, William V., 1186
Tuck, S. Pinckney, 602, 1195
Tugwell, Rexford G., 1236
Tumulty, Joseph, 98–99, 101–102, 121
Tunis, message from FDR on African
  landing, 1191–1192
Turkey, capital moved to Ankara, 201;
  question of U.S. special mission to
  Mohammedans in, 715–716; U.S. efforts to solidify resistance to Axis
  (1941), 928–932; U.S.-British policy
  decisions *re,* 1365–1368;
    entry into war: Soviet proposals
  urging, 1279–1280, 1297, 1301, 1312,
  1368–1369, 1373; joint Allied efforts
  toward, 1368–1369, 1371, 1373, 1375–
  1376; meetings of President Inönü
  with FDR and Churchill, 1365, 1369–

Turkey—*Continued*
1370; lend-lease aid to, 1366; Allied lease of air bases in, 1301, 1312; embargo of strategic materials to Germany, 1371–1372; severance of diplomatic relations with Germany, 1372–1376; decision to enter war, 1370, 1376
Turney, Peter, 31–33
Twenty-one Demands of Japan against China, 270, 271
Twitchell, K. S., 1512
Tydings, Millard, 1719
Tydings-McDuffie Act (1934), 278, 1595
Tyson, Lawrence D., 134

Ukrainian Republic, question of membership in U.N., 1680
Unconditional surrender, announced and defined by FDR, 1570–1571, 1572; CH views on, 1570; British views, 1570, 1572, 1573; Soviet views, 1572, 1573; question of public definition, 1573–1574; British and Soviet pressure to modify definition for Axis satellites, 1575–1577, 1579–1580; U.S. General Staff suggested tripartite statement to weaken German morale, 1578–1579, 1580–1582
Under Secretary of State, 160, 184, 187, 509–510, 1230 (*see also* Phillips, William; Stettinius, Edward R., Jr.; Welles, Sumner)
Underwood, Oscar, 63, 64, 67, 68, 70–72, 92, 108
Underwood Tariff Act (1913), 70–72, 73–74, 75–76, 84, 91, 332, 358
Union of South Africa, concern over U.S. neutrality bill, 694, 694–695
U.S.S.R.: Siberia, 117, 271, 299; disarmament policy, 293, 304, 306; League of Nations membership, 304, 709–710; intervention in Spain, 482, 489–490, 512; Litvinov replaced as Foreign Commissar by Molotov, 656; Soviet desire to check aggression, 658; signatory to United Nations Declaration, 1115, 1120, 1121–1124; dissolution of Comintern, 1251–1252; press censorship, 1278–1279; lack of freedom of religion, 1288–1289; isolationism, 1297, 1310; position on uncondi-

U.S.S.R.—*Continued*
tional surrender principle, 1572–1582; U.S. diplomatic recognition: Soviet desire for, 292–295; U.S. study of question, 172, 294–299; prerequisites to, 294, 297, 300; FDR invitation for exploratory conversations, 297–298; terms of proposed agreements, 299–300; conversations with Litvinov, 300–302; U.S. recognition, 212, 276, 302; failure of U.S. to obtain debt settlement, 303–304;
subsequent relations with U.S., 306–307: Communist propaganda in U.S., 292, 305–306, 741, 1251, 1288–1289; trade with U.S., 304–305, 659, 660, 743–744, 807–810, 970–971; *City of Flint* incident, 704–705, 709; U.S. moral embargo, 706–707, 744, 969; restrictions on U.S. consular officers and rudeness of Soviet officials, 707–709; U.S. aviation engineers return to U.S., 707; Soviet grievances, 708–709, 743–745, 807–810, 970–972; lend-lease aid, 976–977, 981, 1176, 1272–1273, 1461–1462; U.S. credit, 977; appointment of Litvinov as Ambassador to U.S., 981; U.S. oil shipments, 1017 1018; noncooperation with U.S. against Japan, 1111–1113; air bases in U.S.S.R., 1111, 1112, 1302; pressure on U.S. and Britain for second front, 1173, 1174, 1179–1180, 1249, 1264, 1278, 1279, 1280, 1306; refusals of Stalin to meet with FDR, 1249–1250, 1252; U.S. press attacks on CH as anti-Russian, 1253, 1255; U.S. Embassy building in Moscow, 1277; change in Soviet foreign policy, 1459–1460; U.S. relations with and policy toward, (1933–39) · 657–660, (1940) 743–745, (1941) 972–973, (1943) 1250–1251, (1944) 1436, 1449, 1459–1471, 1665, 1739;
relations with Great Britain (*see* Great Britain: relations with U.S.S.R.);
attack on Poland (*see* Poland: Soviet attack);
in the Baltic: demands on and occupation of Estonia, Latvia, and Lithuania, 701, 810, 812; war with

U.S.S.R.—*Continued*
Finland (*see* Finland: war with
U.S.S.R.);
relations with Germany: Anti-
Comintern Pact between Germany,
Japan, and Italy, 488, 489, 556, 634,
639, 717, 908, 980; nonaggression pact,
655–657, 701, 717, 720–721, 969; relations, 707, 806, 807, 810–811, 969;
invasion of U.S.S.R., 967–968, 973;
nonapplication of U.S. Neutrality Act
to U.S.S.R., 973; U.S. aid to U.S.S.R.,
973, 974, 976–977; Japanese attempts
to bring about separate peace between U.S.S.R. and Germany, 1263–
1264, 1310, 1462; German allegation
of death of 10,000 Polish officers at
hands of Russians, 1267; Soviet victories, 1297–1298;
relations with Italy: request to
U.S. and Britain for information on
developments in Italy, 1283, 1549,
1556–1557; for Italian war vessels,
1284, 1301–1302; member, Advisory
Council for Italy, 1283–1284, 1551;
U.S.S.R. accepts as cobelligerent, 1551;
establishment of diplomatic relations
with Italy, 1449, 1463, 1556–1557,
1567–1568;
southeastern Europe: occupation of
Rumania, 745, 807, 810, 1451; pressure for Turkish entrance into war,
1279–1280, 1297, 1301, 1312, 1368–
1369, 1373–1376; British proposal for
spheres of influence in Balkans, 1451–
1459, 1470; armistice terms with Rumania, Bulgaria, and Hungary, 1459,
1461;
Iran: consent for Iran to sign
United Nations Declaration, 1253;
use as supply route to U.S.S.R., 1498,
1500, 1502–1503, 1506; invasion of
Iran with British, 976, 1500, 1501–
1502, 1506; Anglo-Soviet treaty
(1942), 1502, 1505, 1506; Tehran
Declaration on Iran, 1505, 1506–1507,
1510; demands for oil concessions in
Iran, 1509;
Far East: relations with Japan
(*see* Japan: relations with U.S.S.R.);
relations with China, 1257; objections
to China's inclusion in Four-Nation

U.S.S.R.—*Continued*
Declaration, 1256–1257, 1265, 1279,
1281, 1282, 1299, 1301, 1302, 1312;
Indo-China, 1597; advances in Far
East, 1671;
postwar policy: pressure for territorial commitments prior to peace
conference, 1165–1174, 1177; postwar
intentions, 1247–1249; signatory to
Four-Nation Declaration (*see* Four-
Nation Declaration); reconstruction,
1303; postwar treatment of Germany,
1607, 1608, 1609, 1613, 1616–1617,
1618, 1619, 1620–1621, 1622; exchange
of views with U.S. and Britain on
international organization, 1650–1651;
participant in Dumbarton Oaks discussions, 1459, 1469, 1470, 1671–1685,
1700–1707; desire to participate in
U.N., 1469, 1665; question of admission of constituent republics to U.N.,
1679–1680;
see also Moscow Conference; Tehran Conference; Yalta Conference
United Nations, early preparatory work
for:
need for an international organization, 731–732, 1177–1178, 1238–1239,
1280–1281, 1288, 1294, 1307, 1321,
1322–1323, 1625–1626, 1634, 1638;
called for by Four-Nation Declaration
(*see* Four-Nation Declaration); postwar planning in State Department,
732, 1626–1630, 1631, 1632, 1638,
1647, 1650; creation and functions of
Advisory Committee on Postwar Foreign Policy, 1631–1639; interest of
other governments, 1475–1476, 1625–
1626, 1631, 1650–1651;
nonpartisan Congressional support,
1258–1263, 1314, 1315, 1630, 1635,
1639, 1655, 1656, 1657–1670, 1676,
1695–1698, 1711; exclusion from 1944
presidential campaign, 1656, 1657,
1666, 1669, 1670, 1686–1695, 1699;
CH views on: Soviet participation,
1468–1470, 1659, 1664–1665; development of favorable public opinion,
1659, 1662–1663, 1711; insistence on
establishment prior to conclusion of
peace treaties, 1660, 1661, 1665–1666,
1667–1668, 1698; defense of veto

United Nations—*Continued*
power, 1662–1664; opposition to regional organizations within, 1666–1667; appraisal and plea for support, 1736–1737, 1741;
United Nations, structure and functions of organization (provisions of proposed Charter):
envisaged on regional basis, 1639–1647, 1649; on universal basis, 1647; method of initiating establishment of, 1651–1652; selection of name, 1683, 1685; of location, 1681–1682;
Security Council, composition, 1652, 1674, 1678; functions, 1677, 1694; method of voting in, 1652, 1678, 1682–1683, 1685; question of voting by parties to dispute, 1459, 1469, 1653, 1674, 1677–1678, 1680, 1683, 1685, 1700–1702, 1705, 1706; veto power of permanent Council members, 1653, 1683, 1685, 1701;
Assembly functions, 1653, 1677, 1684, 1694; Military Staff Committee functions, 1684; International Court, 1653; president of organization, 1653, 1674, 1695–1696; director general, 1654, 1695–1696; inclusion of economic and social council, 1643, 1653, 1673, 1677, 1680–1681, 1683–1684, 1708;
membership of "associated nations," 1425, 1678–1679; of Soviet republics, 1679–1680; suspension or expulsion of members, 1683, the role of small nations, 1686–1689, 1691; question of Vatican membership, 1711–1712;
question of provisions for international police force, 1653, 1682, 1684; ratification in cases of application of force under, 1691, 1695–1697, 1698; trusteeship system, 1234–1238, 1304–1305, 1466, 1638–1639, 1653, 1706–1707;
see also Dumbarton Oaks Conference; San Francisco
United Nations, CH the "Father of," 1718, 1723, 1728
United Nations Commission for the Investigation of War Crimes, 1185
United Nations Day, 1221

United Nations Declaration (Jan. 1, 1942), conception and drafting, 1114–1116; presentation of drafts to President and Cabinet, 1117; question of constitutionality, 1117–1118; British, Chinese, and Soviet approval, 1119–1124; signing, 1124–1125, 1570, 1632; CH statement, 1125; adherence by nongovernmental authorities, 1125–1126, 1163, 1242–1243; Argentine objection regarding, 1144; French adherence, 1243; Iran signature, 1253; adherence, 1505; Iraq adherence, 1504
United Nations Relief and Rehabilitation Agreement, 1657
United States. *See specific subject; for relations with other countries, see individual countries*
Uruguay, efforts to end Chaco War, 336, 337–338, 347; mediation in Spanish War, 480; support of Argentina at Lima Conference, 606; scuttling of *Graf von Spee* in Montevideo harbor, 690, 691–692; proposal for protest on invasion of Low Countries, 764; center of Nazi subversive activity, 820; defense against possible invasion from Argentina, 1395; support of Allied cause in the war, 1425; Montevideo Conference (*see* Montevideo)

Vandenberg, Arthur H., 637, 1262, 1657, 1658, 1676, 1695, 1696–1697
Vansittart, Sir Robert, 380, 400
Vargas, Getulio, 601, 607–608, 609, 941, 1145, 1340–1341
Variety Clubs of America Humanitarian Award to CH, 1719
Vatican, U.S. establishment of relations with, 713–715; peace appeal to Mussolini, 778, 779; U.S. instructions to mission to, 941; question of asylum for Axis leaders, 1360, 1361; efforts to prevent bombing of Rome, 1560–1563; question of membership in U.N., 1711–1712; *see also* Pope Pius XII
Velloso, Pedro Leão, 1407
Versailles Treaty, 103, 112–113, 127, 223, 230, 233, 243
Vertrees, John J., 33
Vice Presidency, FDR nominee (1920), 104; nomination of John Garner

Vice Presidency—*Continued*
(1932), 153–154; candidacy of Henry
A. Wallace (1940), 859, 861; CH refusal to consider candidacy (1940),
860–861, (1944) 1714
Vichy Government. *See* France, Vichy
Victor Emmanuel III, of Italy, 655, 661,
662, 664; U.S. objections to, 1550,
1569; refusal to abdicate, 1552, 1554;
transfers powers to Prince Humbert,
1555, 1558, 1563; abdication, 1568–
1569
Victory Bond Act (1919), 125
Victory clubs to aid Democratic Party
(1920), 114, 116
Villarroel, Gualberto, 1388, 1398
Vincent, Sténio, 345
Vinson-Trammell Act, 287
Virginia, University of, FDR's stab-in-
the-back address, 784–785
Vishinski, Andrei A., 1376, 1502
Vladivostok, U.S. shipments to Soviet
Union via, 1020–1021

Wadleigh, Julian, 1630
Wadsworth, George, 1543, 1545
Wadsworth, James W., 1262, 1263
Wagner, Robert F., 139, 1531
Wakasugi, Kaname, 1034, 1061
Walden, George S., 423–424
Walker, Frank C., 209, 984, 985, 991,
994
Walker, John E., 65
Wallace, Henry A., 357, 1599, 1697,
1719; missions abroad, 200, 1585–
1586; infringement on State Depart-
ment duties as head of BEW, 204,
1154–1157, 1347, 1379; CH appraisal,
209; candidate for Vice President
(1940), 859, 861
Walsh, James Edward, 984, 985, 989,
991, 1003
Walsh, Thomas J., 114–115, 132, 152
Wang, C. T., 557
Wang Ching-wei puppet government in
China, 724–725, 894, 914, 1086
War, renunciation, 234, 503 (*see also*
Peace); local hostilities an international threat, 225, 425, 482–483;
"methods short of war," 612, 614,
615;

War—*Continued*
prevention: effect of trade agreements in, 363–364, 365; neutrality,
409 (*see also* Isolationism; Neutrality
policy); efforts in Western Hemisphere, 499–501, 503; Ludlow resolution for war referendum, 563; Johnson resolution, 573–574; *see also*
World War
War Council, Supreme. *See* Supreme
War Council
War Council, U.S., repeated warnings
by CH of imminent danger to U.S.
from Japan, 1079–1080, 1087; non-
participation by CH after Pearl Harbor, 1109–1110
War crimes. *See* Atrocities
War debts, CH views, 125, 126; opposition to cancellation in 1932 Democratic platform, 153; CH proposal for
adjustment, 155; U.S.-British discussion (1933), 160; payment of, 171;
FDR–Ramsay MacDonald conference,
247; CH disinterest, 247; stricken
from London Economic Conference
agenda, 247, 250, 256; general situation (1933–35), 380–381; Great
Britain, 381–382; France, 385; Johnson Act (1934), 303, 382; CH proposal for bond issues by debtors,
382; Congressional arguments, 381;
payments by Finland, 382; Italy, 785
War Department, objection to international supervision of arms, 233; informed of international situation,
864–865, 866; warned of Japanese attacks, 984, 1080, 1087; membership on
War Council, 1109; negotiations for
agreement on French civil administration, 1432–1433; instructions to U.S.
forces in India, 1489; position on
British and Soviet troops in Iran, 1506;
position on postwar treatment of
Germany, 1602, 1607, 1609–1610; *see
also* Army, U.S.; Joint Chiefs of
Staff; National defense; Stimson,
Henry L.
War Refugee Board, 1539, 1540
Warren, Avra, 1398
Warren, Charles, 404, 460
Warren, George, 198

Washington, George, on secrecy in conduct of foreign relations, 213–214; on commercial policy, 360

Washington Disarmament Conference (1921–22), 116, 222, 271

Washington Naval Treaty (1922), 288–290, 444, 447, 448

Wasson, Thomas C., 852, 1040

Watterson, Henry, 67

Weddell, Alexander W., 182, 319, 327, 494; as U.S. Ambassador to Spain, 617, 875–880, 940, 1188, 1190

Wei Tao-ming, 1258, 1671, 1672

Weizmann, Chaim, 1531, 1533

Welch, Richard J., 1636

Welles, Sumner, Ambassador to Cuba, 313, 315; Assistant Secretary of State, 313, 341, 343, 345;
Under Secretary of State, 184, 202, 979, 1013–1014; appointment, 509–510; views and proposals on: international peace meeting in 1937, 546–549; Italian possession of Ethiopia, 581–582; Czech crisis, 591, 593, 596, 615; Munich agreement, 596; European war, 671, 672; Western Hemisphere neutrality zone, 945; Monroe Doctrine, 959–960; Atlantic Charter, 976; international situation (1941), 1058; U.N. Declaration, 1121; Board of Economic Warfare, 1156; U.S. troops in Northern Ireland, 1355; Chile and Argentina, 1383, 1409; India, 1484; conferences with Soviet Ambassador, 812, 968, 970, 971; participation in postwar planning, 732, 1595, 1626–1627, 1631–1632, 1635, 1638, 1639–1640;
international conferences and missions, 494, 688, 721, 737–740, 777, 1017–1018, 1143–1150, 1253, 1254–1255;
divergency of policy with CH, 1227–1230; resignation as Under Secretary of State, 1230–1231, 1256

Wendelin, Eric C., 475, 480

West Africa. See Dakar

West India Conference, 1237

West Indies. See British West Indies; Netherlands West Indies

Western Hemisphere, neutrality zone, 689–692, 945; U.S. and inter-American

Western Hemisphere—Continued
policy on European possessions in, 791, 804, 814–817, 822–826, 1629–1630; defense, 935–936; see also American republics; Canada; Monroe Doctrine

Weygand, Maxime, appointed French supreme army commander, 770; Delegate-General in French North Africa, 853; support of U.S. in Africa, 853–854, 949–951, 956, 961, 1039–1040, 1043–1044; influence against Darlan agreement with Germany, 963, 966; dismissal as Delegate-General, 1038, 1042–1043; refusal to return to North Africa to cooperate with Allies, 1127

Whale oil, imports from Norway, 376

Wheat, U.S. relief shipments to Spain, 875–882; to unoccupied France, 952–955, 957

Wheeler, Burton K., 217

Wheeler, Leslie A., 822

Whiskey, stilling in Tennessee, 4–5; U.S. claims against Canada for alleged non-payment of excise taxes, 206–207

White, Harry D., 207, 822, 1604, 1605, 1614, 1636

White, Wallace H., 1635, 1658, 1695, 1697

White, William Allen, 833

White House Correspondents Association, FDR address, 925, 1571

White Russian Republic, question of membership in U.N., 1680

Whitney, Alexander F., 494

Wickard, Claude R., 1512, 1531

Wikawa, Tadao, 1003, 1014

Wiley, John C., 810

Wilhelmina, Queen, 712, 762, 765, 1051

William and Mary College, CH address, 390

Williams, John Sharp, 50, 81, 108

Willkie, Wendell, 833, 862–864, 866–868, 1182–1183, 1437, 1690, 1697

Willson, Russell, 1675, 1705

Wilson, Charles E., 1522

Wilson, Edwin C., 181, 821, 1244, 1675

Wilson, Sir Henry Maitland, 1551, 1554, 1557, 1563, 1564

Wilson, Sir Horace, 662

Wilson, Hugh R., 182–183, 379–380, 671, 672, 674; as U.S. Ambassador to

Wilson, Hugh R.—*Continued*
  Germany, 170, 572, 589, 599, 600;
  postwar planning, 732, 1626–1627,
  1694, 1695, 1711
Wilson, Joseph R., 68
Wilson, William L., 49
Wilson, Woodrow, election and inauguration as President (1912), 67–73;
  denounces lobbying, 72; desire for
  peace, 75, 87; actions as President,
  80, 89, 96–97, 99–100, 107, 125, 198;
  Fourteen Points, 82, 1266, 1540; war
  message (1917), 87–88; opposition in
  Congress, 98, 102–104, 112; question
  of attendance at Paris Peace Conference, 101–102; fight for League, 102–
  104, 118; 1920 elections, 105; opposition to regional basis for world organization, 116; interest in rebuilding
  Democratic Party, 117–121; views on
  neutrality, 408; illness and death, 104,
  117; CH appraisal, 120–121, 404;
    FDR address to Woodrow Wilson
  Foundation, 339–340, 386–387
Wilson Tariff Act (1894), 48, 66
Winant, John G., as U.S. Ambassador
  to Great Britain, 926, 976, 1153, 1165,
  1167, 1171, 1330, 1358–1359, 1373–
  1374, 1431, 1479, 1483–1485, 1595
Wise, Stephen S., 1536
Witz, Frances. *See* Hull, Frances Witz
Wolfram to Germany, U.S.-British ef-
  forts to effect embargo on Spanish
  exports, 1328–1333; on Portuguese
  exports, 1333, 1335, 1336–1339
Wolverton, Charles A., 1636
Woman suffrage, 115, 119–120
Woodring, Harry, 208, 416
Woodrow Wilson Foundation, FDR ad-
  dress to, 339–340, 386–387
Woods, Sam E., 967–968
Woodson, Walter B., 840
World Congress of the International
  Chamber of Commerce (Brussels
  1925), CH as delegate, 125
World Court, 153, 177, 212, 215, 387–389,
  1178, 1631, 1647, 1651, 1653, 1681
World order under law, 173, 291, 731,
  732, 1296; *see also* Peace
World organizations, proposals for dur-
  ing World War I, 75, 86; during
  World War II (*see* United Nations)

World War I, no premonition of in
  1912, 69, 70; causes, 75; effect on
  trade, 75–76; on income-tax principle,
  76; failure of U.S. citizenry to grasp
  import, 76–77; financing of, 89–93,
  94–100, 124–125; effects on U.S., 89–
  90; German peace overtures, 97; neutral rights after, 409, 463; lack of
  Allied common agreement on war
  aims, 1115–1116; Supreme War Council, 1117
World War II, forecasts and warnings
  of danger to U.S., 203, 231, 651–652,
  864–865, 866, 1057–1058, 1079–1080,
  1087, 1088, 1098; summary of FDR
  and CH efforts to prevent, 665–667;
  peace moves and feelers, 710–712, 844–
  845, 1179, 1297, 1573; economic effects on American republics, 827–
  828; second front, 1110, 1173, 1174,
  1179–1180, 1249, 1264, 1278, 1279,
  1280, 1306; crises in 1940 and 1942,
  1730; *see also* Embargo; National defense; Neutrality policy; Postwar
  planning; *and individual countries*
Wright, J. Butler, 319
Wrong, Hume, 1129
Wynne, Cyril, 219

Yahya, Imam, 1535
Yalta Conference (1945), 1458, 1467,
  1587, 1720; Stalin's promise *re* declaration of war on Japan, 1310; question of Soviet republics' membership
  in U.N., 1680; agreement on voting
  procedure in U.N Council, 1705
Yamada, Lieut., 1012
Yarnell, Harry E., 540
Yemen, 1535, 1546–1547
Yen, W. W., 723–724
Yonai, Mitsumasa, 728, 902
Yugoslavia, efforts to resist German invasion, 928–933; freezing of credits
  in U.S., 932; Politicomilitary Commission in Algiers, 1275; Inter-Allied
  Advisory Council for Italy, 1284,
  1551; British sphere of influence,
  1453

Zeeland, Paul van, 529
Zionist Organization, World, 1531, 1533
Zog, King of Albania, 618